# FORD TEMPO AND MERCURY TOPAZ
# 1984-94 REPAIR MANUAL

| | |
|---|---|
| President, Chilton Enterprises | David S. Loewith |
| Senior Vice President | Ronald A. Hoxter |
| Publisher and Editor-In-Chief | Kerry A. Freeman, S.A.E. |
| Executive Editors | Dean F. Morgantini, S.A.E., W. Calvin Settle, Jr., S.A.E. |
| Managing Editor | Nick D'Andrea |
| Special Products Manager | Ken Grabowski, A.S.E., S.A.E. |
| Senior Editors | Jacques Gordon, Michael L. Grady, Debra McCall, Kevin M. G. Maher, Richard J. Rivele, S.A.E., Richard T. Smith, Jim Taylor, Ron Webb |
| Project Managers | Martin J. Gunther, Will Kessler, A.S.E., Richard Schwartz |
| Production Manager | Andrea Steiger |
| Product Systems Manager | Robert Maxey |
| Director of Manufacturing | Mike D'Imperio |
| Editor | Gordon L. Tobias, S.A.E. |

D1456218

## CHILTON BOOK COMPANY

ONE OF THE **DIVERSIFIED PUBLISHING COMPANIES,**
A PART OF **CAPITAL CITIES/ABC,INC.**

Manufactured in USA
© 1995 Chilton Book Company
Chilton Way, Radnor, PA 19089
ISBN 0-8019-8670-2
Library of Congress Catalog Card No. 94-069441
2345678901   5432109876

# Contents

# Contents

## SAFETY NOTICE

Proper service and repair procedures are vital to the safe, reliable operation of all motor vehicles, as well as the personal safety of those performing repairs. This manual outlines procedures for servicing and repairing vehicles using safe, effective methods. The procedures contain many NOTES, CAUTIONS, and WARNINGS which should be followed along with standard procedures to eliminate the possibility of personal injury or improper service which could damage the vehicle or compromise its safety.

It is important to note that the repair procedures and techniques, tools and parts for servicing motor vehicles, as well as the skill and experience of the individual performing the work vary widely. It is not possible to anticipate all of the conceivable ways or conditions under which vehicles may be serviced, or to provide cautions as to all of the possible hazards that may result. Standard and accepted safety precautions and equipment should be used when handling toxic or flammable fluids, and safety goggles or other protection should be used during cutting, grinding, chiseling, prying, or any other process that can cause material removal or projectiles.

Some procedures require the use of tools specially designed for a specific purpose. Before substituting another tool or procedure, you must be completely satisfied that neither your personal safety, nor the performance of the vehicle will be endangered.

Although information in this manual is based on industry sources and is complete as possible at the time of publication, the possibility exists that some car manufacturers made later changes which could not be included here. While striving for total accuracy, Chilton Book Company cannot assume responsibility for any errors, changes or omissions that may occur in the compilation of this data.

## PART NUMBERS

Part numbers listed in this reference are not recommendation by Chilton for any product by brand name. They are references that can be used with interchange manuals and aftermarket supplier catalogs to locate each brand supplier's discrete part number.

## SPECIAL TOOLS

Special tools are recommended by the vehicle manufacturer to perform their specific job. Use has been kept to a minimum, but where absolutely necessary, they are referred to in the text by the part number of the tool manufacturer. These tools can be purchased, under the appropriate part number, from your local dealer or regional distributor, or an equivalent tool can be purchased locally from a tool supplier or parts outlet. Before substituting any tool for the one recommended, read the SAFETY NOTICE at the top of this page.

## ACKNOWLEDGMENTS

The Chilton Book Company expresses appreciation to Ford Motor Company for their generous assistance.

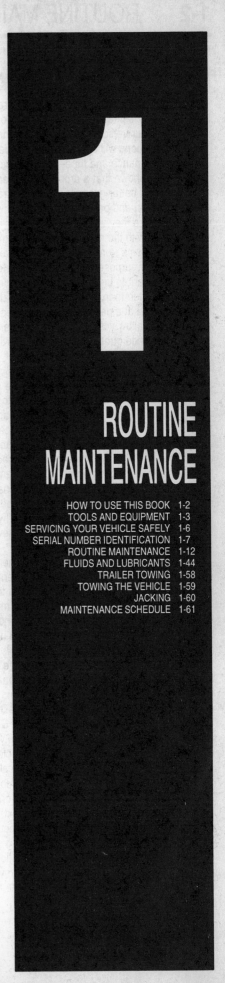

# 1

# ROUTINE MAINTENANCE

## HOW TO USE THIS BOOK

Chilton's Repair Manual for 1984–94 Ford Tempo and Mercury Topaz is intended to teach you about the inner workings of your vehicle and save you money on its upkeep. The first 2 sections will be used most frequently, since they contain maintenance and tune–up information and procedures. Studies have shown that a properly tuned and maintained engine can get better gas mileage (which translates into lower operating costs) and periodic maintenance will catch minor problems before they turn into major repair bills. The other sections deal with the more complex systems of your vehicle. Operating systems from engine through brakes are covered.

A secondary purpose of this book is a reference guide for owners who want to understand their vehicle and/or their mechanics better. In this case, no tools at all are required. Knowing just what a particular repair job requires in parts and labor time will allow you to evaluate whether or not you're getting a fair price quote and help decipher itemized bills from a repair shop.

Before attempting any repairs or service on your vehicle, read through the entire procedure outlined in the appropriate section. This will give you the overall view of what tools and supplies will be required. Read ahead and plan ahead. Each operation should be approached logically and all procedures thoroughly understood before attempting any work. Special tools that may be required can often be rented from local automotive jobbers or places specializing in renting tools and equipment.

All sections contain adjustments, maintenance, removal and installation procedures, and overhaul procedures. When overhaul is not considered practical, we tell you how to remove the failed part and then how to install the new or rebuilt replacement.

Two basic mechanic's rules should be mentioned here. First, whenever the LEFT side of the vehicle or engine is referred to, it is meant to specify the DRIVER'S side of the vehicle. Conversely, the RIGHT side of the vehicle means the PASSENGER'S side. Second, all screws and bolts are removed by turning counterclockwise, and tightened by turning clockwise (left loosen, right tighten).

Safety is always the MOST important rule. Constantly be aware of the dangers involved in working on or around any vehicle and take proper precautions to avoid the risk of personal injury or damage to the vehicle. See the section in this section, Servicing Your Vehicle Safely, and the SAFETY NOTICE on the acknowledgment page before attempting any service procedures, and pay attention to the instructions provided. There are 3 common mistakes in mechanical work:

1. Incorrect order of assembly, disassembly or adjustment. When taking something apart or putting it together, doing things in the wrong order usually just costs you extra time; beside, damage can occur to an individual component or the vehicle. Read the entire procedure before beginning disassembly. Do everything in the order in which the instructions say, even if you can't immediately see a reason for it. When you're taking apart something that is very intricate (for example a carburetor), you might want to draw a picture of how it looks when assembled in order to make sure you get everything back in its proper position. We will supply exploded views whenever possible, but sometimes the job requires more attention to detail than an illustration provides. When making adjustments (especially tune–up adjustments), do them in order. One adjustment often affects another.

2. Overtorquing (or undertorquing) nuts and bolts. While it is more common for overtorquing to cause damage, undertorquing can cause a fastener to vibrate loose causing serious damage, especially when dealing with aluminum parts. Pay attention to torque specifications and utilize a torque wrench in assembly. If a torque figure is not available remember that, if you are using the right tool to do the job, you will probably not have to strain yourself to get a fastener tight enough. The pitch of most threads is so slight that the tension you put on the wrench will be multiplied many times in actual force on what you are tightening. A good example of how critical torque is can be seen in the case of spark plug installation, especially where you are putting the plug into an aluminum cylinder head. Too little torque can fail to crush the gasket, causing leakage of combustion gases and consequent overheating of the plug and engine parts. Too much torque can damage the threads or distort the plug, which changes the spark gap at the electrode. Since more and more manufacturers are using aluminum in their engine and chassis parts to save weight, a torque wrench should be in any serious do–it–yourselfers tool box.

There are many commercial chemical products available for ensuring that fasteners won't come loose, even if they are not torqued just right (a very common brand is Loctite®). If you're worried about getting something together tight enough to hold, but loose enough to avoid mechanical damage during assembly, one of these products may offer substantial insurance. Read the label on the package and make sure the product is compatible with the materials, fluids, etc. involved before choosing one.

3. Crossthreading. This occurs when a part such as a bolt is screwed into a nut or casting at the wrong angle and forced, causing the threads to become damaged. Crossthreading is more likely to occur if access is difficult. It helps to clean and lubricate fasteners, and to start threading the part to be installed, using your fingers. If you encounter resistance, unscrew the part and start over again at a different angle until it can be inserted and turned several times without much effort. Keep in mind that many parts, especially spark plugs, use tapered threads so that gentle turning will automatically bring the part you're threading to the proper angle if you don't force it, or resist a change in angle. Don't put a wrench on the part until it's been turned in a couple of times by hand. If you suddenly encounter resistance and the part has not seated fully, don't force it. Pull it back out and make sure it's clean and threaded properly.

Always take your time and be patient; once you have some experience, working on your vehicle will become an enjoyable hobby.

## TOOLS AND EQUIPMENT

♦ **See Figures 1, 2, 3, 4, 5, 6, 7, 8, 9, 10, 11 and 12**

Naturally, without the proper tools and equipment it is impossible to properly service your vehicle. It would be impossible to catalog each tool that you would need to perform each or every operation in this book. It would also be unwise for the amateur to rush out and buy an expensive set of tools and the theory that he may need one or more of them at sometime. The best approach is to proceed slowly, gathering together a good quality set of tools that are used most frequently. Don't be misled by the low cost of bargain tools. It is far better to spend a little more for better quality. Forged wrenches, 6 or 12–point sockets and fine tooth ratchets are by far preferable to their less expensive counterparts. As any good mechanic can tell you, there are few worse experiences than trying to work on any vehicle with bad tools. Your monetary savings will be far outweighed by frustration and mangled knuckles.

Certain tools, plus a basic ability to handle them, are required to get started. A basic mechanics tool set, a torque wrench and a Torx® bits set. Torx® bits are hexlobular drivers which fit both inside and outside on special Torx® head fasteners used in various places on modern vehicles. Begin accumulating those tools that are used most frequently; those associated with routine maintenance and tune–up. In addition to the normal assortment of screwdrivers and pliers you should have the following tools for routine maintenance jobs (your vehicle is equipped with metric fasteners):

1. SAE/Metric wrenches, sockets and combination open end/box end wrenches in sizes from 1/8 in. (3mm) to 3/4 in. (19mm) and a spark plug socket (13/16 in. or 5/8 in.). If possible, buy various length socket drive extensions. The metric sockets available in the U.S. will all fit the ratchet handles and extensions which you may already have (1/4 in., 3/8 in., and 1/2 in. drive).
2. Jackstands for support.
3. Oil filter wrench.
4. Oil filter spout for pouring oil.
5. Grease gun for chassis lubrication.
6. Hydrometer for checking the battery.
7. A container for draining oil.
8. Many rags (paper or cloth) for wiping up the inevitable mess.

In addition to the above items there are several others that are not absolutely necessary, but handy to have around. These include a hydraulic floor jack, oil–dry, a transmission funnel and the usual supply of lubricants, antifreeze and fluids, although these can be purchased as needed. This is a basic list for routine maintenance, but only your personal needs and desires can accurately determine your list of necessary tools.

The second list of tools is for tune–ups. While the tools involved here are slightly more sophisticated, they need not be outrageously expensive. There are several inexpensive tach/dwell meters on the market that are every bit as good for the average mechanic as an expensive professional model. Just be sure that it works on 4, 6 and 8 cylinder engines. A basic list of tune–up equipment could include:

9. Tach/dwell meter.
10. Spark plug wrench.
11. Timing light (a DC light that works from the vehicle's battery is best, although an AC light that plugs into 110V house current will suffice at some sacrifice in brightness).
12. Wire spark plug gauge/adjusting tools.

Here again, be guided by your own needs. While not absolutely necessary, an ohmmeter can be useful in determining whether or not a spark plug wire is any good by measuring its resistance. In addition to these basic tools, there are several other tools and gauges you may find useful. These include:

13. A compression gauge. The screw–in type is slower to use, but eliminates the possibility of a faulty reading due to escaping pressure.
14. A manifold vacuum gauge.
15. A test light.
16. An induction meter. This is used for determining whether or not there is current in a wire. These are handy for use if a wire is broken somewhere in a wiring harness.

➡ **As a final note, you will probably find a torque wrench necessary for all but the most basic work. The beam type models are perfectly adequate, although the newer click (breakaway) type are more precise, and you don't have to crane your neck to see a torque reading in awkward situations. The breakaway torque wrenches are more expensive and should be recalibrated periodically.**

Torque specification for each fastener will be given in the procedure in any case that a specific torque value is required. If no torque specifications are given, use the following values as a guide, based upon fastener size:

- Bolts marked 6T
- 6mm bolt/nut—5–7 ft. lbs. (6.7–9.4 Nm)
- 8mm bolt/nut —12–17 ft. lbs. (16.2–23.0 Nm)
- 10mm bolt/nut—23–34 ft. lbs. (31.1–46.0 Nm)
- 12mm bolt/nut—41–59 ft. lbs. (55.5–66.4 Nm)
- 14mm bolt/nut—56–76 ft. lbs. (75.9–103.0 Nm)

**Bolts marked 8T**

- 6mm bolt/nut —6–9 ft. lbs. (8.1–12.2 Nm)
- 8mm bolt/nut —13–20 ft. lbs. (17.6–27.1 Nm)
- 10mm bolt/nut —27–40 ft. lbs. (36.6–54.2 Nm)
- 12mm bolt/nut —46–69 ft. lbs. (62.3–93.5 Nm)
- 14mm bolt/nut—75–101 ft. lbs. (101,6–136.9 Nm)

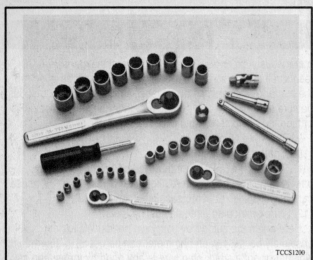

TCCS1200

**Fig. 1 All but the most basic procedures will require an assortment of ratchets and sockets**

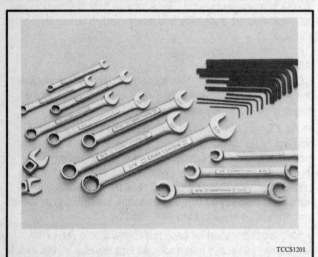

TCCS1201

**Fig. 2 In addition to ratchets, a good set of wrenches and hex keys will be necessary**

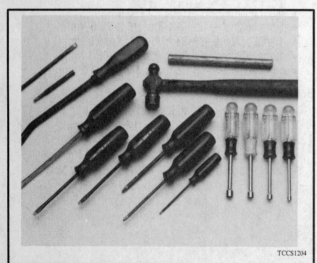

TCCS1204

**Fig. 3 Various screwdrivers, a hammer, chisels and prybars are necessary to have in your toolbox**

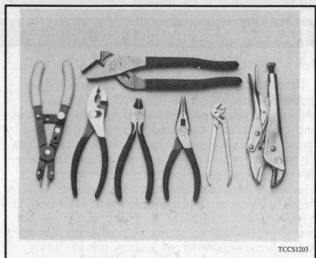

TCCS1203

**Fig. 4 An assortment of pliers will be handy, especially for old rusted parts and stripped bolt heads**

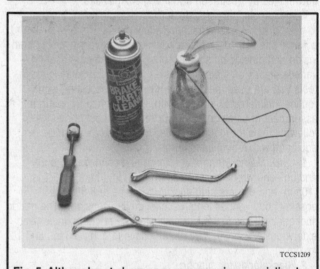

TCCS1209

**Fig. 5 Although not always necessary, using specialized brake tools will save time**

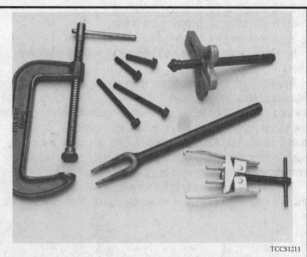

TCCS1211

**Fig. 6 Various pullers, clamps and separator tools are useful for the repair of many components**

Fig. 7 A few inexpensive lubrication tools will make regular service easier

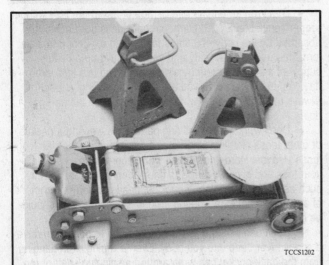

Fig. 8 A hydraulic floor jack and a set of jackstands are essential for safely lifting and supporting the vehicle

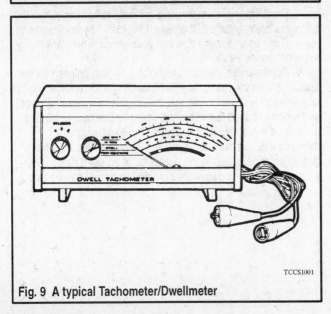

Fig. 9 A typical Tachometer/Dwellmeter

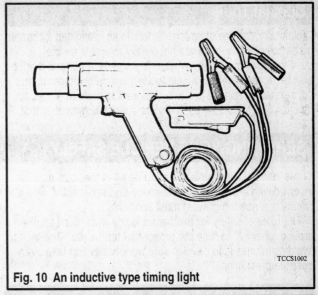

Fig. 10 An inductive type timing light

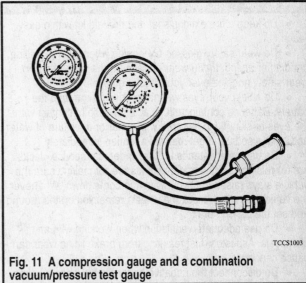

Fig. 11 A compression gauge and a combination vacuum/pressure test gauge

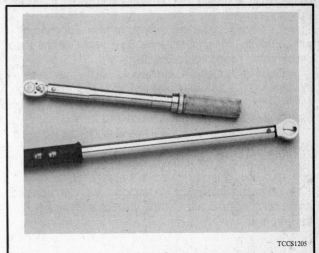

Fig. 12 Many repairs will require the use of a torque wrench to assure the components are properly tightened

## Special Tools

Normally, the use of special factory tools is avoided for repair procedures, since these are not readily available for the do–it–yourself mechanic. When it is possible to perform the job with more commonly available tools, it will be pointed out, but occasionally a special tool was designed to perform a specific function and should be used. Before substituting another tool, you should be convinced that neither your safety nor the performance of the vehicle will be compromised. Where possible, an illustration of the special tool will be provided so that an equivalent tool may be used.

Some special tools are available commercially from major tool manufacturers. Others can be purchased through your Ford dealer or local parts supplier.

## SERVICING YOUR VEHICLE SAFELY

It is virtually impossible to anticipate all of the hazards involved with automotive maintenance and service, but care and common sense will prevent most accidents.

The rules of safety for mechanics range from "don't smoke around gasoline" to "use the proper tool for the job." The trick to avoiding injuries is to develop safe work habits and take every possible precaution.

### Do's

• Do keep a fire extinguisher and first aid kit within easy reach.

• Do wear safety glasses or goggles when cutting, drilling, grinding or prying. If you wear glasses for the sake of vision, wear safety goggles over your regular glasses.

• Do shield your eyes whenever you work around the battery. Batteries contain sulfuric acid. In case of contact with the eyes or skin, flush the area with water or a mixture of water and baking soda and get medical attention immediately.

• Do use safety stands for any under–car service. Jacks are for raising vehicles; safety stands are for making sure the vehicle stays raised until you want it to come down. Whenever the vehicle is raised, block the wheels remaining on the ground and set the parking brake.

• Do use adequate ventilation when working with any chemicals. Asbestos dust resulting from brake lining wear can cause cancer.

• Do disconnect the negative battery cable when working on the electrical system. The primary ignition system produces extremely high voltage.

• Do follow manufacturer's directions whenever working with potentially hazardous materials. Both brake fluid and some antifreeze are poisonous if taken internally.

• Do properly maintain your tools. Loose hammerheads, mushroomed punches and chisels, frayed or poorly grounded electrical cords, excessively worn screwdriver, spread wrenches (open end), cracked sockets can cause accidents.

• Do use the proper size and type of tool for the job being done.

• Do when possible, pull on a wrench handle rather than push on it, and adjust your stance to prevent a fall.

• Do be sure that adjustable wrenches are tightly adjusted on the nut or bolt and pulled so that the face is on the side of the fixed jaw.

• Do select a wrench or socket that fits the nut or bolt. The wrench or socket should sit straight, not cocked.

• Do strike squarely with a hammer to avoid glancing blows.

• Do set the parking brake and block the drive wheels if the work requires that the engine is running.

### Don'ts

• Don't run an engine in a garage or anywhere else without proper ventilation EVER! Carbon monoxide is poisonous. It is absorbed by the body 400 times faster than oxygen. It takes a long time to leave the body and you can build up a deadly supply of it in you system by simply breathing in a little every day. You may not realize you are slowly poisoning yourself. Always use power vents, windows, fans or open the garage doors.

• Don't work around moving parts while wearing a necktie or other loose clothing. Short sleeves are much safer than long, loose sleeves. Hard–toed shoes with neoprene soles protect your toes and give a better grip on slippery surfaces. Jewelry such as watches, fancy belt buckles, beads or body adornment of any kind is not safe working around a car. Long hair should be hidden under a hat or cap.

• Don't use pockets as toolboxes. A fall or bump can drive a screwdriver deep into you body. Even a wiping cloth hanging from the back pocket can wrap around a spinning shaft or fan.

• Don't smoke when working around gasoline, cleaning solvent or other flammable material.

• Don't smoke when working around the battery. When the battery is being charged, it gives off explosive hydrogen gas.

• Don't use gasoline to wash your hands. There are many excellent soaps available.

• Don't service the air conditioning system unless you are equipped with the necessary tools, training and certification. The refrigerants, R–12 and R–134a, if available, are extremely cold and when exposed to the air, will instantly freeze any surface they come in contact with, including eyes. Although the refrigerant is normally nontoxic, R–12 and R–134a become a deadly poisonous gas in the presence of an open flame. One good whiff of the vapors from burning refrigerant can be fatal.

## SERIAL NUMBER IDENTIFICATION

### Model

▶ See Figure 13

The vehicle can be identified by the 6th and 7th character of the Vehicle Identification Number (VIN). This 2 digit identification code will provide such information as body type, series and line.

### Vehicle

▶ See Figures 14, 15, 16, 17 and 18

The Vehicle Identification Number (VIN) is located on the instrument panel close to the windshield on the driver's side of the vehicle. It is visible from outside the vehicle. This 17 character label contains such information as manufacturer name, month and year of manufacture, type of restraint system, body type, engine, etc. The VIN is used for title and registration purposes.

A Vehicle Certification Label (VCL) is also affixed on the left front door lock panel or door pillar. This label contains such information as gross vehicle weight, paint code, tire pressure, trans. and axle type, etc. The VCL is also used for warranty identification of the vehicle.

---

**LINE, SERIES, BODY TYPE FOR PASSENGER CARS**

**(VIN POSITIONS 6 AND 7)**

1FABP 36 F2PZ100001

| VIN Code | Line | Series | Body Type | Body Code |
|---|---|---|---|---|
| **Make — Ford** | | | | |
| 31 | Tempo | GL | 2-Dr. Sedan | GL2 |
| 32 | Tempo | LX | 2-Dr. Sedan | LX2 |
| 33 | Tempo | GLS | 2-Dr. Sedan | ZS2 |
| 36 | Tempo | GL | 4-Dr. Sedan | GL4 |
| 37 | Tempo | LX | 4-Dr. Sedan | LX4 |
| 38 | Tempo | GLS | 4-Dr. Sedan | 4S4 |
| **Make — Mercury** | | | | |
| 31 | Topaz | GS Front Wheel drive | 2-Dr. Sedan | GS2 |
| 33 | Topaz | XR5 Front Wheel Drive | 2-Dr. Sedan | XR2 |
| 36 | Topaz | GS Front Wheel Drive | 4-Dr. Sedan | GS4 |
| 37 | Topaz | LT Front Wheel Drive | 4-Dr. Sedan | LS4 |
| 38 | Topaz | LTS Front Wheel Drive | 4-Dr. Sedan | LT4 |

86701001

Fig. 13 Line, series and body type identification codes

---

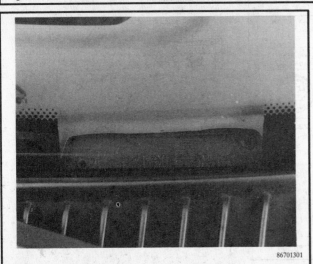

86701301

Fig. 14 The VIN is located on the left side of the instrument panel and is visible through the windshield

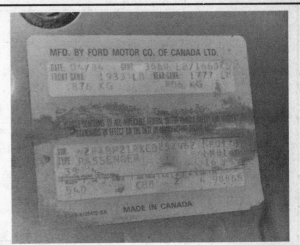

86701302

Fig. 15 The VCL is affixed to the inside of the left driver's door

## VEHICLE IDENTIFICATION CHART

| \ Engine Code | | | | | | Model Year | |
|---|---|---|---|---|---|---|---|
| Code | Liters | Cu. In. (cc) | Cyl. | Fuel Sys. | Eng. Mfg. | Code | Year |
| H | 2.0 | 122 (2000) | 4 | DSL | Mazda | E | 1984 |
| R | 2.3 | 140 (2300) | 4 | 1BBL | Ford | F | 1985 |
| X | 2.3 | 140 (2300) | 4 | CFI | Ford | G | 1986 |
| S | 2.3 | 140 (2300) | 4 | CFI | Ford | H | 1987 |
| U | 3.0 | 181 (2971) | 6 | MFI | Ford | J | 1988 |
|  |  |  |  |  |  | K | 1989 |
|  |  |  |  |  |  | L | 1990 |
|  |  |  |  |  |  | M | 1991 |
|  |  |  |  |  |  | N | 1992 |
|  |  |  |  |  |  | O | 1993 |
|  |  |  |  |  |  | P | 1994 |

BBL - Barrel carburetor

MFI - Multiport fuel injection

DSL - Diesel

CFI - Central fuel injection

MFI - Multiport fuel injection

86701666

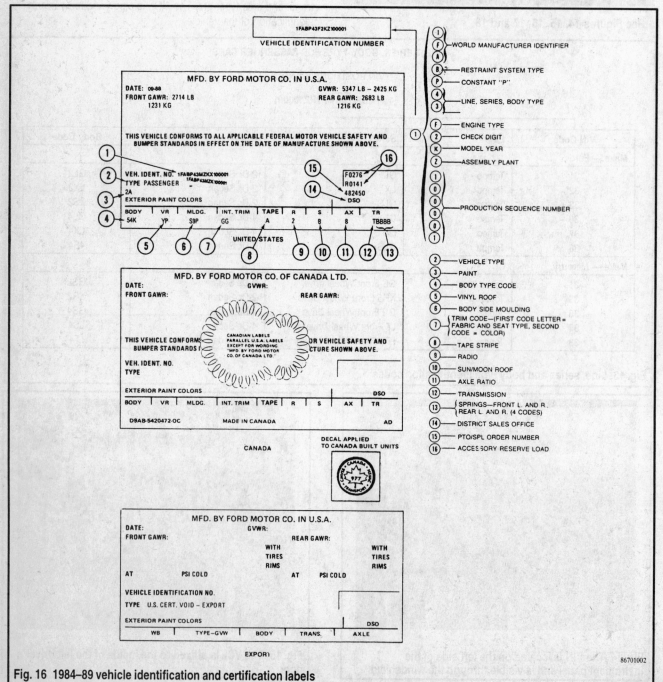

Fig. 16  1984–89 vehicle identification and certification labels

86701002

**Certification Label (Typical)**

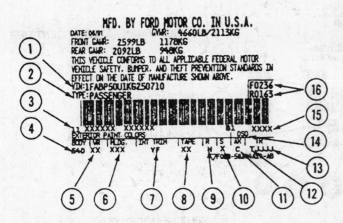

1FABP43F2KZ100001

VEHICLE IDENTIFICATION NUMBER

MFD. BY FORD MOTOR CO. IN U.S.A.
DATE: 06/91   GVWR:  4660LB/2113KG
FRONT GAWR: 2599LB   1178KG
REAR GAWR: 2092LB   948KG
THIS VEHICLE CONFORMS TO ALL APPLICABLE FEDERAL MOTOR
VEHICLE SAFETY, BUMPER, AND THEFT PREVENTION STANDARDS IN
EFFECT ON THE DATE OF MANUFACTURE SHOWN ABOVE.
VIN:1FABP5OU1KG250710           F0236
TYPE:PASSENGER                  R0163

1 XXXXX  XXXXX          B1    XXXX
EXTERIOR PAINT COLORS              DSO
BODY │VR │MLDG. │INT TRIM │TAPE │R │S │AX │ TR
540  XX   XXX      YF       XX   M  X  C  TJJJJ
                            ▽F0EB-5&204A10-AB

**UNITED STATES**

MFD. BY FORD MOTOR CO. OF CANADA LTD.
DATE: 06/91   GVWR:  3682LB/1670KG
FRONT GAWR: 1999LB   906KG
REAR GAWR: 1812LB   821KG
THIS VEHICLE CONFORMS TO ALL APPLICABLE FEDERAL MOTOR
VEHICLE SAFETY, BUMPER, AND THEFT PREVENTION STANDARDS IN
EFFECT ON THE DATE OF MANUFACTURE SHOWN ABOVE.
VIN:2FABP35X4KB218512           F0075
TYPE:PASSENGER                  R0095

1C                    B5    XXXX
EXTERIOR PAINT COLORS              DSO
BODY │VR │MLDG. │INT TRIM │TAPE │R │S │AX │ TR
540  XX   B5A      CG       XX   9  X  6  BMMDD
**MADE IN CANADA**    ▽F0EB-5&204A10-BB

DECAL APPLIED          CANADA
TO CANADA BUILT UNITS

MFD. BY FORD MOTOR CO. IN U.S.A.
DATE: 06/91   GVWR:  4900LB/2222KG
FRONT GAWR: 2557LB   1159KG
REAR GAWR: 2430LB   1102KG

VIN:1FABP5O44KA253107           F0052
TYPE:U.S.CERT VOID-EXPORT       R0164

4S                    90    
EXTERIOR PAINT COLORS              DSO
BODY │VR │MLDG. │INT TRIM │TAPE │R │S │AX │ TR
740  XX   ACN      MA       A    M  X  Z  TJJGG
                            ▽F0ED-5&204A10-AB

**UNITED STATES EXPORT LABEL SHOWN
(CANADIAN EXPORT LABEL TYPICAL)**

NOTE: X'S ON LABELS ARE
SHOWN IN PLACE OF ACTUAL
NUMBERS TO REPRESENT
TYPICAL LABELS ONLY.

1 ⎫
F ⎬ WORLD MANUFACTURER IDENTIFIER
A ⎭
B   RESTRAINT SYSTEM TYPE
P   CONSTANT "P"
4 ⎫
3 ⎬ LINE, SERIES, BODY TYPE
F   ENGINE TYPE
2   CHECK DIGIT
M   MODEL YEAR
Z   ASSEMBLY PLANT
1 ⎫
0 ⎪
0 ⎬ PRODUCTION SEQUENCE NUMBER
0 ⎪
0 ⎪
1 ⎭
2   VEHICLE TYPE
3   PAINT
4   BODY TYPE CODE
5   VINYL ROOF
6   BODY SIDE MOULDING
7   TRIM CODE—(FIRST CODE LETTER = FABRIC AND SEAT TYPE, SECOND CODE = COLOR)
8   TAPE STRIPE
9   RADIO
10  SUN/MOON ROOF
11  AXLE RATIO
12  TRANSMISSION
13  SPRINGS—FRONT L. AND R. REAR L. AND R. (4 CODES)
14  DISTRICT SALES OFFICE
15  PTO/SPL ORDER NUMBER
16  ACCESSORY RESERVE LOAD

86701003

**Fig. 17  1990–93 vehicle identification and certification labels**

Certification Label (Typical)

### 1FABP43F2RZ100001

**VEHICLE IDENTIFICATION NUMBER**

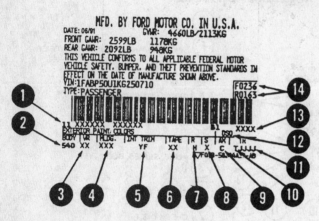

UNITED STATES

CANADA

**DECAL APPLIED TO CANADA BUILT UNITS**

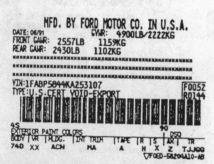

UNITED STATES EXPORT LABEL SHOWN
(CANADIAN EXPORT LABEL TYPICAL)

NOTE: X'S ON LABELS ARE
SHOWN IN PLACE OF ACTUAL
NUMBERS TO REPRESENT
TYPICAL LABELS ONLY.

|  |  |
|---|---|
| I | |
| F | WORLD MANUFACTURER IDENTIFIER |
| A | |
| B | RESTRAINT SYSTEM TYPE |
| P | MANUFACTURER SPECIFICATION |
| 4 | LINE, SERIES, BODY TYPE |
| 3 | |
| F | ENGINE TYPE |
| 2 | CHECK DIGIT |
| R | VEHICLE MODEL YEAR |
| Z | ASSEMBLY PLANT |
| 1 | |
| 0 | |
| 0 | |
| 0 | PRODUCTION SEQUENCE NUMBER |
| 0 | |
| 0 | |
| 1 | |

1 EXTERIOR PAINT COLOR CODES

2 BODY TYPE CODES

3 VINYL ROOF CODES

4 MOULDING CODES

5 INTERIOR TRIM CODES — (FIRST CODE LETTER = FABRIC AND SEAT TYPE, SECOND CODE = COLOR)

6 TAPE STRIPE CODES

7 RADIO TYPE CODES

8 SUN ROOF/MOON ROOF CODES

9 AXLE RATIO CODES

10 TRANSMISSION/TRANSAXLE CODES

11 SUSPENSION SPRING CODES

12 DISTRICT CODES

13 SPECIAL ORDER CODES

14 ACCESSORY RESERVE LOAD CODES

86701004

**Fig. 18 1994 vehicle identification and certification labels**

## ENGINE IDENTIFICATION

| Year | Model | Engine Displacement Liters (cc) | Engine Series (ID/VIN) | Fuel System | No. of Cylinders | Engine Type |
|---|---|---|---|---|---|---|
| 1984 | Tempo/Topaz | 2.0 (2000) | H | DSL | 4 | SOHC |
| | Tempo/Topaz | 2.3 (2300) | R | 1BBL | 4 | OHV |
| 1985 | Tempo/Topaz | 2.0 (2000) | H | DSL | 4 | SOHC |
| | Tempo/Topaz | 2.3 (2300) | R | 1BBL | 4 | OHV |
| | Tempo/Topaz | 2.3 (2300) | X | CFI | 4 | OHV |
| | Tempo/Topaz | 2.3 (2300) | S | CFI | 4 | OHV |
| 1986 | Tempo/Topaz | 2.0 (2000) | H | DSL | 4 | SOHC |
| | Tempo/Topaz | 2.3 (2300) | R | 1BBL | 4 | SOHC |
| | Tempo/Topaz | 2.3 (2300) | S | CFI | 4 | OHV |
| | Tempo/Topaz | 2.3 (2300) | X | CFI | 4 | SOHC |
| 1987 | Tempo/Topaz | 2.0 (2000) | H | DSL | 4 | SOHC |
| | Tempo/Topaz | 2.3 (2300) | R | 1BBL | 4 | OHV |
| | Tempo/Topaz | 2.3 (2300) | S | CFI | 4 | OHV |
| | Tempo/Topaz | 2.3 (2300) | X | CFI | 4 | OHV |
| 1988 | Tempo/Topaz | 2.3 (2300) | X | MFI | 4 | SOHC |
| | Tempo/Topaz | 2.3 (2300) | S | MFI | 4 | SOHC |
| 1989 | Tempo/Topaz | 2.3 (2300) | X | MFI | 4 | SOHC |
| | Tempo/Topaz | 2.3 (2300) | S | MFI | 4 | SOHC |
| 1990 | Tempo/Topaz | 2.3 (2300) | X | MFI | 4 | SOHC |
| | Tempo/Topaz | 2.3 (2300) | S | MFI | 4 | SOHC |
| 1991 | Tempo/Topaz | 2.3 (2300) | X | MFI | 4 | SOHC |
| | Tempo/Topaz | 2.3 (2300) | S | MFI | 4 | SOHC |
| 1992 | Tempo/Topaz | 2.3 (2300) | X | MFI | 4 | SOHC |
| | Tempo/Topaz | 3.0 (2971) | U | MFI | 6 | OHV |
| 1993 | Tempo/Topaz | 2.3 (2300) | X | MFI | 4 | SOHC |
| | Tempo/Topaz | 3.0 (2971) | U | MFI | 6 | OHV |
| 1994 | Tempo/Topaz | 2.3 (2300) | X | MFI | 4 | OHV |
| | Tempo/Topaz | 3.0 (2971) | U | MFI | 6 | OHV |

BBL - Barrel carburetor

MFI - Multiport fuel injection

CFI - Central fuel injection

DSL - Diesel

SOHC - Single overhead camshaft

OHV - Overhead valve

86701777

## Engine

The 8th character of the VIN designates the engine type installed in the vehicle.

## Transaxle

♦ **See Figure 19**

The transaxle code is found on the Vehicle Certification Label (VCL), affixed to the left (driver's) side door lock post. The code is located in the lower right hand corner of the VCL. This code designates the transaxle type installed in the vehicle. An identification tag is also affixed to the transaxle assembly.

## Drive Axle

The drive axle code is found in the lower right hand corner of the vehicle certification label. This code designates the transaxle ratio.

## Transfer Case—All Wheel Drive (AWD)

The transfer case identification code is usually affixed or stamped along the bottom of the transaxle case.

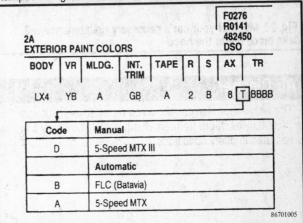

Fig. 19 Transaxle identification code location on the Vehicle Certification Label

## TRANSAXLE APPLICATION CHART

| Year | Model | Transaxle Identification | Transaxle Type |
|------|-------|--------------------------|----------------|
| 1984 | Tempo/Topaz | 5 | 5-speed MTX |
| 1984-85 | Tempo/Topaz | 9 | 4-speed MTX |
| 1984-92 | Tempo/Topaz | B | ATX (Batavia) |
| 1985 | Tempo/Topaz | O | ATX (Toyo Koqyo) |
| 1985-93 | Tempo/Topaz | D | 5-speed |
| 1988-90 | Tempo/Topaz | K | ATX (Mazda) |
| 1991-94 | Tempo/Topaz | B | FLC (Batavia) |
| 1994 | Tempo/Topaz | A | 5-speed MTX |
| 1994 | Tempo/Topaz | D | 5-speed MTX III |

86701a44

## ROUTINE MAINTENANCE

▶ See Figure 20

86701303

**Fig. 20 Much of your car's necessary maintenance will take place under the hood**

## Air Cleaner

The air cleaner element should be replaced every 30 months or 30,000 miles. More frequent changes are necessary if the car is operated in dusty conditions.

## REMOVAL & INSTALLATION

### 2.0 Engine

▶ See Figure 21

1. Loosen the clamps that attach the resonator outlet tube to the engine and disconnect the resonator outlet tube from the intake manifold.
2. Unfasten the air cleaner cover retaining clips and remove the air cleaner cover, resonator and tube unit.
3. Remove the air filter element.
4. Inspect the inside surfaces of the cover and tray for traces of dirt leakage past the cleaner element as a result of damaged seals, incorrect element use, or inadequate tightness of the cover retaining clips. Wipe around the sealing surface with a cloth.

**To Install:**

5. Insert new filter element into air filter tray making sure the new filter fits securely, but does not distort the filter element.
6. Attach the air cleaner cover using the retaining clips, as well as the resonator tube assembly, making sure to tightening the clamps to 12–20 ft. lbs. (1.4–2.3 Nm).
7. Start engine and check for leaks.

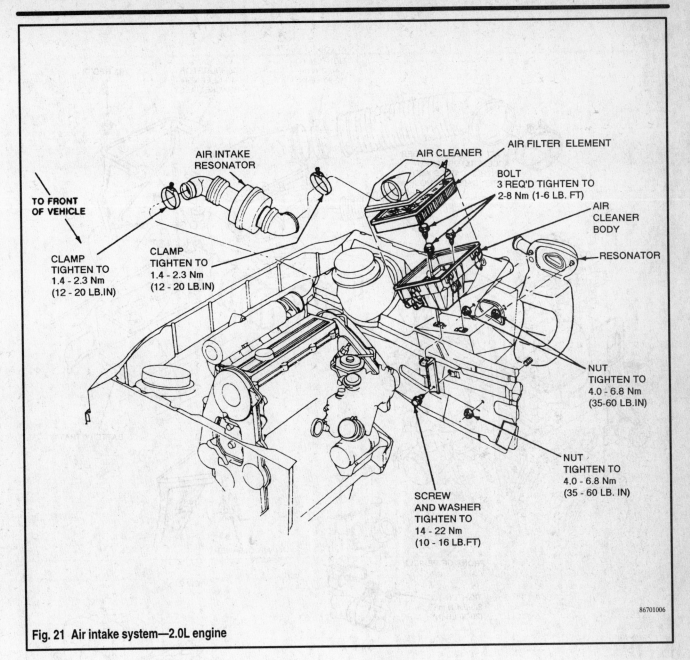

Fig. 21 Air intake system—2.0L engine

## 2.3 Engine

♦ **See Figures 22, 23, 24 and 25**

1. Loosen the clamps that attach the outlet tube from the intake manifold to the air cleaner assembly.

2. Disconnect the fresh air zip tube, and if equipped, the PCV hose attached to the outlet tube or air filter tray and engine valve cover.

3. If applicable, remove the mass flow sensor wire harness from the air cleaner assembly.

4. Unfasten any retaining clips or screws which secure the air filter assembly to the air filter tray.

5. Slowly, lift air cleaner assembly up and away enough to remove air filter element.

6. Inspect the inside surfaces of the tray for traces of dirt leakage. Wipe sealing surface with a clean cloth.

**To Install:**

7. Insert new air filter element into air filter tray. Make sure the new element fits securely, but does not distort the filter itself.

8. Connect air filter assembly to air filter tray by aligning tabs. Reconnect retaining clips, or insert and tighten retaining screws to 22–32 inch lbs. (2.4–3.6 Nm).

9. Connect PCV hose and fresh air zip tube. Make sure outlet tube from intake manifold is secure. Position all clamps and tighten to 24–35 inch lbs. (2.7–4.0 Nm).

10. Reconnect mass flow sensor wire harness to air cleaner assembly.

11. Start engine and check for leaks.

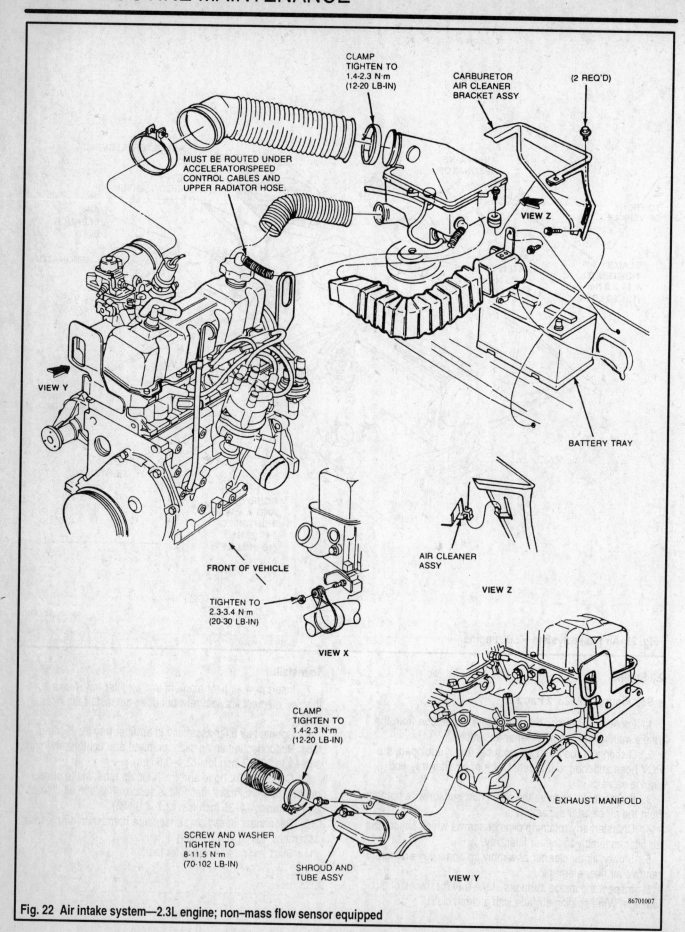

CLAMP
TIGHTEN TO
1.4-2.3 N·m
(12-20 LB-IN)

CARBURETOR
AIR CLEANER
BRACKET ASSY

(2 REQ'D)

MUST BE ROUTED UNDER
ACCELERATOR/SPEED
CONTROL CABLES AND
UPPER RADIATOR HOSE.

VIEW Z

VIEW Y

BATTERY TRAY

FRONT OF VEHICLE

TIGHTEN TO
2.3-3.4 N·m
(20-30 LB-IN)

VIEW X

AIR CLEANER
ASSY

VIEW Z

CLAMP
TIGHTEN TO
1.4-2.3 N·m
(12-20 LB-IN)

EXHAUST MANIFOLD

SCREW AND WASHER
TIGHTEN TO
8-11.5 N·m
(70-102 LB-IN)

SHROUD AND
TUBE ASSY

VIEW Y

86701007

**Fig. 22 Air intake system—2.3L engine; non–mass flow sensor equipped**

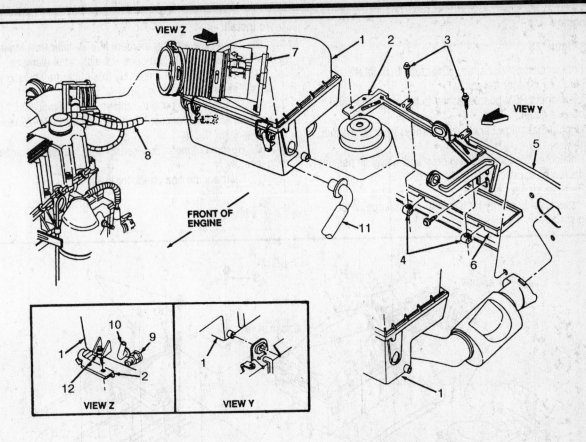

1 Engine air cleaner
2 Engine air cleaner bracket
3 Screw and washer - 4.2 x
   19.0 hex HD (3 req'd)
4 Nut - M4.2 x 1.41 U (2 req'd)
5 LH fender wall
7 Mass air flow (MAF) sensor

8 PCV inlet tube
9 Intake air temp. (IAT) sensor
10 Engine air cleaner inlet hose
   adapter
11 Pulse air hose
12 Air cleaner mounting grommet

Fig. 23 Air intake system—2.3L engine; mass flow sensor equipped

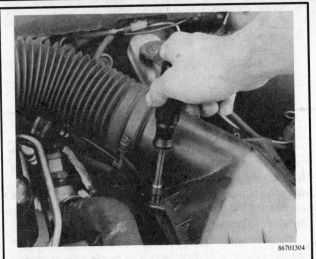

Fig. 24 Remove any retaining clips or screws to access the air filter

Fig. 25 Carefully lift housing and move to one side to expose filter

### 3.0 Engine

▶ **See Figure 26**

1. Loosen clamps that attach outlet tube from intake manifold to air cleaner assembly.
2. Disconnect PCV hose attached to the outlet tube and engine valve cover.
3. Unplug mass flow sensor wire harness from air cleaner assembly.
4. Unlatch air cleaner retaining clips and slowly lift assembly up and away to expose air filter element.
5. Remove air filter element .
6. Inspect inside of tray for traces of dirt leakage. Wipe sealing surface with a clean cloth.

**To Install:**

7. Insert new air filter element into air filter tray. Make sure the filter fits securely, but does not distort the element.
8. Connect air filter assembly to air filter tray by aligning the tabs. Fasten the retaining clips.
9. Connect PCV hose to outlet tube from manifold. Make sure outlet tube is secure. Tight all clamps to 24–25 inch lbs. (2.7–4.0 Nm).
10. Reconnect mass flow sensor wire harness to air filter assembly.
11. Start engine and check for leaks.

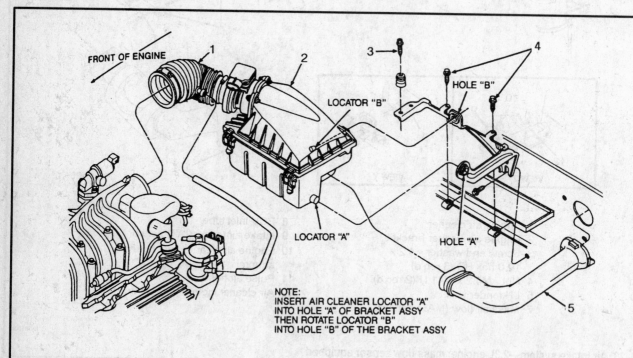

FRONT OF ENGINE 1 2 3 4

HOLE "B"

LOCATOR "B"

LOCATOR "A"

HOLE "A"

NOTE:
INSERT AIR CLEANER LOCATOR "A"
INTO HOLE "A" OF BRACKET ASSY
THEN ROTATE LOCATOR "B"
INTO HOLE "B" OF THE BRACKET ASSY

5

1  Air cleaner outlet tube
2  Engine air cleaner
3  Screw - M6.3 x 1.81 x 32 hex wash HD tap (2 req'd)
4  Screw - M4.2 x 1.41 x 19 hex wash HD tap (2 req'd)
5  Engine air cleaner intake tube

86701009

**Fig. 26  Air intake system—3.0L engine**

## Fuel Filter

The fuel filter should be replaced, immediately, upon evidence of dirt in the fuel system. Regular replacement of the fuel filter should be every 30,000 miles. If the engine seems to be suffering from fuel starvation, remove the filter and blow through it with compressed air to see if it is clogged. If air won't pass through the filter easily, or if dirt is visible in the inlet passage, replace the filter.

➥ A backup wrench is an open end wrench of the proper size used to hold a fuel filter or fitting in position while a fuel line is removed. A flared wrench is a special hex wrench with a narrow open end allowing the fuel line nut to be gripped tightly. A regular open end wrench may be substituted if used carefully so the fitting is not rounded.

The fuel filter on non–EFI models contains a screen to minimize the amount of contaminants entering the carburetor via the fuel system. The fuel filter on the non–EFI models is attached to the carburetor.

The EFI fuel filter provides extremely fine filtration to protect the small metering orifices of the injector nozzles. The filter is a one–piece construction which cannot be cleaned. If the filter becomes clogged or restricted, it should be replaced with a new filter. The filter is mounted on the right fender apron.

### ❋❋CAUTION

**Do not smoke or carry an open flame of any type when working on or near any fuel–related component. Highly flammable mixtures are always present and may be ignited, resulting in possible injury.**

## REMOVAL & INSTALLATION

### Carbureted Engines

▶ **See Figures 27, 28 and 29**

On these vehicles, the fuel filter is located on the fuel line to the carburetor. Special care should be taken when removing and installing the fuel filter, not to bend or distort the fuel line in any way.

1. Remove gas cap to relieve any pressure that may be present in the fuel system.

2. Remove the air cleaner bonnet assembly.
3. Using a backup wrench on the return line fitting on the top of the fuel filter, remove the fuel line with a flare nut wrench.
4. Using a backup wrench on the fuel filter inlet fitting, remove the fuel line from the fuel filter with a flare nut wrench.
5. Using a backup wrench on the fuel filter outlet fitting, loosen the fuel line and remove the fuel filter from the engine with a flare nut wrench.

**To Install:**

6. Apply a drop of engine oil to all the fuel line nuts and flared ends.
7. Position the fuel filter with flow arrow on the filter directed towards the fuel line going to the carburetor.
8. Finger–tighten the fittings at the fuel filter outlet, inlet and return line into the top of the filter.
9. Using a backup wrench on the fuel filter fittings, tighten the fuel lines in the following sequence:

    a. Tighten the outlet and inlet line nuts to 15–18 ft. lbs. (20.0–24.0 Nm)

    b. Tighten the nut on the return line at the top of the filter to 6–9 ft. lbs. (15–18 Nm).

10. Inspect the fuel lines and carefully adjust if they are interfering with the carburetor, air pump, or fuel filter housing.
11. Start the engine and check for fuel leaks at all the connections. Retighten if necessary.
12. If removed, install the air filter bonnet assembly.

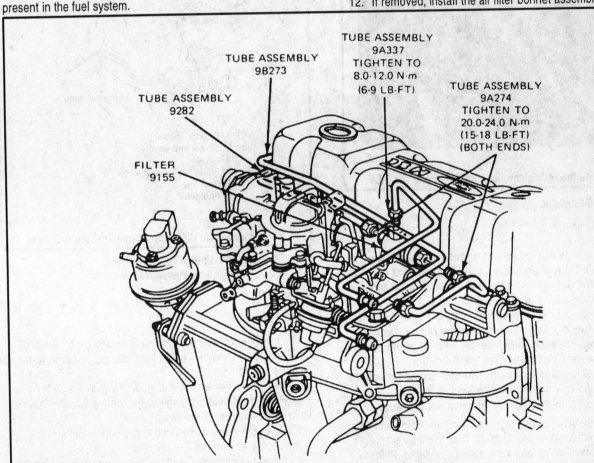

**Fig. 27 The fuel filter and lines are located behind the valve cover on carbureted vehicles**

**Fig. 28 Carefully loosen each of the three fittings to the fuel filter**

**Fig. 29 Once the fittings are loosened, remove the filter**

## Fuel Injected Engines

▶ See Figure 30

➡ If the vehicle is equipped with a pressure relief valve, install an EFI/CFI fuel pressure gauge T80L 9974 B or equivalent and depressurize the fuel system. If the vehicle is not equipped with a pressure relief valve, the fuel filter connection should be covered with a shop rag or towel to prevent the fuel from spraying during the removal procedure. It is also possible to reduce the amount of pressure in the fuel system by locating the inertia switch (usually located in the luggage compartment) and disconnecting the electrical connection on the inertia switch. Next crank the engine for 15 seconds to reduce the system pressure.

Fuel injected vehicles use steel fuel lines and nylon fuel hose assemblies with push connect fittings. This type of system requires special removal and installation procedures. Refer to the procedure "Push Connector Fittings" when necessary.

### ✳✳CAUTION

The fuel filter connections at both ends of the filter, should be covered with a shop rag or towel when separating the connection to prevent the fuel from spraying out during the removal procedure, and dripping on the exhaust manifold below.

1. Disconnect the negative battery cable.
2. Properly relieve the fuel system of any pressure.
3. Remove the push connect fittings according to the "Push Connector Fittings" removal and installation procedure. Install new retainer clips in each connector fitting.

➡ The flow arrow direction should be noted to ensure proper flow of fuel through the replacement filter.

4. Remove the filter from the bracket by loosening the filter retaining clamp enough to allow the filter to pass through.

**To install:**

5. Install the filter into the bracket, ensuring the proper direction of flow, as noted earlier. Tighten the clamp to 15–25 inch lbs. (1.7–2.8 Nm).
6. Install push connect fittings at both ends of the filter.

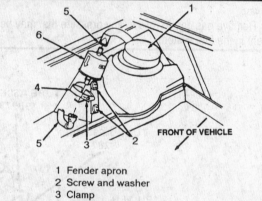

1 Fender apron
2 Screw and washer
3 Clamp
4 Fuel filter bracket assy
5 Fuel line
6 Fuel filter

**Fig. 30 Location and direction of fuel injected fuel filter**

7. Connect the negative battery cable.
8. Start the engine and inspect for leaks.

### Diesel Engine

▶ See Figure 31

The fuel filter/conditioner must be serviced (water purged) at each engine oil change (7500 miles) interval. To purge water from the system:

1. Make sure the engine and ignition switch are OFF.
2. Place a suitable container under the fuel filter/conditioner water drain tube under the car.
3. Open the water drain valve at the bottom of the filter/conditioner element 2½–3 turns.
4. Pump the prime pump at the top of the filter for 10 to 15 strokes, or until all of the water is purged from the filter, and clear diesel fuel is apparent.

➡ **If the water/fuel will not drain from the tube, open the drain valve one more turn or until the water/fuel starts to flow.**

5. Close the drain valve and tighten.
6. Start the engine and check for leaks.

### To replace the filter/conditioner:

7. Make sure that the engine and ignition are OFF.
8. Disconnect the water level sensor harness located at the bottom of the filter element.
9. Using an appropriate filter strap wrench loosen and remove the filter element from the top mounting bracket. Clean filter mounting surface.
10. Carefully unscrew the water drain valve/sensor probe from the bottom of the element. Wipe the probe with a clean dry cloth.
11. Unsnap the sensor probe pigtail from the bottom of the filter element and wipe with a clean dry rag.
12. Snap cleaned probe pigtail onto the new filter element.
13. Lubricate the two O–rings on the water sensor probe with a light film of oil. Slowly screw the probe into the bottom of the new filter element.

14. Lubricate the sealing gasket of the new filter with oil. Screw the filter element onto the mount adapter. Hand tighten, then back off to the point where the gasket is just touching the adapter. Retighten by hand and an additional $1/2$–$5/8$ turn.
15. Reconnect the water level sensor harness.
16. Prime the fuel system by pumping the primer handle until pressure is felt when pumping.
17. Start the engine and check for fuel leaks.

## Fuel and A/C Push Connect Fittings

Push connect fittings utilize two different retaining clips. The fittings used with $5/16$ in. (8mm) diameter tubing use a "hairpin clip." The fittings used with $1/4$ in. (6mm) and $1/2$ in. (12.7mm) diameter tubing use a "duck bill" clip. Each type of fitting requires a different procedure for removal.

Push connect fitting disassembly must be accomplished prior to fuel component removal (filter, pump, etc.) except for the fuel tank where removal is necessary for access to the push connects.

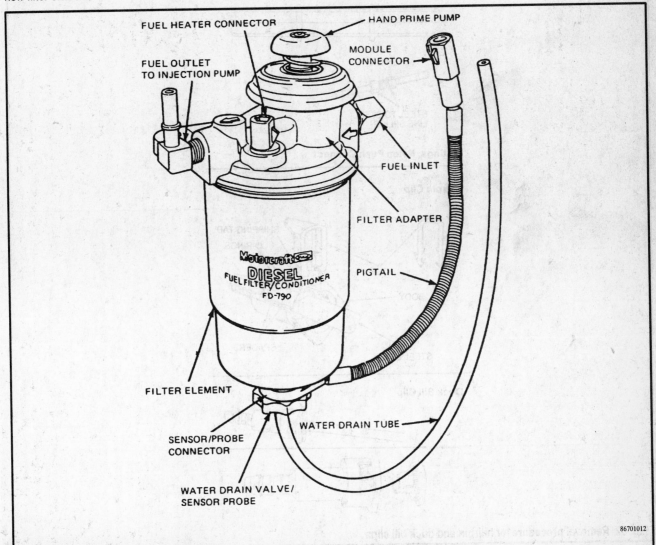

Fig. 31  Diesel engine fuel filter/conditioner

## REMOVAL & INSTALLATION

### ⁵/₁₆ IN. FITTINGS (HAIRPIN CLIP)

▶ **See Figure 32**

1. Inspect the internal portion of the fitting for dirt accumulation. If more than a light coating is present, clean the fitting before disassemble.

2. Using your hands, slowly pry the two clip legs apart about ¹/₈ in. (3mm) and push entire clip toward the center of the tube. Complete removal is accomplished by lightly pulling from the triangular end of the clip and working it clear of the tube and fitting.

➡ **Do not use any tools.**

3. Grasp the fitting and hose assembly and pull in an outward direction to separate the fitting from the steel tube. For particularly difficult connections, a slight twist of the fitting may be required to break any adhesion and permit effortless removal.

4. Examine fittings and tube for dust or dirt. Clean all ends with a cloth before reconnecting.

5. Inspect clips for damage or wear, and replace any clips which are not perfect. If undamaged, reinstall clip by inserting into two adjacent openings with the triangular portion pointing away from the fitting opening. To fully engage the body of the clip, the legs should be locked on the outside of the tube. Piloting with an index finger may be necessary.

6. To reinstall the fitting onto the tube, align both ends up and push the fitting onto the tube end. When the fitting is engaged, a definite click will be heard. Pull on fitting to ensure a proper engagement.

### ½ in. and ¼ in. Fittings (Duck Bill Clip)

▶ **See Figures 32 and 33**

These fittings consist of a body, spacers, O–rings and a duck bill retaining clip. The clip maintains the fitting juncture. When disassembly is required, one of the two following methods should be followed:

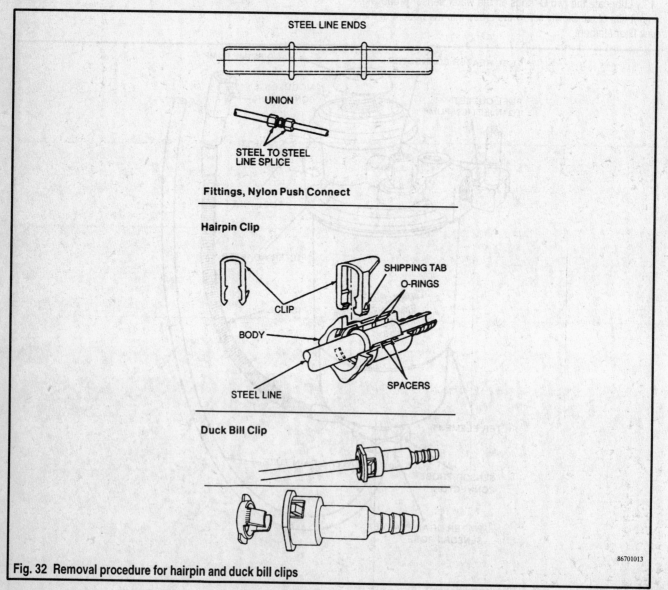

**Fig. 32 Removal procedure for hairpin and duck bill clips**

86701013

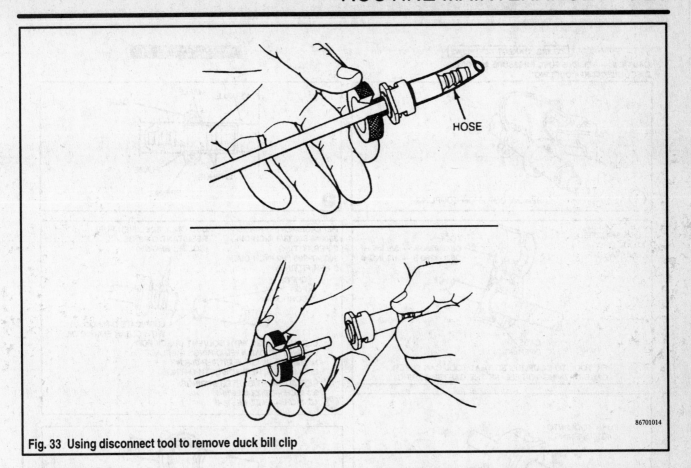

HOSE

86701014

**Fig. 33  Using disconnect tool to remove duck bill clip**

### ¼ IN. FITTINGS

Using disassembly tool T82L 9500 or equivalent, to separate the tube from the fitting, align the slot on the tool with either tab on the clip and insert the tool. This disengages the duck bill from the tube. Holding the tool and the tube with one hand, slowly pull the fitting away from the tube. Inspect and clean both tube and fitting. Also inspect internal retaining clip, and replace if necessary.

➡ **Only moderate effort is required if the tube has been properly disengaged. Use hands only. Some fuel tubes have a secondary bead which aligns with the outer surface of the clip. These beads can make tool insertion difficult. If there is extreme difficulty, use the disassembly method which follows.**

### ½ IN. FITTING AND ALTERNATE METHOD FOR ¼ IN. FITTING

This method of removal disengages the retaining clip from the fitting body. Use a pair of narrow pliers with a jaw width of 0.2 in. (5mm) or less, 6 in. (153mm), locking pliers are ideal.

Align the jaws of the pliers with the openings in the side of the fitting case, and slowly compress the portion of the retaining clip that engages into the fitting case. This disengages the retaining clip from the case. Make sure that both sides of the clip have been disengaged. If so, pull the fitting off the tube.

➡ **Only moderate effort is required if the retaining clip has been properly disengaged. Use hands only.**

The retaining clip will remain on the tube. Disengage the clip from the tube bead and remove. Replace the retaining clip if it appears to be damaged or worn.

Slight ovaling of the ring of the clip will usually occur. If there are no visible cracks and the ring will pinch back to its circular configuration, it is not damaged. If there is any doubt, replace the clip.

Install the clip into the body by inserting one of the retaining clip's serrated edges into one of the window openings. Push on the other side until the clip snaps into place. Slide the remaining end of the line back into the clip.

**Spring Lock Coupling**

▶ See Figure 34

➡ **To disassemble this type of coupler, coupler tool D87L–9280–A for ³⁄₈ in. diameter line, or D87L–9280–B for 1/2 in. diameter line is needed. Equivalent type respective tools are available.**

The spring lock coupling is a line coupling held together by a garter spring inside a circular cage. When the coupling is connected together, the flared end of the female fitting slips behind the garter spring inside the cage of the male fitting. The garter spring and cage then prevent the flared end of the female fitting from pulling out of the cage. This coupling system is used for fuel, A/C and power steering lines.

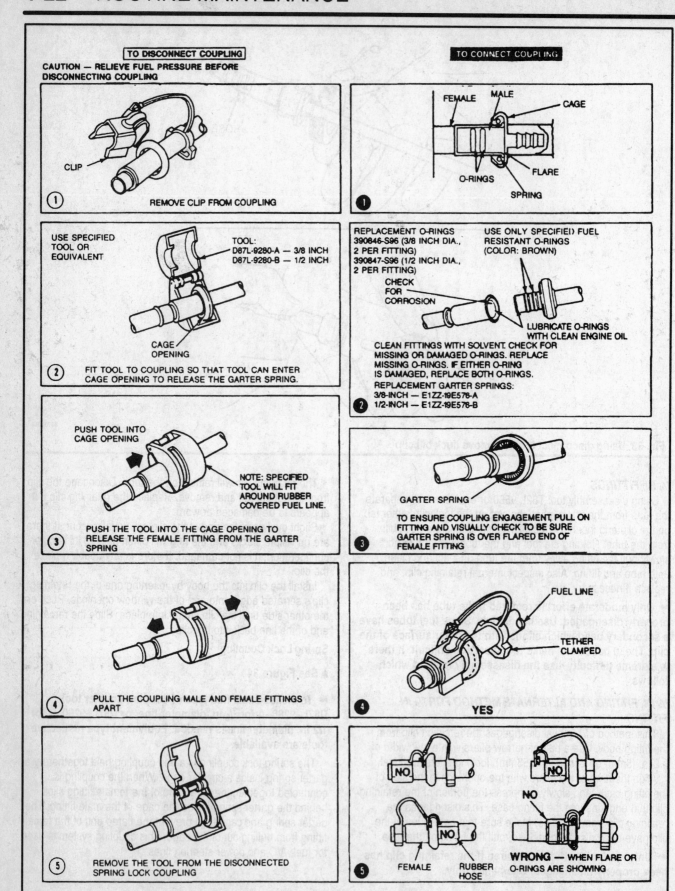

**TO DISCONNECT COUPLING**

CAUTION — RELIEVE FUEL PRESSURE BEFORE DISCONNECTING COUPLING

CLIP

① REMOVE CLIP FROM COUPLING

USE SPECIFIED TOOL OR EQUIVALENT

TOOL:
D87L-9280-A — 3/8 INCH
D87L-9280-B — 1/2 INCH

CAGE OPENING

② FIT TOOL TO COUPLING SO THAT TOOL CAN ENTER CAGE OPENING TO RELEASE THE GARTER SPRING.

PUSH TOOL INTO CAGE OPENING

NOTE: SPECIFIED TOOL WILL FIT AROUND RUBBER COVERED FUEL LINE.

③ PUSH THE TOOL INTO THE CAGE OPENING TO RELEASE THE FEMALE FITTING FROM THE GARTER SPRING

④ PULL THE COUPLING MALE AND FEMALE FITTINGS APART

⑤ REMOVE THE TOOL FROM THE DISCONNECTED SPRING LOCK COUPLING

**TO CONNECT COUPLING**

FEMALE    MALE    CAGE

O-RINGS    FLARE

SPRING

① 

REPLACEMENT O-RINGS
390846-S96 (3/8 INCH DIA., 2 PER FITTING)
390847-S96 (1/2 INCH DIA., 2 PER FITTING)

CHECK FOR CORROSION

USE ONLY SPECIFIED FUEL RESISTANT O-RINGS (COLOR: BROWN)

LUBRICATE O-RINGS WITH CLEAN ENGINE OIL

CLEAN FITTINGS WITH SOLVENT. CHECK FOR MISSING OR DAMAGED O-RINGS. REPLACE MISSING O-RINGS. IF EITHER O-RING IS DAMAGED, REPLACE BOTH O-RINGS.
REPLACEMENT GARTER SPRINGS:
3/8-INCH — E1ZZ-19E576-A
1/2-INCH — E1ZZ-19E576-B

②

GARTER SPRING

TO ENSURE COUPLING ENGAGEMENT, PULL ON FITTING AND VISUALLY CHECK TO BE SURE GARTER SPRING IS OVER FLARED END OF FEMALE FITTING

③

FUEL LINE

TETHER CLAMPED

④ YES

NO    NO

NO

FEMALE    RUBBER HOSE

WRONG — WHEN FLARE OR O-RINGS ARE SHOWING

⑤

86701015

**Fig. 34 Removal procedure for spring lock couplings**

Two O–rings are used to seal between the 2 halves of the coupling. These O–rings are made of special material and must be replaced with an O–ring made of the same material. To disconnect the coupling do the following:

1. Discharge any pressure or fluid from the line. If present, pry up on safety clip with a small screwdriver.

2. Then fit Coupling Tool ($^3/_8$ in. or $^1/_2$ in.) or equivalent to the coupling.

3. Fit the tool to the coupling so that the tool can enter the cage opening to release the garter spring.

4. Push the tool toward the garter spring to release the female fitting from the coupling.

5. Slowly, pull the male and female fittings apart. Remove the tool from the disconnected spring lock coupling. Inspect the condition of the O–rings, and replace if needed.

6. Be sure to check for a missing or damaged garter spring. If damaged, remove the spring with a small hooked wire and install a new spring.

7. If replacing any O–rings, lubricate the O–rings with clean engine oil. Slide new O–rings on fitting with a twisting motion.

8. Carefully push both ends of line together until tight.

9. To ensure coupling engagement, pull on the fitting and visually check to be sure the garter spring is over the flared end of the female fitting.

10. Reinstall safety clip if present. Start car and check for leaks.

## PCV Valve

♦ See Figures 35 and 36

➡ Most models do not use a PCV (positive crankcase ventilation) valve. Instead, an internal baffle and an orifice control the flow of crankcase gases. But there are some later model 2.3L engines that have a PCV valve incorporated into the emission system. (See Section 4 for more details on emission controls.)

The PCV valve is located on top of the valve cover or on the intake manifold. Its primary function is to purge harmful vapors from the crankcase, via a system of vacuum and fresh air drawn through the crankcase. Proper operation of the PCV valve depends on a sealed engine.

Signals of a malfunctioning PCV system include rough idling, oil present in the air cleaner, oil leaks or excessive oil sludging.

A simple way to check the PCV valve is to remove it from its rubber grommet, and shake it. If it rattles, it is functioning. If not, replace it. In any event, the PCV valve should be replaced even 30 months or 30,000 miles. When checking a PCV valve, it is also a good idea to inspect the hose attached to it as well as the grommet. If there are any cracks in the hose, replace it as well.

### REMOVAL & INSTALLATION

1. Remove the valve, with the hose still attached from the rubber grommet using a rocking both and forth motion

2. Loosen or remove the hose clamp securing the PCV valve to the hose. Use a twisting motion to remove the valve from the hose. Inspect the the hose and grommet, and replace if needed.

3. Coat both ends of the PCV valve with oil, install the new valve into the hose, sliding the clamp into position, and finally install the valve into the rubber grommet.

4. Start the car and check for any air leaks.

Fig. 35  Remove valve with a back and forth motion

Fig. 36  Remove any breather hosing attached to the PCV valve

## Evaporative Emission Canister

♦ See Figures 37, 38 and 39

To prevent gasoline vapors from being vented into the atmosphere, an evaporative emission system is utilized to capture the vapors and store them in a charcoal filled canister.

### SERVICING THE EMISSION CANISTER

Since the canister is purged of vapors when the engine is operating, no real maintenance is required. However, the canister should be visually inspected for cracks, loose connections or other potential problems. Replacement is simply a matter of disconnecting the hoses, loosening the mount and replacing the canister.

**Fig. 37 Remove any hardware that attaches the canister to the vehicle**

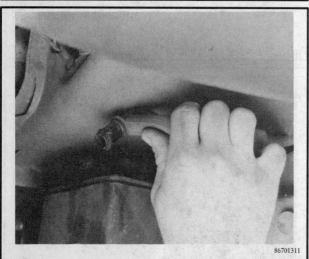

**Fig. 38 Carefully remove any hoses attached to the canister**

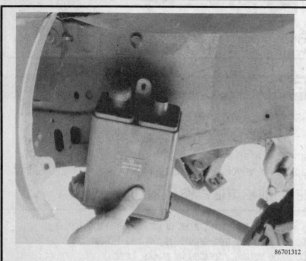

**Fig. 39 With everything disconnected, the canister can be removed**

## Battery

### GENERAL MAINTENANCE

◗ **See Figures 40, 41, 42, 43, 44 and 45**

Your vehicle may be equipped with a maintenance–free battery, in which case the need for periodic checking and adding of fluid is greatly reduced, or not necessary at all. To check if your car has a maintenance free battery, fist check the labeling on the battery. Also, the absence of filler caps would indicate a maintenance free battery.

A maintenance free battery can be either a sealed or non–sealed type. A non–maintenance free battery is always a non–sealed type unit. A sealed battery is one in which you can not open the battery to access the cells. This means the fluid levels cannot be adjusted. With a non–sealed battery, the top(s) can be removed so the cell fluid level can be adjusted.

To determine which type of battery you have, consult the battery label first. This will tell you whether the unit is maintenance free or non–maintenance free. Look for individual round caps on the top of the unit, or a single long rectangular cap, which will identify the battery as a non–sealed unit.

➡ **Batteries normally produce explosive gases which can cause personal injury. Therefore, do not allow flames, sparks or lighted tobacco to come near the battery. Always shield your face and protect your eyes. Also, always provide ventilation.**

**Fluid Level**

*SEALED BATTERY*

Although the battery in your vehicle may be a sealed, maintenance–free battery, it still is a good idea to check the fluid level. To do this, look at the side of the battery. The level in all the cells should be just below the top of the battery. If the level is not, refer to the testing section to determine battery strength.

*NON–SEALED BATTERY*

Check the battery electrolyte level at least once a month, or more often in hot weather or during periods of extended car operation. The level can be checked through the case on translucent battery cases. On other batteries, the cell cap(s) must be removed. The electrolyte level in each cell should be kept filled to the split ring inside, or the line marked on the outside of the case.

If the level is low, add only distilled water, or colorless, odorless drinking water, through the opening until the level is correct. Each cell is completely separate from the others, so each must be checked and filled individually.

If water is added in freezing weather, the car should be driven several miles to allow the water to mix with the electrolyte. Otherwise, the battery could freeze.

**Cables**

➡ **When unfastening battery cables, always disconnect the negative cable first.**

Once a year, the battery terminals and cable clamps should be cleaned and checked. Loosen the clamps and remove the cables. On cables that are difficult to remove, try twisting the cable back and forth, or purchase a battery cable puller. This tool is inexpensive and extremely useful on stuck cables.

Clean the cable clamps and the battery posts with a wire brush or battery post and terminal cleaner, until all corrosion, grease, etc. is removed and metal surface is shiny. It is especially important to clean the inside of the clamp thoroughly. Even a small deposit of foreign material or oxidation can inhibit full battery power.

Before reinstalling the cables, loosen the battery hold down clamp or strap, and remove the battery to inspect the battery tray. Clear it of any debris, and check it for soundness. Rust should be wire brushed away, and the metal given a coat of anti–rust paint. Once the tray is clean, replace the battery and fasten all hardware. Be careful not to overtighten the clamp, this could crack the battery case.

On many batteries, a white powdery substance develops. This oxidation is both bad for the battery as well as the car. This oxidation takes power away from the battery, because this powder contains battery acid. This oxidation is bad for the car because of the acidic nature of the powder, which can eat through plastic, rubber, paint and metal. The most effective solution to this problem, is to remove the battery, clean with water, and apply a layer of baking soda to all surfaces of the battery.

➡ **Wear safety goggles and heavy clothing. This acid can burn eyes, clothing and skin.**

This baking soda will react with the acid and bubble. This bubbling effect is actually neutralizing the oxidation. Continue to wash and add baking soda until the bubbling stops. Perform the same steps to the battery tray as well as the area around the battery. Allow all areas to dry before reinstalling the battery.

After the clamps and terminals are clean, reinstall the cables, positive cable first, then negative cable.

➡ **Keep flame or sparks away from the battery; it gives off explosive hydrogen gas. Battery electrolyte contains sulfuric acid. If you should splash any on your skin or in your eyes, flush the affected areas with plenty of clear water; if it lands in your eyes, get medical help immediately.**

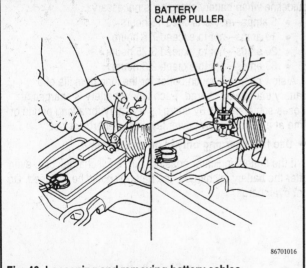

Fig. 40  Loosening and removing battery cables

Do not hammer or excessive force on the clamps when installing. Tighten the clamps securely, but do not distort them. Give the clamps and terminals a thin external coat of grease after installation, to retard corrosion.

Check the cables at the same time that the terminals are cleaned. If the cable insulation is cracked or broken, or if the ends are frayed, the cable should be replace with a new cable of the same length and gauge.

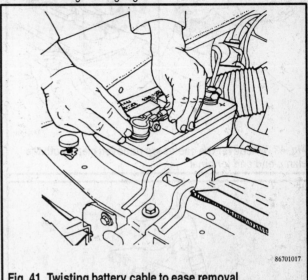

Fig. 41  Twisting battery cable to ease removal

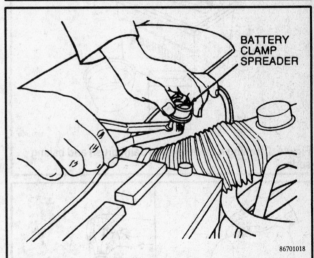

Fig. 42  With cable removed use clamp spreader to enlarge cable terminal opening

## TESTING

Tests are made on a battery to determine the state of charge and also its capacity or ability to crank an engine. The ultimate result of these tests is to show that the battery is good, needs recharging, or must be replaced.

### Visual Inspection

Before attempting to test any battery, it is important to thoroughly examine it to determine if it has been damaged in any way.

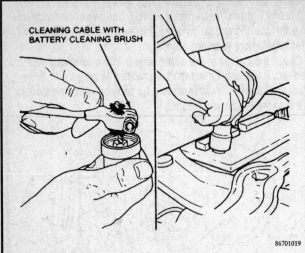

**Fig. 43 Whenever the cables are removed clean both the clamp end and terminal**

**Fig. 44 Cleaning a battery with a paint brush and baking soda**

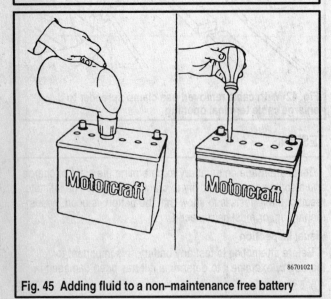

**Fig. 45 Adding fluid to a non–maintenance free battery**

To inspect the battery, remove the cable clamps. Disconnect the negative cable. Check for dirty or corroded connections as well as loose battery posts. Also, check for a broken or cracked case or cover. If a defective, loose or broken post or cracked case or cover is found, replace the battery.

Many batteries contains a visual test indicator which can give a color signal when an adequate charge level exists, and when charging is required. Consult the battery label, or battery manufacturer for color levels.

### Capacity Test

A battery capacity test should follow the "Visual Inspection." A high rate discharge tester (Rotunda Battery Starter Tester 02 0204 or equivalent) in conjunction with a voltmeter is used for this test. Follow the instructions supplied with the tester. If the battery is below minimum voltage for the capacity test, charge the battery for 20 minutes at 35 amperes and repeat the capacity test. If the battery fails a second time, it should be replaced.

### Load Test

Another useful test for checking battery output is a load test. To perform this test, a load tester will need to be purchased. This is available at most automotive parts stores. In this test, the battery is loaded to represent a "draw" or reduction in output. This test's advantage is that it indicates the available output remaining after a significant drop in output. This test is extremely useful in colder weather because it can help show how a battery will perform on a cold morning.

## CHARGING

If it has been determined that your battery needs charging, either by sight glass inspection or testing, charge only until the appropriate dot appears or maximum charge is reached. Never over charge a battery.

➡ **Whenever a battery is being charged, it is giving off hydrogen gas. Charge the battery in a well ventilated area, and never smoke around a battery.**

### Charging Rate

The following specifications should be used as a general guideline when battery charging is necessary:

- 5 amps—not to exceed 15 hours
- 10 amps—not to exceed 7.5 hours
- 20 amps—not to exceed 3.75 hours
- 30 amps—not to exceed 2.5 hours.

A slow charge is much better for the long term life of a battery than a fast charge. Each time a battery is charged, it looses some energy. By charging a battery for a long period of time at a relatively low power level, less energy is lost.

➡ **Use fast charging only in an emergency.**

If the battery indicator does not turn a full charge color, even after the battery is charged, the battery should be replaced. Do not overcharge.

## Specific Gravity

♦ See Figure 46

➡ **If your battery is not a maintenance–free type, a specific gravity test can be performed.**

At least once a year, the specific gravity of your battery should be checked. If the individual cells of the battery are healthy, the gravity reading level of each cell will be between 1.20 and 1.26.

The specific gravity can be checked with the use of an hydrometer, an inexpensive instrument available at most auto parts stores. The hydrometer has a squeeze bulb at one end and a nozzle at the other. Battery electrolyte is drawn into the hydrometer until a float is lifted from its seat. The specific gravity is then read by noting the position of the float. Generally, if after charging, the specific gravity between any two cells varies more than 50 points (0.050), one or more cells are weak, and the battery should be replaced.

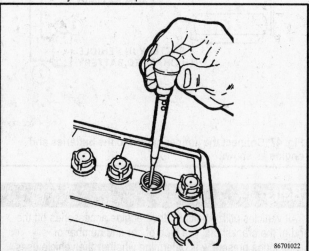

**Fig. 46  The specific gravity of the battery can be checked with a simple hydrometer**

## REPLACEMENT

When it becomes necessary to replace the battery, refer to the owner's manual for battery specifications. There are many batteries available, and not all of them will fit your car. Depending on an individuals needs and budget, will determine whether the battery is a maintenance free type or not.

Because today's cars utilize computers and equipment that most memorize information about a particular car, it is a good idea to provide some power to these pieces while changing a battery. Most automotive parts stores sell a product that uses a small radio battery and plugs into a cigarette lighter, and allows these electronic items to maintain their information. It also allows the clock and radio to maintain the correct time and channel memory.

The procedure is as follows:
1. First, disconnect the negative battery cable, followed by the positive cable.
2. Remove the battery hold–downs and heat shields, as required.
3. Remove the battery from the vehicle.

4. Inspect and clean if needed the battery tray and clamps.

**To install:**
5. Install the replacement battery into the vehicle.
6. Clean the battery posts and install the battery hold–downs and heat shields, as required
7. Reconnect the positive cable first, followed by the the negative cable.
8. After installing the cables, apply a small quantity of grease to each battery post to help prevent corrosion.

## JUMP STARTING A DEAD BATTERY

♦ See Figure 47

Whenever a vehicle must be jump started, precautions must be taken in order to prevent the possibility of personal injury. Remember that batteries contain a small amount of explosive hydrogen gas which is a by–product of the battery charging.

Sparks should always be avoided when working around batteries, especially when attaching jumper cables. To minimize the possibility of accidentally sparks, follow the procedures very carefully.

### ✳✳CAUTION

**NEVER hook the batteries up in a series circuit or the entire electrical system will short circuit, especially the starter.**

**Precautions**
• Be sure both batteries are of the same voltage. Most vehicles covered by this manual and on the road today function on a 12 volt charging system.
• Be sure that both batteries are the same polarity, that is they are grounded similarly (usually through the negative battery terminal). Many early British cars and some antique vehicles were actually positive grounded.
• Be sure the the vehicles are not touching or a short could occur.
• On serviceable batteries, be sure the vent cap holes are not obstructed.
• Do not smoke or allow sparks anywhere near the batteries.
• In cold weather, make sure the battery electrolyte is not frozen. This can occur more readily in a battery that has been in a state of discharge.
• Do not allow electrolyte to contact your skin or clothing.

**Jump Starting Procedure**
1. Make sure that the voltages of the 2 batteries are the same. Most batteries and charging systems are of the 12 volt variety.
2. Pull the jumping vehicle(with the good battery) into a position so the jumper cables can reach the dead battery and the vehicle's engine. Make sure the the vehicles do NOT touch.
3. Place the transmissions/transaxles of both cars in NEUTRAL or PARK, and firmly set the brake.

➡ **If necessary, for safety reasons, both vehicles hazard lights may be operated throughout the entire procedure without significantly increasing the difficulty of jumping the dead battery.**

4. Turn all lights and accessories off on both cars. Make sure the ignition switch on both vehicles is turned to the OFF position.

5. Cover the battery cell caps with a rag, but do not cover the terminals.

6. Make sure the terminals on both batteries are clean and free of corrosion, or proper electrical connections will be impeded. If necessary, clean the battery terminals before proceeding.

7. Identify the positive (+) and negative (–) terminals on both battery posts.

8. Connect the first jumper cable to the positive (+) terminal of the dead battery, then connect the other end of the cable tot the positive (+) terminal of the booster battery (good) battery.

9. Connect one end of the other jumper cable to the negative (–) terminal of the booster battery and the other cable clamp to an engine bolt head, alternator bracket or other solid, metal point on the dead batteries engine. Try to pick a ground on the engine that is positioned away from the battery in order to minimize the possibility of the 2 clamps touching, should one loosen during the procedure. DO NOT connect this clamp to the negative (–) terminal of the dead battery.

### ✳✳WARNING

**Be careful to keep the jumper cables away from moving parts like cooling fans and belts on both engines.**

10. Making sure that the cables are routed safely, start the donor vehicle's engine. Run the engine at moderate speed for several minutes to allow the dead battery a chance to receive some initial charge.

11. With the donor vehicle running, try to start the car with the dead battery. Crank the engine for no more than 10 seconds at a time and let the starter cool for at least 20 seconds between tries. If the car does not start in 3 attempts, it is likely that something else is also wrong or the battery needs additional time to charge.

12. Once the vehicle is started, allow it to run at idle for a few seconds to make sure that it is running correctly.

13. Turn on headlights, blower and rear defroster of both cars to reduce the severity of voltage spikes and subsequent risk of damage to the vehicle's electrical system when the cables are removed.

14. Carefully disconnect the cables in the reverse order of connection. Start with the negative (–) cable that is attached to the engine ground, then the negative cable on the donor battery. Disconnect the positive (+) cable from the formerly dead battery, then the positive (+) cable from the donor battery. Be careful

when disconnecting the cables from the positive terminals not to allow the cable ends to touch any metal surface or sparks will occur.

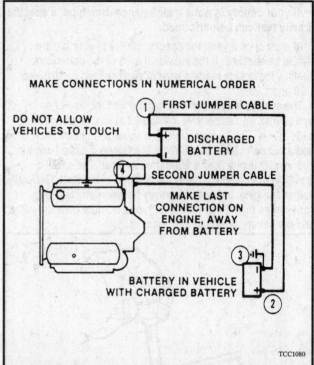

MAKE CONNECTIONS IN NUMERICAL ORDER

DO NOT ALLOW VEHICLES TO TOUCH

① FIRST JUMPER CABLE
DISCHARGED BATTERY

SECOND JUMPER CABLE
MAKE LAST CONNECTION ON ENGINE, AWAY FROM BATTERY

③

BATTERY IN VEHICLE WITH CHARGED BATTERY

②

TCC1080

**Fig. 47 Connect the jumper cables to the batteries and engine as shown**

### Belts

All vehicles utilize belts to drive engine accessories off the end of the crankshaft. The type of car and number of accessories present, will determine whether the vehicle uses standard V–type belts, a cog belts or some variation of a rib belt. In either case, these belts must be properly adjusted at all times. Loose belt(s) will result in slippage which may cause noise or improper accessory operation.

### INSPECTION

◆ **See Figures 48, 49, 50 and 51**

Inspect all drive belts for excessive wear, cracks, glazed condition and frayed or broken cords. Replace any drive belt showing the above condition(s). Belts should be inspected at least 2 times per year, but it is always a good idea to take a look at them whenever the hood is open. Also, refer to your owner's manual for recommended change intervals.

➡ **If a drive belt continually gets cut, the crankshaft pulley might have a sharp projection on it. Have the pulley replaced if this condition exists.**

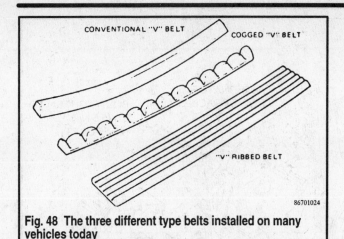

**Fig. 48  The three different type belts installed on many vehicles today**

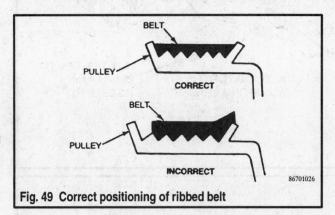

**Fig. 49  Correct positioning of ribbed belt**

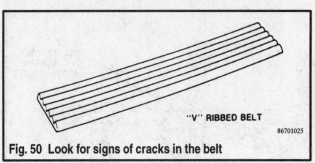

**Fig. 50  Look for signs of cracks in the belt**

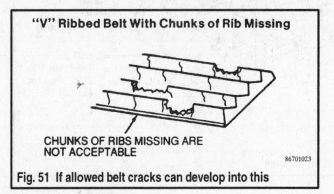

**Fig. 51  If allowed belt cracks can develop into this**

## ADJUSTMENT

Based upon on the production year, the Tempo/Topaz utilized serpentine, cogged and V–belts on their gasoline and diesel engines. Some engines used only a single type of belt, while other engines used a combination. Before replacing any belts, check to see which type of belt(s) your vehicle requires.

The following should be observed when belt tension adjustment and/or replacement is necessary:

• Due to the tight working space in the engine compartment, it may be necessary to disconnect some spark plug wires when adjusting or replacing drive belts. If a spark plug wire is disconnected it is necessary to coat the terminal of the lead with silicone grease (Part number D7AZ19A331A or the equivalent) before it is attached.

• On vehicles equipped with both power steering and air pumps, the belt tension on the air pump cannot be adjusted until the power steering belt has been adjusted or replaced.

### V–Belt & Cogged V–Belt

▶ **See Figures 52, 53, 54, 55, 56 and 57**

One method of cogged and V–belt adjustment requires the use of a tension gauge. Since most people do not have the necessary gauge, a deflection method of adjustment can be used instead. Locate a midway point on the belt between two pulleys. Push down on the belt with one finger and measure the deflection. For belts with a distance of 12 in. (305mm) or less between the pulleys, $1/8$–$1/4$ in. (3–6mm) is a desirable deflection measurement. For belts with a distance greater than 12 in. (305mm) between the pulleys, $1/8$–$3/8$ in. (3–9mm) is an acceptable measurement. Keep in mind that too tight an adjustment will quickly wear the accessories bearings, while too loose and adjustment may cause a whipping action and subsequent accessory damage as well.

On some gasoline 2.3L engines using a cogged belt, a 4–inch C–clamp can be used to help adjust the alternator belt. Place the bottom jaw of the C–clamp under the alternator adjustment boss and the upper jaw in the notch at the top of the alternator bracket. By screwing in the C–clamp the belt tension is changed.

To adjust the deflection of other cogged or V–belts, proceed as follows:

1. Loosen the accessory adjustment and pivot bolts.
2. If equipped with a slider idler pulley, loosen the adjusting bolt.
3. Carefully pry against the accessory, using a suitable prytool, in order to gain the proper belt tension. Idler pulleys are adjusted using the nut located just beneath the pulley itself. To tighten the belt, turn the nut to the right, to loosen, turn nut to the left.
4. Tighten the accessory or idler pulley adjustment bolts. Release any pressure on the prybar. Tighten all pivot bolts.
5. Check the belt tension and reset, if necessary.

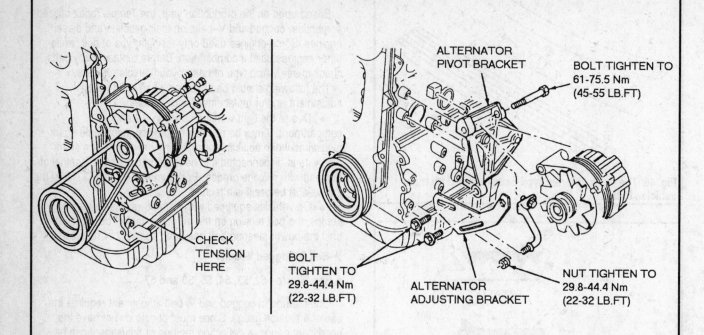

ALTERNATOR PIVOT BRACKET

BOLT TIGHTEN TO 61-75.5 Nm (45-55 LB.FT)

CHECK TENSION HERE

BOLT TIGHTEN TO 29.8-44.4 Nm (22-32 LB.FT)

ALTERNATOR ADJUSTING BRACKET

NUT TIGHTEN TO 29.8-44.4 Nm (22-32 LB.FT)

86701027

Fig. 52 Belt tension adjustment—alternator only—2.0L engines

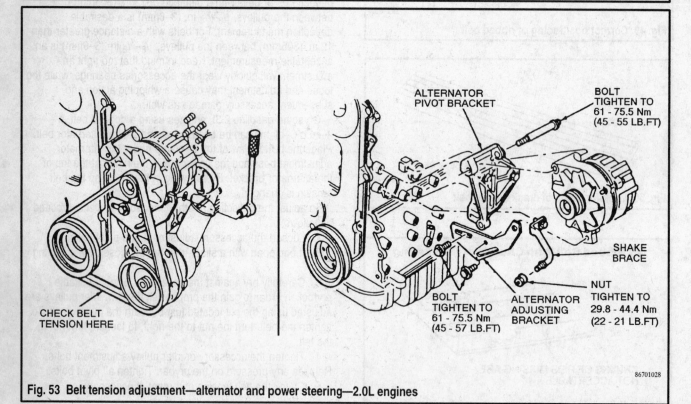

ALTERNATOR PIVOT BRACKET

BOLT TIGHTEN TO 61 - 75.5 Nm (45 - 55 LB.FT)

SHAKE BRACE

CHECK BELT TENSION HERE

BOLT TIGHTEN TO 61 - 75.5 Nm (45 - 57 LB.FT)

ALTERNATOR ADJUSTING BRACKET

NUT TIGHTEN TO 29.8 - 44.4 Nm (22 - 21 LB.FT)

86701028

Fig. 53 Belt tension adjustment—alternator and power steering—2.0L engines

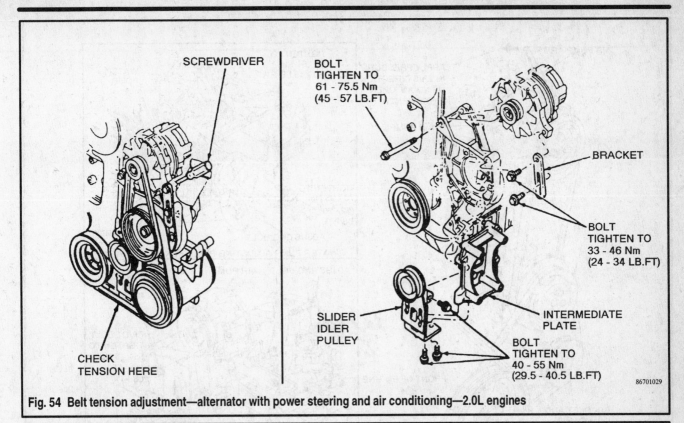

Fig. 54 Belt tension adjustment—alternator with power steering and air conditioning—2.0L engines

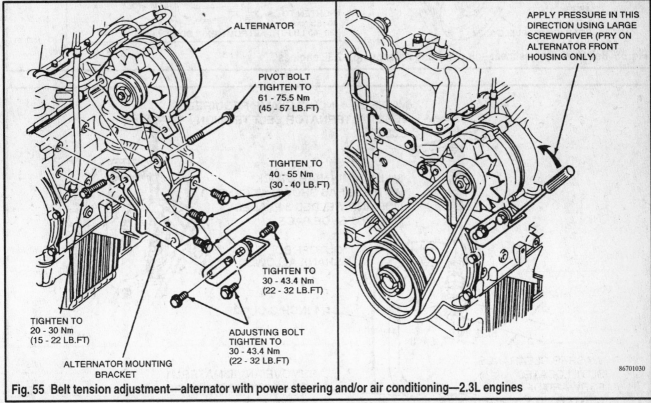

Fig. 55 Belt tension adjustment—alternator with power steering and/or air conditioning—2.3L engines

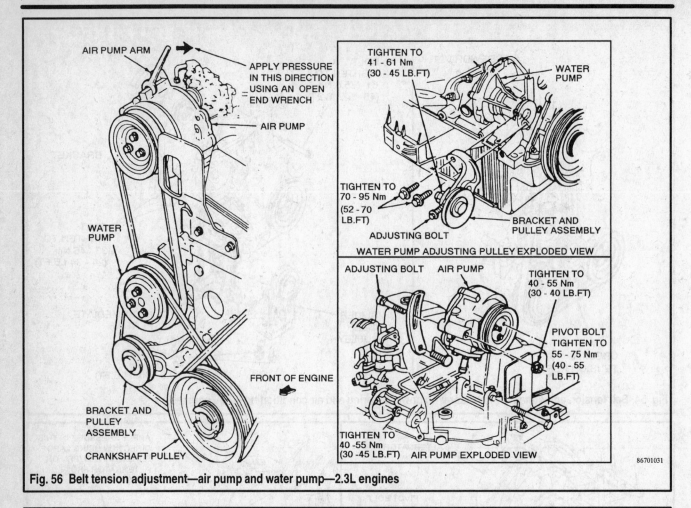

Fig. 56 Belt tension adjustment—air pump and water pump—2.3L engines

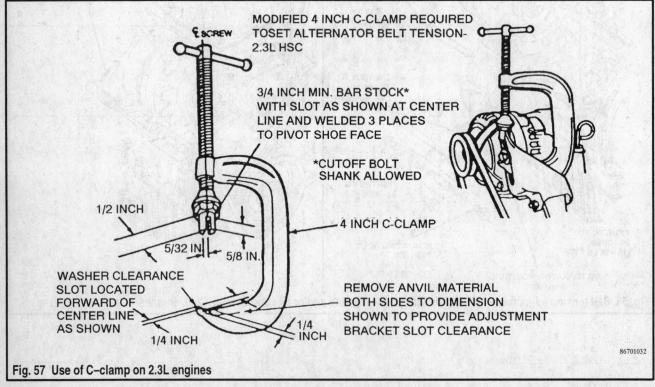

Fig. 57 Use of C—clamp on 2.3L engines

### Ribbed Serpentine Belt

▶ **See Figures 58, 59 and 60**

Belt tension on engines using ribbed or serpentine belts is maintained by an automatic tensioner and does not require adjustment. Movement of the automatic tensioner pulley is not a sign of a malfunctioning tensioner. The movement is required to maintain a constant belt tension with cyclical engine and accessory loads.

When re–tensioning a loose serpentine belt, it is important that the belt not be allowed to relax and unseat from the drive and accessory pulleys.

## REMOVAL & INSTALLATION

Depending on the engine and types of accessories installed, certain belts may require removal for access to other belts. When removing belts of different lengths, either tag the belt, or remember the order and location of the belts. Many vehicles come with a diagram in the engine compartment which covers belt routing, in the event the order is forgotten.

### V–Belt & Cogged V–Belt

1. Loosen adjustment and pivot bolts.
2. Remove the belt by pivoting the particular accessory (alternator, power steering pump, air box, etc.) to decrease belt tension. Slide the belt off the pulley and remove it from the engine.
3. Inspect the belt for wear or damage. If the belt is torn, check pulley for any sharp edges, and determine if edge can be filed or the pulley must be replaced.

### To install:

4. Determine correct belt for respective unit.
5. Install the new bolt on the drive unit and either move the unit toward or away from the engine to create tension on the belt.
6. Snug the mounting and/or adjusting bolt to hold the driven unit secure, but do not completely tighten.
7. Use the above procedure checking the deflection of the belt.
8. Start car and check for loose or noisy belts. Readjust if necessary.

### Ribbed Serpentine Belt

Depending on the year, type of engine and level of accessories installed on the engine, certain vehicles utilize either V–belts and or cogged V–belts in addition to ribbed belts. As a result, one or more of these belts move have to be removed to enable you to remove the ribbed belt.

The use of an 18 in. (457mm) or longer $^3/_8$ in. drive socket extension will be needed to remove and install a ribbed belt.

1. Determine whether the engine utilizes multiple belts, and remove those belts needed to expose the ribbed belt.
2. Insert the $^3/_8$ in. extension into the belt tensioner, and push away to relieve tension on the belt. Remove the belt from the tensioner.

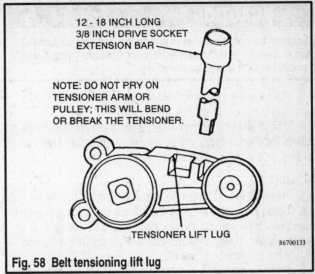

Fig. 58 Belt tensioning lift lug

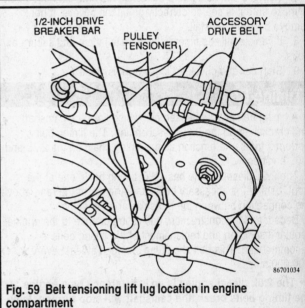

Fig. 59 Belt tensioning lift lug location in engine compartment

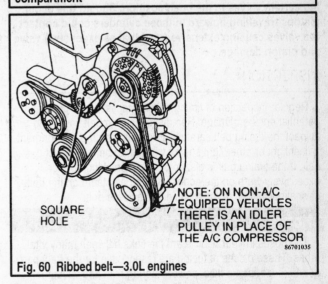

Fig. 60 Ribbed belt—3.0L engines

## ✻✻CAUTION

Because the belt tensioner is spring loaded, use extreme care in moving it. If the extension is not securely positioned, it could break free and cause injury.

3. Remove the extension from the belt tensioner. Finish removing the ribbed belt from the engine.

4. Check all belts for torn areas. If tears are present, inspect pulleys for sharp edges, and determine whether the edge can be filed, or the pulley must be replaced.

**To Install:**

5. Reinstall ribbed belt on to all pulleys except belt tensioner.

6. Using the extension, insert it into the belt tensioner and push away from you. Carefully install the ribbed belt on the tensioner, and slowly allow the extension to move toward you as tension is placed on the belt.

7. Remove extension from belt tensioner. Inspect ribbed belt to make sure it is seated correctly on all the pulleys. If not, remove belt and reinstall.

8. If vehicle utilizes other belts, reinstall them and secure all bolts.

9. Start car and check for loose or noisy belts.

## Timing Belt

A timing belt is a rubberized belt which links the camshaft and crankshaft on the 2.0L diesel engine. The timing belt performs the same function as the timing chain on the 2.3L and 3.0L engines.

The 2.0L diesel engine has TWO timing belts, one at the front, behind the accessory belts, and another at the rear, above the connection between the transaxle and the engine.

Because of its construction, and its importance to the engine, regular inspection and replacement of the timing belts is recommended. This belt should be changed at least every 100,000 miles.

➡ **The 2.0L diesel engine is an interference type engine. If the timing belts break, the camshaft will stop turning, leaving certain valves in the open position. Should this occur, pistons travelling upward in those cylinders could contact the valves causing extensive (read that as expensive) valve and piston damage.**

### INSPECTION

Regular inspection of timing belts is necessary to prevent potential engine damage. Remove the timing belt cover and inspect the timing belt carefully. Depending on the environment, a flashlight or other light source will help to better inspect the belt. If the timing belt is glazed or shiny, cracking, torn or excessively worn on the edges, missing any teeth on the belt, or soaked with oil or other liquid, replace the belt.

## Hoses

The hoses in your vehicle are the links between many vital areas. These pieces of tubing are responsible for the transport of antifreeze, brake fluid, power steering fluid and vacuum pressure, just to name a few. Because of their importance, and the environment with which they exist, routine inspection is recommended.

### INSPECTION

## ✻✻CAUTION

Do not inspect hose while vehicle is running or engine is hot. Injury may result.

Because the materials used to construct hosing are as numerous as the length and width of the automotive hoses available, the potential lifespan of a hose varies greatly. Also, temperature and degree of pressure effect hose life.

Inspection of hosing is as simple as a squeeze. Plastic hose, like that used in vacuum systems, should be hard but not brittle. Breather hose should be soft, but not cracked. At no time, should a hose be damp, as if fluid was soaking through. If there is a question about the condition of a hose, be safe, and replace it.

When inspecting your hoses, take the time to also check the connectors (elbow, right angle, T-fitting, etc.) between many of these hoses. They are as important as the hose, and are effected by many of the same elements as hosing.

## Cooling System Hoses

## ✻✻CAUTION

When working on or around the cooling system or the front of the vehicle, be aware that the cooling fan motor can automatically turn ON. The cooling fan motor is controlled by a temperature switch and may come ON while the engine is OFF. It will continue to run until the correct temperature is reached. Before working on or around the fan, disconnect the negative battery cable or the fan wiring harness.

◆ **See Figures 61, 62 and 63**

The cooling hoses used in your vehicle are subjected to both high and low temperatures as well as changes in pressure. For this reason, it is important to check the condition of cooling hoses regularly, and replace those that appear to be weakening.

86701313

**Fig. 61 Remove the radiator cap**

Fig. 62 Loosen draincock to allow coolant to drain out

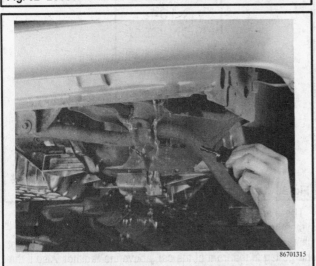

Fig. 63 Allow coolant to drain completely before reinstalling the draincock

### ✳✳CAUTION

Under no circumstances should you check or repair any cooling system hose while the car is running or after prolonged periods of use. Not only is the cooling system under pressure at this time, but the hoses will be hot. The potential for injury is high. Always allow the engine to cool before servicing these hoses.

### INSPECTION

Whenever the hoses are being checked, make sure there is adequate enough light to see all the hoses. This includes upper and lower hoses. Visually inspect each hose for signs of swelling, cracks or frayed ends due to weak clamps. If the engine is sufficiently cool, put your hand around each hose and squeeze. The hose should be firm. In the event the hose is soft, swollen, cracked of frayed, replace that length of hose.

### REMOVAL & INSTALLATION

→ **Make sure the engine is cool, and any system pressure has been reduced.**

1. Remove radiator cap, to relieve any pressure.
2. Open the hood and cover the fenders to protect them from scratches.
3. Disconnect the negative (ground) cable at the battery.
4. Place a suitable drain pan under the cooling system hose that is to be replaced to catch any fluid that may come out. Always dispose of any waste fluid properly.
5. Loosen any clamps which are holding the hose in place.
6. Using a back and forth motion, slowly begin removing the hose. Take your time. Some hoses are harder to remove than others.

### ✳✳CAUTION

Cats and dogs are attracted to ethylene glycol antifreeze, and could drink any that is left uncovered or in puddles on the ground. This will prove fatal in sufficient quantity. Always drain the coolant into a sealable container. Coolant should be reused unless it is contaminated or several years old.

7. Remove the hose. Clean fittings or ends that the new hose will attach to. Check to make sure the new and old hose are alike.

**To Install:**

8. Moisten interior edges of new hose with antifreeze to help installation. Slowly insert hose over ends, working back and forth until secure.
9. Install clamps and tighten. Add antifreeze to radiator. Leave cap off.
10. Install Negative battery cable.
11. Start engine, allow to run for 10 to 15 minutes. If antifreeze level falls, add more fluid. Once level has stabilized, install cap. Check for leaks.

## Constant Velocity (CV) Joint Boots

Because these vehicles are either front wheel or all wheel drive equipped, they vehicles do not utilize a solid axle system to drive the wheels. Instead, a shafts with flexible joints at both ends are incorporated into the vehicle. These flexible joints are called Constant Velocity (CV) joints. The advantage of this system is that steerability and independent suspension travel are maintained, while power is being delivered to the wheel.

### INSPECTION

♦ **See Figures 64 and 65**

There is no regular maintenance service to be performed on a CV–joint. But regular inspection of the rubber boot and clamps surrounding the CV–joint is recommended. Verify that the boots have no cracks, tears or splits. Also look for signs of grease on the inside of the wheel, or around the engine, this is a sure indication of a torn CV–boot. In the event a boot is torn, repair it, or have it repaired as soon as possible. If a CV–joint is not serviced quickly, the grease will leak out, dry and ruin the joint.

The grease used in CV–joints is a Moly type grease designed to withstand the high temperatures that are created within the joint. This grease does not need replacing, unless the boot is torn and the grease is contaminated with dust, water and dirt.

TCCS1010

**Fig. 64 An example of a CV–boot in good condition**

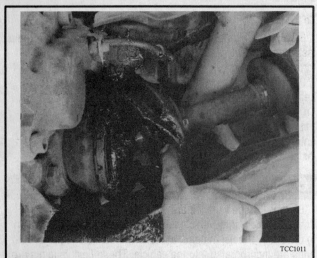

TCC1011

**Fig. 65 An example of a torn CV–boot in need of replacement**

## Air Conditioning System

➡ **Many 1994 Tempo/Topaz covered by this manual are equipped with the new refrigerant (R–134a) to which the automotive industry is slowly changing over to prevent R–12 ozone damage. This new refrigerant is not available to the public in most areas and it is usually illegal to service a vehicle with this refrigerant (or R–12) unless certified. If you have a 1994 Tempo/Topaz, it is important to determine which A/C system the vehicle utilizes, and if it has R–134a the vehicle should be taken to a qualified technician for all A/C system service.**

## IDENTIFYING TYPE OF AIR CONDITIONING SYSTEM

◆ **See Figures 66 and 67**

Until model year 1994, all Tempo/Topaz vehicles used R–12 in their A/C systems. Starting in 1994, Ford began offering some vehicles with R–134a instead of R–12. Because in this year there are cars that use R–12 as well as R–134a, and because these two refrigerants and their respective components are not interchangeable, it is very important to identify which type of system is in your car.

```
R-134a
NON-CFC

R-134a
NON-CFC

R-134a
NON-CFC

R-134a
NON-CFC
```

86701036

**Fig. 66 An example of an R–134a refrigerant tag**

There are several different ways to tell which type of A/C system is installed in your car. The fist way is to look for the stickers in the engine compartment. There is an A/C refrigerant charge tag in the front of the car, above the radiator. Also if the car uses R–134a, there will be gold stickers placed along the various A/C lines. Several will be around the compressor, there are some before the condenser, and there is one before the accumulator.

## SAFETY WARNINGS

### ✳✳WARNING

**R–12 refrigerant is a chlorofluorocarbon which, when released into the atmosphere, contributes to the depletion of the ozone layer. Consult the laws in your area before servicing the air conditioning system. In many states it is illegal to perform repairs involving refrigerant unless the work is done by a certified technician.**

➡ **Due to environmental concerns, when the A/C system is drained, the refrigerant must be collected using a refrigerant recovery/recycling equipments satisfying SAE J1990 and J2210 specifications. R–12 and R–134a must never be removed without the appropriate equipment.**

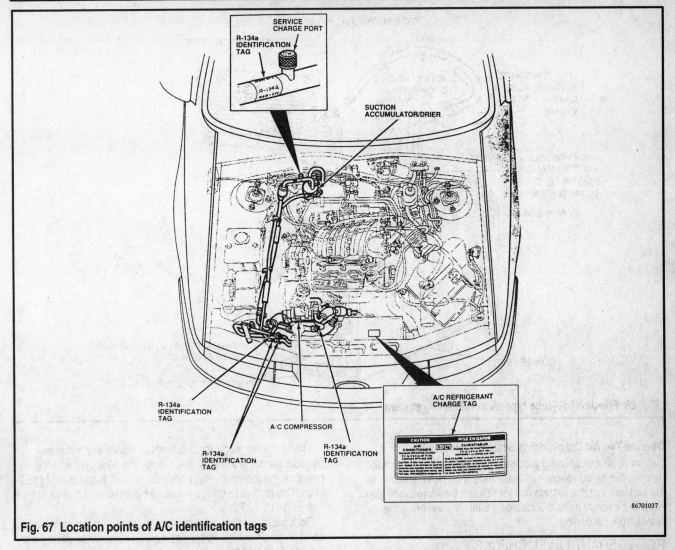

**Fig. 67 Location points of A/C identification tags**

86701037

• Do not smoke when servicing the refrigeration system of any car.

• Always wear safety goggles when servicing any part of the refrigerant system.

• Avoid inhaling the fumes from any leak detector.

• Keep service tools and work area clean.

Although R–12 and R–134a systems may appear similar in appearance, there are differences in design and function which require the use of different tools.

➡ **Do not use R–12 tools on R–134a A/C systems.**

## SYSTEM INSPECTION

▶ **See Figure 68**

Generally it is possibly to detect air conditioning system failures by a careful visual inspection. This includes check for broken belts, broken lines or hoses, obstructed condenser air passage or even disconnected wires.

### Checking For Oil Leaks

Refrigerant leaks show up as oily areas on the various components because the compressor oil is transported around the entire system along with the refrigerant. Look for only spots on all the hoses and lines, and especially on the hose and tubing connections. If there are oily deposits, the system may have a leak, and you should have it checked by a qualified technician.

➡ **A small area of oil on the front of the compressor is normal and no cause for alarm.**

### Keeping the Condenser Clear

Periodically inspect the front of the condenser for bent fins or foreign material (dirt, bugs, leaves, etc.). If any cooling fins are bent, straighten them carefully with needle nose pliers, or a condenser comb which is available at most auto parts stores. You can remove any debris with a stiff bristle brush or compressed air.

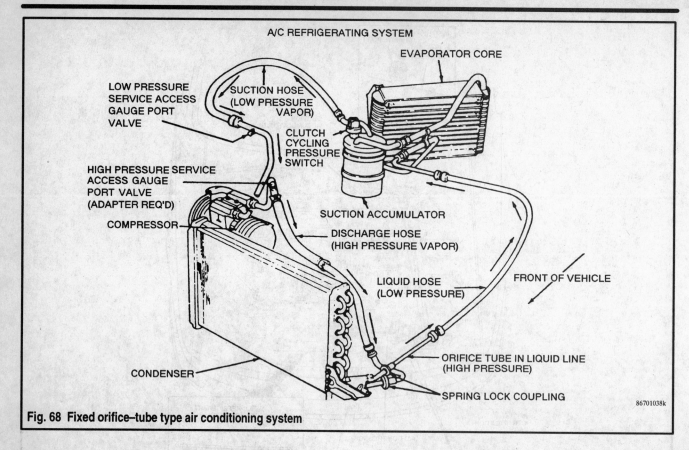

**Fig. 68 Fixed orifice–tube type air conditioning system**

### Operate The Air Conditioning System Periodically

A lot of air conditioning problems can be avoided by simply running the air conditioner at least once a week, regardless of the season. Let the system run for at least 5 minutes, and you'll keep the internal parts lubricated as well as preventing the hoses from hardening.

## REFRIGERANT LEVEL CHECKS

The only way to accurately check the refrigerant level is to measure the system evaporator pressures with a manifold gauge set, although rapid on/off cycling of the compressor clutch usually indicates that the air conditioning system is low on refrigerant. Have a qualified shop check the system pressures. The normal refrigerant capacity for 1984–87 is 40–42 oz., for 1988–93 models is 35–37 oz. and 1994 models the capacity is 31–33 oz.

In most engine compartments, there is a sticker which details the capacity of the A/C system. This sticker now also indicates whether the A/C system uses R–12 or R–134a type refrigerant.

## GAUGE SETS

◗ **See Figures 69 and 70**

➡ **Do not use gauge sets as a means for discharging the A/C system**

Most of the service work performed in air conditioning requires the use of a set of 2 gauges, one for the high (Head) pressure side of the system, the other for the low (Suction) side.

The low side gauge records both pressure and vacuum. Vacuum readings are calibrated from 0 to 30 in. Hg and the pressure graduations read from 0 to no less than 60 psi (413.7 kPa). The high side gauge measures pressure from 0 to at least 600 psi (413.7 kPa).

Both gauges are threaded into a manifold that contains two hand shut–off valves. Proper manipulation of these valves and the use of the attached test hoses allow the user to perform the following services:

1. Test high and low side pressures.
2. Remove air, moisture and contaminated refrigerant.
3. Purge the system (of refrigerant).
4. Charge the system.

The manifold valves are designed so that they have no direct effect on the gauge readings, but serve only to provide for, or cut off, flow of refrigerant through the manifold. During all testing and hook–up operations, the valves are kept in a close position to avoid disturbing the refrigerant system. The valves are opened only to purge the system of refrigerant or to change it.

### Connecting the Manifold Gauge Set

➡ **Many states require any type of A/C work be done only by certified technicians. Heavy penalties are attached to those who do not follow the law.**

The following procedure is for the connection of a manifold gauge set to the service gauge port valves. If charge station type equipment is used, consult the equipment manufacturer's instructions.

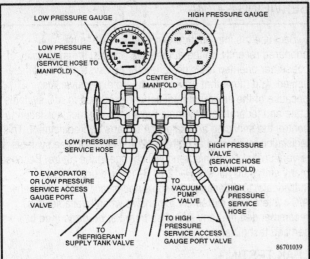

Fig. 69 An example of an air conditioning manifold gauge set

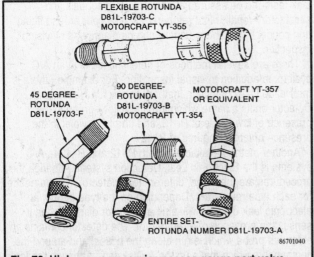

Fig. 70 High pressure service access gauge port valve adapters

The high and low service gauge ports for a 2.0L engine are located in the refrigerant lines near the compressor. An adaptor (YT–354 or equivalent) is required on the high service gauge port. For the 2.3L and 3.0L engines, the low service port is located near the accumulator, the high service port is located close to the compressor. An adaptor (YT–354 or equivalent) is required on the high service port.

1. Make sure both the valves on the gauge are turned to their closed position.

2. Remove the valve caps (if present) from the high and low service ports. Install the adaptor on the high service port. If the manifold gauge hoses do not have valve pins, adaptors T71P–19703–S and R or equivalent must be installed on to the hoses.

3. Connect the high and low pressure hose to their respective ports, making sure each is installed correctly, and seated secure. By turning the valve on each gauge, an associated high or low reading will be given.

4. Before removing the gauges, make sure each valve is closed. Slowly unscrew the fitting, and replace the valve caps. If

there are no valve caps, consider purchasing them at an automotive parts store.

## DISCHARGING THE SYSTEM

### ❄❄CAUTION

Perform in well ventilated area. The compressed refrigerant used in the air conditioning system expands and evaporates into the atmosphere at a temperature of –21.7°F (–29.8°C) or less. This will freeze any surface (including your eyes) that it contacts. In addition, the refrigerant decomposes into a poisonous gas in the presence of flame.

➡ An approved R–12 recovery/recycling machine that meets SAE standards should be employed when discharging the A/C system.

1. Operate the A/C system for at least 10 minutes.

2. Attach the charging hoses, checking for proper connections and sealing. Shut off the A/C system and engine.

3. Connect the center hose of the gauge to the approved recovery/recycling machine.

4. Open the low side valve slightly. Open the high side valve slightly.

➡ Too rapid a purging process will be identified by the appearance of an oily foam. If this occurs, close both hand valves a small amount until the condition stops.

5. Close both valves when the pressures read 0, and all the refrigerant has left the system.

➡ The A/C system should always be discharged before removing any hoses or components of the A/C system.

The discharging of an R–134a A/C system is similar to an R–12 system, with the exception that the equipment required for the job must be designed exclusively for R–134a A/C systems. Many states prohibit the servicing of any A/C systems without proper certification.

➡ R–12 and R–134a tools are not interchangeable.

## EVACUATING THE SYSTEM

1. Attach the charging hoses, checking for proper connections and sealing. Ensure that all refrigerant has been discharged from the system.

2. When all the pressure has been released from the system, connect the center charging hose to a vacuum pump.

3. Close both valves on the gauge, if already not done. Start the vacuum pump.

4. With the vacuum pump running, open the low pressure valve until fully open.

5. Continue to evacuate the system with the vacuum pump until the low pressure gauge reads between 29.4–30.0 in Hg (99.4–101.1 kPa). Continue to run vacuum pump for additionally 30 minutes after desired low pressure reading is reached.

6. Turn manifold gauges fully off, then turn off vacuum pump off. observe low pressure gauge for five minutes to be sure there is no change in pressure level. If there is a change,

perform a leak test. If there is no change, the A/C system can be charged.

➡ **R–12 and R–134a tools are not interchangeable.**

The procedures for evacuating an R–134a type A/C system are similar to an R–12 system, except that the tools required to do the work must be designed for an R–134a A/C system. Many states prohibit the servicing of A/C systems without proper certification.

## CHARGING

### ✳✳CAUTION

**Refrigerant decomposes into a poisonous gas in the presence of a flame. Do not smoke while performing A/C service.**

The refrigerant charge level of the air conditioning system is critical to optimum performance. An under–charged or over–charged system will adversely affect A/C performance. To determine the correct amount of refrigerant, consult the A/C refrigerant label in the engine compartment.

The following procedure for charging an A/C system uses an A/C recovery/recycling machine. Because many of these machines are different, consult the manufacturers literature for details.

➡ **In many states, only certified technicians can service or charge A/C systems.**

1. Determine the correct amount of refrigerant needed in your A/C system.

2. Connect respective low and high pressure hoses from the station to the vehicle's A/C system. Depending on the station being used, an adaptor may be needed on the high pressure valve from the car. Check for correct hook–up and secure fit.

3. Disconnect the wire harness from the clutch cycling pressure switch and install a jumper wire across the 2 terminals.

4. Slowly at first, open the low side valve on the station to add refrigerant. Make sure there are no leaks.

5. Watch the gauges on the station, until no more refrigerant is drawn into the A/C system. start the car, insert a temperature probe into one of the vents, and turn the A/C system ON. Position the blower on HIGH.

6. Continue to add refrigerant until the desired vehicle refrigerant weight is reached. Close the valves at the station, and slowly remove. There may be a slight loose of refrigerant as the lines are removed. Reinstall protective caps on the high and low side valves. If originally missing, purchase some at an automotive parts store. Reconnect the wire harness to the clutch cycling pressure switch.

7. Continue to operate the A/C system, checking the temperature probe to make sure that the interior is truly cooling down.

The procedure for charging an A/C system with R–134a is similar, with the exception that R–134a requires a different set of tools and equipment. Many states require proper certification when working with R–134a.

## SERVICING R–134A

Because the introduction and use of R–134a has only appeared recently on the automotive market, the availability of consumer oriented tools designed for this system is extremely limited, and those that are available are expensive. Also because of the environmental concerns related to A/C systems, state and federal governments have impose strict legislation to control the servicing and sale of A/C parts and equipment. This legislation is directed at both R–12 and R–134a type systems. It is very unlikely that this trend will change in the future. Because many states do not sell R–12 or R–134a to uncertified individuals, and because the tools necessary to service many A/C systems are extremely expensive when available, it is recommended that any A/C system repair be performed by certified technicians.

## LEAK TESTING

Any A/C system that has lost its refrigerant charge should be leak tested to be assured of an accurate diagnosis and satisfactory repair. Most refrigerant leaks occur around fitting and connections. These usually can be diagnosed by visual inspection.

There are several methods of detecting leaks in an A/C system, in addition to visual inspection. For example , there is the Halide Leak Detection method, in which a Halide Leak Detector emits a flame which turns a yellow–green in the presence of low levels of R–12, and purple or violet in the presence of large amounts of R–12.

Another method available to both R–12 and R–134a A/C systems is the Electronic Leak Detection system. Although the procedures are the same, different leak detectors will be needed for each type refrigerant. Depending on the type of unit, an electronic leak detector will emit a sound or display when it senses the presence of a refrigerant. The detector contains an extended probe which is run along the hoses, and around the components which make up the A/C system. Although the tools are relatively expensive, they are simple and legal to use, and could save you money in A/C service charges.

## Windshield Wiper Blades

◆ **See Figure 71**

At least twice a year, check the windshield washer spray and wiper operation. Check and replace worn wiper blades. Worn blades can contribute to poor frontal vision, by not adequately removing rain or snow from the front windshield. This in turn could increase your chances of having an accident. In areas where winter are harsh, consider changing to winter wiper blades during this season. These blades remove ice and snow better, while their rubber coated frame will not freeze to the windshield as easily as regular wiper blades do.

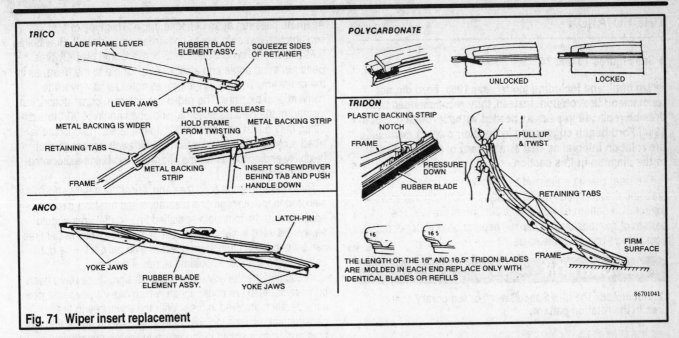

**Fig. 71 Wiper insert replacement**

## REMOVAL & INSTALLATION

1. Turn the ignition switch to ON position.

2. Turn the wiper control ON. Cycle the wiper arm assembly, then turn the ignition switch OFF when the wiper arm assembly is at a position on the windshield where removal can be accomplished without difficulty.

3. To remove the blade: Pull the wiper arm up and away from the windshield. Grasp the wiper blade assembly and pull away from the mounting pin of the wiper arm. Or pull back on the spring lock, where the arm is connected to the blade, and pull the wiper blade assembly from the wiper arm.

4. Inspect the wiper arm to make sure the plastic or metal wiper frame is secure. Check the tabs which hold the blade insert tight, and make sure they are in good condition.

5. Install the new wiper blade using the hardware provided with the product, or depending on the type system used, push the new blade on the wiper arm, or push the spring lock and install to wiper arm. Make sure the new blades are secure.

6. Check the operation of the wipers.

## Tires and Wheels

♦ See Figure 72

The tires and wheels are an important part of any vehicle, because not only do they allow the power from the engine to be transmitted to the road, they also provide for a smooth ride, stable handling, and traction in harsh weather. It is a good practice to perform regular wheel and tire inspection, as follows:

- Check your tires whenever you stop for fuel. Look for under-inflated or unusually worn tires.

- At least once a month check all tire pressure. Check the tire pressure when the tires are cool, not after a long drive.

- At regular interval, check the wheel lugs, and also check the pressure in the spare tire.

All tires today are equipped with built-in tread wear indicator bars that show up as $1/2$ in. (12.7mm) wide smooth bands

across the tire when $1/16$ in. (1.5mm) of tread remains. The appearance of tread wear indicators means that the tires should be replaced. In fact, many states have laws prohibiting the use of tires with less than $1/16$ in. (1.5mm) of tread remaining.

You can check you own tread depth with an inexpensive tire depth gauge, or by using a Lincoln head penny. Push the base of the gauge down between two treads. Remove the gauge, and read the number at the top of the gauge. Most gauges record the measurement in both $1/16$ in. (1.5mm) as well as $1/32$ in. (0.80mm) increments. If the tire has less than $1/16$ in. (1.5mm), the tire should be replaced.

To check tire depth using a penny, slip the penny into several tread grooves. If you can see the top of Lincoln's head in 2 adjacent grooves, the tires have less than $1/16$ in. (1.5mm) tread left and should be replaced. You can measure snow tires in the same manner by using the tails side of the Lincoln penny. If you see the top of the Lincoln memorial, it's time to replace the snow tires.

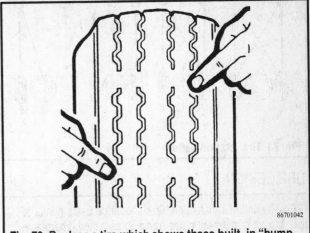

**Fig. 72 Replace a tire which shows these built-in "bump strips"**

## TIRE ROTATION

◆ **See Figures 73 and 74**

➡ **Up until, and including model year 1983, Ford did not recommend tire rotation. Instead, they recommended that tires be replaced in pairs as needed without rotation. But in 1984, Ford began suggesting in the their owners manuals a tire rotation interval as well as a pattern of rotation similar to the diagram in this section.**

Tire wear can be equalized by switching the position of the tires about every 6,000 miles. Including a conventional spare in the rotation pattern can give up to 20% more tire life. The pattern of tire rotation you use will depend on whether or not your vehicle has a usable spare.

### ✳✳CAUTION

**Do not include the new SpaceSaver® or temporary spare tires in the rotation pattern.**

There are certain exceptions when rotating tires. These should be kept in mind when determining rotation patterns. For example, studded snow tires should never be rotated. This is because studded snow tires can ruin front wheel bearings if moved to the front of the car, as well as the studs potentially coming loose if the rotational direction is changed. Special attention should also be paid in rotating tires which are directional. Because these tires are designed to function only in one direction, particular attention must be paid to make sure the rotational direction is correctly maintained.

Because of the advances in tire technology, and especially radial tire technology, the belief that radial tires should not be cross–rotated no longer holds true.

➡ **Whenever tires are removed from the car, mark them, so you can maintain the same direction of rotation.**

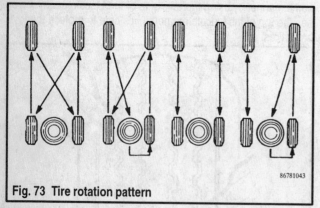

86781043

**Fig. 73 Tire rotation pattern**

## TIRE DESIGN

For maximum satisfaction, tires should be used in sets of five. Mixing of different types (radial, bias/belted, fiberglass belted) should be avoided. Conventional bias tires are constructed so that the cords run bead–to–bead at an angle.

Alternate plies run at an opposite angle. This type of construction gives rigidity to both tread and sidewall. Bias/belted tires are similar in construction to conventional bias ply tires. Belts run at an angle and also at a 90° angle to the bead, as in the radial tire. Tread life is improved considerably over the conventional bias tire. The radial tire differs in construction, but instead of the carcass plies running at an angle of 90° to each other, they run at an angle of 90° to the bead. This gives the tread a great deal of rigidity and the sidewall a great deal of flexibility and accounts for the characteristic bulge associated with radial tires.

Remember that the tire sizes and wheel diameters should be selected to maintain ground clearance and tire load capacity equivalent to the minimum specified tire. Radial tires should always be used in sets of five, but in an emergency radial tires can be used with caution on the rear axle only. If this is done, both tires on the rear should be of radial design.

In addition the the advances in tire design, there have been improvements in tire construction, which has introduced a new consideration involved in tires. With the advances in tire construction, all tires including snow, all season, truck and car tires are given a speed rating which indicates the maximum speed at which a vehicle can be driven with those tires in normal weather conditions. This speed rating is given in the form of a letter which can be found on the side wall of a tire. At no time should a car be able to out–perform the tires which it equipped with. What this means, for example, is that a race car should not have tires that are meant to be driven at a maximum of 35 mph, when in fact it is capable of going 80 mph. In this case, the tires are unsafe.

When buying new tires, here are some additional points to consider, especially if you are considering a switch to larger tires or a different profile series;

1. All 4 tires must be of the same construction type. This rule should not be violated, radial, bias and bias belted tires should not be mixed.

2. The wheels should be the correct width for the tire. Tire dealers have charts of tire and rim compatibility. A mismatch will cause sloppy handling and rapid tire wear. The tread width should match the rim width (inside bead to inside bead) within an inch. For radial tires, the rim should be 80% or less of the tire (not tread) width.

3. The height (mounted diameter) of the new tires can change the speedometer accuracy, engine speed at a given road speed, fuel mileage, acceleration and ground clearance. Tire manufacturers furnish full measurement specifications.

4. The spare tire should be usable, at least for short distance and low speed operations, with any new tires.

5. There should not be any body interference when loaded, on bumps or in turns.

## TIRE STORAGE

Store the tires at proper inflation pressures, never over–inflated. All tires should be kept in a cool, dry place. If they are stored in the garage or basement, do not let them stand on a concrete floor; set them horizontally on strips of wood.

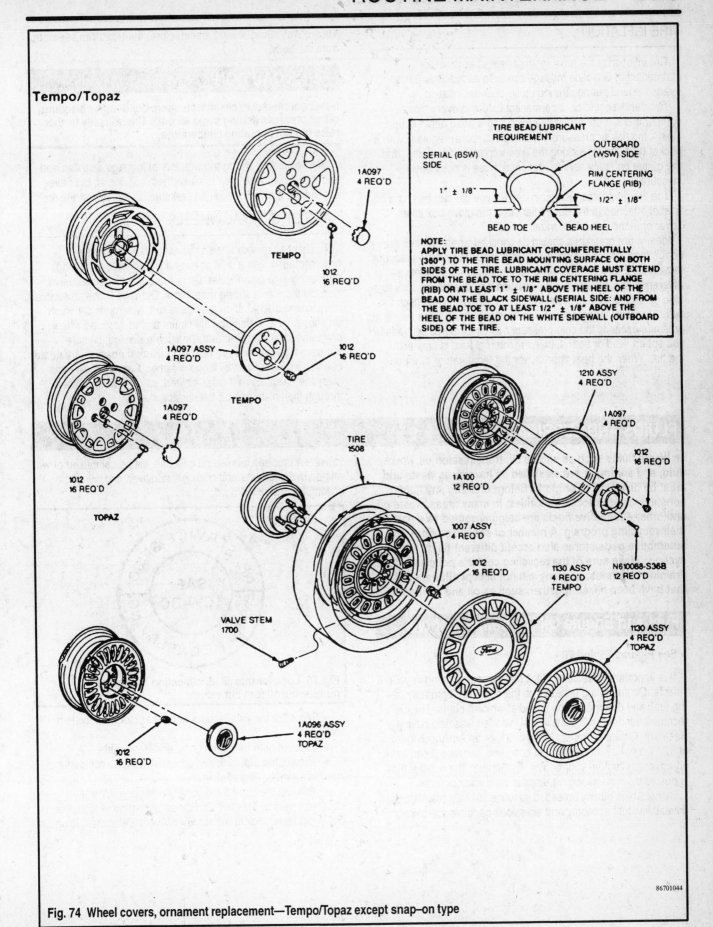

Tempo/Topaz

TIRE BEAD LUBRICANT REQUIREMENT

SERIAL (BSW) SIDE

OUTBOARD (WSW) SIDE

RIM CENTERING FLANGE (RIB)

1" ± 1/8"

1/2" ± 1/8"

BEAD TOE

BEAD HEEL

NOTE:
APPLY TIRE BEAD LUBRICANT CIRCUMFERENTIALLY (360°) TO THE TIRE BEAD MOUNTING SURFACE ON BOTH SIDES OF THE TIRE. LUBRICANT COVERAGE MUST EXTEND FROM THE BEAD TOE TO THE RIM CENTERING FLANGE (RIB) OR AT LEAST 1" ± 1/8" ABOVE THE HEEL OF THE BEAD ON THE BLACK SIDEWALL (SERIAL SIDE: AND FROM THE BEAD TOE TO AT LEAST 1/2" ± 1/8" ABOVE THE HEEL OF THE BEAD ON THE WHITE SIDEWALL (OUTBOARD SIDE) OF THE TIRE.

1A097
4 REQ'D

TEMPO

1012
16 REQ'D

1A097 ASSY
4 REQ'D

1012
16 REQ'D

TEMPO

1A097
4 REQ'D

1012
16 REQ'D

TOPAZ

1210 ASSY
4 REQ'D

1A097
4 REQ'D

1012
16 REQ'D

TIRE
1508

1A100
12 REQ'D

1007 ASSY
4 REQ'D

1012
16 REQ'D

1130 ASSY
4 REQ'D
TEMPO

N610068-S36B
12 REQ'D

VALVE STEM
1700

1130 ASSY
4 REQ'D
TOPAZ

1A096 ASSY
4 REQ'D
TOPAZ

1012
16 REQ'D

Ford

Fig. 74  Wheel covers, ornament replacement—Tempo/Topaz except snap–on type

86701044

## TIRE INFLATION

Tire inflation is the most ignored item of automotive maintenance. Gasoline mileage can drop as much as 0.8% for every 1 pound per square inch (psi) of under inflation.

Two items should be a permanent fixture in every glove compartment: a tire pressure gauge and a tread depth gauge. Check the tire air pressure (including the spare) regularly with a pocket type gauge. Kicking the tires won't tell you a thing, and the gauge on many service station air hose is notoriously inaccurate.

The tire pressures recommended for you car can be found on a label attached to the door pillar or on the glove box inner cover or in the owner's manual.

Ideally, tire pressures should be checked when the tires are cool. When the air becomes heated it expands and the pressure increases. Every 10° rise (or drop) in temperature means a difference of 1 psi, which also explains why the tire appears to lose air on a very cold night. When it is impossible to check the ties cold, allow for pressure build–up due to heat. If the hot pressure exceeds the cold pressure by more than 15 psi, reduce you speed, lead or both. Otherwise internal heat is created in the tire. When the heat approaches the temperature at which the tire was cured, during manufacture, the tread can separate from the body.

### ✳✳CAUTION

**Never counteract excessive pressure build–up by bleeding off air pressure (letting some air out). This will only further raise the tire operating temperature.**

Before starting a long trip with lots of luggage, you can add about 2–4 psi to the tires to make them run cooler, but never exceed the maximum inflation pressure on the side of the tire.

## CARE OF SPECIAL WHEELS

To clean aluminum wheels, wheel covers and wheel ornamentation, use a mild soap and water solution, rinsing thoroughly with clean water. Do not use steel wool, abrasive type cleaners or a strong detergents. Damage to the protective coating and discoloration may be result. Automatic car wash brushes may also damage aluminum and styled road wheel protective coatings. Before using such a service, be sure abrasive type brushes are not being used. If possible, try not to use these type wheels in winter weather. Road salt will eat away the finish. Even if clear–coated, salt will work its way through the finish, and pit the surface.

## FLUIDS AND LUBRICANTS

➡ **Waste fluids such as engine oil, transmission oil, brake fluid, and antifreeze are classified as hazardous waste and must be disposed of properly. Before draining any fluids, consult with your local authorities; in many areas, waste oil and other automotive fluids are being accepted as a part of their recycling program. A number of service stations and automotive parts stores also accept different fluids for re-cycling . Make sure of the recycling center's policies before draining any fluids, as many will not accept different fluids that have been mixed together, such as oil and antifreeze.**

### Fuel and Engine Oil Recommendations

◆ **See Figures 75 and 76**

It is important to use fuel of the proper octane rating in your vehicle. Octane rating is based on the anti–knock property of the fuel, and determines the speed at which it burns. The fuel recommended for your vehicle is "Unleaded Gasoline having a Research Octane Number (RON) of 91, or an Antiknock Index of 87." Do not get these number confused, because it can have an adverse effect on your engine. Remember, the number that is posted on most gasoline pumps is the antiknock index.

Using a high quality unleaded gasoline will help maintain the driveability, fuel economy and emissions performance of your vehicle. A properly formulated gasoline will be comprised of well refined hydrocarbons and chemical additives and will accomplish the following.

**Fig. 75 Look for this oil identification label when purchasing oil for your vehicle**

• Minimize varnish, lacquer and other induction system deposits.

• Prevent gum formation or other deterioration.

• Protect the fuel tank and other fuel system components from corrosion or degradation.

• Provide the correct seasonally and geographically adjusted volatility. This will provide easy starting in the winter and avoid vapor lock in the summer. Avoid fuel system icing.

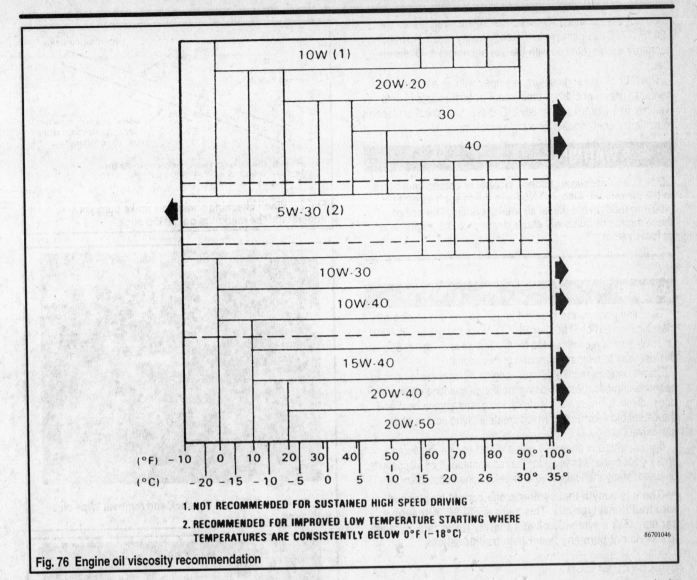

**Fig. 76 Engine oil viscosity recommendation**

In addition, the fuel will be free of water deposits and other impurities. Some driveability deterioration on multi–port electronically fuel injected vehicles can be traced to continuous use of certain gasoline which may have insufficient amounts of detergent additives to provide adequate deposit control protection. Many manufacturers recommend using two or three different blend gasoline at regular intervals.

## DIESEL ENGINE

Fuel makers produce two grades of diesel fuel, No. 1 and No. 2, for use in automotive diesel engines. Generally speaking, No. 2 fuel is recommended over No. 1 for driving in temperatures above 20°F (–7°C). In fact, in many areas, No. 2 diesel is the only fuel available. By comparison, No. 2 diesel fuel is less volatile than No. 1 fuel, and gives better fuel economy. No. 2 fuel is also a better injection pump lubricant.

Two important characteristics of diesel fuel are the cetane number, and the viscosity rate. The cetane number of a diesel fuel refers to the ease with which a diesel fuel ignites. High cetane numbers mean that the fuel will ignite with relative ease or that it ignites well at low temperatures. Naturally, the lower the cetane number, the higher the temperature must be to ignite the fuel. Most commercial fuels have cetane numbers that range from 35 to 65. No. 1 diesel fuel generally has a higher cetane rating than No. 2 fuel.

Viscosity is the ability of a liquid, in this case diesel fuel, to flow. Using straight No. 2 diesel fuel below 20°F (–7°C) can cause problems, because this fuel tends to become cloudy, meaning wax crystals begin to form in the fuel. 20°F (–7°C) is often called the cloud point for No. 2 fuel. In extremely cold weather, No. 2 fuel can stop flowing altogether. In either case, fuel flow is restricted, which can result in a poor starting conditions or poor engine performance. Fuel manufacturers often winterize No. 2 diesel fuel by using various fuel additives and blends (no. 1 diesel fuel, kerosene, etc.) to lower its winter time viscosity. Generally speaking, though, No. 1 diesel fuel is more satisfactory in extremely cold weather.

➡ **The 2.0L diesel engine in the Tempo/Topaz is designed to use number 2–D diesel fuel. Use of number 1–D diesel fuel in temperatures +20°F (–7°C) is acceptable, but not necessary.**

Do not use number 1–D diesel fuel in temperatures above +20°F (–7°C) as damage to the engine may result. Also fuel economy will be reduced with the use of number 1–D diesel fuel.

The 2.0L diesel engines are equipped with an electric fuel heater to prevent cold fuel problems. For best results in cold weather use winterized number 2–D diesel fuel which is blended to minimize cold weather operation problems.

## ✳✳WARNING

**DO NOT add gasoline, gasohol, alcohol or cetane improvers to the diesel fuel. Also, DO NOT use fluids such as ether (starting fluid) in the diesel air intake system. The use of these liquids or fluids will cause damage to the engine and/or fuel system.**

## Engine

Gasoline engines are required to use engine oil meeting API classification SH or SH/CC or SH/CD. Viscosity grades 5W–30 or 10W–30 are recommended for the Tempo and Topaz. See the viscosity to temperature chart in this section.

Diesel engines require different engine oil from those used in gasoline engines. Besides doing the things gasoline engine oil does, diesel oil must also deal with increased engine heat and the diesel blow–by gases, which create sulfuric acid, a high corrosive.

If your vehicle is equipped with a diesel engine, be sure to check your owner's manual for the recommended oil viscosity to be used. Many manuals have a diesel engine supplement.

➡ There is a myth that synthetic oils cannot be blended with traditional type oils. This myth is FALSE. Although a car may leak a synthetic oil at a slightly faster rate, synthetic oils do not burn any faster than traditional oils.

### OIL LEVEL CHECK

◆ **See Figures 77, 78 and 79**

It is a good idea to check the engine oil level every time you fill your gas tank.

1. Be sure your vehicle is on level surface. Shut off the engine and wait for at least 5 minutes to allow the oil to drain back into the oil pan.

2. Remove the engine oil dipstick and wipe with a clean rag.

3. Reinsert the dipstick and push it down until it is fully seated in the tube.

4. Remove and check the oil level indicated on the dipstick. If the oil level is below the lower mark, add one quart. Wait several minutes, and check level again. Add enough oil until level is at the top mark on the dip stick. Remember, add oil in small amounts. It is easy to add more oil, but much harder to take it away.

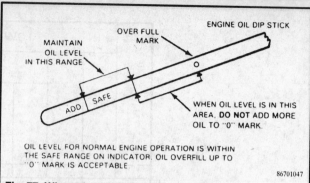

Fig. 77 When checking engine oil, make sure you understand the markings on the dip stick

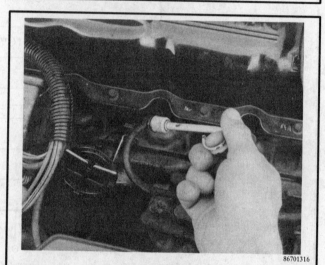

Fig. 78 Locate oil level dip stick and remove. Wipe clean with a rag

Fig. 79 Make sure the oil level is between the levels. Add oil if necessary

### OIL AND FILTER CHANGE

♦ **See Figures 80, 81, 82, 83 and 84**

The recommended engine oil and filter service interval on your vehicle is every 3 months or 3000 miles (whichever comes first). If the vehicle is operated in severe conditions, more frequent intervals may be required.

1. Make sure the engine is at normal operating temperature (this promotes complete draining of the old oil). Make sure engine is OFF.

**✳✳CAUTION**

The EPA warns that prolonged contact with used engine oil may cause a number of skin disorders, including cancer! You should make every effort to minimize your exposure to used engine oil. Protective gloves should be worn when changing the oil. Wash your hands and any other exposed skin areas as soon as possible. Soap and water, or waterless hand cleaner should be used.

2. Apply the parking brake and block the rear wheels. Raise and support the vehicle safely.

**✳✳CAUTION**

Use only jackstands or a lift, if available.

3. Place a suitable drain pan (approximately a gallon and a half capacity) under the engine oil pan drain plug. Using the proper size socket and rachet or wrench if necessary, loosen and remove the plug. Allow all the old oil to drain out. Wipe the pan and the drain plug with a clean rag. Inspect the drain plug gasket for signs of distorting, replace if necessary.

4. Reinstall drain plug by hand and tighten with a wrench. DO NOT OVERTIGHTEN.

5. Move the drain pan underneath the engine oil filter. Use a strap wrench or equivalent tool to loosen the oil filter (do not remove yet), allowing the oil to drain. Once drained, unscrew the filter completely by hand. Use a rag, if necessary, to keep from burning your fingers. When the filter comes loose from the engine, turn the mounting base upside down to avoid spilling the remaining oil.

6. Wipe the engine filter mount clean with a rag. Coat the rubber gasket on the new oil filter with clean engine oil, applying it with a finger. Carefully start the filter onto the threaded mount. Turn the filter until it touches the engine mounting surface. Tighten the filter, by hand, an additional 1/2 turn or as recommended by the filter manufacturer.

7. Lower the vehicle. Refill the crankcase with four quarts of engine oil. Replace the filler cap and start the engine. Allow the engine to idle, checking for any oil leaks. Shut off the engine, wait for at least five minutes, and check the oil level with the dipstick. Add oil if necessary.

➡ Store the used oil in a suitable container made for that purpose, until you can find a service station or garage that will accept the used oil for recycling.

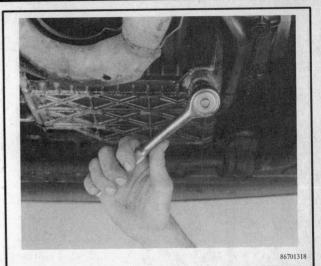

Fig. 80 With car properly supported, loosen oil pan nut

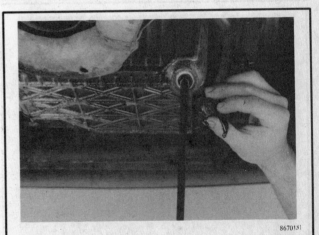

Fig. 81 Allow oil to drain into a pan. Dispose of oil properly

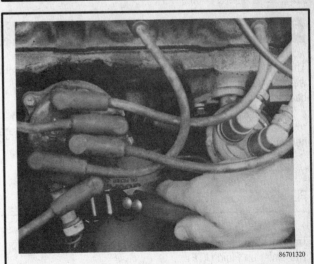

Fig. 82 With a filter strap, remove the oil filter from the engine

TCCS1901

**Fig. 83 Before installing a new oil filter, coat the rubber gasket with clean oil**

86701321

**Fig. 84 Adding engine oil**

## Manual Transaxle

The manual transaxle is a front wheel drive powertrain unit. The transmission and differential are housed in a two piece light weight aluminum alloy housing which is bolted directly to the back of the engine.

The transaxle is fully synchronized in all forward gears with reverse provided by a sliding gear. All gears, except reverse, are helical cut for quiet operation.

The manual transaxle and engine assembly are mounted transversely in the vehicle.

## FLUID RECOMMENDATIONS

- 1984–88 manual transaxles—Type F Automatic Transmission Fluid (ATF) or Motorcraft Dexron®II Automatic Transmission Fluid (ATF).
- 1989–94 manual transaxles—Type F Automatic Transmission Fluid (ATF) or MERCON® Automatic Transmission Fluid (ATF).

➡ In some areas, Dexron fluid may only be available in a type 3. There is little difference between type 2, and type 3 and each may be interchanged.

## FLUID LEVEL CHECK

◆ **See Figures 85 and 86**

Each time the engine oil is changed, the fluid level of the transaxle should be checked. The vehicle must be evenly supported on jackstands (front and back) or on a lift, if available. To check the fluid, make sure the engine is OFF, remove the filler plug, (round headed plug) located on the upper front (driver's side) of the transaxle with a $9/16$ in. wrench or a $3/8$ inch extension and rachet.

➡ The filler plug/bolt has a hex–head or it has a flat surface with a cut–in $3/8$ in. square box. Do not mistake any other bolts for the filler. Damage to the transaxle could occur if the wrong plug/bolt is removed.

86701322

**Fig. 85 With the vehicle properly supported locate the transaxle fill and check plug**

86701324

**Fig. 86 Loosening the plug/bolt**

The oil level should be even with the edge of the filler hole or within ¼ in. (6mm) of the hole. If the oil level is not as specified, add the recommended lubricant until the proper level is reached.

➡ A rubber bulb syringe, such as a turkey baster, will be helpful in adding the recommended lubricant.

## DRAIN AND REFILL

♦ See Figures 87 and 88

Changing the fluid in a manual transaxle is not necessary under normal operating conditions. However, the fluid levels should be checked at normal intervals. The only two ways to drain the oil from the transaxle is by removing it and then turning the transaxle on its side to drain fully, or by using a suction tool. When refilling the transaxle, the lubricant level should be even with the edge of the filler hole or within ¼ inch (6mm) of the hole.

Fig. 87 Loosen the transaxle drain plug/bolt

Fig. 88 Allow transaxle fluid to drain completely

## Automatic Transaxle

The automatic transaxle is a front wheel drive powertrain unit. The transmission and differential are housed is a compact one–piece case and bolted to the back of the engine.

The automatic transaxle and engine assembly are mounted transversely in the vehicle.

## FLUID RECOMMENDATIONS

- 1984–85 automatic transaxles—Motorcraft Dexron®II Automatic Transmission Fluid (ATF).
- 1986–87 automatic transaxles—Motorcraft Type H Automatic Transmission Fluid (ATF).
- 1988–94 automatic transaxles—Motorcraft MECRON® Automatic Transmission Fluid (ATF).

➡ In some areas, Dexron fluid may only be available in a type 3. There is little deference between type 2, and type 3.

## FLUID LEVEL CHECK

A dipstick is provided in the engine compartment to check the level of the automatic transaxle.

1. Position the vehicle on level surface.
2. Apply the parking brake and place the transaxle selector lever in the P position.
3. Operate the engine until it reaches normal operating temperature.
4. Move the selector lever through all detent positions, then return to the P position. DO NOT TURN OFF THE ENGINE DURING THE FLUID LEVEL CHECK.
5. Clean all dirt from the dipstick cap before removing the dipstick. Remove the dipstick and wipe clean. Reinsert the dipstick making sure it is fully seated. Pull the dipstick out of the tube and check the fluid level. The fluid level should be between the FULL and ADD marks.

If necessary, add enough fluid through the dipstick tube/filler to bring the level to the FULL mark on the dipstick. If fluid needs to be added, pour in small amounts, and check regularly. Use only the specified lubricant.

➡ Do not overfill. Make sure the dipstick is fully seated.

## DRAIN AND REFILL

♦ See Figures 89 and 90

If your vehicle is equipped with an automatic transaxle, and the region in which you live has severe cold weather, a multi–viscosity automatic transaxle fluid should be used. Ask your auto parts retailer about the availability of an MV type Automatic Transaxle Fluid.

If you operate you vehicle under severe conditions, such as in a dusty environment or tow a trailer regularly, have extended idling or low speed operation, it may be necessary to change the ATF fluid at regular intervals such as 20 months or 20,000 miles or even more often.

Because the automatic transaxle does not have a drain plug, the entire drain pan must be removed. Therefore, when this procedure is done, a new pan gasket will need to be installed.

➡ **Use of fluid other than specified could result in transaxle malfunctions and/or failure.**

1. Make sure vehicle is OFF, and in the P position. Set the parking brake.

2. Raise the vehicle and safely support it on jackstands, or use a lift if available. If raising the front, make sure rear wheels have blocks behind them.

3. Place a suitable drain pan underneath the transaxle oil pan.

4. Loosen slightly each oil pan retaining bolt in order. After all the bolts have been loosened, loosen each bolt more until fluid begins to drain into the pan.

5. Remove all the retaining bolts except 2 from one end, so that the pan will tip, and the rest of the fluid will drain out.

6. Remove the oil pan. Thoroughly clean the pan. Remove the old gasket, making sure that the gasket mounting surface is clean.

7. Install the new gasket around the pan. Carefully align the pan and gasket to the transaxle body. Slowly re-attach the retaining bolts, making sure that the new gasket is neither torn, or distorted during the procedure. Once all the retaining bolts are attached, tighten each by hand.

8. With all the retaining bolts installed, torque each bolt to 12–17 ft. lbs. (16–23 Nm) in an alternate order.

9. Add 7 quarts of appropriate automatic transaxle fluid. Lower vehicle, start and run car until warm, and check level. Add fluid until required level is reached. Check for leaks around pan gasket.

## PAN AND FILTER SERVICE

Because there in no drain plug for automatic transaxles, it is a good idea to incorporate a pan and filter service, with a fluid change.

1. Make sure vehicle is OFF, and in the P position. Set the parking brake.

2. Raise the vehicle and safely support it on jackstands, or use a lift if available. If raising the front, make sure rear wheels have blocks behind them.

3. Place a suitable drain pan underneath the transaxle oil pan.

4. Loosen slightly each oil pan retaining bolt in order. After all the bolts have been loosened, loosen each bolt more until fluid begins to drain into the pan.

5. Remove all the retaining bolts except 2 from one end, so that the pan will tip, and the rest of the fluid will drain out.

6. Remove the oil pan. Thoroughly clean the pan. Remove the old gasket, making sure that the gasket mounting surface is clean.

7. Remove the transaxle filter screen retaining bolt. Carefully remove the screen from the transaxle body, making sure that the O–ring was removed.

8. Install a new filter screen and O–ring. Hand tighten the retaining bolts at first, then torque to 7–9 ft. lbs. (9–12 Nm)

9. Install the new gasket around the pan. Carefully align the pan and gasket to the transaxle body. Slowly re-attach the retaining bolts, making sure that the new gasket is neither torn,

or distorted during the procedure. Once all the retaining bolts are attached, tighten each by hand.

10. With all the retaining bolts installed, torque each bolt to 12–17 ft. lbs. (16–23 Nm) in an alternate order.

11. Add 7 quarts of appropriate automatic transaxle fluid. Lower vehicle, start and run car until warm, and check level. Add fluid until required level is reached. Check for leaks around pan gasket.

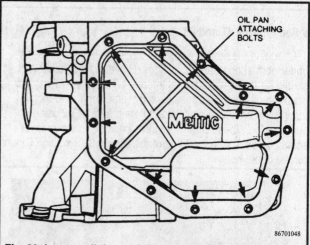

**Fig. 89 Loosen all the retaining bolts to remove transaxle pan**

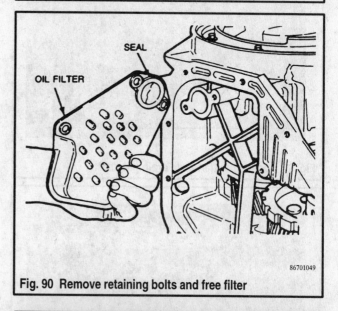

**Fig. 90 Remove retaining bolts and free filter**

## Transfer Case

### FLUID RECOMMENDATIONS

The fluid requirements of the transfer case are the same as those of the transaxle, namely ATF or Dexron®, Type H, or Mecron®, depending on the year. Consult your owner's manual for exact type.

In adding, or changing transaxle fluid, take into account that the specification for transaxle fluid would also include the transfer case, in the event a transfer case was an installed option.

## LEVEL CHECK

Because there is no actual plug for checking transfer case fluid level, and also because both the transaxle and transfer case share the same fluid, transfer fluid level, can be checked by checking the level of the transaxle. An increase or decrease in transfer case fluid level will have a direct effect on transaxle fluid level.

## DRAIN AND REFILL

Changing the lubricant in the transfer case is not practical under normal conditions. Should it become necessary to drain the lubricant from the transfer case, proceed as follows:

1. Raise the vehicle and safely support it on jackstands or a lift, if available. If raising the front of the car, make sure the rear wheels are blocked properly.

2. Loosen the 2 rear engine mount bolts, far enough to gain access to the transfer case cup plug. DO NOT REMOVE BOLTS.

3. Place a suitable drain pan underneath the transfer case assembly.

4. Using a screwdriver, carefully pry up on the cup plug. Using a twisting motion, remove the cup plug. Clean the cup plug with a clean rag. If not too distorted, the plug can be reused. If distorted purchase a new plug.

5. After all the lubricant has been drained from the transfer case assembly, reinstall the cup plug.

6. Tighten the 2 rear engine mount bolts.

7. Lower the vehicle and refill the transaxle with the appropriate transaxle fluid. Start the car, allowing it to warm to a normal temperature. Check the fluid level, as well as for any possible leaks. Add fluid if necessary.

## Cooling System

The cooling system of any car is very important to the proper functioning and longevity of the vehicle. Not only does the system help dissipate the high temperatures present in the engine, it also provides the heat with which warms the interior of the car in the winter seasons.

## FLUID RECOMMENDATIONS

The antifreeze used in vehicles today is designed to lower the freezing point while increasing the boiling point of the water inside the cooling system, in addition to providing needed protection against corrosion of the cooling system components. Because these temperature levels are directly related to the concentration of antifreeze to water, it is important that not only is the amount of fluid critical to the car, be also the concentration of water to antifreeze.

In addition to the conventional ethylene glycol type of antifreeze, there are several brands which are environmentally safe. For example, several brands use propylene glycol, which is claimed to be safer for animals, and is biodegradable.

Unfortunately, it is more expensive to produce, and therefore is slightly more expensive to purchase.

➡ **Cats and dogs are attracted to ethylene glycol antifreeze, and are quite likely to drink any that is left uncovered or in puddles on the ground. This will prove fatal in sufficient quantity. Always drain the coolant into a sealable container. Coolant should be reused unless it is contaminated or several years old.**

Whenever you add engine coolant use equal parts of water and Ford Premium Cooling System Fluid E2FZ 19549 AA or equivalent (antifreeze) that meets ford specifications. Do not use alcohol or methanol antifreeze, or mix them with specified coolant. Be aware that propylene glycol and ethylene glycol type antifreeze are NOT compatible. When replacing one type for the other, the entire cooling system must be flushed.

➡ **A coolant mixture of less than 40% (approximately 3.0 quarts) engine coolant concentrate may result in engine corrosion and over-heating.**

The optimum concentration level is 50%, that is a mixture of 1 part water to 1 part antifreeze. The factory installed solution of Ford cooling system fluid and water will protect your vehicle to −35°F (−37°C). Check the freezing protection rating of the coolant at least once a year, just before winter. This can be done using an antifreeze concentration tester. This tester can be purchased at any automotive parts store.

Maintain a protection rating consistent with the lowest temperature in which you operate your vehicle or at least −20°F (−29°C) to prevent engine damage as a result of freezing and to ensure proper engine operating temperature. Rust and corrosion inhibitors tend to deteriorate with time, changing the coolant every 3 years or 30,000 miles is recommended for proper protection of the cooling system.

➡ **Ford Motor Company does not authorize the use of recycled engine coolant, nor do they sanction the use of any machines or devices that recycle engine coolant. Recycled engine coolant is not equivalent to the factory fill OEM coolant, the Ford premium cooling system fluid (E2FZ 19549 AA) or the Ford heavy duty low silicate cooling fluid (E6HZ 19549 A). The quality of engine coolant degenerates with use. Recycling used engine coolant is very difficult to do without exposing the used coolant to additional foreign substances. Merely adding an additive to the coolant will not restore it. Always use new engine coolant that meets the Ford Motor coolant specifications for the engine being serviced.**

## ✳✳CAUTION

**The disposal of all used engine coolant must always be done in accordance with all applicable Federal, State and Local laws and regulations.**

## FLUID LEVEL CHECK

▶ **See Figure 91**

The cooling system of your vehicle contains, among other items, a radiator and a expansion tank. When the engine is running, heat is generated. The rise in temperature causes the coolant in the radiator to expand, and as a result internal pressure builds up. When a certain pressure is reached, a pressure relief valve in the radiator filler cap (pressure cap) is lifted from its seat and allows coolant to flow through the radiator filler neck, down a hose, and into the expansion reservoir.

When the system temperature and pressure are reduced in the radiator, the water in the expansion reservoir is siphoned back into the radiator.

**Fig. 91  Radiator expansion tank**

Check the level in the coolant recovery reservoir at least one month. With engine cold, the level must be maintained at or above the ADD mark. At normal operating temperatures, the coolant level should be at the FULL HOT mark. If the level is below the recommended level a 50/50 mixture of coolant (antifreeze) and water should be added to the reservoir. If the reservoir is empty, add the coolant to the radiator and then fill the reservoir to the required level.

➡ **Never fill a warm or hot radiator with cold fluid. This immediate change in temperature could crack the radiator.**

### ✳✳CAUTION

**The cooling fan motor is controlled by a temperature switch. The fan may come on and run when the engine is off. It will continue to run until the correct temperature is reached. Avoid getting your fingers, etc. caught in the fan blades.**

**Never remove the radiator cap under any circumstances when the engine is operating. Before removing the cap, switch off the engine and wait until it has cooled. Even then, use extreme care when removing the cap from a hot radiator. Wrap a thick cloth around the cap and turn it slowly to the first stop. Step back while the pressure is released from the cooling system. When you are sure all the pressure has been released, press down on the cap, still with a cloth, turn and remove it.**

Check the coolant level in the radiator and antifreeze reservoir at least once a month, only when the engine is cool. Whenever coolant checks are made, check the condition of the radiator cap rubber seal. Make sure it is clean and free of any dirt particles. Rinse off with water if necessary. When replacing cap on radiator, also make sure that the radiator filler neck seat is clean. Check that overflow hose in the reservoir is not kinked and is inserted to within ½ in. (13mm) of bottom of the bottle.

Anytime you add coolant to the radiator, use a 50/50 mixture of coolant and water. If you have to add coolant more than once a month, or if you have to add more than one quart at a time, have the cooling system checked for leaks.

## DRAIN AND REFILL

▶ **See Figures 92, 93, 94 and 95**

**Draining The Cooling System**

To drain the coolant, place a suitable container under the radiator, connect an 18 in. (457mm) long, $3/8$ in. (9.5mm) inside diameter hose to the nipple on the drain valve located on the bottom of the radiator. With the engine cool, set the heater control to the maximum heat position, remove the radiator cap and open the drain valve allowing the coolant to drain into the container. When all of the coolant is drained, remove the 3/8 in. hose and close the drain valve.

There may be some coolant left in the engine block cavities. To drain the block, locate the engine block coolant drain plug on the front side of the engine above the oil pan. Loosen plug and allow coolant to drain out. Prior to reinstalling any coolant plugs or drain valves be sure to coat the threads with a suitable thread sealer or Teflon® tape.

**Fig. 92  Radiator draincock**

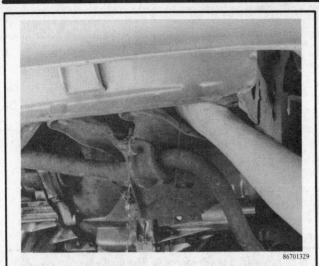

**Fig. 93 Wait until all the coolant has flowed out before reinstalling draincock**

**Fig. 94 With everything tightened fill the radiator with coolant**

**Fig. 95 Fill the reservoir with coolant if needed**

### ✳✳CAUTION

Cats and dogs are attracted to ethylene glycol antifreeze, and are quite likely to drink any that is left uncovered or in puddles on the ground. This will prove fatal in sufficient quantity. Always drain the coolant into a sealable container. Coolant should be reused unless it is contaminated or several years old.

➡ If there is any evidence of rust or scaling in the cooling system the system should be flushed thoroughly before refilling.

#### Refilling The Cooling System

1. Install engine block drain plug if removed, and close the radiator draincock. In a clean plastic container, mix a solution of 1 part antifreeze to 1 part distilled water. Pour this mixture into the radiator. Continue doing this until radiator is full.

➡ Be sure to wait several minutes as the coolant level in the radiator drops, continue to slowly add coolant until the radiator remains full (approximately 10–15 minutes are required to fill the system). A coolant mixture of less than 30% (approximately 2.1 quarts) engine coolant concentrate may result in engine corrosion and over–heating.

2. Reinstall the radiator cap to the pressure relief position by installing the cap to the fully installed position and then backing off to the first stop.

3. Start and idle the engine until the upper radiator hose is warm and slightly hard to in feel.

4. Shut OFF engine. Cautiously remove the radiator cap by placing a thick cloth over the cap and slowly turning the cap and removing it. If needed, add water until the radiator is full. Reinstall the radiator cap fully when complete.

5. Check the level of coolant in the reservoir, and add if below the FULL HOT level.

6. Start engine again, and check for leaks. This is also a good time to make sure the heating system is working. Turn the heater control to full heat and see how warm the interior gets.

#### Flushing and Cleaning the System

1. Drain the cooling system as outlined earlier. Add warm water until the radiator is full.

2. Reinstall the radiator cap to the pressure relief position by installing the cap to the fully installed position and then backing off to the first stop.

3. Start and idle the engine until the upper radiator hose is warm and slightly hard to the feel.

4. Shut engine off. With a thick cloth over the radiator cap, slowly remove the cap. Drain the water by opening the radiator draincock. Be careful because the water will be hot.

5. Repeat the above procedure until nearly clear water comes out of the radiator. Allow remaining water to drain and then close the radiator draincock.

6. Disconnect the overflow hose from the radiator filler neck. Remove the coolant reservoir from the fender apron and empty the fluid. Flush the reservoir with clean water, drain and install the reservoir and overflow hose.

7. Refill the coolant system as outlined earlier, being careful to check the levels in both the radiator and reservoir.

➡ **If the radiator has been removed, it is possible to back flush the system as follows:**

8. Back flush the radiator using the above procedures. Ensuring that the radiator cap is tightly in position, turn the radiator upside down. Position a high pressure water washer in the bottom hose location and back–flush. These can be rented at most rental organizations. Be careful not to exceed the internal pressure of 20 psi (4.9 kPa).

9. Remove the thermostat housing and thermostat. Back flush the engine by positioning a high pressure hose into the engine through the thermostat location and back flush the engine.

➡ **If the radiator is showing signs of rust and wear, it may be a good idea to thoroughly clean and get the cooling fins free of debris. Then using a suitable high temperature rust proof engine paint, paint the exterior of the radiator assembly.**

## Brake Master Cylinder

The braking system of most vehicles is a closed system utilizing fluid pressure to drive pistons in the calipers, cylinders or both, which in turn engages the pads or shoes to slow the vehicle down. In the event there is air or a leak in the brake system, the braking pressure is reduced therefore decreasing the possible brake braking efficiency. If there is water or condensation in the brake lines or reservoir, the bake system is also adversely effected. Therefore, it is important to check and maintain your brake system.

### FLUID RECOMMENDATION

The brake fluid to be used in these vehicles should be of a DOT 3 , or higher classification. The number associated with brake fluid corresponds to its respective boiling point. In general, the higher the number, the higher the boiling point.

### FLUID LEVEL CHECK

▶ **See Figure 96**

The brake master cylinder is located under the hood, on the driver's side firewall. Before removing the master cylinder reservoir cap, make sure the vehicle is on a level surface. Wipe the cover and around the master cylinder clean, before removing the cap. Depending on the type of reservoir you may have to either pry the retaining clip off to the side, or turn a cap to remove the master cylinder cover.

Once the cap is removed, if the level of the brake fluid inside is within ¼ in. (6mm) of the top, the fluid level is OK. If the level is less than half the volume of the reservoir, check the brake system for leaks. Leaks in the brake system most commonly occur at the wheel cylinders or at the front calipers, or a cracked rubber brake line leading to either a front or rear brake.

When checking the fluid level, make sure the rubber gasket inside the cap is in good working condition. The rubber should be soft, with no visible cracks. If there is any question, replace it. This cap not only prevents dirt from entering the reservoir, it also helps maintain system pressure when the fluid level goes down.

86701332

**Fig. 96 Brake master cylinder and reservoir**

Never over fill a brake reservoir. The fluid will only leak out, and this can cause debris to enter the system, not to mention that brake fluid is a hazardous fluid, and can easily strip paint off a car.

On the later vehicles, check the brake fluid by visually inspecting the fluid level through the translucent master cylinder reservoir. It should be between the MIN and the MAX level marks embossed on the side of the reservoir. If the level is found to be low, remove the reservoir cap and fill to the MAX level with DOT 3 brake fluid.

The brake fluid level will decrease with accumulated mileage. This is a normal condition associated with the wear of the disc brake linings. If the fluid is excessively low, it would be advisable to have the brake system checked.

➡ **To avoid the possibility of brake failure that could result in property damage or personal injury, do not allow the master cylinder to run dry. Never reuse brake fluid that has been drained from the hydraulic system or fluid that has been allowed to stand in an open container for an extended period of time.**

## Power Steering Pump Reservoir

The power steering system incorporated into most Tempo/Topaz is a hydraulically driven system which enables the driver to maneuver the vehicle with ease because the pressure created is used to drive gears which converts the turning action into a mechanical force.

By maintaining the proper power steering fluid level, the driver is ensured that enough fluid is available to adequately driver the power steering system. Whenever the engine oil level is checked, also check the power steering fluid level.

### FLUID RECOMMENDATION

Use only power steering fluid that meets Ford Specifications such as Motorcraft Type F Automatic Transmission and Power Steering Fluid or an equivalent type F fluid which displays a Ford registration number (2P– followed by six numerals). Whenever the dipstick is inserted, always make sure it is properly seated and locked.

## FLUID LEVEL CHECK

▶ **See Figures 97, 98, 99 and 100**

Make sure the vehicle is parked on level ground. Run the engine until it reaches normal operating temperature. While the engine is idling, turn the steering wheel all the way to the right and then left several times. Shut the engine OFF. Open the hood and remove the power steering pump dipstick. Wipe the dipstick clean and reinstall into the pump reservoir. Withdraw the dipstick and note the fluid level shown. The level must show between the cold full mark and the hot full mark. Add fluid if necessary, but do not overfill. Remove any excess fluid with a suction bulb or suction gun.

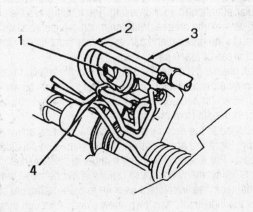

1 Power steering pressure switch
2 Return line
3 Pressure line
4 Strap

CIII, 2.3L

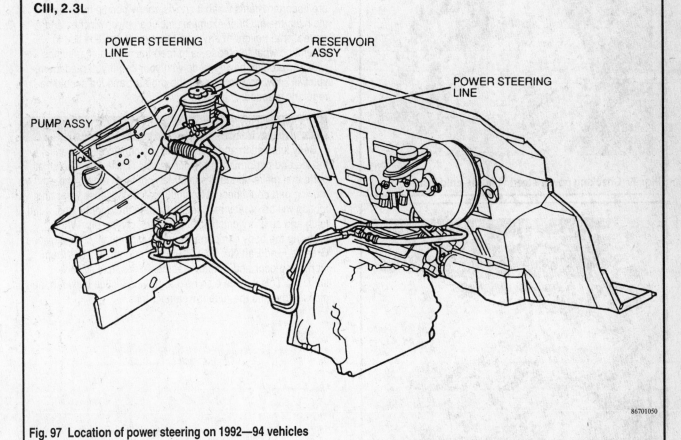

**Fig. 97 Location of power steering on 1992—94 vehicles**

86701050

Fig. 98 Checking power steering fluid—hot level

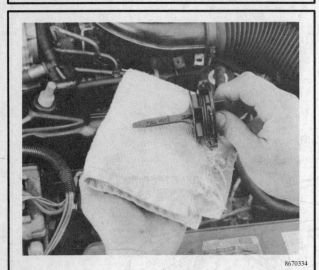

Fig. 99 Checking power steering fluid—cold level

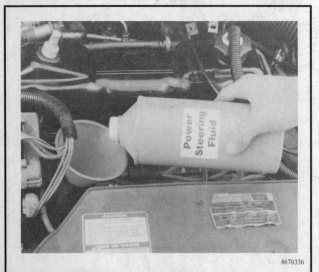

Fig. 100 Adding power steering fluid

## Chassis Greasing

◆ See Figure 101

Although not as important as on cars of the past, chassis greasing is still considered essential to the life and performance of your vehicle. Today, fewer areas of the chassis need the attention of grease, but those areas that do require grease should be checked and greased at least twice a year, and more often if the vehicle is operating in dust areas or under heavy–duty conditions. When greasing the chassis, use Long Life Lubricant (Ford Part No. C1AZ 19590 B or equivalent). Pay particular attention to your greasing. Too much grease is almost as bad as too little grease. With too much grease, road dirt is attached to the grease, and can eventually work its way into the contact areas of many parts.

When greasing a chassis, look for areas that move frequently, like control arms, ball joints and sway bars. When you are driving, listen for squeaks and other noises from the chassis that could benefit from grease.

In addition to the areas that the manufacturer recommends greasing, there are areas of the car that should be considered for grease. For example, with the number of "aftermarket" products today, many could use grease either because of their movement, or their infrequent use. An excellent example of this point is the individuals who own snow plows. Although these are important items when it snows, many people forget to maintain them. Other examples include power winches and recreational trailers of any type. An excellent guide line to determine what to grease, is to read the manual that comes with any product having to do with your car. If you read them, you will know how to care for the product, and if it should be regularly greased.

## Body Lubrication and Maintenance

Body lubrication and maintenance is considered essential to the life and performance of your vehicle. Think of all the small parts that make up today's car. Many of them move, and any moving part could benefit from lubrication, because wear and friction will be greatly reduced. Lubricate the door hinges, hood latch and auxiliary catch, lock cylinders, pivots, etc. When greasing the body components, use a high quality Polyethylene Grease (Ford Part No. D7AZ 19584 A or equivalent). When lubricating door and window weather–strips, use silicone lubricant. This service also help to reduce friction between the glass frame and the rubber weather strips.

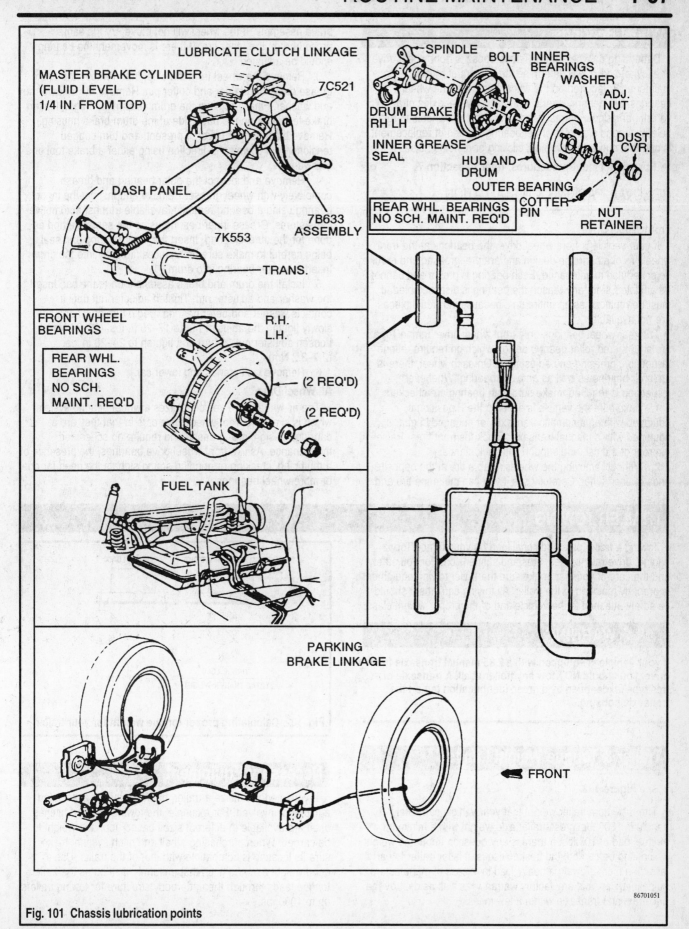

**Fig. 101 Chassis lubrication points**

## Wheel Bearings

Depending on whether the Tempo/Topaz is front wheel drive or all wheel drive, will determine the amount of routine maintenance required on the wheel bearings. The wheel bearings, are bearing inserts found at all wheel axles of a vehicle, and under normal conditions allow the wheels to rotate quietly. A good sign of a wheel bearing in need of replacement, is one that makes a thumping, clicking or grinding noise.

➡ **For replacement procedures, refer to section 7.**

### REMOVAL, PACKING & INSTALLATION

#### Front Wheel Drive

If your vehicle is front wheel drive, the bearings at the front wheels re of a cartridge design and are pre–greased and require no scheduled maintenance. Each bearing is preset and cannot be adjusted. If for any reason the bearing is disassembled, it must be replaced as an entire unit, because individual pieces are not available.

The rear wheel bearings on a front wheel drive Tempo/Topaz are a tampered roller bearing design which do require retinue inspection, greasing and adjustment. On each wheel, there is an inner bearing as well as an outer bearing. Whenever inspection is required, make sure both bearing are checked.

1. Make sure the vehicle is either in the P position if equipped with an automatic transaxle, or engaged in gear if equipped with a manual transaxle. Block the front tires. Raise the rear of the car, and support with jack stands.

2. Without removing the wheels, grab a tire at the opposite ends of each other. Carefully see if you can move the tire and brake assemble. If the wheel will not move, try the same procedure on the other tire. If there is movement the bearing should be adjusted.

3. Remove the wheel from the axle, then remove the brake grease cap, nut retainer and cotter pin. Remove the adjuster nut and washer. Finally remove the drum assemble. If tight, loosen brake tensioner on the back side of the drum brake housing. Remove black rubber cover, if present, and turn cogged tensioner in a downward direction using either a brake tool or a screwdriver.

4. Remove and inspect the outer bearing and grease completely with wheel grease. Remove and inspect the inner bearing using a bearing remover, available at most automotive parts stores. Grease inner bearing using the same method as done for the outer bearing. Insert the inner bearing and seal, being careful to make sure both pieces fit tightly into the drum. Insert the outer bearing into drum.

5. Install the drum and brake assemble on to the car. Insert the washer and adjuster nut. Tighten adjuster nut until it contacts washer and outer bearing. Begin turning wheel, and slowly tighten the adjuster nut to 17–25 ft. lbs. (23–34 Nm). Loosen adjuster nut ½ turn and tighten to 24–28 in lbs. (2.7–3.2 Nm).

6. Remove jack stands and lower car.

#### All Wheel Drive

The all wheel drive vehicle utilizes a wheel bearing system which is similar to front wheel drive cars in that they are a cartridge design, pre–greased and require no scheduled maintenance. As like front wheel drive bearings, the presence of a thumping, cracking or grinding sound signals the need for one or more wheel bearings.

## TRAILER TOWING

Towing a trailer puts additional load on your Tempo/Topaz engine, drivetrain, brakes, tires and suspension. For you safety and the care of your car, make sure the trailer towing equipment is properly matched to the trailer. All towing equipment should be safely attached to the vehicle and of the proper weight class.

### ❋❋WARNING

**If your vehicle is equipped with a 2.85 manual transaxle final drive, you should NOT tow any trailer at all. A transaxle of this type is identified by a green identification tag on the transaxle housing.**

## Trailer & Tongue Weight Limits

▶ **See Figure 102**

The maximum trailer weight that your vehicle can safely handle is 1000 lbs. gross trailer axle weight with a minimum tongue load of 100 lbs. If there is any question about the weight which is to be carried, the best advise is, it is far better to carry less than more. Towing a heavy load in excess of manufacturer guidelines can void any factory warranty, as well as destroy the drivetrain and transaxle within a few miles.

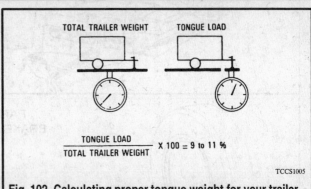

Fig. 102 Calculating proper tongue weight for your trailer

## Necessary Equipment

If you intend to utilize a trailer, be aware of the associated equipment involved. For example, the towing ball and hitches used are available in different sizes based upon the weight to be carried. When purchasing a ball and hitch system, make sure its location is compatible with that of the trailer. Use a good weight carrying hitch that uniformly distributes the trailer tongue loads through the underbody structure for towing trailers up to 1000 lbs.

Under no circumstances should a single or multi–clamp type hitch be installed on your vehicle, damage to the bumper will result. Nor should any hitch which attaches to the axle be used. Underbody mounted hitches are acceptable if installed properly. Never attach safety chains to the bumper.

Whenever the trailer is being used, make sure all parts are secure and in good working order. This includes the lights, the tire pressures, and hardware.

Because most trailer use some type of tail lighting system, make sure the wiring harness used to attach these light is installed properly, with connections that are secure and present no danger of shorting out. Also make sure that the harness does not drag on the ground or crimp when run from the vehicle to the trailer.

If you intend to tow a trailer long distances, it is highly recommended that you install an auxiliary oil cooler for both the power steering and automatic transaxle systems because of the added strain placed upon the associated components. Also if you are towing a full load of 1000 lbs, do not drive at speeds higher than 55 mph. With this much weight, not only will it be difficult to attain and maintain this speed, it will take a greater distance to stop the vehicle should you need to in a hurry.

## General Recommendations

Before starting on a trip, practice turning, stopping and backing up in an area away from other traffic (such as a deserted shopping center parking lot) to gain experience in handling the extra weight and length of the trailer. Take enough time to get the feel of the vehicle/ trailer combination under a variety of situations.

Skillful backing up requires practice. Back up slowly with an assistant acting as a guide and watching for obstructions. Use both rear view mirrors. Place your hand at the bottom of the steering wheel and move it in the direction you want the rear of the trailer to swing. Make small corrections, instead of exaggerated ones,as a slight movement of the steering wheel will result in a much larger movement of the rear of the trailer.

Allow considerably more room for stopping when a trailer is attached to the vehicle. If the trailer is equipped with brakes, lead with the trailer brakes when approaching a stop. Trailer brakes are also handy for correcting side sway. Just touch them for a moment without using the vehicle brakes, and the trailer should settle down and track straight again.

To assist in obtaining good handling with the car/trailer combination, it is important that the trailer tongue load be maintained at approximately 10–15% of the loaded trailer weight.

Checking everything before starting out on the road, then stop after you've traveled about 50 miles and double–check the trailer hitch and electrical connections to make sure everything is still correct. Listen for sounds like chains dragging on the ground, and check your rear view mirrors frequently to make sure the trailer is still attached and tracking properly. Check the trailer wheel lugs to make sure they are tight and never attempt to tow the trailer with a spare saver tire installed on the vehicle.

Remember that the car/trailer combination is more sensitive to cross winds and slow down when crossing tall bridges and open expanses in gusty wind situations. Exceeding the speed limit while towing a trailer is not only illegal, it is foolish.

Because the trailer wheels are closer than the towing vehicle's wheels to the inside of a turn, drive slightly beyond the normal turning point when negotiating a sharp turn at a corner. Allow extra distance for passing other vehicles and downshift if necessary for better acceleration. Allow at least the equivalent of 1 vehicle and trailer length combined for each 10 mph of road speed.

Finally, remember to check the height of the loaded car/trailer, allowing for luggage racks, antenna, etc. mounted on the roof and take note of low bridges or parking garage clearances.

## TOWING THE VEHICLE

▶ **See Figures 103 and 104**

➡ **If your Tempo/Topaz is all wheel drive, your vehicle CANNOT be towed using a conventional tow truck. All wheel drive vehicles must be towed using a "flatbed" tow vehicle or the car must be towed using a dolly type system. This is because both front and rear axles drive the car, and a tow truck could cause internal transaxle damage.**

## Preparatory Steps

Release the parking brake, and place the transaxle in NEUTRAL. As a rule, the vehicle being towed, should be pulled with the driving wheels OFF the ground. This means in a front wheel drive car, the front wheels should be off the ground. If the driving wheels cannot be raised off the ground, place them on a dolly.

➡ **It is recommended that your vehicle be towed from the front, unless conditions do not allow it. Towing the vehicle backwards with the front wheels on the ground, may cause internal damage to the transaxle.**

When the vehicle is being towed, the steering wheel must be clamped in the straight–ahead position with a steering wheel clamping device designed for towing service use, such as those provided by towing system manufacturers.

➡ **J–hooks should not be used to tow a vehicle. The manufacturer recommends that T–hooks be used when towing the vehicle.**

In the event your vehicle requires towing, do not try to take on this job yourself, leave it up to a professional. At no time should you attempt to have your vehicle towed by using a strap and another vehicle. Not only is it dangerous, in many areas it is illegal.

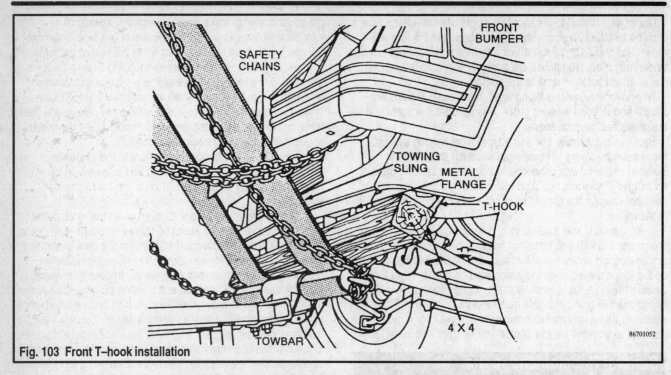

**Fig. 103 Front T–hook installation**

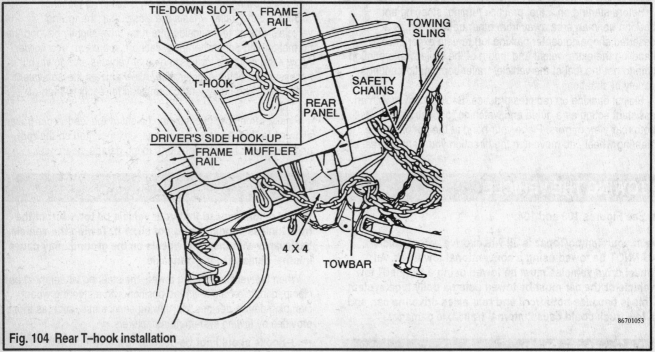

**Fig. 104 Rear T–hook installation**

## JACKING

▶ **See Figure 105**

➡ **Whenever a vehicle is raised above the ground, use extreme caution. If one end of the car is being lifted, always block the other to prevent any wheel movement. Finally, never raise a car on any surface that is not flat.**

When using a floor jack, the front of the vehicle may be raised by positioning the floor jack under the front body rail behind the suspension arm–to–body bracket. The front, as well as either side of the rear end may be lifted by positioning the floor jack under the rocker flange at the contact points used for the jack supplied with the vehicle. The rear of the vehicle may be raised by positioning the floor jack forward of the tie rod bracket or by positioning the floor jack under either rear lower control arm.

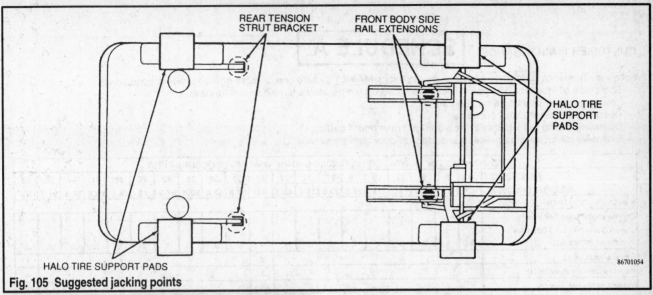

**Fig. 105  Suggested jacking points**

## ✳✳WARNING

**Under no circumstances should the vehicle ever be lifted by the front or rear control arms, halfshafts or CV–joints. Severe damage to the vehicle could result.**

On vehicles equipped with All Wheel Drive (AWD), the vehicle must be in 2 wheel drive or rotation from the wheel being removed could be transferred to one or more of the other wheels, causing the vehicle to move or fall off the jack.

➡ **The service jack provided with the vehicle is only intended to be used during emergencies, such as changing a flat tire. Never use the service jack to hoist the vehicle for any other service. Refer to the owner's manual when using the jack supplied with the vehicle.**

## MAINTENANCE SCHEDULES

◆ **See Figures 106, 107 and 108**

The maintenance schedules which follow are meant as a general guideline with which you can determine the service needed on your vehicle. It is important to stay as close to the mileage interval suggested between service changes. Of course, there is no harm performing a service early, but it is not recommended to prolong a service interval.

The maintenance schedules are broken into two categories, one for normal conditions, the second for more severe driving environments. Schedule B is for normal driving conditions, schedule A is for severe driving conditions.

CUSTOMER MAINTENANCE    **SCHEDULE B**

Follow maintenance [Schedule B] if, generally, you drive your vehicle on a daily basis for more than 10 miles (16 km) and NONE OF THE DRIVING CONDITIONS SHOWN IN SCHEDULE A APPLY TO YOUR DRIVING HABITS.

| PERFORM AT THE MONTHS OR DISTANCES SHOWN, WHICHEVER OCCURS FIRST | | | | | | | | |
|---|---|---|---|---|---|---|---|---|
| MILES (000) | 7.5 | 15 | 22.5 | 30 | 37.5 | 45 | 52.5 | 60 |
| KILOMETERS (000) | 12 | 24 | 36 | 48 | 60 | 72 | 84 | 96 |
| **EMISSION CONTROL SERVICE** | | | | | | | | |
| Change engine oil and oil filter — every 6 months or 7500 miles, whichever occurs first | x | x | x | x | x | x | x | x |
| Replace spark plugs | | | | x | | | | x |
| Change crankcase filter (1) | | | | X(1) | | | | X(1) |
| Inspect accessory drive belt(s) | | | | x | | | | x |
| Replace air cleaner filter (1) | | | | X(1) | | | | X(1) |
| Replace engine coolant (every 36 months) OR | | | | x | | | | x |
| Check engine coolant protection, hoses and clamps | | | | ANNUALLY | | | | |
| **GENERAL MAINTENANCE** | | | | | | | | |
| Check exhaust heat shields | | | | x | | | | x |
| Inspect disc brake pads and rotors (front) (2) | | | | X(2) | | | | X(2) |
| Inspect brake linings and drums (rear) (2) | | | | X(2) | | | | X(2) |
| Inspect and repack rear wheel bearings. | | | | x | | | | x |
| Rotate tires | x | | x | | x | | x | |

**Fig. 106  Maintenance schedule for normal driving conditions**

## CUSTOMER MAINTENANCE  | SCHEDULE A |

Follow maintenance | Schedule A | if your driving habits **MAINLY** include one or more of the following conditions:
- Short trips of less than 10 miles (16 km) when outside temperatures remain below freezing.
- Towing a trailer, or using a car-top carrier.
- Operating in severe dust conditions.
- Operating during hot weather in stop-and-go "rush hour" traffic.
- Extensive idling, such as police, taxi or door-to-door delivery service.

| PERFORM AT THE MONTHS OR DISTANCES SHOWN, WHICHEVER OCCURS FIRST | | | | | | | | | | | | | | | | | | | | |
|---|---|---|---|---|---|---|---|---|---|---|---|---|---|---|---|---|---|---|---|---|
| MILES (000) | 3 | 6 | 9 | 12 | 15 | 18 | 21 | 24 | 27 | 30 | 33 | 36 | 39 | 42 | 45 | 48 | 51 | 54 | 57 | 60 |
| KILOMETERS (000) | 4.8 | 9.6 | 14.4 | 19.2 | 24 | 28.8 | 33.6 | 38.4 | 43.2 | 48 | 52.8 | 57.6 | 62.4 | 67.2 | 72 | 76.8 | 81.6 | 86.4 | 91.2 | 96 |
| **EMISSION CONTROL SERVICE** | | | | | | | | | | | | | | | | | | | | |
| Change engine oil and oil filter (every 3 months) OR 3,000 miles whichever occurs first | X | X | X | X | X | X | X | X | X | X | X | X | X | X | X | X | X | X | X | X |
| Replace spark plugs | | | | | | | | | | X | | | | | | | | | | X |
| Inspect accessory drive belt(s) | | | | | | | | | | X | | | | | | | | | | X |
| Replace air cleaner filter (1) | | | | | | | | | | X(1) | | | | | | | | | | X(1) |
| Replace crankcase emission filter (1) | | | | | | | | | | X(1) | | | | | | | | | | X(1) |
| Replace engine coolant EVERY 36 months OR | | | | | | | | | | X | | | | | | | | | | X |
| Check engine coolant protection, hoses and clamps | ANNUALLY | | | | | | | | | | | | | | | | | | | |
| **GENERAL MAINTENANCE** | | | | | | | | | | | | | | | | | | | | |
| Inspect exhaust heat shields | | | | | | | | | | X | | | | | | | | | | X |
| Change automatic transaxle fluid | | | | | | | | | | (2) | | | | | | | | | | (2) |
| Inspect disc brake pads and rotors (front) (3) | | | | | | | | | | X(3) | | | | | | | | | | X(3) |
| Inspect brake linings and drums (rear) (3) | | | | | | | | | | X(3) | | | | | | | | | | X(3) |
| Inspect and repack rear wheel bearings | | | | | | | | | | X | | | | | | | | | | X |
| Rotate tires | | X | | | X | | | X | | | X | | | | X | | | | | |

(1) If operating in severe dust, more frequent intervals may be required, consult your dealer.

(2) Change automatic transmission fluid if your driving habits frequently include one or more of the following conditions:
- Operation during hot weather (above 90°F, 32°C), carrying heavy loads and in hilly terrain.
- Towing a trailer or using a car-top carrier.
- Police, taxi or door-to-door delivery service.

(3) If your driving includes continuous stop-and-go driving or driving in mountainous areas, more frequent intervals may be required.

86701056

**Fig. 107 Maintenance schedule for severe driving conditions**

| Item | Part Name | Ford Part No. | Ford Specification |
|---|---|---|---|
| *Hinges, Hinge Checks and Pivots | Polyethylene Grease | D7AZ-19584-A | ESB-M1C106-B |
| Hood Latch and Auxiliary Catch | Polyethylene Grease | D7AZ-19584-A | ESB-M1C106-B |
| Lock Cylinders | Lock Lubricant | D8AZ-19587-A | ESB-M2C20-A |
| Steering Gear Housing (Manual) | Steering Gear Grease | D8AZ-19578-A | ESA-M1C175-A |
| Steering Gear (Power) | Grease | C3AZ-19578-A | ESW-M1C87-A |
| Steering-Power (Pump Reservoir) | Motorcraft Auto. Trans. Fluid — Type F | XT-1-QF | ESW-M2C33-F |
| Speedometer Cable | Speedometer Cable Lube | D2AZ-19581-A | ESF-M1C160-A |
| Engine Coolant | Cooling System Fluid | E2FZ-19549-A | ESE-M97B44-A |
| Front Wheel Bearings and Hubs Front Wheel Bearing Seals Rear Wheel Bearings | Long Life Lubricant | C1AZ-19590-B | ESA-M1C75-B |
| Brake Master Cylinder | H.D. Brake Fluid | C6AZ-19542-A | ESA-M6C25-A |
| Brake Master Cylinder Push Rod and Bushing | Motorcraft SAE 10W-30 Engine Oil | XO-10W30-QP | ESE-M2C153-B |
| Drum Brake Shoe Ledges | Disc Brake Caliper Slide Grease | D7AZ-19590-A | ESA-M1C172-A |
| Parking Brake Cable | Polyethylene Grease | D0AZ-19584-A | ESB-M1C93-B |
| Brake Pedal Pivot Bushing | Motorcraft SAE 10W-30 Engine Oil | XO-10W30-QP | ESE-M2C153-B |
| Tire Mounting Bead (of Tire) | Tire Mounting Lube | D9AZ-19583-A | ESA-M1B6-A |
| Clutch Pedal Pivot Bushing | Motorcraft SAE 10W-30 Engine Oil | XO-10W30-QP | ESE-M2C153-B |
| Clutch Pedal Quadrant and Pawl Pivot Holes | | | |
| Clutch Cable Connection Transmission End | Long Life Lubricant | C1AZ-19590-B | ESA-M1C75-B |
| Clutch Release Lever — At Fingers (Both Sides and Fulcrum) | | | |
| Clutch Release Bearing Retainer | | | |

*For                door hinges, use Disc Brake Caliper slide grease D7AZ-19590-A
DEXRON* is a registered trademark of General Motors Corporation

86701057

**Fig. 108  Vehicle lubrication chart**

## CAPACITIES

| Year | Model | Engine ID/VIN | Engine Displacement Liters (cc) | Engine Oil with Filter | Transmission (pts.) | | | Transfer Case (pts.) | Drive Axle | | Fuel Tank (gal.) | Cooling System (qts.) |
|------|-------|---------------|--------------------------------|------------------------|------|------|------|----------------------|------------|------|------------------|-----------------------|
| | | | | | 4-Spd | 5-Spd | Auto. | | Front (pts.) | Rear (pts.) | | |
| 1984 | Tempo/Topaz | H | 2.0 (2000) | 7.2 | 5.3 | 6.1 | 16.6 | - | 1 | - | 14.0 | 6.5 |
| | Tempo/Topaz | R | 2.3 (2300) | 5.0 | 5.3 | 6.1 | 16.6 | - | 1 | - | 14.0 [2] | 6.5 |
| 1985 | Tempo/Topaz | H | 2.0 (2000) | 7.2 | 5.3 | 6.1 | 16.6 | - | 1 | - | 14.0 | 6.5 |
| | Tempo/Topaz | R | 2.3 (2300) | 5.0 | 5.3 | 6.1 | 16.6 | - | 1 | - | 14.0 [2] | 6.5 |
| | Tempo/Topaz | S | 2.3 (2300) | 5.0 | 5.3 | 6.1 | 16.6 | - | 1 | - | 14.0 | 8.4 |
| | Tempo/Topaz | X | 2.3 (2300) | 5.0 | 5.3 | 6.1 | 16.6 | - | 1 | - | 14.0 | 8.4 |
| 1986 | Tempo/Topaz | H | 2.0 (2000) | 7.2 | 5.3 | 6.1 | 16.6 | - | 1 | - | 14.0 | 6.5 |
| | Tempo/Topaz | R | 2.3 (2300) | 5.0 | 5.3 | 6.1 | 16.6 | - | 1 | - | 14.0 [2] | 6.5 |
| | Tempo/Topaz | S | 2.3 (2300) | 5.0 | 5.3 | 6.1 | 16.6 | - | 1 | - | 14.0 | 8.4 |
| | Tempo/Topaz | X | 2.3 (2300) | 5.0 | 5.3 | 6.1 | 16.6 | - | 1 | - | 14.0 | 8.4 |
| 1987 | Tempo/Topaz | H | 2.0 (2000) | 7.2 | 5.3 | 6.1 | 16.6 | - | 1 | - | 14.0 | 6.5 |
| | Tempo/Topaz | R | 2.3 (2300) | 5.0 | 5.3 | 6.1 | 16.6 | - | 1 | - | 14.0 [2] | 6.5 |
| | Tempo/Topaz | S | 2.3 (2300) | 5.0 | 5.3 | 6.1 | 16.6 | - | 1 | - | 14.0 | 8.4 |
| | Tempo/Topaz | X | 2.3 (2300) | 5.0 | 5.3 | 6.1 | 16.6 | - | 1 | - | 14.0 | 8.4 |
| 1988 | Tempo/Topaz | S | 2.3 (2300) | 5.0 | - | 6.2 | [4] | - | 1 | 1.3 | [2] | [3] |
| | Tempo/Topaz | X | 2.3 (2300) | 5.0 | 5.3 | 6.1 | [4] | - | 1 | 1.3 | [2] | [3] |
| 1989 | Tempo/Topaz | S | 2.3 (2300) | 5.0 | - | 6.2 | [4] | - | 1 | 1.3 | [2] | [3] |
| | Tempo/Topaz | X | 2.3 (2300) | 5.0 | 5.3 | 6.1 | [4] | - | 1 | 1.3 | [2] | [3] |
| 1990 | Tempo/Topaz | S | 2.3 (2300) | 5.0 | - | 6.2 | [4] | - | 1 | 1.3 | [2] | [3] |
| | Tempo/Topaz | X | 2.3 (2300) | 5.0 | 5.3 | 6.1 | [4] | - | 1 | 1.3 | [2] | [3] |
| 1991 | Tempo/Topaz | S | 2.3 (2300) | 5.0 | - | 6.2 | [4] | - | 1 | 1.3 | [2] | [3] |
| | Tempo/Topaz | X | 2.3 (2300) | 5.0 | 5.3 | 6.1 | [4] | - | 1 | 1.3 | [2] | [3] |
| 1992 | Tempo/Topaz | X | 2.3 (2300) | 5.0 | - | 6.1 | 16.6 | - | 1 | - | [2] | [3] |
| | Tempo/Topaz | U | 3.0 (2971) | 4.5 | - | 6.1 | 16.6 | - | 1 | - | 15.9 | [3] |
| 1993 | Tempo/Topaz | X | 2.3 (2300) | 5.0 | - | 6.1 | 16.6 | - | 1 | - | [2] | [3] |
| | Tempo/Topaz | U | 3.0 (2971) | 4.5 | - | 6.1 | 16.6 | - | 1 | - | 15.9 | [3] |
| 1994 | Tempo/Topaz | X | 2.3 (2300) | 5.0 | - | 6.4 | 17.2 [5] | - | 1 | - | 15.9 | [3] |
| | Tempo/Topaz | U | 3.0 (2971) | 4.5 | - | 6.4 | 17.2 [5] | - | 1 | - | 15.9 | [3] |

NOTES
1 Included in transaxle capacity
2 Standard tank: 13 gals.
  Except AWD models: 15.4 gals.
3 Manual transmission: 6.6 qts.
  Manual transaxle with A/C: 7.3 qts
  Automatic transmission: 7.3 qts.
  Automatic transaxle with A/C: 7.8 qts
4 AWD models: 20.0 pts
5 Includes torque converter

86701799

## Troubleshooting Basic Air Conditioning Problems

| Problem | Cause | Solution |
| --- | --- | --- |
| There's little or no air coming from the vents (and you're sure it's on) | • The A/C fuse is blown<br>• Broken or loose wires or connections<br>• The on/off switch is defective | • Check and/or replace fuse<br>• Check and/or repair connections<br><br>• Replace switch |
| The air coming from the vents is not cool enough | • Windows and air vent wings open<br>• The compressor belt is slipping<br>• Heater is on<br>• Condenser is clogged with debris<br>• Refrigerant has escaped through a leak in the system<br>• Receiver/drier is plugged | • Close windows and vent wings<br>• Tighten or replace compressor belt<br>• Shut heater off<br>• Clean the condenser<br>• Check system<br><br>• Service system |
| The air has an odor | • Vacuum system is disrupted<br>• Odor producing substances on the evaporator case<br>• Condensation has collected in the bottom of the evaporator housing | • Have the system checked/repaired<br>• Clean the evaporator case<br><br>• Clean the evaporator housing drains |
| System is noisy or vibrating | • Compressor belt or mountings loose<br>• Air in the system | • Tighten or replace belt; tighten mounting bolts<br>• Have the system serviced |
| Sight glass condition<br>   Constant bubbles, foam or oil streaks<br>   Clear sight glass, but no cold air<br>   Clear sight glass, but air is cold<br>   Clouded with milky fluid | <br>• Undercharged system<br><br>• No refrigerant at all<br>• System is OK<br>• Receiver drier is leaking dessicant | <br>• Charge the system<br><br>• Check and charge the system<br><br>• Have system checked |
| Large difference in temperature of lines | • System undercharged | • Charge and leak test the system |
| Compressor noise | • Broken valves<br>• Overcharged<br><br>• Incorrect oil level<br><br><br>• Piston slap<br>• Broken rings<br>• Drive belt pulley bolts are loose | • Replace the valve plate<br>• Discharge, evacuate and install the correct charge<br>• Isolate the compressor and check the oil level. Correct as necessary.<br>• Replace the compressor<br>• Replace the compressor<br>• Tighten with the correct torque specification |
| Excessive vibration | • Incorrect belt tension<br>• Clutch loose<br>• Overcharged<br><br>• Pulley is misaligned | • Adjust the belt tension<br>• Tighten the clutch<br>• Discharge, evacuate and install the correct charge<br>• Align the pulley |
| Condensation dripping in the passenger compartment | • Drain hose plugged or improperly positioned<br>• Insulation removed or improperly installed | • Clean the drain hose and check for proper installation<br>• Replace the insulation on the expansion valve and hoses |

86701888

## Troubleshooting Basic Air Conditioning Problems (cont.)

| Problem | Cause | Solution |
| --- | --- | --- |
| Frozen evaporator coil | · Faulty thermostat<br>· Thermostat capillary tube improperly installed<br><br>· Thermostat not adjusted properly | · Replace the thermostat<br>· Install the capillary tube correctly<br><br>· Adjust the thermostat |
| Low side low—high side low | · System refrigerant is low<br><br>· Expansion valve is restricted | · Evacuate, leak test and charge the system<br>· Replace the expansion valve |
| Low side high—high side low | · Internal leak in the compressor—worn | · Remove the compressor cylinder head and inspect the compressor. Replace the valve plate assembly if necessary. If the compressor pistons, rings or |
| Low side high—high side low (cont.) | | cylinders are excessively worn or scored replace the compressor |
| | · Cylinder head gasket is leaking<br><br>· Expansion valve is defective<br>· Drive belt slipping | · Install a replacement cylinder head gasket<br>· Replace the expansion valve<br>· Adjust the belt tension |
| Low side high—high side high | · Condenser fins obstructed<br>· Air in the system<br><br>· Expansion valve is defective<br>· Loose or worn fan belts | · Clean the condenser fins<br>· Evacuate, leak test and charge the system<br>· Replace the expansion valve<br>· Adjust or replace the belts as necessary |
| Low side low—high side high | · Expansion valve is defective<br>· Restriction in the refrigerant hose | · Replace the expansion valve<br>· Check the hose for kinks—replace if necessary |
| Low side low—high side high | · Restriction in the receiver/drier<br>· Restriction in the condenser | · Replace the receiver/drier<br>· Replace the condenser |
| Low side and high normal (inadequate cooling) | · Air in the system<br><br>· Moisture in the system | · Evacuate, leak test and charge the system<br>· Evacuate, leak test and charge the system |

86701889

## Troubleshooting Basic Wheel Problems

| Problem | Cause | Solution |
|---|---|---|
| The car's front end vibrates at high speed | · The wheels are out of balance<br>· Wheels are out of alignment | · Have wheels balanced<br>· Have wheel alignment checked/adjusted |
| Car pulls to either side | · Wheels are out of alignment<br><br>· Unequal tire pressure<br>· Different size tires or wheels | · Have wheel alignment checked/adjusted<br>· Check/adjust tire pressure<br>· Change tires or wheels to same size |
| The car's wheel(s) wobbles | · Loose wheel lug nuts<br>· Wheels out of balance<br>· Damaged wheel<br><br><br>· Wheels are out of alignment<br><br>· Worn or damaged ball joint<br>· Excessive play in the steering linkage (usually due to worn parts)<br>· Defective shock absorber | · Tighten wheel lug nuts<br>· Have tires balanced<br>· Raise car and spin the wheel. If the wheel is bent, it should be replaced<br>· Have wheel alignment checked/adjusted<br>· Check ball joints<br>· Check steering linkage<br><br>· Check shock absorbers |
| Tires wear unevenly or prematurely | · Incorrect wheel size<br><br>· Wheels are out of balance<br>· Wheels are out of alignment | · Check if wheel and tire size are compatible<br>· Have wheels balanced<br>· Have wheel alignment checked/adjusted |

86701444

## Troubleshooting Basic Tire Problems

| Problem | Cause | Solution |
|---|---|---|
| The car's front end vibrates at high speeds and the steering wheel shakes | · Wheels out of balance<br>· Front end needs aligning | · Have wheels balanced<br>· Have front end alignment checked |
| The car pulls to one side while cruising | · Unequal tire pressure (car will usually pull to the low side)<br>· Mismatched tires<br><br>· Front end needs aligning | · Check/adjust tire pressure<br><br>· Be sure tires are of the same type and size<br>· Have front end alignment checked |
| Abnormal, excessive or uneven tire wear<br><br>See "How to Read Tire Wear" | · Infrequent tire rotation<br><br>· Improper tire pressure<br><br>· Sudden stops/starts or high speed on curves | · Rotate tires more frequently to equalize wear<br>· Check/adjust pressure<br><br>· Correct driving habits |
| Tire squeals | · Improper tire pressure<br>· Front end needs aligning | · Check/adjust tire pressure<br>· Have front end alignment checked |

86701445

## Tire Size Comparison Chart

| "Letter" sizes | | | Inch Sizes | Metric-inch Sizes | | |
| "60 Series" | "70 Series" | "78 Series" | 1965–77 | "60 Series" | "70 Series" | "80 Series" |
|---|---|---|---|---|---|---|
| | | Y78-12 | 5.50-12, 5.60-12<br>6.00-12 | 165/60-12 | 165/70-12 | 155-12 |
| | | W78-13 | 5.20-13 | 165/60-13 | 145/70-13 | 135-13 |
| | | Y78-13 | 5.60-13 | 175/60-13 | 155/70-13 | 145-13 |
| | | | 6.15-13 | 185/60-13 | 165/70-13 | 155-13, P155/80-13 |
| A60-13 | A70-13 | A78-13 | 6.40-13 | 195/60-13 | 175/70-13 | 165-13 |
| B60-13 | B70-13 | B78-13 | 6.70-13 | 205/60-13 | 185/70-13 | 175-13 |
| | | | 6.90-13 | | | |
| C60-13 | C70-13 | C78-13 | 7.00-13 | 215/60-13 | 195/70-13 | 185-13 |
| D60-13 | D70-13 | D78-13 | 7.25-13 | | | |
| E60-13 | E70-13 | E78-13 | 7.75-13 | | | 195-13 |
| | | | 5.20-14 | 165/60-14 | 145/70-14 | 135-14 |
| | | | 5.60-14 | 175/60-14 | 155/70-14 | 145-14 |
| | | | 5.90-14 | | | |
| A60-14 | A70-14 | A78-14 | 6.15-14 | 185/60-14 | 165/70-14 | 155-14 |
| | B70-14 | B78-14 | 6.45-14 | 195/60-14 | 175/70-14 | 165-14 |
| | C70-14 | C78-14 | 6.95-14 | 205/60-14 | 185/70-14 | 175-14 |
| D60-14 | D70-14 | D78-14 | | | | |
| E60-14 | E70-14 | E78-14 | 7.35-14 | 215/60-14 | 195/70-14 | 185-14 |
| F60-14 | F70-14 | F78-14, F83-14 | 7.75-14 | 225/60-14 | 200/70-14 | 195-14 |
| G60-14 | G70-14 | G77-14, G78-14 | 8.25-14 | 235/60-14 | 205/70-14 | 205-14 |
| H60-14 | H70-14 | H78-14 | 8.55-14 | 245/60-14 | 215/70-14 | 215-14 |
| J60-14 | J70-14 | J78-14 | 8.85-14 | 255/60-14 | 225/70-14 | 225-14 |
| L60-14 | L70-14 | | 9.15-14 | 265/60-14 | 235/70-14 | |
| | A70-15 | A78-15 | 5.60-15 | 185/60-15 | 165/70-15 | 155-15 |
| B60-15 | B70-15 | B78-15 | 6.35-15 | 195/60-15 | 175/70-15 | 165-15 |
| C60-15 | C70-15 | C78-15 | 6.85-15 | 205/60-15 | 185/70-15 | 175-15 |
| | D70-15 | D78-15 | | | | |
| E60-15 | E70-15 | E78-15 | 7.35-15 | 215/60-15 | 195/70-15 | 185-15 |
| F60-15 | F70-15 | F78-15 | 7.75-15 | 225/60-15 | 205/70-15 | 195-15 |
| G60-15 | G70-15 | G78-15 | 8.15-15/8.25-15 | 235/60-15 | 215/70-15 | 205-15 |
| H60-15 | H70-15 | H78-15 | 8.45-15/8.55-15 | 245/60-15 | 225/70-15 | 215-15 |
| J60-15 | J70-15 | J78-15 | 8.85-15/8.90-15 | 255/60-15 | 235/70-15 | 225-15 |
| | K70-15 | | 9.00-15 | 265/60-15 | 245/70-15 | 230-15 |
| L60-15 | L70-15 | L78-15, L84-15 | 9.15-15 | | | 235-15 |
| | M70-15 | M78-15 | | | | 255-15 |
| | | N78-15 | | | | |

NOTE: Every size tire is not listed and many size comaprisons are approximate, based on load ratings. Wider tires than those supplied new with the vehicle should always be checked for clearance

86701446

# 2

# ENGINE PERFORMANCE AND TUNE-UP

## TUNE-UP PROCEDURES

### Spark Plugs

Spark plugs are used in all gasoline engines to ignite the mixture of air and fuel introduced into the cylinder. The controlled burning and expansion of the gases that result, forces the piston down, turning the crankshaft, which provides the locomotion that turn the wheels.

Ford recommends that spark plugs be changed every 30,000 miles (48,300 km). In severe driving environments, these intervals should be more frequent. Severe driving conditions would include:

1. Extended periods of idling or low speed operation, such as off–road or door–to–door deliveries.

2. Driving short distances of less than 10 miles (16 km) where the average temperature is below 10°F (–12°C) for 60 days or more.

3. Vehicle frequently operated in excessive dusty conditions.

Under normal operation, plug gap increases about 0.001 in. (0.025mm) for every 1000–2500 miles (1600–4000 km). As the gap increases, the plug's voltage requirement also increases. As the spark plug voltage demand increases,it takes as much as two to three times as much voltage to fire a plug at higher speeds.

When a spark plugs is removed, the condition of the plugs a good indicator of the engine's operating conditions. A small deposit of light tan or gray material on a spark plug that has been used for any period of time is considered normal. Any other color, or abnormal amounts of deposit, indicate that there is something amiss in the engine.

The gap between the center electrode and the side or ground electrode can be expected to increase no more than 0.001 in. (0.025mm) every 1000 miles (1600 km) under normal driving conditions. If a plug fouls, investigate and correct the cause of the fouling and either clean or replace the plug.

There are several reasons why a spark plug would foul and you can determine the fault just by observing the plug.

### SPARK PLUG HEAT RANGE

Spark plug heat range is the ability of the spark plug to dissipate heat. The longer the insulator (or the farther it extends into the engine), the hotter the plug will operate; the shorter the insulator, the cooler it will operate. A plug that absorbs little heat and remains too cool will quickly accumulate deposits of oil and carbon, because it is not hot enough to burn it off. This leads to plug fouling and consequently to misfiring. A plug that absorbs too much heat will have few deposits, but, due to the excessive heat, the electrodes will burn away more quickly and in some instances, pre–ignition may result. Pre–ignition takes place when plug tips get so hot that they glow sufficiently enough to ignite the fuel/air mixture before the actual spark occurs. This early ignition will usually cause a pinging sound during low speeds and heavy loads.

The general rule of thumb in choosing the correct heat range when picking a spark plug is as follows:

1. Cooler plug—if most of your driving is long distance, high speed travel.

2. Hotter plug—if most of your driving involves short distances or heavy stop and go traffic.

Original equipment plugs can be termed "Compromise Plugs." Most drivers never have the need for changing their plugs from the factory recommended heat range.

### REMOVAL & INSTALLATION

◆ **See Figures 1, 2, 3, 4, 5, 6, 7, 8 and 9**

Because the Tempo and Topaz utilize a variety of engines, it is a good idea to determine what type of engine your vehicle uses, and how many spark plugs are required.

The 2.0L diesel engine requires NO spark plugs at all. This is based on the unique nature of the diesel engine. The 2.3L engine requires 4 spark plugs because it is four cylinder, and the 3.0L engine requires 6 spark plugs because it has six cylinders.

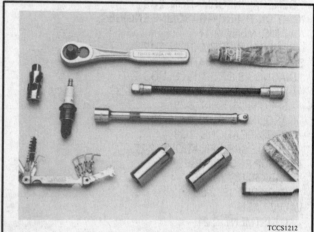

TCCS1212

**Fig. 1 A variety of tools and gauges are needed for spark plug service**

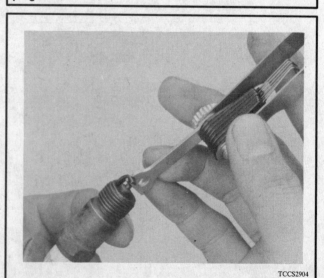

TCCS2904

**Fig. 2 Adjusting the spark plug gap**

➡ The spark plugs used in your vehicle, require the use of a deep plug socket for removal and installation. A special purpose spark plug wire puller is also recommended. The puller has a cupped jaw that grips the plug wire boot and makes the job of twisting and pulling the wire from the plug easier. This tool is available at most automotive parts stores.

1. Determine engine type and number of spark plugs needed to complete the job.

2. Disconnect the negative battery cable.

3. Locate each spark plug, and remove any air cleaner parts necessary to access the plug.

4. Starting at one end of the engine and working toward the other, identify and tag the individual spark lug wires, then remove the plug wire, using the spark plug wire removal tool. If you do not have the wire removal tool, you can remove the wire by grabbing the wire as close to the plug as possible, and moving the wire back and forth until the wire separates from the plug.

➡ It is not recommended to remove more than one plug wire at a time. The order of the wires are important to the proper running of the engine.

5. After removing the wire, blow out the cavity where the spark plug meets the wire with air or clean it out with a small brush.

6. Remove the spark plug with a plug socket and ratchet. Turn the socket counterclockwise slowly at first to remove the plug. Be sure to hold the socket straight on the plug to avoid breaking the insulator (a deep socket designed for spark plugs has a rubber cushion built–in to help prevent plug damage).

7. Once the plug is removed, compare it with the spark plug illustrations to determine if there are any potential engine problems.

## To install:

8. If the old plugs are to be reused, clean and re–gap them. If new spark plugs are to be installed, check the gap. Use a feeler gauge to check plug gap. The correct size gauge should pass through the electrode with a slight drag. If you're in doubt, try the next smaller and one size larger measurements. The smaller gauge should go through easily, while the larger should be unable to pass through at all. If adjustment is necessary use the bending tool on the end of the gauge. When adjusting the gap, always bend the side of the electrode. Use great care in adjusting any gap, the electrode is delicate and can be damaged easily.

➡ The correct spark plug gap is 0.039–0.043 in. (1.0–1.09mm)

9. Apply a small amount of anti–seize or squirt a drop of penetrating oil on the plug threads. Using your hand, insert the plug into the engine plug hole and turn clockwise until tight. In the event you cannot get your hand in, use a small piece of hose, and insert the end of the spark plug into the hose and use it as an extension to install and tighten the plug.

10. With the spark plug hand tight, use a torque wrench and torque the plug to the correct torque specifications. DO NOT OVERTIGHTEN.

11. Install the plug wire firmly over the spark plug after coating the inside of the terminal with a thin coat of dielectric compound (Motorcraft D7AZ–19A331–A or the equivalent).

12. Proceed to the next spark plug until complete.

13. Reconnect the battery cable.

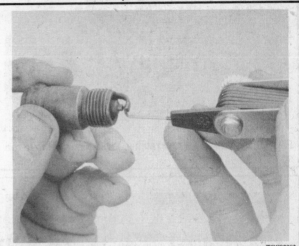

TCCS2903

**Fig. 3  Checking the spark plug gap with a feeler gauge**

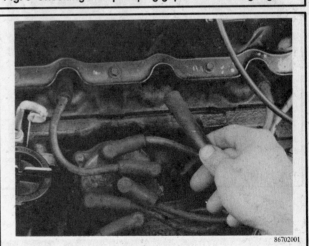

86702001

**Fig. 4  Carefully remove the spark plug wire. Use either your hand or a spark plug puller**

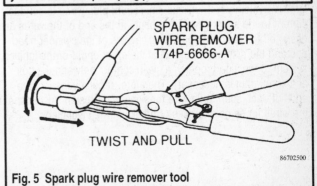

SPARK PLUG
WIRE REMOVER
T74P-6666-A

TWIST AND PULL

86702500

**Fig. 5  Spark plug wire remover tool**

86702002

**Fig. 6 Using a socket and ratchet, loosen and remove the spark plug**

86702003

**Fig. 7 With the spark plug removed, inspect it carefully**

## Spark Plug Wires

The gasoline Tempo/Topaz is equipped with an electronic ignition system which utilizes 8mm spark plug wires to conduct current to the spark plugs. The boots at the end of the wires are designed to cover the spark plug cavities at the cylinder head end and the distributor contact at the other end. For the ignition system to function properly, a clean contact between the coil and spark plug is necessary. Therefore, regularly inspect the ends of each spark plug wire for signs of corrosion. Also inspect the wires for signs of cracks or breaks in the insulation.

**✳✳CAUTION**

Because the coil and ignition system is capable of producing a large amount of current, never service any ignition component with the car running.

### TESTING SPARK PLUG WIRES

Most spark plugs today are of a resistor type. This means that for them to function correctly, there must be a resistance level between the start of the wire and it's end. With this level of resistance, the spark is of a greater intensity, and therefore the engine is more productive because the combustion is more efficient.

To test the resistance of a spark plug wire, it is necessary to use a multi–meter. This tool is available at most automotive parts stores. Although it is not a cheap tool, it is useful for many electrical situations. It is the only way to test the functionality of resistor plug wires.

➡ **When testing plug wires, remove, test and replace one wire at a time.**

1. Remove the spark plug wire, using a twisting motion, from both the spark plug and distributor cap.

2. Using your multi–meter, set to ohms, connect individual probe ends to respective ends of the plug wire. Record the readings registered on the meter.

3. The correct resistance should be between 4000–7000 ohms per foot. If the resistance is not within this range, replace the wire.

4. Continue until all the wires, including the coil wire has been tested.

### REMOVAL & INSTALLATION

◆ **See Figures 5, 10 and 11**

➡ **To avoid confusion when removing or replacing spark plug wires, always remove and tag the wires one at a time.**

1. Carefully inspect the wires before removing them from the spark plug, coil or distributor cap. Look for visible damage such as cuts, pinches, cracks or torn boots. Replace any wires that show sign of damage. If the boot is damaged, it may be possible to replace it by itself.

2. Carefully grasp and twist the boot back and forth while pulling away from the spark plug. A spark plug wire removal tool (T74P–6666–A or equivalent) can make the job easier.

➡ **Do not pull on the wire directly, it may become separated from the connector inside the boot.**

3. Once removed, inspect the inside connection of the spark plug wire. It should be clean metal, usually copper. If corroded, clean with a small wire brush or replace completely.

### GAP BRIDGED

IDENTIFIED BY DEPOSIT BUILD—UP CLOSING GAP BETWEEN ELECTRODES.

CAUSED BY OIL OR CARBON FOULING. REPLACE PLUG, OR, IF DEPOSITS ARE NOT EXCESSIVE THE PLUG CAN BE CLEANED.

### OIL FOULED

IDENTIFIED BY WET BLACK DEPOSITS ON THE INSULATOR SHELL BORE ELECTRODES.

CAUSED BY EXCESSIVE OIL ENTERING COMBUSTION CHAMBER THROUGH WORN RINGS AND PISTONS, EXCESSIVE CLEARANCE BETWEEN VALVE GUIDES AND STEMS, OR WORN OR LOOSE BEARINGS. CORRECT OIL PROBLEM. REPLACE THE PLUG.

### CARBON FOULED

IDENTIFIED BY BLACK, DRY FLUFFY CARBON DEPOSITS ON INSULATOR TIPS, EXPOSED SHELL SURFACES AND ELECTRODES.

CAUSED BY TOO COLD A PLUG, WEAK IGNITION, DIRTY AIR CLEANER, DEFECTIVE FUEL PUMP, TOO RICH A FUEL MIXTURE, IMPROPERLY OPERATING HEAT RISER OR EXCESSIVE IDLING. CAN BE CLEANED.

### NORMAL

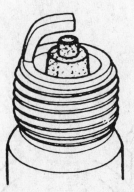

IDENTIFIED BY LIGHT TAN OR GRAY DEPOSITS ON THE FIRING TIP

### PRE-IGNITION

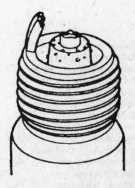

IDENTIFIED BY MELTED ELECTRODES AND POSSIBLY BLISTERED INSULATOR. METALIC DEPOSITS ON INSULATOR INDICATE ENGINE DAMAGE.

CAUSED BY WRONG TYPE OF FUEL, INCORRECT IGNITION TIMING OR ADVANCE, TOO HOT A PLUG, BURNT VALVES OR ENGINE OVERHEATING. REPLACE THE PLUG.

### OVERHEATING

IDENTIFIED BY A WHITE OR LIGHT GRAY INSULATOR WITH SMALL BLACK OR GRAY BROWN SPOTS AND WITH BLUISH-BURNT APPEARANCE OF ELECTRODES.

CAUSED BY ENGINE OVER-HEATING, WRONG TYPE OF FUEL, LOOSE SPARK PLUGS, TOO HOT A PLUG, LOW FUEL PUMP PRESSURE OR INCORRECT IGNITION TIMING. REPLACE THE PLUG.

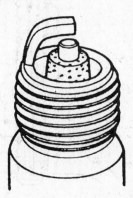

### FUSED SPOT DEPOSIT

IDENTIFIED BY MELTED OR SPOTTY DEPOSITS RESEMBLING BUBBLES OR BLISTERS.

CAUSED BY SUDDEN ACCELERATION. CAN BE CLEANED IF NOT EXCESSIVE, OTHERWISE REPLACE PLUG.

TCCS2002

**Fig. 8  Visual inspection will tell you a lot about your spark plugs**

**Tracking Arc**
High voltage arcs between a fouling deposit on the insulator tip and spark plug shell. This ignites the fuel/air mixture at some point along the insulator tip, retarding the ignition timing which causes a power and fuel loss.

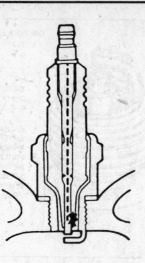

**Wide Gap**
Spark plug electrodes are worn so that the high voltage charge cannot arc across the electrodes. Improper gapping of electrodes on new or "cleaned" spark plugs could cause a similar condition. Fuel remains unburned and a power loss results.

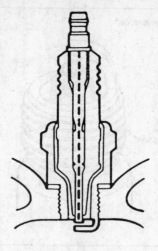

**Flashover**
A damaged spark plug boot, along with dirt and moisture, could permit the high voltage charge to short over the insulator to the spark plug shell or the engine. A buttress insulator design helps prevent high voltage flashover.

**Fouled Spark Plug**
Deposits that have formed on the insulator tip may become conductive and provide a "shunt" path to the shell. This prevents the high voltage from arcing between the electrodes. A power and fuel loss is the result.

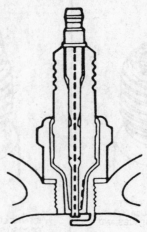

**Bridged Electrodes**
Fouling deposits between the electrodes "ground out" the high voltage needed to fire the spark plug. The arc between the electrodes does not occur and the fuel air mixture is not ignited. This causes a power loss and exhausting of raw fuel.

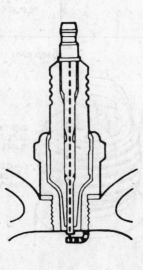

**Cracked Insulator**
A crack in the spark plug insulator could cause the high voltage charge to "ground out." Here, the spark does not jump the electrode gap and the fuel air mixture is not ignited. This causes a power loss and raw fuel is exhausted.

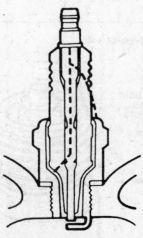

TCCS2001

**Fig. 9 Spark plug wear can also tell you about engine condition**

## Diagnosis of Spark Plugs

| Problem | Possible Cause | Correction |
| --- | --- | --- |
| Brown to grayish-tan deposits and slight electrode wear. | • Normal wear. | • Clean, regap, reinstall. |
| Dry, fluffy black carbon deposits. | • Poor ignition output. | • Check distributor to coil connections. |
| Wet, oily deposits with very little electrode wear. | • "Break-in" of new or recently overhauled engine.<br>• Excessive valve stem guide clearances.<br>• Worn intake valve seals. | • Degrease, clean and reinstall the plugs.<br>• Refer to Section 3.<br>• Replace the seals. |
| Red, brown, yellow and white colored coatings on the insulator. Engine misses intermittently under severe operating conditions. | • By-products of combustion. | • Clean, regap, and reinstall. If heavily coated, replace. |
| Colored coatings heavily deposited on the portion of the plug projecting into the chamber and on the side facing the intake valve. | • Leaking seals if condition is found in only one or two cylinders. | • Check the seals. Replace if necessary. Clean, regap, and reinstall the plugs. |
| Shiny yellow glaze coating on the insulator. | • Melted by-products of combustion. | • Avoid sudden acceleration with wide-open throttle after long periods of low speed driving. Replace the plugs. |
| Burned or blistered insulator tips and badly eroded electrodes. | • Overheating. | • Check the cooling system.<br>• Check for sticking heat riser valves. Refer to Section 1.<br>• Lean air-fuel mixture.<br>• Check the heat range of the plugs. May be too hot.<br>• Check ignition timing. May be over-advanced.<br>• Check the torque value of the plugs to ensure good plug-engine seat contact. |
| Broken or cracked insulator tips. | • Heat shock from sudden rise in tip temperature under severe operating conditions. Improper gapping of plugs. | • Replace the plugs. Gap correctly. |

TCCS1200

**To install:**

4. Before installing the spark plug wire, coat the inside of the boot and terminal with a thin coat of dielectric compound (Motorcraft D7AZ–19A331–A or the equivalent). Install the wires in their correct order, making certain they fit firmly over the spark plug, coil or distributor.

5. With all the wires connected, including the wire between the coil and the distributor cap, secure all loose wires using the factory holder installed in the engine compartment.

6. Start the vehicle to make sure the work was done properly.

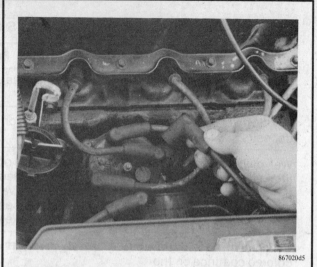

Fig. 11 Spark plug wire removed using twisting motion

**Spark Plug Boot Replacement**

If it is necessary to replace a boot on a particular wire, use the following procedure:

1. Carefully twist or cut off the old boot. Apply a thin coat of dielectric compound (Motorcraft D7AZ–19A331–A or the equivalent) to the area of the wire that will contact the new boot.

2. Slowly work the new boot over the spark plug wire, using a twisting motion. (A tool is available for this job. The special tool number is T74P–6666–A).

3. With the wire and boot secure, reconnect plug wire to plug or cap. Start vehicle to make sure connection is adequate.

Fig. 10 Spark plug wire and boot; distributor side

## FIRING ORDER

▶ See Figure 12

➡ To avoid confusion, when replacing spark plug wires, remove and tag the wires one at a time.

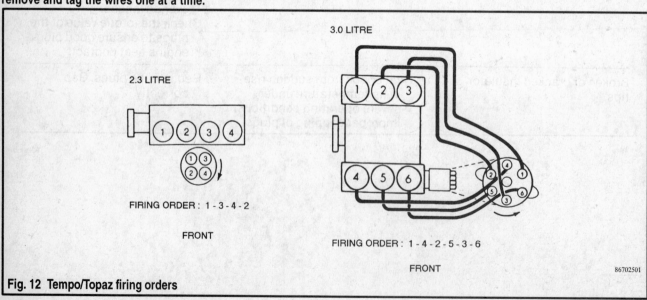

2.3 LITRE

FIRING ORDER : 1 - 3 - 4 - 2

FRONT

3.0 LITRE

FIRING ORDER : 1 - 4 - 2 - 5 - 3 - 6

FRONT

Fig. 12 Tempo/Topaz firing orders

## ELECTRONIC IGNITION—GASOLINE ENGINE

### Description & Operation

▶ See Figures 13, 14, and 15

The gasoline engine equipped Tempo /Topaz utilizes Ford's Thick Film Ignition (TFI–IV) System. This ignition system features an extended reach 14mm tapered seat spark plug, a multi–point rotor, a universal distributor (which eliminates the conventional centrifugal and vacuum advance mechanisms) and provisions for fixed octane adjustment. The TFI–IV system module has 6 pins and uses an E–Core ignition coil, named after the shape of the laminations making up the core. This type ignition system was used in the Tempo/Topaz from 1984 through 1992.

There are 2 types of TFI–IV ignition systems:
• PUSH START: This TFI–IV system first appeared on the 1984 Tempo/Topaz and was used on the 2.3L High Swirl Combustion (HSC) engine. It featured a "push start" mode which allowed manual transmission vehicles to be push started. Automatic transmission vehicles must not be push started because they were not equipped with this.
• COMPUTER CONTROLLED DWELL: This second TFI–IV system appeared on the 1990 model and features an EEC–IV controlled ignition coil charge time.

All TFI–IV ignition systems have a distributor base–mounted TFI ignition module and a hall effect stator assembly. The distributor also contains a provision to change the basic distributor calibration with the use of a replaceable octane rod. The replacement of a rod allows for a retard rate of either the standard 0° to 3° or 6°. No other calibration changes are possible.

The operation of the distributor is accomplished through the Hall Effect stator assembly which causes the ignition coil to be switched off and on by the EEC–IV computer or TFI–IV modules. The vane switch within this assembly consists of a Hall sensor on one side and a permanent magnet on the other side.

A rotary armature, made of ferrous metal, is used to trigger the Hall Effect switch. When the window of the armature is between the magnet and the Hall Effect device, a magnetic flux field is completed from the magnet through the Hall Effect device back to the magnet. As the vane passes through the opening, the flux lines are shunted through the vane and back to the magnet. A voltage is produced while the vane passes through the opening. When the vane clears the opening, the window causes the signal to go to 0 volts. In the EEC–IV system, the signal is used for crankshaft position sensing and the computation of the desired spark advance based on the engine demand and calibration. The voltage distribution is accomplished through a conventional rotor, cap and ignition wires.

In this system, the TFI–IV module supplies voltage to the Profile Ignition Pick–up (PIP) sensor, which in turn sends the crankshaft position information to the TFI–IV module. The TFI–IV module then sends this information to the EEC–IV module, which determines the spark timing and sends an electronic signal to the TFI–IV ignition module to trigger the coil and produce a spark to fire the spark plug.

Starting with the 1993 Tempo/Topaz the TFI ignition system was updated. In reality, very little changed between the new and the old systems. The principles and components remained similar. The only real update was the departure of the TFI Module and the replacement with an ignition control module.

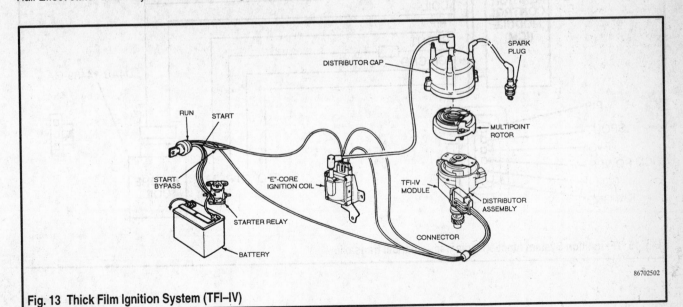

Fig. 13 Thick Film Ignition System (TFI–IV)

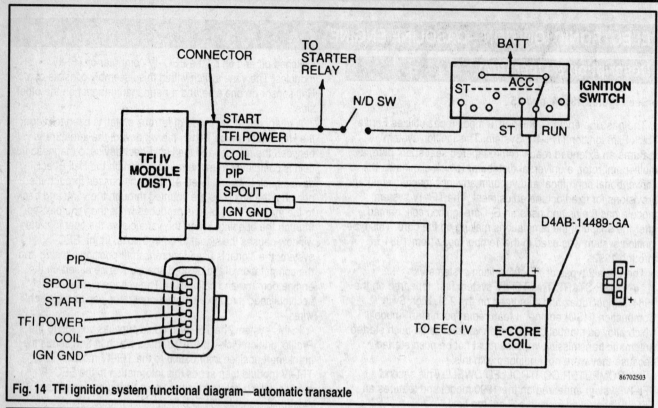

Fig. 14 TFI ignition system functional diagram—automatic transaxle

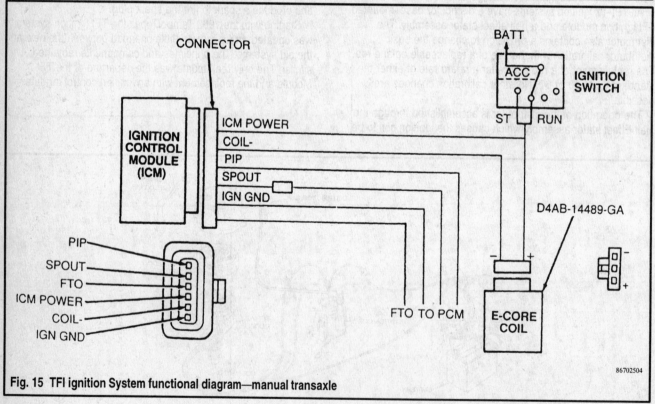

Fig. 15 TFI ignition System functional diagram—manual transaxle

## Diagnosis & Testing

### SERVICE PRECAUTIONS

• Always turn the key OFF and isolate both ends of a circuit whenever testing for short or continuity

• Never measure voltage or resistance directly at the processor module connector.

• Always disconnect solenoids and switches from the harness before measuring for continuity, resistance or energizing by way of a 12 voltage source.

• When unfastening connectors, inspect for damaged or pushed–out pins, corrosion, loose or broken wires or any other unusual condition. If there is something wrong, fix or replace before continuing with any diagnosis.

### PRELIMINARY CHECKS

1. Inspect the engine compartment to ensure that all vacuum lines and spark plug wires are properly routed and securely connected.

2. Examine all wiring harnesses and connectors for insulation damage, burn or melted marks or loose connections. Check that the module is securely fastened to the side of the distributor.

3. Be certain that the battery is fully charged and that all accessories are turned OFF.

### IGNITION COIL SECONDARY VOLTAGE

1. Connect a spark tester between the ignition coil wire and a good engine ground.

2. Crank the engine and check for spark at the tester.

3. If no spark occurs, check the following:

   a. Measure the resistance of the ignition coil secondary wire (high voltage wire). The resistance should not exceed 7000 ohms per foot (30cm).

   b. Inspect the ignition coil for damage, cracks or carbon tracking.

   c. Check that the distributor shaft is rotating when the engine is being cranked.

4. If the results of a, b, and c are okay, go to the next section, "Ignition Coil Primary Circuit Switching."

5. If a spark did occur, inspect the top, bottom and edges of the rotor blade tip. Service any part if necessary.

6. If the engine still does not start, go to the "Wiring Harness" test section.

### IGNITION COIL PRIMARY CIRCUIT SWITCHING

▶ See Figure 16

1. Push the connector tabs and separate the wiring harness connector from the ignition module. Inspect the harness and connector for signs of dirt, corrosion or burn marks. Service if necessary.

2. If okay, reconnect harness. Attach a 12 volt test light between the coil tach terminal connection and a good engine ground. Crank the engine and check for the test light to turn on.

3. If the test lamp flashes, go to the Ignition Coil test section.

4. If the test lamp did not light, go to next section.

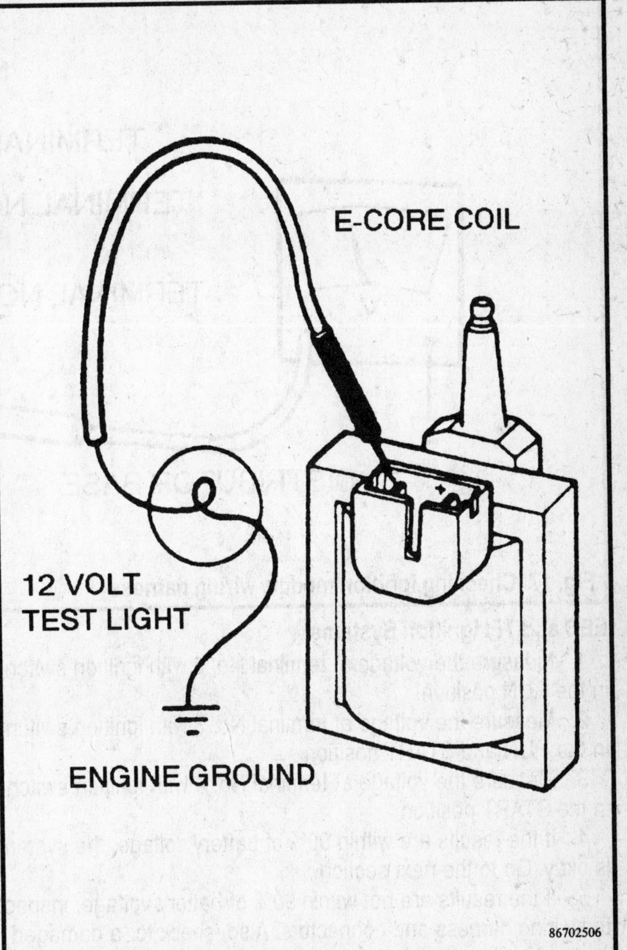

**Fig. 16 Checking for ignition with a test light**

### WIRING HARNESS

▶ See Figure 17

1. Push the connector tabs and separate the wiring harness connector from the ignition module. Inspect for dirt, corrosion or damage. Service, if necessary.

2. Disconnect the wire at the S terminal of the starter relay.

3. Using a voltmeter, attach the negative (–) lead of the meter to the distributor base. Using a small pin attached to the positive (+) lead of the meter, measure the voltage outputs of the harness as follows:

➡ **Do not allow the pin inserted into the harness to contact electrical ground (–) while performing this test.**

**Non–EEC Ignition Systems**

1. Measure the voltage at terminal No. 1 with ignition switch in the RUN position.

2. Measure the voltage at terminal No. 2 with ignition switch in the RUN position.

3. Measure the voltage at terminal No. 3 with ignition switch in the RUN and START position.

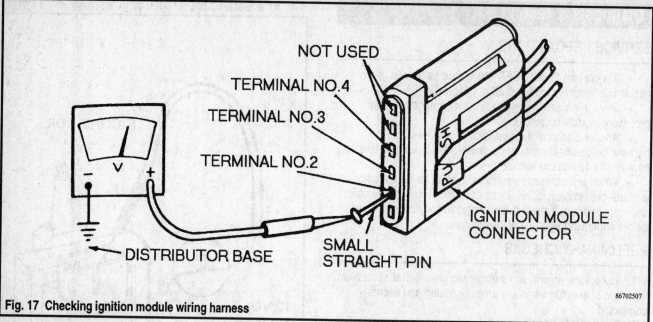

**Fig. 17 Checking ignition module wiring harness**

### EEC and TFI Ignition Systems

1. Measure the voltage at terminal No. 2 with ignition switch in the RUN position.

2. Measure the voltage at terminal No. 3 with ignition switch in the RUN and START position.

3. Measure the voltage at terminal No. 4 with ignition switch in the START position

4. If the results are within 90% of battery voltage, the system is okay. Go to the next section.

5. If the results are not within 90% of battery voltage, inspect the wiring harness and connectors. Also, check for a damaged or worn ignition switch.

6. Turn the ignition switch OFF. Remove the pin from the plug.

7. Reconnect the wire at the S terminal of the starter relay.

### EEC–IV—TFI–IV Ignition Systems

1. Push the connector tabs and separate the wiring harness connector from the ignition module. Inspect for dirt, corrosion or damage. Service, if necessary.

2. Disconnect the pin–in–line connector and check for spark.

3. If a spark occurs, check the IMS wire for continuity. If okay, the problem is in the EEC system.

4. If no spark occurs, remove the distributor module from the distributor.

5. Install a new TFI–IV module.

### IGNITION COIL

▶ See Figures 18 and 19

1. Verify that the ignition switch is in the OFF position.

2. Remove the primary connector, clean and inspect for dirt or corrosion. Service if necessary.

3. Measure the resistance between the positive (+) and negative (–) terminals of the primary connector with an ohmmeter. Resistance should be 0.3–1.0 ohms.

4. Measure resistance from the coil negative (–) terminal of the primary connector and the high voltage terminal of the coil. Resistance should be 8000–11500 ohms.

5. Replace the coil if either readings are not within the given specifications.

### STATOR ASSEMBLY & MODULE

1. Remove the distributor from the engine compartment

2. Remove the ignition module from the distributor body.

3. Inspect the distributor ground screw, stator assembly wires and terminals.

4. Measure the resistance of the stator assemble.

   a. If the resistance is 650–1300 ohms, replace the ignition module.

   b. If the resistance is less than 650 ohms, or greater than 1300 ohms, replace the stator assembly.

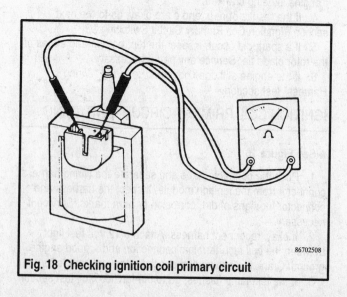

**Fig. 18 Checking ignition coil primary circuit**

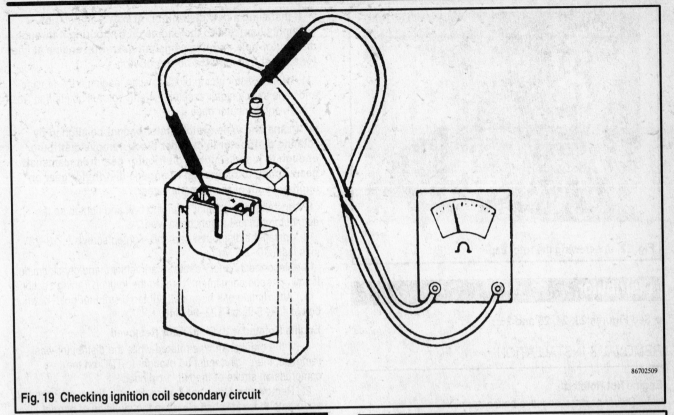

**Fig. 19 Checking ignition coil secondary circuit**

## Distributor Cap & Rotor

### REMOVAL & INSTALLATION

▶ See Figures 20, 21 and 22

➡ The Tempo/Topaz utilize two different type rotor caps. These caps are NOT interchangeable.

1. Disconnect the negative battery cable.
2. Release the distributor cap retaining screws and lift the cap from the distributor assembly.
3. With the distributor cap removed, determine whether the rotor cap is a screw type, or a pull up type. Proceed as follows
    a. If the rotor cap is round, then it is a screw type cap.
    b. If the cap is small and straight, then it is a pull up type.
4. Based upon the identification above, remove the rotor cap.

**To install:**

5. Place the rotor into position and either push down to secure, or install the retaining screws.
6. Properly fit the cap onto the distributor by aligning the marks on the side of the cap, and secure the retaining screws. Tighten screws to 18–23 inch lbs. (2.0–2.6 Nm).
7. Reconnect the negative battery cable.

**Fig. 20 Unscrew the distributor cap**

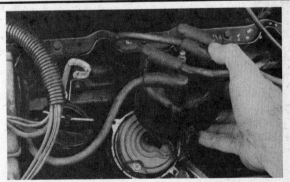

**Fig. 21 Lift cap and determine which type of rotor is installed**

86702008
**Fig. 22 Unscrewing the rotor cap**

## Distributor

♦ See Figures 23, 24, 25 and 26

### REMOVAL & INSTALLATION

#### Engine Not Rotated

1. Disconnect the negative battery terminal.
2. Turn the engine over until No. 1 cylinder is at TDC of the compression stroke.
3. Remove the distributor cap. Remove the wire harness connected to the side of the distributor.
4. Mark the position of the distributor base in relation to the engine block with white paint or other suitable marking material, for reference when reinstalling the distributor.
5. Loosen and remove the distributor hold–down bolt and clamp.
6. Carefully begin lifting the distributor up and out. Once the shaft is clear of the engine compartment, inspect the shaft for cracks in the O–seal, the condition of the shaft drive gear and any other part which could lead to distributor problems in the future.

#### To install:

7. Check to make sure the engine is still at TDC. Inspect distributor shaft hole to make sure it is free of dirt.
8. Rotate distributor shaft until the painted mark on rotor is pointing toward painted mark on engine block made during removal.
9. Continue rotating rotor slightly so leading edge of the vane is centered in vane the switch stator assembly.
10. Dip entire distributor gear in engine assembly lubricant D9AZ–19579–D or equivalent.

➡ If installing a new distributor, ALWAYS add engine assembly lubricant to the engine oil by pouring it through distributor hole onto the camshaft gear. Run engine at idle for at least five minutes before driving.

11. Rotate distributor in block to align leading edge of vane and vane switch stator assembly. Verify rotor is pointing at No. 1 mark on distributor base.

➡ If vane and vane switch stator cannot be aligned by rotating distributor in cylinder block, remove distributor enough to just disengage distributor gear from camshaft gear. Rotate rotor enough to engage distributor gear on another tooth of the camshaft gear.

12. Install the distributor retaining bolt and tighten so the distributor can just barely be moved.
13. Install the distributor cap and, tighten screws to 18–23 inch lbs. (2.0–2.6 Nm).
14. Reconnect battery cable. Start vehicle, and check timing. If timing needs adjustment, refer to the Ignition Timing section.
15. After timing has been set, tighten distributor hold–down bolt to 17–25 ft. lbs. (23–34 Nm).

#### Engine Rotated with Distributor Removed

1. If the crankshaft was rotated while the distributor was removed, the engine must be brought to TDC on the compression stroke of the No. 1 cylinder.
2. Remove the No. 1 spark plug. Place a finger over the hole and rotate the crankshaft slowly in the direction of normal rotation until engine compression is felt.
3. When engine compression is felt at the spark plug hole, indicating that the piston is approaching TDC, continue to turn the crankshaft until the timing mark on the pulley is aligned with the 0 mark on the engine front cover.
4. Turn the distributor shaft until the ignition rotor is at the No. 1 firing position.
5. Rotate distributor shaft so the blade on rotor is pointing toward paint mark on distributor base made during removal.
6. Continue rotating rotor slightly so leading edge of the vane is centered in vane switch stator assembly. Verify rotor is pointing at No. 1 mark on distributor base.

➡ If vane and vane switch stator cannot be aligned by rotating distributor in cylinder block, remove distributor enough to just disengage distributor gear from camshaft gear. Rotate rotor enough to engage distributor gear on another tooth of the camshaft gear.

7. Install the distributor retaining bolt and tighten so the distributor can just barely be moved.
8. Install the rotor and distributor cap and connect all wiring. Tighten distributor cap to 18–23 inch lbs. (2.0–2.6 Nm).
9. Reconnect battery cable. Start vehicle, and check timing. If timing needs adjustment, refer to the Ignition Timing section.
10. After timing has been set, tighten distributor hold–down bolt to 17–25 ft. lbs. (23–34 Nm).

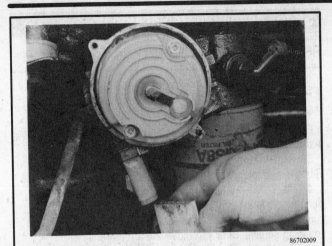

**Fig. 23 Unplug module wire harness**

**Fig. 24 Paint alignment marks on both the rotor cap and engine block**

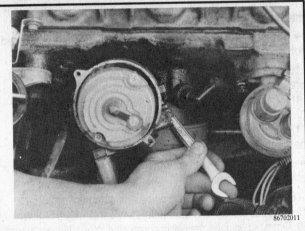

**Fig. 25 Loosen and remove distributor retaining bolt**

**Fig. 26 Carefully remove distributor**

## Ignition Module Replacement

### REMOVAL & INSTALLATION

▶ **See Figures 27 and 28**

1. Disconnect the negative battery cable.
2. Remove the distributor from the engine.
3. Place the distributor on a workbench and remove the the module retaining screws. Carefully pull the right side of the module down towards the base of the distributor mounting flange, then back up to disengage the module terminals from the connector in the distributor base. The module may be pulled toward the flange and away from the distributor.

➡ **Do not attempt to lift the module from the mounting surface, except as explained in Step 3. Any other way will cause the pins to break at the distributor module connector. To install:**

4. Coat the baseplate of the ignition module uniformly with a $1/32$ in. (0.8mm) of silicone dielectric compound WA–10 or equivalent.
5. Position the module on the distributor base mounting flange. Carefully position the module toward the distributor bowl and engage the 3 connector pins securely.
6. Install the retaining screws. Tighten to 15–35 inch lbs. (1.7–4.0 Nm), starting with the upper right screw.
7. Install the distributor into the engine, making sure all the marks align properly. Install the retaining bolt and tighten to 17–25 ft. lbs. (23–34 Nm). Attach cap and wires.
8. Reconnect the negative battery cable.
9. Recheck the initial timing. Adjust, if necessary.

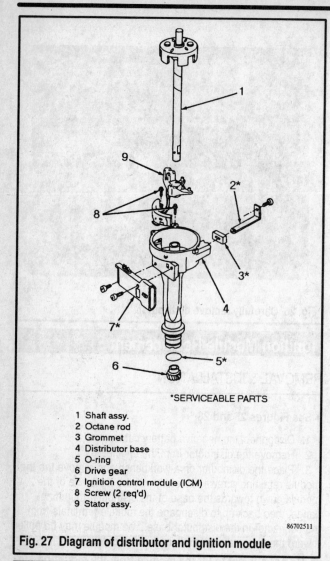

\*SERVICEABLE PARTS

1 Shaft assy.
2 Octane rod
3 Grommet
4 Distributor base
5 O-ring
6 Drive gear
7 Ignition control module (ICM)
8 Screw (2 req'd)
9 Stator assy.

86702511

**Fig. 27 Diagram of distributor and ignition module**

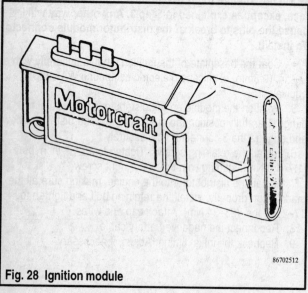

86702512

**Fig. 28 Ignition module**

## Stator Assembly Replacement

### REMOVAL & INSTALLATION

▶ **See Figure 29**

1. Disconnect the negative battery cable.
2. Mark the distributor and engine block for orientation during installation.
3. Remove the distributor assembly from the engine. Remove the rotor. Carefully, remove the module from the base.
4. Mark the armature and distributor gear for orientation during installation.
5. Hold the distributor drive gear and remove the armature retaining screws. Slowly, remove the armature.
6. Remove the distributor gear retaining pin.
7. Place the distributor assembly in a press. Carefully, press off the distributor gear from the shaft. Use bearing removal tool D84L–950–A or equivalent.
8. Once the gear is removed, clean and polish the shaft with emery paper. Wipe clean so that the shaft slides out freely from the distributor base. Remove the shaft.
9. Remove the stator assembly retaining screws, and remove the stator.

**To install:**

10. Position the stator assembly over the bushing and press down to secure. Place the stator connector in position. The tab should fit in the notch on the base and the fastening eyelets aligned with the screw holes. Be certain the wires are positioned away from any moving parts.
11. Install the stator retaining screws, and tighten to 15–35 inch lbs. (1.7–4.0 Nm).
12. Apply a light coat of engine oil to the distributor shaft beneath the armature. Carefully install the shaft.
13. Position a ½ in. deep socket over the shaft and place in the arbor press.
14. Place the distributor gear on the shaft end. Make certain the mark on the armature aligns correctly with the gear.

➡ **The hole in the shaft and gear must be properly aligned ton ensure ease of the roll pin installation.**

15. Place a ⅝ in. deep socket over the shaft and gear, and press the gear slowly onto the shaft. Install the roll pin.
16. Install the armature and tighten to 25–35 inch lbs. (2.8–4.0Nm).
17. Rotate the distributor shaft while checking for free–play between the shaft and base.

➡ **If the armature contacts the stator, the entire distributor should be replaced.**

18. Wipe the back of the module and its mounting surface clean. Coat the base of the module uniformly with a ¹/₃₂ in. (0.79mm) of silicone dielectric compound WA–10 or equivalent.
19. Invert the distributor base so the stator connector is in full view. Carefully insert the module. Be certain the 3 module pins are inserted into the stator connector and are secure.

20. Install the module retaining screws and tighten to 15–35 inch lbs. (1.7–4.0 Nm).

21. Install the distributor assembly into the engine block, making sure the marks made earlier are correctly aligned. Install the retaining bolt and tighten. Finally, install the cap and check to make sure everything is secure.

22. Reconnect the negative battery cable.

23. Check the initial timing. Adjust if necessary.

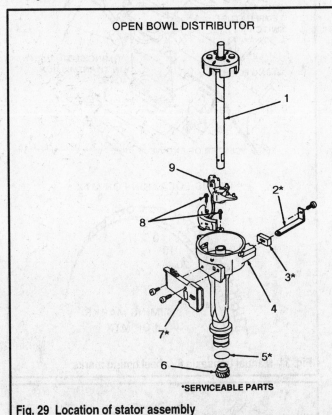

OPEN BOWL DISTRIBUTOR

1  Shaft assy
2  Octane rod
3  Grommet
4  Distributor base
5  O-ring
6  Drive gear
7  Ignition control module (ICM)
8  Screws (2 req'd)
9  Stator assy

*SERVICEABLE PARTS

86702513

**Fig. 29  Location of stator assembly**

# IGNITION TIMING—GASOLINE ENGINE

## General Information

Gasoline engine ignition timing is the measurement, in degrees, of crankshaft position at the instant the spark plug fires. Ignition timing is adjusted by rotating the distributor in either a clockwise or counterclockwise direction. Timing directly effects vital engine function like gas mileage, engine performance and driveability.

Timing is checked by using a timing light that triggers in relation to spark firing. This flashing light in turn is then pointed toward timing marks on the exterior of the engine to determine relative timing condition. The timing is advanced or retarded by turning the distributor. This turning of the distributor effects the rate at which the spark plugs fire. The timing marks on gasoline Tempo/Topaz engines can be found on the harmonic balancer/crank pulley, located on the right side of the engine, as well as through a hole on the transmission case. Before attempting to adjust the engine timing, make sure these timing marks are clean and easy to read.

## Adjustment

♦ See Figures 30, 31, 32 and 33

➡ Do not change the ignition timing by the use of a different octane rod without having the proper authority to do so as federal emission requirements will be affected.

1. Park the vehicle on a level surface. Firmly apply the parking brake and block the wheels to prevent accidental movement.

2. Place transmission in PARK or NEUTRAL. Make sure no accessories are on, and that the A/C and heater are in the OFF position.

3. Locate the timing marks on the harmonic balancer/crank pulley on the front of the engine. These marks resemble grooves in the balancer/pulley. Once you have found them, mark them with white paint for easy identification. In addition, if equipped with a manual transaxle, timing marks can be found on the

flywheel, and on the converter assembly if equipped with an automatic transaxle. These marks are visible as grooves through the hole in the transmission case. To view the mark on the flywheel/converter assembly, the cover plate must be removed. If the cover plate is dirty, clean area with a wire brush before removing.

4. Connect an inductive timing light to the engine using the tool manufacturer's instructions. Make sure the wires will not get caught in any moving parts when the engine is started.

5. Connect a tachometer according to the manufacturer's instructions. Make sure no wires can get caught in any moving parts when the engine is running.

6. Disconnect the in-line spout connector between the distributor and the control module in the interior of the vehicle. The spout is located near the distributor, and can be identified by the single wire connector.

7. Loosen the distributor retaining bolt.

8. Start the engine and allow it to idle until normal operating temperature is reached.

9. Using the timing light, point the light at the harmonic balancer/crank pulley to check the timing. The light could also be pointed at the flywheel/converter assembly to check the timing. Check to see whether the groove and pointer align evenly. If they do not, the timing should be adjusted.

10. If the timing needs adjustment rotate the distributor in either direction until the timing marks align correctly.

11. Once the timing is set, reconnect the spout connector and check with the timing light to make sure the timing is now advancing past the initial setting.

12. With everything functioning properly, the timing light and tachometer can be disconnected and removed from the engine compartment.

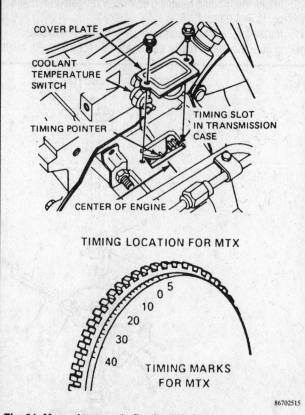

TIMING LOCATION FOR MTX

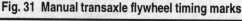

**Fig. 31 Manual transaxle flywheel timing marks**

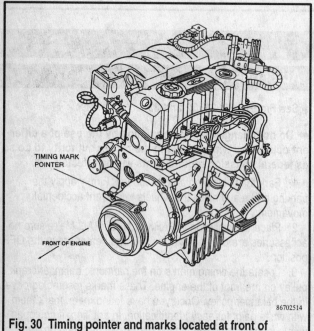

**Fig. 30 Timing pointer and marks located at front of engine**

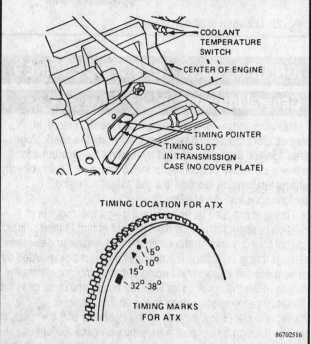

**Fig. 32 Automatic Transaxle Converter Assembly Timing Marks**

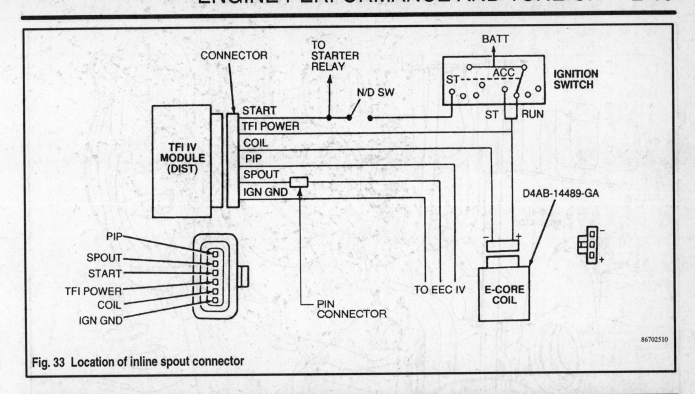

**Fig. 33 Location of inline spout connector**

## IGNITION TIMING—DIESEL ENGINE

### General Information

Because of its unique design, the diesel engine does not utilize spark plugs, rotor or distributor. In fact, the diesel engine uses no sparking method at all. For this reason, the proper functioning of the diesel engine is not dependent upon timing and spark delivery, like a gas engine, instead the diesel engine relays on the injection pump to deliver the correct amount of fuel at the desired time. For this reason, diesel timing is more correctly referred to as injection timing.

With the diesel engine's unique characteristics, comes the requirement that different tools and equipment are needed to perform many of the service procedures. This is the case with injection timing. In this situation, no timing light is used, instead a dial indicator is used. Some of the tools necessary to service a diesel vehicle are available at local parts stores or through rental businesses, but before tackling any diesel procedure, make sure the tools are available.

### Adjustment

▶ See Figures 34 and 35

➡ **Engine coolant temperature must be above 176°F (80°C) before injection timing can be checked or adjusted.**

1. Park the vehicle on a level surface. Firmly apply parking brake and block the wheels to prevent accidental movement.

2. Place transmission in NEUTRAL. Make sure no accessories are on, and that the A/C and heater are in OFF position.

3. Locate and remove injection pump distributor head plug bolt and sealing washer. This can be accessed from the left side of the pump assembly.

4. With the bolt and washer removed, install the Static Timing Gauge Adaptor with Metric Dial Indicator or equivalent. Make sure that indicator plunger is in contact with injection pump plunger.

5. Remove the timing mark cover from transmission housing. If the cover is dirty, clean with a wire brush before removing. Align timing mark with pointer on rear engine cover plate.

6. Rotate crankshaft pulley slowly counterclockwise until dial indicator pointer stops moving. This is approximately 30°–50° BTDC.

7. Adjust dial indicator to zero.

➡ **Make sure that dial indicator pointer does not move from zero. Slowly rotate crankshaft left and right to make sure.**

8. Turn the crankshaft clockwise until the timing marks align with indicator pin. At this point, the dial indicator should read 0.0392–0.0408 in. (0.98–1.02mm). If the reading is not within this specification, adjust the timing as follows:

   a. Loosen injection pump attaching bolt and nut.

   b. Rotate the injection pump toward the engine to advance the timing, and away from the engine to retard the timing. Rotate the pump until the dial indicator reads 0.0392–0.408 in. (0.98–1.02mm).

   c. When the desired specification has been reached, tighten the injection pump attaching bolt and nut to 13–20 ft. lbs. (18–27 Nm).

9. Remove the dial indicator and adaptor. Install the injection pump distributor head plug, then tighten to 10–14.5 ft. lbs. (13.5–19.5 Nm).

10. Connect the negative battery cable. Start the vehicle and check for fuel leaks, or a weak idle. Adjust if necessary.

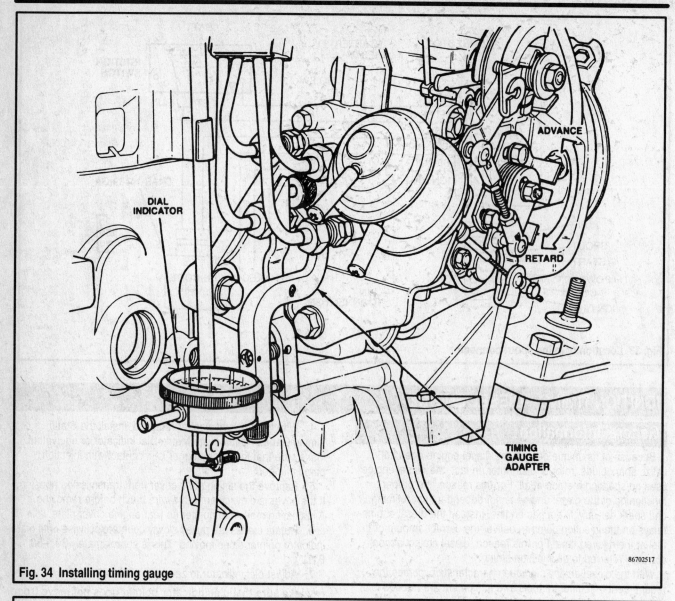

**Fig. 34 Installing timing gauge**

86702517

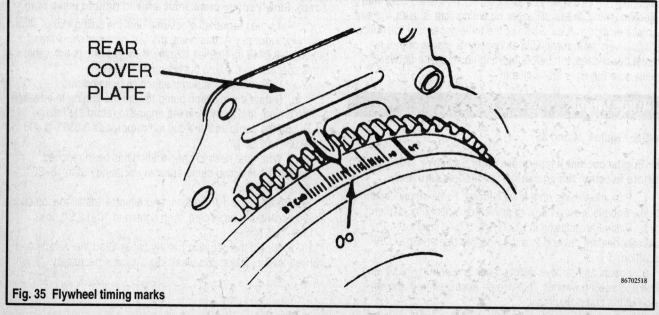

**Fig. 35 Flywheel timing marks**

86702518

## VALVE LASH

Valve adjustment determines how far the valves enter the cylinder and how long they remain open and/or closed. If valve clearance is too large, part of the lift of the camshaft will be used in removing the excessive clearance. Consequently, the valve will not be opening as far as it could. This condition has two effects: the valve train components will emit a tapping sound as they take up the excessive clearance and the engine will perform poorly because the valves don't open fully and allow the proper amount of gases to flow into and out of the engine.

If the valve clearance is too small, the intake valve and the exhaust valves will open too far and they will not fully seat on the cylinder head when they close. When a valve seats itself on the cylinder head, it does two things: it seals the combustion chamber so that none of the gases in the cylinder escape and it cools itself by transferring some of the heat it absorbs from the combustion in the cylinder to the cylinder head and to the engine's cooling system. If the valve clearance is too small, the engine will run poorly because of the gases escaping from the combustion chamber. The valves will also become overheated and will warp, since they cannot transfer heat unless they are touching the valve seat in the cylinder head.

## Adjustment

### GASOLINE ENGINES

The intake and exhaust valves in the Tempo and Topaz are driven by the camshaft. The energy created by the turning of the camshaft drives a series of hydraulic lash adjusters and stamped steel rocker arms. As these rocker arms move back and forth, the individual valve attached to the rocker arm opens and closes. The newly introduced lash adjusters eliminated the need for periodic valve lash adjustments.

It is not uncommon for vehicles equipped with hydraulic lifters to develop a valve tap noise from the top of the engine. Usually this noise is created due to air in the hydraulic assembly. In most cases, the procedure below will eliminate this condition. In the event the noise continues, more involved mechanical repairs may be necessary. Refer to section 3 for engine and valve repairs.

To eliminate valve tap noise proceed as follows;

1. Park the vehicle on a level surface. Engage the parking brake fully. Place blocks behind the tires.

2. Make sure the vehicle is in either PARK or NEUTRAL. Start the car, and allow to run until normal operating temperature is reached.

3. Once normal operating temperature is reached, run the car at 2000 rpm for 20 minutes.

4. After 20 minutes, shut vehicle off for 2 minutes, then start car and allow to idle for 1–2 minutes.

### DIESEL ENGINES

▶ See Figures 36, 37 and 38

Because the diesel engine does not utilize a hydraulic lifter assembly, the valve lash should be checked at regular intervals. The camshaft is supported by 5 machined bearing bores in the cylinder head. The number 1 and 5 bearing caps are different designs and are easily recognized from each other. The number 2, 3 and 4 bearing caps are identical and are numbered accordingly. The bearing caps have arrows cast into the top surface, and must be installed with the arrow to the front of the engine.

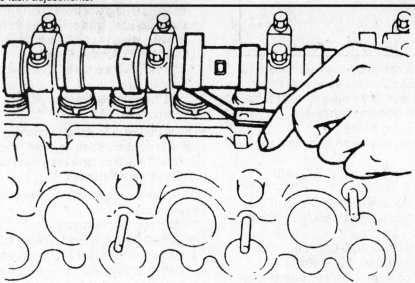

86702519

**Fig. 36  Checking valve clearance**

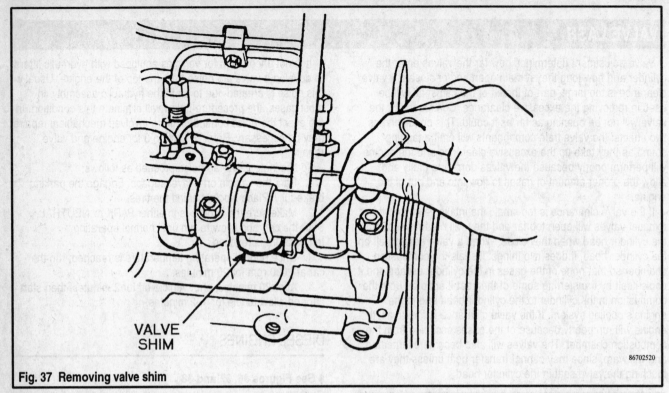

VALVE
SHIM

86702520

**Fig. 37 Removing valve shim**

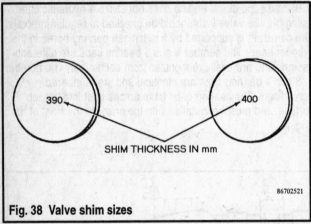

390 ──── 400

SHIM THICKNESS IN mm

86702521

**Fig. 38 Valve shim sizes**

The valves are adjusted by changing the valve shims located on top of the cam follower. Each shim has a stamped number located on the bottom of the shim. In the event the number has worn off, use a micrometer to measure the thickness.

To adjust valve lash, proceed as follows:

1. Disconnect breather hose from the intake manifold and remove camshaft cover.

2. Rotate crankshaft until No. 1 piston is at TDC on the compression stroke.

3. Using a feeler gauge, check the valve shim–to–cam lobe clearance for No. 1 and No. 2 intake valves, and No. 1 and No. 3 exhaust valves.
   - Intake Valves: 0.008–0.011 in. (0.20–0.30mm).
   - Exhaust Valves: 0.011–0.015 in. (0.30–0.40mm).

4. Rotate crankshaft one complete revolution. Measure valve clearance for No. 3 and No. 4 intake valves, and No. 2 and No. 4 exhaust valves.

5. If a valve clearance is out of specifications, adjust as follows:

➡ **On diesel engines, valve adjustment is accomplished through the installation of shims between the camshaft and valve spring assembly.**

   a. Rotate the crankshaft until the lobe of the valve to be adjusted is down.

   b. Install cam follower retainer, T84P–6513–B or equivalent.

   c. Rotate crankshaft until the cam lobe is on the base circle.

   d. Using O–ring pick tool T71P–19703–C or equivalent, pry the valve adjusting shim out of the cam follower.

   e. Valve shims are available in thicknesses ranging from 0.13–0.18 in. (3.40mm–4.60mm).

   f. If the valve was too tight, install a new shim, of the appropriate size.

   g. If the valve was too loose, install a new shim of the appropriate size.

➡ **Shim thickness is stamped on valve shim. Install new shim with numbers down, to avoid wearing the numbers off the shim. If numbers have been worn off, use a micrometer to measure shim thickness.**

6. Rotate crankshaft until cam lobe is down and remove cam follower retainer.

7. Recheck valve clearance.

8. Repeat Steps 4, 5 and 6 for each valve to be adjusted.

9. Make sure the camshaft cover gasket is fully seated in the camshaft cover and install valve cover. Tighten bolts to 5–7 ft. lbs. (7–10 Nm).

10. Connect breather hose.

11. Start car to check idle and performance of engine.

## IDLE SPEED AND MIXTURE ADJUSTMENTS

### Curb Idle Speed

#### 2.3L HSC ENGINE WITH 1946C & 6149FB CARBURETOR

▶ See Figures 39 and 40

➡ With A/C on, idle speed is non–adjustable.

1. Park Vehicle on level surface.
2. Place the transaxle in PARK or NEUTRAL.
3. Set the parking brake and block the wheels. Connect a tachometer to the engine according to manufacturers specifications.
4. Disconnect the throttle kicker vacuum line and plunger.
5. Bring the engine to normal operating temperature. (Cooling fan should cycle at least once).
6. Place the air conditioning selector in the OFF position.
7. Activate the cooling fan by grounding the control wire with a jumper wire.
8. Check/adjust curb idle speed. If adjustment is required, turn curb idle adjusting screw.
9. Increase the engine rpm momentarily. Readjust if necessary.
10. Reconnect the cooling fan wiring.
11. Turn the ignition key to the OFF position.
12. Reconnect the vacuum line to the throttle kicker.
13. If the vehicle is equipped with an automatic transaxle and curb idle adjustment exceeds 50 rpm, an automatic transaxle linkage adjustment may be necessary.
14. Remove all test equipment and reinstall the air cleaner assembly.

#### 2.3L HSC ENGINE WITH 6149FB CARBURETOR & THROTTLE POSITION SENSOR (TPS)

➡ This adjustment is not required as part of a normal engine idle speed check/adjustment. Use if engine continues to run after ignition key is turned to OFF position.

1. Park vehicle on level surface.
2. Place the transaxle in PARK or NEUTRAL. Set the parking brake and block the wheels.
3. Connect a tachometer to the engine according to manufacturer specifications.
4. Bring the engine to normal operating temperature.
5. Disconnect the throttle kicker vacuum line and plunger.
6. Place the air conditioning selector to OFF position.
7. Disconnect the electrical lead to the TPS, and verify that plunger collapses. Check or adjust engine idle speed to specification.
8. Adjust the TPS Off idle speed to factory specification.
9. Shut the engine off, reconnect TPS electrical lead and throttle kicker vacuum line.
10. Remove all test equipment and reinstall the air cleaner assembly.

### FUEL INJECTED ENGINES

Starting in model year 1985, the Tempo/Topaz was available with fuel injected engines. With this fuel delivery system, idle adjustment is automatically performed by the idle air control assemble attached to the throttle body. Therefore no idle adjustment is necessary.

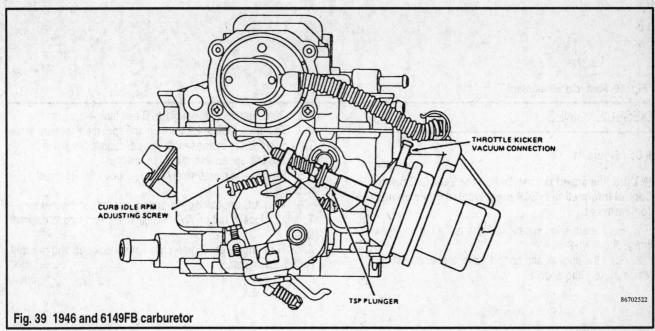

THROTTLE KICKER VACUUM CONNECTION

CURB IDLE RPM ADJUSTING SCREW

TSP PLUNGER

86702522

**Fig. 39  1946 and 6149FB carburetor**

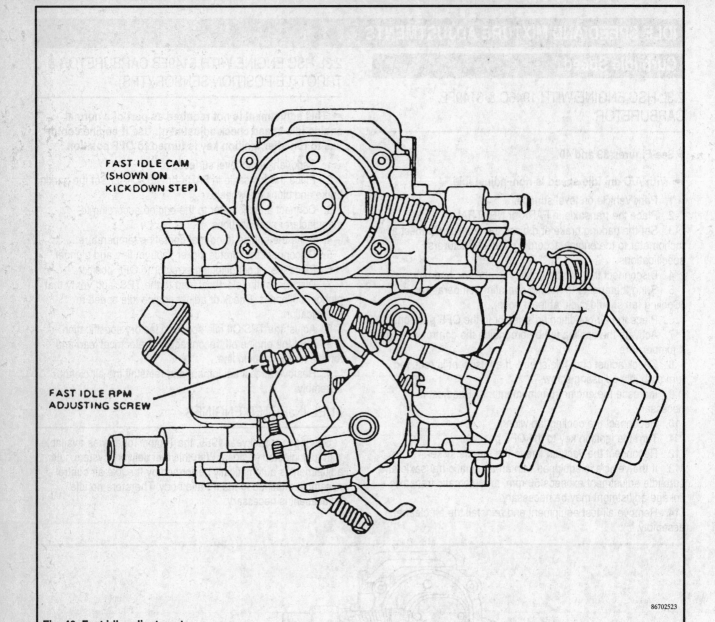

FAST IDLE CAM
(SHOWN ON
KICKDOWN STEP)

FAST IDLE RPM
ADJUSTING SCREW

86702523

**Fig. 40 Fast idle adjustment**

## DIESEL ENGINES

▶ See Figure 41

➡ Curd idle speed is specified on the Vehicle Emission Control Information (VECI) decal located in the engine compartment.

1. Put transmission in neutral. Engage the parking brake firmly, chock wheels.

2. Start the engine, and bring it up to normal operating temperature. Stop engine.

3. Remove timing cover plate. Clean flywheel surface.

4. To adjust, loosen lock nut on idle speed adjustment screw. Turn clockwise to increase idle speed, counterclockwise to decrease idle speed. Hand tighten lock nut.

5. Rev engine momentarily and recheck idle. Readjust if necessary.

6. Turn A/C on. Check idle speed, and adjust if necessary. To adjust, loosen nut on A/C throttle kicker and turn to desired level.

7. Turn engine off. Tighten idle speed lock nut, and reinstall timing cover plate.

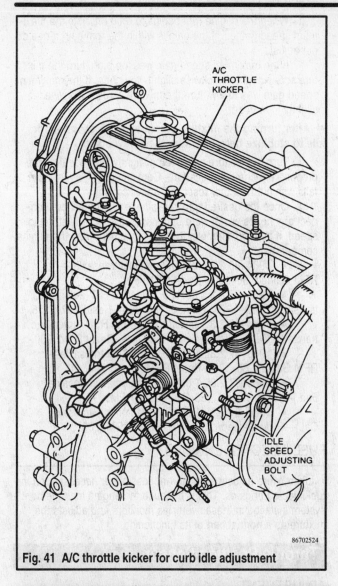

A/C THROTTLE KICKER

IDLE SPEED ADJUSTING BOLT

86702524

**Fig. 41 A/C throttle kicker for curb idle adjustment**

## Fast Idle Speed

### 2.3L HSC ENGINE WITH 1949 AND 6149FB CARBURETOR

1. Park vehicle on a level surface.
2. Place the transaxle in PARK or NEUTRAL. Set the parking brake and block the wheels.
3. Connect a tachometer to the engine, according to manufacturers specifications.
4. Start the engine, and bring it up to normal operating temperature with the carburetor set on the second step of fast idle cam.
5. Return the throttle to normal idle position.
6. Place the air conditioning selector in the OFF position.
7. Disconnect the vacuum hose at the EGR valve and plug it.
8. Place the fast idle adjusting screw on the second lowest step of the fast idle cam.
9. Check the fast idle speed, and adjust the fast idle screw to factory specification if necessary.

10. Increase the engine rpm momentarily, and allow the engine to return to idle. Turn ignition key to OFF position.
11. Remove the plug from the EGR vacuum hose and reconnect. Disconnect the tachometer.

### 2.3L ENGINES WITH 6149FB CARBURETOR & THROTTLE POSITION SENSOR (TPS)

1. Park vehicle on a level surface.
2. Engage the parking brake fully. Block the wheels. Place the transaxle in NEUTRAL.
3. Connect a tachometer to the engine, according to manufacturers specifications.
4. Start engine and allow to reach normal operating temperature. Make sure all accessories are OFF, then shut the engine OFF.
5. Unplug the spout in-line connector. Start the engine, then check the ignition timing is set to factory specifications if necessary.
6. Turn the ignition switch OFF.
7. Remove the PCV hose and install special orifice T86P-9600-A or an equivalent orifice with a 0.200 in (5mm) diameter opening. Disconnect the idle speed control air bypass valve assembly connector.
8. Start the engine and run at 2500 rpm for approximately 30 seconds, and allow engine to return to idle.
9. Place the transmission in DRIVE for automatic transaxle or NEUTRAL for manual transaxle. Check to see that the idle speed is within specifications. If the idle speed is not within specifications, go on to the next Step.
10. Make sure that the cooling fan is OFF. Turn the throttle plate adjusting screw until the idle is within specifications.

➡ **Adjustments must be made within 2 minutes after returning to idle speed.**

11. Turn the engine OFF and reconnect the ignition timing in-line spout connector. Remove the orifice from the PCV line and reinstall the PCV line. Reconnect the idle speed control air bypass valve assembly connection. Remove the tachometer. Make sure that the throttle plate is not binding in the bore or that the linkage is preventing the throttle plate from returning.
12. To verify proper adjustment, run the engine at 2500 rpm for approximately 30 seconds and return it to idle. Be sure to refer to the under hood emission/calibration sticker for the engine idle rpm specification.

### FUEL INJECTED ENGINES

1. Park the vehicle on a level surface. Block the tires for safety.
2. Place the transaxle in NEUTRAL. Connect a tachometer to the engine according to the manufactures instructions.
3. With all accessories OFF, start the engine and allow it to reach normal operating temperature, then turn the engine OFF.
4. Disconnect the air idle bypass valve wire connector. Start the engine and allow it the run at 1500 rpm for approximately 20 seconds, then return it to idle.
5. Place the transmission in NEUTRAL (automatic transaxle) or DRIVE (manual transaxle). Start the engine and check that the idle speed is 500-550 rpm. If the idle speed is not within this range, proceed as follows:

a. With the cooling fan OFF, turn the throttle plate adjusting screw until the idle speed is with 500–550 rpm.

b. If the idle speed was adjusted, repeat the above steps in order.

6. Once the correct idle speed has been set, turn OFF the engine, then connect the air bypass valve wire connector.

## Idle Mixture

### CARBURETOR EQUIPPED ENGINES

➡ **The following procedure is not recommended for DIYer's. The carburetor must be removed in order to gain access to the tamper resistant plugs that cover the mixture screw. It should also be noted that a propane enrichment kit will be needed to perform this operation.**

1. Remove the carburetor from the engine and drain any remaining fuel from the fuel bowl.

2. Drill a $3/32$ in. (2.4mm) hole through both the steel and the plastic tamper resistant plugs.

3. Using a hack saw, cut through the metal cup in a lengthwise direction and insert a suitable tool to twist the metal so as to expose the inner tamper resistant plug.

4. Install a screw extractor into the hole and remove the steel and or plastic plugs. Reinstall the carburetor assembly on the engine. Adjust the idle speed mixture as follows:

a. Connect a tachometer and timing light to the engine. Make sure that the hot idle compensator is closed, if equipped.

b. Disconnect the fuel evaporative system purge hose at the air cleaner assembly and plug the fitting on the air cleaner.

c. Disconnect the fresh air duct from the air cleaner and insert the hose from the propane tank ¾ of the way into the air cleaner duct. Be sure to leave all vacuum lines attached to the air cleaner. The air cleaner can be positioned off to the side, but it must be complete and in place when making this adjustment.

d. If the emission system is equipped with air injection, the air injection dump valves should be altered as follows:

• If the valve has 2 vacuum fittings, disconnect and plug the hoses. If there is only 1 vacuum fitting, disconnect and plug the hose and then run another vacuum hose from the fitting to manifold vacuum.

• If equipped with an automatic transmission, disconnect and plug the vacuum line at ISC motor. Connect a vacuum pump to the ISC and apply enough vacuum to retract the ISC plunger clear of the throttle linkage.

e. Remove the PCV valve from the valve cover and allow it to draw fresh air. Run the engine briefly at 2500 rpm.

f. With the engine at normal operating temperature and idling, and the transmission in NEUTRAL (manual transaxle) or DRIVE (automatic transaxle), begin to slowly open the valve on the propane bottle and watch for the engine rpm to rise.

➡ **The propane bottle must be held in a vertical position during this adjustment.**

g. When the engine rpm begins to drop off, note the maximum speed gained. If the gain is within the rpm gain range do not adjust.

h. If the maximum speed gain was too high, turn the mixture screw counterclockwise slightly to richen. If the maximum speed gain was to low, turn the mixture screw clockwise slightly to lean out.

➡ **After turning the mixture screw, allow 15 seconds for idle to stabilize before turning the screw again.**

i. Turn the mixture screw left or right while repeating the propane enrichment procedure. Continue until the rpm level falls within the factory reset rpm specifications.

j. Once the desired rpm levels have been reached, connect any hoses which were unfastened earlier. Adjust the idle speed, if needed. Remove the test equipment from the engine compartment.

• 1984–85 2.3 1 bbl HO (manual transaxle)—RPM Gained: 60–100—Reset RPM: 80.

• 1984–85 2.3 1 bbl HO 2.3L 1 bbl HO (automatic transaxle Fed.)—RPM Gained: 150–200—Reset RPM: 175.

• 1984–85 2.3 1 bbl HO 2.3L 1 bbl HSC (automatic transaxle Cal.)—RPM Gained: 160–240—Reset RPM: 200.

• 1986–87 2.3L 1 bbl OHC (manual transaxle—RPM Gained: 60–100—Reset RPM: 80.

• 1986–87 2.3L 1 bbl OHC (automatic transaxle Fed.)—RPM Gained: 150–20—Reset RPM: 175.

• 1986–87 2.3L 1 bbl OHC (automatic transaxle Cal.)—RPM Gained: 160–240—Reset RPM: 200.

### FUEL INJECTED ENGINES

Idle mixture adjustments are not possible or necessary on the fuel injected engines. This is because the engine management system installed in theses vehicles monitors and adjusts the mixture as a normal part of its functioning.

## Throttle Position Sensor

### ADJUSTMENT

The Throttle Position Sensor (TPS) being used on the gasoline fuel injected Tempo/Topaz uses, a rotary tang to control the throttle shaft blade. When removing or installing a TPS, be careful not to bent any of these tangs.

To test or adjust a TPS, a digital volt/ohmmeter is needed. Proceed as follows:

1. Connect a suitable digital volt/ohmmeter to terminal A (output terminal) and terminal B (ground) of the TPS.

2. Turn the ignition switch to the ON position and check the voltage reading at closed throttle. If the voltage reading is not 0.0–1.1 volts, loosen the TPS mounting screws and rotate the TPS until the correct voltage is obtained.

3. If the correct TPS voltage cannot be obtained, replace the TPS.

4. Slowly open the throttle and observe the digital volt/ohmmeter. The voltage should gradually increase to 4.0 volts at wide open throttle.

## Chilton Tip

### 1984 TEMPO & TOPAZ WITH CARBURETOR

Some carbureted models of this particular year Tempo/Topaz may exhibit signs of poor acceleration at steady speeds when the engine is warm. This could be caused by an inoperative fuel control solenoid. There is a new replacement fuel control solenoid, E43Z–9B998–A, available which is designed to correct this condition. To check the condition of the fuel solenoid, proceed as follows:

1. Disconnect the electrical connector from the solenoid. Place a vacuum T valve with a vacuum gauge into the $5/32$ vacuum hose between the solenoid and the carburetor.

2. Start the engine and let it run at idle speed. Read the vacuum gauge. The gauge should read between 1.0–1.5 in. Hg of vacuum. Now apply a 12 volt source to the fuel control solenoid.

3. With 12 volts applied to the solenoid, the vacuum gauge should read between 4.0–5.5 in. Hg of vacuum. If the vacuum gauge readings do not agree with these specifications, replace the fuel control solenoid with a new replacement fuel control solenoid E43Z–9B998–A available at your local Ford or Lincoln/Mercury dealer.

## TORQUE SPECIFICATIONS

| Component | U.S. | Metric |
|---|---|---|
| Spark Plugs | | |
| 1984–85: | 10–15 ft. lbs. | 7–20 Nm |
| 1986–94: | 7–15 ft. lbs. | 9–20 Nm |
| Distributor Hold-down Bolts | 17–25 ft. lbs. | 23–34 Nm |
| Distributor Cap Hold-down Screws | 18–23 inch lbs. | 2.0–2.6 Nm |
| Distributor Rotor Hold-down Screws | 25–35 inch lbs. | 2.8–3.9 Nm |
| TFI Ignition Module Mounting Screws | | |
| 1984–85 | 9–16 inch lbs. | 1.1–1.8 Nm |
| 1986 | 25–35 inch lbs. | 2.8–3.9 Nm |
| 1987–94 | 16–35 inch lbs. | 1.8–4 Nm |
| Octane Rod Retaining Screw | | |
| 1984–85 | 15–36 inch lbs. | 1.8–4.3 Nm |
| 1986–87 | 25–35 inch lbs. | 2.8–3.9 Nm |
| 1988–94 | 15–35 inch lbs. | 1.7–4.0 Nm |

NOTE: Do not over-tighten spark plugs. Excessive tightening can result in stripping the threads in the cylinder head.

NOTE: Do not under-tighten spark plugs. Insufficient tightness can permit the plug to loosen; subsequent overheating will cause preignition and result in engine damage.

86702889

## DIESEL ENGINE TUNE-UP SPECIFICATIONS

| Year | Engine ID/VIN | Engine Displacement cu. in. (cc) | Valve Clearance Intake (in.) | Valve Clearance Exhaust (in.) | Intake Valve Opens (deg.) | Injection Pump Setting (deg.) | Injection Nozzle Pressure (psi) New | Injection Nozzle Pressure (psi) Used | Idle Speed (rpm) | Cranking Compression Pressure (psi) |
|------|------|------|------|------|------|------|------|------|------|------|
| 1985 | H | 2.0 (2000) | 0.010 [1] | 0.014 | 13 | TDC [2] | 1990-2105 | 1849-1990 | 675-775 | 390-435@2000 |
| 1986 | H | 2.0 (2000) | 0.010 [1] | 0.014 | 13 | TDC [2] | 1990-2105 | 1849-2100 | 675-775 | 390-435@2000 |
| 1987 | H | 2.0 (2000) | 0.010 [1] | 0.014 | 13 | TDC [2] | 1990-2105 | 1849-2100 | 675-775 | 390-435@2000 |

NOTE: The Vehicle Emission Control Information label often reflects specification changes made during production. The label figures must be used if they differ from those in this chart

TDC - Top dead center

[1] Valve clearance specifications are set cold

[2] With engine hot

86702777

## GASOLINE ENGINE TUNE-UP SPECIFICATIONS

| Year | Engine ID/VIN | Engine Displacement Liters (cc) | Spark Plugs Gap (in.) | Ignition Timing (deg.) MT | Ignition Timing (deg.) AT | Fuel Pump (psi) | Idle Speed (rpm) MT | Idle Speed (rpm) AT | Valve Clearance In. | Valve Clearance Ex. |
|------|------|------|------|------|------|------|------|------|------|------|
| 1984 | R | 2.3 (2300) | 0.044 | 10B | 10B | 4-6 | 800 | 750 | HYD | HYD |
| 1985 | R | 2.3 (2300) | 0.044 | 10B | 10B | 4-6 | 800 | 750 | HYD | HYD |
|  | X | 2.3 (2300) | 0.044 | 10B | 10B | 35-45 | 725 | 570 | HYD | HYD |
|  | S | 2.3 (2300) | 0.044 | 10B | 10B | 35-45 | 725 | 570 | HYD | HYD |
| 1986 | R | 2.3 (2300) | 0.044 | 10B | 10B | 4-6 | 800 | 750 | HYD | HYD |
|  | S | 2.3 (2300) | 0.044 | 10B | 10B | 35-45 | 725 | 570 | HYD | HYD |
|  | X | 2.3 (2300) | 0.044 | 10B | 10B | 35-45 | 725 | 570 | HYD | HYD |
| 1987 | R | 2.3 (2300) | 0.044 | 10B | 10B | 4-6 | 800 | 750 | HYD | HYD |
|  | S | 2.3 (2300) | 0.034 | 10B | 10B | 36-42 | 775 | 725 | HYD | HYD |
|  | X | 2.3 (2300) | 0.044 | 10B | 10B | 35-45 | 725 | 570 | HYD | HYD |
| 1988 | S | 2.3 (2300) | 0.044 | 10B | 10B | 45-60 | 975 | 975 | HYD | HYD |
|  | X | 2.3 (2300) | 0.044 | 10B | 10B | 45-60 | 975 | 875 | HYD | HYD |
| 1989 | S | 2.3 (2300) | 0.044 | 10B | 10B | 45-60 | 975 | 975 | HYD | HYD |
|  | X | 2.3 (2300) | 0.044 | 10B | 10B | 45-60 | 975 | 875 | HYD | HYD |
| 1990 | S | 2.3 (2300) | 0.044 | 10B | 10B | 45-60 | 975 | 975 | HYD | HYD |
|  | X | 2.3 (2300) | 0.044 | 10B | 10B | 45-60 | 975 | 875 | HYD | HYD |
| 1991 | S | 2.3 (2300) | 0.054 | 10B | 10B | 45-60 | 975 | 975 | HYD | HYD |
|  | X | 2.3 (2300) | 0.054 | 10B | 10B | 45-60 | 975 | 875 | HYD | HYD |
| 1992 | X | 2.3 (2300) | 0.054 | 10B | 10B | 45-60 | 975 | 875 | HYD | HYD |
|  | U | 3.0 (2980) | 0.044 | 10B | 10B | 35-45 | - | 625 | HYD | HYD |
| 1993 | X | 2.3 (2300) | 0.054 | 10B | 10B | 45-60 | 975 | 875 | HYD | HYD |
|  | U | 3.0 (2980) | 0.044 | 10B | 10B | 35-45 | - | 625 | HYD | HYD |
| 1994 | X | 2.3 (2300) | 0.054 | 10B | 10B | 45-60 [2] | [1] | [1] | HYD | HYD |
|  | U | 3.0 (2980) | 0.044 | 10B | 10B | 30-45 [2] | [1] | [1] | HYD | HYD |

NOTE: The Vehicle Emission Control Information label often reflects specification changes made during production. The label figures must be used if they

B - Before top dead center

HYD - Hydraulic

[1] Refer to Vehicle Emission Control Information label

[2] Fuel pressure with engine running, pressure regulator vacuum hose connected

86702a88

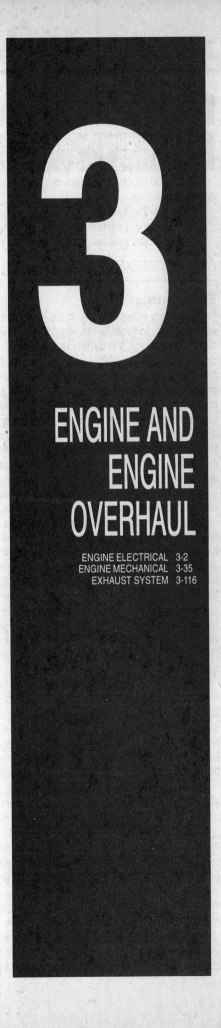

# 3

# ENGINE AND ENGINE OVERHAUL

# ENGINE ELECTRICAL

## Understanding the Engine Electrical System

The engine electrical system can be broken down into three separate systems:

1. The starting system.
2. The charging system.
3. The ignition system.

## BATTERY AND STARTING SYSTEM

### Basic Operating Principles

The battery is the first link in the chain of mechanisms which work together to provide cranking of the automobile engine. In most modern cars, the battery is a lead/acid electrochemical device consisting of six 2v subsections connected in series so the unit is capable of producing approximately 12v of electrical pressure. Each subsection, or cell, consists of a series of positive and negative plates held a short distance apart in a solution of sulfuric acid and water. The two types of plates are of dissimilar metals. This causes a chemical reaction, and it is this reaction which produces current flow from the battery when its positive and negative terminals are connected to an electrical appliance such as a lamp or motor. The continued transfer of electrons would eventually convert the sulfuric acid in the electrolyte to water, and make the two plates identical in chemical composition. As electrical energy is removed from the battery, its voltage output tends to drop. Thus, measuring battery voltage and battery electrolyte composition are two ways of checking the ability of the unit to supply power. During engine cranking, electrical energy is removed from the battery. However, if the charging circuit is in good condition and the operating conditions are normal, the power removed from the battery will be replaced by the generator (or alternator) which will force electrons back through the battery, reversing the normal flow, and restoring the battery to its original chemical state.

The battery and starting motor are linked by very heavy electrical cables designed to minimize resistance to the flow of current. Generally, the major power supply cable that leaves the battery goes directly to the starter, while other electrical system needs are supplied by a smaller cable. During starter operation, power flows from the battery to the starter and is grounded through the car's frame and the battery's negative ground strap.

The starting motor is a specially designed, direct current electric motor capable of producing a very great amount of power for its size. One thing that allows the motor to produce a great deal of power is its tremendous rotating speed. It drives the engine through a tiny pinion gear (attached to the starter's armature), which drives the very large flywheel ring gear at a greatly reduced speed. Another factor allowing it to produce so much power is that only intermittent operation is required of it. Thus, little allowance for air circulation is required, and the windings can be built into a very small space.

The starter solenoid is a magnetic device which employs the small current supplied by the starting switch circuit of the ignition switch. This magnetic action moves a plunger which mechanically engages the starter and electrically closes the heavy switch which connects it to the battery. The starting switch circuit consists of the starting switch contained within the ignition switch, a transmission switch (neutral safety switch if equipped with an automatic transmission, clutch switch if equipped with a manual transmission), and the wiring necessary to connect these in series with the starter solenoid or relay.

A pinion, which is a small gear, is mounted to a one-way drive clutch. This clutch is splined to the starter armature shaft. When the ignition switch is moved to the START position, the solenoid plunger slides the pinion toward the flywheel ring gear via a collar and spring. If the teeth on the pinion and flywheel match properly, the pinion will engage the flywheel immediately. If the gear teeth butt one another, the spring will be compressed and will force the gears to mesh as soon as the starter turns far enough to allow them to do so. As the solenoid plunger reaches the end of its travel, it closes the contacts that connect the battery and starter then the engine is cranked.

As soon as the engine starts, the flywheel ring gear begins turning fast enough to drive the pinion at an extremely high rate of speed. At this point, the one-way clutch allows the pinion to spin faster than the starter shaft so that the starter will not operate at excessive speed. When the ignition switch is released from the starter position, the solenoid is de-energized, a spring contained within the solenoid assembly pulls the gear out of mesh and interrupts the current flow to the starter.

Some starters employ a separate relay, mounted away from the starter, to switch the motor and solenoid current ON and OFF. The relay thus replaces the solenoid electrical switch, buy does not eliminate the need for a solenoid mounted on the starter used to mechanically engage the starter drive gears. The relay is used to reduce the amount of current the starting switch must carry.

## CHARGING SYSTEM

### Basic Operating Principles

The automobile charging system provides electrical power for operation of the vehicle's ignition and starting systems and all the electrical accessories. The battery serves as an electrical surge or storage tank, storing (in chemical form) the energy originally produced by the engine driven generator. The system also provides a means of regulating generator output to protect the battery from being overcharged and to avoid excessive voltage to the accessories.

The storage battery is a chemical device incorporating parallel lead plates in a tank containing a sulfuric acid/water solution. Adjacent plates are slightly dissimilar, and the chemical reaction of the two dissimilar plates produces electrical energy when the battery is connected to a load such as the starter motor. The chemical reaction is reversible, so that when the generator is producing a voltage (electrical pressure) greater than that produced by the battery, electricity is forced into the battery, and the battery is returned to its fully charged state.

The vehicle's generator is driven mechanically, through V-belts, by the engine crankshaft. It consists of two coils of fine wire, one stationary (the stator), and one movable (the rotor). The rotor may also be known as the armature, and consists of fine wire wrapped around an iron core which is mounted on a shaft. The electricity which flows through the two coils of wire (provided initially by the battery in some cases) creates an intense magnetic field around both rotor and stator, and the interaction between the two fields creates voltage, allowing the generator to power the accessories and charge the battery.

There are two types of generators: earlier vehicles used the Direct Current (DC) type. The current produced by the DC generator is produced in the armature and carried off the spinning armature by stationary brushes contacting the commutator. The commutator is a series of smooth metal contact plates on the end of the armature. The commutator plates, which are separated from one another by a very short gap, are connected to the armature circuits so that current will flow in one direction only in the wires carrying the generator output. The generator stator consists of two stationary coils of wire which draw some of the output current of the generator to form a powerful magnetic field and create the interaction of fields which generates the voltage. The generator field is wired in series with the regulator.

Newer automobiles use alternating current generators or alternators, because they are more efficient, can be rotated at higher speeds, and have fewer brush problems. In an alternator, the field rotates while all the current produced passes only through the stator winding. The brushes bear against continuous slip rings rather than a commutator. This causes the current produced to periodically reverse the direction of its flow. Diodes (electrical one–way switches) block the flow of current from traveling in the wrong direction. A series of diodes is wired together to permit the alternating flow of the stator to be converted to a pulsating, but unidirectional flow at the alternator output. The alternator's field is wired in series with the voltage regulator.

The regulator consists of several circuits. Each circuit has a core, or magnetic coil of wire, which operates a switch. Each switch is connected to ground through one or more resistors. The coil of wire responds directly to system voltage. When the voltage reaches the required level, the magnetic field created by the winding of wire closes the switch and inserts a resistance into the generator field circuit, thus reducing the output. The contacts of the switch cycle open and close many times each second to precisely control voltage.

While alternators are self–limiting as far as maximum current is concerned, DC generators employ a current regulating circuit which responds directly to the total amount of current flowing through the generator circuit rather than to the output voltage. The current regulator is similar to the voltage regulator except that all system current must flow through the energizing coil on its way to the various accessories.

## IGNITION SYSTEM

For detailed descriptions of the ignition systems and diagnosis and testing procedures, as well as removal and installation of additional ignition system components, please refer to Section 2.

## Ignition Coil

▶ **See Figure 1**

The ignition coil provides the electricity which the spark plugs use to ignite the air/fuel mixture in the combustion chamber. As it's name implies, it is a coil which initially receives a nominal 12 volt signal of current and increases the output to thousands of volts.

## ✳✳CAUTION

**Because of the extremely high voltage output of most coils, great care most be taken in diagnosing or servicing the coil.**

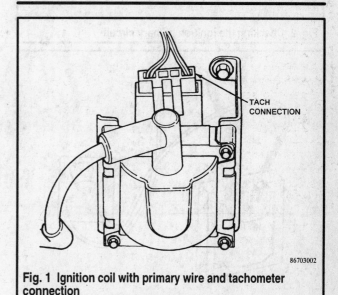

Fig. 1 Ignition coil with primary wire and tachometer connection

## TESTING

▶ **See Figures 2 and 3**

1. Verify that the ignition switch is in the OFF position.
2. Remove the primary connector using spark plug wire pullers or a twisting motion with your hand. Inspect for dirt or corrosion, and clean if necessary.
3. Measure the resistance between the positive and negative terminals of the primary wire harness with an ohmmeter. Resistance should measure 0.3–1.0 ohms.
4. Measure the resistance from the negative (–) terminal of the wire harness to the high voltage terminal of the coil. Resistance should be between 8000–11,500 ohms
5. Replace the coil, if either readings are not within the given specifications.

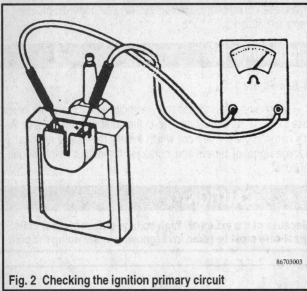

Fig. 2 Checking the ignition primary circuit

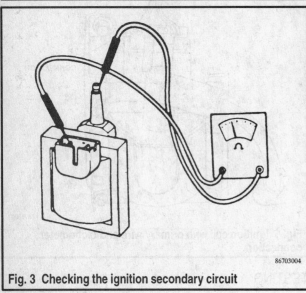

Fig. 3 Checking the ignition secondary circuit

## REMOVAL & INSTALLATION

▶ See Figures 4, 5 and 6

1. Disconnect the negative battery cable.
2. Remove the ignition coil wiring harness, at the coil. Using spark plug pullers or your hand, remove the high voltage coil lead attached to the coil.
3. Unscrew the ignition coil retaining bolts and remove the coil assembly.

**To install:**

4. Place the ignition coil into position and install the retaining screws.
5. Reconnect the ignition coil high voltage wire and wiring harness.
6. Reconnect the negative battery cable.
7. Start vehicle to verify proper operation.

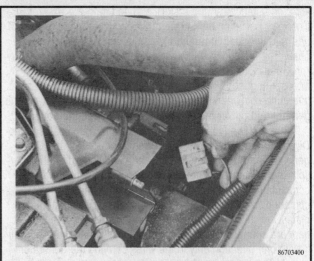

Fig. 4 Remove the high voltage wire and wire harness from the coil

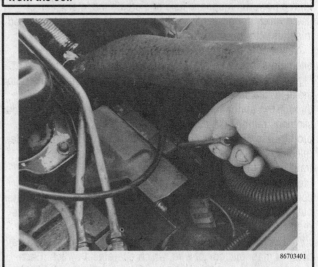

Fig. 5 Remove the retaining bolts which secure the coil to the side of the engine

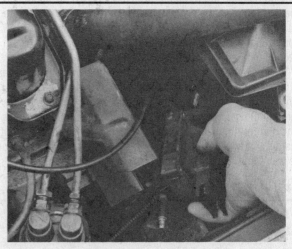

Fig. 6 Remove the coil from the vehicle

## Ignition Module

### REMOVAL & INSTALLATION

◗ See Figures 7 and 8

1. Disconnect the negative battery cable.
2. It is recommended that you remove the distributor assembly from the engine.
3. Place the distributor on the workbench and remove the the module retaining screws. Pull the right side of the module down the distributor mounting flange and back up to disengage the module terminals from the connector in the distributor base. The module may be pulled toward the flange and away from the distributor.

➡ Do not attempt to lift the module from the mounting surface, except as explained in Step 3, as pins will break at the distributor module connector.

To install:

4. Coat the baseplate of the new ignition module uniformly with a $1/32$ in. (0.8mm) coating of silicone dielectric compound WA–10 or equivalent.
5. Position the module on the distributor base mounting flange. Carefully position the module toward the distributor bowl and engage the 3 connector pins securely.
6. Install the retaining screws. Tighten to 15–35 inch lbs. (1.7–4.0 Nm), starting with the upper right screw.
7. Install the distributor into the engine.
8. Reconnect the negative battery cable.
9. Start vehicle. Recheck the initial timing. Adjust, if necessary.

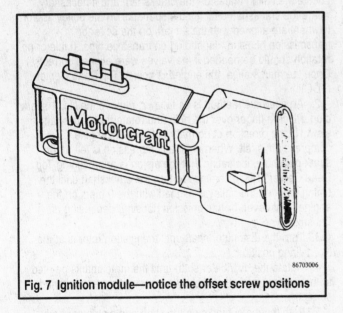

86703006

Fig. 7 Ignition module—notice the offset screw positions

## OPEN BOWL DISTRIBUTOR

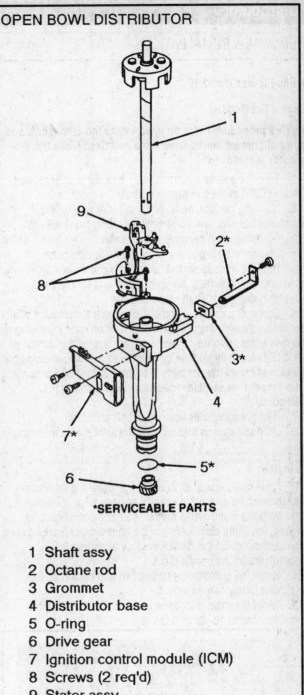

*SERVICEABLE PARTS

1 Shaft assy
2 Octane rod
3 Grommet
4 Distributor base
5 O-ring
6 Drive gear
7 Ignition control module (ICM)
8 Screws (2 req'd)
9 Stator assy

86703005

Fig. 8 Distributor with ignition module attached to the side

## Distributor

### REMOVAL & INSTALLATION

▶ See Figures 9 and 10

#### Engine Not Rotated

➡ **This procedure is for engines where the crankshaft and other alignment marks have remained fixed while the distributor is removed.**

1. Turn the engine over until No. 1 cylinder is at Top Dead Center (TDC) of the compression stroke.

2. Mark the position of the No. 1 cylinder wire on the distributor base for reference when installing the distributor.

3. Disconnect the negative battery cable.

4. Disconnect the primary wiring from the distributor.

5. Remove the cap screws and lift the distributor cap straight off to prevent damage to the rotor blade and spring. Remove rotor from distributor shaft and armature.

6. Scribe or paint an alignment mark on the distributor shaft and body, showing the position of the ignition rotor in relation to the distributor assembly. Place another mark on the outside of the distributor body and the cylinder head or block, showing the position of the distributor body in relation to the head or block. These marks are used for reference when installing the distributor.

7. Remove distributor hold–down bolt and clamp.

8. Lift distributor up and out until the shaft clears mounting hole.

#### To install:

9. If the distributor shaft has moved, rotate the distributor until the matchmarks on the shaft and body align correctly.

10. With the matchmarks on the shaft and distributor body aligned, lower the distributor into the engine block, making sure the matchmarks on the distributor body align with the matchmarks on the engine block.

11. Install the distributor retaining bolt and tighten so the distributor barely can be moved.

12. Install the rotor, distributor cap and all wiring. Tighten distributor cap to 18–23 inch lbs. (2.0–2.6 Nm).

**Fig. 9 Loosen the distributor retaining bolt**

**Fig. 10 Lift the distributor out**

13. Start vehicle and set initial timing according to the procedures in Section 2.

14. After timing has been set, tighten the distributor hold–down bolt to 17–25 ft. lbs. (23–34 Nm).

#### Engine Rotated

➡ **If the crankshaft was rotated while the distributor was removed, the engine must be brought to Top Dead Center (TDC) on the compression stroke of the No. 1 cylinder.**

1. Remove the valve cover(s). Locate the cylinder No. 1 intake and exhaust valve assembly. Rotate the crankshaft until the No. 1 valves are as close to closed as possible. At this point the camshaft is close to or at its lowest point on the lobe. Locate the timing marks on the crankshaft, and if necessary rotate the crankshaft until the timing marks on the pulley and/or flywheel are aligned with the 0 mark on the cover or transmission housing, depending on transaxle type. (Little or no rotation should be needed if the valves were aligned correctly.) Once the marks align, the engine is now at Top Dead Center (TDC).

2. An alternate method is as follows: remove the No. 1 spark plug. Place a finger over the hole and rotate the crankshaft slowly in the direction of normal rotation, until engine compression is felt. When engine compression is felt at the spark plug hole, indicating that the piston is approaching Top Dead Center (TDC), continue to turn the crankshaft until the timing mark on the pulley is aligned with the 0 mark on the engine front cover, or transmission housing, depending on transaxle type.

3. Turn the distributor shaft until the ignition rotor is at the No. 1 firing position.

4. Rotate the distributor shaft until the matchmarks painted to the distributor shaft and body prior to removal are aligned correctly.

5. With the matchmarks on the shaft and distributor body aligned, lower the distributor into the engine block, making sure the matchmarks on the distributor body align with the matchmarks on the engine block. Verify rotor is pointing at No. 1 mark on distributor base.

6. Install the distributor retaining bolt and tighten so the distributor can just barely be moved.

7. Install the rotor and distributor cap and connect all wiring. Tighten distributor cap to 18–23 inch lbs. (2.0–2.6 Nm).

8. Start vehicle and set initial timing according to the procedures in section 2.

9. After timing has been set, tighten distributor hold–down bolt to 17–25 ft. lbs. (23–34 Nm).

## Alternator

The alternator is the primary source of electrical energy for the vehicle once the car is started. Not only is it a source of energy for radios, cruise control and diagnostic modules, it is also responsible for recharging the battery. It is a belt driven device, which initially produces alternating current that is transformed to direct current through diodes in the unit. A regulator automatically adjusts the alternator field current to maintain the output voltage within a given limit.

## PRECAUTIONS

There are several precautions which must be strictly observed in order to avoid damaging the unit. They are:

• Always observe proper polarity of the battery connections: be especially careful when jump starting the car. (See Section 1 for jump starting procedures).

• Never ground or short out the alternator or alternator regulator terminals.

• Never operate the alternator with any of its or the battery's lead wires disconnected.

• Always remove the battery or at least disconnect the ground cable while charging.

• Always disconnect the battery ground cable while repairing or replacing an electrical component.

• Never use a fast battery charger to jump start a dead battery.

• Never attempt to polarize an alternator.

• Never subject the alternator to excessive heat or dampness (for instance, steam cleaning the engine).

• Never use arc welding equipment on the car with the alternator connected.

## TESTING

▶ **See Figures 11, 12, 13, 14, 15 and 16**

There are several tests that can be done with inexpensive equipment. The first thing to do is to see if the discharge warning light on the dashboard illuminates when the ignition switch is turned ON. If it does not, and the battery keeps going dead, check for a blown fuse, a burned out indicator bulb, or a bad connection.

➡ **If a battery/alternator tester is available, connect the tester to the vehicle charging system as per the manufacturer's instructions.**

If the warning light does not illuminate with the ignition switch ON, but does stay on with the engine running, check the following:

• Proper electrolyte level (specific gravity) in the battery
• Loose or missing alternator belt
• Loose or corroded battery cable
• A shorted or open wire

If everything checks out, but the charge light is still on, the alternator itself is probably at fault. This does not mean the entire unit needs to be replaced. Many times the voltage regulator may be defective and cause a no charge condition. Check the alternator and regulator operation by performing the following tests.

## ✳✳CAUTION

**Keep all wires and tools away from moving engine parts. Serious personal injury and damage to the car could result.**

There are several different types of alternators used on the Tempo/Topaz. One is the side terminal alternator which uses an externally mounted voltage regulator. The other is an external fan alternator which has the voltage regulator mounted in the rear of the alternator housing (integral). All 1992–94 vehicles are equipped with an internal fan/integral voltage regulator type alternator.

When performing charging system tests, turn off all lights and electrical components. Place the transmission in P and apply the parking brake.

To ensure accurate meter indications, the battery terminal posts and battery cable clamps must be clean and tight.

## ✳✳WARNING

**Do not make jumper wire connections except as instructed. Incorrect jumper wire connections can damage the regulator or fuse links.**

**Preliminary Inspection**

1. Make sure the battery cable connections are clean and tight.

2. Check all alternator and regulator wiring connections. Make sure all connections are clean and secure.

3. Check the alternator belt tension. Adjust, if necessary.

4. Check the fuse link between the starter relay and alternator. Replace if burned out.

5. Make sure the fuses/fuse links to the alternator are not burned or damaged. This could cause an open circuit or high resistance, resulting in erratic or intermittent charging problems.

6. If equipped with a heated windshield, make sure the wiring connections to the alternator output control relay are correct and tight.

7. If equipped with a heated windshield, make sure the connector to the heated windshield module is properly seated and there are no broken wires.

## PINPOINT TEST A: CHARGING SYSTEM — DIAGNOSIS

| | TEST STEP | RESULT | ▶ | ACTION TO TAKE |
|---|---|---|---|---|
| A1 | LAMP CHECK NO. 1 <br> • Engine OFF. <br> • Key in OFF position. <br> • **Is charging system indicator on?** | Yes <br><br> No | ▶ <br><br> ▶ | GO to A4. <br><br> GO to A2. |

86703009

**Fig. 11 Alternator diagnosis chart**

| | TEST STEP | RESULT | ▶ | ACTION TO TAKE |
|---|---|---|---|---|
| A2 | LAMP CHECK NO. 2 <br> • Engine OFF. <br> • Key in RUN position. <br> • **Is charging system indicator on?** | Yes <br><br> No | ▶ <br><br> ▶ | GO to A3. <br><br> GO to A5. |
| A3 | LAMP CHECK NO. 3 <br> • Key in RUN position. <br> • Engine running. <br> • **Is charging system indicator on?** | No <br><br> Yes | ▶ <br><br> ▶ | Lamp test complete. <br><br> GO to A9. |
| A4 | IMPROPER 'I' CIRCUIT WIRING <br> • Key in OFF position. <br> • Check for voltage at 'I' circuit. <br> • **Is voltage present?** | Yes <br><br><br><br> No | ▶ <br><br><br><br> ▶ | CHECK for voltage feed from always hot circuit to 'I' circuit. <br><br> CHECK for damaged or improper wiring to charging system indicator lamp at instrument cluster. |
| A5 | INOPERATIVE CHARGING SYSTEM INDICATOR LAMP <br> • Key in ON position. <br> • Engine OFF. <br> • Disconnect regulator connector and ground 'I' terminal. <br> • **Is charge indicator on?** | Yes <br><br> No | ▶ <br><br> ▶ | GO to A7. <br><br> GO to A6. |

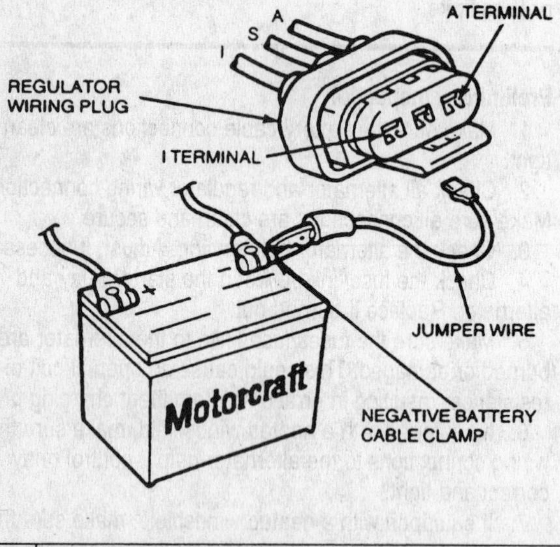

REGULATOR WIRING PLUG — A TERMINAL — I TERMINAL — JUMPER WIRE — NEGATIVE BATTERY CABLE CLAMP — Motorcraft

| | TEST STEP | RESULT | ▶ | ACTION TO TAKE |
|---|---|---|---|---|
| A6 | RESISTANCE / BULB TEST <br> • Check for voltage at 'I' terminal of regulator connector. <br> • **Is voltage present?** | Yes <br><br><br> No | ▶ <br><br><br> ▶ | CHECK for burned out charging system indicator lamp or high resistance in lamp circuit. <br><br> CHECK for an open in 'I' circuit wiring. |

86703010

**Fig. 12 Alternator diagnosis chart**

**PINPOINT TEST A: CHARGING SYSTEM — DIAGNOSIS (Continued)**

| TEST STEP | RESULT ▶ | ACTION TO TAKE |
|---|---|---|
| **A7**   STATOR VOLTAGE FAULT<br>• Reconnect voltage regulator.<br>• Engine OFF.<br>• Check voltage 'S' terminal.<br>• **Is voltage present?** | Yes<br><br>No | ▶ GO to **A8**.<br>▶ REPLACE regulator. |
| 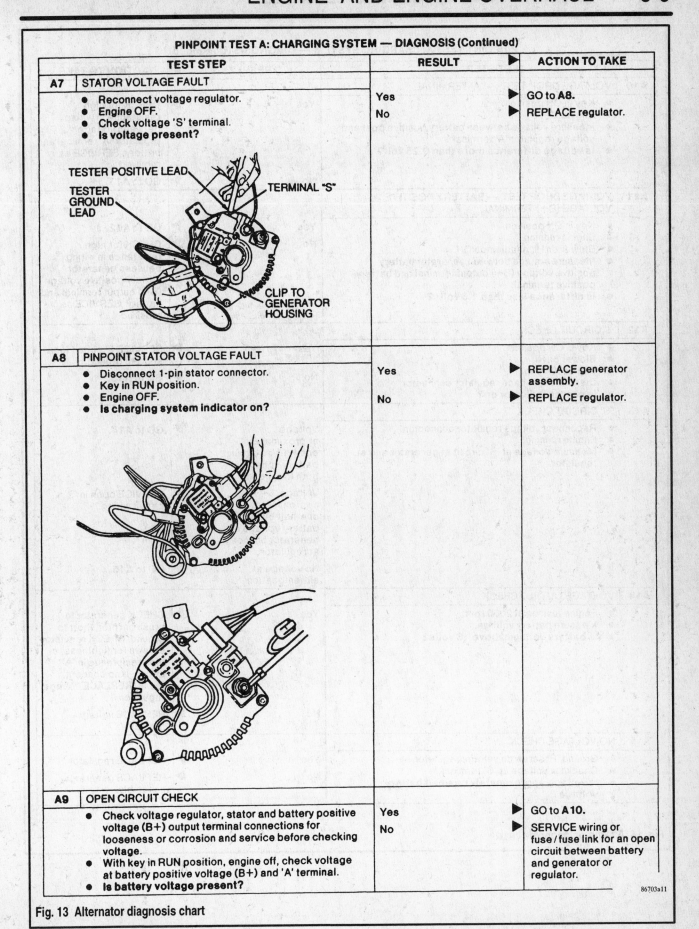 | | |
| **A8**   PINPOINT STATOR VOLTAGE FAULT<br>• Disconnect 1-pin stator connector.<br>• Key in RUN position.<br>• Engine OFF.<br>• **Is charging system indicator on?** | Yes<br><br><br>No | ▶ REPLACE generator assembly.<br>▶ REPLACE regulator. |
| **A9**   OPEN CIRCUIT CHECK<br>• Check voltage regulator, stator and battery positive voltage (B+) output terminal connections for looseness or corrosion and service before checking voltage.<br>• With key in RUN position, engine off, check voltage at battery positive voltage (B+) and 'A' terminal.<br>• **Is battery voltage present?** | Yes<br>No | ▶ GO to **A10**.<br>▶ SERVICE wiring or fuse / fuse link for an open circuit between battery and generator or regulator. |

86703a11

**Fig. 13 Alternator diagnosis chart**

**PINPOINT TEST A: CHARGING SYSTEM — DIAGNOSIS (Continued)**

| TEST STEP | RESULT ▶ | ACTION TO TAKE |
|---|---|---|
| **A10** VOLTAGE DROP TEST — 'A' TERMINAL | | |
| • Key in ON position.<br>• Engine OFF.<br>• Measure voltage between battery positive post and voltage regulator 'A' terminal.<br>• **Is voltage difference more than 0.25 volt?** | Yes ▶ | CHECK for high resistance in wiring between voltage regulator 'A' terminal and battery. SERVICE as required. |
| | No ▶ | GO to **A11.** |
| **A11** VOLTAGE DROP TEST — BATTERY POSITIVE VOLTAGE (B+) TERMINAL | | |
| • Key in ON position.<br>• Engine running.<br>• Blower on HI, headlamps ON.<br>• Measure voltage between generator battery positive voltage (B+) output terminal and battery positive terminal.<br>• **Is difference less than 1.5 volts?** | Yes ▶ | GO to **A12.** |
| | No ▶ | CHECK for high resistance in wiring between generator battery positive voltage (B+) output terminal and battery. SERVICE as required. |
| **A12** 'I' CIRCUIT CHECK | | |
| • Key in ON position.<br>• Blower on HI.<br>• Engine running.<br>• Disconnect voltage regulator connector.<br>• **Is charge indicator on?** | Yes ▶ | SERVICE 'I' circuit for a short to ground. |
| | No ▶ | GO to **A13.** |
| **A13** 'S' CIRCUIT CHECK | | |
| • Reconnect voltage regulator connector.<br>• Engine running.<br>• Measure voltage at 'S' circuit at generator and at regulator. | Voltage approximately one-half 'A' circuit battery voltage at both locations ▶ | GO to **A14.** |
| | Voltage approximately one-half 'A' circuit battery voltage at generator but not at regulator ▶ | SERVICE open in 'S' circuit wiring. |
| | No voltage at either location ▶ | GO to **A15.** |
| **A14** VOLTAGE OUTPUT CHECK | | |
| • Engine running at 2000 rpm.<br>• Measure battery voltage.<br>• **Is battery voltage above 16 volts?** | Yes ▶ | CHECK generator for brush or rotor short to ground. CHECK regulator screws for tightness, or high resistance in 'A' circuit. If no concern found, REPLACE voltage regulator. |
| | No ▶ | REPLACE voltage regulator. |
| **A15** NO VOLTAGE CHECK | | |
| • Ground 'F' screw on voltage regulator.<br>• Check for voltage at 'S' terminal.<br>• **Is voltage approximately one-half battery voltage?** | Yes ▶ | REPLACE regulator. |
| | No ▶ | REPLACE generator assembly. |

86703a12

**Fig. 14 Alternator diagnosis chart**

**PINPOINT TEST B: CHARGING SYSTEM TEST — IGR GENERATOR**

| | TEST STEP | RESULT | ▶ | ACTION TO TAKE |
|---|---|---|---|---|
| **B1** | PRELIMINARY CHECKS | | | |
| | ● Preliminary Checks:<br>— Fuse link<br>— Battery terminals and cable clamps<br>— Wiring and ground connections to generator, regulator and engine<br>— Generator belt tension<br>● **Are components OK?** | Yes<br><br>No | ▶<br><br>▶ | GO to **B2**.<br><br>SERVICE and / or REPLACE as necessary. GO to **B2**. |
| **B2** | BASE VOLTAGE AND NO LOAD TEST | | | |
| | ● Connect voltmeter to battery posts. Read battery voltage — this is base reading.<br>● Start engine, run at 1500 rpm with no electrical load. Voltage should increase but not more than 3 volts.<br>● **Does voltage increase more than 3 volts?** | No<br>No increase<br>Yes | ▶<br>▶<br>▶ | GO to **B3**.<br>GO to **B5**.<br>GO to **B12**. |
| **B3** | LOAD TEST | | | |
| | ● Increase engine speed to 2000 rpm.<br>● Turn heater-A / C blower and headlamps on HI.<br>● **Is voltage a minimum of 0.5 volt over base voltage?** | Yes<br><br>No | ▶<br><br>▶ | GO to **B4**.<br><br>GO to **B5**. |
| **B4** | BATTERY DRAIN TEST — KEY OFF | | | |
| | ● Concern can still be battery drain. Turn OFF ignition, install test lamp in series with positive battery cable and check to isolate problem circuit.<br>● **Is there a battery drain?** | Yes<br><br><br>No | ▶<br><br><br>▶ | CHECK vehicle circuits for drain.<br><br>REFER to Section 14-01. |
| **B5** | UNDER-VOLTAGE TEST | | | |
| | ● Disconnect regulator.<br>● Check resistance between regulator 'A' and 'F' terminals on regulator.<br>● **Is resistance more than 2.4 ohms?** | Yes<br><br>No | ▶<br><br>▶ | GO to **B6**.<br><br>CHECK generator for shorted field circuit and REPLACE generator assembly if required. If generator is OK, REPLACE regulator. GO to **B2**. |
| **B6** | 'A' TERMINAL VOLTAGE CHECK | | | |
| | ● Reconnect regulator.<br>● Measure 'A' terminal voltage.<br>● **Is there battery voltage?** | Yes<br>No | ▶<br>▶ | GO to **B7**.<br>SERVICE 'A' circuit wiring. |
| **B7** | 'F' TERMINAL VOLTAGE CHECK — IGNITION OFF | | | |
| | ● Voltage regulator connected.<br>● Key OFF.<br>● Measure regulator 'F' terminal voltage with ignition off.<br>● **Is there battery voltage?** | Yes<br><br>No | ▶<br><br>▶ | GO to **B8**.<br><br>REPLACE generator assembly. GO to **B2**. |
| **B8** | 'F' TERMINAL VOLTAGE CHECK — IGNITION IN RUN | | | |
| | ● Turn ignition to RUN position (engine not running).<br>● Measure regulator 'F' terminal voltage.<br>● **Is voltage more than 1.5 volts?** | Yes<br>No | ▶<br>▶ | GO to **B9**.<br>GO to **B10**. |
| **B9** | 'I' CIRCUIT TESTS | | | |
| | ● Perform 'I' circuit tests.<br>● **Is circuit OK?** | Yes<br><br>No | ▶<br><br>▶ | REPLACE regulator. GO to **B2**.<br>SERVICE 'I' circuit wiring. GO to **B2**. |
| **B10** | JUMPERED LOAD TEST | | | |
| | ● Repeat Load Test measuring voltage to generator battery positive voltage (B+) output terminal from battery negative clamp.<br>● **Does voltage rise 0.5 volt or more?** | Yes<br><br><br>No | ▶<br><br><br>▶ | SERVICE generator to starter relay wiring. GO to **B2**.<br>GO to **B11**. |

86703013

**Fig. 15 Alternator diagnosis chart**

**PINPOINT TEST B: CHARGING SYSTEM TEST — IGR GENERATOR (Continued)**

| TEST STEP | RESULT | | ACTION TO TAKE |
|---|---|---|---|
| **B11** LOAD TEST REPEAT — 'F' TERMINAL | | | |
| • Connect a jumper wire from generator rear housing to regulator 'F' terminal. | Yes | ▶ | REPLACE regulator. GO to **B2**. |
| • Repeat load test measuring voltage at battery positive voltage (B+) output terminal. | No | ▶ | REPLACE generator assembly. GO to **B2**. |
| • **Does voltage rise 0.5 volt or more?** | | | |
| **B12** OVER-VOLTAGE TEST | | | |
| • Turn ignition to RUN position (engine not running). | Yes | ▶ | GO to **B13**. |
| • Measure voltage at regulator 'A' terminal and starter solenoid. | No | ▶ | SERVICE A circuit wiring. GO to **B2**. |
| • **Is voltage difference 0.5 volt or less?** | | | |
| **B13** REGULATOR GROUND CHECK | | | |
| • Check for loose regulator ground screws. | Yes | ▶ | GO to **B14**. |
| • **Is ground OK?** | No | ▶ | SERVICE ground screws. GO to **B2**. |
| **B14** ENGINE GROUND CHECK | | | |
| • Check for bad engine ground. | Yes | ▶ | GO to **B15**. |
| • **Is ground OK?** | No | ▶ | SERVICE engine ground. GO to **B2**. |
| **B15** GENERATOR GROUND CHECK | | | |
| • Check generator ground. | Yes | ▶ | GO to **B16**. |
| • **Is ground OK?** | No | ▶ | SERVICE generator ground. GO to **B2**. |
| **B16** REPEAT NO LOAD TEST | | | |
| • Start engine, run at 1500 rpm with no electrical load. | No | ▶ | GO to **B3**. |
| • Voltage should increase but not more than 3 volts. | Yes | ▶ | GO to **B17**. |
| • **Does voltage increase more than 3 volts?** | | | |
| **B17** 'A' AND 'F' VOLTAGE CHECKS | | | |
| • Turn ignition OFF. | Yes | ▶ | REPLACE regulator. GO to **B2**. |
| • Measure voltage at regulator 'A' and 'F' terminals. | | | |
| • Terminal voltages should be the same as battery voltage. | No | ▶ | REPLACE generator assembly. GO to **B2**. |
| • **Is there battery voltage at both terminals?** | | | |

86703014

**Fig. 16 Alternator diagnosis chart**

**Alternator With External Regulator**

♦ See Figure 17

### CHARGING SYSTEM INDICATOR LIGHT TEST

1. If the charging system indicator light does not come on with the ignition key in the RUN position and the engine not running, check the ignition switch–to–regulator I terminal wiring for an open circuit or burned out charging system indicator light. Replace the light, if necessary.

2. If the charging system indicator light does not come on, unplug the electrical connector at the regulator and connect a jumper wire between the I terminal of the connector and the negative battery cable clamp.

3. The charging system indicator light should go on with the ignition switch in the RUN position.

4. If the light does not go on, check the light for continuity and replace, if necessary.

5. If the light is not burned out, there is an open circuit between the ignition switch and the regulator.

6. Check the 500 ohm resistor at the indicator light.

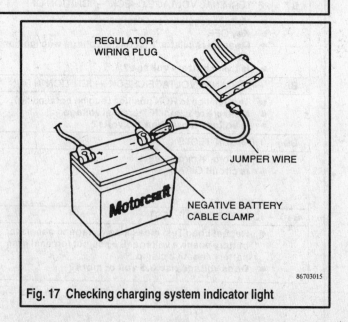

**Fig. 17 Checking charging system indicator light**

## BASE VOLTAGE TEST

▶ **See Figure 18**

1. Connect the negative and positive leads of a voltmeter to the negative and positive battery cable clamps.

2. Make sure the ignition switch is in the OFF position and all electrical loads (lights, radio, etc.) are OFF.

3. Record the battery voltage shown on the voltmeter; this is the base voltage.

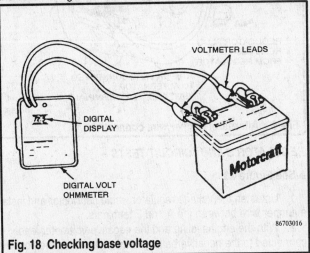

**Fig. 18 Checking base voltage**

## NO-LOAD TEST

1. Connect a suitable tachometer to the engine using the manufacturers specifications.

2. Start the engine and bring the engine speed to 1500 rpm. With no other electrical loads (doors closed, foot off the brake pedal), the reading on the voltmeter should increase, but no more than 2.5 volts above the base voltage.

➡ **The voltage reading should be taken when the voltage stops rising. This may take a few minutes.**

3. If the voltage increases as in Step 2, perform the Load Test.

4. If the voltage continues to rise, perform the Over Voltage Tests.

5. If the voltage does not rise to the proper level, perform the Under Voltage Tests.

## LOAD TEST

1. With the engine running, turn the blower speed switch to the HIGH SPEED position and turn the headlights on to HIGH BEAM.

2. Raise the engine speed to approximately 2000 rpm. The voltmeter reading should be a minimum of 0.5 volts above the base voltage. If not, perform the Under Voltage Tests.

➡ **If the voltmeter readings in the No-Load Test and Load Test are as specified, the charging system is operating properly. Go to the following tests if one or more of the voltage readings is different. Also check for any battery drain.**

## OVER VOLTAGE TESTS

▶ **See Figure 19**

1. If the voltmeter reading was more than 2.5 volts above the base voltage in the No-Load Test, connect a jumper wire

between the voltage regulator base and the alternator frame or housing. Repeat the No-Load Test.

2. If the over voltage condition disappears, check the ground connections on the alternator, regulator and from the engine to the dash panel and to the battery. Clean and securely tighten the connections.

3. If the over voltage condition still exists, disconnect the voltage regulator wiring connector from the voltage regulator. Repeat the No-Load Test.

4. If the over voltage condition disappears (voltmeter reads base voltage), replace the voltage regulator.

5. If the over voltage condition still exists with the voltage regulator wiring connector unplugged, check for a short between A and F terminal screws holding the regulator in place and service, as necessary. Then fasten the voltage regulator wiring connector.

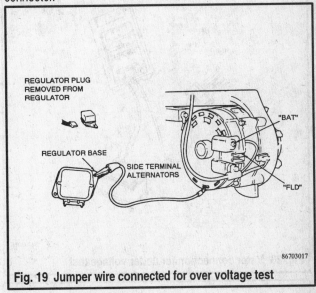

**Fig. 19 Jumper wire connected for over voltage test**

## UNDER VOLTAGE TESTS

▶ **See Figures 20, 21 and 22**

1. If the voltage reading was not more than 0.5 volts above the base voltage, Unfasten the wiring connector from the voltage regulator and connect an ohmmeter from the F terminal of the connector to ground. The ohmmeter should indicate more than 2.4 ohms.

2. If the ohmmeter reading is less than 2.4 ohms, service the grounded field circuit in the wiring harness or alternator and repeat the Load Test.

### ✳✳WARNING

**Do not replace the voltage regulator before a shorted rotor coil or field circuit has been serviced. Damage to the regulator could result.**

3. If the ohmmeter reading is more than 2.4 ohms, connect a jumper wire from the A to F terminals of the wiring connector and repeat the Load Test. If the voltmeter now indicates more than 0.5 volts above the base voltage, the regulator or wiring is damaged or worn. Perform the S and I Circuit Tests and service the wiring or regulator, as required.

4. If the voltmeter still indicates an under voltage problem, remove the jumper wire from the voltage regulator connector and leave the connector unfastened from the regulator.

5. Disconnect the FLD terminal on the alternator and pull back the protective cover from the BAT terminal. Connect a jumper wire between the FLD and BAT terminals and repeat the Load Test.

6. If the voltmeter indicates a 0.5 volts or more increase above base voltage, perform the S and I Circuit Tests and service the wiring or regulator, as indicated.

7. If the voltmeter still indicates under voltage, shut the engine OFF and move the positive voltmeter lead to the BAT terminal of the alternator. If the voltmeter now indicates the base voltage, service the alternator. If the voltmeter indicates 0 volts, service the alternator–to–starter relay wire.

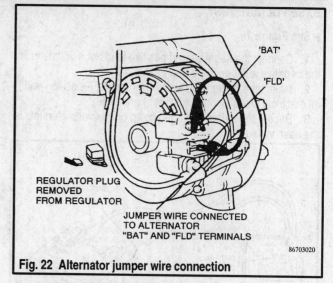

Fig. 22 Alternator jumper wire connection

### REGULATOR S AND I CIRCUIT TESTS

▶ See Figure 23

1. Unfasten the voltage regulator wiring connector and install a jumper wire between the A and F terminals.

2. With the engine idling and the negative voltmeter lead connected to the negative battery terminal, connect the positive voltmeter lead to the S terminal and then to the I terminal of the regulator wiring connector.

3. The S circuit voltage reading should be approximately 1/2 the I circuit reading. If the voltage readings are correct, remove the jumper wire. Replace the voltage regulator and repeat the Load Test.

4. If there is no voltage present, service the faulty wiring circuit. Connect the positive voltmeter lead to the positive battery terminal.

5. Remove the jumper wire from the regulator wiring connector and connect the connector to the regulator. Repeat the Load Test

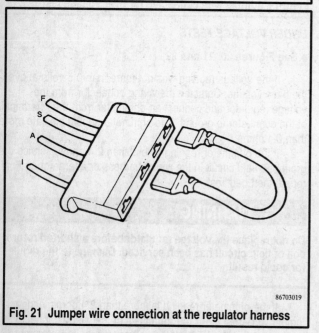

Fig. 20 Meter connection for under voltage test

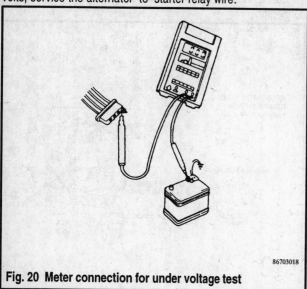

Fig. 21 Jumper wire connection at the regulator harness

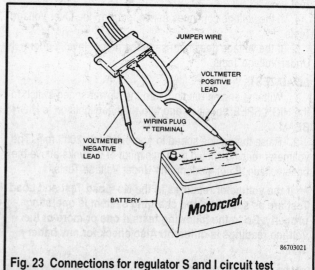

Fig. 23 Connections for regulator S and I circuit test

## FUSE LINK CONTINUITY

1. Make sure the battery is okay (See Section 1).

2. Turn on the headlights or any accessory. If the headlights or accessory do not operate, the fuse link is probably burned out.

3. On some vehicles there are several fuse links. Proceed as in Step 2 to test other fuse links.

4. To test the fuse link that protects the alternator, check for voltage at the BAT terminal of the alternator, using a voltmeter. If there is no voltage, the fuse link is probably burned out.

## Alternator With Integral Regulator/External Fan

### CHARGING SYSTEM INDICATOR LIGHT TEST

▶ See Figure 24

Two conditions can cause the charging system indicator light to come on when your car is running: no alternator output, caused by a damaged alternator, regulator or wiring, or an over voltage condition, caused by a shorted alternator rotor, regulator or wiring.

In a normally functioning system, the charging system indicator light will be OFF when the ignition switch is in the OFF position, ON when the ignition switch is in the RUN position and the engine not running, and OFF when the ignition switch is in the RUN position and the engine is running.

1. If the charging system indicator light does not come on, unplug the wiring connector from the regulator.

2. Install a jumper wire between the connector I terminal and the negative battery cable clamp.

3. Turn the ignition switch to the RUN position, but leave the engine OFF. If the charging system indicator light does not come on, check for a light socket resistor. If there is a resistor, check the contact of the light socket leads to the flexible printed circuit. If they are good, check the indicator light for continuity and replace if burned out. If the light checks out good, perform the Regulator I Circuit Test.

4. If the indicator light comes on, remove the jumper wire and reconnect the wiring connector to the regulator. Connect the negative voltmeter lead to the negative battery cable clamp and connect the positive voltmeter lead to the regulator A terminal screw. Battery voltage should be indicated. If battery voltage is not indicated, service the A circuit wiring.

5. If battery voltage is indicated, clean and tighten the ground connections to the engine, alternator and regulator. Tighten loose regulator mounting screws to 15–26 inch lbs. (1.7–2.8 Nm).

6. Turn the ignition switch to the RUN position with the engine OFF. If the charging system indicator light still does not come on, replace the regulator.

### BASE VOLTAGE TEST

▶ See Figure 25

1. Connect the negative and positive leads of a voltmeter to the negative and positive battery cable clamps.

2. Make sure the ignition switch is in the OFF position and all electrical loads (lights, radio, etc.) are OFF.

3. Record the battery voltage shown on the voltmeter; this is the base voltage.

### NO–LOAD TEST

1. Connect a suitable tachometer to the engine.

2. Start the engine and bring the engine speed to 1500 rpm. With no other electrical loads (doors closed, foot off the brake pedal), the reading on the voltmeter should increase, but no more than 2.5 volts above the base voltage.

➡ The voltage reading should be taken when the voltage stops rising. This may take a few minutes.

3. If the voltage increases as in Step 2, perform the Load Test.

4. If the voltage continues to rise, perform the Over Voltage Tests.

5. If the voltage does not rise to the proper level, perform the Under Voltage Tests.

### LOAD TEST

1. With the engine running, turn the blower speed switch to the high speed position and turn the headlights on to high beam.

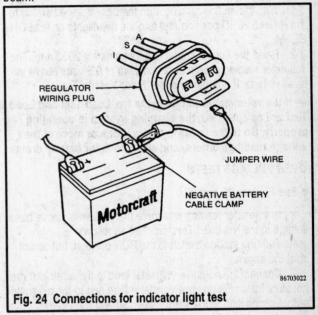

**Fig. 24 Connections for indicator light test**

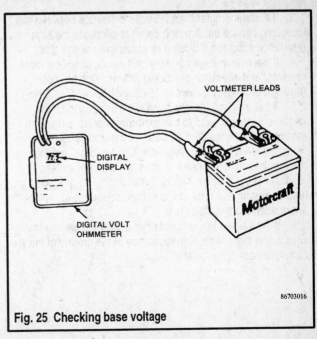

**Fig. 25 Checking base voltage**

## NO–LOAD TEST

1. Connect a suitable tachometer to the engine using the manufacturers specifications.

2. Start the engine and bring the engine speed to 1500 rpm. With no other electrical loads (doors closed, foot off the brake pedal), the reading on the voltmeter should increase, but no more than 2.5 volts above the base voltage.

➡ **The voltage reading should be taken when the voltage stops rising. This may take a few minutes.**

3. If the voltage increases as in Step 2, perform the Load Test.

4. If the voltage continues to rise, perform the Over Voltage Tests.

5. If the voltage does not rise to the proper level, perform the Under Voltage Tests.

## LOAD TEST

1. With the engine running, turn the blower speed switch to the HIGH SPEED position and turn the headlights on to HIGH BEAM.

2. Raise the engine speed to approximately 2000 rpm. The voltmeter reading should be a minimum of 0.5 volts above the base voltage. If not, perform the Under Voltage Tests.

➡ **If the voltmeter readings in the No–Load Test and Load Test are as specified, the charging system is operating properly. Go to the following tests if one or more of the voltage readings differs, and also check for battery drain.**

## OVER VOLTAGE TESTS

▶ **See Figures 26 and 27**

If the voltmeter reading was more than 2.5 volts above base voltage in the No–Load Test, proceed as follows:

1. Turn the ignition switch to the RUN position, but do not start the engine.

2. Connect the negative voltmeter lead to the alternator rear housing. Install the positive voltmeter lead first to the alternator output connection at the starter solenoid and then to the regulator A screw head.

3. If there is greater than 0.5 volts difference between the 2 locations, service the A wiring circuit to eliminate the high resistance condition indicated by excessive voltage drop.

4. If the over voltage condition still exists, check for loose regulator and alternator grounding screws. Tighten loose regulator grounding screws to 15–26 inch lbs. (1.7–2.8 Nm).

5. If the over voltage condition still exists, connect the negative voltmeter lead to the alternator rear housing. With the ignition switch in the OFF position, connect the positive voltmeter lead first to the regulator A screw head and then to the regulator F screw head. If there are different voltage readings at the 2 screw heads, a malfunctioning grounded brush lead or a grounded rotor coil is indicated; service or replace the entire alternator/regulator unit.

6. If the same voltage is obtained at both screw heads in Step 5 and there is no high resistance in the ground of the A+ circuit, replace the regulator.

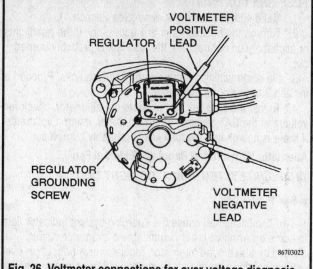

**Fig. 26 Voltmeter connections for over voltage diagnosis**

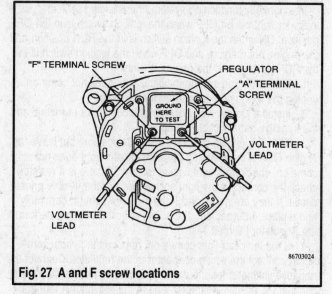

**Fig. 27 A and F screw locations**

## UNDER VOLTAGE TESTS

▶ **See Figures 28, 29 and 30**

If the voltmeter reading was not more than 0.5 volts above base voltage, proceed as follows:

1. Unplug the electrical connector from the regulator. Connect an ohmmeter between the regulator A and F terminal screws. The ohmmeter reading should be more than 2.4 ohms. If it is less than 2.4 ohms, the regulator has failed. also check the alternator for a shorted rotor or field circuit. Perform the Load Test after servicing.

## ✳✳WARNING

Do not replace the voltage regulator before a shorted rotor coil or field circuit has been serviced. Damage to the regulator could result.

2. If the ohmmeter reading is greater than 2.4 ohms, fasten the regulator wiring connector and plug the negative voltmeter lead to the alternator rear housing. Connect the positive voltmeter lead to the regulator A terminal screw. The voltmeter should indicate battery voltage. If there is no voltage, service the A wiring circuit and then perform the Load Test.

3. If the voltmeter indicates battery voltage, connect the negative voltmeter lead to the alternator rear housing. With the ignition switch in the OFF position, connect the positive voltmeter lead to the regulator F terminal screw. The voltmeter should indicate battery voltage. If there is no voltage, there is an open field circuit in the alternator. Service or replace the alternator, then perform the Load Test after servicing.

4. If the voltmeter indicates battery voltage, connect the negative voltmeter lead to the alternator rear housing. Turn the ignition switch to the RUN position, leaving the engine OFF, and connect the positive voltmeter lead to the regulator F terminal screw. The voltmeter should read 1.5 volts or less. If more than 1.5 volts is indicated, perform the I circuit tests and service the I circuit if needed. If the I circuit is normal, replace the regulator, if needed, and perform the Load Test after servicing.

5. If 1.5 volts or less is indicated, unplug the alternator wiring connector. Install a set of 12 gauge jumper wires between the alternator B+ terminal blades and the mating wiring connector terminals. Perform the Load Test, but connect the positive voltmeter lead to one of the B+ jumper wire terminals. If the voltage increases more than 0.5 volts above base voltage, service the alternator–to–starter relay wiring. Repeat the Load Test, measuring voltage at the battery cable clamps after servicing.

6. If the voltage does not increase more than 0.5 volts above base voltage, connect a jumper wire from the alternator rear housing to the regulator F terminal. Repeat the Load Test with the positive voltmeter lead connected to one of the B+ jumper wire terminals. If the voltage increases more than 0.5 volts, replace the regulator. If the voltage does not increase more than 0.5 volts, service or replace the alternator.

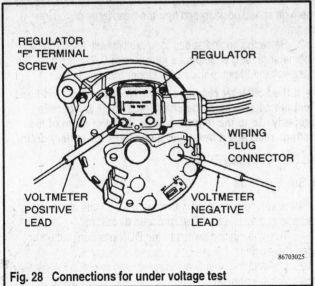

**Fig. 28  Connections for under voltage test**

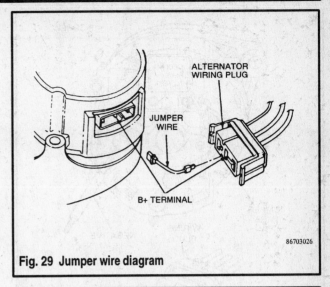

**Fig. 29  Jumper wire diagram**

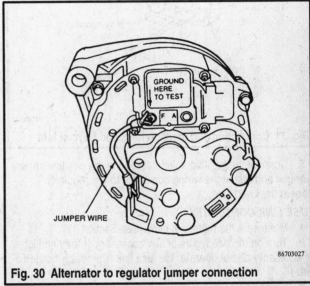

**Fig. 30  Alternator to regulator jumper connection**

### *REGULATOR S AND I CIRCUIT TEST*

▶ **See Figure 31**

1. Fasten the wiring connector from the regulator. Plug a jumper wire between the regulator A terminal and the wiring connector A lead and install a jumper wire between the regulator F screw and the alternator rear housing.

2. With the engine idling and the negative voltmeter lead connected to the negative battery terminal, connect the positive voltmeter lead first to the S terminal and then to the I terminal of the regulator wiring connector.

3. The S circuit voltage should be approximately 1/2 that of the I circuit. If the voltage readings are correct, remove the jumper wire. Replace the regulator and install the regulator wiring connector. Perform the Load Test.

4. If there is no voltage present, remove the jumper wire and service the faulty wiring circuit or alternator.

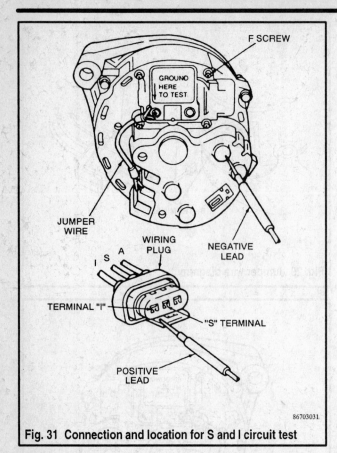

Fig. 31 Connection and location for S and I circuit test

5. Connect the positive voltmeter lead to the positive battery terminal and fasten the wiring connector to the regulator. Repeat the Load Test.

### FUSE LINK CONTINUITY

1. Make sure the battery is okay (See Section 1).
2. Turn on the headlights or any accessory. If the headlights or accessory do not operate, the fuse link is probably burned out.
3. On some vehicles there are several fuse links. Proceed as in Step 2 to test other fuse links.
4. To test the fuse link that protects the alternator, check for voltage at the BAT terminal of the alternator and A terminal of the regulator, using a voltmeter. If there is no voltage, the fuse link is probably burned out.

### FIELD CIRCUIT DRAIN

In all of the Field Circuit Drain test steps, connect the negative voltmeter lead to the alternator rear housing.

1. With the ignition switch in the OFF position, connect the positive voltmeter lead to the regulator F terminal screw. The voltmeter should read battery voltage if the system is operating normally. If less than battery voltage is indicated, go to Step 2.
2. Unplug the wiring connector from the regulator and connect the positive voltmeter lead to the wiring connector I terminal. There should be no voltage indicated. If voltage is indicated, service the I lead from the ignition switch to identify and eliminate the voltage source.
3. If there was no voltage indicated in Step 2, connect the positive voltmeter lead to the wiring connector S terminal. No voltage should be indicated. If no voltage is indicated, replace the regulator.

4. If there was voltage indicated in Step 3, unplug the wiring connector from the alternator rectifier harness. Connect the positive voltmeter lead to the regulator wiring connector S terminal. If voltage is indicated, service the S lead to the alternator connector to eliminate the voltage source. If no voltage is indicated, the alternator rectifier assembly is faulty.

### Alternator With Integral Regulator/Internal Fan

#### BASE VOLTAGE TEST

◆ See Figure 25

1. Connect the negative and positive leads of a voltmeter to the negative and positive battery cable clamps.
2. Make sure the ignition switch is in the OFF position and all electrical loads (lights, radio, etc.) are OFF.
3. Record the battery voltage shown on the voltmeter; this is the base voltage.

➡ Turn the headlights ON for 10–15 seconds to remove any surface charge from the battery, then wait until the voltage stabilizes, before performing the base voltage test.

#### NO–LOAD TEST

1. Connect a suitable tachometer to the engine.
2. Start the engine and bring the engine speed to 1500 rpm. With no other electrical loads (doors closed, foot off the brake pedal), the reading on the voltmeter should increase, but no more than 3 volts above the base voltage.

➡ The voltage reading should be taken when the voltage stops rising. This may take a few minutes.

3. If the voltage increases as in Step 2, perform the Load Test.
4. If the voltage continues to rise, perform the Over Voltage Tests.
5. If the voltage does not rise to the proper level, perform the Under Voltage Tests.

#### LOAD TEST

1. With the engine running, turn the blower speed switch to the high speed position and turn the headlights on to high beam.
2. Raise the engine speed to approximately 2000 rpm. The voltmeter reading should be a minimum of 0.5 volts above the base voltage. If not, perform the Under Voltage Tests.

➡ If the voltmeter readings in the No–Load Test and Load Test are as specified, the charging system is operating properly. Go to the following tests if one or more of the voltage readings differs, and also check for battery drain.

#### OVER VOLTAGE TESTS

◆ See Figure 32

If the voltmeter reading was more than 3 volts above base voltage in the No–Load Test, proceed as follows:

1. Turn the ignition switch to the RUN position, but do not start the engine.
2. Connect the negative voltmeter lead to ground. Connect the positive voltmeter lead first to the alternator output connection at the starter solenoid (1992) or load distribution point (1993) and then to the regulator A screw head.

3. If there is greater than 0.5 volts difference between the 2 locations, service the A wiring circuit to eliminate the high resistance condition indicated by excessive voltage drop.

4. If the over voltage condition still exists, check for loose regulator and alternator grounding screws. Tighten loose regulator grounding screws to 16–24 inch lbs. (1.7–2.8 Nm).

5. If the over voltage condition still exists, connect the negative voltmeter lead to ground. Turn the ignition switch to the OFF position and connect the positive voltmeter lead first to the regulator A screw head and then to the regulator F screw head. If there are different voltage readings at the 2 screw heads, a malfunctioning regulator grounded brush lead or a grounded rotor coil is indicated; replace the regulator/brush set or the entire alternator.

6. If the same voltage reading, battery voltage, is obtained at both screw heads in Step 5, then there is no short to ground through the alternator field/brushes. Replace the regulator.

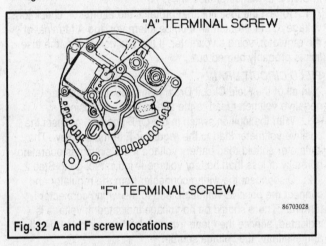

**Fig. 32  A and F screw locations**

86703028

### UNDER VOLTAGE TESTS

♦ See Figures 32, 33 and 34

If the voltmeter reading was not more than 0.5 volts above base voltage, proceed as follows:

1. Unplug the wiring connector from the regulator and connect an ohmmeter between the regulator A and F terminal screws. The ohmmeter should read more than 2.4 ohms. If the ohmmeter reads less than 2.4 ohms, check the alternator for shorted rotor to field coil or for shorted brushes. Replace the brush holder or the entire alternator assembly. Perform the Load Test after replacement.

### ✳✳WARNING

**Do not replace the regulator if a shorted rotor coil or field circuit has been diagnosed, or regulator damage could result. Replace the alternator assembly.**

2. If the ohmmeter reading is greater than 2.4 ohms, install the regulator wiring connector and plug the negative voltmeter

lead to ground. Connect the positive voltmeter lead to the regulator A terminal screw; battery voltage should be indicated. If there is no voltage, service the A wiring circuit and then perform the Load Test.

3. If battery voltage is indicated in Step 2, connect the negative voltmeter lead to ground. Turn the ignition switch to the OFF position, then connect the positive voltmeter lead to the regulator F terminal screw. Battery voltage should be indicated on the voltmeter. If there is no voltage, replace the alternator and then perform the Load Test.

4. If battery voltage is indicated in Step 3, connect the negative voltmeter lead to ground. Turn the ignition switch to the RUN position, but leave the engine OFF. Connect the positive voltmeter lead to the regulator F terminal screw; the voltmeter reading should be 2 volts or less. If more than 2 volts is indicated, perform the I circuit tests and service the I circuit, if needed. If the I circuit tests normal, replace the regulator, if needed, then perform the Load Test.

5. If 2 volts or less is indicated in Step 4, perform the Load Test, but connect the positive voltmeter lead to the alternator output stud. If the voltage increases more than 0.5 volts above base voltage, service the alternator–to–starter relay (1992) or alternator–to–load distribution point (1993) wiring. Repeat the Load Test, measuring the voltage at the battery cable clamps after servicing.

6. If the voltage does not increase more than 0.5 volts above base voltage in Step 5, perform the Load Test and measure the voltage drop from the battery to the A terminal of the regulator (regulator connected). If the voltage drop exceeds 0.5 volts, service the wiring from the A terminal to the starter relay (1992) or load distribution point (1993).

7. If the voltage drop does not exceed 0.5 volts, connect a jumper wire from the alternator rear housing to the regulator F terminal. Repeat the Load Test with the positive voltmeter lead connected to the alternator output stud. If the voltage increases more than 0.5 volts, replace the regulator. If voltage does not increase more than 0.5 volts, replace the alternator.

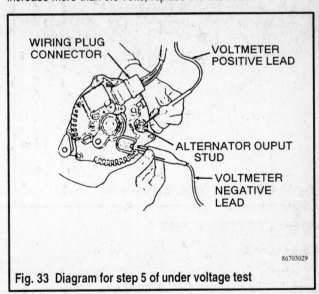

86703029

**Fig. 33  Diagram for step 5 of under voltage test**

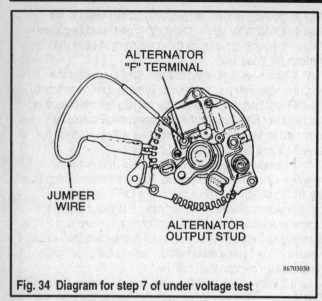

**Fig. 34 Diagram for step 7 of under voltage test**

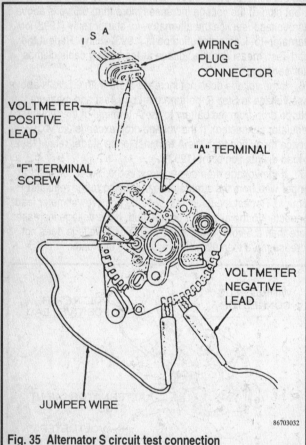

**Fig. 35 Alternator S circuit test connection**

## ALTERNATOR S CIRCUIT TEST

▶ See Figure 35

1. Unplug the wiring connector from the regulator. Connect a jumper wire from the regulator A terminal to the wiring connector A lead. Connect a jumper wire from the regulator F screw to the alternator rear housing.

2. With the engine idling and the negative voltmeter lead connected to ground, connect the positive voltmeter lead first to the S terminal and then to the A terminal of the regulator wiring connector. The S circuit voltage should be approximately 1/2 the A circuit voltage. If the voltage readings are normal, remove the jumper wire, replace the regulator and fasten the wiring connector. Repeat the Load Test.

3. If there is no voltage present, remove the jumper wire and service the damaged or worn wiring circuit or alternator.

4. Connect the positive voltmeter lead to the positive battery terminal. Secure the wiring connector to the regulator and repeat the Load Test.

### FUSE LINK CONTINUITY

1. Make sure the battery is okay (See Section 1).

2. Turn on the headlights or any accessory. If the headlights or accessory do not operate, the fuse link is probably burned out.

3. On some vehicles there are several fuse links. Proceed as in Step 2 to test other fuse links.

4. To test the fuse link that protects the alternator, check for voltage at the BAT terminal of the alternator and A terminal of the regulator, using a voltmeter. If there is no voltage, the fuse link is probably burned out.

### FIELD CIRCUIT DRAIN

In all of the Field Circuit Drain test steps, connect the negative voltmeter lead to the alternator rear housing.

1. With the ignition switch in the OFF position, connect the positive voltmeter lead to the regulator F terminal screw. The voltmeter should read battery voltage if the system is operating normally. If less than battery voltage is indicated, go to Step 2.

2. Disconnect the wiring connector from the regulator and connect the positive voltmeter lead to the wiring connector I terminal. There should be no voltage indicated. If voltage is indicated, service the I lead from the ignition switch to identify and eliminate the voltage source.

3. If there was no voltage indicated in Step 2, connect the positive voltmeter lead to the wiring connector S terminal. No voltage should be indicated. If no voltage is indicated, replace the regulator.

4. If there was voltage indicated in Step 3, disconnect the 1–pin S terminal connector. Again, connect the positive voltmeter lead to the regulator wiring connector S terminal. If voltage is indicated, service the S lead wiring to eliminate the voltage source. If no short is found, replace the alternator.

## REMOVAL & INSTALLATION

▶ See Figures 36, 37, 38 and 39

1. Disconnect the negative battery cable.

2. If equipped with a pulley cover shield, remove the shield at this time.

3. Unplug alternator wiring harness. Inspect for cracks or damage to the plug end or harness. Repair if necessary.

➡ **Based upon the amount and type of accessories present in the vehicle, other belts may have to be removed to gain access to the alternator.**

4. If equipped with V–belts or ribbed V–belts, loosen the necessary pivot bolts enough to slacken the alternator or other equipment and remove the belt. If numerous belts are used, tag the belt to remember the order for reassembly. Completely

remove the adjustment bracket to alternator bolt (and nut, if equipped) as well as the alternator pivot bolt.

5.  If equipped with a serpentine belt, use the appropriate tools to relieve tension on the tensioner pulley and remove the belt. Loosen and remove the alternator pivot bolt.

6.  Remove the alternator.

**To install:**

7.  Position the alternator onto the necessary bracket system and install the pivot bolt. Do not tighten the bolt at this time.

8.  If equipped with a serpentine belt, Relieve tension on the pulley enough to reinstall the serpentine belt. Make sure the ribs in the belt align correctly with the pulleys.

9.  If equipped with V–belts or ribbed V–belts, loosely install the belts on their respective accessaries. Begin tensioning each belt until individual deflection is 160 lbs (73 kg) for new belts and 140 ft. lbs. (64 kg) for used belts, using a belt tensioning gauge. Tighten adjuster bolts to 30 ft. lbs. (41 Nm), tighten pivot bolts to 50 ft. lbs. (68 Nm).

10.  Fasten the alternator wiring harness. Install the pulley shield, if equipped and connect the negative battery cable.

11.  Start vehicle and check for belt squeak as well as proper alternator voltage output.

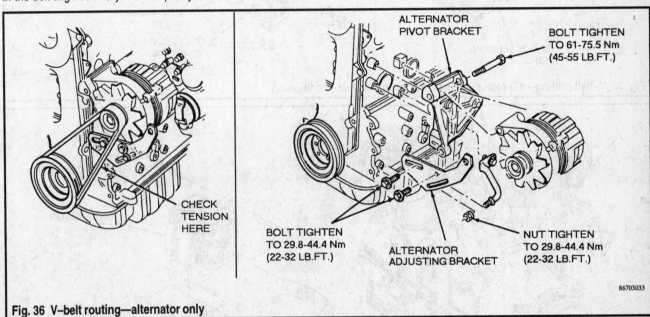

**Fig. 36  V–belt routing—alternator only**

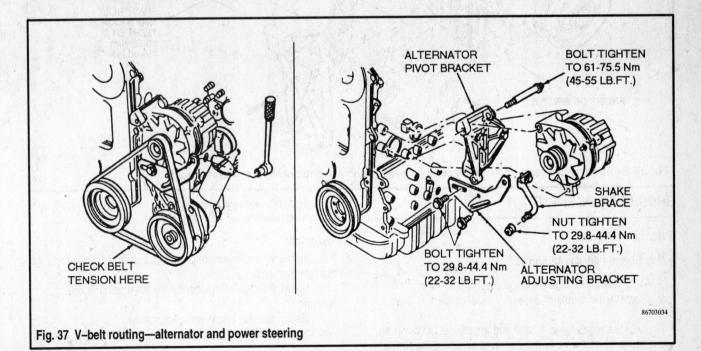

**Fig. 37  V-belt routing—alternator and power steering**

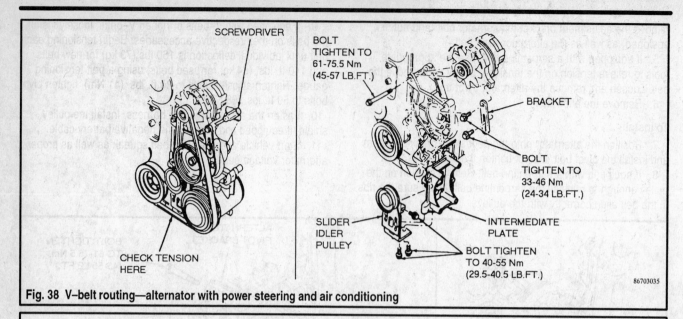

**Fig. 38 V–belt routing—alternator with power steering and air conditioning**

Labels in figure:
- SCREWDRIVER
- CHECK TENSION HERE
- BOLT TIGHTEN TO 61-75.5 Nm (45-57 LB.FT.)
- BRACKET
- BOLT TIGHTEN TO 33-46 Nm (24-34 LB.FT.)
- SLIDER IDLER PULLEY
- INTERMEDIATE PLATE
- BOLT TIGHTEN TO 40-55 Nm (29.5-40.5 LB.FT.)
- 86703035

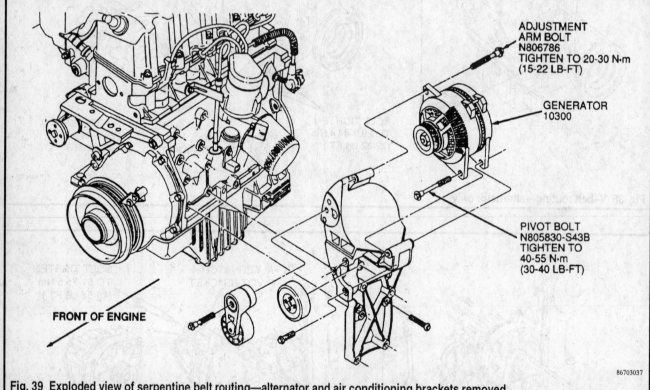

**Fig. 39 Exploded view of serpentine belt routing—alternator and air conditioning brackets removed**

Labels in figure:
- ADJUSTMENT ARM BOLT N806786 TIGHTEN TO 20-30 N·m (15-22 LB-FT)
- GENERATOR 10300
- PIVOT BOLT N805830-S43B TIGHTEN TO 40-55 N·m (30-40 LB-FT)
- FRONT OF ENGINE
- 86703037

## BRUSH REPLACEMENT

### External Fan Type

▶ **See Figures 40, 41, 42 and 43**

1. Disconnect the negative battery cable.
2. Remove the regulator assembly as described, in this section.
3. Hold the regulator in 1 hand and pry off the tab covering the A screw head. Remove the 2 screws attaching the regulator to the brush holder.

4. Separate the regulator, retaining nuts, brushes and brush springs from the brush holder.

**To install:**

5. Install the replacement brush springs and brushes. Install the retaining nuts.
6. Install the regulator assembly to the alternator rear housing.
7. Reconnect the negative battery cable.
8. Start vehicle and check alternator voltage output. ="AA30

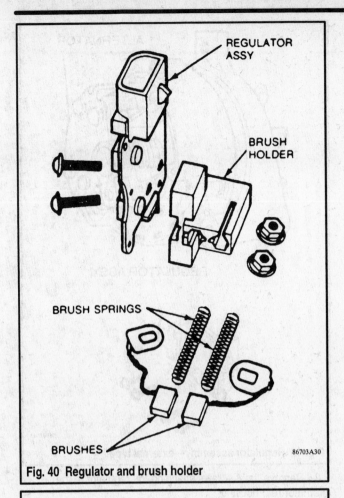

Fig. 40 Regulator and brush holder

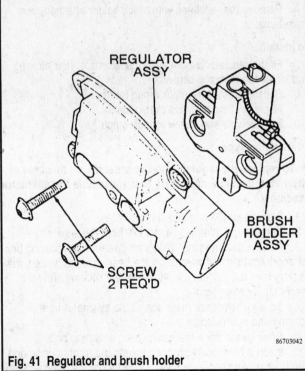

Fig. 41 Regulator and brush holder

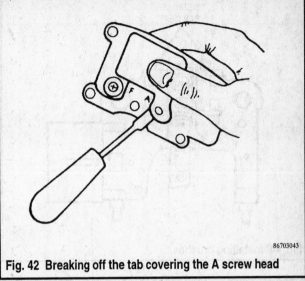

Fig. 42 Breaking off the tab covering the A screw head

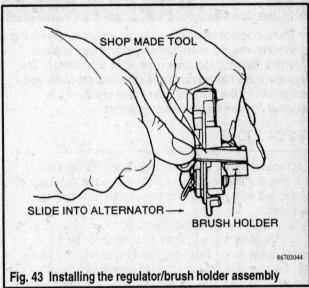

Fig. 43 Installing the regulator/brush holder assembly

**Internal Fan Type**

◆ See Figure 44

1. Disconnect the negative battery cable.
2. Remove the alternator assembly from the engine.
3. Remove the regulator assembly from the alternator, as described in this section.
4. Using a soldering iron, remove the solder from the brush pigtails and remove the brushes.

**To install:**

5. Install the new brush springs.
6. Solder the brushes to the pigtail so that the wear limit line of the brush projects 0.08–0.12 in. (2–3mm) out from the end of the brush holder.
7. Install the regulator assembly.
8. Install the alternator to the engine.
9. Reconnect the negative battery cable.
10. Start vehicle and check voltage output.

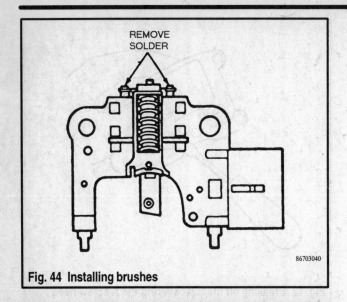

Fig. 44 **Installing brushes**

## Regulator

➡ **Three different types of regulators are used, depending on models, engine, alternator output and type of dash mounted charging indicator used (light or ammeter). The regulators are 100 percent solid state and are calibrated and preset by the manufacturer. No readjustment is required or possible on these regulators.**

### PRECAUTIONS

Whenever system components are being replaced the following precautions should be followed so that the charging system will work properly and the components will not be damaged.

● Always use the proper alternator.
● The electronic regulators are color coded for identification. Never install a different coded regulator for the one being replaced. General coding identification follows, if the regulator removed does not have the color mentioned, identify the output of the alternator and method of charging indication, then consult a parts department to obtain the correct regulator. A black coded regulator is used in systems which use a signal lamp for charging indication. Gray coded regulators are used with an ammeter gauge. Neutral coded regulators are used on models equipped with a diesel engine. The special neutral regulator must be used on vehicles equipped with a diesel engine to prevent glow plug failure. Neutral regulator are colored white.
● Models using a charging lamp indicator are equipped with a 500 ohm resistor on the back of the instrument panel.

### REMOVAL & INSTALLATION

◗ **See Figure 45**

#### External Fan Type

1. Disconnect the negative battery cable.
2. Disconnect the wiring harness from the alternator/regulator assembly.

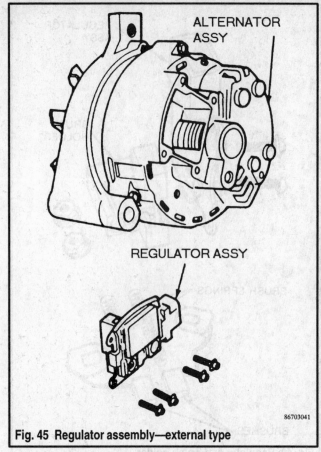

Fig. 45 **Regulator assembly—external type**

3. Remove the 4 screws attaching the regulator to the alternator rear housing.
4. Remove the regulator, with brush holder attached, from the alternator.

**To install:**

5. Fit the regulator assembly to the alternator rear housing and install the retaining screws.
6. Reconnect the alternator wiring harness.
7. Reconnect the negative battery cable.
8. Start vehicle and check voltage output.

#### Internal Fan Type

➡ **To replace the regulator and/or brushes, on this type of alternator, it will be necessary to disassemble the alternator assembly.**

1. Disconnect the negative battery cable.
2. Remove the alternator assembly from the engine.
3. Place a soldering iron (200 watt class) on the bearing box for approximately 3–4 minutes. If the bearing is not heated, the bearing may not pull out, because the rear bearing and rear bracket fit together tightly.
4. Scribe a reference mark across the alternator front housing and rear housing.
5. Remove the front–to–rear housing attaching bolts.
6. Insert a flat–tipped prytool between the front housing and rear housing and separate them. Do not force the prytool in too far, because the stator may be scratched.

7. Remove the regulator from the rectifier, using a soldering iron.

**To install:**

8. Place the regulator into position and re–solder the assembly.

9. Assemble the front and rear housings, while aligning the reference marks made during the initial disassemble.

10. Install the front housing–to–rear housing attaching bolts.

11. Install the alternator to the engine.

12. Reconnect the negative battery cable.

13. Start vehicle and check voltage output.

## FUSE LINK

The fuse link is a short length of insulated wire contained in the alternator wiring harness, between the alternator and the starter relay. The fuse link is several wire gauge sizes smaller than the other wires in the harness. If a booster battery is connected incorrectly in the car battery or if some component of the charging system is shorted to ground, the fuse link melts and protects the alternator. The fuse link is attached to the starter relay. The insulation on the wire reads: Fuse Link.

A melted fuse link can usually be identified by cracked or bubbled insulation. If it is difficult to determine if the fuse link is melted, connect a test light to both ends of the wire. If the fuse link is not melted, the test light will illuminate showing that an open circuit does not exist in the wire.

**Replacement**

1. Disconnect the negative battery cable.

2. Disconnect the eyelet end of the link from the starter relay.

3. Cut the other end of the link from the wiring harness at the splice.

4. Connect the eyelet end of the new fuse link to the starter relay.

➡ **When replacing fuse link, replace with the original gauge fuse link. Do not replace with standard wire.**

5. Splice the open end of the new fuse link into the wiring harness.

6. Solder the splice with rosin core solder and wrap the splice in electrical tape. This splice must be soldered.

7. Connect the negative battery cable.

8. Start the vehicle to make sure the repair is complete.

## Battery

### REMOVAL & INSTALLATION

◆ **See Figures 46 and 47**

➡ **Vehicles equipped with a diesel engine, have the battery located in the trunk.**

1. Loosen the battery cable bolts and spread the ends of the battery cable terminals.

2. Disconnect the negative battery cable first.

3. Disconnect the positive battery cable.

4. Remove the battery hold–down.

5. Wearing heavy gloves and goggles, clean the cable terminals and battery with baking soda and water, and terminal cleaning brush. Remove the battery from under the hood. Be careful not to tip the battery and spill any acid on yourself or the car during removal.

**To install:**

6. Wearing heavy gloves and goggles, place the battery in its holder under the hood. Use care not to spill the acid.

7. Install the battery hold–down. When tightening hold–down, do not over tighten , because the plastic battery case may break and spill the acid. This would ruin the battery.

8. Install the positive battery cable first.

9. Install the negative battery cable.

10. Apply a light coating of grease to the cable ends. This will seal and protect the connectors.

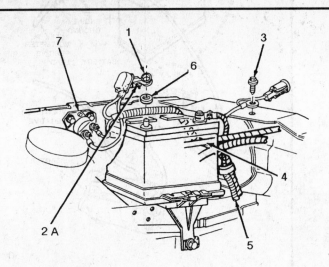

1 Battery to starter relay cable assy.
2 Battery terminal bolt
3 Screw
4 Battery
5 Cable assy.
6 Felt washer (saturate with oil prior to installation)
7 Starter motor relay assy.
A Tighten to 7-9 Nm(62-80 lb.in.)

86703045

**Fig. 46 Battery location in engine compartment—gas engine**

## 2.0L Diesel Engine

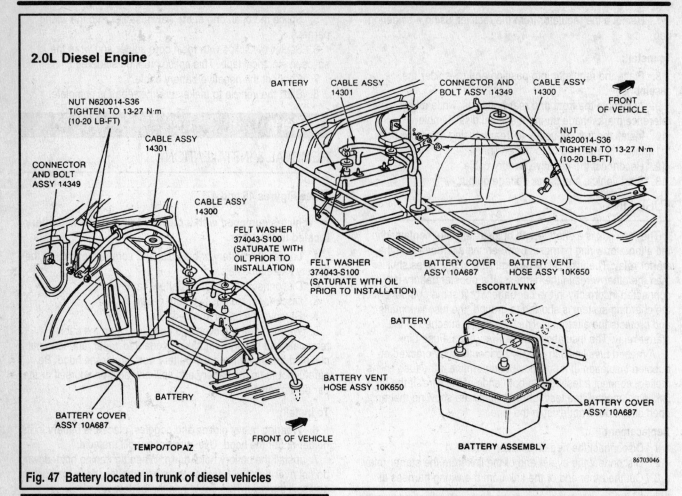

Fig. 47 Battery located in trunk of diesel vehicles

# Starter

## TESTING

▶ See Figures 48, 49, 50 and 51

Before performing any advanced testing of the starter, check the condition of the wires running to and from the starter as well as the connections at the battery and starter. Many times, a starting problem can be traced to one of these areas. For example, a weak ground can make a starter act as if it is faulty.

Place the transmission in N or P. Firmly set the parking brake and block the drive wheels. Disconnect the vacuum line to the Thermactor bypass valve, if equipped, before performing any cranking tests. After tests, run the engine for 3 minutes before connecting the vacuum line.

### Starter Cranks Slowly

1. Connect jumper cables as shown in the Jump Starting procedure in Section 1. If, with the aid of the booster battery, the starter now cranks normally, check the condition of the battery. Recharge or replace the battery, as necessary. Clean the cables and battery posts and make sure connections are tight.

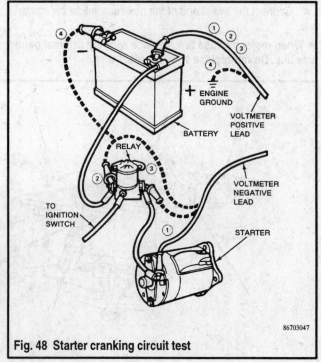

Fig. 48 Starter cranking circuit test

2. If Step 1 does not correct the problem, clean and tighten the connections at the starter relay and battery ground on the engine. You should not be able to rotate the eyelet terminals easily, by hand. Also make sure the positive cable is not shorted to ground.

3. If the starter still cranks slowly, it must be replaced.

## Starter Relay Operates But Starter Doesn't Crank

1. Connect jumper cables as shown in the Jump Starting procedure in Section 1. If, with the aid of the booster battery, the starter now cranks normally, check the condition of the battery. Recharge or replace the battery, as necessary. Clean the cables and battery posts and make sure connections are tight.

2. If Step 1 does not correct the problem, clean and tighten the connections at the starter and relay. Make sure the wire strands are secure in the eyelets.

3. On 1989 and earlier vehicles, if the starter still doesn't crank, it must be replaced.

4. On 1990–94 vehicles with starter mounted solenoid: Connect a jumper cable across terminals B and M of the starter solenoid. If the starter does not operate, replace the starter. If the starter does operate, replace the solenoid.

### ✳✳CAUTION

**Making the jumper connections could cause a spark. Battery jumper cables or equivalent, should be used due to the high current in the starting system.**

## Starter Doesn't Crank—Relay Chatters or Doesn't Click

1. Connect jumper cables as shown in the Jump Starting procedure in Section 1. If, with the aid of the booster battery, the starter now cranks normally, check the condition of the battery. Recharge or replace the battery, as necessary. Clean the ground cable and battery posts and make sure connections are tight.

2. If Step 1 does not correct the problem, remove the push–on connector from the relay (red with blue stripe wire). Make sure the connection is clean and secure and the relay bracket is properly grounded.

3. If the connections are good, check the relay operation with a jumper wire. Remove the push–on connector from the relay and, using a jumper wire, jump from the now exposed terminal on the starter relay to the main terminal (battery side or battery positive post). If this corrects the problem, check the ignition switch, neutral safety switch or clutch switch depending on which type of transaxle is equipped in the vehicle, and the wiring in the starting circuit for open or loose connections.

4. If a jumper wire across the relay does not correct the problem, replace the relay.

## Starter Spins But Doesn't Crank Engine

5. Remove the starter.

6. Check the armature shaft for corrosion and clean or replace, as necessary.

7. If there is no corrosion, replace the starter drive.

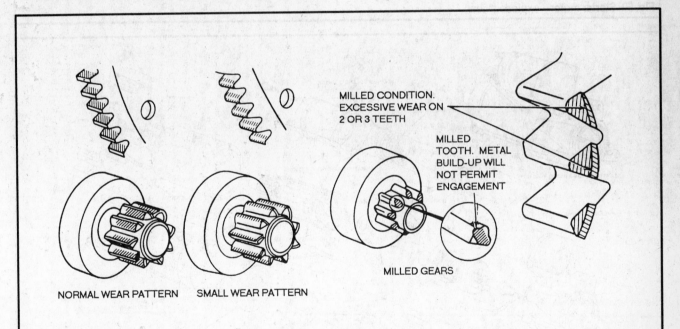

MILLED CONDITION. EXCESSIVE WEAR ON 2 OR 3 TEETH

MILLED TOOTH. METAL BUILD-UP WILL NOT PERMIT ENGAGEMENT

MILLED GEARS

NORMAL WEAR PATTERN    SMALL WEAR PATTERN

86703050

**Fig. 49 Starter gear wear chart**

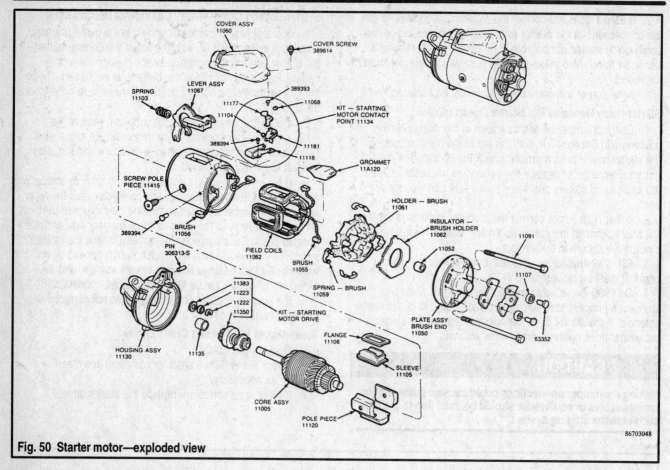

**Fig. 50 Starter motor—exploded view**

86703048

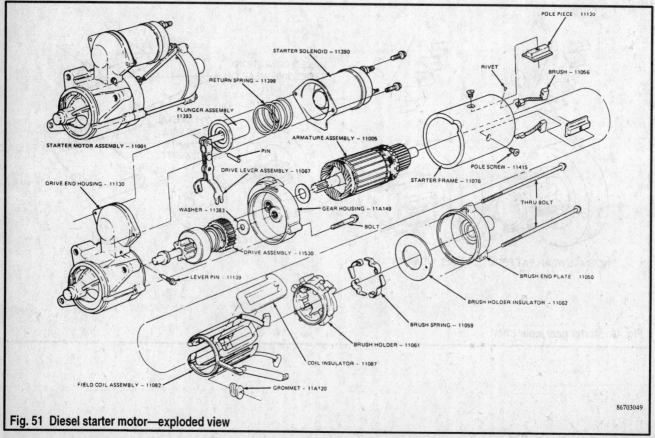

**Fig. 51 Diesel starter motor—exploded view**

86703049

## REMOVAL & INSTALLATION

### Gasoline Engines

▶ See Figures 52, 53, 54, 55, 56 and 57

1. Park vehicle on level surface. Block the rear wheels.
2. Disconnect the negative battery cable.
3. Raise and support the vehicle safely on jackstands.
4. Disconnect the electrical harness from the starter motor.
5. Remove the 2 bolts attaching the rear starter support bracket, remove the retaining nut from the rear of the starter motor and remove the support bracket.
6. On models that are equipped with a manual transaxle, remove the 3 nuts that attach the roll restricter brace to the starter mounting studs at the transaxle, then remove the brace.
7. On models that are equipped with an automatic transaxle, remove the nose bracket mounted on the starter studs.
8. On models equipped with a manual transaxle, remove the 3 starter mounting studs and the starter motor.
9. On models equipped with a automatic transaxle, remove the 2 starter mounting studs and the starter motor.

### To install:

10. Position the starter to the transaxle housing. Install the attaching studs or bolts. Tighten the fasteners to 30–40 ft. lbs. (41–54 Nm).
11. On vehicles equipped with a roll restricter brace, install the brace on the starter mounting studs at the transmission housing. Install the cable support on the top of the brace. Attach the 3 retaining bolts.
12. Position the starter rear support bracket to the starter. Attach the 2 attaching bolts. Connect the starter cable at the starter terminal.
13. Lower the vehicle and connect the negative battery cable.
14. Start vehicle to make sure starter functions properly.

Fig. 53 Remove the rear starter bracket

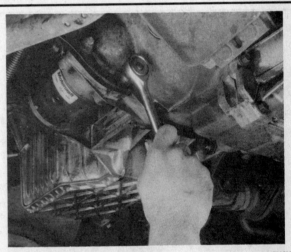

Fig. 54 Loosen nuts holding the nose bracket

Fig. 52 Remove the cable attached to starter

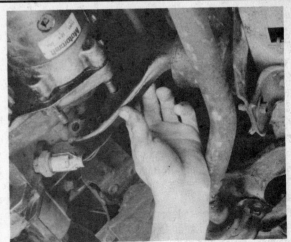

Fig. 55 Remove the nose bracket

Fig. 56 Loosen studs holding the starter

Fig. 57 Remove the starter

**Diesel Engines**

♦ See Figure 51

1. Park vehicle on level surface. Block rear wheels.
2. Disconnect the negative battery cable. Battery is located in trunk compartment. Disconnect positive cable at starter.
3. Raise and support the vehicle safely.
4. Disconnect the electrical harness from the starter motor, solenoid and relay assembly at fender apron.
5. Remove upper starter mounting stud bolt.
6. Disconnect vacuum hose on vacuum pump.
7. Loosen an remove 3 starter support bracket screws and bracket.
8. Disconnect power steering hose bracket.
9. Remove ground strap from starter stud bolt. Remove remaining starter stud bolts
10. Remove vacuum pump bracket.
11. Remove starter.

**To install:**

12. Position the starter to the transaxle housing. Install the vacuum pump bracket.
13. Install the 2 lower starter mounting studs followed by the starter support bracket. Tighten bolts to 30–40 ft. lbs. (41–54 Nm).
14. Reconnect the cable support bracket and the ground strap. Connect power steering hose bracket.
15. Reinstall the hose for the vacuum pump.
16. Install upper starter mounting stud bolt. Tighten to 30–40 ft. lbs. (41–54 Nm).
17. Reinstall starter cable. Connect ground cable at battery in trunk.
18. Start vehicle to check starter operation.

## SOLENOID REPLACEMENT

➡ A solenoid is mounted to the starter, and delivers the current which drives the starter. A relay is mounted to one of the interior fenders, in most cases, on the passenger side, and is the triggering source for the solenoid.

1. Disconnect the negative battery cable.
2. Remove the starter.
3. Remove the positive brush connector from the solenoid M terminal.
4. Remove the solenoid retaining screws and remove the solenoid.
5. Attach the solenoid plunger rod to the slot in the lever and tighten the solenoid retaining screws to 45–54 inch lbs. (5.1–6.1 Nm).
6. Attach the positive brush connector to the solenoid M terminal and tighten the retaining nut to 80–120 inch lbs. (9.0–13.5 Nm).
7. Install the starter and connect the negative battery terminal.
8. Start vehicle to check the repair.

## RELAY REPLACEMENT

♦ See Figures 58, 59, 60, 61 and 62

➡ A solenoid is mounted to the starter, and delivers the current which drives the starter. A relay is mounted to one of the interior fenders, in most cases, on the passenger side, and is the triggering source for the solenoid.

1. Disconnect the negative battery cable.
2. Label and disconnect the wires from the relay.
3. Remove the relay retaining bolts and remove the relay.

**To install:**

4. Install the relay to the fender wall with the retaining screws.
5. Connect the heavy gauge leads and tighten the nuts.
6. Connect the thin lead to the stud.
7. Connect the negative battery cable.
8. Test the vehicle to make sure the relay works correctly.

Fig. 58 Remove the thin gauged trigger wire

Fig. 59 Remove the the nuts securing the heavy gauge wire

Fig. 60 Remove all the wires from the unit

Fig. 61 Unfasten the retaining bolts securing the relay to the fender wall

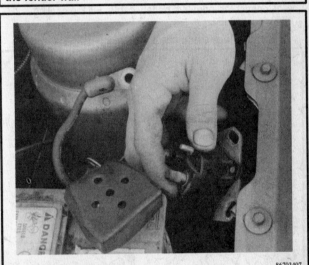

Fig. 62 Remove the relay from the vehicle

## Sending Units and Sensors

### REMOVAL & INSTALLATION

**Coolant Temperature Sender/Switch**

▶ See Figures 63, 64, and 65

On all Tempo/Topaz vehicles, the coolant temperature sender unit is located in the same region as the coolant thermostat. Refer to the diagrams for exact locations.

➡ **On some automatic transaxle equipped vehicles, there are numerous sender units in the same location as the coolant sender. When servicing any of these pieces, do not confuse the different units.**

1. If vehicle has recently been driven, allow to cool down before working with cooling system.
2. Disconnect the negative battery cable.
3. Relieve any coolant system pressure that may be present.

4. Drain the cooling system into a suitable container.

### ✳✳CAUTION

**When draining coolant, keep in mind that cats and dogs are attracted to ethylene glycol antifreeze, and are quite likely to drink any in an uncovered container or in puddles on the ground. This can prove fatal. Always drain the coolant into a sealable container. Coolant should be reused unless contaminated or several years old.**

5. Disconnect the electrical connector at the temperature sender/switch.

6. Remove the temperature sender/switch.

**To install:**

7. Apply pipe sealant or teflon tape to the threads of the new sender/switch.

8. Install the temperature sender/switch, tightening to 12–17 ft. lbs. (16–24 Nm). Connect the electrical connector.

9. Connect the negative battery cable. Fill the cooling system.

10. Run the engine and check for leaks.

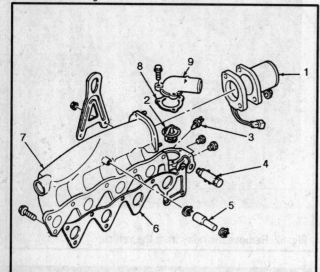

1 Air inlet
2 Thermostat
3 Temperature sensor
4 Vacuum temperature switch
5 Hose
6 Intake gasket
7 Intake manifold
8 Gasket
9 Thermostat housing

86703057

**Fig. 63 Coolant temperature sender—2.0L Diesel engine**

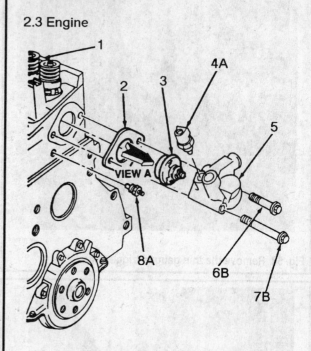

2.3 Engine

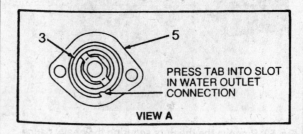

PRESS TAB INTO SLOT IN WATER OUTLET CONNECTION

**VIEW A**

1 Cylinder head
2 Gasket
3 Thermostat assy
4A Engine coolant temperature sensor
5 Water outlet connection
6B Bolt (M8 X 1.25 X 53.0)
7B Bolt (M8 X 1.25 X 101.0)
8A Water temperature indicator sender assy

A Tighten to 11-24 Nm (9-17 lb.ft.)
B Tighten to 20-30 Nm (15-22 lb.ft.)

86703058

**Fig. 64 Coolant temperature sender—2.3L engine**

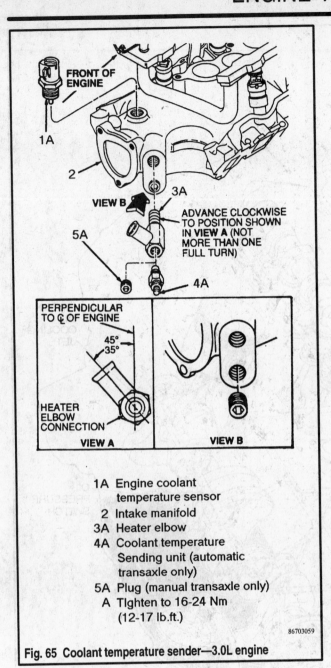

Fig. 65 Coolant temperature sender—3.0L engine

1A  Engine coolant
     temperature sensor
2   Intake manifold
3A  Heater elbow
4A  Coolant temperature
     Sending unit (automatic
     transaxle only)
5A  Plug (manual transaxle only)
A   TIghten to 16-24 Nm
     (12-17 lb.ft.)

86703059

## Oil Pressure Sender/Switch

▶ See Figures 66 and 67

### ✳✳WARNING

The pressure switch used with the oil pressure warning light is not interchangeable with the sending unit used with the oil pressure gauge. If the incorrect part is installed the oil pressure indicating system will be inoperative and the sending unit or gauge could be damaged.

Determines the placement of the oil pressure sender/switch, based on engine type. Refer to the diagrams for actual locations.

1. Disconnect the negative battery cable.
2. Place a suitable container under the switch/sender to catch any oil that may drip from the engine.
3. Unplug the electrical connector and remove the oil pressure sender/switch.

**To install:**

4. Apply pipe sealant to the threads of the new sender/switch.
5. Install the oil pressure sender/switch and tighten to 9–11 ft. lbs. (12–16 Nm).
6. Install the electrical connector to the sender/switch and connect the negative battery cable.
7. Run the engine, then check for leaks and proper operation.
8. Add engine oil if necessary.

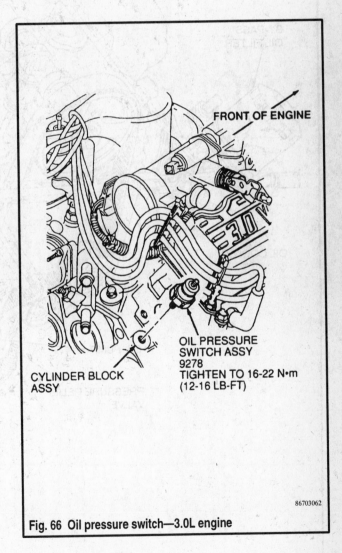

Fig. 66  Oil pressure switch—3.0L engine

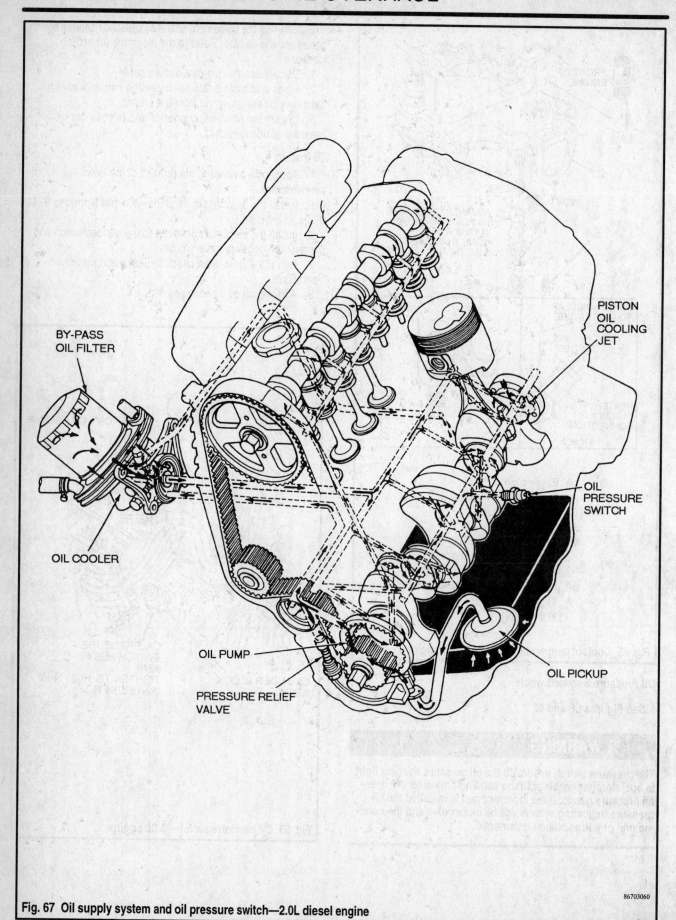

**BY-PASS
OIL FILTER**

**PISTON
OIL
COOLING
JET**

**OIL
PRESSURE
SWITCH**

**OIL COOLER**

**OIL PICKUP**

**OIL PUMP**

**PRESSURE RELIEF
VALVE**

86703060

**Fig. 67 Oil supply system and oil pressure switch—2.0L diesel engine**

**Electric Fan Switch**

◆ **See Figure 68**

Starting with model year 1985, the Tempo/Topaz utilized a coolant temperature switch that ALSO controls the electric fan. On these models, the electric fan turns on when the coolant temperature rises above 210°F (84.7°C), or when the air conditioning system is engaged, if equipped. The electric fan will shut off below 193°F (75°C) or after the air conditioning system is turned off.

On the 1984 model Tempo/Topaz, 2 different cooling fan control systems were used, depending on whether the vehicle was equipped with air conditioning. If the vehicle was equipped with A/C, the cooling fan functions were controlled through the cooling fan controller and cooling fan relay. If the vehicle was equipped with a diesel engine, whether it came with or without A/C, it also utilized the control system just mentioned.

If the vehicle was gasoline powered, and came without A/C, the cooling fan was controlled through the use of a separate fan switch.

➡ **If your vehicle is equipped with a fan controller, and functioning problems are suspected, it is recommended that the vehicle be taken to a dealer for service. This is because several different control units are used on the Tempo/Topaz, and control units are not interchangeable.**

1. Disconnect the negative battery cable.
2. Place a suitable container under the front of the car to catch any antifreeze that may spill.
3. Unfasten the electrical connector and remove the fan switch.

**To install:**

4. Apply pipe sealant to the threads of the new sender/switch.
5. Install the switch and tighten to 9–11 ft. lbs. (12–16 Nm).
6. Connect the electrical connector to the sender/switch and connect the negative battery cable.
7. Run the engine, then check for leaks and proper operation.
8. Check and adjust the cooling level if necessary.

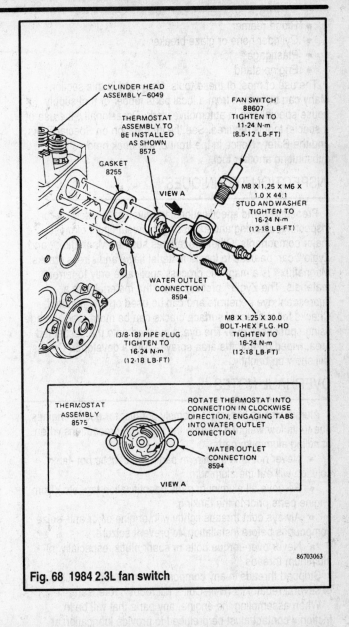

**Fig. 68 1984 2.3L fan switch**

## ENGINE MECHANICAL

## Engine Overhaul Tips

Most engine overhaul procedures are fairly standard. In addition to specific parts replacement procedures and complete specifications for each individual engine, this section is also a guide to acceptable rebuilding procedures. Examples of standard rebuilding practice are shown and should be used along with specific details concerning your particular engine.

Competent and accurate machine shop services will help insure maximum performance, reliability and engine life. In most instances, it is more profitable for the do–it–yourself mechanic to remove, clean and inspect the component, buy the necessary parts and deliver them to a shop for actual machine work.

On the other hand, much of the rebuilding work (crankshaft, block, bearings, piston rods, and other components) is well within the scope of the do–it–yourself mechanic.

### TOOLS

The tools required for an engine overhaul or parts replacement will depend on the depth of your involvement. With a few exceptions, they will be the tools found in any mechanic's tool kit (see Section 1). More in–depth work will require some or all of the following:

- A dial indicator (reading in thousandths) mounted on a universal base
- Micrometers and telescope gauges
- Jaw and screw–type pullers
- Scraper
- Valve spring compressor
- Ring groove cleaner
- Piston ring expander and compressor

- Ridge reamer
- Cylinder hone or glaze breaker
- Plastigage®
- Engine stand

The use of most of these tools is covered in this section. Many can be rented from a local parts jobber or tool supply house specializing in automotive work. Occasionally, the use of a special tool is required. See the information on Special Tools and the Safety Notice in the front of this book before substituting another tool.

## INSPECTION TECHNIQUES

Procedures and specifications are given in this section for inspecting, cleaning and assessing the wear limits of most major components. Other procedures such as Magnaflux® and Zyglo® can be used to locate material flaws and stress cracks. Magnaflux® is a magnetic process applicable only to ferrous materials. The Zyglo® process coats the material with a fluorescent dye penetrate and can be used on any material. Checks for suspected surface cracks can be more readily made using spot check dye. The dye is sprayed onto the suspected area, wiped off and the area sprayed with a developer. Cracks will show up brightly.

## OVERHAUL NOTES

Aluminum has become extremely popular for use in engines, due to its low weight. Observe the following precautions when handling aluminum parts:

- Never hot tank aluminum parts; the caustic hot-tank solution will eat the aluminum.
- Remove all aluminum parts (identification tag, etc.) from engine parts prior to the tanking.
- Always coat threads lightly with engine oil or anti-seize compounds before installation, to prevent seizure.
- Never over-torque bolts or spark plugs, especially in aluminum threads.

Stripped threads in any component can be repaired using any of several repair kits (Heli-Coil®, Microdot®, Keenserts®,etc.)

When assembling the engine, any parts that will be in frictional contact must be prelubed to provide lubrication at initial start-up. Any product specifically formulated for this purpose can be used, but engine oil is NOT recommended as a prelube.

When semi-permanent (locked, but removable) installation of bolts or nuts is desired, threads should be cleaned and coated with Loctite® or other similar, commercial non-hardening sealant.

## REPAIRING DAMAGED THREADS

◆ **See Figures 69, 70, 71, 72 and 73**

Several methods of repairing damaged threads are available. Heli-Coil® (shown here), Heli-Coil® (shown here), Keenserts® and Microdot® are among the most widely used. All involve basically the same principle, namely drilling out stripped threads, tapping the hole and installing a prewound insert. This method makes welding, plugging and oversize fasteners unnecessary.

Two types of thread repair inserts are usually supplied: a standard type for most Inch Coarse, Inch Fine, Metric Course and Metric Fine thread sizes and a spark lug type to fit most spark plug port sizes. Consult the individual manufacturer's catalog to determine exact applications. Typical thread repair kits will contain a selection of prewound threaded inserts, a tap (corresponding to the outside diameter threads of the insert) and an installation tool. Spark plug inserts usually differ because they require a tap equipped with pilot threads and a combined reamer/tap section. Most manufacturers also supply blister packed thread repair inserts separately in addition to a master kit containing a variety of taps and inserts plus installation tools.

Before attempting a repair to a threaded hole, remove any snapped, broken or damaged bolts or studs. Penetrating oil can be used to free frozen threads. The offending item can be removed with locking pliers or with a screw or stud extractor. After the hole is clear, the thread can be repaired, as shown in the series of accompanying illustrations and in the manufacturer's instructions.

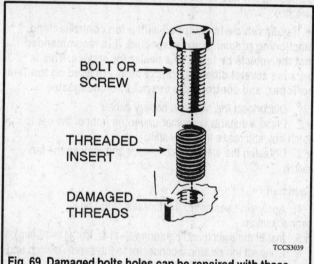

BOLT OR SCREW

THREADED INSERT

DAMAGED THREADS

TCCS3039

**Fig. 69 Damaged bolts holes can be repaired with these thread inserts**

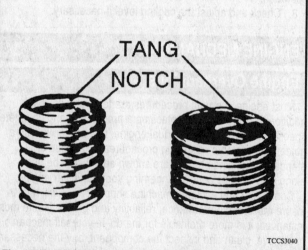

TANG

NOTCH

TCCS3040

**Fig. 70 Standard thread repair insert (left), and spark plug threads insert (right)**

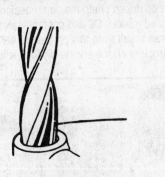

Fig. 71 Drill out the damaged threads with the specified drill. Be sure to drill completely through the hole or to the bottom of a blind hole

TCCS3041

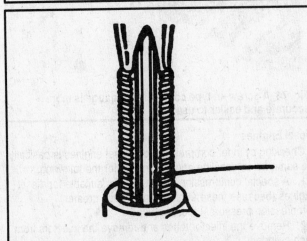

Fig. 72 Using the kit, tap the hole in order to receive the thread insert. Keep the tap well oiled and back it out frequently to avoid clogging the threads

TCCS3042

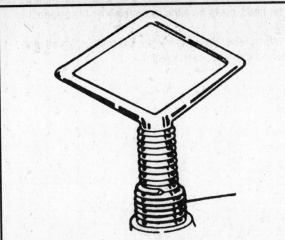

Fig. 73 Screw the threaded insert onto the installer tool until the tang engages the slot. Thread the insert into the hole until it is 1/4 or 1/2 turn below the top surface, then remove the tool and break off the tang using a punch

TCCS3043

**CHECKING ENGINE COMPRESSION**

## Compression Comparison Chart

| Maximum PSI | Minimum PSI | Maximum PSI | Minimum PSI |
|---|---|---|---|
| 250 | 187 | 190 | 142 |
| 248 | 186 | 188 | 141 |
| 246 | 184 | 186 | 140 |
| 244 | 183 | 184 | 138 |
| 242 | 181 | 182 | 136 |
| 240 | 180 | 180 | 135 |
| 238 | 178 | 178 | 133 |
| 236 | 177 | 176 | 132 |
| 234 | 175 | 174 | 131 |
| 232 | 174 | 172 | 129 |
| 230 | 172 | 170 | 127 |
| 228 | 171 | 168 | 126 |
| 226 | 169 | 166 | 124 |
| 224 | 168 | 164 | 123 |
| 222 | 166 | 162 | 121 |
| 220 | 165 | 160 | 120 |
| 218 | 163 | 158 | 118 |
| 216 | 162 | 156 | 117 |
| 214 | 160 | 154 | 115 |
| 212 | 157 | 152 | 114 |
| 210 | 156 | 150 | 113 |
| 208 | 154 | 148 | 111 |
| 204 | 153 | 146 | 110 |
| 202 | 151 | 144 | 108 |
| 200 | 150 | 142 | 107 |
| 198 | 148 | 140 | 105 |
| 196 | 147 | 138 | 104 |
| 194 | 15 | 136 | 102 |
| 192 | 144 | 134 | 101 |

86703902

**Gasoline Engines**

▶ See Figure 74

A noticeable lack of engine power, excessive oil consumption and/or poor fuel mileage measured over an extended period are all indicators of internal engine wear. Worn piston rings, scored or worn cylinder bores, blown head gaskets, sticking or burnt valves and worn valve seats are all possible culprits here. A check of each cylinder's compression will help you locate the problems.

As mentioned in the Tools and Equipment section of Section 1, a screw–in type compression gauge is more accurate that the type you simply hold against the spark plug hole, although it takes slightly longer to use. It's worth it to obtain a more accurate reading.

1. Warm the engine to normal operating temperature.

2. Remove all spark plugs.

3. Disconnect the high tension lead from the ignition coil.

4. On fuel injected vehicles, disconnect all fuel injector electrical connections.

5. On carburetor equipped vehicles, fully open the throttle either by operating the carburetor throttle linkage by hand, or by having an assistant push the accelerator pedal to the floor.

6. Screw the compression gauge into No. 1 spark plug hole until the fitting is snug.

➡ **Be careful not to crossthread the plug hole. On aluminum cylinder heads use extra care, as the threads in these heads are easily ruined. Using some type of anti–seize on the compression gauge threads is a good idea.**

7. Have an assistant depress the accelerator pedal fully. Then, while you read the compression gauge, ask the assistant to crank the engine enough so that at least 5 complete compression strokes are made within the engine.

8. Read the compression gauge at the end of each series of cranks, and record the highest of these readings. Repeat this procedure for each of the engine's cylinders. Maximum compression should be 175–185 psi. A cylinder's compression pressure is usually acceptable if it is between 75%–80% of maximum. The difference between each cylinder should be no more than 12–14 psi (82–95 kPa). Refer to the chart to compare maximum and minimum compression rates.

9. If a cylinder is unusually low, pour a tablespoon of clean engine oil into the cylinder, through the spark plug hole and repeat the compression test. If the compression comes up after adding the oil, it appears that the cylinder's piston rings or bore are worn or damaged. If the pressure remains low, the valves may not be seating properly (a valve job could be needed), or the head gasket may be blown near that cylinder. If

compression in any two adjacent cylinders is low, and if the addition of oil doesn't help the compression, there is leakage past the head gasket. Oil and coolant water in the combustion chamber can result from this problem. There may be evidence of water droplets on the engine dipstick when a head gasket has blown.

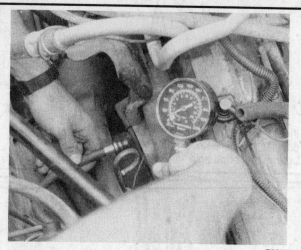

TCCS3801

**Fig. 74  A screw–in type compression gauge is more accurate and easier to use**

### Diesel Engines

Checking cylinder compression on diesel engines is basically the same as on gasoline engines except for the following:

1. A special compression gauge adaptor suitable for diesel engines (because these engines have much greater compression pressures) must be used

2. Remove the injector tubes and remove the injectors from each cylinder.

➡ **Don't forget to remove the washer underneath each injector. Otherwise, it may get lost when the engine is cranked.**

3. When fitting the compression gauge adaptor to the cylinder head, make sure the gauge bleeder (if equipped) is closed.

4. When reinstalling the injector assemblies, install new washers underneath each injector.

## GENERAL ENGINE SPECIFICATIONS

| Year | Engine ID/VIN | Engine Displacement Liters (cc) | Fuel System Type | Net Horsepower @ rpm | Net Torque @ rpm (ft. lbs.) | Bore x Stroke (in.) | Compression Ratio | Oil Pressure @ rpm |
|---|---|---|---|---|---|---|---|---|
| 1984 | H | 2.0 (2000) | DSL | 52@4000 | 82@2400 | 3.39x3.39 | 22.7:1 | 55-60@2000 |
| | R | 2.3 (2300) | 1 BBL | 84@4600 | 118@2600 | 3.70x3.30 | 9.0:1 | 55-70@2000 |
| 1985 | H | 2.0 (2000) | DSL | 52@4000 | 82@2400 | 3.39x3.39 | 22.7:1 | 55-60@2000 |
| | R | 2.3 (2300) | 1 BBL | 84@4600 | 118@2600 | 3.70x3.30 | 9.0:1 | 55-70@2000 |
| | X | 2.3 (2300) | CFI | 100@4600 | 125@3200 | 3.70x3.30 | 9.0:1 | 55-70@2000 |
| | S | 2.3 (2300) | CFI | 100@4600 | 125@3200 | 3.70x3.30 | 9.0:1 | 55-70@2000 |
| 1986 | H | 2.0 (2000) | DSL | 52@4000 | 82@2400 | 3.39x3.39 | 22.7:1 | 55-60@2000 |
| | R | 2.3 (2300) | 1 BBL | 84@4600 | 118@2600 | 3.70x3.30 | 9.0:1 | 55-70@2000 |
| | S | 2.3 (2300) | CFI | 100@4600 | 125@3200 | 3.70x3.30 | 9.0:1 | 55-70@2000 |
| | X | 2.3 (2300) | CFI | 100@4600 | 125@3200 | 3.70x3.30 | 9.0:1 | 55-70@2000 |
| 1987 | H | 2.0 (2000) | DSL | 52@4000 | 82@2400 | 3.39x3.39 | 22.7:1 | 55-60@2000 |
| | R | 2.3 (2300) | 1 BBL | 84@4600 | 118@2600 | 3.70x3.30 | 9.0:1 | 55-70@2000 |
| | S | 2.3 (2300) | CFI | 100@4600 | 125@3200 | 3.70x3.30 | 9.0:1 | 55-70@2000 |
| | X | 2.3 (2300) | CFI | 100@4600 | 125@3200 | 3.70x3.30 | 9.0:1 | 55-70@2000 |
| 1988 | S | 2.3 (2300) | MFI | 100@4400 | 130@2600 | 3.70x3.30 | 9.0:1 | 55-70@2000 |
| | X | 2.3 (2300) | MFI | 98@4400 | 124@2200 | 3.70x3.30 | 9.0:1 | 55-70@2000 |
| 1989 | S | 2.3 (2300) | MFI | 100@4400 | 130@2600 | 3.70x3.30 | 9.0:1 | 55-70@2000 |
| | X | 2.3 (2300) | MFI | 98@4400 | 124@2200 | 3.70x3.30 | 9.0:1 | 55-70@2000 |
| 1990 | S | 2.3 (2300) | MFI | 100@4400 | 130@2600 | 3.70x3.30 | 9.0:1 | 55-70@2000 |
| | X | 2.3 (2300) | MFI | 98@4400 | 124@2200 | 3.70x3.30 | 9.0:1 | 55-70@2000 |
| 1991 | S | 2.3 (2300) | MFI | 100@4400 | 130@2600 | 3.70x3.30 | 9.0:1 | 55-70@2000 |
| | X | 2.3 (2300) | MFI | 98@4400 | 124@2200 | 3.70x3.30 | 9.0:1 | 55-70@2000 |
| 1992 | U | 3.0 (2971) | MFI | 140@4800 | 160@3000 | 3.50x3.10 | 9.3:1 | 55-70@2000 |
| | X | 2.3 (2300) | MFI | 98@4400 | 124@2200 | 3.70x3.30 | 9.0:1 | 55-70@2000 |
| 1993 | U | 3.0 (2971) | MFI | 140@4800 | 160@3000 | 3.50x3.10 | 9.3:1 | 55-70@2000 |
| | X | 2.3 (2300) | MFI | 98@4400 | 124@2200 | 3.70x3.30 | 9.0:1 | 55-70@2000 |
| 1994 | X | 2.3 (2300) | MFI | 98@4400 | 124@2200 | 3.68x3.30 | 9.0:1 | 55-70@2000 |
| | U | 3.0 (2971) | MFI | 140@4800 | 160@3000 | 3.50x3.15 | 9.3:2 | 55-70@2500 |

BBL - Barrel carburetor

MFI - Multiport fuel injection

CFI - Central fuel injection

DSL-Diesel

86703901

## VALVE SPECIFICATIONS

| Year | Engine ID/VIN | Engine Displacement Liters (cc) | Seat Angle (deg.) | Face Angle (deg.) | Spring Test Pressure (lbs. @ in.) | Spring Installed Height (in.) | Stem-to-Guide Clearance (In.) | | Stem Diameter (in.) | |
|------|------|------|------|------|------|------|------|------|------|------|
| | | | | | | | Intake | Exhaust | Intake | Exhaust |
| 1984 | H | 2.0 (2000) | 45 | 45.5 | NA | 1.776 | 0.0016-0.0029 | 0.0018-0.0031 | 0.3138 | 0.3138 |
| | R | 2.3 (2300) | 45 | 45.5 | 182@1.10 | 1.490 | 0.0018 | 0.0023 | 0.3415 | 0.3411 |
| 1985 | H | 2.0 (2000) | 45 | 45.5 | NA | 1.776 | 0.0016-0.0029 | 0.0018-0.0031 | 0.3138 | 0.3138 |
| | R | 2.3 (2300) | 45 | 45.5 | 182@1.10 | 1.490 | 0.0018 | 0.0023 | 0.3415 | 0.3411 |
| | X | 2.3 (2300) | 45 | 45.5 | 182@1.10 | 1.490 | 0.0018 | 0.0023 | 0.3415 | 0.3411 |
| | S | 2.3 (2300) | 45 | 45.5 | 182@1.10 | 1.490 | 0.0018 | 0.0023 | 0.3415 | 0.3411 |
| 1986 | H | 2.0 (2000) | 45 | 45.5 | NA | 1.776 | 0.0016-0.0029 | 0.0018-0.0031 | 0.3138 | 0.3138 |
| | R | 2.3 (2300) | 45 | 45.5 | 182@1.10 | 1.490 | 0.0018 | 0.0023 | 0.3415 | 0.3411 |
| | X | 2.3 (2300) | 45 | 45.5 | 182@1.10 | 1.490 | 0.0018 | 0.0023 | 0.3415 | 0.3411 |
| | S | 2.3 (2300) | 45 | 45.5 | 182@1.10 | 1.490 | 0.0018 | 0.0023 | 0.3415 | 0.3411 |
| 1987 | H | 2.0 (2000) | 45 | 45.5 | NA | 1.776 | 0.0016-0.0029 | 0.0018-0.0031 | 0.3138 | 0.3138 |
| | R | 2.3 (2300) | 45 | 45.5 | 182@1.10 | 1.490 | 0.0018 | 0.0023 | 0.3415 | 0.3411 |
| | X | 2.3 (2300) | 45 | 45.5 | 182@1.10 | 1.490 | 0.0018 | 0.0023 | 0.3415 | 0.3411 |
| | S | 2.3 (2300) | 45 | 45.5 | 182@1.10 | 1.490 | 0.0018 | 0.0023 | 0.3415 | 0.3411 |
| 1988 | X | 2.3 (2300) | 45 | 45.5 | 182@1.10 | 1.490 | 0.0018 | 0.0023 | 0.3415 | 0.3411 |
| | S | 2.3 (2300) | 45 | 45.5 | 182@1.10 | 1.490 | 0.0018 | 0.0023 | 0.3415 | 0.3411 |
| 1989 | X | 2.3 (2300) | 45 | 45.5 | 182@1.10 | 1.490 | 0.0018 | 0.0023 | 0.3415 | 0.3411 |
| | S | 2.3 (2300) | 45 | 45.5 | 182@1.10 | 1.490 | 0.0018 | 0.0023 | 0.3415 | 0.3411 |
| 1990 | X | 2.3 (2300) | 45 | 45.5 | 182@1.10 | 1.490 | 0.0018 | 0.0023 | 0.3415 | 0.3411 |
| | S | 2.3 (2300) | 45 | 45.5 | 182@1.10 | 1.490 | 0.0018 | 0.0023 | 0.3415 | 0.3411 |
| 1991 | X | 2.3 (2300) | 45 | 45.5 | 182@1.10 | 1.490 | 0.0018 | 0.0023 | 0.3415 | 0.3411 |
| | S | 2.3 (2300) | 45 | 45.5 | 182@1.10 | 1.490 | 0.0018 | 0.0023 | 0.3415 | 0.3411 |
| 1992 | X | 2.3 (2300) | 45 | 45.5 | 182@1.10 | 1.490 | 0.0018 | 0.0023 | 0.3415 | 0.3411 |
| | U | 3.0 (2971) | 45 | 44 | 185@1.11 | 1.850 | 0.0001-0.0027 | 0.0015-0.0032 | 0.3126 | 0.3121 |
| 1993 | X | 2.3 (2300) | 45 | 44 | 128-141@1.12 | 1.520 | 0.0010-0.0027 | 0.0015-0.0032 | 0.3416-0.3423 | 0.3411-0.3418 |
| | U | 3.0 (2971) | 45 | 44 | 185@1.11 | 1.850 | 0.0001-0.0027 | 0.0015-0.0032 | 0.3126 | 0.3121 |
| 1994 | X | 2.3 (2300) | 44-45 | 44-45 | 128-141@1.12 | 1.520 | 0.0018 | 0.0023 | 0.3416-0.3423 | 0.3411-0.3418 |
| | U | 3.0 (2971) | 45 | 44 | 180@1.06 | 1.580 | 0.0001-0.0027 | 0.0015-0.0032 | 0.3126-0.3129 | 0.3121-0.3134 |

86703903

## CAMSHAFT SPECIFICATIONS

All measurements given in inches.

| Year | Engine ID/VIN | Engine Displacement Liters (cc) | Journal Diameter | | | | | Elevation | | Bearing Clearance | Camshaft End Play |
|---|---|---|---|---|---|---|---|---|---|---|---|
| | | | 1 | 2 | 3 | 4 | 5 | In. | Ex. | | |
| 1984 | H | 2.0 (1993) | 1.2582-1.2589 | 1.2582-1.2589 | 1.2582-1.2589 | 1.2582-1.2589 | 1.2582-1.2589 | NA | NA | 0.0010-0.0026 | 0.0008-0.0059 |
| | R | 2.3 (2300) | 2.006-2.008 | 2.006-2.008 | 2.006-2.008 | 2.006-2.008 | 2.006-2.008 | 0.249 | 0.239 | 0.001-0.003 | 0.009 |
| 1985 | H | 2.0 (1993) | 1.2582-1.2589 | 1.2582-1.2589 | 1.2582-1.2589 | 1.2582-1.2589 | 1.2582-1.2589 | NA | NA | 0.0010-0.0026 | 0.0008-0.0059 |
| | R | 2.3 (2300) | 2.006-2.008 | 2.006-2.008 | 2.006-2.008 | 2.006-2.008 | 2.006-2.008 | 0.249 | 0.239 | 0.001-0.003 | 0.009 |
| | S | 2.3 (2300) | 2.006-2.008 | 2.006-2.008 | 2.006-2.008 | 2.006-2.008 | 2.006-2.008 | 0.249 | 0.239 | 0.001-0.003 | 0.009 |
| | X | 2.3 (2300) | 2.006-2.008 | 2.006-2.008 | 2.006-2.008 | 2.006-2.008 | 2.006-2.008 | 0.249 | 0.239 | 0.001-0.003 | 0.009 |
| 1986 | H | 2.0 (1993) | 1.2582-1.2589 | 1.2582-1.2589 | 1.2582-1.2589 | 1.2582-1.2589 | 1.2582-1.2589 | NA | NA | 0.0010-0.0026 | 0.0008-0.0059 |
| | R | 2.3 (2300) | 2.006-2.008 | 2.006-2.008 | 2.006-2.008 | 2.006-2.008 | 2.006-2.008 | 0.249 | 0.239 | 0.001-0.003 | 0.009 |
| | S | 2.3 (2300) | 2.006-2.008 | 2.006-2.008 | 2.006-2.008 | 2.006-2.008 | 2.006-2.008 | 0.249 | 0.239 | 0.001-0.003 | 0.009 |
| | X | 2.3 (2300) | 2.006-2.008 | 2.006-2.008 | 2.006-2.008 | 2.006-2.008 | 2.006-2.008 | 0.249 | 0.239 | 0.001-0.003 | 0.009 |
| 1987 | H | 2.0 (1993) | 1.2582-1.2589 | 1.2582-1.2589 | 1.2582-1.2589 | 1.2582-1.2589 | 1.2582-1.2589 | NA | NA | 0.0010-0.0026 | 0.0008-0.0059 |
| | R | 2.3 (2300) | 2.006-2.008 | 2.006-2.008 | 2.006-2.008 | 2.006-2.008 | 2.006-2.008 | 0.249 | 0.239 | 0.001-0.003 | 0.009 |
| | S | 2.3 (2300) | 2.006-2.008 | 2.006-2.008 | 2.006-2.008 | 2.006-2.008 | 2.006-2.008 | 0.249 | 0.239 | 0.001-0.003 | 0.009 |
| | X | 2.3 (2300) | 2.006-2.008 | 2.006-2.008 | 2.006-2.008 | 2.006-2.008 | 2.006-2.008 | 0.249 [1] | 0.239 | 0.001-0.003 | 0.009 |
| 1988 | X | 2.3 (2300) | 2.006-2.008 | 2.006-2.008 | 2.006-2.008 | 2.006-2.008 | 2.006-2.008 | 0.249 | 0.239 | 0.001-0.003 | 0.009 |
| | S | 2.3 (2300) | 2.006-2.008 | 2.006-2.008 | 2.006-2.008 | 2.006-2.008 | 2.006-2.008 | 0.249 | 0.239 | 0.001-0.003 | 0.009 |
| 1989 | X | 2.3 (2300) | 2.006-2.008 | 2.006-2.008 | 2.006-2.008 | 2.006-2.008 | 2.006-2.008 | 0.249 [2] | 0.239 | 0.001-0.003 | 0.009 |
| | S | 2.3 (2300) | 2.006-2.008 | 2.006-2.008 | 2.006-2.008 | 2.006-2.008 | 2.006-2.008 | 0.249 [2] | 0.239 | 0.001-0.003 | 0.009 |
| 1990 | X | 2.3 (2300) | 2.006-2.008 | 2.006-2.008 | 2.006-2.008 | 2.006-2.008 | 2.006-2.008 | 0.245-0.249 | 0.235-0.239 | 0.001-0.003 | 0.009 |
| | S | 2.3 (2300) | 2.006-2.008 | 2.006-2.008 | 2.006-2.008 | 2.006-2.008 | 2.006-2.008 | 0.258-0.262 | 0.258-0.262 | 0.001-0.003 | 0.009 |
| 1991 | X | 2.3 (2300) | 2.006-2.008 | 2.006-2.008 | 2.006-2.008 | 2.006-2.008 | NA | 0.245-0.249 | 0.235-0.239 | 0.001-0.003 | 0.009 |
| | S | 2.3 (2300) | 2.006-2.008 | 2.006-2.008 | 2.006-2.008 | 2.006-2.008 | NA | 0.258-0.262 | 0.258-0.262 | 0.001-0.003 | 0.009 |

86703904

## CAMSHAFT SPECIFICATIONS

All measurements given in inches.

| | Engine | Engine Displacement | Journal Diameter | | | | | Elevation | | Bearing | Camshaft |
|---|---|---|---|---|---|---|---|---|---|---|---|
| 1992 | X | 2.3 (2300) | 2.006-2.008 | 2.006-2.008 | 2.006-2.008 | 2.006-2.008 | NA | 0.245-0.249 | 0.235-0.239 | 0.001-0.003 | 0.009 |
| 1992 | U | 3.0 (2980) | 2.0074-2.0084 | 2.0074-2.0084 | 2.0074-2.0084 | 2.0074-2.0084 | NA | 0.255-0.260 | 0.255-0.260 | 0.001-0.003 | 0.009 |
| 1993 | X | 2.3 (2300) | 2.006-2.008 | 2.006-2.008 | 2.006-2.008 | 2.006-2.008 | NA | 0.245-0.249 | 0.235-0.239 | 0.001-0.003 | 0.009 |
| | U | 3.0 (2980) | 2.0074-2.0084 | 2.0074-2.0084 | 2.0074-2.0084 | 2.0074-2.0084 | NA | 0.255-0.260 | 0.255-0.260 | 0.001-0.003 | 0.009 |
| 1994 | X | 2.3 (2300) | 2.0060-2.0080 | 2.0060-2.0080 | 2.0060-2.0080 | 2.0060-2.0080 | 2.0060-2.0080 | 0.2450-0.2499 | 0.2350-0.2390 | 0.0010-0.0030 | 0.009 |
| | U | 3.0 (2980) | 2.0074-2.0084 | 2.0074-2.0084 | 2.0074-2.0084 | 2.0074-2.0084 | 2.0074-2.0084 | 0.2550-0.2600 | 0.2550-0.2600 | 0.001-0.003 | 0.001-0.005 |

NA - Not Available

1 Endplay is controlled by button and spring on camshaft end
2 HO engine, Intake: 0.2780
2 HO engine, Exhaust: 0.2780

86703905

## CRANKSHAFT AND CONNECTING ROD SPECIFICATIONS

All measurements are given in inches.

| Year | Engine ID/VIN | Engine Displacement Liters (cc) | Crankshaft | | | | Connecting Rod | | |
|------|---------------|-------------------------------|------------|---|---|---|----------------|---|---|
| | | | Main Brg. Journal Dia. | Main Brg. Oil Clearance | Shaft End-play | Thrust on No. | Journal Diameter | Oil Clearance | Side Clearance |
| 1984 | H | 2.0 (2000) | 2.3598-2.3605 | 0.0012-0.0020 | 0.0011-0.0016 | 3 | 2.0055-2.0061 | 0.0010-0.0020 | 0.0043-0.0103 |
| | R | 2.3 (2300) | 2.2489-2.2490 | 0.0008-0.0015 | 0.004-0.008 | 3 | 2.1232-2.1240 | 0.0008-0.0015 | 0.0035-0.0105 |
| 1985 | H | 2.0 (2000) | 2.3598-2.3605 | 0.0012-0.0020 | 0.0011-0.0016 | 3 | 2.0055-2.0061 | 0.0010-0.0020 | 0.0043-0.0103 |
| | R | 2.3 (2300) | 2.2489-2.2490 | 0.0008-0.0015 | 0.004-0.008 | 3 | 2.1232-2.1240 | 0.0008-0.0015 | 0.0035-0.0105 |
| | S | 2.3 (2300) | 2.2489-2.2490 | 0.0008-0.0015 | 0.004-0.008 | 3 | 2.1232-2.1240 | 0.0008-0.0015 | 0.0035-0.0105 |
| | X | 2.3 (2300) | 2.2482-2.2490 | 0.0008-0.0015 | 0.004-0.008 | 3 | 2.1232-2.1240 | 0.0008-0.0015 | 0.0035-0.0105 |
| 1986 | H | 2.0 (2000) | 2.3598-2.3605 | 0.0012-0.0020 | 0.0011-0.0016 | 3 | 2.0055-2.0061 | 0.0010-0.0020 | 0.0043-0.0103 |
| | R | 2.3 (2300) | 2.2482-2.2490 | 0.0008-0.0015 | 0.004-0.008 | 3 | 2.1232-2.1240 | 0.0008-0.0015 | 0.0035-0.0105 |
| | S | 2.3 (2300) | 2.3982-2.3990 | 0.0008-0.0015 | 0.004-0.008 | 3 | 2.1232-2.1240 | 0.0008-0.0015 | 0.0035-0.0105 |
| | X | 2.3 (2300) | 2.2482-2.2490 | 0.0008-0.0015 | 0.004-0.008 | 3 | 2.1232-2.1240 | 0.0008-0.0015 | 0.0035-0.0105 |
| 1987 | H | 2.0 (2000) | 2.3598-2.3605 | 0.0012-0.0020 | 0.0011-0.0016 | 3 | 2.0055-2.0061 | 0.0010-0.0020 | 0.0043-0.0103 |
| | R | 2.3 (2300) | 2.2482-2.2490 | 0.0008-0.0015 | 0.004-0.008 | 3 | 2.1232-2.1240 | 0.0008-0.0015 | 0.0035-0.0105 |
| | S | 2.3 (2300) | 2.2482-2.2490 | 0.0008-0.0015 | 0.004-0.008 | 3 | 2.1232-2.1240 | 0.0008-0.0015 | 0.0035-0.0105 |
| | X | 2.3 (2300) | 2.2482-2.2490 | 0.0008-0.0015 | 0.004-0.008 | 3 | 2.1232-2.1240 | 0.0008-0.0015 | 0.0035-0.0105 |
| 1988 | X | 2.3 (2300) | 2.2482-2.2490 | 0.0008-0.0015 | 0.004-0.008 | 3 | 2.1232-2.1240 | 0.0008-0.0015 | 0.0035-0.0105 |
| | S | 2.3 (2300) | 2.2482-2.2490 | 0.0008-0.0015 | 0.004-0.008 | 3 | 2.1232-2.1240 | 0.0008-0.0015 | 0.0035-0.0105 |
| 1989 | X | 2.3 (2300) | 2.2482-2.2490 | 0.0008-0.0015 | 0.004-0.008 | 3 | 2.1232-2.1240 | 0.0008-0.0015 | 0.0035-0.0105 |
| | S | 2.3 (2300) | 2.2482-2.2490 | 0.0008-0.0015 | 0.004-0.008 | 3 | 2.1232-2.1240 | 0.0008-0.0015 | 0.0035-0.0105 |
| 1990 | X | 2.3 (2300) | 2.2482-2.2490 | 0.0008-0.0015 | 0.004-0.008 | 3 | 2.1232-2.1240 | 0.0008-0.0015 | 0.0035-0.0105 |
| | S | 2.3 (2300) | 2.2482-2.2490 | 0.0008-0.0015 | 0.004-0.008 | 3 | 2.1232-2.1240 | 0.0008-0.0015 | 0.0035-0.0105 |
| 1991 | X | 2.3 (2300) | 2.2482-2.2490 | 0.0008-0.0015 | 0.004-0.008 | 3 | 2.1232-2.1240 | 0.0008-0.0015 | 0.0035-0.0105 |
| | S | 2.3 (2300) | 2.2482-2.2490 | 0.0008-0.0015 | 0.004-0.008 | 3 | 2.1232-2.1240 | 0.0008-0.0015 | 0.0035-0.0105 |
| 1992 | X | 2.3 (2300) | 2.2482-2.2490 | 0.0008-0.0015 | 0.004-0.008 | 3 | 2.1232-2.1240 | 0.0008-0.0015 | 0.0035-0.0105 |

86703906

## CRANKSHAFT AND CONNECTING ROD SPECIFICATIONS

All measurements are given in inches.

| Year | Engine ID/VIN | Engine Displacement Liters (cc) | Crankshaft | | | | Connecting Rod | | |
|------|---------------|--------------------------------|------------|--|--|--|----------------|--|--|
| | | | Main Brg. Journal Dia. | Main Brg. Oil Clearance | Shaft End-play | Thrust on No. | Journal Diameter | Oil Clearance | Side Clearance |
| 1992 | U | 3.0 (2971) | 2.5182-2.5190 | 0.0010-0.0014 | 0.004-0.008 | 3 | 2.1240 | 0.0010-0.0014 | 0.006-0.014 |
| 1993 | X | 2.3 (2300) | 2.2482-2.2490 | 0.0008-0.0015 | 0.004-0.008 | 3 | 2.1232-2.1240 | 0.0008-0.0015 | 0.0035-0.0105 |
| | U | 3.0 (2971) | 2.5189-2.5190 | 0.0010-0.0014 | 0.004-0.008 | 3 | 2.1240 | 0.0010-0.0014 | 0.006-0.014 |
| 1994 | X | 2.3 (2300) | 2.2482-2.2490 | 0.0008-0.0015 | 0.004-0.008 | 3 | 2.1232-2.1240 | 0.0008-0.0015 | 0.0035-0.0105 |
| | U | 3.0 (2971) | 2.5190-2.5198 | 0.0010-0.0014 | 0.004-0.008 | 3 | 2.1253-2.1261 | 0.0010-0.0014 | 0.006-0.014 |

86703907

## PISTON AND RING SPECIFICATIONS
All measurements are given in inches.

| Year | Engine ID/VIN | Engine Displacement Liters (cc) | Piston Clearance | Ring Gap Top Compression | Ring Gap Bottom Compression | Ring Gap Oil Control | Ring Side Clearance Top Compression | Ring Side Clearance Bottom Compression | Ring Side Clearance Oil Control |
|---|---|---|---|---|---|---|---|---|---|
| 1984 | H | 2.0 (2000) | 0.0013-0.0020 | 0.0079-0.0157 | 0.0079-0.0157 | 0.0079-0.0157 | 0.0020-0.0035 | 0.0016-0.0031 | SNUG |
| | R | 2.3 (2300) | 0.0013-0.0021 | 0.008-0.016 | 0.008-0.016 | 0.015-0.055 | 0.002-0.004 | 0.002-0.004 | SNUG |
| 1985 | H | 2.0 (2000) | 0.0013-0.0020 | 0.0079-0.0157 | 0.0079-0.0157 | 0.0079-0.0157 | 0.0020-0.0035 | 0.0016-0.0031 | SNUG |
| | R | 2.3 (2300) | 0.0013-0.0021 | 0.008-0.016 | 0.008-0.016 | 0.015-0.055 | 0.002-0.004 | 0.002-0.004 | SNUG |
| | S | 2.3 (2300) | 0.0013-0.0021 | 0.008-0.016 | 0.008-0.016 | 0.015-0.055 | 0.002-0.004 | 0.002-0.004 | SNUG |
| | X | 2.3 (2300) | 0.0013-0.0021 | 0.008-0.016 | 0.008-0.016 | 0.015-0.055 | 0.002-0.004 | 0.002-0.004 | SNUG |
| 1986 | H | 2.0 (2000) | 0.0013-0.0020 | 0.0079-0.0157 | 0.0079-0.0157 | 0.0079-0.0157 | 0.0020-0.0035 | 0.0016-0.0031 | SNUG |
| | R | 2.3 (2300) | 0.0013-0.0021 | 0.008-0.016 | 0.008-0.016 | 0.015-0.055 | 0.002-0.004 | 0.002-0.004 | SNUG |
| | S | 2.3 (2300) | 0.0013-0.0021 | 0.008-0.016 | 0.008-0.016 | 0.015-0.055 | 0.002-0.004 | 0.002-0.004 | SNUG |
| | X | 2.3 (2300) | 0.0013-0.0021 | 0.008-0.016 | 0.008-0.016 | 0.015-0.055 | 0.002-0.004 | 0.002-0.004 | SNUG |
| 1987 | H | 2.0 (2000) | 0.0013-0.0020 | 0.0079-0.0157 | 0.0079-0.0157 | 0.0079-0.0157 | 0.0020-0.0035 | 0.0016-0.0031 | SNUG |
| | R | 2.3 (2300) | 0.0013-0.0021 | 0.008-0.016 | 0.008-0.016 | 0.015-0.055 | 0.002-0.004 | 0.002-0.004 | SNUG |
| | S | 2.3 (2300) | 0.0030-0.0038 | 0.010-0.020 | 0.010-0.020 | 0.015-0.055 | 0.002-0.004 | 0.002-0.004 | SNUG |
| | X | 2.3 (2300) | 0.0013-0.0021 | 0.008-0.016 | 0.008-0.016 | 0.015-0.055 | 0.002-0.004 | 0.002-0.004 | SNUG |
| 1988 | S | 2.3 (2300) | 0.0013-0.0021 | 0.008-0.016 | 0.008-0.016 | 0.015-0.055 | 0.002-0.004 | 0.002-0.004 | SNUG |
| | X | 2.3 (2300) | 0.0013-0.0021 | 0.008-0.016 | 0.008-0.016 | 0.015-0.055 | 0.002-0.004 | 0.002-0.004 | SNUG |
| 1989 | S | 2.3 (2300) | 0.0013-0.0021 | 0.008-0.016 | 0.008-0.016 | 0.015-0.055 | 0.002-0.004 | 0.002-0.004 | SNUG |
| | X | 2.3 (2300) | 0.0013-0.0021 | 0.008-0.016 | 0.008-0.016 | 0.015-0.055 | 0.002-0.004 | 0.002-0.004 | SNUG |
| 1990 | S | 2.3 (2300) | 0.0012-0.0021 | 0.008-0.016 | 0.008-0.016 | 0.015-0.055 | 0.002-0.004 | 0.002-0.004 | SNUG |
| | X | 2.3 (2300) | 0.0012-0.0021 | 0.008-0.016 | 0.008-0.016 | 0.015-0.055 | 0.002-0.004 | 0.002-0.004 | SNUG |
| 1991 | X | 2.3 (2300) | 0.0013-0.0021 | 0.008-0.016 | 0.008-0.016 | 0.015-0.055 | 0.002-0.004 | 0.002-0.004 | SNUG |
| | S | 2.3 (2300) | 0.0013-0.0021 | 0.008-0.016 | 0.008-0.016 | 0.015-0.055 | 0.002-0.004 | 0.002-0.004 | SNUG |
| 1992 | X | 2.3 (2300) | 0.0013-0.0021 | 0.008-0.016 | 0.008-0.016 | 0.015-0.055 | 0.002-0.004 | 0.002-0.004 | SNUG |

86703908

## PISTON AND RING SPECIFICATIONS
All measurements are given in inches.

| Year | Engine ID/VIN | Engine Displacement Liters (cc) | Piston Clearance | Ring Gap | | | Ring Side Clearance | | |
|------|------|------|------|------|------|------|------|------|------|
| | | | | Top Compression | Bottom Compression | Oil Control | Top Compression | Bottom Compression | Oil Control |
| 1992 | U | 3.0 (2971) | 0.0014-0.0022 | 0.010-0.020 | 0.010-0.020 | 0.010-0.049 | 0.0012-0.0031 | 0.0012-0.0031 | SNUG |
| 1993 | X | 2.3 (2300) | 0.0013-0.0021 | 0.008-0.016 | 0.008-0.016 | 0.015-0.055 | 0.002-0.004 | 0.002-0.004 | SNUG |
| | U | 3.0 (2971) | 0.0014-0.0022 | 0.010-0.020 | 0.010-0.020 | 0.010-0.049 | 0.0012-0.0031 | 0.0012-0.0031 | SNUG |
| 1994 | X | 2.3 (2300) | 0.0011-0.0022 | 0.008-0.016 | 0.008-0.016 | 0.015-0.055 | 0.0020-0.0040 | 0.0020-0.0040 | SNUG |
| | U | 3.0 (2971) | 0.0014-0.0022 | 0.010-0.020 | 0.010-0.020 | 0.010-0.049 | 0.0012-0.0031 | 0.0012-0.0031 | SNUG |

86703909

## TORQUE SPECIFICATIONS
### All readings in ft. lbs.

| Year | Engine ID/VIN | Engine Displacement Liters (cc) | Cylinder Head Bolts | Main Bearing Bolts | Rod Bearing Bolts | Crankshaft Damper Bolts | Flywheel Bolts | Manifold Intake | Manifold Exhaust | Spark Plugs | Lug Nut |
|---|---|---|---|---|---|---|---|---|---|---|---|
| 1984 | H | 2.0 (2000) | 2 | 61-65 | 51-54 | 115-123 | 54-64 | 15-23 | 20-30 | [3] | 95 |
|  | R | 2.3 (2300) | 4 | 51-56 | 21-26 | 140-170 | 54-64 | 15-23 | [5] | 5-10 | 95 |
| 1985 | H | 2.0 (2000) | 2 | 61-65 | 51-54 | 115-123 | 54-64 | 15-23 | 20-30 | [3] | 95 |
|  | R | 2.3 (2300) | 4 | 51-56 | 21-26 | 140-170 | 54-64 | 15-23 | [5] | 5-10 | 95 |
|  | X | 2.3 (2300) | 4 | 51-56 | 21-26 | 140-170 | 54-64 | 15-23 | [5] | 5-10 | 95 |
|  | S | 2.3 (2300) | 4 | 51-56 | 21-26 | 140-170 | 54-64 | 15-23 | [5] | 5-10 | 95 |
| 1986 | H | 2.0 (2000) | 1 | 61-65 | 51-54 | 115-123 | 54-64 | 15-23 | 20-30 | [2] | 95 |
|  | R | 2.3 (2300) | 3 | 51-56 | 21-26 | 140-170 | 54-64 | 15-23 | [5] | 5-10 | 95 |
|  | X | 2.3 (2300) | 3 | 51-56 | 21-26 | 140-170 | 54-64 | 15-23 | [5] | 5-10 | 95 |
|  | S | 2.3 (2300) | 3 | 51-56 | 21-26 | 140-170 | 54-64 | 15-23 | [5] | 5-10 | 95 |
| 1987 | H | 2.0 (2000) | 1 | 61-65 | 51-54 | 115-123 | 54-64 | 15-23 | 20-30 | [2] | 95 |
|  | R | 2.3 (2300) | 3 | 51-56 | 21-26 | 140-170 | 54-64 | 15-23 | [5] | 5-10 | 95 |
|  | S | 2.3 (2300) | 3 | 51-56 | 21-26 | 140-170 | 54-64 | 15-23 | [5] | 5-10 | 95 |
|  | X | 2.3 (2300) | 3 | 51-56 | 21-26 | 140-170 | 54-64 | 15-23 | [5] | 5-10 | 95 |
| 1988 | X | 2.3 (2300) | 3 | 51-56 | 21-26 | 140-170 | 54-64 | 15-23 | [5] | 5-10 | 95 |
|  | S | 2.3 (2300) | 3 | 51-56 | 21-26 | 140-170 | 54-64 | 15-23 | [5] | 5-10 | 95 |
| 1989 | X | 2.3 (2300) | 3 | 51-56 | 21-26 | 140-170 | 54-64 | 15-23 | [5] | 5-10 | 95 |
|  | S | 2.3 (2300) | 3 | 51-56 | 21-26 | 140-170 | 54-64 | 15-23 | [5] | 5-10 | 95 |
| 1990 | X | 2.3 (2300) | 3 | 51-56 | 21-26 | 140-170 | 54-64 | 15-23 | [5] | 5-10 | 95 |
|  | S | 2.3 (2300) | 3 | 51-56 | 21-26 | 140-170 | 54-64 | 15-23 | [5] | 5-10 | 95 |
| 1991 | S | 2.3 (2300) | 3 | 51-56 | 21-26 | 140-170 | 54-64 | 15-23 | [5] | 5-10 | 95 |
|  | X | 2.3 (2300) | 3 | 51-56 | 21-26 | 140-170 | 54-64 | 15-23 | [5] | 5-10 | 95 |
| 1992 | X | 2.3 (2300) | 3 | 51-56 | 21-26 | 140-170 | 54-64 | 15-23 | [5] | 5-10 | 95 |
|  | U | 3.0 (2971) | 7 | 65-81 | [1] | 141-169 | 54-64 | [2] | [5] | 5-10 | 95 |
| 1993 | X | 2.3 (2300) | 3 | 51-56 | 21-26 | 140-170 | 54-64 | 15-23 | [5] | 5-10 | 95 |
|  | U | 3.0 (2971) | 7 | 65-81 | [1] | 141-169 | 54-64 | [2] | [5] | 5-10 | 95 |
| 1994 | X | 2.3 (2300) | 2 | 51-56 | 21-26 | 80-100 | 54-64 | [17] | [4] | 5-10 | 95 |
|  | U | 3.0 (2971) | 6 | 55-63 | 26 | 93-121 | 54-64 | [1] | 15-22 | 7-15 | 95 |

1 Do not reuse cylinder head bolts. Always install new ones, as directed:
  Step 1: Tighten bolts, in sequence, to 44 ft. lbs.
  Step 2: Loosen all bolts approximately two turns, then retighten, in sequence, to 44 ft. lbs.
  Step 3: Turn all bolts an additional 90 degrees
  Step 4: Repeat Step 3
2 Step 1: Tighten to 22 ft. lbs.
  Step 2: Tighten another 90-105 degrees
  Step 3: Repeat Step 2
3 Tighten glow plugs 11-15 ft. lbs.
4 Step 1: 52-59 ft. lbs.
  Step 2: 70-76 ft. lbs.
5 Step 1: 5-7 ft. lbs.
  Step 2: 20-30 ft. lbs.
6 Step 1: 50-60 ft. lbs.
  Step 2: 80-90 ft. lbs.
7 Step 1: 50-60 ft. lbs.
  Step 2: 75-85 ft. lbs.
17 Step 1: 11-13 ft. lbs.
  Step 2: 22-25 ft. lbs.

86703910

## Engine

### SAFETY PRECAUTIONS

- Always disconnect the negative battery terminal to prevent sparks that may result from short–circuiting,
- Smoking must not be allowed when working around flammable liquids.
- Always keep a $CO_2$ fire extinguisher close at hand, in case of fire.
- Dry sand, cat litter or other similar oil absorbent substance must be available to soak up any spillage from oil or other liquid.
- The fuel system, on vehicles equipped with Electronic Fuel Injection (EFI), is under pressure. In order to reduce the chance of personal injury, follow the fuel pressure relief procedures in Section 5, and cover all fittings with shop towels before disconnecting.
- The air conditioning system (if equipped) must be discharged prior to engine removal. The refrigerant is contained under high pressure and is very dangerous when released. The system should be discharged by a certified professional using the proper recovery equipment.
- A special engine support bar is necessary. The bar is used to support the engine/transaxle while disconnecting the various engine mounts Ford Part No. T81P–6000–A. A suitable support can be constructed using angle iron, a heavy J–hook and some strong chain.
- When draining coolant, keep in mind that cats and dogs are attracted to ethylene glycol antifreeze, and are quite likely to drink any that is left in an uncovered container. Always drain the coolant into a sealable container.
- The EPA warns that prolonged contact with used engine oil may cause a number of skin disorders, including cancer! You should make every effort to minimize your exposure to used engine oil. Protective gloves should be worn when changing the oil. Wash your hands and any other exposed skin areas as soon as possible after exposure to used engine oil. Soap and water, or waterless hand cleaner should be used.

### REMOVAL & INSTALLATION

➡ The following procedures are for engine and transaxle removal and installation as an assembly. The engine and transaxle assembly are removed together as a unit from underneath the vehicle. Steps should be taken to safely raise and support the vehicle for power train removal and installation.

#### 2.0L Engine

➡ Before beginning the removal procedure, have the A/C system discharged by a certified technician.

1. Mark position of hood hinges and remove from vehicle.
2. Unfasten the negative cable from the battery. The battery is in the trunk.
3. Remove the air cleaner assembly.
4. Position a large sealable container under the lower radiator hose. Loosen the clamp and remove the hose, so the coolant can drain into the container. If the coolant is less than 2 years old, or appears in good condition, consider reusing it. Once the coolant has completely drained out, remove the upper radiator hose.

➡ When draining coolant, keep in mind that cats and dogs are attracted to ethylene glycol antifreeze, and are quite likely to drink any that is left in an uncovered container. Always drain the coolant into a sealable container.

5. Disconnect cooling fan harness. Loosen radiator shroud, and remove fan and shroud as an entire unit. Once removed, the radiator can come out.
6. Remove starter cable from starter.
7. If equipped with air conditioning, have the A/C system evacuated by a qualified professional. Once empty, remove the lines attached to the compressor.
8. Tag and label all vacuum hoses. Once marked, disconnect as needed. Unplug engine harness and glow plug relay harness at the dash panel. Disconnect alternator harness on right fender wall.
9. Remove clutch cable from shift lever on transaxle.
10. Disconnect injection pump throttle linkage. Loosen and plug fuel supply and return lines on engine.
11. Disconnect power steering pressure and return lines at the power steering pump, if equipped. Remove power steering bracket at cylinder head.
12. Install support tool D79P–6000–A or equivalent to existing engine lifting eyes.
13. Raise vehicle, and properly support with jackstands.
14. Unfasten bolt attaching exhaust pipe bracket to the oil pan.
15. Remove the two exhaust pipe to exhaust manifold attaching nuts. Pull exhaust system out of rubber insulating grommets and set aside.
16. Remove speedometer cable from transaxle.
17. Put drain pan under heater hoses, remove one hose from the water pump inlet tube, and remove another hose from from the oil cooler.
18. Remove the bolts attaching the control arms to the vehicle body. Unfasten the stabilizer bar bracket retaining bolts, and remove the brackets.
19. Loosen and remove the halfshafts from both sides of the vehicle.
20. If equipped with a manual transaxle, remove shift stabilizer attaching bolts. Remove the shift mechanism to shift shaft attaching nut and bolt at the transaxle.
21. Remove the left rear insulator mount bracket from the body by removing the 2 nuts.
22. Remove the left front insulator to transaxle mounting bolts. Remove the roll restricter from the right front stabilizer bar bracket.
23. Lower vehicle carefully. Do not allow front wheels to touch the ground. Install engine lifting equipment to the 2 lifting eyes on the engine.
24. Remove the jackstands supporting the engine.
25. Remove right rear insulator intermediate bracket bolts. Unfasten the intermediate bracket to insulator attaching nuts and the nut at the bottom of the double ended stud attaching the intermediate bracket to the engine bracket. Once all the hardware is unfastened, remove the bracket.

26. With everything loosened, slowly lower engine and transaxle to the ground.

**To Install:**

27. Raise vehicle and support with jackstands.

28. With engine and transaxle positioned directly under the engine compartment, slowly begin to lower the vehicle down. Do not lower enough such that the front wheels touch the ground.

29. Install an engine lift and begin raising the engine into the vehicle.

30. Install right rear insulator intermediate attaching nuts and intermediate bracket to the engine bracket bolts. Install the nut on the bottom of the double ended stud attaching the intermediate bracket to the engine bracket. Tighten to 75–100 ft. lbs. (100–135 Nm).

31. Install engine support tool D79P–6000–A or equivalent to lifting eyes. With engine properly supported, remove the engine lift.

32. Raise the vehicle, and support with jackstands.

33. Position transaxle jack or equivalent under engine and raise engine/transaxle into mounted position.

34. Install left front insulator to bracket nut and tighten to 45–65 ft. lbs. (61–68 Nm). Install left rear insulator bracket to body. Tighten nuts to 45–65 ft. lbs. (61–68 Nm).

35. Install lower radiator hose and retaining bracket and bolt.

36. Install shift stabilizer bar to transaxle attaching bolt. Tighten to 23–35 ft. lbs. (31–47 Nm). Install roll restricter to engine bracket and stabilizer bar bracket with attaching bolts and tighten.

37. Install shifty mechanism to input shift shaft on the transaxle. Tighten nut and bolt 7–10 ft. lbs. (9–13 Nm) .

38. Place radiator in engine compartment and secure. Install lower radiator hose and tighten clamps. Connect heater hoses to water pump and oil cooler. Install speedometer cable to transaxle.

39. Position exhaust system to engine and into insulator rubber grommets. Install exhaust pipe to exhaust manifold bolts. Install exhaust pipe bracket to oil pan bolt. Tighten all hardware.

40. Place control arm and stabilizer bars into position. Install control arm attaching bolts, and stabilizer bar brackets. Install and tighten bracket hardware.

41. Reinstall both left and right halfshafts. When secure, lower vehicle and remove engine support tool.

42. Connect all wiring harnesses including the alternator, glow plug relay harness and main harness. At the same time, reconnect all vacuum hoses.

43. Reconnect A/C line to the compressor, but do not charge the system until the engine job is complete.

44. Connect the fuel supply and return lines to the injection pump. Connect injection pump throttle cable.

45. Install power steering pressure and return lines. Install bracket at cylinder head.

46. Fasten clutch cable to shift lever and adjust if necessary.

47. Connect battery cable to starter.

48. Install radiator shroud and fan assembly. Tighten all hardware and connect coolant fan connection. Reconnect upper radiator hose. With all clamps tight, add coolant to the system.

49. Connect negative cable to battery.

50. Install air cleaner assembly.

51. Position hood on hinges, and align properly. Tighten all hardware.

52. Check all fluid levels, including oil, transmission and antifreeze.

53. Start engine, then check timing and idle, bleed the coolant system, check the transaxle fluid level, if equipped with automatic transaxle. Check for leaks.

54. If engine function correctly, take vehicle to certified professional to have air conditioning system charged to proper levels.

### 2.3L Engine

*1984–90 MODELS*

➡ **To remove the engine, the air conditioning system must be disconnected. Therefore, before starting the project, you must have the A/C system evacuated by a qualified professional.**

1. Park the vehicle on a level open surface.

2. Mark the position of the lines on the underside of the hood and remove the hood.

3. Disconnect the battery cables from the battery, negative cable first. Remove the air cleaner assembly.

4. Remove the radiator cap and disconnect the lower radiator hose from the radiator to drain the cooling system into a sealable container. If the coolant is less than two years old, and in good condition, try to reuse it.

5. With the cooling system empty, remove the upper and lower radiator hoses. On models equipped with an automatic transaxle, disconnect and plug the oil cooler lines from the rubber connectors at the radiator.

6. Disconnect and remove the coil from the cylinder head. Disconnect the cooling fan wiring harness. Remove the radiator shroud and electric fan as an entire assembly.

7. Remove the air conditioner hoses from the compressor. Label and unfasten all electrical harness connections, linkage and vacuum lines from the engine.

8. On automatic transaxle models disconnect the TV (throttle valve) linkage at the transaxle. On manual transaxle models disconnect the clutch cable from the lever at the transaxle.

9. Unfasten accelerator cable.

10. Disconnect the fuel supply and return lines. Plug the fuel line from the gas tank. Disconnect the thermactor pump discharge hose at the pump.

11. Disconnect the power steering lines at the pump. Remove the hose support bracket from the cylinder head.

12. Remove coil, tension wire for coil and bracket.

13. Install an engine support (Ford Tool D88L–6000–A or equivalent) to the engine lifting eye.

14. Raise and safely support the car on jackstands.

15. Remove the starter cable from the starter motor terminal. Drain the engine oil and the transaxle lubricant. Dispose of properly.

16. Disconnect the hose from the catalytic converter. Remove the bolts retaining the exhaust pipe bracket to the oil pan.

17. Remove the exhaust pipe to exhaust manifold attaching nuts. Remove the pipes from the mounting bracket insulators and position out of the way.

18. Disconnect the speedometer cable from the transaxle. Remove the heater hoses from the water pump inlet and intake manifold connector.

19. Remove the water intake tube bracket from the engine block. Remove the two clamp attaching bolts from the bottom of the oil pan. Remove the water pump inlet tube.

20. Remove the bolts attaching the control arms to the body. Remove the stabilizer bar bracket retaining bolts and remove the brackets.

21. Remove the halfshafts (drive axles) from the transaxle. Plug transaxle with shipping plugs or equivalent.

22. On models equipped with a manual transaxle, remove the roll restricter nuts from the transaxle and pull the roll restricter away from the mounting bracket.

23. On models equipped with a manual transaxle, remove the shift stabilizer bar to transaxle attaching bolts. Remove the shift mechanism to shift shaft attaching nut and bolt at the transaxle

24. On models equipped with an automatic transaxle, disconnect the shift cable clip from the transaxle lever. Remove the manual shift linkage bracket bolts from the transaxle and remove the bracket.

25. Remove the left rear insulator mount bracket from the body by removing the retaining nut.

26. Remove the left front insulator to transaxle mounting bolts.

27. Lower the car and support with stands so that the front wheels are just above the ground. Do not allow the wheels to touch the ground.

28. Connect an engine sling to the lifting brackets provided. Connect a hoist to the sling and apply slight tension. Remove engine support tool used previously in step 13.

29. Remove the right hand insulator intermediate bracket to engine bracket bolts, intermediate bracket to insulator attaching nuts and the nut on the bottom of the double ended stud which attaches the intermediate bracket and engine bracket. Remove the bracket.

30. Slowly, lower the engine and transaxle assembly to the ground.

31. Raise and support the car at a height suitable from assembly to be removed.

**To install:**

32. Raise the engine and transaxle assembly and lower it into the vehicle

33. Install the right hand insulator intermediate bracket to engine bracket bolts, intermediate bracket to insulator attaching nuts and the nut on the bottom of the double ended stud which attaches the intermediate bracket and engine bracket. Install the bracket.

34. Connect an engine sling to the lowering brackets provided. Connect a hoist to the sling and apply slight tension. Install and support sling.

35. Raise the car and support with stands so that the front wheels are just above the ground. Do not allow the wheels to touch the ground.

36. Install the left front insulator to transaxle mounting bolts.

37. Install the left rear insulator mount bracket to the body by removing the retaining nuts.

38. On models equipped with an automatic transaxle, reconnect the shift cable clip to the transaxle lever. Install the manual shift linkage bracket bolts to the transaxle and install the bracket.

39. On models equipped with a manual transaxle, install the shift stabilizer bar to the transaxle attaching bolts. Then install the shift mechanism to shift shaft attaching nut and bolt at the transaxle. Position and secure the roll restricter nuts to the transaxle and pull the roll restricter to the mounting bracket.

40. Remove the shipping plugs and install the halfshafts (drive axles) to the transaxle.

41. Install the bolts attaching the control arms to the body. Install the stabilizer bar bracket retaining bolts and install the bracket.

42. Install the water intake tube bracket to the engine block. Install the two clamp attaching bolts to the bottom of the oil pan. Install the water pump inlet tube.

43. Reconnect the speedometer cable to the transaxle. Install the heater hoses to the water pump inlet and intake manifold connector.

44. Install the exhaust pipe to exhaust manifold mounting nuts. Install the pipes to the mounting bracket insulators.

45. Reconnect the hose to the catalytic converter. Install the bolts retaining the exhaust pipe bracket to the oil pan.

46. Install the starter cable to the starter motor terminal. Refill the engine oil and the transaxle lubricant.

47. Lower the car from the jackstands.

48. Remove the engine support sling.

49. Reconnect the power steering lines at the pump. Install the hose support bracket to the cylinder head.

50. Reconnect the fuel supply and return lines. Reconnect the thermactor pump discharge hose at the pump.

51. On automatic transaxle models, reconnect the Throttle Valve (TV) linkage at the transaxle.

52. On manual transaxle models reconnect the clutch cable to the lever at the transaxle.

53. Install the hoses to the A/C compressor. Fasten all electrical harness connections, linkage and vacuum lines to the engine.

54. Reconnect and install the coil to the cylinder head. Reconnect the cooling fan wiring harness. Install the radiator shroud and electric fan as an assembly.

55. Install the upper and lower radiator hoses. On models equipped with an automatic transaxle, reconnect the oil cooler lines to the rubber connectors at the radiator, if equipped.

56. Reconnect the lower radiator hose to the radiator. Refill the cooling system.

57. Reconnect the battery cables to the battery. Install the air cleaner assembly.

58. Install the hood.

59. Start the vehicle and check for a properly running engine, Inspect for any fluid leaks or other problem areas.

60. Have a qualified professional recharge the system.

***1991–94 MODELS***

➡ **To remove the engine, the air conditioning system must be disconnected. Therefore, before starting the project, you must have the A/C system evacuated by a qualified professional.**

1. Park the vehicle on a level open surface.

2. Mark position of hood hinges and remove hood.

3. Remove negative ground cable from battery.

4. Relieve the fuel system pressure. Remove the air cleaner assembly.

5. Remove lower radiator hose and allow coolant to drain into a sealable container. If the coolant is less than 2 years old or in good condition, consider reusing it.

6. Remove upper radiator hose. Disconnect and plug the transaxle cooler lines and rubber hoses below the radiator, if equipped with automatic transaxle.

7. Remove the high tension wire to the coil, then the coil and bracket, Unplug the coolant fan at the electrical connection.

8. Remove the radiator shroud and cooling fan as an entire assembly. Remove radiator from vehicle.

9. Disconnect the A/C pressure and suction lines from the compressor.

10. Identify, tag and disconnect all electrical and vacuum lines as necessary.

11. Disconnect Throttle Valve (TV) linkage or clutch cable at transaxle.

12. Disconnect accelerator linkage and fuel lines.

13. Disconnect the power steering lines at steering pump. Remove the bracket at the cylinder head, if equipped.

14. Install 2 engine lifting eyes and fasten engine support tool to engine lifting eyes.

15. Raise and safely support the vehicle.

16. Remove battery cable from starter and remove hose from catalytic converter.

17. Remove bolt attaching the exhaust pipe bracket to the oil pan and unfasten the 2 exhaust pipe to manifold attaching nuts.

18. Remove the exhaust inlet pipe–to–exhaust manifold retaining nuts, pull exhaust system out of rubber insulating grommets and set aside.

19. Remove speedometer cable from transaxle.

20. Remove the heater hose from water pump inlet tube and the other from the steel tube on intake manifold.

21. Remove water pump inlet tube bolt at the engine block and clamp bolts at the underside of the oil pan. Remove the inlet tube.

22. Remove bolts attaching the control arms to the car body. Remove the stabilizer bar retaining bolts, and remove the brackets.

23. Remove the halfshaft assemblies from the transaxle. Plug the holes with shipping plugs or an equivalent.

24. On manual transaxle equipped vehicles, remove the roll restricter nuts from the transaxle. Pull the roll restricter from it's mounting bracket. Remove the shift stabilizer bar attaching bolts. Also remove the shift mechanism attached to the shaft at the transaxle.

25. On automatic transaxle equipped, disconnect the shift cable clip from the lever on the transaxle. Remove the shift linkage bracket bolts from the transaxle and remove the bracket.

26. Remove the left rear insulator mounting bracket from the body bracket.

27. Remove the left front insulator to transaxle mounting bolts.

28. Lower the vehicle carefully. Install engine lifting equipment to the 2 lifting eyes on engine.

➡ **When lowering the vehicle, do not allow the front wheels to touch the ground.**

29. Remove the engine support tool.

30. Remove right rear insulator intermediate bracket-to–engine bracket bolts, intermediate bracket-to–insulator attaching nuts and the nut on the bottom of the double ended stud which attaches the intermediate bracket-to–engine bracket. Remove bracket.

31. Carefully lower engine and transaxle as entire assembly to the floor.

**To install:**

32. Raise and safely support the vehicle on jackstands.

33. Position engine and transaxle assembly directly below engine compartment.

34. Slowly lower vehicle over engine and transaxle assembly.

➡ **Do not allow the front wheels to touch the ground.**

35. Install an engine lift to both existing engine lifting eyes on engine. Raise engine and transaxle assembly up through engine compartment and position accordingly.

36. Install right rear insulator intermediate attaching nuts to intermediate bracket. Tighten to 55–75 ft. lbs. (75–100 Nm). Attach intermediate bracket to engine bracket bolts. Tighten to 52–70 ft. lbs. (70–95 Nm). Install nut on bottom of double–ended stud that attaches the intermediate bracket–to–engine bracket. Tighten to 60–90 ft. lbs. (80–120 Nm).

37. Install engine support tool D88L–6000 to engine lifting eyes. With engine supported using tool, loosen and remove lifting equipment.

38. Raise and safely support the vehicle.

39. Position a transaxle jack or equivalent under engine and transaxle. Raise engine and transaxle assembly into mounted position.

40. Install insulator–to–bracket nut. Tighten to 45–65 ft. lbs. (61–68 Nm).

41. If equipped with a manual transaxle, position roll restricter onto starter studs. Install nuts attaching roll restricter to transaxle. Tighten to 25–39 ft. lbs. (35–50 Nm).

42. Install starter cable to starter.

43. Install radiator, lower radiator hose and retaining bracket and bolt.

44. If equipped with manual transaxle, install shift stabilizer bar–to–transaxle attaching bolt. Tighten to 23–35 ft. lbs. (31–47 Nm).

45. If equipped with manual transaxle, install shift mechanism–to–input shift shaft (on transaxle) bolt and nut. Tighten to 7–10 ft. lbs. (9–13 Nm).

46. If equipped with an automatic transaxle, install manual shift linkage bracket bolts to transaxle. Install cable clip to lever on transaxle.

47. Install lower radiator hose to radiator.

48. Install speedometer cable to transaxle.

49. Position exhaust system up and into insulating rubber grommets located at rear of vehicle.

50. Install exhaust pipe–to–exhaust manifold studs. Install exhaust pipe bracket–to–oil pan bolt.

51. Connect pulse air hose to catalytic converter.

52. Place stabilizer bar and control arm assembly into position. Install control arm–to–body attaching bolts. Install stabilizer bar brackets and tighten all fasteners.

53. Install halfshaft assemblies on both sides of the vehicle.

54. Slowly lower vehicle.

55. Remove engine support tool.

56. Connect any remaining electrical and vacuum lines.

57. Install heater hose.

58. If equipped, install the air conditioning discharge and suction lines to compressor.

59. Connect the fuel supply and return lines to engine.

60. Connect accelerator cable.

61. Install power steering pressure and re turn lines.

62. If equipped with an automatic transaxle, connect TV linkage at transaxle.

63. If equipped with a manual transaxle, connect clutch cable to shift lever on transaxle. Check clutch adjustment.

64. Install radiator shroud and coolant fan assembly.

65. If equipped with automatic transaxle, connect transaxle cooler lines to rubber hoses below radiator.

66. Fill cooling system.

67. Connect battery ground cable.

68. Install air cleaner assembly.

69. Check engine compartment to make sure all connections are made, all hardware is secure and the vehicle is ready to be driven.

70. Install hood and align hinges. Tighten bolts.

71. Check all fluid levels.

72. Start engine. Check for leak, poor timing or other problems.

73. Once the vehicle is functioning properly, have the A/C system charged by a certified professional.

### 3.0L Engine

➡ To remove the engine, the air conditioning system must be disconnected. Therefore, before starting the project, you must have the A/C system evacuated by a qualified professional.

1. Disconnect the negative battery cable.

2. Drain engine coolant into a sealable container by loosening radiator draincock. The lower radiator hose can also be remove to accomplish this job. Loosen the clamp, then remove the hose from the fitting and allow the coolant to flow into a container.

3. Remove the vehicle hood.

4. Relieve any fuel pressure that may be present in the fuel system. Disconnect all fuel lines.

5. Remove the upper radiator hose.

6. Tag then disconnect all wiring harnesses and connectors.

7. Tag and disconnect all vacuum lines and crankcase venting hoses.

8. Remove the power steering high pressure and return lines. Remove power steering reservoir.

9. If equipped with air conditioning, remove any A/C line from the condenser (not the compressor), leaving the manifold lines attached to the compressor. Remove the bolt secure the A/C line to the engine block.

10. Loosen and remove the accelerator linkage, transaxle throttle valve linkage and speed control cable, if equipped. Disconnect the speedometer cable.

11. If equipped with automatic transaxle, remove the transmission oil cooler lines from the radiator and plug the ends.

12. Remove the lower radiator hose as well as the power steering lines located toward the rear of the transaxle.

13. Raise the vehicle and support with jackstands.

14. Drain the engine into a proper container. Dispose of oil in a safe manner.

15. Remove the heater hoses

16. Remove the exhaust inlet pipe by supporting the entire exhaust system and removing the bolts.

17. Remove the front wheels. Remove the tie rod ends from the spindles. Disconnect the lower ball joint and pull down on the control arm to disengage them from the spindle.

18. Remove both halfshafts from the vehicle.

19. Lower vehicle slightly.

20. Unfasten the coil high tension wire, if not already completed, and remove the bracket and coil.

21. Install engine lifting eyes (D81L–6001–D or equivalent). Install suitable engine lifting device and begin unloading the engine weight from the vehicle body.

22. Remove engine through–bolts from the engine mounts. Refer to the next section, Engine mount for more detail.

23. Carefully lift the engine out and away from the car. Be sure as you remove the engine/transaxle assembly, you clear the master cylinder. Once remove place assembly on floor.

### To install:

24. Raise and safely support the vehicle on jackstands.

25. Install a suitable engine lift to both existing engine lifting eyes. Lift engine and transaxle assembly and position assembly over engine compartment.

26. Slowly lower assembly into compartment until engine mounts align. Install engine through–bolts on engine mounts and tighten. Tighten through–bolts to 30–40 ft. lbs. (40–55 Nm).

27. Remove engine lifting equipment and lifting eyes.

28. Position the ignition coil, coil/bracket and install with the attaching bolts. Connect high tension wire.

29. Install halfshafts to transaxle. Position spindle so outer CV–joint goes through center of spindle. Loosely install retaining nut. Connect lower ball joint and tie rod ends to the spindle. the wheels and tires can be installed at this time.

30. Install the A/C line bracket to the engine block using the retaining bolts and tighten.

31. Support the exhaust system and connect the inlet pipe.

32. Reconnect heater hoses, power steering lines at the rear of the transaxle, and the transmission oil cooler lines, if equipped.

33. Install the radiator, along with the upper and lower radiator hoses and coolant recovery/reservoir tank

34. Connect the speedometer cable, accelerator linkage, transaxle throttle valve linkage and speed control cable, if equipped.

35. Fasten both A/C line to the condenser. Attach brackets where necessary.

36. Install the high pressure line and return line on the power steering pump. At the same time, install the power steering reservoir.

37. Reconnect all the vacuum lines and crankcase ventilation hoses removed earlier. Connect all the wiring harnesses removed during the disassembly.

38. Install the fuel lines, making sure the connections are secure.

39. Install hood by aligning marks and installing the bolts.

40. Reconnect battery.

41. Add fluids where needed. This includes oil, transmission and antifreeze,

42. Start vehicle and check for poor idle, fluid leaks or areas that need adjustments.

43. With the work complete, if equipped with air conditioning, take the car to a certified professional and have the A/C system charged.

## Engine Mounts

## REMOVAL & INSTALLATION

### 2.0L Engine

#### RIGHT FRONT ENGINE MOUNT

▶ **See Figure 75**

1. Disconnect negative battery cable from battery in the trunk.

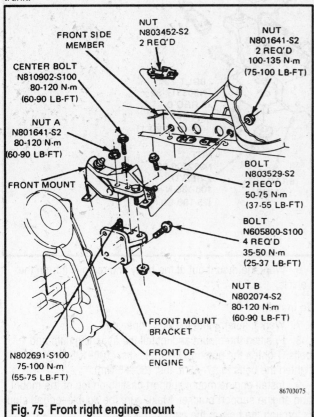

**Fig. 75  Front right engine mount**

2. Support the engine using a floor jack and block of wood. Raise engine enough to unload any weight upon the engine.

3. Remove the 2 nut securing the engine mount to the vehicle body. One nut is accessible from the engine compartment, but the remaining nut is only accessible from under the vehicle. Remove the center bolt from the engine mount.

4. Slowly lower the engine enough to improve clearance.

5. Working from the inside front wheel well, remove the 2 nuts holding the engine mount to the fender apron.

6. Remove the 2 bolts attaching the engine to the right front rail.

7. Slide the engine mount toward the engine until the studs clear the fender, then remove the mount.

**To install:**

8. Position engine mount on right front member and loosely install the 2 attaching bolts.

9. From inside the wheel well, install the 2 attaching nuts and tighten to 75–100 ft. lbs. (100–135 Nm). Tighten the 2 bolts to 37–55 ft. lbs. (50–75 Nm).

10. Raise engine slowly until the engine bracket contacts the engine mount. Some adjustment using a prybar or other tool may be necessary.

11. Install 2 final nuts and center engine bolt and tighten to 60–90 ft. lbs. (80–120 Nm).

12. Lower vehicle and remove the jack and block of wood.

#### TRANSMISSION MOUNTS

▶ **See Figures 76 and 77**

1. Disconnect negative battery cable from battery in the trunk.

2. Support transmission using a floor jack and block of wood. Raise engine enough to unload any weight upon the engine.

3. Remove 3 bolts attaching the front mount to the transmission. Raise the engine enough to unload any weight.

4. Remove the nut attaching the mount to the left stabilizer bar bracket and remove the mount.

5. Remove the 2 nuts attaching the rear mount to the bracket.

6. Remove the 2 bolts attaching the mount to the transmission and r remove the mount.

**To install:**

7. Position front mount on the stabilizer bar bracket and install the 3 bolts attaching the mount to the transmission. Tighten bolts to 25–37 ft. lbs. (35–50 Nm).

8. Install attaching nut to the stabilizer bar bracket and tighten nut to 45–65 ft. lbs. (61–68 Nm).

9. Position rear mount on the transmission and install the 2 attaching bolts. Tighten bolts to 30–45 ft. lbs. (41–61 Nm).

10. Install 2 nuts attaching the mount to the bracket and tighten to 45–65 ft. lbs. (61–88 Nm).

11. Lower vehicle and remove the jack and block of wood.

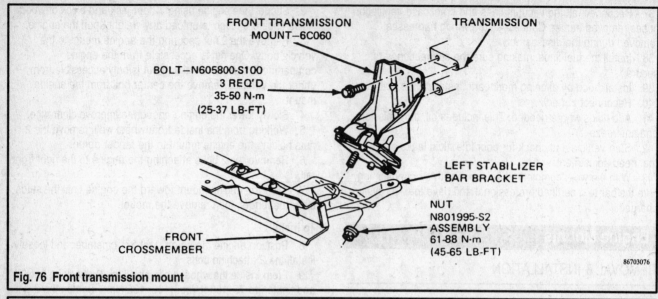

**Fig. 76 Front transmission mount**

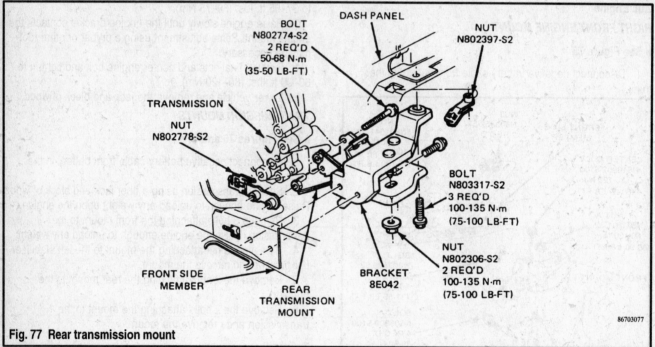

**Fig. 77 Rear transmission mount**

### 1984–90 2.3L Engine

#### FRONT RIGHT ENGINE MOUNT

♦ See Figure 78

1. Disconnect the negative battery cable.
2. Place a floor jack and a block of wood under the engine oil pan. Raise the engine enough to take the load off of the mount.
3. Remove the lower support bracket attaching nut, (bottom of the double ended stud).
4. Remove the insulator–to–support bracket attaching nuts and bolts. Do not remove the nut on top of the double ended stud.
5. Remove the insulator support bracket from the vehicle. Remove the insulator attaching nuts through the right hand front wheel opening.

6. Work the mount out of the body and remove it from the vehicle.

**To install:**

7. Work insulator into the body opening.
8. Position the mount and install the attaching nuts and bolts. Tighten the nuts to 75–100 ft. lbs. (100–135 Nm) and tighten the bolts to 37–55 ft. lbs. (50–75 Nm).
9. Install engine mount support casting on top of the mount and engine support bracket. Make sure the double–edged stud is through the hole in the engine bracket.
10. Tighten the attaching nuts to 52–70 ft. lbs. (70–95 Nm). Install and tighten lower support bracket nut to 60–90 ft. lbs. (80–120 Nm).
11. Lower engine. Connect negative battery cable.
12. Test drive vehicle and adjust if necessary.

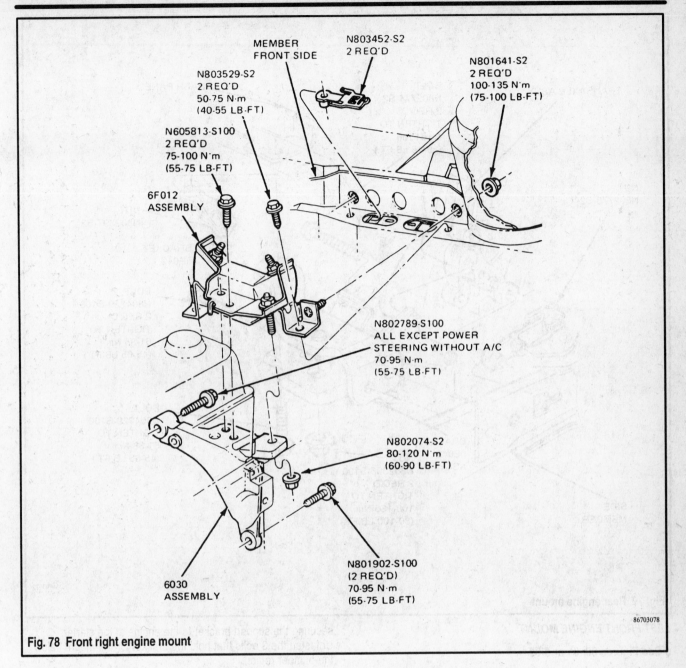

**Fig. 78 Front right engine mount**

N803529-S2
2 REQ'D
50-75 N·m
(40-55 LB-FT)

MEMBER
FRONT SIDE

N803452-S2
2 REQ'D

N801641-S2
2 REQ'D
100-135 N·m
(75-100 LB-FT)

N605813-S100
2 REQ'D
75-100 N·m
(55-75 LB-FT)

6F012
ASSEMBLY

N802789-S100
ALL EXCEPT POWER
STEERING WITHOUT A/C
70-95 N·m
(55-75 LB-FT)

N802074-S2
80-120 N·m
(60-90 LB-FT)

N801902-S100
(2 REQ'D)
70-95 N·m
(55-75 LB-FT)

6030
ASSEMBLY

86703078

## REAR ENGINE MOUNT

▶ See Figure 79

1. Disconnect the negative battery cable.
2. Raise the vehicle and support safely. Place a transaxle jack and a block of wood under the transaxle.
3. Raise the transaxle enough to take the load off of the engine mount.
4. Remove the engine mount attaching nuts from the support bracket. Remove the 2 through–bolts and remove the mount from the transaxle.

**To install:**

5. Install the mount over the left rear transaxle housing and support bracket stud.

6. Install the 2 through–bolts and tighten to 30–45 ft. lbs. (41–61 Nm).
7. Install the 2 support bracket attaching nuts. Tighten to 80–100 ft. lbs. (108–136 Nm).
8. Lower vehicle and remove floor jack. Connect negative battery cable.
9. test drive vehicle and adjust if necessary.

➡ **To remove the left rear support bracket, remove the left rear engine mount. Then remove the support bracket attaching bolts. When installing the support bracket, torque the attaching bolts to 45–65 ft. lbs. (61–88 Nm).**

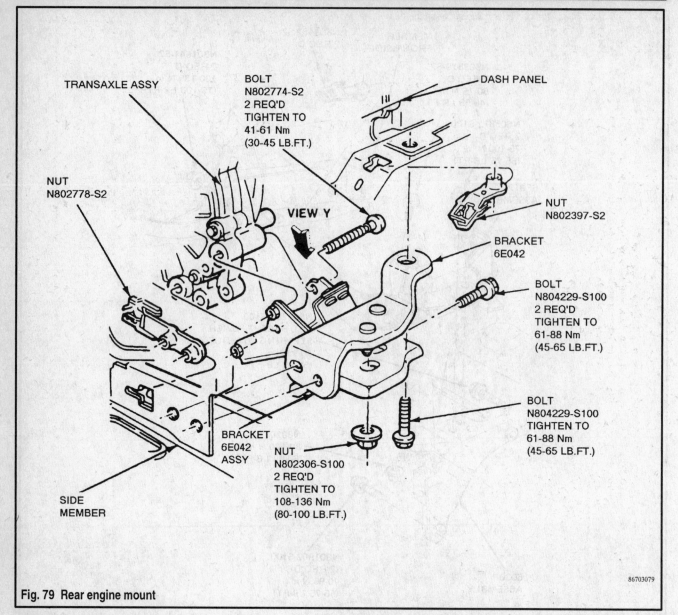

TRANSAXLE ASSY

BOLT
N802774-S2
2 REQ'D
TIGHTEN TO
41-61 Nm
(30-45 LB.FT.)

DASH PANEL

NUT
N802778-S2

VIEW Y

NUT
N802397-S2

BRACKET
6E042

BOLT
N804229-S100
2 REQ'D
TIGHTEN TO
61-88 Nm
(45-65 LB.FT.)

BOLT
N804229-S100
TIGHTEN TO
61-88 Nm
(45-65 LB.FT.)

BRACKET
6E042
ASSY

NUT
N802306-S100
2 REQ'D
TIGHTEN TO
108-136 Nm
(80-100 LB.FT.)

SIDE
MEMBER

86703079

**Fig. 79 Rear engine mount**

*LEFT FRONT ENGINE MOUNT*

♦ **See Figures 80, 81 and 82**

➡ **Depending on the type of transmission equipped on the vehicle will determine which front engine mount is needed for the car. Refer to the diagrams as well as a visual inspection of the mount on your vehicle to determine requirements.**

1. Disconnect the negative battery cable. Raise and support the vehicle safely. Place a transaxle jack and a block of wood under the transaxle. Raise the transaxle enough to take the load off of the engine mount.

2. On all transaxle type EXCEPT for the 1984 4–speed manual transaxle, remove the engine mount–to–support bracket attaching nut. Unfasten the attaching bolts and remove the engine mount from the vehicle from the vehicle.

3. If your vehicle is equipped with a 1984 4–speed manual transaxle, an additional mount is installed. Remove the 3 nuts

securing the support bracket to the engine at the starter. Unfasten the 3 bolts that hold the bracket for the mount below the bumper region.

4. Remove the mount.
To install;

5. On all transaxle type vehicles, position the replacement mount between the support bracket and transaxle. Torque the bolts to 25–37 ft. lbs. (35–50 Nm).

6. If equipped with a 1984 4–speed manual transaxle, install the support bracket and bolts to the body portion below the bumper. Tighten the bolts to 13–19 ft. lbs. (18–26 Nm).

7. Install engine mount nut and tighten to 80–100 ft. lbs. (108–136 Nm).

8. If equipped with 1984 4–speed equipped, install the nut and tighten to 45–65 ft. lbs. (35–50 Nm). Install the additional bracket, then secure using the attachment nuts, tightening to 25–44 ft. lbs. (35–50 Nm).

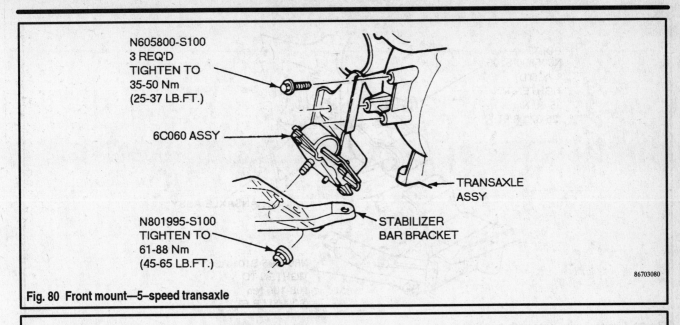

N605800-S100
3 REQ'D
TIGHTEN TO
35-50 Nm
(25-37 LB.FT.)

6C060 ASSY

TRANSAXLE ASSY

N801995-S100
TIGHTEN TO
61-88 Nm
(45-65 LB.FT.)

STABILIZER BAR BRACKET

Fig. 80 Front mount—5–speed transaxle

86703080

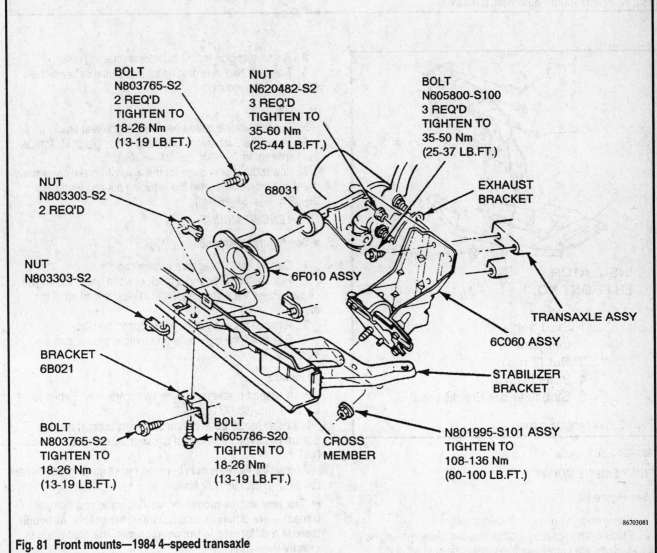

BOLT
N803765-S2
2 REQ'D
TIGHTEN TO
18-26 Nm
(13-19 LB.FT.)

NUT
N620482-S2
3 REQ'D
TIGHTEN TO
35-60 Nm
(25-44 LB.FT.)

BOLT
N605800-S100
3 REQ'D
TIGHTEN TO
35-50 Nm
(25-37 LB.FT.)

NUT
N803303-S2
2 REQ'D

68031

EXHAUST BRACKET

NUT
N803303-S2

6F010 ASSY

TRANSAXLE ASSY

6C060 ASSY

BRACKET
6B021

STABILIZER BRACKET

BOLT
N803765-S2
TIGHTEN TO
18-26 Nm
(13-19 LB.FT.)

BOLT
N605786-S20
TIGHTEN TO
18-26 Nm
(13-19 LB.FT.)

CROSS MEMBER

N801995-S101 ASSY
TIGHTEN TO
108-136 Nm
(80-100 LB.FT.)

Fig. 81 Front mounts—1984 4–speed transaxle

86703081

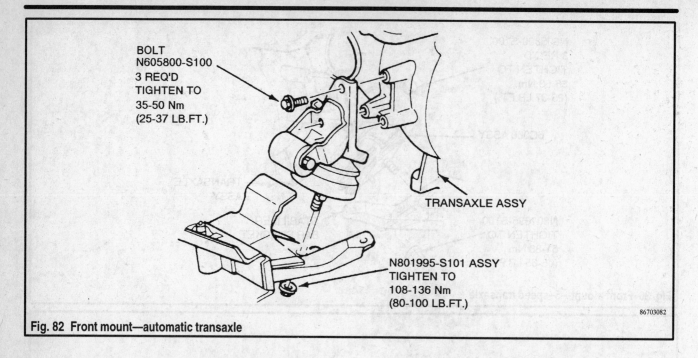

BOLT
N605800-S100
3 REQ'D
TIGHTEN TO
35-50 Nm
(25-37 LB.FT.)

TRANSAXLE ASSY

N801995-S101 ASSY
TIGHTEN TO
108-136 Nm
(80-100 LB.FT.)

**Fig. 82 Front mount—automatic transaxle**

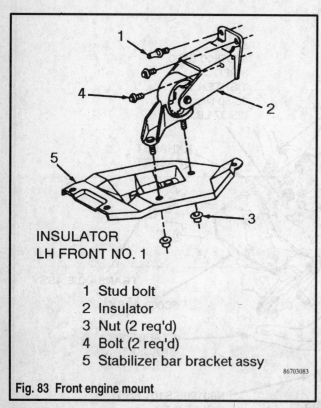

INSULATOR
LH FRONT NO. 1

1 Stud bolt
2 Insulator
3 Nut (2 req'd)
4 Bolt (2 req'd)
5 Stabilizer bar bracket assy

**Fig. 83 Front engine mount**

**1991–94 2.3L Engine**

***FRONT ENGINE MOUNT***

▶ **See Figure 83**

1. Disconnect the negative battery cable.
2. Place a floor jack and a block of wood under the engine oil pan. Raise the engine enough to take the load off of the mounts.

3. Remove engine mount to bracket retaining nuts.
4. Remove the 2 retaining bolts, and 1 stud between the engine and the mount.

**To install:**

5. Position engine mount between engine and bracket.
6. Install the 2 retaining bolts , and the single stud. Torque the hardware to 26–33 ft. lbs (34–46 Nm).
7. Lower the jack enough for the mount to make contact with the support bracket. Install the retaining nut and torque to 26–33 ft. lbs. (34–46 Nm).

***REAR ENGINE MOUNT***

▶ **See Figures 84 and 85**

1. Disconnect the negative battery cable.
2. Place a floor jack and a block of wood under the engine oil pan. Raise the engine enough to take the load off of the mounts.
3. Remove retaining bolts from support bracket.
4. Remove 2 through–bolts and remove mount from transaxle.

**To install:**

5. If support bracket was removed, instal now. Torque to 51–67 ft. lbs. (68–92 Nm).
6. Install mount between transaxle and support bracket. Secure two through–bolts and torque to 30–40 ft. lbs. (40–55 Nm).
7. Install 2 retaining nuts between mount and bracket. Torque to 73–97 ft. lbs. (98–132 Nm).

➡ **The rear engine mount for an automatic and manual transaxle are different, and not interchangeable. Although there is a difference in the components, the procedure is exactly the same.**

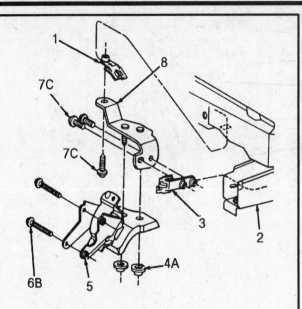

1 Nut
2 Body assy
3 Nut
4A Nuts (2 req'd)
5 Insulator
6B Bolt (2 req'd)
7C Bolt (3 req'd)
8 Support bracket assy
A Tighten to 97.7-132.3 Nm (73-97 lb.ft.)
B Tighten to 40.3-54.7 Nm (30-40 lb.ft.)
C Tighten to 68-92 Nm (51-67 lb.ft.)

86703084

**Fig. 84 Rear engine mount—manual transaxle**

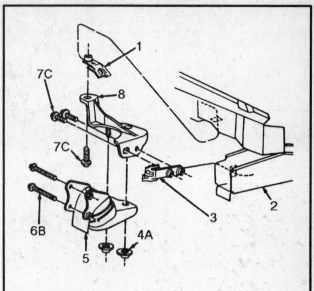

1 Nut
2 Body assy
3 Nut
4A Nut (2 req'd)
5 Insulator
6B Bolt (2 req'd)
7C Bolt (3 req'd)
8 Support bracket assy
A Tighten to 97.7-132.3 Nm (73-97 lb.ft.)
B Tighten to 40.3-54.7 Nm (30-40 lb.ft.)
C Tighten to 68-92 Nm (51-67 lb.ft.)

86703a85

**Fig. 85 Rear engine mount—automatic transaxle**

## RIGHT FRONT ENGINE MOUNT

▶ **See Figure 86**

1. Disconnect the negative battery cable.
2. Place a floor jack and a block of wood under the engine oil pan. Raise the engine enough to take the load off of the mounts.
3. Remove retaining nuts located at the bottom of the double ended stud.
4. Unfasten the lower attaching nuts through the right front wheel opening.
5. Remove the lower retaining bolts through the engine compartment.
6. Remove the 2 attaching bolts between the mount and bracket.

**To install:**

7. Position mount into body opening and into place.
8. Once in position, loosely install the retaining nuts, followed by the bolts. Torque the nuts to 73–97 ft. lbs. (98–132 Nm). Torque the bolts to 40–53 ft. lbs. (53–72 Nm)

### 1992–94 3.0L Engine

#### FRONT ENGINE MOUNT

The parts, tools and procedure for this job are exactly the same as for the 1991–94 2.3L engine. Please refer to the above procedure for details.

#### REAR ENGINE MOUNT

The parts, tools and procedure for this job are exactly the same as for the 1991–94 2.3L engine. Please refer to the above procedure for details.

#### RIGHT FRONT ENGINE MOUNT

▶ **See Figure 86**

1. Disconnect the negative battery cable.
2. Place a floor jack and a block of wood under the engine oil pan. Raise the engine enough to take the load off of the mounts.
3. Remove retaining nuts located at the bottom of the double ended stud.
4. Unfasten the lower attaching nuts through the right front wheel opening.

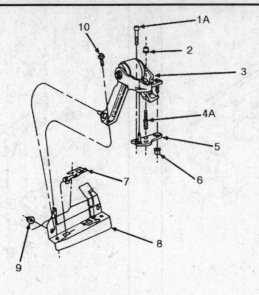

1A Bolt
2 Nut (2 req'd)
3 Insulator
4A Bolt (2 req'd)
5 Bracket assy
6 Nut
7 Nut (2 req'd)
8 Body assy
9 Nut (2 req'd)
10 Bolt (2req'd)
A Tighten to 29.7-40.3 Nm
(22-29 lb.ft.)

86703087

**Fig. 86 Right front engine mount**

5. Remove the lower retaining bolts through the engine compartment.
6. Remove the 2 attaching bolts between the mount and bracket.

## To install:

7. Position mount into body opening and into place.
8. Once in position, loosely install the retaining nuts, followed by the bolts. Torque the nuts to 73–97 ft. lbs. (98–132 Nm). Torque the bolts to 40–53 ft. lbs. (53–72 Nm)

## Rocker Arm (Valve) Cover

### REMOVAL & INSTALLATION

♦ See Figures 87, 88, 89, 90, 91, 92 and 93

➡ The 3.0L engine uses two rocker covers, as opposed to the 2.0L and the 2.3L engine which use only one.

1. Disconnect the negative battery cable.
2. Place fender covers or other protective device on the fenders.
3. Remove the PCV hose and oil filler cap. Set them aside.
4. Disconnect the throttle linkage cable and speed control cable, if equipped.

5. Remove ignition wires and wire separator.
6. If removing 3.0L engine cover . the following additional parts will need to be removed;
   a. Fuel injector harness stand–offs.
   b. Throttle body.
   c. Loosen lower EGR tube.
7. Remove either the nuts or bolts securing the cover to the top of the engine.
8. Lift the cover(s) off of the cylinder head. You may need to tap on the cover with a plastic tipped hammer to free the cover from the gasket.
9. Completely clean the engine mounting surface as well as the cover. Allow to dry before installing gasket.

## To install:

10. Coat the rocker arm gasket surface and the UP side of the gasket with a quality Silicone sealant or oil resistance sealer F1AZ–19562–A or equivalent.

➡ Install gasket within five minutes to prevent sealer from shrinking

11. Install the rocker arm cover by using a straight down approach.
12. If using original bolts to secure cover, apply small amount of Loctite® or equivalent to bolts before tightening. Tighten each bolt to 71–106 inch lbs. (8–12 Nm).

13. If using nuts to secure the covers( 3.0L engine) refer to diagram of order of tightening the nuts. Tighten each nut, in order, 8–10 ft. lbs. (10–14 Nm).

14. Connect throttle body, fuel injector harness or EGR tube, if equipped.

15. Connect throttle linkage cable and speed control cable, if equipped.

16. Connect the PCV hose and install the oil filler cap.

17. Reconnect the negative battery cable,

18. Start the engine and check for leaks.

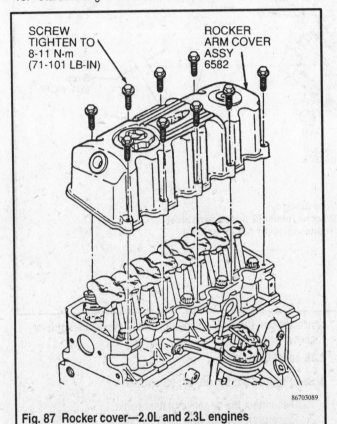

SCREW TIGHTEN TO 8-11 N·m (71-101 LB-IN)

ROCKER ARM COVER ASSY 6582

Fig. 87 Rocker cover—2.0L and 2.3L engines

Fig. 88 Loosen and remove the rocker arm retaining bolts

Fig. 89 Remove the rocker arm cover

Fig. 90 Remove any old gasket material. Some are easier than others

Fig. 91 Clean the cylinder head surface free of any remaining gasket material. Try to keep any from falling into the engine cavity

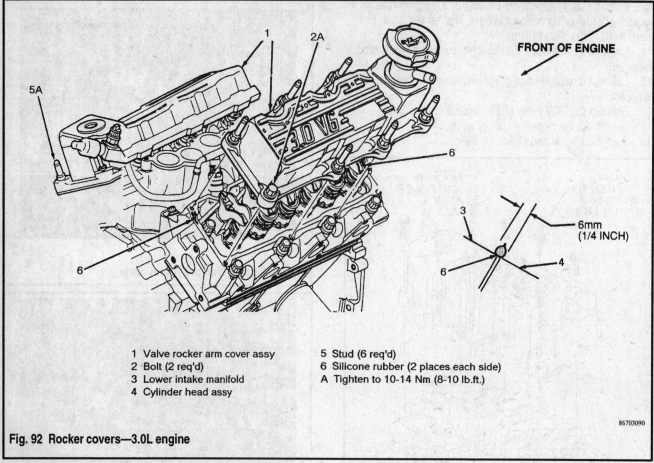

1 Valve rocker arm cover assy
2 Bolt (2 req'd)
3 Lower intake manifold
4 Cylinder head assy

5 Stud (6 req'd)
6 Silicone rubber (2 places each side)
A Tighten to 10-14 Nm (8-10 lb.ft.)

86703090

**Fig. 92 Rocker covers—3.0L engine**

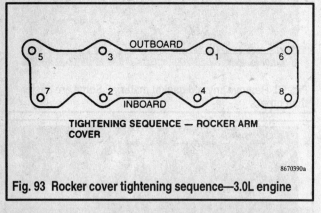

TIGHTENING SEQUENCE — ROCKER ARM
COVER

8670390a

**Fig. 93 Rocker cover tightening sequence—3.0L engine**

## Rocker Arms/Shafts

### REMOVAL & INSTALLATION

#### 2.0L Engine

The 2.0L engine is equipped with the camshaft mounted on top of the valves and springs. Because of this design characteristic, the 2.0L engine does not have rocker arms or rocker shafts.

#### 2.3L and 3.0L Engine

▶ **See Figures 94, 95, 96, 97, 98 and 99**

1. Disconnect the negative battery cable.
2. Place protective covers on the fenders.
3. Remove the rocker arm (valve) cover according to the above procedure.
4. Loosen and remove the rocker arm bolt, fulcrum and rocker arm. Keep all parts in order so they can be reinstalled to their original position.
5. Clean all parts thoroughly. Check that all oil passages are open.

**To install:**

6. Before installation, coat the valve tips, rocker arm and fulcrum contact areas with Lubriplate® or equivalent prelube.
7. Install the rocker arm, fulcrum and rocker arm bolt. Tighten fulcrum bolt to 20–26 ft. lbs. (26–38 Nm).
8. Install the rocker arm (valve) cover.
9. Connect the negative battery cable, start the engine and check for leaks.

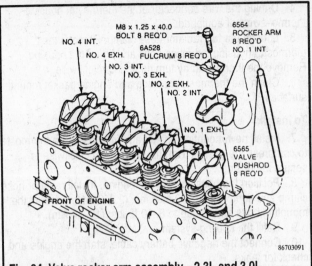

Fig. 94 Valve rocker arm assembly—2.3L and 3.0L engines

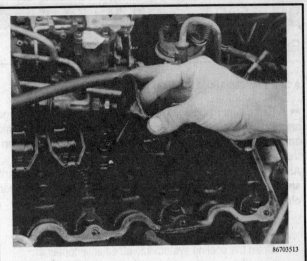

Fig. 97 With the bolts loosened, remove the rocker arm and inspect carefully

Fig. 95 Loosen and remove the rocker cover retaining bolts

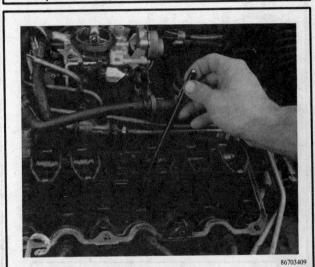

Fig. 98 Remove the rocker arm shaft

Fig. 96 Remove the retaining bolt from the rocker arm

Fig. 99 Tighten the retaining bolts

## Thermostat

### REMOVAL & INSTALLATION

▶ **See Figures 100, 101, 102, 103, 104 and 105**

➡ **When draining coolant, keep in mind that cats and dogs are attracted to ethylene glycol antifreeze, and could drink any that is left in an uncovered container or in puddles on the ground. This will prove fatal in sufficient quantity. Always drain the coolant into a sealable container. Coolant should be reused unless it is contaminated or several years old.**

1. Disconnect the negative battery cable.
2. Place protective covers on the front fenders.
3. Drain the cooling system into a sealable container.

4. Unplug the wire connector at the thermostat housing thermo–switch if equipped.
5. Loosen the top radiator hose clamp. Remove the thermostat housing mounting bolts and lift up the housing. Remove the thermostat by turning counterclockwise.
6. Clean the thermostat housing and engine gasket mounting surfaces.

**To install:**

7. Install new mounting gasket and fully insert the thermostat to compress the gasket. Turn the thermostat clockwise to secure in housing.
8. Position the housing onto the engine. Install radiator hose clamp and tighten to 20–30 inch lbs. (2.3–3.4 Nm). Install the mounting bolts and torque to 8–10 ft. lbs. (10–14 Nm).
9. Refill the cooling system.
10. Connect the negative battery cable, start the engine and check for leaks.

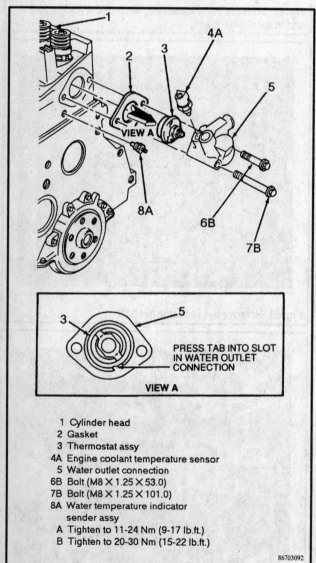

1 Cylinder head
2 Gasket
3 Thermostat assy
4A Engine coolant temperature sensor
5 Water outlet connection
6B Bolt (M8 × 1.25 × 53.0)
7B Bolt (M8 × 1.25 × 101.0)
8A Water temperature indicator
  sender assy
A Tighten to 11-24 Nm (9-17 lb.ft.)
B Tighten to 20-30 Nm (15-22 lb.ft.)

86703092

**Fig. 100 Engine thermostat—2.0L engine**

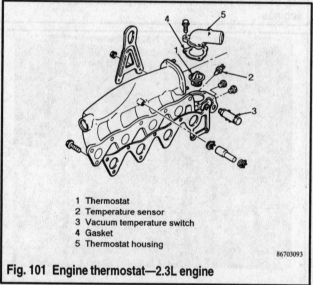

1 Thermostat
2 Temperature sensor
3 Vacuum temperature switch
4 Gasket
5 Thermostat housing

86703093

**Fig. 101 Engine thermostat—2.3L engine**

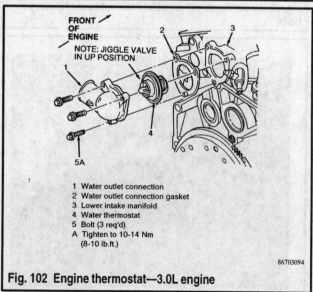

1 Water outlet connection
2 Water outlet connection gasket
3 Lower intake manifold
4 Water thermostat
5 Bolt (3 req'd)
A Tighten to 10-14 Nm
  (8-10 lb.ft.)

86703094

**Fig. 102 Engine thermostat—3.0L engine**

**Fig. 103 Remove the harness from the housing**

**Fig. 104 With the retaining bolts removed, take the thermostat and housing out of the engine compartment, and place on a clean surface**

**Fig. 105 Remove the thermostat from the housing. Remember the direction in which it was installed**

## Intake Manifold

### REMOVAL & INSTALLATION

➡ When removing the intake manifold, the cooling system must be drained. When draining coolant, keep in mind that cats and dogs are attracted to ethylene glycol antifreeze, and could drink any that is left in an uncovered container or in puddles on the ground. This will prove fatal in sufficient quantity. Always drain the coolant into a sealable container. Coolant should be reused unless it is contaminated or several years old.

**2.0L Engine**

➡ **See Figures 106, 107, 108, 109 and 110**

1. Disconnect the negative battery cable
2. Disconnect air inlet duct from the intake manifold and install the protective cap (T84P–9394–A or equivalent) in the intake manifold.
3. Unplug the glow plug resister electrical connection.
4. Remove the breather hose.
5. Drain the cooling system into a sealable container.
6. Disconnect the upper radiator hose at the thermostat housing as well as any other hoses attached to the housing.
7. Disconnect the wire connection at the temperature sensors.
8. Unfasten the attachment bolts securing the intake manifold to the cylinder head and remove the manifold.

**To install:**

9. Clean the intake manifold and cylinder head gasket mating surfaces. Install the intake manifold using a new gasket and torque the attachment bolts to 12–16 ft. lbs. (16–23 Nm).
10. Connect temperature sensor connectors.
11. Install lower coolant hose to the thermostat housing, as well as any other hose attached to the housing. Attach the upper radiator hose to this piece. Fasten housing to engine using a new gasket and torquing the hardware to 5–7 ft. lbs. (7–10 Nm).
12. Connect the breather hose.
13. Plug in the glow plug resister electrical connection.
14. Remove intake manifold protective cap and install air duct.
15. Fill and bleed the cooling system.
16. Connect negative battery cable. Start vehicle and check for leaks.

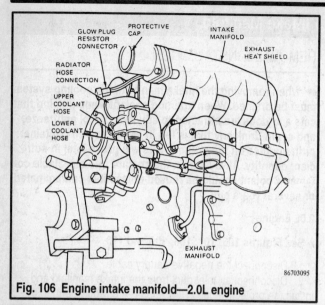

Fig. 106 Engine intake manifold—2.0L engine

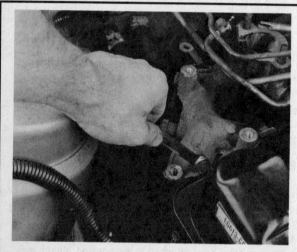

Fig. 107 Remove the upper manifold bolts

Fig. 108 Remove the lower attaching bolts

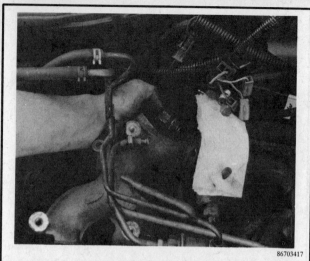

Fig. 109 Loosen and remove the breather line

Fig. 110 With all the hardware unfastened, remove the manifold from the engine

**2.3L Engine**

◆ See Figures 107, 108, 109, 110 and 111

1. Disconnect the negative battery cable.
2. Place protective covers on each fender.
3. Drain the cooling system into a suitable sealable container.
4. Remove air cleaner assembly and heat stove tube at the heat shield.
5. Remove the accelerator cable and any necessary throttle linkage.
6. Disconnect the speed control cable, if equipped.
7. Remove required vacuum lines and any electrical connectors
8. Disconnect fuel supply and fuel return lines at the rubber connector. Be careful because the fuel system is under pressure. Place a rag over the fuel line when disconnecting the lines.
9. Unfasten the EGR tube at the EGR valve.

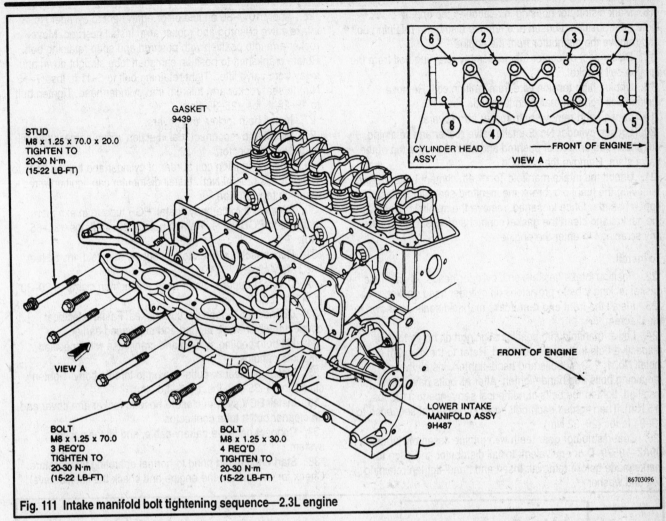

**Fig. 111 Intake manifold bolt tightening sequence—2.3L engine**

STUD
M8 x 1.25 x 70.0 x 20.0
TIGHTEN TO
20-30 N·m
(15-22 LB-FT)

GASKET
9439

BOLT
M8 x 1.25 x 70.0
3 REQ'D
TIGHTEN TO
20-30 N·m
(15-22 LB-FT)

BOLT
M8 x 1.25 x 30.0
4 REQ'D
TIGHTEN TO
20-30 N·m
(15-22 LB-FT)

VIEW A

FRONT OF ENGINE

LOWER INTAKE
MANIFOLD ASSY
9H487

CYLINDER HEAD
ASSY

FRONT OF ENGINE

VIEW A

86703096

10. Unbolt the intake manifold attachment bolts and remove the manifold. Remove the gasket and clean the gasket contact surfaces.

**To install:**

11. Install intake manifold with gasket and retaining bolts. Refer to the diagram for the correct tightening order. Torque the retaining bolts to 15–22 ft. lbs. (20–30 Nm).

12. Plug in the oxygen sensor wire to the wire connector.

13. Connect the EGR tube to EGR valve.

14. Connect the fuel supply and return lines.

15. Install vacuum lines.

16. Install the air cleaner assembly and heat stove tubing.

17. Install accelerator cable and speed control cable, if equipped.

18. Connect negative battery cable, and fill the cooling system.

19. Start engine and bring to normal operating temperature. Check for leaks. Stop the engine and check the coolant level.

### 3.0L Engine

▶ **See Figures 107, 108, 109, 110, 112 and 113**

1. Disconnect the negative battery cable.

2. Place protective covers on each fender.

3. Drain the cooling system into a suitable sealable container.

4. Remove PCV system closure hose from rocker arm cover and air cleaner outlet tube.

5. Remove air cleaner outlet tube from throttle body and air cleaner.

6. Carefully relieve fuel system pressure at fuel supply manifold schrader valve.

7. Remove fuel line safety clips and disconnect the fuel lines.

8. Identify and tag vacuum lines. After being marked unfasten and move out of position.

9. Identify and tag any wire connector around the manifold. this includes the Throttle Position (TP) sensor, distributor and ignition coil connectors and coolant temperature connectors.

10. Unfasten upper radiator hose from thermostat housing.

11. Loosen EGR tube retaining nuts and remove EGR valve to exhaust manifold tube.

12. Remove throttle body.

13. Disconnect the wire harness for the fuel injectors. Remove them from the rocker arm cover studs as well as from each injector.

14. Remove heater hose.

15. Identify, mark and disconnect the spark plug wires.

16. Mark distributor housing in relation to the engine block. Note rotor position. Loosen and remove distributor retaining bolt and remove the distributor from the engine.

17. Disconnect oil cooler tube assembly retaining bolt from the ignition coil bracket.

18. Unplug high tension wire from ignition coil. Remove ignition coil from left rear cylinder head.

19. Loosen and remove both rocker arm covers.

20. Loosen cylinder No. 3 intake valve rocker arm retaining nut and rotate arm off of pushrod and away from the top of the valve stem. Remove the pushrod.

21. Unbolt the intake manifold Torx® attachment bolts. Before removing the manifold, break the manifold seal with a plastic tipped hammer Once loosened, remove the manifold. Remove the gasket and clean the gasket contact surfaces. Do not allow any scrapings to enter the engine.

**To install:**

22. Position intake gaskets onto cylinder heads. Align intake gasket locking tabs to provisions on cylinder head gasket.

23. Install the front and rear intake manifold seals as shown in the diagram.

24. Lower manifold into position aligning bolt holes to their respective hole in the cylinder head. Refer to the diagram and install No. 1, 2, 3, 4, bolts and hand–tighten. Install the remaining bolts and hand–tighten. After all bolts have been installed, tighten the bolts in numerical sequence to 11 ft. lbs. (15 Nm). Then tighten each bolt again in numerical sequence to 19–24 ft. lbs (26–32 Nm).

25. Coat distributor gear teeth with engine assembly lubricant D9AZ–19579–D or equivalent. Install distributor and align to marks made before removal. Insert and hand–tighten retaining bolt and washer.

26. Apply 10W–30 engine oil or equivalent to cylinder No. 3 intake valve pushrod and rocker arm. Install pushrod. Move rocker arm into position with pushrod and snug retaining bolt. Rotate crankshaft to position camshaft lobe straight down and away from valve lifter. Tight retaining bolt to 5–11 ft. lbs. (7–15 Nm) to seat rocker arm fulcrum into cylinder head. Tighten bolt to 19–28 ft. lbs. (26–38 Nm) .

27. Install both rocker arm covers.

28. Install and reconnect fuel injection wiring harness to each respective connector.

29. Position ignition coil at rear of cylinder and tighten bolts to 15–22 ft. lbs (20–30 Nm). Install distributor cap, ignition wires and high tension wire.

30. Connect throttle body. Install EGR tube from exhaust manifold to EGR valve. Tighten nuts to 26–48 ft. lbs. (35–65 Nm).

31. Reconnect fuel lines to fuel supply manifold. Install fuel line safety clips.

32. Connect upper radiator hose and tighten clamp to 20–30 inch lbs. (2.3–3.4 Nm).

33. Connect all tagged vacuum hoses. Fasten electrical connector which were tagged and unplugged earlier.

34. Fill both cooling system and crankcase with specified amounts of fluids.

35. Install air cleaner outlet tubing to throttle body. Tighten clamp to 24–35 inch lbs. ( 2.7–4.0 Nm).

36. Install PCV system closure hose to rocker arm cover and air cleaner outlet tube connector.

37. Connect negative battery cable, and fill the cooling system.

38. Start engine and bring to normal operating temperature. Check for leaks. Stop the engine and check the coolant level.

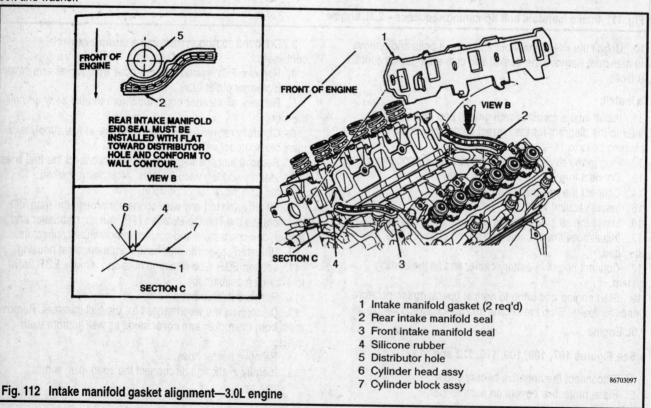

REAR INTAKE MANIFOLD END SEAL MUST BE INSTALLED WITH FLAT TOWARD DISTRIBUTOR HOLE AND CONFORM TO WALL CONTOUR.

VIEW B

SECTION C

FRONT OF ENGINE

1 Intake manifold gasket (2 req'd)
2 Rear intake manifold seal
3 Front intake manifold seal
4 Silicone rubber
5 Distributor hole
6 Cylinder head assy
7 Cylinder block assy

**Fig. 112  Intake manifold gasket alignment—3.0L engine**

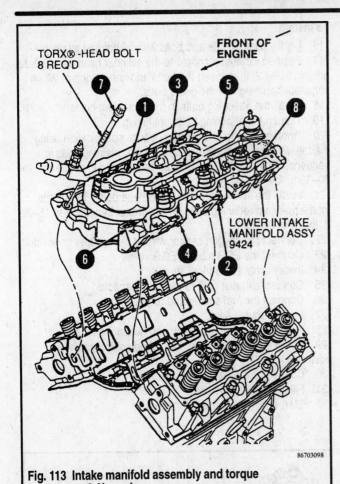

**Fig. 113 Intake manifold assembly and torque sequence—3.0L engine**

- TORX® -HEAD BOLT 8 REQ'D
- FRONT OF ENGINE
- LOWER INTAKE MANIFOLD ASSY 9424

86703098

## Exhaust Manifold

### REMOVAL & INSTALLATION

#### 2.0L Engine

◆ See Figure 114

1. Disconnect the negative battery cable.
2. Place protective covers on each fender.
3. Remove nuts attaching the muffler inlet pipe to the exhaust manifold.
4. Remove the bolts holding the heat shield to the exhaust manifold.
5. Unfasten the nuts securing the exhaust manifold to the cylinder head section of the engine.
6. Carefully remove the exhaust manifold.
7. Clean the surfaces of the exhaust manifold and cylinder head section where the manifold attaches to the engine.

#### To install:

8. Lightly coat all nuts and bolts with oil before installing.
9. Install exhaust manifold using a new gasket. Attach nuts and tighten to 16–20 ft. lbs. (22–27 Nm).
10. Install heat shield to exhaust manifold and tighten bolts to 12–16 ft. lbs. (16–23 Nm).
11. Connect muffler inlet pipe to the exhaust manifold and torque nuts to 25–35 ft. lbs. (34–47 Nm).
12. Run engine and check for exhaust leaks. Adjust if necessary.

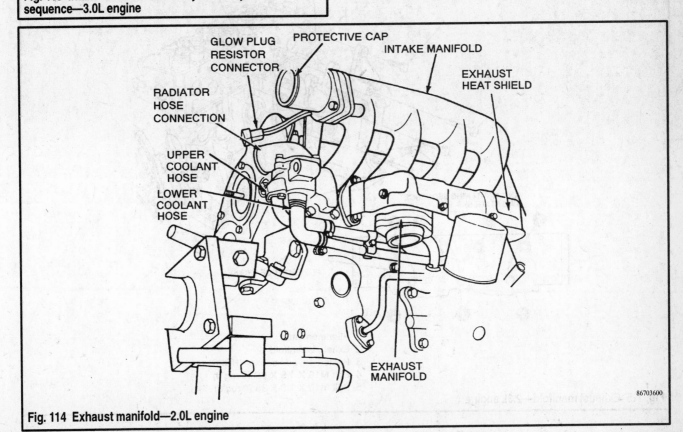

- GLOW PLUG RESISTOR CONNECTOR
- PROTECTIVE CAP
- INTAKE MANIFOLD
- EXHAUST HEAT SHIELD
- RADIATOR HOSE CONNECTION
- UPPER COOLANT HOSE
- LOWER COOLANT HOSE
- EXHAUST MANIFOLD

86703600

**Fig. 114 Exhaust manifold—2.0L engine**

## 2.3L Engine

▶ See Figure 115

➥ When draining coolant, keep in mind that cats and dogs to ethylene glycol antifreeze, and could drink any that is left in an uncovered container or in puddles on the ground. This will prove fatal in sufficient quantity. Always drain the coolant into a sealable container. Coolant should be reused unless it is contaminated or several years old.

1. Disconnect the negative battery cable.
2. Place protective covers on each fender.
3. Drain the cooling system.
4. Remove the accelerator cable and position to the si
5. Remove air cleaner assembly and heat stove tube at heat shield
6. Identify, tag and disconnect all necessary vacuum line.
7. Disconnect the exhaust pipe–to–exhaust manifold retaining nut.
8. Remove exhaust manifold heat shield.
9. Disconnect the oxygen sensor wire at the connector
10. Disconnect the throttle linkage.
11. Disconnect the speed control cable, if equipped.
12. Disconnect the fuel supply and return lines at the rubber connect.
13. Disconnect EGR tube from the EGR valve.
14. Remove the intake manifold.
15. Remove the exhaust manifold retaining nuts. Remove the exhaust manifold from the vehicle.

**To install:**

16. Lightly coat all nuts and bolts with oil before installing.
17. Position exhaust manifold to the cylinder head using guide bolts in holes 2, then insert the bolts and hand–tighten. When complete hand–tighten the guide bolts.
18. Install the attaching bolts in the remaining holes.
19. Tighten the attaching bolts until snug.
20. Tighten all exhaust manifold bolts to specification using the following tightening procedure: torque retaining bolts in sequence to 5–7 ft. lbs. (7–10 Nm) then tighten in sequence, to 20–30 ft. lbs. (27–41 Nm).
21. Install the intake manifold gasket and bolts. Torque the intake manifold retaining bolts, in the proper sequence to 15–22 ft. lbs. (20–30 Nm).
22. Connect the oxygen sensor wire at their proper connector.
23. Connect the EGR tube to EGR valve.
24. Install exhaust manifold studs.
25. Connect exhaust pipe to exhaust manifold
26. Connect the fuel supply and return lines.
27. Install vacuum lines.
28. Install air cleaner assembly and heatstove tube.
29. Install accelerator cable and speed control cable, if equipped.
30. Connect the negative battery cable.
31. Fill the cooling system.
32. Start engine and check for leaks.

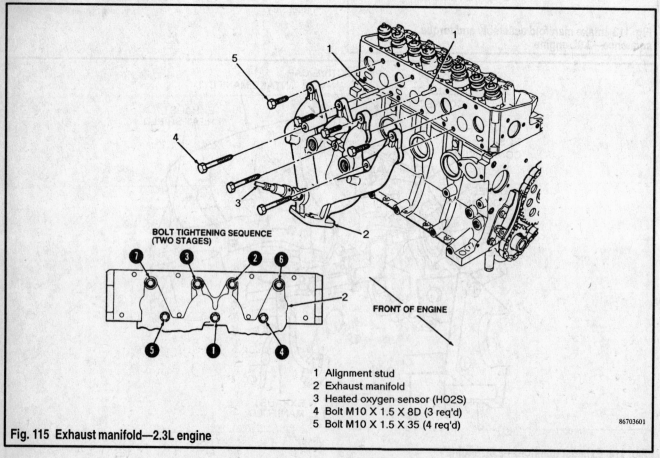

BOLT TIGHTENING SEQUENCE
(TWO STAGES)

FRONT OF ENGINE

1 Alignment stud
2 Exhaust manifold
3 Heated oxygen sensor (HO2S)
4 Bolt M10 X 1.5 X 8D (3 req'd)
5 Bolt M10 X 1.5 X 35 (4 req'd)

86703601

**Fig. 115 Exhaust manifold—2.3L engine**

**3.0L Engine**

▶ **See Figure 116**

➡ **Because of the design of the 3.0L engine, there are 2 exhaust manifolds.**

1. Disconnect the negative battery cable.
2. Place protective covers on each fender.
3. Drain the cooling system.
4. Loosen and remove the nuts securing the shields to the manifolds.
5. Carefully rotate or remove the dipstick tube away from the left exhaust manifold.
6. Disconnect the pressure feedback sender hose connection to the EGR valve attached the exhaust manifold tube on the right exhaust manifold.
7. Loosen and remove the EGR tube nuts at the exhaust manifold and EGR valve, and remove the tube on the right manifold.
8. Disconnect the water pump assembly if removing the right manifold.
9. Remove the exhaust inlet pipe retaining nuts on one or both manifolds.

10. Remove the exhaust manifold retaining bolts/studs. Carefully remove the manifold.
11. Clean the manifold and cylinder head surface.

**To install:**

12. Lightly coat all nuts and bolts with oil before installing.
13. Position exhaust manifold to cylinder head surface, and install retaining bolts/studs. Torque bolts/nuts to 15–22 ft. lbs. (20–30 Nm).
14. Install exhaust manifold inlet pipe and tighten attaching nuts to 25–34 ft. lbs. (34–46 Nm).
15. Connect water pump housing, if removed.
16. Install and tighten EGR tube, if removed.
17. Secure pressure feedback sender connector if removed.
18. Rotate or install oil dipstick tube, if removed.
19. Install the heat shield to the exhaust manifold and torque to 12–15 ft. lbs. (16–20 Nm).
20. Fill cooling system.
21. Connect negative battery cable.
22. Run engine and check for exhaust leaks. Adjust if necessary.

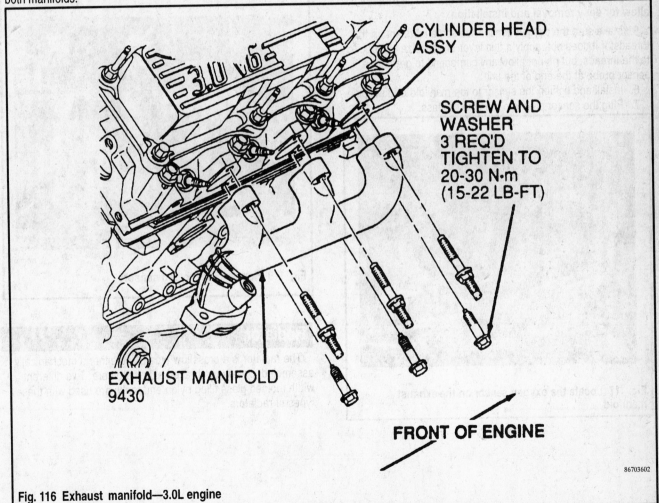

CYLINDER HEAD ASSY

SCREW AND WASHER 3 REQ'D TIGHTEN TO 20-30 N·m (15-22 LB-FT)

EXHAUST MANIFOLD 9430

FRONT OF ENGINE

86703602

**Fig. 116 Exhaust manifold—3.0L engine**

## Oxygen Sensor

### REMOVAL & INSTALLATION

⊳ See Figures 117, 118 and 119

### ✳✳CAUTION

**Make sure that the vehicle has not been driven for at least 20 minutes to allow the manifold to cool down. Otherwise the manifold could burn a hand while attempting to remove the sensor.**

1. Locate the oxygen sensor in the exhaust manifold, or downpipe.
2. Unplug the harness for the sensor.
3. Using a flare wrench or a socket made for removing oxygen sensors, loosen the oxygen sensor.
4. Remove the oxygen sensor.

**To install:**

➥ Most oxygen sensors have a lubricant on the threads to allow for easy removal and installation.

5. Make sure the oxygen sensor has some lubricant on the threads. If it does not, apply a thin layer of antiseize compound to the threads, but do not allow any compound to get on the sensor probe at the end of the unit.
6. Install and tighten the sensor to the manifold or downpipe.
7. Plug the sensor plug into the wire harness.

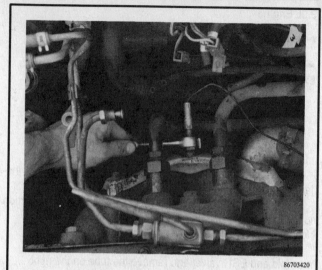

Fig. 118 With the plug already unfastened, loosen the sensor

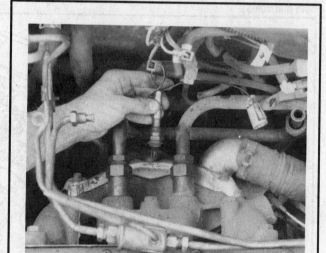

Fig. 119 Remove the oxygen sensor

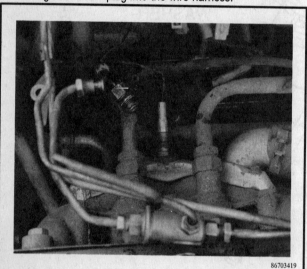

Fig. 117 Locate the oxygen sensor on the exhaust manifold

## Radiator

The radiator is a crossflow type using either a mechanically assembled, or vacuum brazed aluminum core. Two different width molded glass filled nylon end tanks are used with these types of radiators.

The radiator and fan shroud mounting brackets are an integral part of the unit, EXCEPT on the 2,0L engine, and those vehicles equipped with factory installed air conditioning. These vehicles do not have the shroud lower mounting tab on the outlet tank.

## REMOVAL & INSTALLATION

▶ See Figures 120, 121, 122, 123, 124, 125, 126, 127, 128 and 129

➡ When draining coolant, keep in mind that cats and dogs are attracted to ethylene glycol antifreeze, and could drink any left in an uncovered container or in puddles on the ground. This will prove fatal in sufficient quantity. Always drain the coolant into a sealable container. Coolant should be reused unless it is contaminated or several years old.

1. Disconnect the negative battery cable.
2. Place protective covers on each fender.
3. Drain the cooling system.
4. If equipped, remove the plastic shield over the radiator.
5. Disconnect the electric cooling fan motor wires and air conditioning discharge line, if equipped.
6. Disconnect the overflow hose from the radiator filler neck.
7. Remove the upper hose from the radiator and engine block.
8. Remove the 2 fasteners retaining the upper end of the fan shroud to the radiator and sight shield.

➡ If equipped with air conditioning, remove the nut and screw retaining the upper end of the fan shroud to the radiator at the cross support and nut and screw at the inlet end of the tank.

9. Remove the fan shroud, by carefully pulling the unit up and out of the vehicle.
10. Remove the 2 nuts retaining the top of the radiator to the radiator support. If the stud loosens, make sure it is tightened before the radiator is installed.
11. Remove the clamp which secure the lower radiator hose to the radiator.
12. Tilt the top of the radiator rearward to allow for clearance with the upper mounting stud and lift the radiator from the vehicle. Make sure the mounts do not stick to the radiator lower mounting brackets.

### To install:

13. Make sure the lower radiator isomounts are installed over the bolts on the radiator support.

14. Position the unit to the radiator support, making sure the radiator lower brackets are positioned correctly on the lower mounts.
15. Position the top of the radiator to the mounting studs on the radiator support and install the 2 retaining nuts. Tighten to 5–7 ft. lbs. (7–9.5 Nm).
16. Connect the radiator lower hose to the engine water pump inlet tube. Install constant tension clamp between alignment marks on the hose.
17. Position the fan shroud to the radiator lower mounting bosses. On vehicles with air conditioning, insert the lower edge of the shroud into the clip at the lower center of the radiator. Install the 2 nuts and bolts retainers in the upper end of the fan shroud. Tighten the nuts to 35–41 inch lbs. (3.9–4.6 Nm). Do not overtighten.
18. Connect the electric cooling fan motor wires to the wire harness.
19. Connect the upper hose to the radiator inlet tank fitting as well as to the engine block, then install the constant tension hose clamp.
20. Connect the overflow hose to the nipple just below the radiator filler neck.
21. Install the air intake tube or sight shield.
22. Connect the negative battery cable.
23. Refill the cooling system. Start the engine and allow to come to normal operating temperature. Check for leaks. Confirm the operation of the electric cooling fan.

86703422

**Fig. 120 Remove the screws securing the shield over the radiator**

Fig. 121 Remove the shield

Fig. 124 Remove the hose from the engine block

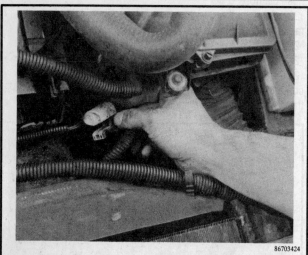

Fig. 122 Disconnect the fan plug from the electric fan on the radiator shroud

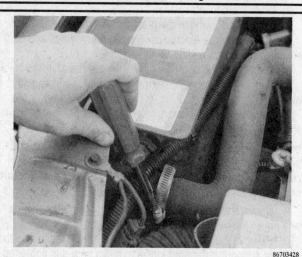

Fig. 125 Remove the hose from the upper position of the radiator

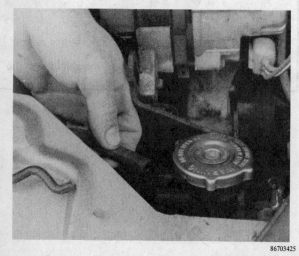

Fig. 123 Remove the overflow tank hose from the radiator

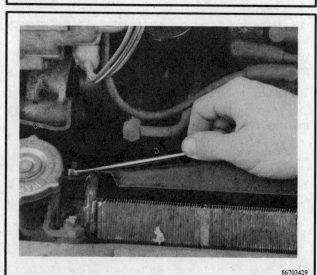

Fig. 126 Remove the fan shroud nuts

**Fig. 127  Carefully lift the fan and shroud out of the engine compartment**

**Fig. 128  Remove the upper radiator retaining bolts**

**Fig. 129  With the lower hardware loosened, and the lower hose disconnected, remove the radiator from the engine compartment**

## Electric Cooling Fan

The electro–drive cooling fan system consists of a fan and electric motor attached to a fan shroud located behind the radiator. The system utilizes a coolant temperature switch which is usually mounted in the thermostat housing. Vehicles that are equipped with air conditioning, have a cooling fan controller and a cooling fan relay for the cooling fan system. On vehicles with a standard heater, the engine cooling fan is powered through the cooling fan relay.

The electro–drive cooling fan is wired to operate only when the ignition switch is in the RUN position. A thermal switch mounted in the thermostat housing activates the fan when the cool ant reaches a specified temperature. When the temperature is approximately 210°F (85°C) the thermal switch closes thus starting the fan.

The electric fan also operates when the air conditioner (if equipped) is turned on. When the temperature drops to between 185–193°F (85–90°C) the thermal switch opens and the fan shuts off.

Since the fan is governed by temperature the engine does not have to be ON for the fan to operate. If any underhood operations must be performed on a warm engine, disconnect the wiring harness to the fan.

### COMPONENT LOCATION

#### Cooling Fan Controller

The cooling fan controller is located either behind the left side of the instrument panel, or mounted on the right hand cowl panel under the dash panel.

#### Cooling Fan Controller Module

The cooling fan control module can be found behind the right side of the dash panel.

#### Cooling Fan Relay

The cooling fan relay is located in the air conditioning cooling fan control module.

### TESTING

1. Make sure the vehicle is correctly filled with coolant.
2. Check the fuse or circuit breaker for power to the cooling fan motor.
3. Remove the connector at the cooling fan motor. Connect a jumper wire and apply battery voltage to the positive terminal of the cooling fan motor.
4. Using an ohmmeter, check for continuity in the cooling fan motor.

➡ **Remove the cooling fan connector at the fan motor before performing continuity checks. Perform continuity check of the motor windings only. The cooling fan control circuit is connected electrically to the Electronic Control Module (ECM) through the cooling fan relay center. Ohmmeter battery voltage must not be applied to the Electronic Control Module (ECM).**

5. Ensure proper continuity of the cooling fan motor ground circuit at the chassis ground connector.

## REMOVAL & INSTALLATION

▶ **See Figures 120, 121, 122, 126 and 127**

1. Disconnect the negative battery cable.
2. Place protective covers on each fender.
3. Drain the cooling system.
4. Unplug the wiring connector from the fan motor. Disconnect the wire loom from the clip on the shroud by pushing down on the lock fingers and pulling the connector from the motor end.
5. Remove the fasteners retaining the fan motor and shroud assembly and remove the unit from the vehicle.
6. Remove the retaining clip from the motor shaft and remove the fan.

➡ **A metal burr may be present on the motor shaft after the retaining clip has been removed. If necessary, remove the burr to facilitate fan removal.**

7. Unbolt and withdraw the fan motor from the shroud.

**To install:**

8. Install the fan motor in the fan shroud. Install the retaining nuts and washers or screws and tighten to 44–66 inch lbs. (5.0–7.5 Nm).
9. Position the fan assembly on the motor shaft and install the retaining clip.
10. Position the fan, motor and shroud as an assembly in the vehicle. Install the retaining nuts or screws and tighten the nuts to 31–41 inch lbs. (3.5–4.6 Nm).
11. Install the fan motor wire loom in the clip provided on the fan shroud. Connect the wiring connector to the fan motor. Be sure the lock fingers on the connector snap firmly into place.
12. Fill the cooling system with antifreeze.
13. Reconnect the battery cable.
14. Check the fan for proper operation. Make sure the coolant level is correct.

# Water Pump

## REMOVAL & INSTALLATION

➡ **When draining coolant, keep in mind that cats and dogs are attracted to ethylene glycol antifreeze, and could drink any that is left in an uncovered container or in puddles on the ground. This will prove fatal in sufficient quantity. Always drain the coolant into a sealable container. Coolant should be reused unless it is contaminated or several years old.**

### 2.0L Engine

▶ **See Figure 130**

1. Disconnect the negative battery cable.
2. Place protective covers on each fender.
3. Drain the cooling system.
4. Remove front timing belt upper cover.
5. Loosen and remove the front timing belt.
6. Disconnect the lower radiator and heater hoses from the water pump.
7. Remove the coolant tube from the thermostat housing.
8. Unfasten the 3 bolts attaching the water pump to the crankcase, and remove the water pump.
9. Clean any remaining gasket material that may remain on the engine surface, or thermostat housing.

**To install:**

10. Install the water pump using a new gasket. Tighten bolts to 23–34 ft. lbs. (32–47 Nm).
11. Connect the coolant tube from the thermostat housing to the water pump, using a new gasket. Torque the bolts to 5–7 ft. lbs. (7–10 Nm).
12. Fasten the heater and lower radiator hoses to the water pump unit.

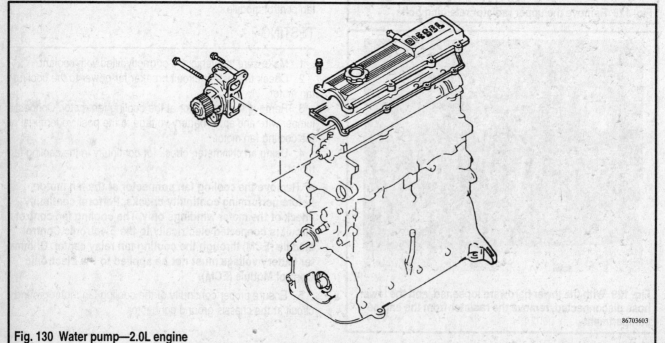

**Fig. 130 Water pump—2.0L engine**

86703603

13. Fill the vehicle cooling system.

14. Run engine and check for coolant leaks. When engine is cool, check coolant level. Add if necessary.

15. Install front timing belt upper cover.

### 2.3L and 3.0L Engine

▶ **See Figures 131 and 132**

1. Disconnect the negative battery cable.
2. Place protective covers on each fender.
3. Drain the cooling system.
4. If equipped with an air pump, remove it as follows:

   d. Loosen thermactor pump adjusting bolt and remove belt.

   e. Remove thermactor pump hose clamp located below the thermactor pump.

   f. Remove the thermactor pump bracket bolts.

   g. Remove thermactor pump and bracket as an assembly.

5. Loosen the water pump idler pulley and remove the belt from the water pump pulley.
6. Disconnect the heater hose at the water pump or the water pump inlet tube. Disconnect the water pump inlet tube, if equipped.
7. Clean any remaining gasket material that may remain on the engine surface.

**To install:**

8. Coat the new gasket on both sides with a water resistant sealer and position on the cylinder block.
9. Install the water pump retaining bolts and tighten to 15–22 ft. lbs. (20–30 Nm).
10. Connect the water pump inlet tube, if equipped.
11. Connect the heater hose.
12. Install water pump belt on the pulley and adjust the tension. Install thermactor pump and bracket, if equipped.
13. Connect the negative battery cable.

14. Fill the cooling system. Operate the engine until normal operating temperature is reached. Check for leaks and recheck the coolant level.

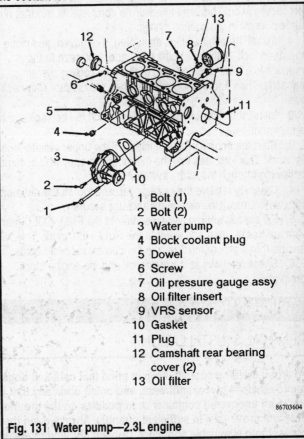

| | |
|---|---|
| 1 | Bolt (1) |
| 2 | Bolt (2) |
| 3 | Water pump |
| 4 | Block coolant plug |
| 5 | Dowel |
| 6 | Screw |
| 7 | Oil pressure gauge assy |
| 8 | Oil filter insert |
| 9 | VRS sensor |
| 10 | Gasket |
| 11 | Plug |
| 12 | Camshaft rear bearing cover (2) |
| 13 | Oil filter |

86703604

**Fig. 131 Water pump—2.3L engine**

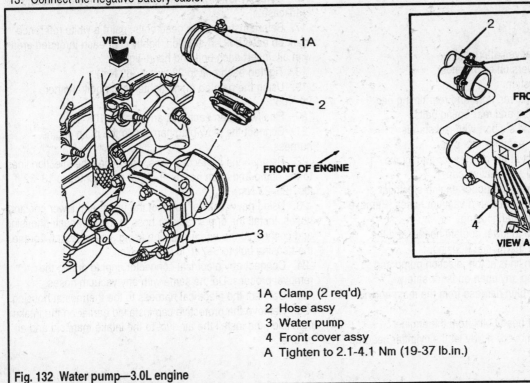

1A Clamp (2 req'd)
2 Hose assy
3 Water pump
4 Front cover assy
A Tighten to 2.1-4.1 Nm (19-37 lb.in.)

86703605

**Fig. 132 Water pump—3.0L engine**

## COOLING SYSTEM BLEEDING

When the entire cooling system is drained, the following procedure should be used to ensure a complete fill and that no air is present in the cooling system.

1. Install the engine block drain plug, if removed, and close the draincock. With the engine OFF, add antifreeze to the radiator to a level of 50 percent of the total cooling system capacity. Then add water until it reaches the radiator filler neck seat.

2. Install the radiator cap to the first notch to keep spillage to a minimum.

3. Start the engine and let it idle until the upper radiator hose is warm. This indicates that the thermostat is open and coolant is flowing through the entire system.

4. Carefully remove the radiator cap and top off the radiator with water. Install the cap on the radiator securely.

5. Fill the coolant recovery reservoir to the FULL COLD mark with antifreeze, then add water to the FULL HOT mark. This will ensure that a proper mixture is in the coolant recovery bottle.

6. Check for leaks at the draincock and the engine block drain plug.

## Cylinder Head

### REMOVAL & INSTALLATION

➡ When draining coolant, keep in mind that cats and dogs are to ethylene glycol antifreeze, and could drink any that is left in an uncovered container or in puddles on the ground. This will prove fatal in sufficient quantity. Always drain the coolant into a sealable container. Coolant should be reused unless it is contaminated or several years old.

#### 2.0L Engine

♦ See Figure 133

1. Disconnect the negative battery cable.
2. Place protective covers on each fender.
3. Drain the cooling system.
4. Remove rocker arm cover, front and rear timing belt covers, as well as both front and rear timing belts.
5. Raise the vehicle, and support with jackstands.
6. Disconnect exhaust manifold inlet pipe.
7. Remove air inlet duct at the air cleaner and intake manifold. For safety, install a protective cap.
8. Identify, tag and unplug any upper engine electrical connections as well as any associated vacuum hoses. Remove the connector to the thermostat housing.
9. Unfasten the upper and lower coolant hoses, and the upper radiator hose to the thermostat housing.
10. Remove the injection lines at the injection pump and nozzles on the engine. Cap any open ends for safety.
11. Disconnect the glow plug harness from the main engine harness.
12. Remove the cylinder head bolts from the engine.
13. With all the bolts removed, slowly lift the cylinder head up and away from the engine.

➡ Do not lay the cylinder head flat. Damage to spark plugs or gasket surfaces may result.

14. With the head removed, perform the following steps before reinstalling the unit:
   a. Remove each glow plug.
   b. Remove the pre–chamber cups from each cylinder using a brass drift.
   c. Check for cylinder head for flatness. Using a straight edge, place on head. If there is any non–flat areas, the head should be replaced If there are any questions, take the unit to a machine shop for a professional diagnosis.

➡ Because the 2.0L engine is constructed of case hardened metal, this type of cylinder head cannot be resurfaced. Therefore, if there is any warpage in a 2.0L head, the unit must be replaced.

   d. Install pre–chambers in the cylinder head, making sure the locating pins are aligned correctly with the slots provided.
   e. Install the glow plugs and tighten to 11–15 ft. lbs. (15–20 Nm). Connect the remaining glow plug harness to each individual plug and tighten each nut to 5–7 ft. lbs. (7–10 Nm).
   f. Blow out the head bolt threads with compressed air.
   g. Measure each cylinder head bolt. If the measurement is more than 4.51 inches (114.5mm) replace the head bolt.
   h. Rotate the camshaft in the cylinder head until the cam lobe for No. 1 cylinder have BOTH valve closed. Then rotate the crankshaft clockwise until No. 1 piston is halfway up the cylinder bore toward Top Dead Center (TDC). This is to prevent accidental contact between the valves and the piston.

**To install:**

15. Position a new head gasket on the crankcase making sure the cylinder head oil feed hole is not blocked.
16. Carefully lower the cylinder head on to the gasket and crankcase.
17. Before installing the head bolts, paint a white reference mark on each bolt. In addition, lightly coat each threaded area with oil. Insert each bolt and hand–tighten.
18. Tighten each bolt to 22 ft. lbs. (30 Nm).
19. Using the painted mark, tighten each bolt another 90–105°.
20. Finally, tighten each bolt another 90–105°.
21. Connect the glow plug harness to the main engine harness.
22. Remove the protective caps, and install the injection lines to the pump and each nozzle. Tighten the capnuts to 18–22 ft. lbs. (25–29 Nm).
23. Using new gaskets, connect the upper and lower coolant hoses. Install the upper radiator hose to the thermostat housing and connect to the engine section using a new gasket. Torque the housing bolt to 5–7 ft. lbs. (7–10 Nm).
24. Connect any electrical connector unplug during the removal process. Do the same with any vacuum hoses.
25. Connect the electrical harness to the thermostat housing.
26. Remove the protective cap installed earlier on the intake manifold, and install the air duct to the intake manifold and air cleaner.

27. Secure the muffler inlet pipe to the exhaust manifold. Tighten the nuts to 25–35 ft. lbs (34–47 Nm).

28. Lower vehicle to ground.

29. Install and adjust the front and rear timing belts.

30. Connect the front and rear timing belt covers. Tighten bolts to 5–7 ft. lbs. (7–10 Nm).

31. Check and adjust the valves, if necessary. Install rocker arm cover and tighten bolts to 5–7 ft. lbs. (7–10 Nm).

32. Fill cooling system with antifreeze.

33. Connect battery ground.

34. Start engine and check for leaks or noises. Stop vehicle and check fluid levels.

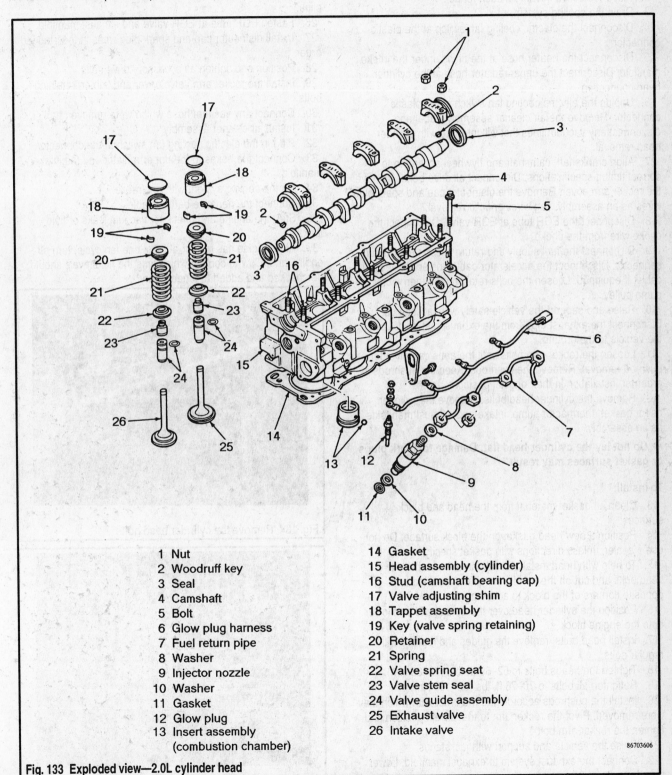

| | |
|---|---|
| 1 Nut | 14 Gasket |
| 2 Woodruff key | 15 Head assembly (cylinder) |
| 3 Seal | 16 Stud (camshaft bearing cap) |
| 4 Camshaft | 17 Valve adjusting shim |
| 5 Bolt | 18 Tappet assembly |
| 6 Glow plug harness | 19 Key (valve spring retaining) |
| 7 Fuel return pipe | 20 Retainer |
| 8 Washer | 21 Spring |
| 9 Injector nozzle | 22 Valve spring seat |
| 10 Washer | 23 Valve stem seal |
| 11 Gasket | 24 Valve guide assembly |
| 12 Glow plug | 25 Exhaust valve |
| 13 Insert assembly (combustion chamber) | 26 Intake valve |

**Fig. 133 Exploded view—2.0L cylinder head**

86703606

## 2.3L Engine

### 1984–86 MODELS

♦ See Figures 134, 135 and 136

1. Disconnect the negative battery cable.
2. Place protective covers on each fender.
3. Drain the cooling system.
4. Disconnect the electric cooling fan switch at the plastic connector.
5. Disconnect the heater hose at the fitting under the intake manifold. Disconnect the upper radiator hose at the cylinder head connection.
6. Unplug the electric cooling fan switch at the plastic connector. Remove the air cleaner assembly. Label and disconnect any vacuum lines that will interfere with cylinder head removal.
7. Align crankshaft, camshaft and flywheel according to correct timing specifications. Disconnect all drive belts. Remove the rocker arm cover. Remove the distributor cap and spark plug wires as an assembly. Tag wires prior to removal.
8. Disconnect the EGR tube at EGR valve. Disconnect the choke wire from the choke.
9. Disconnect the fuel supply and return lines at the rubber connector. Disconnect the accelerator cable and speed control cable, if equipped. Loosen the bolts retaining the thermactor pump pulley.
10. Raise and support the vehicle safely with jackstands. Disconnect the exhaust pipe from the exhaust manifold. Lower the vehicle to the ground.
11. Loosen the rocker arm bolts until the arms can pivot for pushrod removal. Remove the pushrods. Keep the pushrods in order for installation in their original positions.
12. Remove the cylinder head bolts. Remove the cylinder head, gasket, thermactor pump, intake and exhaust manifolds as an assembly.

➡ Do not lay the cylinder head flat. Damage to spark plugs or gasket surfaces may result.

**To install:**

13. Clean all gasket material from the head and block surfaces.
14. Position a new head gasket on the block surface. Do not use a sealer, unless directions with gasket specify.
15. To help with head installation alignment, purchase two head bolts and cut off the heads. Install the modified bolts at opposite corners of the block to act as guides.
16. Position the cylinder head over the guide bolts and lower onto the engine block.
17. Install head bolts, remove the guides and replace with regular bolts.
18. Tighten the heads bolts to 52–59 ft. lbs. (70–80 Nm).
19. Retighten all bolts to 70–76 ft. lbs (95–103 Nm).
20. Install the pushrods according to the order with which they were removed. Pivot the rocker arm to the correct position and tighten the rocker arm bolt
21. Raise the vehicle and support with jackstands.
22. Connect the exhaust system to exhaust manifold. Lower vehicle to the ground

23. Check that the crankshaft is aligned correctly in relation to the camshaft. Install front and rear drive belts belt. Check tension.
24. Connect accelerator cable and speed control cable , if equipped.
25. Connect fuel supply and return lines. Instal fuel line safety clips.
26. Fasten EGR tube at EGR valve and exhaust manifold.
27. Install distributor cap and spark plug wires in their tagged order.
28. Position and tighten all accessory drive belts.
29. Install the rocker arm valve cover and tighten retaining bolts.
30. Connect any vacuum hose which were removed earlier.
31. Install air cleaner assembly.
32. Plug in the electric cooling fan switch at the connector.
33. Connect the hoses to the upper radiator and the intake manifold.
34. Fill the cooling system with antifreeze.
35. Connect the negative battery cable.
36. Start the engine and check for vacuum leaks or fluid leaks.
37. After engine has run for at least one fan cycle, turn off engine and allow to cool, at which time the fluid levels should be checked and added to if necessary.

Fig. 134 Remove the cylinder head bolts

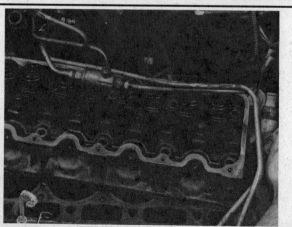

Fig. 135 Lift the head out of the engine

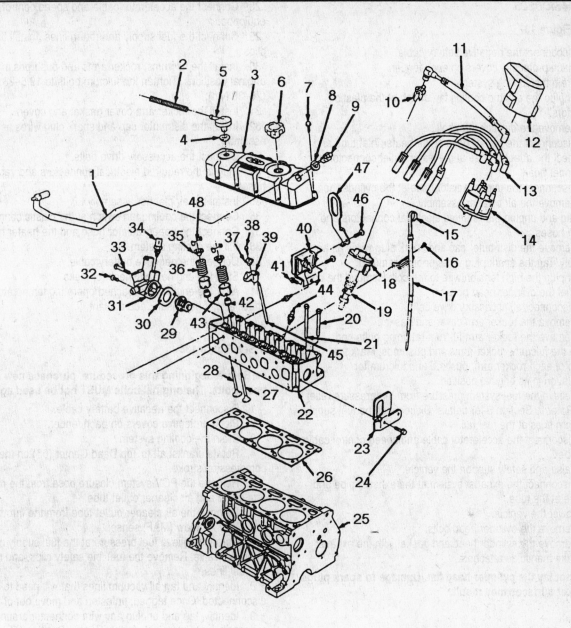

| | | |
|---|---|---|
| 1 Crankcase vent hose | 17 Oil tube indicator | 33 Bolt |
| 2 Hose | 18 Rotor assy | 34 Engine coolant temp. sensor |
| 3 Rocker arm cover | 19 Distributor assy | 35 Valve spring retainer |
| 4 Grommet | 20 Bolt (5) | 36 Valve spring |
| 5 Closure filter | 21 Bolt (5) | 37 Rocker arm fulcrum |
| 6 Oil fill cap | 22 Cylinder head | 38 Bolt (8) |
| 7 Bolt assembly (9) | 23 Lifting eye | 39 Rocker arm |
| 8 Grommet | 24 Bolt (2) | 40 Coil and bracket |
| 9 PCV valve assy | 25 Block assy | 41 Bolt (2) |
| 10 Coil mounting strap | 26 Gasket | 42 Valve seal |
| 11 Coil wire suppressor | 27 Exhaust valve | 43 Valve spring damper |
| 12 Distributor boot | 28 Intake valve | 44 Spark plug |
| 13 Spark plug wire assy | 29 Thermostat | 45 Push rod |
| 14 Distributor cap | 30 Gasket | 46 Bolt |
| 15 Oil level indicator | 31 Water outlet connector | 47 Lifting eye |
| 16 Bolt (1) | 32 Bolt | 48 Key valve |

**Fig. 136 Cylinder head—2.3L engine**

86703607

*1987–94 MODELS*

◆ **See Figure 137**

1. Disconnect the negative battery cable.
2. Place protective covers on each fender.
3. Drain the cooling system.
4. Unplug the electric cooling fan switch at the plastic connectors.
5. Remove the dipstick tube bolt.
6. Disconnect the heater hose at the heater inlet tube and disconnect the adapter hose at the water outlet connector on the cylinder head.
7. Disconnect the upper radiator hose at the cylinder head.
8. Remove the air cleaner assembly.
9. Tag and unplug the required electrical connectors and vacuum hoses.
10. Remove the distributor cap and spark plug wires as an assembly. Tag the spark plug wires prior to removal.
11. Unplug the high tension wire to the coil. Remove the coil bracket at the cylinder head bolt.
12. Disconnect all accessory drive belts.
13. Remove the rocker arm cover and gasket.
14. Remove the rocker arm fulcrum retaining bolts and remove the fulcrum, rocker arms and pushrods. Mark the location of each rocker arm, pushrod and fulcrum for reinstallation in its original position.
15. Relieve the fuel system pressure from the pressure relief valve. Refer to Section 5 for details. Disconnect the fuel supply and return lines at the fuel rail.
16. Disconnect the accelerator cable and speed control cable, if equipped.
17. Raise and safely support the vehicle.
18. Disconnect the exhaust system at the exhaust pipe and the hose at the tube.
19. Lower the vehicle.
20. Remove the cylinder head bolts.
21. Remove the cylinder head and gasket with the exhaust and intake manifolds attached.

➡ **Do not lay the cylinder head flat. Damage to spark plugs or gasket surfaces may result.**

**To install:**

22. Clean all gasket material from the mating surfaces of the cylinder head and engine block.
23. Position the head gasket on the cylinder block.

➡ **Before installing the cylinder head, thread 2 cylinder head alignment studs T84P-6065-A, or use 2 old head bolts with the bolt heads cut off, into the block at opposite corners.**

24. Install the cylinder head over the alignment studs onto the cylinder block. Start and hand–tighten several head bolts until snug. Remove the alignment studs and install the remaining head bolts. Tighten the bolts in 2 steps, first to 52–59 ft. lbs. (70–80 Nm) and then to 70–76 ft. lbs. (95–103 Nm).
25. Raise and safely support the vehicle.
26. Connect the exhaust system at the exhaust pipe and the hose to the metal tube.
27. Lower the vehicle.

28. Connect the accelerator cable and speed control cable, if equipped.
29. Connect the fuel supply and return lines. Install the safety clips
30. Install the fulcrums, rocker arms and pushrods in their original positions. Tighten the fulcrum bolts to 19.5–26.5 ft. lbs. (26–36 Nm).
31. Install the rocker arm cover gasket and cover.
32. Install the distributor cap and spark plug wires as an assembly.
33. Connect the accessory drive belts.
34. Plug in the required electrical connectors and vacuum hoses.
35. Install the air cleaner assembly.
36. Connect the cooling fan switch at the plastic connector.
37. Connect the upper radiator hose and the heater hose.
38. Fill the cooling system.
39. Connect the negative battery cable.
40. Start the engine and check for leaks.
41. After the engine has reached operating temperature, check and, if necessary, add coolant.

### 3.0L Engine

◆ **See Figure 138**

➡ **Before beginning this procedure, purchase new cylinder head bolts. The original bolts MUST not be used again.**

1. Disconnect the negative battery cable.
2. Place protective covers on each fender.
3. Drain the cooling system.
4. Rotate crankshaft to Top Dead Center (0°) on the compression stroke.
5. Remove the PCV system closure hose from the rocker arm cover and air cleaner outlet tube.
6. Remove the air cleaner outlet tube from the throttle body and Mass Air Flow (MAF) sensor.
7. Carefully relieve fuel pressure at the fuel supply manifold Schrader valve. Remove the fuel line safety clips, and remove the fuel lines.
8. Identify and tag all vacuum lines that will need to be disconnected. Once tagged, unfasten and move out of the way.
9. Identify, tag and unplug any wire connector around the cylinder head. These include the Throttle Position (TP) sensor, idle air control valve, distributor, ignition coil and coolant temperature sending unit electrical connectors.
10. Unfasten the upper radiator hose from the thermostat housing. Remove the heater hose.
11. Loosen the EGR tube retaining nuts and remove EGR valve to exhaust manifold tube.
12. Remove the throttle body.
13. Disconnect the fuel injector wiring harness retaining stand off from the rocker arm cover stud. Carefully unplug the electrical connection to each injector. Once completely unplugged, remove the harness from the engine.
14. Mark and remove each spark plug wire. Mark distributor housing in relation to engine block. Note rotor position in relation to distributor. Remove distributor retaining bolt and washer. Carefully remove distributor.

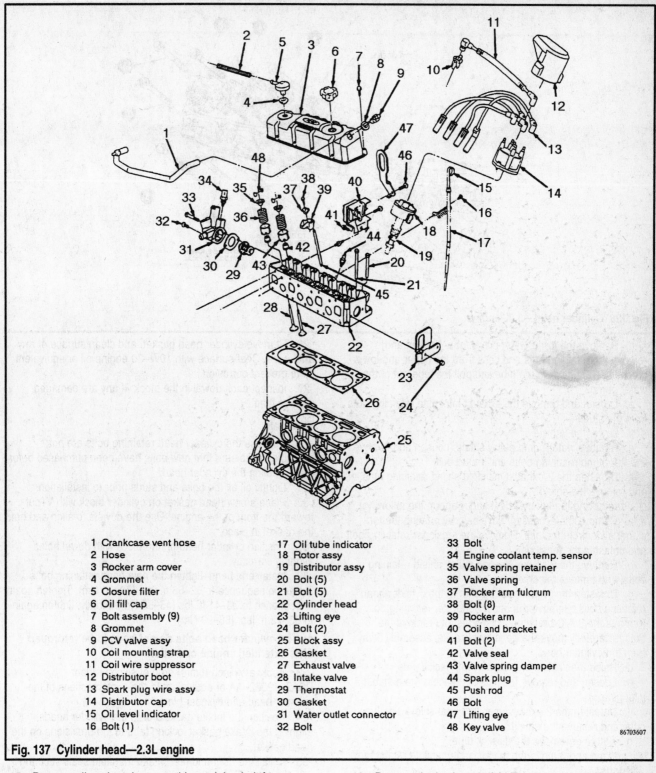

1  Crankcase vent hose
2  Hose
3  Rocker arm cover
4  Grommet
5  Closure filter
6  Oil fill cap
7  Bolt assembly (9)
8  Grommet
9  PCV valve assy
10  Coil mounting strap
11  Coil wire suppressor
12  Distributor boot
13  Spark plug wire assy
14  Distributor cap
15  Oil level indicator
16  Bolt (1)

17  Oil tube indicator
18  Rotor assy
19  Distributor assy
20  Bolt (5)
21  Bolt (5)
22  Cylinder head
23  Lifting eye
24  Bolt (2)
25  Block assy
26  Gasket
27  Exhaust valve
28  Intake valve
29  Thermostat
30  Gasket
31  Water outlet connector
32  Bolt

33  Bolt
34  Engine coolant temp. sensor
35  Valve spring retainer
36  Valve spring
37  Rocker arm fulcrum
38  Bolt (8)
39  Rocker arm
40  Coil and bracket
41  Bolt (2)
42  Valve seal
43  Valve spring damper
44  Spark plug
45  Push rod
46  Bolt
47  Lifting eye
48  Key valve

86703607

**Fig. 137 Cylinder head—2.3L engine**

15. Remove oil cooler tube assembly retaining bolt from ignition coil bracket.

16. Remove ignition coil from rear of left cylinder head.

17. Remove both rocker arm covers.

18. Loosen cylinder No. 3 intake valve rocker arm retaining nut and rotate the arm off of the pushrod and away from the top of the valve stem. When completely rotated, remove the pushrod.

19. Remove the intake manifold Torx® retaining bolts. Before removing intake manifolds, break the seal between the manifold and the cylinder with a plastic tipped hammer.

20. If removing the right cylinder head, perform the following;

a. Remove the accessary drive belt, by moving the drive belt tensioner away from the belt.

b. Remove the water pump to front cover hose .

c. Raise and support the vehicle on jackstands.

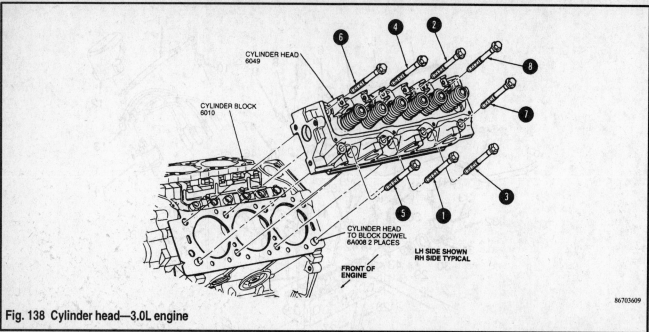

CYLINDER HEAD
6049

CYLINDER BLOCK
6010

CYLINDER HEAD
TO BLOCK DOWEL
6A008 2 PLACES

FRONT OF
ENGINE

LH SIDE SHOWN
RH SIDE TYPICAL

86703609

**Fig. 138 Cylinder head—3.0L engine**

d. Remove the lower water pump tube. Loosen and remove the retaining nuts and bolts from the upper and lower brackets. Gentle grasp the tube and pull the tube out of the water pump.

e. Loosen and remove the exhaust inlet pipe retaining nuts from the studs.

f. Lower the vehicle

g. Remove water pump pulley shield. Loosen and remove 2 water pump retaining bolts and 1 stud bolt.

h. Unfasten the 3 exhaust manifold shield retaining nuts, and remove the shield.

21. If removing the left cylinder head, perform the following:

a. Remove the accessary drive belt, by rotating the tensioner away from the belt. Remove the tensioner retaining bolt and unfasten the tensioner.

b. Remove the 2 power steering pulley shield retaining bolts, and remove the shield.

c. Unfasten the 3 generator bracket to the cylinder head retaining bolts. Remove the upper generator retaining bolt. Remove the 3 A/C brace retaining bolts and remove the brace. Carefully move the generator bracket assembly away from the cylinder head.

d. Raise the vehicle and support with jackstands.

e. Loosen and remove the nuts that secure the exhaust inlet pipe.

f. Unfasten the 2 exhaust manifold heat shield attaching nuts, and remove the shield.

g. Rotate or remove the dipstick tube.

22. Loosen and remove the the exhaust manifold retaining bolts/studs.

23. Loosen the rocker arm fulcrum retaining bolts enough to allow the rocker arm to be lifted off the pushrod and rotated to one side. Remove pushrods and mark location of each.

24. Loosen and remove cylinder head retaining bolts, then discard the bolts as new bolts MUST be used during assembly.

25. Remove cylinder head assembly. If difficult to remove, carefully hit the head with a plastic tipped hammer. Pull the head perpendicular to cylinder block mating surface.

26. Remove cylinder head gasket, and clean surface of any antifreeze. Coat surface with 10W–30 engine oil or equivalent oil to prevent corrosion.

27. Inspect each dowel in the block. If any are damaged, replace them.

**To install:**

28. Because the cylinder head retaining bolts are not reusable, make sure that new bolts have been purchased before reassembling the cylinder head.

29. Lightly oil all the bolts and studs prior to installation.

30. Place a new head gasket on cylinder block with V–cut toward the front of the engine. Use the dowels to align and hold the gasket in place.

31. Position cylinder head on the block with dowel holes aligning correctly.

32. Install and hand–tighten the new head retaining bolts . Torque in sequence to 52–66 ft. lbs. (70–90 Nm). Tighten again in sequence to 33–41 ft. lbs (45–55 Nm). Finally, tighten again to 63–73 ft. lbs. (85–99 Nm).

➡ **The cylinder head bolts do not have to be retorqued after extended engine operation.**

33. Apply a ¼ inch (6mm) drop of silicon rubber D6AZ–19562–AA or equivalent to the 4 intersections of the cylinder head and cylinder block.

34. Position the intake gaskets onto the cylinder heads, aligning the intake gasket locking tabs to the provisions on the head gasket.

35. Install the front and rear intake manifold seals securing with the retaining hardware.

36. Lubricate the removed pushrods and rocker arms with D9AZ–19579–D or equivalent engine lubricant. Install pushrods into position snugging them with the rocker arm. Rotate the crankshaft 360° in a clockwise direction. Tighten the rocker arm retaining bolt to 5–11 ft. lbs. (7–15 Nm). Rotate crankshaft 120° in a clockwise direction. Tighten remainder of the rocker arms to

the above mentioned amounts. Finally tighten all rocker arm bolts to 19–28 ft. lbs (26–38 Nm).

37. Install rocker arm gaskets and covers. Tighten the retaining bolts.

38. If right cylinder head was removed, perform the following;

a. Install exhaust manifold. Tighten bolts and studs to 15–22 ft. lbs. (20–30 Nm). Install the heat shield, and tighten nuts to 12–15 ft. lbs. (16–20 Nm).

b. Install water pump to bracket. Tighten bolts and stud to 15–22 ft. lbs. (20–30 Nm).

c. Install water pump pulley shield, and tighten nut to 7–10 ft. lbs. (9–14 Nm).

d. Connect heater hose to fitting at rear of water pump. Secure firmly.

e. Raise vehicle and support with jackstands.

f. Install water pump inlet tube lubricating water pump end with silicone lubricant COAZ–19553–AA or equivalent. Install retaining nut to water pump inlet tube bracket and stud bolt and tighten to 5 ft. lbs. (7 Nm). Install lower tube bracket retaining bolt and tighten to 71–106 inch lbs. (8–12 Nm).

g. Fasten exhaust inlet pipe and tighten nuts to 25–34 ft. lbs. (34–46 Nm).

h. Lower vehicle.

i. Install water pump to front cover hose. Tighten clamp to 19–37 inch lbs. (2.1–4.1 Nm).

j. Install accessory belt and tension.

39. If left cylinder head was removed, perform the following;

a. Install exhaust manifold and tighten retaining bolts and studs to 15–22 ft. lbs. (20–30 Nm).

b. Rotate or install oil dipstick tube and secure with retaining nut torqued to 11–15 ft. lbs. (15–20 Nm).

c. Install manifold heat shield and tighten to 12–15 ft. lbs. (16–20 Nm).

d. Install exhaust inlet pipe, torquing nuts to 25–34 ft. lbs. (34–46 Nm).

e. Align generator bracket to cylinder head. Install the 3 generator bracket bolts and tighten to 30–41 ft. lbs. (40–55 Nm).

f. Position A/C brace and install upper generator bolt. Tighten the long bolt to 30–41 ft. lbs. (40–55 Nm), and the remaining bolts to 15–22 ft. lbs. (20–30 Nm).

g. Install belt tensioner and torque bolt to 30–41 ft. lbs. (40–55 Nm).

h. Install accessory belt and tension.

i. Fasten power steering pulley shield and tighten bolts to 6–8 ft. lbs. (8.5–11 Nm).

40. Install fuel injector wire harness to each injector and secure to rocker arm studs.

41. Position ignition coil to rear left cylinder head and torque bolts to 29–41 ft. lbs. (40–55 Nm).

42. Fasten oil cooler tube assembly bracket to the ignition coil bracket. Install and tighten the hardware to 15–22 ft. lbs. (20–30 Nm).

43. Secure and fasten distributor cap and wires noting their correct order. Connect wire harness to rocker arm cover studs.

44. Install throttle body, using a new gasket.

45. Fasten EGR valve and tube to exhaust manifold tightening nut to 26–48 ft. lbs. (36–65 Nm).

46. Connect fuel lines to the supply rail. Secure with safety clips.

47. Install upper radiator and heater hoses, tighten clamps to 20–30 inch lbs. (2.3–3.4 Nm).

48. Connect vacuum lines to their marked locations.

49. Plug in the electrical connections removed earlier.

50. Fill cooling system with antifreeze.

51. Drain and replace the engine oil.

52. Install air cleaner outlet tube to the throttle body and Mass Air Flow (MAF) sensor. Tighten clamps to 24–35 inch lbs. (2.7–4.0 Nm).

53. Install PCV system closure hose to the rocker arm cover.

54. Connect negative battery cable.

55. Start engine and check for leaks, poor timing or idle. Allow engine to cool, and check and add fluid if needed.

## CLEANING AND INSPECTION

1. Place the head on a workbench and remove any manifolds that are still connected. If still installed, remove all rocker arm retaining parts and rocker arms.

2. Turn the cylinder head over so that the mounting surface is facing up and support evenly on wooden blocks.

➡ **If an aluminum cylinder head, exercise care when cleaning.**

3. Use a scraper and remove all of the gasket material stuck to the head mounting surface. Mount a wire carbon removal brush in an electric drill. With the valves installed to protect the valve seats, clean away the carbon on the valves and head combustion chambers. After the valves are removed, clean the valve guide bores. Use cleaning solvent to remove dirt, grease and other deposits from the valves.

➡ **When scraping or decarbonizing the cylinder head take care not to damage or nick the gasket mounting surface.**

4. Number the valve heads with a permanent felt–tip marker for cylinder location.

## RESURFACING

➡ **If a 2.3L or 3.0L cylinder head is found to be warped, it will be necessary to have it resurface by a machine shop. If a 2.0L cylinder head is found to be warped, it is not possible to resurfaces this head. Therefore a replacement head will have to be purchased.**

### Inspection

Place a straightedge across the gasket surface of the head. Using feeler gauges, determine the clearance at the center and along the length between the head and the straightedge. Measure clearance at the center and along the lengths of both diagonals. If warpage exceeds 0.003 in. (0.076mm) in a 6 in. (152mm) span, or 0.006 in. (0.15mm) over the total length the cylinder head must be resurfaced. Replace the head if it is cracked.

➡ **Do not plane or grind more than 0.010 in. (0.254mm) from the original cylinder head gasket surface.**

## Valves

### REMOVAL & INSTALLATION

◆ **See Figure 139**

#### 2.0L Engine

A valve spring compressor is needed to remove the valve assemblies. Valve spring compressors are available at most auto parts and auto tool shops. A small magnet is very helpful for removing the keepers (keys) and spring seats.

1. Remove the cylinder head from the engine and place on a work bench.

2. Remove camshaft bearing cap No.1, then No.3, and No. 5. No. 1 cylinder is closest to the right side of the vehicle (passenger side).

3. For camshaft bearing cap No. 2 and No. 4, proceed as follows:

   a. Loosen one of the 2 nuts on each bearing cap 2–3 turns only.

   b. Then, loosen the remaining nut on each bearing cap 2–3 turns.

   c. Continue this alternating sequence until the nuts are loose.

4. Remove remaining bearing caps and remove the camshaft.

5. Remove each valve shim.

6. Install the spring compressor so that the fixed side of the tool is flat against the valve head in the combustion chamber, and the opposite end toward the spring retainer.

7. Compress the spring assembly.

➡ **As the spring is compressed, the keepers (keys) will be revealed. Remove them from the valve stem with a magnet as they are easily fumbled and lost.**

8. Remove the keys, spring retainer, spring, seal and valve from the cylinder head. Keep the assemblies intact so they will be re–installed in their original positions.

9. Remove the remaining valves from the cylinder head, keeping all parts together.

10. Clean and inspect the valve components, as outlined in this Section.

#### To install:

11. Install the valve into the cylinder head. Assemble the seal, spring and spring retainer.

➡ **Always use new valve seals.**

12. Install the spring compressor, and compress the spring retainer until the keeper (key) groove on the valve stem is fully revealed. Then, install the the keepers (keys).

13. It may be necessary to apply a little grease to the grooves on the valve stem to hold the keepers (keys) until the spring compressor is released.

14. Slowly release the spring compressor until the spring retainer covers the keepers (keys). Remove the spring compressor tool.

➡ **Lightly tap the end of each valve stem with a rubber mallet to ensure proper fit of the retainers and keepers.**

15. Install the remaining valve assemblies to the cylinder head.

16. Install valve shims.

17. Install the camshaft into position, and locate bearing cap No. 2 and No. 4 by loosely tightening each nut. Once all 4 nut are hand–tight, go back with a socket and tighten each nut 2–3 turns. Continue this sequence until the bearing caps are seated.

18. Install bearing caps No. 1, No. 3 and No. 5. Tighten nuts as above. With all the nuts seated, torque each nut to 15–19 ft. lbs. (20–27 Nm).

19. Install the cylinder head.

20. Before starting engine, adjust valves using the cold specification. Check valve adjustment regularly. Always check the valves when the engine is cold.

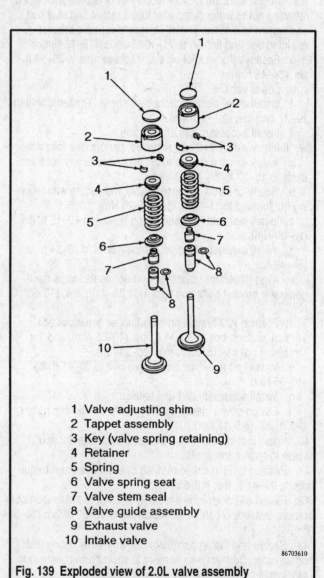

1 Valve adjusting shim
2 Tappet assembly
3 Key (valve spring retaining)
4 Retainer
5 Spring
6 Valve spring seat
7 Valve stem seal
8 Valve guide assembly
9 Exhaust valve
10 Intake valve

86703610

**Fig. 139 Exploded view of 2.0L valve assembly**

**2.3L and 3.0L Engine**

▶ See Figures 140, 141, 142, 143 and 144

A valve spring compressor is needed to remove the valve assemblies. Valve spring compressors are available at most auto parts and auto tool shops. A small magnet is very helpful for removing the keepers (keys) and spring seats.

1. Remove the cylinder head from the engine and place on a work bench.

2. Remove rocker arm fulcrum retaining bolts, as well as fulcrums and rocker arms.

3. Install the spring compressor so that the fixed side of the tool is flat against the valve head in the combustion chamber, and the opposite end toward the spring retainer.

4. Compress the spring assembly.

➡ As the spring is compressed, the keepers (keys) will be revealed. Remove them from the valve stem with a magnet as they are easily fumbled and lost.

5. Remove the keys, spring retainer, spring, seal and valve from the cylinder head. Keep the assemblies intact so they will be re–installed in their original positions.

6. Remove the remaining valves from the cylinder head, keeping all parts together.

7. Clean and inspect the valve components, as outlined in this Section.

**To install:**

8. Install the valve into the cylinder head. Assemble the seal, spring and spring retainer.

➡ Always use new valve seals.

9. Install the spring compressor, and compress the spring retainer until the keeper (key) groove on the valve stem is fully revealed. Then, install the the keepers (keys).

10. It may be necessary to apply a little grease to the grooves on the valve stem to hold the keepers (keys) until the spring compressor is released.

11. Slowly release the spring compressor until the spring retainer covers the keepers (keys). Remove the spring compressor tool.

➡ Lightly tap the end of each valve stem with a rubber mallet to ensure proper fit of the retainers and keepers.

12. Install the remaining valve assemblies to the cylinder head.

13. After installing the valve spring, measure the distance between the spring mounting pad and the lower edge of the spring retainer. Compare the measurement to specifications. If the installed height is incorrect, add shims washers between the spring mounting pad and the spring. Use only washers designed for valve springs, available at at most automotive parts stores.

14. Position rocker arms and fulcrums on cylinder head and hand–tighten fulcrum bolts.

15. Rotate camshaft at least one full turn, and torque fulcrum bolts to 20–26 ft. lbs. (26–38 Nm).

16. Install the cylinder head.

Fig. 140 Using a spring compressor to compress the spring

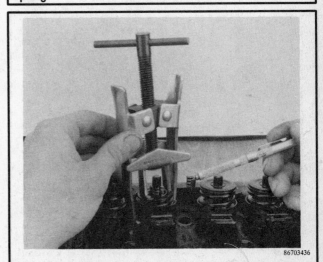

Fig. 141 With the spring compressed, the keys can be removed using a magnet

Fig. 142 With the keys removed, lift the spring out

**Fig. 143 When the valve is removed, the seal can be pulled from the head and discarded**

**Fig. 144 Always properly tighten the rocker arm retaining bolts when any valve work is completed**

## VALVE INSPECTION

### ◗ See Figure 145

Before inspecting the valve or any part of the valve assembly, wash each valve piece, one at a time, in a suitable solvent. Allow the parts to dry completely. Then, inspect all components.

Begin by inspecting the valve stem for bends, and/or grooves at the end of the stem. Proceed to the valve face and edge where you should look for burnt signs identified by a discoloration, grooves, scores, warpage or cracks.

➡ **Minor pits or grooves may be removed.**

Discard any valves that are severely damaged, or are questionable in any way. If the face runout cannot be corrected, refinishing, or if the stem diameter is not within specifications, discard the valve.

Check the valve stems for bends and any wear which may show up as a "step" between two parts of the stem.

Check the valve stem to valve guide clearance. If a dial indicator is not available, a visual inspection can give a relatively good idea if a guide, valve stem, or both need attention. Insert the valve into the guide until the valve head is slightly away from the valve seat. Wiggle the valve sideways. A small amount of wobble is normal, excessive wobble means a worn guide and/or valve stem.

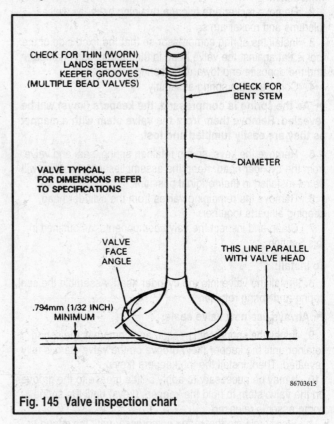

CHECK FOR THIN (WORN) LANDS BETWEEN KEEPER GROOVES (MULTIPLE BEAD VALVES)

CHECK FOR BENT STEM

VALVE TYPICAL, FOR DIMENSIONS REFER TO SPECIFICATIONS

DIAMETER

VALVE FACE ANGLE

THIS LINE PARALLEL WITH VALVE HEAD

.794mm (1/32 INCH) MINIMUM

**Fig. 145 Valve inspection chart**

## REFACING

Before beginning any refacing, determine if the valve is usable.

The valve refacing operation should be closely coordinated with the valve seat refacing portion so that the finished angles of the valve face and valve seat will be to specifications and provide a compression–tight fit.

➡ **Be sure that the refacer grinding wheels are properly dressed.**

Grind the valve seat to specified degree angle. Remove only enough stock to clean up pits and grooves or to correct the valve seat runout. After the seat has been refaced, use a seat width scale or a machinist scale to measure the seat width. Narrow the seat, if necessary, to bring it to within specification. If the valve seat width exceeds the maximum limit, remove enough stock from the top edge and/or bottom edge of the seat to reduce the width to specification.

Reface the valve, if the valve face runout is excessive, and/or pits or grooves are evident. Remove only enough stock to clean up pits and grooves or to correct the runout.

➡ **If the edge of the valve head is less than 32 in. (0.794mm) thick after grinding, replace the valve as the valve will run too hot in the engine.**

## Valve Stem Seals

### REMOVAL & INSTALLATION

#### 2.0L Engine

♦ **See Figure 139**

##### *CYLINDER HEAD REMOVED*

1. Remove cylinder head.
2. Remove the valve spring retainer, valve spring and spring seat.
3. Install a valve stem seal remover T72J–6571 or equivalent over the valve stem. Tap the remover lightly with a hammer to fully seat the tool.
4. Install slide hammer T50T–100–A or equivalent and remove the seal.

**To install:**

5. Position a new valve stem seal using Valve stem seal installer T84P–6571–A or equivalent.
6. Install valve spring, valve spring and valve spring retainer.
7. Position and secure cylinder head.

##### *CYLINDER HEAD INSTALLED*

1. Disconnect the negative battery cable.
2. Place protective covers on each fender.
3. Drain the cooling system.
4. Remove the rocker arm cover
5. Remove the spark plug from the cylinder where the seals are to be replaced.
6. Rotate the crankshaft until the piston is at Top Dead Center (Top Dead Center (TDC)) with both valves closed.
7. Refer to the valve removal procedure, and remove the camshaft.
8. Install a suitable adapter in the spark plug hole and connect an air supply line. Apply air into the cylinder chamber.

➡ **If the air pressure does not hold the valves closed, there is most likely valve or valve seat damage, and the cylinder head must be removed to address this problem.**

9. Compress the valve assembly using valve spring compressor T91–6565–A or equivalent. Once compressed, remove the keeper, seal, retainer and valve spring.
10. Make sure the piston is at Top Dead Center (TDC). Remove the air pressure from the spark plug adapter and inspect the valve stem for damage. Rotate the valve and check the valve stem tip for eccentric movement. Move the valve up and down in the guide through its normal travel and check for binding.

**To install:**

11. If the valve is okay, apply clean engine oil to the valve stem and hold the valve closed. Apply air pressure to cylinder. Install a new valve seal using seal replacer tool T91–6571–A or equivalent.
12. Position valve spring and retainer over the valve stem, and install keeper.
13. If replacing other seals, move on to next cylinder, otherwise, install camshaft and torque according to the earlier procedure.

#### 2.3L and 3.0L Engines

♦ **See Figure 146**

##### *CYLINDER HEAD REMOVED*

1. Remove cylinder head.
2. Remove rocker cover retaining bolts. Remove rocker arm cover.
3. Remove rocker arm bolts, fulcrums, rocker arms and pushrods.
4. Using a spring compressor, remove the valve keepers followed by the valve spring retainer, valve spring and spring seat.
5. Gentle remove valve stem seal using pliers or other device. Inspect valve for wear and replace if necessary.

**To install:**

6. Apply light coat of oil to valve stem. Position new valve stem seal and push on valve stem. If difficult to install use stem seal installer T91P–656–A or equivalent.
7. Install spring, retainer and other parts on valve. Compress spring and install keepers.
8. If replacing other seals, move to next valve assembly.
9. Once complete, install pushrods, fulcrum, rocker arm and rocker arm bolts. Fasten cylinder head to block and tighten bolts.
10. Install rocker arm cover and assemble engine compartment.

##### *CYLINDER HEAD INSTALLED*

1. Disconnect the negative battery cable.
2. Place protective covers on each fender.
3. Drain the cooling system.
4. Remove the rocker arm cover
5. Remove the spark plug from the cylinder where the seals are to be replaced.
6. Rotate the crankshaft until the piston is at Top Dead Center (TDC) with both valves closed.
7. Remove rocker arm bolts, fulcrums, rocker arms and pushrods.
8. Install a suitable adapter in the spark plug hole and connect an air supply line. Apply air into the cylinder chamber.

➡ **If the air pressure does not hold the valves closed, there is most likely valve or valve seat damage, and the cylinder head must be removed to address this problem.**

9. Compress the valve assembly using valve spring compressor T91–6565–A or equivalent. Once compressed, remove the keeper, seal, retainer and valve spring.

10. Make sure the piston is at Top Dead Center (TDC). Remove the air pressure from the spark plug adapter and inspect the valve stem for damage. Rotate the valve and check the valve stem tip for eccentric movement. Move the valve up and down in the guide through its normal travel and check for binding.

**To install:**

11. If the valve is okay, apply clean engine oil to the valve stem and hold the valve closed. Apply air pressure to cylinder. Install a new valve seal using seal replacer tool T91–6571–A or equivalent.

12. Position valve spring and retainer over the valve stem, and install keeper.

13. If replacing other seals, move on to next cylinder.

14. Once complete, install pushrods, fulcrum, rocker arm and rocker arm bolts.

15. Install rocker arm cover.

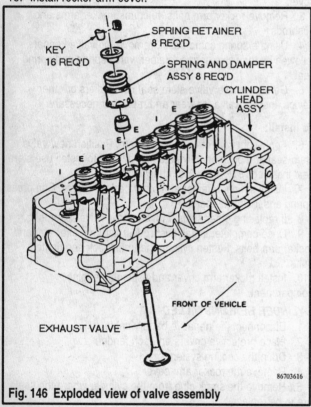

**Fig. 146 Exploded view of valve assembly**

## Valve Springs

### REMOVAL & INSTALLATION

#### 2.0L Engine

1. Remove rocker arm cover.

2. Remove bearing cap No. 1, No. 3 and No. 5. No. 1 bearing cap is located on the right side of the engine (passenger side).

3. Loosen one nut on bearing cap No. 2 about two or three turns as well as one of the nuts on bearing cap No. 4. Go back to bearing cap No. 2 and do the same to the other nut, followed by the nut on bearing cap No. 4. Continue this alternating

sequence until all four nuts are loose. Once loose, remove bearing caps, and the camshaft.

4. Remove the spring retainer from the spring assembly.

5. Using a spring compressor, press down on the spring assembly and remove the valve keeper.

6. Remove the spring and inspect. Replace if excessively worn.

**To install:**

7. Assemble valve seats and spring and position in cylinder head.

8. Compress the spring assembly and install the keeper. Install the spring retainer on top of each spring assembly.

9. Position camshaft and install bearing caps No. 2 and No. 4, and hand–tighten the nuts.

➡ **Camshaft bearing caps are to be installed with the arrow pointer toward the front of the engine.**

10. Tighten 2–3 turns in sequence the nuts on bearing caps No. 2 and No. 4. Continue this until bearing caps are seated.

11. Install bearing caps No. 1, No. 3 and No. 5, tightening the nuts until each cap is seated.

12. Torque the nuts on each bearing cap to 15–19 ft. lbs. (20–27 Nm).

13. Install rocker arm cover and tighten bolts to 5–7 ft. lbs. (7–10 Nm).

#### 2.3L and 3.0L Engines

1. Remove the rocker arm covers.

2. Remove the rocker arm bolt, fulcrum, rocker arm and pushrods.

3. Using a spring compressor, press down on the spring assembly and remove the valve keeper from the assembly.

4. With the valve assembly removed from the cylinder head, dismantle the retainer and sleeve to expose the spring.

5. Inspect the spring and replace if necessary.

**To install:**

6. Position the retainers on the top and bottom of the spring, and secure in the spring sleeve.

7. Install the spring assembly in the cylinder head in it's original location.

8. Compress the assembly and install the keepers.

9. Install any other spring assemblies using the same methods.

10. Install the pushrod, rocker arm, fulcrum and rocker arm bolt. Torque bolt to 20 –26 ft. lbs. (26–38 Nm).

11. Install rocker arm covers and secure with retaining bolts, tightening to 71–106 inch lbs (8–12 Nm) for 2.3L engine. and 8–10 ft. lbs (10–14 Nm) for 3.0L engines.

### INSPECTION

◆ **See Figures 147 and 148**

Place the valve spring on a flat surface next to a carpenters square. Measure the height of the spring, and rotate the spring against the edge of the square to measure distortion. If the spring height varies (by comparison) by more than $1/16$ in. (1.6mm) or if the distortion exceeds $1/16$ in. (1.6mm), replace the spring.

Have the valve springs tested for spring pressure at the installed and compressed height (installed height minus valve lift) using a valve spring tester. Springs should be within one pound, plus or minus each other. Replace any spring not within this range.

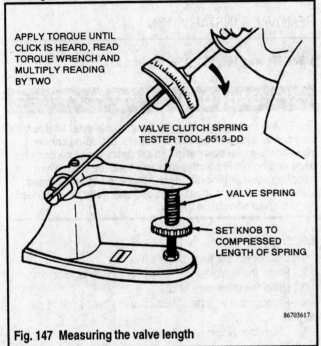

APPLY TORQUE UNTIL CLICK IS HEARD, READ TORQUE WRENCH AND MULTIPLY READING BY TWO

VALVE CLUTCH SPRING TESTER TOOL-6513-DD

VALVE SPRING

SET KNOB TO COMPRESSED LENGTH OF SPRING

86703617

**Fig. 147 Measuring the valve length**

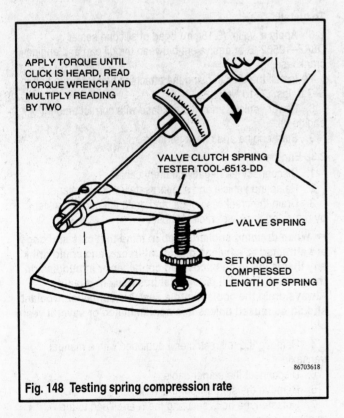

APPLY TORQUE UNTIL CLICK IS HEARD, READ TORQUE WRENCH AND MULTIPLY READING BY TWO

VALVE CLUTCH SPRING TESTER TOOL-6513-DD

VALVE SPRING

SET KNOB TO COMPRESSED LENGTH OF SPRING

86703618

**Fig. 148 Testing spring compression rate**

## Valve Seats

Because of the design and the material used to construct the cylinder head of the 2.0L, 2.3L and 3.0L engines, the valve seats cannot be replaced. Instead, assuming the wear is not too great, the valve seat must be refaced using a grinding stone or cutting tool.

The valve seat refacing operation should be closely coordinated with the valve refacing portion because the finished angles of the valve face and valve seat must be to specifications to provide a compression–tight fit. Because of the close tolerances involved, it is recommended this procedure be completed by a machine shop.

➡ **Be sure that the refacer grinding wheels are properly dressed.**

Grind the valve seat to specified degree angle. Remove only enough stock to clean up pits and grooves or to correct the valve seat runout. After the seat has been refaced, use a seat width scale or a machinist scale to measure the seat width. Narrow the seat, if necessary, to bring it to within specification. If the valve seat width exceeds the maximum limit, remove enough stock from the top edge and/or bottom edge of the seat to reduce the width to specification.

## Valve Guides

◆ **See Figure 149**

If a valve guide is determined to be worn during the valve inspection procedure, there are 3 possible repair alternatives: knurling, reaming to oversize, or complete replacement.

If guide wear is minimal, the correct inside diameter can be restored by knurling. This process involves using a special tool to raise a spiral ridge on the inside of the guide while it is installed in the cylinder head. This effectively reduces the inside diameter of the guide. A reamer is then utilized and passed through the guide to make the inside diameter smooth and uniform, and restore the guide to its original inside diameter. Knurling is only an alternative if there is minimum guide wear.

The valve guide can also be reamed oversized, necessitating the use of a valve with a corresponding oversized valve stem.

The final alternative, complete guide replacement is a precision process, requiring special equipment. Because of the experience and tools needed to complete the job, valve guide replacement should be left to an automotive machine shop.

### VALVE GUIDE REAMING

◆ **See Figure 149**

If valve guide reaming is needed, ram the valve guide from the next oversize valve stem. A hand reaming kit can be purchased at most automotive parts and/or auto tool shops.

When replacing a standard size valve with an oversize valve, always use the reamer in sequence (smallest oversize first, and then the smallest, etc.) so as not to overload the reamers.

➡ **Always reface the valve seat after the valve guide has been reamed.**

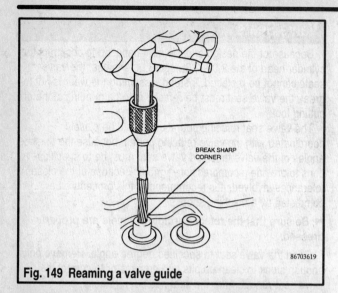

**Fig. 149 Reaming a valve guide**

BREAK SHARP CORNER

86703619

## Valve Lifters

### REMOVAL & INSTALLATION

1. Disconnect the negative battery cable.
2. Place protective cover on each fender.
3. Remove the coolant from the engine.
4. Remove the cylinder head and any related parts.
5. On a 2.0L engine, remove the shim and lifter assembly. f removing multiple lifters, tag and number the lifters.
6. On 2.3L and 3.0L engines, remove the lifter. Identify, tag and place the lifters in a rack so they can be installed in the original position.
7. If the lifters are stuck in their bores by excessive varnish or gum, it may be necessary to use a hydraulic lifter puller tool to remove the lifters. Rotate the lifters back and forth to loosen any gum and varnish which may have formed. Keep the assemblies intact until they are to be cleaned.
8. Inspect the lifters for any pitting or scoring. Replace any showing these signs.

**To install:**

9. On a 2.0L engine, slide the lifter and shim into place.
10. On 2.3L and 3.0L engines, install the new or cleaned hydraulic lifters through the pushrod openings with a magnet.
11. Install the cylinder head and related parts.
12. Connect the negative battery cable.

### OVERHAUL

➡ The lifter assemblies should be keep in proper sequence so that they can be installed in their original position. If any part of the lifter assembly needs replacing, the entire assembly should be replaced.

1. Remove the plunger cap retainer, from the lifter assembly.
2. Remove the plunger cap, plunger sub assembly and return spring from the lifter body.

➡ Disassemble each lifter separately so as not to intermix.

3. Thoroughly clean all the parts in clean solvent, then wipe with a lint–free cloth.

4. Inspect the lifter assembly and discard if any part shows pitting, scoring, galling, excessive wear or evidence of non–rotation.

## Oil Pan

### REMOVAL & INSTALLATION

➡ See Figures 150, 151, 152, 153 and 154

### ✳✳CAUTION

The EPA warns that prolonged contact with used engine oil may cause a number of skin disorders, including cancer! You should make every effort to minimize your exposure to used engine oil. Protective gloves should be worn when handling used engine oil. Clean hands and other exposed skin area as soon as possible. Soap and water, or waterless hand cleaner should be used.

**2.0L Engine**

1. Disconnect the negative battery cable.
2. Raise the vehicle and support safely with jackstands.
3. Drain the crankcase of oil.
4. Remove the attaching bolts securing the oil pan to the engine.
5. Clean the oil and gasket mating surface completely, and allow to dry.

**To install:**

6. Apply a $1/8$ in. (3.18mm) bead of silicone sealer D6AZ–19562–B or equivalent between the oil pan and engine crankcase.
7. Install the oil pan using the attaching bolts. Torque bolt to 5–7 ft. lbs. (7–10 Nm).
8. Lower vehicle, and fill crankcase with correct amount of engine oil.
9. Start engine and check for leaks.

**2.3L Engine**

1. Disconnect the negative battery cable.
2. Raise the vehicle and support safely with jackstands.
3. Drain the crankcase of oil, and drain the cooling system by removing the lower radiator hose.

➡ When draining coolant, keep in mind that cats and dogs are attracted to ethylene glycol antifreeze, and could drink any that is left in an uncovered container or in puddles on the ground. This will prove fatal in sufficient quantity. Always drain the coolant into a sealable container. Coolant should be reused unless it is contaminated or several years old.

4. Remove the roll restricter if equipped with a manual transaxle.
5. Disconnect the starter cable.
6. Remove the starter from the vehicle
7. Unfasten the bolts securing the rear oil pan to the transaxle case.
8. If equipped with a manual transaxle, remove the secondary air injection tube at the check valve.

9. Remove the heater supply tube located at the lower water pump inlet tube assembly.

10. Loosen the bolts and remove the brackets at the block and water pump inlet tube and A/C compressor line at the pan.

11. Using a prybar between the engine and body of car, flex engine enough the remove oil pan.

12. Clean the oil and gasket mating surface completely, and allow to dry.

13. Clean both mating surfaces of oil pan and cylinder block making certain all traces of RTV sealant are removed. Ensure that the block rails, front cover and rear cover retainer are also clean.

14. Remove and clean oil pump pick–up tube and screen assembly. After cleaning, install tube and screen assembly.

**To install:**

15. Apply a bead of RTV E8AZ–19562–A sealer or equivalent, in the oil pan groove. Completely fill oil pan groove with sealer. Sealer bead should be 0.200 in. (5mm) wide and 0.080–0.150 in. (2.0–3.8mm) high (above oil pan surface) in all areas except the half–rounds. The half–rounds should have a bead 0.200 in. (5mm) wide and 0.150–0.200 in. (3.8–5.1mm) high, above the oil pan surface.

➡ **Applying RTV in excess of the specified amount will not improve the sealing of the oil pan, and could cause the oil pickup screen to become clogged with sealer. Use ad equate ventilation when applying sealer.**

16. Install oil pan to cylinder block within 5 minutes to prevent skinning over. RTV needs to cure completely before coming in contact with any engine oil. Ideally, about 1 hour at ambient temperature between 65–75°F (18–24°C) is recommended as a drying time.

17. Install oil pan bolts lightly until the 2 oil pan–to–transmission bolts can be installed.

18. Install 2 oil pan–to–transaxle bolts. Tighten to 30–39 ft. lbs. (40–54 Nm) to align oil pan with transaxle. Loosen bolts 1/2 turn.

19. Tighten all oil pan flange bolts to 15–22 ft. lbs. (20–30 Nm).

20. Tighten 2 oil pan–to–transmission bolts to 30–39 ft. lbs. (40–54 Nm).

21. Install brackets for A/C compressor line and water pump inlet tube.

22. If equipped with a manual transaxle, fasten the air injection tube.

23. Install the starter and cable.

24. Lower vehicle.

25. Install engine oil and coolant.

26. Connect the negative battery cable.

27. Start engine and check for coolant and oil leaks.

### 3.0L Engine

1. Disconnect the negative battery cable.

2. Raise the vehicle and support safely with jackstands.

3. Drain the crankcase of oil.

4. Remove the oil level dipstick. If equipped with a low oil level sensor, unplug electrical harness at the sensor.

5. Disconnect the starter cable, and remove the starter from the vehicle.

6. Disconnect the heated oxygen sensor wire harness from the exhaust. Unbolt and remove catalytic converter and pipe assembly.

7. If equipped with an automatic transaxle, remove torque converter access plate.

8. If equipped with a manual transaxle, remove the left and right transaxle support plates.

9. Remove the heater supply tube located at the lower water pump inlet tube assembly.

10. Loosen and remove oil pan oil pan retaining bolts. Make sure internal pan baffle does not snag on oil pump pickup tube and screen.

11. With oil pan removed from engine, scrap and discard oil pan gasket. Clean oil pan and engine mating surfaces.

**To install:**

12. Secure gasket to oil pan using gasket and trim adhesive D7AZ–19B508–B or equivalent. Position the oil pan to the engine crankcase and secure with retaining bolts.

➡ **Do not allow sealer to cure longer than 4 minutes prior to oil pan installation.**

13. Tighten oil pan 4 corner bolts to 7–10 ft. lbs. (10–14 Nm).

14. Tighten remaining bolts to 7–10 ft. lbs. (10–14 Nm).

15. If equipped with an automatic transaxle, install torque converter access plate.

16. If equipped with a manual transaxle, Install the left and right transaxle plates.

17. Install the catalytic converter pipe assembly, and oxygen sensor.

18. Install the starter and cable.

19. If equipped with low oil level sensor, connect wire harness to sensor plug.

20. Lower vehicle.

21. Install engine oil, oil dipstick and coolant.

22. Connect negative battery cable.

23. Start engine and check for coolant and oil leaks.

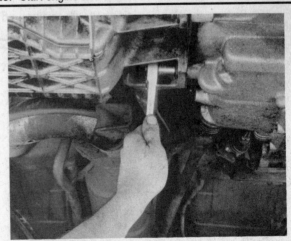

**Fig. 150 If needed, remove the bolt securing the oil pan to the transaxle. On some early vehicles, this was not installed**

86703439

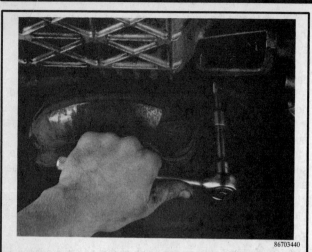

Fig. 151 Remove any brackets which could prevent the removal of the oil pan. Also remove the retaining bolts closest to the transaxle

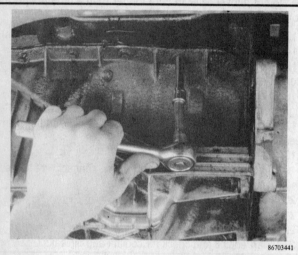

Fig. 152 Remove the other retaining bolts which surround the oil pan

Fig. 153 Slowly lower the oil pan and remove. Be careful, some oil may still be in the bottom of the pan

Fig. 154 Remove the oil pan gasket. Some will be stuck to the engine block, while some will be attached to the pan

## Oil Pump

### REMOVAL & INSTALLATION

▶ **See Figures 155, 156 and 157**

#### 2.0L Engine

1. Disconnect the negative battery cable
2. Raise and safely support the vehicle on jackstands
3. Remove oil pan according to the earlier procedure.
4. Remove the accessary drive belts.
5. Loosen and disconnect the front timing belt, crankshaft pulley, front timing belt tensioner and crankshaft front oil seal.
6. Remove the bolts attaching the oil pump to the crankcase and remove the pump. Remove the crankshaft front oil seal.
7. Clean any gasket or sealer present on the oil pump assembly as well as the crankcase mating surface.

#### To install:

8. Apply a $1/8$ in. (3.18mm) bead of silicone sealer D6AZ-19562-B or equivalent to the oil pump to crankcase mating surface.
9. Install a new O-ring.
10. Install the oil pump making sure the inner gears engage with the splines on the crankshaft. Install and tighten the 10mm retaining bolts to 23–34 ft. lbs. (32–47 Nm), and the 8mm retaining bolts to 12–16 ft. lbs. (16–23 Nm).
11. Install a new crankshaft front oil seal.
12. Position, connect and tighten the front timing belt, timing belt tensioner and crankshaft pulley.
13. Install and tighten the accessary belts.
14. Position and tighten the oil pan.
15. Connect negative battery cable.
16. Fill the crankcase. Start engine and check for leaks.

#### 2.3L Engine

1. Disconnect the negative battery cable
2. Raise and safely support the vehicle on jackstands

3. Remove oil pan.

4. Remove the oil pump attaching bolts and remove oil pump and intermediate driveshaft.

**To install:**

5. Prime oil pump by filling inlet port with engine oil. Rotate pump shaft until oil flows from outlet port.

6. If screen and cover assembly have been removed, replace gasket. Clean screen and reinstall screen and cover assembly and tighten the attaching nuts to 15–22 ft. lbs. (20–30 Nm).

7. Position intermediate driveshaft into distributor socket.

8. Insert intermediate driveshaft into oil pump. Install pump and shaft as an assembly.

➡ **Do not attempt to force the pump into position if it will not seat. The shaft hex may be mis–aligned with the distributor shaft. To align, remove the oil pump and rotate the intermediate driveshaft into a new position.**

9. Tighten the oil pump attaching bolts to 15–22 ft. lbs. (20–30 Nm).

10. Install oil pan with new gasket.

11. Connect negative battery cable.

12. Fill the crankcase. Start the engine and check for leaks.

### 3.0L Engine

1. Disconnect the negative battery cable
2. Raise and safely support the vehicle on jackstands
3. Remove oil pan from the engine.
4. Remove retaining bolt and remove oil pump.

➡ **When the oil pump is removed, the intermediate shaft will remain in the pump. If replacing oil pump or shaft, pull shaft from pump and check the retaining clip for damage. Replace if necessary.**

**To install:**

5. Insert oil pump intermediate shaft into hex drive hole in oil pump assembly until retainer "clicks" into place.

6. Install oil pump assembly through rear bearing cap. Position pump over locating pins and install retaining bolts, torquing to 30–41 ft. lbs. (40–55 Nm).

7. Install the oil pan.

8. Connect the negative battery cable.

9. Fill the crankcase with oil. Start the engine and check for leaks.

**Fig. 155 With the oil pan removed, the oil pump is easily visible**

**Fig. 156 Loosen and remove the retaining bolts**

**Fig. 157 Remove the pump from the engine block**

## INSPECTION AND OVERHAUL

➡ **The oil pump internal components are not serviceable. If any components are out of specifications, the pump assembly must be replaced.**

1. Remove the oil pump from the vehicle.

2. Inspect the inside of the pump housing for damage or excessive wear.

3. Check the mating surface for wear. Minor scuff marks are normal, but if the cover, gears or housing are excessively worn, scored or grooved, replace the pump.

4. On a 2.0L engine, check the oil pump to crankcase assembly for wear on the gears. If worn, replace.

5. Inspect the rotor for nicks, burrs or score marks. Replace if necessary.

6. Measure the inner–to–outer rotor tip clearance. With a feeler gauge inserted and the rotors removed from the pump housing, clearance must not exceed 0.012 in. (0.30mm).

7. With the rotor assembly installed, place a straightedge across the rotor assembly and housing. Measure the rotor

clearance, between the the inner and outer rotors. The clearance should be 0.004 in. (0.101mm).

8. Check the relief valve spring tension. If the spring is worn or damaged, replace the pump. Check the relief valve piston for freedom of movement in the bore.

## Timing Belt Cover

➡ The only Tempo/Topaz engine which utilizes timing belts is the 2.0L diesel. This engine actually uses timing belt at BOTH end of the engine.

### REMOVAL & INSTALLATION

#### Front Cover

◆ **See Figure 158**

The front timing belt cover is that cover in the engine compartment between the right side of the body and the engine assembly.

1. Disconnect the negative battery cable
2. Raise and safely support the vehicle on jackstands
3. Remove any accessory belts installed.
4. Remove the crankshaft pulley using tool T77F–4220–B1 or equivalent.
5. Remove the retaining bolts securing the timing belt cover over the cam sprocket, water pump and belt tensioner. With the bolts unfastened, remove the cover.
6. Loosen and remove the retaining bolts securing the timing belt cover between the cam sprocket and the crankshaft.

**To install:**

7. Position timing belt cover between cam sprocket and crankshaft. Secure with retaining bolts and tighten to 5–7 ft. lbs. (7–10 Nm).
8. Position upper timing belt cover and install retaining bolts tightening to 5–7 ft. lbs. (7–10 Nm).
9. Install and torque crankshaft pulley to 17–24 ft. lbs. (23–33 Nm).
10. Install accessory belts. Check tension to make sure none are too tight.
11. Lower vehicle.
12. Start vehicle and listen for any noise indicating a loose belt or mis–aligned cover.

#### Rear Cover

◆ **See Figure 158**

The rear timing belt cover is that cover located between the transaxle and engine.

1. Disconnect the negative battery cable
2. Raise and safely support the vehicle on jackstands
3. Loosen and remove the retaining bolts securing the inner timing belt cover. Remove the cover.

**To install:**

4. Position the inner timing belt cover and secure with retaining bolts tightening to 5–7 ft. lbs. (7–10 Nm).
5. Lower vehicle.
6. Start vehicle and listen for any noise indicating a loose belt or misaligned cover.

## Timing Chain Front Cover

### REMOVAL & INSTALLATION

#### 2.3L Engine

◆ **See Figure 159**

1. Remove the engine and transaxle from the vehicle as an assembly and position in a suitable holding fixture. Remove the dipstick and tube.
2. Remove accessory drive pulley, if equipped, Remove any accessory belts. Remove the crankshaft pulley attaching bolt and washer and remove the pulley using tool T77F–4220–B1 or equivalent.
3. Remove front cover attaching bolts from the cover. Pry the top of the front cover away from the engine block.
4. Clean any gasket material from the surface.
5. Check timing chain and sprockets for excessive wear. If the timing chain and sprockets are worn, replace with new parts.
6. Check timing chain tensioner blade for wear depth. If the wear depth exceeds specification, replace tensioner.
7. Remove the oil pan.

➡ Oil pan removal is recommended to ensure proper sealing to front cover.

**To install:**

8. Clean and inspect all parts before installation. Clean the oil pan, cylinder block and front cover of gasket material and dirt.
9. Apply oil resistant sealer to a new front cover gasket and position gasket into front cover.
10. Position front cover alignment tool T84P–6019–C or equivalent, onto the end of the crankshaft, ensuring the crank key is aligned with the keyway in the tool. Bolt the front cover to the engine and torque bolts to 6–9 ft. lbs. (8–12 Nm). Remove the front cover alignment tool when complete.
11. Replace the front cover seal with new. Lubricate the hub of the crankshaft pulley with polyethylene grease to prevent damage to the seal during installation and initial engine start. Install crankshaft pulley and hand–tighten bolt.
12. Install the oil pan.
13. Install the accessory drive pulley, if equipped. Install any accessary belts removed earlier.
14. Torque crankshaft pulley attaching bolt and washer. Tighten to 140–170 ft. lbs. (190–230 Nm).
15. Remove engine from work stand and install in vehicle.

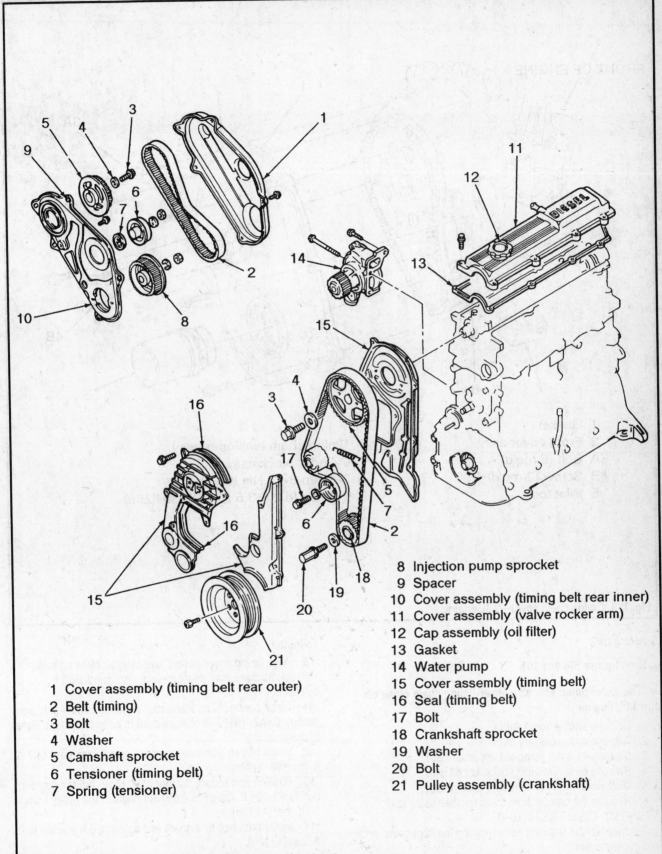

8 Injection pump sprocket
9 Spacer
10 Cover assembly (timing belt rear inner)
11 Cover assembly (valve rocker arm)
12 Cap assembly (oil filter)
13 Gasket
14 Water pump
15 Cover assembly (timing belt)
16 Seal (timing belt)
17 Bolt
18 Crankshaft sprocket
19 Washer
20 Bolt
21 Pulley assembly (crankshaft)

1 Cover assembly (timing belt rear outer)
2 Belt (timing)
3 Bolt
4 Washer
5 Camshaft sprocket
6 Tensioner (timing belt)
7 Spring (tensioner)

86703620

**Fig. 158 Exploded view of 2.0L front and rear timing belt covers**

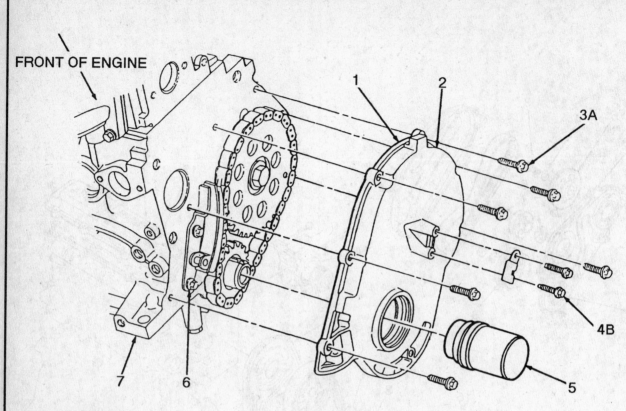

FRONT OF ENGINE

1 Gasket
2 Front cover assy
3A Bolt (6 req'd)
4B Screw (2 req'd)
5 Pilot tool

6 Timing chain tensioner assy
7 Cylinder block assy
A Tighten 8-12 Nm (6-9 lb.ft.)
B Tighten to 2.5-3.5 Nm (23-30 lb.in.)

86703621

**Fig. 159 Timing chain cover—2.3L engine**

## 3.0L Engine

♦ See Figures 160 and 161

➡ The water pump acts as a lower timing chain cover on the 3.0L engine

1. Remove engine from vehicle.
2. Remove any accessory belts.
3. Disconnect water pump to front cover hose.
4. Remove oil pan retaining bolts and oil pan.
5. Disconnect both belt tensioner assemblies.
6. Remove the damper from the crankshaft using tool T58P–6316–D and T82L–6316–B.
7. Unfasten the retaining bolts securing the front cover, and remove the cover.
8. Carefully clean any gasket material from the timing chain cover, oil pan and engine.

To install:

9. Align timing cover gasket over cylinder block dowels.
10. Install crankshaft seal protector onto crankshaft if available.
11. Install timing cover. Hand start retaining bolts. Apply pipe sealant D8AZ–19554–A or equivalent to bolts 1, 2 and 3. Refer to diagram.
12. Install oil pan with retaining bolts and tighten bolts to 7–10 ft. lbs. (10–14 Nm).
13. Position and secure damper and pulley. Tighten damper bolt to 93–121 ft. lbs. (125–165 Nm). Tighten the pulley bolts to 26 ft. lbs. (48 Nm).
14. Install both belt tensioners and tighten the hardware to 35 ft. lbs. (48 Nm).
15. Connect and tighten the accessory belts.
16. Install the water pump to front cover hose.

Tighten retaining bolts as shown.

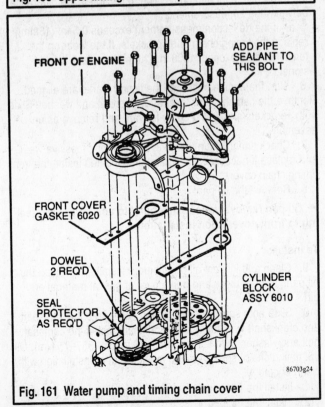

| Hole No. | Part No. | Bolt Size | Torque |
|---|---|---|---|
| 1-2 | N605907-S100 | M8 x 1.25 x 33 | 20-30 N-m (15-22 Lb-Ft) |
| 3-4-5-6-7-8-9-10-11-12-13 Front Cover Assy | N606543-S100 | M8 - 1.25 x 53 | 20-30 N-m (15-22 Lb-Ft) |

86703623

**Fig. 160 Upper timing chain/damper cover**

FRONT OF ENGINE

ADD PIPE SEALANT TO THIS BOLT

FRONT COVER GASKET 6020

DOWEL 2 REQ'D

SEAL PROTECTOR AS REQ'D

CYLINDER BLOCK ASSY 6010

86703g24

**Fig. 161 Water pump and timing chain cover**

## Front Cover Oil Seal

### REMOVAL & INSTALLATION

#### 2.3L Engine

➡ The removal and installation of the front cover oil seal on these engines can only be accomplished with the engine removed from the vehicle.

1. Remove the engine from the vehicle and position in a suitable holding fixture.
2. Remove bolt and washer at crankshaft pulley.
3. Remove the crankshaft pulley, using tool T77F-4220-B1 or equivalent.
4. Using tool T74P-6700-A or equivalent, remove the front cover oil seal.

**To install:**

5. Coat a new seal with Multi-Purpose Long-Life Lubricant C1AZ-19590-B or equivalent. Using tool T83T-4676-A or equivalent, install the seal into the cover. Drive the seal in until it is fully seated. Check the seal after installation to be sure the spring is properly positioned in the seal.
6. Install crankshaft pulley, attaching bolt and washer. Tighten the crankshaft pulley bolt to 140-170 ft. lbs. (190—230 Nm).

#### 3.0L Engine

➡ The removal and installation of the front oil seal on these engines is best accomplished with the engine removed from the vehicle.

1. Remove the engine from the vehicle and position in a suitable holding fixture.
2. Remove any accessary belts.
3. Remove the bolt and washer at crankshaft pulley.
4. Remove the crankshaft pulley, using tool T77F-4220-B1 or equivalent.
5. Remove the front oil seal. A prytool may be used if needed.
6. Inspect the housing and seal surface for damage, nick or burrs which may cause the new seal to fail. Service or replace components as necessary. Clean crankshaft and housing of all dirt.

**To install:**

7. Coat the seal lip with clean engine oil and install seal using vibration damper and seal installer T82L-6316-A or equivalent.
8. Install crankshaft pulley, attaching bolt and washer. Torque the crankshaft pulley bolt to 93-121 ft. lbs. (125-165 Nm).
9. Install any accessary belts removed earlier.
10. Install engine if all necessary work has been completed.

## Timing Belts

♦ See Figure 158

➡ The only Tempo/Topaz engine which utilizes a timing belt is the 2.0L diesel. This engine has a timing belt at the front and rear of the engine.

The timing belt is a cogged type rubber and cloth constructed belt which functions as the link between the upper cylinder head of the engine and the lower engine block. It is very close in appearance and construction to an accessory belt, with the exception that it is cogged.

Because of its material construction, the timing belt should be checked regularly, and replaced at least every 60000 miles (9661 km).

➡ Because the Tempo/Topaz 2.0L engine is a non–free-wheeling type (i.e., one in which that if the timing belt breaks, the valves will contact the pistons) it is very important that the timing belt be changed according to schedule, and checked regularly.

### REMOVAL & INSTALLATION

#### Front Timing Belt

1. Remove both timing belt covers.
2. Rotate the engine clockwise until the timing marks on the flywheel and front camshaft sprocket are aligned with their respective pointers.
3. Loosen the tensioner pulley lockbolt and slide the timing belt off the water pump and camshaft sprockets.

**To install:**

4. With the flywheel timing mark at Top Dead Center (TDC), and the camshaft aligned with it's respective timing mark, install the front timing belt.
5. Position and tighten the belt tensioner. Adjust until the tension is 33–44 ft. lbs. (147–196 Nm) using tensioner tool 021–00028 or equivalent. Once correct tension has bee reached, tighten lockbolt to 23–34 ft. lbs. (32–47 Nm).
6. Rotate the engine clockwise 2 revolution and make sure the respective marks on the flywheel and camshaft sprocket are correct. Adjust if necessary.
7. Install and secure both timing belt covers.

#### Rear Timing Belt

1. Remove the rear timing belt cover according to the earlier procedure.
2. Remove the flywheel timing mark cover from the clutch housing.
3. Rotate the crankshaft until the flywheel timing mark is at Top Dead Center (TDC) on No. 1 cylinder.
4. Check that the injection pump and camshaft sprocket are correctly aligned with their respective timing marks.
5. Loosen tensioner locknut and with a flat prytool inserted into the slot, rotate the tensioner clockwise to relieve belt tension. When the tension is loose enough, remove the timing belt.

**To install:**

6. Position the timing belt taking care not to alter the crank, injection pump or cam from their timing marks.

7. With everything properly aligned, begin to increase the tension on the timing belt using a prytool.
8. Once the timing belt is tensioned, rotate the engine 2 revolutions and check the timing marks on the flywheel and camshaft sprocket. Adjust if necessary.
9. Install timing belt cover and secure with the retaining bolts.

## Timing Chain and Sprockets

### REMOVAL & INSTALLATION

#### 2.3L Engine

♦ See Figure 162

➡ This procedure is easiest with the engine removed from the vehicle.

1. Disconnect negative battery cable.
2. Remove engine and transaxle from vehicle as an assembly and position in a suitable holding fixture.
3. Remove the dipstick.
4. Remove front timing chain cover from the engine.
5. Check timing chain deflection as follows:
    a. Rotate crankshaft counterclockwise, as viewed from the front of the engine, to take up slack on the left side of chain.
    b. Make a reference mark on the block at approximately mid–point of chain. Measure from this point to the chain.
    c. Rotate the crankshaft in the opposite direction to take up any slack on the right side of the chain. Force the left side of chain out with your fingers and measure the distance between the reference point and chain. The deflection is the difference between the 2 measurements.
    d. If the deflection measurement exceeds 0.5 in. (13mm), replace the timing chain and sprockets. If the wear on the tensioner face exceeds 0.06 in. (1.5mm), replace the tensioner.
6. Turn the engine over until the timing marks are aligned. Remove the camshaft sprocket attaching bolt and washer. Slide both sprockets and timing chain forward and remove as an assembly.
7. Check timing chain vibration damper for excessive wear and replace if necessary. The damper is located inside the front timing chain cover.
8. Remove the oil pan.

➡ Oil pan removal is recommended to ensure proper sealing to front cover upon installation.

**To install:**

9. Clean and inspect all parts before installation. Clean the oil pan, cylinder block and front cover of gasket material and dirt.
10. Slide both sprockets and timing chain onto the camshaft and crankshaft with timing marks aligned. Install the camshaft bolt and washer, then tighten to 41–56 ft. lbs. (557–75 Nm). Oil the timing chain, sprockets and tensioner after installation with clean engine oil.
11. Install the front cover.
12. Install the oil pan.
13. Install the accessory drive pulley, if equipped

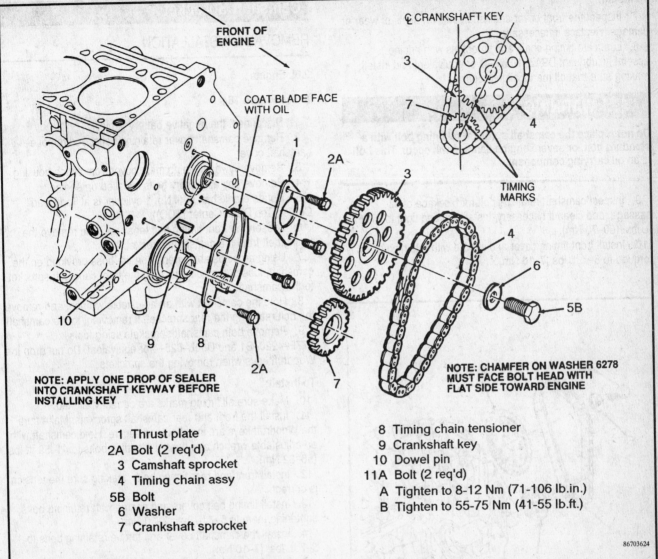

FRONT OF ENGINE

COAT BLADE FACE WITH OIL

CRANKSHAFT KEY

TIMING MARKS

NOTE: APPLY ONE DROP OF SEALER INTO CRANKSHAFT KEYWAY BEFORE INSTALLING KEY

NOTE: CHAMFER ON WASHER 6278 MUST FACE BOLT HEAD WITH FLAT SIDE TOWARD ENGINE

1  Thrust plate
2A Bolt (2 req'd)
3  Camshaft sprocket
4  Timing chain assy
5B Bolt
6  Washer
7  Crankshaft sprocket

8  Timing chain tensioner
9  Crankshaft key
10 Dowel pin
11A Bolt (2 req'd)
A  Tighten to 8-12 Nm (71-106 lb.in.)
B  Tighten to 55-75 Nm (41-55 lb.ft.)

86703624

**Fig. 162 Exploded view of 2.3L timing chain and sprocket**

14. Install crankshaft pulley attaching bolt and washer. Tighten to 140–170 ft. lbs. (190–230 Nm).

15. Remove engine from workstand and install in vehicle.

16. Connect negative battery cable.

### 3.0L Engine

◆ See Figure 163

1. Remove the timing chain cover as outlined earlier.

2. Check camshaft end–play as follows;

   a. Push camshaft toward rear of engine. Install dial indicator with bracket 014–00282 or equivalent such that the indicator point is on the camshaft sprocket retaining screw.

   b. Zero the dial indicator. Pull camshaft forward and release. Compare dial indicator reading with specifications. If end–play is in excess of 0.005 in. (0.127mm), replace the thrust plate.

3. Check timing chain deflection as follows:

   a. Rotate crankshaft counterclockwise, as viewed from the front of the engine, to take up slack on the left side of chain.

   b. Make a reference mark on the block at approximately mid–point of chain. Measure from this point to the chain.

   c. Rotate the crankshaft in the opposite direction to take up any slack on the right side of the chain. Force the left side of chain out with your fingers and measure the distance between the reference point and chain. The deflection is the difference between the 2 measurements.

   d. If the deflection measurement exceeds 0.5 in. (13mm), replace the timing chain and sprockets. If the wear on the tensioner face exceeds 0.06 in. (1.5mm), replace the tensioner.

4. Remove camshaft sprocket retaining bolt and washer.

5. Remove timing chain and sprockets by pulling pieces forward.

6. Carefully clean any gasket material from the front cover and cylinder block. Remove any silicone from the cylinder block and oil pan.

**To install:**

7. Inspect the front cover crankshaft seal for signs of wear or damage. Replace if necessary.

8. Lubricate timing chain and sprockets with engine assembly lubricant D9AZ–19579–D or equivalent and install, making sure that all marks align properly.

### ✳✳WARNING

Do not replace the camshaft sprocket retaining bolt with a standard bolt, or severe engine damage will occur. This bolt is an oil carrying component.

9. Inspect camshaft retaining bolt for blockage of oil passage, and clean if necessary. Install bolt and tight to 37–52 ft. lbs. (50–70 Nm).

10. Install front timing cover and secure with retaining bolts torqued to 5–7 ft. lbs (7–10 Nm).

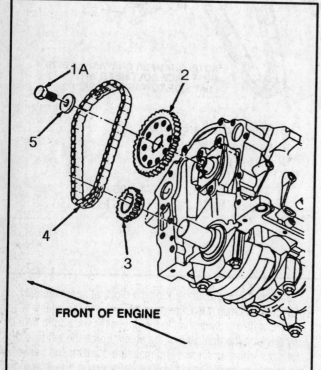

**FRONT OF ENGINE**

1A Bolt
2 Camshaft sprocket
3 Crankshaft sprocket
4 Timing chain lubricate with oil
5 Washer-camshaft sprocket
A Tighten to 50-70 Nm (37-51 lb.ft.)

86703625

**Fig. 163 Exploded view of 3.0L timing chain and sprocket**

## Camshaft Sprocket

### REMOVAL & INSTALLATION

#### 2.0L Engine

▶ See Figure 164

1. Disconnect the negative battery cable.
2. Remove camshaft cover retaining bolts, and remove camshaft cover.
3. Remove flywheel timing mark cover from clutch housing.
4. Remove any accessary belts installed on engine.
5. Rotate crankshaft until No. 1 cylinder is at Top Dead Center (Top Dead Center (TDC)).
6. Loosen the front timing belt tensioner, and remove the timing belt from the camshaft sprocket.
7. Using an adjustable wrench on the boss provided on the camshaft, loosen the bolt attaching the front camshaft sprocket to the camshaft.
8. Hold the camshaft with an adjustable wrench, and remove the bolt retaining the rear sprocket, if removing, to the camshaft.
9. Remove both camshaft sprockets using tools T77F–4220–B1 and D80L–625–4 or equivalent. Do not drop the Woodruff keys when removing the sprockets.

**To install:**

10. Make sure all timing marks are correctly aligned.
11. Install the front and rear camshaft sprockets. Make sure the Woodruff keys are installed and secure. Hold camshaft with an adjustable wrench and tighten retaining bolts to 41–59 ft. lbs. (56–82 Nm).
12. Install front and rear timing belts, making sure the tension is correct.
13. Install timing belt covers and secure with retaining bolts tightening them to 5–7 ft. lbs. (7–10 Nm).
14. Install the camshaft cover and torque retaining bolts to 5–7 ft. lbs. (7–10 Nm).
15. Install any accessary belts which were removed earlier.
16. Connect the negative the battery cable.

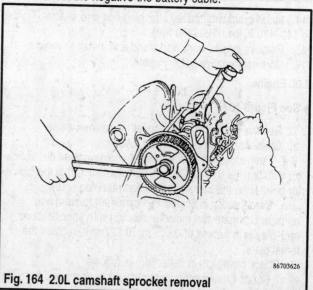

86703626

**Fig. 164 2.0L camshaft sprocket removal**

## 2.3L Engine

▶ See Figure 162

1. Remove the engine from the vehicle and position in a suitable holding fixture.
2. Remove the drive belts and pulleys.
3. Remove the cylinder head.
4. Remove the crankshaft pulley.
5. Remove the oil pan.
6. Remove the timing chain front cover and gasket.
7. Remove the camshaft sprocket retaining bolt.
8. Remove the timing chain, sprockets and timing chain tensioner.
9. Remove camshaft sprocket with a pulley puller or equivalent tool. Be careful not to loose the Woodruff key.

### To install:

10. Clean and inspect all parts before installation.
11. Position the Woodruff key, camshaft sprocket and retaining bolt.
12. Tighten attaching bolt to 71–106 ft. lbs (96–144 Nm).
13. Install the timing chain, sprockets and timing chain tensioner according to the proper procedure.
14. Install the cylinder front cover and crank shaft pulley.
15. Install the accessory drive belt pulley assembly.
16. Install cylinder head.
17. Install engine in vehicle.

## 3.0L Engine

▶ See Figure 163

1. Disconnect the negative battery cable.
2. Remove the engine from the vehicle .
3. Remove the drive belts and pulleys.
4. Rotate crankshaft to Top Dead Center (TDC) on the compression stroke.
5. Remove the front cover assembly.
6. Remove damper retaining bolt and washer. Remove damper.
7. Remove camshaft sprocket bolt and retaining washer.
8. Remove timing chain and sprocket using a pulley puller. Be careful not to loose the Woodruff key.

### To install:

9. Position the Woodruff key and camshaft pulley with the timing chain.
10. Install the retaining bolt and torque to 37–52 ft. lbs. (50–70 Nm).
11. Fasten damper washer and bolt. Tighten bolt to specification.
12. Install the front cover tightening the bolts to 8–10 ft. lbs. (10–14 Nm).
13. Install drive belt pulleys and belts. Check to make sure belt tension is to specification.
14. Install engine in vehicle.
15. Connect battery cable.

## Camshaft

### REMOVAL & INSTALLATION

#### 2.0L Engine

▶ See Figure 165

1. Disconnect the negative battery cable.
2. Remove camshaft cover retaining bolts, and remove camshaft cover.
3. Remove flywheel timing mark cover from clutch housing.
4. Remove any accessary belts installed on engine.
5. Rotate crankshaft until No. 1 cylinder is at Top Dead Center (TDC).
6. Remove both front and rear timing belt covers.
7. Loosen the front timing belt tensioner, and remove the timing belt from the camshaft sprocket.
8. Using an adjustable wrench on the boss provided on the camshaft, loosen the bolt attaching the front camshaft sprocket to the camshaft.
9. Hold the camshaft with an adjustable wrench, and remove the bolt retaining the rear sprocket to the camshaft.
10. Remove both camshaft sprockets using tools T77F–4220–B1 and D80L–625–4 or equivalent. Do not drop the Woodruff keys when removing the sprockets.
11. Remove No.1, No. 3 and No. 5 camshaft bearing caps.

➡ Failure to follow these procedures can result in damage to the cylinder head and/or camshaft.

12. For bearing caps No. 2 and No. 4 loosen nuts as follows;
    a. Loosen one nut on one cap 2–3 turns.
    b. Loosen a nut on the other bearing cap 2–3 turns.
    c. Return to the original bearing cap and loosen 2–3 turns.
    d. Continue process until both bearing caps are loose and can be removed.
13. Check camshaft and shims for signs of wear. Replace if necessary.

#### To install:

➡ Camshaft bearings are to be installed with the arrows pointing toward the front of the engine. No. 2, 3 and 4 bearing caps have their numbers cast in the top surface. No. 1 and 5 bearing caps are not marked, however No. 1 has a slot to fit over the camshaft thrust flange.

14. Make sure all timing marks are correctly aligned.
15. Position the camshaft in the cylinder head and instal No. 2 and No. 4 bearing cap as follows;
    a. Place bearing cap over camshaft and tighten one nut 2–3 turns.
    b. Proceed to the other bearing cap and do the same.
    c. Proceeding in sequence, continue until these bearing cap are seated.

16. Install bearing caps No. 1, 3 and 5, tightening all the nuts to 15–19 ft. lbs (20–27 Nm).

17. Tighten the nuts on bearing caps No. 2 and 4 to the above amounts.

18. Install the front and rear camshaft sprockets. Hold camshaft with an adjustable wrench and tighten retaining bolts to 41–59 ft. lbs. (56–82 Nm).

19. Install front and rear timing belts, making sure the tension is correct.

20. Adjust valves, if necessary.

21. Install timing belt covers and secure with retaining bolts tightening them to 5–7 ft. lbs. (7–10 Nm).

22. Install the camshaft cover and torque retaining bolts to 5–7 ft. lbs. 7–10 Nm).

23. Install any accessary belts which were removed earlier.

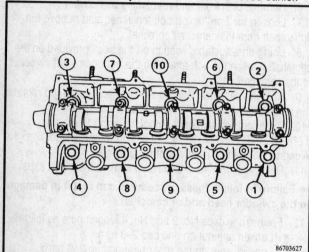

**Fig. 165 Camshaft bearing removal sequence—2.0L engine**

## 2.3L Engine

▶ See Figure 166

➡ When draining coolant, keep in mind that cats and dogs are attracted to ethylene glycol antifreeze, and could drink any that is left in an uncovered container or in puddles on the ground. This will prove fatal in sufficient quantity. Always drain the coolant into a sealable container. Coolant should be reused unless it is contaminated or several years old.

1. Disconnect the negative battery cable.

2. Drain the cooling system and crankcase. Properly relieve the fuel system pressure.

3. Remove the engine from the vehicle and position in a suitable holding fixture. Remove the engine oil dipstick and tube.

4. Remove the drive belts and pulleys.

5. Remove the cylinder head.

6. Mark and remove the distributor body from the engine.

7. Using a magnet, remove the hydraulic lifters and label them so they can be installed in their original positions. If the lifters are stuck in the bores by excessive varnish, etc., use a suitable puller to remove the assembly.

8. Remove the crankshaft pulley.

9. Remove the oil pan.

10. Remove the timing chain front cover and gasket.

11. Check the camshaft end–play as follows:

   a. Push the camshaft toward the rear of the engine and install a dial indicator tool, so the indicator point is on the camshaft sprocket attaching screw.

   b. Zero the dial indicator. Position a small prybar or equivalent, between the camshaft sprocket or gear and the engine block.

   c. Pull the camshaft forward and release it. Compare the dial indicator reading with the camshaft end–play specification of 0.009 in. (0.228mm).

   d. If the camshaft end–play is over the amount specified, replace the thrust plate.

12. Remove the timing chain, sprockets and timing chain tensioner.

13. Remove camshaft thrust plate. Carefully remove the camshaft by pulling it toward the front of the engine. Use caution to avoid damaging bearings, journals and lobes.

### To install:

14. Clean and inspect all parts before installation.

15. Lubricate camshaft lobes and journals with heavy engine oil. Carefully slide the cam shaft through the bearings in the cylinder block.

16. Install the thrust plate. Tighten attaching bolts to 6–9 ft. lbs (8–12 Nm).

17. Install the timing chain, sprockets and timing chain tensioner according to the proper procedure.

18. Install the cylinder front cover and crank shaft pulley.

19. Clean the oil pump inlet tube screen, oil pan and cylinder block gasket surfaces. Prime oil pump by filling the inlet opening with oil and rotate the pump shaft until oil emerges from the outlet tube. Install oil pump, oil pump inlet tube screen and oil pan.

20. Install the accessory drive belts and pulley assembly.

21. Lubricate the lifters and lifter bores with heavy engine oil. Install lifters into their original bores.

22. Install cylinder head.

23. Position No. 1 piston at Top Dead Center (TDC) after the compression stroke. Position distributor in the block with the rotor at the No. 1 firing position. Install distributor retaining clamp.

24. Install engine in vehicle.

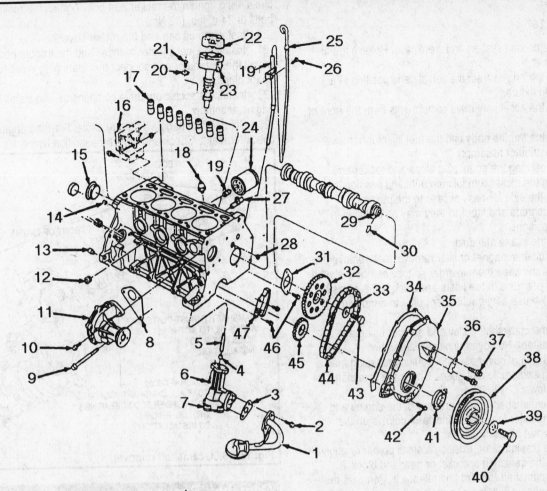

1 Oil pump screen and cover
2 Bolt (2)
3 Gasket
4 Oil pump dowel
5 Oil pump shaft
6 Bolt (2)
7 Oil pump
8 Gasket
9 Bolt (1)
10 Bolt (2)
11 Water pump
12 Block coolant plug
13 Dowel
14 Screw
15 Camshaft rear bearing cover (2)
16 Bracket coil
17 Tappet assy (8)
18 Oil pressure gauge assy
19 Oil filter insert
20 Distributor clamp
21 Bolt (1)
22 Rotor assy
23 Distributor assy
24 Oil filter

25 Oil lever indicator
26 Bolt
27 VRS sensor
28 Plug
29 Camshaft
30 Dowel pin
31 Camshaft thrust plate
32 Washer
33 Camshaft sprocket
34 Gasket
35 Timing chain cover
36 Timing pointer
37 Screw (2)
38 Crankshaft pulley
39 Washer
40 Bolt (1)
41 Oil seal
42 Bolt (6)
43 Bolt (1)
44 Timing chain
45 Crankshaft sprocket
46 Bolt (2)
47 Tensioner assy

86703628

**Fig. 166 Exploded view of 2.3L block with camshaft**

### 3.0L Engine

**♦ See Figure 167**

1. Drain the cooling system and crankcase. Relieve the fuel system pressure.

2. Remove the engine from the vehicle and position in a suitable holding fixture.

3. Remove the accessory drive components from the front of the engine.

4. Remove the throttle body and the fuel injector harness. Remove the distributor assembly.

5. Remove and tag the spark plug wires and rocker arm covers. Loosen the rocker arm fulcrum nuts and position the rocker arms to the side for easy access to the pushrods. Remove the pushrods and label so they may be installed in their original positions.

6. Remove the intake manifold.

7. Using a suitable magnet or lifter removal tool, remove the hydraulic lifters and keep them in order so they can be installed in their original positions. If the lifters are stuck in the bores by excessive varnish use a hydraulic lifter puller to remove the lifters.

8. Remove the crankshaft pulley and damper using a suitable removal tool. Remove the oil pan assembly.

9. Remove the front cover assembly. Align the timing marks on the camshaft and crankshaft gears. Check the camshaft end–play as follows:

   a. Push the camshaft toward the rear of the engine and install a dial indicator tool, so the indicator point is on the camshaft sprocket attaching screw.

   b. Zero the dial indicator. Position a small prybar or equivalent, between the camshaft sprocket or gear and block.

   c. Pull the camshaft forward and release it. Compare the dial indicator reading with the camshaft end–play service limit specification of 0.005 in. (0.13mm).

   d. If the camshaft end–play is over the amount specified, replace the thrust plate.

10. Remove the timing chain and sprockets.

11. Remove the camshaft thrust plate. Carefully remove the camshaft by pulling it toward the front of the engine. Remove it slowly to avoid damaging the bearings, journals and lobes.

### To install:

12. Clean and inspect all parts before installation.

13. Lubricate camshaft lobes and journals with heavy engine oil. Carefully insert the camshaft through the bearings in the cylinder block.

14. Install the thrust plate. Tighten the retaining bolts to 7 ft. lbs. (10 Nm).

15. Install the timing chain and sprockets. Check the camshaft sprocket bolt for blockage of drilled oil passages prior to installation and clean, if necessary.

16. Install the front timing cover and crankshaft damper and pulley.

17. Lubricate the lifters and lifter bores with a heavy engine oil. Install the lifters into their original bores.

18. Install the intake manifold assembly.

19. Lubricate the pushrods and rocker arms with heavy engine oil. Install the pushrods and rocker arms into their original positions. Rotate the crankshaft to set each lifter on its base

circle, then tighten the rocker arm bolt. Tighten the rocker arm bolts to 24 ft. lbs. (32 Nm).

20. Install the oil pan and the rocker covers.

21. Install the fuel injector harness and the throttle body. Install the distributor and connect the spark plug wires to the spark plugs.

22. Install the accessory drive components and install the engine assembly.

23. Connect the negative battery cable. Start the engine and check for leaks. Check and adjust the ignition timing.

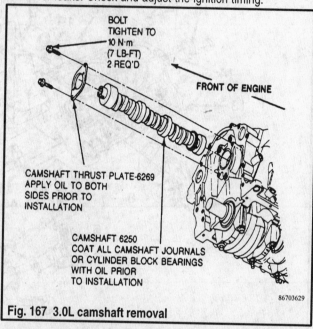

BOLT TIGHTEN TO 10 N·m (7 LB-FT) 2 REQ'D

FRONT OF ENGINE

CAMSHAFT THRUST PLATE-6269 APPLY OIL TO BOTH SIDES PRIOR TO INSTALLATION

CAMSHAFT 6250 COAT ALL CAMSHAFT JOURNALS OR CYLINDER BLOCK BEARINGS WITH OIL PRIOR TO INSTALLATION

86703629

**Fig. 167 3.0L camshaft removal**

## Camshaft Bearings

### REMOVAL & INSTALLATION

#### 2.3L and 3.0L Engine

**♦ See Figure 168**

The camshaft bearings are available prefinished to size and require no reaming for standard 0.015 in. (0.38mm) undersize journal diameters.

1. Disconnect the negative battery cable.

2. Remove the engine from the vehicle. Place the engine on a work stand and remove the camshaft, crankshaft and rear bearing bore plug.

3. Remove the camshaft bearing, using tool T65L–6250–A or equivalent.

4. Select the proper size expanding collet and backup nut and assemble on the expanding mandrel. With the expanding collet collapsed, install the collet assembly in the camshaft bearing. Tighten the backup nut on the expanding mandrel until the collet fits the camshaft bearing.

5. Assembly the puller screw and extension, if necessary, and install on the expanding mandrel. Wrap a cloth around the threads of the puller screw to protect the bearing or journal. Tighten the puller nut against the thrust bearing and pulling plate to remove the camshaft bearing. Hold the end of the puller screw to prevent it from turning

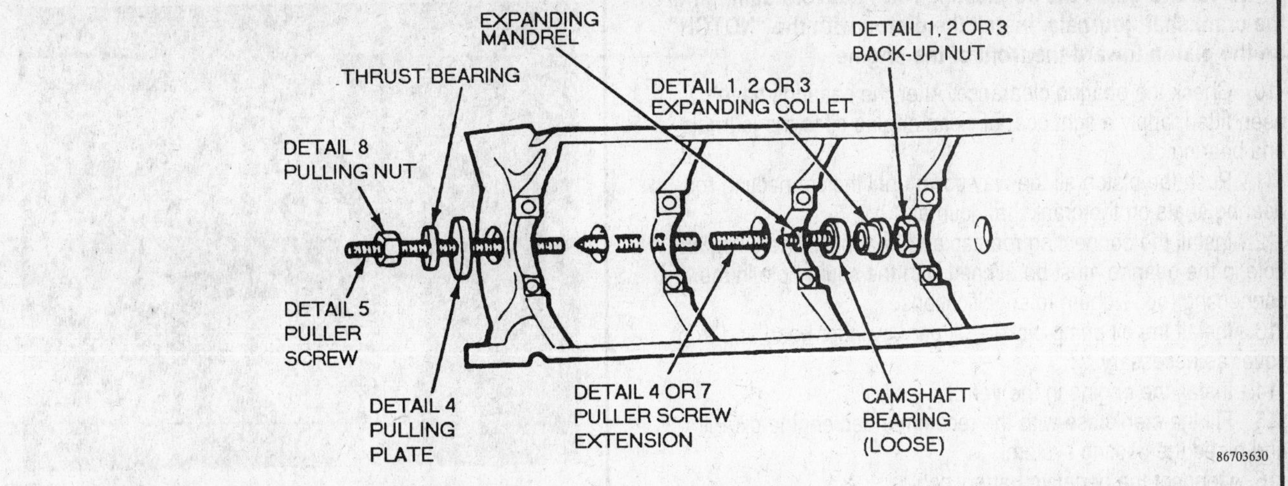

Fig. 168 Camshaft bearing tool—2.3L and 3.0L engines

6. Repeat Step 5 for each bearing. To remove the front bearing, install the puller from the rear of the block.

**To install:**

7. Position the new bearings at the bearing bores and press them in place with the cam bearing tool. Be sure to center the pulling plate and puller screw to avoid damage to the bearing.

➡ **Failure to use the correct expanding collet can cause severe bearing damage. Be sure to align the oil holes in the bearings and install below the front face of the cylinder block. Check the oil passage for obstructions by squirting oil into the opening in the cylinder block and observing flow through the oil hole at the rear camshaft bearing.**

8. Install a new bearing bore plug.
9. Install the camshaft, flywheel and related parts.
10. Install the engine.

## Pistons and Connecting Rods

### REMOVAL & INSTALLATION

◆ **See Figures 169, 170, 171, 172 and 173**

➡ **When draining coolant, keep in mind that cats and dogs are attracted to ethylene glycol antifreeze, and could drink any that is left in an uncovered container or in puddles on the ground. This will prove fatal in sufficient quantity. Always drain the coolant into a sealable container. Coolant should be reused unless it is contaminated or several years old.**

### ✳✳CAUTION

**The EPA warns that prolonged contact with used engine oil may cause a number of skin disorders, including cancer! You should make every effort to minimize your exposure to used engine oil. Protective gloves should be worn when changing the oil. Wash your hands and any other exposed skin areas as soon as possible after exposure to used engine oil. Soap and water, or waterless hand cleaner should be used.**

➡ **Although, in most cases, the pistons and connecting rods can be removed from the engine (after the cylinder head and oil pan are removed) while the engine is still in the vehicle, it is much easier to remove the engine from the vehicle.**

1. Disconnect the negative battery cable.
2. Drain the cooling system and engine crankcase of fluids.
3. Remove the engine from the vehicle.
4. Remove the cylinder head(s), oil pan and front cover (if necessary).

➡ **Mark the connecting rods and bearing caps so they can be installed in the proper cylinders.**

5. Remove the connecting rod bearing caps and bearings.

➡ **Because the top piston ring does not travel to the very top of the cylinder bore, a ridge is built up between the end of the travel and the top of the cylinder. Pushing the piston and connecting rod assembly past the ridge may be difficult and may cause damage to the piston. If necessary, ridge ream the top of the cylinder sleeve before removing the piston assembly.**

6. Push the piston assembly out of the cylinder.

**To install:**

➡ **If new piston rings are to be installed, remove the cylinder wall glaze. Follow the instructions of the tool manufacturer. Clean the cylinder bores with soap and water solution after deglazing or honing. Properly dry and oil the cylinder walls immediately after cleaning.**

7. Oil the piston rings, piston and cylinder walls with clean engine oil.
8. Position the piston ring gaps approximately 90 degrees apart.
9. Install a suitable piston ring compressor on the piston and push the piston in with a hammer handle, until it is slightly below the top of the cylinder.

➡ **Be sure to guide the connecting rods to avoid damaging the crankshaft journals. Install the piston with the "NOTCH" on the piston toward the front of the engine.**

10. Check the bearing clearance. After the bearings have been fitted, apply a light coat of clean engine oil to the journals and bearing.

11. Push the piston all the way down until the connecting rod bearing seats on the crankshaft journals.

12. Install the connecting rod cap and bearings. The oil squirt hole in the bearing must be aligned with the squirt hole in the connecting rod. Tighten to specifications.

13. Install the oil pump pickup, oil pan, cylinder head and front cover as necessary.

14. Install the engine in the vehicle.

15. Fill the crankcase with the recommended engine oil. Fill and bleed the cooling system.

16. Connect the negative battery cable.

17. Run the engine and check for leaks.

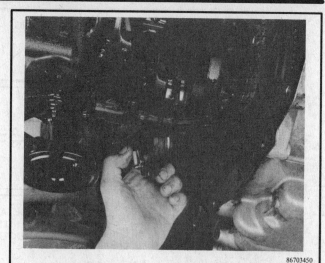

Fig. 171 Remove the bearing cap from the studs

Fig. 169 Loosen and remove the connecting rod bearing cap nut

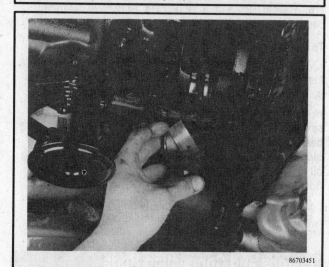

Fig. 172 Bearing cap with bearing

Fig. 170 Using a brass punch, loosen the bearing cap

Fig. 173 When the job is complete torque the bearing cap

## CLEANING AND INSPECTION

1. Use a piston ring expander and remove the rings from the piston.

2. Clean the ring grooves using an appropriate cleaning tool. Exercise care to avoid cutting too deep into the piston.

3. Clean all varnish and carbon from the piston with a safe solvent. Do not use a wire brush or caustic solution on the piston.

4. Inspect the pistons for scuffing, scoring, cracks, pitting or excessive ring groove wear. If wear is evident, the piston must be replaced.

5. Have the piston and connecting rod assembly checked by a machine shop for correct alignment, piston pin wear and piston diameter . If the piston has collapsed it will have to be replace or knurled to restore original diameter. Connecting rod bushing replacement, piston pin fitting and piston changing can be handled by the machine shop.

## CYLINDER BORE

Check the cylinder bore for wear using a telescope gauge and a micrometer, measure the cylinder bore diameter perpendicular to the piston pin at a point 2.5 in. (63.5mm) below the top of the engine block. Measure the piston skirt perpendicular to the piston pin. The difference between the two measurements is the piston clearance. If the clearance is within specifications, finish honing or glaze breaking is all that is required. If clearance is excessive a slightly oversize piston may be required. If greatly oversize, the engine will have to be bored and oversized pistons installed.

## PISTON RING REPLACEMENT

◗ **See Figures 174 and 175**

1. Take the new piston rings and compress them, one at a time into the cylinder that they will be used in. Press the ring about 0.98 in. (25mm) below the top of the cylinder block using an inverted piston.

2. Use a feeler gauge and measure the distance between the ends of the ring. This is called measuring the ring end–gap. Compare the reading to the one called for in the specifications table. If the measurement is too small, when the engine heats up the ring ends will butt together and cause damage. File the ends of the ring with a fine file to obtain necessary clearance.

➡ **If inadequate ring end–gap is utilized, ring breakage will result.**

3. Inspect the ring grooves on the piston for excessive wear or taper. If necessary, have the grooves recut for use with a standard ring and spacer. The machine shop can handle the job for you.

4. Check the ring grooves by rolling the new piston ring around the groove to check for burrs or carbon deposits. If any are found, remove with a fine file. Hold the ring in the groove and measure side clearance with a feeler gauge. If the clearance is excessive, spacer(s) will have to be added.

➡ **Always add spacers above the piston ring.**

5. Install the ring on the piston, lower oil ring first. Use a ring installing tool (piston ring expander) on the compression rings.

Consult the instruction sheet that comes with the rings to be sure they are installed with the correct side up. A mark on the ring usually faces upward.

6. When installing oil rings, first, install the expanding ring in the groove. Hold the ends of the ring butted together (they must not overlap) and install the bottom rail (scraper) with the end about 25mm away from the butted end of the control ring. Install the top rail about 25mm away from the butted end of the control but on the opposite side from the lower rail. Be careful not to scrap the piston when installing oil control rings.

7. Install the two compression rings. The lower ring first.

8. Arrange the rings in a staggered order such that the ends do not overlap on top of each other. Install a ring compressor and insert the piston and rod assembly into the engine.

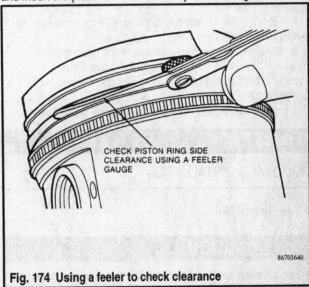

**Fig. 174 Using a feeler to check clearance**

**Fig. 175 Cleaning the piston grooves**

## PISTON PIN REPLACEMENT

1. Matchmark the piston head and the connecting rod for reassembly.

2. Position the piston assembly in a piston pin removal tool.

3. Following the tool manufacturers instructions, press the piston pin from the piston.

4. Check the piston pin bore for damage, replace defective components as required. Check the piston pin for damage, replace as required.

5. Installation is the reverse of the removal procedure.

## ROD BEARING REPLACEMENT

1. Remove the engine from the vehicle. Position the engine assembly in a suitable holding fixture.

2. Remove the oil pan. Remove the oil pump, as required.

3. Rotate the crankshaft so that you can remove the rod bearing cap. Matchmark the rod bearing cap so that it can be reinstalled properly.

4. Remove the rod bearing cap. Remove the upper half of the bearing from its mounting.

5. Carefully remove the lower half of the bearing from its mounting. It may be necessary to pull the piston down in the cylinder chamber to gain more access to the bearing and complete the procedure.

6. Installation is the reverse of the removal procedure.

## Freeze Plugs

### REMOVAL & INSTALLATION

▶ See Figure 176

### ✳✳CAUTION

**When draining coolant, keep in mind that cats and dogs to ethylene glycol antifreeze, and could drink any that is left in an uncovered container or in puddles on the ground. This will prove fatal in sufficient quantity. Always drain the coolant into a sealable container. Coolant should be reused unless it is contaminated or several years old.**

1. Disconnect the negative battery cable. Drain the cooling system.

2. Remove the necessary components to gain access to the freeze plug that requires service.

3. As required, raise and support the vehicle safely.

4. Using a punch or a slide hammer, remove and discard the old freeze plug.

**To install:**

5. If using a new metal freeze plug, position it over the opening in the block. Lightly tap it in place until it sits flush with the bore in the block.

6. If using the rubber type freeze plug, position it over the opening in the block and using the proper tool, lock it in place.

7. Install all the removed components. Lower the vehicle, as required.

8. Fill the cooling system and check for leaks.

9. Connect the negative battery cable.

## Block Heaters

Block heaters are used to keep the oil in the crankcase warm during periods of extremely cold temperatures. These items are useful in regions where the temperature is below the freezing point for extended periods.

Because the oil in the engine becomes thicker as the weather gets colder, the friction needed to warm and move the oil increases. This puts an added strain on the battery when starting the vehicle. The block heater keeps the oil warm, therefore reducing the chance for it to thicken.

Block heater use household electricity to function. When using a block heater, plug the heater in before going to bed, and unplug before starting the vehicle.

### REMOVAL & INSTALLATION

1. Disconnect the negative battery cable. Drain the cooling system.

2. Remove the necessary components to gain access to the engine block heater.

3. As required, raise and support the vehicle safely.

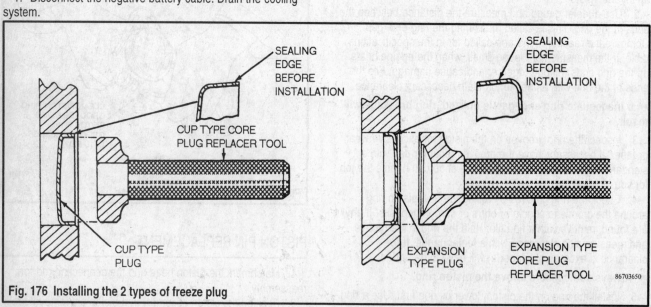

Fig. 176 Installing the 2 types of freeze plug

SEALING EDGE BEFORE INSTALLATION

CUP TYPE CORE PLUG REPLACER TOOL

CUP TYPE PLUG

SEALING EDGE BEFORE INSTALLATION

EXPANSION TYPE PLUG

EXPANSION TYPE CORE PLUG REPLACER TOOL

86703650

4. Carefully remove the engine block heater from its mounting on the engine block.

5. Installation is the reverse of the removal procedure.

## Rear Main Seal

### REMOVAL & INSTALLATION

▶ **See Figures 177, 178, 179, 180 and 181**

1. Disconnect the negative battery cab

2. Remove the transaxle from the vehicle.

3. Install a suitable flywheel holding tool and remove the flywheel retaining bolts. Remove the flywheel

4. Remove the rear cover plate.

5. With an awl, punch a hole into the seal metal surface between the lip and block. Use a slide hammer with a threaded end and remove the seal.

**To install:**

6. Inspect the crankshaft seal area for any damage which may cause the seal to leak. If there is damage evident, service or replace the crankshaft as necessary

7. Clean the seal mounting surfaces. Coat the crankshaft and seal with engine oil and press into place.

8. Using a suitable seal installer, install the new rear seal cover. Install the cover plate.

9. Install the flywheel and using a suitable flywheel holding tool, torque the flywheel retaining bolts to 131–137 ft. lbs. (180–190 Nm).

10. Install the clutch and transaxle assemblies. Connect the negative battery. Start the engine and check for oil leaks.

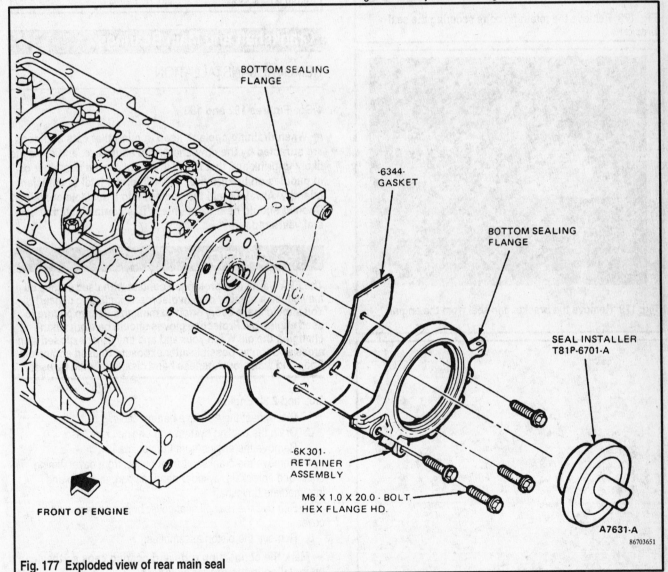

**Fig. 177 Exploded view of rear main seal**

Fig. 178 Remove the retaining bolts securing the seal bracket

Fig. 179 Remove the bracket and seal from the engine

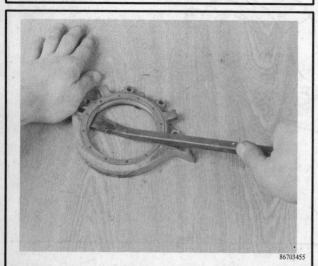

Fig. 180 Prying the seal out

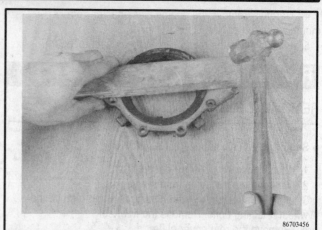

Fig. 181 Using a hammer and a smooth piece of wood to install a new seal

## Crankshaft and Main Bearings

### REMOVAL & INSTALLATION

♦ See Figures 182 and 183

➡ When draining coolant, keep in mind that cats and dogs are attracted by the ethylene glycol antifreeze, and are quite likely to drink any that is left in an uncovered container or in puddles on the ground. This will prove fatal in sufficient quantity. Always drain the coolant into a sealable container. Coolant should be reused unless it is contaminated or several years old.

### ✳✳CAUTION

The EPA warns that prolonged contact with used engine oil may cause a number of skin disorders, including cancer! You should make every effort to minimize your exposure to used engine oil. Protective gloves should be worn when changing the oil. Wash your and and any other exposed skin areas as soon as possible after exposure to used engine oil. Soap and water, or waterless hand cleaner should be used.

#### 2.0L and 2.3L Engine

1. Disconnect the negative battery cable.
2. Drain the cooling system and engine crankcase.
3. Remove the engine from the vehicle.
4. Remove the crankshaft front pulley, front cover, timing chain and sprockets, cylinder head, oil pan, oil pump and intermediate driveshaft.
5. Remove the rear oil seal cover bolts and remove the cover.
6. Remove the piston assemblies.

➡ Mark the connecting rods and bearing caps so they can be installed in the proper cylinders.

7. Remove the main bearing caps and bearing.
8. Carefully lift the crankshaft out of the crankcase, so No. 3 thrust bearing surfaces are not damaged.

9. Remove the main bearing inserts from the engine block and bearing caps.

➡ **For cleaning purposes, the oil gallery and coolant drain plugs can be removed.**

**To install:**

10. Wash the cylinder block thoroughly to remove all foreign material and dry before assembling other components. Check to ensure all oil holes are fully open and clean. Check to ensure the bearing inserts and bearing bores are clean. Clean the mating surfaces of the crankcase and each main bearing cap.

11. Install the main bearings in the cylinder block. Note that the center front bearing is a thrust bearing and the front upper bearing has a small "V" notch on the parting line face.

12. Lubricate the bearings with clean engine oil.

13. Carefully lower the crankshaft into place. Be careful not to damage the bearing surfaces.

14. Check the clearance of each main bearing as outlined in this section.

15. After the bearing has been fitted, apply a light coat of engine oil to the journal and bearings. Install the bearing cap in their original locations . (refer to numbers on caps). The caps must be installed with the arrows pointing to ward the front of the engine. Oil the bolts and tighten to specifications. Repeat the procedure for the remaining bearings.

➡ **Turn the crankshaft to check for turning torque. The turning torque should not exceed 4.5 ft. lbs. (6 Nm).**

16. Install the pistons and connecting rod caps. Check clearance of each bearing, as out lined in this section.

17. After the connecting rod bearings have been fitted, apply a light coat of engine oil to the journal and bearings.

18. Turn the crankshaft throw to the bottom of its stroke. Pull the piston all the way down until the rod bearing seats on the crankshaft journal.

➡ **Guide the rod to prevent crankshaft journal and oil cooling jet damage.**

19. Install the connecting rod cap. Align the marks on the rods with the marks on the cap, and tighten the nut.

20. After the piston and connecting rod assemblies have been installed, check the side clearance between the connecting rods on each connecting rod crankshaft journal.

21. Install the rear crankshaft seal and cover. Tighten the bolts to 5–7 ft. lbs. (7–10 Nm).

22. Install the intermediate driveshaft, oil pump, timing chain and sprockets, front cover, crankshaft pulley and cylinder head.

23. Install the engine in the vehicle.

24. Fill the crankcase with the recommended engine oil. Fill and bleed the cooling system.

25. Connect the negative battery cable.

26. Run the engine and check for leaks.

### 3.0L Engine

1. With the engine removed from the vehicle and placed on a workstand, loosen the idler pulley and the alternator belt adjusting bolt.

2. Remove the oil pan and gasket.

3. Remove the front cover assembly.

4. Check the timing chain deflection. Remove the timing chain and sprockets.

5. Invert the engine on the workstand. Remove the flywheel. Remove the oil pump inlet and the oil pump assembly.

6. Ensure all bearing caps (main and connecting rod) are marked so that they can be installed in their original positions. Turn the crankshaft until the connecting rod from which the cap is being removed is up. Remove the connecting rod cap. Push the connecting rod and piston assembly up in the cylinder. Repeat the procedure for the remaining connecting rod assemblies.

7. Remove the main bearing caps.

8. Carefully lift the crankshaft out of the block so that the upper thrust bearing surfaces are not damaged.

**To install:**

➡ **If the bearings are to be reused they should be identified to ensure that they are installed in their original positions.**

9. Remove the main bearing inserts from the block and bearing caps.

10. Remove the connecting rod bearing inserts from the connecting rods and caps.

11. Inspect all the machined surfaces on the crankshaft for nicks, scratches, scores, etc., which could cause premature bearing wear.

12. If the crankshaft main bearing journals have been refinished to a definite undersize, install the correct undersize bearings, usually in 0.25mm, 0.50mm, 0.80mm undersize.

➡ **Ensure the bearing inserts and the bearing bores are clean. Foreign material under the inserts will distort the bearing and cause a failure.**

13. Place the upper main bearing inserts in position in the bores with the tang fitted in the slot provided.

14. Install the lower main bearing inserts in the bearing caps.

15. Carefully lower the crankshaft into place.

16. Check the clearance of each main bearing. Select fit the bearings for proper clearance.

17. After the bearings have been fitted, apply a light coat of Oil Conditioner part No. D9AZ–19578–CO or heavy engine oil, SAE 50 weight, to the journals bearings and rear seal surface. Install all the bearing caps. Apply RTV to the gap between the rear main bearing and the block. Take care to keep RTV from the parting surfaces between the block and the cap.

➡ **Ensure the main bearing caps are installed in their original positions and orientation.**

18. Lubricate the journal with oil conditioner or heavy engine oil 50 SAE weight. Install the thrust bearing cap with the bolts finger–tight. Pry the crankshaft forward against the thrust surface of the upper half of the bearing. Hold the crankshaft cap to the rear. This will align the thrust surfaces of both halves of the bearing to be positioned properly. Retain the forward pressure on the crankshaft. Tighten the cap bolts to 65–81 ft. lbs. (85–105 Nm).

19. Check the crankshaft end–play with a dial indicator mounted on the front of the engine.

20. If the end–play exceeds specification, replace the upper and lower thrust bearings. If the end–play is less than specification, inspect the thrust bearing faces for damage, dirt or improper alignment. Install the thrust bearing and align the faces. Recheck the end–play.

21. Install the new bearing inserts in the connecting rods and caps. Check the clearance of each bearing by using a piece of Plastigage®

22. If the bearing clearances are to specification, apply a light coat of Oil Conditioner part No. D9AZ–19579–C or heavy engine oil, SAE 50 weight, to the journals and bearings.

23. Turn the crankshaft throw to the bottom of the stroke. Push the piston all the way down until the rod bearings seat on the crankshaft journal.

24. Install the connecting rod cap.

25. After the piston and connecting rod assemblies have been installed, check all the connecting rod crankshaft journal clearances using a piece of Plastigage®

26. Turn the engine on the work stand so that the front end is up. Install the timing chain, sprockets, front cover, new oil seal and crankshaft pulley.

27. Turn the engine on the work stand so that the rear end is up. Install the rear oil seal.

28. Clean the oil pan, oil pump and the oil pump screen assembly.

29. Prime the oil pump by filling the inlet opening with oil and rotating the pump shaft until the oil emerges from the outlet opening. Install the oil pump, baffle and oil pan.

30. Position the flywheel on the crankshaft. Tighten to 54–64 ft. lbs. (70–83 Nm).

31. Turn the engine on work stand so that the engine is in the normal upright position. Install the accessory drive pulley. Install and adjust the accessory drive belts to specification.

32. Install the torque converter, as required.

33. Remove the engine from the work stand. Install the engine in the vehicle.

## CLEANING AND INSPECTION

1. Handle the crankshaft with care to avoid possible fractures or damage to the finish surface.

2. Clean the crankshaft with solvent, and blow out all passages with compressed air.

3. Inspect the main and connecting rod journals for cracks, scratches, grooves or scores.

4. Measure the diameter of each journal at least 4 places to determine out–of–round, taper or undersize conditions.

5. Dress minor scores with an oil stone. If the journals are severely marred or exceed the service limit, they should be refinished to size for the next undersize bearing. If the journal will not clean up to maximum undersize bearing available, replace the crankshaft.

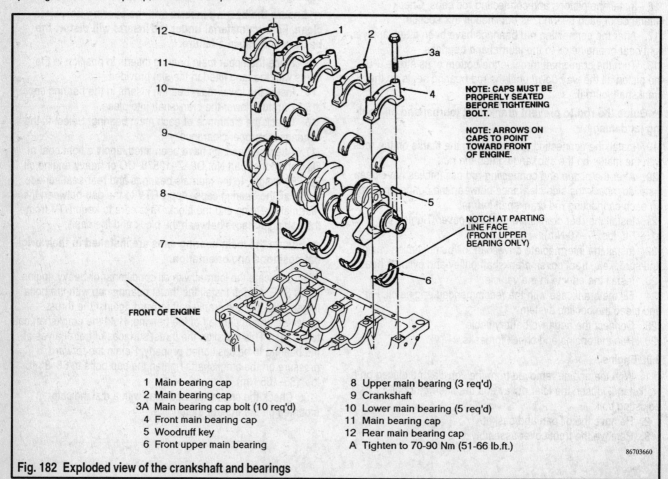

NOTE: CAPS MUST BE PROPERLY SEATED BEFORE TIGHTENING BOLT.

NOTE: ARROWS ON CAPS TO POINT TOWARD FRONT OF ENGINE.

NOTCH AT PARTING LINE FACE (FRONT UPPER BEARING ONLY)

FRONT OF ENGINE

1  Main bearing cap
2  Main bearing cap
3A Main bearing cap bolt (10 req'd)
4  Front main bearing cap
5  Woodruff key
6  Front upper main bearing
8  Upper main bearing (3 req'd)
9  Crankshaft
10 Lower main bearing (5 req'd)
11 Main bearing cap
12 Rear main bearing cap
A  Tighten to 70-90 Nm (51-66 lb.ft.)

86703660

**Fig. 182 Exploded view of the crankshaft and bearings**

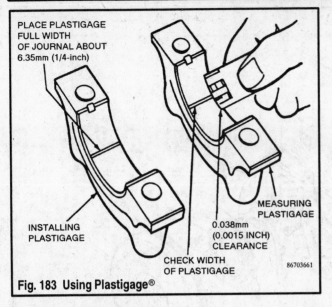

PLACE PLASTIGAGE FULL WIDTH OF JOURNAL ABOUT 6.35mm (1/4-inch)

INSTALLING PLASTIGAGE

MEASURING PLASTIGAGE

0.038mm (0.0015 INCH) CLEARANCE

CHECK WIDTH OF PLASTIGAGE

86703661

**Fig. 183 Using Plastigage®**

## CRANKSHAFT END–PLAY

1. Force the crankshaft toward the rear of the engine.
2. Install a dial indicator so that the contact point rests against the crankshaft end and the indicator axis is parallel to the crankshaft axis.
3. Zero the dial indicator. Push the crank shaft forward and note the reading on the dial.
4. If the end–play exceeds specification, replace the No. 3 main bearing.

## FITTING BEARINGS WITH PLASTIGAGE®

▶ **See Figure 183**

1. Clean the crankshaft journals. Check to ensure the journals and thrust bearing faces and free of nicks, burrs or bearing puck–up that would cause premature bearing wear.
2. When fitting a main bearing, position a jack under the counterweight adjoining the bearing which is being checked. Support the crankshaft with the jack so its weight will not compress the Plastigage® and provide an erroneous reading.

➡ **Do not place the jack under the front post of the crankshaft.**

3. Place a piece of Plastigage® on the bearing surface across full width of the bearing cap and about ¼ in. (6mm) off center.
4. Install the cap and tighten bolts to specification cation. Do not turn the crankshaft while the Plastigage® is in place.
5. Remove the cap. Using the Plastigage® scale, check width of the Plastigage® at widest point to get minimum clearance. Check narrow est point to get maximum clearance. Difference between readings is taper of journal.
6. After the bearing has been fitted, apply a light coat of engine oil to the journal and bearings. Install the bearing cap.

Tighten to specifications. Repeat the procedure for the remaining bearings.

## BEARING OIL CLEARANCE

Remove the cap from the bearing to be checked. Using a clean, dry rag, thoroughly clean all oil from the crankshaft journal and bearing insert.

➡ **Plastigage® is soluble in oil, therefore, oil on the journal or bearing could result in false readings.**

Place a piece of Plastigage® along the full width of the bearing insert, reinstall cap, and torque to specifications.

Remove the bearing cap, and determine bearing clearance by comparing width of the bearing insert, reinstall cap, and torque to specifications.

➡ **Do not rotate crankshaft with Plastigage® installed. If the bearing insert and journal appear intact, and are within tolerances, no further main bearing service is required. If the bearing or journal appear defective, cause of failure should be determined before replacement.**

## CRANKSHAFT REPAIRS

If a journal is damaged on the crankshaft, repair is possible by having the crankshaft machined to a standard undersize.

In most cases, however, since the engine must be removed from the car and disassembled, some thought should be given to replacing the damaged crankshaft with a reground shaft kit. A reground crankshaft kit contains the necessary main and rod bearings for installation. The shaft has been ground and polished to undersize specifications and will usually hold up well if installed correctly.

## Flywheel

### REMOVAL & INSTALLATION

▶ **See Figure 184**

1. Disconnect the negative battery cable.
2. Remove the transaxle and clutch assemblies. Remove the rear cover plate, if so equipped.
3. Install a suitable flywheel holding tool and remove the flywheel retaining bolts. Remove the flywheel.

**To install:**

4. Inspect the flywheel for cracks, heat checks or other damage that would make it unfit for further service. Replace the flywheel with a new one, if required.
5. Install the flywheel and using a suitable flywheel holding tool, torque the flywheel retaining bolts to 54–64 ft. lbs. (73–87 Nm).
6. Install the transaxle assemblies. Rear cover plate, if so equipped.
7. Reconnect the negative battery. Start the engine and check for proper starter gear–to–flywheel meshing.

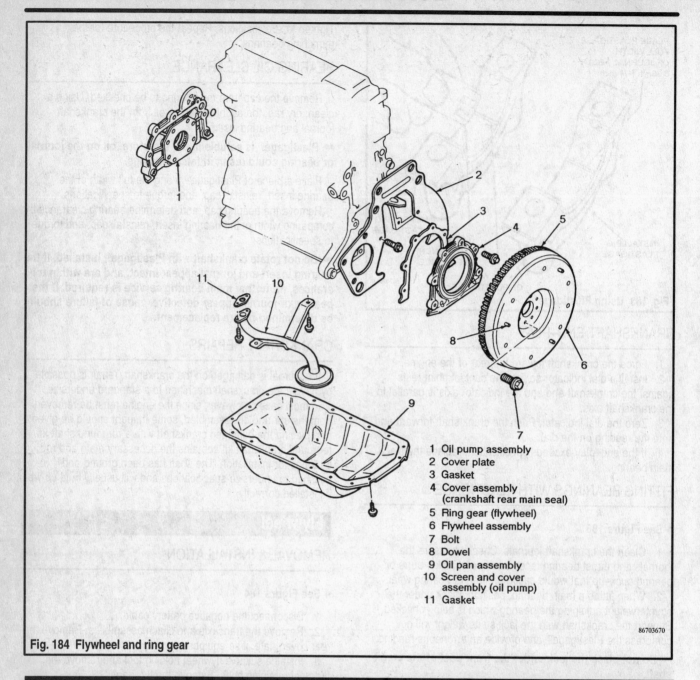

1 Oil pump assembly
2 Cover plate
3 Gasket
4 Cover assembly
   (crankshaft rear main seal)
5 Ring gear (flywheel)
6 Flywheel assembly
7 Bolt
8 Dowel
9 Oil pan assembly
10 Screen and cover
   assembly (oil pump)
11 Gasket

86703670

**Fig. 184 Flywheel and ring gear**

# EXHAUST SYSTEM

## Safety Precautions

For a number of reasons, exhaust system work can be the most dangerous among the type of work you can do on your car. Always observe the following precautions:

• Support the car extra securely. Not only will you often be working directly under it, but you'll frequently be using a lot of force, say, heavy hammer blows, to dislodge rusted parts. This can cause a car that's improperly supported to shift and possibly fall.

• Wear goggles. Exhaust system parts are always rusty. Metal chips can be dislodged, even when you're only turning rusted bolts. Attempting to pry pipes apart with a chisel makes the chips fly even more frequently.

• If you're using a cutting torch, keep it a great distance from either the fuel tank or lines. Stop what you're doing and feel the temperature of the fuel bearing pipes on the tank frequently. Even slight heat can expand and/or vaporize fuel, resulting in accumulated vapor, or even a liquid leak, near your torch.

• Watch where your hammer blows fall and make sure you hit squarely. You could easily tap a brake or fuel line when you hit an exhaust system part with a glancing blow. Inspect all lines and hoses in the area where you've been working.

## ❋❋CAUTION

**Be very careful when working on or near the catalytic converter. External temperatures can reach 1,500°F (816°C) and more, causing severe burns. Removal or installation should be performed only on a cold exhaust system.**

## Special Tools

A number of special exhaust system tools can be rented from auto supply houses or local stores that rent special equipment. A common one is a tail pipe expander, designed to enable you to join pipes of identical diameter.

It may also be quite helpful to use solvents designed to loosen rusted bolts or flanges. Soaking rusted parts the night before you do the job can speed the work of freeing rusted parts considerably. Remember that these solvents are often flammable. Apply only to parts after they are cool!

Inspect inlet pipes, outlet pipes and mufflers for cracked joints, broken welds and corrosion damage that would result in a leaking exhaust system. It is normal for a certain amount of moisture and staining to be present around the muffler seams. The presence of soot, light surface rust or moisture does not indicate a faulty muffler. Inspect the clamps, brackets and insulators for cracks and stripped or badly corroded bolt threads. When flat joints are loosened and/or disconnected to replace a shield pipe or muffler, replace the bolts and flange nuts if there is reasonable doubt that its service life is limited.

The exhaust system, including brush shields, must be free of leaks, binding, grounding and excessive vibrations. These conditions are usually caused by loose or broken flange bolts, shields, brackets or pipes. If any of these conditions exist, check the exhaust system components and alignment. Align or replace as necessary. Brush shields are positioned on the underside of the catalytic converter and should be free from bends which would bring any part of the shield in contact with the catalytic converter or muffler. The shield should also be clear of any combustible material such as dried grass or leaves.

Coat all of the exhaust connections and bolt threads with anti–seize compound to prevent corrosion from making the next disassembly difficult.

## Gasoline Engines

▶ **See Figures 185 and 186**

The converter contains 2 separate ceramic honeycombs coated with different catalytic material. The front catalyst is coated with a rhodium/platinum catalyst designed to control Oxides of Nitrogen (NOx), unburned Hydrocarbons (HC) and Carbon Monoxide (CO). This is therefore called a Three way Catalytic Converter (TWC). The rear catalyst is coated with platinum/palladium and is called a Conventional Oxidation Catalyst (COC).

The TWC converter operates on the exhaust gases as they arrive from the engine. As the gases flow from the TWC to the COC converter, they mix with the air in the secondary air system into the mixing chamber between the two ceramic honeycombs. This air is required for optimum operating conditions for the oxidation of the HC and CO on the COC converter. Air is diverted upstream of the TWC during cold start to provide faster catalyst light off and better HC/CO control.

The factory installed exhaust system uses a one–piece converter system. The exhaust system is usually serviced in 4 pieces. The rear section of the muffler inlet pipe (intermediate muffler inlet) is furnished separate from the muffler.

➡ **The operating temperature of the exhaust system is very high. Never attempt to service any part of the system until it has cooled. Be especially careful when working around the catalytic converter. The temperature of the converter rise to high level after only a few minutes of operating temperature.**

## Muffler and Outlet Pipe Assembly

### REMOVAL & INSTALLATION

#### Gasoline Engine

1. Raise the vehicle and support on jackstands.
2. Remove the U–bolt assembly and the rubber insulators from the hanger brackets and remove the muffler assembly. Slide the muffler assembly toward the rear of the car to disconnect it from the converter.
3. Replace parts as needed.

**To install:**

4. Position the muffler assembly under the car and slide it forward onto the converter outlet pipe. Check that the slot in the muffler and the tab on the converter are fully engaged.
5. Install the rubber insulators on the hanger assemblies. Install the U–bolt and tighten the nuts.
6. Check the system for leaks. Lower the vehicle.

#### Catalytic Converter and/or Pipe Assembly

1. Raise the vehicle and support on jackstands.
2. Remove the front catalytic converter flange fasteners, loosen the rear U–bolt connection and disconnect the air hoses.
3. Separate the catalytic converter inlet and outlet connections. Remove the converter.

**To install:**

4. Install the converter to the muffler.
5. Install the converter and muffler assembly to the inlet pipe/flex joint. Connect the air hoses and position the U–bolt.
6. Align the exhaust system into position and, starting at the front of the system, tighten all the nuts and bolts.
7. Check the system for leaks. Lower the vehicle.

#### Diesel Engine

The 4–cylinder 2.0L diesel engine is made up of the rear section of the muffler inlet pipe, intermediate muffler, center pipe and downpipe. Because this is a diesel engine, there is no catalytic converter.

➡ The operating temperature of the exhaust system is very high. Never attempt to service any part of the system until it has cooled. Be especially careful when working around the catalytic converter. The temperature of the converter rise to high level after only a few minutes of operating temperature.

## Muffler Assembly

### REMOVAL & INSTALLATION

1. Raise the vehicle and support on jackstands.

2. Remove the U–bolt assembly and the rubber insulators from the hanger brackets and remove the muffler assembly. Slide the muffler assembly toward the rear of the car to disconnect it from the converter.

3. Replace parts as needed.

**To install:**

4. Position the muffler assembly under the car and slide it forward onto the converter outlet pipe. Check that the slot in the muffler and the tab on the converter are fully engaged.

5. Install the rubber insulators on the hanger assemblies. Install the U–bolt and tighten

6. Check the system for leaks. Lower the vehicle.

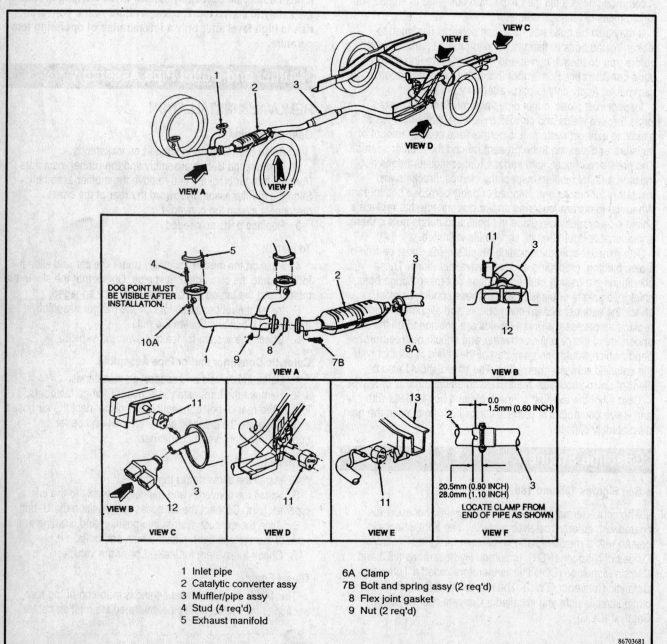

1 Inlet pipe
2 Catalytic converter assy
3 Muffler/pipe assy
4 Stud (4 req'd)
5 Exhaust manifold
6A Clamp
7B Bolt and spring assy (2 req'd)
8 Flex joint gasket
9 Nut (2 req'd)

DOG POINT MUST BE VISIBLE AFTER INSTALLATION.

0.0
1.5mm (0.60 INCH)
20.5mm (0.80 INCH)
28.0mm (1.10 INCH)
LOCATE CLAMP FROM END OF PIPE AS SHOWN

VIEW A   VIEW B   VIEW C   VIEW D   VIEW E   VIEW F

**Fig. 185 Exhaust system—3.0L engine**

86703681

Typical factory-installed exhaust systems are shown in the following illustration.

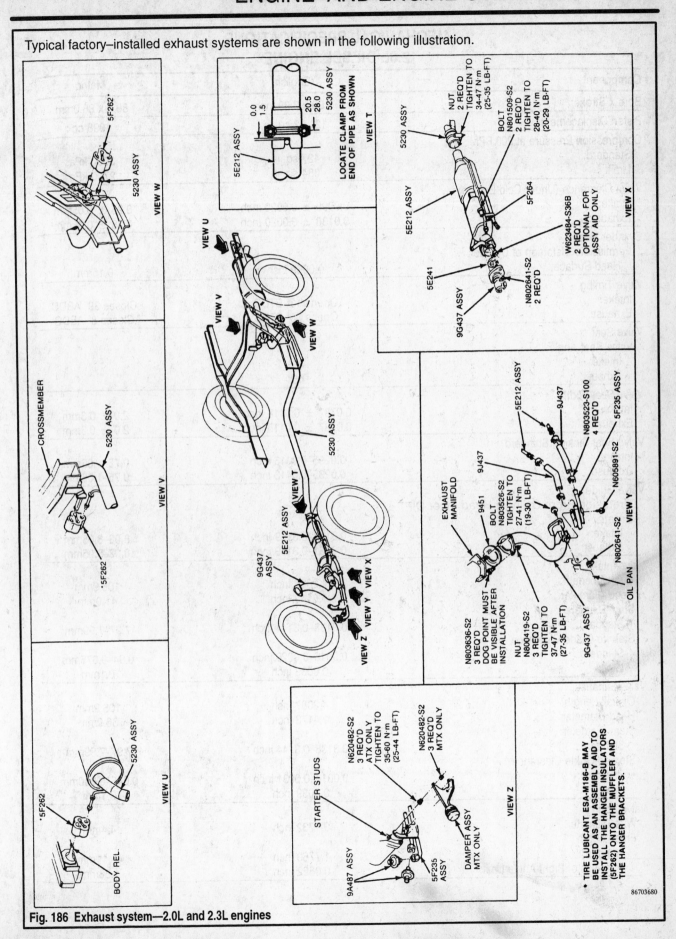

Fig. 186 Exhaust system—2.0L and 2.3L engines

## MECHANICAL SPECIFICATIONS
## 2.0L DIESEL ENGINE

| Component | English | Metric |
|---|---|---|
| Bore x Stroke: | 3.39 x 3.39 inch | 86.0 x 86.0mm |
| Piston Displacement: | 121.92 cu. in. | 1998 cc |
| Compression Pressure at 200 RPM | | |
|   Standard: | 427 sq. in. | 3000 kPa |
|   Limit: | 384 sq. in. | 2700 kPa |
| Valve Clearance (Under Cold Engine) | | |
|   Intake: | 0.0098 ± 0.0020 inch | 0.25 ± 0.05mm |
|   Exhaust: | 0.0138 ± 0.0020 inch | 0.35 ± 0.05mm |
| Cylinder Head | | |
|   Permissible Distortion of Cylinder | | |
|     Head Surface: | 0.0059 inch | 0.15mm |
| Valve Timing | | |
|   Intake: | Opens 13° BTDC | Closes 39° ABDC |
|   Exhaust: | Opens 60° BTDC | Closes 8° ABDC |
| Valve Seat | | |
|   Valve Seat Angle | | |
|     Intake: | 45° | |
|     Exhaust: | 45° | |
| Valve Seat Width | | |
|   Intake: | 0.0787 ± 0.0118 inch | 2.0 ± 0.3mm |
|   Exhaust: | 0.0787 ± 0.0118 inch | 2.0 ± 0.3mm |
| Valve Seat Sinking Standard | | |
|   Intake: | 0.0295–0.0413 inch | 0.75–1.05mm |
|   Exhaust: | 0.0295–0.0413 inch | 0.75–1.05mm |
| Valve Guide | | |
|   Protusion From Cylinder Head Inner Di-ameter | | |
|     Intake: | 0.3161–0.3169 inch | 8.03–8.05mm |
|     Exhaust: | 0.3161–0.3169 inch | 8.03–8.05mm |
| Valve-Intake | | |
|   Overall Length: | 4.2087 inch | 106.9mm |
|   Head Diameter: | 1.6142 inch | 41.0mm |
|   Stem Diameter | | |
|     Standard: | 0.3138–0.3144 inch | 7.97–7.99mm |
|   Stem-to-Guide Clearance | | |
|     Standard: | 0.0016–0.0029 inch | 0.04–0.075mm |
|     Limit: | 0.0039 inch | 0.1mm |
| Valve-Exhaust | | |
|   Overall Length: | 4.2087 inch | 106.9mm |
|   Head Diameter: | 1.4173 inch | 36.0mm |
|   Stem Diameter | | |
|     Standard: | 0.3138–0.3144 inch | 7.97–7.99mm |
|   Stem-to-Guide Clearance | | |
|     Standard: | 0.0018–0.0031 inch | 0.045–0.080mm |
|     Limit: | 0.0039 inch | 0.1mm |
| Valve Spring | | |
|   Wire Diameter: | 0.1732 inch | 4.4mm |
|   Free Length | | |
|     Standard: | 1.7760 inch | 45.11mm |
|   Trueness of Right Angle Limit: | 0.0622 inch | 1.58mm |

86703920

## MECHANICAL SPECIFICATIONS
## 2.0L DIESEL ENGINE

| Component | English | Metric |
|---|---|---|
| **Camshaft** | | |
| Cam Lobe Height | | |
| Standard | | |
| Intake: | 1.7444 inch | 44.306mm |
| Exhaust: | 1.7835 inch | 45.300mm |
| Wear Limit | | |
| Intake: | 1.7284 inch | 43.900mm |
| Exhaust: | 1.7677 inch | 44.900mm |
| Camshaft Run-Out | | |
| Standard: | 0.0006 inch | 0.015mm |
| Limit: | 0.0039 inch | 0.10mm |
| Journal Diameter | | |
| Standard: | 1.2582–1.2589 inch | 31.959–31.975mm |
| Oil Clearance | | |
| Standard: | 0.0010–0.0026 inch | 0.025–0.066mm |
| Limit: | 0.0039 inch | 0.1mm |
| End Play | | |
| Standard: | 0.0008–0.0059 inch | 0.02–0.15mm |
| Limit: | 0.0079 inch | 0.2mm |
| **Connecting Rod** | | |
| Permissible Bend or Twist Limit* | | |
| Small End Bore** | | |
| Piston Pin and Small End Bushing Clearance | | |
| Standard: | 0.0006–0.103 inch | 0.110–0.262mm |
| Limit: | 0.0020 inch | 0.05mm |
| End Play | | |
| Standard: | 0.0043–0.0103 inch | 0.110–0.262mm |
| Limit: | 0.0020 inch | 0.05mm |
| Bearing Oil Clearance | | |
| Standard: | 0.0010–0.0022 inch | 0.027–0.055mm |
| Limit: | 0.0031 inch | 0.08mm |
| Available Undersize Bearing*** | | |
| *: | 0.0063 inch per 3.9371 inch | 0.16mm per 100mm |
| **: | 0.9848–0.9854 inch | 25.014–25.030mm |
| ***: | 0.0098 inch | 0.25mm |
| **Piston and Piston Pin** | | |
| Diameter: | 3.3842–3.3852 inch | 85.957–85.983mm |
| Piston and Cylinder Clearance | | |
| Standard: | 0.0013–0.0020 inch | 0.032–0.050mm |
| Limit: | 0.0059 inch | 0.15mm |
| Ring Groove Width | | |
| Top: | 0.0803–0.0811 inch | 2.040–2.060mm |
| Second: | 0.0799–0.0807 inch | 2.030–2.050mm |
| Oil: | 0.1583–0.1591 inch | 4.020–4.040mm |
| Clearance Between Piston Ring and Ring Groove | | |
| Top: | 0.0020–0.0035 inch | 0.05–0.09mm |
| Second: | 0.0016–0.0031 inch | 0.04–0.08mm |
| Limit: | 0.0079 inch | 0.2mm |
| Piston Pin | | |
| Diameter: | 1.0234–0.9843 inch | 25.994–25.000mm |

86703921

## MECHANICAL SPECIFICATIONS
## 2.0L DIESEL ENGINE

| Component | English | Metric |
|---|---|---|
| Crankshaft and Main Bearing | | |
| Main Journal Diameter | | |
| Standard: | 2.3598–2.3605 inch | 59.937–59.955mm |
| Wear Limit: | 2.3578–2.3585 inch | 59.887–59.905mm |
| Grinding Limit: | 0.0295 inch | 0.75mm |
| Crankpin Diameter | | |
| Standard: | 2.0055–2.0061 inch | 50.940–50.955mm |
| Wear Limit: | 2.0036–2.0042 inch | 50.890–50.905mm |
| Grinding Limit: | 0.0295 inch | 0.75mm |
| Main Journal Bearing Clearance | | |
| Standard: | 0.0012–0.0020 inch | 0.031–0.050mm |
| Wear Limit: | 0.0031 inch | 0.08mm |
| Crankshaft End Play | | |
| Standard: | 0.0016–0.0111 inch | 0.040–0.282mm |
| Limit: | 0.0118 inch | 0.30mm |
| Cylinder Block | | |
| Bore Diameter | | |
| Standard: | 3.3859–3.3867 inch | 86.000–86.022mm |
| Wear Limit: | 0.0059 inch | 0.15mm |
| Flywheel | | |
| Run-Out Limit: | 0.0079 inch | 0.2mm |

86703922

## GASOLINE ENGINE TORQUE SPECIFICATIONS

| Component | English | Metric |
|---|---|---|
| Fuel Pump Bolts: | 15–20 ft. lbs. | 20–28 Nm |
| Crankshaft Pulley Bolt: | 140–170 ft. lbs. | 190–230 Nm |
| Spark Plugs: | 5.5–10.5 ft. lbs. | 7–14 Nm |
| Carburetor Nuts: | 12–15 ft. lbs. | 16–20 Nm |
| Flywheel Bolts: | 54–64 ft. lbs. | 73–87 Nm |
| RH No. 34 Intermediate Bracket Bolt: | 55–75 ft. lbs. | 75–100 Nm |
| RH No. 3A Insulator Nuts: | 75–100 ft. lbs. | 100–135 Nm |
| LH Front No. 1 Insulator-to-Transaxle Bolts: | 25–37 ft. lbs. | 35–50 Nm |
| LH Front No. 1 Insulator-to-Bracket Nut: | 75–100 ft. lbs. | 100–135 Nm |
| LH Rear No. 4 Insulator-to-Body Bolts: | 75–100 ft. lbs. | 100–135 Nm |
| LH Rear No. 4 Insulator-to-Transaxle Bolts: | 35–50 ft. lbs. | 50–68 Nm |
| Oil Pan Drain Plug: | 15–25 ft. lbs. | 20–34 Nm |
| Oil Pan-to-Transaxle Bolts: | 30–39 ft. lbs. | 40–50 Nm |
| *: 70–76 ft. lbs. | Tighten in 2 Steps 51.6–59 ft. lbs. 95–103 Nm | 70–80 Nm |
| **: 20–30 ft. lbs. | Tighten in 2 Steps 5–7 ft. lbs. 27–41 Nm | 7–10 Nm |
| ***: 19–26 ft. lbs. | Tighten in 2 Steps 4–7 ft. lbs. 26–38 Nm | 6–10 Nm |

86703778

## Troubleshooting Basic Charging System Problems

| Problem | Cause | Solution |
| --- | --- | --- |
| Noisy alternator | • Loose mountings<br>• Loose drive pulley<br>• Worn bearings<br>• Brush noise<br>• Internal circuits shorted (High pitched whine) | • Tighten mounting bolts<br>• Tighten pulley<br>• Replace alternator<br>• Replace alternator<br>• Replace alternator |
| Squeal when starting engine or accelerating | • Glazed or loose belt | • Replace or adjust belt |
| Indicator light remains on or ammeter indicates discharge (engine running) | • Broken fan belt<br>• Broken or disconnected wires<br>• Internal alternator problems<br>• Defective voltage regulator | • Install belt<br>• Repair or connect wiring<br>• Replace alternator<br>• Replace voltage regulator |
| Car light bulbs continually burn out—battery needs water continually | • Alternator/regulator overcharging | • Replace voltage regulator/alternator |
| Car lights flare on acceleration | • Battery low<br>• Internal alternator/regulator problems | • Charge or replace battery<br>• Replace alternator/regulator |
| Low voltage output (alternator light flickers continually or ammeter needle wanders) | • Loose or worn belt<br>• Dirty or corroded connections<br>• Internal alternator/regulator problems | • Replace or adjust belt<br>• Clean or replace connections<br>• Replace alternator or regulator |

86703979

## Troubleshooting Engine Mechanical Problems

| Problem | Cause | Solution |
|---|---|---|
| External oil leaks | • Fuel pump gasket broken or improperly seated | • Replace gasket |
| | • Cylinder head cover RTV sealant broken or improperly seated | • Replace sealant; inspect cylinder head cover sealant flange and cylinder head sealant surface for distortion and cracks |
| | • Oil filler cap leaking or missing | • Replace cap |
| External oil leaks | • Oil filter gasket broken or improperly seated | • Replace oil filter |
| | • Oil pan side gasket broken, improperly seated or opening in RTV sealant | • Replace gasket or repair opening in sealant; inspect oil pan gasket flange for distortion |
| | • Oil pan front oil seal broken or improperly seated | • Replace seal; inspect timing case cover and oil pan seal flange for distortion |
| | • Oil pan rear oil seal broken or improperly seated | • Replace seal; inspect oil pan rear oil seal flange; inspect rear main bearing cap for cracks, plugged oil return channels, or distortion in seal groove |
| | • Timing case cover oil seal broken or improperly seated | • Replace seal |
| | • Excess oil pressure because of restricted PCV valve | • Replace PCV valve |
| | • Oil pan drain plug loose or has stripped threads | • Repair as necessary and tighten |
| | • Rear oil gallery plug loose | • Use appropriate sealant on gallery plug and tighten |
| | • Rear camshaft plug loose or improperly seated | • Seat camshaft plug or replace and seal, as necessary |
| | • Distributor base gasket damaged | • Replace gasket |
| Excessive oil consumption | • Oil level too high | • Drain oil to specified level |
| | • Oil with wrong viscosity being used | • Replace with specified oil |
| | • PCV valve stuck closed | • Replace PCV valve |
| | • Valve stem oil deflectors (or seals) are damaged, missing, or incorrect type | • Replace valve stem oil deflectors |
| | • Valve stems or valve guides worn | • Measure stem-to-guide clearance and repair as necessary |
| | • Poorly fitted or missing valve cover baffles | • Replace valve cover |
| | • Piston rings broken or missing | • Replace broken or missing rings |
| | • Scuffed piston | • Replace piston |
| | • Incorrect piston ring gap | • Measure ring gap, repair as necessary |
| | • Piston rings sticking or excessively loose in grooves | • Measure ring side clearance, repair as necessary |
| | • Compression rings installed upside down | • Repair as necessary |
| | • Cylinder walls worn, scored, or glazed | • Repair as necessary |
| | • Piston ring gaps not properly staggered | • Repair as necessary |
| | • Excessive main or connecting rod bearing clearance | • Measure bearing clearance, repair as necessary |

## Troubleshooting Engine Mechanical Problems (cont.)

| Problem | Cause | Solution |
|---|---|---|
| No oil pressure | • Low oil level | • Add oil to correct level |
| | • Oil pressure gauge, warning lamp or sending unit inaccurate | • Replace oil pressure gauge or warning lamp |
| | • Oil pump malfunction | • Replace oil pump |
| | • Oil pressure relief valve sticking | • Remove and inspect oil pressure relief valve assembly |
| | • Oil passages on pressure side of pump obstructed | • Inspect oil passages for obstruction |
| | • Oil pickup screen or tube obstructed | • Inspect oil pickup for obstruction |
| | • Loose oil inlet tube | • Tighten or seal inlet tube |
| Low oil pressure | • Low oil level | • Add oil to correct level |
| | • Inaccurate gauge, warning lamp or sending unit | • Replace oil pressure gauge or warning lamp |
| | • Oil excessively thin because of dilution, poor quality, or improper grade | • Drain and refill crankcase with recommended oil |
| | • Excessive oil temperature | • Correct cause of overheating engine |
| | • Oil pressure relief spring weak or sticking | • Remove and inspect oil pressure relief valve assembly |
| | • Oil inlet tube and screen assembly has restriction or air leak | • Remove and inspect oil inlet tube and screen assembly. (Fill inlet tube with lacquer thinner to locate leaks.) |
| | • Excessive oil pump clearance | • Measure clearances |
| | • Excessive main, rod, or camshaft bearing clearance | • Measure bearing clearances, repair as necessary |
| High oil pressure | • Improper oil viscosity | • Drain and refill crankcase with correct viscosity oil |
| | • Oil pressure gauge or sending unit inaccurate | • Replace oil pressure gauge |
| | • Oil pressure relief valve sticking closed | • Remove and inspect oil pressure relief valve assembly |
| Main bearing noise | • Insufficient oil supply | • Inspect for low oil level and low oil pressure |
| | • Main bearing clearance excessive | • Measure main bearing clearance, repair as necessary |
| | • Bearing insert missing | • Replace missing insert |
| | • Crankshaft end play excessive | • Measure end play, repair as necessary |
| | • Improperly tightened main bearing cap bolts | • Tighten bolts with specified torque |
| | • Loose flywheel or drive plate | • Tighten flywheel or drive plate attaching bolts |
| | • Loose or damaged vibration damper | • Repair as necessary |

86703889

## Troubleshooting Engine Mechanical Problems (cont.)

| Problem | Cause | Solution |
|---|---|---|
| Connecting rod bearing noise | • Insufficient oil supply | • Inspect for low oil level and low oil pressure |
| | • Carbon build-up on piston | • Remove carbon from piston crown |
| | • Bearing clearance excessive or bearing missing | • Measure clearance, repair as necessary |
| | • Crankshaft connecting rod journal out-of-round | • Measure journal dimensions, repair or replace as necessary |
| | • Misaligned connecting rod or cap | • Repair as necessary |
| | • Connecting rod bolts tightened improperly | • Tighten bolts with specified torque |
| Piston noise | • Piston-to-cylinder wall clearance excessive (scuffed piston) | • Measure clearance and examine piston |
| | • Cylinder walls excessively tapered or out-of-round | • Measure cylinder wall dimensions, rebore cylinder |
| | • Piston ring broken | • Replace all rings on piston |
| | • Loose or seized piston pin | • Measure piston-to-pin clearance, repair as necessary |
| | • Connecting rods misaligned | • Measure rod alignment, straighten or replace |
| | • Piston ring side clearance excessively loose or tight | • Measure ring side clearance, repair as necessary |
| | • Carbon build-up on piston is excessive | • Remove carbon from piston |
| Valve actuating component noise | • Insufficient oil supply | • Check for:<br>(a) Low oil level<br>(b) Low oil pressure<br>(c) Plugged push rods<br>(d) Wrong hydraulic tappets<br>(e) Restricted oil gallery<br>(f) Excessive tappet to bore clearance |
| | • Push rods worn or bent | • Replace worn or bent push rods |
| | • Rocker arms or pivots worn | • Replace worn rocker arms or pivots |
| | • Foreign objects or chips in hydraulic tappets | • Clean tappets |
| | • Excessive tappet leak-down | • Replace valve tappet |
| | • Tappet face worn | • Replace tappet; inspect corresponding cam lobe for wear |
| | • Broken or cocked valve springs | • Properly seat cocked springs; replace broken springs |
| | • Stem-to-guide clearance excessive | • Measure stem-to-guide clearance, repair as required |
| | • Valve bent | • Replace valve |
| | • Loose rocker arms | • Tighten bolts with specified torque |
| | • Valve seat runout excessive | • Regrind valve seat/valves |
| | • Missing valve lock | • Install valve lock |
| | • Push rod rubbing or contacting cylinder head | • Remove cylinder head and remove obstruction in head |
| | • Excessive engine oil (four-cylinder engine) | • Correct oil level |

86703890

## Troubleshooting the Cooling System

| Problem | Cause | Solution |
|---|---|---|
| High temperature gauge indication—overheating | • Coolant level low | • Replenish coolant |
| | • Fan belt loose | • Adjust fan belt tension |
| | • Radiator hose(s) collapsed | • Replace hose(s) |
| | • Radiator airflow blocked | • Remove restriction (bug screen, fog lamps, etc.) |
| | • Faulty radiator cap | • Replace radiator cap |
| | • Ignition timing incorrect | • Adjust ignition timing |
| | • Idle speed low | • Adjust idle speed |
| | • Air trapped in cooling system | • Purge air |
| | • Heavy traffic driving | • Operate at fast idle in neutral intermittently to cool engine |
| | • Incorrect cooling system component(s) installed | • Install proper component(s) |
| | • Faulty thermostat | • Replace thermostat |
| | • Water pump shaft broken or impeller loose | • Replace water pump |
| | • Radiator tubes clogged | • Flush radiator |
| | • Cooling system clogged | • Flush system |
| | • Casting flash in cooling passages | • Repair or replace as necessary. Flash may be visible by removing cooling system components or removing core plugs. |
| | • Brakes dragging | • Repair brakes |
| | • Excessive engine friction | • Repair engine |
| | • Antifreeze concentration over 68% | • Lower antifreeze concentration percentage |
| | • Missing air seals | • Replace air seals |
| | • Faulty gauge or sending unit | • Repair or replace faulty component |
| | • Loss of coolant flow caused by leakage or foaming | • Repair or replace leaking component, replace coolant |
| | • Viscous fan drive failed | • Replace unit |
| Low temperature indication—undercooling | • Thermostat stuck open | • Replace thermostat |
| | • Faulty gauge or sending unit | • Repair or replace faulty component |
| Coolant loss—boilover | • Overfilled cooling system | • Reduce coolant level to proper specification |
| | • Quick shutdown after hard (hot) run | • Allow engine to run at fast idle prior to shutdown |
| | • Air in system resulting in occasional "burping" of coolant | • Purge system |
| | • Insufficient antifreeze allowing coolant boiling point to be too low | • Add antifreeze to raise boiling point |
| | • Antifreeze deteriorated because of age or contamination | • Replace coolant |
| | • Leaks due to loose hose clamps, loose nuts, bolts, drain plugs, faulty hoses, or defective radiator | • Pressure test system to locate source of leak(s) then repair as necessary |
| Coolant loss—boilover | • Faulty head gasket | • Replace head gasket |
| | • Cracked head, manifold, or block | • Replace as necessary |
| | • Faulty radiator cap | • Replace cap |
| Coolant entry into crankcase or cylinder(s) | • Faulty head gasket | • Replace head gasket |
| | • Crack in head, manifold or block | • Replace as necessary |

86703891

## Troubleshooting the Cooling System (cont.)

| Problem | Cause | Solution |
|---|---|---|
| Coolant recovery system inoperative | • Coolant level low<br>• Leak in system<br><br>• Pressure cap not tight or seal missing, or leaking<br>• Pressure cap defective<br>• Overflow tube clogged or leaking<br>• Recovery bottle vent restricted | • Replenish coolant to FULL mark<br>• Pressure test to isolate leak and repair as necessary<br>• Repair as necessary<br><br>• Replace cap<br>• Repair as necessary<br>• Remove restriction |
| Noise | • Fan contacting shroud<br><br>• Loose water pump impeller<br>• Glazed fan belt<br>• Loose fan belt<br>• Rough surface on drive pulley<br>• Water pump bearing worn<br><br>• Belt alignment | • Reposition shroud and inspect engine mounts<br>• Replace pump<br>• Apply silicone or replace belt<br>• Adjust fan belt tension<br>• Replace pulley<br>• Remove belt to isolate. Replace pump.<br>• Check pulley alignment. Repair as necessary. |
| No coolant flow through heater core | • Restricted return inlet in water pump<br>• Heater hose collapsed or restricted<br>• Restricted heater core<br>• Restricted outlet in thermostat housing<br>• Intake manifold bypass hole in cylinder head restricted<br>• Faulty heater control valve<br>• Intake manifold coolant passage restricted | • Remove restriction<br><br>• Remove restriction or replace hose<br>• Remove restriction or replace core<br>• Remove flash or restriction<br><br>• Remove restriction<br><br>• Replace valve<br>• Remove restriction or replace intake manifold |

**NOTE:** *Immediately after shutdown, the engine enters a condition known as heat soak. This is caused by the cooling system being inoperative while engine temperature is still high. If coolant temperature rises above boiling point, expansion and pressure may push some coolant out of the radiator overflow tube. If this does not occur frequently it is considered normal.*

86703892

## Troubleshooting the Serpentine Drive Belt

| Problem | Cause | Solution |
|---|---|---|
| Tension sheeting fabric failure (woven fabric on outside circumference of belt has cracked or separated from body of belt) | • Grooved or backside idler pulley diameters are less than minimum recommended<br>• Tension sheeting contacting (rubbing) stationary object<br>• Excessive heat causing woven fabric to age<br>• Tension sheeting splice has fractured | • Replace pulley(s) not conforming to specification<br><br>• Correct rubbing condition<br><br>• Replace belt<br><br>• Replace belt |
| Noise (objectional squeal, squeak, or rumble is heard or felt while drive belt is in operation) | • Belt slippage<br>• Bearing noise<br>• Belt misalignment<br>• Belt-to-pulley mismatch<br>• Driven component inducing vibration<br>• System resonant frequency inducing vibration | • Adjust belt<br>• Locate and repair<br>• Align belt/pulley(s)<br>• Install correct belt<br>• Locate defective driven component and repair<br>• Vary belt tension within specifications. Replace belt. |

## Troubleshooting the Serpentine Drive Belt (cont.)

| Problem | Cause | Solution |
|---|---|---|
| Rib chunking (one or more ribs has separated from belt body) | • Foreign objects imbedded in pulley grooves<br>• Installation damage<br>• Drive loads in excess of design specifications<br>• Insufficient internal belt adhesion | • Remove foreign objects from pulley grooves<br>• Replace belt<br>• Adjust belt tension<br><br>• Replace belt |
| Rib or belt wear (belt ribs contact bottom of pulley grooves) | • Pulley(s) misaligned<br>• Mismatch of belt and pulley groove widths<br>• Abrasive environment<br>• Rusted pulley(s)<br>• Sharp or jagged pulley groove tips<br>• Rubber deteriorated | • Align pulley(s)<br>• Replace belt<br><br>• Replace belt<br>• Clean rust from pulley(s)<br>• Replace pulley<br>• Replace belt |
| Longitudinal belt cracking (cracks between two ribs) | • Belt has mistracked from pulley groove<br>• Pulley groove tip has worn away rubber-to-tensile member | • Replace belt<br><br>• Replace belt |
| Belt slips | • Belt slipping because of insufficient tension<br>• Belt or pulley subjected to substance (belt dressing, oil, ethylene glycol) that has reduced friction<br>• Driven component bearing failure<br>• Belt glazed and hardened from heat and excessive slippage | • Adjust tension<br><br>• Replace belt and clean pulleys<br><br><br>• Replace faulty component bearing<br>• Replace belt |
| "Groove jumping" (belt does not maintain correct position on pulley, or turns over and/or runs off pulleys) | • Insufficient belt tension<br>• Pulley(s) not within design tolerance<br>• Foreign object(s) in grooves | • Adjust belt tension<br>• Replace pulley(s)<br><br>• Remove foreign objects from grooves |
| "Groove jumping" (belt does not maintain correct position on pulley, or turns over and/or runs off pulleys) | • Excessive belt speed<br><br>• Pulley misalignment<br>• Belt-to-pulley profile mismatched<br>• Belt cordline is distorted | • Avoid excessive engine acceleration<br>• Align pulley(s)<br>• Install correct belt<br>• Replace belt |
| Belt broken (Note: identify and correct problem before replacement belt is installed) | • Excessive tension<br><br>• Tensile members damaged during belt installation<br>• Belt turnover<br>• Severe pulley misalignment<br>• Bracket, pulley, or bearing failure | • Replace belt and adjust tension to specification<br>• Replace belt<br><br>• Replace belt<br>• Align pulley(s)<br>• Replace defective component and belt |
| Cord edge failure (tensile member exposed at edges of belt or separated from belt body) | • Excessive tension<br>• Drive pulley misalignment<br>• Belt contacting stationary object<br>• Pulley irregularities<br>• Improper pulley construction<br>• Insufficient adhesion between tensile member and rubber matrix | • Adjust belt tension<br>• Align pulley<br>• Correct as necessary<br>• Replace pulley<br>• Replace pulley<br>• Replace belt and adjust tension to specifications |

## Troubleshooting the Serpentine Drive Belt (cont.)

| Problem | Cause | Solution |
|---|---|---|
| Sporadic rib cracking (multiple cracks in belt ribs at random intervals) | · Ribbed pulley(s) diameter less than minimum specification | · Replace pulley(s) |
| | · Backside bend flat pulley(s) diameter less than minimum | · Replace pulley(s) |
| | · Excessive heat condition causing rubber to harden | · Correct heat condition as necessary |
| | · Excessive belt thickness | · Replace belt |
| | · Belt overcured | · Replace belt |
| | · Excessive tension | · Adjust belt tension |

86703952

## Troubleshooting Basic Starting System Problems

| Problem | Cause | Solution |
|---|---|---|
| Starter motor rotates engine slowly | · Battery charge low or battery defective | · Charge or replace battery |
| | · Defective circuit between battery and starter motor | · Clean and tighten, or replace cables |
| | · Low load current | · Bench-test starter motor. Inspect for worn brushes and weak brush springs. |
| | · High load current | · Bench-test starter motor. Check engine for friction, drag or coolant in cylinders. Check ring gear-to-pinion gear clearance. |
| Starter motor will not rotate engine | · Battery charge low or battery defective | · Charge or replace battery |
| | · Faulty solenoid | · Check solenoid ground. Repair or replace as necessary. |
| | · Damage drive pinion gear or ring gear | · Replace damaged gear(s) |
| | · Starter motor engagement weak | · Bench-test starter motor |
| | · Starter motor rotates slowly with high load current | · Inspect drive yoke pull-down and point gap, check for worn end bushings, check ring gear clearance |
| | · Engine seized | · Repair engine |
| Starter motor drive will not engage (solenoid known to be good) | · Defective contact point assembly | · Repair or replace contact point assembly |
| | · Inadequate contact point assembly ground | · Repair connection at ground screw |
| | · Defective hold-in coil | · Replace field winding assembly |
| Starter motor drive will not disengage | · Starter motor loose on flywheel housing | · Tighten mounting bolts |
| | · Worn drive end busing | · Replace bushing |
| | · Damaged ring gear teeth | · Replace ring gear or driveplate |
| | · Drive yoke return spring broken or missing | · Replace spring |
| Starter motor drive disengages prematurely | · Weak drive assembly thrust spring | · Replace drive mechanism |
| | · Hold-in coil defective | · Replace field winding assembly |
| Low load current | · Worn brushes | · Replace brushes |
| | · Weak brush springs | · Replace springs |

86703955

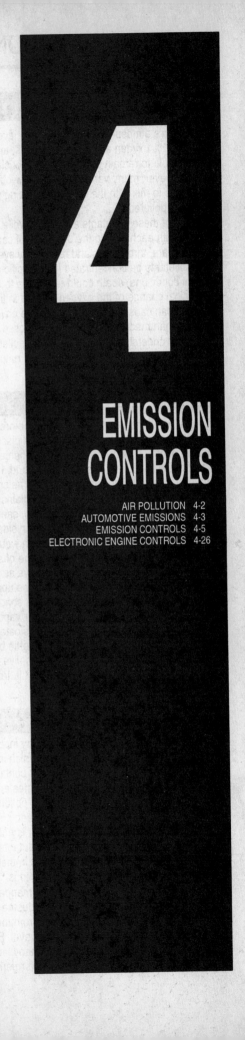

# 4

# EMISSION CONTROLS

## AIR POLLUTION

The earth's atmosphere, at or near sea level, consists of 78% nitrogen, 21% oxygen and 1% other gases, approximately. If it were possible to remain in this state, 100% clean air would result. However, many varied causes allow other gases and particulates to mix with the clean air, causing it to become unclean or polluted.

Certain of these pollutants are visible while others are invisible, with each having the capability of causing distress to the eyes, ears, throat, skin and respiratory system. Should these pollutants be concentrated in a specific area and under the right conditions, death could result due to the displacement or chemical change of the oxygen content in the air. These pollutants can cause much damage to the environment and to the many man made objects that are exposed to the elements.

To better understand the causes of air pollution, the pollutants can be categorized into 3 separate types, natural, industrial and automotive.

## Natural Pollution

Natural pollution not present on earth before man appeared and is still a factor to be considered when discussing air pollution, although it causes only a small percentage of the present overall pollution existing in our world. It is the direct result of decaying organic matter, windborne smoke and particulates from such natural events as plains and forest fires (ignited by heat or lightning), volcanic ash, sand and dust which can spread over a large area of the countryside.

Such a phenomenon of natural pollution would include volcanic eruptions, with the resulting plume of smoke, steam and volcanic ash blotting out the sun's rays as it spreads and rises higher into the atmosphere, where the upper air currents catch and carry the smoke and ash, while condensing the steam back into water vapor. As the water vapor, smoke and ash travel on their journey, the smoke dissipates into the atmosphere while the ash and moisture settle back to earth in a trail hundred of miles long. In some cases, lives are lost and millions of dollars of property damage result. Ironically, man can only stand by and watch it happen.

## Industrial Pollution

Industrial pollution is caused primarily by industrial processes, the burning of coal, oil and natural gas, which in turn produces smoke and fumes. Because burning fuels contain much sulfur, the principal ingredients of smoke and fumes are sulfur dioxide ($SO_2$) and particulate matter. This type of pollutant occurs most severely during still, damp and cool weather, such as at night. Even in its less severe form, this pollutant is not confined to just cities. Because of air movements, the pollutants move for miles over the surrounding countryside, leaving in their path a barren and unhealthy environment for all living things.

Working with Federal, State and Local mandated regulations, and by carefully monitoring emissions, industries have greatly reduced the amount of pollutant emitted from their industrial sources, striving to obtain an acceptable level. Because of the mandated industrial emission clean up, many land areas and streams in or around the cities that were formerly barren of vegetation and life, have now begun to move back in the direction of nature's intended balance.

## Automotive Pollution

The third major source of air pollution is automotive emissions. The pollutants from the internal combustion engine were not an appreciable problem years ago because of the small number of registered vehicles and the nation's small highway system. However, during the early 1950s, the trend of the American people was to move from the cities to the surrounding suburbs. This caused an immediate problem in transportation because the majority of the suburbs were not afforded mass transit conveniences. This lack of transportation created an attractive market for the automobile manufacturers, which resulted in a dramatic increase in the number of vehicles produced and sold, along with a marked increase in highway construction between cities and the suburbs. Multi–vehicle families emerged with much emphasis placed on individual vehicle per family member. As the increase in vehicle ownership and usage occurred, so did the pollutant levels in and around the cities, as the suburbanites drove daily to their businesses and employment in the city and its fringe area, returning at the end of the day to their homes in the suburbs.

It was noted that a fog and smoke type haze was being formed and at times, remained in suspension over the cities taking time to dissipate. At first this "smog," derived from the words "smoke" and "fog," was thought to result from industrial pollution but it was determined that automobile emissions shared the blame. It was discovered that as normal automobile emissions were exposed to sunlight for a period of time, complex chemical reactions would take place.

It was found the smog was a photo chemical layer and was developed when certain oxides of nitrogen (NOx) and unburned hydrocarbons (HC) from the automobile emissions were exposed to sunlight and was more severe when the smog would remain stagnant over an area in which a warm layer of air would settle over the top of a cooler air mass at ground level, trapping and holding the automobile emissions, instead of the emissions being dispersed and diluted through normal air flows. This type of air stagnation was given the name "Temperature Inversion."

## Temperature Inversion

In normal weather situations, surface air is warmed by the heat radiating from the earth's surface and the sun's rays and will rise upward, into the atmosphere, to be cooled through a convection type heat expands with the cooler upper air. As the warm air rises, the surface pollutants are carried upward and dissipated into the atmosphere.

When a temperature inversion occurs, we find the higher air is no longer cooler, but is warmer than the surface air, causing the cooler surface air to become trapped and unable to move. This warm air blanket can extend from above ground level to a few hundred or even a few thousand feet into the air. As the surface air is trapped, so are the pollutants, causing a severe smog condition. Should this stagnant air mass extend to a few thousand feet high, enough air movement with the inversion takes place to allow the smog layer to rise above ground level but the pollutants still cannot dissipate. This inversion can remain for days over an area, with only the smog level rising or lowering from ground level to a few hundred feet high. Meanwhile, the pollutant levels increase, causing eye irritation, respirator problems, reduced visibility, plant damage and in some cases, disease.

This inversion phenomenon was first noted in the Los Angeles, California area. The city lies in a basin type of terrain and during certain weather conditions, a cold air mass is held in the basin while a warmer air mass covers it like a lid.

Because this type of condition was first documented as prevalent in the Los Angeles area, this type of smog was named Los Angeles Smog, although it occurs in other areas where a large concentration of automobiles are used and the air remains stagnant for any length of time.

## Internal Combustion Engine Pollution

Consider the internal combustion engine as a machine in which raw materials must be placed so a finished product comes out. As in any machine operation, a certain amount of wasted material is formed. When we relate this to the internal combustion engine, we find that by putting in air and fuel, we obtain power from this mixture during the combustion process to drive the vehicle. The by–product or waste of this power is, in part, heat and exhaust with which we must dispose of.

## AUTOMOTIVE EMISSIONS

Before emission controls were mandated on the internal combustion engines, other sources of engine pollutants were discovered, along with the exhaust emission. It was determined the engine combustion exhaust produced 60% of the total emission pollutants, fuel evaporation from the fuel tank and carburetor vents produced 20%, with the another 20% being produced through the crankcase as a by–product of the combustion process.

## Exhaust Emissions

The exhaust gases emitted into the atmosphere are a combination of burned and unburned fuel. To understand their composition we must review some basic chemistry.

When the air/fuel mixture is introduced into the engine, we are mixing air, composed of nitrogen (78%), oxygen (21%) and other gases (1%) with the fuel, which is 100% hydrocarbons (HC), in a semi–controlled ratio. As the combustion process is accomplished, power is produced to move the vehicle while the heat of combustion is transferred to the cooling system. The exhaust gases are then composed of nitrogen, a diatomic gas ($N_2$), the same as was introduced in the engine, carbon dioxide ($CO_2$), the same gas that is used in beverage carbonation and water vapor ($H_2O$). The nitrogen ($N_2$), for the most part passes through the engine unchanged, while the oxygen ($O_2$) reacts (burns) with the hydrocarbons (HC) and produces the carbon dioxide ($CO_2$) and water vapors ($H_2O$). If this chemical process

## HEAT TRANSFER

The heat from the combustion process can rise to over 4000°F (2204°C). The dissipation of this heat is controlled by a ram air effect, the use of cooling fans to cause air flow and having a liquid coolant solution surrounding the combustion area and transferring the heat of combustion through the cylinder walls and into the coolant. The coolant is then directed to a thin–finned, multi–tubed radiator, from which the excess heat is transferred to the outside air by 1 or all of the 3 heat transfer methods, conduction, convection or radiation.

Cooling of the combustion area is an important part in the control of exhaust emissions. To understand the behavior of the combustion and transfer of its heat, consider the air/fuel charge. It is ignited and the flame front burns progressively across the combustion chamber until the burning charge reaches the cylinder walls. Some of the fuel in contact with the walls is not hot enough to burn, thereby snuffing out or quenching the combustion process. This leaves unburned fuel in the combustion chamber. This unburned fuel is then forced out of the cylinder along with the exhaust gases and into the exhaust system.

Many attempts have been made to minimize the amount of unburned fuel in the combustion chambers due to quenching, by increasing the coolant temperature and lessening the contact area of the coolant around the combustion area. Design limitations within the combustion chambers prevent the complete burning of the air/fuel charge, so a certain amount of the unburned fuel is still expelled into the exhaust system, regardless of modifications to the engine.

would be the only process to take place, the exhaust emissions would be harmless. However, during the combustion process, other pollutants are formed and are considered dangerous. These pollutants are carbon monoxide (CO), hydrocarbons (HC), oxides of nitrogen (NOx) oxides of sulfur (SOx) and engine particulates.

## HYDROCARBONS

Hydrocarbons (HC) are essentially unburned fuel that has not been fully combusted during the ignition process or has escaped into the atmosphere through fuel evaporation. The main sources of incomplete combustion are rich air/fuel mixtures, low engine temperatures and improper spark timing. The main sources of hydrocarbon emission through fuel evaporation on most vehicles used to be from the vehicle's fuel tank and carburetor bowl. This has changed with the introduction of sealed fuel tanks and the growing use of fuel injected vehicles.

To reduce combustion hydrocarbon emission, engine modifications were made to minimize dead space and surface area in the combustion chamber. In addition the air/fuel mixture was made more lean through improved carburetion, fuel injection and by the addition of external controls to aid in further combustion of the hydrocarbons outside the engine. Two such methods were the addition of an air injection system, to inject fresh air into the exhaust manifolds and the installation of a catalytic converter, a unit that is able to burn traces of hydrocarbons without affecting the internal combustion process or fuel economy.

To control hydrocarbon emissions through fuel evaporation, modifications were made to the fuel tank and carburetor bowl to allow storage of the fuel vapors during periods of engine shut–down, and at specific times during engine operation, to purge and burn these same vapors by blending them with the air/fuel mixture.

## CARBON MONOXIDE

Carbon monoxide is formed when not enough oxygen is present during the combustion process to convert carbon (C) to carbon dioxide ($CO_2$). An increase in the carbon monoxide (CO) emission is normally accompanied by an increase in the hydrocarbon (HC) emission because of the lack of oxygen to completely burn all of the fuel mixture.

Carbon monoxide (CO) also increases the rate at which the photo chemical smog is formed by speeding up the conversion of nitric oxide (NO) to nitrogen dioxide ($NO_2$). To accomplish this, carbon monoxide (CO) combines with oxygen ($O_2$) and nitrogen dioxide ($NO_2$) to produce carbon dioxide ($CO_2$) and nitrogen dioxide ($NO_2$). ($CO + O_2 + NO = CO_2 + NO_2$).

The dangers of carbon monoxide, which is an odorless, colorless toxic gas are many. When carbon monoxide is inhaled into the lungs and passed into the blood stream, oxygen is replaced by the carbon monoxide in the red blood cells, causing a reduction in the amount of oxygen being supplied to the many parts of the body. This lack of oxygen causes headaches, lack of coordination, reduced mental alertness and, should the carbon monoxide concentration be high enough, death could result.

## NITROGEN

Normally, nitrogen is an inert gas. When heated to approximately 2500°F (1371°C) through the combustion process, this gas becomes active and causes an increase in nitric oxide (NOx) emissions.

Oxides of nitrogen (NOx) are composed of approximately 97–98% nitric oxide ($NO_2$). Nitric oxide is a colorless gas but when it is passed into the atmosphere, it combines with oxygen and forms nitrogen dioxide ($NO_2$). The nitrogen dioxide then combines with chemically active hydrocarbons (HC) and when in the presence of sunlight, causes the formation of photo chemical smog.

## OZONE

To further complicate matters, some of the nitrogen dioxide ($NO_2$) is broken apart by the sunlight to form nitric oxide and oxygen. ($NO_2 + sunlight = NO + O$). This single atom of oxygen then combines with diatomic (meaning 2 atoms) oxygen ($O_2$) to form ozone ($O_3$). Ozone is 1 of the smells associated with smog. It has a pungent and offensive odor, irritates the eyes and lung tissues, affects the growth of plant life and causes rapid deterioration of rubber products. Ozone can be formed by sunlight as well as electrical discharge into the air.

The most common discharge area on the automobile engine is the secondary ignition electrical system, especially when inferior quality spark plug cables are used. As the surge of high

voltage is routed through the secondary cable, the circuit builds up an electrical field around the wire, acting upon the oxygen in the surrounding air to form the ozone. The faint glow along the cable with the engine running that may be visible on a dark night, is called the "corona discharge." It is the result of the electrical field passing from a high along the cable, to a low in the surrounding air, which forms the ozone gas. The combination of corona and ozone has been a major cause of cable deterioration. Different types and better quality insulating materials have lengthened the life of the electrical cables.

Although ozone at ground level can be harmful, ozone is beneficial to the earth's inhabitants. By having a concentrated ozone layer called the "ozonosphere," between 10 and 20 miles (16–32 km) up in the atmosphere much of the ultra violet radiation from the sun's rays are absorbed and screened. If this ozone layer was not present, much of the earth's surface would be burned, dried and unfit for human life.

## OXIDES OF SULFUR

Oxides of sulfur (SOx) were initially ignored in the exhaust system emissions, since the sulfur content of gasoline as a fuel is less than of 1%. Because of this small amount, it was felt that it contributed very little to the overall pollution problem. However, because of the difficulty in solving the sulfur emissions in industrial pollutions and the introduction of catalytic converter to the automobile exhaust systems, a change was mandated. The automobile exhaust system, when equipped with a catalytic converter, changes the sulfur dioxide ($SO_2$) into the sulfur trioxide ($SO_3$).

When this combines with water vapors ($H_2O$), a sulfuric acid mist ($H_2SO_4$) is formed. It is a very difficult pollutant to handle and is extremely corrosive. This sulfuric acid mist that is formed, is the same mist that rises from the vents of an automobile storage battery when an active chemical reaction takes place within the battery cells.

When a large concentration of vehicles equipped with catalytic converters are operating in an area, this acid mist will rise and be distributed over a large ground area causing land, plant, crop, paint and building damage.

## PARTICULATE MATTER

A certain amount of particulate matter is present in the burning of any fuel, with carbon constituting the largest percentage of the particulates. In gasoline, the remaining percentage of particulates is the burned remains of the various other compounds used in its manufacture. When a gasoline engine is in good internal condition, the particulate emissions are low but as the engine wears internally, the particulate emissions increase. By visually inspecting the tail pipe emissions, a determination can be made as to where an engine defect may exist. An engine with light gray smoke emitting from the tail pipe normally indicates an increase in the oil consumption through burning due to internal engine wear. Black smoke would indicate a defective fuel delivery system, causing the engine to operate in a rich mode. Regardless of the color of the smoke, the internal part of the engine or the fuel delivery system should be repaired to a "like new" condition to prevent excess particulate emissions.

Diesel and turbine engines emit a darkened plume of smoke from the exhaust system because of the type of fuel used. Emission control regulations are mandated for this type of emission and more stringent measures are being used to prevent excess emission of the particulate matter. Electronic components are being introduced to control the injection of the fuel at precisely the proper time of piston travel, to achieve the optimum in fuel ignition and fuel usage. Other particulate after–burning components are being tested to achieve a cleaner particular emission.

Good grades of engine lubricating oils should be used, meeting the manufacturers specification. "Cut–rate" oils can contribute to the particulate emission problem because of their low "flash" or ignition temperature point. Such oils burn prematurely during the combustion process causing emissions of particulate matter.

The cooling system is an important factor in the reduction of particulate matter. With the cooling system operating at a temperature specified by the manufacturer, the optimum of combustion will occur. The cooling system must be maintained in the same manner as the engine oiling system, as each system is required to perform properly in order for the engine to operate efficiently for a long time.

## Crankcase Emissions

Crankcase emissions are made up of water, acids, unburned fuel, oil fumes and particulates. The emissions classified as hydrocarbons (HC) are formed by the small amount of unburned, compressed air/fuel mixture entering the crankcase from the combustion area during the compression and power strokes, between the cylinder walls and piston rings. The head of the compression and combustion help to form the remaining crankcase emissions.

Since the first engines, crankcase emissions were allowed to the air through a road draft tube, mounted on the lower side of the engine block. Fresh air came in through an open oil filler cap or breather. The air passed through the crankcase mixing with blow–by gases. The motion of the vehicle and the air blowing past the open end of the road draft tube caused a low pressure area at the end of the tube. Crankcase emissions were simply drawn out of the road draft tube into the air.

To control the crankcase emission, the road draft tube was deleted. A hose and/or tubing was routed from the crankcase to the intake manifold so the blow–by emission could be burned with the air/fuel mixture. However, it was found that intake manifold vacuum, used to draw the crankcase emissions into the manifold, would vary in strength at the wrong time and not allow the proper emission flow. A regulating type valve was needed to control the flow of air through the crankcase.

Testing, showed the removal of the blow–by gases from the crankcase as quickly as possible, was most important to the longevity of the engine. Should large accumulations of blow–by gases remain and condense, dilution of the engine oil would occur to form water, soots, resins, acids and lead salts, resulting in the formation of sludge and varnishes. This condensation of the blow–by gases occurs more frequently on vehicles used in numerous starting and stopping conditions, excessive idling and when the engine is not allowed to attain normal operating temperature through short runs. The crankcase purge control or PCV system will be described in detail later in this section.

## Fuel Evaporative Emissions

Gasoline fuel is a major source of pollution, before and after it is burned in the automobile engine. From the time the fuel is refined, stored, pumped and transported, again stored until it is pumped into the fuel tank of the vehicle, the gasoline gives off unburned hydrocarbons (HC) into the atmosphere. Through redesigning of the storage areas and venting systems, the pollution factor has been diminished but not eliminated, from the refinery standpoint. However, the automobile still remained the primary source of vaporized, unburned hydrocarbon (HC) emissions.

Fuel pumped from an underground storage tank is cool but when exposed to a warmer ambient temperature, will expand. Before controls were mandated, an owner could fill the fuel tank with fuel from an underground storage tank and park the vehicle for some time in warm area, such as a parking lot. As the fuel would warm, it would expand and should no provisions or area be provided for the expansion, the fuel would spill out the filler neck and onto the ground, causing hydrocarbon (HC) pollution and creating a severe fire hazard. To correct this condition, the vehicle manufacturers added overflow plumbing and/or gasoline tanks with built in expansion areas or domes.

However, this did not control the fuel vapor emission from the fuel tank and the carburetor bowl. It was determined that most of the fuel evaporation occurred when the vehicle was stationary and the engine not operating. Most vehicles carry 5–25 gallons (19–95 liters) of gasoline. Should a large concentration of vehicles be parked in one area, such as a large parking lot, excessive fuel vapor emissions would take place, increasing as the temperature increases.

To prevent the vapor emission from escaping into the atmosphere, the fuel system is designed to trap the fuel vapors while the vehicle is stationary, by sealing the fuel system from the atmosphere. A storage system is used to collect and hold the fuel vapors from the carburetor and the fuel tank when the engine is not operating. When the engine is started, the storage system is then purged of the fuel vapors, which are drawn into the engine and burned with the air/fuel mixture. The components of the fuel evaporative system will be described in detail later in this section.

## EMISSION CONTROLS

There are 3 basic sources of automotive pollution in the modern internal combustion engine. They are the crankcase with its accompanying blow–by vapors, the fuel system with its evaporation of unburned gasoline and the combustion chambers with their resulting exhaust emissions. Pollution arising from the incomplete combustion of fuel generally falls into three categories: hydrocarbons (HC), carbon monoxide (CO) and oxides of nitrogen (NOx).

Some gasoline engines are equipped with an air pump system, positive crankcase ventilation, exhaust gas recirculation, electronic ignition, catalytic converter, thermostatically controlled air cleaner, and an evaporative emissions system. Electronic engine controls are used on various engines, depending on model and year.

If a gasoline vehicle is equipped with a belt driven air pump system, clean air is injected into either the exhaust manifold, or downstream into the catalytic converter, depending on engine conditions. The oxygen contained in the injected air supports continued combustion of the hot carbon monoxide (CO) and hydrocarbon (HC) gases, reducing their release into the atmosphere.

On some gasoline engines equipped with a carburetor, a back pressure modulated EGR may be mounted next to the carburetor on the intake manifold. Vacuum applied to the EGR diaphragm raises the pintle valve from its seat, allowing hot exhaust gases to be drawn into the intake manifold with the intake charge. The exhaust gases reduce peak combustion temperature; lower temperatures reduce the formation of oxides of nitrogen (NOx).

A dual bed catalytic converter is mounted in the exhaust system, ahead of the muffler on most gasoline engines. Catalytic converters use noble metals (platinum and palladium) and extreme heat, sometimes as high as 1,200°F (650°C) to catalytically oxidize HC and CO gases into $H_2O$ and $CO_2$.

The Thermactor system is used as a fresh air (and therefore, oxygen) supply on some gasoline engines. The thermostatically controlled air cleaner housing is able to draw fresh air from 2 sources: cool air from outside the car (behind the grille), or warm air obtained from a heat stove encircling the exhaust manifold. A warm air supply is desirable during cold engine operation. Because it promotes better atomization of the air/fuel mixture, while cool air promotes better combustion in a hot engine.

Instead of venting gasoline vapors from the carburetor float bowl into the atmosphere, an evaporative emission system captures the vapors and stores them in a charcoal filled canister, located ahead of the left front wheel arch. When the engine is running, a purge control solenoid allows fresh air to be drawn through the canister. The fresh air and vapors are then routed to the carburetor, to be mixed with the intake charge.

## Crankcase Ventilation System

### OPERATION

▶ See Figure 1

The Positive Crankcase Ventilation (PCV) system incorporated into the gasoline and diesel engine cycles crankcase gases back through the engine where they are burned. The PCV valve regulates the amount of ventilating air and blow-by gas to the intake manifold and also prevents backfire from traveling into the crankcase. The PCV valve should always be

mounted in a vertical position. On some engine applications, the PCV system is connected with the evaporative emission system.

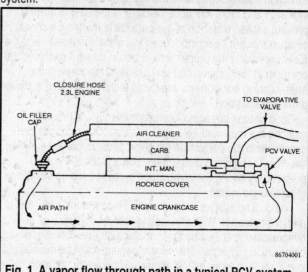

Fig. 1  A vapor flow through path in a typical PCV system

## TESTING

▶ See Figure 2

**Stuck PCV Valve Check**

1. With the engine OFF. Remove the PCV valve from the grommet and hose.
2. Shake the PCV valve.
   a. Inspect the base of the valve for any obstructions.
   b. If the valve rattles when shaken, re-connect it.
   c. If it does not rattle, replace it.
3. Start the engine and allow it to idle. Disconnect the hose from the air cleaner and check for vacuum at the hose. This can be accomplished by placing a finger over the hose, or using a vacuum gauge with the correct fitting to create an air-tight seal around the hose. If vacuum exists the system is functioning normally.
4. If vacuum does not exist, the hose may be broken, the system may be plugged or the evaporative valve is leaking. Disconnect the evaporative hose, cap the tee and recheck the system. If the vacuum exists, the PCV system is functioning. Check the evaporative emission system.
5. If vacuum still does not exist at the PCV, check for vacuum back through the system (filler cap, hoses). Also check the torque of the bolts securing the rocker cover. A loose rocker cover could cause a vacuum lose. Service the defective components as required.
6. Reconnect the PCV valve into the hose and grommet, and check for proper operation.

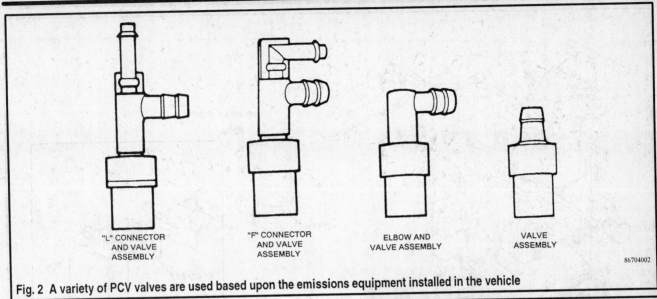

"L" CONNECTOR AND VALVE ASSEMBLY

"F" CONNECTOR AND VALVE ASSEMBLY

ELBOW AND VALVE ASSEMBLY

VALVE ASSEMBLY

86704002

**Fig. 2  A variety of PCV valves are used based upon the emissions equipment installed in the vehicle**

## REMOVAL & INSTALLATION

▶ **See Figures 3 and 4**

1. Remove the valve, with the hose still attached from the rubber grommet using a rocking back and forth motion
2. Loosen or remove the hose clamp securing the PCV valve to the hose. Use a twisting motion to remove the valve from the hose. Inspect the the hose and grommet, and replace if needed.

### To install:

3. Coat both ends of the PCV valve with oil, install the new valve into the hose, sliding the clamp into position, and finally install the valve into the rubber grommet.
4. Start the car and check for any air leaks.

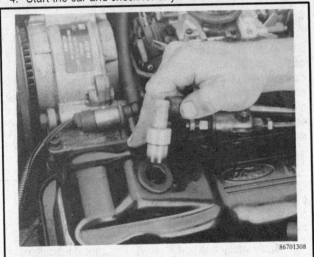

86701308

**Fig. 3  Remove the PCV valve from the retaining grommet with a back and forth motion . . .**

86701309

**Fig. 4  . . . then remove any breather hose which is attached to the PCV valve**

## Evaporative Emission Controls

### OPERATION

▶ **See Figures 5 and 6**

#### Canister Purging

Purging the carbon canister removes the fuel vapor stored in the carbon. With an EEC–IV controlled EVAP system, the flow of vapors from the canister to the engine is controlled by a Canister Purge solenoid (CANP) or vacuum controlled purge valve. Purging occurs when the engine is at operating temperature and off idle.

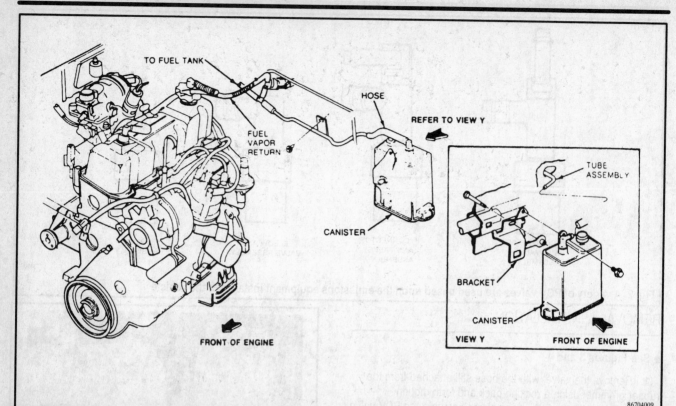

Fig. 5 Canister venting system—2.3L engine

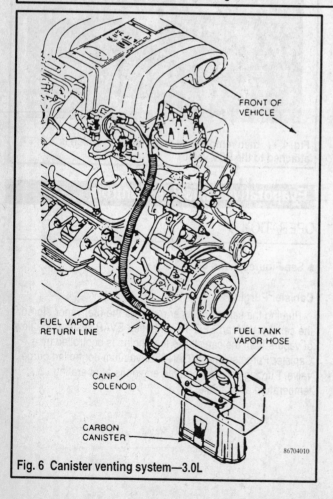

Fig. 6 Canister venting system—3.0L

### Fuel Tank Venting

Trapped fuel vapors inside the sealed fuel tank are vented through a vapor valve assembly in the top of the fuel tank. These vapors leave the valve assembly through a single vapor line and continue to the canister, for storage, until such time as they are purged to the engine for burning.

### Carburetor Venting

In carburetor equipped vehicles, trapped fuel, which might otherwise pass directly into the atmosphere, is collected in the carburetor fuel bowl. These vapors are vented to the carbon canister when the engine is stopped through the combined efforts of the canister purge valve and solenoid, as well as the carburetor fuel bowl solenoid and thermal vent valves. When the engine is started and normal operating engine temperature is reached, the vapors will be drawn into the engine for burning.

## TESTING

▶ See Figure 7

### Purge Control Valve

1. Apply vacuum to port A (only). This should indicate no flow. If flow occurs, replace the valve.
2. Apply vacuum to port B (only). This should indicate no flow. The valve should be closed. If flow occurs, replace the valve.
3. Apply and maintain 16 in. Hg (54 kPa) vacuum to port A, and apply vacuum to port B. Air should pass.

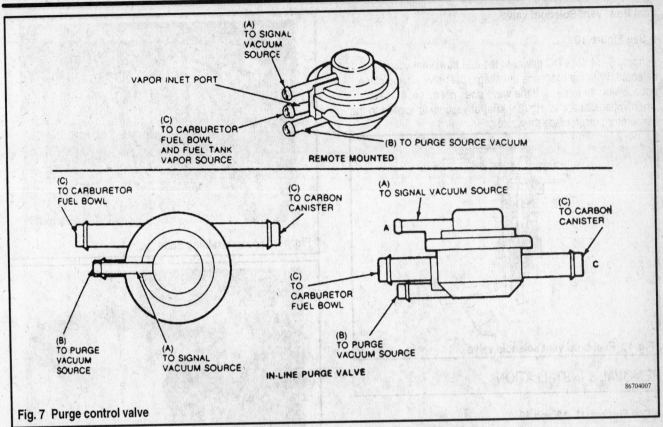

**Fig. 7 Purge control valve**

## Thermostatic Bowl Vent Valve

### ♦ See Figure 8

1. Check for vacuum at the vent valve when the engine is at a normal operating temperature. Air should flow between the carburetor port and canister port, when no vacuum is applied to the vacuum signal nipple.

2. When vacuum is applied to the vent valve, air should not pass between the ports.

3. At an engine temperature of 90°F (32°C) or less, the valve should not flow air, or be restrictive to air flow.

## Vacuum Bowl Vent Valve

### ♦ See Figure 9

The vacuum bowl vent valve should allow an air flow between the carburetor port and the canister port when no vacuum is applied to the vacuum signal nipple. No air flow should occur air with a vacuum applied at the vacuum signal nipple.

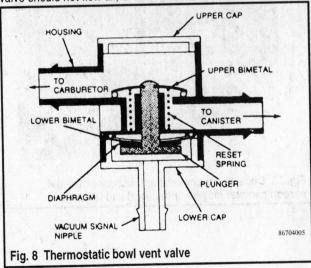

**Fig. 8 Thermostatic bowl vent valve**

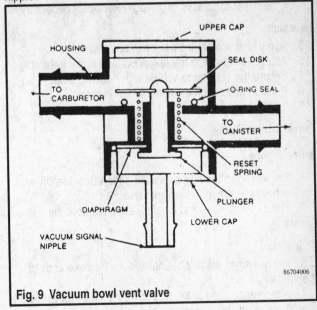

**Fig. 9 Vacuum bowl vent valve**

### Fuel Bowl Vent Solenoid Valve

◆ **See Figure 10**

Apply 9–14 volts DC power to the fuel bowl vent valve solenoid. With the presence of voltage, the valve should close, not allowing air to pass. If the valve does not close, or leaks when voltage and 1 in. Hg (3.4 kPa) of vacuum is applied to the carburetor port, replace the valve.

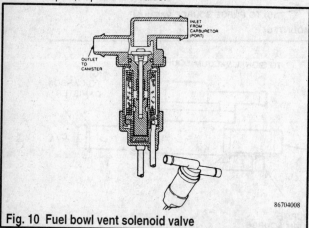

Fig. 10 Fuel bowl vent solenoid valve

## REMOVAL & INSTALLATION

◆ **See Figures 11, 12 and 13**

### Carbon Canister

1. Raise vehicle and support safely with jack stands.
2. Loosen the retaining screws securing the mud shield above the left front tire. Remove the shield
3. Remove any retaining bolts securing the canister to vehicle.
4. Identify and tag any hoses which are attached to canister. Check the hoses for cracks or damage. Replace if necessary.

**To install:**

5. Apply engine oil to the hose end on canister.
6. Attach each hose to the respective end of the assembly.
7. Secure the canister to vehicle with retaining bolts.
8. Position and attach the screws to mud shield.
9. Lower the vehicle.

### Purge Control Valve

◆ **See Figure 7**

1. Loosen any hose clamps securing the valve. Identify and tag the hoses attached to the vent valve.
2. Rotate each hose, and carefully separate from the assembly.

**To install:**

3. Apply a small amount of engine oil to the hose ends of the vent valve.
4. Attach each hose to the respective nipple of the assembly.
5. Tighten any hose clamps.

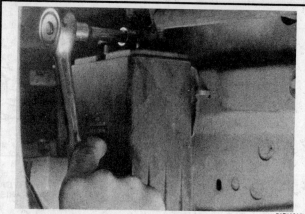

Fig. 11 Loosen retaining bolts . . .

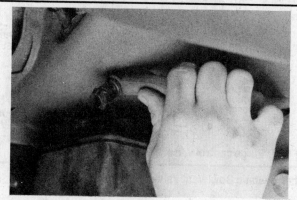

Fig. 12 . . . then tag and disconnect the hoses

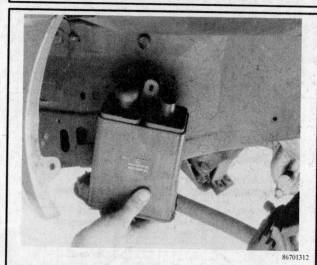

Fig. 13 Once all attachments are disconnected, the carbon canister may be unfastened and removed

### Thermostatic Bowl Vent Valve

▶ See Figure 8

1. Loosen any hose clamps securing the valve. Identify and tag the hoses attached to the vent valve.
2. Rotate each hose, and carefully separate from the assembly.

**To install:**

3. Apply a small amount of engine oil to the hose ends of the vent valve.
4. Attach each hose to the respective nipple of the assembly.
5. Tighten any hose clamps.

### Vacuum Bowl Vent Valve

▶ See Figure 9

1. Loosen any hose clamps securing the valve. Identify and tag the hoses attached to the vent valve.
2. Rotate each hose, and carefully separate from the assembly.

**To install:**

3. Apply a small amount of engine oil to the hose ends of the vent valve.
4. Attach each hose to the respective nipple of the assembly.
5. Tighten any hose clamps.

### Fuel Bowl Vent Solenoid Valve

▶ See Figure 10

1. Disconnect the wire harness attached to the assembly.
2. Loosen any hose clamps.
3. Identify and tag all hoses.
4. Rotate each hose, and carefully separate the assembly.

**To install:**

5. Apply a small amount of engine oil to the hose ends of the assembly.
6. Attach each hose to the respective end of the assembly.
7. Tighten any equipped hose clamps.
8. Connect wire harness to assembly.

## Exhaust Gas Recirculation System

### OPERATION

The Exhaust Gas Recirculation (EGR) system is designed reintroduce exhaust gas into the combustion cycle, thereby lowering combustion temperatures and reducing the formation of Nitrous Oxides (NOx). The amount of exhaust gas reintroduced and the timing of the cycle varies by calibration and is controlled by various factors such as engine speed, altitude, engine vacuum, exhaust system backpressure, coolant temperature and throttle angle.

A malfunctioning EGR valve can cause 1 or more of the following:

- Detonation
- Rough idle or stalls on deceleration
- Hesitation or surge
- Abnormally low power at wide–open throttle

### Integral Backpressure Transducer EGR Valve

This poppet–type or tapered (pintle) valve cannot be opened by vacuum until the bleed hole is closed by exhaust backpressure. Once the valve opens, it seeks a level dependent upon exhaust backpressure flowing through the orifice and in so doing, oscillates at that level. The higher the signal vacuum and exhaust backpressure, the more the valve opens.

### Backpressure Variable Transducer EGR Valve

This exhaust gas recirculation system combines a ported EGR valve with a backpressure variable transducer in order to control nitrous oxides. The amount of exhaust gas reintroduced and the timing of the cycle varies by engine calibration and is controlled by various factors such as engine speed, altitude, engine vacuum, exhaust system backpressure, coolant temperature and throttle angle. The typical system consists of 3 components, a vacuum regulator, an EGR valve and a flow control orifice. The regulator modulates the vacuum signal to the EGR valve using 2 backpressure inputs. One input is the standard vehicle backpressure. The other is backpressure downstream of the flow control orifice. The control chamber sensor point is in the EGR tube. The flow control orifice is integral to the upstream EGR tube connector.

### PFE and DPFE EGR Systems

▶ See Figures 14, 15, 16, 17 and 18

The Pressure Feedback Electronic (PFE) is a subsonic closed loop EGR system that controls the EGR flow rate by monitoring the pressure drop across a remotely located sharp–edged orifice. With a PFE system, the EGR valve only serves as a pressure regulator, rather than a flow metering device.

The Differential Pressure Feedback Electronic (DPFE) EGR system operates in the same manner as the PFE system, with the exception that it also monitors exhaust pressure in the exhaust system. This allows for a more accurate control of the recirculation gases.

### Electronic EGR System

▶ See Figures 19 and 20

An electronic EGR valve is required in the Electronic Engine Control (EEC) systems where EGR flow is controlled according to computer demands by means of an EGR Valve Position (EVP) sensor attached to the valve. The valve is controlled according to signals sent from the EGR Vacuum Regulator (EVR). The EVP sensor, mounted on the valve, sends an electrical signal of its position to the Electronic Control Assembly (ECA).

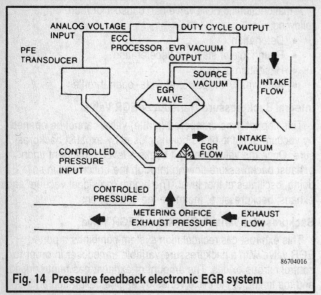

Fig. 14  Pressure feedback electronic EGR system

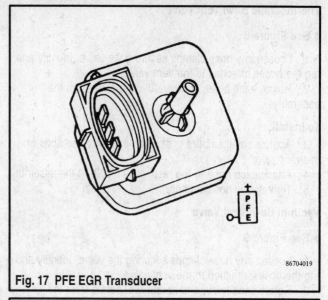

Fig. 17  PFE EGR Transducer

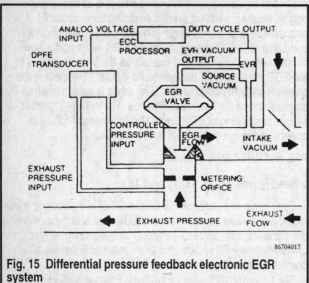

Fig. 15  Differential pressure feedback electronic EGR system

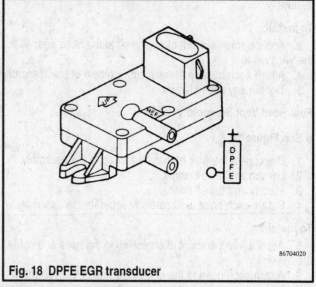

Fig. 18  DPFE EGR transducer

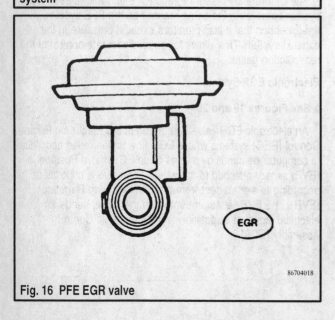

Fig. 16  PFE EGR valve

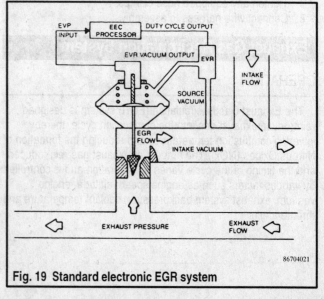

Fig. 19  Standard electronic EGR system

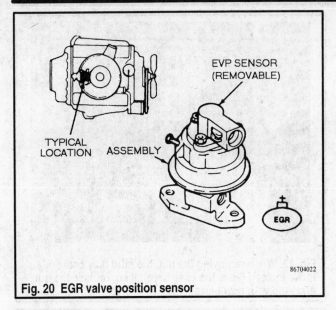

**Fig. 20 EGR valve position sensor**

## TESTING

### Integral Backpressure Transducer EGR Valve

▶ See Figure 21

1. Check that all vacuum lines are properly routed, all connections are secured and the vacuum hoses are not cracked, crimped or broken.

2. With the EGR valve at rest, air should flow freely when vacuum is applied to the signal vacuum nipple of the valve. Also the valve should not hold any vacuum at this time. If the valve does holds vacuum, clean or replace it, and perform the test again.

3. With the vehicle at idle, there should be no vacuum going to the EGR valve. If there is, check for correct hose routing.

4. With the engine at normal operating temperature, and the engine running at 3000 rpm, there should be vacuum going to the EGR valve. If there in no vacuum, check back through the vacuum lines from the EGR to source. Replace, as necessary.

### Backpressure Variable Transducer EGR Valve

▶ See Figure 22

1. Apply a minimum of 2.5 psi (5.0 in. Hg) of vacuum individually to the 3 ports of the EGR valve.

2. The middle and bottom ports should hold vacuum, while the top port should not hold vacuum.

3. If the previous results are not achieved, replace the valve.

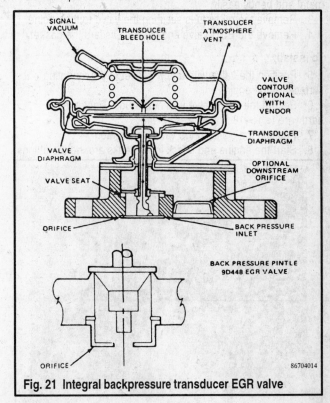

**Fig. 21 Integral backpressure transducer EGR valve**

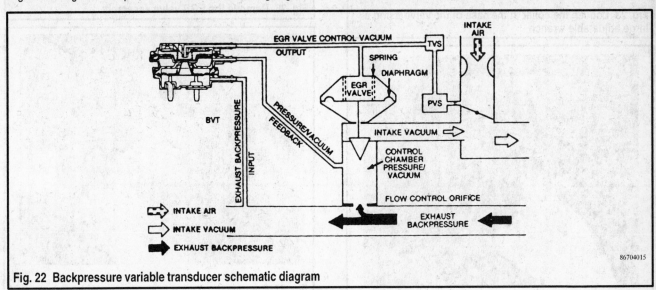

**Fig. 22 Backpressure variable transducer schematic diagram**

## REMOVAL & INSTALLATION

▶ **See Figure 23, 24, 25, 26, 27 and 28**

1. Locate the EGR valve at the rear of the engine compartment by the firewall. It can be found bolted to the engine, next to the brake booster.

2. Using a suitable adjustable wrench, loosen the connection at the base of the valve. Loosen the collar, and push the fitting down. Do not move the tube. In most vehicles, this tube is thin metal and bends easily.

3. Remove the nuts/studs securing the valve to the engine.

4. Remove the EGR valve and gasket. Discard the gasket.

**To install:**

5. Position the valve with a new gasket to the mounting surface on the engine.

6. Secure the EGR valve with nuts/studs. Tighten the hardware to 15–18 ft. lbs. (20–24 Nm).

7. Position the collar to the valve and tighten.

8. Start the engine and check for air leaks around the fittings.

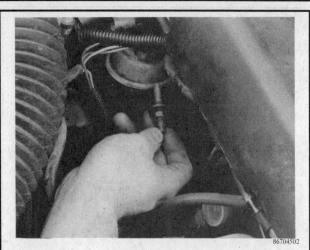

**Fig. 25 When removing the nut, the stud may come loose instead (as is the case here); If so, replace the nut and stud with new parts**

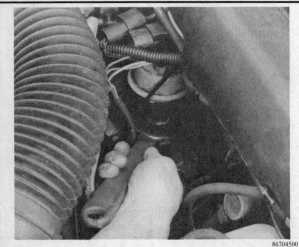

**Fig. 23 Loosen the collar at the base of the valve using a large adjustable wrench**

**Fig. 26 Remove the EGR valve assembly**

**Fig. 27 Remove the gasket from the assembly and discard**

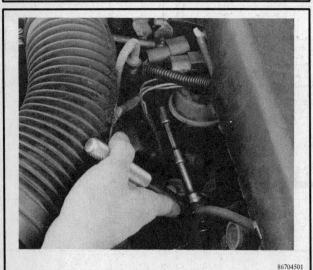

**Fig. 24 Remove the nuts/studs securing the valve**

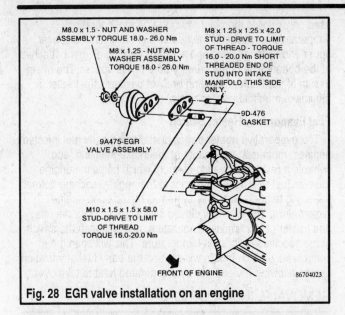

**Fig. 28 EGR valve installation on an engine**

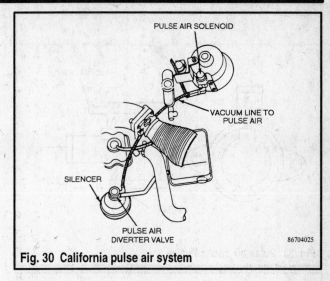

**Fig. 30 California pulse air system**

# Pulse Air System

## OPERATION

▶ **See Figures 29 and 30**

Some fuel injected 2.3L engines are equipped with an air injection system called Pulse Air or Thermactor II. This system does not use an air pump. Instead, the system uses natural pulses, (present in the exhaust system), to pull air into the exhaust manifold and catalyst through air tubes. The pulse air valve is installed to the exhaust manifold, and connects the catalyst to the to the air cleaner silencer with a hose.

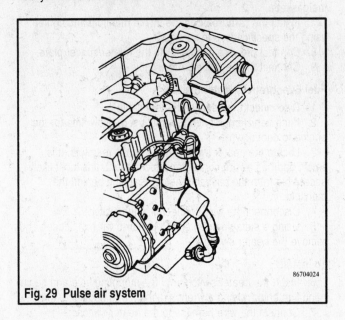

**Fig. 29 Pulse air system**

## TESTING

▶ **See Figures 31 and 32**

1. Visually inspect the thermactor hoses, control and check valves for leaks that may be caused by a backflow of exhaust gas. If the holes are found, the check valve may be faulty.
2. The valve should allow free flow of air in only 1 direction (see illustrations). Exhaust gases should be blocked in the opposite direction.
3. Remove the inlet hose from the valve. At idle and normal operating temperature, air should be drawn into the valve.
4. With the vacuum line removed, the airflow should stop. If these conditions are met, the valve is operating properly.
5. If not, check for vacuum at the valve. If vacuum is present, but no air flows, check the pulse air check valve, silencer filter and air cleaner for blocked or restricted passages.
6. If vacuum is present and no blocked or restricted passages are found, replace the valve.

## REMOVAL & INSTALLATION

▶ **See Figures 31 and 32**

**Pulse air control valve—all models**

1. Remove the clamp that secures the hose to the assembly.
2. Rotate and remove vacuum and inlet hoses
3. Carefully remove the control valve from the engine by unscrewing it from the threaded collar on the manifold.

**To install:**

4. Coat the threaded end of the control valve with engine oil. Thread the control valve into place on the exhaust manifold.
5. Lubricate hose ends of valve. Fasten hoses to assembly.
6. Tighten the hose clamps.

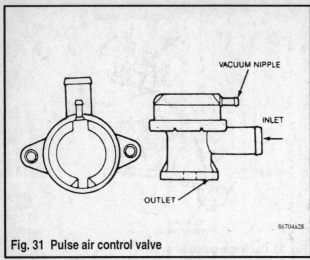

**Fig. 31 Pulse air control valve**

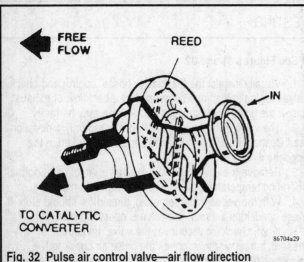

**Fig. 32 Pulse air control valve—air flow direction**

## Mixture Enhancement Systems

In some carburetor equipped and early fuel injected vehicles, heater elements are incorporated into the engine and emission systems to provide for better cold air/fuel mixture when the vehicle is initially started.

When a car is first started, the atomization rate between the outside air and fuel is very poor. By heating the mixture as it enters the engine, (through the use of the heating element), the atomization rate is improved, allowing for better fuel utilization and less automotive emissions during cold engine operation. These heater elements will continue to run until the normal operating temperature is reached, when the heat of the engine is sufficient for proper fuel atomization.

## OPERATION

### Heater/Spacer Assembly

The heater/spacer assembly is a twelve volt grid type element mounted below the carburetor to heat the air/fuel mixture for better fuel mixture when the engine is cold. This assembly is used only prior to the point when the normal operating temperature is reached. The heater unit consists of a spacer, upper and lower gaskets and a 12 volt heating element attached to the bottom side of the primary bore of the spacer. The offset design of the heater mounting bracket positions the heater in the intake manifold inlet opening.

### Fuel Evaporative Heater Switch

The evaporative heater switch, installed on early fuel injected engines, mounts at the bottom of the intake manifold, and controls a relay and heating element which helps the engine atomize fuel at a better rate prior to the engine reaching normal operating temperature. This system is based upon engine temperature. The normally closed switch will activate the relay and heater at low engine temperature, and will open the switch at the specified calibration temperature. This will open the control relay, which in turn will shut off the early fuel atomization heater, allowing the engines own generated heat to take over.

## REMOVAL & INSTALLATION

### Heater/Spacer Assembly

1. Disconnect the negative battery cable.
2. Locate the wire connector attached to the heater element between the carburetor and intake manifold, and disconnect.
3. Remove the carburetor as outlined in section 3.
4. With the carburetor removed, lift the heater/spacer plate off the manifold.
5. Clean all gasket material from both mounting surfaces of the heater/spacer as well as the carburetor and intake manifold.

### To install:

6. Position the heater/spacer plate on the intake manifold with new gaskets between the plate. Do not use any sealant on the gaskets.
7. Install the carburetor on the intake manifold and tighten using the specifications in section 3.
8. Connect the wire connector to the heater/spacer plate.
9. Connect the negative battery cable.

### Fuel Evaporative Heater Switch

1. Disconnect the negative battery cable.
2. If the vehicle has been recently used, allow time for the engine to cool down.
3. Locate the heater switch on the intake manifold. It is small, and has a wire connector attached to it. It is most likely accessible from the passenger side, reaching behind the manifold.
4. Disconnect the wire connector to the switch.
5. Using a suitable open ended or flared wrench, loosen and remove the heater switch.

### To install:

6. Insert the heater switch in to the mounting hole and begin hand tightening. Using a wrench, tighten one additional turn.
7. Connect the wire harness to the heater switch.
8. Connect the negative battery cable.

## EGR SYSTEM — SYMPTOMS DIAGNOSIS

| SYMPTOM | POSSIBLE SOURCE | ACTION |
|---|---|---|
| • Rough Idle Cold | • EGR valve malfunction. | • Run EEC-IV Quick Test |
| | • EGR flange gasket leaking. | • Replace flange gasket and tighten valve attaching nuts or bolts to specification. |
| | • EGR valve attaching nuts or bolts loose or missing. | • Replace flange gasket and tighten valve attaching nuts or bolts to specification. |
| | • EGR or VCV malfunction. | • Perform EGR or VCV diagnosis. |
| | • Load control (WOT) valve malfunction. | • Perform load control (WOT) valve diagnosis. |
| | • Vacuum leak at EVP sensor. | • Replace O-ring seal and tighten EVP sensor attaching nuts to specification. |
| | • EGR valve contamination. | • Clean EGR valve. |
| • Rough Idle Hot | • EGR valve malfunction. | • Run EEC-IV Quick Test |
| | • EGR flange gasket leaking. | • Replace flange gasket and tighten valve attaching nuts or bolts to specification. |
| | • EGR valve attaching nuts or bolts loose or missing. | • Replace flange gasket and tighten valve attaching nuts or bolts to specification. |
| | • Load control (WOT) valve malfunction. | • Perform load control (WOT) valve diagnosis. |
| | • Vacuum leak at EVP sensor. | • Replace O-ring seal and tighten EVP sensor attaching nuts to specification. |
| | • EGR valve contamination. | • Clean EGR valve. |

86704f00

| SYMPTOM | POSSIBLE SOURCE | ACTION |
|---|---|---|
| • Rough Running, Surge, Hesitation, Poor Part Throttle Performance — Cold | • EGR valve malfunction. | • Perform EGR valve diagnosis. |
| | • EGR flange gasket leaking. | • Replace flange gasket and tighten valve attaching nuts or bolts to specification. |
| | • EGR valve attaching nuts or bolts loose or missing. | • Replace flange gasket and tighten valve attaching nuts or bolts to specification. |
| | • EGR solenoid malfunction. | • Run EEC-IV Quick Test |
| | • EGR or VCV malfunction. | • Perform EGR or VCV diagnosis. |
| | • Load control (WOT) valve malfunction. | • Perform load control (WOT) valve diagnosis. |
| | • Vacuum leak at EVP sensor. | • Replace O-ring seal and tighten EVP sensor attaching nuts to specification. |
| | • EGR valve contamination. | • Clean EGR valve. |
| • Rough Running, Surge, Hesitation, Poor Part Throttle Performance — Hot | • EGR valve malfunction. | • Perform EGR valve diagnosis. |
| | • EGR flange gasket leaking. | • Replace flange gasket and tighten valve attaching nuts or bolts to specification. |
| | • EGR valve attaching nuts or bolts loose or missing. | • Replace flange gasket and tighten valve attaching nuts or bolts to specification. |
| | • EGR or VCV malfunction. | • Perform EGR or VCV diagnosis. |
| | • EGR valve contamination. | • Clean EGR valve and if necessary, replace EGR valve. |
| | • Load control (WOT) valve malfunction. | • Perform load control (WOT) valve diagnosis. |
| | • Vacuum leak at EVP sensor. | • Replace O-ring seal and tighten EVP sensor attaching nuts to specification. |
| | • Insufficient exhaust back pressure to activate valve. | • Check exhaust system for leaks. |

86704f01

## EGR SYSTEM – SYMPTOMS DIAGNOSIS – CONTINUED

| SYMPTOM | POSSIBLE SOURCE | ACTION |
|---|---|---|
| • Engine Stalls On Deceleration — Hot and Cold | • EGR valve malfunction. | • Perform EGR valve diagnosis. |
| | • EGR flange gasket leaking. | • Replace flange gasket and tighten valve attaching nuts or bolts to specification. |
| | • EGR valve attaching nuts or bolts loose or missing. | • Replace flange gasket and tighten valve attaching nuts or bolts to specification. |
| | • EGR solenoid malfunction. | • Run EEC-IV Quick Test |
| | • EGR or VCV malfunction. | • Perform EGR or VCV diagnosis. |
| | • EGR valve contamination. | • Clean EGR valve and if necessary, replace EGR valve. |
| | • Load control (WOT) valve malfunction. | • Perform load control (WOT) valve diagnosis. |

| SYMPTOM | POSSIBLE SOURCE | ACTION |
|---|---|---|
| • Engine Spark Knock or Ping | • EGR malfunction. | • Perform EGR valve diagnosis. |
| | • EGR flange gasket leaking. | • Replace flange gasket and tighten valve attaching nuts or bolts to specification. |
| | • EGR valve attaching nuts or bolts loose or missing. | • Replace flange gasket and tighten valve attaching nuts or bolts to specification. |
| | • EGR solenoid malfunction. | • Run EEC-IV Quick Test |
| | • EGR or VCV malfunction. | • Perform EGR or VCV diagnosis. |
| | • Blocked or restricted passages in valve or spacer. | • Clean passages in EGR spacer and EGR valve. |
| | • Vacuum leak at EVP sensor. | • Replace O-ring seal and tighten EVP sensor attaching nuts to specification. |
| | • Insufficient exhaust back pressure to actuate valve. | • Check exhaust system for leaks. |
| • Engine Stalls At Idle — Cold | • EGR valve malfunction. | • Perform EGR valve diagnosis. |
| | • EGR flange gasket leaking. | • Replace flange gasket and tighten valve attaching nuts or bolts to specification. |
| | • EGR valve attaching nuts or bolts loose or missing. | • Replace flange gasket and tighten valve attaching nuts or bolts to specification. |
| | • EGR solenoid malfunction. | • Run EEC-IV Quick Test |
| | • EGR or PVS malfunction. | • Perform EGR or PVS diagnosis. |
| | • EGR valve contamination. | • Clean EGR valve. |
| | • Load control (WOT) valve malfunction. | • Perform load control (WOT) valve diagnosis. |

86704f02

## EGR SYSTEM — SYMPTOMS DIAGNOSIS—CONTINUED

| SYMPTOM | POSSIBLE SOURCE | ACTION |
|---|---|---|
| • Engine Starts But Will Not Run — Engine Hard To Start Or Will Not Start | • EGR valve malfunction. | • Perform EGR valve diagnosis. |
| | • EGR flange gasket leaking. | • Replace flange gasket and tighten valve attaching nuts or bolts to specification. |
| | • EGR valve attaching nuts or bolts loose or missing. | • Replace flange gasket and tighten valve attaching nuts or bolts to specification. |
| | • EGR solenoid malfunction. | • Run EEC-IV Quick Test |
| | • EGR or VCV malfunction. | • Perform EGR or VCV diagnosis. |
| | • EGR valve contamination. | • Clean EGR valve. |
| | • Vacuum leak at EVP sensor. | • Replace O-ring seal and tighten EVP sensor attaching nuts to specification. |
| • Poor Fuel Economy | • EGR valve malfunction. | • Perform EGR valve diagnosis. |
| | • EGR flange gasket leaking. | • Replace flange gasket and tighten valve attaching nuts or bolts to specification. |
| | • EGR valve attaching nuts or bolts loose or missing. | • Replace flange gasket and tighten attaching nuts or bolts to specification. |
| | • EGR solenoid malfunction. | • Run EEC-IV Quick Test |
| | • EGR or PVS malfunction. | • Perform EGR or PVS diagnosis. |
| | • Blocked or restricted EGR passages in valve or spacer. | • Clean passages in EGR spacer and replace EGR valve. |
| | • Load control (WOT) valve malfunction. | • Perform load control (WOT) valve diagnosis. |
| | • Vacuum leak at EVP sensor. | • Replace O-ring seal and tighten EVP sensor attaching nuts to specification. |
| | • Insufficient exhaust back pressure to activate valve. | • Check exhaust system for leaks. |

86704503

## EGR SYSTEM — FUNCTIONAL DIAGNOSIS INTEGRAL BACK PRESSURE (IBP) TRANSDUCER EGR VALVE

| TEST STEP | RESULT ▶ | | ACTION TO TAKE |
|---|---|---|---|
| **IBP1** CHECK SYSTEM INTEGRITY | | | |
| **WARNING** <br><br> **DO NOT USE ROTUNDA EGR CLEANER (021-80056) ON THIS VALVE.** <br> • Check vacuum hoses and connections for looseness, pinching, leakage, splitting, blockage and proper routing. <br> • Inspect EGR valve for loose attaching bolts or damaged flange gasket. <br> • **Does system appear to be in good condition and vacuum hoses properly routed?** | Yes <br><br> No | ▶ <br><br> ▶ | GO to **IBP2**. <br><br> SERVICE EGR system as required. RE-EVALUATE symptom. |
| **IBP2** CHECK EGR VALVE FUNCTION | | | |
| • Install a tachometer, Rotunda 059-00010 or equivalent. <br> • Plug the tailpipe(s) to increase the exhaust system back pressure, leaving a half-inch diameter opening to allow exhaust gases to escape. <br> • Remove and plug the vacuum supply hose from the EGR valve nipple. <br> • Start engine, idle with transmission in NEUTRAL, and observe idle speed. If necessary, adjust idle speed <br> • Tee into a manifold vacuum source and apply direct manifold vacuum to the EGR valve vacuum nipple. <br> **NOTE: Vacuum applied to the EGR valve may bleed down if not applied continuously.** <br> • **Does idle speed drop more than 100 rpm with vacuum continuously applied and return to normal (± 25 rpm) after the vacuum is removed?** | Yes <br><br><br><br><br><br> NO | ▶ <br><br><br><br><br><br> ▶ | The EGR system is OK. UNPLUG and RECONNECT the EGR valve vacuum supply hose. REMOVE tailpipe plug(s). <br><br> REPLACE the EGR valve. RE-EVALUATE symptom. |

86704f04

## EGR SYSTEM — FUNCTIONAL DIAGNOSIS   PFE EGR VALVE

| TEST STEP | RESULT ▶ | | ACTION TO TAKE |
|---|---|---|---|
| **PEV1** CHECK SYSTEM INTEGRITY<br><br>• Check vacuum hoses and connections for looseness, pinching, leakage, splitting, blockage and proper routing.<br><br>• Inspect EGR valve for loose attaching bolts or damaged flange gasket.<br><br>• **Does system appear to be in good condition and vacuum hoses properly routed?** | Yes<br><br>No | ▶<br><br>▶ | GO to PEV2 .<br><br>SERVICE EGR system as required. RE-EVALUATE symptom |
| **PEV2** CHECK EGR VACUUM AT IDLE<br><br>• Run engine until normal operating temperature is reached.<br><br>• With engine running at idle, disconnect EGR vacuum supply at the EGR valve and check for a vacuum signal.<br><br>NOTE: **The EVR solenoid has a constant internal leak. You may notice a small vacuum signal. This signal should be less than 1.0 in-Hg at idle.**<br><br>• **Is EGR vacuum signal less than 1.0 in-Hg at idle?** | Yes<br><br>No | ▶<br><br>▶ | GO to PEV3 .<br><br>RECONNECT EGR vacuum hose. INSPECT EVR solenoid for leakage. RUN EEC-IV Quick Test |

86704505

### EGR SYSTEM – FUNCTIONAL DIAGNOSIS    PFE EGR VALVE – CONTINUED

| TEST STEP | RESULT ▶ | ACTION TO TAKE |
|---|---|---|
| **PEV3** CHECK EGR VALVE FUNCTION | | |
| • Install a tachometer, Rotunda 059-00010 or equivalent.<br><br>• Disconnect the Idle Air Bypass Valve (9F715) electrical connector (EFI engines only).<br><br>• Remove and plug the vacuum supply hose from the EGR valve nipple.<br><br>• Start engine, idle with transmission in NEUTRAL, and observe idle speed. If necessary, adjust idle speed<br><br>• Slowly apply 5-10 inches of vacuum to the EGR valve nipple using a hand vacuum pump, Rotunda 021-00014 or equivalent.<br><br>• **Does idle speed drop more than 100 rpm with vacuum applied and return to normal (± 25 rpm) after the vacuum is removed?** | Yes ▶<br><br><br><br><br><br><br>NO ▶ | The EGR system is OK. UNPLUG and RECONNECT the EGR valve vacuum supply hose. RECONNECT the idle air bypass valve connector.<br><br>INSPECT the EGR valve for blockage or contamination. CLEAN the valve using Rotunda 021-80056 EGR valve cleaner. INSPECT valve for vacuum leakage. REPLACE if necessary. |

86704506

## EGR SYSTEM — FUNCTIONAL DIAGNOSIS   ELECTRONIC EGR (EEGR) VALVE

| TEST STEP | RESULT ▶ | ACTION TO TAKE |
|---|---|---|
| **EEGR1  CHECK SYSTEM INTEGRITY**<br><br>• Check vacuum hoses and connections for looseness, pinching, leakage, splitting, blockage, and proper routing.<br>• Inspect EGR valve for loose attaching bolts or damaged flange gasket.<br>• **Does system appear to be in good condition and vacuum hoses properly routed?** | Yes ▶<br><br>NO ▶ | GO to **EEGR2** .<br><br>SERVICE EGR system as required. RE-EVALUATE symptom. |
| **EEGR2  CHECK EGR VACUUM AT IDLE**<br><br>• Run engine until normal operating temperature is reached.<br>• With engine running at idle, disconnect EGR vacuum supply at the EGR valve and check for a vacuum signal.<br>**NOTE: The EVR solenoid has a constant internal leak. You may notice a small vacuum signal. This signal should be less than 1.0 in-Hg at idle.**<br>• **Is EGR vacuum signal less than 1.0 in-Hg at idle?** | Yes ▶<br><br>No ▶ | GO to **EEGR3** .<br><br>RECONNECT EGR vacuum hose. INSPECT EVR solenoid for leakage. RUN EEC-IV Quick Test |

86704507

## EGR SYSTEM – FUNCTIONAL DIAGNOSIS
## ELECTRONIC EGR (EEGR) VALVE– CONTINUED

| TEST STEP | RESULT ▶ | ACTION TO TAKE |
|---|---|---|
| **EEGR3**  **CHECK EGR VALVE FUNCTION**<br><br>• Install a tachometer, Rotunda 059-00010 or equivalent.<br><br>• Disconnect the Idle Air Bypass Valve (9F715) electrical connector (EFI engines only).<br><br>• Remove and plug the vacuum supply hose from the EGR valve nipple.<br><br>• Start engine, idle with transmission in NEUTRAL, and observe idle speed. If necessary, adjust idle speed<br><br>• Slowly apply 5-10 inches of vacuum to the EGR valve nipple using a hand vacuum pump, Rotunda 021-00014 or equivalent.<br><br>• **Does idle speed drop more than 100 rpm with vacuum applied and return to normal (± 25 rpm) after the vacuum is removed?** | Yes ▶<br><br><br><br><br><br><br><br><br><br>No ▶ | The EGR system is OK. UNPLUG and RECONNECT the EGR valve vacuum supply hose. RECONNECT the idle air bypass valve connector. If you were sent here from EEC Pinpoint Tests for EVP/ EGR code, then REPLACE EVP sensor.<br><br>INSPECT the EGR valve for blockage or contamination. CLEAN the valve using Rotunda 021-80056 EGR valve cleaner. INSPECT valve for vacuum leakage. REPLACE if necessary. |

86704508

## EGR SYSTEM — FUNCTIONAL DIAGNOSIS
## VALVE AND TRANSDUCER ASSEMBLY

| TEST STEP | RESULT ▶ | ACTION TO TAKE |
|---|---|---|
| **VTA1** CHECK SYSTEM INTEGRITY<br><br>• Check vacuum hoses and connections for looseness, pinching, leakage, splitting, blockage and proper routing.<br>• Inspect EGR valve assembly for loose bolts or damaged flange gasket.<br>• **Does system appear to be in good condition and vacuum hoses properly routed?** | Yes ▶<br><br>No ▶ | GO to **VTA2**.<br><br>SERVICE EGR system as required. RE-EVALUATE symptom. |
| **VTA2** CHECK EGR VALVE FUNCTION<br><br>• Install a tachometer, Rotunda 059-00010 or equivalent.<br>• Plug the tailpipe(s) to increase the exhaust system back pressure, leaving a half-inch diameter opening to allow exhaust gases to escape.<br>• Remove and plug the vacuum supply hose from the Exhaust Back Pressure Transducer nipple. Do not disconnect the transducer from the EGR valve.<br>• Start engine, idle with transmission in NEUTRAL, and observe idle speed. If necessary, adjust idle speed<br>• Tee into a manifold vacuum source and apply direct manifold vacuum to the Back Pressure Transducer vacuum nipple.<br>NOTE: Vacuum applied to the transducer may bleed down if not applied continuously.<br>• **Does idle speed drop more than 100 rpm with vacuum continuously applied and return to normal (± 25 rpm) after the vacuum is removed?** | Yes ▶<br><br><br><br><br><br>No ▶ | The EGR system is OK. UNPLUG and RECONNECT the transducer vacuum supply hose. REMOVE tailpipe plug(s).<br><br>INSPECT the EGR valve assembly for blockage, sand (grit) in pick-up tube, or contamination. CLEAN the valve using Rotunda 021-80056 EGR valve cleaner. INSPECT EGR valve assembly for vacuum leakage. REPLACE as necessary. |

86704509

## ELECTRONIC ENGINE CONTROLS

### General Information

The EEC–IV system uses a microprocessor to receive and process information from a number of sensors and other electronic components. The processor contains a specific calibration for maintaining optimum emissions, fuel economy and driveability. By comparing the input signals to its own calibrated program, the processor generates output signals to the various relays solenoids and actuators through the engine compartment.

The EEC–IV processor, located under the instrument panel, to the left of the steering column, communicates service information to the outside world by way of the "Self–Test" service codes. These codes are two–digit numbers signaling that an input has been received which is not within the parameters of the computer program. When the EEC–IV module receives an input telling it that a system is malfunctioning, it alerts the driver by turning on the "Check Engine" light in the instrument panel. If equipped with the proper tools, the driver can retrieve the necessary information from the EEC–IV module, or take the vehicle to an individual who has the proper equipment to retrieve the data.

### System Diagnosis

#### TESTING

In addition to alerting the driver to potential problems based upon information received, the EEC–IV module is capable of performing a diagnostic test on itself and other electronic systems or components of the vehicle.

➡ **A basic working knowledge of the EEC–IV system is critical to efficient troubleshooting of the symptoms. Often a mechanical fault will cause a good EEC–IV system to react abnormally. When performing diagnosis on the EEC system, follow all tests and steps in the order listed below.**

#### Quick Test

The quick test is a functional test of the EEC–IV system. It consists of the basic preparatory steps to be followed, in diagnosing the EEC–IV system.

➡ **The Quick Test steps must be carefully followed, otherwise misdiagnosis or replacement of non-faulty components may result.**

The Quick Test does not have to be initiated. It is an automatic procedure incorporated into the EEC–IV module.

Before hooking up any test equipments to the EEC system, the following checks should be made.

1. Check the condition of the air cleaner and ducting.
2. Check all engine vacuum hoses for leaks and proper routing per the Vehicle Emission Control Information (VECI) decal.
3. Check the EEC–IV system wiring harness for proper electrical connections, routing or corrosion.
4. Check the processor, sensors and actuators for physical damage.
5. Apply the parking brake. Place the shift lever in PARK or NEUTRAL, depending on transaxle type.
6. Turn the ignition switch ON.

➡ **Check that the engine coolant is at specified level.**

7. Operate the engine until normal operating temperature is reached.
8. Turn the ignition switch OFF.
9. Service any items, if required.
10. When complete, proceed to "Equipment Hook–Up".

#### Self–Test Description

The processor stores the self–test program in its permanent memory. When activated, it checks the EEC–IV system by testing its memory and processing capability. The self–test also verifies if the various sensors and actuators are connected and operating properly.

The self–test is divided into 3 specialized tests:
- Key On, Engine Off (KOEO), is a static check of the processor inputs and outputs
- Engine Running is a dynamic check with the engine in operation
- Continuous Testing, checks the sensor inputs for opens and shorts while the vehicle is in operation.

The KOEO and Engine Running tests are functional tests which only detect faults present at the time of the self–test. Continuous testing is an ongoing test that stores fault information for retrieval at a later time, during the self–test.

#### Equipment Hook–Up

##### USING AN ANALOG VOLTMETER (VOM)

▶ See Figure 33

1. Turn the ignition key OFF.
2. Set the analog VOM to read 0–15 volts DC.
3. Connect a jumper wire from the Self–Test Input (STI) to pin 2 (signal return) on the self test connector.
4. Connect the VOM from battery (+) to pin (4) of the Self–Test Output (STO) in the self–test connector.
5. After the equipment is properly connected, proceed to the "Key On, Engine Off Self–Test."

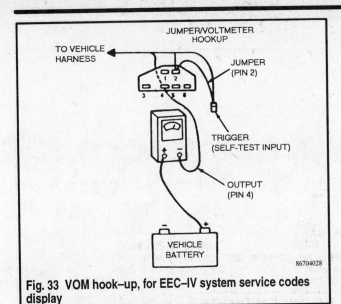

**Fig. 33 VOM hook-up, for EEC-IV system service codes display**

### USING A STAR TESTER

1. Turn the ignition OFF.
2. Connect the color coded wires of the tester according to the manufacturers instructions.
3. Ground the adaptor cable. Refer to the manufacturers instructions for exact cable.
4. Proceed with the "Key On, Engine Off Self-Test" or other tests according to the manufacturer instruction provided with the star tool.

### USING THE CHECK ENGINE LIGHT

If you are running an EEC-IV Self Test and wish to use the the check engine light to read the codes, no special equipment is required.

Although this is a convenient method of reading some codes, it does become complicated when multiple codes are stored and need to be retrieved.

➡ **This method of code retrieval can only be used for the self tests modes.**

Jump the Self Test Input (STI) wire to ground.

#### Key On, Engine Off Self-Test

1. Check that the vehicle being tested has been properly prepared, according to the Quick Test preparations.
2. Activate the self-test by by turning the key to ON.
3. Connect the STI wire to ground.
4. Observe and record all service codes indicated. When more than 1 service code is received, always start with the first code received.
5. After the repairs are made, turn the key to the OFF position, wait 10 seconds, then turn to the ON position, and wait ten seconds. Finally, the vehicle can be switched OFF.

#### Engine Running Self-Test

1. Turn the engine OFF, and wait 10 seconds.

2. Activate the self-test by starting the engine, allowing it to run at 2000 rpm for at least 2 minutes.
3. Turn the engine OFF.
4. Turn key to ON, and wait 10 seconds.
5. Run engine at idle, and read codes.
6. Observe and record all service codes indicated. When more than 1 service code is received, always start with the first code received.
7. After the repairs are made, turn the key to the OFF position, wait 10 seconds, then turn to the ON position, and wait ten seconds. Finally, the vehicle can be switched OFF.

#### Continuous Monitor Mode (Wiggle Test)

The Wiggle Test checks input signals from the individual input switches to the ECC-IV module.

➡ **Turn engine OFF. Allow the engine to cool before starting the test.**

1. Make sure all electrical devices are **OFF**.
2. Turn the ignition key ON.
3. Connect the STI wire to ground.
4. Test all switches individually, and record the results.
5. The STO will be activated whenever a fault is detected. The fault will be indicated on the VOM by a deflection of 10.5 volts or greater.
6. Observe and record all service codes indicated. When more than 1 service code is received, always start with the first code received.
7. After the repairs are made, turn the key to the OFF position, wait 10 seconds, then turn to the ON position, and wait ten seconds. Finally, the vehicle can be switched OFF.

## READING CODES

▶ **See Figure 34**

When service codes are reported on the analog voltmeter or Check Engine light, it will be represented by sweeping movements of the voltmeter's needle across the dial face or a blink of the light. All service codes are represented by 2-digit numbers. For example, Code 23, will be represented by 2 needle pulses (sweeps)/blinks, then after a 2 second pause, the needle will pulse/blink 3 times.

Continuous test codes are separated from the functional codes by a 6-second delay, a single half-second sweep, and another 6-second delay. These codes will be produced on the VOM in the same manner as the functional codes.

## CLEARING CODES

To clear any codes stored in memory, disconnect the negative battery cable. With the negative battery cable off, depress the brake pedal for 5-10 seconds. Finally, to complete the procedure, reconnect the battery cable.

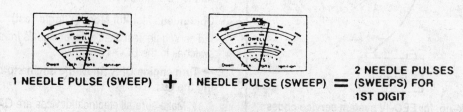

2-SECOND PAUSE BETWEEN DIGITS

1 NEEDLE PULSE (SWEEP) + 1 NEEDLE PULSE (SWEEP) = 2 NEEDLE PULSES (SWEEPS) FOR 1ST DIGIT

:23 SERVICE CODE

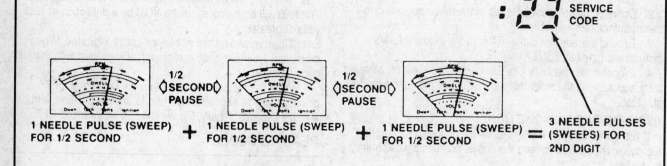

1 NEEDLE PULSE (SWEEP) FOR 1/2 SECOND + 1 NEEDLE PULSE (SWEEP) FOR 1/2 SECOND + 1 NEEDLE PULSE (SWEEP) FOR 1/2 SECOND = 3 NEEDLE PULSES (SWEEPS) FOR 2ND DIGIT

1/2 SECOND PAUSE    1/2 SECOND PAUSE

**4-SECOND PAUSE BETWEEN SERVICE CODES, WHEN MORE THAN ONE CODE IS INDICATED**

Fig. 34 Analog VOM functional service code format

86704029

## Tempo/Topaz ECA Service Codes: 1984-94

| Trouble Code: | | Explanation: |
|---|---|---|
| 11 | ORC | System PASS |
| 12 | R | Cannot control RPM during KOER Self Test high RPM check |
| 13 | R | Cannot control RPM during KOER Selft Test low RPM check |
| 14 | C | PIP circuit failure |
| 15 | O | PCM Read Only Memory (ROM) test failed |
| 15 | C | PCM Keep Alive Memory (KAM) test failed |
| 16 | R | RPM too low to perform HO2S test |
| 18 | R | SPOUT circuit open |
| 18 | C | IDM circuit failure/SPOUT circuit grounded |
| 19 | O | Failure in PCM internal voltage |
| 21 | OR | ECT out of Self Test range |
| 22 | ORC | MAP/BARO out of Self Test range |
| 23 | OR | TP out of Self Test range |
| 24 | OR | IAT out of Selft Test range |
| 26 | OR | MAF out of Selft Test range |
| 29 | C | Insufficient input from the Vehicle Speed Sensor (VSS) |
| 31 | ORC | EVP circuit below minimum voltage |
| 32 | ORC | EVP voltage below closed limit |
| 33 | RC | EGR valve opening not detected |
| 34 | ORC | EVP voltage above closed limit |
| 35 | ORC | EVP circuit above maximum voltage |
| 41 | R | HO2S circuit indicates system lean (right HO2S) |
| 41 | C | No HO2S switch detected (right HO2S) |
| 42 | R | HO2S circuit indicates system rich (right HO2S) |
| 44 | R | Secondary Air Injection system inoperative (right side) |
| 45 | R | Secondary Air Injection upstream during Self Test |
| 46 | R | Secondary Air Injection not bypassed during Self Test |
| 51 | OC | ECT indicated -40C (-40F)/circuit open |
| 53 | OC | TP circuit above maximum voltage |
| 54 | OC | IAT indicated -40C (-40F)/ circuit open |
| 56 | OC | MAF circuit above maximum voltage |
| 61 | OC | ECT indicated 123C (254F)/circuit grounded |
| 63 | OC | TP circuit below minimum voltage |
| 64 | OC | IAT indicated 123C (254F)/circuit grounded |
| 66 | C | MAF circuit below minimum voltage |
| 67 | O | Park/Neutral Position (PNP) switch circuit open-A/C ON during Self Test |
| 77 | R | Breif WOT not sensed during Self Test/Operator error |
| 79 | O | A/C on /Defrost on during Self Test |
| 81 | O | Secondary Air Injection Diverter (AIRD) solenoid circuit failure |
| 82 | O | Secondary Air Injection Bypass (AIRB) solenoid circuit failure |
| 84 | O | EGR Vacuum Regulator (EVR) circuit failure |
| 85 | O | Canister Purge (CANP) circuit failure |
| 87 | OC | Fuel pump primary circuit failure |
| 91 | R | HO2S circuit indicates system lean (left HO2S) |

86704348

### Tempo/Topaz ECA Service Codes: 1984-94

| Trouble Code: | | Explanation: |
|---|---|---|
| 91 | C | No HO2S switching detected (left HO2S) |
| 92 | R | HO2S circuit indicates system rich (left HO2S) |
| 94 | R | Secondary Air Injection system inoperative (left side) |
| 95 | OC | Fuel pump secondary circuit failure |
| 96 | OC | Fuel pump secondary circuit failure |
| 98 | R | Hard fault present-FMEM mode |
| No Code | | Unable to indicate Self Test or unable to output DTC's |
| Code not listed | | DTC's displayed are not applicable to the vehicle being tested |

867043

## Symptom Diagnosis

For each symptom, visual and mechanical checks listed in a suggested order. When the results indicate service or repairs be performed on either the fuel or ignition system, the appropriate section in this manual should be referred to.

➡ **Refer to Section 2 for Ignition system diagnosis and Section 5 for Fuel System diagnosis.**

Although the possible causes listed below are based upon mechanical experience, they are only suggestions. When diagnosing a driveability problem, attempt to use every test available to you to prevent a misdiagnosis, or the replacement of a perfectly good part.

### SYMPTOMS & POSSIBLE CAUSES

#### No Start—but Cranks

*POSSIBLE FUEL SYSTEM CAUSES*
- Fuel pump inertia switch
- Fuel contamination/quality in gas tank or fuel lines
- Clogged fuel filter

*POSSIBLE IGNITION SYSTEM CAUSES*
- Cracked or worn distributor cap, adapter and/or rotor
- Worn spark plug and/or plug wires
- Defective ignition switch and/or wiring
- No voltage ignition coil
- Worn ignition module

*POSSIBLE POWER AND ELECTRICAL GROUND CAUSES*
- Low battery voltage due to cable connection
- Defective starter and/or starter circuit
- Weak electrical connections, wires and/or harnesses

*POSSIBLE AIR/VACUUM CAUSES*
- Leaking or worn vacuum lines

*OTHER CAUSES*
- Engine coolant level
- Defective thermostat and/or fan switch
- EGR valve stuck open
- Moisture entry into the EEC–IV module
- Poor camshaft timing and cylinder compression

#### Stalls at Idle—Poor Running

*POSSIBLE IGNITION SYSTEM CAUSES*
- Cracked or worn distributor cap, adapter and/or rotor
- Worn spark plug and/or plug wires
- Defective ignition switch and/or wiring
- No voltage ignition coil
- Worn ignition module

*POSSIBLE FUEL SYSTEM CAUSES*
- Fuel pump inertia switch
- Fuel contamination/quality in gas tank or fuel lines
- Clogged fuel filter

*POSSIBLE POWER AND ELECTRICAL GROUND CAUSES*
- Low battery voltage due to cable connection
- Defective starter and/or starter circuit
- Weak electrical connections, wires and/or harnesses

*POSSIBLE AIR/VACUUM CAUSES*
- Leaking or worn vacuum lines

*OTHER CAUSES*
- Engine coolant level
- Defective thermostat and/or fan switch
- EGR valve stuck open
- Moisture entry into the EEC–IV module
- Poor camshaft timing and cylinder compression

#### Idle Fluctuates

*POSSIBLE FUEL SYSTEM CAUSES*
- Fuel pump inertia switch
- Fuel contamination/quality in gas tank or fuel lines
- Clogged fuel filter

*POSSIBLE AIR/VACUUM CAUSES*
- Leaking or worn vacuum lines
- Dirty air filter

*POSSIBLE IGNITION SYSTEM CAUSES*
- Cracked or worn distributor cap, adapter and/or rotor
- Worn spark plug and/or plug wires
- Defective ignition switch and/or wiring
- No voltage ignition coil
- Worn ignition module

### POSSIBLE POWER AND ELECTRICAL GROUND CAUSES

- Low battery voltage due to cable connection
- Defective starter and/or starter circuit
- Weak electrical connections, wires and/or harnesses

### OTHER CAUSES

- Engine coolant level
- Defective thermostat and/or fan switch
- EGR valve stuck open
- Moisture entry into the EEC–IV module
- Poor camshaft timing and cylinder compression

## Surges

### POSSIBLE AIR/VACUUM CAUSES

- Leaking or worn vacuum lines
- Dirty air filter

### POSSIBLE FUEL SYSTEM CAUSES

- Fuel pump inertia switch
- Weak fuel pressure
- Fuel contamination/quality in gas tank or fuel lines
- Clogged fuel filter

### POSSIBLE IGNITION SYSTEM CAUSES

- Cracked or worn distributor cap, adapter and/or rotor
- Worn spark plug and/or plug wires
- Defective ignition switch and/or wiring
- No voltage ignition coil
- Worn ignition module

### POSSIBLE POWER AND ELECTRICAL GROUND CAUSES

- Low battery voltage due to cable connection
- Defective starter and/or starter circuit
- Weak electrical connections, wires and/or harnesses

### OTHER CAUSES

- Engine coolant level
- Defective thermostat and/or fan switch
- Clogged PCV valve
- EGR valve stuck open
- Exhaust System Blockage
- Poor camshaft timing and cylinder compression

## Poor Acceleration

### POSSIBLE IGNITION SYSTEM CAUSES

- Cracked or worn distributor cap, adapter and/or rotor

- Worn spark plug and/or plug wires
- Defective ignition switch and/or wiring
- No voltage ignition coil
- Worn ignition module

### POSSIBLE POWER AND ELECTRICAL GROUND CAUSES

- Low battery voltage due to cable connection
- Defective starter and/or starter circuit
- Weak electrical connections, wires and/or harnesses

### POSSIBLE AIR/VACUUM CAUSES

- Leaking or worn vacuum lines
- Dirty air filter

### OTHER CAUSES

- Engine coolant level
- Defective thermostat and/or fan switch
- Clogged PCV valve
- EGR valve stuck open
- Exhaust System Blockage
- Poor camshaft timing and cylinder compression

## Engine Knock

### POSSIBLE AIR/VACUUM CAUSES

- Leaking or cracked vacuum lines

### POSSIBLE IGNITION SYSTEM CAUSES

- Cracked or worn distributor cap, adapter and/or rotor
- Worn spark plug and/or plug wires
- Defective ignition switch and/or wiring
- Advanced/retarded ignition
- No voltage ignition coil
- Worn ignition module

### POSSIBLE POWER AND ELECTRICAL GROUND CAUSES

- Low battery voltage due to cable connection
- Defective starter and/or starter circuit
- Weak electrical connections, wires and/or harnesses

### OTHER CAUSES

- Engine coolant level
- Defective thermostat and/or fan switch
- Clogged PCV valve
- EGR valve stuck open
- Exhaust System Blockage
- Poor camshaft timing and cylinder compression

## VACUUM DIAGRAMS

# CALIBRATION: 4—37A—R00

## MODEL YEAR: 1984

## CAR ENGINE: 2.0L

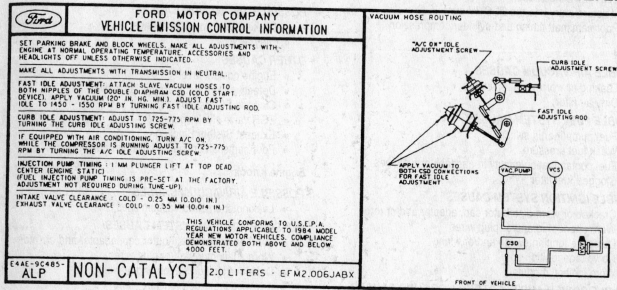

**FORD MOTOR COMPANY**
**VEHICLE EMISSION CONTROL INFORMATION**

SET PARKING BRAKE AND BLOCK WHEELS. MAKE ALL ADJUSTMENTS WITH ENGINE AT NORMAL OPERATING TEMPERATURE. ACCESSORIES AND HEADLIGHTS OFF UNLESS OTHERWISE INDICATED.

MAKE ALL ADJUSTMENTS WITH TRANSMISSION IN NEUTRAL.

FAST IDLE ADJUSTMENT: ATTACH SLAVE VACUUM HOSES TO BOTH NIPPLES OF THE DOUBLE DIAPHRAM CSD (COLD START DEVICE). APPLY VACUUM (20" IN. HG. MIN.). ADJUST FAST IDLE TO 1450 - 1550 RPM BY TURNING FAST IDLE ADJUSTING ROD.

CURB IDLE ADJUSTMENT: ADJUST TO 725-775 RPM BY TURNING THE CURB IDLE ADJUSTING SCREW.

IF EQUIPPED WITH AIR CONDITIONING, TURN A/C ON. WHILE THE COMPRESSOR IS RUNNING ADJUST TO 725-775 RPM BY TURNING THE A/C IDLE ADJUSTING SCREW.

INJECTION PUMP TIMING : 1 MM PLUNGER LIFT AT TOP DEAD CENTER (ENGINE STATIC) (FUEL INJECTION PUMP TIMING IS PRE-SET AT THE FACTORY. ADJUSTMENT NOT REQUIRED DURING TUNE-UP).

INTAKE VALVE CLEARANCE : COLD - 0.25 MM (0.010 IN.)
EXHAUST VALVE CLEARANCE : COLD - 0.35 MM (0.014 IN.)

THIS VEHICLE CONFORMS TO U.S.E.P.A. REGULATIONS APPLICABLE TO 1984 MODEL YEAR NEW MOTOR VEHICLES. COMPLIANCE DEMONSTRATED BOTH ABOVE AND BELOW 4000 FEET.

E4AE-9C485-ALP   NON-CATALYST   2.0 LITERS · EFM2.0D6JABX

VACUUM HOSE ROUTING

"A/C ON" IDLE ADJUSTMENT SCREW — CURB IDLE ADJUSTMENT SCREW — FAST IDLE ADJUSTING ROD — APPLY VACUUM TO BOTH CSD CONNECTIONS FOR FAST IDLE ADJUSTMENT — VAC. PUMP — VCS — CSD — VCV — FRONT OF VEHICLE

## FUEL INJECTION PUMP SPECIFICATIONS

Model:
Part Number:

Nippondenso VE-4
RF33-13-800A
RF33-13-800B (Alternate)

## COLD START SYSTEM

The dual vacuum can cold start device increases engine speed and injection pump timing as shown:

| Cold Start Device Stage | Engine Coolant Temperature | Injection Pump Timing | Engine Speed |
|---|---|---|---|
| Stage 1 & Stage 2 | Above 60°C | 8° BTDC | 1450–1550 RPM (Adjustment) |
| Stage 1 | Above 60°C | 5° BTDC | 800–1000 RPM (Check) |
| None | Above 60°C | 0° TDC | 725–775 RPM (Adjustment) |

8670420

# CALIBRATION: 5—37A—R00

**MODEL YEAR: 1985**                     **CAR ENGINE: 2.0L**

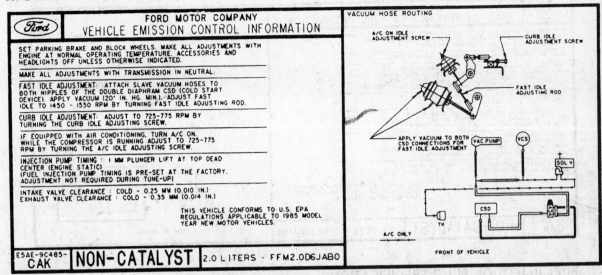

**FORD MOTOR COMPANY**
**VEHICLE EMISSION CONTROL INFORMATION**

SET PARKING BRAKE AND BLOCK WHEELS. MAKE ALL ADJUSTMENTS WITH ENGINE AT NORMAL OPERATING TEMPERATURE. ACCESSORIES AND HEADLIGHTS OFF UNLESS OTHERWISE INDICATED.

MAKE ALL ADJUSTMENTS WITH TRANSMISSION IN NEUTRAL.

FAST IDLE ADJUSTMENT: ATTACH SLAVE VACUUM HOSES TO BOTH NIPPLES OF THE DOUBLE DIAPHRAM CSD (COLD START DEVICE). APPLY VACUUM (20" IN. HG. MIN.). ADJUST FAST IDLE TO 1450 - 1550 RPM BY TURNING FAST IDLE ADJUSTING ROD.

CURB IDLE ADJUSTMENT: ADJUST TO 725-775 RPM BY TURNING THE CURB IDLE ADJUSTING SCREW.

IF EQUIPPED WITH AIR CONDITIONING, TURN A/C ON. WHILE THE COMPRESSOR IS RUNNING ADJUST TO 725-775 RPM BY TURNING THE A/C IDLE ADJUSTING SCREW.

INJECTION PUMP TIMING : 1 MM PLUNGER LIFT AT TOP DEAD CENTER (ENGINE STATIC)
(FUEL INJECTION PUMP TIMING IS PRE-SET AT THE FACTORY. ADJUSTMENT NOT REQUIRED DURING TUNE-UP)

INTAKE VALVE CLEARANCE : COLD - 0.25 MM (0.010 IN.)
EXHAUST VALVE CLEARANCE : COLD - 0.35 MM (0.014 IN.)

THIS VEHICLE CONFORMS TO U.S. EPA REGULATIONS APPLICABLE TO 1985 MODEL YEAR NEW MOTOR VEHICLES.

E5AE-9C485-CAK  **NON-CATALYST**  2.0 LITERS - FFM2.0D6JAB0

VACUUM HOSE ROUTING

A/C ON IDLE ADJUSTMENT SCREW — CURB IDLE ADJUSTMENT SCREW

FAST IDLE ADJUSTING ROD

APPLY VACUUM TO BOTH CSD CONNECTIONS FOR FAST IDLE ADJUSTMENT

VAC PUMP   VCS   SOL V   CSD   TK   A/C ONLY   FRONT OF VEHICLE

## FUEL INJECTION PUMP SPECIFICATIONS

Model:            Nippondenso VE-4
Part Number:      RF42-13-800

## COLD START SYSTEM

The dual vacuum can cold start device increases engine speed and injection pump timing as shown:

| Cold Start Device Stage | Engine Coolant Temperature | Injection Pump Timing | Engine Speed |
|---|---|---|---|
| Stage 1 & Stage 2 | Above 60°C | 8° BTDC | 1450–1550 RPM (Adjustment) |
| Stage 1 | Above 60°C | 5° BTDC | 800–1000 RPM (Check) |
| None | Above 60°C | 0°TDC | 725–775 RPM (Adjustment) |

86704202

## CALIBRATION: 4—37B—R00

**MODEL YEAR: 1985**

**CAR ENGINE: 2.0L**

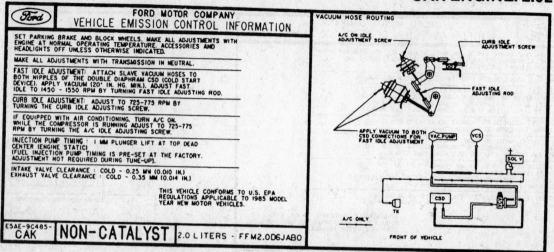

## FUEL INJECTION PUMP SPECIFICATIONS

Model: Nippondenso VE-4

Part Number:
RF10-13-800B
RF10-13-800C (Alt.)
RF10-13-800D (Alt.)
RF10-13-800E (Alt.)

## COLD START SYSTEM

The dual vacuum can cold start device increases engine speed and injection pump timing as shown:

| Cold Start Device Stage | Engine Coolant Temperature | Injection Pump Timing | Engine Speed |
|---|---|---|---|
| Stage 1 & Stage 2 | Above 60 °C | 8° BTDC | 1450–1550 RPM (Adjustment) |
| Stage 1 | Above 60 °C | 5° BTDC | 800–1000 RPM (Check) |
| None | Above 60 °C | 0°TDC | 725–775 RPM (Adjustment) |

86704203

# CALIBRATION: 7—37B—R00

**MODEL YEAR: 1987**

**ENGINE: 2.0L DIESEL**

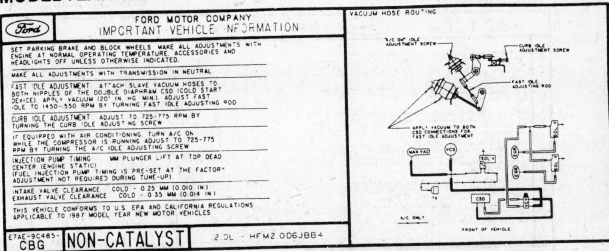

VACUUM HOSE ROUTING

FORD MOTOR COMPANY
IMPORTANT VEHICLE INFORMATION

SET PARKING BRAKE AND BLOCK WHEELS. MAKE ALL ADJUSTMENTS WITH ENGINE AT NORMAL OPERATING TEMPERATURE. ACCESSORIES AND HEADLIGHTS OFF UNLESS OTHERWISE INDICATED.

MAKE ALL ADJUSTMENTS WITH TRANSMISSION IN NEUTRAL.

FAST IDLE ADJUSTMENT: ATTACH SLAVE VACUUM HOSES TO BOTH NIPPLES OF THE DOUBLE DIAPHRAM CSD (COLD START DEVICE). APPLY VACUUM (20" IN HG MIN.). ADJUST FAST IDLE TO 1450-1550 RPM BY TURNING FAST IDLE ADJUSTING ROD

CURB IDLE ADJUSTMENT: ADJUST TO 725-775 RPM BY TURNING THE CURB IDLE ADJUSTING SCREW

IF EQUIPPED WITH AIR CONDITIONING, TURN A/C ON WHILE THE COMPRESSOR IS RUNNING ADJUST TO 725-775 RPM BY TURNING THE A/C IDLE ADJUSTING SCREW.

INJECTION PUMP TIMING     MM PLUNGER LIFT AT TOP DEAD CENTER (ENGINE STATIC) (FUEL INJECTION PUMP TIMING IS PRE-SET AT THE FACTORY ADJUSTMENT NOT REQUIRED DURING TUNE-UP).

INTAKE VALVE CLEARANCE     COLD - 0.25 MM (0.010 IN.)
EXHAUST VALVE CLEARANCE    COLD - 0.35 MM (0.014 IN.)

THIS VEHICLE CONFORMS TO U.S. EPA AND CALIFORNIA REGULATIONS APPLICABLE TO 1987 MODEL YEAR NEW MOTOR VEHICLES

E7AE-9C485-CBG   **NON-CATALYST**   2.0L - HFM2.006JBB4

## CALIBRATION PARTS LIST

| NAME | DESCRIPTION | PART NUMBER |
|---|---|---|
| FUEL INJECTOR | | ND-3410 |
| | | RF66-13-H50 |
| FUEL INJECTION PUMP | | RF67-13-800E |
| LOAD TIMER | | PIA Fuel Inj. Pump |
| COLD START DEVICE | | PIA Fuel Inj. Pump |
| VACUUM CONTROL VALVE | 4-Port, Thermo Valve Start/EGR . | RF67-13-980A |
| ALTITUDE COMPENSATOR | | PIA Fuel Inj. Pump |
| QUICK START SYSTEM CONTROL UNIT | Glow Plug | RF10-18-701B |
| WATER TEMPERATURE SWITCH | Glow Plug | RF67-18-840 |
| NEUTRAL SWITCH | Glow Plug | E4ER-7A247-AA |
| EGR CONTROL UNIT | | RF67-18-941B |
| | | E7EE-9F480-AA |
| EGR VALVE | | RF66-20-300 |
| SOLENOID VALVE | EGR | RF67-18-745A |
| FIFTH GEAR SWITCH | EGR | E5EC-7L238-AA |
| THROTTLE POSITION SENSOR | EGR | PIA Fuel Inj. Pump |
| TACH SENSOR | EGR | PIA Fuel Inj. Pump |
| CLUTCH SWITCH | w/o Speed Control Glow Plug | E4EB-12B537-AA |
| CLUTCH SWITCH | w/Speed Control Glow Plug | E4EB-12B537-BA |
| SWITCH AND BRACKET ASSY. | Gear Shift Position Sensor | E5FZ-7L238-A |
| SWITCH ASSY. | Transmission Neutral Sensing | E4FZ-7A247-A |
| SWITCH | Coolant Temp. Control Vacuum | E73Z-8A564-A |
| SWITCH | Glow Plug Control | E73Z-9A444-A |
| VALVE ASSY. | EGR Solenoid Vacuum | E73Z-9D474-A |

## CALIBRATION PARTS LIST CONT'D

| NAME | DESCRIPTION | PART NUMBER |
|---|---|---|
| VALVE ASSY. | EGR | E73Z-9D475-A |
| CONTROL ASSY. | EGR Valve | E7FZ-9F480-A |
| CONTROL ASSY. | Engine Idle | E43Z-9L513-B |
| NOZZLE HOLDER ASSY. | Fuel Injector | E73Z-9E527-A |
| PUMP ASSY. | Fuel Injection | E73Z-9A543-A |
| MOTOR ASSY. | Fuel Cold Start Vacuum | E43Z-9F785-B |
| POTENTIOMETER ASSY. | Throttle Position Sensor | E7FZ-9B989-B |
| MODULE | Glow Plug Control | E73Z-12B533-A |
| SWITCH AND WIRE ASSY. | Engine Idle Control —w/o Speed Control | E4FZ-12B537-A |
| SWITCH AND WIRE ASSY. | Engine Idle Control —with Speed Control | E4FZ-12B537-B |
| SENSOR ASSY. | Tachometer | E7FZ-17B384-A |

86704204

## CALIBRATION: 4—05H—R00

**MODEL YEAR: 1984**

**ENGINE: 2.3L**

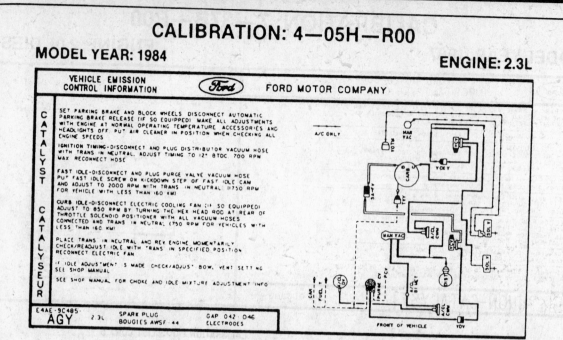

VEHICLE EMISSION CONTROL INFORMATION — FORD — FORD MOTOR COMPANY

**C A T A L Y S T   C A T A L Y S E U R**

SET PARKING BRAKE AND BLOCK WHEELS DISCONNECT AUTOMATIC PARKING BRAKE RELEASE (IF SO EQUIPPED) MAKE ALL ADJUSTMENTS WITH ENGINE AT NORMAL OPERATING TEMPERATURE ACCESSORIES AND HEADLIGHTS OFF PUT AIR CLEANER IN POSITION WHEN CHECKING ALL ENGINE SPEEDS

IGNITION TIMING-DISCONNECT AND PLUG DISTRIBUTOR VACUUM HOSE WITH TRANS IN NEUTRAL ADJUST TIMING TO 12° BTDC 700 RPM MAX RECONNECT HOSE

FAST IDLE-DISCONNECT AND PLUG PURGE VALVE VACUUM HOSE PUT FAST IDLE SCREW ON KICKDOWN STEP OF FAST IDLE CAM AND ADJUST TO 2000 RPM WITH TRANS IN NEUTRAL (1750 RPM FOR VEHICLE WITH LESS THAN 160 KM)

CURB IDLE-DISCONNECT ELECTRIC COOLING FAN (IF SO EQUIPPED) ADJUST TO 850 RPM BY TURNING THE HEX HEAD ROD AT REAR OF THROTTLE SOLENOID POSITIONER WITH ALL VACUUM HOSES CONNECTED AND TRANS IN NEUTRAL (750 RPM FOR VEHICLES WITH LESS THAN 160 KM)

PLACE TRANS IN NEUTRAL AND REV ENGINE MOMENTARILY CHECK/READJUST IDLE WITH TRANS IN SPECIFIED POSITION RECONNECT ELECTRIC FAN

IF IDLE ADJUSTMENT IS MADE CHECK/ADJUST BOWL VENT SETTING SEE SHOP MANUAL

SEE SHOP MANUAL FOR CHOKE AND IDLE MIXTURE ADJUSTMENT INFO

E4AE-9C485-AGY  2.3L  SPARK PLUG BOUGIES AWSF-44  GAP .042-.046 ELECTRODES

A/C ONLY

FRONT OF VEHICLE

## CALIBRATION: 4—05H—R10

**MODEL YEAR: 1984**

**ENGINE: 2.3L**

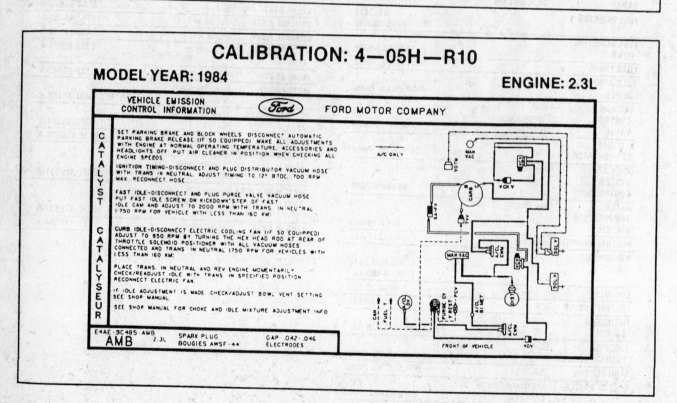

VEHICLE EMISSION CONTROL INFORMATION — FORD — FORD MOTOR COMPANY

**C A T A L Y S T   C A T A L Y S E U R**

SET PARKING BRAKE AND BLOCK WHEELS DISCONNECT AUTOMATIC PARKING BRAKE RELEASE (IF SO EQUIPPED) MAKE ALL ADJUSTMENTS WITH ENGINE AT NORMAL OPERATING TEMPERATURE ACCESSORIES AND HEADLIGHTS OFF PUT AIR CLEANER IN POSITION WHEN CHECKING ALL ENGINE SPEEDS

IGNITION TIMING-DISCONNECT AND PLUG DISTRIBUTOR VACUUM HOSE WITH TRANS IN NEUTRAL ADJUST TIMING TO 12° BTDC 700 RPM MAX RECONNECT HOSE

FAST IDLE-DISCONNECT AND PLUG PURGE VALVE VACUUM HOSE PUT FAST IDLE SCREW ON KICKDOWN STEP OF FAST IDLE CAM AND ADJUST TO 2000 RPM WITH TRANS IN NEUTRAL (1750 RPM FOR VEHICLE WITH LESS THAN 160 KM)

CURB IDLE-DISCONNECT ELECTRIC COOLING FAN (IF SO EQUIPPED) ADJUST TO 850 RPM BY TURNING THE HEX HEAD ROD AT REAR OF THROTTLE SOLENOID POSITIONER WITH ALL VACUUM HOSES CONNECTED AND TRANS IN NEUTRAL (750 RPM FOR VEHICLES WITH LESS THAN 160 KM)

PLACE TRANS IN NEUTRAL AND REV ENGINE MOMENTARILY CHECK/READJUST IDLE WITH TRANS IN SPECIFIED POSITION RECONNECT ELECTRIC FAN

IF IDLE ADJUSTMENT IS MADE CHECK/ADJUST BOWL VENT SETTING SEE SHOP MANUAL

SEE SHOP MANUAL FOR CHOKE AND IDLE MIXTURE ADJUSTMENT INFO

E4AE-9C485-AMB  2.3L  SPARK PLUG BOUGIES AWSF-44  GAP .042-.046 ÉLECTRODES

A/C ONLY

FRONT OF VEHICLE

86704206

## CALIBRATION: 4—06H—R00

**MODEL YEAR: 1984**  **ENGINE: 2.3L**

VEHICLE EMISSION CONTROL INFORMATION  FORD MOTOR COMPANY

**C A T A L Y S T  C A T A L Y S E U R**

SET PARKING BRAKE AND BLOCK WHEELS DISCONNECT AUTOMATIC PARKING BRAKE RELEASE (IF SO EQUIPPED) MAKE ALL ADJUSTMENTS WITH ENGINE AT NORMAL OPERATING TEMPERATURE. ACCESSORIES AND HEADLIGHTS OFF PUT AIR CLEANER IN POSITION WHEN CHECKING ALL ENGINE SPEEDS

IGNITION TIMING-DISCONNECT AND PLUG DISTRIBUTOR VACUUM HOSE WITH TRANS IN "D". ADJUST TIMING TO 12° BTDC. 700 RPM MAX RECONNECT HOSE

FAST IDLE-DISCONNECT AND PLUG EGR VACUUM HOSE DISCONNECT AND PLUG PURGE VALVE VACUUM HOSE PUT FAST IDLE SCREW ON KICKDOWN STEP OF FAST IDLE CAM AND ADJUST TO 2200 RPM WITH TRANS IN NEUTRAL (1950 RPM FOR VEHICLE WITH LESS THAN 160 KM) RECONNECT HOSES

CURB IDLE-DISCONNECT ELECTRIC COOLING FAN (IF SO EQUIPPED) ADJUST TO 800 RPM BY TURNING THE HEX HEAD ROD AT REAR OF TSP (THROTTLE SOLENOID POSITIONER) WITH ALL VACUUM HOSES CONNECTED AND TRANS IN "D" (700 RPM FOR VEHICLES WITH LESS THAN 160 KM)

PLACE TRANS IN NEUTRAL AND REV ENGINE MOMENTARILY CHECK/READJUST IDLE WITH TRANS IN SPECIFIED POSITION RECONNECT ELECTRIC FAN

IF IDLE ADJUSTMENT IS MADE, CHECK/ADJUST BOWL VENT SETTING SEE SHOP MANUAL

SEE SHOP MANUAL FOR CHOKE AND IDLE MIXTURE ADJUSTMENT INFO

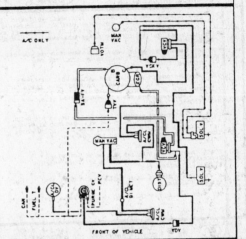

E4AE-9C485-**AHB**   2.3L   SPARK PLUG BOUGIES AWSF-44   GAP .042-.046 ÉLECTRODES

---

## CALIBRATION: 4—06H—R10

**MODEL YEAR: 1984**  **ENGINE: 2.3L**

VEHICLE EMISSION CONTROL INFORMATION  FORD MOTOR COMPANY

**C A T A L Y S T  C A T A L Y S E U R**

SET PARKING BRAKE AND BLOCK WHEELS DISCONNECT AUTOMATIC PARKING BRAKE RELEASE (IF SO EQUIPPED) MAKE ALL ADJUSTMENTS WITH ENGINE AT NORMAL OPERATING TEMPERATURE. ACCESSORIES AND HEADLIGHTS OFF PUT AIR CLEANER IN POSITION WHEN CHECKING ALL ENGINE SPEEDS.

IGNITION TIMING-DISCONNECT AND PLUG DISTRIBUTOR VACUUM HOSE WITH TRANS IN "D". ADJUST TIMING TO 12° BTDC. 700 RPM MAX RECONNECT HOSE.

FAST IDLE-DISCONNECT AND PLUG EGR VACUUM HOSE DISCONNECT AND PLUG PURGE VALVE VACUUM HOSE PUT FAST IDLE SCREW ON KICKDOWN STEP OF FAST IDLE CAM AND ADJUST TO 2200 RPM WITH TRANS IN NEUTRAL. (1950 RPM FOR VEHICLE WITH LESS THAN 160 KM) RECONNECT HOSES.

CURB IDLE-DISCONNECT ELECTRIC COOLING FAN (IF SO EQUIPPED) ADJUST TO 800 RPM BY TURNING THE HEX HEAD ROD AT REAR OF TSP (THROTTLE SOLENOID POSITIONER) WITH ALL VACUUM HOSES CONNECTED AND TRANS IN "D" (700 RPM FOR VEHICLES WITH LESS THAN 160 KM)

PLACE TRANS IN NEUTRAL AND REV ENGINE MOMENTARILY CHECK/READJUST IDLE WITH TRANS IN SPECIFIED POSITION RECONNECT ELECTRIC FAN

IF IDLE ADJUSTMENT IS MADE. CHECK/ADJUST BOWL VENT SETTING SEE SHOP MANUAL

SEE SHOP MANUAL FOR CHOKE AND IDLE MIXTURE ADJUSTMENT INFO

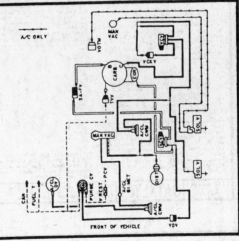

E4AE-9C485-**AMC**   2.3L   SPARK PLUG BOUGIES AWSF-44   GAP .042-.046 ÉLECTRODES

86704208

## CALIBRATION: 4—06H—R11

**MODEL YEAR: 1984**

**ENGINE: 2.3L**

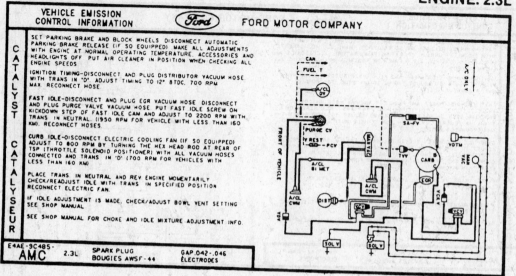

VEHICLE EMISSION CONTROL INFORMATION　Ford　FORD MOTOR COMPANY

**CATALYST CATALYSEUR**

SET PARKING BRAKE AND BLOCK WHEELS DISCONNECT AUTOMATIC PARKING BRAKE RELEASE (IF SO EQUIPPED) MAKE ALL ADJUSTMENTS WITH ENGINE AT NORMAL OPERATING TEMPERATURE, ACCESSORIES AND HEADLIGHTS OFF. PUT AIR CLEANER IN POSITION WHEN CHECKING ALL ENGINE SPEEDS.

IGNITION TIMING-DISCONNECT AND PLUG DISTRIBUTOR VACUUM HOSE WITH TRANS IN 'D'. ADJUST TIMING TO 12° BTDC, 700 RPM MAX. RECONNECT HOSE.

FAST IDLE-DISCONNECT AND PLUG EGR VACUUM HOSE DISCONNECT AND PLUG PURGE VALVE VACUUM HOSE PUT FAST IDLE SCREW ON KICKDOWN STEP OF FAST IDLE CAM AND ADJUST TO 2200 RPM WITH TRANS IN NEUTRAL. (1950 RPM FOR VEHICLE WITH LESS THAN 160 KM). RECONNECT HOSES.

CURB IDLE-DISCONNECT ELECTRIC COOLING FAN (IF SO EQUIPPED) ADJUST TO 800 RPM BY TURNING THE HEX HEAD ROD AT REAR OF TSP (THROTTLE SOLENOID POSITIONER) WITH ALL VACUUM HOSES CONNECTED AND TRANS IN 'D' (700 RPM FOR VEHICLES WITH LESS THAN 160 KM).

PLACE TRANS IN NEUTRAL AND REV ENGINE MOMENTARILY CHECK/READJUST IDLE WITH TRANS IN SPECIFIED POSITION RECONNECT ELECTRIC FAN.

IF IDLE ADJUSTMENT IS MADE, CHECK/ADJUST BOWL VENT SETTING SEE SHOP MANUAL.

SEE SHOP MANUAL FOR CHOKE AND IDLE MIXTURE ADJUSTMENT INFO.

E4AE-9C485-
**AMC**　2.3L　SPARK PLUG BOUGIES AWSF-44　GAP.042-.046 ÉLECTRODES

## CALIBRATION: 4—06N—R00

**MODEL YEAR: 1984**

**ENGINE: 2.3L**

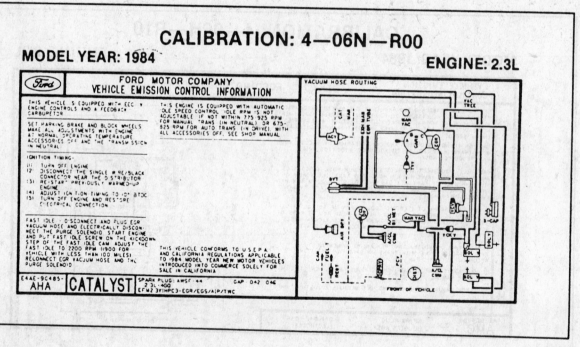

Ford　FORD MOTOR COMPANY VEHICLE EMISSION CONTROL INFORMATION

THIS VEHICLE IS EQUIPPED WITH EEC IV ENGINE CONTROLS AND A FEEDBACK CARBURETOR

SET PARKING BRAKE AND BLOCK WHEELS MAKE ALL ADJUSTMENTS WITH ENGINE AT NORMAL OPERATING TEMPERATURE ACCESSORIES OFF AND THE TRANSMISSION IN NEUTRAL

IGNITION TIMING:
(1) TURN OFF ENGINE
(2) DISCONNECT THE SINGLE WIRE/BLACK CONNECTOR NEAR THE DISTRIBUTOR
(3) RE-START PREVIOUSLY WARMED-UP ENGINE
(4) ADJUST IGNITION TIMING TO 10° BTDC
(5) TURN OFF ENGINE AND RESTORE ELECTRICAL CONNECTION

FAST IDLE - DISCONNECT AND PLUG EGR VACUUM HOSE AND ELECTRICALLY DISCONNECT THE PURGE SOLENOID START ENGINE AND PUT FAST IDLE SCREW ON THE KICKDOWN STEP OF THE FAST IDLE CAM ADJUST THE FAST IDLE TO 2200 RPM (1900 FOR VEHICLE WITH LESS THAN 100 MILES) RECONNECT EGR VACUUM HOSE AND THE PURGE SOLENOID

THIS ENGINE IS EQUIPPED WITH AUTOMATIC IDLE SPEED CONTROL IDLE RPM IS NOT ADJUSTABLE IF NOT WITHIN 775-925 RPM FOR MANUAL TRANS (IN NEUTRAL) OR 675-825 RPM FOR AUTO TRANS (IN DRIVE) WITH ALL ACCESSORIES OFF. SEE SHOP MANUAL

THIS VEHICLE CONFORMS TO USEPA AND CALIFORNIA REGULATIONS APPLICABLE TO 1984 MODEL YEAR NEW MOTOR VEHICLES INTRODUCED INTO COMMERCE SOLELY FOR SALE IN CALIFORNIA

E4AE-9C485-
**AHA**　**CATALYST**　SPARK PLUG: AWSF-44 2.3L/4GO EFM2 3V1HPC3-EGR/EGS/AIP/TWC　GAP .042-.046

VACUUM HOSE ROUTING

86704209

## CALIBRATION: 4—25A—R10

**MODEL YEAR: 1984**　　　　　　　　　　　　　　　　**ENGINE: 2.3L**

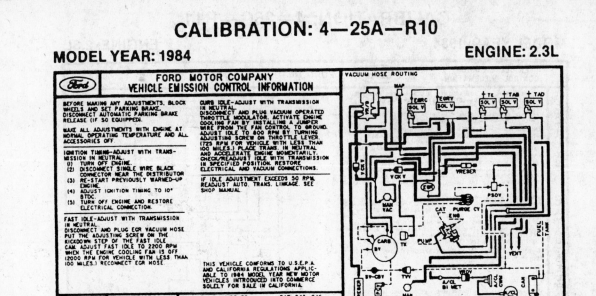

## CALIBRATION: 4—25D—R12

**MODEL YEAR: 1984**　　　　　　　　　　　　　　　　**ENGINE: 2.3L**

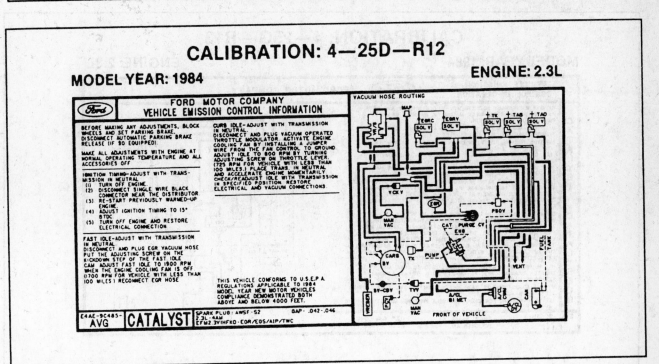

86704210

## CALIBRATION: 4—25G—R11

**MODEL YEAR: 1984**

**ENGINE: 2.3L**

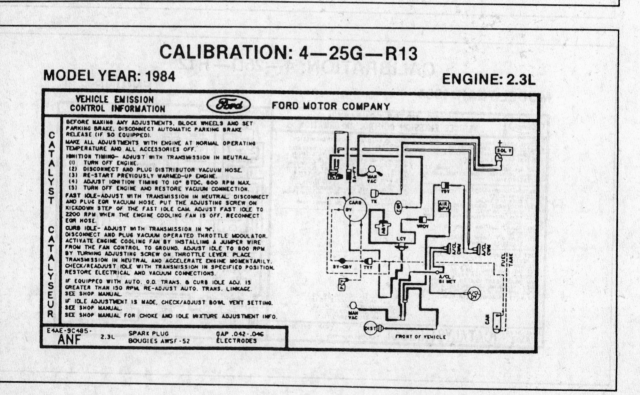

## CALIBRATION: 4—25G—R13

**MODEL YEAR: 1984**

**ENGINE: 2.3L**

86704211

## CALIBRATION: 4—25D—R13
**MODEL YEAR: 1984**     **ENGINE: 2.3L**

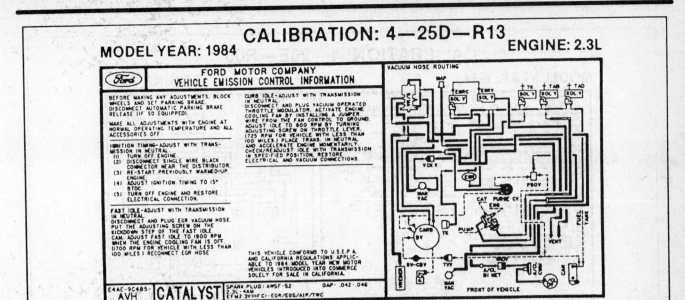

## MODEL YEAR: 1984   CALIBRATION: 4—25E—R01   ENGINE: 2.3L

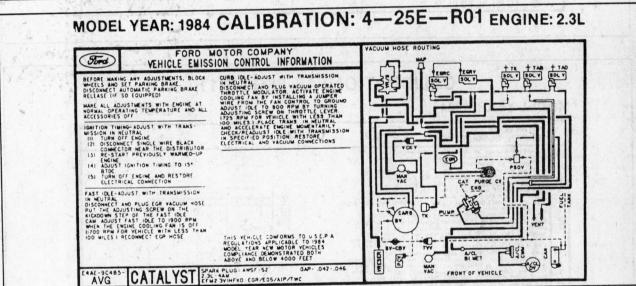

## MODEL YEAR: 1984   CALIBRATION: 4—25F—R00   ENGINE: 2.3L

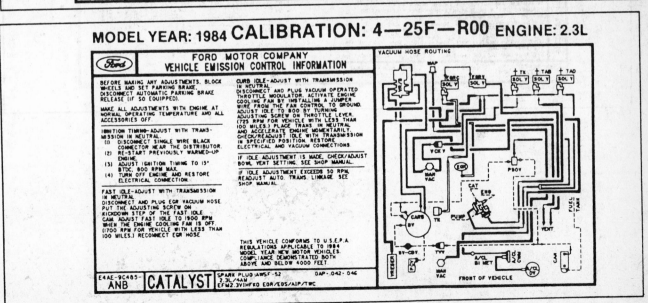

86704212

### CALIBRATION: 4—26E—R00

**MODEL YEAR: 1984**                                   **ENGINE: 2.3L**

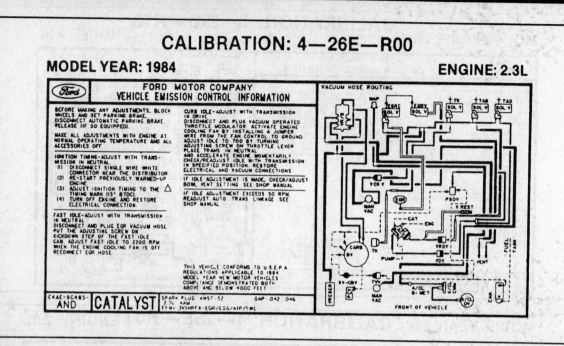

### CALIBRATION: 4—26G—R11

**MODEL YEAR: 1984**                                   **ENGINE: 2.3L**

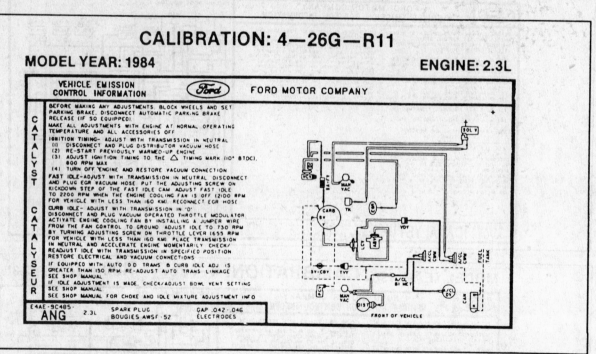

86704213

**MODEL YEAR: 1984**    **CALIBRATION: 4—26J—R28**    **ENGINE: 2.3L**

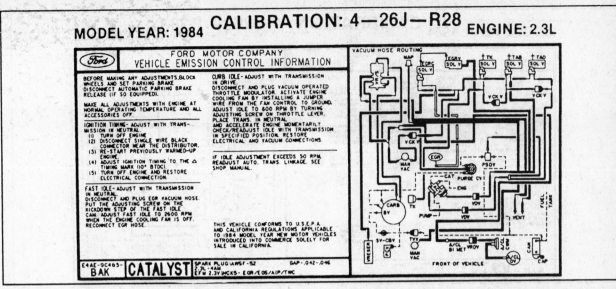

**MODEL YEAR: 1984**    **CALIBRATION: 4—26K—R22**    **ENGINE: 2.3L**

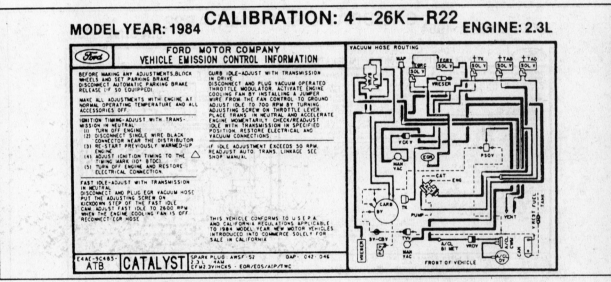

**MODEL YEAR: 1984**    **CALIBRATION: 4—26K—R24**    **ENGINE: 2.3L**

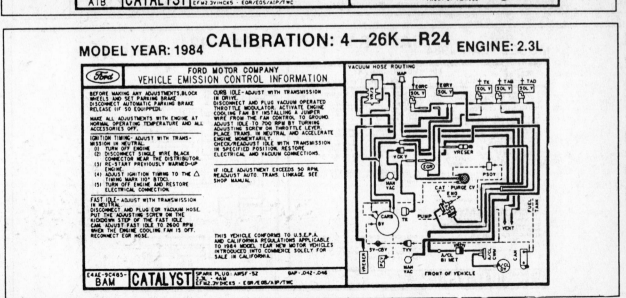

86704215

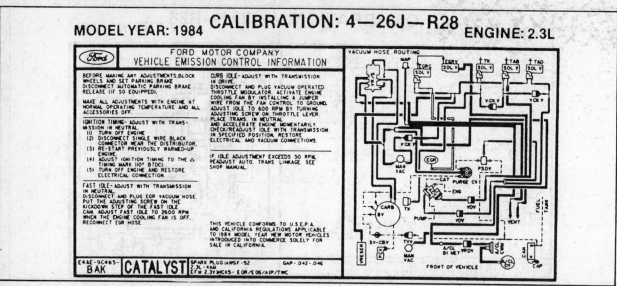

MODEL YEAR: 1984   CALIBRATION: 4—26J—R28   ENGINE: 2.3L

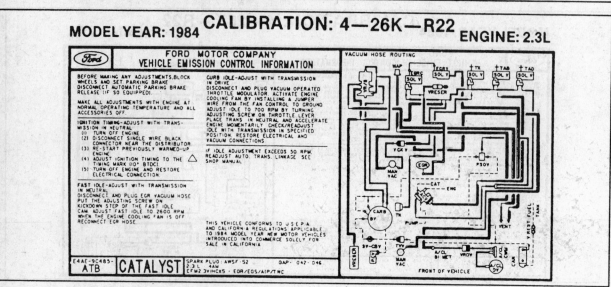

MODEL YEAR: 1984   CALIBRATION: 4—26K—R22   ENGINE: 2.3L

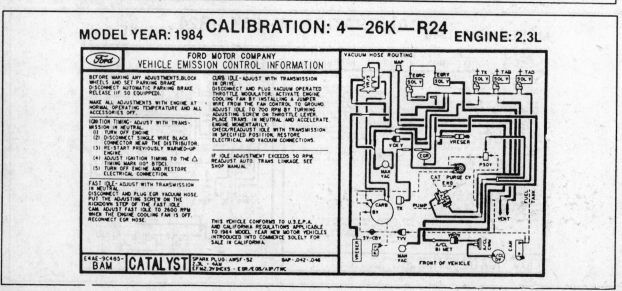

MODEL YEAR: 1984   CALIBRATION: 4—26K—R24   ENGINE: 2.3L

86704215

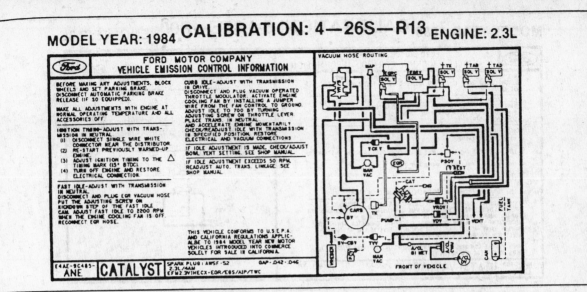

**MODEL YEAR: 1984  CALIBRATION: 4—26S—R13  ENGINE: 2.3L**

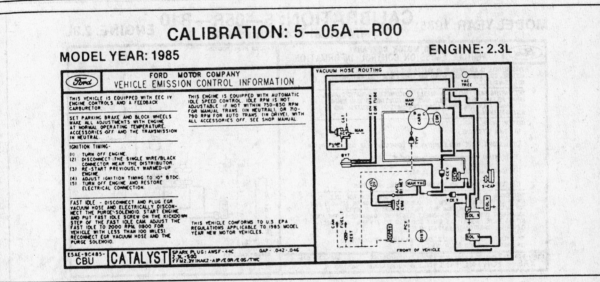

**CALIBRATION: 5—05A—R00**

**MODEL YEAR: 1985**

**ENGINE: 2.3L**

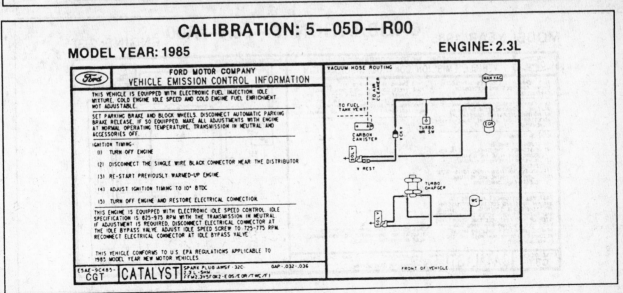

**CALIBRATION: 5—05D—R00**

**MODEL YEAR: 1985**

**ENGINE: 2.3L**

86704216

**MODEL YEAR: 1985  CALIBRATION: 5—05E—R00  ENGINE: 2.3L**

### FORD MOTOR COMPANY
### VEHICLE EMISSION CONTROL INFORMATION

THIS VEHICLE IS EQUIPPED WITH ELECTRONIC FUEL INJECTION. IDLE MIXTURE, COLD ENGINE IDLE SPEED AND COLD ENGINE FUEL ENRICHMENT NOT ADJUSTABLE.

SET PARKING BRAKE AND BLOCK WHEELS. DISCONNECT AUTOMATIC PARKING BRAKE RELEASE. IF SO EQUIPPED. MAKE ALL ADJUSTMENTS WITH ENGINE AT NORMAL OPERATING TEMPERATURE, TRANSMISSION IN NEUTRAL AND ACCESSORIES OFF.

IGNITION TIMING-
(1) TURN OFF ENGINE
(2) DISCONNECT THE SINGLE WIRE BLACK CONNECTOR NEAR THE DISTRIBUTOR.
(3) RE-START PREVIOUSLY WARMED-UP ENGINE.
(4) ADJUST IGNITION TIMING TO 10° BTDC
(5) TURN OFF ENGINE AND RESTORE ELECTRICAL CONNECTION.

THIS ENGINE IS EQUIPPED WITH ELECTRONIC IDLE SPEED CONTROL. IDLE SPECIFICATION IS 825-975 RPM FOR MANUAL TRANSMISSION OR 925-1075 RPM FOR AUTOMATIC TRANSMISSION WITH THE TRANSMISSION IN NEUTRAL. IF ADJUSTMENT IS REQUIRED, DISCONNECT ELECTRICAL CONNECTOR AT THE IDLE BYPASS VALVE. ADJUST IDLE SPEED SCREW TO 725-775 RPM. RECONNECT ELECTRICAL CONNECTOR AT IDLE BYPASS VALVE.

THIS VEHICLE CONFORMS TO U.S. EPA REGULATIONS APPLICABLE TO 1985 MODEL YEAR NEW MOTOR VEHICLES.

E5AE-9C485-CGY | CATALYST | SPARK PLUG: AWSF-32C  2.3L-5HM  FFM2.3Y5FOX2-E05/EGR/TWC | GAP-.032-.036

VACUUM HOSE ROUTING

FRONT OF VEHICLE

---

**MODEL YEAR: 1985  CALIBRATION: 5—05R—R10**
**(Manual Transmission)**
**ENGINE: 2.3L**

### FORD MOTOR COMPANY
### VEHICLE EMISSION CONTROL INFORMATION

THIS VEHICLE IS EQUIPPED WITH ELECTRONIC FUEL INJECTION. IDLE MIXTURE, COLD ENGINE IDLE SPEED AND COLD ENGINE FUEL ENRICHMENT NOT ADJUSTABLE.

SET PARKING BRAKE AND BLOCK WHEELS. DISCONNECT AUTOMATIC PARKING BRAKE RELEASE. IF SO EQUIPPED. MAKE ALL ADJUSTMENTS WITH ENGINE AT NORMAL OPERATING TEMPERATURE, TRANSMISSION IN NEUTRAL AND ACCESSORIES OFF.

IGNITION TIMING-
(1) TURN OFF ENGINE
(2) DISCONNECT THE SINGLE WIRE BLACK CONNECTOR NEAR THE DISTRIBUTOR.
(3) RE-START PREVIOUSLY WARMED-UP ENGINE.
(4) ADJUST IGNITION TIMING TO 13° BTDC
(5) TURN OFF ENGINE AND RESTORE ELECTRICAL CONNECTION.

THIS ENGINE IS EQUIPPED WITH ELECTRONIC IDLE SPEED CONTROL. IDLE SPECIFICATION IS 825-975 RPM FOR MANUAL TRANSMISSION OR 925-1075 RPM FOR AUTOMATIC TRANSMISSION WITH THE TRANSMISSION IN NEUTRAL. IF ADJUSTMENT IS REQUIRED, DISCONNECT ELECTRICAL CONNECTOR AT THE IDLE BYPASS VALVE. ADJUST IDLE SPEED SCREW TO 725-775 RPM. RECONNECT ELECTRICAL CONNECTOR AT IDLE BYPASS VALVE.

THIS VEHICLE CONFORMS TO U.S. EPA REGULATIONS APPLICABLE TO 1985 MODEL YEAR NEW MOTOR VEHICLES.

E5RO-9C485-XAS | CATALYST | SPARK PLUG: AWSF-32C  2.3L-5HM  FFM2.3Y5FOX2-E05/EGR/TWC | GAP-.032-.036

VACUUM HOSE ROUTING

FRONT OF VEHICLE

---

**MODEL YEAR: 1985  CALIBRATION: 5—06A—R00  ENGINE: 2.3L**

### FORD MOTOR COMPANY
### VEHICLE EMISSION CONTROL INFORMATION

THIS VEHICLE IS EQUIPPED WITH EEC IV ENGINE CONTROLS AND A FEEDBACK CARBURETOR

SET PARKING BRAKE AND BLOCK WHEELS MAKE ALL ADJUSTMENTS WITH ENGINE AT NORMAL OPERATING TEMPERATURE, ACCESSORIES OFF AND THE TRANSMISSION IN NEUTRAL

IGNITION TIMING-
(1) TURN OFF ENGINE.
(2) DISCONNECT THE SINGLE WIRE/BLACK CONNECTOR NEAR THE DISTRIBUTOR
(3) RE-START PREVIOUSLY WARMED-UP ENGINE.
(4) ADJUST IGNITION TIMING TO 10° BTDC
(5) TURN OFF ENGINE AND RESTORE ELECTRICAL CONNECTION.

FAST IDLE-DISCONNECT AND PLUG EGR VACUUM HOSE AND ELECTRICALLY DISCONNECT THE PURGE SOLENOID START ENGINE AND PUT FAST IDLE SCREW ON THE KICKDOWN STEP OF THE FAST IDLE CAM. ADJUST THE FAST IDLE TO 2200 RPM (1900 FOR VEHICLE WITH LESS THAN 100 MILES). RECONNECT EGR VACUUM HOSE AND THE PURGE SOLENOID.

THIS ENGINE IS EQUIPPED WITH AUTOMATIC IDLE SPEED CONTROL. IDLE RPM IS NOT ADJUSTABLE IF NOT WITHIN 750-850 RPM FOR MANUAL TRANS. (IN NEUTRAL), OR 710-790 RPM FOR AUTO TRANS. (IN DRIVE). WITH ALL ACCESSORIES OFF. SEE SHOP MANUAL

THIS VEHICLE CONFORMS TO U.S. EPA REGULATIONS APPLICABLE TO 1985 MODEL YEAR NEW MOTOR VEHICLES

E5AE-9C485-CBY | CATALYST | SPARK PLUG: AWSF-44C  2.3L-500  FFM2.3Y1HAK2-AIP/EGR/EOS/TWC | GAP-.042-.046

VACUUM HOSE ROUTING

FRONT OF VEHICLE

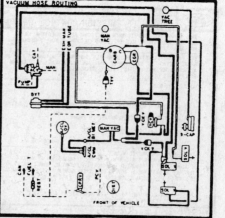
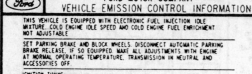

86704217

## MODEL YEAR: 1985  CALIBRATION: 5—06E—R00  ENGINE: 2.3L

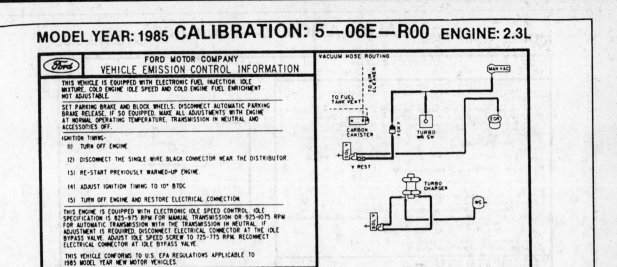

## CALIBRATION: 5—06N—R00

**MODEL YEAR: 1985**                    **ENGINE: 2.3L**

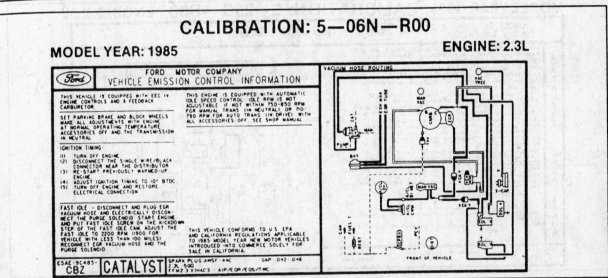

## CALIBRATION: 5—25C—R01

**MODEL YEAR: 1985**                    **ENGINE: 2.3L**

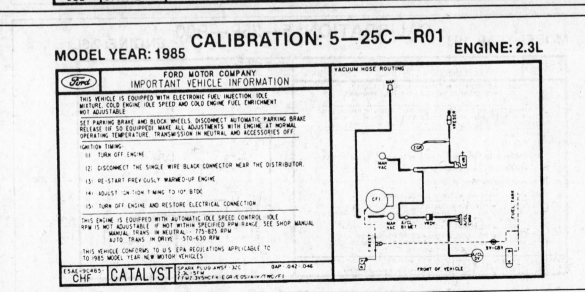

86704218

## MODEL YEAR: 1985  CALIBRATION: 5—25F—R00  ENGINE: 2.3L

**FORD MOTOR COMPANY**
**IMPORTANT VEHICLE INFORMATION**

THIS VEHICLE IS EQUIPPED WITH ELECTRONIC FUEL INJECTION MIXTURE. COLD ENGINE IDLE SPEED AND COLD ENGINE FUEL ENRICHMENT NOT ADJUSTABLE

SET PARKING BRAKE AND BLOCK WHEELS DISCONNECT AUTOMATIC PARKING BRAKE RELEASE (IF SO EQUIPPED) MAKE ALL ADJUSTMENTS WITH ENGINE AT NORMAL OPERATING TEMPERATURE TRANSMISSION IN NEUTRAL AND ACCESSORIES OFF

IGNITION TIMING
(1) TURN OFF ENGINE
(2) DISCONNECT THE SINGLE WIRE BLACK CONNECTOR NEAR THE DISTRIBUTOR
(3) RE-START PREVIOUSLY WARMED-UP ENGINE
(4) ADJUST IGNITION TIMING TO 10° BTDC
(5) TURN OFF ENGINE AND RESTORE ELECTRICAL CONNECTION

THIS ENGINE IS EQUIPPED WITH AUTOMATIC IDLE SPEED CONTROL IDLE RPM IS NOT ADJUSTABLE. IF NOT WITHIN SPECIFIED RPM RANGE SEE SHOP MANUAL
MANUAL TRANS IN NEUTRAL - 725-775 RPM
AUTO TRANS IN DRIVE - 570-630 RPM

THIS VEHICLE CONFORMS TO U.S. EPA REGULATIONS APPLICABLE TO 1985 MODEL YEAR NEW MOTOR VEHICLES

E5AE-9C485-CEV  **CATALYST**  SPARK PLUG: AWSF-52C 2.3L SFM  GAP .042-.046  FFM2 JV5HCF4·EGR/EGS/AIP/TWC

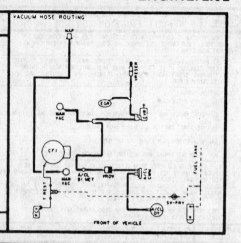

VACUUM HOSE ROUTING

FRONT OF VEHICLE

## MODEL YEAR: 1985  CALIBRATION: 5—25G—R00  ENGINE: 2.3L

**VEHICLE EMISSION CONTROL INFORMATION**  **FORD MOTOR COMPANY**

**CATALYST  CATALYST  CATALYSEUR**

BEFORE MAKING ANY ADJUSTMENTS, BLOCK WHEELS AND SET PARKING BRAKE. DISCONNECT AUTOMATIC PARKING BRAKE RELEASE (IF SO EQUIPPED).
MAKE ALL ADJUSTMENTS WITH ENGINE AT NORMAL OPERATING TEMPERATURE AND ALL ACCESSORIES OFF.
IGNITION TIMING- ADJUST WITH TRANSMISSION IN NEUTRAL
(1) TURN OFF ENGINE.
(2) DISCONNECT AND PLUG DISTRIBUTOR VACUUM HOSE
(3) RE-START PREVIOUSLY WARMED-UP ENGINE
(4) ADJUST IGNITION TIMING TO 10° BTDC, 800 RPM MAX
(5) TURN OFF ENGINE AND RESTORE VACUUM CONNECTION
FAST IDLE- ADJUST WITH TRANSMISSION IN NEUTRAL. DISCONNECT AND PLUG EGR VACUUM HOSE. PUT THE ADJUSTING SCREW ON KICKDOWN STEP OF THE FAST IDLE CAM. ADJUST FAST IDLE TO 2200 RPM WHEN THE ENGINE COOLING FAN IS OFF. RECONNECT EGR HOSE.
CURB IDLE- ADJUST WITH TRANSMISSION IN 'N'
DISCONNECT AND PLUG VACUUM OPERATED THROTTLE MODULATOR ACTIVATE ENGINE COOLING FAN BY INSTALLING A JUMPER WIRE FROM THE FAN CONTROL TO GROUND ADJUST IDLE TO 800 RPM BY TURNING ADJUSTING SCREW ON THROTTLE LEVER PLACE TRANSMISSION IN NEUTRAL AND ACCELERATE ENGINE MOMENTARILY CHECK/READJUST IDLE WITH TRANSMISSION IN SPECIFIED POSITION RESTORE ELECTRICAL AND VACUUM CONNECTIONS

IF EQUIPPED WITH AUTO. O.D. TRANS & CURB IDLE ADJ IS GREATER THAN 150 RPM, RE-ADJUST AUTO. TRANS. LINKAGE SEE SHOP MANUAL.
SEE SHOP MANUAL FOR CHOKE AND IDLE MIXTURE ADJUSTMENT INFO

E5AE-9C485-CHH  2.3L  SPARK PLUG/BOUGIES AWSF-52  GAP/ÉLECTRODES 042-046

FRONT OF VEHICLE

## MODEL YEAR: 1985  CALIBRATION: 5—25P—R00  ENGINE: 2.3L

**FORD MOTOR COMPANY**
**VEHICLE EMISSION CONTROL INFORMATION**

THIS VEHICLE IS EQUIPPED WITH ELECTRONIC FUEL INJECTION. IDLE MIXTURE, COLD ENGINE IDLE SPEED AND COLD ENGINE FUEL ENRICHMENT NOT ADJUSTABLE

SET PARKING BRAKE AND BLOCK WHEELS DISCONNECT AUTOMATIC PARKING BRAKE RELEASE (IF SO EQUIPPED) MAKE ALL ADJUSTMENTS WITH ENGINE AT NORMAL OPERATING TEMPERATURE. TRANSMISSION IN NEUTRAL AND ACCESSORIES OFF.

IGNITION TIMING
(1) TURN OFF ENGINE
(2) DISCONNECT THE SINGLE WIRE BLACK CONNECTOR NEAR THE DISTRIBUTOR
(3) RE-START PREVIOUSLY WARMED-UP ENGINE
(4) ADJUST IGNITION TIMING TO 10° BTDC
(5) TURN OFF ENGINE AND RESTORE ELECTRICAL CONNECTION

THIS ENGINE IS EQUIPPED WITH AUTOMATIC IDLE SPEED CONTROL. IDLE RPM IS NOT ADJUSTABLE. IF NOT WITHIN SPECIFIED RPM RANGE, SEE SHOP MANUAL
MANUAL TRANS. IN NEUTRAL - 775-825 RPM
AUTO TRANS IN DRIVE - 570-630 RPM

THIS VEHICLE CONFORMS TO U.S. EPA AND CALIFORNIA REGULATIONS APPLICABLE TO 1985 MODEL YEAR NEW MOTOR VEHICLES INTRODUCED INTO COMMERCE SOLELY FOR SALE IN CALIFORNIA.

E5AE-9C485-CHE  **CATALYST**  SPARK PLUG AWSF-32C 2.3L SFM  GAP .042-.046  FFM2 JV5HCH6·EGR/EGS/AIV/TWC/FI

VACUUM HOSE ROUTING

FRONT OF VEHICLE

86704219

## CALIBRATION: 5—25Q—R00

**MODEL YEAR: 1985**                    **ENGINE: 2.3L**

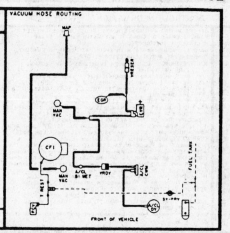

FORD MOTOR COMPANY
VEHICLE EMISSION CONTROL INFORMATION

THIS VEHICLE IS EQUIPPED WITH ELECTRONIC FUEL INJECTION. IDLE MIXTURE, COLD ENGINE IDLE SPEED AND COLD ENGINE FUEL ENRICHMENT NOT ADJUSTABLE.

SET PARKING BRAKE AND BLOCK WHEELS. DISCONNECT AUTOMATIC PARKING BRAKE RELEASE (IF SO EQUIPPED) MAKE ALL ADJUSTMENTS WITH ENGINE AT NORMAL OPERATING TEMPERATURE, TRANSMISSION IN NEUTRAL AND ACCESSORIES OFF

IGNITION TIMING-

(1) TURN OFF ENGINE

(2) DISCONNECT THE SINGLE WIRE BLACK CONNECTOR NEAR THE DISTRIBUTOR

(3) RE-START PREVIOUSLY WARMED-UP ENGINE

(4) ADJUST IGNITION TIMING TO 10° BTDC

(5) TURN OFF ENGINE AND RESTORE ELECTRICAL CONNECTION

THIS ENGINE IS EQUIPPED WITH AUTOMATIC IDLE SPEED CONTROL IDLE RPM IS NOT ADJUSTABLE. IF NOT WITHIN SPECIFIED RPM RANGE, SEE SHOP MANUAL
MANUAL TRANS. IN NEUTRAL:- 725-775 RPM
AUTO TRANS IN DRIVE - 570-630 RPM

THIS VEHICLE CONFORMS TO U.S. EPA AND CALIFORNIA REGULATIONS APPLICABLE TO 1985 MODEL YEAR NEW MOTOR VEHICLES. INTRODUCED INTO COMMERCE SOLELY FOR SALE IN CALIFORNIA.

E5AE-9C485-CEY | CATALYST | SPARK PLUG: AWSF-52C 2.3L-5FM GAP: 042-046 FFM2.3V5HCMG-EGR/EGS/AIP/TWC

VACUUM HOSE ROUTING

## CALIBRATION: 5—26E—R00

**MODEL YEAR: 1985**                    **ENGINE: 2.3L**

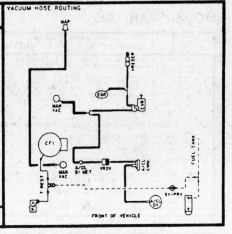

FORD MOTOR COMPANY
IMPORTANT VEHICLE INFORMATION

THIS VEHICLE IS EQUIPPED WITH ELECTRONIC FUEL INJECTION, IDLE MIXTURE, COLD ENGINE IDLE SPEED AND COLD ENGINE FUEL ENRICHMENT NOT ADJUSTABLE

SET PARKING BRAKE AND BLOCK WHEELS. DISCONNECT AUTOMATIC PARKING BRAKE RELEASE (IF SO EQUIPPED) MAKE ALL ADJUSTMENTS WITH ENGINE AT NORMAL OPERATING TEMPERATURE, TRANSMISSION IN NEUTRAL AND ACCESSORIES OFF

IGNITION TIMING-

(1) TURN OFF ENGINE

(2) DISCONNECT THE SINGLE WIRE BLACK CONNECTOR NEAR THE DISTRIBUTOR

(3) RE-START PREVIOUSLY WARMED-UP ENGINE

(4) ADJUST IGNITION TIMING TO 10° BTDC

(5) TURN OFF ENGINE AND RESTORE ELECTRICAL CONNECTION

THIS ENGINE IS EQUIPPED WITH AUTOMATIC IDLE SPEED CONTROL IDLE RPM IS NOT ADJUSTABLE IF NOT WITHIN SPECIFIED RPM RANGE. SEE SHOP MANUAL
MANUAL TRANS. IN NEUTRAL:- 725-775 RPM
AUTO TRANS IN DRIVE - 570-630 RPM

THIS VEHICLE CONFORMS TO U.S EPA REGULATIONS APPLICABLE TO TO 1985 MODEL YEAR NEW MOTOR VEHICLES

E5AE-9C485-CEV | CATALYST | SPARK PLUG: AWSF-52C 2.3L-5FM GAP: 042-046 FFM2.3V5HCF4-EGR/EGS/AIP/TWC

VACUUM HOSE ROUTING

86704220

## CALIBRATION: 5—26G—R00

**MODEL YEAR: 1985**                                    **ENGINE: 2.3L**

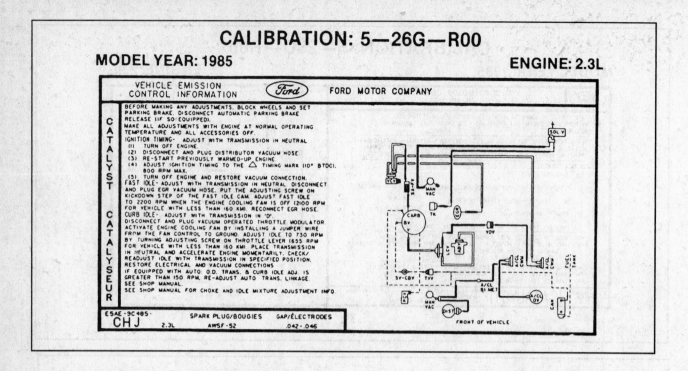

VEHICLE EMISSION CONTROL INFORMATION — Ford — FORD MOTOR COMPANY

C A T A L Y S T   C A T A L Y S E U R

BEFORE MAKING ANY ADJUSTMENTS, BLOCK WHEELS AND SET PARKING BRAKE, DISCONNECT AUTOMATIC PARKING BRAKE RELEASE (IF SO EQUIPPED).
MAKE ALL ADJUSTMENTS WITH ENGINE AT NORMAL OPERATING TEMPERATURE AND ALL ACCESSORIES OFF.
IGNITION TIMING- ADJUST WITH TRANSMISSION IN NEUTRAL
(1) TURN OFF ENGINE.
(2) DISCONNECT AND PLUG DISTRIBUTOR VACUUM HOSE.
(3) RE-START PREVIOUSLY WARMED-UP ENGINE.
(4) ADJUST IGNITION TIMING TO THE △ TIMING MARK (10° BTDC). 800 RPM MAX.
(5) TURN OFF ENGINE AND RESTORE VACUUM CONNECTION.
FAST IDLE- ADJUST WITH TRANSMISSION IN NEUTRAL DISCONNECT AND PLUG EGR VACUUM HOSE. PUT THE ADJUSTING SCREW ON KICKDOWN STEP OF THE FAST IDLE CAM. ADJUST FAST IDLE TO 2200 RPM WHEN THE ENGINE COOLING FAN IS OFF (2100 RPM FOR VEHICLE WITH LESS THAN 160 KM). RECONNECT EGR HOSE.
CURB IDLE- ADJUST WITH TRANSMISSION IN "D".
DISCONNECT AND PLUG VACUUM OPERATED THROTTLE MODULATOR. ACTIVATE ENGINE COOLING FAN BY INSTALLING A JUMPER WIRE FROM THE FAN CONTROL TO GROUND. ADJUST IDLE TO 730 RPM BY TURNING ADJUSTING SCREW ON THROTTLE LEVER (655 RPM FOR VEHICLE WITH LESS THAN 160 KM). PLACE TRANSMISSION IN NEUTRAL AND ACCELERATE ENGINE MOMENTARILY. CHECK/READJUST IDLE WITH TRANSMISSION IN SPECIFIED POSITION. RESTORE ELECTRICAL AND VACUUM CONNECTIONS.
IF EQUIPPED WITH AUTO. O.D. TRANS. & CURB IDLE ADJ. IS GREATER THAN 150 RPM, RE-ADJUST AUTO. TRANS. LINKAGE. SEE SHOP MANUAL.
SEE SHOP MANUAL FOR CHOKE AND IDLE MIXTURE ADJUSTMENT INFO.

E5AE-9C485- **CHJ**  2.3L   SPARK PLUG/BOUGIES  AWSF-52   GAP/ÉLECTRODES  .042-.046

FRONT OF VEHICLE

## CALIBRATION: 5—26J—R01

**MODEL YEAR: 1985**                                    **ENGINE: 2.3L**

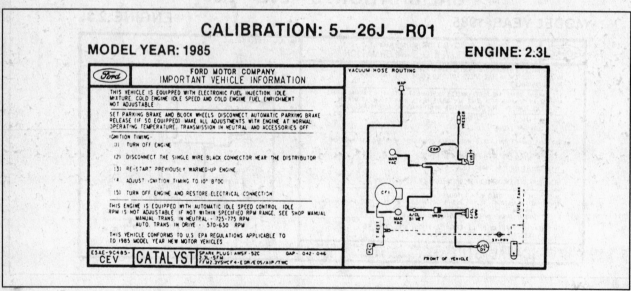

Ford — FORD MOTOR COMPANY — IMPORTANT VEHICLE INFORMATION        VACUUM HOSE ROUTING

THIS VEHICLE IS EQUIPPED WITH ELECTRONIC FUEL INJECTION. IDLE MIXTURE, COLD ENGINE IDLE SPEED AND COLD ENGINE FUEL ENRICHMENT NOT ADJUSTABLE.

SET PARKING BRAKE AND BLOCK WHEELS. DISCONNECT AUTOMATIC PARKING BRAKE RELEASE (IF SO EQUIPPED). MAKE ALL ADJUSTMENTS WITH ENGINE AT NORMAL OPERATING TEMPERATURE, TRANSMISSION IN NEUTRAL AND ACCESSORIES OFF.

IGNITION TIMING-
(1) TURN OFF ENGINE.
(2) DISCONNECT THE SINGLE WIRE BLACK CONNECTOR NEAR THE DISTRIBUTOR.
(3) RE-START PREVIOUSLY WARMED-UP ENGINE.
(4) ADJUST IGNITION TIMING TO 10° BTDC.
(5) TURN OFF ENGINE AND RESTORE ELECTRICAL CONNECTION.

THIS ENGINE IS EQUIPPED WITH AUTOMATIC IDLE SPEED CONTROL. IDLE RPM IS NOT ADJUSTABLE. IF NOT WITHIN SPECIFIED RPM RANGE, SEE SHOP MANUAL.
   MANUAL TRANS. IN NEUTRAL - 725-775 RPM
   AUTO. TRANS. IN DRIVE - 570-630 RPM

THIS VEHICLE CONFORMS TO U.S. EPA REGULATIONS APPLICABLE TO TO 1985 MODEL YEAR NEW MOTOR VEHICLES.

E5AE-9C485- **CEV** | **CATALYST** | SPARK PLUG: AWSF-52C  GAP .042-.046  2.3L-5FM  FFM2.3V5HCF4-EGR/EOS/AIP/TWC

FRONT OF VEHICLE

86704221

## CALIBRATION: 5—26R—R01

**MODEL YEAR: 1985**  **ENGINE: 2.3L**

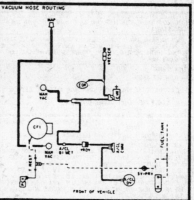

## CALIBRATION: 5—05A—R00

**MODEL YEAR: 1986**  **ENGINE: 2.3L**

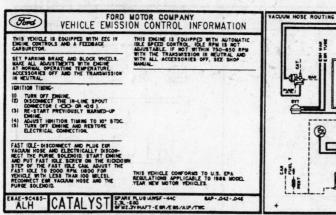
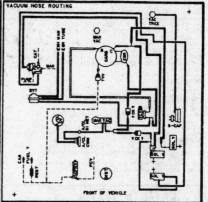

## CALIBRATION: 5—05E—R00

**MODEL YEAR: 1986**  **ENGINE: 2.3L T/C**

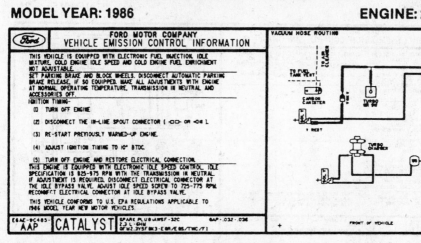

86704222

MODEL YEAR: 1986    **CALIBRATION: 5—05R—R10**    ENGINE: 2.3L T/C

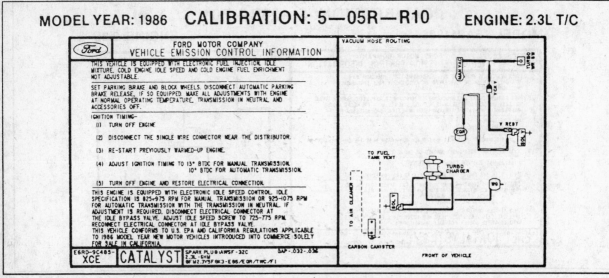

MODEL YEAR: 1986

**CALIBRATION: 5—05S—R01**

ENGINE: 2.3L T/C

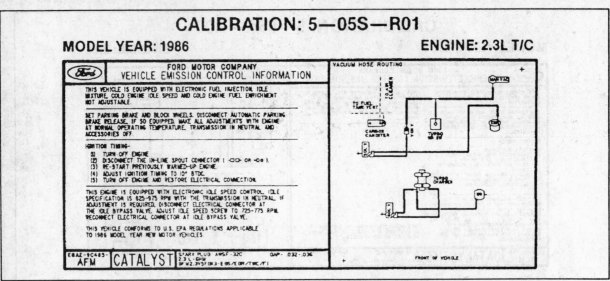

MODEL YEAR: 1986

**CALIBRATION: 5—06A—R00**

ENGINE: 2.3L

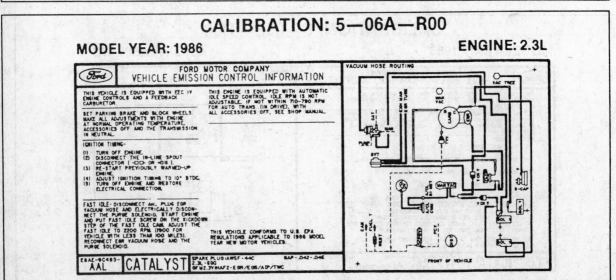

86704223

# CALIBRATION: 5—06N—R00

**MODEL YEAR: 1986**

**ENGINE: 2.3L**

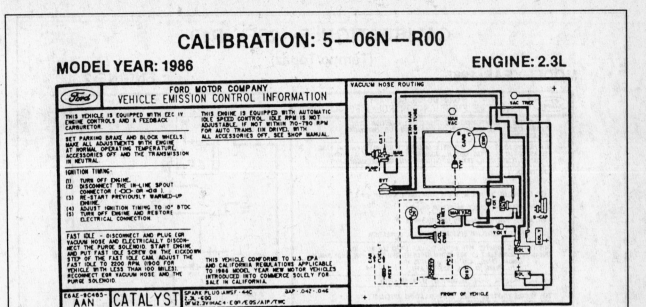

# CALIBRATION: 5—25C—R01

**MODEL YEAR: 1986**

**ENGINE: 2.3L**

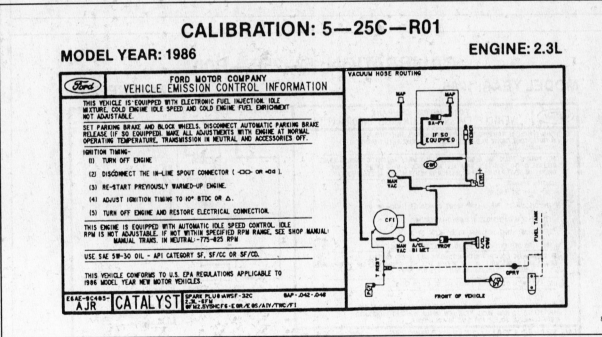

86704224

## CALIBRATION: 5—25F—R10

### (Tempo/Topaz)

**MODEL YEAR: 1986**

**ENGINE: 2.3L**

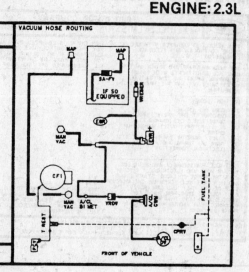

**FORD MOTOR COMPANY**
**VEHICLE EMISSION CONTROL INFORMATION**

THIS VEHICLE IS EQUIPPED WITH ELECTRONIC FUEL INJECTION. IDLE MIXTURE, COLD ENGINE IDLE SPEED AND COLD ENGINE FUEL ENRICHMENT NOT ADJUSTABLE.

SET PARKING BRAKE AND BLOCK WHEELS. DISCONNECT AUTOMATIC PARKING BRAKE RELEASE (IF SO EQUIPPED). MAKE ALL ADJUSTMENTS WITH ENGINE AT NORMAL OPERATING TEMPERATURE, TRANSMISSION IN NEUTRAL AND ACCESSORIES OFF.

IGNITION TIMING-

(1) TURN OFF ENGINE

(2) DISCONNECT THE IN-LINE SPOUT CONNECTOR ( -OO- OR -Od ).

(3) RE-START PREVIOUSLY WARMED-UP ENGINE.

(4) ADJUST IGNITION TIMING TO 10° BTDC OR △.

(5) TURN OFF ENGINE AND RESTORE ELECTRICAL CONNECTION.

THIS ENGINE IS EQUIPPED WITH AUTOMATIC IDLE SPEED CONTROL. IDLE RPM IS NOT ADJUSTABLE. IF NOT WITHIN SPECIFIED RPM RANGE, SEE SHOP MANUAL:
MANUAL TRANS. IN NEUTRAL -725-775 RPM
AUTO. TRANS. IN DRIVE -625-675 RPM

USE SAE 5W-30 OIL - API CATEGORY SF, SF/CC OR SF/CD.

THIS VEHICLE CONFORMS TO U.S. EPA REGULATIONS APPLICABLE TO 1986 MODEL YEAR NEW MOTOR VEHICLES.

E6AE-9C485-AJT | CATALYST | SPARK PLUG:AWSF-52 | GAP-.042-.046
2.3L-6FM
BFM2.5VSHCFS-EOR/EOS/AIY/TWC/FI

---

## CALIBRATION: 5—25P—R00

**MODEL YEAR: 1986**

**ENGINE: 2.3L**

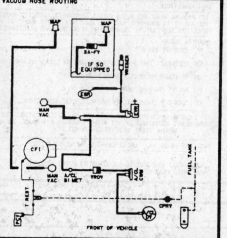

**FORD MOTOR COMPANY**
**VEHICLE EMISSION CONTROL INFORMATION**

THIS VEHICLE IS EQUIPPED WITH ELECTRONIC FUEL INJECTION. IDLE MIXTURE, COLD ENGINE IDLE SPEED AND COLD ENGINE FUEL ENRICHMENT NOT ADJUSTABLE.

SET PARKING BRAKE AND BLOCK WHEELS. DISCONNECT AUTOMATIC PARKING BRAKE RELEASE (IF SO EQUIPPED). MAKE ALL ADJUSTMENTS WITH ENGINE AT NORMAL OPERATING TEMPERATURE, TRANSMISSION IN NEUTRAL AND ACCESSORIES OFF.

IGNITION TIMING-

(1) TURN OFF ENGINE

(2) DISCONNECT THE IN-LINE SPOUT CONNECTOR ( -OO- OR -Od ).

(3) RE-START PREVIOUSLY WARMED-UP ENGINE.

(4) ADJUST IGNITION TIMING TO 10° BTDC OR △.

(5) TURN OFF ENGINE AND RESTORE ELECTRICAL CONNECTION.

THIS ENGINE IS EQUIPPED WITH AUTOMATIC IDLE SPEED CONTROL. IDLE RPM IS NOT ADJUSTABLE. IF NOT WITHIN SPECIFIED RPM RANGE, SEE SHOP MANUAL:
MANUAL TRANS. IN NEUTRAL -775-825 RPM

USE SAE 5W-30 OIL - API CATEGORY SF, SF/CC OR SF/CD.

THIS VEHICLE CONFORMS TO U.S. EPA AND CALIFORNIA REGULATIONS APPLICABLE TO 1986 MODEL YEAR NEW MOTOR VEHICLES INTRODUCED INTO COMMERCE SOLELY FOR SALE IN CALIFORNIA.

E6AE-9C485-AJS | CATALYST | SPARK PLUG:AWSF-32C | GAP-.042-.046
2.3L-6FM
BFM2.5VSHCH0-EOR/EOS/AIY/TWC/FI

86704224

## CALIBRATION: 6—05R—R00

**MODEL YEAR: 1986**                                **ENGINE: 2.3L T/C**

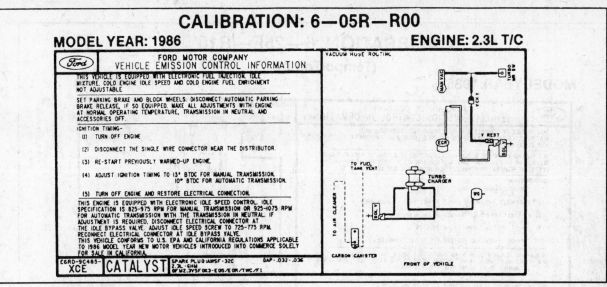

FORD MOTOR COMPANY
VEHICLE EMISSION CONTROL INFORMATION

THIS VEHICLE IS EQUIPPED WITH ELECTRONIC FUEL INJECTION. IDLE MIXTURE, COLD ENGINE IDLE SPEED AND COLD ENGINE FUEL ENRICHMENT NOT ADJUSTABLE.

SET PARKING BRAKE AND BLOCK WHEELS. DISCONNECT AUTOMATIC PARKING BRAKE RELEASE, IF SO EQUIPPED. MAKE ALL ADJUSTMENTS WITH ENGINE AT NORMAL OPERATING TEMPERATURE, TRANSMISSION IN NEUTRAL AND ACCESSORIES OFF.

IGNITION TIMING-
(1) TURN OFF ENGINE
(2) DISCONNECT THE SINGLE WIRE CONNECTOR NEAR THE DISTRIBUTOR.
(3) RE-START PREVIOUSLY WARMED-UP ENGINE.
(4) ADJUST IGNITION TIMING TO 13° BTDC FOR MANUAL TRANSMISSION. 10° BTDC FOR AUTOMATIC TRANSMISSION.
(5) TURN OFF ENGINE AND RESTORE ELECTRICAL CONNECTION.

THIS ENGINE IS EQUIPPED WITH ELECTRONIC IDLE SPEED CONTROL. IDLE SPECIFICATION IS 825-975 RPM FOR MANUAL TRANSMISSION OR 925-1075 RPM FOR AUTOMATIC TRANSMISSION WITH THE TRANSMISSION IN NEUTRAL. IF ADJUSTMENT IS REQUIRED, DISCONNECT ELECTRICAL CONNECTOR AT THE IDLE BYPASS VALVE. ADJUST IDLE SPEED SCREW TO 725-775 RPM. RECONNECT ELECTRICAL CONNECTOR AT IDLE BYPASS VALVE.
THIS VEHICLE CONFORMS TO U.S. EPA AND CALIFORNIA REGULATIONS APPLICABLE TO 1986 MODEL YEAR NEW MOTOR VEHICLES INTRODUCED INTO COMMERCE SOLELY FOR SALE IN CALIFORNIA.

E6RD-9C485-XCE | CATALYST | SPARK PLUG:AWSF-32C 2.3-6HM 0AP-.032-.036 0FM2.3Y5FOK3-EOS/EGR/TWC/FI

---

## CALIBRATION: 6—06A—R10

**MODEL YEAR: 1986**                                **ENGINE: 2.3L**

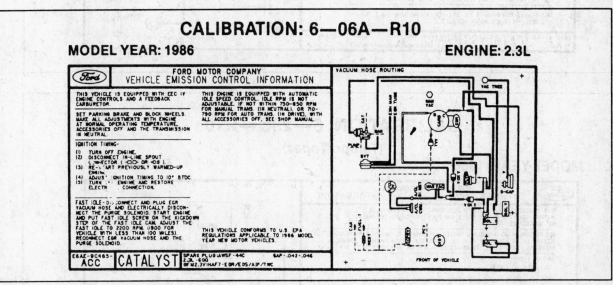

FORD MOTOR COMPANY
VEHICLE EMISSION CONTROL INFORMATION

THIS VEHICLE IS EQUIPPED WITH EEC IV ENGINE CONTROLS AND A FEEDBACK CARBURETOR.

SET PARKING BRAKE AND BLOCK WHEELS. MAKE ALL ADJUSTMENTS WITH ENGINE AT NORMAL OPERATING TEMPERATURE, ACCESSORIES OFF AND THE TRANSMISSION IN NEUTRAL.

IGNITION TIMING-
(1) TURN OFF ENGINE.
(2) DISCONNECT IN-LINE SPOUT CONNECTOR.
(3) RE-START PREVIOUSLY WARMED-UP ENGINE.
(4) ADJUST IGNITION TIMING TO 10° BTDC.
(5) TURN OFF ENGINE AND RESTORE ELECTRICAL CONNECTION.

FAST IDLE-DISCONNECT AND PLUG EGR VACUUM HOSE AND ELECTRICALLY DISCONNECT THE PURGE SOLENOID. START ENGINE AND PUT FAST IDLE SCREW ON THE KICKDOWN STEP OF THE FAST IDLE CAM. ADJUST FAST IDLE TO 2200 RPM (1800 FOR VEHICLE WITH LESS THAN 100 MILES). RECONNECT EGR VACUUM HOSE AND THE PURGE SOLENOID.

THIS ENGINE IS EQUIPPED WITH AUTOMATIC IDLE SPEED CONTROL. IDLE RPM IS NOT ADJUSTABLE. IF NOT WITHIN 750-850 RPM FOR MANUAL TRANS. (IN NEUTRAL), OR 710-790 RPM FOR AUTO TRANS. (IN DRIVE), WITH ALL ACCESSORIES OFF, SEE SHOP MANUAL.

THIS VEHICLE CONFORMS TO U.S. EPA REGULATIONS APPLICABLE TO 1986 MODEL YEAR NEW MOTOR VEHICLES.

E6AE-9C485-ACC | CATALYST | SPARK PLUG:AWSF-44C 2.3-600 0AP-.042-.046 0FM2.3Y1HAF7-EGR/EOS/AIP/TWC

---

## CALIBRATION: 6—06A—R11

**MODEL YEAR: 1986**                                **ENGINE: 2.3L**

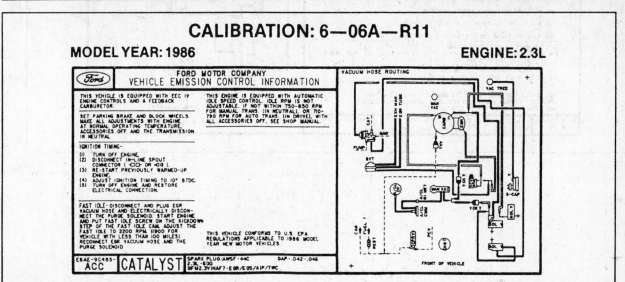

FORD MOTOR COMPANY
VEHICLE EMISSION CONTROL INFORMATION

THIS VEHICLE IS EQUIPPED WITH EEC IV ENGINE CONTROLS AND A FEEDBACK CARBURETOR.

SET PARKING BRAKE AND BLOCK WHEELS. MAKE ALL ADJUSTMENTS WITH ENGINE AT NORMAL OPERATING TEMPERATURE, ACCESSORIES OFF AND THE TRANSMISSION IN NEUTRAL.

IGNITION TIMING-
(1) TURN OFF ENGINE.
(2) DISCONNECT IN-LINE SPOUT CONNECTOR.
(3) RE-START PREVIOUSLY WARMED-UP ENGINE.
(4) ADJUST IGNITION TIMING TO 10° BTDC.
(5) TURN OFF ENGINE AND RESTORE ELECTRICAL CONNECTION.

FAST IDLE-DISCONNECT AND PLUG EGR VACUUM HOSE AND ELECTRICALLY DISCONNECT THE PURGE SOLENOID. START ENGINE AND PUT FAST IDLE SCREW ON THE KICKDOWN STEP OF THE FAST IDLE CAM. ADJUST THE FAST IDLE TO 2200 RPM (1800 FOR VEHICLE WITH LESS THAN 100 MILES). RECONNECT EGR VACUUM HOSE AND THE PURGE SOLENOID.

THIS ENGINE IS EQUIPPED WITH AUTOMATIC IDLE SPEED CONTROL. IDLE RPM IS NOT ADJUSTABLE. IF NOT WITHIN 750-850 RPM FOR MANUAL TRANS. (IN NEUTRAL), OR 710-790 RPM FOR AUTO TRANS. (IN DRIVE), WITH ALL ACCESSORIES OFF, SEE SHOP MANUAL.

THIS VEHICLE CONFORMS TO U.S. EPA REGULATIONS APPLICABLE TO 1986 MODEL YEAR NEW MOTOR VEHICLES.

E6AE-9C485-ACC | CATALYST | SPARK PLUG:AWSF-44C 2.3-600 0AP-.042-.046 0FM2.3Y1HAF7-EGR/EOS/AIP/TWC

86704227

## CALIBRATION: 6—25F—R10
### (Tempo/Topaz)

**MODEL YEAR: 1986**　　　　　　　　　　　　　**ENGINE: 2.3L**

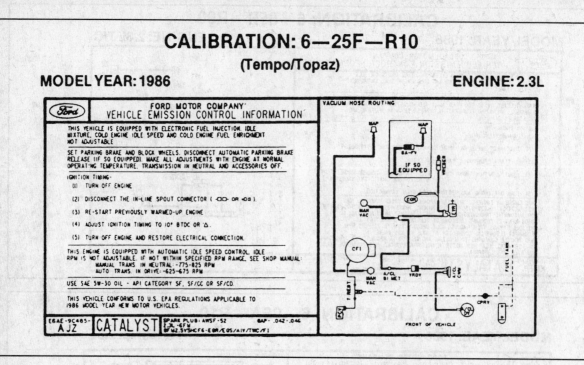

## CALIBRATION: 6—25Q—R10
### (Tempo/Topaz)

**MODEL YEAR: 1986**　　　　　　　　　　　　　**ENGINE: 2.3L**

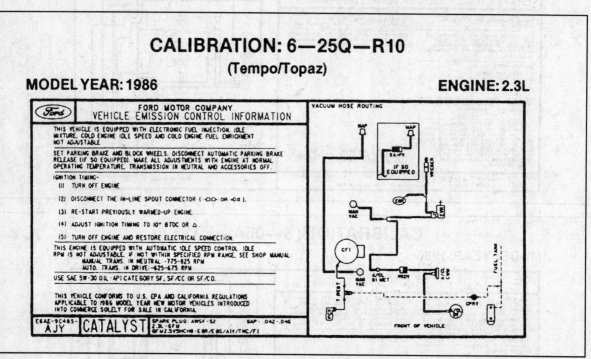

86704228

## CALIBRATION: 6—26E—R00

**MODEL YEAR: 1986**                    **ENGINE: 2.3L**

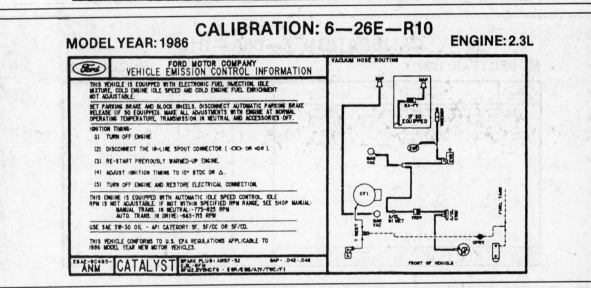

## CALIBRATION: 6—26E—R10

**MODEL YEAR: 1986**                    **ENGINE: 2.3L**

## CALIBRATION: 6—26R—R11

**MODEL YEAR: 1986**                    **ENGINE: 2.3L**

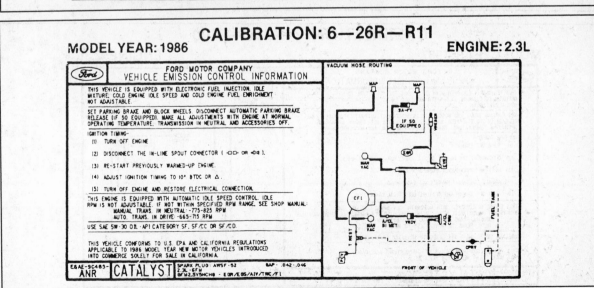

## CALIBRATION: 7—06A—R00

**MODEL YEAR: 1987**     **ENGINE: 2.3L**

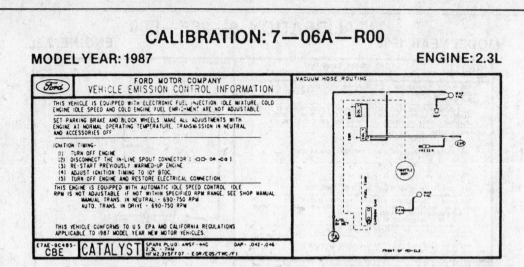

## CALIBRATION: 7—06A—R10

**MODEL YEAR: 1987**     **ENGINE: 2.3L**

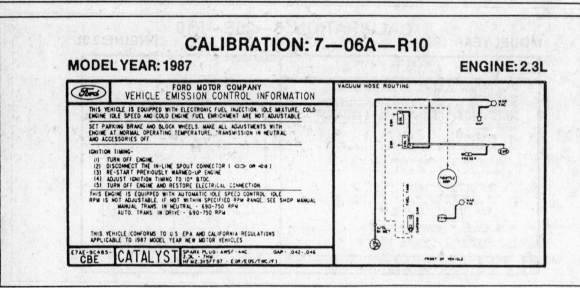

## CALIBRATION: 7—25C—R00

**MODEL YEAR: 1987**     **ENGINE: 2.3L**

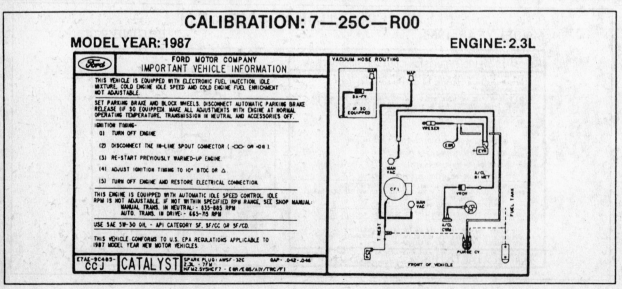

86704231

## CALIBRATION: 7—25C—R10

**MODEL YEAR: 1987**                    **ENGINE: 2.3L**

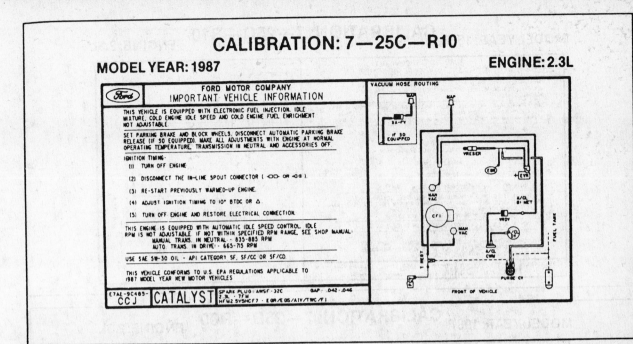

## CALIBRATION: 7—25F—R00

**MODEL YEAR: 1987**                    **ENGINE: 2.3L**

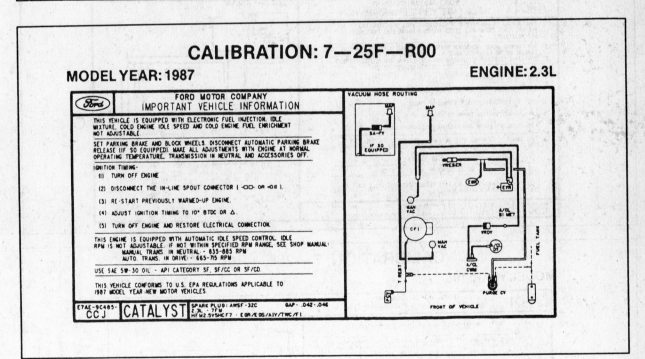

86704232

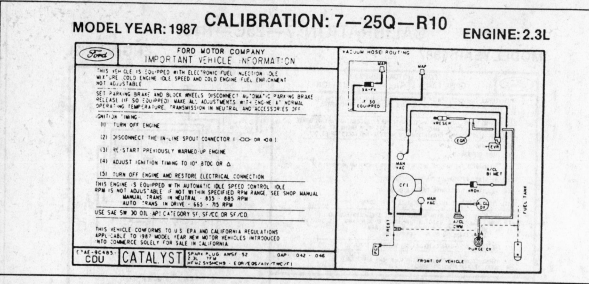

**MODEL YEAR: 1987    CALIBRATION: 7—25Q—R10    ENGINE: 2.3L**

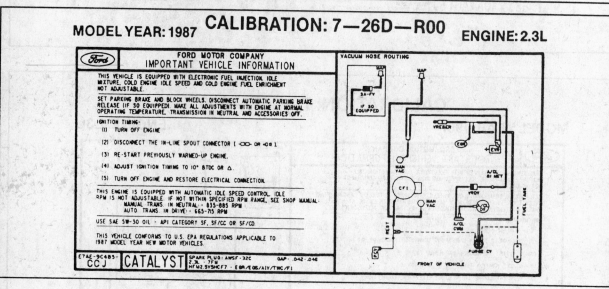

**MODEL YEAR: 1987    CALIBRATION: 7—26D—R00    ENGINE: 2.3L**

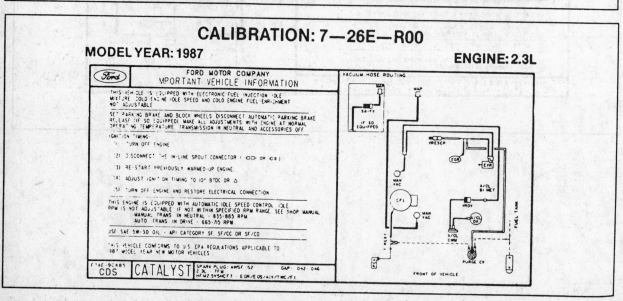

**CALIBRATION: 7—26E—R00**

**MODEL YEAR: 1987    ENGINE: 2.3L**

86704235

## ENGINE: 2.3L

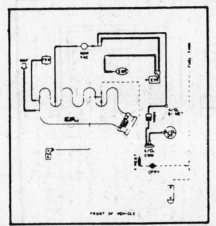

1988 2.3L Tempo/Topaz, 50 states (Calib.8–25C–R00)

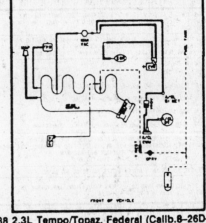

1988 2.3L Tempo/Topaz, Federal (Calib.8–26D–R10)

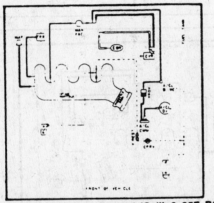

1988 2.3L Tempo/Topaz, Federal (Calib.8–25F–R00)

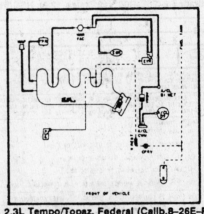

1988 2.3L Tempo/Topaz, Federal (Calib.8–26E–R00)

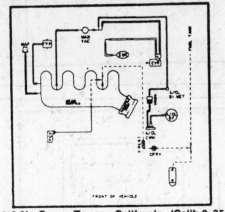

1988 2.3L Tempo/Topaz, California (Calib.8–25Q–R00)

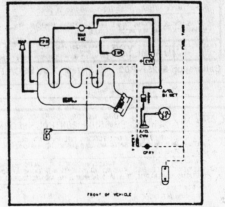

1988 2.3L Tempo/Topaz, California (Calib.8–26R–R00)

86704238

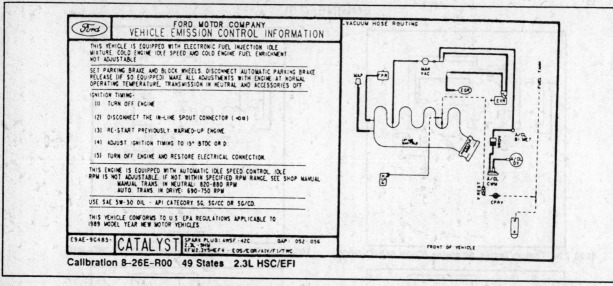

**Calibration 8–26E–R00    49 States    2.3L HSC/EFI**

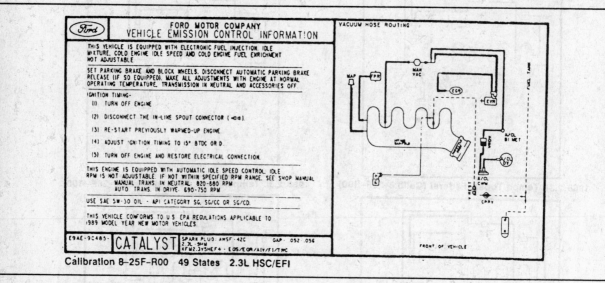

**Calibration 8–25F–R00    49 States    2.3L HSC/EFI**

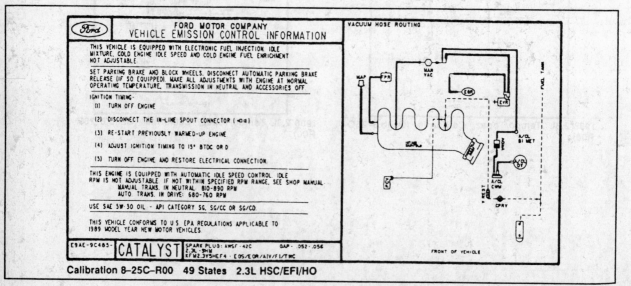

**Calibration 8–25C–R00    49 States    2.3L HSC/EFI/HO**

86704239

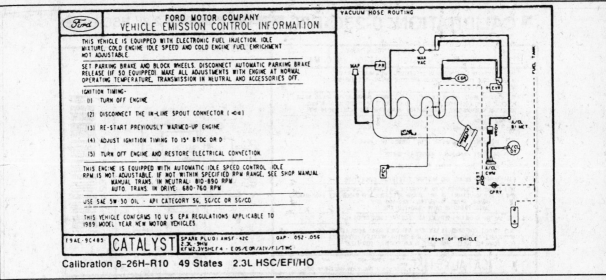

**Calibration 8-26H-R10   49 States   2.3L HSC/EFI/HO**

## ■ CALIBRATION: 0-25P-R00 ▬▬▬ 2.3L HSC-EFI-HO ■

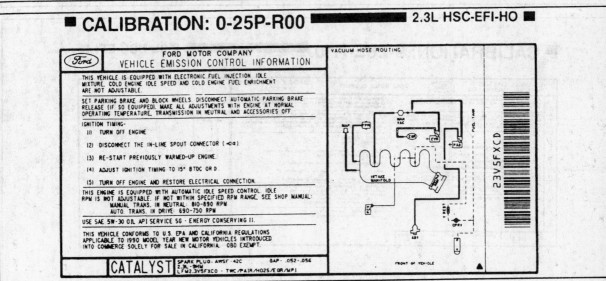

## ■ CALIBRATION: 9-26D-R10 ▬▬▬ 2.3L HSC-EFI-HO ■

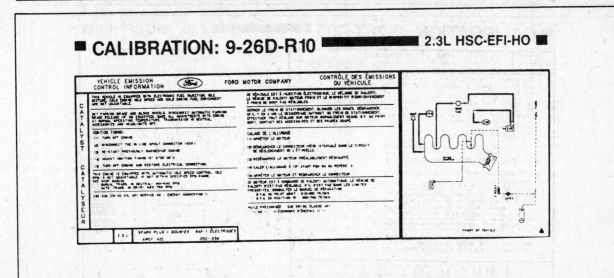

### ■ CALIBRATION: 0-25Q-R00 ■ 2.3L HSC-EFI ■

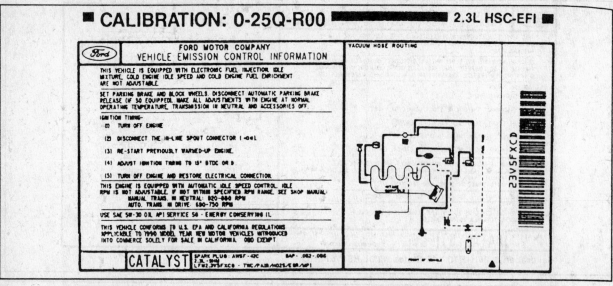

### ■ CALIBRATION: 9-26E-R10 ■ 2.3L HSC-EFI ■

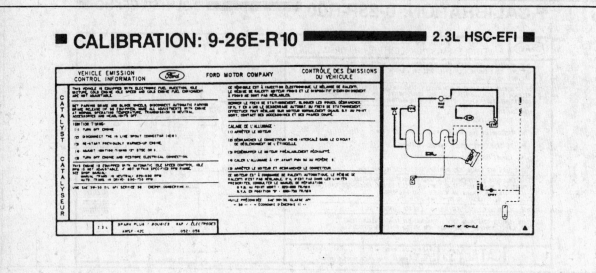

### ■ CALIBRATION: 0-26T-R00 ■ 2.3L HSC-EFI-HO ■

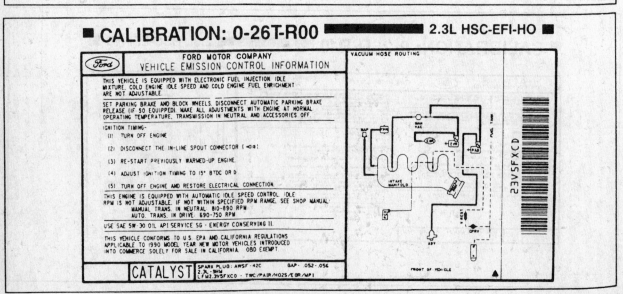

86704241

## CALIBRATION: 9-25C-R10 ■■■■■ 2.3L HSC-EFI-HO ■■

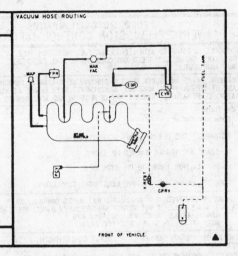

FORD MOTOR COMPANY
VEHICLE EMISSION CONTROL INFORMATION

THIS VEHICLE IS EQUIPPED WITH ELECTRONIC FUEL INJECTION. IDLE MIXTURE, COLD ENGINE IDLE SPEED AND COLD ENGINE FUEL ENRICHMENT ARE NOT ADJUSTABLE.

SET PARKING BRAKE AND BLOCK WHEELS. DISCONNECT AUTOMATIC PARKING BRAKE RELEASE (IF SO EQUIPPED). MAKE ALL ADJUSTMENTS WITH ENGINE AT NORMAL OPERATING TEMPERATURE, TRANSMISSION IN NEUTRAL AND ACCESSORIES OFF.

IGNITION TIMING-

(1) TURN OFF ENGINE

(2) DISCONNECT THE IN-LINE SPOUT CONNECTOR ( ◁◁ ).

(3) RE-START PREVIOUSLY WARMED-UP ENGINE.

(4) ADJUST IGNITION TIMING TO 15° BTDC OR D.

(5) TURN OFF ENGINE AND RESTORE ELECTRICAL CONNECTION.

THIS ENGINE IS EQUIPPED WITH AUTOMATIC IDLE SPEED CONTROL. IDLE RPM IS NOT ADJUSTABLE. IF NOT WITHIN SPECIFIED RPM RANGE, SEE SHOP MANUAL
MANUAL TRANS. IN NEUTRAL: 810-890 RPM
AUTO. TRANS. IN DRIVE: 680-760 RPM

USE SAE 5W-30 OIL API SERVICE SG - ENERGY CONSERVING II.

THIS VEHICLE CONFORMS TO U.S. EPA REGULATIONS APPLICABLE TO 1990 MODEL YEAR NEW MOTOR VEHICLES.

CATALYST | SPARK PLUG: AWSF-42C  GAP .052-.056
2.3L-9HM
LFW2.3V5HXF9 - TWC·OC/PAIR/HO2S/EGR/WPI

## CALIBRATION: 9-26D-R10 ■■■■■ 2.3L HSC-EFI-HO ■

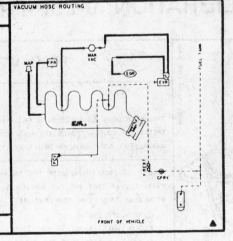

FORD MOTOR COMPANY
VEHICLE EMISSION CONTROL INFORMATION

THIS VEHICLE IS EQUIPPED WITH ELECTRONIC FUEL INJECTION. IDLE MIXTURE, COLD ENGINE IDLE SPEED AND COLD ENGINE FUEL ENRICHMENT ARE NOT ADJUSTABLE.

SET PARKING BRAKE AND BLOCK WHEELS. DISCONNECT AUTOMATIC PARKING BRAKE RELEASE (IF SO EQUIPPED). MAKE ALL ADJUSTMENTS WITH ENGINE AT NORMAL OPERATING TEMPERATURE, TRANSMISSION IN NEUTRAL AND ACCESSORIES OFF.

IGNITION TIMING-

(1) TURN OFF ENGINE

(2) DISCONNECT THE IN-LINE SPOUT CONNECTOR ( ◁◁ ).

(3) RE-START PREVIOUSLY WARMED-UP ENGINE.

(4) ADJUST IGNITION TIMING TO 15° BTDC OR D.

(5) TURN OFF ENGINE AND RESTORE ELECTRICAL CONNECTION.

THIS ENGINE IS EQUIPPED WITH AUTOMATIC IDLE SPEED CONTROL. IDLE RPM IS NOT ADJUSTABLE. IF NOT WITHIN SPECIFIED RPM RANGE, SEE SHOP MANUAL
MANUAL TRANS. IN NEUTRAL: 810-890 RPM
AUTO. TRANS. IN DRIVE: 680-760 RPM

USE SAE 5W-30 OIL API SERVICE SG - ENERGY CONSERVING II.

THIS VEHICLE CONFORMS TO U.S. EPA REGULATIONS APPLICABLE TO 1990 MODEL YEAR NEW MOTOR VEHICLES.

CATALYST | SPARK PLUG: AWSF-42C  GAP .052-.056
2.3L-9HM
LFW2.3V5HXF9 - TWC·OC/PAIR/HO2S/EGR/WPI

86704243

## ■ CALIBRATION: 0-25C-R12 ███████ ▌ 2.3L HSC-EFI-HO ▌

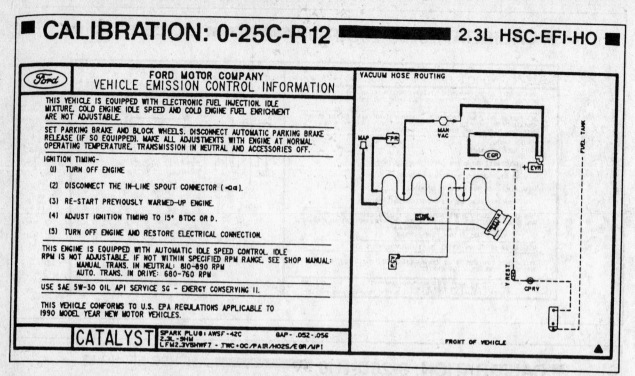

**FORD MOTOR COMPANY**
**VEHICLE EMISSION CONTROL INFORMATION**

THIS VEHICLE IS EQUIPPED WITH ELECTRONIC FUEL INJECTION. IDLE MIXTURE, COLD ENGINE IDLE SPEED AND COLD ENGINE FUEL ENRICHMENT ARE NOT ADJUSTABLE.

SET PARKING BRAKE AND BLOCK WHEELS. DISCONNECT AUTOMATIC PARKING BRAKE RELEASE (IF SO EQUIPPED). MAKE ALL ADJUSTMENTS WITH ENGINE AT NORMAL OPERATING TEMPERATURE, TRANSMISSION IN NEUTRAL AND ACCESSORIES OFF.

IGNITION TIMING-
(1) TURN OFF ENGINE
(2) DISCONNECT THE IN-LINE SPOUT CONNECTOR ( ◄◄ ).
(3) RE-START PREVIOUSLY WARMED-UP ENGINE.
(4) ADJUST IGNITION TIMING TO 15° BTDC OR D.
(5) TURN OFF ENGINE AND RESTORE ELECTRICAL CONNECTION.

THIS ENGINE IS EQUIPPED WITH AUTOMATIC IDLE SPEED CONTROL. IDLE RPM IS NOT ADJUSTABLE. IF NOT WITHIN SPECIFIED RPM RANGE, SEE SHOP MANUAL:
    MANUAL TRANS. IN NEUTRAL: 810-890 RPM
    AUTO. TRANS. IN DRIVE: 680-760 RPM

USE SAE 5W-30 OIL API SERVICE SG - ENERGY CONSERVING II.

THIS VEHICLE CONFORMS TO U.S. EPA REGULATIONS APPLICABLE TO 1990 MODEL YEAR NEW MOTOR VEHICLES.

**CATALYST** | SPARK PLUG: AWSF-42C    GAP - .052-.056
2.3L - SHM
LFM2.3V5HWF7 . TWC·OC/PAIR/HO2S/EGR/API

VACUUM HOSE ROUTING

FRONT OF VEHICLE

## ■ CALIBRATION: 0-25P-R11 ███████ ▌ 2.3L HSC-EFI-HO ▌

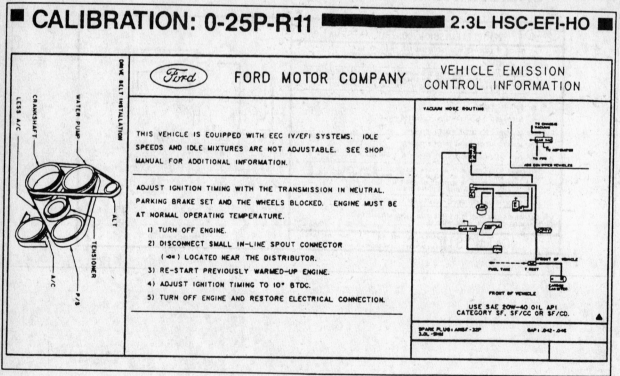

DRIVE BELT INSTALLATION

LESS A/C
CRANKSHAFT
WATER PUMP
A/C
TENSIONER
P/S
ALT

**FORD MOTOR COMPANY**    VEHICLE EMISSION CONTROL INFORMATION

THIS VEHICLE IS EQUIPPED WITH EEC IV/EFI SYSTEMS.  IDLE SPEEDS AND IDLE MIXTURES ARE NOT ADJUSTABLE.  SEE SHOP MANUAL FOR ADDITIONAL INFORMATION.

ADJUST IGNITION TIMING WITH THE TRANSMISSION IN NEUTRAL, PARKING BRAKE SET AND THE WHEELS BLOCKED.  ENGINE MUST BE AT NORMAL OPERATING TEMPERATURE.

1) TURN OFF ENGINE.
2) DISCONNECT SMALL IN-LINE SPOUT CONNECTOR
   ( ◄◄ ) LOCATED NEAR THE DISTRIBUTOR.
3) RE-START PREVIOUSLY WARMED-UP ENGINE.
4) ADJUST IGNITION TIMING TO 10° BTDC.
5) TURN OFF ENGINE AND RESTORE ELECTRICAL CONNECTION.

VACUUM HOSE ROUTING

FRONT OF VEHICLE

USE SAE 20W-40 OIL API CATEGORY SF, SF/CC OR SF/CD.

SPARK PLUG: AWSF-32P    GAP: .042-.046
2.3L - SHM

86704244

## ■ CALIBRATION: 0-25Q-R11    ■ 2.3L HSC-EFI ■

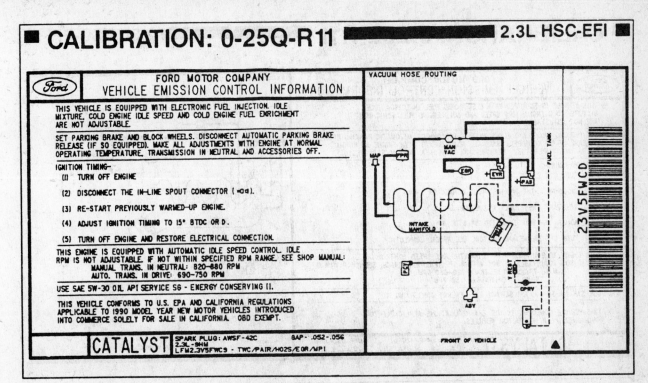

**FORD MOTOR COMPANY**
**VEHICLE EMISSION CONTROL INFORMATION**

THIS VEHICLE IS EQUIPPED WITH ELECTRONIC FUEL INJECTION. IDLE MIXTURE, COLD ENGINE IDLE SPEED AND COLD ENGINE FUEL ENRICHMENT ARE NOT ADJUSTABLE.

SET PARKING BRAKE AND BLOCK WHEELS. DISCONNECT AUTOMATIC PARKING BRAKE RELEASE (IF SO EQUIPPED). MAKE ALL ADJUSTMENTS WITH ENGINE AT NORMAL OPERATING TEMPERATURE, TRANSMISSION IN NEUTRAL AND ACCESSORIES OFF.

IGNITION TIMING-

(1)  TURN OFF ENGINE

(2)  DISCONNECT THE IN-LINE SPOUT CONNECTOR ( ◁◁ ).

(3)  RE-START PREVIOUSLY WARMED-UP ENGINE.

(4)  ADJUST IGNITION TIMING TO 15° BTDC OR D.

(5)  TURN OFF ENGINE AND RESTORE ELECTRICAL CONNECTION.

THIS ENGINE IS EQUIPPED WITH AUTOMATIC IDLE SPEED CONTROL. IDLE RPM IS NOT ADJUSTABLE. IF NOT WITHIN SPECIFIED RPM RANGE, SEE SHOP MANUAL:
    MANUAL TRANS. IN NEUTRAL: 820-880 RPM
    AUTO. TRANS. IN DRIVE: 690-750 RPM

USE SAE 5W-30 OIL API SERVICE SG - ENERGY CONSERVING II.

THIS VEHICLE CONFORMS TO U.S. EPA AND CALIFORNIA REGULATIONS APPLICABLE TO 1990 MODEL YEAR NEW MOTOR VEHICLES INTRODUCED INTO COMMERCE SOLELY FOR SALE IN CALIFORNIA.  OBD EXEMPT.

**CATALYST** SPARK PLUG: AWSF-42C   GAP- .052-.056
2.3L-9HM
LFM2.3V5FWC9 - TWC/PAIR/HO2S/EGR/MPI

VACUUM HOSE ROUTING

23V5FWCD

FRONT OF VEHICLE

## ■ CALIBRATION: 0-26D-R12    ■ 2.3L HSC-EFI-HO ■

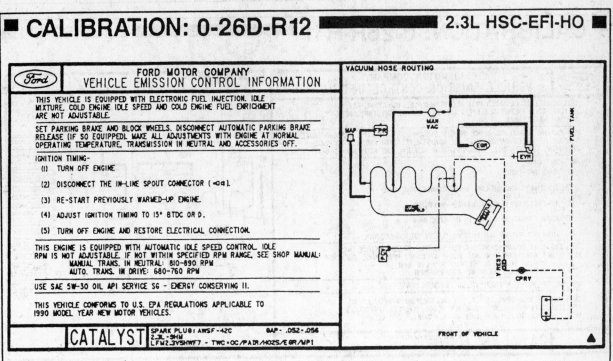

**FORD MOTOR COMPANY**
**VEHICLE EMISSION CONTROL INFORMATION**

THIS VEHICLE IS EQUIPPED WITH ELECTRONIC FUEL INJECTION. IDLE MIXTURE, COLD ENGINE IDLE SPEED AND COLD ENGINE FUEL ENRICHMENT ARE NOT ADJUSTABLE.

SET PARKING BRAKE AND BLOCK WHEELS. DISCONNECT AUTOMATIC PARKING BRAKE RELEASE (IF SO EQUIPPED). MAKE ALL ADJUSTMENTS WITH ENGINE AT NORMAL OPERATING TEMPERATURE, TRANSMISSION IN NEUTRAL AND ACCESSORIES OFF.

IGNITION TIMING-

(1)  TURN OFF ENGINE

(2)  DISCONNECT THE IN-LINE SPOUT CONNECTOR ( ◁◁ ).

(3)  RE-START PREVIOUSLY WARMED-UP ENGINE.

(4)  ADJUST IGNITION TIMING TO 15° BTDC OR D.

(5)  TURN OFF ENGINE AND RESTORE ELECTRICAL CONNECTION.

THIS ENGINE IS EQUIPPED WITH AUTOMATIC IDLE SPEED CONTROL. IDLE RPM IS NOT ADJUSTABLE. IF NOT WITHIN SPECIFIED RPM RANGE, SEE SHOP MANUAL:
    MANUAL TRANS. IN NEUTRAL: 810-890 RPM
    AUTO. TRANS. IN DRIVE: 680-760 RPM

USE SAE 5W-30 OIL API SERVICE SG - ENERGY CONSERVING II.

THIS VEHICLE CONFORMS TO U.S. EPA REGULATIONS APPLICABLE TO 1990 MODEL YEAR NEW MOTOR VEHICLES.

**CATALYST** SPARK PLUG: AWSF-42C   GAP- .052-.056
2.3L-9HM
LFM2.3V5HWF7 - TWC·OC/PAIR/HO2S/EGR/MPI

VACUUM HOSE ROUTING

FRONT OF VEHICLE

86704245

# ■ CALIBRATION: 0-26E-R11 ■ 2.3L HSC-EFI ■

### FORD MOTOR COMPANY
### VEHICLE EMISSION CONTROL INFORMATION

THIS VEHICLE IS EQUIPPED WITH ELECTRONIC FUEL INJECTION. IDLE MIXTURE, COLD ENGINE IDLE SPEED AND COLD ENGINE FUEL ENRICHMENT ARE NOT ADJUSTABLE.

SET PARKING BRAKE AND BLOCK WHEELS. DISCONNECT AUTOMATIC PARKING BRAKE RELEASE (IF SO EQUIPPED). MAKE ALL ADJUSTMENTS WITH ENGINE AT NORMAL OPERATING TEMPERATURE, TRANSMISSION IN NEUTRAL AND ACCESSORIES OFF.

IGNITION TIMING-

(1) TURN OFF ENGINE

(2) DISCONNECT THE IN-LINE SPOUT CONNECTOR ( ◁◁ ).

(3) RE-START PREVIOUSLY WARMED-UP ENGINE.

(4) ADJUST IGNITION TIMING TO 15° BTDC OR D.

(5) TURN OFF ENGINE AND RESTORE ELECTRICAL CONNECTION.

THIS ENGINE IS EQUIPPED WITH AUTOMATIC IDLE SPEED CONTROL. IDLE RPM IS NOT ADJUSTABLE. IF NOT WITHIN SPECIFIED RPM RANGE, SEE SHOP MANUAL:
    MANUAL TRANS. IN NEUTRAL: 820-880 RPM
    AUTO. TRANS. IN DRIVE: 690-750 RPM

USE SAE 5W-30 OIL API SERVICE SG - ENERGY CONSERVING II.

THIS VEHICLE CONFORMS TO U.S. EPA REGULATIONS APPLICABLE TO 1990 MODEL YEAR NEW MOTOR VEHICLES.

CATALYST | SPARK PLUG: AWSF-42C    GAP- .052-.056
2.3L -9HW
LFM2.3V5HWF7 - TWC-OC/PAIR/HO2S/EGR/MPI

VACUUM HOSE ROUTING

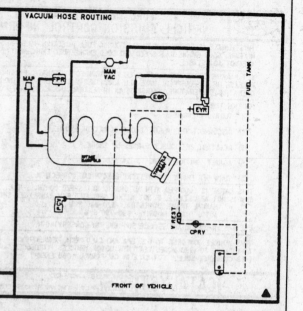

FRONT OF VEHICLE

---

# ■ CALIBRATION: 0-26R-R11 ■ 2.3L HSC-EFI ■

### FORD MOTOR COMPANY
### VEHICLE EMISSION CONTROL INFORMATION

THIS VEHICLE IS EQUIPPED WITH ELECTRONIC FUEL INJECTION. IDLE MIXTURE, COLD ENGINE IDLE SPEED AND COLD ENGINE FUEL ENRICHMENT ARE NOT ADJUSTABLE.

SET PARKING BRAKE AND BLOCK WHEELS. DISCONNECT AUTOMATIC PARKING BRAKE RELEASE (IF SO EQUIPPED). MAKE ALL ADJUSTMENTS WITH ENGINE AT NORMAL OPERATING TEMPERATURE, TRANSMISSION IN NEUTRAL AND ACCESSORIES OFF.

IGNITION TIMING-

(1) TURN OFF ENGINE

(2) DISCONNECT THE IN-LINE SPOUT CONNECTOR ( ◁◁ ).

(3) RE-START PREVIOUSLY WARMED-UP ENGINE.

(4) ADJUST IGNITION TIMING TO 15° BTDC OR D.

(5) TURN OFF ENGINE AND RESTORE ELECTRICAL CONNECTION.

THIS ENGINE IS EQUIPPED WITH AUTOMATIC IDLE SPEED CONTROL. IDLE RPM IS NOT ADJUSTABLE. IF NOT WITHIN SPECIFIED RPM RANGE, SEE SHOP MANUAL:
    MANUAL TRANS. IN NEUTRAL: 820-880 RPM
    AUTO. TRANS. IN DRIVE: 690-750 RPM

USE SAE 5W-30 OIL API SERVICE SG - ENERGY CONSERVING II.

THIS VEHICLE CONFORMS TO U.S. EPA AND CALIFORNIA REGULATIONS APPLICABLE TO 1990 MODEL YEAR NEW MOTOR VEHICLES INTRODUCED INTO COMMERCE SOLELY FOR SALE IN CALIFORNIA. OBD EXEMPT.

CATALYST | SPARK PLUG: AWSF-42C    GAP- .052-.056
2.3L -9HW
LFM2.3V5FWC9 - TWC/PAIR/HO2S/EGR/MPI

VACUUM HOSE ROUTING

FRONT OF VEHICLE

23V5FWCD

86704246

## ■ CALIBRATION: 0-26S-R00 ███████  2.3L HSC-EFI-HO ■

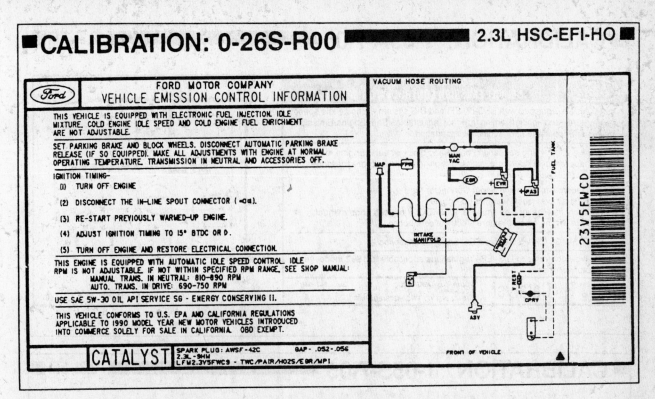

### FORD MOTOR COMPANY
### VEHICLE EMISSION CONTROL INFORMATION

THIS VEHICLE IS EQUIPPED WITH ELECTRONIC FUEL INJECTION. IDLE MIXTURE, COLD ENGINE IDLE SPEED AND COLD ENGINE FUEL ENRICHMENT ARE NOT ADJUSTABLE.

SET PARKING BRAKE AND BLOCK WHEELS. DISCONNECT AUTOMATIC PARKING BRAKE RELEASE (IF SO EQUIPPED). MAKE ALL ADJUSTMENTS WITH ENGINE AT NORMAL OPERATING TEMPERATURE, TRANSMISSION IN NEUTRAL AND ACCESSORIES OFF.

IGNITION TIMING-

(1) TURN OFF ENGINE

(2) DISCONNECT THE IN-LINE SPOUT CONNECTOR (-�‹�‹).

(3) RE-START PREVIOUSLY WARMED-UP ENGINE.

(4) ADJUST IGNITION TIMING TO 15° BTDC OR D.

(5) TURN OFF ENGINE AND RESTORE ELECTRICAL CONNECTION.

THIS ENGINE IS EQUIPPED WITH AUTOMATIC IDLE SPEED CONTROL. IDLE RPM IS NOT ADJUSTABLE. IF NOT WITHIN SPECIFIED RPM RANGE, SEE SHOP MANUAL:
   MANUAL TRANS. IN NEUTRAL: 810-890 RPM
   AUTO. TRANS. IN DRIVE: 690-750 RPM

USE SAE 5W-30 OIL API SERVICE SG - ENERGY CONSERVING II.

THIS VEHICLE CONFORMS TO U.S. EPA AND CALIFORNIA REGULATIONS APPLICABLE TO 1990 MODEL YEAR NEW MOTOR VEHICLES INTRODUCED INTO COMMERCE SOLELY FOR SALE IN CALIFORNIA. OBD EXEMPT.

**CATALYST**  SPARK PLUG: AWSF-42C    GAP - .052-.056
2.3L-SHM
LFM2.3V5FWC9 - TWC/PAIR/HO2S/EGR/MPI

VACUUM HOSE ROUTING

23V5FWCD

## ■ CALIBRATION: 0-26T-R12 ███████  2.3L HSC-EFI-HO ■

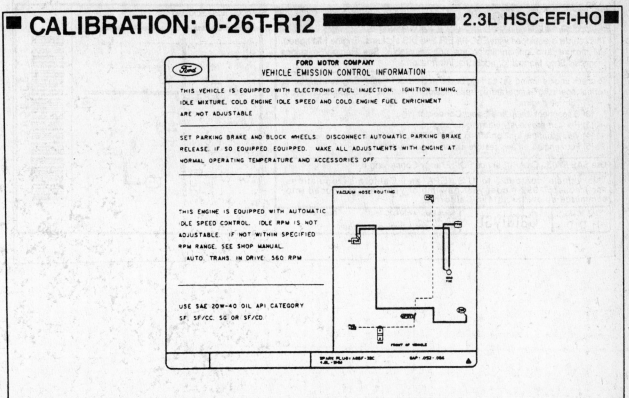

### FORD MOTOR COMPANY
### VEHICLE EMISSION CONTROL INFORMATION

THIS VEHICLE IS EQUIPPED WITH ELECTRONIC FUEL INJECTION. IGNITION TIMING, IDLE MIXTURE, COLD ENGINE IDLE SPEED AND COLD ENGINE FUEL ENRICHMENT ARE NOT ADJUSTABLE.

SET PARKING BRAKE AND BLOCK WHEELS. DISCONNECT AUTOMATIC PARKING BRAKE RELEASE, IF SO EQUIPPED EQUIPPED. MAKE ALL ADJUSTMENTS WITH ENGINE AT NORMAL OPERATING TEMPERATURE AND ACCESSORIES OFF.

THIS ENGINE IS EQUIPPED WITH AUTOMATIC IDLE SPEED CONTROL. IDLE RPM IS NOT ADJUSTABLE. IF NOT WITHIN SPECIFIED RPM RANGE, SEE SHOP MANUAL.
   AUTO. TRANS. IN DRIVE: 560 RPM

USE SAE 20W-40 OIL API CATEGORY SF, SF/CC, SG OR SF/CD.

VACUUM HOSE ROUTING

FRONT OF VEHICLE

SPARK PLUG: AGSF-32C    GAP: .052-.084
4.6L-1990

## ■ CALIBRATION: 1-05A-R05 ■■■■■■ 2.3L EFI ■

**Ford Motor Company**
**VEHICLE EMISSION CONTROL INFORMATION**

This vehicle is equipped with EEC-IV, EFI and DIS systems. Engine idle speed, idle mixture, and ignition timing are not adjustable. See Engine/Emissions Diagnosis Shop Manual for additional information.

To check engine timing set parking brake and block wheels. Engine must be at normal operating temperature, transmission in neutral, and accessories off.

(1) Turn off engine
(2) Disconnect the in-line Spout Connector (=0□ ).
(3) Re-start previously warmed-up engine.
(4) Verify that the ignition timing is 10°BTDC. If not see shop manual.
(5) Turn engine off and restore electrical connection.

Use SAE 5W-30 Oil API Service SG - Energy Conserving II.

This vehicle conforms to U.S. EPA regulations applicable to 1992 model year new motor vehicles.

| F2AE-9C485- | Catalyst | Spark Plug  AWSF-32C | Gap: .042-.046 |
| HDB | | 2.3L-9HM NFM2.3V5FYF7-TWC/HO2S/EGR/MPI | |

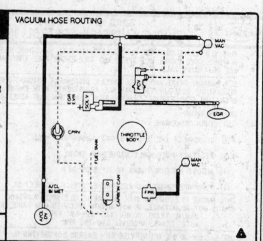

VACUUM HOSE ROUTING

## ■ CALIBRATION: 1-05S-R05 ■■■■■■ 2.3L EFI ■

**Ford Motor Company**
**VEHICLE EMISSION CONTROL INFORMATION**

This vehicle is equipped with EEC-IV, EFI and DIS systems. Engine idle speed, idle mixture, and ignition timing are not adjustable. See Engine/Emissions Diagnosis Shop Manual for additional information.

To check engine timing set parking brake and block wheels. Engine must be at normal operating temperature, transmission in neutral, and accessories off.

(1) Turn off engine
(2) Disconnect the in-line Spout Connector (=0□ ).
(3) Re-start previously warmed-up engine.
(4) Verify that the ignition timing is 10°BTDC. If not see shop manual.
(5) Turn engine off and restore electrical connection.

Use SAE 5W-30 Oil API Service SG - Energy Conserving II.

This vehicle conforms to U.S. EPA and California regulations applicable to 1992 model year new motor vehicles introduced into commerce solely for sale in California.

| F2AE-9C485- | Catalyst | Spark Plug  AWSF-32C | Gap: .042-.046 |
| HDD | | 2.3L-9HM NFM2.3V5FYC4-TWC/HO2S/EGR/MPI | |

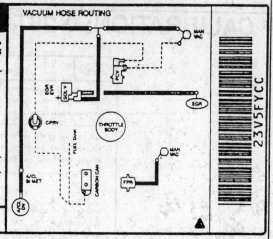

VACUUM HOSE ROUTING

23V5FYCC

86704248

### ■ CALIBRATION: 1-06A-R05

**2.3L EFI**

**Ford Motor Company**
**VEHICLE EMISSION CONTROL INFORMATION**

This vehicle is equipped with EEC-IV, EFI and DIS systems. Engine idle speed, idle mixture, and ignition timing are not adjustable. See Engine/Emissions Diagnosis Shop Manual for additional information.

To check engine timing set parking brake and block wheels. Engine must be at normal operating temperature. transmission in neutral, and accessories off.

(1) Turn off engine.
(2) Disconnect the in-line Spout Connector (=▯◁ ).
(3) Re-start previously warmed-up engine.
(4) Verify that the ignition timing is 10° BTDC. If not see shop manual.
(5) Turn engine off and restore electrical connection.

Use SAE 5W-30 Oil API Service SG · Energy Conserving II.

This vehicle conforms to U.S. EPA regulations applicable to 1992 model year new motor vehicles.

| F2AE-9C485- H D B | Catalyst | Spark Plug AWSF-32C 2.3L-9HM NFM2.3V5FYF7-TWC/HO2S/EGR/MPI | Gap .042-.046 |
|---|---|---|---|

VACUUM HOSE ROUTING

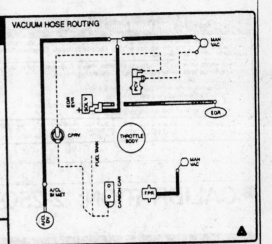

### ■ CALIBRATION: 1-06S-R05

**2.3L EFI**

**Ford Motor Company**
**VEHICLE EMISSION CONTROL INFORMATION**

This vehicle is equipped with EEC-IV, EFI and DIS systems. Engine idle speed, idle mixture, and ignition timing are not adjustable. See Engine/Emissions Diagnosis Shop Manual for additional information.

To check engine timing set parking brake and block wheels. Engine must be at normal operating temperature, transmission in neutral, and accessories off.

(1) Turn off engine.
(2) Disconnect the in-line Spout Connector (=▯◁ ).
(3) Re-start previously warmed-up engine.
(4) Verify that the ignition timing is 10° BTDC. If not see shop manual.
(5) Turn engine off and restore electrical connection.

Use SAE 5W-30 Oil API Service SG · Energy Conserving II.

This vehicle conforms to U.S. EPA and California regulations applicable to 1992 model year new motor vehicles introduced into commerce solely for sale in California.

| F2AE-9C485- H D D | Catalyst | Spark Plug AWSF-32C 2.3L-9HM NFM2.3V5FYC4-TWC/HO2S/EGR/MPI | Gap .042-.046 |
|---|---|---|---|

VACUUM HOSE ROUTING

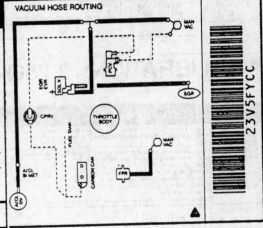

23V5FYCC

### ■ CALIBRATION: 2-25F-R10

**2.3L HSC-EFI**

**Ford Motor Company**

VEHICLE EMISSION CONTROL INFORMATION

This vehicle is equipped with EEC-IV, EFI systems. Engine idle speed, idle mixture, and ignition timing are not adjustable. See Engine/Emissions Diagnosis Shop Manual for additional information.

To check engine timing set parking brake and block wheels. Engine must be at normal operating temperature, transmission in neutral, and accessories off.

(1) Turn off engine
(2) Disconnect the in-line Spout Connector =▯◁ ).
(3) Re-start previously warmed-up engine
(4) Verify that the ignition timing is 10° BTDC. If not see shop manual.
(5) Turn engine off and restore electrical connection.

Use SAE 5W-30 Oil API Service SG · Energy Conserving II.

This vehicle conforms to U.S. EPA regulations applicable to 1992 model year new motor vehicles.

| F2AE-9C485- H K F | Catalyst | Spark Plug AWSF-42C 2.3L-2HM NFM2.3V5HWF9 TWC-OC/PAIR/HO2S/EGR/SMPI | Gap .052-.056 |
|---|---|---|---|

VACUUM HOSE ROUTING

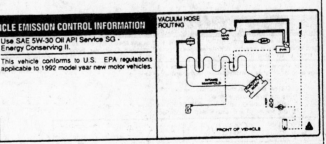

86704249

## ■ CALIBRATION: 2-25F-R11 ■■■■■■■■■ 2.3L HSC-EFI ■

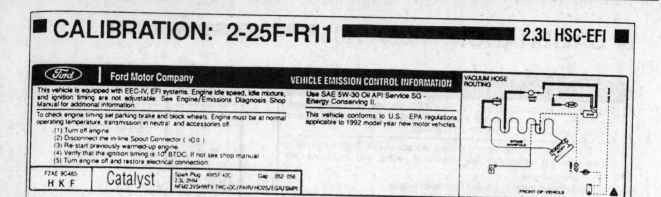

**Ford | Ford Motor Company**

This vehicle is equipped with EEC-IV, EFI systems. Engine idle speed, idle mixture, and ignition timing are not adjustable. See Engine/Emissions Diagnosis Shop Manual for additional information.

To check engine timing set parking brake and block wheels. Engine must be at normal operating temperature, transmission in neutral, and accessories off.

(1) Turn off engine
(2) Disconnect the in-line Spout Connector ( ⊐ )
(3) Re-start previously warmed-up engine
(4) Verify that the ignition timing is 10° BTDC. If not see shop manual
(5) Turn engine off and restore electrical connection.

**VEHICLE EMISSION CONTROL INFORMATION**

Use SAE 5W-30 Oil API Service SG - Energy Conserving II.

This vehicle conforms to U.S. EPA regulations applicable to 1992 model year new motor vehicles.

F2AE 9C485 | Catalyst | Spark Plug AWSF-42C  Gap 052-056
H K F | | 2.3L-2HM  NFM2 3V5HWF9 TWC-OC/PAIR/HO2S/EGR/SMPI

## ■ CALIBRATION: 2-25Q-R10 ■■■■■■■■ 2.3L HSC-EFI ■

**Ford | Ford Motor Company**

This vehicle is equipped with EEC-IV, EFI systems. Engine idle speed, idle mixture, and ignition timing are not adjustable. See Engine/Emissions Diagnosis Shop Manual for additional information.

To check engine timing set parking brake and block wheels. Engine must be at normal operating temperature, transmission in neutral, and accessories off.

(1) Turn off engine
(2) Disconnect the in-line Spout Connector ( ⊐ )
(3) Re-start previously warmed-up engine
(4) Verify that the ignition timing is 10° BTDC. If not see shop manual
(5) Turn engine off and restore electrical connection.

**VEHICLE EMISSION CONTROL INFORMATION**

Use SAE 5W-30 Oil API Service SG - Energy Conserving II.

This vehicle conforms to U.S. EPA and California regulations applicable to 1992 model year new motor vehicles introduced into commerce solely for sale in California.

23V5FWCD

F2AE 9C485 | Catalyst | Spark Plug AWSF-42C  Gap 052-056
H K H | | 2.3L-2HM  NFM2 3V5FWCG-TWC/PAIR/HO2S/EGR/SMPI

## ■ CALIBRATION: 2-25Q-R11 ■■■■■■■ 2.3L HSC-EFI ■

**Ford | Ford Motor Company**

This vehicle is equipped with EEC-IV, EFI systems. Engine idle speed, idle mixture, and ignition timing are not adjustable. See Engine/Emissions Diagnosis Shop Manual for additional information.

To check engine timing set parking brake and block wheels. Engine must be at normal operating temperature, transmission in neutral, and accessories off.

(1) Turn off engine
(2) Disconnect the in-line Spout Connector ( ⊐ )
(3) Re-start previously warmed-up engine
(4) Verify that the ignition timing is 10° BTDC. If not see shop manual
(5) Turn engine off and restore electrical connection.

**VEHICLE EMISSION CONTROL INFORMATION**

Use SAE 5W-30 Oil API Service SG - Energy Conserving II.

This vehicle conforms to U.S. EPA and California regulations applicable to 1992 model year new motor vehicles introduced into commerce solely for sale in California.

23V5FWCD

F2AE 9C485 | Catalyst | Spark Plug AWSF-42C  Gap 052-056
H K H | | 2.3L-2HM  NFM2 3V5FWCG-TWC/PAIR/HO2S/EGR/SMPI

## ■ CALIBRATION: 2-26E-R05 ■■■■■■■ 2.3L HSC-EFI ■

**Ford | Ford Motor Company**

This vehicle is equipped with EEC-IV, EFI systems. Engine idle speed, idle mixture, and ignition timing are not adjustable. See Engine/Emissions Diagnosis Shop Manual for additional information.

To check engine timing set parking brake and block wheels. Engine must be at normal operating temperature, transmission in neutral, and accessories off.

(1) Turn off engine
(2) Disconnect the in-line Spout Connector ( ⊐ )
(3) Re-start previously warmed-up engine
(4) Verify that the ignition timing is 10° BTDC. If not see shop manual
(5) Turn engine off and restore electrical connection.

**VEHICLE EMISSION CONTROL INFORMATION**

Use SAE 5W-30 Oil API Service SG - Energy Conserving II.

This vehicle conforms to U.S. EPA regulations applicable to 1992 model year new motor vehicles.

F2AE 9C485 | Catalyst | Spark Plug AWSF-42C  Gap 052-056
H K F | | 2.3L-2HM  NFM2 3V5HWF9 TWC-OC/PAIR/HO2S/EGR/SMPI

86704250

# ■ CALIBRATION: 2-26E-R11

**2.3L HSC-EFI**

### Ford | Ford Motor Company

**VEHICLE EMISSION CONTROL INFORMATION**

This vehicle is equipped with EEC-IV, EFI systems. Engine idle speed, idle mixture, and ignition timing are not adjustable. See Engine/Emissions Diagnosis Shop Manual for additional information.

To check engine timing set parking brake and block wheels. Engine must be at normal operating temperature, transmission in neutral, and accessories off.
(1) Turn off engine
(2) Disconnect the in-line Spout Connector.
(3) Re-start previously warmed-up engine
(4) Verify that the ignition timing is 10° BTDC. If not see shop manual
(5) Turn engine off and restore electrical connection.

Use SAE 5W-30 Oil API Service SG - Energy Conserving II.

This vehicle conforms to U.S. EPA regulations applicable to 1992 model year new motor vehicles.

F2AE-9C485-
**H K F**   Catalyst

Spark Plug  AWSF 42C   Gap  052-056
2.3L-2HM
NFM2 3V5HWF9-TWC-/OC/PAIR/HO2S/EGR/SMPI

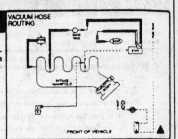

VACUUM HOSE ROUTING — FRONT OF VEHICLE

---

# ■ CALIBRATION: 2-26R-R05

**2.3L HSC-EFI**

### Ford | Ford Motor Company

**VEHICLE EMISSION CONTROL INFORMATION**

This vehicle is equipped with EEC-IV, EFI systems. Engine idle speed, idle mixture, and ignition timing are not adjustable. See Engine/Emissions Diagnosis Shop Manual for additional information.

To check engine timing set parking brake and block wheels. Engine must be at normal operating temperature, transmission in neutral, and accessories off
(1) Turn off engine
(2) Disconnect the in-line Spout Connector.
(3) Re-start previously warmed up engine
(4) Verify that the ignition timing is 10° see shop manual
(5) Turn engine off and restore electrical connection.

Use SAE 5W-30 Oil API Service SG - Energy Conserving II.

This vehicle conforms to U.S. EPA and California regulations applicable to 1992 model year new motor vehicles introduced into commerce solely for sale in California

23V5FWCD

F2AE-9C485-
**H K H**   Catalyst

Spark Plug  AWSF 42C   Gap  052-056
2.3L-2HM
NFM2 3V5FWC0-TWC/PAIR/HO2S/EGR/SMPI

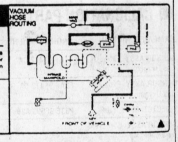

VACUUM HOSE ROUTING — FRONT OF VEHICLE

---

# ■ CALIBRATION: 2-26R-R11

**2.3L HSC-EFI**

### Ford | Ford Motor Company

**VEHICLE EMISSION CONTROL INFORMATION**

This vehicle is equipped with EEC-IV, EFI systems. Engine idle speed, idle mixture, and ignition timing are not adjustable. See Engine/Emissions Diagnosis Shop Manual for additional information.

To check engine timing set parking brake and block wheels. Engine must be at normal operating temperature, transmission in neutral, and accessories off
(1) Turn off engine
(2) Disconnect the in-line Spout Connector.
(3) Re-start previously warmed up engine
(4) Verify that the ignition timing is 10° see shop manual
(5) Turn engine off and restore electrical connection.

Use SAE 5W-30 Oil API Service SG - Energy Conserving II.

This vehicle conforms to U.S. EPA and California regulations applicable to 1992 model year new motor vehicles introduced into commerce solely for sale in California

23V5FWCD

F2AE-9C485-
**H K H**   Catalyst

Spark Plug  AWSF 42C   Gap  052-056
2.3L-2HM
NFM2 3V5FWC0-TWC/PAIR/HO2S/EGR/SMPI

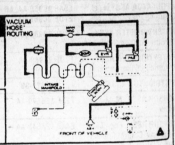

VACUUM HOSE ROUTING — FRONT OF VEHICLE

86704251

# ■ CALIBRATION: 2-55F-R00 ■■■■■■ 3.0L EFI ■

**Ford Motor Company**
**IMPORTANT VEHICLE INFORMATION**

This vehicle is equipped with EEC-IV, EFI systems. Engine idle speed, idle mixture, and ignition timing are not adjustable. See Engine/Emissions Diagnosis Shop Manual for additional information.

To check engine timing set parking brake and block wheels. Engine must be at normal operating temperature, transmission in neutral, and accessories off.

(1) Turn off engine.
(2) Disconnect the in-line Spout Connector ( =◻◻ ).
(3) Re-start previously warmed-up engine.
(4) Verify that the ignition timing is 10° BTDC. If not see shop manual.
(5) Turn engine off and restore electrical connection.

Use SAE 5W-30 Oil API Service SG - Energy Conserving II.

This vehicle conforms to U.S. EPA regulations applicable to 1992 model year new light-duty trucks and is certified for sale in California.

| F2AE-9C485-<br>H G A | Catalyst | Spark Plug: AWSF-32P<br>3.0L-9HM<br>NFM3.0T5FZF0-TWC/HO2S/SMPI | Gap: .042-.046 |

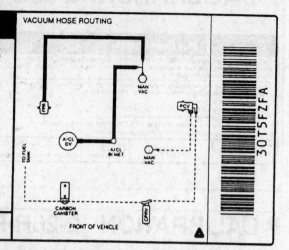

VACUUM HOSE ROUTING

30T5FZFA

# ■ CALIBRATION PARTS LIST ■■■■■ CODE: HGA ■

| NAME/DESCRIPTION | ENGINEERING NO. | SERVICE NO. |
|---|---|---|
| **SENSOR ASSY,** Exhaust Gas Oxygen | F1UF 9F472-CA | F1UZ 9F472-C |
| **SENSOR ASSY,** Exhaust Gas Oxygen | F2AF 9F472-CA | F2AZ 9F472-C |
| **INJECTOR ASSY,** Fuel | F03E 9F593-A2B | F03Z 9F593-A |
| **SENSOR ASSY,** Carburetor Air Cleaner Air Temperature Control | | D7FZ 9E607-A |
| **MOTOR ASSY,** Carburetor Air Cleaner Vacuum | | D4FZ 9D612-A |
| **VALVE ASSY,** Throttle Air By-Pass | F23E 9F715-CA | F2TZ 9F715-C |
| **SENSOR ASSY,** Speed | E3AF 9E731-AB | E3AZ 9E731-A |
| **REGULATOR ASSY,** Fuel Charging Pressure | E6AE 9C968-AA, AB<br>E7DE 9C968-BA | E6AZ 9C968-A |
| **POTENTIOMETER ASSY,** Throttle Position Sensor | E7DF 9B989-AA | E7DZ 9B989-A |
| **POTENTIOMETER ASSY,** Throttle Position Sensor | F2DF 9B989-AA | F2DZ 9B989-A |
| **DISTRIBUTOR ASSY** | F27E 12127-BB | F2TZ 12127-B |
| **SENSOR ASSY,** Mass Airflow | F23F 12B579-AA | F2TZ 12B579-A |
| **SENSOR ASSY,** Engine Electronic Control Coolant Temperature | E4AF 12A648-AA | E1AZ 12A648-A |
| **PROCESSOR AND CALIBRATOR ASSY,** EEC-IV | F27F 12A650-AA | F2TZ 12A650-RAA |
| **SENSOR ASSY,** Air Charge Temperature | E4AF 12A697-AA | E1AZ 12A697-A |

86704252

## ■ CALIBRATION: 2-55T-R00 ■■■■■ 3.0L EFI ■

**Ford Motor Company**
**IMPORTANT VEHICLE INFORMATION**

This vehicle is equipped with EEC-IV, EFI systems. Engine idle speed, idle mixture, and ignition timing are not adjustable. See Engine/Emissions Diagnosis Shop Manual for additional information.

To check engine timing set parking brake and block wheels. Engine must be at normal operating temperature, transmission in neutral, and accessories off.

(1) Turn off engine.
(2) Disconnect the in-line Spout Connector ( =▯▯ ).
(3) Re-start previously warmed-up engine.
(4) Verify that the ignition timing is 10° BTDC. If not see shop manual.
(5) Turn engine off and restore electrical connection.

Use SAE 5W-30 Oil API Service SG - Energy Conserving II.

This vehicle conforms to U.S. EPA and California regulations applicable to 1992 model year new light-duty trucks introduced into commerce solely for sale in California.

| F2AE-9C485-<br>H G G | Catalyst | Spark Plug: AWSF-32P<br>3.0L-9HM<br>NFM3.0T5FFD3-TWC/HO2S/SMPI | Gap: .042-.046 |

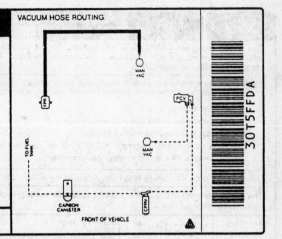

VACUUM HOSE ROUTING

MAN VAC — PCV — MAN VAC — CARBON CANISTER — CPRV — FRONT OF VEHICLE

30T5FFDA

## ■ CALIBRATION PARTS LIST ■■■■■ CODE: HGG ■

| NAME/DESCRIPTION | ENGINEERING NO. | SERVICE NO. |
|---|---|---|
| **SENSOR ASSY,** Exhaust Gas Oxygen | F1UF 9F472-AA | F1UZ 9F472-A |
| **SENSOR ASSY,** Exhaust Gas Oxygen | F2AF 9F472-AA | F2AZ 9F472-A |
| **INJECTOR ASSY,** Fuel | F03E 9F593-A2B | F03Z 9F593-A |
| **VALVE ASSY,** Throttle Air By-Pass | F23E 9F715-CA | F2TZ 9F715-C |
| **REGULATOR ASSY,** Fuel Charging Pressure | E6AE 9C968-AA, AB<br>E7DE 9C968-BA | E6AZ 9C968-A |
| **POTENTIOMETER ASSY,** Throttle Position Sensor | E7DF 9B989-AA | E7DZ 9B989-A |
| **POTENTIOMETER ASSY,** Throttle Position Sensor | F2DF 9B989-AA | F2DZ 9B989-A |
| **DISTRIBUTOR ASSY** | F27E 12127-BB | F2TZ 12127-B |
| **SENSOR ASSY,** Mass Airflow | F27F 12B579-AA | F2TZ 12B579-B |
| **SENSOR ASSY,** Engine Electronic Control Coolant Temperature | E4AF 12A648-AA | E1AZ 12A648-A |
| **PROCESSOR AND CALIBRATOR ASSY,** EEC-IV | F27F 12A650-DA | F2TZ 12A650-RDA |
| **SENSOR ASSY,** Air Charge Temperature | E4AF 12A697-AA | E1AZ 12A697-A |

86704254

# ■ CALIBRATION: 2-56F-R00 ■■■■■■ 3.0L EFI ■

| **Ford** | **Ford Motor Company** **IMPORTANT VEHICLE INFORMATION** |
|---|---|

This vehicle is equipped with EEC-IV, EFI systems. Engine idle speed, idle mixture, and ignition timing are not adjustable. See Engine/Emissions Diagnosis Shop Manual for additional information.

To check engine timing set parking brake and block wheels. Engine must be at normal operating temperature, transmission in neutral, and accessories off.

   (1) Turn off engine.
   (2) Disconnect the in-line Spout Connector ( =0d ).
   (3) Re-start previously warmed-up engine.
   (4) Verify that the ignition timing is 10° BTDC. If not see shop manual.
   (5) Turn engine off and restore electrical connection.

Use SAE 5W-30 Oil API Service SG - Energy Conserving II.

This vehicle conforms to U.S. EPA regulations applicable to 1992 model year new light-duty trucks.

| F2AE-9C485- **H F Y** | Catalyst | Spark Plug: AWSF-32P 3.0L-9HM NFM3.0T5FZF0-TWC/HO2S/SMPI | Gap: .042-.046 |
|---|---|---|---|

VACUUM HOSE ROUTING

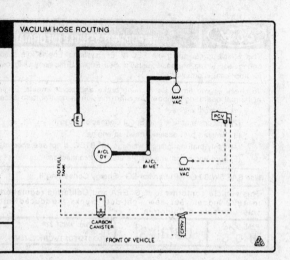

FRONT OF VEHICLE

# ■ CALIBRATION PARTS LIST ■■■■■■■ CODE: HFY ■

| NAME/DESCRIPTION | ENGINEERING NO. | SERVICE NO. |
|---|---|---|
| **SENSOR ASSY**, Exhaust Gas Oxygen | F1UF 9F472-CA | F1UZ 9F472-C |
| **SENSOR ASSY**, Exhaust Gas Oxygen | F2AF 9F472-CA | F2AZ 9F472-C |
| **INJECTOR ASSY**, Fuel | F03E 9F593-A2B | F03Z 9F593-A |
| **SENSOR ASSY**, Carburetor Air Cleaner Air Temperature Control | | D7FZ 9E607-A |
| **MOTOR ASSY**, Carburetor Air Cleaner Vacuum | | D4FZ 9D612-A |
| **VALVE ASSY**, Throttle Air By-Pass | F23E 9F715-CA | F2TZ 9F715-C |
| **SENSOR ASSY**, Speed | E3AF 9E731-AB | E3AZ 9E731-A |
| **REGULATOR ASSY**, Fuel Charging Pressure | E6AE 9C968-AA, AB E7DE 9C968-BA | E6AZ 9C968-A |
| **POTENTIOMETER ASSY**, Throttle Position Sensor | E7DF 9B989-AA | E7DZ 9B989-A |
| **POTENTIOMETER ASSY**, Throttle Position Sensor | F2DF 9B989-AA | F2DZ 9B989-A |
| **DISTRIBUTOR ASSY** | F27E 12127-BB | F2TZ 12127-B |
| **SENSOR ASSY**, Mass Airflow | F23F 12B579-AA | F2TZ 12B579-A |
| **SENSOR ASSY**, Engine Electronic Control Coolant Temperature | E4AF 12A648-AA | E1AZ 12A648-A |
| **PROCESSOR AND CALIBRATOR ASSY**, EEC-IV | F29F 12A650-AA | F29Z 12A650-AA |
| **SENSOR ASSY**, Air Charge Temperature | E4AF 12A697-AA | E1AZ 12A697-A |

86704255

## ■ CALIBRATION: 2-56J-R00 ■■■■■■■■■■ 3.0L EFI ■

**Ford Motor Company**
**IMPORTANT VEHICLE INFORMATION**

This vehicle is equipped with EEC-IV, EFI systems. Engine idle speed, idle mixture, and ignition timing are not adjustable. See Engine/Emissions Diagnosis Shop Manual for additional information.

To check engine timing set parking brake and block wheels. Engine must be at normal operating temperature, transmission in neutral, and accessories off.

(1) Turn off engine.
(2) Disconnect the in-line Spout Connector ( ═☐╢ ).
(3) Re-start previously warmed-up engine.
(4) Verify that the ignition timing is 10° BTDC. If not see shop manual.
(5) Turn engine off and restore electrical connection.

Use SAE 5W-30 Oil API Service SG - Energy Conserving II.

This vehicle conforms to U.S. EPA regulations applicable to 1992 model year new light-duty trucks.

| F2AE-9C485- H G B | Catalyst | Spark Plug: AWSF-32P 3.0L-9HM NFM3.0T5FZEX-TWC/HO2S/SMPI | Gap: .042-.046 |
|---|---|---|---|

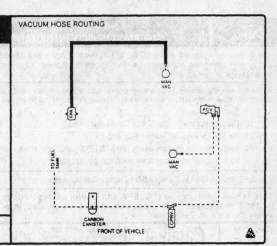

VACUUM HOSE ROUTING

## ■ CALIBRATION PARTS LIST ■■■■■■■■■■ CODE: HGB ■

| NAME/DESCRIPTION | ENGINEERING NO. | SERVICE NO. |
|---|---|---|
| SENSOR ASSY, Exhaust Gas Oxygen | F1UF 9F472-AA | F1UZ 9F472-A |
| SENSOR ASSY, Exhaust Gas Oxygen | F2AF 9F472-AA | F2AZ 9F472-A |
| INJECTOR ASSY, Fuel | F03E 9F593-A2B | F03Z 9F593-A |
| VALVE ASSY, Throttle Air By-Pass | F23E 9F715-CA | F2TZ 9F715-C |
| REGULATOR ASSY, Fuel Charging Pressure | E6AE 9C968-AA, AB E7DE 9C968-BA | E6AZ 9C968-A |
| POTENTIOMETER ASSY, Throttle Position Sensor | E7DF 9B989-AA | E7DZ 9B989-A |
| POTENTIOMETER ASSY, Throttle Position Sensor | F2DF 9B989-AA | F2DZ 9B989-A |
| DISTRIBUTOR ASSY | F27E 12127-BB | F2TZ 12127-B |
| SENSOR ASSY, Mass Airflow | F27F 12B579-AA | F2TZ 12B579-B |
| SENSOR ASSY, Engine Electronic Control Coolant Temperature | E4AF 12A648-AA | E1AZ 12A648-A |
| PROCESSOR AND CALIBRATOR ASSY, EEC-IV | F29F 12A650-CA | F29Z 12A650-CA |
| SENSOR ASSY, Air Charge Temperature | E4AF 12A697-AA | E1AZ 12A697-A |

86704256

## ■ CALIBRATION: 2-56T-R00 ■■■■■■■ 3.0L EFI ■

**Ford Motor Company**
**IMPORTANT VEHICLE INFORMATION**

This vehicle is equipped with EEC-IV, EFI systems. Engine idle speed, idle mixture, and ignition timing are not adjustable. See Engine/Emissions Diagnosis Shop Manual for additional information.

To check engine timing set parking brake and block wheels. Engine must be at normal operating temperature, transmission in neutral, and accessories off.

    (1) Turn off engine.
    (2) Disconnect the in-line Spout Connector ( =◻◁ ).
    (3) Re-start previously warmed-up engine.
    (4) Verify that the ignition timing is 10° BTDC. If not see shop manual.
    (5) Turn engine off and restore electrical connection.

Use SAE 5W-30 Oil API Service SG - Energy Conserving II.

This vehicle conforms to U.S. EPA and California regulations applicable to 1992 model year new light-duty trucks introduced into commerce solely for sale in California.

| F2AE-9C485- H G G | Catalyst | Spark Plug: AWSF-32P 3.0L-9HM NFM3.0T5FFD3-TWC/HO2S/SMPI | Gap: .042-.046 |

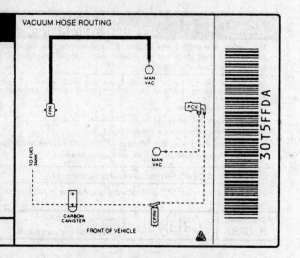

VACUUM HOSE ROUTING

FRONT OF VEHICLE

30T5FFDA

## ■ CALIBRATION PARTS LIST ■■■■■■■■■■ CODE: HGG ■

| NAME/DESCRIPTION | ENGINEERING NO. | SERVICE NO. |
|---|---|---|
| **SENSOR ASSY**, Exhaust Gas Oxygen | F1UF 9F472-AA | F1UZ 9F472-A |
| **SENSOR ASSY**, Exhaust Gas Oxygen | F2AF 9F472-AA | F2AZ 9F472-A |
| **INJECTOR ASSY**, Fuel | F03E 9F593-A2B | F03Z 9F593-A |
| **VALVE ASSY**, Throttle Air By-Pass | F23E 9F715-CA | F2TZ 9F715-C |
| **REGULATOR ASSY**, Fuel Charging Pressure | E6AE 9C968-AA, AB E7DE 9C968-BA | E6AZ 9C968-A |
| **POTENTIOMETER ASSY**, Throttle Position Sensor | E7DF 9B989-AA | E7DZ 9B989-A |
| **POTENTIOMETER ASSY**, Throttle Position Sensor | F2DF 9B989-AA | F2DZ 9B989-A |
| **DISTRIBUTOR ASSY** | F27E 12127-BB | F2TZ 12127-B |
| **SENSOR ASSY**, Mass Airflow | F27F 12B579-AA | F2TZ 12B579-B |
| **SENSOR ASSY**, Engine Electronic Control Coolant Temperature | E4AF 12A648-AA | E1AZ 12A648-A |
| **PROCESSOR AND CALIBRATOR ASSY**, EEC-IV | F29F 12A650-DA | F29Z 12A650-DA |
| **SENSOR ASSY**, Air Charge Temperature | E4AF 12A697-AA | E1AZ 12A697-A |

86704257

## ALTERNATE METHOD

▶ **See Figure 26**

1. Locate the inertia switch in the luggage compartment, then unplug the switch electrical connector.

2. Crank the engine for a minimum of 15 seconds. Pressure in the fuel system is now reduced.

➡ **Always place a shop cloth around the fitting prior to loosening to absorb any fuel that may spill out.**

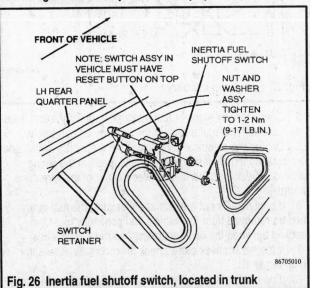

FRONT OF VEHICLE

NOTE: SWITCH ASSY IN VEHICLE MUST HAVE RESET BUTTON ON TOP

INERTIA FUEL SHUTOFF SWITCH

LH REAR QUARTER PANEL

NUT AND WASHER ASSY TIGHTEN TO 1-2 Nm (9-17 LB.IN.)

SWITCH RETAINER

86705010

**Fig. 26  Inertia fuel shutoff switch, located in trunk**

## Electric Fuel Pump

▶ **See Figures 27 and 28**

The fuel pump, used on the Tempo/Topaz fuel injected engine, is mounted on a fuel sender assembly inside the fuel tank. The fuel tank has an internal pump cavity in which the fuel pump and sender assembly rest. This design provides satisfactory operation during most vehicle operating conditions (Ex: Steep altitudes with low tank fill level).

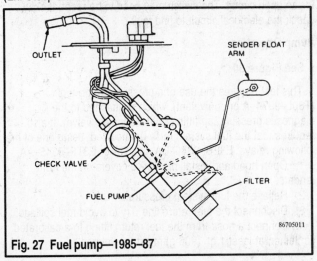

OUTLET

SENDER FLOAT ARM

CHECK VALVE

FILTER

FUEL PUMP

86705011

**Fig. 27  Fuel pump—1985–87**

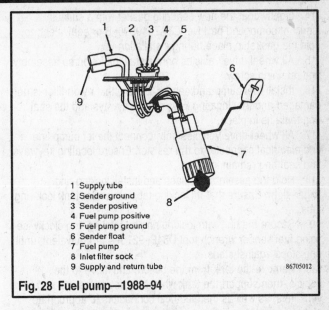

1 Supply tube
2 Sender ground
3 Sender positive
4 Fuel pump positive
5 Fuel pump ground
6 Sender float
7 Fuel pump
8 Inlet filter sock
9 Supply and return tube

86705012

**Fig. 28  Fuel pump—1988–94**

## REMOVAL & INSTALLATION

### ✳✳WARNING

**Extreme caution should be taken when removing the fuel tank from the vehicle! Ensure that all removal procedures are conducted in a well ventilated area! Have a sufficient amount of absorbent material in the vicinity of the work area to quickly contain fuel spillages should they occur. Never store waste fuel in an open container as it presents a serious fire hazard!**

1. Disconnect the negative battery cable.

2. Relieve the fuel system pressure.

3. Remove the fuel from the fuel tank by pumping out through the filler. Use care to prevent combustion from fuel spillage.

4. Raise and support the vehicle safely.

5. Disconnect and remove the fuel filler tube.

6. On all wheel drive vehicles, remove the exhaust system and rear axle assembly.

7. Support the fuel tank and remove the fuel tank support straps.

8. Lower the fuel tank partially and tag the fuel lines. Unplug the electrical connectors, then the vent lines from the tank. Finally, remove the fuel tank from the vehicle.

9. Clean any dirt from around the fuel pump attaching flange so that it will not enter the fuel tank during removal and installation.

10. Turn the fuel pump locking ring counterclockwise, and remove the locking ring.

11. Remove the fuel pump and bracket assembly.

12. Remove the seal gasket and discard.

**To install:**

13. Clean fuel pump mounting flange and fuel tank mounting surface and seal ring groove.

14. Lightly coat the new seal ring gasket with a suitable lubricant compound part No. C1AZ–19590–B or equivalent, to hold the gasket in place during installation.

15. All wheel drive vehicles only, install the jet pump assembly and retaining screw.

16. Install fuel pump and sender. Ensure that nylon filter is not damaged and that locating keys are in keyways and the seal ring remains in place.

17. All wheel drive vehicles only, connect the jet pump line and electrical connector to the resistor. Ensure locating keyways and seal ring remain in place.

18. Hold the assembly in place and install locking ring finger–tight. Ensure that all locking tabs are under tank lock ring tabs.

19. Secure the unit with locking ring by rotating ring clockwise using fuel sender wrench tool D84P–9275–A or equivalent, until ring stops against stops.

20. Remove the tank from the bench, and move to the vehicle, then support the tank while plugging in the fuel and vent lines, as well as the electrical connectors to appropriate places.

21. Install tank in vehicle and secure with retaining straps.

22. All wheel drive vehicles only, install rear axle assembly and exhaust system.

23. Lower the vehicle and refill the tank. Check for any leaks.

24. Connect the negative battery cable.

25. Check fuel pressure.

26. Remove the pressure gauge, start the engine and recheck for fuel leaks. Correct all fuel leaks immediately.

**All Wheel Drive Jet Pump**

➡ The jet pump is an additional feature equipped on these vehicles. It is designed to provide adequate fuel supply during extreme conditions. The jet pump is installed next to the fuel pump.

1. Lower the fuel tank as explained.
2. Loosen fuel pump using an appropriate wrench.
3. Partially lift out the sending unit. Unplug the jet pump line and electrical connector to the resister.
4. Remove the fuel pump and bracket.
5. Remove the jet pump retaining screws.
6. Remove jet pump.

**To install:**

7. Install jet pump assembly using retaining screws tightened to 10–15 ft. lbs. (14–20 Nm).
8. Install the fuel pump.
9. Plug in the electrical connector and the pump line.
10. Install the fuel tank.

## TESTING

**Electrical Circuit**

◗ See Figure 29

1. Check that the tank contains an adequate supply of fuel.
2. Make certain the ignition switch is OFF.

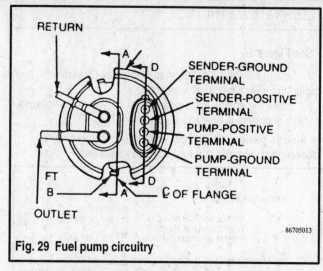

**Fig. 29  Fuel pump circuitry**

3. Check for any signs of fuel leakage at all fittings and lines.
4. Locate the inertia switch in the luggage compartment.
5. Unplug the electrical connector from the inertia switch and connect a continuity tester to one of the leads at the wiring harness. Check for continuity between either of the wires and ground.
6. If continuity is not present at either wire, the fuel tank must be removed from the vehicle and continuity must be checked between the wiring harness and the switch leads.
7. If the leads check okay, check for continuity across the pump terminals.
8. If no continuity is present across terminals, then replace the fuel pump and sender assembly.
9. If continuity is present across the pump terminals, check the ground circuit or the connections to the pump form the body connector.
10. Reconnect the inertia switch. Attach a voltmeter to the wiring harness on the pump side of the switch. (This would be the side which did indicate continuity.)
11. Observe the voltmeter reading, when the ignition key is turned to the ON position. The voltmeter should read over 10 volts for 1 second and then return to zero (0) volts.
12. If the voltage is not as specified, check the inertia switch for an open circuit. The switch may need to be reset. If okay, check the electrical circuit to find fault.

**Pump Operation**

◗ See Figure 30

This test requires the use of a pressure gauge tool (T80L–9974–A or equivalent), which is attached to the diagnostic pressure tap fitting (fuel diagnostic valve). It also requires that the fuel system relay be modified, using one of the following relays: E3EB–9345–BA, CA, DA or E3TF–9345–AA.

1. Open hood and install protective covers on the front fenders.
2. Relieve the fuel system pressure.
3. Disconnect the fuel return line. Try to avoid fuel spillage.
4. Connect a hose from the fuel return fitting to a calibrated container, at least 1 qt. (906 g) minimum volume.

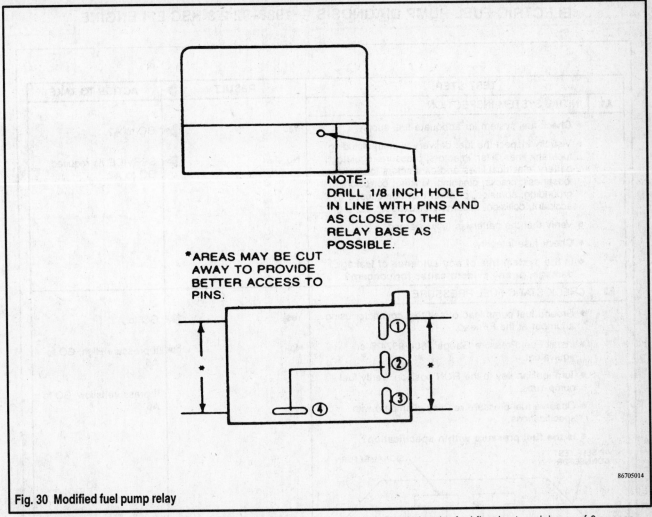

NOTE:
DRILL 1/8 INCH HOLE
IN LINE WITH PINS AND
AS CLOSE TO THE
RELAY BASE AS
POSSIBLE.

*AREAS MAY BE CUT
AWAY TO PROVIDE
BETTER ACCESS TO
PINS.

86705014

**Fig. 30 Modified fuel pump relay**

5. Attach the pressure gauge between the fuel charging unit (Central) or the fuel rail (Multiport) and the fuel filter.

6. Locate the fuel pump relay (behind the glove box or near the EEC module around the steering column) and remove it. The ground lead should be brought outside the vehicle and located nearby.

7. Using the appropriate relay indicated above, modify the relay case by drilling a 1/8 in. (3.1mm) hole and cutting the skirt as indicated in the diagram.

8. Add a 16–18 gauge jumper wire between pins 2 and 4, as outlined in the diagram.

9. Add 8 feet 2 m) of flexible wire through the hole in the case to point B, as shown. Add a ground to the end of the added wire.

➡ **The leads should be soldered in place and as close to the base as possible, to permit insertion of the relay into socket with minimum interference.**

10. Energize the fuel pump by jumper the ground lead from the relay for 10 seconds. Check the fuel pressure while energized. If there is no pressure, check that there is voltage pass the inertia switch. Correct, if necessary.

   a. The gauge should indicate a reading between 13–16 psi (90–110 kPa).

   b. Check that the fuel flow is at a minimum of 6 ounces (178 ml) in 10 seconds and fuel pressure remains at a minimum of 11.6 psi (80 kPa) immediately after shutdown.

   c. If these conditions are met, the pump is operating properly.

   d. If both pressure and flow conditions are met, but pressure will not maintain after shutdown, check for a leaking regulator or injector. If both check okay, replace the fuel pump.

11. After testing, replace the modified fuel pump relay with the original relay.

Generally any faults related to the electric fuel pump will result in a loss or reduction of fuel flow and/or pressure.

➡ **Exercise care when disconnecting fuel lines or when installing gauges, to avoid fuel spillage.**

Unless otherwise stated, turn OFF the fuel pump relay at the conclusion of any tests, by disconnecting the jumper or by turning the ignition switch OFF.

➡ **On vehicles equipped with all wheel drive, the following conditions may be an indication that the jet pump is not functioning properly.**

• Vehicle stumbles during right turns when fuel level is low.
• Fuel gauge indicates a low level of fuel, but there is no fuel in the line.
• Complaints of erratic fuel fill readings.

## ELECTRIC FUEL PUMP DIAGNOSIS — 1988–92 2.3 HSC EFI ENGINE

| TEST STEP | RESULT | ► | ACTION TO TAKE |
|---|---|---|---|
| **A1** INITIAL SYSTEM INSPECTION | | | |
| • Check fuel system for adequate fuel supply. | Yes | ► | GO to **A2**. |
| • Visually inspect the fuel delivery system including fuel tank lines, filter, injectors, pressure regulator, battery, electrical lines and connectors for leakage, looseness, cracks, pinching, kinking, corrosion, grounding, abrasion, or other damage caused by accident, collision, assembly or usage. | No | ► | SERVICE as required. GO to **A2**. |
| • Verify that the battery is fully charged. | | | |
| • Check fuse integrity. | | | |
| • **Is the system free of any evidence of leakage, damage, or any evident cause for concern?** | | | |
| **A2** CHECK STATIC FUEL PRESSURE | | | |
| • Ground fuel pump lead of self-test connector using a jumper at the FP lead. | Yes | ► | GO to **A3**. |
| • Install Fuel Pressure Gauge T80L-9974-B or equivalent. | No | ► | If pressure High, GO to **A5**. |
| • Turn ignition key to the RUN position. Verify fuel pump runs. | | | |
| • Observe fuel pressure reading. Compare with specifications. | | | If pressure is low, GO to **A6**. |
| • **Is the fuel pressure within specification?** | | | |

VIP SELF TEST CONNECTOR

SIGNAL RETURN

SELF TEST OUT

FP (FUEL PUMP) LEAD (SHORT END OF CONNECTOR)

| TEST STEP | RESULT | ► | ACTION TO TAKE |
|---|---|---|---|
| **A3** CHECK STATIC LEAKDOWN | | | |
| • Run fuel pump for 10 seconds and note pressure (Ground FP lead of self test connector and turn ignition switch to the RUN position). | Yes | ► | GO to **A4**. |
| • Turn off pump and monitor pressure for 60 seconds. (Disconnect ground or turn ignition switch to the OFF position). | No | ► | GO to **A10**. |
| • **Does fuel line pressure remain within 34 kPa (5 psi) of shut off pressure for 60 seconds?** | | | |

86705015

## ELECTRIC FUEL PUMP DIAGNOSIS — CONTINUED — 1988–92 2.3 HSC EFI ENGINE

| | TEST STEP | RESULT | ▶ | ACTION TO TAKE |
|---|---|---|---|---|
| **A4** | CHECK VEHICLE UNDER LOAD CONDITIONS | | | |
| | • Remove and block vacuum line to pressure regulator. | Yes | ▶ | Fuel system is OK. DISCONNECT all test connections, RECONNECT vacuum line to regulator. |
| | • Run vehicle at idle and then increase engine speed to 2000 RPM or more in short bursts. | | | |
| | • **Does fuel system pressure remain within chart limits?** | No | ▶ | GO to **A12**. |
| | NOTE: Operating vehicle under load (road test) should give same results. | | | |
| **A5** | CHECK FUEL PRESSURE | | | |
| | • Disconnect return line at fuel pressure regulator. Connect outlet of regulator to appropriate receptacle to catch return fuel. | Yes | ▶ | CHECK return fuel line for restrictions. SERVICE as required. REPEAT A2. GO to A3. |
| | • Turn on fuel pump (ground FP lead and turn ignition to the ON position) and monitor pressure. | | | |
| | • **Is fuel pressure within chart limits?** | No | ▶ | SERVICE or REPLACE fuel regulator as required. REPEAT A2. GO to A3. |
| **A6** | CHECK FUEL PUMP OPERATION | | | |
| | • Turn on fuel pump (ground FP lead and turn ignition to the RUN position). | Yes | ▶ | GO to **A9**. |
| | • Raise vehicle on hoist and use stethoscope to listen at fuel tank to monitor fuel pump noise, or listen at filler neck for fuel pump sound. | No | ▶ | GO to **A7**. |
| | • Is fuel pump running? | | | |
| **A7** | CHECK INERTIA SWITCH AND FUEL PUMP GROUND CONNECTOR | | | |
| | • Check if inertia switch is tripped. | Yes | ▶ | GO to **A8**. |
| | • Check fuel pump ground connection in vehicle. | No | ▶ | SERVICE switch or ground connection as required. REPEAT A2 and GO to A3. |
| | • **Is inertia switch and ground connection OK?** | | | |

86705016

## ELECTRIC FUEL PUMP DIAGNOSIS — CONTINUED — 1988–92 2.3 HSC EFI ENGINE

| TEST STEP | RESULT | ► | ACTION TO TAKE |
|---|---|---|---|
| **A8** CHECK VOLTAGE AT FUEL PUMP | | | |
| • Check for continuity through fuel pump to ground by connecting meter to pump power wire lead as close to pump as possible.<br><br>• Check voltage as close to fuel pump as possible (turn on pump as outlined in A6).<br><br>• Is voltage within 0.5 Volts of battery voltage and is there continuity through pump? | Yes | ► | REPLACE fuel pump. REPEAT A2. If pressure OK GO to A3. If presure not OK CHECK fuel pump connector for oversize connectors or other sources of open electrical circuit. SERVICE as required. REPEAT A3. |
| | No | ► | If voltage not present, CHECK fuel pump relay, EEC relay, and wiring for problem. If no ground, CHECK connection at fuel tank, etc. SERVICE as required. REPEAT A2 and A3. |
| **A9** CHECK FUEL PRESSURE REGULATOR | | | |
| • Replace fuel filter (if not replaced previously) and recheck pressure as in A2. If pressure not OK, continue. If pressure OK, go to A3.<br><br>• Open return line at pressure regulator. Attach return fitting from regulator to suitable container to catch gasoline.<br><br>• Turn on fuel pump as in A2.<br><br>• **Is fuel being returned from regulator with low pressure in system?** | Yes | ► | SERVICE or REPLACE regulator as required. REPEAT A2 and A3. |
| | No | ► | RECHECK systems for pressure restrictions. SERVICE as required. If no problem found, REPLACE fuel pump. GO to A2 and A3. |
| **A10** CHECK FUEL PRESSURE FOR LEAKS | | | |
| • Open return line at pressure regulator and attach suitable container to catch return fuel. Line should be clear to observe fuel flow.<br><br>• Run fuel pump as in A2.<br><br>• Turn off fuel pump by removing ground from self test connector or turning ignition to the OFF position.<br><br>• Observe fuel return flow from regulator and system pressure when pump is off.<br><br>• **Is there return flow when pump is turned off and system pressure is dropping?** | Yes | ► | REPLACE regulator. REPEAT A2 and A3. If OK, GO to A4. If not OK, REPEAT A2 and follow procedure. |
| | No | ► | GO to A11. |

86705017

## ELECTRIC FUEL PUMP DIAGNOSIS — CONTINUED — 1988-92 2.3 HSC EFI ENGINE

| TEST STEP | | RESULT ▶ | ACTION TO TAKE |
|---|---|---|---|
| **A11** | **CHECK FUEL PUMP CHECK VALVE** | | |
| | • Open pressure line from fuel pump and attach pressure gauge to line and block line to allow pressure build up. | Yes ▶ | CHECK injectors for leakage or regulator for internal leakage. SERVICE as required. Fuel pump check valve is OK. GO to **A4**. |
| | • Operate pump momentarily as in A2 and bring pressure to about system pressure. | | |
| | • Observe fuel pressure for one minute. | | |
| | • **Does pressure remain within 34 kPa (5 psi) of starting pressure over one minute period?** | No ▶ | CHECK lines and fittings from pump to rail for leakage, if none found REPLACE pump assembly. REPEAT **A2**. When OK GO to **A4**. |
| **A12** | **CHECK FUEL FILTER FOR RESTRICTIONS** | | |
| | • Replace fuel line filter (if not previously replaced during this procedure) and repeat test A5. | Yes ▶ | System is OK. DISCONNECT all test connections and RECONNECT all loosened or removed parts and lines. |
| | • **Does system pressure remain within chart limits?** | No ▶ | CHECK pressure lines for kinks or restrictions. CHECK at fuel pump for low voltage. CHECK for wrong size injectors (too large). If no problem found, REPLACE pump and REPEAT **A4**. If problem found, SERVICE as required. REPEAT **A4**. |

86705018

## Throttle Body

### REMOVAL & INSTALLATION

#### 1985-87 Models

➡ On the Central Fuel Injected (CFI) engine, the throttle body is part of the fuel charging assembly. Please refer to the fuel charging procedure found later in this section.

#### 1988-94 Models

▶ See Figure 31

1. Disconnect the negative battery cable.
2. Disconnect air intake system.
3. Disconnect the idle air control valve wire harness.
4. Unplug the throttle position sensor wire harness, if equipped.
5. Remove the 4 throttle body retaining bolts.
6. Unfasten the throttle control cable and speed control cable, if equipped. Disconnect the Throttle Valve (TV) control rod, if equipped with an automatic transaxle.

7. Remove the throttle control cable bracket, and place out of the way
8. Carefully pry the throttle body away from the upper manifold.
9. Remove the gasket from the throttle body. Clean both the throttle body and manifold surface.

**To install:**

10. Install gasket to the throttle body.
11. Secure throttle body to manifold using retaining bolts torqued to 12–14 ft. lbs. (16–20 Nm).
12. Install throttle cable bracket with retaining nuts, tightening to 12–14 ft. lbs. (16–20 Nm).
13. Connect throttle position sensor and idle air harnesses.
14. Connect air intake system, and secure.
15. Install throttle control cable, TV cable and speed control cable, if equipped.
16. Connect negative battery cable.
17. Start vehicle and check for air leaks. Adjust idle if necessary.

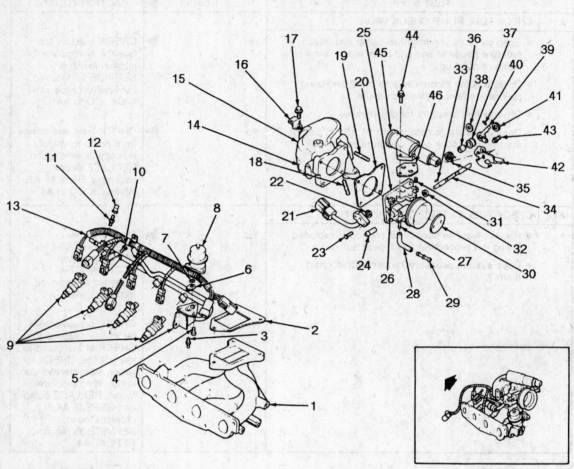

1 Intake lower manifold
2 Intake manifold upper gasket
3 1/4 flareless x 1/8 external pipe connector
4 M5 x .8 x 10 socket head screw
5 Fuel injecton fuel supply manifold assembly
6 Fuel pressure regulator gasket
7 5/16 x .070 "O" ring seal
8 Fuel pressure regulator assembly
9 Fuel injector assembly
10 M8 x 1.25 x 20 hex flange head bolt
11 Fuel pressure relief valve assembly
12 Fuel presssure relief cap
13 Fuel charging wiring harness
14 Carburetor identification decal
15 Intake upper manifold
16 Wiring harness retainer
17 M8 x 1.25 x 30 hex flange head bolt
18 M6 x 1.0 x 1.0 x 40 stud
19 M8 x 1.25 x 1.25 x 47.5 stud
20 Air intake charge to intake manifold gasket
21 Throttle position potentiometer
22 Carburetor throttle shaft bushing
23 Screw and washer assembly M4 x 22

24 Emission inlet tube
25 Air intake charge throttle body
26 M8 x 1.25 nut
27 Tube
28 Vacuum hose
29 Connector
30 Air intake charge throttle plate
31 M4 x .7 x 8 screw
32 Throttle control shaft seal
33 Spring coiled 1/16 x .42 pin
34 Shaft
35 Throttle return spring
36 Accelerator pump overtravel spring bushing
37 Throttle control linkage bearing
38 Throttle control torsion spring (MTX only) spacer
39 Carburetor transmission linkage lever
40 M5 x .8 x 16.25 slot head screw
41 Carburetor throttle shaft spacer
42 Carburetor throttle lever
43 Carburetor throttle lever ball
44 M6 x 1.0 x 20 hex flange head bolt
45 Throttle air bypass valve assembly
46 Air bypass valve gasket

86705022

**Fig. 31 Exploded view of the multiport fuel injection system**

## IDLE AIR CONTROL VALVE REPLACEMENT

**♦ See Figures 32 and 33**

1. Disconnect the idle air control valve wire harness.
2. Remove the 2 retaining screws, and remove the valve.
3. Remove gasket and discard. Clean surface of mounting surface.

**To install:**

4. Install gasket and valve to manifold and secure with screws. Tighten to 71–97 inch lbs. (8–11 Nm).
5. Plug in the electrical connector to the valve.

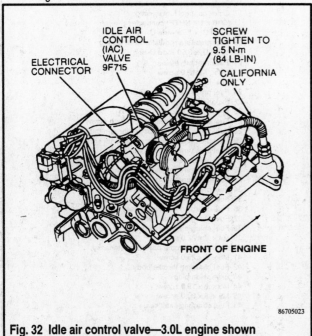

**Fig. 32 Idle air control valve—3.0L engine shown**

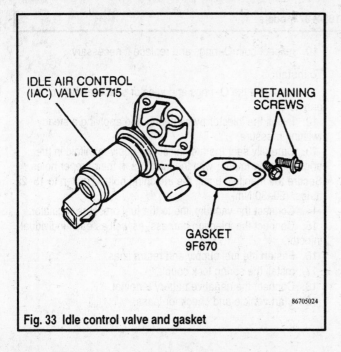

**Fig. 33 Idle control valve and gasket**

## THROTTLE PLATE ADJUSTMENT

**♦ See Figure 34**

1. Start vehicle and allow to reach normal operating temperature.
2. Connect a tachometer according to the tachometer manufacturer's specification.

**➡ When adjusting throttle plate position, perform service in a well ventilated area.**

3. Access the adjuster screw hole from the rear of the throttle body. To increase the idle, turn screw clockwise. To lower the idle, turn screw counterclockwise. Vehicle idle should be 850–1100 rpm.

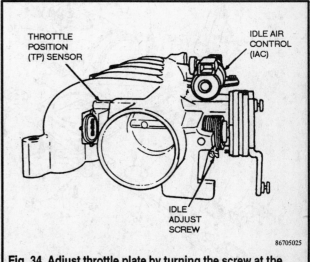

**Fig. 34 Adjust throttle plate by turning the screw at the rear of the throttle body**

## Fuel Injectors

### REMOVAL & INSTALLATION

**♦ See Figure 35**

**1985–87 Models**

1. Disconnect the negative battery cable.
2. Remove the fuel injector retaining screw and retainer.
3. Remove the injector and O–rings. Discard both O–rings

**To install:**

4. Lubricate the new O–ring and injector seat area with clean engine oil.
5. Install the lower O–ring on the injector.
6. Lubricate the upper O–ring. Clean and lubricate the throttle body O–ring seat.
7. Install the injector by centering and applying a steady downward pressure with a slight rotational force.
8. Install the injector retainer and retaining screw. Tighten to 18–22 inch lbs. (2.0–2.5 Nm).
9. Connect the negative battery terminal.
10. Start vehicle and check for leaks.

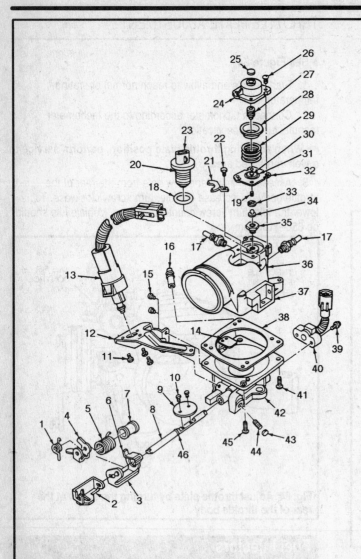

1 Engine idle speed-up control actuator spring
2 Carb. transmision linkage lever
3 Carb. throttle lever ball
4 Carb. idle speed-up control lever
5 Carb. throttle return spring
6 Carburetor throttle lever
7 Throttle control linkage bearing
8 Air intake charge throttle shaft
9 Air intake charge throttle plate
10 M4 x .7 x 8.0 screw
11 M4.2 x 1.41 x 15.9 (selftapping screw)
12 Engine throttle positioner bracket
13 Throttle control actuator assy.
14 Engine air distribution plate
15 M5 x .8 x 14.0 screw
16 Carburetor emission inlet tube
17 Quick connect fuel injection
   (5/16 x 1/4 NPTF) connector
18 20.4 I.D x 1.78 wide O-ring
19 Fuel pressure regulator valve spring
20 18.6 I.D. x 3.50 wide O-ring
21 Fuel injector retainer
22 M4 x .7 x 12.0 screw
23 Fuel injector assy.
24 Fuel pressure regulator cover
25 Expansion plug
26 M4 x .7 x 16.0 screw
27 Fuel pressure regulator adjusting screw
28 Fuel pressure regulator diaphragm cup
29 Fuel pressure regulator diaphragm spring
30 Fuel pressure regulator valve body
31 Fuel pressure regulator diaphragm retainer
32 Fuel pressure regulator diaphragm
33 Fuel pressure regulator valve retainer
34 Fuel pressure regulator valve assy.
35 Fuel pressure regulator outlet tube
36 Fuel charging main body assy.
37 Fuel charging main body
38 Fuel charging body gasket
39 M4 x .7 x 22.0 screw
40 Carburetor throttle potentiometer assy.
41 M5 x .8 x 25.0 screw
42 Fuel charging throttle body
43 Expansion plug
44 M5 x .8 x 19.0 screw
45 M5 x .8 x 30.0 screw
46 Fuel charging shaft seal

86705021

**Fig. 35 Exploded view of a Central Fuel Injected (CFI) system—1984–87 models**

### 1988–94 Models

▶ See Figures 36 and 37

1. Disconnect the negative battery cable.
2. Relieve the fuel system of pressure.
3. Remove the upper intake manifold. Refer to Section 3 for details.
4. Remove the spring lock coupler.
5. Disconnect the fuel supply and return lines.
6. Remove the vacuum line from the pressure regulator.
7. Unplug the fuel injector harness, and remove from each individual injector.
8. Remove the bolts securing the fuel injector supply manifold assembly to the intake manifold. Remove the supply manifold.
9. Grasp the supply manifold in one hand and the injector in the other. Slowly and carefully remove the injector by rocking back and forth.

10. Inspect both O–rings and replace if necessary.

**To install:**

11. Lubricate the O–rings and injector seat area with clean engine oil.
12. Install the injector by centering and applying a steady twisting pressure.
13. Carefully seat the fuel injection supply manifold in the engine compartment , with the injectors in their proper holes. Secure the manifold using the attaching bolts. Tighten to 15–22 ft. lbs. (20–30 Nm).
14. Connect the vacuum line to the fuel pressure regulator.
15. Connect the injection harness, as well as each individual injector.
16. Fasten the fuel supply and return lines.
17. Install the spring lock coupler.
18. Connect the negative battery terminal.
19. Start vehicle and check for leaks.

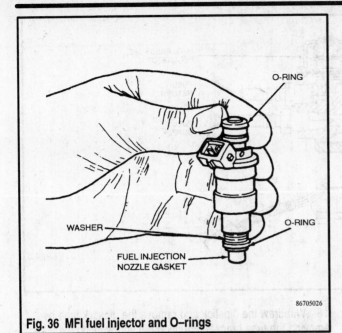

**Fig. 36 MFI fuel injector and O-rings**

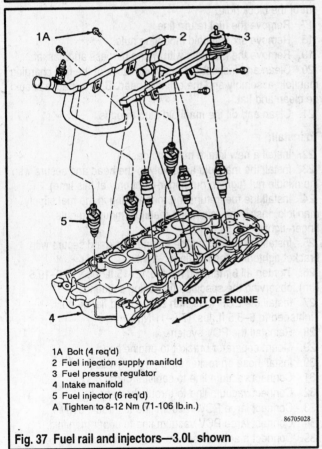

1A Bolt (4 req'd)
2 Fuel injection supply manifold
3 Fuel pressure regulator
4 Intake manifold
5 Fuel injector (6 req'd)
A Tighten to 8-12 Nm (71-106 lb.in.)

86705028

**Fig. 37 Fuel rail and injectors—3.0L shown**

## TESTING FUEL INJECTORS

Because the fuel injectors use a pulsed electrical signal, it is possible to test them for correct functioning. Unfortunately, the equipment necessary to do this is beyond the budget of most weekend mechanics.

If you feel that one or more of the injectors are not functioning properly, it is recommended that the individual injectors, or the entire fuel supply manifold with the injectors be taken to an authorized dealer for testing.

### Fuel Charging Assembly

The fuel charging system in the modern fuel injected vehicle is responsible for collecting a certain amount of fuel in the engine compartment, an creating the pressure needed by this type of fuel system to atomize the fuel so it will enter the cylinder chamber as a fine mist as opposed to a stream like the carbureted fuel systems. The fuel charging system helps ensure that the available fuel is used in a more efficient manner.

## REMOVAL & INSTALLATION

### 1985–87 Models

▶ See Figures 35 and 38

1. Open the hood and install protective covers on the front fenders.
2. Release the fuel system pressure.
3. Disconnect the negative battery cable.
4. Remove the air tube clamp at the fuel charging assembly air inlet.
5. Disconnect the throttle cable, and also the transaxle throttle valve lever on automatic transaxle vehicles.
6. Unplug the electrical connector at the Idle Speed Control (ISC), Throttle Position (TP) sensor and fuel injector.
7. Unfasten the fuel inlet and outlet connections, and PCV vacuum line at the fuel charging assembly.
8. Remove the 2 fuel charging assembly retaining nuts and remove the fuel charging assembly.
9. Remove the mounting gasket form the intake manifold.

### To install:

10. Clean the mounting surface and position a new gasket on the intake manifold.
11. Position the fuel charging assembly on the intake manifold and install the retaining nuts. Tighten to 71–106 inch lbs. (8–12 Nm).
12. Plug in all electrical connectors, fuel and vacuum lines.
13. Connect the throttle cable, and throttle valve lever, if equipped.
14. Connect the negative battery cable.
15. Start the engine and check for leaks.

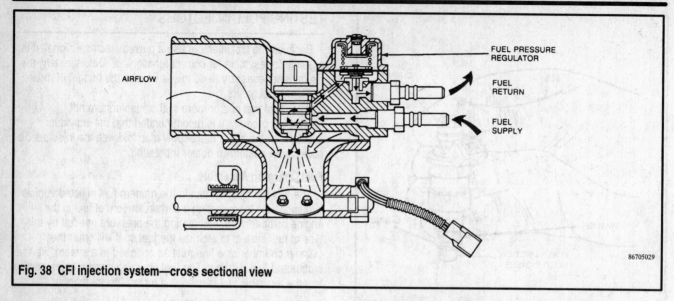

AIRFLOW

FUEL PRESSURE REGULATOR

FUEL RETURN

FUEL SUPPLY

86705029

**Fig. 38 CFI injection system—cross sectional view**

**1988–94 Models**

1. Open the hood and install protective covers on the front fenders.
2. Make sure that ignition key is in OFF position.
3. Disconnect the negative battery lead and secure it out of the way.
4. Drain the oil and engine coolant from the vehicle.
5. Remove fuel cap to relieve fuel tank pressure.
6. Release pressure from the fuel system at the fuel pressure relief valve on the fuel injection manifold assembly. Use tool T80L–9974–A or equivalent. To gain access to the fuel pressure relief valve, the valve cap must first be removed.
7. On 1988 vehicles, unfasten the push–connect fuel supply line and fuel return hose, using the Fuel Line Coupling Disconnect Tool D87L–9280–A or B or equivalent. Also, unplug the injector wiring harness and air bypass connector from the EEC harness.
8. Remove the retaining clip from the spring–lock coupling by hand only. Do not use any sharp tool or prytool as it may damage the spring–lock coupling.
9. Remove the engine air cleaner outlet tube between the vane air meter and air throttle body by loosening the 2 clamps.
10. Disconnect and remove the accelerator and speed control cables (if so equipped) from the accelerator mounting bracket and throttle lever.
11. Identify and tag the top manifold vacuum fitting connections including the rear vacuum line to the dash panel and the front vacuum line to the air cleaner and fuel pressure regulator.
12. Unfasten the PCV system by disconnecting the hoses from the connectors on the throttle body and intake manifold, throttle body port hose, canister purge line and the PCV hose at the rocker cover.
13. Unbolt the PCV separator support bracket from cylinder head and remove PCV system.
14. Disconnect the EGR vacuum line at the EGR valve.
15. Disconnect the EGR tube from the upper intake manifold by removing the 2 flange nuts.

16. Withdraw the dipstick and remove the dipstick tube by removing the tube bracket mounting nut and working the tube out of the block hole.
17. Remove the fuel return line.
18. Remove six manifold mounting nuts.
19. Remove the manifold with wiring harness and gasket.
20. Clean and inspect the mounting faces of the fuel charging manifold assembly and the cylinder head. Both surfaces should be clean and flat.
21. Clean and oil the manifold stud threads.

**To install:**

22. Install a new intake manifold gasket.
23. Install the manifold assembly to the head and secure with the middle nut (tighten nut finger–tight only at this time).
24. Install the fuel return line to the fitting in the fuel supply manifold. Install the remaining manifold mounting nuts, finger–tight.
25. Install the dipstick in the engine block and secure with bracket tightening the nut finger–tight.
26. Tighten all 6 manifold nuts to 12–15 ft. lbs. (15.6–19.5 Nm), observing the specified tightening sequence.
27. Install the EGR tube with 2 oil coated flange nuts. Tightened to 6–8.5 ft. lbs. (7.8–11 Nm).
28. Reinstall the PCV system.
29. Mount separator bracket to engine head.
30. Install hose on rocker cover, tighten clamp.
31. Connect vacuum line to canister purge.
32. Connect vacuum line to throttle body port.
33. Connect large PCV vacuum line to throttle body.
34. Connect large PCV vacuum line to upper manifold.
35. Connect manifold vacuum connections including rear connection to vacuum tree and the front connection to the fuel pressure regulator and air cleaner.
36. Connect accelerator and speed control cables (if so equipped).
37. Install air supply tube and tighten clamps to 25 inch lbs. (2.8 Nm).

38. Connect the wiring harness at the ECT sensor in heater supply tube, and electronic engine control harness.

39. Connect the fuel supply hose from the fuel filter to the fuel rail.

40. Connect the fuel return line.

41. Connect negative battery cable.

42. Install engine coolant using the prescribed fill procedure.

43. Start engine and allow to run at idle until engine temperature is stabilized. Check for coolant, oil and fuel leaks.

44. If necessary, reset idle speed.

## OVERHAUL

➡ **To prevent damage to the throttle plates, the fuel charging assembly should be placed on a work stand during disassembly and assembly procedures. If a proper stand is not available, use 4 bolts, 21/2 inches long, as legs. Install nuts on the bolts above and below the throttle body.**

The following is a step–by–step sequence of operations for completely overhauling the fuel charging assembly. Most components may be serviced without a complete disassembly of the fuel charging assembly. To replace individual components follow only the applicable steps.

Use a separate container for the parts of each component to insure proper assembly. The automatic transaxle throttle valve lever must be adjusted whenever the fuel charging assembly is removed for service or replacement.

1. Remove the air cleaner stud. The air cleaner stud must be removed to separate the upper body from the throttle body.

2. Turn the fuel charging assembly over and remove the 4 screws from the bottom of the throttle body.

3. Separate throttle body from main body. Set throttle body aside and cover with a clean cloth.

4. Carefully remove and discard the gasket.

5. Remove the pressure regulator retaining screws.

6. Remove the pressure regulator. Inspect the condition of gasket and O–ring. Replace if necessary.

7. Unplug the electrical connectors at each injector. Pull the connectors outward.

➡ **Pull the connector and the wire. Tape to identify the connectors. They must be installed on the same injector as removed.**

8. Loosen, DO NOT REMOVE, the wiring harness retaining screw with the multi–connector as well as the 10–pin connector.

9. Remove the fuel injector retainer screws.

10. One at a time, pull each of the injectors out of upper body. Identify each injector.

➡ **Each injector has a small O–ring at its top. If the O–ring does not come out with the injector, carefully pick the O–ring out of the cavity in the throttle body.**

11. Remove fuel diagnostic valve assembly.

12. Note the position of index mark on choke cap housing.

13. Remove the choke cap retaining ring, choke cap, and gasket, if so equipped.

14. Remove the thermostat lever screw, and lever, if equipped.

15. If equipped with a control diaphragm, hold the diaphragm cover tightly in position, while removing the retaining screws. Carefully, remove the cover, spring, and pull–down diaphragm.

16. Remove fast idle retaining nut, if so equipped.

17. Remove throttle position sensor connector bracket retaining screw.

18. Remove throttle position sensor retaining screws and slide throttle position sensor off the throttle shaft.

19. Remove the throttle positioner retaining screw, and remove the throttle positioner.

**To assemble:**

20. Install the fuel pressure diagnostic valve and cap. Tighten valve to 48–84 inch lbs. (5–9 Nm). Tighten cap to 5–10 inch lbs. (0.6–2 Nm).

21. Lubricate the new O–rings and install on each injector (use a light grade oil).

22. Identify injectors and install them in their appropriate locations. Use a light twisting, pushing motion to install.

23. With injectors installed, install injector retainer into position.

24. Install injector retainer screw, and tighten to 36–60 inch lbs. (4–7 Nm).

25. Install injector wiring harness in upper body. Snap harness into position.

26. If equipped with a single 10–pin connector, tighten injector wiring harness retaining screws to 8–10 inch lbs. (1 Nm).

27. Snap the electrical connectors into position on injectors.

28. Lubricate new fuel pressure regulator O–ring with light oil. Install O–ring and new gasket on regulator.

29. Install pressure regulator in upper body. Tighten retaining screws to 27–40 inch lbs. (3–4 Nm).

30. Depending upon CFI assembly, install either the throttle positioner, or the ISC DC Motor.

31. Hold throttle position sensor so wire faces up.

32. Slide throttle position sensor on throttle shaft.

33. Rotate throttle position sensor clockwise until aligned with screw holes on throttle body. Install retaining screws and tighten to 11–16 inch lbs. (1–2 Nm).

34. Install throttle position wiring harness bracket retaining screw. Tighten screw to 18–22 inch lbs. (2–3 Nm).

35. Install the E–clip, fast idle lever, spring and retaining nut, if equipped.

36. Tighten fast idle retaining nut to 16–20 inch lbs. (1–2 Nm).

37. Install the pull down control diaphragm, control modulator spring and cover. Hold the cover in position and install the retaining screws, and tighten to 13–19 inch lbs. (1–2 Nm).

38. Install fast idle cam, if equipped.

39. Install thermostat lever and retaining screws, if equipped. Tighten to 13–19 inch lbs. (1–2 Nm).

40. Install choke cap gasket, choke cap, and retaining ring, if equipped.

➡ **Be sure the choke cap bimetal spring is properly inserted between the fingers of the thermostat lever and choke cap index mark is properly aligned.**

41. Install choke cap retaining screws, tighten to 13–18 inch lbs. (1–2 Nm).

42. Install fuel charging gasket on upper body. Be sure gasket is positioned over bosses. Place throttle body in position on upper body.

43. Install the upper body to throttle body retaining screws. Tighten to specifications.

44. Install air cleaner stud. Tighten stud to 70–95 inch lbs. (8–11 Nm).

## Fuel Pressure Regulator

### REMOVAL & INSTALLATION

♦ See Figure 39

**1985–87 Models**

1. Disconnect the negative battery cable.

2. Relieve the system of fuel pressure. Refer to the section earlier on pressure relief methods.

➡ **The fuel pressure regulator cover is spring loaded. Apply downward pressure when removing.**

3. Remove the fuel pressure regulator retaining screws.

4. Remove the cover assembly, cup, spring and diaphragm assembly.

5. Remove the regulator valve seat.

**To install:**

6. Install the fuel pressure regulator valve seat.

7. Install the fuel pressure regulator diaphragm assembly, spring and spring cup cover.

8. Apply downward pressure to the cover and install the retaining screws.

9. Connect the negative battery cable.

10. Start vehicle and check for fuel leaks.

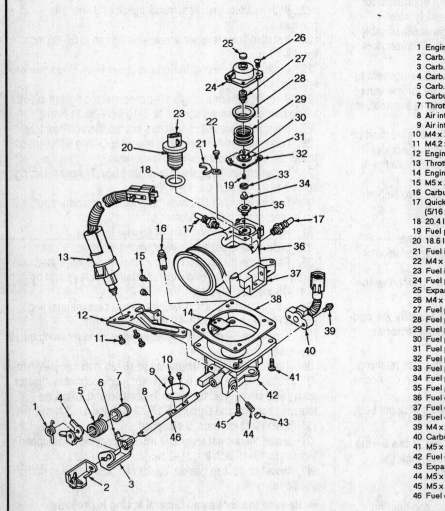

1 Engine idle speed-up control actuator spring
2 Carb. transmision linkage lever
3 Carb. throttle lever ball
4 Carb. idle speed-up control lever
5 Carb. throttle return spring
6 Carburetor throttle lever
7 Throttle control linkage bearing
8 Air intake charge throttle shaft
9 Air intake charge throttle plate
10 M4 x .7 x 8.0 screw
11 M4.2 x 1.41 x 15.9 (selftapping screw)
12 Engine throttle positioner bracket
13 Throttle control actuator assy.
14 Engine air distribution plate
15 M5 x .8 x 14.0 screw
16 Carburetor emission inlet tube
17 Quick connect fuel injection (5/16 x 1/4 NPTF) connector
18 20.4 I.D. x 1.78 wide O-ring
19 Fuel pressure regulator valve spring
20 18.6 I.D. x 3.50 wide O-ring
21 Fuel injector retainer
22 M4 x .7 x 12.0 screw
23 Fuel injector assy.
24 Fuel pressure regulator cover
25 Expansion plug
26 M4 x .7 x 16.0 screw
27 Fuel pressure regulator adjusting screw
28 Fuel pressure regulator diaphragm cup
29 Fuel pressure regulator diaphragm spring
30 Fuel pressure regulator valve body
31 Fuel pressure regulator diaphragm retainer
32 Fuel pressure regulator diaphragm
33 Fuel pressure regulator valve retainer
34 Fuel pressure regulator valve assy.
35 Fuel pressure regulator outlet tube
36 Fuel charging main body assy.
37 Fuel charging main body
38 Fuel charging body gasket
39 M4 x .7 x 22.0 screw
40 Carburetor throttle potentiometer assy.
41 M5 x .8 x 25.0 screw
42 Fuel charging throttle body
43 Expansion plug
44 M5 x .8 x 19.0 screw
45 M5 x .8 x 30.0 screw
46 Fuel charging shaft seal

86705030

**Fig. 39 Fuel pressure regulator—CFI injection systems**

**1988–94 Models**

▶ **See Figure 40**

1. Disconnect the negative battery cable.
2. Relieve the system of fuel pressure. Refer to the section earlier on pressure relief methods.
3. Remove the Allen bolts retaining the fuel supply manifold shield. Remove the shield.
4. Disconnect the vacuum line at the fuel pressure regulator.
5. Remove the Allen head screws from the regulator housing, and discard.
6. Remove fuel pressure regulator assembly, gasket and O–ring. Discard the gasket and O–ring

**To install:**

7. Lubricate new O–ring with clean engine oil. Ensure gasket surface of fuel pressure regulator and supply manifold are clean.
8. Install the new O–ring and gasket to the fuel pressure regulator, and install regulator on fuel supply manifold using the Allen head screws. Tighten to 27–40 inch lbs. (3.0–4.5 Nm).
9. Install the vacuum line to the fuel pressure regulator
10. Install the fuel pressure regulator shield using the Allen head bolts. Torque to 15–22 ft. lbs. (20–30 Nm).
11. Connect the negative battery cable.
12. Start vehicle and check for fuel leaks.

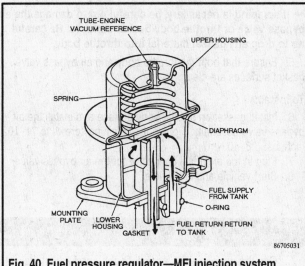

Fig. 40 Fuel pressure regulator—MFI injection system

## Fuel Pressure Relief Valve

### REMOVAL & INSTALLATION

▶ **See Figure 41**

1. Disconnect the negative battery cable.
2. Remove the pressure relief valve cap.
3. Relieve fuel pressure by removing fuel tank filler cap, and releasing the fuel pressure from the relief valve on the fuel supply manifold.
4. Using a suitable deep well socket, remove the fuel pressure relief valve from the supply manifold.

5. Clean the opening where the relief valve attaches.

**To install:**

6. Install the pressure relief valve with a suitable deep well socket. Tighten valve to 48–84 inch. lbs. (6–10 Nm).
7. Install and tighten pressure relief cap to 4–6 inch. lbs. (0.5–0.7 Nm).
8. Connect negative battery cable.
9. Start vehicle and check for leaks.

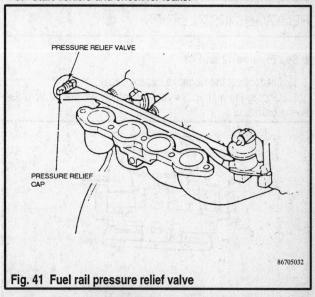

Fig. 41 Fuel rail pressure relief valve

## Throttle Position Sensor

### REMOVAL & INSTALLATION

1. Disconnect the negative battery terminal.
2. Disconnect the throttle position sensor from the wire harness.
3. Make scribe marks on the throttle body and on throttle position sensor to indicate the proper alignment during installation.
4. Remove the sensor retaining screws. Remove the sensor from the engine compartment.

**To install:**

### ✳✳CAUTION

**Slide the rotary tangs into position over the throttle shaft blade, then rotate throttle position sensor clockwise enough to properly align the installation marks. Failure to install the throttle position sensor in this manner may result in excessive idle speeds.**

5. Install the sensor, aligning the marks, using the retaining screws tightening to 25–34 inch. lbs. (2.8–3.8 Nm). Ensure that the rotary tangs on the sensor are in proper alignment, and the connector is pointing down.

➡ **If the sensor is being replaced, the alignment marks must be transfer from the original unit to the new unit.**

6. Connect the wire harness to the sensor.
7. Connect the negative battery terminal.
8. Start vehicle and check idle speed. If high, check alignment marks before adjusting idle.

## Air Bypass Valve

### REMOVAL & INSTALLATION

▶ **See Figures 42 and 43**

1. Disconnect the negative battery cable.
2. Unplug the air bypass valve assembly connector from the wiring harness.

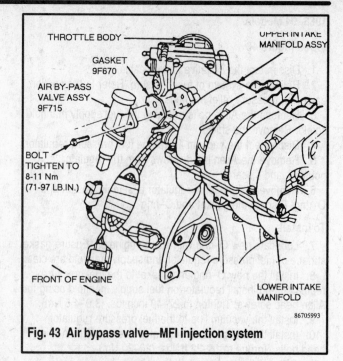

Fig. 43 Air bypass valve—MFI injection system

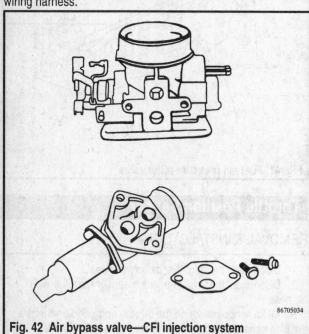

Fig. 42 Air bypass valve—CFI injection system

3. Remove the 2 air bypass valve retaining screws.
4. Remove the air bypass valve and gasket.

➡ **If scraping is necessary, be careful not to damage the air bypass valve or throttle body gasket surfaces. Be careful no to drop any gasket material into throttle body.**

5. Ensure that both the throttle body and air bypass valve gasket surfaces are clean.

**To install:**

6. Install gasket on throttle body surface and install the air bypass valve assembly. Tighten the retaining screws to 71–102 inch lbs. (28–40 Nm).
7. Plug in the electrical connector for the air bypass valve.
8. Start vehicle and check idle.

## DIESEL FUEL SYSTEM

### Injection Lines

### REMOVAL & INSTALLATION

▶ **See Figures 44 and 45**

1. Disconnect the negative battery located in the trunk of the vehicle.
2. Remove the brackets which secure the entire fuel line system.
3. Using a suitable flare wrench, loosen the nut securing the line at the injection pump as well as at the cylinder injector.
4. Carefully remove the line. Check the O–ring at both ends of the line. If cracked, replace the ring.

5. Cap the open injector, as well as the open end at the injection pump.

**To install:**

6. Remove the caps, and fit the fuel line with O–rings installed at each end into the opening at the fuel injection pump and injector.
7. hand–tighten the securing nuts. Tighten nuts to 10 ft. lbs. (14 Nm) with a suitable wrench.
8. Install the fuel line securing brackets.
9. Connect the negative battery cable.
10. Start vehicle and check for leaks.

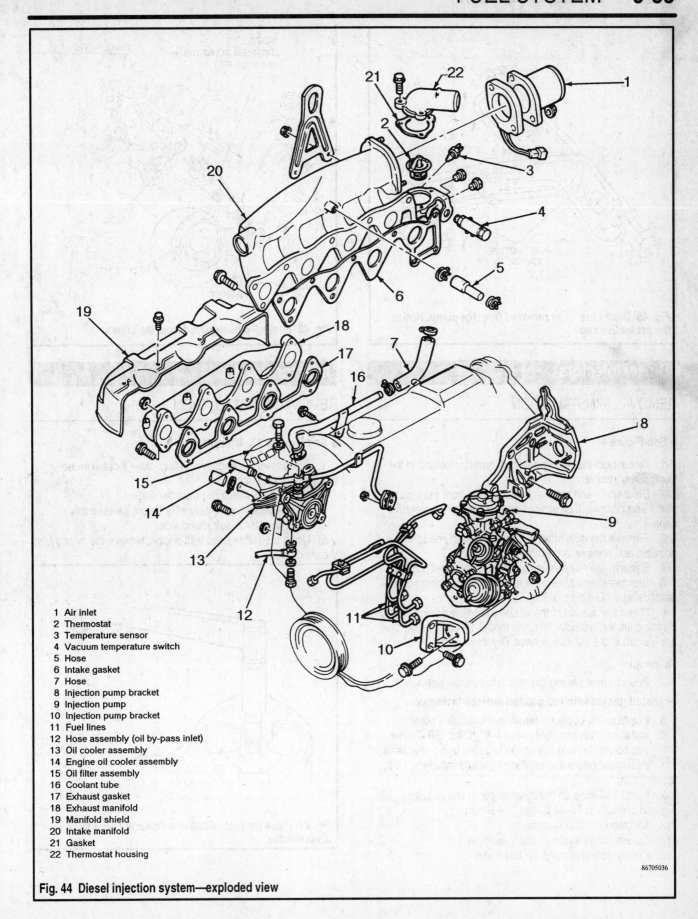

1  Air inlet
2  Thermostat
3  Temperature sensor
4  Vacuum temperature switch
5  Hose
6  Intake gasket
7  Hose
8  Injection pump bracket
9  Injection pump
10  Injection pump bracket
11  Fuel lines
12  Hose assembly (oil by-pass inlet)
13  Oil cooler assembly
14  Engine oil cooler assembly
15  Oil filter assembly
16  Coolant tube
17  Exhaust gasket
18  Exhaust manifold
19  Manifold shield
20  Intake manifold
21  Gasket
22  Thermostat housing

86705036

**Fig. 44  Diesel injection system—exploded view**

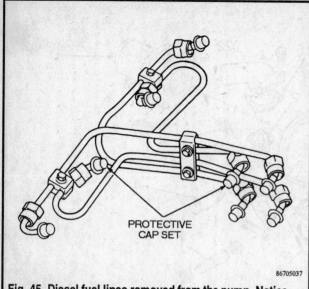

**Fig. 45 Diesel fuel lines removed from the pump. Notice the protective caps**

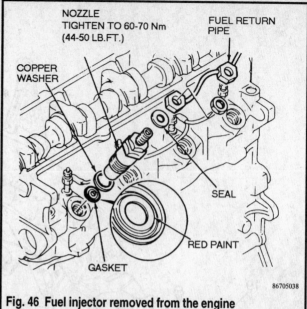

**Fig. 46 Fuel injector removed from the engine**

## Diesel Injectors

### REMOVAL & INSTALLATION

♦ **See Figure 46**

1. Disconnect the negative battery terminal located in the trunk compartment.
2. Disconnect and remove injection lines from the injection pump and nozzles. Cap all lines and fittings using protective caps.
3. Remove the nuts attaching the fuel return line to the nozzles, and remove the return line and seals.
4. Remove the nozzles using a 27mm deep well socket.
5. Remove the nozzles gaskets and washers from nozzle seat, using an O–ring pick tool.
6. Clean the outside of the nozzle assemblies using a nozzle cleaning kit, for example, Rotunda model 14–0301 or equivalent, and a suitable solvent. Dry thoroughly.

**To install:**

7. Position new sealing gaskets in the nozzle seats.

➡ **Install gasket with red painted surface facing up.**

8. Position new copper washers in the nozzles bores.
9. Install nozzles and tighten to 44–51 ft. lbs. (60–70 Nm).
10. Position fuel return line on the nozzles, using new seals.
11. Install fuel return line retaining nuts and tighten to 10 ft. lbs. (13 Nm).
12. Install fuel lines on the injection pump and nozzles. Tighten capnuts to 18–22 ft. lbs. (25–29 Nm).
13. Air bleed the fuel system.
14. Connect the negative battery terminal.
15. Run engine and check for fuel leaks.

## Injector Nozzles

### REMOVAL & INSTALLATION

♦ **See Figures 47, 48 and 49**

1. Disconnect the negative battery cable located in the luggage compartment.
2. Remove the injector(s) from the engine.
3. Clean entire injector assembly before disassembly.
4. Place injector in soft jawed vise.
5. Using a suitable deep well socket, remove the nozzle from the injector.

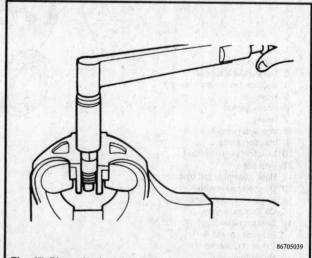

**Fig. 47 Place the fuel nozzle in a vise and carefully disassemble**

6. Place the nozzle on a clean cloth and remove the internal parts in order on the cloth.

7. Clean all parts in a suitable cleaning solution. Wash nozzle and needle valve in light oil.

8. Visually inspect all parts, and replace any if necessary.

**To install:**

9. Install needle valve, nozzle spacer, pushrod pressure spring, adjuster spring and nozzle holder into the retaining nut.

10. Tighten nozzle to injector body.

11. Install injector into engine.

12. Start vehicle and check for fuel leaks.

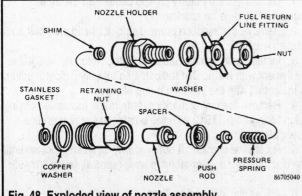

**Fig. 48 Exploded view of nozzle assembly**

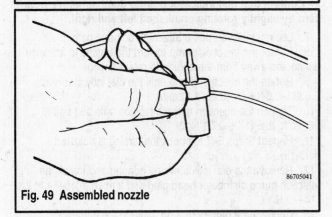

**Fig. 49 Assembled nozzle**

## AIR BLEEDING

In the event the injection lines are loosened or removed, the system must be bleed to remove any air that may have entered the line. If air enters a diesel fuel injection system, the vehicle looses performance.

1. Start vehicle and allow to reach operating temperature.

2. While the vehicle is running, loosen the capnut at the top of the of each injector slightly. Do not loosen the nut more than 1 full revolution. This will allow any air present in the fuel line to escape.

3. Start at one end of the engine and proceed to the other end until the job is complete.

## Fuel Pump

The fuel pump in the diesel engine is a mechanical type located in the engine compartment. The pump draws fuel from the fuel tank as the cam lobes activate the pump action.

## REMOVAL & INSTALLATION

➡ **The fuel pump is located in the engine compartment, bolted to the left hand side of the cylinder head.**

1. Disconnect the negative battery cable located in the luggage compartment.

2. Loosen the fuel lines at the fuel pump. Remove the lines and cap the ends.

3. Loosen and remove the mounting bolts securing the pump to the engine. Remove the pump.

4. Remove and discard the gasket. Make sure the mounting surfaces are clean.

**To install:**

5. Position a new gasket between the engine surface and the fuel pump. Secure the fuel pump using the mounting bolts. Tighten bolts to 11–19 ft. lbs. (15–25 Nm).

6. Install and tighten the fuel inches to the fuel pump.

7. Connect the negative battery cable.

8. Start vehicle and check for leaks.

9. Air bleed the fuel system if necessary.

## Fuel Cutoff Solenoid

### REMOVAL & INSTALLATION

1. Disconnect the negative battery cable located in the luggage compartment.

2. Remove the connector from the fuel cutoff solenoid.

3. Remove fuel cutoff solenoid and discard the O–ring.

**To install:**

4. Install fuel cutoff solenoid using a new O–ring. Tighten to 30–33 ft. lbs. (40–45 Nm).

5. Plug in the electrical connector.

6. Connect the battery ground cable.

7. Run engine and check for fuel leaks.

## Injection Pump

### REMOVAL & INSTALLATION

1. Disconnect the negative battery cable located in the trunk.

2. Disconnect air inlet duct from the air cleaner and intake manifold. Install protective cap in intake manifold.

3. Remove rear timing belt cover and flywheel timing mark cover.

4. Remove rear timing belt.

5. Disconnect throttle cable and speed control cable, if so equipped.

6. Disconnect vacuum hoses at the altitude compensator and cold start diaphragm.

7. Unplug the fuel cutoff solenoid connector.

8. Disconnect the fuel supply and fuel return hoses at injection pump. Place protective caps on the open ends.

9. Remove injection lines at the injection pump and nozzles. Cap all lines and fittings.

10. Rotate the injection pump sprocket until timing marks are aligned. Install 2 bolts into the holes to hold the injection pump sprocket securely. Remove the sprocket retaining nut.

11. Remove injection pump sprocket using Gear Puller T77F–4220–B1 and Adapter LD80L–625–4 or equivalent, using 2 bolts installed in the threaded holes in the sprocket.

12. Remove the bolt attaching the injection pump to the pump front bracket.

13. Remove the nuts attaching the injection pump to the pump rear bracket and remove the pump.

**To install:**

14. Install injection pump in position on the pump bracket.

15. Install the pump–to–rear bracket attaching nuts and tighten to 23–34 ft. lbs. (23–47 Nm).

16. Install bolt attaching the pump to the front bracket and tighten to 12–16 ft. lbs. (16–23 Nm).

17. Install injection pump sprocket. Hold the sprocket in place using the procedure described in Step 10, above. Install the sprocket retaining nut and tighten to 51–58 ft. lbs. (70 –80 Nm).

18. Remove protective caps and install the fuel lines at the injection pump and nozzles. Tighten the fuel line capnuts to 18–22 ft. lbs. (25–29 Nm).

19. Connect the fuel supply and fuel return hoses at the injection pump.

20. Plug in the fuel cutoff solenoid connector.

21. Connect the vacuum lines to the cold start diaphragm and altitude compensator.

22. Connect throttle cable and speed control cable, if so equipped.

23. Install and adjust the rear timing belt.

24. Remove the protective cap and install the air inlet duct to the intake manifold and air cleaner.

25. Connect battery ground cable to battery.

26. Air bleed fuel system as outlined.

27. Check and adjust the injection pump timing.

28. Run engine and check for fuel leaks.

29. Check and adjust engine idle.

## Injection Timing

### CHECKING

➡ **Engine coolant temperature must be above 176°F (80°C) before the injection timing can be checked and/or adjusted.**

1. Disconnect the battery ground cable from the battery located in luggage compartment.

2. Remove the injection pump distributor head plug bolt and sealing washer.

3. Install Static Timing Gauge Adapter, Rotunda 14–0303 or equivalent with Metric Dial Indicator, so that the indicator pointer is in contact with the injection pump plunger.

4. Remove the timing mark cover from the transaxle housing. Align timing mark (TDC) with the pointer on the rear engine cover plate.

5. Rotate the crankshaft pulley slowly, counterclockwise until the dial indicator pointer stops moving (approximately 30°–50° BTDC).

6. Adjust dial indicator to Zero.

➡ **Confirm that dial indicator pointer does not move from zero by slightly rotating crankshaft left and right.**

7. Turn crankshaft clockwise until crankshaft timing mark aligns with indicator p in. Dial indicator should read 0.0392–0.0408 in. (0.98–1.02mm). If reading is not within specification, timing adjustment is needed.

### ADJUSTING

➡ **Engine coolant temperature must be above 176°F (80°C) before the injection timing can be checked and/or adjusted.**

1. Disconnect the battery ground cable from the battery located in luggage compartment.

2. Remove the injection pump distributor head plug bolt and sealing washer.

3. Install Static Timing Gauge Adapter, Rotunda 14–0303 or equivalent with Metric Dial Indicator, so that the indicator pointer is in contact with the injection pump plunger.

4. Remove the timing mark cover from the transaxle housing. Align timing mark (TDC) with the pointer on the rear engine cover plate.

5. Rotate the crankshaft pulley slowly, counterclockwise until the dial indicator pointer stops moving (approximately 30°–50° BTDC).

6. Adjust dial indicator to Zero.

➡ **Confirm that dial indicator pointer does not move from zero by slightly rotating crankshaft left and right.**

7. Loosen injection pump attaching bolt and nuts.

8. Rotate the injection pump toward the engine to advance timing and away from the engine to retard timing.

9. Rotate the injection pump until the dial indicator reads 0.0392–0.0408 in. (0.98–1.02mm).

10. Tighten the injection pump attaching nuts and bolt to 13–20 ft. lbs. (17.6–27.1 Nm).

11. Repeat Steps 5–7 to check that timing is adjusted correctly.

12. Remove the dial indicator and adapter and install the injection pump distributor head plug and tighten to 10–14 ft. lbs. (14–19 Nm).

13. Connect the battery ground cable to the battery.

14. Run the engine, check and adjust idle rpm, if necessary. Check for fuel leaks.

## Glow Plugs

◆ **See Figure 50**

The diesel start/glow plug control circuit applies power to the glow plugs which heat the combustion chambers, so that the cold diesel engine can be started.

### PLUG CONTROL

The solid state diesel control module is mounted under the left hand side of the instrument panel. It controls glow plug pre–glow time, after–glow time and the operation of the wait–to–start indicator.

When the ignition switch is placed in the RUN position, the wait indicator lamp lights and the pre–glow No. 1 relay and the after–glow No. 2 relay go into operation. Voltage from the ignition switch is applied through pin 6 of the control module and then to the relays through pins 2 and 3. The contacts of the pre–glow relay close and the power is applied from fusible link S (located at the left hand side of the engine above the starter) to operate the glow plugs. The plugs will then start to heat up.

With power applied to the glow plugs, voltage is return through circuit 472 yellow wire with a black tracer to the control module at pin No. 11. After 3 seconds the wait–to–start indicator goes out and stays out. The glow plugs are now warm enough for the engine to be started. After 3 more seconds the pre–glow relay opens. Power is now applied through the after–glow relay and the dropping resistor (located in the air intake at the engine manifold) to keep the glow plugs operating at a reduced voltage.

➡ **The after–glow and the pre–glow relays are located at the top center area of the dash panel, which could be either underneath the instrument panel or the center of the firewall.**

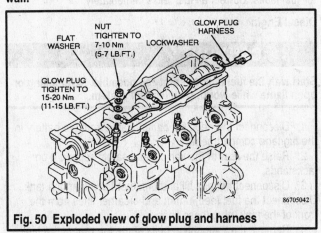

**Fig. 50 Exploded view of glow plug and harness**

## STARTING

Power is applied through heavy gauge wires to the starter relay located on the left hand front fender apron, then to the starter solenoid. When the wait–to–start indicator light goes out, the ignition switch can be turned to the START position. At this point, power is applied to the starter relay. The relay applies power to the solenoid coil, which in turn closes the contacts to apply battery power to the starter motor.

Even after the wait–to–start indicator goes out, the glow plugs must be kept hot because the combustion chambers may not be hot enough to keep the engine running smoothly. To compensate for this, the after–glow relay continues power to the glow plugs until one of the following conditions occurs:

1. The vehicle moves.
2. The coolant temperature rises above 86°F (30°C).
**or**
3. The glow plug voltage goes above 5.7 volts.

Vehicle movement is defined as a clutch switch closed (not depressed) and the neutral switch closed (transaxle in any position except neutral). This means pin 10 of the diesel control module is grounded.

The coolant temperature is measured by the thermoswitch. Whenever the coolant temperature is above 86°F (30°C), the

thermoswitch is opened and there is no voltage on pin No. 8. This will prevent the entire glow plug circuit from operating because the engine is hot enough to start and run without the glow plugs working.

If the voltage on the glow plugs is over 5.7 volts, they may overheat and burn out. Therefore, if over 5.7 volts is detected at pin 11 (with the pre–glow relay off), then the after–glow relay is shut off.

When the ignition is in the START position, 12 volts is supplied to pin No. 7 of the module. This causes the pre–glow relay to cycle on and off to keep the glow plugs hot. The pre–glow relay will cycle only during cranking.

Power from fusible link B (which is connected to the starter relay) is applied to the fuel solenoid with the ignition switch in the START or RUN position. The fuel solenoid opens the fuel line to permit the engine to run. When the ignition switch is in the OFF position, the solenoid cuts off fuel flow and stops the engine.

## STARTING DIAGNOSIS

### Visual Inspection

Remove the wire harness from each individual injector and check the harness for signs of cracks in the insulation. Also check the connection going to the glow plug. Use a multimeter and check for continuity from both ends of the harness. Replace if excessive cracks, loose connector or poor continuity are present.

With the glow plugs removed, check the glow end of each plug. They should be uniform, and have no cracks or rough edges. Replace any that do not meet these specifications.

### Electrical Inspection

1. Determine that the quick start and after–glow fuse in the fuse panel is functioning properly.
2. Disconnect the wire from each individual glow plug.
3. Turn ignition to the ON position.
4. Using a multimeter, test for current at each individual connector to the glow plugs. Replace harness if current is not present in one or more injector terminals.
5. Connect the wire harness to the injectors.

## REMOVAL & INSTALLATION

1. Disconnect battery ground cable from the battery, located in the luggage compartment.
2. Disconnect glow plug harness from the individual glow plugs.
3. Using a 12mm deep well socket, remove the glow plugs.

**To install:**

4. Install glow plugs, using a 12mm deep well socket. Tighten the glow plugs to 11–15 ft. lbs. (15–20 Nm).
5. Connect glow plug harness to the glow plugs. Tighten the nuts to 5–7 ft. lbs. (7–9 Nm).
6. Connect battery ground cable to the battery located in the luggage compartment.
7. Start vehicle and check for smooth a idle.

# FUEL TANK

## Tank Assembly

### REMOVAL & INSTALLATION

♦ See Figure 51

**Gasoline Engines**

### ✳✳CAUTION

**Extreme caution should be taken when removing the fuel tank from the vehicle. Ensure that all removal procedures are conducted in a well ventilated area. Have a sufficient amount of absorbent material in the vicinity of the work area to quickly contain fuel spillages should they occur. Never store waste fuel in an open container as it presents a serious fire hazard.**

1. Relieve the fuel system pressure.
2. Disconnect the negative battery cable.
3. Remove the fuel from the fuel tank by pumping it out through the filler neck. Clean up any fuel spillage immediately.
4. Raise and support the vehicle safely and remove the fuel filler tube (neck). On all wheel drive vehicles, remove the exhaust system and rear axle assembly.
5. Support the fuel tank and remove the fuel tank straps, lower the fuel tank enough to be able to remove the fuel lines, electrical connectors and vent lines from the tank.
6. Remove the fuel tank from under the vehicle and place it on a suitable work bench. Remove any dirt around the fuel pump attaching flange.
7. Turn the fuel pump locking ring counterclockwise and remove the lock ring.
8. Remove the fuel pump from the fuel tank and discard the flange gasket.
9. On all wheel drive vehicles, partially raise the sender unit and disconnect the jet pump line and resistor electrical connector. Remove the fuel pump and bracket assembly with seal gasket. Remove the seal gasket and replace with new. Remove the jet pump assembly.

**To install:**

10. Clean fuel pump mounting flange and fuel tank mounting surface and seal ring groove.
11. Lightly coat the new seal ring gasket with a suitable lubricant compound part No. C1AZ–19590–B or equivalent, to hold the gasket in place during installation.
12. All wheel drive vehicles only, install jet pump assembly and retaining screw.
13. Install fuel pump and sender. Ensure that nylon filter is not damaged and that locating keys are in keyways and seal ring remains in place.
14. All wheel drive vehicles only, connect jet pump line and electrical connector to resistor. Ensure locating keyways and seal ring remain in place.

15. Hold assembly in place and install locking ring finger–tight. Ensure that all locking tabs are under tank lock ring tabs.
16. Secure unit with locking ring by rotating ring clockwise using fuel sender wrench tool D84P–9275–A or equivalent, until ring stops against stops.
17. Remove tank from bench to vehicle and support tank while connecting fuel lines, vent line and electrical connectors to appropriate places.
18. Install tank in vehicle and secure with retaining straps.
19. All wheel drive vehicles only, install rear axle assembly and exhaust system.
20. Lower vehicle and install fuel in tank. Check for leaks.
21. Connect negative battery cable.
22. Check fuel pressure.
23. Remove the pressure gauge, start the engine and recheck for fuel leaks. Correct all fuel leaks immediately.

**Diesel Engine**

### ✳✳CAUTION

**Start with the fuel tank as empty as possible. No smoking or open flame while working on the fuel system.**

1. Disconnect the negative battery cable from the battery in the luggage compartment.
2. Raise the rear of the vehicle and safely support it on jackstands.
3. Disconnect the gas fill and breather lines from the tank. Disconnect the fuel feed, return and breather lines from the front of the tank, plug these lines.
4. Remove the 2 mounting bolts at the top rear of the tank while supporting the tank on a piece of wood and a floor jack. Lower and remove the gas tank.

**To install:**

5. Raise the fuel tank to the vehicle, and secure by installing the mounting bolts at the rear of the tank.
6. Connect the gas fill, breather hose, fuel fill and return lines.
7. Lower the vehicle.
8. Connect the negative battery cable.
9. Start vehicle and check for leaks.

### SENDING UNIT REPLACEMENT

On all Tempo/Topaz models, the fuel gauge sender is located in the fuel tank.

But the year, fuel delivery method and fuel used in the vehicle will determine the type of fuel sender incorporated into the vehicle.

Carbureted vehicles use a mechanical fuel pump at the engine. As a result this vehicle uses an electrical sender unit in the fuel tank. Diesel vehicles also use a mechanical fuel pump in the engine compartment and also use an electrical pump in the tank.

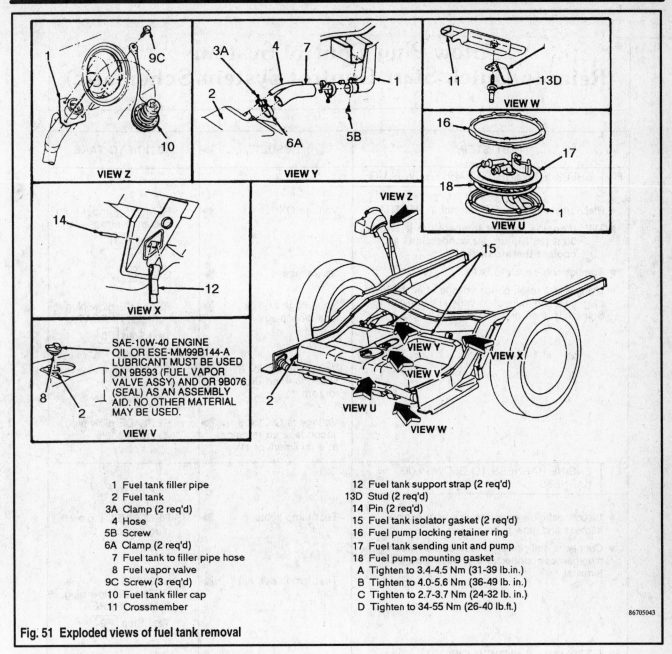

1  Fuel tank filler pipe
2  Fuel tank
3A Clamp (2 req'd)
4  Hose
5B Screw
6A Clamp (2 req'd)
7  Fuel tank to filler pipe hose
8  Fuel vapor valve
9C Screw (3 req'd)
10 Fuel tank filler cap
11 Crossmember

12  Fuel tank support strap (2 req'd)
13D Stud (2 req'd)
14  Pin (2 req'd)
15  Fuel tank isolator gasket (2 req'd)
16  Fuel pump locking retainer ring
17  Fuel tank sending unit and pump
18  Fuel pump mounting gasket
A   Tighten to 3.4-4.5 Nm (31-39 lb.in.)
B   Tighten to 4.0-5.6 Nm (36-49 lb. in.)
C   Tighten to 2.7-3.7 Nm (24-32 lb. in.)
D   Tighten to 34-55 Nm (26-40 lb.ft.)

86705043

**Fig. 51 Exploded views of fuel tank removal**

Fuel injected vehicles utilize a more complicated fuel sender unit. This type of fuel registry unit incorporates the fuel pump with the fuel sender. The sender unit is not individually serviceable from the pump. Also the sender uses a magnetic method of delivering information as opposed to an electrical method used by carbureted and diesel vehicles.

Before replacing a fuel sending unit, determine whether a sender, or a sender/pump unit is needed to complete the procedure.

1. Disconnect the negative battery terminal.
2. Remove the fuel from the fuel tank.
3. Remove the tank from the vehicle.
4. Disconnect the fuel sender/pump sender wire harness.
5. Using the appropriate tools, remove the sending/pump sender unit from the vehicle, by turning the collar counterclockwise. Carefully lift the sender/pump sender out of the tank.

6. Check the gasket used to seal and secure the sender/pump sender, and replace if necessary.

**To install:**

7. Carefully install the sender/pump sender into the fuel tank with a new gasket. Use care not to bend the rod with the float at the end, this could effect fuel gauge accuracy.
8. Tighten the collar using the appropriate tool.
9. Connect the wire harness to the sender/pump sender.
10. Position and secure the fuel tank to the vehicle.
11. Lower vehicle, add fuel, connect the negative battery terminal and check for proper fuel gauge function.

# Glow Plug Control System
## (Refer to Quick Start Control System Schematic)

| TEST STEP | RESULT ▶ | ACTION TO TAKE |
|---|---|---|
| **F0** CHECK VOLTAGE TO EACH GLOW PLUG | | |
| • Place transmission gear selector in NEUTRAL.<br>**NOTE: If engine coolant temperature is above 30°C (86°F), jumper connections at coolant thermoswitch.**<br>• Turn ignition switch to RUN.<br>• Using a voltmeter, check voltage at each glow plug lead. Minimum of 11 volts at each lead for 6 seconds, then drops to 4.2 to 5.3 volts. | Voltage OK ▶ | REMOVE jumper from coolant thermoswitch. GO to F13 . |
| | No voltage ▶ | GO to F1 . |
| | No voltage at 3 or less glow plugs ▶ | REPLACE glow plug harness. REPEAT Test Step F0 . |
| | Voltage is OK for 6 seconds, then drops to zero ▶ | GO to F6 . |
| | Voltage is OK for 6 seconds, then remains at a minimum of 11V ▶ | REPLACE glow plug control module. |
| **F1** ENGINE HARNESS TO GLOW PLUG HARNESS | | |
| • Disconnect glow plug harness from engine harness and glow plugs.<br>• Connect a self-powered test lamp between glow plug harness connector and each glow plug terminal. | Test lamp lights ▶ | RECONNECT glow plug harness. GO to F2 . |
| | Test lamp does not light ▶ | SERVICE or REPLACE glow plug harness. REPEAT Test Step F0 . |
| **F2** TERMINAL 6 (POWER CIRCUIT) | | |
| • Connect a 12 volt test lamp between glow plug control module terminal No. 6 and ground.<br>• Turn ignition switch to RUN. | Test lamp lights ▶ | GO to F3 . |
| | Test lamp does not light ▶ | SERVICE and/or REPLACE ignition switch and/or wiring as necessary. REPEAT Test Step F0 . |

86705300

## Glow Plug Control System

| TEST STEP | RESULT ▶ | ACTION TO TAKE |
|---|---|---|
| **F3** TERMINAL 2 (NO. 1 GLOW PLUG RELAY SIGNAL) <br><br>• Connect a 12 volt test lamp between glow plug control module terminal No. 2 (signal) and ground. <br>• Turn ignition switch to RUN. | Test lamp lights for 6 seconds ▶ <br><br> Test lamp does not light ▶ | GO to **F4**. <br><br> REPLACE quick start control unit. REPEAT Test Step **F3**. |
| **F4** NO. 1 GLOW PLUG RELAY WIRING <br><br>• Connect a 12 volt test lamp between No. 1 glow plug relay signal terminal and ground. <br>• Turn ignition to RUN. | Test lamp lights for 6 seconds ▶ <br><br> Test lamp does not light ▶ | GO to **F5**. <br><br> SERVICE or REPLACE wiring between quick start control unit terminal 2 and No. 1 glow plug relay. REPEAT Test Step **F4**. |
| **F5** NO. 1 GLOW PLUG RELAY <br><br>• Connect a voltmeter between No. 1 glow plug relay output terminal (to glow plugs) and ground. <br>• Turn ignition switch to RUN. | 11 volts or more for 6 seconds ▶ <br><br> Less than 11 volts ▶ | GO to **F12**. <br><br> REPLACE No. 1 glow plug relay. REPEAT Test Step **F5**. |
| **F6** TERMINAL NO. 3 (NO. 2 GLOW PLUG RELAY SIGNAL) <br><br>• Connect a 12 volt test lamp between glow plug control module terminal No. 3 (signal) and ground. <br>• Turn ignition switch to RUN. | Test lamp lights ▶ <br><br> Test lamp does not light ▶ | GO to **F8**. <br><br> GO to **F7**. |

# Glow Plug Control System

| TEST STEP | RESULT ▶ | ACTION TO TAKE |
|---|---|---|
| **F7** CLUTCH SWITCH/NEUTRAL SWITCH | | |
| • Using a self-powered test lamp, check the functioning of clutch and neutral switch in both open and closed positions.<br>• With transmission in gear and clutch pedal released, both switches should be open.<br>• With transmission in Neutral and clutch pedal depressed, both switches should be closed. | ⓄⓀ ▶<br><br>⨂ⓄⓀ ▶ | GO to F8.<br><br>REPLACE malfunctioning clutch or neutral switch. REPEAT Test Step F7. |
| **F8** NO. 2 GLOW PLUG RELAY WIRING | | |
| • Connect a 12 volt test lamp between No. 2 glow plug relay signal terminal and ground.<br>• Place transmission gear selector in Neutral.<br>• Turn ignition switch to RUN. | Test lamp lights ▶<br><br>Test lamp does not light ▶ | GO to F9.<br><br>SERVICE or REPLACE wiring between glow plug control module terminal No. 3 and No. 2 glow plug relay. REPEAT Test Step F8. |
| **F9** NO. 2 GLOW PLUG RELAY | | |
| • Connect a 12 volt test lamp between No. 2 glow plug relay output terminal (to glow plugs) and ground.<br>• Turn ignition to RUN. | Test lamp lights ▶<br><br>Test lamp does not light ▶ | GO to F10.<br><br>REPLACE No. 2 glow plug relay. REPEAT Test Step F9. |
| **F10** DROPPING RESISTOR WIRING | | |
| • Disconnect dropping resistor from wiring harness.<br>• Connect a 12 volt test lamp between the dropping resistor input terminal on wiring harness and ground.<br>• Turn ignition to RUN. | Test lamp lights ▶<br><br>Test lamp does not light ▶ | GO to F11.<br><br>SERVICE or REPLACE wiring between No. 2 glow plug relay and dropping resistor. REPEAT Test Step F10. |

86705302

# Glow Plug Control System

| TEST STEP | RESULT ▶ | ACTION TO TAKE |
|---|---|---|
| **F11   DROPPING RESISTOR**<br><br>• Connect an ohmmeter to the connector terminals on the resistor.<br>• Set multiply by knob to X1.<br>• Ohmmeter should indicate less than 1 ohm. | (OK) ▶<br><br><br><br>(not OK) ▶ | RECONNECT dropping resistor to wiring harness. GO to [F12].<br><br>REPLACE dropping resistor. REPEAT Test Step [F11]. |
| **F12   GLOW PLUG HARNESS**<br><br>• Connect a 12 volt test lamp between any glow plug terminal and ground.<br>• Turn ignition to RUN. | Test lamp lights ▶<br><br>Test lamp does not light ▶ | GO to [F0].<br><br>SERVICE or REPLACE wiring from No. 1 glow plug relay to glow plug harness. REPEAT Test Step [F12]. |
| **F13   GLOW PLUGS**<br><br>• Disconnect leads from each glow plug.<br>• Connect one lead of ohmmeter to glow plug terminal and one lead to a good ground.<br>• Set ohmmeter multiply by knob to X1.<br>• Test each glow plug. | Meter indicates less than one ohm ▶<br><br><br><br>Meter indicates one ohm or more ▶ | Problem is not in glow plug system.<br><br><br><br>REPLACE glow plug. REPEAT Test Step [F13]. |

86705303

## TORQUE SPECIFICATIONS – CARBURETOR

| Component | U.S. | Metric |
|---|---|---|
| Air Horn Attaching Screws: | 45 inch lbs. | 5 Nm |
| Carburetor-to-intake Manifold Attaching Nuts: | 20 ft. lbs. | 27 Nm |
| Choke Lever Screws: | 10 inch lbs. | 1.1 Nm |
| Fuel Inlet Fitting: | 150 inch lbs. | 17 Nm |
| Fuel Lines-to-Fuel Pump Outlet Fittings: | 15–18 ft. lbs. | 20–24 Nm |
| Fuel Pump-to-Engine Block: | 11–19 ft. lbs. | 15–25 Nm |
| Main System Feedback | | |
|   Valve: | 20 inch lbs. | 2.3 Nm |
|   Diaphragm and Actuator: | 4–5 inch lbs. | .45–.55 Nm |
| Pulldown Diaphragm Retaining Screws: | 45 inch lbs. | 5 Nm |
| Throttle Position Sensor Retaining Screws: | 45 inch lbs. | 5 Nm |
| Vacuum Gradient Power Enrichment | | |
|   Valve: | 20 inch lbs. | 2.3 Nm |
|   Diaphragm and Actuator: | 8 inch lbs. | .9 Nm |
| WOT Pullover Enrichment Valve: | 20 inch lbs. | 2.3 Nm |

86705666

# 6

# CHASSIS ELECTRICAL

## UNDERSTANDING AND TROUBLESHOOTING ELECTRICAL SYSTEMS

Most vehicles covered by this manual (all cars which are equipped with fuel injected and all feedback carbureted engines) utilize one or more on–board computer. These electronic components (with no moving parts) should theoretically last the life of the vehicle, provided nothing external happens to damage the circuits or memory chips.

While it is true that electronic components should never wear out, in the real world malfunctions do occur. It is also true that any computer–based system is extremely sensitive to electrical voltages and cannot tolerate careless or haphazard testing or service procedures. An inexperienced individual can literally do major damage looking for a minor problem by using the wrong kind of test equipment or connecting test leads or connectors with the ignition switch ON. When selecting test equipment, make sure the manufacturers instructions state that the tester is compatible with whatever type of electronic control system is being serviced. Read all instructions carefully and double check all test points before installing probes or making any test connections.

The following section outlines basic diagnosis techniques for dealing with computerized automotive control systems. Along with a general explanation of the various types of test equipment available to aid in servicing modern electronic automotive systems, basic repair techniques for wiring harnesses and connectors is given. Read the basic information before attempting any repairs or testing on any computerized system, to provide the background of information necessary to avoid the most common and obvious mistakes that can cost both time and money. Although the replacement and testing procedures are simple in themselves, the systems are not, and unless one has a thorough understanding of all components and their function within a particular computerized control system, the logical test sequence these systems demand cannot be followed. Minor malfunctions can make a big difference, so it is important to know how each component affects the operation of the overall electronic system to find the ultimate cause of a problem without replacing good components unnecessarily. It is not enough to use the correct test equipment; the test equipment must be used correctly.

### Safety Precautions

### ✳✳CAUTION

**Whenever working on or around any computer based microprocessor control system, always observe these general precautions to prevent the possibility of personal injury or damage to electronic components.**

• Never install or remove battery cables with the key ON or the engine running. Jumper cables should be connected with the key OFF to avoid power surges that can damage electronic control units. Engines equipped with computer controlled systems should avoid both giving and getting jump starts due to the possibility of serious damage to components from arcing in the engine compartment when connections are made with the ignition ON.

• Always remove the battery cables before charging the battery. Never use a high output charger on an installed battery or attempt to use any type of "hot shot (24 volt) starting aid.

• Exercise care when inserting test probes into connectors to insure good connections without damaging the connector or spreading the pins. Always probe connectors from the rear (wire) side, NOT the pin side, to avoid accidental shorting of terminals during test procedures.

• Never remove or attach wiring harness connectors with the ignition switch ON, especially to an electronic control unit.

• Do not drop any components during service procedures and never apply 12 volts directly to any component (like a solenoid or relay) unless instructed specifically to do so. Some component electrical windings are designed to safely handle only 4 or 5 volts and can be destroyed in seconds if 12 volts are applied directly to the connector.

• Remove the electronic control unit if the vehicle is to be placed in an environment where temperatures exceed approximately 176°F (80°C), such as a paint spray booth or when arc or gas welding near the control unit location in the vehicle.

### Organized Troubleshooting

When diagnosing a specific problem, organized troubleshooting is a must. The complexity of a modern automobile demands that you approach any problem in a logical, organized manner. There are certain troubleshooting techniques that are standard:

1. Establish when the problem occurs. Does the problem appear only under certain conditions? Were there any noises, odors, or other unusual symptoms?

2. Isolate the problem area. To do this, make some simple tests and observations; then eliminate the systems that are working properly. Check for obvious problems such as broken wires, dirty connections or split or disconnected vacuum hoses. Always check the obvious before assuming something complicated is the cause.

3. Test for problems systematically to determine the cause once the problem area is isolated. Are all the components functioning properly? Is there power going to electrical switches and motors? Is there vacuum at vacuum switches and/or actuators? Is there a mechanical problem such as bent linkage or loose mounting screws? Doing careful, systematic checks will often turn up most causes on the first inspection without wasting time checking components that have little or no relationship to the problem.

4. Test all repairs after the work is done to make sure that the problem is fixed. Some causes can be traced to more than one component, so a careful verification of repair work is important to pick up additional malfunctions that may cause a problem to reappear or a different problem to arise. A blown fuse, for example, is a simple problem that may require more than another fuse to repair. If you don't look for a problem that caused a fuse to blow, for example, a shorted wire may go undetected.

Experience has shown that most problems tend to be the result of a fairly simple and obvious cause, such as loose or corroded connectors or air leaks in the intake system; making careful inspection of components during testing essential to quick and accurate troubleshooting. Special, hand held computerized testers designed specifically for diagnosing the EEC–IV system are available from a variety of after market sources, as well as from the vehicle manufacturer, but care should be taken that any test equipment being used is designed to diagnose that particular computer controlled system accurately without damaging the control unit (ECU) or components being tested.

➡ **Pinpointing the exact cause of trouble in an electrical system can sometimes only be accomplished by the use of special test equipment. The following describes commonly used test equipment and explains how to put it to best use in diagnosis. In addition to the information covered below, the manufacturer's instructions booklet provided with the tester should be read and clearly understood before attempting any test procedures.**

## Test Equipment

### JUMPER WIRES

Jumper wires are simple, yet extremely valuable, pieces of test equipment. Jumper wires are merely wires that are used to bypass sections of a circuit. The simplest type of jumper wire is merely a length of multistrand wire with an alligator clip at each end. Jumper wires are usually fabricated from lengths of standard automotive wire and whatever type of connector (alligator clip, spade connector or pin connector) that is required for the particular vehicle being tested. The well equipped tool box will have several different styles of jumper wires in several different lengths. Some jumper wires are made with three or more terminals coming from a common splice for special purpose testing. In cramped, hard-to-reach areas it is advisable to have insulated boots over the jumper wire terminals in order to prevent accidental grounding, sparks, and possible fire, especially when testing fuel system components.

Jumper wires are used primarily to locate open electrical circuits, on either the ground (–) side of the circuit or on the hot (+) side. If an electrical component fails to operate, connect the jumper wire between the component and a good ground. If the component operates only with the jumper installed, the ground circuit is open. If the ground circuit is good, but the component does not operate, the circuit between the power feed and component is open. You can sometimes connect the jumper wire directly from the battery to the hot terminal of the component, but first make sure the component uses 12 volts in operation. Some electrical components, such as fuel injectors, are designed to operate on about 4 volts and running 12 volts directly to the injector terminals can burn out the wiring. By inserting an inline fuse holder between a set of test leads, a fused jumper wire can be used for bypassing open circuits. Use a 5 amp fuse to provide protection against voltage spikes. When in doubt, use a voltmeter to check the voltage input to the component and measure how much voltage is being applied normally. By moving the jumper wire successively back from the lamp toward the power source, you can isolate the area of the circuit where the open is located. When the component stops

functioning, or the power is cut off, the open is in the segment of wire between the jumper and the point previously tested.

### ✳✳CAUTION

**Never use jumpers made from wire that is of lighter gauge than used in the circuit under test. If the jumper wire is of too small gauge, it may overheat and possibly melt. Never use jumpers to bypass high resistance loads (such as motors) in a circuit. Bypassing resistances, in effect, creates a short circuit which may, in turn, cause damage and fire. Never use a jumper for anything other than temporary bypassing of components in a circuit.**

### 12 VOLT TEST LIGHT

The 12 volt test light is used to check circuits and components while electrical current is flowing through them. It is used for voltage and ground tests. Twelve volt test lights come in different styles but all have three main parts; a ground clip, a probe, and a light. The most commonly used 12 volt test lights have pick–type probes. To use a 12 volt test light, connect the ground clip to a good ground and probe wherever necessary with the pick. The pick should be sharp so that it can penetrate wire insulation to make contact with the wire, without making a large hole in the insulation. The wrap–around light is handy in hard to reach areas or where it is difficult to support a wire to push a probe pick into it. To use the wrap around light, hook the wire to probed with the hook and pull the trigger. A small pick will be forced through the wire insulation into the wire core.

### ✳✳CAUTION

**Do not use a test light to probe electronic ignition spark plug or coil wires. Never use a pick–type test light to probe wiring on computer controlled systems unless specifically instructed to do so. Any wire insulation that is pierced by the test light probe should be taped and sealed with silicone after testing.**

Like the jumper wire, the 12 volt test light is used to isolate opens in circuits. But, whereas the jumper wire is used to bypass the open to operate the load, the 12 volt test light is used to locate the presence of voltage in a circuit. If the test light glows, you know that there is power up to that point; if the 12 volt test light does not glow when its probe is inserted into the wire or connector, you know that there is an open circuit (no power). Move the test light in successive steps back toward the power source until the light in the handle does glow. When it does glow, the open is between the probe and point previously probed.

➡ **The test light does not detect that 12 volts (or any particular amount of voltage) is present; it only detects that some voltage is present. It is advisable before using the test light to touch its terminals across the battery posts to make sure the light is operating properly.**

## SELF–POWERED TEST LIGHT

The self–powered test light usually contains a 1.5 volt penlight battery. One type of self–powered test light is similar in design to the 12 volt test light. This type has both the battery and the light in the handle and pick–type probe tip. The second type has the light toward the open tip, so that the light illuminates the contact point. The self–powered test light is dual purpose piece of test equipment. It can be used to test for either open or short circuits when power is isolated from the circuit (continuity test). A powered test light should not be used on any computer controlled system or component unless specifically instructed to do so. Many engine sensors can be destroyed by even this small amount of voltage applied directly to the terminals.

### Open Circuit Testing

To use the self–powered test light to check for open circuits, first isolate the circuit from the vehicle's 12 volt power source by disconnecting the battery or wiring harness connector. Connect the test light ground clip to a good ground and probe sections of the circuit sequentially with the test light. (start from either end of the circuit). If the light is out, the open is between the probe and the circuit ground. If the light is on, the open is between the probe and end of the circuit toward the power source.

### Short Circuit Testing

By isolating the circuit both from power and from ground, and using a self–powered test light, you can check for shorts to ground in the circuit. Isolate the circuit from power and ground. Connect the test light ground clip to a good ground and probe any easy–to–reach test point in the circuit. If the light comes on, there is a short somewhere in the circuit. To isolate the short, probe a test point at either end of the isolated circuit (the light should be on). Leave the test light probe connected and open connectors, switches, remove parts, etc., sequentially, until the light goes out. When the light goes out, the short is between the last circuit component opened and the previous circuit opened.

➡ **The 1.5 volt battery in the test light does not provide much current. A weak battery may not provide enough power to illuminate the test light even when a complete circuit is made (especially if there are high resistances in the circuit). Always make sure that the test battery is strong. To check the battery, briefly touch the ground clip to the probe; if the light glows brightly the battery is strong enough for testing. Never use a self–powered test light to perform checks for opens or shorts when power is applied to the electrical system under test. The 12 volt vehicle power will quickly burn out the 1.5 volt light bulb in the test light.**

## VOLTMETER

A voltmeter is used to measure voltage at any point in a circuit, or to measure the voltage drop across any part of a circuit. It can also be used to check continuity in a wire or circuit by indicating current flow from one end to the other. Voltmeters usually have various scales on the meter dial and a selector switch to allow the selection of different voltages. The voltmeter has a positive and a negative lead. To avoid damage to the meter, always connect the negative lead to the negative (–) side of circuit (to ground or nearest the ground side of the circuit) and connect the positive lead to the positive (+) side of the circuit (to the power source or the nearest power source). Note that the negative voltmeter lead will always be black and that the positive voltmeter will always be some color other than black (usually red). Depending on how the voltmeter is connected into the circuit, it has several uses.

A voltmeter can be connected either in parallel or in series with a circuit and it has a very high resistance to current flow. When connected in parallel, only a small amount of current will flow through the voltmeter current path; the rest will flow through the normal circuit current path and the circuit will work normally. When the voltmeter is connected in series with a circuit, only a small amount of current can flow through the circuit. The circuit will not work properly, but the voltmeter reading will show if the circuit is complete or not.

### Available Voltage Measurement

Set the voltmeter selector switch to the 20V position and connect the meter negative lead to the negative post of the battery. Connect the positive meter lead to the positive post of the battery and turn the ignition switch ON to provide a load. Read the voltage on the meter or digital display. A well charged battery should register over 12 volts. If the meter reads below 11.5 volts, the battery power may be insufficient to operate the electrical system properly. This test determines voltage available from the battery and should be the first step in any electrical trouble diagnosis procedure. Many electrical problems, especially on computer controlled systems, can be caused by a low state of charge in the battery. Excessive corrosion at the battery cable terminals can cause a poor contact that will prevent proper charging and full battery current flow.

Normal battery voltage is 12 volts when fully charged. When the battery is supplying current to one or more circuits it is said to be "under load. When everything is off the electrical system is under a "no–load condition. A fully charged battery may show about 12.5 volts at no load; will drop to 12 volts under medium load; and will drop even lower under heavy load. If the battery is partially discharged the voltage decrease under heavy load may be excessive, even though the battery shows 12 volts or more at no load. When allowed to discharge further, the battery's available voltage under load will decrease more severely. For this reason, it is important that the battery be fully charged during all testing procedures to avoid errors in diagnosis and incorrect test results.

### Voltage Drop

When current flows through a resistance, the voltage beyond the resistance is reduced (the larger the current, the greater the reduction in voltage). When no current is flowing, there is no voltage drop because there is no current flow. All points in the circuit which are connected to the power source are at the same voltage as the power source. The total voltage drop always equals the total source voltage. In a long circuit with many connectors, a series of small, unwanted voltage drops due to corrosion at the connectors can add up to a total loss of voltage which impairs the operation of the normal loads in the circuit.

### INDIRECT COMPUTATION OF VOLTAGE DROPS

1. Set the voltmeter selector switch to the 20 volt position.

2. Connect the meter negative lead to a good ground.

3. Probe all resistances in the circuit with the positive meter lead.

4. Operate the circuit in all modes and observe the voltage readings.

## DIRECT MEASUREMENT OF VOLTAGE DROPS

5. Set the voltmeter switch to the 20 volt position.

6. Connect the voltmeter negative lead to the ground side of the resistance load to be measured.

7. Connect the positive lead to the positive side of the resistance or load to be measured.

8. Read the voltage drop directly on the 20 volt scale.

Too high a voltage indicates too high a resistance. If, for example, a blower motor runs too slowly, you can determine if there is too high a resistance in the resistor pack. By taking voltage drop readings in all parts of the circuit, you can isolate the problem. Too low a voltage drop indicates too low a resistance. If, for example, a blower motor runs too fast in the MED and/or LOW position, the problem can be isolated in the resistor pack by taking voltage drop readings in all parts of the circuit to locate a possibly shorted resistor. The maximum allowable voltage drop under load is critical, especially if there is more than one high resistance problem in a circuit because all voltage drops are cumulative. A small drop is normal due to the resistance of the conductors.

## HIGH RESISTANCE TESTING

1. Set the voltmeter selector switch to the 4 volt position.

2. Connect the voltmeter positive lead to the positive post of the battery.

3. Turn on the headlights and heater blower to provide a load.

4. Probe various points in the circuit with the negative voltmeter lead.

5. Read the voltage drop on the 4 volt scale. Some average maximum allowable voltage drops are:

- FUSE PANEL—0.7 volts
- IGNITION SWITCH—0.5 volts
- HEADLIGHT SWITCH—0.7 volts
- IGNITION COIL (+)—0.5 volts
- ANY OTHER LOAD—1.3 volts

➡ **Voltage drops are all measured while a load is operating; without current flow, there will be no voltage drop.**

# OHMMETER

The ohmmeter is designed to read resistance (ohms) in a circuit or component. Although there are several different styles of ohm meters, all will usually have a selector switch which permits the measurement of different ranges of resistance (usually the selector switch allows the multiplication of the meter reading by 10, 100, 1000, and 10,000). A calibration knob allows the meter to be set at zero for accurate measurement. Since all ohmmeters are powered by an internal battery (usually 9 volts), the ohm meter can be used as a self-powered test light. When the ohm meter is connected, current from the ohm meter flows through the circuit or component being tested. Since the ohmmeter's internal resistance and voltage are known

values, the amount of current flow through the meter depends on the resistance of the circuit or component being tested.

The ohmmeter can be used to perform continuity test for opens or shorts (either by observation of the meter needle or as a self-powered test light), and to read actual resistance in a circuit. It should be noted that the ohm meter is used to check the resistance of a component or wire while there is no voltage applied to the circuit. Current flow from an outside voltage source (such as the vehicle battery) can damage the ohmmeter, so the circuit or component should be isolated from the vehicle electrical system before any testing is done. Since the ohmmeter uses its own voltage source, either lead can be connected to any test point.

➡ **When checking diodes or other solid state components, the ohm meter leads can only be connected one way in order to measure current flow in a single direction. Make sure the positive (+) and negative (−) terminal connections are as described in the test procedures to verify the one-way diode operation.**

In using the meter for making continuity checks, do not be concerned with the actual resistance readings. Zero resistance, or any resistance readings, indicate continuity in the circuit. Infinite resistance indicates an open in the circuit. A high resistance reading where there should be none indicates a problem in the circuit. Checks for short circuits are made in the same manner as checks for open circuits except that the circuit must be isolated from both power and normal ground. Infinite resistance indicates no continuity to ground, while zero resistance indicates a dead short to ground.

## Resistance Measurement

The batteries in an ohmmeter will weaken with age and temperature, so the ohmmeter must be calibrated or "zeroed before taking measurements. To zero the meter, place the selector switch in its lowest range and touch the two ohmmeter leads together. Turn the calibration knob until the meter needle is exactly on zero.

➡ **All analog (needle) type ohmmeters must be zeroed before use, but some digital ohmmeter models are automatically calibrated when the switch is turned on. Self-calibrating digital ohmmeters do not have an adjusting knob, but its a good idea to check for a zero readout before use by touching the leads together. All computer controlled systems require the use of a digital ohmmeter with at least 10 megohms impedance for testing. Before any test procedures are attempted, make sure the ohmmeter used is compatible with the electrical system or damage to the on-board computer could result.**

To measure resistance, first isolate the circuit from the vehicle power source by disconnecting the battery cables or the harness connector. Make sure the key is OFF when disconnecting any components or the battery. Where necessary, also isolate at least one side of the circuit to be checked to avoid reading parallel resistances. Parallel circuit resistances will always give a lower reading than the actual resistance of either of the branches. When measuring the resistance of parallel circuits, the total resistance will always be lower than the smallest resistance in the circuit. Connect the meter leads to both sides to the proper ohm scale for the circuit being tested to avoid misreading the ohmmeter test value.

**✳✳CAUTION**

Never use an ohmmeter with power applied to the circuit. Like the self-powered test light, the ohmmeter is designed to operate on its own power supply. The normal 12 volt automotive electrical system current could damage the meter.

## AMMETERS

An ammeter measures the amount of current flowing through a circuit in units called amperes or amps. Amperes are units of electron flow which indicate how fast the electrons are flowing through the circuit. Since Ohms Law dictates that current flow in a circuit is equal to the circuit voltage divided by the total circuit resistance, increasing voltage also increases the current level (amps). Likewise, any decrease in resistance will increase the amount of amps in a circuit. At normal operating voltage, most circuits have a characteristic amount of amperes, called "current draw which can be measured using an ammeter. By referring to a specified current draw rating, measuring the amperes, and comparing the two values, one can determine what is happening within the circuit to aid in diagnosis. An open circuit, for example, will not allow any current to flow so the ammeter reading will be zero. More current flows through a heavily loaded circuit or when the charging system is operating.

An ammeter is always connected in series with the circuit being tested. All of the current that normally flows through the circuit must also flow through the ammeter; if there is any other path for the current to follow, the ammeter reading will not be accurate. The ammeter itself has very little resistance to current flow and therefore will not affect the circuit, but it will measure current draw only when the circuit is closed and electricity is flowing. Excessive current draw can blow fuses and drain the battery, while a reduced current draw can cause motors to run slowly, lights to dim and other components to not operate properly. The ammeter can help diagnose these conditions by locating the cause of the high or low reading.

## MULTIMETERS

Different combinations of test meters can be built into a single unit designed for specific tests. Some of the more common combination test devices are known as Volt/Amp testers, Tach/Dwell meters, or Digital Multimeters. The Volt/Amp tester is used for charging system, starting system or battery tests and consists of a voltmeter, an ammeter and a variable resistance carbon pile. The voltmeter will usually have at least two ranges for use with 6, 12 and 24 volt systems. The ammeter also has more than one range for testing various levels of battery loads and starter current draw and the carbon pile can be adjusted to offer different amounts of resistance. The Volt/Amp tester has heavy leads to carry large amounts of current and many later models have an inductive ammeter pickup that clamps around the wire to simplify test connections. On some models, the ammeter also has a zero-center scale to allow testing of charging and starting systems without switching leads or polarity. A digital multimeter is a voltmeter, ammeter and ohmmeter combined in an instrument which gives a digital

readout. These are often used when testing solid state circuits because of their high input impedance (usually 10 megohms or more).

The tach/dwell meter combines a tachometer and a dwell (cam angle) meter and is a specialized kind of voltmeter. The tachometer scale is marked to show engine speed in rpm and the dwell scale is marked to show degrees of distributor shaft rotation. In most electronic ignition systems, dwell is determined by the control unit, but the dwell meter can also be used to check the duty cycle (operation) of some electronic engine control systems. Some tach/dwell meters are powered by an internal battery, while others take their power from the car battery in use. The battery powered testers usually require calibration much like an ohmmeter before testing.

## SPECIAL TEST EQUIPMENT

A variety of diagnostic tools are available to help troubleshoot and repair computerized engine control systems. The most sophisticated of these devices are the console type engine analyzers that usually occupy a garage service bay, but there are several types of aftermarket electronic testers available that will allow quick circuit tests of the engine control system by plugging directly into a special connector located in the engine compartment or under the dashboard. Several tool and equipment manufacturers offer simple, hand held testers that measure various circuit voltage levels on command to check all system components for proper operation. Although these testers are usually expensive, consider that the average computer control unit can cost just as much and the money saved by not replacing perfectly good sensors or components in an attempt to correct a problem could justify the purchase price of a special diagnostic tester the first time it's used.

These computerized testers can allow quick and easy test measurements while the engine is operating or while the car is being driven. In addition, the on-board computer memory can be read to access any stored trouble codes; in effect allowing the computer to tell you where it hurts and aid trouble diagnosis by pinpointing exactly which circuit or component is malfunctioning. In the same manner, repairs can be tested to make sure the problem has been corrected. The biggest advantage these special testers have is their relatively easy hookups that minimize or eliminate the chances of making the wrong connections and getting false voltage readings or damaging the computer accidentally.

➡ It should be remembered that these testers check voltage levels in circuits! they don't detect mechanical problems or failed components if the circuit voltage fails within the preprogrammed limits stored in the tester PROM unit. Also, most of the hand held testers are designed to work only on one or two systems made by a specific manufacturer.

A variety of after market testers are available to help diagnose different computerized control systems. Owatonna Tool Company (OTC), for example, markets a device called the OTC Monitor which plugs directly into the assembly line diagnostic link (ALDL). The OTC tester makes diagnosis a simple matter of pressing the correct buttons and, by changing the internal PROM or inserting a different diagnosis cartridge, it will work on any model from full size to subcompact, over a wide range of

PROM or inserting a different diagnosis cartridge, it will work on any model from full size to subcompact, over a wide range of years. An adapter is supplied with the tester to allow connection to all types of ALDL links, regardless of the number of pin terminals used. By inserting an updated PROM into the OTC tester, it can be easily updated to diagnose any new modifications of computerized control systems,

## Wiring Harnesses

The average automobile contains about 1/2 mile of wiring, with hundreds of individual connections. To protect the many wires from damage and to keep them from becoming a confusing tangle, they are organized into bundles, enclosed in plastic or taped together and called wire harnesses. Different wiring harnesses serve different parts of the vehicle. Individual wires are color coded to help trace them through a harness where sections are hidden from view.

A loose or corroded connection or a replacement wire that is too small for the circuit will add extra resistance and an additional voltage drop to the circuit. A ten percent voltage drop can result in slow or erratic motor operation, for example, even though the circuit is complete. Automotive wiring or circuit conductors can be in any one of three forms:

1. Single strand wire
2. Multistrand wire
3. Printed circuitry

Single strand wire has a solid metal core and is usually used inside such components as alternators, motors, relays and other devices. Multistrand wire has a core made of many small strands of wire twisted together into a single conductor. Most of the wiring in an automotive electrical system is made up of multistrand wire, either as a single conductor or grouped together in a harness. All wiring is color coded on the insulator, either as a solid color or as a colored wire with an identification stripe. A printed circuit is a thin film of copper or other conductor that is printed on an insulator backing. Occasionally, a printed circuit is sandwiched between two sheets of plastic for more protection and flexibility. A complete printed circuit, consisting of conductors, insulating material and connectors for lamps or other components is called a printed circuit board. Printed circuitry is used in place of individual wires or harnesses in places where space is limited, such as behind instrument panels.

## WIRE GAUGE

Since computer controlled automotive electrical systems are very sensitive to changes in resistance, the selection of properly sized wires is critical when systems are repaired. The wire gauge number is an expression of the cross section area of the conductor. The most common system for expressing wire size is the American Wire Gauge (AWG) system.

Wire cross section area is measured in circular mils. A mil is 1/1000 in. (0.001 in.); a circular mil is the area of a circle one mil in diameter. For example, a conductor 1/4 in. in diameter is 0.250 in. or 250 mils. The circular mil cross section area of the wire is 250 squared or 62,500 circular mils. Imported car models usually use metric wire gauge designations, which is simply the cross section area of the conductor in square millimeters (mm).

Gauge numbers are assigned to conductors of various cross section areas. As gauge number increases, area decreases and the conductor becomes smaller. A 5 gauge conductor is smaller than a 1 gauge conductor and a 10 gauge is smaller than a 5 gauge. As the cross section area of a conductor decreases, resistance increases and so does the gauge number. A conductor with a higher gauge number will carry less current than a conductor with a lower gauge number.

➡ **Gauge wire size refers to the size of the conductor, not the size of the complete wire. It is possible to have two wires of the same gauge with different diameters because one may have thicker insulation than the other.**

12 volt automotive electrical systems generally use 10, 12, 14, 16 and 18 gauge wire. Main power distribution circuits and larger accessories usually use 10 and 12 gauge wire. Battery cables are usually 4 or 6 gauge, although 1 and 2 gauge wires are occasionally used. Wire length must also be considered when making repairs to a circuit. As conductor length increases, so does resistance. An 18 gauge wire, for example, can carry a 10 amp load for 10 feet without excessive voltage drop; however if a 15 foot wire is required for the same 10 amp load, it must be a 16 gauge wire.

An electrical schematic shows the electrical current paths when a circuit is operating properly. It is essential to understand how a circuit works before trying to figure out why it doesn't. Schematics break the entire electrical system down into individual circuits and show only one particular circuit. In a schematic, no attempt is made to represent wiring and components as they physically appear on the vehicle; switches and other components are shown as simply as possible. Face views of harness connectors show the cavity or terminal locations in all multi–pin connectors to help locate test points.

If you need to backprobe a connector while it is on the component, the order of the terminals must be mentally reversed. The wire color code can help in this situation, as well as a keyway, lock tab or other reference mark.

➡ **Wiring diagrams are not included in this book. As vehicles have become more complex and available with longer option lists, wiring diagrams have grown in size and complexity. It has become almost impossible to provide a readable reproduction of a wiring diagram in a book this size. Information on ordering wiring diagrams from the vehicle manufacturer can be found in the owner's manual.**

## WIRING REPAIR

Soldering is a quick, efficient method of joining metals permanently. Everyone who has the occasion to make wiring repairs should know how to solder. Electrical connections that are soldered are far less likely to come apart and will conduct electricity much better than connections that are only "pig–tailed together. The most popular (and preferred) method of soldering is with an electrical soldering gun. Soldering irons are available in many sizes and wattage ratings. Irons with higher wattage ratings deliver higher temperatures and recover lost heat faster. A small soldering iron rated for no more than 50 watts is recommended, especially on electrical systems where excess heat can damage the components being soldered.

crevices. When soldering, always use a resin flux or resin core solder which is non–corrosive and will not attract moisture once the job is finished. Other types of flux (acid core) will leave a residue that will attract moisture and cause the wires to corrode. Tin is a unique metal with a low melting point. In a molten state, it dissolves and alloys easily with many metals. Solder is made by mixing tin with lead. The most common proportions are 40/60, 50/50 and 60/40, with the percentage of tin listed first. Low priced solders usually contain less tin, making them very difficult for a beginner to use because more heat is required to melt the solder. A common solder is 40/60 which is well suited for all–around general use, but 60/40 melts easier, has more tin for a better joint and is preferred for electrical work.

### Soldering Techniques

Successful soldering requires that the metals to be joined be heated to a temperature that will melt the solder–usually 360–460°F (182–238°C). Contrary to popular belief, the purpose of the soldering iron is not to melt the solder itself, but to heat the parts being soldered to a temperature high enough to melt the solder when it is touched to the work. Melting flux–cored solder on the soldering iron will usually destroy the effectiveness of the flux.

➡ **Soldering tips are made of copper for good heat conductivity, but must be "tinned" regularly for quick transference of heat to the project and to prevent the solder from sticking to the iron. To "tin" the iron, simply heat it and touch the flux–cored solder to the tip; the solder will flow over the hot tip. Wipe the excess off with a clean rag, but be careful as the iron will be hot.**

After some use, the tip may become pitted. If so, simply dress the tip smooth with a smooth file and "tin the tip again. An old saying holds that "metals well cleaned are half soldered." Flux–cored solder will remove oxides but rust, bits of insulation and oil or grease must be removed with a wire brush or emery cloth. For maximum strength in soldered parts, the joint must start off clean and tight. Weak joints will result in gaps too wide for the solder to bridge.

If a separate soldering flux is used, it should be brushed or swabbed on only those areas that are to be soldered. Most solders contain a core of flux and separate fluxing is unnecessary. Hold the work to be soldered firmly. It is best to solder on a wooden board, because a metal vise will only rob the piece to be soldered of heat and make it difficult to melt the solder. Hold the soldering tip with the broadest face against the work to be soldered. Apply solder under the tip close to the work, using enough solder to give a heavy film between the iron and the piece being soldered, while moving slowly and making sure the solder melts properly. Keep the work level or the solder will run to the lowest part and favor the thicker parts, because these require more heat to melt the solder. If the soldering tip overheats (the solder coating on the face of the tip burns up), it should be retinned. Once the soldering is completed, let the soldered joint stand until cool. Tape and seal all soldered wire splices after the repair has cooled.

## WIRE HARNESS AND CONNECTORS

The on–board computer wire harness electrically connects the control unit to the various solenoids, switches and sensors used by the control system. Most connectors in the engine compartment or otherwise exposed to the elements are protected against moisture and dirt which could create oxidation and deposits on the terminals. This protection is important because of the very low voltage and current levels used by the computer and sensors. All connectors have a lock which secures the male and female terminals together, with a secondary lock holding the seal and terminal into the connector. Both terminal locks must be released when disengaging computer connectors.

These special connectors are weather–proof and all repairs require the use of a special terminal and the tool required to service it. This tool is used to remove the pin and sleeve terminals. If removal is attempted with an ordinary pick, there is a good chance that the terminal will be bent or deformed. Unlike standard blade type terminals, these terminals cannot be straightened once they are bent. Make certain that the connectors are properly seated and all of the sealing rings in place when connecting leads. On some models, a hinge–type flap provides a backup or secondary locking feature for the terminals. Most secondary locks are used to improve the connector reliability by retaining the terminals if the small terminal lock tangs are not positioned properly.

Molded–on connectors require complete replacement of the connection. This means splicing a new connector assembly into the harness. All splices in on–board computer systems should be soldered to insure proper contact. Use care when probing the connections or replacing terminals in them as it is possible to short between opposite terminals. If this happens to the wrong terminal pair, it is possible to damage certain components. Always use jumper wires between connectors for circuit checking and never probe through weatherproof seals.

Open circuits are often difficult to locate by sight because corrosion or terminal misalignment are hidden by the connectors. Merely wiggling a connector on a sensor or in the wiring harness may correct the open circuit condition. This should always be considered when an open circuit or a failed sensor is indicated. Intermittent problems may also be caused by oxidized or loose connections. When using a circuit tester for diagnosis, always probe connections from the wire side. Be careful not to damage sealed connectors with test probes.

All wiring harnesses should be replaced with identical parts, using the same gauge wire and connectors. When signal wires are spliced into a harness, use wire with high temperature insulation only. With the low voltage and current levels found in the system, it is important that the best possible connection at all wire splices be made by soldering the splices together. It is seldom necessary to replace a complete harness. If replacement is necessary, pay close attention to insure proper harness routing. Secure the harness with suitable plastic wire clamps to prevent vibrations from causing the harness to wear in spots or contact any hot components.

➡ **Weatherproof connectors cannot be replaced with standard connectors. Instructions are provided with replacement connector and terminal packages. Some wire harnesses have mounting indicators (usually pieces of colored tape) to mark where the harness is to be secured.**

In making wiring repairs, it is important that you always replace damaged wires with wires that are the same gauge as the wire being replaced. The heavier the wire, the smaller the prevent vibrations from causing the harness to wear in spots or contact any hot components.

➡ **Weatherproof connectors cannot be replaced with standard connectors. Instructions are provided with replacement connector and terminal packages. Some wire harnesses have mounting indicators (usually pieces of colored tape) to mark where the harness is to be secured.**

In making wiring repairs, it is important that you always replace damaged wires with wires that are the same gauge as the wire being replaced. The heavier the wire, the smaller the gauge number. Wires are color–coded to aid in identification and whenever possible the same color coded wire should be used for replacement. A wire stripping and crimping tool is necessary to install solderless terminal connectors. Test all crimps by pulling on the wires; it should not be possible to pull the wires out of a good crimp.

Wires which are open, exposed or otherwise damaged are repaired by simple splicing. Where possible, if the wiring harness is accessible and the damaged place in the wire can be located, it is best to open the harness and check for all possible damage. In an inaccessible harness, the wire must be bypassed with a new insert, usually taped to the outside of the old harness,

When replacing fusible links, be sure to use fusible link wire, NOT ordinary automotive wire. Make sure the fusible segment is of the same gauge and construction as the one being replaced and double the stripped end when crimping the terminal connector for a good contact. The melted (open) fusible link segment of the wiring harness should be cut off as close to the harness as possible, then a new segment spliced in as described. In the case of a damaged fusible link that feeds two harness wires, the harness connections should be replaced with two fusible link wires so that each circuit will have its own separate protection.

➡ **Most of the problems caused in the wiring harness are due to bad ground connections. Always check all vehicle ground connections for corrosion or looseness before performing any power feed checks to eliminate the chance of a bad ground affecting the circuit.**

### Repairing Hard Shell Connectors

Unlike molded connectors, the terminal contacts in hard shell connectors can be replaced. Weatherproof hard–shell connectors with the leads molded into the shell have non–replaceable terminal ends. Replacement usually involves the use of a special terminal removal tool that depress the locking fangs (barbs) on the connector terminal and allow the connector to be removed from the rear of the shell. The connector shell should be replaced if it shows any evidence of burning, melting, cracks, or breaks. Replace individual terminals that are burnt, corroded, distorted or loose.

➡ **The insulation crimp must be tight to prevent the insulation from sliding back on the wire when the wire is pulled. The insulation must be visibly compressed under the crimp tabs, and the ends of the crimp should be turned in for a firm grip on the insulation.**

The wire crimp must be made with all wire strands inside the crimp. The terminal must be fully compressed on the wire strands with the ends of the crimp tabs turned in to make a firm grip on the wire. Check all connections with an ohmmeter to insure a good contact. There should be no measurable resistance between the wire and the terminal when connected.

## SUPPLEMENTAL RESTRAINT SYSTEM (SRS or AIR BAG)

### General Information

▶ **See Figure 1**

The Supplemental Restraint System (SRS or Air Bag), is designed to provide addition protection for the driver in addition to that which is provided by the use of a seat belt.

The system is made up of two basic systems. They are the driver's side air bag and the electrical components made up of the impact sensors, backup power supply and electronic air bag diagnostic monitor assembly.

Special attention should be applied when working on a vehicle equipped with an air bag. If for any reason the indicator light in the dash should come on, consult an authorized dealer immediately for complete diagnostic service.

### SYSTEM OPERATION

The Supplemental Restraint System (SRS or Air Bag) provides increased protection for the driver in an accident. The word "supplemental is key, as the air bag is designed to be used in addition to the seat belts. In the event of an accident, the air bag will be the most effective if the vehicle occupant(s) is held in position by the seat belts.

### SYSTEM COMPONENTS

The air bag consists of two subsystems: the driver's air bag, and the electrical system, which includes the impact sensors and electronic diagnostic monitor.

➡ **For removal and installation procedures, refer to section 8.**

#### Air Bag Module

▶ **See Figure 2**

The air bag module consists of: the inflator, bag assembly, a mounting plate or housing, and a trim cover.

➡ **The air bag module components cannot be serviced. The air bag module is only serviced as a complete assembly.**

#### *INFLATOR*

Inside the inflator is an igniter. When the impact sensors detects a crash and the sensor contacts close, battery power flows to the igniter, which then converts the electrical energy to thermal (heat) energy, igniting the sodium azide/copper oxide gas inside the air bag. The combustion process produces nitrogen gas, which inflates the air bag.

## AIR BAG

The driver's air bag is constructed of neoprene coated nylon. Fill volume of the air bag is 2.3 cubic feet.

## MOUNTING PLATE/HOUSING

A mounting plate and retainer ring attach and seal the driver air bag to the inflator. The mounting plate is used to attach the trim cover and to mount the entire module to the steering wheel.

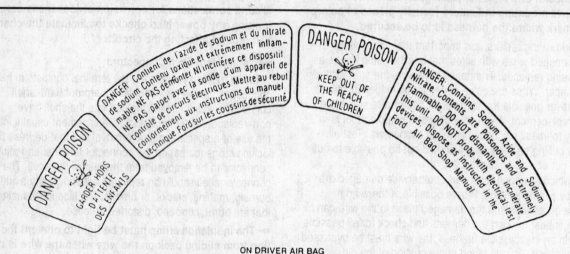

DANGER POISON
KEEP OUT OF THE REACH OF CHILDREN

DANGER: Contains Sodium Azide and Sodium Nitrate. Contents are Poisonous and Extremely Flammable. DO NOT dismantle or incinerate this unit. DO NOT probe with electrical test devices. Dispose as instructed in the Ford Air Bag Shop Manual.

DANGER: Contient de l'azide de sodium et du nitrate de sodium Contenu toxique et extrêmement inflammable NE PAS démonter NI incinérer ce dispositif NE PAS palper avec la sonde d'un appareil de contrôle de circuits électriques Mettre au rebut conformément aux instructions du manuel technique Ford sur les coussins de sécurité

DANGER POISON
GARDER HORS D'ATTEINTE DES ENFANTS

**ON DRIVER AIR BAG**

### ⚠WARNING

**DO NOT TAMPER WITH OR DISCONNECT THE AIR BAG SYSTEM WIRING.** You could inflate the bag(s) or make it inoperative which may result in injury. See Shop Manual.

### ⚠ AVERTISSEMENT

**NE PAS MANIPULER NI DÉBRANCHER LE CÂBLAGE ÉLECTRIQUE DU DISPOSITIF D'UN SAC GONFLABLE.** Cela pourrait gonfler lè sac gonflable ou le mettre hors service et entraîner des blessures. Voir le manuel de réparation.

F40B-5400014-AA

This vehicle has an AIR BAG for the driver.

### ⚠ WARNING  YOU NEED YOUR SAFETY BELT, EVEN WITH AN AIR BAG, AND HERE'S WHY:

- Air bags are not designed to inflate in rollovers or in rear, side, or low speed frontal crashes.

- Air bags inflate with great force, faster than the blink of an eye. If you're too close to an inflating air bag, it could seriously injure you. Safety belts help keep you in position for air bag inflation in a crash.

REGULAR MAINTENANCE OF THE AIR BAG SYSTEM IS NOT REQUIRED. If the air bag readiness light comes on while you're driving, or doesn't come on when you first start your vehicle, see your dealer for service.

See your Owner Guide for more information.

Ce véhicule est équipé d'un SAC GONFLABLE pour le conducteur.

### ⚠ AVERTISSEMENT  IL FAUT CONTINUER À BOUCLER SA CEINTURE DE SÉCURITÉ POUR LES RAISONS SUIVANTES:

- Les sacs gonflables ne sont pas conçus pour se déployer lors d'un capotage, d'impacts latéraux ou à l'arrière, ou de collisions frontales à faibles vitesses.

- Les sacs gonflables se déploient en un clin d'œil et avec grande force. Si vous êtes trop près d'un sac gonflable qui se déploie, vous pourriez subir de graves blessures. La ceinture de sécurité aide à maintenir la position de l'occupant lors du déploiement d'un sac gonflable à la suite d'une collision.

LE SYSTÈME DE RETENUE À SAC GONFLABLE N'EXIGE PAS D'ENTRETIEN PÉRIODIQUE. Si le témoin «air bag» s'allume en cours de route ou ne s'allume pas lorsque le contact est établi initialement, faire vérifier le système par un concessionnaire.

Pour plus de détails, consulter le Guide du propriétaire.

86706001

**Fig. 1 Air bag warning labels**

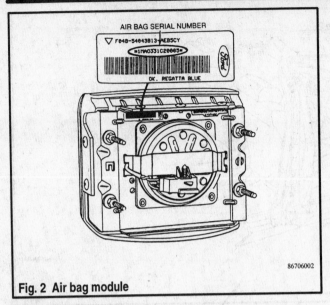

**Fig. 2  Air bag module**

### TRIM COVER

When the driver air bag is activated, tear seams moulded into the steering wheel trim cover separate to allow air bag inflation.

### Diagnostic Monitor

▸ See Figure 3

The diagnostic monitor continually monitors all air bag system components and wiring connections for possible faults. If a fault is detected, a code will be displayed on the air bag warning light, located on the instrument cluster.

The diagnostic monitor illuminates the air bag light for approximately 6 seconds when the ignition switch is turned ON, then turns it off. This indicates that the air bag light is operational. If the air bag light does not illuminate, or if it stays on or flashes at any time, a fault has been detected by the diagnostic monitor.

➡ **If a system fault exists and the air bag light is malfunctioning, an audible tone will be heard indicating the need for service.**

Performing system diagnostics is the main purpose of the diagnostic monitor. The diagnostic monitor does not deploy the air bags in the event of a crash.

### Sensors

▸ See Figures 4, 5, 6 and 7

The sensor is an electrical switch that reacts to impacts according to direction and force. It can discriminate between impacts that do or do not require air bag deployment. When an impact occurs that requires air bag deployment, the sensor contacts close and complete the electrical circuit necessary for system operation.

Four crash sensors are used on air bag equipped vehicles: a dual crash and safing sensor located at the hood latch support, a crash sensor at each of the right and left fender aprons, and a safing sensor at the left–hand cowl side in the passenger compartment.

At least 2 crash sensors, one safing and one front, must be activated to inflate the air bag.

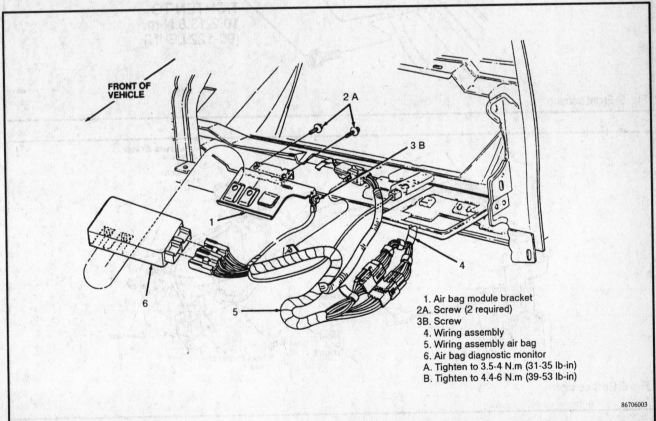

1. Air bag module bracket
2A. Screw (2 required)
3B. Screw
4. Wiring assembly
5. Wiring assembly air bag
6. Air bag diagnostic monitor
A. Tighten to 3.5-4 N.m (31-35 lb-in)
B. Tighten to 4.4-6 N.m (39-53 lb-in)

**Fig. 3  Air bag diagnostic module**

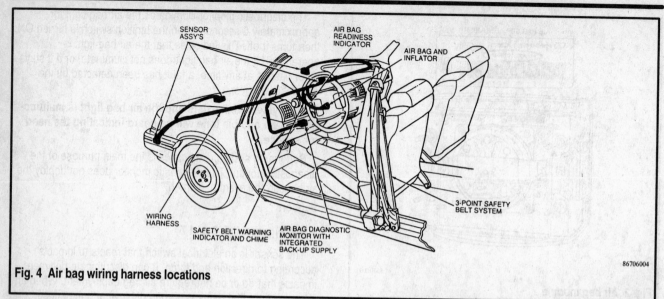

Fig. 4  Air bag wiring harness locations

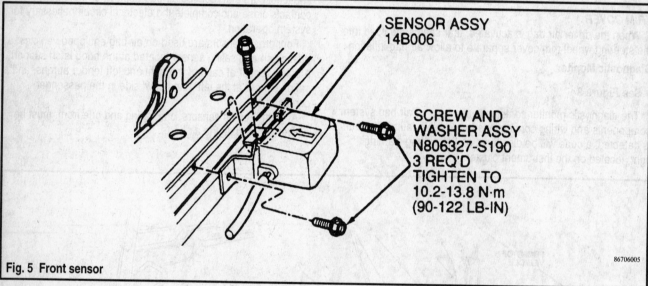

Fig. 5  Front sensor

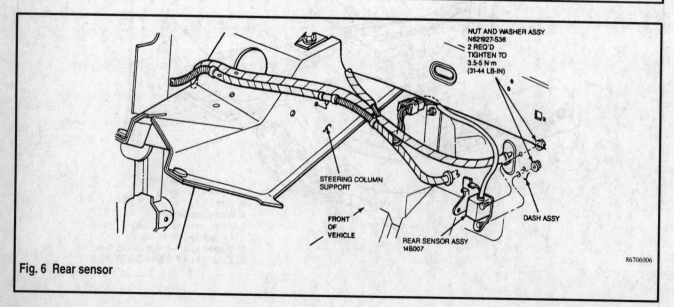

Fig. 6  Rear sensor

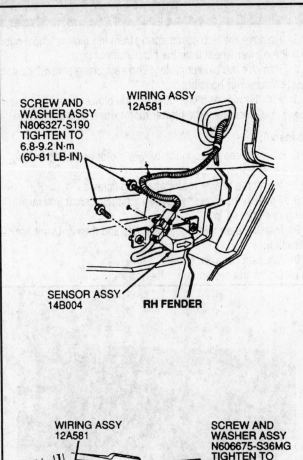

SCREW AND
WASHER ASSY
N806327-S190
TIGHTEN TO
6.8-9.2 N·m
(60-81 LB-IN)

WIRING ASSY
12A581

SENSOR ASSY
14B004

RH FENDER

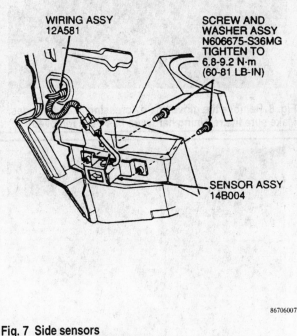

WIRING ASSY
12A581

SCREW AND
WASHER ASSY
N606675-S36MG
TIGHTEN TO
6.8-9.2 N·m
(60-81 LB-IN)

SENSOR ASSY
14B004

86706007

**Fig. 7 Side sensors**

## SERVICE PRECAUTIONS

• Always wear safety glasses when servicing an air bag vehicle, and when handling an air bag.

• Never attempt to service the steering wheel or steering column on an air bag equipped vehicle without first properly disarming the air bag system. The air bag system should be properly disarmed whenever ANY service procedure in this manual indicates that you should do so.

• When carrying a live air bag module, always make sure the bag and trim cover are pointed away from your body. In the unlikely event of an accidental deployment, the bag will then deploy with minimal chance of injury.

• When placing a live air bag on a bench or other surface, always face the bag and trim cover up, away from the surface. This will reduce the motion of the air bag if is accidentally deployed.

• If you should come in contact with a deployed air bag, be advised that the air bag surface may contain deposits of sodium hydroxide, which is a product of the gas generant combustion and is irritating to the skin. Always wear gloves and safety glasses when handling a deployed air bag, and wash your hands with mild soap and water afterwards.

➡ **For removal and installation procedures, refer to section 8.**

## DISARMING THE SYSTEM

1. Disconnect the negative battery cable.
2. Disengage the electrical connector from the backup power supply.

➡ **The backup power supply allows air bag deployment if the battery or battery cables are damaged in an accident before the crash sensors close. The power supply is a capacitor that will leak down in approximately 15 minutes after the battery is disconnected or in 1 minute if the battery positive cable is grounded. It is located in the instrument panel and is combined with the diagnostic monitor. The backup power supply must be disconnected before any air bag related service is performed.**

3. Remove the nut and washer assemblies retaining the driver air bag module to the steering wheel.
4. Disconnect the driver air bag module connector and attach a jumper wire to the air bag terminals on the clockspring.
5. Connect the backup power supply and negative battery cable.

## REACTIVATING THE SYSTEM

➡ **For removal and installation procedures, refer to section 8.**

1. Disconnect the negative battery cable and the backup power supply.
2. Remove the jumper wire from the air bag terminals on the clockspring assembly and reconnect the air bag connector.
3. Position the driver air bag on the steering wheel with the nut and washer assemblies. Tighten the nuts to 24–32 inch lbs. (2.7–3.7 Nm).
4. Connect the backup power supply and negative battery cable. Verify the air bag light.

## HEATING SYSTEM

### Blower Motor

#### REMOVAL & INSTALLATION

♦ See Figures 8, 9, 10, 11, 12, 13 and 14

➡ When draining the coolant, keep in mind that cats and dogs are attracted to ethylene glycol antifreeze, and could drink any that is left in an uncovered container or in puddles on the ground. This will prove fatal in sufficient quantity. Always drain the coolant into a sealable container. Coolant should be reused unless it is contaminated or several years old.

#### With Air Conditioning

1. Disconnect the negative battery cable.
2. Remove the glove compartment door and glove compartment by removing the retaining screws and bolts. Push the sides of the glove box in to free the drawer from dash panel.
3. Loosen the instrument panel at the lower right hand of the glove compartment opening. This is on it necessary if the panel is in the way of the motor housing.
4. Remove the retaining screws securing the ducting around the blower motor.
5. Remove the clip securing the blower motor fan blade to the motor arm. Remove the fan blade from the motor.
6. Remove the blower motor mounting plate from the evaporator case by unscrewing the retaining screws.
7. Rotate the motor until the mounting plate clears the edge of the glove compartment opening and remove the motor.
8. Remove the wire harness from the rear of the motor.
9. Inspect the fan blade for broken edges or cracks. Replace if needed.

#### To install:

10. Connect the wire harness to the rear of the blower motor.
11. Install the motor into the case and secure with the retaining screws.
12. Position and fasten the fan blade to the blower motor arm. Secure with the clip.
13. Secure the blower motor outer housing to the duct assembly with the retaining screws.
14. Install the instrument panel at the lower right hand side if removed earlier.
15. Install the glove compartment door and glove compartment.
16. Connect the negative battery cable.
17. Run blower motors to make the motor works correctly.

#### Without Air Conditioning

1. Disconnect the negative battery cable.
2. Remove the right ventilator assembly.

3. Remove the hub clamp spring from the blower wheel hub. Pull the blower wheel from the blower motor shaft.
4. Remove the blower motor flange attaching screws located inside the blower housing.
5. Pull the blower motor out from the blower housing (heater case) and disconnect the blower motor wires from the motor.

#### To install:

6. Connect the wires to the blower motor and position the motor in the blower housing.
7. Install the blower motor attaching screws.
8. Position the blower wheel on the motor shaft and install the hub clamp spring.
9. Install the air inlet duct assembly and the right ventilator assembly.
10. Connect negative battery cab
11. Check the system for proper operation.

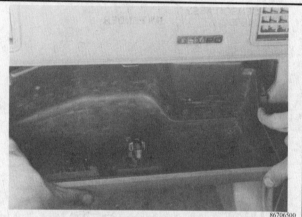

**Fig. 8 Remove the glove box by pressing in on the sides. Make sure the retaining hardware has been removed**

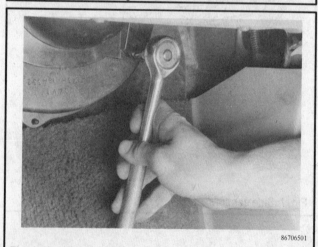

**Fig. 9 Remove the case retaining screws**

Fig. 10 Use a suitable pair of pliers to remove the clip from the fan blade

Fig. 11 Remove the fan blade from the blower motor arm

Fig. 12 Remove the retaining screws securing the blower motor to the interior housing

Fig. 13 Turn the motor and remove

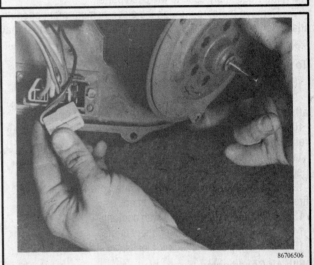

Fig. 14 Unplug the wire harness from the rear of the motor

## Heater Core

Vehicles may be equipped with either a brass or aluminum heater core. All replacement cores are copper/brass. It is important to positively identify the type of core being used because aluminum cores use different heater core–to–heater case seals than the copper/brass cores. Having the proper seal is necessary for proper heating system performance.

Identification can be made by looking at one of the core tubes after one of the hoses has been disconnected. An aluminum core will have a colored tube. A brass core will have a brass colored tube.

If the vehicle is equipped with a copper/brass core, the old core seal may be used for the replacement core, providing that it is not damaged.

If the vehicle is equipped with an aluminum core, a new seal will be required for the replacement core.

## REMOVAL & INSTALLATION

◆ See Figures 15, 16 and 17

➥ In some cases removal of the instrument panel may be helpful or necessary.

### Without Air Conditioning

1. Disconnect the negative battery cable.
2. Drain the coolant system.
3. Disconnect the heater hoses from the core tubes at the firewall, inside the engine compartment. Plug the core tubes to prevent coolant spillage when the core is removed.
4. Open the glove compartment. Remove the glove compartment and liner, by removing the retaining screws.
5. Remove the core access plate retaining screws, and remove the access plate.
6. Working under the hood, remove the two nuts attaching the heater assembly case to the dash panel.
7. Remove the core through the glove compartment opening. Place some towels on the floor to catch any antifreeze that may come out of the core.

### To install:

8. Install the core through the glove compartment opening.
9. Working under the hood, install the two retaining nuts attaching the heater assembly case to the dash panel.
10. Install the core access plate and seal, securing with the retaining screws.
11. Fasten the glove compartment liner and door with the necessary hardware.
12. Reconnect the heater hoses to the core tubes at the firewall, inside the engine compartment.
13. Refill the cooling system with coolant.
14. Reconnect the negative battery cable.
15. Start vehicle and check for leaks.

### With Air Conditioning

1. Disconnect the negative battery cable.
2. Drain the cooling system into a suitable container.
3. Disconnect the heater hoses from the heater core.
4. Working inside the vehicle, remove the floor duct from the plenum by unfastening 2 retaining screws.
5. Remove the four screws attaching the heater core cover to the plenum. Remove the cover and finally the heater core.

### To install:

6. Install the heater core and install the cover. Install the four screws attaching the heater core cover to the plenum.
7. Working inside the vehicle, Install the floor duct to the plenum using the 2 retaining screws.
8. Reconnect the heater hoses to the heater core.
9. Reconnect the negative battery cable.
10. Refill the cooling system.
11. Start vehicle and check for leaks.

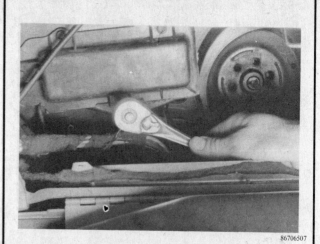

Fig. 15 With the glove box removed, unfasten the retaining screws from the plate securing the heater core in place

Fig. 16 Remove the plate and clean

Fig. 17 With the clamps and retainers removed, slide the heater core from the housing

## Control Cables

### ADJUSTMENT

♦ See Figure 18

**1984–88 Models**

1. Remove negative battery cable.
2. Remove the control panel from the instrument panel. Refer to the next section, control panel removal and installation for the correct procedure.
3. Remove the cable from the control assembly.
4. Insert the blade of a small screwdriver into the wire end loop (crank arm end) of the respective function control or temperature control cable.
5. Grip the self–adjusting clip with pliers and slide it down the control wire, away from the end loop, approximately 1.0 in. (25.4mm).
6. Install the cable to the control unit.
7. Move the control levers to the top of the slot, temperature warm, or function defrost, to position the self adjusting clip.
8. Install control panel and secure with retaining screws.
9. Connect battery cable.
10. Check ventilation system for proper operation.

**1989–94 Models**

1. Remove the negative battery cable.
2. Disconnect the control cable housing end retainer from the heater case.
3. Grip the self–adjusting clip and cable with pliers and slide the clip down the control wire away from the end approximately 11/2 in. (38mm).
4. Install cable to control assembly.
5. Move control lever to full position to adjust self–adjusting clip.
6. Connect negative battery cable.
7. Check for proper operation.

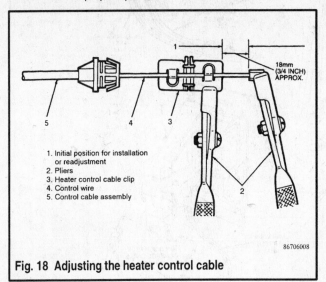

1. Initial position for installation or readjustment
2. Pliers
3. Heater control cable clip
4. Control wire
5. Control cable assembly

18mm (3/4 INCH) APPROX.

86706008

**Fig. 18 Adjusting the heater control cable**

### REMOVAL & INSTALLATION

**1984–88 Models**

1. Remove negative battery terminal.
2. Remove instrument cluster trim panel.
3. Remove any wire harnesses connected to the control assembly.
4. Move function lever to OFF position, and disconnect cable end retainer clip from heater case.
5. Move temperature control lever to COOL position and disconnect cable end retainer clip from heater case.
6. Remove 4 retainer screws securing control panel to instrument panel.
7. Identify and tag the control cables.
8. Remove the function control cable assembly from the vehicle through the control assembly housing in the instrument panel, using care not to hook any wiring.
9. Remove the temperature control cable assembly from the vehicle through the control assembly housing in the instrument panel, using care not to hook any wiring.

**To install:**

10. Position self adjusting clip on control cable, if not already completed.
11. Insert the self–adjusting clip end of the function and/or temperature control cable through the control assembly opening of the instrument panel and down to the bottom of the left side of the heater case.
12. Move function lever to OFF, or temperature lever to COOL position.
13. Insert cable wire end into the hole in either the function lever or temperature lever arm, depending on which cable is being installed. Connect the cable to the control assembly.
14. Connect any wire harnesses removed earlier.
15. Position the control assembly to the instrument panel and secure with 4 retaining screws.
16. Connect the self–adjusting clip of the cable to the cam pin on the bottom of the heater case.
17. Slide the cable housing and retainer into the cable bracket and engage the tabs to secure.
18. Move control levers to ensure they move freely.
19. Install the instrument panel trim.
20. Connect battery cable.
21. Check system to make sure ventilation system works correctly.

**1989–94 Models**

➡ Because of the design of the heater/defroster system, there is only one cable control assembly.

1. Remove negative battery terminal.
2. Move temperature lever to COOL position, and disconnect cable end retainer clip from heater case.
3. Remove the retaining screws attaching the passenger heater floor duct, and remove the duct.
4. Insert the end of a small Phillips head screwdriver in to the 0.14 in. (3.5mm) holes in the control assembly bezel and

apply inboard force to the control assembly to depress the springs.

5. Remove control assembly from register housing.
6. Remove any wire harness connection attached to the control assembly.
7. Disconnect temperature control cable housing from the mounting bracket.
8. Remove the twist–off cap from the temperature control lever and remove the cable.

**To install:**

9. Position self adjusting clip on control cable, if not already completed.
10. Insert the self–adjusting clip end of the temperature control cable through the control assembly opening of the instrument panel and down to the bottom of the left side of the heater case.
11. Move temperature lever to COOL position.
12. Connect temperature cable housing to the control bracket.
13. Connect any wire harnesses removed earlier.
14. Install twist–off cap by pushing it on.
15. Align the locking tabs on the control bracket with the metal slide track on the instrument panel.
16. Slide temperature cable housing end retainer into the heater case cable bracket and push to secure the cable housing to the bracket.

17. Connect the self–adjusting clip at the temperature cable to the temperature door crank arm.
18. Connect battery cable.
19. Check system to make sure ventilation system works correctly.

## Control Panel

### REMOVAL & INSTALLATION

**1984–88 Models**

▶ **See Figure 19**

1. Remove negative battery cable.
2. Remove the instrument panel finish trim around the control panel.
3. Remove the 4 retaining screws securing the the control assembly to the instrument panel.
4. Carefully pull the control assembly out of the instrument panel.
5. Disconnect the wire harnesses for the blower motor and dimmer light on the unit.
6. Identify and tag the control assembly cables. Remove the temperature control and function control cable from the control assembly.

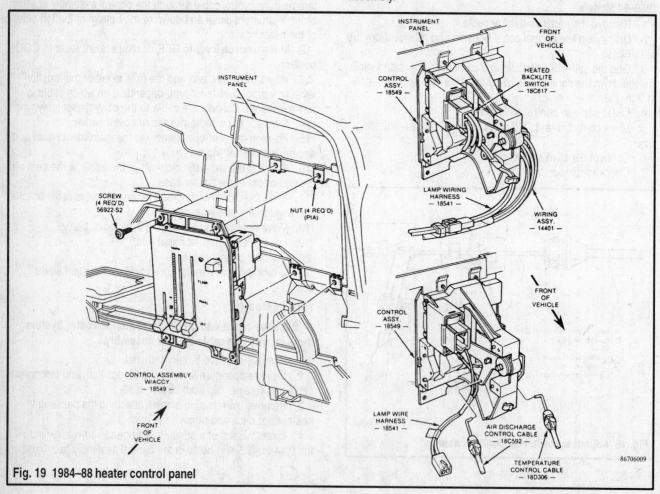

Fig. 19 1984–88 heater control panel

**To install:**

7.  Attach the temperature control and function control cables to their correct location.

8.  Connect the wire harness for the blower switch and dimmer light on the control assembly.

9.  Position control assembly in instrument panel and secure with retaining screws.

10.  Install the instrument panel finish trim.

11.  Attach battery cable.

12.  Check ventilation system for proper operation.

### 1989–94 Models

▶ **See Figures 20 and 21**

1.  Move the temperature control lever to the COOL position.

2.  Disconnect the temperature control housing end retainer from the air conditioning case bracket using the proper tool.

3.  Insert the ends of two 1/8 in. (3mm) diameter prying tools into the 3.5mm holes in the bezel.

4.  Apply a light inboard force on the tools to depress the spring clips and release the control assembly from the register housing.

5.  Pull the control assembly from the register housing and move the control lever to the COOL position.

6.  Disconnect the temperature cable housing from the control mounting bracket using the proper tool.

7.  Remove the twist off cap from the temperature control lever and remove the temperature control cable.

8.  Remove the temperature control wire from the lever.

9.  Disengage the electrical connectors from the control assembly.

10.  Detach the vacuum harness (2 spring and nuts) and remove the control assembly from the instrument panel.

**To install:**

11.  Position the control assembly near the instrument panel opening and connect the vacuum harness with the spring nuts and engage the electrical connectors.

12.  Move the temperature control lever to the COOL position.

13.  Connect the temperature control cable to the control assembly.

14.  Position the control assembly onto the register housing.

15.  Align the control bracket metal locking tabs with the metal slide track in the instrument panel.

16.  Slide the control assembly down the metal track until the spring clips snap and lock the control assembly into the register housing.

17.  Move the temperature control lever to the COOL position.

18.  Connect the temperature control cable self–adjusting clip to the temperature door crank a

19.  Slide the cable housing end retainer into the plenum cable bracket and engage the tabs.

20.  Move the function selector lever to the WARM position and adjust the cable.

21.  Check the operation of all the control function levers.

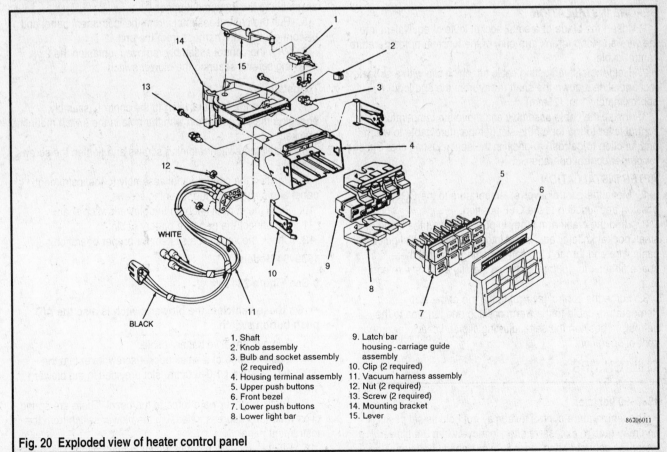

1. Shaft
2. Knob assembly
3. Bulb and socket assembly (2 required)
4. Housing terminal assembly
5. Upper push buttons
6. Front bezel
7. Lower push buttons
8. Lower light bar
9. Latch bar housing - carriage guide assembly
10. Clip (2 required)
11. Vacuum harness assembly
12. Nut (2 required)
13. Screw (2 required)
14. Mounting bracket
15. Lever

WHITE

BLACK

86706011

**Fig. 20  Exploded view of heater control panel**

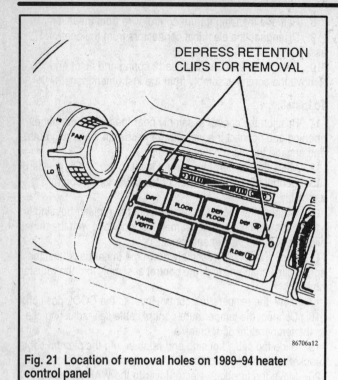

DEPRESS RETENTION CLIPS FOR REMOVAL

86706a12

**Fig. 21 Location of removal holes on 1989–94 heater control panel**

## Cable Preset & Self–Adjustment

### BEFORE INSTALLATION

1. Insert the blade of a small pocket knife of equivalent into the wire and loop (crank arm end) of the function or temperature control cable.

2. Hold the self–adjusting cable attaching clip with a suitable tool and slide it down the shaft (away from the end loop) approximately 1 in. (25mm).

3. Install the cable assembly and move the temperature control lever to the top of the slot (temperature cable to warm and function to defrost) to position the self adjusting clip. Check for proper control operation.

### AFTER INSTALLATION

1. Move the control lever(s) temperature to the COOL position and function to the OFF position.

2. Hold the crank arm firmly in position, insert the blade of a small pocket knife or equivalent into the wire loop and pull the cable wire end through the self–adjusting clip until there is a space about 1 in. (50mm) between the clip and the wire end loop.

3. Force the control lever(s) to the top of the slot (temperature cable to the warm position and function to defrost) to position the self–adjusting clip and check for proper control operation.

## CHILTON TIPS

### 1989–90 Vehicles

The temperature control lever may not hold its set position and may require excessive effort to move when the blower motor fan control switch is set for high speed operation. This occurs because the temperature door does not have an assist

spring. To install a temperature door assist spring, use the following procedure.

1. Reach up behind the instrument panel. Locate the temperature control cable where it attaches to the temperature blend door control arm.

2. Slide the cable spring clip and cable as an assembly off the end of the door control arm.

3. Install the temperature door assist spring (part #F03Z–19760–A).

4. After the assist spring is properly seated, slide the spring clip, with the cable attached, onto the door control arm.

5. Adjust the cable as required. Make sure that the door travels the full distance between the maximum heat and cool range.

## Blower Switch

### REMOVAL & INSTALLATION

#### 1984–88

♦ See Figure 22

1. Remove the negative battery cable

2. Remove blower switch knob from switch lever by carefully pulling the knob straight out.

3. Remove the instrument cluster opening finish panel.

4. Unfasten the 4 retaining screws securing the control assembly to the instrument panel.

5. Pull the control assembly from the instrument panel and disconnect the wire harness from the unit.

6. With the control assembly removed, unfasten the 2 retaining screws securing the blower switch

**To install:**

7. Position the blower switch to the control assembly, engaging the alignment pin with the hole in the switch mounting bracket.

8. Install the switch retaining screws and tighten the screws securely.

9. Position the control panel assembly to the instrument panel and secure with the retaining screws.

10. Push the control knob on the blower switch shaft.

11. Reconnect the negative battery cable.

12. Check the ventilation system for proper operation.

#### 1989–94 Models

♦ See Figure 23

➥ On these vehicles, the blower switch is also the A/C push button switch.

13. Remove negative battery cable.

14. Insert the end of a small pocket screwdriver into the 0.0394–0.2362 in. ( 1.0–6.0mm) slot provided in the blower switch bezel.

15. Apply a light upward force to the bezel. There are spring clips which will depress, releasing the blower switch from the instrument panel.

16. Pull blower switch out of the instrument panel. Disconnect the wire harness from the control assembly.

**To install:**

17. Connect the wire harness to blower switch.

18. Position blower switch on instrument panel, and push gently until spring snaps into place.

19. Reconnect the negative battery cable.

20. Check ventilation system for proper operation.

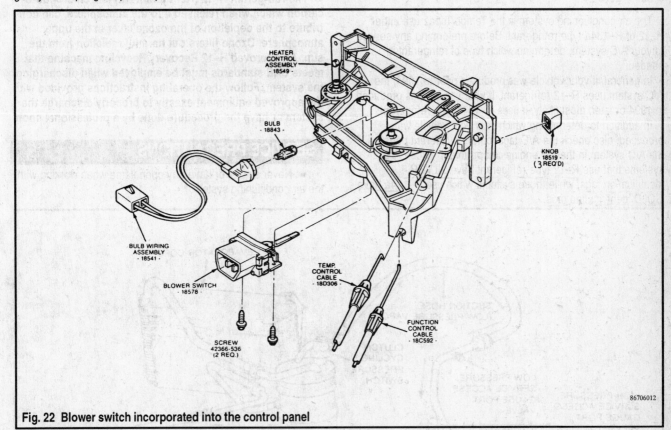

**Fig. 22 Blower switch incorporated into the control panel**

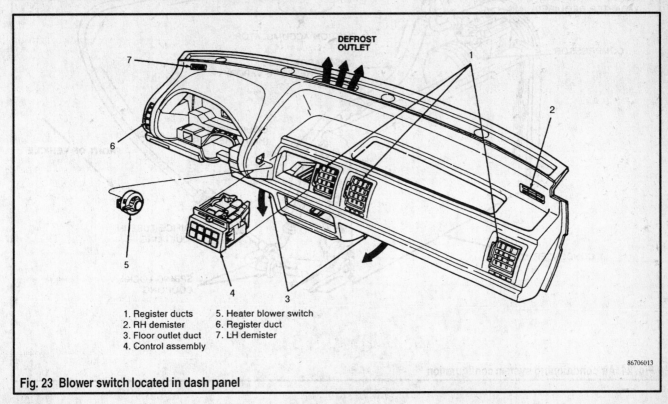

1. Register ducts
2. RH demister
3. Floor outlet duct
4. Control assembly
5. Heater blower switch
6. Register duct
7. LH demister

**Fig. 23 Blower switch located in dash panel**

## AIR CONDITIONING

▶ **See Figure 24**

The air conditioning system in the Tempo/Topaz use either R–12 or R–134a type refrigerant. Before preforming any service to your A/C system, determine which type of refrigerant is needed.

In general, if your vehicle was produced prior to 1994, the A/C system uses R–12 refrigerant. If your vehicle was produced in 1994 or later, most likely, it uses R–134a type refrigerant.

In addition to determining which year your vehicle was produced, also check the A/C tags found on different parts of the A/C system in the the engine compartment. Those A/C systems that use R–12 type refrigerant have SILVER identification tags, while those systems which use R–134a have GOLD identification tags.

➡ The refrigerant R–12 (Refrigerant–12) is a chlorofluoro-carbon which,when released into the atmosphere, can contribute to the depletion of the ozone layer in the upper atmosphere. Ozone filters out harmful radiation from the sun. An approved R–12 Recovery/Recycling machine that meets SAE standards must be employed when discharging the system. Follow the operating instructions provided with the approved equipment exactly to properly discharge the system or have the procedure done by a professional shop.

## SERVICE PRECAUTIONS

- Never smoke or have any open flame when working with the air conditioning system.

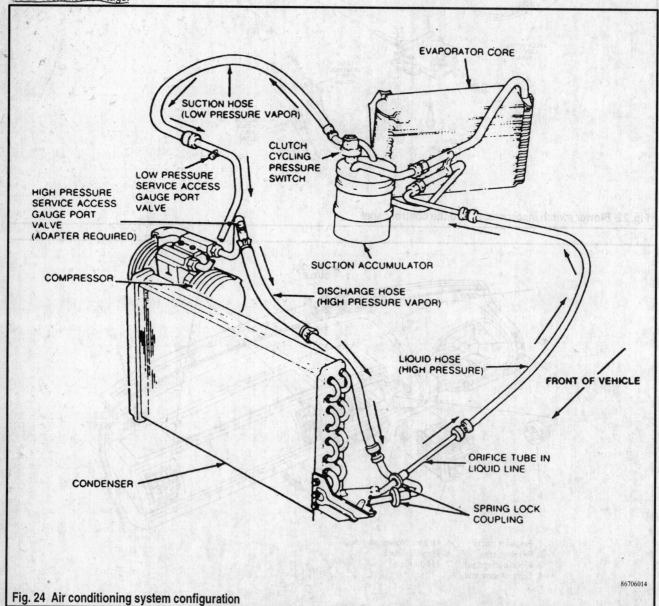

Fig. 24 Air conditioning system configuration

• Never open or loosen a connection before discharging the system properly.

• When loosening a connection, if any residual pressure is evident, allow it to leak off before opening the fitting fully.

• Keep service tools and work area clean.

• Before disconnecting a component from the system, clean the outside of the fittings thoroughly.

• A system which has been opened to replace a component or one which has discharged through leakage must be evacuated before charging the system.

• Immediately after disconnecting a component from the system, seal the open fittings with a cap or plug.

• Before connecting an open fitting, always install a new seal ring. Coat the seal with refrigerant oil before connecting.

➡ **Because of the potential risk to the environment, many regions of the country have tight regulations as to the service or repair of A/C systems. Before serving any part of the A/C system, check with the local authorities as to what regulations apply.**

## Compressor

### REMOVAL & INSTALLATION

➡ **The procedures outlined below are the same whether your vehicle uses an R–12 or an R–134a filled A/C system.**

### ✳✳WARNING

**Although the repair procedures are the same, R–12 and R–134a parts are NOT interchangeable.**

#### 2.0L and 2.3L Engines

➡ **Whenever the compressor is replaced, the suction accumulator/drier must also be replaced.**

1. Disconnect the negative battery cable
2. Properly discharge the refrigerant system.
3. If required, remove the alternator from the engine compartment.
4. Disconnect the compressor clutch wires at the field coil connector on the compressor.
5. Remove the discharge line from the manifold and tube assembly using the proper spring–lock coupling disconnect tool. Refer to Section 1 for more detail on tool use.
6. On 2.3L engines, remove the suction line from the suction manifold using a backup wrench on each fitting. On 2.0L engines, remove the suction manifold and tube assembly from the compressor , by unfastening the retaining bolts. Cap or plug suction parts to prevent the entrance of dirt or moisture.
7. Loosen 2 idler attaching screws and release the compressor belt tension.
8. Raise and safely support the vehicle on jackstands. Remove the 4 bolts attaching the compressor to the mounting bracket.
9. Remove the 2 screws attaching the heater water return tube to the underside of the en}engine support.
10. Remove the compressor from the underside of the vehicle.

**To install:**

➡ **A new service replacement compressor contains 8 oz. (240 ml) of refrigerant oil. Prior to installing the replacement compressor, drain the refrigerant oil from the removed compressor into a calibrated container. Then, drain the refrigerant oil from the new compressor into a clean calibrated container. If the amount of oil drained from the removed compressor was between 3–5 oz. (90–148 ml), pour the same amount of clean refrigerant oil into the new compressor. If the amount of oil that was removed from the old compressor is greater than 5 oz. (148 ml), pour 5 oz. (148 ml) of clean refrigerant oil into the new compressor. If the amount of refrigerant oil that was removed from the old compressor is less than 3 oz. (90 ml), pour 3 oz. (90 ml) of clean refrigerant oil into the new compressor.**

11. Position the compressor to the compressor bracket and install the 4 bolts. Tighten to 13–19 ft. lbs. (18–26 Nm).
12. Attach 2 screws attaching the heater water return tube to the underside of the engine support.
13. Attach the compressor belt and tighten the 2 idler screws.
14. On 2.3L engines, install the suction line to the suction manifold using a backup wrench on each fitting. Use new O–rings lubricated with clean refrigerant oil. On 2.0L engines, position manifolds and tube assembly to compressor and install the retaining bolts and tighten. Use new O–rings lubricated with clean refrigerant oil.
15. Install the discharge line spring lock fitting to the manifold and tube assembly. Use new O–rings lubricated with clean refrigerant oil.
16. Connect the compressor clutch wire connector to the field coil connector at the compressor.
17. Connect negative battery cable.
18. Leak test, evacuate and charge the system according to the proper procedure.
19. Check the system for proper operation.

#### 3.0L Engine

➡ **Whenever the compressor is replaced, the suction accumulator/drier must also be replaced.**

1. Disconnect the negative battery cable
2. Properly discharge the refrigerant system.
3. If required, remove the alternator from the engine compartment.
4. Disconnect the compressor clutch wires at the field coil connector on the compressor.
5. Remove the discharge line from the manifold and tube assembly using the proper spring–lock coupling disconnect tool. Refer to Section 1 for more detail on tool use.
6. Remove the suction line from the suction manifold using a spring–lock coupling disconnect tool.
7. Loosen and remove any accessary drive belts.
8. Raise and safely support the vehicle on jackstands. Remove the 4 bolts attaching the compressor to the mounting bracket.
9. Remove the 2 screws attaching the heater water return tube to the underside of the en}engine support.
10. Remove the compressor from the underside of the vehicle.

**To install:**

11. Position the compressor to the compressor bracket and install the 4 bolts. Tighten to 13–19 ft. lbs. (18–26 Nm).

12. Attach 2 screws attaching the heater water return tube to the underside of the engine support.

13. Attach any accessary drive belts removed and tighten to specification.

14. Install the suction line to the suction manifold. Use new O–rings lubricated with clean refrigerant oil.

15. Install the discharge line spring lock fitting to the manifold and tube assembly. Use new O–rings lubricated with clean refrigerant oil.

16. Connect the compressor clutch wire connector to the field coil connector at the compressor.

17. Connect negative battery cable.

18. Leak test, evacuate and charge the system according to the proper procedure.

19. Check the system for proper operation.

## Condenser

### REMOVAL & INSTALLATION

▶ See Figure 25

### ✳✳CAUTION

When draining the coolant, keep in mind that cats and dogs are attracted to ethylene glycol antifreeze, and could drink any that is left in an uncovered container or in puddles on the ground. This will prove fatal in sufficient quantity. Always drain the coolant into a sealable container. Coolant should be reused unless it is contaminated or several years old.

➡ The procedures outlined below are the same whether your vehicle uses an R–12 or an R–134a filled A/C system.

### ✳✳WARNING

Although the repair procedures are the same, R–12 and R–134a parts are NOT interchangeable.

➡ Whenever the condenser is replace, the suction accumulator/drier must also be replaced.

#### 2.0L and 2.3L Engines

1. Disconnect the negative battery cable.
2. Drain the cooling system into a suitable container.
3. Remove the ignition coil from the engine, if require. Discharge the air conditioning system.
4. Unfasten the fan shroud retaining screw and nut and remove the fan shroud. Disconnect the fan motor electrical connection.
5. Disconnect the A/C discharge line retaining clip from the radiator fan shroud.
6. Disconnect the upper and lower radiator hoses.

7. If equipped with an automatic transaxle, disconnect and cap the transaxle oil cooler lines from the transaxle.
8. Remove the radiator–to–support attaching nuts and carefully remove the radiator from the vehicle.
9. Disconnect the liquid line and compressor discharge line from the condenser using tool T81P–19623–G or equivalent.
10. Remove the condenser–to–bracket retaining screws and remove the condenser from the vehicle.

**To install:**

11. Add 1 oz. (30 ml) of clean refrigerant oil to a new replacement condenser. Place the condenser into position and install the condenser–to–bracket retaining screws.
12. Using new O–rings lubricated with clean refrigerant oil, connect the liquid line and compressor discharge line to the condenser.
13. Place the radiator into position and install the radiator–to–support attaching nuts.
14. Attach the upper and lower radiator hoses to the radiator and tighten each clamp.
15. Remove cap and connect the transaxle oil cooler lines.
16. Install and secure the fan shroud to the radiator. Connect the fan motor electrical connector.
17. Install the ignition coil.
18. Connect the A/C discharge hose retainer to the top corner of the fan shroud.
19. Connect the negative battery cable.
20. Fill the cooling system.
21. Leak test, evacuate and charge the A/C system. Check the system for proper operation.

#### 3.0L Engines

1. Disconnect the negative battery cable.
2. Drain the cooling system into a suitable container.
3. Remove the ignition coil from the engine.
4. Discharge the air conditioning system properly.
5. Unfasten the fan shroud retaining screw and nut and remove the fan shroud. Disconnect the fan motor electrical connection.
6. Disconnect the A/C discharge line retaining clip from the radiator fan shroud.
7. Disconnect the upper and lower radiator hoses.
8. If equipped with an automatic transaxle, disconnect and cap the transaxle oil cooler lines from the transaxle.
9. Remove the radiator–to–support attaching nuts and carefully remove the radiator from the vehicle.
10. Disconnect the liquid line and compressor discharge line from the condenser using tool T81P–19623–G or equivalent.
11. Remove the condenser–to–bracket retaining screws and remove the condenser from the vehicle.

**To install:**

12. Add 1 oz. (30 ml) of clean refrigerant oil to a new replacement condenser. Place the condenser into position and install the condenser–to–bracket retaining screws.
13. Using new O–rings lubricated with clean refrigerant oil, connect the liquid line and compressor discharge line to the condenser.

14.  Place the radiator into position and install the radiator–to–support attaching nuts.

15.  Attach the upper and lower radiator hoses to the radiator and tighten each clamp.

16.  Remove cap and connect the transaxle oil cooler lines.

17.  Install and secure the fan shroud to the radiator. Connect the fan motor electrical connector.

18.  Install the ignition coil.

19.  Connect the A/C discharge hose retainer to the top corner of the fan shroud.

20.  Connect the negative battery cable.

21.  Fill the cooling system.

22.  Leak test, evacuate and charge the A/C system. Check the system for proper operation.

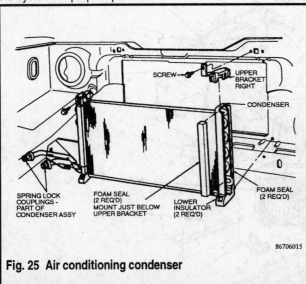

**Fig. 25  Air conditioning condenser**

## Evaporator Case

### REMOVAL & INSTALLATION

▶ **See Figure 26**

#### 2.0L and 2.3L Engines

1.  Disconnect the negative battery cable.

2.  Drain the radiator into a suitable container.

3.  Discharge the air conditioning system properly.

4.  Disconnect the heater hoses from the heater core. Plug the heater core tubes or blow any coolant from the heater core with low pressure air.

5.  Disconnect the liquid line and the accumulator/drier inlet tube from the evaporator core at the dash panel. Cap the refrigerant lines and evaporator core to prevent the entrance of dirt and moisture.

6.  Remove the instrument panel and lay on front seat.

7.  Disconnect the wire harness connector from the blower motor resistor.

8.  Remove 1 screw attaching the bottom of the evaporator case to the dash panel.

9.  Remove the instrument panel brace from the cowl top panel.

10.  Remove 2 nuts attaching the evaporator case to the dash panel in the engine compartment.

11.  Loosen the sound insulation from the cowl top panel in the area around the air inlet opening.

12.  Remove the 2 screws attaching the support bracket and the brace to the cowl top panels.

**To install:**

13.  Position the evaporator case onto the dash and cowl top panels at the air inlet opening. Install the 2 screws to attach the support bracket and brace the to the cowl top panel.

14.  In the engine compartment, attach the evaporator case to dash panel using 2 retaining nuts. Once positioned, check the evaporative drain tube for a good seal, and no obstructions.

15.  Position the sound insulation around the air inlet duct on the cowl top pan.

16.  Install the instrument panel.

17.  Attach the bottom of the evaporator case to the dash panel, using retaining screw.

18.  Connect the heater core hoses.

19.  Lubricate new liquid and suction line O–rings with clean refrigerant oil and connect these lines to the evaporator core.

20.  Fill the radiator with coolant.

21.  Connect the battery negative cable.

22.  Leak test, evacuate and charge the air conditioning system.

23.  Check the system for proper operation.

#### 3.0L Engine

1.  Disconnect the negative battery cable.

2.  Drain the radiator into a suitable container.

3.  Discharge the air conditioning system properly.

4.  Disconnect the heater hoses from the heater core. Plug the heater core tubes or blow any coolant from the heater core with low pressure air.

5.  Disconnect the liquid line and the accumulator/drier inlet tube from the evaporator core at the dash panel. Cap the refrigerant lines and evaporator core to prevent the entrance of dirt and moisture.

6.  Remove the instrument panel and lay on front seat.

7.  Disconnect the wire harness connector from the blower motor resistor.

8.  Remove 1 screw attaching the bottom of the evaporator case to the dash panel.

9.  Remove the instrument panel brace from the cowl top panel.

10.  Remove 2 nuts attaching the evaporator case to the dash panel in the engine compartment.

11.  Loosen the sound insulation from the cowl top panel in the area around the air inlet opening.

12.  Remove the 2 screws attaching the support bracket and the brace to the cowl top panels.

**To install:**

13.  Position the evaporator case onto the dash and cowl top panels at the air inlet opening. Install the 2 screws to attach the support bracket and brace the to the cowl top panel.

14.  In the engine compartment, attach the evaporator case to dash panel using 2 retaining nuts. Once positioned, check the evaporative drain tube for a good seal, and no obstructions.

1. Motor assembly
2. Screw (4 required)
3. Screw (2 required)
4. Screw
5. A/C vacuum harness plastic clip (2 required)
6. Vacuum harness assembly
7. Tank and hose assembly
8. Screw (2 required)
9. Upper A/C evaporator case
10. A/C evaporator seal
11. A/C temperature control door assembly
12. A/C blower motor resistor assembly
13. Lower A/C evaporator case
14. Heater core seal (copper/brass)
15. Lower heater core cover
16. Rope sealer
17. Heater core assembly (aluminum)
18. Staple (seal to case ) (2 required)
19. A/C evaporator drain tube seal
20. Spring nut (4 required)
21. A/C tube to dash seal
22. Heater to dash seal
23. A/C evaporator core assembly
24. Carriage bolt (2 required)
25. A/C damper door shaft
26. A/C recirc air duct
27. A/C air inlet door assembly
28. A/C air inlet duct
29. Vent air inlet duct gasket
30. Blower motor shaft retainer
31. A/C blower wheel
32. Gasket
33. A/C vacuum motor assembly

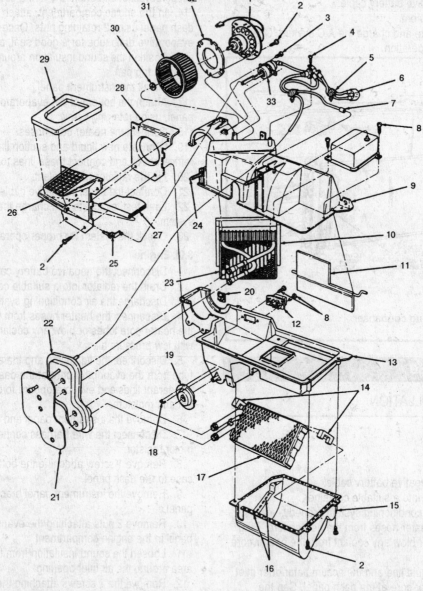

**Fig. 26 Exploded view of air conditioning evaporator case**

86706016

15. Position the sound insulation around the air inlet duct on the cowl top pan.

16. Install the instrument panel.

17. Attach the bottom of the evaporator case to the dash panel, using retaining screw.

18. Connect the heater core hoses.

19. Lubricate new liquid and suction line O–rings with clean refrigerant oil and connect these lines to the evaporator core. tighten to 16–22 ft. lbs. (1.8–2.5 Nm).

20. Fill the radiator with coolant.

21. Connect the battery negative cable.

22. Leak test, evacuate and charge the air conditioning system.

23. Check the system for proper operation.

## Evaporator Core

### REMOVAL & INSTALLATION

▶ See Figures 27 and 28

➡ When draining the coolant, keep in mind that cats and dogs are attracted to ethylene glycol antifreeze, and could drink any that is left in an uncovered container or in puddles on the ground. This will prove fatal in sufficient quantity. Always drain the coolant into a sealable container. Coolant should be reused unless it is contaminated or several years old.

➡ Whenever the evaporator core is removed, the suction accumulator drier must also be replaced.

#### 2.0L and 2.3L Engines

1. Disconnect the negative battery cable.
2. Drain the coolant from the radiator into a clean container.
3. Properly discharge the refrigerant from the air conditioning system.
4. Remove the evaporator case as outlined earlier.
5. Remove the 4 screws attaching the air inlet duct to the evaporator case and remove the air inlet duct.
6. Remove the evaporator-to-cowl seals from the evaporator tubes.
7. Perform the following:
   e. Drill two 3/16 in. holes in both the upright tabs on the top of the evaporator case.
   f. Using a suitable tool, cut the top from the evaporator case completely
   g. Remove the blower motor resistor from the evaporator case by removing the 2 screws.
   h. Remove the cover from the case and lift the evaporator core from the case.
   i. Use a suitable tool to remove any rough edges from the case that may have been caused by the cutting.

To install:

➡ Add 3 oz. (90 ml) of clean refrigerant oil to a new replacement evaporator core to maintain total system refrigerant oil requirements.

8. Transfer the 2 foam seals to the new core.
9. Position the core in the case and close the cut-out cover.
10. Install a spring nut on each of the 2 tabs. Be sure the hole in the spring nut is aligned with the holes drilled earlier in the flange. Then, install and tighten a screw in each spring nut to secure the cut-out cover.
11. Using caulking cord or an equivalent material, seal around the cut-out line.
12. Install the blower motor resistor using 2 retaining screws.
13. Position and secure the foam seal over the evaporator core and the heater core tubes.
14. Install the evaporator case as outlined earlier.
15. Fill the radiator and cooling system.
16. Connect the negative battery cable.
17. Leak test, evacuate and charge the air conditioning system.

#### 3.0L Engines

1. Disconnect the negative battery cable.
2. Drain the coolant from the radiator into a clean container.
3. Properly discharge the refrigerant from the air conditioning system.
4. Remove the evaporator case as outlined earlier.
5. Remove the 4 screws attaching the air inlet duct to the evaporator case and remove the air inlet duct.
6. Remove the evaporator-to-cowl seals from the evaporator tubes.
7. Using a suitable tool, cut the top from the evaporator case completely
8. Remove the cover from the case and lift the evaporator core from the case.
9. Use a suitable tool to remove any rough edges from the case that may have been caused by the cutting.

To install:

10. Transfer the 2 foam seals to the new core.
11. Position the core in the case and close the cut-out cover.
12. Using caulking cord or an equivalent material, seal around the cut-out line.
13. Position and secure the foam seal over the evaporator core and the heater core tubes.
14. Install the evaporator case as outlined earlier.
15. Fill the radiator and cooling system.
16. Connect the negative battery cable.
17. Leak test, evacuate and charge the air conditioning system.

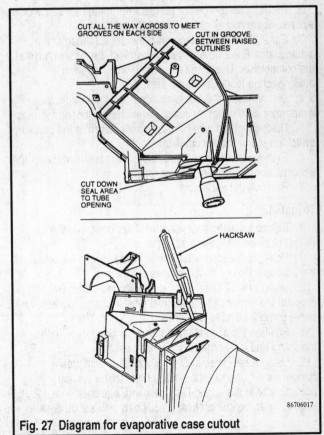

Fig. 27 Diagram for evaporative case cutout

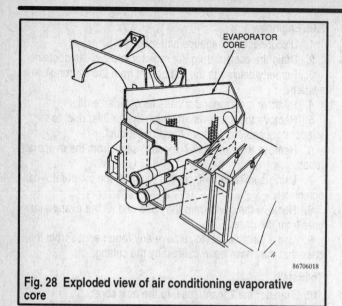

EVAPORATOR CORE

86706018

**Fig. 28 Exploded view of air conditioning evaporative core**

## Accumulator/Drier

### REMOVAL & INSTALLATION

♦ See Figure 29

#### 2.0L and 2.3L Engines

1. Disconnect the negative battery cable.
2. Properly discharge the refrigerant from the air conditioning system, observing all safety precautions.
3. For 2.3L engines, disconnect the suction hose at the accumulator. For 2.0L engines, disconnect the suction hose at the compressor. Use a suitable spring–lock coupler disconnecting tool to separate the lines
4. Disconnect the accumulator/drier inlet tube from the evaporator core outlet by using 2 wrenches to loosen the nuts.
5. Disconnect the wire harness connector from the pressure switch on top of the accumulator.
6. Remove the screws that secure 2 straps which clamp the accumulator/drier to the dash panel.
7. Remove the assembly.

**To install:**

8. Before installing a new accumulator/drier, add 2.0 oz. (60ml) of clean refrigerant oil to the unit.
9. Position the accumulator/drier in the vehicle securing with the 2 straps. Do not attach screws at this time.
10. Using new O–rings lubricated with clean refrigerant oil, connect the accumulator/drier inlet tube to the evaporator core outlet using 2 suitable wrenches.
11. Position the accumulator/drier mounting straps to the mounting and install the retaining screws.
12. Using a new special O–ring lubricated with clean refrigerant oil, connect the suction hose to the suction accumulator at the spring–lock coupling, equipped with a 2.3L engine, or at the compressor if equipped with a 2.0L engine.

➡ Use only O–rings contained in kit E35Y–19D690–A or equivalent. The use of any other O–ring will allow the connection to leak.

13. Install the air pump if equipped.
14. Connect the negative battery cable.
15. Leak test, evacuate and charge the system according to the proper procedure. Observe all safety precautions.
16. Check the system for proper operation.

#### 3.0L Engines

1. Disconnect the negative battery cable.
2. Properly discharge the refrigerant from the air conditioning system, observing all safety precautions.
3. Disconnect the suction hose at the accumulator.
4. Disconnect the accumulator/drier inlet tube from the evaporator core outlet by using a suitable spring–lock coupler disconnect tool.
5. Disconnect the wire harness connector from the pressure switch on top of the accumulator.
6. Remove the screws and nut that secure the accumulator/drier to the dash panel.
7. Remove the assembly.

**To install:**

8. Before installing a new accumulator/drier, add 2.0 oz. (60ml) of clean refrigerant oil to the unit.
9. Position the accumulator/drier in the mounting bracket.
10. Using new O–rings lubricated with clean refrigerant oil, connect the accumulator/drier inlet tube to the evaporator core outlet.
11. Position the accumulator/drier mounting bracket over the evaporator case stud and secure with retaining nut. Tighten to 3–7 ft. lbs. (4–9.5 Nm). Install screw through lower leg of mounting bracket.
12. Using a new special O–ring lubricated with clean refrigerant oil, connect the suction hose to the suction accumulator at the spring–lock coupling.

➡ Use only O–rings contained in kit E35Y–19D690–A or equivalent. The use of any other O–ring will allow the connection to leak.

13. Connect the negative battery cable.
14. Leak test, evacuate and charge the system according to the proper procedure. Observe all safety precautions.
15. Check the system for proper operation.

## Blower Switch

### REMOVAL & INSTALLATION

#### 1984–88 Models

♦ See Figure 30

1. Remove the negative battery cable.
2. Pull the blower switch knob from the blower switch shaft.
3. Remove the instrument cluster opening finish panel.
4. Unscrew the control assembly from the instrument panel.

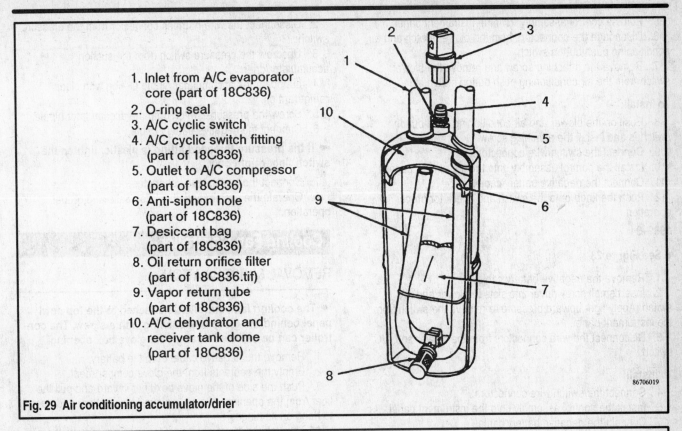

1. Inlet from A/C evaporator core (part of 18C836)
2. O-ring seal
3. A/C cyclic switch
4. A/C cyclic switch fitting (part of 18C836)
5. Outlet to A/C compressor (part of 18C836)
6. Anti-siphon hole (part of 18C836)
7. Desiccant bag (part of 18C836)
8. Oil return orifice filter (part of 18C836.tif)
9. Vapor return tube (part of 18C836)
10. A/C dehydrator and receiver tank dome (part of 18C836)

86706019

**Fig. 29 Air conditioning accumulator/drier**

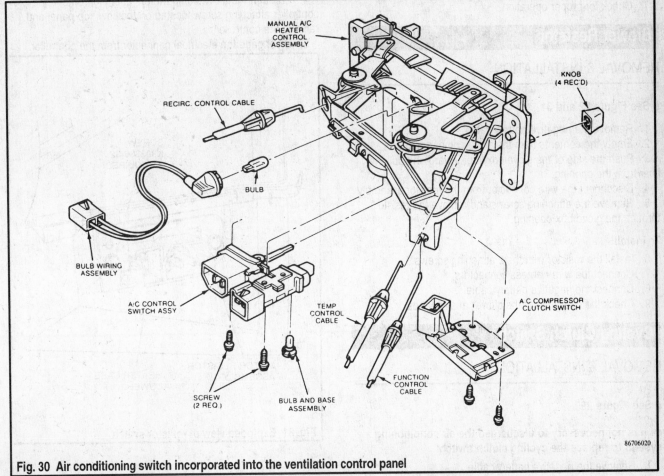

MANUAL A/C HEATER CONTROL ASSEMBLY

KNOB (4 REC'D)

RECIRC. CONTROL CABLE

BULB

BULB WIRING ASSEMBLY

A/C CONTROL SWITCH ASSY

TEMP CONTROL CABLE

A C COMPRESSOR CLUTCH SWITCH

SCREW (2 REQ)

BULB AND BASE ASSEMBLY

FUNCTION CONTROL CABLE

86706020

**Fig. 30 Air conditioning switch incorporated into the ventilation control panel**

5. Pull the control assembly from the instrument panel.

6. Disengage the connectors from the blower switch and air conditioning push button switch.

7. Remove the attaching screw and remove the blower switch from the air conditioning push button switch.

### To install:

8. Position the blower and air conditioning push button switches and install the attaching screw.

9. Connect the switch wire connectors.

10. Install the control assembly onto the instrument panel.

11. Connect the negative battery cable.

12. Push the knob onto the switch and check for proper operation.

### 1989–94

▶ See Figure 23

1. Remove the negative battery cable.

2. Insert small screwdriver into slots in blower and A/C switch. Apply light upward pressure to remove the switch from the instrument panel.

3. Disconnect the wire connectors from the blower and A/C switch.

### To install:

4. Connect the switch wire connectors.

5. Install the control assembly onto the instrument panel.

6. Connect the negative battery cable.

7. Check for proper operation.

## Blower Resistor

### REMOVAL & INSTALLATION

▶ See Figure 22 and 31

1. Remove the negative battery cable.

2. Empty the contents from the glove compartment.

3. Push the side of the glove box liner inward and pull the liner from the opening.

4. Disconnect the wire connector from the resistor assembly.

5. Remove the attaching screws and remove the resistor through the glove box opening.

### To install:

6. Install the resistor with the 2 attaching screws.

7. Connect the wire harness connectors.

8. Connect the negative battery cable.

9. Check the operation of the blower at all speeds.

## Cycling Clutch Switch

### REMOVAL & INSTALLATION

▶ See Figure 29

➡ It is not necessary to discharged the air conditioning system to replace the cycling clutch switch.

1. Remove the negative battery cable.

2. Disconnect the wire harness connector from the pressure switch.

3. Unscrew the pressure switch from the suction accumulator/drier.

4. Lubricate the accumulator nipple O–ring with clean refrigerant oil.

5. Screw the pressure switch onto the accumulator nipple.

6. Connect the negative battery cable.

➡ If the pressure threaded fitting is plastic, tighten the switch finger tight only.

7. Connect the switch wire connector.

8. Operate the system and check for leaks and proper operation.

## Cooling Fan Controller

### REMOVAL & INSTALLATION

➡ The cooling fan controller is attached to the top cowl panel behind the glove box opening with a screw. The controller can be serviced through the glove box opening.

1. Remove the negative cable from the battery.

2. Empty the contents from the glove compartment.

3. Push the side of the glove box liner inward and pull the liner from the opening. Allow the glove compartment and door to hang on its hinges.

4. Through the glove compartment opening, remove the controller attaching screw located on the cowl top panel and remove the controller.

5. Disengage the electrical connector from the controller.

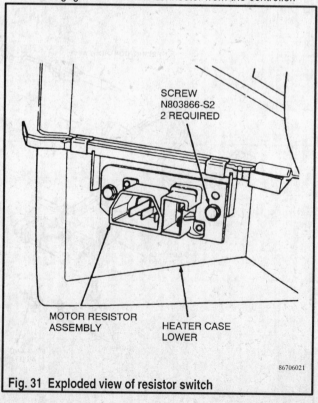

SCREW
N803866-S2
2 REQUIRED

MOTOR RESISTOR
ASSEMBLY

HEATER CASE
LOWER

86706021

**Fig. 31 Exploded view of resistor switch**

**To install:**

6. Engage the electrical connector to the controller.

7. Position the controller to the top cowl panel and engage the mounting tab in the hole and install the attaching screws.

8. Install the glove box liner.

9. Connect the negative battery cable.

10. Check system for proper operation.

## Fixed Orifice Tube

The fixed orifice tube is located in the liquid line near the condenser and is an integral part of the liquid line. If it is necessary to replace the orifice tube, the liquid line must be replaced, or fixed with orifice tube replacement kit E5VY–190695–A or equivalent. The fixed orifice tube is removed and installed using fixed orifice tube remover/replacer T83L–19990–A or equivalent.

The fixed orifice tube should be replaced whenever a compressor is replaced. If, using a gauge, the high pressure reads extremely high and low pressure is almost a vacuum, the fixed orifice is plugged and must be replaced.

## REMOVAL & INSTALLATION

### Liquid Line

➡ **Whenever a refrigerant line is replaced, it will be necessary to replace the accumulator/drier.**

1. Disconnect the negative battery cable.

2. Properly discharge the refrigerant from the air conditioning system. Observe all safety precautions.

3. Disconnect and remove the refrigerant line using a wrench on each side of the tube O–fittings. If the refrigerant line has a spring–lock coupling, disconnect according to the spring–lock coupling disconnection procedure.

**To install:**

4. Route the new refrigerant line with the protective caps installed.

5. Connect the new refrigerant line into the system using new O–rings lubricated with clean refrigerant oil. Use 2 wrenches when tightening tube O–fittings or perform the spring–lock coupling connect procedure, as necessary.

6. Reconnect negative battery cable.

7. Leak test, evacuate and charge the refrigerant system according to the proper procedure. Observe all safety precautions.

### Fixed Orifice Tube Replacement Kit

1. Disconnect the negative battery cable.

2. Discharge the refrigerant from the air conditioning system according to the proper procedures.

3. Remove the liquid line from the vehicle.

4. Locate the orifice tube by 3 indented notches or a circular depression in the metal portion of the liquid line. Note the angular position of the ends of the liquid line so that it can be reassembled in the correct position.

5. Cut a 21/2 in. (63.5mm) section from the tube at the orifice tube location. Do not cut closer than 1 in. (25.4mm) from the start of the bend in the tube.

6. Remove the orifice tube from the housing using pliers. An orifice tube removal tool cannot be used.

7. Flush the 2 pieces of liquid line to remove any contaminants.

8. Lubricate the O–rings with clean refrigerant oil and assemble the orifice tube kit, with the orifice tube installed, to the liquid line. Make sure the flow direction arrow is pointing toward the evaporator end of the liquid line and the taper of each compressor ring is toward the compressor nut.

➡ **The inlet tube will be positioned against the orifice tube tabs when correctly assembled.**

9. While holding the hex of the tube in a vise, tighten each compression nut to 65–70 ft. lbs. (88–94 Nm) with a crow foot wrench.

10. Assemble the liquid line to the vehicle using new O–rings lubricated with clean refrigerant oil.

11. Connect the negative battery cable.

12. Leak test, evacuate and charge the system according to the proper procedure. Observe all safety precautions.

13. Check the system for proper operation.

## Refrigerant Lines

Refrigerant lines are secured with either a threaded type fitting or a spring–lock connection. Whichever type fitting is used on the line, it is very important to use the correct tools to remove or install one of these lines. If the line is a threaded fitting, use back–up wrenches to loosen and tighten the connection. Spring–lock connectors require a special tool to remove the locking pin inside the tube. Because refrigerant lines can be different diameters, there are different diameter spring–lock tools. Before disassembling a refrigerant line, make sure you correctly match the disconnect tool to the A/C line.

## REMOVAL & INSTALLATION

1. Disconnect the negative battery cable.

2. Discharge the A/C refrigerant from the system using the proper procedure.

3. Determine whether the refrigerant line to be removed is a threaded fitting, or a spring–lock fitting.

4. If removing a threaded line, use a back–up wrench to loosen fitting.

5. If removing a spring–lock fitting, use correct spring–lock tool as necessary.

6. Remove line from vehicle.

**To install:**

7. Route new refrigerant line with protective caps installed.

8. Connect the new line into the A/C system using new O–rings oiled with refrigerant oil. Tighten the connection to 7.0 ft. lbs. (9 Nm) for a self–sealing coupling and 15–20 ft. lbs. (21–27 Nm) for non–self–sealing coupling. Use back–up wrenches to prevent component damage, or use a spring–lock procedure if applicable.

9. Connect the negative battery.
10. Leak test, evacuate and charge the A/C system according to the proper procedures.
11. Check A/C system for the proper operation.

## Vacuum System

▶ **See Figure 32**

### LINES

Until the 1989 model year, the heater/air conditioning system of the Tempo/Topaz was cable controlled through the temperature and function control cables.

The vacuum system incorporated into the vehicle after 1989 includes a vacuum motor and assembly fastened to the floor defrost duct of the ventilation system. This vacuum system is controlled through the climate control panel on the dash.

In the event you question the proper functioning of the vacuum motor as a source of a ventilation problem, make sure it is not a vacuum line fist. Because this system works on a limited number of vacuum lines, testing this system is fairly simple.

1. Remove negative battery cable.
2. Remove the ventilation system control panel from the instrument panel as outlined earlier.
3. Carefully pry the vacuum hose connection away from the control panel.
4. Using a hand pump, test each line to make sure it can hold a vacuum. If the line is unable to hold a vacuum, check for cracks or holes in the line and repair.

**To install:**

5. Fasten the vacuum line connection to the control panel.
6. Push control panel into instrument panel.
7. Connect negative battery cable.
8. Check for prior ventilation system functioning.

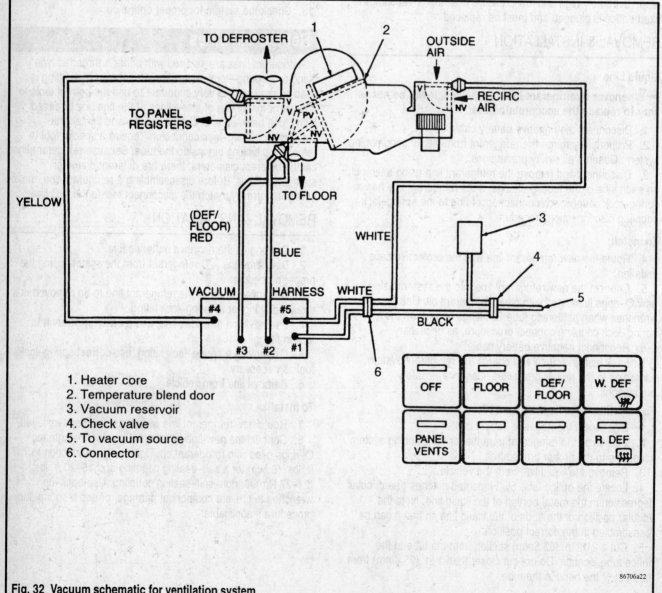

1. Heater core
2. Temperature blend door
3. Vacuum reservoir
4. Check valve
5. To vacuum source
6. Connector

**Fig. 32 Vacuum schematic for ventilation system**

86706a22

## Vacuum Motor

### REMOVAL & INSTALLATION

♦ **See Figure 33**

1. Remove plenum assembly from vehicle.
2. With the plenum assembly removed from the vehicle, turn assembly upside down and remove the floor defroster duct by unfastening the retaining screws.
3. There are two vacuum motors on the duct, one for the floor , the other for the center vent. The procedure to remove them is the same.

4. Unclip the duct door from the vacuum motor. Unplug the vacuum line from the nipple on the vacuum motor.
5. Remove the retaining screws from the vacuum motor, and remove the motor.

**To install:**

6. Position the vacuum motor in the bracket and secure with the retaining screws.
7. Plug the vacuum line into the nipple on the motor.
8. Clip the duct door crank arm to the motor.
9. Install the floor defrost duct to the plenum assembly, and install in vehicle.
10. Connect negative battery cable.
11. Check the system system for proper functioning.

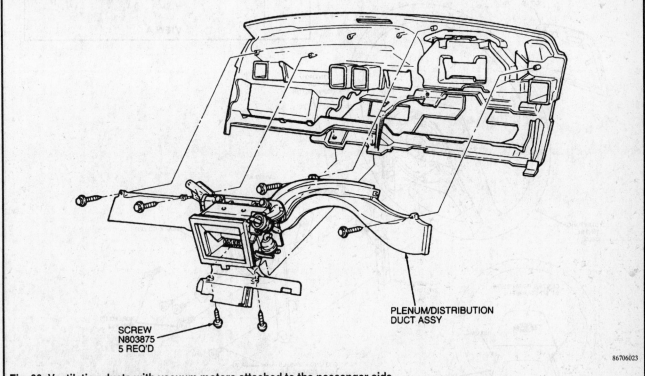

SCREW
N803875
5 REQ'D

PLENUM/DISTRIBUTION
DUCT ASSY

86706023

**Fig. 33 Ventilation ducts with vacuum motors attached to the passenger side**

## CRUISE CONTROL

The cruise control system consists of the operator controls, a servo or throttle acuator assembly, a speed sensor, a clutch, brake and brake light switch, a vacuum dump valve, an amplifier assembly, and the assorted necessary wire harnesses and vacuum hose. To activate the cruise control system, the engine must be running and the vehicle speed must be greater than 30 MPH.

## Control Switches

The switches controlling the cruise control function of the vehicle can be found in the steering wheel. If for any reason one switch becomes defective, the entire switch panel must be replaced.

### REMOVAL & INSTALLATION

♦ **See Figure 34**

➡ **The style of steering wheel may vary between vehicle, but the procedure for control switch removal and installation remains the same.**

1. Remove the negative terminal from the battery.
2. Remove the steering wheel cover pad by unfastening the retaining screws from the back of the wheel.
3. Disconnect the horn wire connectors from the steering wheel cover pad.

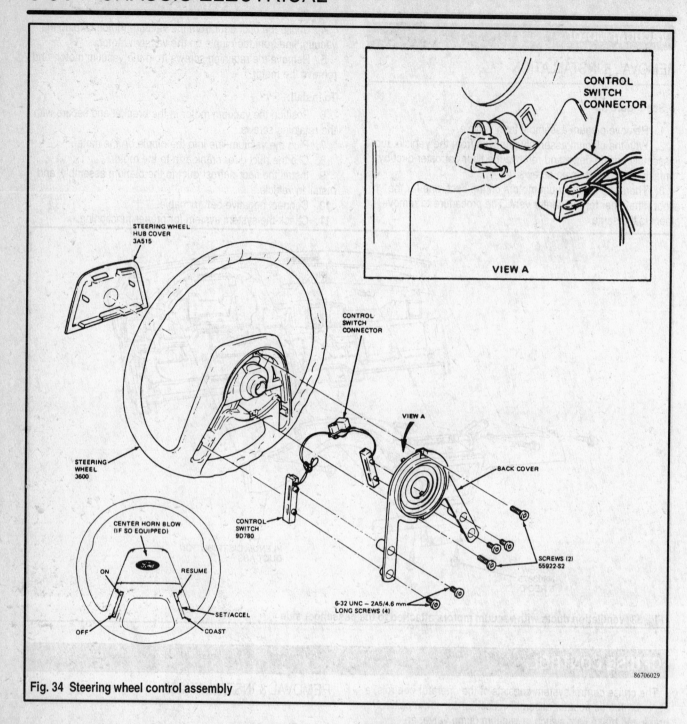

**Fig. 34 Steering wheel control assembly**

4. Remove the entire cruise control switch assembly by unfastening the retaining screws and unplugging the wire connector and removing the switch.

**To install:**

5. Position cruise control switch into steering wheel and secure with retaining screws. Connect wire harness.
6. Carefully attach the horn wire harness to the steering wheel cover pad.
7. Install steering wheel cover pad with retaining hardware.
8. Connect negative battery terminal.
9. Road test vehicle to check cruise control operation.

## Speed Sensor

### REMOVAL & INSTALLATION

#### 1984–88 Models

▶ See Figure 35

1. Disconnect negative battery terminal.
2. Raise and safely support vehicle on jackstands.

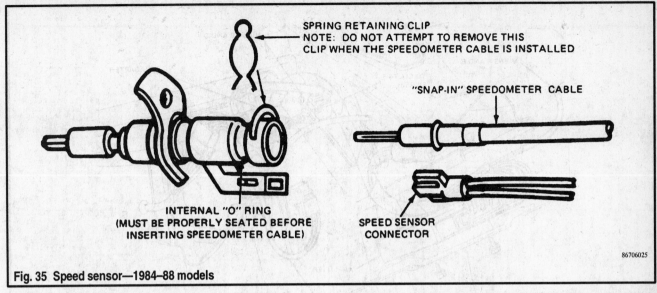

**Fig. 35  Speed sensor—1984–88 models**

3. From underneath the vehicle, unplug the electrical connection at the speed sensor.

4. Remove the bolt retaining the speed sensor mounting clip to the transaxle. Remove the sensor and drive gear from the transaxle.

5. Disconnect the speedometer cable from the speed sensor by carefully pulling the 2 pieces in opposite directions. Discard old O–ring.

**To install:**

6. Clip the speedometer cable and speed sensor together.

7. Install the speed sensor with new O–ring into the transaxle body and secure with the retaining bolt. Tighten bolt to 30–40 inch lbs. (3.4–4.5 Nm).

8. Plug electrical connector to sensor.

9. Lower vehicle.

10. Connect negative battery cable.

11. Road test vehicle to test cruise control operation.

### 1989–94 Models

▶ See Figure 36

1. Disconnect negative battery terminal.

2. Raise and safely support vehicle on jackstands.

3. From underneath the vehicle, unplug the electrical connection at the speed sensor.

4. Remove the nut securing the speed sensor mounting clip to the transaxle. Remove the sensor and drive gear from the transaxle.

5. Disconnect the speedometer cable from the speed sensor by carefully pulling the 2 pieces in opposite directions. Discard the old O–ring.

**To install:**

6. Clip the speedometer cable and speed sensor together.

7. Install the speed sensor with new O–ring into the transaxle body and secure with the retaining nut. Tighten bolt to 30–40 inch lbs. (3.4–4.5 Nm).

8. Plug electrical connector to sensor.

9. Lower vehicle.

10. Connect negative battery cable.

11. Road test vehicle to test cruise control operation.

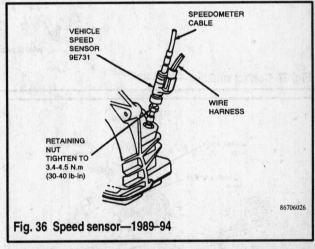

**Fig. 36  Speed sensor—1989–94**

## Amplifier

### REMOVAL & INSTALLATION

#### 1984–88 Models

▶ See Figure 37

➡ **The amplifier assembly is located below the steering column on the instrument panel reinforcement.**

1. Disconnect the negative battery cable.

2. Remove the 2 nuts and bolts securing the amplifier to the mounting bracket.

3. Disconnect the 2 wire harness connections.

**To install:**

4. Connect the 2 wire connectors to the amplifier.

5. Secure the amplifier to the mounting bracket with the 2 nuts and bolts.

6. Connect negative battery cable.

7. Road test the vehicle.

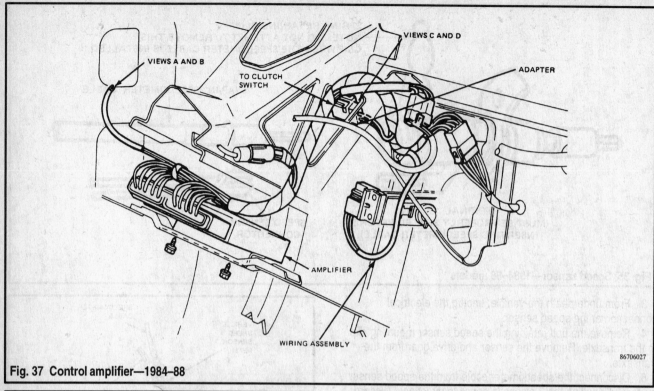

**Fig. 37 Control amplifier—1984–88**

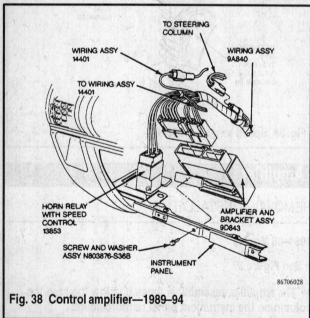

**Fig. 38 Control amplifier—1989–94**

**1989–94 Models**

♦ See Figure 38

➡ The amplifier assembly is located below the steering column on the instrument panel reinforcement.

1. Disconnect the negative battery cable.
2. Remove the knee bolster below the steering column.
3. Remove the 2 nuts and bolts securing the amplifier to the mounting bracket.
4. Disconnect the 2 wire harness connections.

**To install:**

5. Connect the 2 wire connectors to the amplifier.
6. Secure the amplifier to the mounting bracket with the 2 nuts and bolts.
7. Connect negative battery cable.
8. Road test the vehicle.

## Servo Assembly

### REMOVAL & INSTALLATION

**1984–88 Models**

♦ See Figure 39

1. Remove the negative battery cable.
2. Remove the screw and disconnect the speed control actuator cable from the accelerator cable bracket.
3. Disconnect the speed control actuator cable with the adjuster from the accelerator cable.
4. Remove the 2 vacuum hoses as well as the electrical connector from the servo assembly.
5. Remove the 2 nuts securing the servo unit to the mounting bracket. Carefully remove the servo assembly and cable.
6. Remove the 2 nuts holding the cable cover to the servo unit.
7. Pull off the cover and remove the cable assembly.

**To install:**

8. Attach the cable to the servo unit.
9. Secure the cable cover to the servo assembly with the 2 retaining nuts.

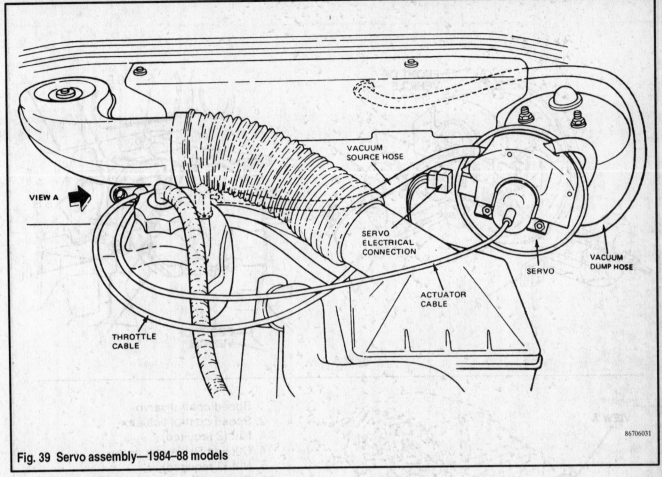

**Fig. 39 Servo assembly—1984–88 models**

10. Attach the servo unit to the mounting bracket with 2 retaining nuts.

11. Feed the acuator cable under the air cleaner duct and snap cable, with adjuster on to the accelerator cable.

12. Connect the acuator cable to the accelerator cable bracket and install the push pin.

13. Engage the electrical connection and vacuum hoses to the assembly.

14. Adjust cable to proper length.

15. Connect negative battery cable.

16. Road test the vehicle.

**1989–94 Models**

▶ **See Figure 40**

1. Remove the negative battery cable.

2. Remove the screw and disconnect the speed control actuator cable from the throttle assembly from the accelerator cable bracket.

   j. On 2.3L engines, disconnect the speed control actuator cable with the adjuster from the accelerator cable.

   k. On 3.0L engines, disconnect the speed control actuator cable from the throttle body nailhead.

3. Disconnect the speed control wire harness located at the right front fender apron.

4. Remove the front bumper.

5. Remove the speed control servo shield assembly, as well as the servo boot assembly.

6. Remove the 2 vacuum hoses from the speed control servo assembly.

7. Remove the 2 nuts holding the servo to its mounting bracket.

8. Carefully remove the speed control servo and cable assembly.

9. Remove the 2 nuts securing the actuator cable cover to the speed control servo. Pull off the cover and remove the cable actuator assembly.

**To install:**

10. Install the actuator cable to the servo unit.

11. Secure the cable cover to the servo assembly with the 2 retaining nuts.

12. Attach the servo unit to the mounting bracket with 2 retaining nuts.

13. Feed the acuator cable through the hole in the right front fender apron.

14. Snap the actuator cable with the adjuster onto the accelerator cable on 2.3L engines and on to the throttle body nailhead if equipped with a 3.0L engine.

15. Connect the actuator cable to the accelerator cable bracket and secure with the retaining screw.

16. Engage the electrical connection and vacuum hoses to the assembly.

17. Install the speed servo control boot.

18. Install the speed control servo control shield.

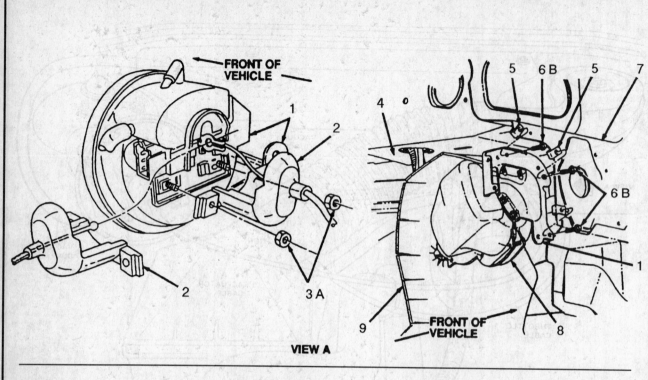

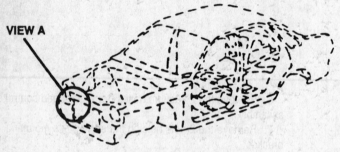

1. Speed control servo
2. Speed control actuator
3A. Nut (2 required)
4. Outside RH fender apron
5. Nut (3 required)
6B. Screw (3 required)
7. Radiator support assembly
8. Speed control servo boot
9. Speed control servo shield
A. Tighten to 4-6 N.m (35-53 lb-in)
B. Tighten to 7.6-10.4 N.m (67-92 lb-in)

86706030

**Fig. 40 Servo assembly—1989–94 models**

19. Position and secure the front bumper.
20. Adjust cable to proper length.
21. Connect negative battery cable.
22. Road test the vehicle.

## Vacuum Dump Valve

### REMOVAL & INSTALLATION

♦ See Figure 41

➡ **The dump valve is located above the brake pedal.**

1. Remove negative battery cable.

2. Remove the vacuum hose from the valve with a back and forth motion.

3. Inspect the hose for signs of breakage or cracks, replace if necessary.

**To install:**

4. Install valve to bracket
5. Connect vacuum hose to valve
6. Connect negative battery cable.
7. Road test the vehicle.

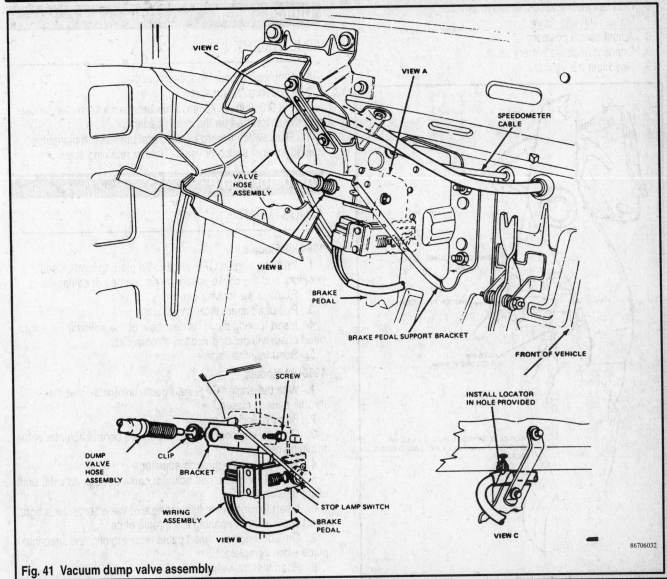

**Fig. 41 Vacuum dump valve assembly**

## ADJUSTMENT

### Evaporator Case

1. Firmly apply the brake.
2. Push dump valve until the collar bottoms against the retaining clip.
3. Place a 0.05–0.10 in. (1.27–2.54mm) shim between the button of the valve and the pad on the brake.
4. Firmly pull brake pedal back allowing dump valve to ratchet backward in retaining clip.

## Clutch Pedal Switch

### REMOVAL & INSTALLATION

▶ See Figure 42

1. Disconnect negative battery cable.
2. Remove screw securing switch.
3. Remove electrical connection from switch.
4. Remove switch from bracket

**To install:**

5. Install switch into bracket

6. Connect electrical connection to switch.
7. Install retaining screw.
8. Adjust switch position.
9. Connect negative battery cable.
10. Road test the vehicle

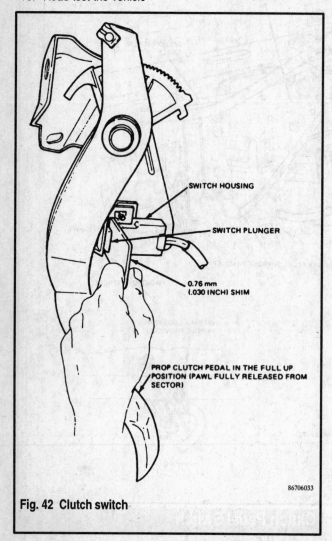

SWITCH HOUSING

SWITCH PLUNGER

0.76 mm
(.030 INCH) SHIM

PROP CLUTCH PEDAL IN THE FULL UP
POSITION (PAWL FULLY RELEASED FROM
SECTOR)

86706033

**Fig. 42 Clutch switch**

## Clutch Switch

### ADJUSTMENT

1. Prop clutch pedal in full–up position.
2. Loosen retaining screw.
3. Put 0.030 in. (0.76mm) shim between switch plunger cap and the striker pad on the clutch pedal.
4. Slide switch toward clutch pedal until switch plunger is seated against switch housing. Tighten retaining screw.

## Actuator Cable

### ADJUSTMENT

**1984–88 Models**

1. With the engine OFF, set throttle plate to total closed position, and the choke linkage is decammed, if equipped.
2. Remove the locking pin.
3. Pull bead chain through adjuster.
4. Insert locking pin in its best hole of the adjuster for a tight bead chain without opening the throttle plate.
5. Road test the vehicle.

**1989–94 Models**

1. With the engine OFF, set throttle linkage so that the throttle plate is closed.
2. Remove locking pin.
3. On 3.0L engines, remove the speed control actuator cable retaining clip.
4. Pull bead chain through adjuster.
5. On 3.0L engines, pull actuator cable through adjuster until slight tension is felt.
6. Insert locking pin in its best hole of the adjuster for a tight bead chain without opening the throttle plate.
7. On 3.0L engines, insert cable retaining clip and snap into place when complete.
8. Road test the vehicle.

## ENTERTAINMENT SYSTEMS

## Receiver/Tape Player

### REMOVAL & INSTALLATION

**1984–88 Models**

▶ See Figures 43, 44, 45 and 46

1. Disconnect the negative battery cable.
2. Remove center instrument trim panel around the stereo unit.
3. Remove the stereo mounting plate attaching screws.
4. Pull stereo unit carefully to disengage it from the lower rear support bracket. Remove from instrument panel as far as possible.

5. Disconnect wiring connectors and antenna cable from the rear of the stereo.

**To install:**

6. Transfer mounting brackets to new radio, if necessary.
7. Connect wiring harnesses and antenna cable to the back of the stereo unit.
8. Position the stereo in the instrument panel, taking care to align the tabs on the bracket with the holes in the instrument panel. Secure unit with retaining screws.
9. Install center trim around stereo.
10. Connect negative battery terminal.
11. Test unit for proper reception on both AM and FM.

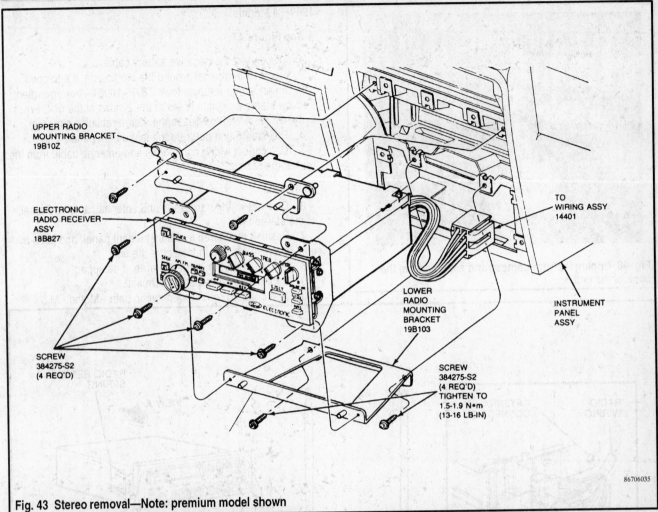

UPPER RADIO
MOUNTING BRACKET
19B10Z

ELECTRONIC
RADIO RECEIVER
ASSY
18B827

SCREW
384275-S2
(4 REQ'D)

LOWER
RADIO
MOUNTING
BRACKET
19B103

SCREW
384275-S2
(4 REQ'D)
TIGHTEN TO
1.5-1.9 N•m
(13-16 LB-IN)

TO
WIRING ASSY
14401

INSTRUMENT
PANEL
ASSY

86706035

Fig. 43 Stereo removal—Note: premium model shown

86706510

Fig. 44 With the trim panel and knobs removed, unscrew
the retaining hardware from all sides of the unit

86706511

Fig. 45 Remove the radio enough to access the wire
harness and antenna cable

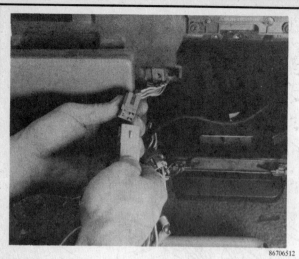

**Fig. 46 Unplug the wire harness and antenna from the back of the unit**

86706512

### 1989–94 Models

▶ See Figure 47

1. Disconnect the negative battery cable.
2. Remove trim panel around the stereo unit, if equipped.
3. Insert stereo removal tools T87P–19061–A or equivalent into the stereo faceplate holes at the 2 sides of the unit. Press in 1.0 in. (25.4mm) to release the stereo retaining clips.
4. Pull stereo unit out from the instrument panel.
5. Disconnect wiring connectors and antenna cable from the rear of the stereo.

#### To install:

6. Connect wiring harnesses and antenna cable to the back of the stereo unit.
7. Position the stereo in the instrument panel, and push in until retaining clip clip in to secure the unit.
8. Install center trim around stereo, if equipped.
9. Connect negative battery terminal.
10. Test unit for proper reception on both AM and FM.

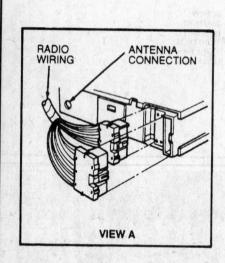

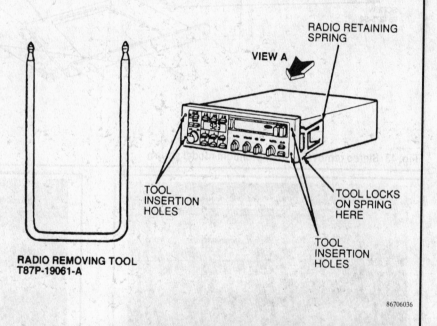

RADIO WIRING
ANTENNA CONNECTION
VIEW A

RADIO REMOVING TOOL
T87P-19061-A

RADIO RETAINING SPRING
VIEW A
TOOL INSERTION HOLES
TOOL LOCKS ON SPRING HERE
TOOL INSERTION HOLES

**Fig. 47 Stereo removal—1989–94 models**

86706036

## RECEPTION ADJUSTMENT

For best FM reception, adjust the antenna to 31 in. (787mm) in height. Fading or weak AM reception may be adjusted by means of the antenna trimmer control. located either on the right rear of front side of the radio chassis. See the owner's manual for position. To adjust the trimmer:

1. Extend the antenna to its maximum height.
2. Tune the radio to a weak station around 1600 KC. Adjust the volume so that the sound is barely audible.
3. Adjust the trimmer to obtain maximum volume.

## Graphic Equalizer

### REMOVAL & INSTALLATION

➡ This option was available on Tempo/Topaz vehicles until 1989.

1. Remove negative battery terminal.
2. Remove 4 retaining screws which secure the console trim panel.
3. Unfasten the 4 equalizer attaching screws.

4. Carefully pull the equalizer out.

5. Disengage the connectors from the rear of the equalizer, and remove unit.

**To install:**

6. Plug connectors into the rear of the equalizer.

7. Position equalizer in the instrument panel, and secure with attaching screws.

8. Position the console trim panel, and secure with retaining screws.

9. Connect negative battery cable.

10. Listen to stereo to ensure equalizer functions correctly.

## Power Amplifier

➡ **The power amplifier for Premium Sound Systems, available on Tempo/Topaz is located on the bottom of the package shelf, accessible from the luggage compartment.**

### REMOVAL & INSTALLATION

▶ **See Figure 48**

1. Disconnect the negative battery cable.

2. Remove the 2 nuts securing the amplifier to the bottom of the package tray in the luggage compartment.

3. Disengage the electrical connectors on the amplifier and remove.

**To install:**

4. Plug connectors into the amplifier.

5. Position amplifier to luggage compartment package tray and secure with retaining nuts.

6. Connect negative battery terminal.

7. Test sound system for proper operation.

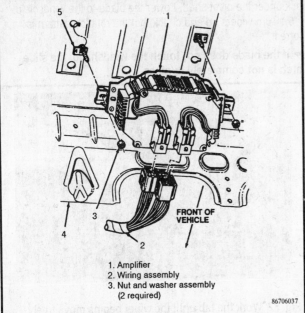

1. Amplifier
2. Wiring assembly
3. Nut and washer assembly (2 required)

86706037

**Fig. 48 Removal of stereo amplifier in trunk compartment**

## Speakers

### REMOVAL & INSTALLATION

**Front**

▶ **See Figure 49**

1. Remove negative battery cable.

2. Remove door panels outlined in Section 10.

3. With the door panel removed, unfasten retaining screws securing the speaker to the door.

4. Unplug the connector at the back of the speaker.

**To install:**

5. Plug wire connector on back of speaker.

6. Position and secure speaker to door with retaining screws.

7. Install door panel.

8. Connect negative battery cable.

9. Listen to stereo to ensure proper functioning of speakers.

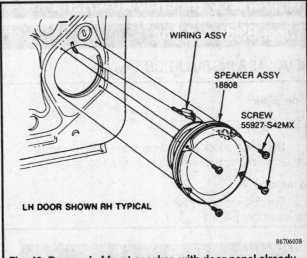

WIRING ASSY

SPEAKER ASSY
18808

SCREW
55927-S42MX

LH DOOR SHOWN RH TYPICAL

86706038

**Fig. 49 Removal of front speaker, with door panel already removed**

**Rear**

▶ **See Figure 50**

1. Remove the negative battery cable.

2. From within the luggage compartment, disconnect connected from the speaker.

3. Pull one end of the speaker rubber retaining strap to disengage the speaker from the tab on the package tray, and remove the speaker.

**To install:**

4. Position speaker and strap assembly in place against package tray. Secure speaker with rubber strap attached to hooks on tray.

5. Connect harness to speaker.

6. Install negative cable to battery.

7. Turn stereo on to ensure speakers work properly.

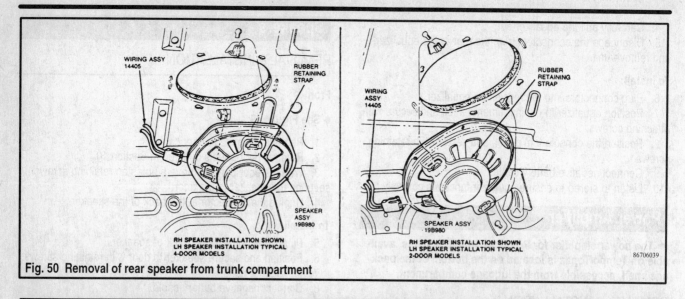

**Fig. 50 Removal of rear speaker from trunk compartment**

## WINDSHIELD WIPERS AND WASHERS

### Wiper Blade and Arm

#### REMOVAL & INSTALLATION

**Wiper Blade**

♦ See Figure 51

1. Depress the lock on the wiper blade body, or mounting bracket which separates the wiper arm and blade.

**To install:**

2. Position and push new blade on to the arm until the blade lock clicks into place.

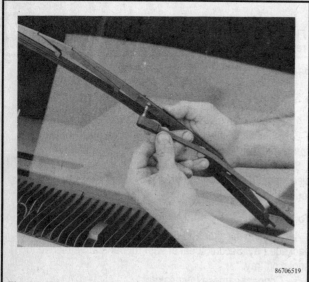

**Fig. 51 Wiper blade removal**

**Wiper Arm**

➡ See Figures 52, 53 and 54

1. Raise the blade end of the arm off the windshield and move the slide latch away from the pivot shaft.

2. The wiper arm should now be unlocked and can be pulled off of the pivot shaft with ease.

**To install:**

3. Position the arm over the pivot pin, hold it down and push the main arm head over the pivot shaft. Make sure the pivot shaft is in the park position.

4. Hold the main arm head on the pivot shaft while raising the blade end of the wiper arm and push the slide latch into the lock under the pivot shaft. Lower the blade to the windshield.

5. Turn wipers on and check that the rotation pattern is correct.

➡ **If the blade does not touch the windshield, the slide latch is not completely in place.**

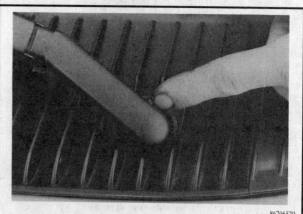

**Fig. 52 Work the tab until the wiper begins move freely from side to side**

Fig. 53 Work the arm side to side with a twisting motion

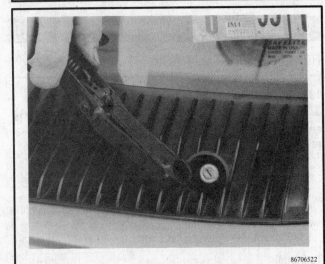

Fig. 54 Pry the arm away from the vehicle

## WIPER ARM AND BLADE ADJUSTMENT

1. With the wiper arm and blade assemblies removed from the pivot shafts turn on the wiper switch and allow the motor to move the pivot shaft three or four cycles, and then turn off the wiper switch. This will place the pivot shafts in the park position.

2. Install the arm and blade assemblies on the pivot shafts to the correct distance between the windshield lower molding or weatherstrip and the blade saddle centerline.

3. Turn wipers on to make sure the rotational pattern is correct.

## Windshield Wiper Motor

### REMOVAL & INSTALLATION

♦ See Figures 55, 56, 57, 58, 59 and 60

1. Disconnect the negative battery cable.

2. Lift the water shield cover from the cowl on the passenger side.

3. Disconnect the power lead from the motor.

4. Remove the linkage retaining clip from the operating arm on the motor by lifting the locking tab up, and pulling the clip away from the pin.

5. Remove the attaching bolts from the motor and bracket assembly and remove the motor from the vehicle.

6. With the motor assembly removed, unscrew the 3 bolts and separate the motor from the mounting bracket.

**To install:**

7. Position the motor on the mounting bracket and install the retaining bolts.

8. Install the operating arm to the motor.

9. Fasten the linkage retaining clip to the operating arm.

10. Engage the electrical lead to the motor.

11. Install the water shield cover to the cowl.

12. Connect the negative battery cable.

13. Turn the wipers on and check for correct operation.

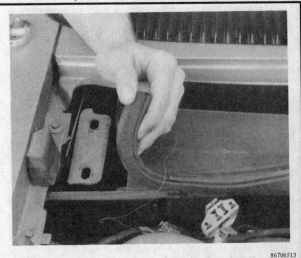

Fig. 55 Remove the stripping from the cowl area

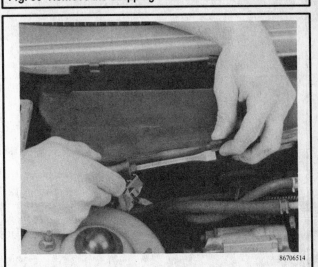

Fig. 56 Pry up the clips securing the protective panel over the wiper motor. When all the clips are removed, lift the panel up and away

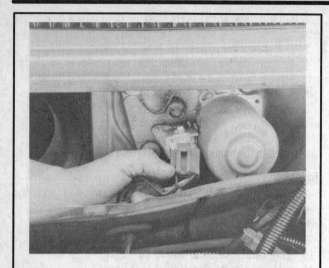

Fig. 57 Unplug the harness from the motor

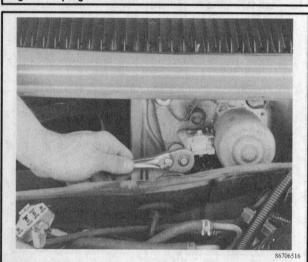

Fig. 58 Remove the bolts securing the motor to the bracket

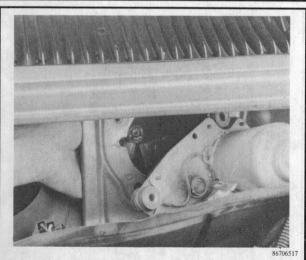

Fig. 59 Pry the wiper attachment arm off the motor assembly

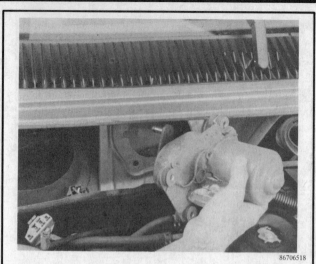

Fig. 60 Remove the motor from the vehicle. Now is a good time to remove any leaves which may be in this area

## Windshield Wiper Switch

### REMOVAL & INSTALLATION

#### 1984–88 Models

➡ The wiper/washer switch is located in the handle, and is an integral part of the switch. It cannot be removed separately.

1. Disconnect the negative battery cable.
2. Remove the upper and lower steering column strouds.
3. Disengage the electrical harness from the handle.
4. Peel the foam seal and remove the 2 screws attaching the switch to the steering column.
5. Remove the wiper/washer switch.

**To install:**

6. Position the switch on the steering column and install the 2 attaching screws. Replace the foam over the switch.
7. Connect the electrical harness to the handle.
8. Install the upper and lower shrouds.
9. Connect the negative battery cable.
10. Check wiper/washer for correct operation.

#### 1989–94 Models

▶ See Figure 61

1. Disconnect the negative battery cable.
2. Insert a suitable prying tool into the small slots on top and bottom of the switch bezel.
3. Push down on the tool to work the top of the switch away from the instrument panel.
4. Work the bottom portion of the switch from the panel and completely remove the switch from the panel opening. Hold the switch and pull the wiring at the rear of the switch until the switch connector can be easily disconnected. Disengage the connector and allow the wiring to hang from the switch mounting opening.

**To install:**

5.  Connect the wiring connector to the new switch and route the wiring back into the mounting opening. Insert the switch into the opening so the graphics are properly aligned.

6.  Push on the switch until the bezel seats against the instrument panel and the clips lock the switch into place.

7.  Connect the negative battery cable.

8.  Turn wipers on and check for correct functioning.

## Interval Governor Module

### REMOVAL & INSTALLATION

▶ **See Figure 62**

1.  Disconnect the negative battery cable.

2.  Remove the steering wheel column strouds to expose piece.

3.  Disengage the connector at the fuse panel.

4.  Remove the 2 retaining screws securing the interval governor assembly to the column bracket.

**To install:**

5.  Position interval governor on steering column brace and install the 2 retaining screws, tightening to 13–17 in. lbs. (1.5–2.0 Nm).

6.  Connect electrical harness to unit.

7.  Install steering wheel strouds.

8.  Connect negative battery terminal.

9.  Check wiper system for proper operation.

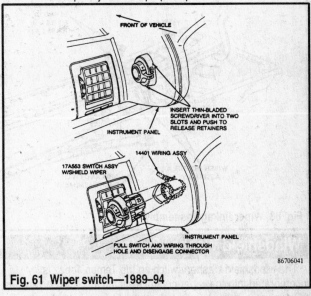

**Fig. 61  Wiper switch—1989–94**

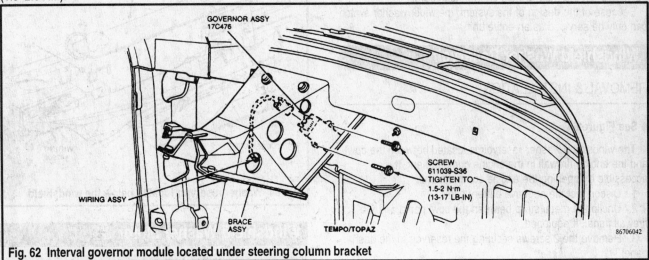

**Fig. 62  Interval governor module located under steering column bracket**

## Wiper Linkage

The wiper linkage is mounted below the cowl panel. It can be reached from the engine compartment pivot shafts and linkage assemblies are connected together with non–removable plastic ball joints. Left and right pivot shafts and linkage are serviced as one unit only.

### REMOVAL & INSTALLATION

▶ **See Figure 63**

1.  Disconnect the negative battery cable.

2.  Remove left and right cowl grilles.

3.  Remove both the windshield wiper arms.

4.  Remove clip on motor drive arm and disconnect the linkage from the motor crank pin.

5.  Unfasten the attaching screws securing the pivot assemblies to the cowl. Remove the linkage and pivot from the engine compartment area.

**To install:**

6.  Position the pivot and linkage assembly in the cowl and install the retaining screws.

7.  Connect the linkage to the crank pin using the retaining clip.

8.  Install both cowl grilles.

9.  Position and secure both wiper arms, taking care to check their position on the windshield.

10.  Connect the negative battery cable.

11.  Check wiper system for correct operation.

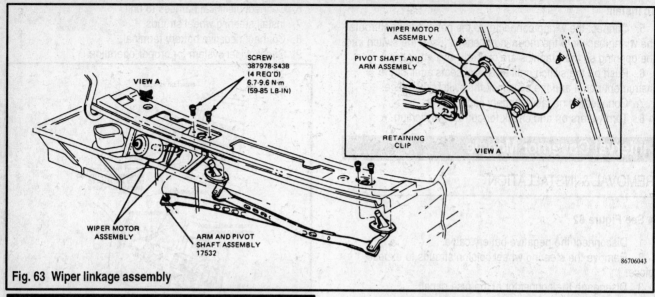

Fig. 63 Wiper linkage assembly

## Windshield Washer Switch

The windshield washer switch on the Tempo/Topaz is incorporated into the wiper control switch. On 1984–88 vehicles, this feature is is the handle behind the steering wheel on the left. On 1989–94 vehicles. the washer function is actuated by pushing in on the wiper switch on the dashboard.

Because of the design of the system, the wiper/washer switch can only be serviced as an entire unit.

## Windshield Washer Reservoir

### REMOVAL & INSTALLATION

◆ See Figure 64

The windshield washer reservoir is located between the cowl and the engine firewall in the engine compartment. It is accessible by opening the engine compartment.

1. Disconnect the negative battery cable.
2. Unclip the metal strap between the cowl panel and the firewall panel, if equipped.
3. Remove the 2 screws securing the reservoir to the dash panel.
4. Remove the reservoir from the engine compartment as far as possible, in order to disconnect the remaining parts.
5. Unplug the harness to the washer motor.
6. Grip the washer pump firmly, turn back and forth, and remove.

**To install:**

7. Lubricate the washer pump seal with a dry lubricant like powdered graphite. Install the washer pump by aligning the projection on the motor end cap with the slot in the reservoir and slide in until tight.
8. Plug the electrical connector into the washer motor.
9. Place the reservoir in the engine compartment and secure with the 2 retaining screws and metal strap clipped to the cowl and firewall panel, if equipped.
10. Connect the negative battery cable.

11. Check the washer system for proper operation.

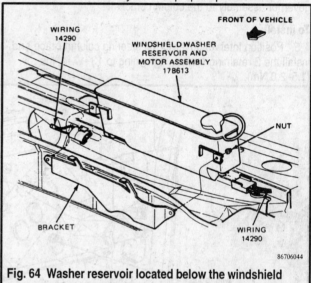

Fig. 64 Washer reservoir located below the windshield

## Windshield Washer Motor

### REMOVAL & INSTALLATION

◆ See Figure 65

1. Disconnect the negative battery cable.
2. Remove the washer reservoir as outline in the reservoir removal procedure.
3. Remove the wire harness from the washer motor.
4. With the reservoir removed from the vehicle, grasp the motor firmly, turn back and forth to loosen the unit in the seal, and pull out.
5. Check the seal between the motor and the reservoir, and replace if necessary.

**To install:**

6. Lubricate the washer pump seal with a dry lubricant like powdered graphite. Install the washer pump by aligning the projection on the motor end cap with the slot in the reservoir and slide in until tight.

7. Plug the electrical connector into the washer motor.

8. Place the reservoir in the engine compartment and secure with the 2 retaining screws and metal strap clipped to the cowl and firewall panel, if equipped.

9. Connect the negative battery cable.

10. Check the washer system for proper operation.

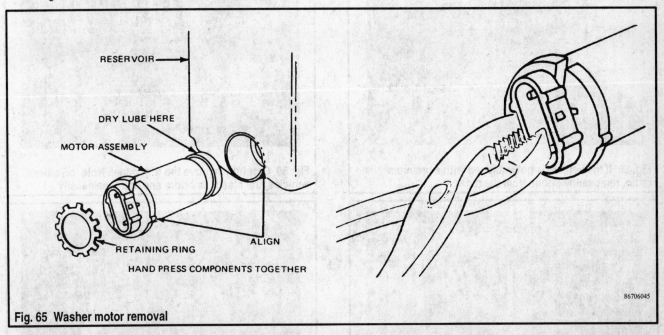

**Fig. 65 Washer motor removal**

## INSTRUMENT CLUSTER

### Instrument Cluster

➡ **Certain years and trim levels will not have as detailed an instrument arrangement as compared to other vehicles.**

#### REMOVAL & INSTALLATION

**1984–88 Models**

▶ **See Figures 66, 67, 68, 69, and 70**

1. Disconnect the negative battery cable.

2. Remove the radio knobs if the vehicle is equipped with a non–premium stereo. You can tell by the 2 knobs on either side of the unit.

3. Remove the instrument cluster finish panel screws and other trim pieces as required, and remove the finish panel.

4. Remove the steering wheel.

5. Remove the upper and lower screws retaining the instrument cluster to the instrument panel.

6. Disconnect the speedometer cable by reaching under the instrument panel and pressing on the flat surface of the speedometer cable quick connector, and pushing away from the speedometer housing.

7. Pull the cluster away from the instrument panel and disengage the electrical feed plug to the cluster from its receptacle in the printed circuit board.

**To install:**

8. Plug the electrical connectors into the instrument cluster at the circuit board.

9. Connect the speedometer cable to the speedometer in the cluster.

10. Position the instrument cluster into the instrument panel and secure with retaining screws at the upper and lower portion of the unit.

11. Install the steering wheel and tighten nut to specification.

12. Install the cluster finish panel, radio knobs and any other trim pieces removed earlier.

13. Connect the negative battery cable.

14. Road test the vehicle to make sure the instruments and warning lamps function correctly.

Fig. 66 If the vehicle is not equipped with a premium radio, remove the knobs from the radio

Fig. 67 Remove the retaining screw above the stereo

Fig. 68 Unscrew the retaining screws below the radio and around the trim panel

Fig. 69 Carefully remove the trim panel. Note, on older vehicles, the plastic is brittle and can break easily

Fig. 70 Remove the screws around the instrument cluster

**1989–94 Models**

▶ **See Figures 71 and 72**

1. Disconnect the negative battery cable.
2. Remove the retaining screws at the bottom of the steering column opening and snap the steering column cover out.
3. Remove the steering column trim shroud.
4. Remove the snap–in lower cluster finish panels.
5. Remove the cluster opening finish panel retaining screws and pull the panel rearward.
6. Disconnect the speedometer cable at the transaxle.
7. Remove the screws retaining the instrument cluster and carefully pull rearward enough to disengage the speedometer cable.
8. Carefully pull the cluster away from the instrument panel. Disconnect the cluster feed plugs from the printed circuit board.

**To install:**

9. Plug the electrical connectors into the instrument cluster at the circuit board.

10. Connect the speedometer cable to the speedometer in the cluster.

11. Position the instrument cluster into the instrument panel and secure with retaining screws at the upper and lower portion of the unit.

12. Connect the speedometer cable to the transaxle.

13. Position and secure the steering wheel stroud as well as the panel below the steering column.

14. Connect the negative battery cable.

15. Road test the vehicle to make sure the instruments and warning lamps function correctly.

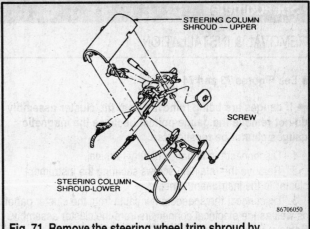

**Fig. 71 Remove the steering wheel trim shroud by removing the screws from the bottom portion**

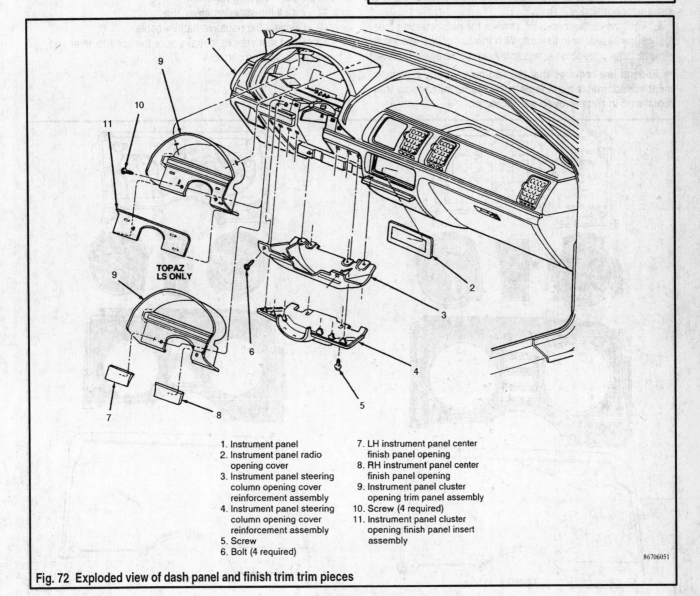

1. Instrument panel
2. Instrument panel radio opening cover
3. Instrument panel steering column opening cover reinforcement assembly
4. Instrument panel steering column opening cover reinforcement assembly
5. Screw
6. Bolt (4 required)
7. LH instrument panel center finish panel opening
8. RH instrument panel center finish panel opening
9. Instrument panel cluster opening trim panel assembly
10. Screw (4 required)
11. Instrument panel cluster opening finish panel insert assembly

**Fig. 72 Exploded view of dash panel and finish trim trim pieces**

## Speedometer

### REMOVAL & INSTALLATION

♦ **See Figures 73 and 74**

➡ **If gauges are being removed from the cluster assembly, do not remove the gauge pointer because the magnetic gauges cannot be recalibrated.**

1. Disconnect the negative battery terminal.
2. Remove the retaining screws securing the instrument cluster to the instrument panel.
3. Disconnect the speedometer cable from the cluster panel, as well as the electrical connectors from the cluster assembly. Remove the instrument cluster.
4. Remove the retaining screws securing the backplate to the instrument housing.
5. With the cluster removed, remove the nuts retaining the fuel gauge assembly to the unit. With the fuel gauge assembly removed, the speedometer assembly can be carefully removed.

➡ **Federal law requires that the odometer in any replacement speedometer must register the same mileage as that registered in the removed speedometer.**

**To install:**

6. Carefully install speedometer assembly into cluster housing.

### ✳✳CAUTION

**The speedometer is calibrated at the factory. excessive rough handling can disturb the calibration.**

7. Install the fuel gauge assembly into the cluster housing and secure with the retaining screws.
8. Position and secure the cluster backplate with retaining screws.
9. Engage the electrical connector to the back of the cluster assembly.
10. Install the cluster assembly into the instrument panel and secure with retaining hardware.
11. Install the speedometer cable.
12. Connect the negative battery cable.
13. Road test vehicle to make sure the speedometer and odometer function correctly.

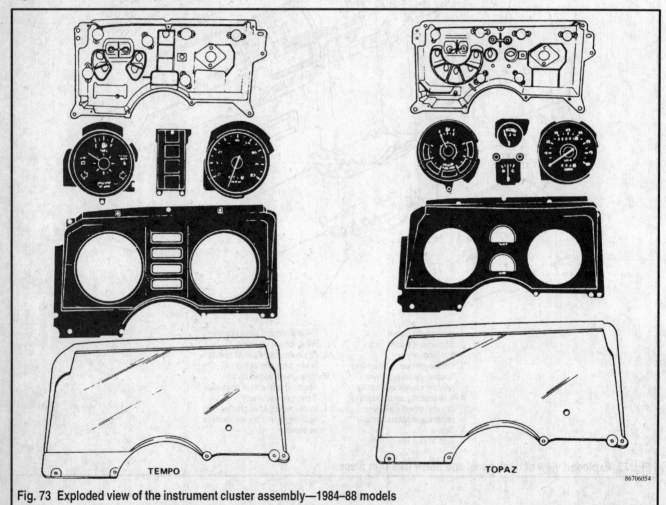

TEMPO          TOPAZ

86706054

**Fig. 73 Exploded view of the instrument cluster assembly—1984–88 models**

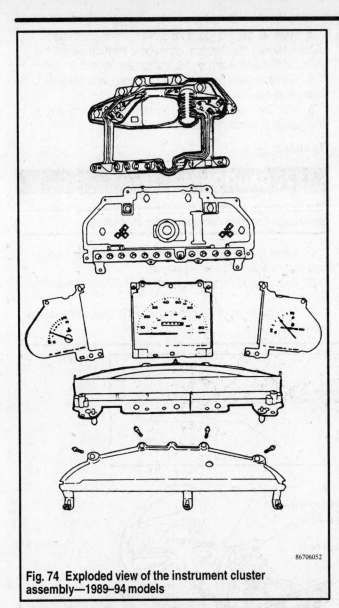

**Fig. 74 Exploded view of the instrument cluster assembly—1989–94 models**

## Tachometer

### REMOVAL & INSTALLATION

➡ **If gauges are being removed from the cluster assembly, do not remove the gauge pointer because the magnetic gauges cannot be recalibrated.**

1. Disconnect the negative battery terminal.
2. Remove the retaining screws securing the instrument cluster to the instrument panel.
3. Disconnect the speedometer cable from the cluster panel, as well as the electrical connectors from the cluster assembly. Remove the instrument cluster.
4. Remove the retaining screws securing the backplate to the instrument panel housing.
5. With the cluster removed, remove the nuts retaining the tachometer assembly to the unit.

**To install:**
6. Carefully install tachometer assembly into cluster housing.

### ✳✳CAUTION

**The tachometer is calibrated at the factory. excessive rough handling can disturb the calibration.**

7. Install the tachometer assembly into the cluster housing and secure with the retaining screws.
8. Position and secure the cluster backplate with retaining screws.
9. Engage the electrical connector to the back of the cluster assembly.
10. Install the cluster assembly into the instrument panel and secure with retaining hardware.
11. Install the speedometer cable.
12. Connect the negative battery cable.
13. Road test vehicle to make sure the instruments function correctly.

## Speedometer Cable

### REMOVAL & INSTALLATION

◆ **See Figure 75**

1. Disconnect the negative battery terminal.
2. Remove the retaining screws securing the instrument cluster to the instrument panel.
3. Remove the retaining screws securing the panel below the steering column, and remove the panel.
4. Disconnect the speedometer cable from the cluster panel.
5. From inside the engine compartment, loosen the retaining nut securing the speedometer cable to the transaxle housing.
6. Disconnect the speed sensor wire harness from the speedometer cable.
7. Remove the speedometer cable from the transaxle housing.
8. Carefully and gently pull the speedometer cable through the firewall into the engine compartment.
9. With the cable removed, check the gear at the transaxle end of the cable for signs of wear, and replace if necessary.

**To install:**
10. Slowly and carefully feed the cable through the firewall into the interior compartment. Feed the cable through the bracket above the steering column. Once it is fed into the interior of the vehicle, loosely secure cable to instrument cluster. Make sure the rubber grommets on the cable are securely in place.
11. Insert the other end of the speedometer cable into the transaxle, and secure with the retaining nut tightening it to 31–40 inch lbs. (3.4–4.5 Nm).
12. Remove the speedometer cable from the instrument cluster in order to engage the electrical connectors to the

instrument cluster. Then install the speedometer cable and tighten.

13. Install the instrument cluster into the dash panel and secure with the retaining screws.

14. Position and tighten with retaining hardware the lower panel below the steering column.

15. Connect the negative battery terminal.

16. Road test vehicle to make sure the speedometer and odometer function correctly.

## Fuel Gauge

### REMOVAL & INSTALLATION

1. Disconnect the negative battery terminal.

2. Remove the retaining screws securing the instrument cluster to the instrument panel.

3. Remove the retaining screws securing the panel below the steering column and remove the panel.

4. Remove the speedometer cable from the instrument cluster. Unplug the electrical connectors from the rear of the instrument cluster. Remove the instrument cluster.

5. Remove the retaining screws securing the backplate to the instrument housing.

6. With the cluster removed, remove the nuts retaining the fuel gauge assembly to the unit.

**To install:**

## ✳✳CAUTION

**The fuel gauge assembly is calibrated at the factory. excessive rough handling can disturb the calibration.**

7. Install the fuel gauge assembly into the cluster housing and secure with the retaining screws.

8. Position and secure the cluster backplate with retaining screws.

9. Plug in the electrical connector to the back of the cluster assembly.

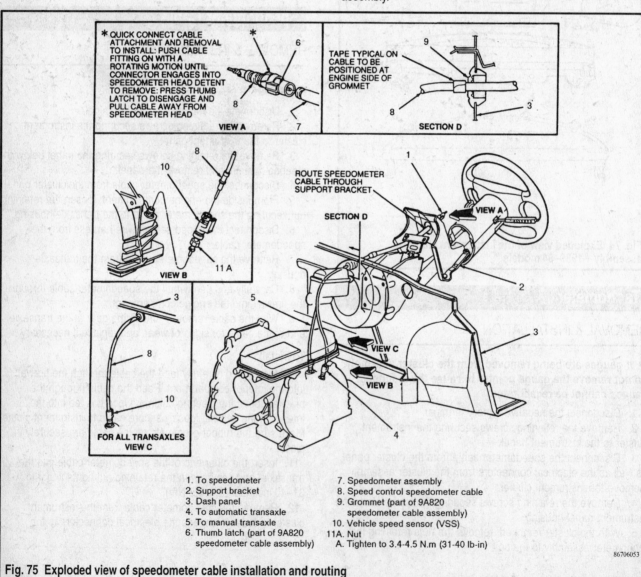

* QUICK CONNECT CABLE ATTACHMENT AND REMOVAL
TO INSTALL: PUSH CABLE FITTING ON WITH A ROTATING MOTION UNTIL CONNECTOR ENGAGES INTO SPEEDOMETER HEAD DETENT
TO REMOVE: PRESS THUMB LATCH TO DISENGAGE AND PULL CABLE AWAY FROM SPEEDOMETER HEAD

VIEW A

TAPE TYPICAL ON CABLE TO BE POSITIONED AT ENGINE SIDE OF GROMMET

SECTION D

VIEW B

ROUTE SPEEDOMETER CABLE THROUGH SUPPORT BRACKET

SECTION D

VIEW A

VIEW C

VIEW B

FOR ALL TRANSAXLES VIEW C

1. To speedometer
2. Support bracket
3. Dash panel
4. To automatic transaxle
5. To manual transaxle
6. Thumb latch (part of 9A820 speedometer cable assembly)
7. Speedometer assembly
8. Speed control speedometer cable
9. Grommet (part of 9A820 speedometer cable assembly)
10. Vehicle speed sensor (VSS)
11A. Nut
A. Tighten to 3.4-4.5 N.m (31-40 lb-in)

86706053

**Fig. 75 Exploded view of speedometer cable installation and routing**

10. Install the cluster assembly into the instrument panel and secure with retaining hardware.

11. Install the speedometer cable.

12. Connect the negative battery cable.

13. Road test vehicle to make sure the instruments and speedometer function correctly.

## Temperature Gauge

### REMOVAL & INSTALLATION

1. Disconnect the negative battery terminal.

2. Remove the retaining screws securing the instrument cluster to the instrument panel.

3. Remove the retaining screws securing the panel below the steering column and remove the panel.

4. Remove the speedometer cable from the instrument cluster. Unplug the electrical connectors from the rear of the instrument cluster. Remove the instrument cluster.

5. Remove the retaining screws securing the backplate to the instrument housing.

6. With the cluster removed, remove the nuts retaining the temperature gauge assembly to the unit.

**To install:**

### ✳✳CAUTION

**The temperature gauge assembly is calibrated at the factory. excessive rough handling can disturb the calibration.**

7. Install the temperature gauge assembly into the cluster housing and secure with the retaining screws.

8. Position and secure the cluster backplate with retaining screws.

9. Engage the electrical connector to the back of the cluster assembly.

10. Install the cluster assembly into the instrument panel and secure with retaining hardware.

11. Install the speedometer cable.

12. Connect the negative battery cable.

13. Road test vehicle to make sure the instruments and speedometer function correctly.

## Printed Circuit Board

➡ **Because of the different configurations of instrument clusters, when replacing a printed circuit board, make sure you purchase one which will function will the equipped gauges in the vehicle.**

### REMOVAL & INSTALLATION

1. Disconnect the negative battery terminal.

2. Remove the retaining screws securing the instrument cluster to the instrument panel.

3. Remove the retaining screws securing the panel below the steering column and remove the panel.

4. Remove the speedometer cable from the instrument cluster. Unplug the electrical connectors from the rear of the instrument cluster. Remove the instrument cluster

5. Remove the retaining screws securing the backplate to the instrument housing. Remove lense and mask on front of cluster if necessary.

6. With the cluster removed, remove the nuts retaining the temperature gauge, speedometer and any other gauge in the cluster assembly.

7. Remove the illumination and indicator bulbs and socket assemblies.

8. Remove and discard the snap–in connector clips.

9. Carefully begin removing the printed circuit board from the assembly. At times a small screwdriver may be needed to remove a portion.

**To install:**

10. Position circuit board over locating pins and carefully press in pins for a secure fit.

11. Install the illumination and indicator bulbs and sockets into position.

12. Install snap–in connectors.

13. Position and secure the speedometer and any other equipped gauge.

14. Install the mask and lense, if removed.

15. Install backplate and secure with retaining screws.

16. Install any electrical connectors previously removed.

17. Install the cluster assembly into the instrument panel and secure with retaining hardware.

18. Install the speedometer cable.

19. Connect the negative battery cable.

20. Road test vehicle to make sure the instruments and speedometer function correctly.

## Headlight Switch

### REMOVAL & INSTALLATION

#### 1984–88 Models

➡ **See Figure 76**

1. Disconnect the negative battery cable.

2. Remove the retaining screws securing the panel below the steering column. Remove panel.

3. Remove the fuse panel bracket retaining screws. Move the fuse panel assembly aside to gain access to the headlight switch.

4. With one hand behind the instrument panel, push the headlight switch out. Unplug the harness from the switch.

**To install:**

5. Connect the wire harness to the headlight switch.

6. Push the switch into the instrument panel until the switch clips in place.

7. Position the fuse panel and secure with retaining screws.

8. Install and secure with retaining screws, the panel below the steering wheel.

9. Connect the negative battery terminal.

10. Road test the vehicle to make sure the instruments and warning lamps function correctly.

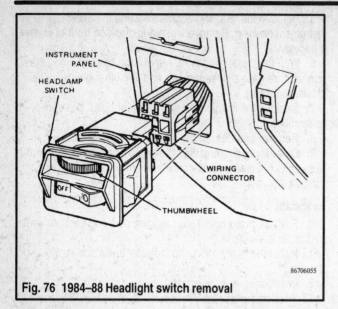

Fig. 76  1984–88 Headlight switch removal

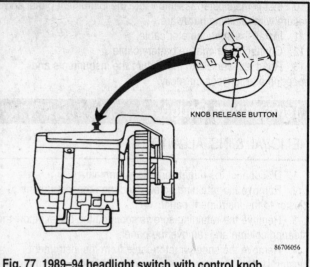

Fig. 77  1989–94 headlight switch with control knob removed. Note the location of the knob release button

## 1989–94 Models

♦ See Figure 77

11. Disconnect the negative battery cable.
12. Remove the left air vent control cable by removing the 2 retaining screws.
13. Remove the fuse panel bracket retaining screws. Move the fuse panel assembly aside to gain access to the headlight switch.
14. Pull headlight to the ON position, and depress the headlight knob and shaft retainer button on the headlight switch and remove the knob and shaft assembly.
15. Remove the headlight switch retaining bezel. Disengage the electrical connector from the switch, and remove the switch from the instrument panel.

**To install:**

16. Connect the wire harness to the headlight switch.
17. Install the headlight switch into the instrument panel. Secure switch with retaining bezel.
18. Install the headlight knob and shaft to the switch and, gentle push shaft until it locks into place
19. Move fuse panel into place and install fuse panel bracket and retaining screws.
20. Install left air vent.
21. Connect the negative battery cable.
22. Road test the vehicle to make sure the instruments and warning lamps function correctly.

## Combination Switch

The combination switch assembly is a multi-function switch comprising turn signal, hazard, headlight dimmer and flash-to-pass functions. The switch lever on the left side of the upper steering column controls the turn signal, headlight dimmer and flash-to-pass functions. The hazard function is controlled by the actuating knob on the bottom part of the steering column.

## REMOVAL & INSTALLATION

1. Disconnect the negative battery cable.
2. Remove the steering column shroud screws and remove the lower steering column shroud.
3. Loosen the steering column attaching nuts enough to allow the removal of the upper trim shroud.
4. Remove the upper shroud.
5. Remove the turn signal switch lever by pulling the lever straight out from the switch. To make removal easier, work the outer end of the lever around with a slight rotary movement before pulling it out.
6. Peel back the foam sight shield from the turn signal switch.
7. Disconnect the turn signal switch electrical connectors.
8. Remove the self-tapping screws that attach the turn signal switch to the lock cylinder housing and disengage the switch from the housing.

**To install:**

9. Align the turn signal switch mounting holes with the corresponding holes in the lock cylinder housing and install self-tapping screws until tight.
10. Apply the foam sight shield to the turn signal switch.
11. Install the turn signal switch lever into the switch by aligning the key on the lever with the keyway in the switch and pushing the lever toward the switch to full engagement.
12. Install the turn signal switch electrical connectors.
13. Install the upper steering column trim shrouds.
14. Torque the steering column attaching nuts to 15–22 ft. lbs. (20–30 Nm).
15. Connect the negative battery cable.
16. Check the steering column and switch assembly for proper operation.

## Clock

♦ See Figure 78

## REMOVAL & INSTALLATION

### 1984–85 Models

1. Disconnect the negative battery cab
2. Remove the cluster opening finish panel screws. Remove the finish panel by rocking upper edge toward the driver's seat.
3. Remove the retaining screws attaching the clock to the instrument panel.
4. Remove the clock from the opening and disengage the electrical connections.

### To install:

5. Engage the electrical connector to the clock. Position the clock in the instrument panel, and secure with the retaining screws.
6. Install the finish panel trim and secure with screws.
7. Connect the negative battery cable.
8. Set time and date.

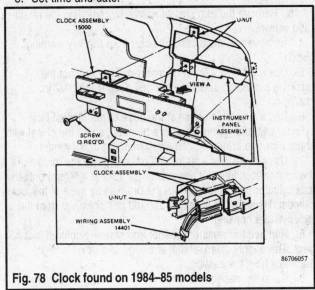

**Fig. 78 Clock found on 1984–85 models**

### 1986–94 Models

➡ **The clock in these models is located in the front headliner between the 2 front seats. to remove the unit, pry the clock module face out of the hole in the instrument panel with a spring hook in the slot at the bottom of the clock and disengage the electrical connector. To install, engage the electrical connector and snap the clock back into the hole.**

9. Disconnect the negative battery cable.
10. Remove the lenses by inserting a suitable tool in one of the notches on the side of the lenses.
11. Remove the screws on the inside of each lens opening.
12. Remove the front screw while supporting the console.
13. Remove the console from the roof. Slide the connector shield off of the electrical connector.

➡ **The shield is moulded to fit securely over the connector. It may be necessary to lift a portion of the shield over the connector ribs before the shield will slide freely.**

14. Disengage the electrical halves. Remove the retaining screws attaching the clock to the console panel.
15. Remove the locators and remove the clock from the opening.

### To install:

16. Position the clock in the console, by aligning the locator pins.
17. Engage the electrical connectors, sliding the shield over the plug when complete, and secure the clock to the console with the retaining screws.
18. Position the console to the headliner and secure by attaching the front screw.
19. Install the screws on the inside of each lense opening, and when complete, install the lense.
20. Connect negative battery cable.
21. Set clock time and date.

## Ignition Lock Cylinder

## REMOVAL & INSTALLATION

### Functional Lock

The following procedure pertains to vehicles that have functional lock cylinders. Functional lock cylinder keys are available for these vehicles or the lock cylinder key numbers are known and the proper key can be made.

1. Disconnect the negative battery cable.
2. If equipped with a tilt steering column, remove the upper extension shroud.
3. Remove the attaching screws and the trim shroud halves.
4. Disconnect the warning buzzer electrical connector. With the key, rotate the cylinder to the RUN position.
5. Take a 1/8 in. (3mm) diameter pin or small wire punch and push on the cylinder retaining pin. The pin is visible through a hole in the mounting surrounding the key cylinder. Push on the pin and withdraw the lock cylinder from the housing.

### To install:

6. Install the lock cylinder by turning it to the RUN position and depressing the retaining pin. Insert the lock cylinder into the housing. Be sure the lock cylinder is fully seated and aligned in the interlocking washer before turning the key to the OFF position. This action will permit the cylinder retaining pin to extend into the cylinder housing hole correctly.
7. Rotate the lock cylinder, using the key, to ensure correct mechanical operation in all positions.
8. Install the electrical connector for the key warning buzzer.
9. Install the lower steering column shroud or trim shroud halves.
10. Connect the negative battery cable.
11. Check for proper start in P or N. Also, make certain the start circuit cannot be actuated in the D and R positions and that the column is locked in the LOCK position.

**Non–Functional Lock**

The following procedure applies to vehicles in which the ignition lock is inoperative and/or the lock cylinder cannot be rotated due to a lost or broken lock cylinder key, the key number is not known or the lock cylinder cap is damaged and/or broken to the extent the lock cylinder cannot be rotated.

1. Make sure the wheels are in the straight ahead position. Disconnect the negative battery cable.

➡ **On most vehicles equipped with an air bag, a backup power supply is included in the system to provide air bag deployment in the event the battery or cables are damaged in an accident before the sensors can close. The power supply is a capacitor that will leak down in approximately 15 minutes after the battery is disconnected or 1 minute if the battery cable positive lead is grounded. If the system is equipped with a backup power supply, it must be disconnected to disarm the system.**

2. If equipped with an air bag, perform the following procedure:

a. Remove the screws retaining the steering column opening cover to the instrument panel and remove the cover.

b. Remove the bolts retaining the bolster and remove the bolster.

c. Disconnect the backup power supply connector

d. Remove the nut and washer assemblies retaining the air bag to the steering wheel.

e. Disconnect the driver air bag electrical connector from the contact assembly connectors and remove the air bag assembly.

### ✳✳CAUTION

**When carrying a live air bag, make sure the bag and trim cover are pointed away from the body. In the unlikely event of an accidental deployment, the bag will then deploy with minimal chance of injury. In addition, when placing a live air bag on a bench or other surface, always face the bag and trim cover up, away from the surface. This will reduce the motion of the module if it is accidentally deployed.**

f. Remove the steering wheel retaining bolt and remove the vibration damper, then reinstall the bolt loosely on the shaft.

g. Loosen the steering wheel on the shaft using a suitable puller.

➡ **Do not use a knock–off type steering wheel puller or strike the retaining bolt with a hammer. This could cause damage to the steering shaft bearings.**

h. Remove and discard the steering wheel retaining bolt and remove the steering wheel.

i. Remove the upper and lower shrouds.

j. Disconnect the air bag clockspring connector from the column harness.

➡ **Before removing the air bag clockspring from the steering shaft, the clockspring must be taped to prevent the clockspring rotor from being turned accidentally and damaging the clockspring.**

k. Remove the screws that secure the clockspring to the retainer plate and remove the clockspring.

3. If not equipped with an air bag, perform the following procedure:

a. Remove the horn pad cover by removing 2 or 4 screws from the back of the steering wheel assembly.

➡ **The emblem assembly is removed after the horn pad cover is removed, by pushing out from the backside of the emblem.**

b. Remove the energy absorbing foam from the wheel assembly, if equipped. Remember to reinstall it when the steering wheel is reassembled.

c. Disconnect the horn pad wiring connector.

d. Loosen the steering wheel retaining bolt 4–6 turns. Do not remove the bolt.

e. Loosen the steering wheel on the shaft using a suitable puller.

➡ **Do not use a knock–off type steering wheel puller or strike the retaining bolt with a hammer. This could cause damage to the steering shaft bearings.**

f. Remove and discard the steering wheel retaining bolt and remove the steering wheel.

g. If equipped with a tilt column, remove the upper extension shroud.

h. Remove the trim shroud halves by removing the retaining screws.

4. Remove the electrical connector from the key warning switch.

5. Using a 1/8 in. (3mm) diameter drill bit, drill out the retaining pin, being careful not to drill deeper than 1/2 in. (12.7mm).

6. Place a suitable chisel at the base of the ignition lock cylinder cap and, using a suitable hammer, strike the chisel with sharp blows to break the cap away from the lock cylinder.

7. Using a 3/8 in. diameter drill bit, drill down the middle of the ignition lock key slot approximately 13/4 in. (44mm) until the lock cylinder breaks loose from the breakaway base of the lock cylinder. Remove the lock cylinder and drill shavings from the lock cylinder housing.

8. Remove the retainer, washer and steering column lock gear. Thoroughly clean all drill shavings and other foreign materials from the casting.

9. Carefully inspect the lock cylinder housing for damage from the foregoing operation. If any damage is evident, the housing must be replaced.

**To install:**

10. Install the ignition lock drive gear, washer and retainer.

11. Install the ignition lock cylinder and check for smooth operation.

12. Engage the electrical connector to the key warning switch.

13. If equipped with an air bag, install the clockspring, steering wheel and air bag module as follows:

a. Place the clockspring onto the steering shaft. Install the 2 retaining screws that secure the clockspring to the retainer plate. Make sure the ground wire is secured with the lower retaining screw. Remove the tape that was installed during the removal procedure.

b. Connect the clockspring wire to the column harness.

c. Install the upper and lower shroud.

d. Install the steering wheel on the steering column, making sure the alignment marks are correct. Install the vibration damper and a new retaining bolt. Tighten the bolt to 23–33 ft. lbs. (31–45 Nm).

e. Connect the air bag module wire to the clockspring connector and place the air bag module on the steering wheel. Install the retaining nuts and tighten to 35–53 inch lbs. (4–6 Nm).

f. Connect the backup power supply connector and install the bolster and steering column opening cover.

g. Connect the negative battery cable and verify the air bag indicator.

14. If not equipped with an air bag, complete the installation as follows:

a. Install the trim shroud halves.

b. Install the steering wheel assembly on the steering column making sure the alignment marks are correct. Install a new retaining bolt and tighten to 23–33 ft. lbs. (31–45 Nm).

c. Connect the horn pad wiring connector. If equipped, install the energy absorbing foam.

d. Install the horn pad cover and the retaining screws. Make sure the wires are not pinched. Tighten the screws to 8–10 inch lbs. (0.9–1.1 Nm).

e. Connect the negative battery cable.

15. Check to make the sure the lock key goes in and comes out of the cylinder easily.

## Ignition Switch

### REMOVAL & INSTALLATION

1. Disconnect the negative battery cable.

2. Remove the steering column upper and lower trim shroud by removing the self–tapping screws. The steering column attaching nuts may have to be loosened enough to allow removal of the upper shroud.

3. Remove the bolts and nuts holding the steering column assembly to the steering column bracket assembly, and lower the steering column to the seat.

4. Disengage the electrical connector from the ignition switch.

5. Rotate ignition lock cylinder to the RUN position.

6. Remove the screws attaching the switch to he lock cylinder housing.

7. Disengage the ignition switch from the actuator pin.

**To install:**

8. Check to see that the actuator pin slot in the ignition switch is in the RUN position.

➡ **A new switch assembly will be pre–set in the RUN position.**

9. Make certain the ignition key lock cylinder is in approximately the RUN position to properly locate the lock actuator pin. The RUN position is achieved by rotating the key lock cylinder approximately 90 degrees from the LOCK position.

10. Install the ignition switch onto the actuator pin. It may be necessary to move the switch slightly back and fourth to align the switch mounting holes with the column lock housing threaded holes.

11. Install the new screws and tighten to 50–70 inch lbs. (5.6–7.9 Nm).

12. Engage the electrical connector to ignition switch.

13. Connect the negative battery cable.

14. Check the ignition switch for proper function including START and ACC positions. Also make certain the steering column is locked when in the LOCK position.

15. Position the top half of the shroud on the steering column.

16. Install the bolts and nuts attaching the steering column assembly to the steering column bracket assembly. Tighten to 15–25 ft. lbs. (20–34 Nm).

17. Position lower shroud to upper shroud and install the self–tapping screws.

## Brake Light (Stoplight) Switch

▶ **See Figure 79**

The mechanical brake light switch assembly is installed on the pin of the brake pedal arm, so that it straddles the master cylinder pushrod.

### REMOVAL & INSTALLATION

1. Disconnect the negative battery cable.

2. Disconnect the wire harness at the connector from the switch.

➡ **The locking tab must be lifted before the connector can be removed.**

3. Remove the hairpin retainer and white nylon washer. Slide the brake light switch and the pushrod away from the pedal. Remove the switch by sliding the switch up.

➡ **The switch side plate nearest the brake pedal is slotted, it is not necessary to remove the brake master cylinder pushrod black bushing and 1 white spacer washer nearest the pedal arm from the brake pedal pin.**

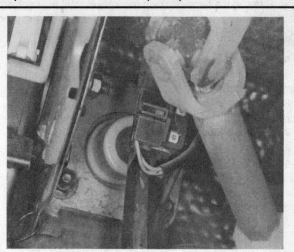

86706528

**Fig. 79 Brake light switch**

**To install:**

4. Position the switch so the U–shaped side is nearest the pedal and directly over/under the pin. The black bushing must be in position in the pushrod eyelet with the washer face on the side closest to the retaining pin.

5. Slide the switch up/down, trapping the master cylinder pushrod and black bushing between the switch side plates. Push the switch and pushrod assembly firmly towards the brake pedal arm. Assemble the outside white plastic washer to the pin and install the hairpin retainer to trap the whole assembly.

➡ **Do not substitute other types of pin retainers. Replace only with production hairpin retainer.**

6. Connect the wire harness connector to the switch.
7. Connect negative battery cable.
8. Check the brake light switch for proper operation}. Stoplights should illuminate with less than 6 lbs. applied to the brake pedal at the pad.

➡ **The brake light switch wire harness must have sufficient length to travel with the switch during full stroke at the pedal.**

## LIGHTING

## Headlights

Two rectangular dual sealed beam headlamps were used on all models from 1984 to 1985 1/2. A dash mounted switch controls them and the steering column dimmer switch controls the high and low beams.

All models after 1985 1/2 are equipped with flush mount headlights. On these models the bulb may be replaced without removing the lens and body assembly.

### REMOVAL & INSTALLATION

**Sealed Beam Type—1984–85 1/2**

▶ **See Figures 80, 81, 82, 83 and 84**

1. Disconnect the negative battery terminal.
2. Remove the headlamp door by removing the retaining screws. After the screws are removed, pull the door slightly forward (certain models have upper locking tabs which disengage by carefully pulling out on the lower edge and pulling downward), and disconnect the parking light (if equipped). Remove the headlight door.
3. Remove the lamp retaining ring screws, pull the headlamp from the connector. unplug the harness at the back of the light.

**To install:**

4. Connect the wire harness to the lamp.
5. Position the headlamp in the ring, with the lettering on the lamp facing upward.
6. Install the lamp and retaining ring with the attaching screws.
7. Install the headlamp door using the retaining screws.
8. Connect the negative battery cable.
9. Turn headlights on and check to make sure the lamp functions correctly on both the low and high beam.

Fig. 80 Remove the screws securing the headlight trim panel

Fig. 81 With the screws removed, lift the panel away from the light

Fig. 82 Remove the screws around the ring which holds the light in place. Do not lose the screws. Be careful that you are removing the small screws and not the large screws which adjust the headlight alignment

Fig. 83 Remove the headlight ring, but hold the headlight in place, or it may fall out

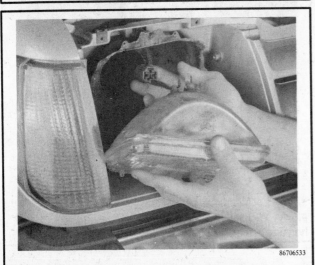

Fig. 84 Remove the plug from the back of the light and remove the light

**Aerodynamic Type—1985 1/2–94**

◗ See Figure 85

➡ The replaceable Halogen headlamp bulb contains gas under pressure. The bulb may shatter if the glass envelope is scratched or the bulb is dropped. Handle the bulb carefully. Grasp the bulb ONLY by its plastic base. Avoid touching the glass envelope. Keep the bulb out of the reach of children.

1. Disconnect the negative battery terminal.
2. Raise the hood and locate the bulb installed in the rear of the headlight body.
3. Remove the electrical connector from the bulb by grasping the wires firmly and snapping the connector rearward.
4. Remove the bulb retaining ring by rotating it counterclockwise (when viewed from the rear) about 1/8 of a turn, then slide the ring off the plastic base.

➡ Keep the bulb retaining ring, it will be reused with the new bulb.

5. Carefully remove the headlight bulb from its socket in the reflector by gently pulling it straight backward out of the socket. DO NOT rotate the bulb during removal.

**To install:**

6. With the flat side of the plastic base of the bulb facing upward, insert the glass envelope of the bulb into the socket. Turn the base slightly to the left or right, if necessary to align the grooves in the forward part of the plastic base with the corresponding locating tabs inside the socket. When the grooves are aligned, push the bulb firmly into the socket until the mounting flange on the base contacts the rear face of the socket.
7. Slip the bulb retaining ring over the rear of the plastic base against the mounting flange. Lock the ring into the socket by rotating the ring counterclockwise. A stop will be felt when the retaining ring is fully engaged.
8. Push the electrical connector into the rear of the plastic until it snaps and locks into position.
9. Connect the negative battery terminal.
10. Turn the headlights on and check for proper operation.

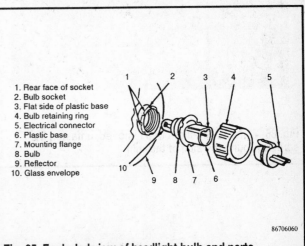

1. Rear face of socket
2. Bulb socket
3. Flat side of plastic base
4. Bulb retaining ring
5. Electrical connector
6. Plastic base
7. Mounting flange
8. Bulb
9. Reflector
10. Glass envelope

Fig. 85 Exploded view of headlight bulb and parts

## Signal & Marker Lights

### REMOVAL & INSTALLATION

**Front Turn Signal and Parking Lights**

**1984–85 Models**

◆ See Figures 86, 87, 88, 89, 90, and 91

1. Disconnect the negative battery cable.
2. Remove the headlamp door.
3. Remove the screws attaching the parking light and pull forward.
4. Remove the bulb socket by twisting and remove the assembly.
5. Unplug the connector from the rear of the socket.
6. Using a counterclockwise motion, remove the bulb.

**To install:**

7. To install, Use a clockwise pushing motion to seat the bulb.
8. Connect the harness to the socket.
9. Install the socket into the parking light by turning the unit clockwise.
10. Position the parking light into place on the vehicle and secure with the retaining screws.
11. Install the headlight door.
12. Connect the negative battery terminal.
13. Turn on light to check for proper functioning.

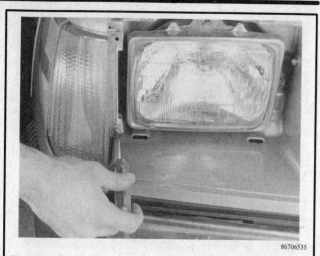

Fig. 87 Remove the screws around the front of the light

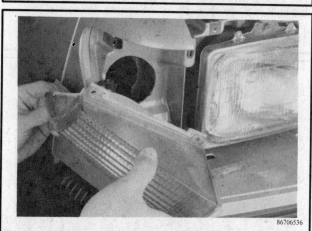

Fig. 88 Remove the light from the vehicle, and using a twisting motion on the bulb base, remove the bulb base and harness

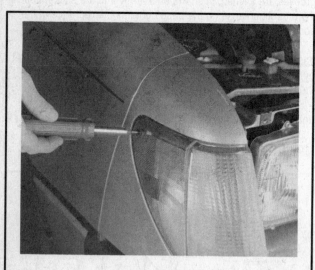

Fig. 86 With the headlight trim removed, unfasten the screws around the side of the light

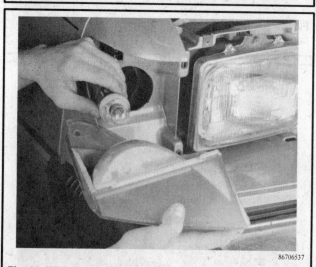

Fig. 89 With the lighting feature removed, place the light housing aside

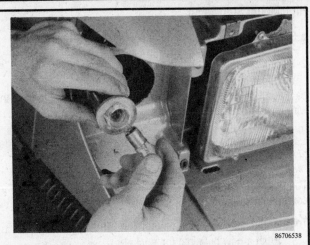

Fig. 90 Using a similar twisting motion, remove the bulb

Fig. 91 Remove the screws around the instrument cluster

**1986–94 Models**

▶ **See Figure 92**

1. Disconnect the negative battery terminal.

2. Remove the screws retaining the parking light to the grille opening panel.

3. Hold the parking light with both hands and pull forward to release the hidden attachment.

4. Remove the bulb socket by twisting and pulling the unit out. Unplug the wire connector.

5. To remove the bulb, twist out.

**To install:**

6. Twist the new bulb in by using the opposite motion from the removal procedure.

7. Plug the connector into the socket using a twisting motion.

8. Carefully push the parking light into position on the vehicle until the hidden tabs click in place.

9. Install the retaining screws.

10. Connect the negative battery cable.

11. Turn both parking lights, then turn signal to test functioning of bulb.

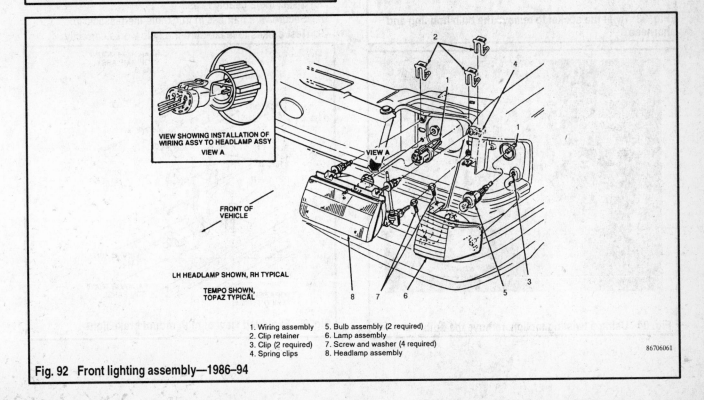

VIEW SHOWING INSTALLATION OF WIRING ASSY TO HEADLAMP ASSY
VIEW A

FRONT OF VEHICLE

LH HEADLAMP SHOWN, RH TYPICAL

TEMPO SHOWN, TOPAZ TYPICAL

1. Wiring assembly
2. Clip retainer
3. Clip (2 required)
4. Spring clips
5. Bulb assembly (2 required)
6. Lamp assembly
7. Screw and washer (4 required)
8. Headlamp assembly

Fig. 92 Front lighting assembly—1986–94

**Rear Turn Signal, Brake and Parking lights**

♦ See Figures 93 and 94

➡ The procedure for replacing these bulbs are the same. Be aware though, many of these bulbs are not interchangeable. Replace bulbs with the exact type.

1. Bulbs can be serviced from the inside of the luggage compartment by removing the luggage compartment rear trim panel, if so equipped.
2. Remove the socket(s) from the lamp body by twisting the socket.
3. Remove the bulb by twisting and pulling out.

**To install:**

4. Install the bulb by twisting into position.
5. Twist the socket into place.
6. Install the trim panel if equipped.
7. Check to make sure the replaced bulb works correctly.

Fig. 93 Twist the socket to remove the bulb housing and harness

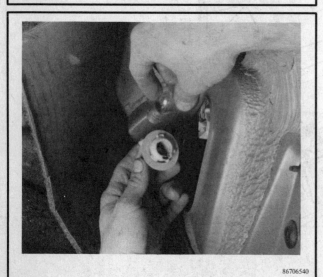

Fig. 94 Using a twisting motion, remove the bulb

**High Mount Stop Lamp**

♦ See Figure 95

**2–Door Models**

1. Locate the wire to the hi–mount brakelamp under the package tray, from inside of the luggage compartment. Twist the wire loose from the plastic housing.
2. Remove the 2 beauty caps from the lamp cover.
3. Remove the screws which can be accessed from the side of the lamp, from the interior of the vehicle.
4. Pull the lamp assembly towards the front of the vehicle. The bulb sockets can then be removed by turning counterclockwise. Pull the bulb from the socket.

**To install:**

5. Push a new bulb into the socket.
6. Twist socket clockwise into light housing.
7. Position lamp and secure with retaining screws.
8. Install the 2 beauty caps.
9. Secure wire harness in trunk into the plastic clip.
10. Test brake to make sure the bulb works correctly.

**4–Door Models**

1. Working from inside the luggage compartment, twist and remove the 2 bulb socket assemblies.
2. From inside the vehicle, remove the 2 screws on the side of the lamp.
3. Slide the lamp assembly toward the front of the vehicle and lift up. Remove the socket from the lamp by twisting counterclockwise. Pull the bulb from the socket.

**To install:**

4. Push the bulb into the socket.
5. Twist socket clockwise into light housing.
6. Position lamp and secure with retaining screws.
7. Install the 2 beauty caps.
8. Secure wire harness in trunk into the plastic clip.
9. Test brakes to make sure the bulb works correctly.

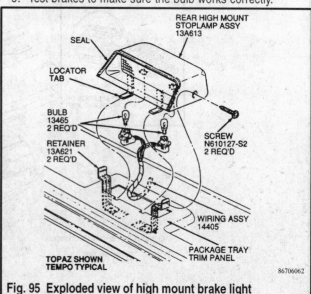

Fig. 95 Exploded view of high mount brake light

### Dome Light

1. Remove the negative battery terminal.
2. Carefully pry the plastic cover off the light.
3. Remove the bulb by pushing the bulb to one end and pulling down.

### To install:

4. Push bulb into place making sure a complete connect between both ends is made.
5. Push cover into place.
6. Connect negative battery cable.
7. Open a door and make sure the dome light comes on.

### License Plate Lights

▶ **See Figures 96, 97 and 98**

1. Remove the negative battery terminal.
2. Remove the 2 retaining screws securing the lense to the vehicle body. Remove the lense.
3. With the lense removed, carefully pull the bulb and socket from the hole.
4. Grasp the socket and pull the bulb from the unit.

### To install:

5. Push a new bulb into place.
6. Carefully push the socket into the hole.
7. Place the lense over the bulb and secure with 2 retaining screws.
8. Connect the negative battery cable.
9. Turn parking lights and to make sure the bulb works correctly.

Fig. 97 Remove the light enough to access the harness and bulb

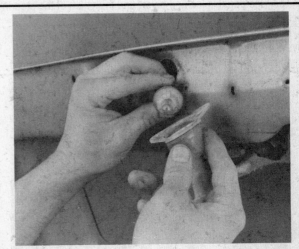

Fig. 98 Remove the light from the housing, and pull the bulb out

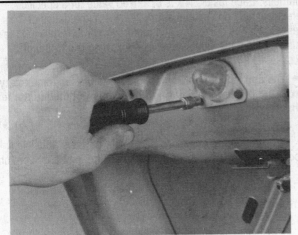

Fig. 96 With the trunk open remove the screws around the light

## TRAILER WIRING

Wiring the car for towing is fairly easy. There are a number of good wiring kits available and these should be used, rather than trying to design your own. All trailers will need brake lights and turn signals as well as tail lights and side marker lights. Most states require extra marker lights for overly wide trailers. Also, most states have recently required back-up lights for trailers,

and most trailer manufacturers have been building trailers with back-up lights for several years.

Additionally, some Class I, most Class II and just about all Class III trailers will have electric brakes. Add to this number an accessories wire, to operate trailer internal equipment or to charge the trailer's battery, and you can have as many as seven wires in the harness.

Determine the equipment on your trailer and buy the wiring kit necessary. The kit will contain all the wires needed, plus a plug adapter set which included the female plug, mounted on the bumper or hitch, and the male plug, wired into, or plugged into the trailer harness.

When installing the kit, follow the manufacturer's instructions. The color coding of the wires is standard throughout the industry.

One point to note: some domestic vehicles, and most imported vehicles, have separate turn signals. On most domestic vehicles, the brake lights and rear turn signals operate with the same bulb. For those vehicles with separate turn signals, you can purchase an isolation unit so that the brake lights won't blink whenever the turn signals are operated, or, you can go to your local electronics supply house and buy four diodes to wire in series with the brake and turn signal bulbs. Diodes will isolate the brake and turn signals. The choice is yours. The isolation units are simple and quick to install, but far more expensive than the diodes. The diodes, however, require more work to install properly, since they require the cutting of each bulb's wire and soldering in place of the diode.

One final point, the best kits are those with a spring loaded cover on the vehicle mounted socket. This cover prevents dirt and moisture from corroding the terminals. Never let the vehicle socket hang loosely; always mount it securely to the bumper or hitch.

## CIRCUIT PROTECTION

### Fuses

▶ See Figure 99

The fuse panel is located below and to the left of the steering column.

Fuses are a one–time circuit protection. If a circuit is overloaded or shorts, the fuse will blow thus protecting the circuit. A fuse will continue to blow until the circuit is repaired.

86706544

Fig. 99 Main fuse box located on driver's side to the left of the steering wheel, above the brake pedal

## REPLACEMENT

1. Access the fuse panel from the left of the steering column.
2. Locate the blown fuse and pull out. DO NOT TWIST.
3. Take note of the ampere number written on the top of the fuse.

**To install:**

4. Push a new fuse of the same ampere into the receptacle, making sure the contact is being made on both sides of the fuse.

### Fuse Link

The fuse link is a short length of special, Hypalon (high temperature) insulated wire, integral with the engine compartment wiring harness and should not be confused with standard wire. It is several wire gauges smaller than the circuit which it protects. Under no circumstances should a fuse link replacement repair be made using a length of standard wire cut from bulk stock or from another wiring harness.

Fusible links are used to prevent major wire harness damage in the event of a short circuit or an overload condition in the wiring circuits that are normally not fused, due to carrying high amperage loads or because of their locations within the wiring harness. Each fusible link is of a fixed value for a specific electrical load and should a fusible link fail, the cause of the failure must be determine and repaired prior to installing a new fusible link of the same value. The following is a listing of fusible links wire gauges and their locations:

➡ **The color coding of replacement fusible links may vary from the production color coding that is outlined in the text that follows.**

**Green 14 Gauge Wire**
- Vehicles equipped with diesel engine, have a fusible link located in the glow plug wiring to protect the glow plug control.

**Black 16 Gauge Wire**
- 1 fusible link located in the wiring for the anti–theft system, if equipped.

**Red 18 Gauge Wire**
- Vehicles equipped with gasoline engines, use 1 fusible link to protect the carburetor circuits, if equipped.

**Brown 18 Gauge Wire**
- One fusible link used to protect the rear window defogger and the fuel door release, if equipped. Also, one fusible link is used to protect the EEC module, if equipped.

**Blue 20 Gauge Wire**
- There is a fusible link located in the wire between the ignition switch and the air conditioning–heater cooling fan. A fusible link is located in the wire between the battery and the engine compartment light. Vehicles equipped with diesel engine,

there is 1 link used to protect the vacuum pump circuit. A fusible link is used to protect the heater fan motor circuit.

➡ **Always disconnect the negative battery cable before servicing the vehicle's electrical system.**

## FUSIBLE LINK REPLACEMENT

◆ **See Figure 100**

1. Disconnect the negative battery terminal.
2. Determine which circuit is damaged, its location and the cause of the open fuse link. If the damaged fuse link is one of three fed by a common No. 10 or 12 gauge feed wire, determine the specific affected circuit.
3. Cut the damaged fuse link from the wiring harness and discard it. If the fuse link is one of three circuits fed by a single feed wire, cut it out of the harness at each splice end and discard it.
4. Identify and procure the proper fuse link and butt connectors for attaching the fuse link to the harness.
5. To repair any fuse link in a 3–link group with one feed:
   a. After cutting the open link out of the harness, cut each of the remaining undamaged fuse links close to the feed wire weld.
   b. Strip approximately 1/2 in. (13mm) of insulation from the detached ends of the two good fuse links, Then insert two wire ends into one end of a butt connector and carefully push one stripped end of the replacement fuse link into the same end of the butt connector and crimp all three firmly together.

➡ **Care must be taken when fitting the three fuse links into the butt connector as the internal diameter is a snug fit for three wires. Make sure to use a proper crimping tool. Pliers, side cutter, etc. will not apply the proper crimp to retain the wires and withstand a pull test. Use a crimping tool available at most automotive parts stores.**

   c. After crimping the butt connector to the three fuse links, cut the weld portion from the feed wire and strip approximately 1/2 in. (13mm) of insulation from the cut end. Insert the stripped end into the open end of the butt connector and crimp very firmly.
   d. To attach the remaining end of the replacement fuse link, strip approximately 1/2 in. (13mm) of insulation from the wire end of the circuit from which the blown fuse link was removed, and firmly crimp a butt connector or equivalent to the stripped wire. Then, insert the end of the replacement link into the other end of the butt connector and crimp firmly.
   e. Using rosin core solder with a consistency of 60 percent tin and 40 percent lead, solder the connectors and the wires at the repairs and insulate completely with electrical tape.
6. To replace any fuse link on a single circuit in a harness, cut out the damaged portion, strip approximately 1/2 in. (13mm) of insulation from the two wire ends and attach the appropriate replacement fuse link to the stripped wire ends with two proper size butt connectors.
7. Solder the connectors and wires and insulate them completely with electrical tape.
8. To repair any fuse link which has an eyelet terminal on one end such as the charging circuit, cut off the open fuse link behind the weld, strip approximately 1/2 in. (13mm) of insulation from the cut end and attach the appropriate new eyelet fuse link to the cut stripped wire with an appropriate size butt connector.
9. Solder the connectors and wires at the repair and insulate completely with electrical tape.
10. Connect the negative battery cable to the battery and test the system for proper operation.

➡ **Do not mistake a resistor wire for a fuse link. The resistor wire is generally longer and has print stating, "Resistor–don't cut or splice."**

When attaching a single No. 16, 17, 18 or 20 gauge fuse link to a heavy gauge wire, always double the stripped wire end of the fuse link before inserting and crimping it into the butt connector for positive wire retention.

## Circuit Breakers

Circuit breakers operate when a circuit overload exceeds its rated amperage. Once operated, they will either blow, or automatically reset after a certain period of time.

Circuit breakers are used to protect the various components of the electrical system, such as headlights and windshield wipers. The circuit breakers are located either in the control switch or mounted on or near the fuse panel.

## LOCATIONS

**Headlights and Highbeam Indicator**
- One 18 amp circuit breaker (22 amp in 1987 vehicles) incorporated in the lighting switch.

**Front and Rear Marker, Side Parking, Rear and License Lamps**
- One 15 amp circuit breaker incorporated in the lighting switch.

**Windshield Wiper**
- One 41/2 amp circuit breaker located in the windshield wiper switch.

**Power Windows**
- Two 20 amp circuit breakers located in the starter relay and the fuse block.

**Power Seats and Power Door Locks**
- One 20 amp circuit breaker located in the fuse block.

## Hazard Flasher

## REMOVAL & INSTALLATION

➡ **The hazard warning flasher is located on the rear side of the fuse panel.**

1. Locate the hazard flasher in the fuse panel.
2. Pull the flasher out. DO NOT TWIST.

**To install:**

3. Push new flasher into place making sure a good contact is made with both terminals.
4. Test flasher to make sure they function properly.

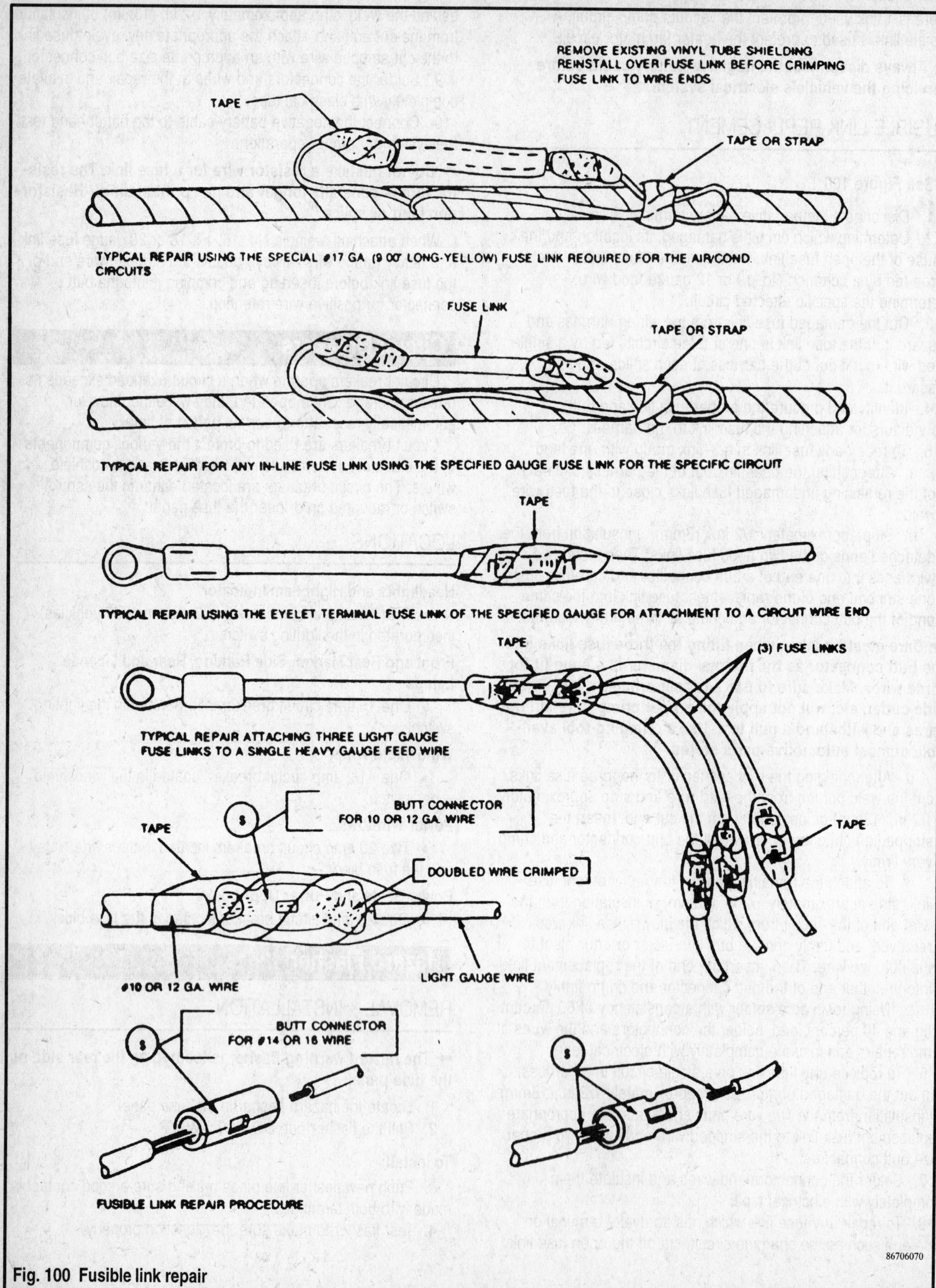

REMOVE EXISTING VINYL TUBE SHIELDING
REINSTALL OVER FUSE LINK BEFORE CRIMPING
FUSE LINK TO WIRE ENDS

TAPE

TAPE OR STRAP

TYPICAL REPAIR USING THE SPECIAL #17 GA. (9.00" LONG-YELLOW) FUSE LINK REQUIRED FOR THE AIR/COND. CIRCUITS

FUSE LINK

TAPE OR STRAP

TYPICAL REPAIR FOR ANY IN-LINE FUSE LINK USING THE SPECIFIED GAUGE FUSE LINK FOR THE SPECIFIC CIRCUIT

TAPE

TYPICAL REPAIR USING THE EYELET TERMINAL FUSE LINK OF THE SPECIFIED GAUGE FOR ATTACHMENT TO A CIRCUIT WIRE END

TAPE

(3) FUSE LINKS

TAPE

TYPICAL REPAIR ATTACHING THREE LIGHT GAUGE
FUSE LINKS TO A SINGLE HEAVY GAUGE FEED WIRE

TAPE

(S) BUTT CONNECTOR
FOR 10 OR 12 GA. WIRE

DOUBLED WIRE CRIMPED

#10 OR 12 GA. WIRE

LIGHT GAUGE WIRE

(S) BUTT CONNECTOR
FOR #14 OR 16 WIRE

(S)

FUSIBLE LINK REPAIR PROCEDURE

86706070

**Fig. 100 Fusible link repair**

## Various Relays

### LOCATION

**Cooling Fan Controller**
- Located behind the left side of the instrument panel.

**Cooling Fan Controller Module**
- Located behind the right side of the instrument panel.

**Cooling Fan Relay**
- Located in the air conditioning cooling fan control module.

**Electronic Control Assembly**
- Located under the left side of the instrument panel.

**Electronic Engine Control Power Relay**
- Located behind the glove box on the right side of the instrument panel.

**Fuel Pump Relay**
- Located behind the glove box.

**Horn Relay**
- Located in the fuse block.

### SPEED CONTROL SYSTEM DIAGNOSIS

| SPEED CONTROL DOES NOT WORK | | |
|---|---|---|
| **TEST STEP** | **RESULT** ▶ | **ACTION TO TAKE** |
| **A0** VERIFY THE CONDITION | | GO to **A1**. |
| **A1** CHECK CONNECTIONS<br>• Check all electrical and vacuum connections. | (OK) ▶<br>(⊘) ▶ | GO to **A2**.<br>SERVICE or REPLACE as required. |
| **A2** CHECK BRAKE LAMP<br>• Press brake pedal.<br>• Check to see that brake lamp is operating. | (OK) ▶<br>(⊘) ▶ | GO to **A3** if manual transmission. If automatic transmission GO to **A4**.<br>SERVICE brake lamp circuit. |
| **A3** CHECK CLUTCH SWITCH (MANUAL TRANSMISSION)<br>• Check clutch switch for proper operation. | (OK) ▶<br>(⊘) ▶ | GO to **A4**.<br>SERVICE as required. |
| **A4** CHECK THROTTLE LINKAGE<br>• Check throttle linkage cable. | (OK) ▶<br>(⊘) ▶ | GO to **A5**.<br>ADJUST or SERVICE as required. |
| **A5** CHECK LINKAGE OPERATION<br>• Check the throttle linkage for proper operation. | (OK) ▶<br>(⊘) ▶ | GO to **A6**.<br>SERVICE as required. |
| **A6** CHECK VACUUM<br>• Check vacuum at servo.<br>NOTE: 2.5 inches of Hg (1.22 psi) is minimum vacuum for normal servo operation. The vacuum source hose is attached to the 5/16 inch, vacuum fitting port. The servo vacuum source hose is connected to the unmarked vacuum reservoir port. | (OK) ▶<br>(⊘) ▶ | GO to **A8**.<br>GO to **A7**. |
| **A7** CHECK DUMP VALVE<br>• Check vacuum dump valve. | (OK) ▶<br>(OK) ▶ | SERVICE or REPLACE vacuum hose as required.<br>SERVICE or ADJUST as required. |

86706100

## SPEED CONTROL SYSTEM DIAGNOSIS — CONTINUED

| SPEED CONTROL DOES NOT WORK (Continued) | | |
|---|---|---|
| **TEST STEP** | **RESULT** ▶ | **ACTION TO TAKE** |
| **A8** PERFORM CONTROL SWITCHES AND CIRCUIT TESTS | | |
| • Perform control switches and circuit tests as described in this Section. | (OK) ▶ | GO to **A9**. |
| | (ⓍK) ▶ | SERVICE or REPLACE switches or circuits as required. |
| **A9** PERFORM SERVO TESTS | | |
| • Perform servo tests as described in this Section. | (OK) ▶ | GO to **A10**. |
| | (ⓍK) ▶ | REPLACE actuator. |
| **A10** PERFORM SENSOR TEST | | |
| • Perform speed sensor test as described in this Section. | (OK) ▶ | GO to **A11**. |
| | (ⓍK) ▶ | REPLACE speed sensor. |
| **A11** PERFORM AMPLIFIER TEST | | |
| • Perform amplifier test as described in this Section (Substitution). | Problem corrected ▶ | INSTALL a new amplifier. |
| | Problem not corrected ▶ | EXAMINE all connectors carefully for proper contact. REPAIR as required. REMOVE substitute amplifier. |

86706101

## SPEED CONTROL SYSTEM DIAGNOSIS—CONTINUED

| TEST STEP | RESULT ▶ | ACTION TO TAKE |
|---|---|---|
| **B0**  VERIFY THE CONDITION | | |
| • Note carefully when intermittent action occurs. | | GO to **B1**. |
| **B1**  INSPECT VISUALLY | | |
| • Perform visual inspection test. | If intermittent action occurs while cruising ▶ | GO to **B2**. |
| | If intermittent action occurs while using control buttons or turning steering wheel ▶ | GO to **B4**. |
| **B2**  CHECK VACUUM TO SERVO | | |
| • Check vacuum supply to servo.<br>NOTE: 2.5 inches of Hg (1.22 psi) is minimum vacuum for normal servo operation. The vacuum source hose is attached to the 5/16 inch engine vacuum-fitting port. | (OK) ▶ | GO to **B3**. |
| | (⊘) ▶ | SERVICE vacuum supply. |
| **B3**  PERFORM SERVO ASSEMBLY TEST | | |
| • Perform servo assembly test. Lightly tap servo body while making test. | (OK) ▶ | SUBSTITUTE known good amplifier if OK — properly INSTALL amplifier. |
| | (⊘) ▶ | REPLACE servo assembly. |
| **B4**  PERFORM CONTROL SWITCHES AND CIRCUIT TEST | | |
| • Perform control switches and circuit tests as described in this Section. | (OK) ▶ | SUBSTITUTE known good amplifier if OK — properly INSTALL amplifier. |
| | (⊘) ▶ | SERVICE circuits, REPLACE horn pad assembly. CLEAN or SERVICE three copper brushes and steering wheel ring. |

SPEED CONTROL OPERATION IS INTERMITTENT

86706102

## SPEED CONTROL SYSTEM DIAGNOSIS—CONTINUED

| SPEED CONTROL OPERATES BUT DOES NOT ACCELERATE OR COAST DOWN PROPERLY | | |
|---|---|---|
| **TEST STEP** | **RESULT** ▶ | **ACTION TO TAKE** |
| **C0** PERFORM VISUAL INSPECTION TEST<br><br>• Visually inspect system. | (OK) ▶<br><br>(OK̸) ▶ | GO to **C1**.<br><br>SERVICE or REPLACE affected circuit. |
| **C1** PERFORM CONTROL SWITCHES AND CIRCUIT TESTS<br><br>• Perform control switches and circuit tests as described in this Section. | (OK) ▶<br><br>(OK̸) ▶ | GO to **C2**.<br><br>SERVICE circuits or REPLACE horn pad assembly. |
| **C2** PERFORM SERVO ASSEMBLY TEST<br><br>• Perform servo assembly test as described in this Section. | (OK) ▶<br><br>(OK̸) ▶ | SUBSTITUTE known good amplifier if OK, REPLACE amplifier.<br><br>REPLACE servo assembly. |

86706103

## SPEED CONTROL SYSTEM DIAGNOSIS—CONTINUED

| TEST STEP | | RESULT ▶ | ACTION TO TAKE |
|---|---|---|---|
| **SPEED CONTINUOUSLY CHANGES UP AND DOWN** | | | |
| **D0** | VERIFY CONDITION | | GO to **D1**. |
| **D1** | CHECK THROTTLE LINKAGE | | |
| | • Check throttle linkage for proper operation and adjustment. | (OK) ▶ | GO to **D2**. |
| | | (ØK) ▶ | SERVICE and ADJUST as required. |
| **D2** | CONTINUITY CHECK | | |
| | • Check continuity of circuits 147, 148 and 149. | (OK) ▶ | GO to **D3**. |
| | | (OK) ▶ | REPAIR or REPLACE wiring as necessary. |
| **D3** | TEST SERVO | | |
| | • Perform servo test as described in this Section. | (OK) ▶ | GO to **D4**. |
| | | (ØK) ▶ | REPLACE as required. |
| **D4** | CHECK SPEEDOMETER CABLES | | |
| | • Check speedometer cables for proper routing, no sharp bends or binding. | (OK) ▶ | GO to **D5**. |
| | | (ØK) ▶ | SERVICE as required. |
| **D5** | CHECK SENSOR | | |
| | • Check sensor for free operation. | (OK) ▶ | GO to **D6**. |
| | | (ØK) ▶ | REPLACE sensor. |
| **D6** | TEST SENSOR | | |
| | • Perform sensor test as described in this Section. | (OK) ▶ | GO to **D7**. |
| | | (ØK) ▶ | REPLACE sensor. |
| **D7** | CHECK DUMP VALVE | | |
| | • Check vacuum dump valve. | (OK) ▶ | GO to **D8**. |
| | | (ØK) ▶ | SERVICE or ADJUST as required. |
| **D8** | TEST AMPLIFIER | | |
| | • Perform amplifier test as described in this Section. | Corrects problem ▶ | REPLACE amplifier. |
| | | Does not correct problem ▶ | CHECK circuit connections for good contacts. REPAIR as required. |

86706104

## SPEED CONTROL SYSTEM DIAGNOSIS – CONTINUED

| SPEED CONTROL DOES NOT DISENGAGE WHEN BRAKES ARE APPLIED | | |
|---|---|---|
| **TEST STEP** | **RESULT** ▶ | **ACTION TO TAKE** |
| **E0**  VERIFY THE CONDITION | | GO to **E1**. |
| **E1**  CHECK STOPLAMPS | | |
| • Apply brakes and observe stop lamps. | (OK) ▶ | GO to **E2**. |
| | (O̶K̶) ▶ | SERVICE stoplamp circuit as required. VERIFY fuses are not open. GO to **E2**. |
| **E2**  CHECK DUMP VALVE | | |
| • Check vacuum dump valve. | (OK) ▶ | GO to **E3**. |
| | (O̶K̶) ▶ | ADJUST or SERVICE as required. |
| **E3**  CHECK SERVO | | |
| • Check servo operation and throttle linkage. | (OK) ▶ | GO to **E4**. |
| | (O̶K̶) ▶ | REPLACE servo. |
| **E4**  TEST AMPLIFIER | | |
| • Perform amplifier test as described in this Section. | Corrects problem ▶ | REPLACE amplifier. |
| | Does not correct problem ▶ | CHECK contacts of electrical connector. SERVICE as required. |

86706105

## SPEED CONTROL SYSTEM DIAGNOSIS—CONTINUED

| SPEED WILL NOT SET IN SYSTEM | | |
| --- | --- | --- |
| TEST STEP | RESULT ▶ | ACTION TO TAKE |
| **F0** VERIFY THE CONDITION | | GO to **F1**. |
| **F1** CHECK THROTTLE LINKAGE<br><br>• Check throttle linkage for proper operation and adjustment. | (OK) ▶ | GO to **F2**. |
| | (OK̸) ▶ | ADJUST or SERVICE as required. |
| **F2** CHECK CONNECTIONS<br><br>• Check system circuit connections. | (OK) ▶ | GO to **F3**. |
| | (OK̸) ▶ | SERVICE as required. |
| **F3** CHECK CONTROL SWITCH<br><br>• Check control switch circuit. | (OK) ▶ | GO to **F4**. |
| | (OK̸) ▶ | SERVICE switch circuit as required. |
| **F4** CHECK DUMP VALVE<br><br>• Check vacuum dump valve. | (OK) ▶ | GO to **F5** for manual transmission, **F6** for automatic transmission. |
| | (OK̸) ▶ | ADJUST or SERVICE as required. |
| **F5** CHECK CLUTCH SWITCH<br><br>• Check clutch switch. | (OK) ▶ | GO to **F6**. |
| | (OK̸) ▶ | SERVICE switch as required. |
| **F6** CHECK STOPLAMPS<br><br>• Check stoplamps, switch and circuit. | (OK) ▶ | GO to **F7**. |
| | (OK̸) ▶ | SERVICE lamps and circuit as required. |
| **F7** CHECK SERVO<br><br>• Check servo for proper operation. | (OK) ▶ | GO to **F8**. |
| | (OK̸) ▶ | REPLACE servo. |
| **F8** CHECK SENSOR<br><br>• Check speed control sensor. | (OK) ▶ | CHECK amplifier, REPLACE as required. |
| | (OK̸) ▶ | REPLACE speed sensor. |

86706106

## SPEED CONTROL SYSTEM DIAGNOSIS—CONTINUED

### SPEED CONTROL SYSTEM DOES NOT DISENGAGE WHEN CLUTCH PEDAL IS DEPRESSED (MANUAL TRANSMISSION ONLY)

| | TEST STEP | RESULT | ACTION TO TAKE |
|---|---|---|---|
| G0 | VERIFY | | |
| | • Verify system disengages when stoplamp switch is activated.<br>• Check clutch switch operation. | (OK) ▶ | SERVICE or REPLACE wire assembly 9A840 as required. |
| | | (OK̸) ▶ | SERVICE or REPLACE as required. |

### SPEED GRADUALLY INCREASES OR DECREASES AFTER SPEED IS SET

| | TEST STEP | RESULT | ACTION TO TAKE |
|---|---|---|---|
| H0 | VERIFY | | |
| | • Verify that engine is properly tuned.<br>• Check accelerator action and actuator cable adjustment. | (OK) ▶ | GO to H1. |
| | | (OK̸) ▶ | ADJUST or CORRECT as required. |
| H1 | CHECK DUMP VALVE | | |
| | • Check vacuum dump valve. | (OK) ▶ | GO to H2. |
| | | (OK̸) ▶ | ADJUST or SERVICE as required. |
| H2 | TEST SERVO | | |
| | • Perform servo test. | (OK) ▶ | PERFORM amplifier test. REPLACE if required. |
| | | (OK̸) ▶ | REPLACE servo. |

86706107

## SPEED CONTROL SYSTEM DIAGNOSIS—CONTINUED

### SPEED CONTROL OPERATES BUT DOES NOT RESUME ACCELERATE OR COAST DOWN PROPERLY

| | TEST STEP | RESULT | ACTION TO TAKE |
|---|---|---|---|
| J0 | VERIFY THE CONDITION | | GO to J1. |
| J1 | CHECK FOLLOWING SWITCHES AND CIRCUITS | | |
| | • Check the Set-Acc switch. Resume switch and slip ring circuits and brush contacts. | (OK) ▶ | GO to J2. |
| | | (OK̸) ▶ | SERVICE the circuit as required. |
| J2 | TEST SERVO | | |
| | • Perform servo test. | (OK) ▶ | GO to I3. |
| | | (OK̸) ▶ | REPLACE servo. |
| J3 | TEST AMPLIFIER | | |
| | • Perform amplifier test as described in this Section. | Corrects problems ▶ | REPLACER amplifier |
| | | Does not correct problem ▶ | CHECK circuit connections for proper contact. SERVICE as required. |

86706108

## Troubleshooting Basic Turn Signal and Flasher Problems

Most problems in the turn signals or flasher system can be reduced to defective flashers or bulbs, which are easily replaced. Occasionally, problems in the turn signals are traced to the switch in the steering column, which will require professional service.

F = Front    R = Rear    ● = Lights off    o = Lights on

| Problem | | Solution |
|---|---|---|
| Turn signals light, but do not flash | 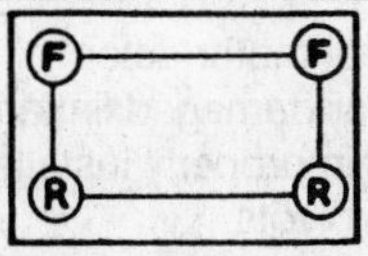 | • Replace the flasher |
| No turn signals light on either side | 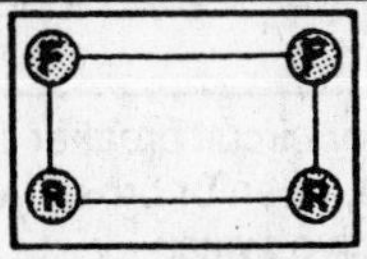 | • Check the fuse. Replace if defective.<br>• Check the flasher by substitution<br>• Check for open circuit, short circuit or poor ground |
| Both turn signals on one side don't work | 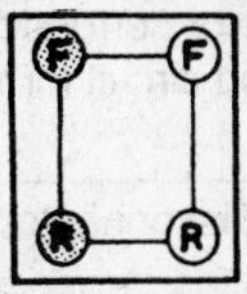 | • Check for bad bulbs<br>• Check for bad ground in both housings |
| One turn signal light on one side doesn't work | 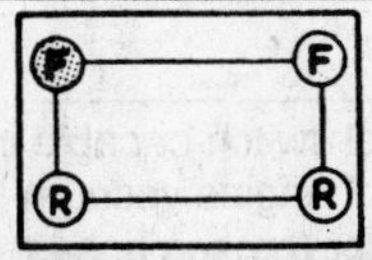 | • Check and/or replace bulb<br>• Check for corrosion in socket. Clean contacts.<br>• Check for poor ground at socket |
| Turn signal flashes too fast or too slow | 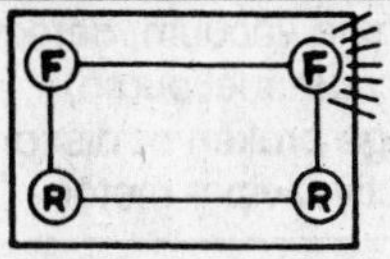 | • Check any bulb on the side flashing too fast. A heavy-duty bulb is probably installed in place of a regular bulb.<br>• Check the bulb flashing too slow. A standard bulb was probably installed in place of a heavy-duty bulb.<br>• Check for loose connections or corrosion at the bulb socket |
| Indicator lights don't work in either direction |  | • Check if the turn signals are working<br>• Check the dash indicator lights<br>• Check the flasher by substitution |

86706110

# Troubleshooting Basic Turn Signal and Flasher Problems

Most problems in the turn signals or flasher system can be reduced to defective flashers or bulbs, which are easily replaced. Occasionally, problems in the turn signals are traced to the switch in the steering column, which will require professional service.

F = Front    R = Rear    ● = Lights off    o = Lights on

| Problem | | Solution |
|---|---|---|
| One indicator light doesn't light |  | • On systems with 1 dash indicator:<br>  See if the lights work on the same side. Often the filaments have been reversed in systems combining stoplights with taillights and turn signals.<br>  Check the flasher by substitution<br>• On systems with 2 indicators:<br>  Check the bulbs on the same side<br>  Check the indicator light bulb<br>  Check the flasher by substitution |

86706111

## Troubleshooting Basic Windshield Wiper Problems

| Problem | Cause | Solution |
| --- | --- | --- |
| **Electric Wipers** | | |
| Wipers do not operate—<br>Wiper motor heats up or hums | • Internal motor defect<br>• Bent or damaged linkage<br>• Arms improperly installed on link-<br>ing pivots | • Replace motor<br>• Repair or replace linkage<br>• Position linkage in park and rein-<br>stall wiper arms |
| **Electric Wipers** | | |
| Wipers do not operate—<br>No current to motor | • Fuse or circuit breaker blown<br>• Loose, open or broken wiring<br>• Defective switch<br>• Defective or corroded terminals<br>• No ground circuit for motor or<br>switch | • Replace fuse or circuit breaker<br>• Repair wiring and connections<br>• Replace switch<br>• Replace or clean terminals<br>• Repair ground circuits |
| Wipers do not operate—<br>Motor runs | • Linkage disconnected or broken | • Connect wiper linkage or replace<br>broken linkage |
| **Vacuum Wipers** | | |
| Wipers do not operate | • Control switch or cable inoperative<br>• Loss of engine vacuum to wiper<br>motor (broken hoses, low<br>engine vacuum, defective<br>vacuum/fuel pump)<br>• Linkage broken or disconnected<br>• Defective wiper motor | • Repair or replace switch or cable<br>• Check vacuum lines, engine<br>vacuum and fuel pump<br><br><br>• Repair linkage<br>• Replace wiper motor |
| Wipers stop on engine acceleration | • Leaking vacuum hoses<br>• Dry windshield<br>• Oversize wiper blades<br><br>• Defective vacuum/fuel pump | • Repair or replace hoses<br>• Wet windshield with washers<br>• Replace with proper size wiper<br>blades<br>• Replace pump |

87606115

## Troubleshooting Basic Lighting Problems

| Problem | Cause | Solution |
|---|---|---|
| **Lights** | | |
| One or more lights don't work, but others do | • Defective bulb(s)<br>• Blown fuse(s)<br>• Dirty fuse clips or light sockets<br>• Poor ground circuit | • Replace bulb(s)<br>• Replace fuse(s)<br>• Clean connections<br>• Run ground wire from light socket housing to car frame |
| Lights burn out quickly | • Incorrect voltage regulator setting or defective regulator<br>• Poor battery/alternator connections | • Replace voltage regulator<br>• Check battery/alternator connections |
| Lights go dim | • Low/discharged battery<br>• Alternator not charging<br><br>• Corroded sockets or connections<br>• Low voltage output | • Check battery<br>• Check drive belt tension; repair or replace alternator<br>• Clean bulb and socket contacts and connections<br>• Replace voltage regulator |
| Lights flicker | • Loose connection<br>• Poor ground<br><br>• Circuit breaker operating (short circuit) | • Tighten all connections<br>• Run ground wire from light housing to car frame<br>• Check connections and look for bare wires |
| Lights "flare"—Some flare is normal on acceleration—if excessive, see "Lights Burn Out Quickly" | • High voltage setting | • Replace voltage regulator |
| Lights glare—approaching drivers are blinded | • Lights adjusted too high<br>• Rear springs or shocks sagging<br>• Rear tires soft | • Have headlights aimed<br>• Check rear springs/shocks<br>• Check/correct rear tire pressure |
| **Turn Signals** | | |
| Turn signals don't work in either direction | • Blown fuse<br>• Defective flasher<br>• Loose connection | • Replace fuse<br>• Replace flasher<br>• Check/tighten all connections |
| Right (or left) turn signal only won't work | • Bulb burned out<br>• Right (or left) indicator bulb burned out<br>• Short circuit | • Replace bulb<br>• Check/replace indicator bulb<br>• Check/repair wiring |
| Flasher rate too slow or too fast | • Incorrect wattage bulb<br>• Incorrect flasher | • Flasher bulb<br>• Replace flasher (use a variable load flasher if you pull a trailer) |
| Indicator lights do not flash (burn steadily) | • Burned out bulb<br>• Defective flasher | • Replace bulb<br>• Replace flasher |
| Indicator lights do not light at all | • Burned out indicator bulb<br>• Defective flasher | • Replace indicator bulb<br>• Replace flasher |

## Troubleshooting Basic Dash Gauge Problems

| Problem | Cause | Solution |
|---|---|---|
| **Coolant Temperature Gauge** | | |
| Gauge reads erratically or not at all | • Loose or dirty connections<br>• Defective sending unit | • Clean/tighten connections<br>• Bi-metal gauge: remove the wire from the sending unit. Ground the wire for an instant. If the gauge registers, replace the sending unit. |
| | • Defective gauge | • Magnetic gauge: disconnect the wire at the sending unit. With ignition ON gauge should register COLD. Ground the wire; gauge should register HOT. |
| **Ammeter Gauge—Turn Headlights ON (do not start engine). Note reaction** | | |
| Ammeter shows charge<br>Ammeter shows discharge<br>Ammeter does not move | • Connections reversed on gauge<br>• Ammeter is OK<br>• Loose connections or faulty wiring<br>• Defective gauge | • Reinstall connections<br>• Nothing<br>• Check/correct wiring<br>• Replace gauge |
| **Oil Pressure Gauge** | | |
| Gauge does not register or is inaccurate | • On mechanical gauge, Bourdon tube may be bent or kinked | • Check tube for kinks or bends preventing oil from reaching the gauge |
| | • Low oil pressure | • Remove sending unit. Idle the engine briefly. If no oil flows from sending unit hole, problem is in engine. |
| | • Defective gauge | • Remove the wire from the sending unit and ground it for an instant with the ignition ON. A good gauge will go to the top of the scale. |
| | • Defective wiring | • Check the wiring to the gauge. If it's OK and the gauge doesn't register when grounded, replace the gauge. |
| | • Defective sending unit | • If the wiring is OK and the gauge functions when grounded, replace the sending unit |
| **All Gauges** | | |
| All gauges do not operate | • Blown fuse<br>• Defective instrument regulator | • Replace fuse<br>• Replace instrument voltage regulator |
| All gauges read low or erratically | • Defective or dirty instrument voltage regulator | • Clean contacts or replace |
| All gauges pegged | • Loss of ground between instrument voltage regulator and car<br>• Defective instrument regulator | • Check ground<br>• Replace regulator |

## Troubleshooting Basic Dash Gauge Problems

| Problem | Cause | Solution |
|---|---|---|
| **Warning Lights** | | |
| Light(s) do not come on when ignition is ON, but engine is not started | • Defective bulb<br>• Defective wire<br><br>• Defective sending unit | • Replace bulb<br>• Check wire from light to sending unit<br>• Disconnect the wire from the sending unit and ground it. Replace the sending unit if the light comes on with the ignition ON. |
| Light comes on with engine running | • Problem in individual system<br>• Defective sending unit | • Check system<br>• Check sending unit (see above) |

86706126

## Troubleshooting the Heater

| Problem | Cause | Solution |
|---|---|---|
| Blower motor will not turn at any speed | • Blown fuse<br>• Loose connection<br>• Defective ground<br>• Faulty switch<br>• Faulty motor<br>• Faulty resistor | • Replace fuse<br>• Inspect and tighten<br>• Clean and tighten<br>• Replace switch<br>• Replace motor<br>• Replace resistor |
| Blower motor turns at one speed only | • Faulty switch<br>• Faulty resistor | • Replace switch<br>• Replace resistor |
| Blower motor turns but does not circulate air | • Intake blocked<br>• Fan not secured to the motor shaft | • Clean intake<br>• Tighten security |
| Heater will not heat | • Coolant does not reach proper temperature<br>• Heater core blocked internally<br>• Heater core air-bound<br>• Blend-air door not in proper position | • Check and replace thermostat if necessary<br>• Flush or replace core if necessary<br>• Purge air from core<br>• Adjust cable |
| Heater will not defrost | • Control cable adjustment incorrect<br>• Defroster hose damaged | • Adjust control cable<br>• Replace defroster hose |

86706130

## WIRING DIAGRAMS

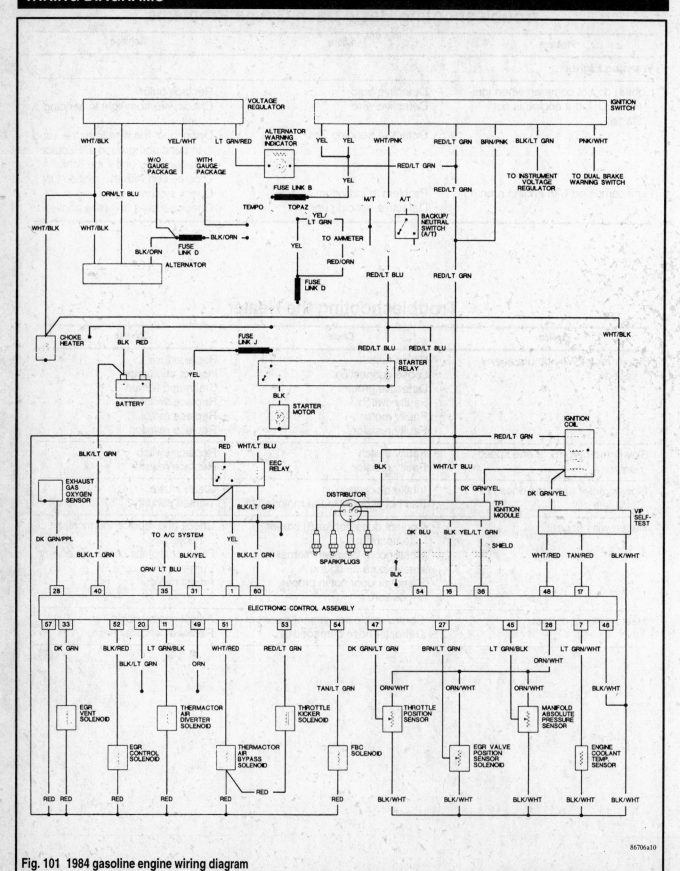

**Fig. 101 1984 gasoline engine wiring diagram**

86706a10

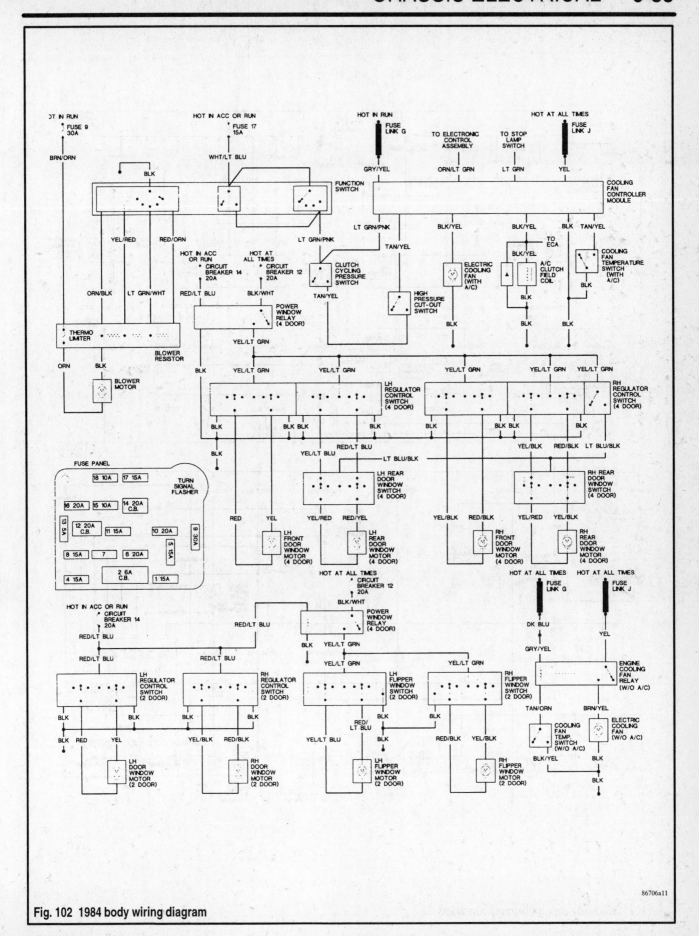

**Fig. 102** 1984 body wiring diagram

86706a11

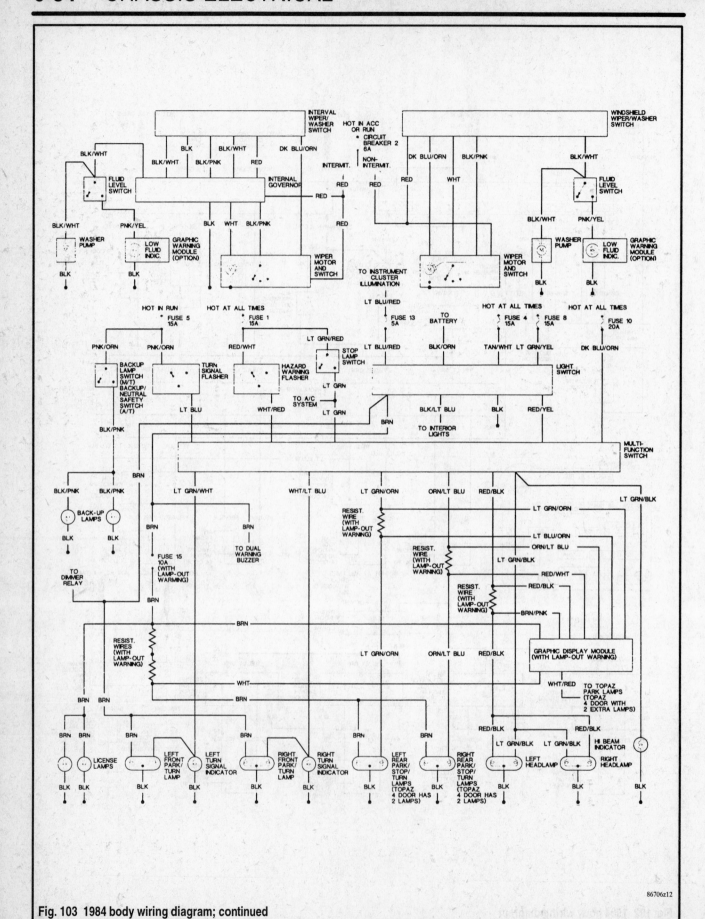

**Fig. 103** 1984 body wiring diagram; continued

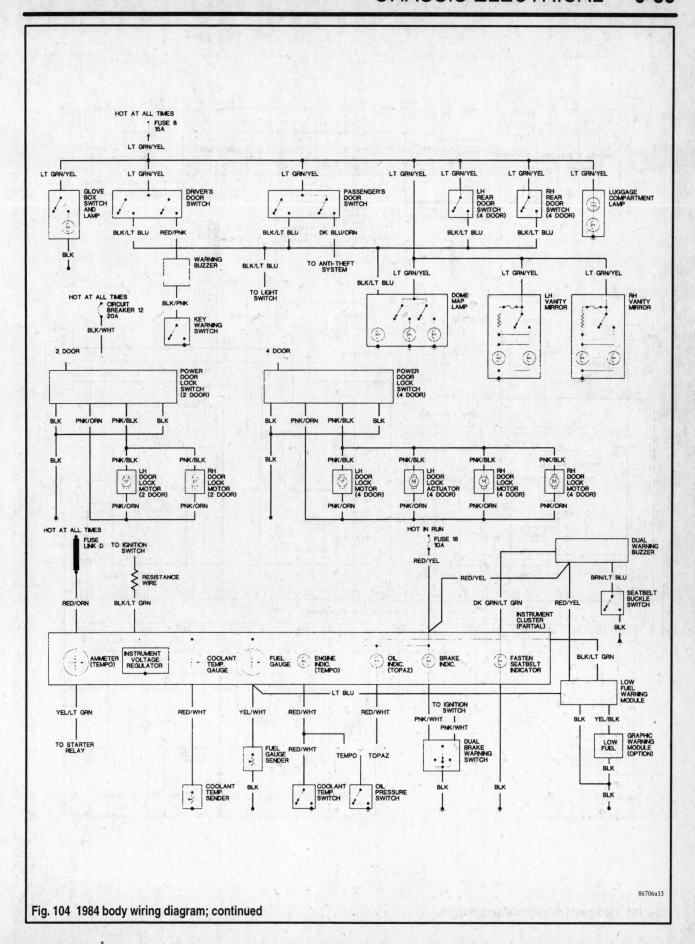

**Fig. 104** 1984 body wiring diagram; continued

86706a13

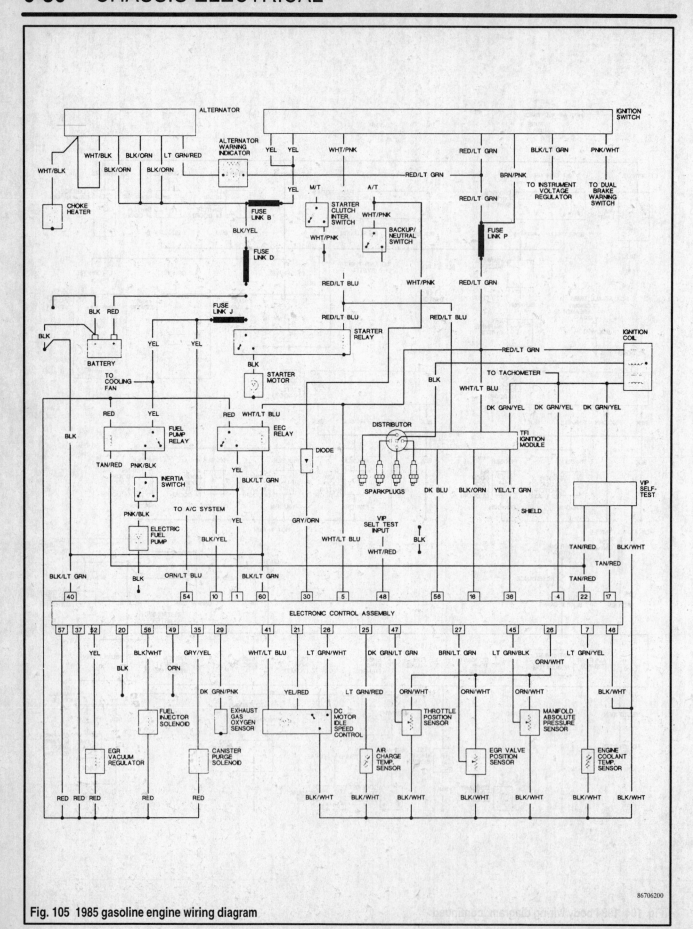

**Fig. 105** 1985 gasoline engine wiring diagram

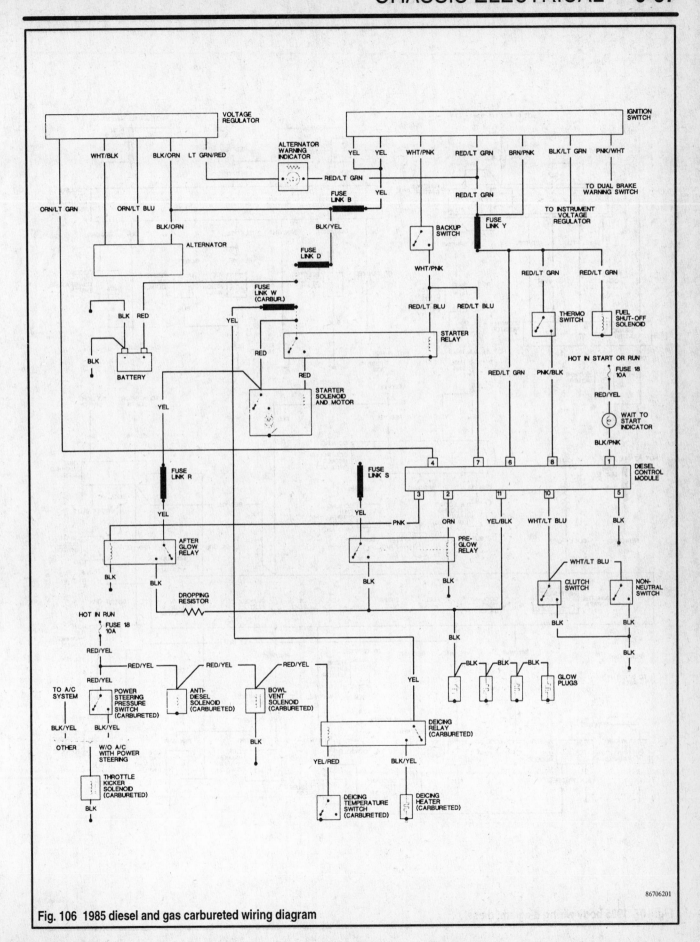

Fig. 106 1985 diesel and gas carbureted wiring diagram

86706201

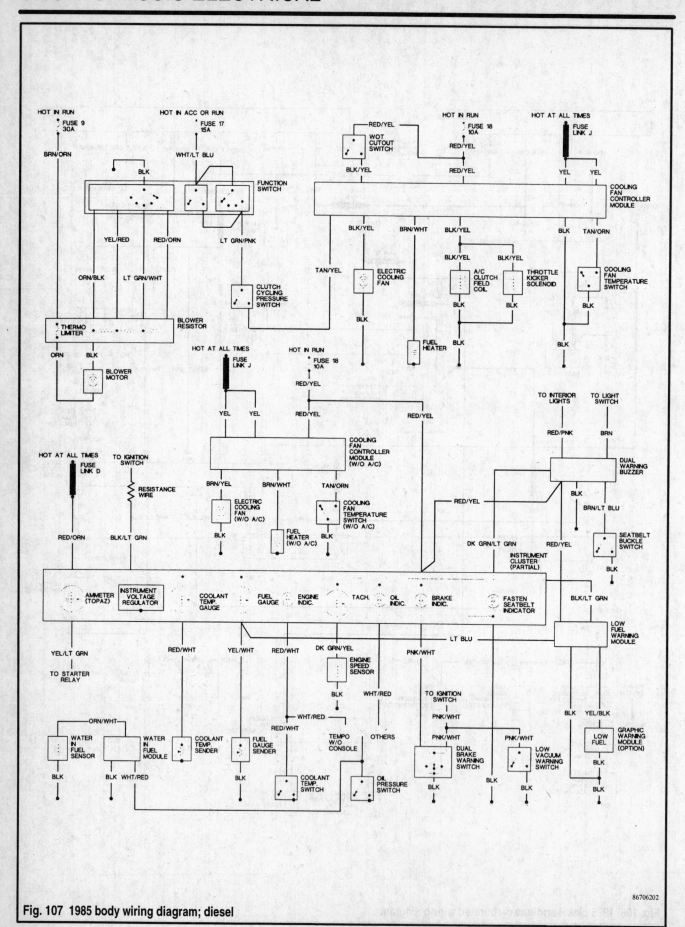

**Fig. 107** 1985 body wiring diagram; diesel

86706202

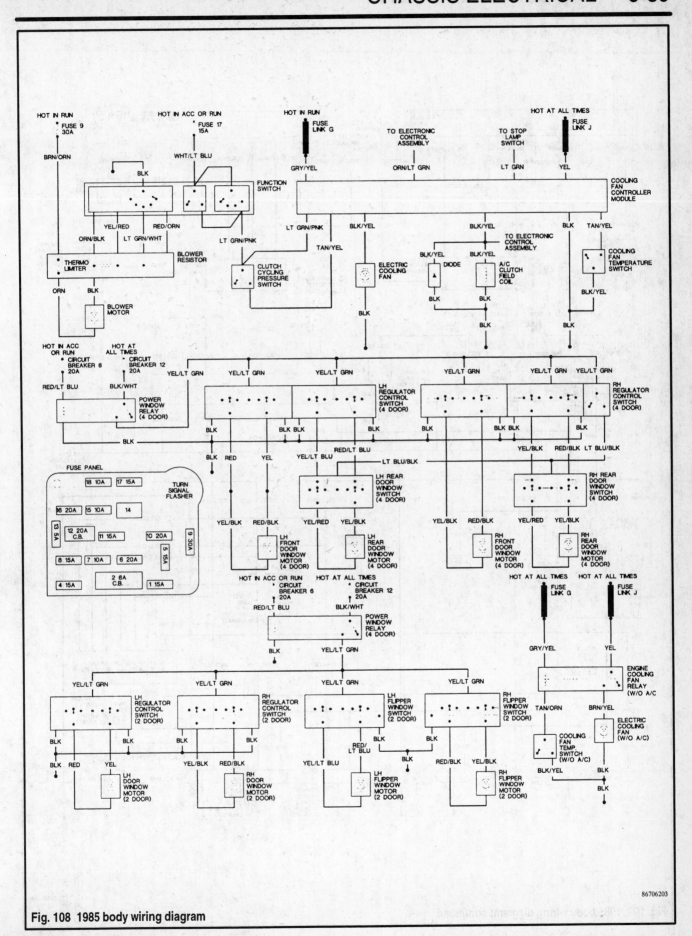

**Fig. 108  1985 body wiring diagram**

86706203

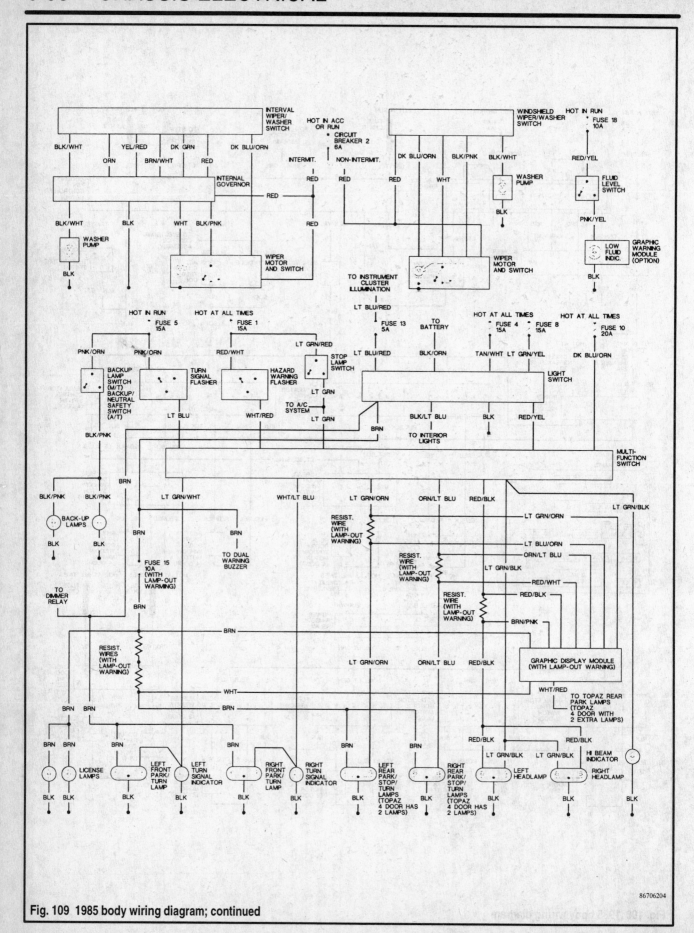

**Fig. 109** 1985 body wiring diagram; continued

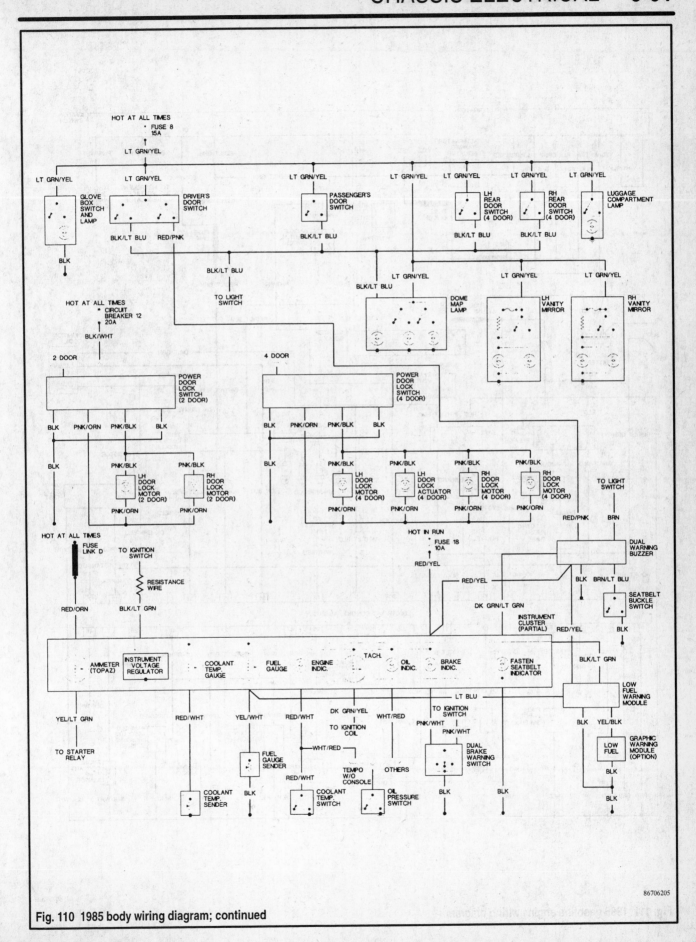

**Fig. 110  1985 body wiring diagram; continued**

86706205

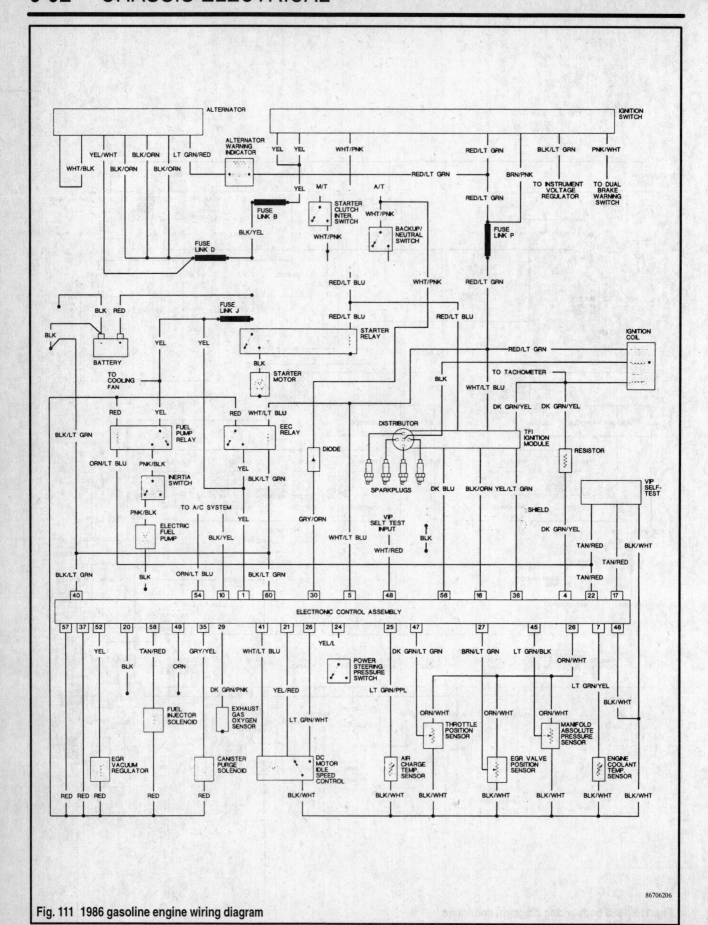

**Fig. 111 1986 gasoline engine wiring diagram**

86706206

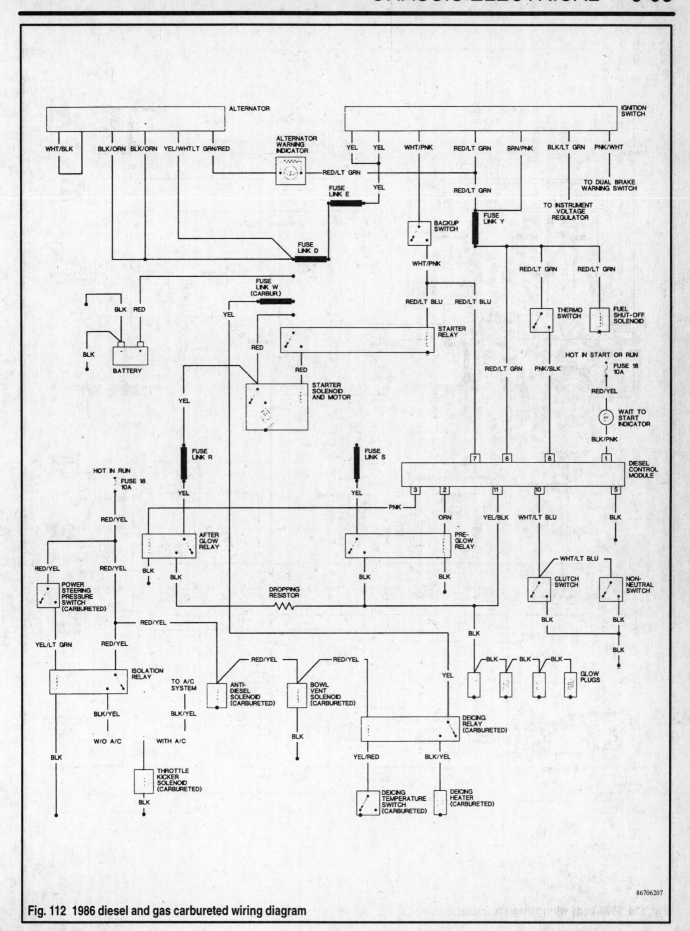

**Fig. 112 1986 diesel and gas carbureted wiring diagram**

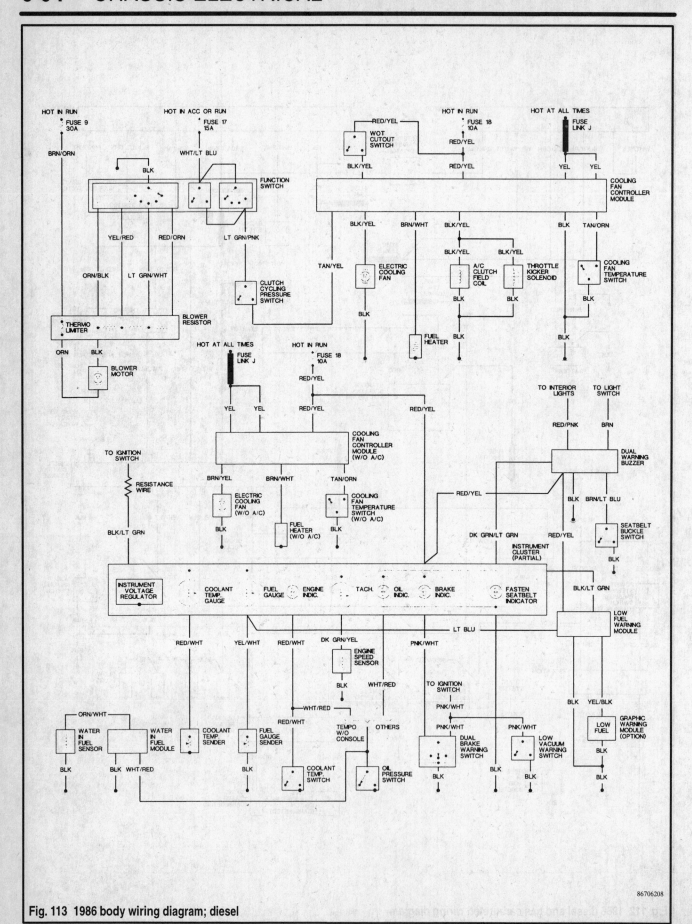

**Fig. 113 1986 body wiring diagram; diesel**

86706208

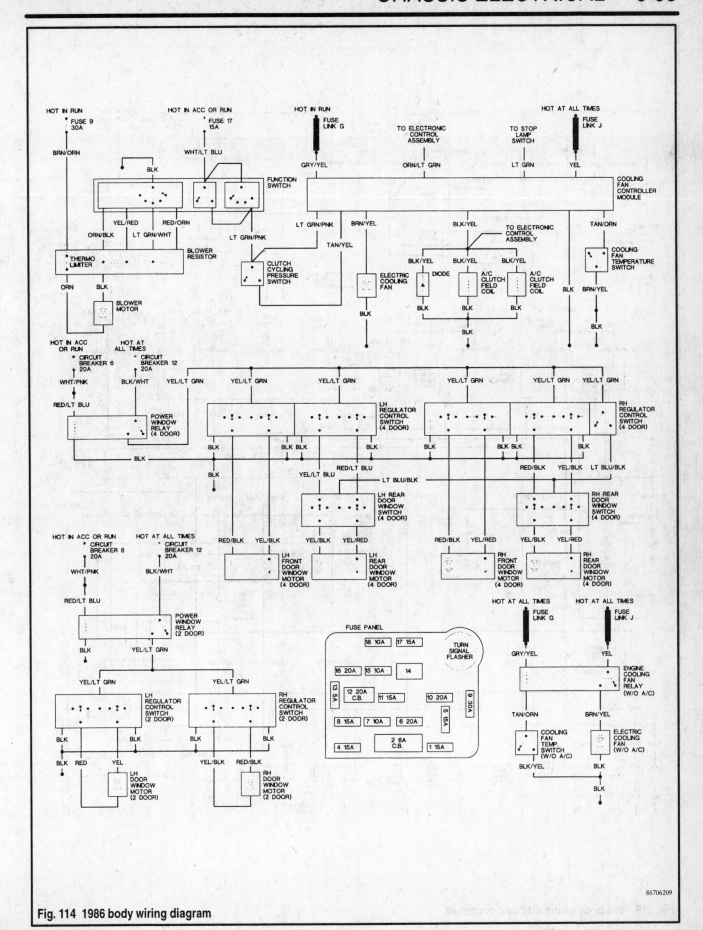

**Fig. 114 1986 body wiring diagram**

86706209

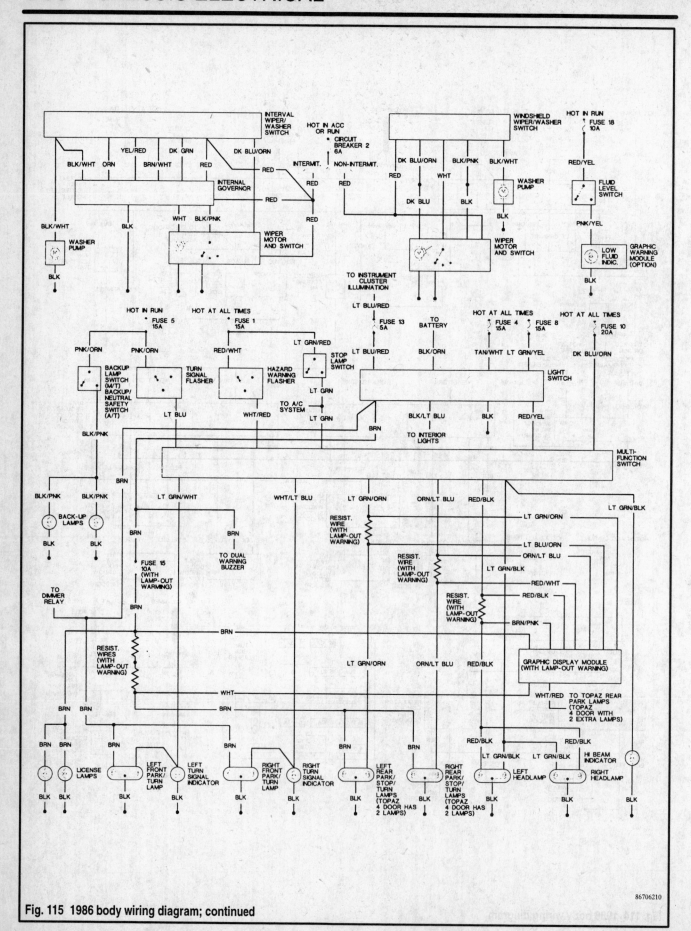

**Fig. 115** 1986 body wiring diagram; continued

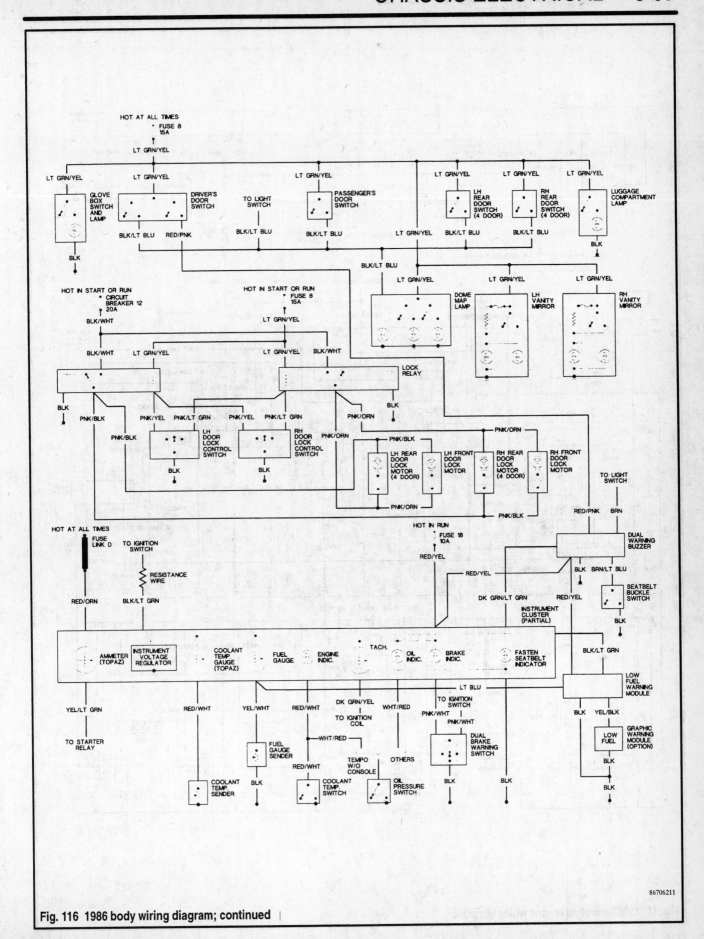

**Fig. 116 1986 body wiring diagram; continued**

86706211

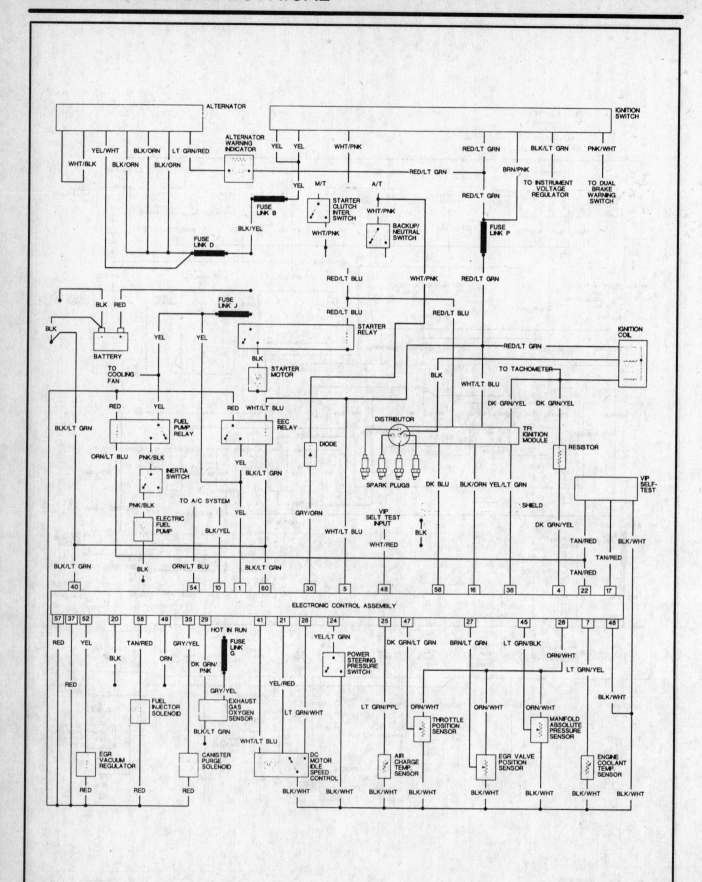

**Fig. 117** 1987 gasoline engine wiring diagram

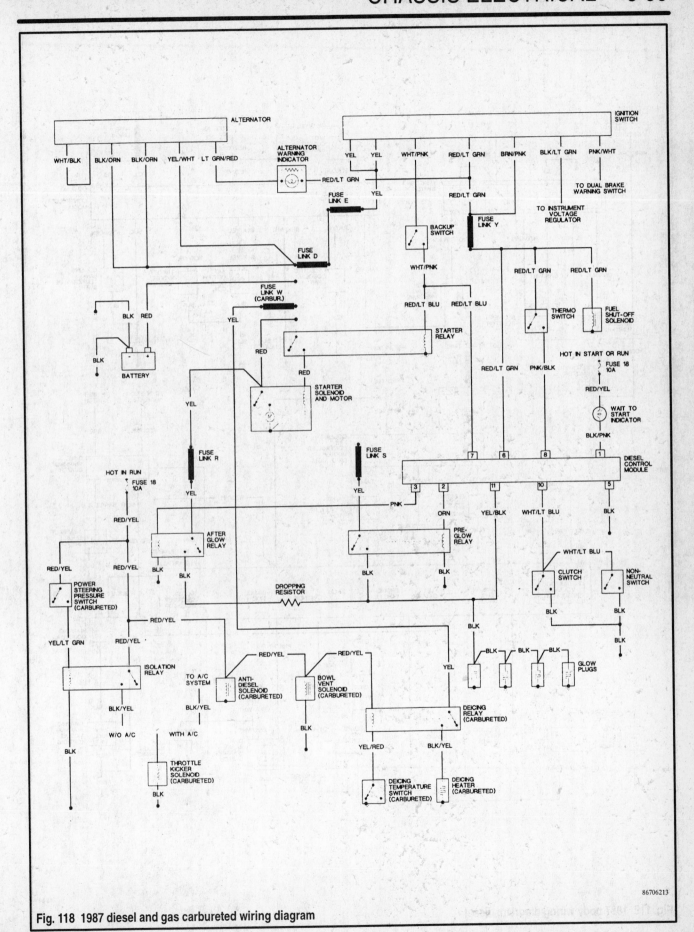

**Fig. 118 1987 diesel and gas carbureted wiring diagram**

86706213

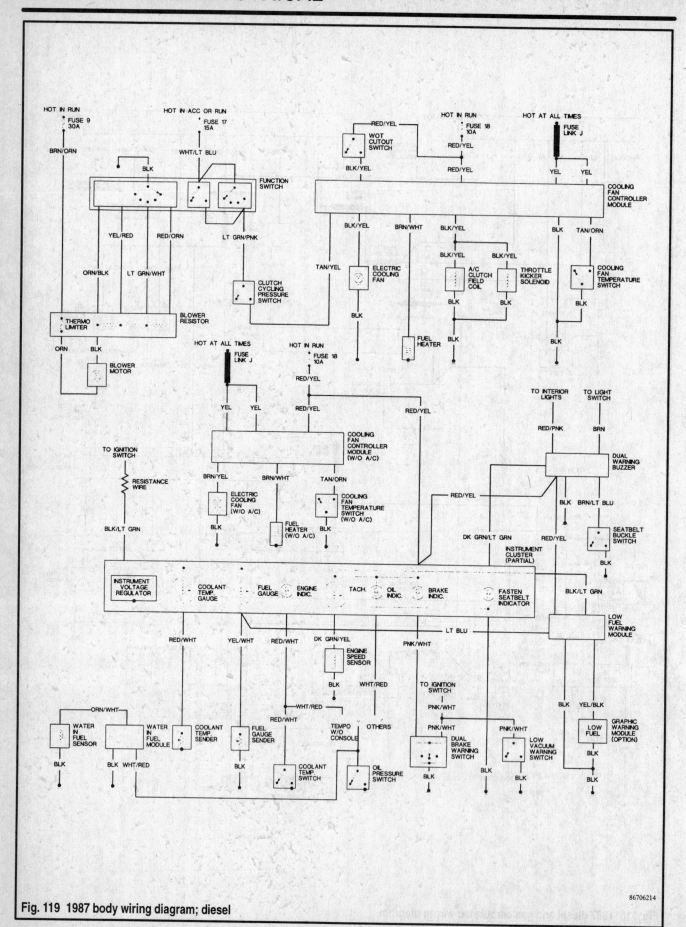

**Fig. 119** 1987 body wiring diagram; diesel

86706214

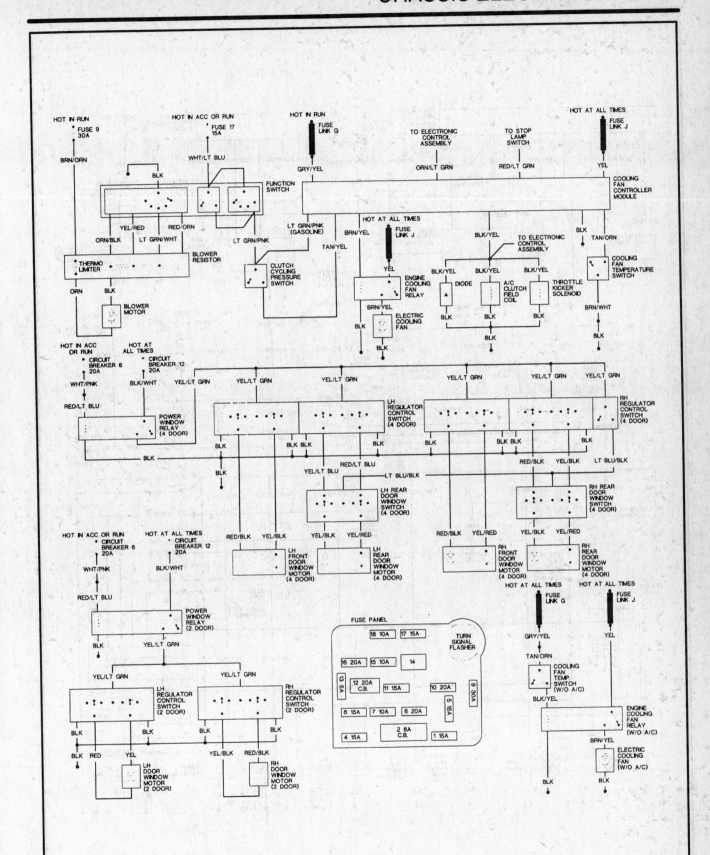

**Fig. 120 1987 body wiring diagram**

86706215

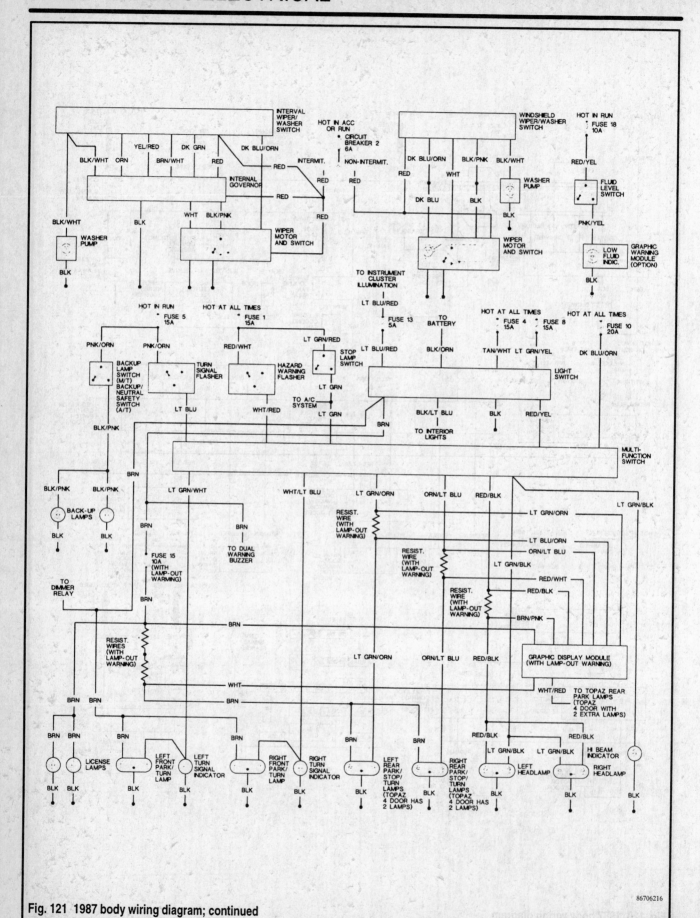

**Fig. 121 1987 body wiring diagram; continued**

86706216

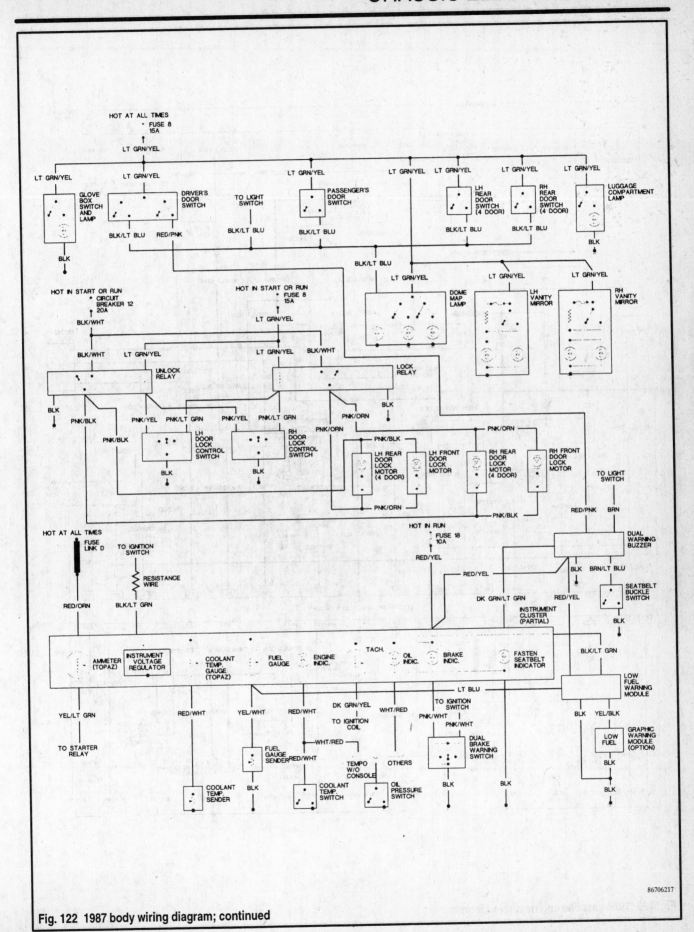

**Fig. 122** 1987 body wiring diagram; continued

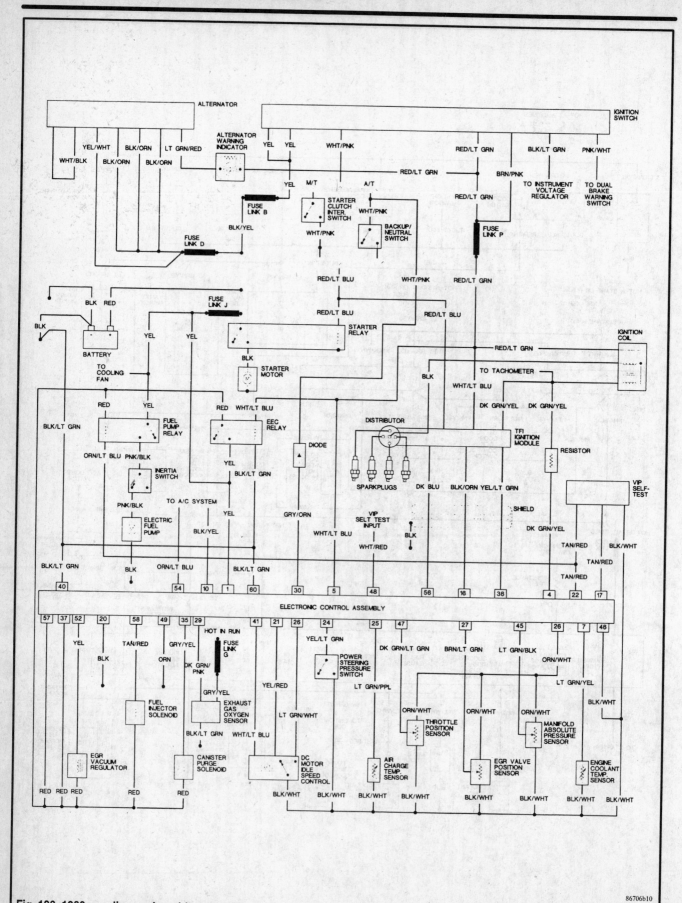

**Fig. 123** 1988 gasoline engine wiring diagram

86706b10

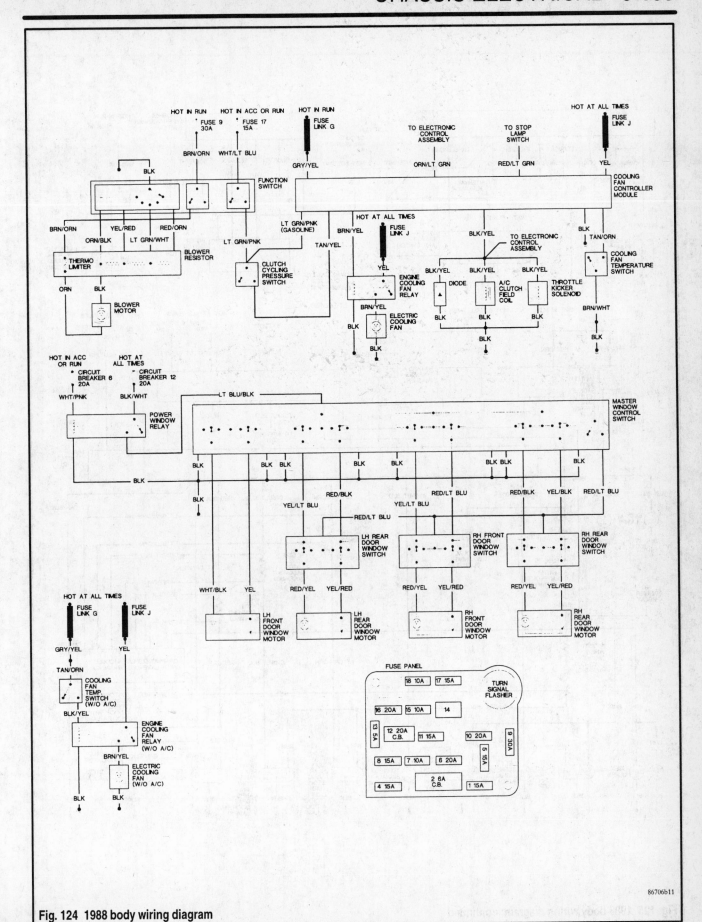

**Fig. 124 1988 body wiring diagram**

86706b11

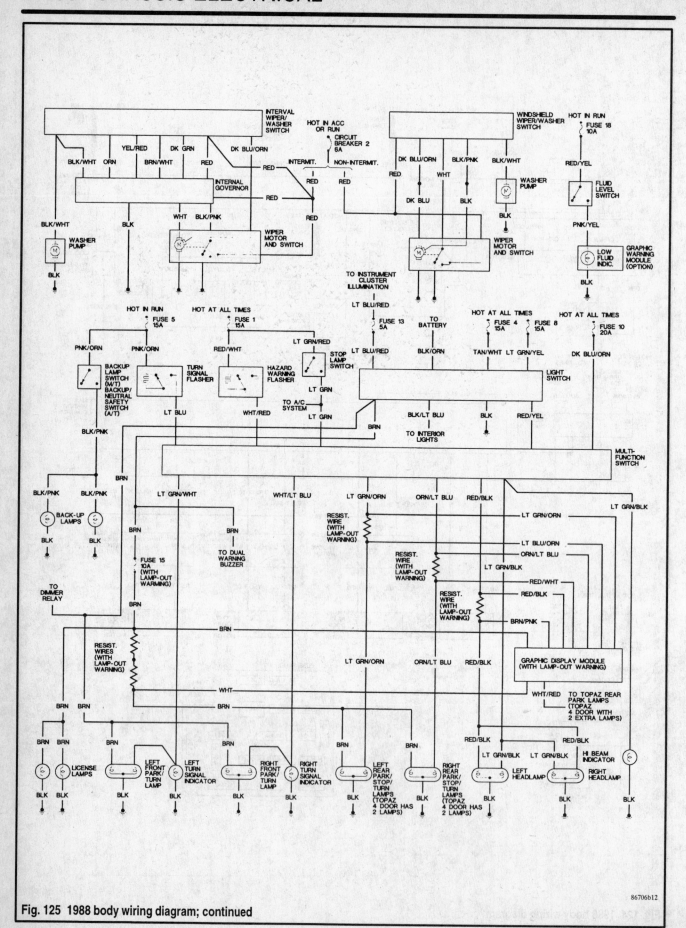

**Fig. 125 1988 body wiring diagram; continued**

86706b12

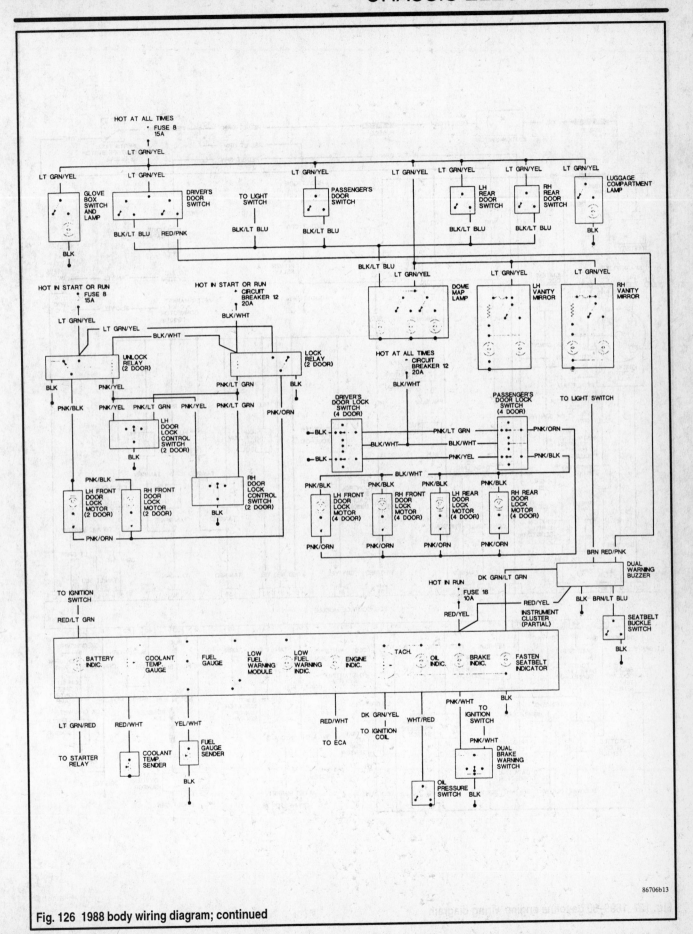

**Fig. 126 1988 body wiring diagram; continued**

86706b13

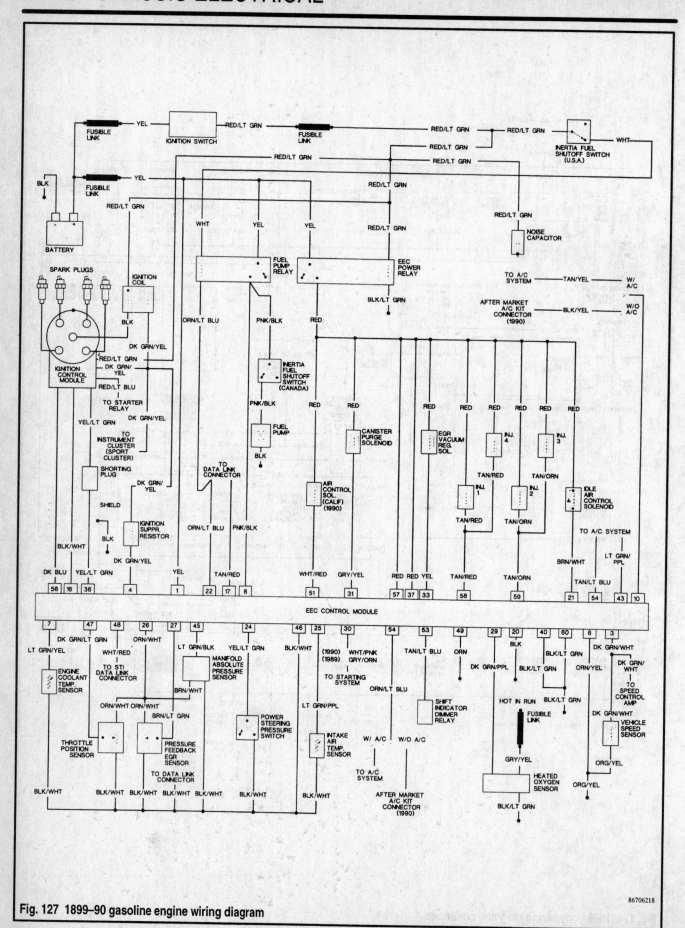

**Fig. 127** 1899–90 gasoline engine wiring diagram

86706218

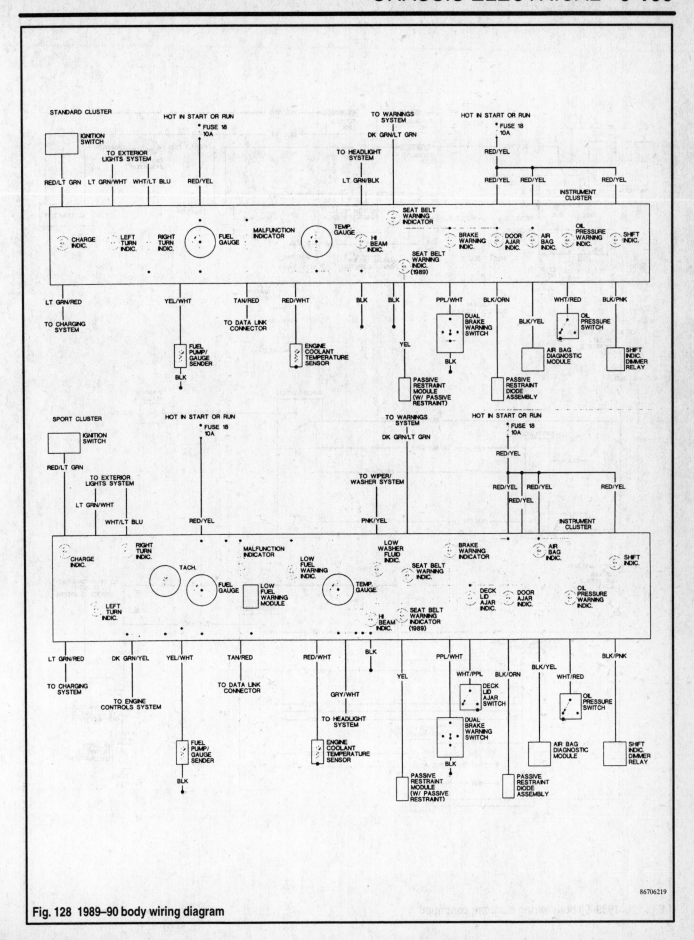

Fig. 128  1989-90 body wiring diagram

86706219

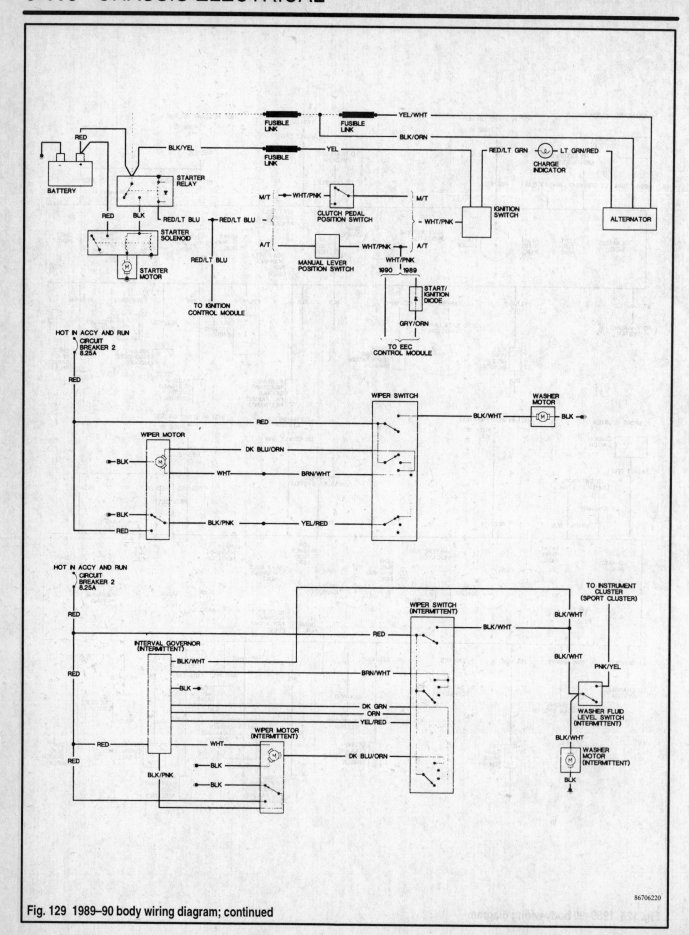

**Fig. 129** 1989–90 body wiring diagram; continued

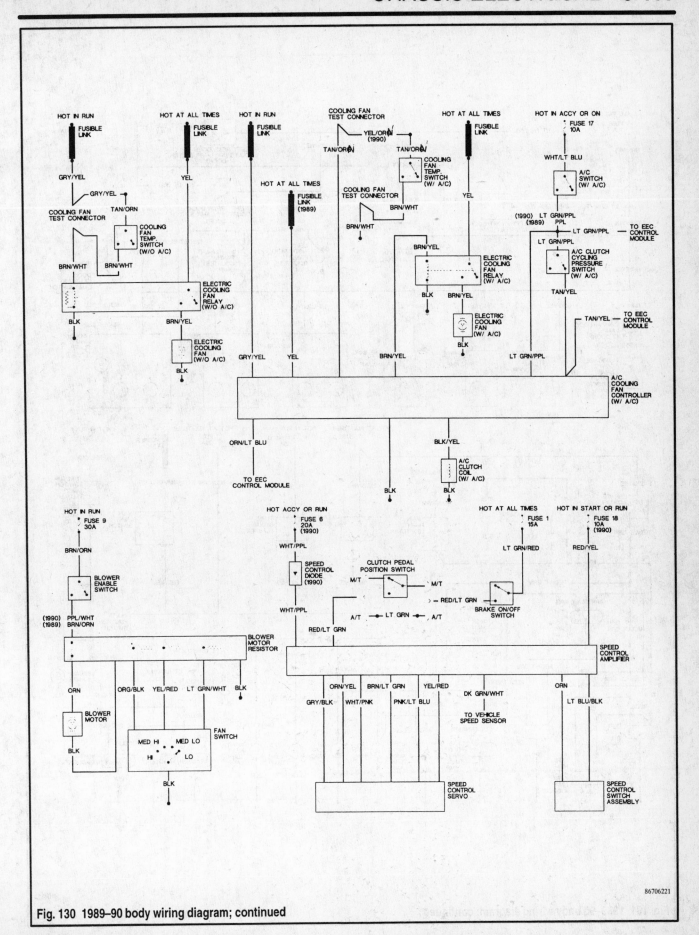

**Fig. 130  1989–90 body wiring diagram; continued**

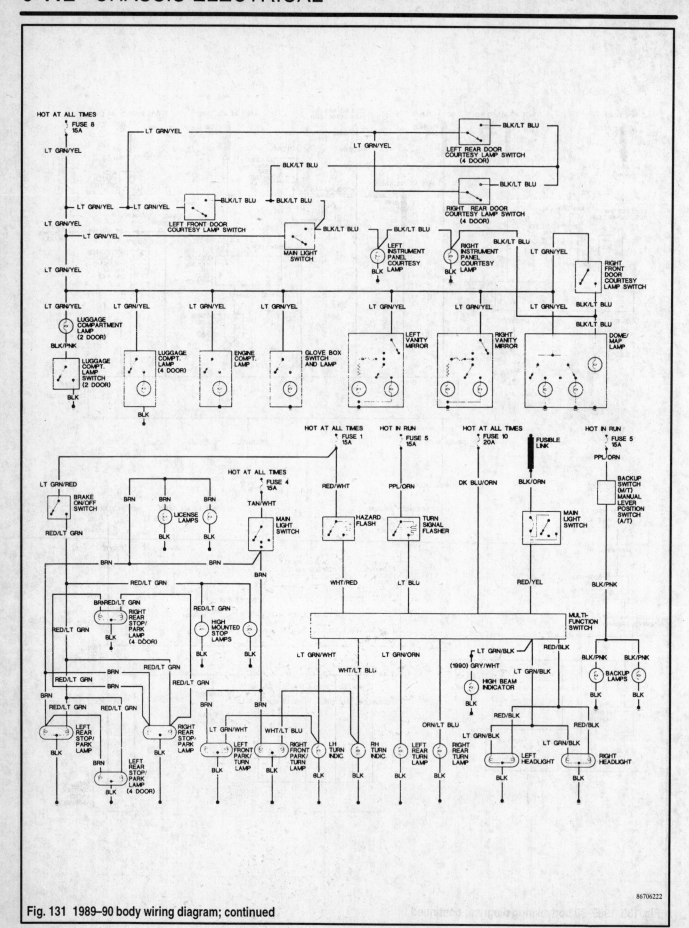

**Fig. 131** 1989–90 body wiring diagram; continued

86706222

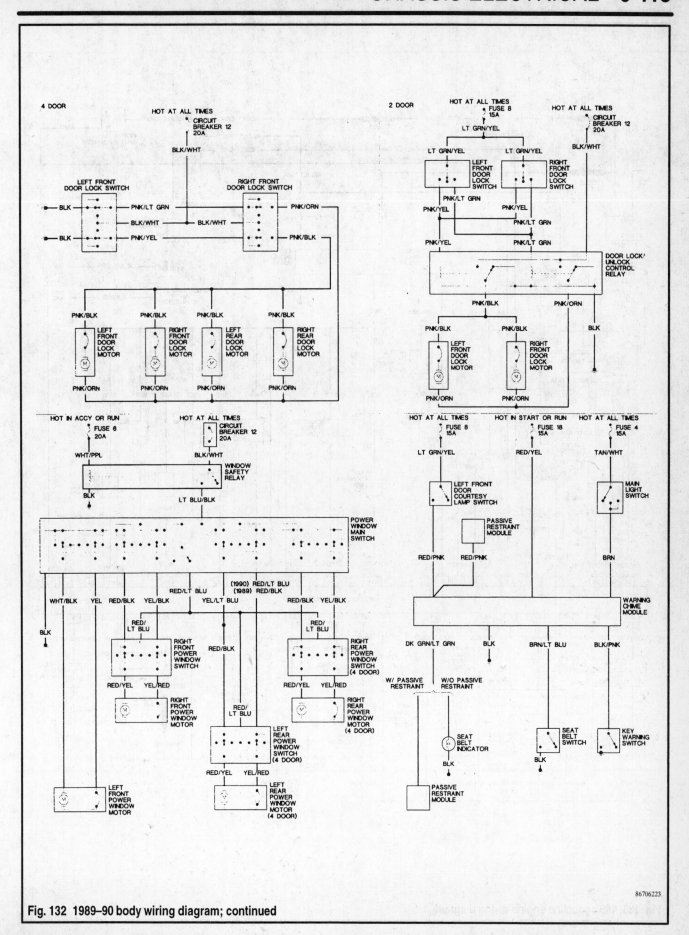

**Fig. 132 1989–90 body wiring diagram; continued**

86706223

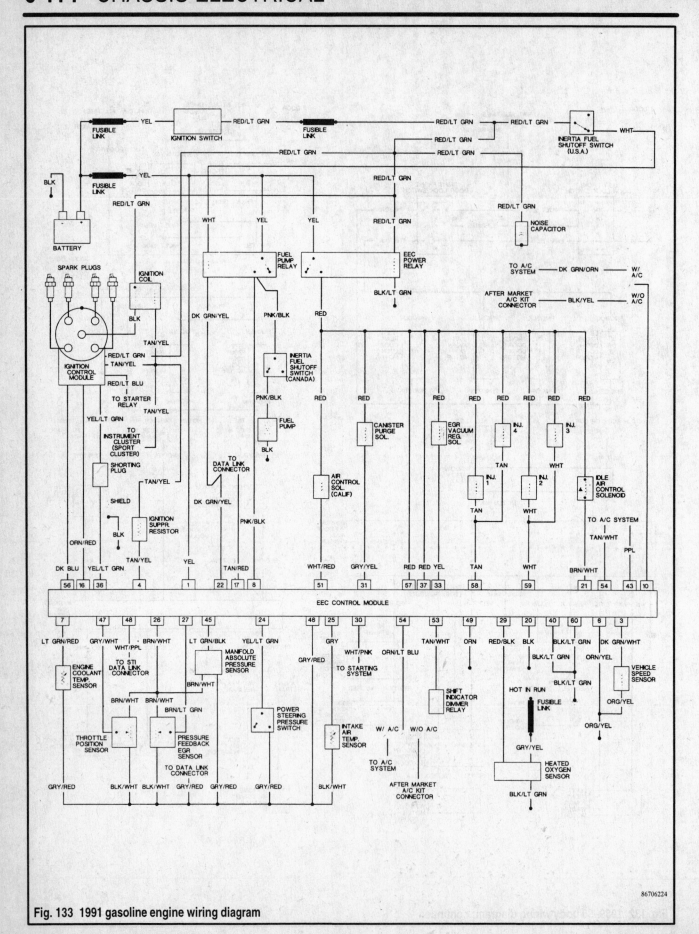

**Fig. 133 1991 gasoline engine wiring diagram**

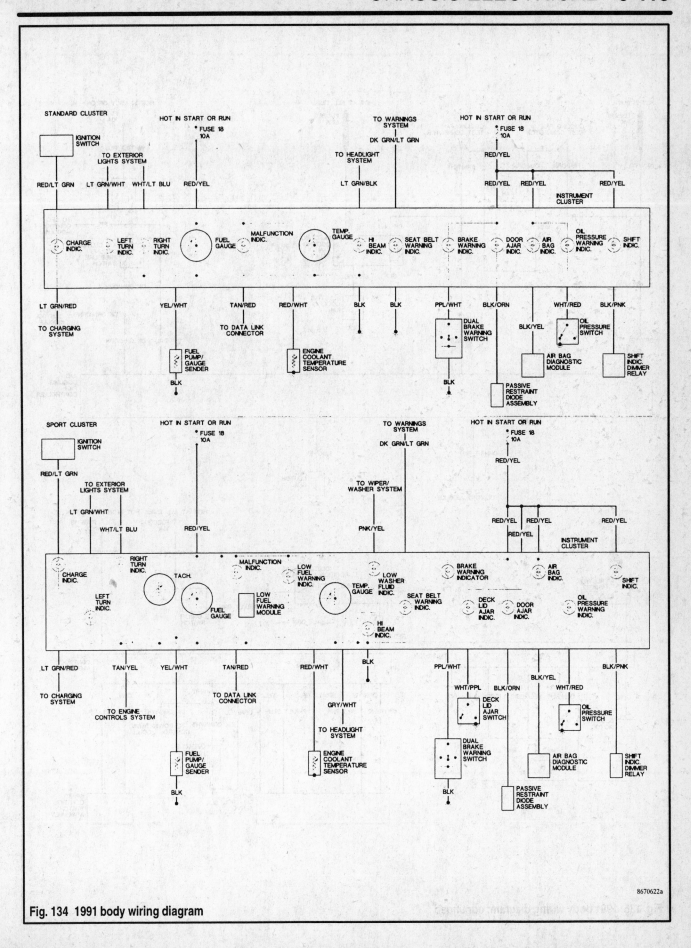

**Fig. 134  1991 body wiring diagram**

8670622a

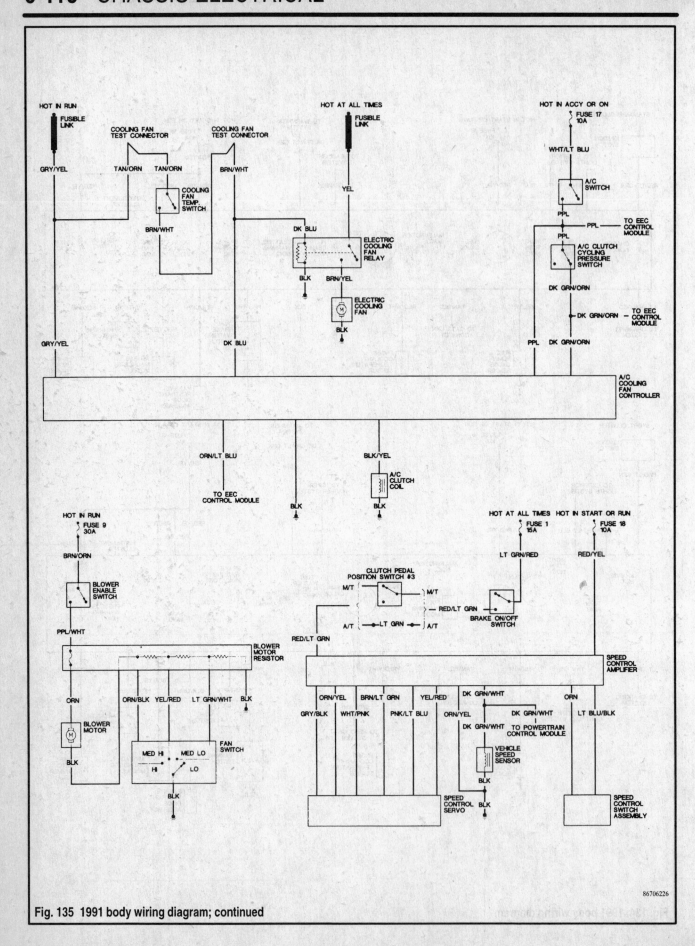

Fig. 135 1991 body wiring diagram; continued

86706226

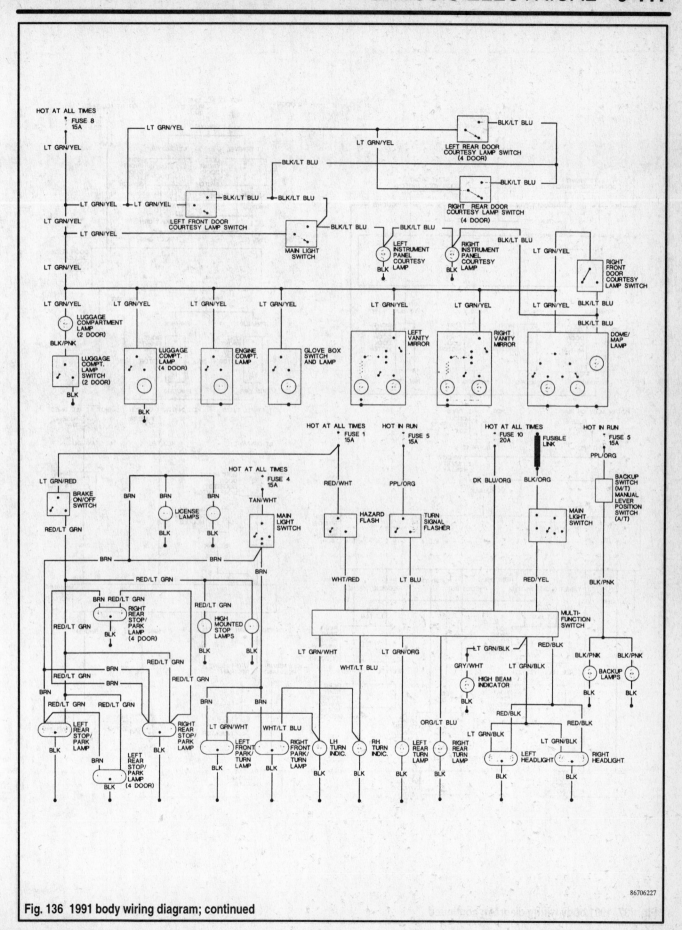

**Fig. 136 1991 body wiring diagram; continued**

86706227

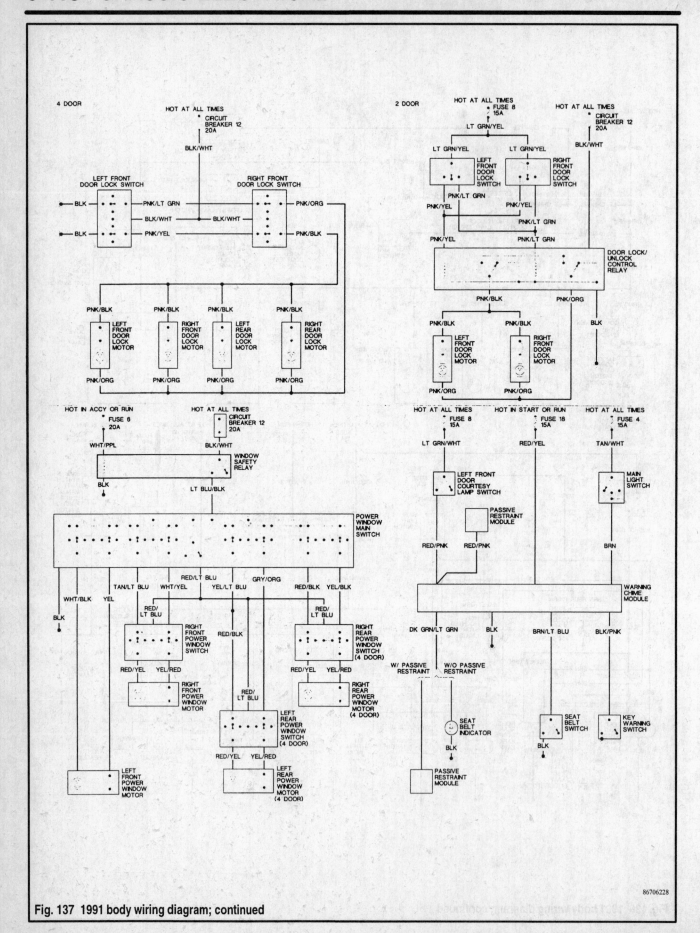

**Fig. 137 1991 body wiring diagram; continued**

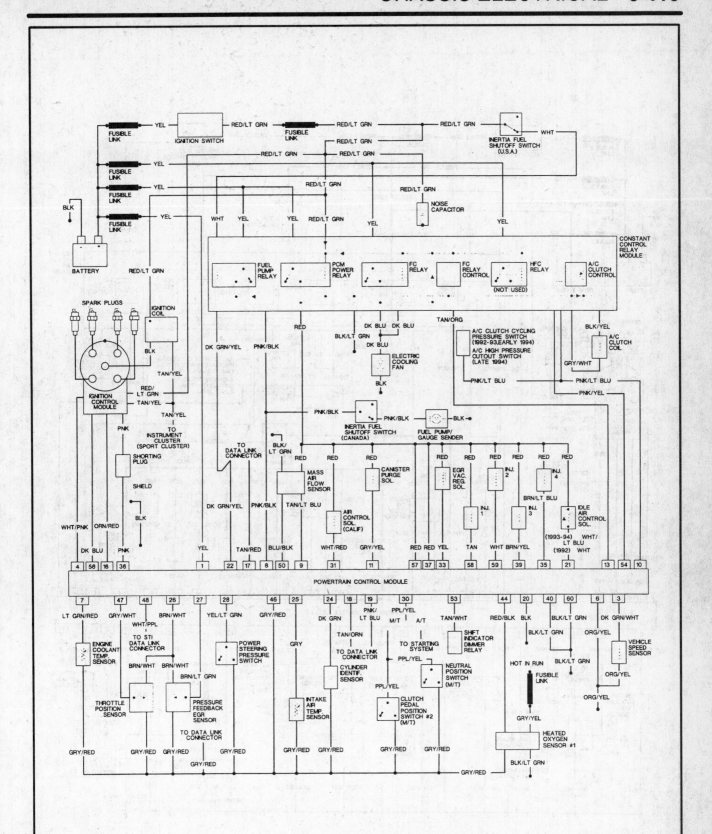

**Fig. 138 1992–94 gasoline engine wiring diagram; 4–cylinder**

86706229

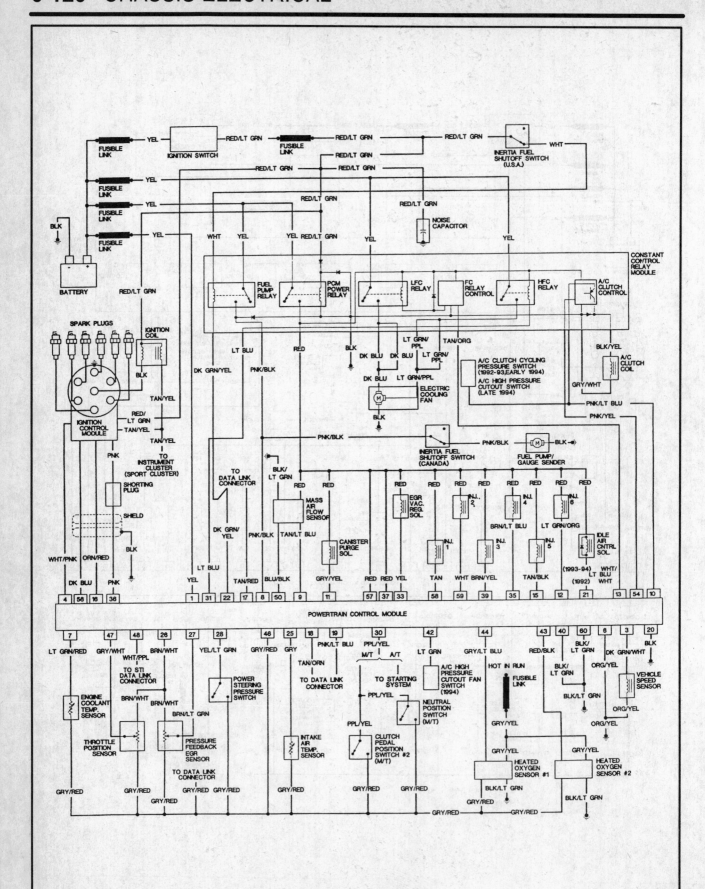

**Fig. 139** 1992–94 gasoline engine wiring diagram; 6–cylinder

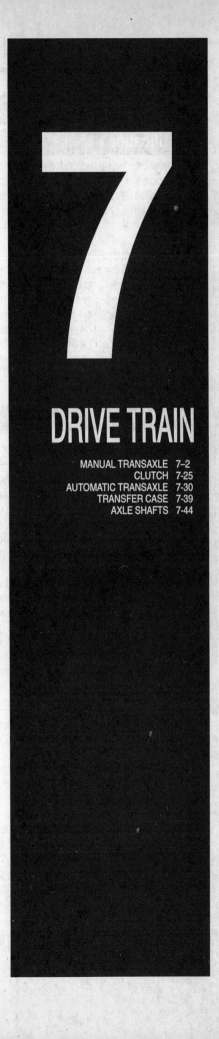

# 7
# DRIVE TRAIN

# MANUAL TRANSAXLE

## Identification

The transaxle unit used on front wheel drive vehicles, is referred too as a transaxle. A 4 or 5–speed fully synchronized Manual Transaxle (MTX) is available, depending on year and model. An internally gated shift mechanism and a single rail shift linkage eliminate the need for periodic shift linkage adjustments. The MTX is designed to use Dexron II automatic transmission/transaxle fluid as a lubricant. Never use gear oil (GL) in place of Dexron II.

The MTX 4–speed and 5–speed transaxles have been used since 1984 with the 5–speed coming out in the later years. The 4–speed manual transaxle is similar in construction to the 5–speed manual transaxle except for the deletion of a 5th gear driveshaft assembly and a 5th gear shift fork assembly. Although similar in appearance, the gear set of the 4–speed transaxle cannot interchange with those of the 5–speed transaxle.

## General Information

### 4–SPEED TRANSAXLE

From the clutch, engine torque is transferred to the mainshaft through the input cluster gear. Each gear on the input cluster is in constant mesh with a matching gear on the mainshaft. It is these matching gear sets which will provide the 4 forward gear ratios. The transaxle gear ratio is determined by the number of teeth on the input cluster gear and the number of teeth on the mainshaft gear.

Reverse is accomplished by sliding a spur gear into mesh with the input cluster shaft gear and the reverse idler gear. The reverse idler gear acts as an idler and reverses the direction of mainshaft rotation. In neutral, none of the gears on the mainshaft are locked to their shafts. Then, no torque from the engine to the input cluster gear shaft is transferred to the differential assembly and to the wheels through the halfshafts.

### 5–SPEED TRANSAXLE

Engine torque is transferred from the clutch to the input cluster gear shaft. The 4 forward gears on the input cluster gear shaft are in constant mesh with a matching gear on the mainshaft. The 4th gear on the input cluster gear shaft is simultaneously meshed with the 5th speed gear on the 5th gear shaft. These meshed gearsets provide the 5 available forward gear ratios.

Both the mainshaft and the 5th gear shaft have a pinion gear, which is constantly engaged with the final drive ring gear of the differential assembly. If a single gear (1st through 4th) on the mainshaft is selected and that gear is locked to the shaft by its shift synchronizer, then the input cluster shaft gear will drive the mainshaft pinion gear; driving the differential final drive ring gear. If the 5th gear is selected, the input cluster shaft 4th gear will drive the 5th gear shaft pinion gear, driving the differential final drive ring gear. At this time, the mainshaft gears will rotate freely.

Reverse is accomplished by sliding a spur gear into mesh with the input cluster shaft gear and the reverse idler gear. The reverse idler gear acts as an idler and reverses the direction of mainshaft rotation.

### METRIC FASTENERS

The metric fastener dimensions are very close to the dimensions of the inch fasteners, and for this reason, replacement fasteners must have the same measurement and strength as those removed.

➡ **Do not attempt to interchange metric fasteners for inch system fasteners. Mismatched or incorrect fasteners can result in damage to the transaxle unit through malfunctions or breakage and possible personal injury.**

## Adjustments

### SHIFT LINKAGE

The external gear shift mechanism consists of a gear shift lever, transaxle shift rod, stabilizer rod and shift housing. Adjustment of the external linkage is not necessary.

### SHIFTER

▶ **See Figure 1**

Because of the design of the shifter mechanism in the Tempo/Topaz, there is no shifter adjustment unless the assembly is worn out or damaged.

## Shift Linkage

### REMOVAL & INSTALLATION

▶ **See Figure 2**

1. Raise the vehicle and safely support on jackstands.
2. From under the vehicle, remove the shift stabilizer assembly hardware.
3. Remove the shift mechanism–to–shift shaft attaching nut and bolt and control selector indicator switch arm. Slide arm out of the way.
4. Remove the shift stabilizer assembly and linkage.

**To install:**

5. Position the shift stabilizer assembly, with linkage to vehicle and secure with nuts. Hand tighten only.
6. Engage the shift mechanism to shift shaft and secure with attaching nut and bolt. Tighten to 7–10 ft. lbs. (9–13 Nm). Be sure to shift the transaxle into 4th gear for a 4–speed or 5th gear for a 5–speed, and align the actuator.
7. Install control selector indicator switch arm and tighten 23–35 ft. lbs. (31–47 Nm).

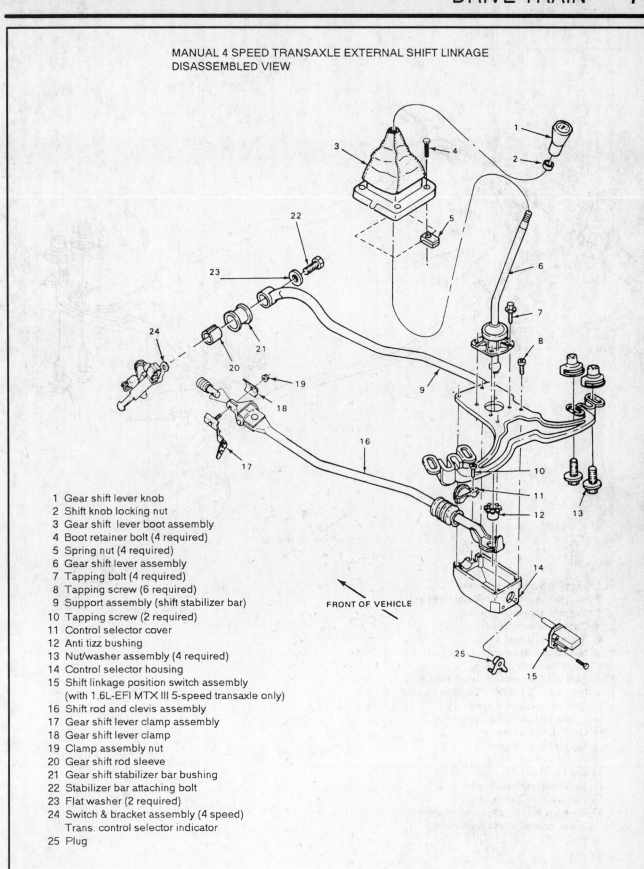

MANUAL 4 SPEED TRANSAXLE EXTERNAL SHIFT LINKAGE
DISASSEMBLED VIEW

FRONT OF VEHICLE

1   Gear shift lever knob
2   Shift knob locking nut
3   Gear shift lever boot assembly
4   Boot retainer bolt (4 required)
5   Spring nut (4 required)
6   Gear shift lever assembly
7   Tapping bolt (4 required)
8   Tapping screw (6 required)
9   Support assembly (shift stabilizer bar)
10  Tapping screw (2 required)
11  Control selector cover
12  Anti tizz bushing
13  Nut/washer assembly (4 required)
14  Control selector housing
15  Shift linkage position switch assembly
      (with 1.6L-EFI MTX III 5-speed transaxle only)
16  Shift rod and clevis assembly
17  Gear shift lever clamp assembly
18  Gear shift lever clamp
19  Clamp assembly nut
20  Gear shift rod sleeve
21  Gear shift stabilizer bar bushing
22  Stabilizer bar attaching bolt
23  Flat washer (2 required)
24  Switch & bracket assembly (4 speed)
      Trans. control selector indicator
25  Plug

867007001

**Fig. 1  Manual transaxle shifter and linkage**

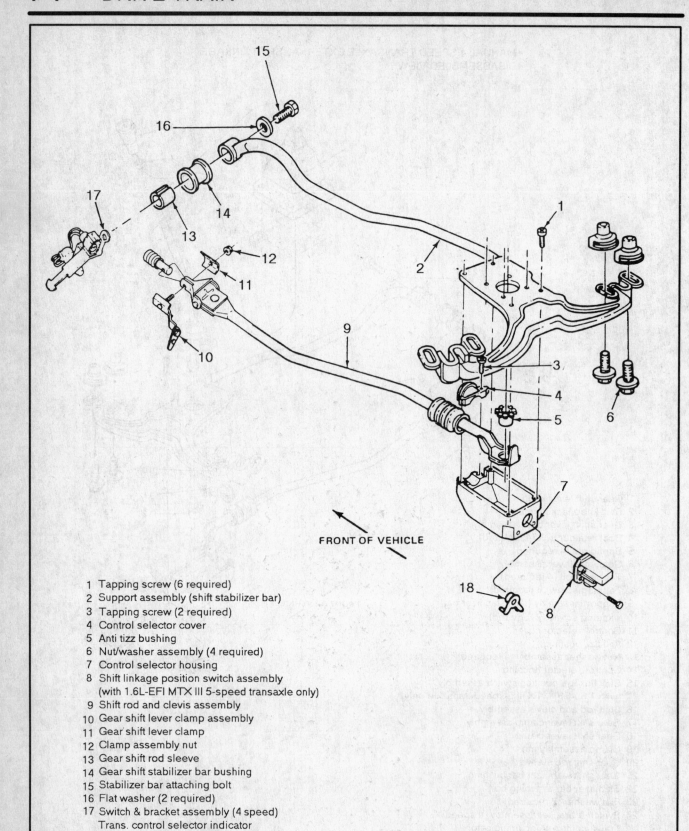

FRONT OF VEHICLE

1 Tapping screw (6 required)
2 Support assembly (shift stabilizer bar)
3 Tapping screw (2 required)
4 Control selector cover
5 Anti tizz bushing
6 Nut/washer assembly (4 required)
7 Control selector housing
8 Shift linkage position switch assembly
   (with 1.6L-EFI MTX III 5-speed transaxle only)
9 Shift rod and clevis assembly
10 Gear shift lever clamp assembly
11 Gear shift lever clamp
12 Clamp assembly nut
13 Gear shift rod sleeve
14 Gear shift stabilizer bar bushing
15 Stabilizer bar attaching bolt
16 Flat washer (2 required)
17 Switch & bracket assembly (4 speed)
   Trans. control selector indicator
18 Plug

86707003

**Fig. 2 Exploded view of transaxle linkage**

8. Tighten the nuts securing the shift stabilizer to 7–10 ft. lbs. (9–13 Nm).

9. Lower the vehicle.

10. Road test the vehicle.

## Shift Handle

### REMOVAL & INSTALLATION

1. Grasp shift handle and turn in a counterclockwise direction and remove.

2. Check condition of threads on shift knob. Clean thread of shift shaft.

**To install:**

3. Place shift handle on shift shaft and turn in clockwise direction until tight.

## Control Selector Housing

### REMOVAL & INSTALLATION

▶ See Figure 3

1. Raise and safely support vehicle on jackstands.

2. From under the vehicle, remove the bolts securing the shift stabilizer and control selector housing to the vehicle.

3. Remove the hardware fastening the support assembly to the transaxle.

4. Remove the nut and bolt securing the shift mechanism to the shift shaft, and move out of the way.

5. Lower the shifter assembly down. Separate the control selector housing from the stabilizer. Inspect rubber of both units, and replace if excessively worn.

**To install:**

6. Position the stabilizer assembly and control selector housing together and mount to underside of vehicle. Tighten nuts to 7–10 ft. lbs. (9–13 Nm).

7. Slide the shift shaft in to the shift mechanism and secure with the nut and bolt. Tighten the hardware to 7–10 ft. lbs. (9–13 Nm). Be sure to shift the transaxle into 4th gear for a 4–speed or 5th gear for a 5–speed, and align the actuator.

8. Position and secure the shift stabilizer, tightening the nut to 23–35 ft. lbs. (31–47 Nm).

9. Lower the vehicle. Test the shifter for a smooth transition between gears. Road test the vehicle.

## Clutch Switch

### REMOVAL & INSTALLATION

▶ See Figure 4

1. Disconnect negative battery cable.

2. Remove the panel below the steering column.

3. Disconnect the wire harness attached to the clutch switch.

4. Remove clutch switch attaching screws and hairpin clip, then remove switch.

**To install:**

5. Install the switch with the self adjusting clip about 1.0 inch (25.4mm) from the end of the rod. The clutch pedal must be fully up (clutch engaged).

6. Insert the eyelet end of rod over the pin on the clutch pedal, and secure with hairpin clip.

7. Align the mounting boss with the hole in the bracket, and secure with the screw.

8. Reset the interlock switch by pressing the clutch pedal to the floor.

9. Connect the wire harness to the switch.

10. Install the panel. Connect negative battery cable.

11. Test by pressing clutch pedal for correct operation

## Back–Up Light Switch

### REMOVAL & INSTALLATION

▶ See Figure 5

1. Disconnect the negative battery cable.

2. Disengage the electrical connector from the back–up switch.

3. Place the transaxle in reverse.

4. Using a 22mm wrench wrench, remove the back–up light switch.

**To install:**

5. Apply Teflon pipe sealant tape to the threads of the new lamp switch in a clockwise direction.

6. Install the switch in the transaxle, and tighten to 12–15 ft. lbs. (16–20 Nm).

7. Connect electrical harness to switch.

8. Connect negative battery cable.

9. Check to make sure reverse lights function correctly

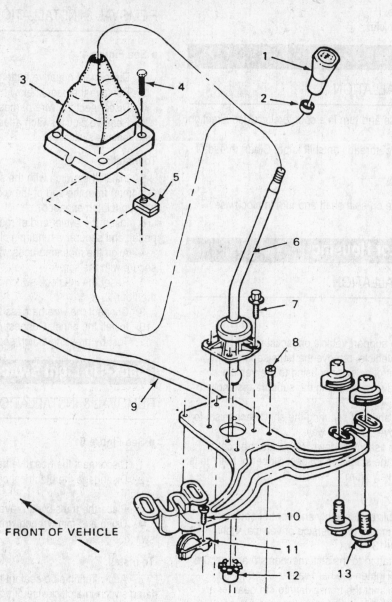

FRONT OF VEHICLE

1 Gear shift lever knob
2 Shift knob locking nut
3 Gear shift lever boot assembly
4 Boot retainer bolt (4 required)
5 Spring nut (4 required)
6 Gear shift lever assembly
7 Tapping bolt (4 required)
8 Tapping screw (6 required)
9 Support assembly (shift stabilizer bar)
10 Tapping screw (2 required)
11 Control selector cover
12 Anti tizz bushing
13 Nut/washer assembly (4 required)

Fig. 3 Exploded view of control selector housing

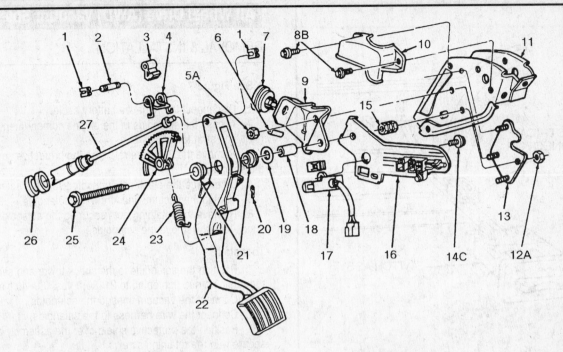

1  Clip (2 req'd)
2  Pin
3  Pawl
4  Pawl tension spring
5A  Nut
6  Stop
7  Insulator
8B  Screw
9  Clutch pedal stop bracket
10  Shield
11  Pedal support
12  Nut
13  Mounting bracket
14C  Screw
15  Pivot spacer nut
16  Clutch pedal position switch
      mounting bracket
17  CPP switch
18  Pivot sleeve
19  Spring washer
20  Clip
21  Pivot bushings (2 req'd)
22  Clutch pedal
23  Gear quadrant tension spring
24  Gear quadrant
25  Pivot bolt
26  Dash panel grommet
27  Clutch cable
 A  Tighten to 34-40 Nm (26-29 lb.ft.)
 B  Tighten to 8-12 Nm (71-106 lb.in.)
 C  Tighten to 0.9-1.36 Nm (8-12 lb.in.)

86707002

**Fig. 4  Exploded view of clutch pedal and clutch switch**

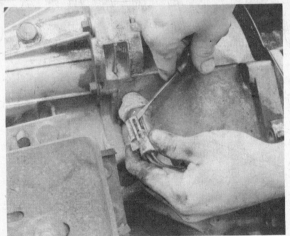

86707500

**Fig. 5  Removing the Back–Up light switch plug from the transaxle**

## All Wheel Drive (AWD) Switch

### REMOVAL & INSTALLATION

▶ **See Figure 6**

1. Disconnect the negative battery cable.
2. Remove the instrument cluster finish panel.
3. Depress the tab on the switch and pull out of the opening
4. Disengage the electrical connector and remove the switch.

**To install:**

5. Connect the wire harness to the switch.
6. Push the switch into place.
7. Position and secure the finish panel.
8. Connect the negative battery cable.
9. Road test the vehicle and test the all wheel drive operation.

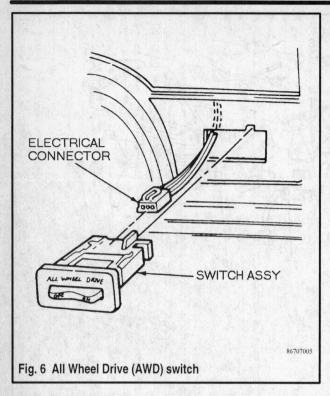

ELECTRICAL
CONNECTOR

ALL WHEEL DRIVE

SWITCH ASSY

86707005

**Fig. 6 All Wheel Drive (AWD) switch**

## All Wheel Drive (AWD) Vacuum Solenoids

### REMOVAL & INSTALLATION

▶ **See Figure 7**

1. Disconnect the negative battery cable.
2. Access the solenoids in the engine compartment on the right side strut tower.
3. Remove the 3 screws retaining the protective cover over the solenoids.
4. Disengage the electrical connector from the solenoids.
5. Unplug the vacuum lines from the solenoids.
6. Remove the retaining nuts securing the solenoids to the shock tower. Remove the solenoids.

**To install:**

7. Position the solenoids to the shock tower and secure with the retaining nut, tightening to 21–30 ft. lbs. (29–40 Nm).
8. Connect the vacuum lines to the solenoids.
9. Connect the wire harness to the solenoids.
10. Position the protective shield over the assembly and secure with the retaining screws.
11. Connect the negative battery cable.
12. Road test the vehicle and test the all wheel drive feature.

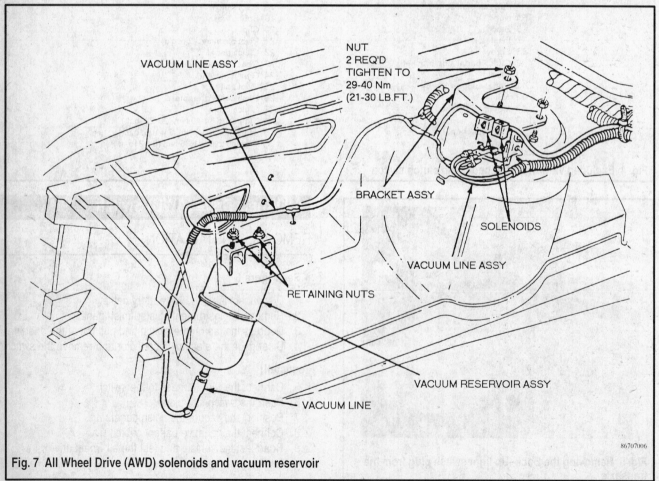

VACUUM LINE ASSY

NUT
2 REQ'D
TIGHTEN TO
29-40 Nm
(21-30 LB.FT.)

BRACKET ASSY

SOLENOIDS

VACUUM LINE ASSY

RETAINING NUTS

VACUUM RESERVOIR ASSY

VACUUM LINE

86707006

**Fig. 7 All Wheel Drive (AWD) solenoids and vacuum reservoir**

## All Wheel Drive (AWD) Vacuum Reservoir

### REMOVAL & INSTALLATION

▶ See Figure 7

1. Disconnect the negative battery cable.
2. Access the reservoir from the right side front fender wheel.
3. Remove the the fender well plastic cover by removing the retaining screws.
4. Remove the retaining nuts securing the reservoir to the vehicle body.
5. Unplug the vacuum line from the reservoir.
6. Remove the reservoir.

**To install:**

7. Connect the vacuum line to the reservoir.
8. Attach the reservoir to the vehicle body and secure with nuts, tightening to 34–38 inch. lbs. (3.8–4.3 Nm).
9. Position the protective shield in the fender and secure with the retaining screws.
10. Connect the negative battery cable.
11. Road test the vehicle and test the all wheel drive feature.

## All Wheel Drive (AWD) Vacuum Servo

### REMOVAL & INSTALLATION

▶ See Figure 8

1. Disconnect the negative battery cable.
2. Raise and support the vehicle on jackstands.
3. Access the servo from under the vehicle, next to the transfer case.
4. Remove the 3 retaining bolts from the shield to the transfer case.
5. Unplug the vacuum lines from the servo.
6. Remove the vacuum line retaining bracket.
7. Remove and discard the 3 E-rings from the servo shift rod.
8. Remove the servo unit from the transfer case by removing the retaining bolts.

**To install:**

9. Position the servo to the transfer case using the retaining bolts. Tighten the bolts to 7–12 ft. lbs. (9–12 Nm).
10. Install 3 new E-rings onto the servo shift rod.
11. Connect the vacuum lines to the servo.
12. Connect the vacuum line retaining bracket. Tighten the hardware to 7–12 ft. lbs. (9–12 Nm).
13. Position the protective shield and secure with the retaining bolts tightening to 7–12 ft. lbs. (9–12 Nm).
14. Connect the negative battery cable.
15. Road test the vehicle and test the all wheel drive feature.

## Speedometer Driven Gear

### REMOVAL & INSTALLATION

▶ See Figure 9

1. Make sure the vehicle is in gear with the hand brake fully engaged.
2. Using a suitable wrench, remove the retaining screw from the speedometer drive gear retainer assemble.
3. Carefully pry on the speedometer retainer to remove both the speedometer gear and retainer assembly from the clutch housing case bore. Be careful not to make contact with teeth on the speedometer gear.
4. Check the condition of the O-ring, and replace if necessary.

**To install:**

5. Lightly grease the O-ring seal on the speedometer driven gear retainer.
6. Align the relief in the retainer with the attaching screw bore and tap the assembly into the bore.
7. Tighten the retaining screw to 12—24 inch lbs. (16–33 Nm).

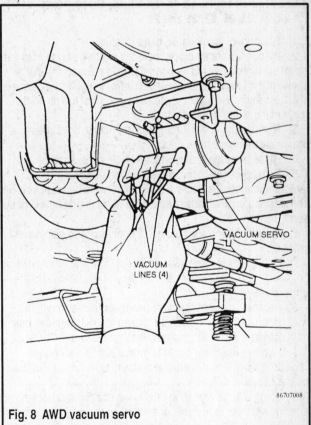

86707008

**Fig. 8 AWD vacuum servo**

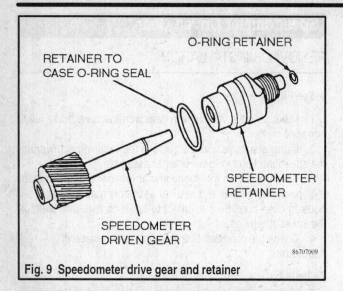

RETAINER TO CASE O-RING SEAL

O-RING RETAINER

SPEEDOMETER RETAINER

SPEEDOMETER DRIVEN GEAR

86707009

**Fig. 9 Speedometer drive gear and retainer**

## Manual Transaxle

### REMOVAL & INSTALLATION

◆ **See Figures 10, 11, 12, 13, 14, 15, 16, 17, 18, 19, 20, 21, 22, 23, 24, 25, 26, 27, 28 and 29**

1. Disconnect the negative battery cable.
2. Wedge a wooden block under the clutch pedal to hold the pedal up slightly beyond its normal position. Grasp the clutch cable, pull it forward and disconnect it from the clutch release shaft assembly. Remove the clutch casing from the rib on the top surface of the transaxle case.
3. Remove the upper 2 transaxle-to-engine bolts. Remove the air cleaner assembly.
4. Raise and safely support the vehicle on jackstands.
5. From underneath the car, support the engine with jackstands or other suitable equipment. This is because you will be removing engine/transaxle mounts, and the engine will need some support.
6. Drain the transaxle fluid into a container and dispose of properly.
7. Unplug the reverse switch harness, and any other harness or vacuum line which may be in the way of the removal of the transaxle assembly.
8. Remove the front stabilizer bar-to-control arm nut and washer, on the driver's side and discard the nut. Remove both front stabilizer bar mounting brackets and discard the bolts.
9. Remove the lower control arm ball joint-to-steering knuckle nut/bolt and discard the nut/bolt; repeat this procedure on the opposite side.
10. Using a large prybar, pry the lower control arm from the steering knuckle; repeat this procedure on the opposite side.

➡ **Be careful not to damage or cut the ball joint boot and do not contact the lower arm.**

11. Remove the front wheels and tires. Remove the nut from the outer CV-joint/halfshaft assembly on both side of the front of the car. Push the halfshaft assembly toward the engine. It may be necessary to use a puller to free the splines in the outer joint.

12. Using a large prybar, pry the inboard CV-joint assemblies from the transaxle.

➡ **Plug the seal opening to prevent lubricant leakage.**

13. Grasp the steering knuckle and swing it and the halfshaft outward from the transaxle; this will disconnect the inboard CV-joint from the transaxle. Inspect the joint boots and replace if needed. Place halfshafts out of the way.
14. Remove the starter studs-to-engine mount hardware. Remove the mount from the vehicle. Unfasten the starter wires. Remove the starter stud bolts and starter.
15. Remove the bolts securing the transaxle to the engine above the starter.
16. Remove the shift mechanism-to-shift shaft nut/bolt, the control selector indicator switch arm and the shift shaft.
17. Remove the shift mechanism stabilizer bar-to-transaxle bolt, control selector indicator switch and bracket assembly.
18. Using a suitable crowfoot or wrench, remove the speedometer cable from the transaxle.
19. Remove the exhaust to the engine/transaxle nuts and bolts.
20. Remove both oil pan-to-clutch housing bolts. Unfasten the hardware securing the exhaust bracket to the engine oil pan.
21. Using a floor jack and a transaxle support, position it under the transaxle and secure the transaxle to it.
22. Remove the insulator-to-body bracket nuts and bolts. When complete, check to make sure all necessary hardware has been removed and no other pieces are preventing the transaxle from being lower out of the car.
23. Slowly, lower the floor jack, until the transaxle clears the rear insulator. Support the engine by placing wood or jackstands under the oil pan.
24. Remove the engine-to-transaxle bolts and lower the transaxle from the vehicle.

➡ **One of the engine-to-transaxle bolts attaches the ground strap and wiring loom stand off bracket.**

**To install:**

25. Raise the transaxle into position and engage the input shaft with the clutch plate. Install the lower engine-to-transaxle bolts and tighten to 28–31 ft. lbs. (38–42 Nm).

➡ **Never attempt to start the engine prior to installing the CV-joints. Damage to the bearings, differential or transaxle side gear for dislocation and/or damage may occur.**

26. Tighten the left front insulator bolts to 25–35 ft. lbs. (34–47 Nm) and the rear insulator bolts to 35–50 ft. lbs. (47–68 Nm).
27. Remove the floor jack and adapter.
28. Using a suitable wrench, install the speedometer cable; be careful not to crossthread the cable nut.
29. Install the oil pan-to-transaxle bolts and tighten to 28–38 ft. lbs. (38–51 Nm).
30. Install the shifter stabilizer bar/control selector indicator switch-to-transaxle bolt and tighten to 23–35 ft. lbs. (31–47 Nm).
31. Install the shift mechanism-to-shift shaft, the switch actuator bracket clamp and tighten the bolt to 7–10 ft. lbs.

(9–13 Nm); be sure to shift the transaxle into 4th gear for a 4–speed or 5th gear for a 5–speed, and align the actuator.

32. Install the starter stud bolts and tighten to 30–40 ft. lbs. (41–54 Nm) and install the engine roll restricter and the attaching nuts.

33. Tighten the attaching nuts to 14–20 ft. lbs. (19–27 Nm).

34. Install the new circlip onto both inner joints of the halfshafts, insert the inner CV–joints into the transaxle and fully seat them; lightly, pry outward to confirm that the retaining rings are seated.

➡ **When installing the halfshafts, be careful not to tear the oil seals.**

35. Install the exhaust bracket and hardware.

36. Connect the lower ball joint to the steering knuckle, insert a new pinch bolt and tighten the new nut to 37–44 ft. lbs. (50–60 Nm); be careful not to damage the boot.

37. Refill the transaxle and lower the vehicle.

38. Install the air cleaner.

39. Install the both upper transaxle–to–engine bolts and tighten to 28–31 ft. lbs. (38–42 Nm).

40. Connect the clutch cable to the clutch release shaft assembly and remove the wooden block from under the clutch pedal. Connect the negative battery cable.

➡ **Prior to starting the engine, set the hand brake and pump the clutch pedal several times to ensure proper clutch adjustment.**

41. Start vehicle and allow to reach normal operating temperature. Check for leaks. Road test the vehicle.

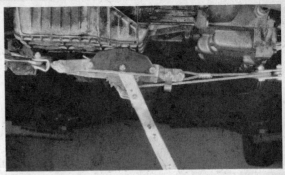

Fig. 11 For safety, support the engine with jackstands, or (like here) tighten a wire come–along under the engine, to keep it from falling when the mounts are removed

Fig. 12 Drain the fluid from the transaxle

Fig. 10 Support the clutch pedal with a wooden block in order to aid in the removal of the clutch cable

Fig. 13 Unplug any necessary wire harnesses, vacuum lines and any components which may prevent the unit from being easily removed

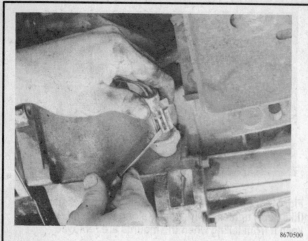

Fig. 14 Unplug the wiring from the reverse switch—it is not necessary to remove the switch itself unless you intend to replace it or the transaxle

Fig. 17 Remove the front engine mount

Fig. 15 Use a puller to free the outer CV-joint

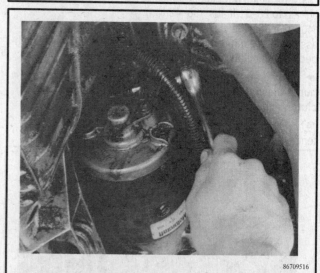

Fig. 18 Remove the starter studs and nuts

Fig. 16 Carefully pry the inner CV-joint out—Be aware that some remaining transaxle fluid may leak

Fig. 19 It may be easier to remove the bolts from the starter instead of from the engine assembly, but DO NOT forget to disconnect the starter wiring

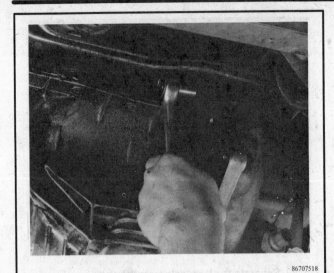

Fig. 20  Remove the retaining bolt above the starter

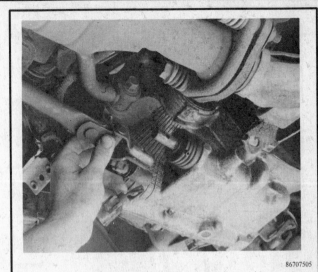

Fig. 23  Separate the shifter from the transaxle

Fig. 21  Loosen the shifter nut and bolt using a wrench . . .

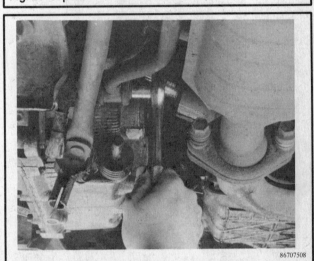

Fig. 24  Remove the stabilizer bar attached to the transaxle

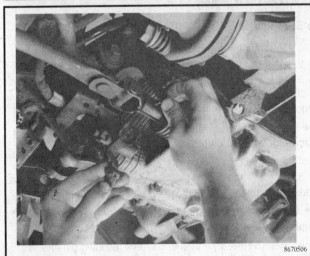

Fig. 22  . . . then remove the nut and bolt to free the linkage

Fig. 25  Unfasten the exhaust hardware

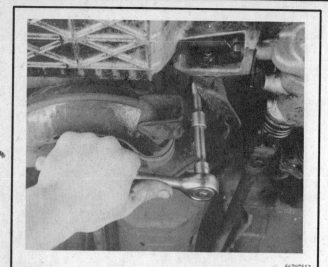

Fig. 26 Remove the oil pan–to–transaxle bolts

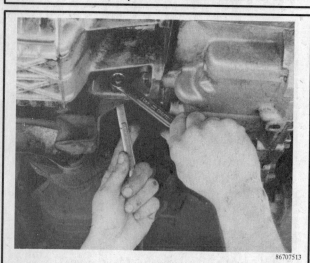

Fig. 27 Remove the exhaust bracket from the engine/transaxle assembly

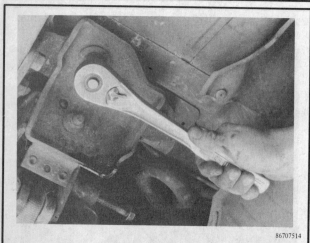

Fig. 28 Remove the engine mounts/insulators, including the rear mount

Fig. 29 Separate the transaxle from the engine and carefully lower the transaxle

## OVERHAUL

### Preparation

When servicing the unit, it is recommended that as each part is disassembled, it be cleaned in solvent and dried with compressed air. Disassembly and reassembly of a unit and its parts must be done on a clean work bench. Also, before installing bolts into aluminum parts, always dip the threads into clean transaxle oil. Anti–seize compound can also be used to prevent bolts from galling the aluminum and seizing. Always use care when tightening not to strip the threads. Take care with the seals when installing them, especially the smaller O–rings. The slightest damage can cause leaks. Aluminum parts are very susceptible to damage so great care should be exercised when handling them. The internal snaprings should be expanded and the external snaprings compressed if they are to be reused. This will help insure proper seating when installed. Be sure to replace any O–ring, gasket, or seal that is removed.

### Transaxle Disassembly

▶ **See Figures 30, 31, 32, 33, 34 and 35**

1. Remove the transaxle assembly from the vehicle.
2. Shift the transaxle into neutral using a drift in the input shaft hole. Pull or push the shaft into the center detent position.
3. Remove the 2 transaxle plugs using T81P–1177–B or equivalent tools from the transaxle. Drain the fluid.

➡ **Place the transaxle on a bench with the clutch housing facing down to facilitate draining and service.**

4. Remove the reverse idler shaft retaining bolt.
5. Remove the detent plunger retaining screw. Then using a magnet, remove the detent spring and the detent plunger.

➡ **Label all parts, as they appear similar to the input shaft plunger and spring contained in the clutch case.**

6. Remove the shift interlock sleeve retaining pin and fill plug.

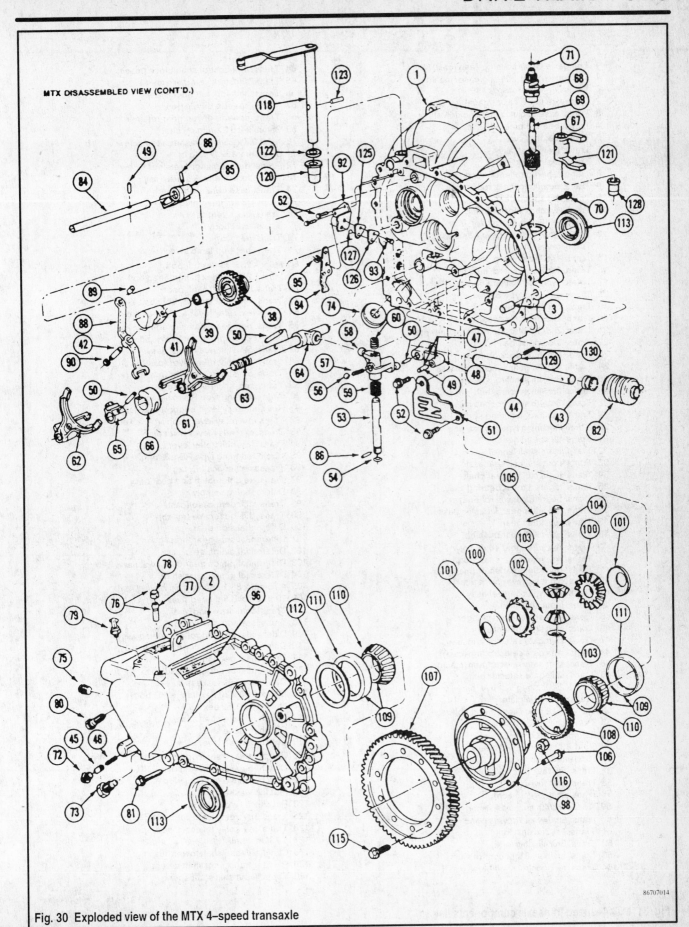

MTX DISASSEMBLED VIEW (CONT'D.)

Fig. 30 Exploded view of the MTX 4–speed transaxle

86707014

| | |
|---|---|
| 1 Transaxle clutch housing case (cast) | 64 Trans. fork control shaft block (mach) |
| 1 Transaxle clutch housing case (mach) | 65 Trans. shift fork selector arm |
| 2 Transaxle trans. case (cast) | 66 Trans. shift fork interlock sleeve |
| 2 Transaxle trans. case (mach) | 67 Trans. speedo driven gear |
| 3 Trans. case to clutch housing dowel | 68 Trans. speedo driven gear retainer |
| 4 Trans. bearing preload shim | 69 25mm x 2.6 'O' ring oil seal |
| 5 Trans. bearing cup | 70 M4 x 0.7 x 25 hex washer head screw |
| 6 Trans. main shaft assy. | 71 5.16mm x 1.6 'O' ring oil |
| 7 Trans. main shaft | 72 Trans. detent plunger retainer screw |
| 8 Trans. tapered roller bearing assy. | 73 Trans. fork interlock sleeve ret. pin |
| 9 Trans. bearing cone & roller assy. | 74 Trans. case ceramic magnet |
| 10 Trans. 1st speed gear | 75 Jis pt 1/2 sq. head plug |
| 11 Trans. synchro. blocking ring | 76 Trans. case vent assy. |
| 12 Trans. 1st/2nd synchronizer assy. | 77 Trans. vent body |
| 13 Trans. 1st/2nd sync. gear & hub assy. | 78 Trans. vent cap |
| 14 Trans. rev. sliding gear | 79 Trans. back-up lamp switch assy. |
| 15 Trans. 1st/2nd synchro. hub | 80 M8 x 1.25 x 33 hex hd. bolt |
| 16 Trans. 1st/2nd synchro. hub insert | 81 M8 x 1.25 x 40 hex flange head bolt |
| 17 Trans. synchro retaining spring | 82 Trans. input shift shaft boot |
| 18 35mm retaining type SB ext. ring | 83 Trans. rev. shift fork control shaft assy. |
| 19 Trans. 2nd speed gear | 84 Trans rev. relay lever actuating shaft |
| 20 Trans. 2nd/3rd thrust washer | 85 Trans. rev. gear actuating arm |
| 21 Trans. 2nd/3rd thrust washer retainer ring | 86 5mm x 20.0 spring slot heavy pin |
| 22 Trans. 3rd speed gear | 87 Trans. 5th shift relay lever assy. |
| 23 Trans. synchro. blocking ring | 88 Trans. 5th shift relay lever (cast) |
| 24 Trans. 3rd/4th gear synchro. assy. | 88 Trans. 5th shift relay lever (mach) |
| 26 Trans. 3rd/4th synchro. sleeve | 89 Trans. rev. shift relay lever pin |
| 27 Trans. 3rd/4th synchro. hub | 90 8mm retaining type RB ext. ring |
| 28 Trans. 3rd/4th synchro. hub insert | 91 Rev shift relay lever support bracket assy. |
| 29 Trans. synchro. retaining spring | 92 Trans rev. relay lever support bracket |
| 30 32mm Retaining type SB ext. ring | 93 Trans. rev. relay lever pivot pin |
| 31 Trans 4th speed gear | 94 Trans. rev. shift relay lever |
| 32 Trans. main shaft funnel | 95 10mm retaining type RB ext. ring |
| 33 Trans input shaft oil seal assy. | 96 Transaxle service I.D. tag |
| 34 Trans. input cluster gear shaft | 97 Transaxe differential and gear assy. |
| 35 Trans. tapered roller bearing assy. | 98 Differential assembly |
| 36 Trans. bearing cone & roller assy. | 99 Trans. diff. gear case (cast) |
| 37 Trans. rev. idler gear & bushing assy. | 99 Trans. diff. gear case (mach) |
| 38 Trans. rev. idler gear | 100 Differential side gear |
| 39 Trans. rev. idler gear bushing | 101 Differential side gear thrust gear |
| 40 Trans. rev. idler gear shaft assy. | 102 Differential pinion gear |
| 41 Trans. rev. idler gear shaft (forging) | 103 Differential pinion gear thrust washer |
| 41 Trans. rev. idler gear shaft (mach) | 104 Differential pinion gear shaft |
| 42 Trans. 5th relay lever pivot pin | 105 4.75mm x 38.1 spring pin |
| 43 Trans. shift shaft oil seal assy. | 106 10 x 32 solid flat head rivet |
| 44 Trans. input shift shaft | 107 Trans. final drive ring gear |
| 45 Trans. shift shaft detent plunger | 108 Trans. speedo drive gear |
| 46 Trans. shift shaft detent spring | 109 Differential tapered roller bearing assy. |
| 47 Trans. shift gate selector arm assy. | 110 Differential bearing cone & roller assy. |
| 48 Trans. shift gate selector arm (cast) | 111 Differential bearing cut |
| 48 Trans. shift gate selector arm (mach) | 112 Differential bearing preload shim |
| 49 Trans. shift gate selector pin | 113 Differential oil seal assy. |
| 50 5mm x 25.0 spring slot hvy. pin | 115 M10 x 1.50 x 30 hex flange HD bolt |
| 51 Trans. shift gate plate | 116 Nut M10 x 1.50 hex |
| 52 M6-1.0 x 22 hex. flange head bolt | 117 Clutch release shaft assy. |
| 53 Trans. shift lever shaft | 118 Clutch release shaft |
| 54 9.2mm x 2.6 'O' ring oil seal | 119 Clutch release lever |
| 55 5mm x 30.0 spring slot heavy pin | 120 Clutch release shaft upper bushing |
| 56 10.319mm ball | 121 Clutch release lever (cast) |
| 57 Trans. 5th rev. inhibitor spring | 122 Clutch release (mach) lever |
| 58 Trans. shift lever (cast) | 122 Flat felt washer |
| 58 Trans. shift lever (mach) | 123 Pin clutch release lever |
| 59 Trans. 3rd/4th shift bias spring | 125 Trans. rev. relay lever ret. spring |
| 60 Trans. 5th/rev kickdown spring | 126 Trans. rev. relay lever ret. sec. spring |
| 61 Trans. 1st/2nd shift fork | 127 8.731mm ball |
| 62 Trans. 3rd/4th shift fork | 128 Clutch release shaft lower bushing |
| 63 Trans. main shift fork control shaft | 129 Plunger trans. shift shaft detent |
| 64 Trans. fork control shaft block (cast) | 130 Trans. input shift shaft spring |

**Fig. 31 MTX4–speed transaxle components list**

86707515

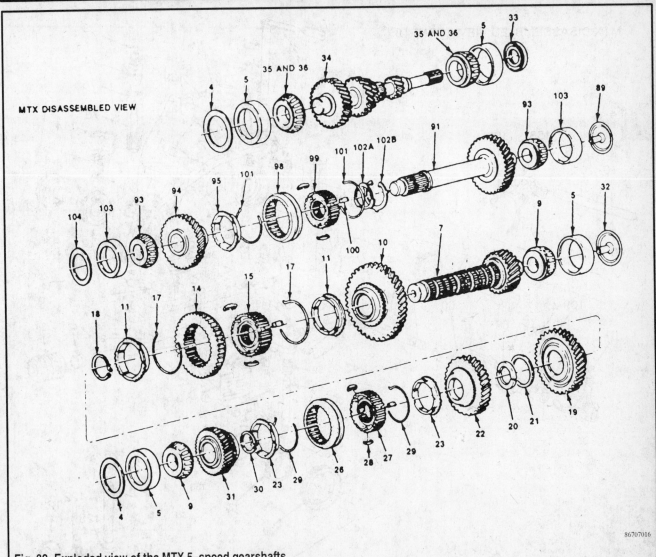

MTX DISASSEMBLED VIEW

Fig. 32  Exploded view of the MTX 5–speed gearshafts

86707016

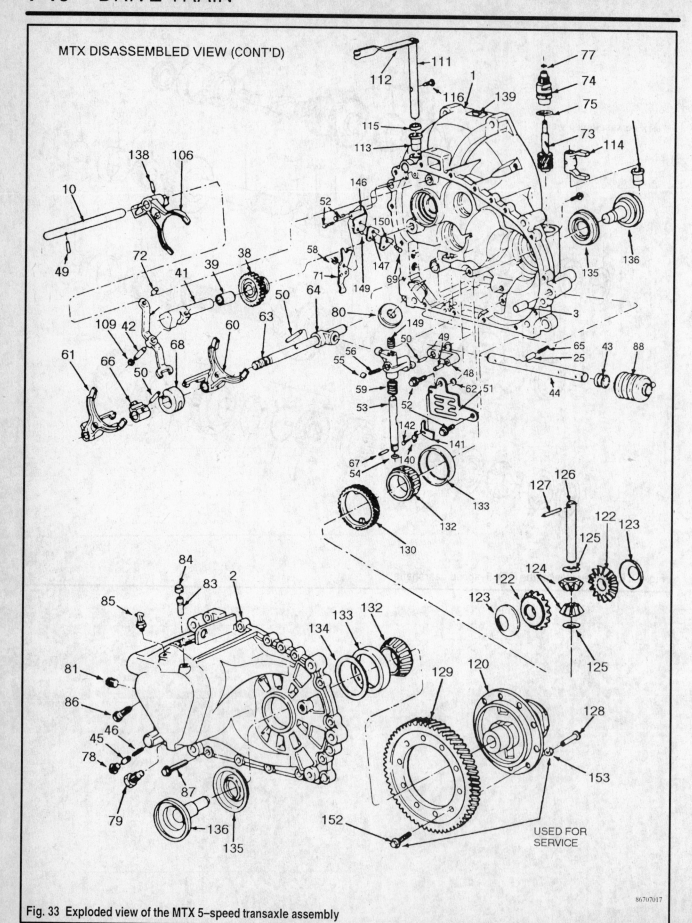

**Fig. 33 Exploded view of the MTX 5-speed transaxle assembly**

1  Transaxle clutch case
2  Transaxle trans. case
3  Trans. case to clutch housing dowel
4  Trans. bearing preload shim
5  Trans. bearing cup
6  Trans. main shaft assy.
7  Trans. main shaft
8  Trans. tapered roller bearing assy.
9  Trans. bearing cone & roller assy.
10  Trans. 1st speed gear
11  Trans. synchro. blocking ring
12  Trans. 1st/2nd synchronizer assy.
13  Trans. 1st/2nd sync. gear & hub assy.
14  Trans. rev. sliding gear
15  Trans. 1st/2nd synchro. hub
16  Trans. 1st/2nd synchro. hub insert
17  Trans. synchro retaining spring
18  35mm retaining type SB ext. ring
19  Trans 2nd speed gear
20  Trans. 2nd/3rd thrust washer
21  Trans. 2nd/3rd thrust washer ref. ring
22  Trans. 3rd speed gear
23  Trans. synchro. blocking ring
24  Trans. 3rd/4th synchronizer assy.
25  Trans. shift shaft detent plunger
26  Trans. 3rd/4th synchro. sleeve
27  Trans. 3rd/4th synchro. hub
28  Trans. 3rd/4th synchro. hub insert
29  Trans. synchro. retaining spring
30  32mm Retaining type SB ext. ring
31  Trans 4th speed gear
32  Trans. main shaft funnel
33  Trans input shaft oil seal assy.
34  Trans. input cluster gear shaft
35  Trans. tapered roller bearing assy.
36  Trans. bearing cone & roller assy.
37  Trans. rev. idler gear & bushing assy.
38  Trans. rev. idler gear
39  Trans. rev. idler gear bushing
40  Trans. rev. idler gear shaft assy.
41  Trans. rev. idler gear shaft
42  Trans. 5th relay lever pivot pin
43  Trans. shift shaft oil seal assy.
44  Trans. input shift shaft
45  Trans. shift shaft detent plunger
46  Trans. shift shaft detent spring
47  Trans. shift gate selector arm assy.
48  Trans. shift gate selector arm
49  Trans. shift gate selector pin
50  5mm x 25.0 spring slot hvy. pin
51  Trans. shift gate plate
52  M6-1.0 x 22 hex. flange head bolt
53  Trans. shift lever shaft
54  9mm x 2.6 'O' ring oil seal
55  10.319mm ball
56  Trans. 5th rev. inhibitor spring
57  Trans. shift lever
58  10mm retaining type RB ext. ring
59  Trans. 3rd/4th shift bias spring
60  Trans. 1st/2nd shift fork

61  Trans. 3rd/4th shift fork
62  Trans. plate & spring assy.
63  Trans. main shift fork control shaft
64  Trans. fork control shaft block
65  Trans. input shift shaft spring
66  Trans. input shift shaft spring
67  5mm x 30.0 spring pin
68  Trans. shift fork interlock sleeve
69  Trans. rev. relay lever pivot pin
71  Trans. rev. shift relay lever
72  Trans. rev. shift relay lever pin
73  Trans. speedo driven gear
74  Trans. speedo driven gear retainer
75  25mm x 2.6 'O' ring oil seal
76  M4 - 0.7 x 25 hex. washer head screw
77  5.16mm x 1.6 'O' ring oil seal
78  Trans. detent plunger ret. screw
79  Trans. fork interlock sleeve ret. pin
80  Trans. case ceramic magnet
81  JIS PT 1/2 sq. hd.
82  Trans. case vent assy.
83  Trans. vent body
84  Trans. vent cap
85  Trans. back-up lamp switch assy.
86  M8-1.25 x 33 hex. head bolt
87  M8-1.25 x 40 hex. flange head bolt
88  Trans. input shift shaft boot
89  Trans. 5th gear shaft funnel
90  Trans. 5th gear shaft assembly
91  Trans. 5th gear drive shaft
92  Trans. tapered roller bearing assy.
93  Trans. bearing cone & roller assy.
94  Trans. 5th speed gear
95  Trans. synchro. blocking ring
96  Trans. 5th synchronizer assy.
98  Trans. 5th synchro. sleeve
99  Trans. 5th synchro. hub
100  Trans. 5th synchro. hub insert
101  Trans. 5th synchro. ret. spring
102A  Trans. 5th synchro. insert retaining spacer
102B  Trans. 5th synchro. insert retainer
103  Trans. bearing cup
104  Trans. bearing preload shim
105  Trans. 5th shift fork control shaft
106  Trans. 5th shift fork
107  Trans. 5th shift relay lever assy.
108  Trans. 5th shift relay lever
109  8mm retaining type RB ext. ring
110  Clutch release shaft assy.
111  Clutch release shaft
112  Clutch release lever
113  Clutch release shaft upper bushing
114  Clutch release lever
115  Flat 17.7 dia. (felt) washer
116  Clutch release lever pin
117  Transaxle differential and gear assy.
118  Differential assy.
120  Diff. gear case
122  Diff. side gear
123  Diff. side gear thrust washer

86707018

**Fig. 34  MTX 5–speed transaxle component list**

INTERNAL SHIFT LINKAGE

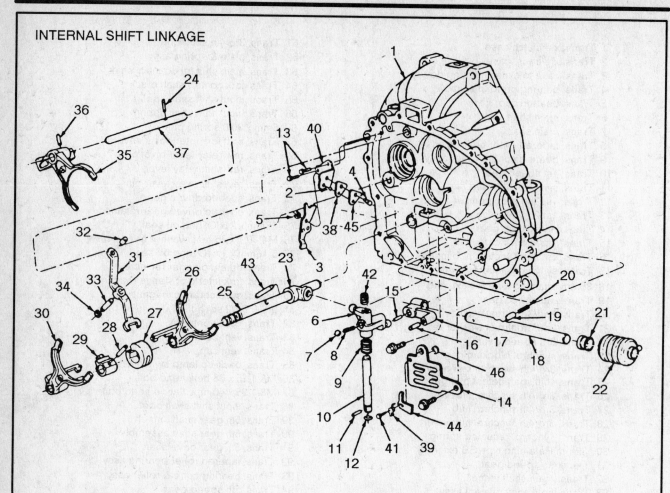

| | |
|---|---|
| 1 Clutch housing case | 24 Shift gate selector pin |
| 2 Ball | 25 Main shift fork control shaft |
| 3 Reverse relay lever | 26 1st/2nd fork |
| 4 Reverse relay lever pivot pin | 27 Fork interlock sleeve |
| 5 External retaining ring | 28 Spring pin |
| 6 Shift lever | 29 Fork selector arm |
| 7 10.319mm ball | 30 3rd/4th fork |
| 8 5th/reverse inhibitor spring | 31 5th shift relay lever |
| 9 3rd/4th shift bias spring | 32 Reverse shift relay lever pin |
| 10 Shift lever shaft | 33 5th relay lever pivot pin |
| 11 Shift lever pin | 34 External retaining ring |
| 12 Shift lever shaft seal | 35 5th fork |
| 13 Shift gate attaching bolts | 36 5th retaining spring pin |
| 14 Shift gate plate | 37 5th fork control shaft |
| 15 Selector arm roll pin | 38 Trans reverse shift relay lever spring |
| 16 Shift gate selector pin | 39 Shift gate pawl spring |
| 17 Shift gate selector arm | 40 Reverse shift relay lever support bracket |
| 18 Input shift shaft | 41 Reverse lockout pawl pivot pin |
| 19 Shift shaft detent plunger | 42 5th/reverse kickdown spring |
| 20 Shift shaft detent spring | 43 Reverse relay lever actuating pin |
| 21 Shift shaft oil seal assembly | 44 Shift gate plate pawl |
| 22 Shift shaft boot | 45 Trans reverse shift relay lever ret., sec. spring |
| 23 Trans input fork control shaft block | 46 C-clip |

**Fig. 35 MTX 5–speed transaxle internal linkage**

86707019

7. Remove the clutch housing–to–transaxle case attaching bolts.

8. Tap the transaxle case with a plastic tipped hammer to break the seal between the case halves. Separate the halves.

➡ **Do not insert pry bars between case halves. Be careful not to drop out the tapered roller bearing cups or shims from the transaxle case housing.**

9. Remove the case magnet.

10. Using a small tool, remove the C–clip retaining ring from the 5th relay lever pivot pin. Remove the 5th gear shift relay lever.

11. Lift the reverse idler shaft and reverse idler gear from the case.

12. Using a punch, drive the spring pin from the shift lever shaft.

13. Using a suitable tool, gently pry on the shift lever shaft so that the hole in the shaft is exposed. Be careful not to damage mainshaft gear teeth or pedestal when prying with tool.

➡ **On vehicles equipped with the 2.0L engine, remove the 2 screws holding the shift lever cover to the shift lever and remove the inhibitor ball and spring**

14. Hold a clean rag over the hole in the lever to prevent the ball and the 5th/reverse inhibitor spring from falling out and remove the shift lever shaft.

15. Remove the inhibitor ball and spring from the hole in the shift lever using a pencil magnet or equivalent. Remove the shift lever, 5th/reverse kickdown spring, and 3–4 bias spring.

16. Remove the mainshaft assembly, input cluster shaft assembly and the main shift control shaft assembly as a complete unit. Be careful not to drop bearings or gears.

17. On 4–speed transaxles, rotate the shaft and remove the reverse actuator arm and shaft assembly from its bore in the case.

18. On 5–speed transaxles, remove the 5th gear shaft assembly and the 5th gear fork assembly from their bores in the case.

19. Lift the differential and final drive gear assembly from the clutch housing case.

20. Remove the 2 bolts retaining the shift relay lever support bracket assembly.

### Mainshaft

#### DISASSEMBLY

1. Remove the slip fit roller bearing on the 4th speed gear end of the shaft. Mark or tag the bearing for proper installation.

2. Remove the 4th speed gear and synchronizer blocker ring.

3. Remove the 3rd/4th synchronizer retaining ring. Slide the 3rd/4th gear synchronizer assembly, blocker ring and 3rd speed gear from the shaft.

4. Remove the 2nd/3rd thrust washer retaining ring and the 2 piece thrust washer.

5. Remove the 2nd speed gear and its blocker ring.

6. Remove the 1st/2nd synchronizer retaining ring. Slide the 1st/2nd synchronizer assembly, blocker ring and 1st speed gear off the shaft.

7. Remove the tapered roller bearing from the pinion end of the mainshaft using a socket or extension and pinion bearing cone remover tool D79L–4621–A or equivalent and an arbor press. Mark or tag bearing.

➡ **Bearings do not have to be removed to disassemble the mainshaft.**

#### INSPECTION

8. Inspect the tapered roller bearing for wear or damage.

9. Check the teeth, splines and journals of the mainshaft for damage.

10. Check all gears for chipped, broken or worn teeth.

11. Check synchronizer sleeves for free movement on their hubs.

12. Inspect the synchronizer blocking rings for wear marks.

#### ASSEMBLY

➡ **Lightly oil the gear bores and other parts with the specified fluid before installation.**

13. Install the bearing on the pinion end of the shaft using a $1^{1}/_{16}$ in. (27mm) socket, pinion bearing cone remover tool D79L–4621–A or equivalent and an arbor press.

14. Slide the 1st speed gear and blocker ring onto the mainshaft. Slide the 1st/2nd synchronizer assembly into place, making sure the shift fork groove on the reverse sliding gear faces the 1st speed gear.

15. When installing the synchronizer, align the 3 grooves in the 1st gear blocker ring with the synchronizer inserts. This allows the synchronizer assembly to seat properly in the blocker ring. Install the synchronizer retaining ring.

16. Install the 2nd speed blocker ring and the 2nd speed gear. Align the 3 grooves in the 2nd gear blocker ring with the synchronizer inserts.

17. Install the thrust washer halves and retaining ring.

18. Slide the 3rd speed gear onto the shaft followed by the 3rd gear synchronizer blocker ring and the 3rd/4th gear synchronizer assembly. Align the 3 grooves in the 3rd gear blocker ring with the synchronizer inserts. Install the synchronizer retaining ring.

19. Install the 4th gear blocker ring and the 4th speed gear. Align the 3 grooves in the 4th gear blocker ring with the synchronizer inserts.

20. Install the slip fit roller bearing on the 4th gear end of the shaft.

21. Make sure bearings are seated against the shoulder of the mainshaft. Make sure bearings are placed on the proper end. Rotate each gear on the shaft to check for binding or roughness. Make sure that the synchronizer sleeves are in the neutral position.

### Input Cluster Shaft Bearing

#### DISASSEMBLY

1. Remove the bearing cone and roller assemblies using a pinion bearing cone remover/installer D79L–4621–A or equivalent, and an arbor press.

2. Mark or tag bearings for proper installation.

3. Thoroughly clean the bearings and inspect their condition.

#### INSPECTION

4. Inspect the tapered roller bearing for wear or damage.

5. Check the teeth, splines and journals of the input shaft for damage.

6. Check all gears for chipped, broken or worn teeth.

#### ASSEMBLY

7. Lightly oil the bearings with the specified transaxle fluid.

8. Using pinion bearing cone remover/installer D79L–4621–A or equivalent and an arbor press, install the bearing on the shaft.

9. Make sure the bearings are pressed on the proper end as marked during the disassembly.

### Synchronizer

#### DISASSEMBLY

1. Note position of the index marks.
2. Remove the synchronizer springs with a small tool. Do not compress the springs more than is necessary.
3. Remove the 3 hub inserts.
4. Slide the hub and sleeve apart.

#### INSPECTION

5. Check the synchronizer sleeves for free movement on their hubs.
6. Check the insert springs.
7. Inspect the synchronizer blocking rings for wear marks.

#### ASSEMBLY

8. Slide the sleeve over the hub. The shorter end of hub shoulder must face the alignment mark on the sleeve.
9. Place the 3 inserts into their slots. Place the tab on the synchronizer spring into the groove of one of the inserts and snap the spring into place.
10. Place the tab of the other spring into the same insert (on the other side of the synchronizer assembly) and rotate the spring in the opposite direction and snap into place.
11. When assembling synchronizers, notice that the sleeve and the hub have an extremely close fit and must be held square to prevent jamming. Do not force the sleeve onto the hub.

### 5TH Gear Shaft Assembly

#### DISASSEMBLY

1. Remove the slip fit bearing from the 5th gear end of the shaft and label it for correct installation.
2. Remove the 5th gear and blocking ring.
3. Remove the 5th gear synchronizer assembly.
4. Remove the press fit bearing from the pinion end of the shaft, using a bearing remover/installer tool D79L–4621–A or equivalent.

#### INSPECTION

5. Inspect the tapered roller bearing for wear or damage.
6. Check all gears for chipped, broken or worn teeth.
7. Check synchronizer sleeves for free movement on their hubs.
8. Inspect the synchronizer blocking rings for wear marks.

#### ASSEMBLY

➡ **Lightly oil the gear bores and other parts with the specified fluid before installation.**

9. Press the bearing onto the pinion gear end of the 5th gear shaft.
10. Install the 5th synchronizer assembly with the plastic insert retainer facing the pinion gear.
11. Install the 5th gear and blocking ring.
12. Install the slip fit bearing on the 5th gear end of the shaft.

### Clutch Housing

#### DISASSEMBLY

1. Remove the 2 control selector plate attaching bolts and remove the plate from the case.
2. With the input shaft in the center detent position, use a drift and drive the spring pin through the selector plate arm assembly and through the input shaft into the recess in the clutch housing case.
3. Remove the shift shaft boot. Using a drift, rotate the input shaft 90 degrees, depressing the detent plunger from the shaft detent notches inside the housing and pull the input shaft out. Remove the input shift selector plate arm assembly and the spring pin.
4. Using a pencil magnet or equivalent, remove the input shaft detent plunger and spring.
5. Using sector shaft seal tool T77F–7288–A or equivalent, remove the transaxle input shaft oil seal assembly.

#### INSPECTION

6. Inspect the clutch housing case for cracks, wear or damaged bearing bores.
7. Inspect for damaged threads in housing.
8. Inspect the clutch housing case mating surfaces for small nicks or burrs that could cause misalignment of the 2 halves.

#### ASSEMBLY

➡ **Lightly oil all parts and bores with the specified fluid.**

9. Lubricate the seal lip of a new shift shaft oil seal. Using sector seal tool T77F–7288–A or equivalent, install a new input shaft oil seal assembly.
10. Install the input shaft detent spring and plunger in the clutch housing case.
11. Using a small drift, force the spring and plunger down into its bore while sliding the input shaft into its bore and over the plunger. Be careful not to cut the shift shaft oil seal when inserting the shaft.
12. Install the selector plate arm in its working position and slide the shaft through the selector plate arm. Align the hole in the selector plate arm with the hole in the shaft and install the spring pin. Install the input shift shaft boot.

➡ **Make sure the notches in the shift shaft face the detent plunger.**

13. Install the control selector plate. The pin in the selector arm must ride in the cutout of the gate in the selector plate. Move the input shaft through the selector plate positions to make sure everything works properly.

### Main Shift Control Shaft

#### DISASSEMBLY

1. Rotate the 3rd/4th shift fork on the shaft until the notch in the fork is located over the interlock sleeve.
2. Rotate the 1st/2nd shift fork on the shaft until the notch in the fork is located over the selector arm finger. With the forks in position, slide the 3rd/4th fork and interlock sleeve off the shaft.
3. Remove the selector arm spring pin.
4. Remove the selector arm and the 1st/2nd shift fork from the shaft.

5. Remove the fork control spring pin.

6. Remove the fork control block from the shift control shaft.

## INSPECTION

Check all components for wear or damage. Check the shift forks for proper alignment on the selector arm.

## ASSEMBLY

➡ **Lightly oil all parts with the specified fluid.**

7. Slide the fork control block onto the shift control shaft. Align the hole in the block with the hole in the shaft and install the fork control block spring pin.

➡ **With pin installed in control block, the offset must point toward the end of the shaft. Also, check the position of the flat on the shaft when installing the control block.**

8. Install the 1st/2nd shift fork and the selector arm on the shaft. The 1st/2nd shift fork is thinner than the 3rd/4th shift fork.

9. Align the hole in the selector arm with the hole in the shaft and install the spring pin.

10. Position the slot in the 1st/2nd fork over the fork selector arm finger.

11. Position the slot in the 3rd/4th fork over the interlock sleeve.

12. Slide the 3rd/4th fork and interlock sleeve onto the main shift control shaft.

13. Align the slot in the interlock sleeve with the splines on the fork selector arm and slide the sleeve and 3rd/4th fork into position. When assembled, the forks should be aligned.

### 5th Gear Shift Control

## DISASSEMBLY

1. Remove the spring pin.

2. Slide the fork from the shaft.

## ASSEMBLY

3. Position the shaft with the hole on the left. Install the 5th gear shift fork so that the protruding arm is positioned toward the long end of the shaft.

4. Install the spring pin.

### Differential

## DISASSEMBLY

1. Remove the left hand differential roller bearing using a suitable tool.

2. Remove the right hand differential bearing cup from the case and install over the right hand differential bearing.

3. With the bearing cup in position, remove the bearing from the speedometer side of the differential using a suitable tool. Failure to use the bearing cup will result in damage to the bearing.

4. Remove the speedometer drive gear from the case.

5. Remove the differential side gears by rotating the gears toward the case window.

6. Remove the pinion shaft retaining pin.

7. Remove the pinion shaft, gears and thrust washer.

8. If the final drive gear is to be replaced, drill out the rivets. To prevent distortion of the case, drill the preformed side of rivet only.

## INSPECTION

Examine the pinion and side gears for scoring, excessive wear, nicks and chips. Worn, scored and damage gears cannot be serviced and must be replaced.

## ASSEMBLY

9. Lubricate all components with the specified fluid before installation.

10. Install the pinion shaft, gears and thrust washer.

11. Install the pinion shaft retaining pin.

12. Install the differential side gears.

13. Install the speedometer drive gear. Install the drive gear with the bevel on the inside diameter facing the differential case.

14. Install the left and right differential roller bearings using a suitable tool.

### Setting Differential Bearing Preload

The differential preload is set at the factory and need not be checked or adjusted unless one of the following components are replaced.

- Transaxle case
- Differential case
- Differential bearings
- Clutch housing

1. Remove the differential seal from the transaxle case.

2. Remove the differential bearing cup from the transaxle case using a suitable tool.

3. Remove the preload shim which is located under the bearing cup.

4. If removed, install the differential in the clutch housing.

5. Install the special tool height gauge spacers on the clutch housing dowels.

6. Position the bearing cup removed from the transaxle case on the differential bearing.

7. Install the differential shim selection special tool over the bearing cup.

8. Position the transaxle case on the height spacer tool and install the 4 bolts supplied with the tool.

9. Tighten the bolts to 17–21 ft. lbs. (23–28 Nm).

10. Rotate the differential several times to ensure seating of the differential bearing.

11. Position the special tool gauge bar across the shim selection tool.

12. Using a feeler gauge, measure the gap between the gauge bar and the selector tool gauge surface.

➡ **This measurement can also be made using a depth micrometer.**

13. Obtain measurements from 3 different positions and take the average of the readings.

14. Check the shim for the correct thickness, then install the shim in the transaxle case.

15. Apply a light film of the specified fluid to the bearing bores in the transaxle case and the clutch housing.

16. Install the bearing cup in the transaxle case using a suitable tool.

17. Check that the cup is fully seated against the shim in the transaxle case and against the shoulder in the clutch housing.

18. Install the differential seal.

**Transaxle Assembly**

➡ Prior to installation, thoroughly clean all parts and inspect their condition. Lightly oil the bores with the specified fluid.

1. Install the shift relay lever support bracket to the case with 2 bolts. Tighten the bolts to 6–9 ft. lbs. (8–12 Nm).

2. Place the differential and the final drive gear assembly into the clutch housing case and align the differential gears.

3. If equipped, install the 5th gear shaft assembly and the fork shaft assembly in the case. Be careful not to damage the 5th gear shaft oil funnel.

4. Position the main control shaft assembly so that the shift forks engage in their respective slots in the synchronizer sleeves on the mainshaft assembly.

5. Bring the mainshaft assembly into mesh with the input cluster shaft assembly. Holding the 3 shafts (input cluster, mainshaft and main shift fork control shaft) in their respective working positions, lower them into their bores in the clutch housing case as a unit. Be careful not to damage the input shaft oil seal or mainshaft oil funnel.

➡ While performing this operation, care should be taken to avoid any movement of the 3rd/4th synchronizer sleeve, which may result in extra travel of the synchronizer sleeve to hub allowing the inserts to pop out of position.

6. Position the shift lever, 3–4 bias spring and 5th/reverse kickdown spring in their working positions (with 1 shift lever ball located in the socket of the input shift gate selector plate arm assembly and the other in the socket of the main shift control shaft block). Install the spring and ball in the 5th/reverse inhibitor shift lever hole.

7. Slide the shift lever shaft (notch down) through the 3rd/4th bias spring and the shift lever. Then, using a small drift, depress the inhibitor ball and spring. Tap the shift shaft through the shift lever, the 5th/reverse gear kickdown spring and then tap into its bore in the clutch housing.

8. Align the shift shaft bore with the case bore and tap the spring pin in, slightly below the case mating surface.

9. Check that the selector pin is in the neutral gate of the control selector plate and the finger of the fork selector arm is partially engaged with the 1st/2nd fork and partially engaged with the 3rd/4th fork.

10. Position reverse idler gear to clutch housing while aligning reverse shift relay lever to the slot in the gear. Slide the reverse idler shaft through the gear and into its bore. Place the reverse idler gear groove in engagement with the reverse relay lever.

11. Install the magnet in its pocket in the clutch housing case.

12. Install the 5th gear relay lever onto the reverse idler shaft, aligning it with the fork interlock sleeve and reverse gear actuating arm slot and install the retaining ring C-clip.

13. Check that the gasket surfaces of the transaxle case and clutch housing are perfectly clean and free of burrs or nicks. Apply a 1/16 in. (1.5mm) wide bead of gasket eliminator E1FZ–19562–A or equivalent to the clutch housing.

14. Install the detent spring and plunger in their bore in the case. Carefully lower the transaxle case over the clutch housing, then using a punch, depress the spring and plunger. Move the transaxle case until the shift control shaft, mainshaft, input cluster shaft and reverse or 5th gear shaft align with their respective bores in the transaxle case.

15. Gently slide the transaxle case over the dowels and flush onto the clutch housing case. Make sure that the case does not bind on the magnet.

16. Apply pipe sealant with Teflon® D8AZ–19554–A or equivalent to the threads of the interlock sleeve retaining pin, in a clockwise direction. Use a drift or equivalent to align the slot in the interlock sleeve with the hole in the transaxle case and install the retaining pin. Tighten to 12–15 ft. lbs. (16–20 Nm).

➡ If the hole in the case does not align with the slot in the interlock sleeve, remove the case half and check for proper installation of the interlock sleeve.

17. Install the transaxle case to clutch housing bolts. Tighten to 13–17 ft. lbs. (18–23 Nm).

18. Use a drift to align the bore in the reverse idler shaft with the retaining screw hole in the transaxle case.

19. Install the reverse idler shaft retaining bolt. Tighten to 16–20 ft. lbs. (22–27 Nm).

20. Apply pipe sealant with Teflon® D8AZ–19554–A or equivalent to the threads of the backup lamp switch in a clockwise direction and install. Tighten the switch to 12–15 ft. lbs. (16–23 Nm).

21. Apply pipe sealant with Teflon® D8AZ–19554–A or equivalent to the treads of the detent plunger retaining screw, in a clockwise direction. If applicable, install detent cartridge spring and plunger. Coat threads of cartridge with pipe sealant D8AZ–19554–A or equivalent. Install the retaining screw and tighten to 6–8 ft. lbs. (8–11 Nm).

22. Tap the differential seal into the transaxle case with a suitable tool.

23. Place the transaxle upright and position a drift through the hole in the input shift shaft. Shift the transaxle into and out of all gears to verify proper installation.

➡ The transaxle will not shift directly into reverse from 5th gear.

24. Install the transaxle fill plugs after the transaxle has been installed in the vehicle and fluid has been added.

# CLUTCH

▶ See Figures 36 and 37

## ✷✷CAUTION

**The clutch driven disc contains asbestos, which has been determined to be a cancer causing agent. Never clean clutch surfaces with compressed air! Avoid inhaling any dust from any clutch surface! When cleaning clutch surfaces, use a commercially available brake cleaning fluid.**

The primary function of the clutch system is to couple and uncouple engine power to the transaxle as desire by the driver. The clutch system also allows engine torque to be applied to the transaxle input shaft gradually, due to mechanical slippage. The car can, consequently, be started smoothly from a full stop.

The transaxle changes the ratio between the rotating speeds of the engine and the wheels by the use of gears. The lower gears allow full engine power to be applied to the rear wheels during acceleration at low speeds.

The clutch driven plate is a thin disc, the center of which is splined to the transaxle input shaft. Both sides of the disc are covered with a layer of material which is similar to brake lining and which is capable of allowing slippage without roughness or excessive noise.

The clutch cover is bolted to the engine flywheel and incorporates a diaphragm spring which provides the pressure to engage the clutch. The cover also houses the pressure plate. The driven disc is sandwiched between the pressure plate and the smooth surface of the flywheel when the clutch pedal is released, thus forcing it to turn at the same speed as the engine crankshaft.

The transaxle contains a mainshaft which passes all the way through the transaxle, from the clutch to the final drive gear in the transaxle. This shaft is separated at one point, so that front and rear portions can turn at different speeds.

Power is transmitted by a countershaft in the lower gears and reverse. The gears of the countershaft mesh with gears on the mainshaft, allowing power to be carried from one to the other. All the countershaft gears are integral with that shaft, while several of the mainshaft gears can either rotate independently of the shaft or be locked to it. Shifting from one gear to the next causes one of the gear to be freed from rotating with the shaft, and locks another to it. Gears are locked and unlocked by internal dog clutches which slide between the center of the gear and the shaft. The forward gears usually employ synchronizers: friction members which smoothly bring gear and shaft to the same speed before the toothed dog clutches are engaged.

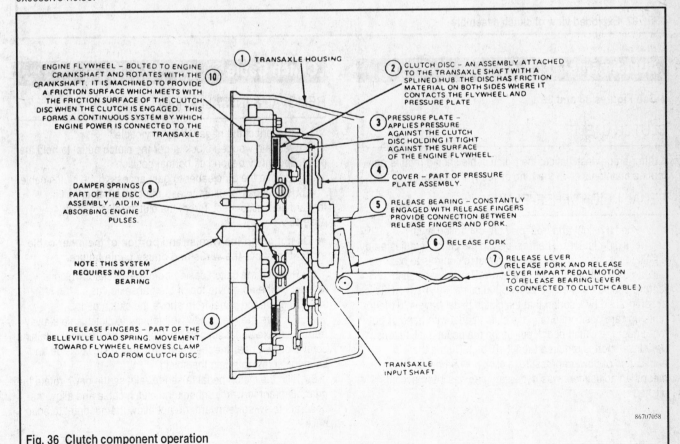

Fig. 36 Clutch component operation

86707058

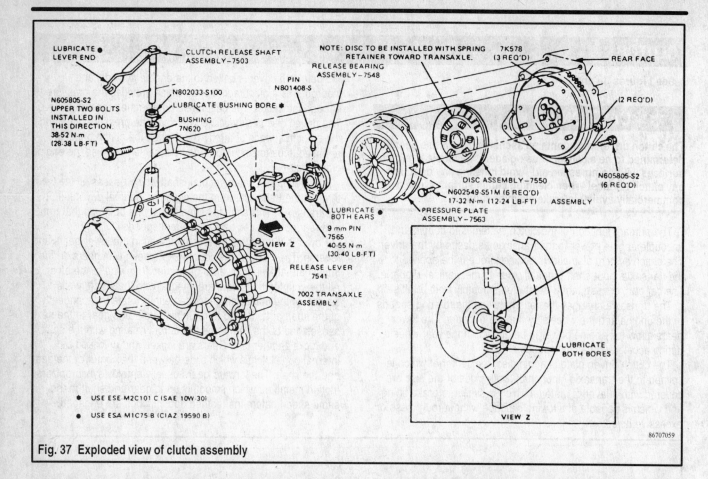

**Fig. 37 Exploded view of clutch assembly**

## Adjustments

♦ **See Figures 38 and 39**

### CLUTCH CABLE

After proper installation, the clutch cable should require only routine maintenance in the form of yearly inspections.

### PEDAL HEIGHT/FREE–PLAY

The pedal height and free–play are controlled by a self–adjusting feature. The free–play in the clutch is adjusted by a built in mechanism that allows the clutch controls to be self–adjusted during normal operation. The self–adjusting feature should be checked every 5000 miles (8051 km). This is accomplished by insuring that the clutch pedal travels to the top of its upward position. Grasp the clutch pedal with hand or put foot under the clutch pedal, pull up on the pedal until it stops. Very little effort is required (about 10 lbs.). During the application of upward pressure, a click may be heard which means an adjustment was necessary and has been accomplished.

## Clutch Cable

### REMOVAL & INSTALLATION

1.  Disconnect the negative battery cable.
2.  Wedge a wooden block under the clutch pedal to hold the pedal up slightly beyond its normal position.
3.  Remove the air cleaner to gain access to the clutch cable.
4.  Using a pair of pliers, grasp the clutch cable, pull it forward and disconnect it from the clutch release shaft assembly.

➡ **Do not grasp the wire strand portion of the inner cable since it may cut the wires and cause cable failure.**

5.  Remove the clutch casing from the insulator which is located on the rib on the top of the transaxle case.
6.  Remove the panel from above the clutch pedal.
7.  Remove the rear screw and move the clutch shield away from the brake pedal support bracket. Loosen the front retaining screw, located near the toe board, rotate the shield aside and snug the screw to retain the shield.
8.  With the clutch pedal raised to release the pawl, rotate the gear quadrant forward, unhook the clutch cable and allow the quadrant to swing rearward; do not allow the quadrant to snap back.

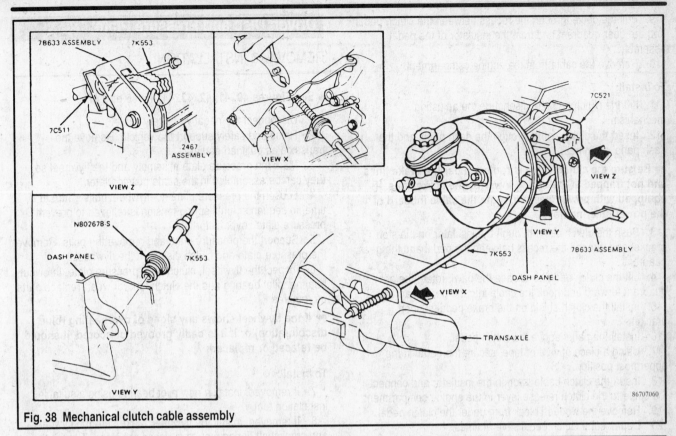

Fig. 38 Mechanical clutch cable assembly

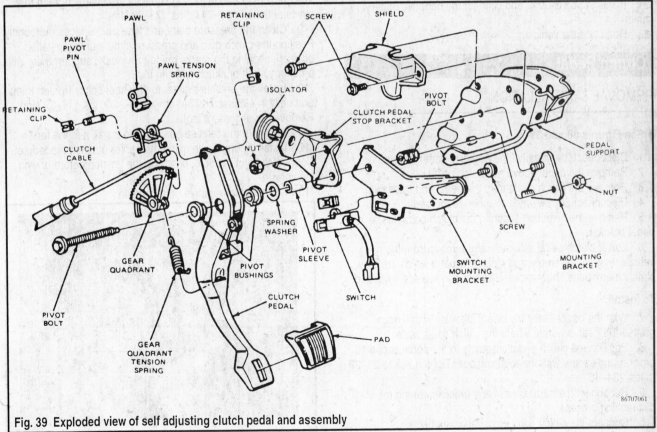

Fig. 39 Exploded view of self adjusting clutch pedal and assembly

9. Pull the cable through the recess between the clutch pedal and the gear quadrant and from the insulator of the pedal assembly.

10. Remove the cable from the engine compartment.

**To install:**

11. Lift the clutch pedal to disengage the adjusting mechanism.

12. Insert the clutch cable through the dash panel and the dash panel grommet.

➡ **Be sure the clutch cable is routed under the brake lines and not trapped at the spring tower by the brake lines. If equipped with power steering, route the cable inboard of the power steering hose.**

13. Push the clutch cable through the insulator on the stop bracket and through the recess between the pedal and the gear quadrant.

14. Lift the clutch pedal to release the pawl, rotate the gear quadrant forward and hook the cable into the gear quadrant.

15. Install the clutch shield on the brake pedal support bracket.

16. Install the panel above the clutch pedal.

17. Using a piece of wire or tape, secure the pedal in the uppermost position.

18. Insert the clutch cable through the insulator and connect the cable to the clutch release lever in the engine compartment.

19. Remove the wooden block from under the clutch pedal.

20. Depress the clutch pedal several times.

21. Install the air cleaner and connect the negative battery cable.

22. Road test the vehicle.

## Clutch Pedal

### REMOVAL & INSTALLATION

▶ **See Figures 38 and 39**

1. Disconnect the negative the negative battery cable.
2. Remove the panel above the clutch pedal.
3. Remove the clutch cable from the pedal and transaxle.
4. Disconnect any switches attached to the pedal.
5. Remove the pivot bolt securing the clutch pedal to the pedal bracket.
6. Lower clutch pedal assembly and remove from the vehicle. Inspect assembly, and clean any parts which are dirty. Notice if any parts show excessive wear and replace if needed.

**To install:**

7. With the pedal assembly clean, lubricate with lithium grease the gear quadrant where the clutch cable rests.

8. Position the clutch pedal assembly to the pedal support bracket and secure with the retaining bolt. Tighten bolt to 26–29 ft. lbs. (34–40 Nm).

9. Reconnect the harnesses of any switches during the dismantling process.

10. Connect the clutch cable to pedal assembly.

11. Install panel below steering column.

12. Connect negative battery terminal.

13. Adjust clutch cable using the earlier procedure.

## Driven Disc and Pressure Plate

### REMOVAL & INSTALLATION

▶ **See Figures 40, 41, 42, 43, 44, 45, 46 and 47**

1. Disconnect the negative battery cable.

2. Raise and safely support the vehicle. Remove the transaxle as outlined earlier.

3. Mark the pressure plate assembly and the flywheel so they can be assembled in the same position later.

4. Loosen the pressure plate–to–flywheel bolts 1 turn at a time, in sequence, until spring tension is relieved to prevent pressure plate cover distortion.

5. Support the pressure plate and remove the bolts. Remove the pressure plate and clutch disc from the flywheel.

6. Inspect the flywheel, clutch disc, pressure plate, throwout bearing, pilot bearing and the clutch fork for wear; replace parts, as required.

➡ **If the flywheel shows any signs of overheating (blue discoloration) or if it is badly grooved or scored, it should be refaced or replaced.**

**To install:**

7. If removed, install a new pilot bearing using a suitable installation tool.

8. If removed, install the flywheel. Make sure the flywheel and crankshaft flange mating surfaces are clean. Tighten the flywheel bolts to 54–64 ft. lbs. (73–86 Nm).

9. Clean the pressure plate and flywheel surfaces thoroughly. Position the clutch disc and pressure plate into the installed position, aligning the marks made previously; support them with a dummy shaft or clutch aligning tool.

10. Install the pressure plate–to–flywheel bolts. Tighten them gradually in a crisscross pattern to 12–24 ft. lbs. (17–32 Nm). Remove the alignment tool.

11. Lubricate the release bearing and install it in the fork.

12. Install the transaxle using the earlier outlined procedure. Connect the clutch cable, checking the tension before driving the vehicle.

13. Connect the negative battery cable.

Fig. 40 Once the retainers are carefully unthreaded, you can remove the pressure plate and clutch disc

Fig. 41 While holding the flywheel in place, remove the retaining bolts

Fig. 42 Remove the flywheel and inspect carefully

Fig. 43 View of the transaxle assembly showing the release mechanism

Fig. 44 Remove the retaining pin securing the bearing

Fig. 45 Remove the bearing

Fig. 46 During installation, use a torque wrench to properly tighten the flywheel retaining bolts

86707528

**Fig. 47 A torque wrench is also necessary when tightening the pressure plate retainers**

## Driveshaft & U–Joints

### REMOVAL & INSTALLATION

**All Wheel Drive (AWD) Vehicles**

➡ **Anytime a U–joint retaining bolt is removed, Loctite® or equivalent, must be used to retain the bolt prior to installation.**

1. Raise the vehicle and safely support on jackstands.
2. To maintain the driveshaft balance, mark the U–joint such that they may be installed in their original position.
3. Remove the front U–joint retaining bolts and straps.
4. Support the driveshaft near the center bearing. Remove the driveshaft center bearing retaining bolts.
5. Slide the driveshaft toward the rear of the vehicle to disengage from the transfer case.
6. Remove there are U–joint bolts and straps retaining the driveshaft from the torque tube yoke flange.
7. Slide the driveshaft toward the front of the vehicle to disengage. Do not allow the splined shafts to contact with excessive force.
8. Remove the center bearing retaining bolts. Remove the driveshaft and retain the bearing cups with tape, if necessary.
9. Inspect the U–joint assemblies for wear and or damage, replace the joint, if necessary

**To install:**

10. Install the driveshaft at the rear torque yoke flange. Ensure that the U–joint is in its original position.
11. Install the U–joint retaining caps and bolts, torquing to 15–17 ft. lbs. (21–23 Nm). Position the front U–joint, installing the caps and bolts, and tightening to 15–17 ft. lbs. (21–23 Nm).
12. Install the center bearing and retaining bolts. tighten bolts to 23–30 ft. lbs. (31–41 Nm). Do not drop the assembled unit, as the impact may cause damage to the U–joint bearing cups.

## Axle Housing

### REMOVAL & INSTALLATION

**All Wheel Drive (AWD) Vehicles**

➡ **Anytime a U–joint retaining bolt is removed, Loctite® or equivalent, must be used to retain the bolt prior to installation.**

1. Disconnect the negative battery cable.
2. Raise and safely support the vehicle on jackstands.
3. Position a hoist or jack under the rear axle housing.
4. Remove the muffler and exhaust assembly from the catalytic converter back to the rear of the vehicle.
5. Remove the rear U–joint retaining bolts and straps securing the driveshaft from the torque tube yoke flange. Remove the driveshaft from the axle yoke and position the driveshaft away from the vehicle, in a clean area.
6. Remove the 4 retaining bolts from the torque tube support bracket. Remove the damper assembly.
7. Disconnect the axle vent hose clip from the body.
8. Remove the axle retaining bolt from the left side differential support bracket.
9. Unfasten the axle retaining bolt from the center differential support bracket.
10. Carefully lower the axle assembly and remove the inboard U–joint retaining bolts and straps from each halfshaft assembly. Remove the halfshaft units and place in a clean area.
11. Remove the rear axle assembly.

**To install:**

12. Position the rear assembly under the vehicle. Slowly raise far enough for the U–joint and halfshaft units to be installed.
13. Position the inboard U–joint to the rear axle assembly. Install the U–joint bolts. Tighten the bolts to 15–17 ft. lbs. (21–23 Nm).
14. Raise the unit into position taking care not to trap or pinch the axle vent hose. Install the bolts securing the differential housing to the left and center support brackets. Tighten the bolts to 70–80 ft. lbs. (95–108 Nm).
15. Attach the vent hose to the body.
16. Position the torque tube, damper and mounting bracket to the crossmember. Install the 4 retaining bolts torquing them to 28–35 ft. lbs. (38–47 Nm). Install the driveshaft with the retaining bolts to the torque tube yoke flange. Tighten hardware to 15–17 ft. lbs. (21–23 Nm).
17. Fasten the exhaust section removed during the removal phase of the procedure.
18. Check and adjust if necessary the rear fluid level.
19. Check to make sure all hardware has been installed and is secure.
20. Lower the vehicle and road test.

## AUTOMATIC TRANSAXLE

♦ **See Figures 48, 49, and 50**

The automatic transaxle (ATX) combines an automatic transmission and differential into a single powertrain component designed for front wheel drive application. The transmission and differential components are housed in a compact, one–piece case.

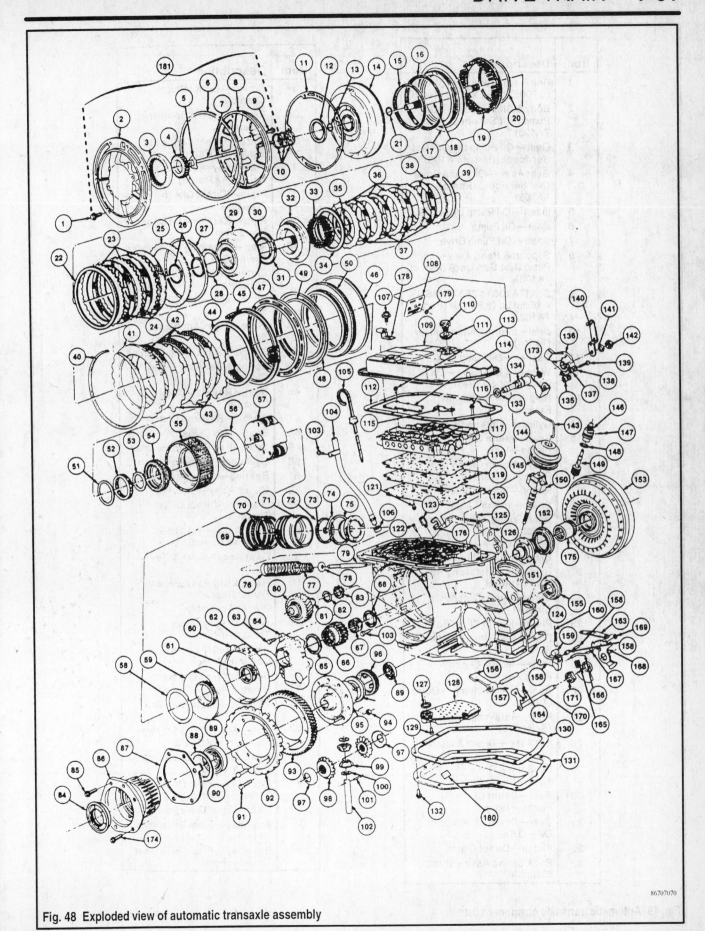

Fig. 48 Exploded view of automatic transaxle assembly

86707070

| Item | Description |
|------|-------------|
| 1 | Bolt & Washer Assy (7A103 to 7005) M6-1 X 40 (7 Req'd) |
| 2 | Body & Sleeve Assy—Oil Pump (Not Serviced) (Part of 7A103) |
| 3 | Gear—Oil Pump Driven (Not Serviced) (Part of 7A103) |
| 4 | Gear Assy—Oil Pump Drive (Not Serviced) (Part of 7A103) |
| 5 | Insert—Oil Pump Drive Gear |
| 6 | Seal—Oil Pump |
| 7 | Shaft—Oil Pump Drive |
| 8 | Support & Bshg Assy—Oil Pump (Not Serviced) (Part of 7A103) |
| 9 | Bolt (7A106 to 7F370)M6-1 x 16mm Lg (5 Req'd) (Part of 7A103) |
| 10 | Seal—Interm Clutch—Inner (Teflon) |
| 11 | Gasket—Oil Pump |
| 12 | Washer & Brg Assy—Oil Pump Support (Selective) |
| 13 | Ring—16.4 Retaining External |
| 14 | Cylinder—Interm Clutch |
| 15 | Seal—Interm Clutch Piston—Inner |
| 16 | Seal—Interm Clutch Piston—Outer |
| 17 | Piston—Interm Clutch |
| 18 | Shaft—Interm Clutch |
| 19 | Ret & Spring Assy—Interm Clutch |
| 20 | Ring-111.76mm Retaining External (7F222 to 7D044) |
| 21 | Ring—17.0 Retaining Rd Wire External |
| 22 | Spring—Rev. Clutch Cushion |
| 23 | Plate—Interm Cl Ext Spline |
| 24 | Plate Assy—Interm Cl Int Spline |
| 25 | Plate—Interm Clutch Pressure |
| 26 | Seal—Interm Clutch—Outer (Teflon) |
| 27 | Ring—Retaining Int (Selective) |
| 28 | Brg Assy—Direct & Interm Clutch |
| 29 | Cyl Shaft & Race Assy—Direct Clutch |
| 30 | Seal—Direct Cl Piston—Inner |
| 31 | Seal—Direct CL Piston Oil—Outer |
| 32 | Piston—Direct Clutch |
| 33 | Ret & Spring Assy—Direct Clutch |

| Item | Description |
|------|-------------|
| 34 | Spring—Direct Clutch Cushion |
| 35 | Ring—59.5mm Retaining, External |
| 36 | Plate—Direct Clutch Ext. Spline (As Req'd) |
| 37 | Plate Assy—Direct Cl Int Spline (As Req'd) |
| 38 | Plate—Direct Clutch Pressure |
| 39 | Ring—Retaining Int Direct (Selective) |
| 40 | Ring—Retaining Int Reverse (Selective) |
| 41 | Plate—Reverse Clutch Pressure |
| 42 | Plate Assy—Rev Cl Int Spline |
| 43 | Plate—Rev Clutch Ext Spline |
| 44 | Spring—Rev Clutch Cushion |
| 45 | Spring & Ret Assy—Rev Clutch |
| 46 | Seal—Reverse Clutch Cylinder |
| 47 | Piston—Reverse Clutch |
| 48 | Seal—Rev Cl Piston—Outer |
| 49 | Seal—Rev Cl Piston—Inner |
| 50 | Cylinder—Reverse Clutch |
| 51 | Bearing—One-Way Clutch |
| 52 | Clutch Assy—One-Way |
| 53 | Washer—Direct Cl Cyl Thrust |
| 54 | Gear Assy—1st-3rd Reverse Speed |
| 55 | Gear Assy—Inter & Rev Cl Rg |
| 56 | Race & Brg Assy—Plant Thrust Rear |
| 57 | Planet Assembly |
| 58 | Washer—Planetary Thrust—Front |
| 59 | Drum & Sun Gear Assy—Low Interm |
| 60 | Band Assy—Low Interm |
| 61 | Bearing Assy—Transfer |
| 62 | Washer—Interm Sun Gr Thrust |
| 63 | Bolt—M8-1.25 x 25.0 Hex Flange Hd (5 Req'd) |
| 64 | Housing—Final Drive Gear (Not Serviced) |
| 65 | Brg Assy—Final Drive Gear Thrust—Rear |
| 66 | Gear—Final Drive Input |
| 67 | Brg Assy—Final Drive Input Gear |
| 68 | Brg Assy—Final Drive Gear Thrust—Front |

**Fig. 49 Automatic transaxle component list**

86707071

| Item | Description |
|------|-------------|
| 69 | Ring—103.5mm Ret Flat Internal |
| 70 | Seal—Low & Interm Band Servo Piston Cover |
| 71 | Cover—Low/Interm Band Servo |
| 72 | Seal—Low/Interm Servo Piston—Small |
| 73 | Ring—15.8mm Retaining External (7D190 to 7D022) |
| 74 | Seal—Low Interm Servo Piston—Large |
| 75 | Piston—Low & Interm Servo |
| 76 | Spring—Low/Interm Servo Piston |
| 77 | Spring—Servo Piston Cushion |
| 78 | Washer—9.7mm x 30 x 2.5 Flat Steel (7F390 to 7D022) |
| 79 | Rod—Low/Interm Servo Piston not Available (Selective) |
| 80 | Gear & Brg Assy—Idler Gear |
| 81 | Shaft—Idler Gear |
| 82 | Seal—22.8 x 1.6 O-Ring |
| 83 | Nut—M25 x 1-12 Point |
| 84 | Seal Assy—Transaxle—Diff |
| 85 | Bolt—M8-1.25 x 30 Hex Flange Hd (5 Req'd) |
| 86 | Retainer—Diff Bearing |
| 87 | Gasket—Diff Bearing Retainer |
| 88 | Shim—Diff Bearing (Selective) |
| 89 | Ball Bearing—Diff (2 Req'd) |
| 90 | Rivet—M10 x 38 Solid Flat Hd (Ref Only—Production) (Not Serviced) |
| 91 | Bolt—M10 x 1.5 x 40 Hex Hd (10 Req'd) Service Only |
| 92 | Gear—Output Shaft Park |
| 93 | Gear—Final Drive Output |
| 94 | Nut—10 x 1.5 Hex Plt—(10 Req'd) Service Only |
| 95 | Diff Housing |
| 96 | Gear—Speedo Drive |
| 97 | Washer—Transaxle Diff Side Gr Thrust |
| 98 | Gear—Transaxle Diff Side |
| 99 | Pinion—Transaxle Diff |
| 100 | Washer—Transaxle Diff Pinion Thrust |
| 101 | Pin—4.75mm x 38.1mm |
| 102 | Shaft—Transaxle Diff Pinion |
| 103 | Bolt—M6-1 x 12 Hex Flange Hd |
| 104 | Tube Assy—Oil Filter |
| 105 | Indicator Assy—Oil Level |
| 106 | Grommet (Seal Filler to Tube to Case) |
| 107 | Bolt—M6-1 x 14mm Lg (10 Req'd) |
| 108 | Identification Tag (Not Serviced) |
| 109 | Cover Assy—Main Control |
| 110 | Vent Assy—Main Control Cover |
| 111 | Grommet—Main Control Cover |
| 112 | Gasket—Main Control Cover |
| 113 | Bolt—M6-1 x 45 Hex Flange Hd (7 Req'd) |
| 114 | Plate—Main Oil Press Reg Exh (Not Serviced) |
| 115 | Plate—Trans (Not Serviced) |
| 116 | Bolt—6-1 x 40 Hex Flange Hd (20 Req'd) |
| 117 | Control Assy—Main |
| 118 | Gasket-Main Control (Bet. 7A092 & 7A008) |
| 119 | Plate-Control Valve Body Sep. (Not Serviced) |
| 120 | Gasket-Main Control (Bet. 7A008 & 7006) |
| 121 | Bolt-M6-1 x 12 Hex Flange Hd. (2 Req'd) |
| 122 | Pin-Timing (2.3L Only) |
| 123 | Connector Assy—Oil Cooler Tube |
| 124 | Screen Assy-Gov. Oil |
| 125 | Pin 3.18mm x 29.65 Dowel Hrdn. |
| 126 | Case and Hsg. Assy |
| 127 | Gasket-Oil Filter |
| 128 | Filter Assy-Oil |
| 129 | Bolt-M6-1 x 14mm Lg. (4 Req'd) |
| 130 | Gasket-Oil Pan |
| 131 | Pan-Oil |
| 132 | Bolt-M8-1.25 x 18 Hex Flange (13 Req'd) |
| 133 | Seal-Manual Control Lever |
| 134 | Lever Assy-Manual Control |
| 135 | Insulator-Gear Shift Arm |
| 136 | Switch Assy Park/Neutral |
| 137 | Washer-# 12 Flat (2 Req'd) |
| 138 | Washer-6.0mm Helical Spg. Lk. (2 Req'd) |
| 139 | Bolt-M6-1 x 40 Hex Flange Hd. (2 Req'd) |
| 140 | Lever Assy-Throttle Valve-Outer |
| 141 | Washer-8mm Lock |
| 142 | Nut-M8 x 1.25 Hex |
| 143 | Clip-Gov. Cover Retaining |
| 144 | Cover-Governor |
| 145 | Seal-77.9mm x 3.40 Rect. Sect. |

86707072

**Fig. 50 Automatic transaxle component list (continued)**

## Fluid Pan and Filter

### REMOVAL & INSTALLATION

◆ See Figures 51 and 52

In normal service it should not be necessary nor is it required to drain and refill the AT fluid. However, under severe operation or dusty conditions the fluid should be changed every 20 months or 20000 miles (32206 km).

1. Raise and support the vehicle safely.
2. Place a suitable drain pan underneath the transaxle oil pan. Loosen the oil pan mounting bolts and allow the fluid to drain until it reaches the level of the pan flange. Remove the attaching bolts, leaving one end attached so that the pan will tip and the rest of the fluid will drain.
3. Remove the oil pan. Thoroughly clean the pan. Remove the old gasket. Make sure that the gasket mounting surfaces are clean.
4. Remove the transaxle filter screen retaining bolt. Remove the screen.

### To install:

5. Install a new filter screen and O–ring.
6. Place a new gasket on the pan and install the pan to the transaxle. Insert and tighten bolts.
7. Lower the vehicle.
8. Fill the transaxle to the correct level.
9. Road test the vehicle.

## Adjustments

### SHIFT LINKAGE

#### 1984–87 Models

1. Place the gear shift selector into D. The shift lever must be in the D position during linkage adjustment.
2. Working at the transaxle, loosen the transaxle lever–to–control cable nut.
3. Move the transaxle lever to the D position, 2nd detent from the most rearward position.
4. Tighten the adjusting nut to 10–15 ft. lbs. (14–20 Nm).
5. Make sure all gears engage correctly and the vehicle will only start in P or D.

#### 1988–94 Models

1. Disconnect the negative battery cable. This will deactivate the shift–lock system.
2. Move the gear selector lever to P.
3. Remove the screw securing the gear selector knob to the gear selector lever. Remove the knob.
4. Remove the shift console as follows:
    f. Remove the rear seat ash tray and position both front seats to the rear–most position.
    g. Remove the 2 front retaining screws from the parking brake console and recline both front seats.
    h. Remove the 2 rear retaining screws from the parking brake console.
    i. With the parking brake engaged, remove the parking brake console.

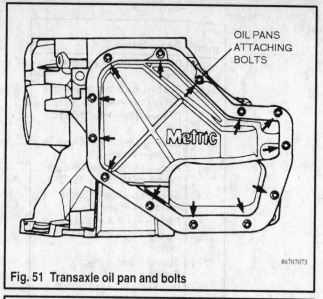

Fig. 51 Transaxle oil pan and bolts

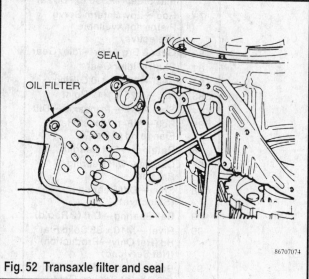

Fig. 52 Transaxle filter and seal

    j. Remove the 2 front retaining screws from the shift console and remove the console.
5. Remove the position indicator mounting screws and disconnect the illumination bulb from the position indicator.
6. Disconnect the shift–lock servo and park range switch electrical connectors.
7. Remove the position indicator.

➡ Make sure the detent spring roller is in the P detent.

8. Loosen the shift control cable bracket mounting bolts.
9. Push the gear selector lever against the P range and hold it.
10. Tighten the shift control cable bracket mounting bolts to 69–95 inch lbs. (8–11 Nm).
11. Lightly press the gear selector pushrod and make sure the guide plate and guide pin clearances are within specifications.
12. Check that the guide plate and guide pin clearances are within the appropriate specifications when the selector lever is shifted to N and OD. If the clearances are not as specified, readjust the shift control cable.
13. Make sure the gear selector operates properly.

14. Connect the illumination bulb to the position indicator.

15. Connect the shift–lock servo and park range switch electrical connectors.

16. Install the position indicator and secure it with the mounting screws.

17. Install the shift console by reversing the removal procedure.

18. Position the gear selector knob onto the gear selector lever and secure the knob with the screw.

19. Connect the negative battery cable.

20. Road test the vehicle.

## THROTTLE LINKAGE

♦ **See Figures 53 and 54**

➥ **The TV linkage adjustment is set at the factory and is critical in establishing automatic transaxle upshift and downshift timing and feel. Any time the engine, transaxle or throttle linkage components are removed, it is recommended that the TV linkage adjustment be reset after the component installation or replacement.**

### 1984–85 Models

The TV control linkage is adjusted at the sliding trunnion block.

1. Adjust the curb idle speed to specification as shown on the under hood decal.

2. After the curb idle speed has been set, shut off the engine. Make sure the choke is completely opened. Check the carburetor throttle lever to make sure it is against the hot en)engine curb idle stop.

3. Set the coupling lever adjustment screw at its approximate midrange. Make sure the TV linkage shaft assembly is fully seated upward into the coupling lever.

## **✳✳CAUTION**

**If adjustment of the linkage is necessary, allow the EGR valve to cool so you won't get burned.**

4. To adjust, loosen the bolt on the sliding block on the TV control rod a minimum of one turn. Clean any dirt or corrosion from the control rod, free–up the trunnion block so that it will slide freely on the control rod.

5. Rotate the transaxle TV control lever up using a finger and light force, to insure that the TV control lever is against its internal stop. With reducing the pressure on the control lever, tighten the bolt on the trunnion block.

6. Check the carburetor throttle lever to be sure it is still against the hot idle stop. If not, repeat the adjustment steps.

### 1986–94 Models

1. Disconnect the negative battery cable.

2. Remove the splash shield from the cable retainer bracket.

3. Loosen the trunnion bolt at the throttle valve rod.

4. Install a plastic clip to bottom the throttle valve rod; be sure the clip does not telescope.

5. Be sure the return spring is connected between the throttle valve rod and the retaining bracket to hold the transaxle throttle valve lever at it's idle position.

6. Make sure the throttle lever is resting on the throttle return control screw.

7. Tighten the throttle valve rod trunnion bolt and remove the plastic clip.

8. Install the splash shield. Connect the negative battery cable and check the vehicle's operation.

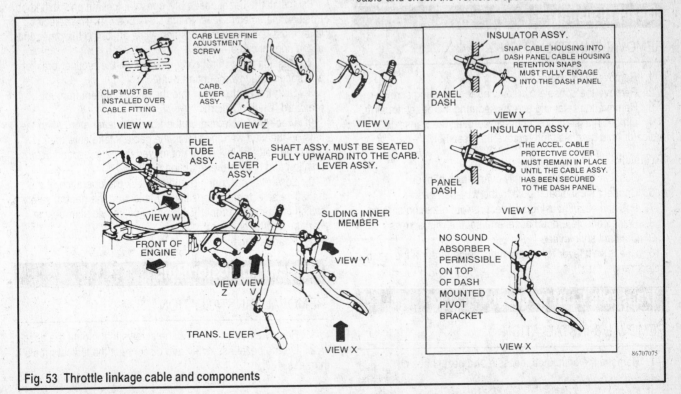

Fig. 53 Throttle linkage cable and components

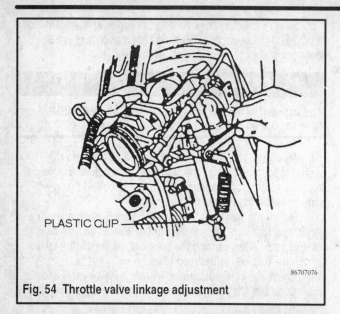

PLASTIC CLIP

86707076

**Fig. 54 Throttle valve linkage adjustment**

## Shift Knob

### REMOVAL & INSTALLATION

1. Hold shift knob and press release button securely.
2. Pull up on shift knob. Be careful the spring loaded release button does not eject from the knob rapidly.

**To install:**

3. Assembly the shift knob, spring and button.
4. Press button in and push on to lever until seated.
5. Run the shifter through the gears to ensure proper functioning.

## Bezel Housing

### REMOVAL & INSTALLATION

1. Remove the shift knob.
2. Remove the console by removing the retaining screws.
3. Remove the retaining screws securing the bezel housing.
4. Lift bezel assembly slightly. Disconnect the transaxle indicator bulb harness, and remove the assembly.

**To install:**

5. Position the bezel assembly over the shift lever.
6. Connect the indicator bulb to the wire harness.
7. Position bezel housing and secure with retaining screws.
8. Place console around bezel and secure with screws.
9. Connect shift lever.
10. Check shift lever for proper functioning through the gear select range.

## Transaxle Control Lever

### REMOVAL & INSTALLATION

1. Remove the shift knob, console and bezel housing.

2. Remove the cable retaining clip from the lever housing assembly. Disconnect the cable.
3. Remove the screw from the interlock cable assembly.
4. Remove the bolts which attach the lever and housing to the floor pan. Remove the assembly.

**To install:**

5. Position the lever and housing to the floor and attach the bolts, tightening to 5–6 ft. lbs. (6–8 Nm).
6. Attach the interlock cable assembly with clip. Secure with screw.
7. Install bezel housing, console and shift lever.
8. Test for proper shift operation.

## Shift Lever Cable

### REMOVAL & INSTALLATION

1. Remove the shift knob, locknut, console, bezel assembly, control cable clip and cable retaining pin.
2. Disengage the rubber grommet from the floor pan by pushing it into the engine compartment. Raise the car and safely support it on jackstands.
3. Remove the retaining nut and control cable assembly from the transaxle lever. Remove the control cable bracket bolts. Pull the cable through the floor.

**To install:**

4. To install the cable, feed the round end through the floor board. Press the rubber grommet into its mounting hole.
5. Position the control cable assembly in the selector lever housing and install the spring clip. Install the bushing and control cable assembly on the selector lever and housing assembly shaft and secure it with the retaining pin.
6. Install the bezel assembly, console, locknut and shift knob. Position the selector lever in the Drive position. The selector lever must be held in this position while attaching the other end of the control cable.
7. Position the control cable bracket on the retainer bracket and secure the tow mounting bolts.
8. Shift the control lever into the second detent from full rearward (Drive position).
9. Place the cable end on the transaxle lever stud. Align the flats on the stud with the slot in the cable. Make sure the transaxle selector lever has not moved from the second detent position and tighten the retaining nut.
10. Lower the car to the ground. Check the operation of the transaxle selector in all positions. Make sure the neutral safety switch is operating properly. (The engine should start only in Park or Neutral position).
11. Road test the vehicle.

## Selector Indicator Bulb

### REMOVAL & INSTALLATION

1. Remove the console and the screws that mount the bezel.
2. Lift the bezel assembly and disconnect the indicator bulb harness.

3. Remove the indicator bulb.

4. Install a new bulb and reverse the removal procedure.

## Neutral Safety Switch

### REMOVAL & INSTALLATION

The mounting location of the neutral safety switch does not provide for adjustment of the switch position when installed. If the engine will not start in P or N or if it will start in R or any of the D ranges, check the control linkage adjustment and/or replace with a known good switch.

1. Set parking brake.

2. Disconnect the battery negative cable.

3. Disconnect the wire connector from the neutral safety switch.

4. Remove the 2 retaining screws from the neutral start switch and remove the switch.

**To install:**

5. Place the switch on the manual shift shaft and loosely install the retaining bolts.

6. Use a No. 43 drill, 0.089 in. (2.26mm) and insert it into the switch to set the contacts.

7. Tighten the retaining screws of the switch, remove the drill and complete the assembly by reversing the removal procedure.

8. Connect negative battery cable.

9. Check the ignition switch for proper starting in P or N. Also make certain that the start circuit cannot be actuated in the D or R position and that the column is locked in the LOCK position.

## Transaxle

### REMOVAL & INSTALLATION

#### 2.0L Engine

1. Disconnect the negative battery cable from the battery.

2. From under the hood, remove the bolts that attach the air manage valve to the AT (automatic transaxle) valve body cover. Disconnect the wiring harness connector from the neutral safety switch.

3. Disconnect the throttle valve linkage and the manual control lever cable. Remove the two transaxle–to–engine upper attaching bolts. The bolts are located below and on either side of the distributor.

4. Loosen the front wheel lugs slightly. Jack up the front of the car and safely support it on jackstands. Remove the wheels.

5. Drain the transaxle fluid. Disconnect the brake hoses from the strut brackets on both sides. Remove the pinch bolts that secure the lower control arms to the steering knuckles. Separate the ball joint from the steering knuckle. Remove the stabilizer bar attaching bracket. Remove the nuts that retain the stabilizer to the control arms. Remove the stabilizer bar. When removing the control arms from the steering knuckles, it will be necessary to bend the plastic shield slightly to gain ball joint clearance for removal.

6. Remove the tie rod ends from the steering knuckles. Use a special tie rod removing tool. Pry the right side halfshaft from the transaxle (see halfshaft removal section).

7. Remove the left side halfshaft from the transaxle. Support both right and left side halfshaft out of the way with wire.

8. Install sealing plugs or the equivalent into the transaxle halfshaft mounting holes.

9. Remove the starter support bracket. Disconnect the starter cable. Remove the starter mounting studs and the starter motor. Remove the transaxle support bracket.

10. Remove the lower cover from the transaxle. Turn the converter for access to the converter mounting nuts. Remove the nuts.

11. Remove the nuts that attach the left front insulator to the body bracket. Remove the bracket to body bolts and remove the bracket.

12. Remove the left rear insulator bracket attaching nut.

13. Disconnect the transaxle cooler lines. Remove the bolts that attach the manual lever bracket to the transaxle case.

14. Position a floor jack with a wide saddle under the transaxle and remove the four remaining transaxle to engine attaching bolts.

15. The torque converter mounting studs must be clear of the engine flywheel before the transaxle can be lowered from the car. Take a small pry bar and place it between the flywheel and the convertor. Carefully move the transaxle away from the engine. When the convertor mounting studs are clear lower the AT about 3 in. (76mm). Disconnect the speedometer cable from the AT. Lower the transaxle to the ground.

➡ **When moving the transaxle away from the engine watch the mount insulator. If it interferes with the transaxle before the converter mounting studs clear the flywheel, remove the insulator.**

**To install:**

16. Installation is the reverse order of the removal procedure. Be sure to pay strict attention to the following:

a. Before installing the halfshaft into the transaxle, replace the circlip on the CV–joint stub shaft. Carefully work the clip over the end of the shaft, spreading it as little as possible.

b. To install the halfshaft into the transaxle, carefully align the splines of the CV–joint with the splines in the differential.

c. Exerting some force, push the CV–joint into the differential until the circlip is felt to seat the differential side gear. Be careful not to damage the differential oil seal.

➡ **A non–metallic, mallet may be used to aid in seating the circlip into the differential side gear groove. If a mallet is necessary, tap only on the outboard CV–joint stub shaft.**

d. Attach the lower ball joint to the steering knuckle, taking care not to damage or cut the ball joint boot. Insert a new service pinch bolt and attach a new nut. Torque the nut to 37–44 ft. lbs. (50–60 Nm). Do not tighten the bolt.

➡ If the stabilizer bar required removal to perform another service procedure in conjunction with the transaxle removal, a disassembled view of the stabilizer bar mounting hardware is provided to aid in the its installation.

### 2.3L and 3.0L Engines

1. Disconnect the negative battery cable.

➡ Due to automatic transaxle case configuration, the right-side halfshaft assembly must be removed first. The differential rotator tool or equivalent, is then inserted into the transaxle to drive the left-side inboard CV-joint assembly from the transaxle.

2. Remove the air cleaner assembly.
3. Disengage the electrical harness connector from the neutral safety switch.
4. Disconnect the throttle valve linkage and the manual lever cable from their levers.

➡ Failure to disconnect the linkage and allowing the transaxle to hang, will fracture the throttle valve cam shaft joint, which is located under the transaxle cover.

5. To prevent contamination, cover the timing window in the converter housing. If equipped, remove the bolts retaining the thermactor hoses.
6. If equipped, remove the ground strap, located above the upper engine mount, and the coil and bracket assembly.
7. Remove both transaxle-to-engine upper bolts; the bolts are located below and on both ides of the distributor. Raise and safely support the vehicle. Remove the front wheels.
8. Remove the control arm-to-steering knuckle nut, at the ball joint.
9. Using a hammer and a punch, drive the bolt from the steering knuckle; repeat this step on the other side. Discard the nut and bolt.

➡ Be careful not to damage or cut ball joint boot. The prybar must not contact lower arm.

10. Using a prybar, disengage the control arm from the steering knuckle; repeat this step on the other side.

➡ Do not hammer on the knuckle to remove the ball joints. The plastic shield installed behind the rotor contains a molded pocket into which the lower control arm ball joint fits. When disengaging the control arm from the knuckle, clearance for the ball joint can be provided by bending the shield back toward the rotor. Failure to provide clearance for the ball joint can result in damage to the shield.

11. Remove the stabilizer bar bracket-to-frame rail bolts and discard the bolts; repeat this step on the other side.
12. Remove the stabilizer bar-to-control arm nut/washer and discard the nut; repeat this step on the other side.
13. Pull the stabilizer bar from of the control arms.
14. Remove the brake hose routing clip-to-suspension strut bracket bolt; repeat this step on the other side.
15. Remove the steering gear tie rod-to-steering knuckle nut and disengage the tie rod from the steering knuckle; repeat this step on the other side.
16. Using a halfshaft removal tool, pry the halfshaft from the right side of the transaxle and support the end of the shaft with a wire.

➡ It is normal for some fluid to leak from the transaxle when the halfshaft is removed.

17. Using a differential rotator tool or equivalent, drive the left-side halfshaft from the differential side gear.
18. Pull the halfshaft from the transaxle and support the end of the shaft with a wire.

➡ Do not allow the shaft to hang unsupported, as damage to the outboard CV-joint may result.

19. Install seal plugs into the differential seals.
20. Remove the starter support bracket and disconnect the starter cable. Remove the starter bolts and the starter. If equipped with a throttle body, remove the hose and bracket bolts on the starter and a bolt at the converter and disconnect the hoses.
21. Remove the transaxle support bracket and the dust cover from the torque converter housing.
22. Remove the torque converter-to-flywheel nuts by turning the crankshaft pulley bolt to bring the nuts into position.
23. Position a suitable transaxle jack under the transaxle and remove the rear support bracket nuts.
24. Remove the left front insulator-to-body bracket nuts, the bracket-to-body bolts and the bracket.
25. Disconnect the transaxle cooler lines.
26. Remove the manual lever bracket-to-transaxle case bolts.
27. Support the engine. Make sure the transaxle is supported and remove the remaining transaxle-to-engine bolts.
28. Make sure the torque converter studs will be clear the flywheel. Insert a prybar between the flywheel and the converter, then, pry the transaxle and converter away from the engine. When the converter studs are clear of the flywheel, lower the transaxle about 2–3 in. (51–76mm).
29. Disconnect the speedometer cable and lower the transaxle.

➡ When moving the transaxle away from the engine, watch the No. 1 insulator. If it contacts the body before the converter studs clear the flywheel, remove the insulator.

### To install:

30. Raise the transaxle and align it with the engine and flywheel. Install the No. 1 insulator, if removed. Tighten the transaxle-to-engine bolts to 25–33 ft. lbs. (34–45 Nm) and the torque converter-to-flywheel bolts to 23–39 ft. lbs. (31–53 Nm).
31. Install the manual lever bracket-to-transaxle case bolts and connect the transaxle cooler lines.
32. Install the left front insulator-to-body bracket nuts and tighten the nuts to 40–50 ft. lbs. (55–70 Nm). Install the bracket-to-body and tighten the bolts to 55–70 ft. lbs. (75–90 Nm).
33. Install the transaxle support bracket and the dust cover to the torque converter housing.
34. If equipped with a throttle body, install the hose and bracket bolts on the starter and a bolt to the converter and connect the hoses. Install the starter and the support bracket; tighten the starter-to-engine bolts to 30–40 ft. lbs. (41–54 Nm). Connect the starter cable.
35. Remove the seal plugs from the differential seals and install the halfshaft by performing the following procedures:

a. Prior to installing the halfshaft in the transaxle, install a new circlip onto the CV–joint stub.

b. Install the halfshaft in the transaxle by carefully aligning the CV–joint splines with the differential side gears. Be sure to push the CV–joint into the differential until the circlip is felt to seat in the differential side gear. Use care to prevent damage to the differential oil seal.

c. Attach the lower ball joint to the steering knuckle, taking care not to damage or cut the ball joint boot. Insert a new pinch bolt and a new nut. While holding the bolt with a 2nd wrench, tighten the nut to 40–54 ft. lbs. (54–74 Nm).

36. Engage the tie rod with the steering knuckle and tighten the nut to 23–35 ft. lbs. (31–47 Nm).

37. Install the brake hose routing clip–to–suspension strut bracket and tighten the bolt to 8 ft. lbs. (11 Nm).

38. Install the stabilizer bar to control arm and using a new nut, tighten it to 98–125 ft. lbs. (133–169 Nm).

39. Install the stabilizer bar bracket–to–frame rail bolts and using new bolts, tighten them to 60–70 ft. lbs. (81–95 Nm).

40. Install the wheels and lower the vehicle. Install the upper transaxle–to–engine bolts and tighten to 25–33 ft. lbs. (34–45 Nm).

41. If equipped, install the ground strap, located above the upper engine mount, and the coil and bracket assembly.

42. If equipped, install the bolts retaining the thermactor hoses. Uncover the timing window in the converter housing.

43. Connect the throttle valve linkage and the manual lever cable to their levers.

44. Engage the electrical harness connector from the neutral safety switch.

45. Install the air cleaner assembly.

46. Connect the negative battery cable and road test the vehicle.

## TRANSFER CASE

▶ See Figure 55

## Identification

The transfer case is actuated by an electrically controlled vacuum servo system. When the all wheel drive switch is placed in the ON position, a relay activates the 4WD solenoid valve. The 4WD solenoid valves allows vacuum to be created in the left hand chamber of the vacuum servo. The vacuum moves the servo rod and sliding collar into engagement with the transfer case output gears, driveshaft and rear axle. When the 2WD switch is turned ON a relay activates the 2WD solenoid valve. Vacuum is created in the right hand chamber of the vacuum servo disengaging the transfer case, driveshaft and rear axle output gears. The transfer case lubrication is integral with the transaxle. The transaxle/transfer case assembly requires 8.3 quarts of Mercon automatic transmission fluid.

### REMOVAL & INSTALLATION

▶ See Figures 56 and 57

1. Disconnect the negative battery cable.
2. Raise and safely support the vehicle.
3. Using a light hammer and a dull chisel, re}move the cup plug from the transfer case and drain the oil.
4. Remove the vacuum line retaining bracket bolt.
5. Remove the driveshaft front retaining bolts and caps; disengage the front driveshaft from the drive yoke.
6. If the transfer case is to be disassembled, check the backlash through the cup plug opening before removal in order to reset to existing backlash at installation. The backlash should be 0.012–0.024 in. (0.3–0.6mm) on a 3 in. (76mm) radius.
7. Remove the vacuum motor shield bolts and the shield unit.

8. Remove the vacuum lines from the vacuum servo.
9. Remove the transfer case–to–transaxle bolts; note and record the length and locations of the bolts.
10. Remove the the transfer case from the vehicle.

**To install:**

11. Position the transfer case to the transaxle.
12. Install the transfer case bolts in the proper positions and tighten the bolts, in sequence, to 23–38 ft. lbs. (31–38 Nm) for 1987, 15–19 ft. lbs. (21–25 Nm) for 1988–89 models, or 12–15 ft. lbs. (16–20 Nm) for 1990–91 models.
13. Install the vacuum motor supply hose connector, vacuum motor shield and tighten the bolts to 7–12 ft. lbs. (9–16 Nm).
14. Install the driveshaft–to–drive yoke, lubricate the bolts with Loctite® and tighten the bolts to 15–17 ft. lbs. (21–23 Nm). Install the vacuum line retaining bracket and tighten the bolt to 7–12 ft. lbs. (9–16 Nm).
15. Refill the transaxle and lower the vehicle. Road test the vehicle and check the performance of the transfer case.

### OVERHAUL

▶ See Figures 58, 59, 60, 61, 62, 63, 64, 65, 66, 67, 68 and 69

**Disassembly**

*CASE COMPONENTS*

1. Remove the negative battery cable.
2. Raise the vehicle and support on jackstands.
3. Drain the oil from the transfer case and remove the case from the vehicle.
4. Remove the case side cover bolts.
5. Clean the gasket material from the case and cover.

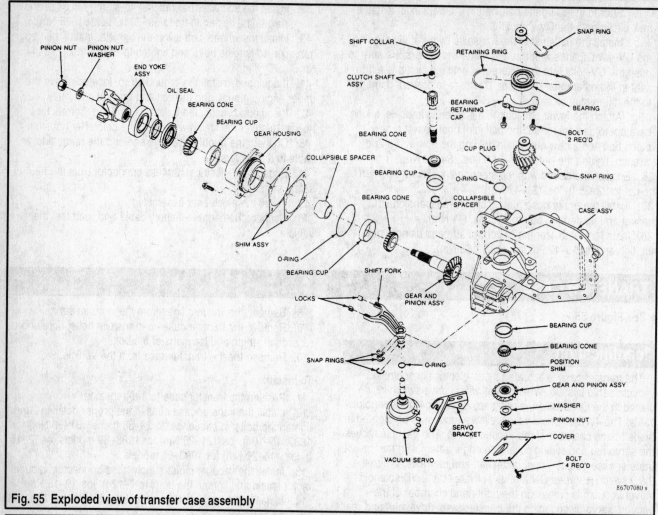

Fig. 55 Exploded view of transfer case assembly

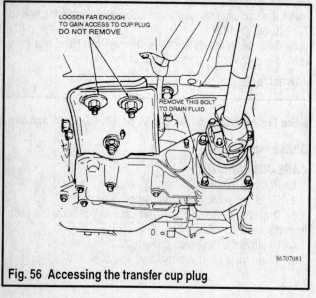

Fig. 56 Accessing the transfer cup plug

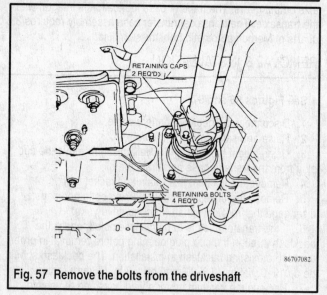

Fig. 57 Remove the bolts from the driveshaft

6. Remove the housing retaining bolts and remove the gear housing assembly.

7. Remove the O–ring and shims. Wire the shim stacks together for reassembly.

8. Remove the snaprings from the vacuum servo shaft and shift fork. Be sure to wear eye protection when removing and installing the snaprings.

9. Remove the shift motor assembly. Unfasten the shift fork and fork clips.

10. Remove the transfer case bearing cap retaining bolts and cap.

11. Rotate the bearing and remove the 2 piece snapring from the bearing.

12. Using a thin prybar, remove the inner snapring which positions the input gear to the ball bearing. Slide the bearing toward the input gear and remove the outer snapring.

13. Remove the cup plug. Slide the input gear toward the ball bearing until the input gear and bearing can be lifted out of the transfer case.

14. Remove the ball bearing from the input gear.

15. Remove the shift collar from the clutch shaft.

16. Remove the pinion nut and washer from the clutch shaft. Use a breaker bar and holding tool T87P–7120–A or equivalent. Tap the clutch shaft from the transfer case, with a soft drift.

17. Remove the pinion gear, outer bearing and shims from the transfer case. Be sure to wire the shims together for reassembly.

18. Remove and discard the clutch shaft collapsible spacer.

19. Mount the transfer case on holding fixture T57L–500–B or equivalent.

20. Install the clutch shaft inner bearing cup removal too T87P–7120–D. Remove the inner and outer bearing, using a suitable slide hammer into the cup remover.

### DRIVE GEAR COMPONENTS

1. Place the gear housing subassembly in a soft jawed vise. Remove the pinion nut, yoke end and washer.

2. Tap on the drive gear with a soft faced hammer to remove from the gear housing.

3. Remove and discard the collapsible spacer.

4. Remove the inner bearing cone from the drive gear, using a suitable press and a pinion bearing cone remover.

5. Mount the drive in a soft jawed vise. Remove the drive gear housing seal, using a roll head prybar or a suitable tool.

6. Remove the inner and outer drive gear bearing cups, using a brass drift and a hammer. Be sure to remove any burrs and wipe the bores clean.

7. Remove the gear housing from the vise. Install the new inner and outer drive bearing cups, using tool T87P–4616–A or equivalent.

To assemble:

8. Clean the drive gear in a suitable solvent, clean and dry completely. Install a new inner bearing cone assembly using pinion bearing cone replacer T62F–4621–A or equivalent. Be sure to install a nut on the end of the drive gear to protect the shaft.

9. Lubricate and install the new outer drive bearing cone. Install a new oil seal, using install tool T87P–7065–B or equivalent. Grease the end of the seal completely.

10. Install a new collapsible spacer on the drive gear stem. Install the drive gear into the gear housing.

11. Install the yoke end, washer and nut.

12. Tighten the pinion nut in small amounts until the rotation effect is 15–32 inch. lbs. (1.7–3.5 Nm) with the new bearing. Do not exceed this specification or a new collapsible spacer will have to be installed.

### CLUTCH SHAFT COMPONENTS

1. Remove the clutch shaft inner bearing using a press and a bearing puller tool D84L–1123–A or equivalent.

2. Mount the clutch shaft in a soft jawed vise.

3. Remove the clutch shaft needle bearings which center the input gears, using pilot bearing preplacer tool T87P–7120–C or equivalent, and a slide hammer.

**To assemble:**

4. Install a new clutch shaft needle bearing, using a hammer and a pilot bearing replacer.

➡ **When installing the needle bearing into the clutch shaft, install; it with the tapered end down, toward the clutch.**

5. Pack the bearing with grease to maintain prior needle position.

6. Install the clutch shaft inner bearing cone, using a press and and bearing puller attachment D84L–1123–A or equivalent.

### Assembly

### Transfer Case

1. Wipe bearing bores clean. Install the inner and outer bearing cups, using bearing cup replacer T87P–7120–B or equivalent.

2. Install a new new collapsible spacer on the clutch shaft. Install the clutch shaft into the transfer case. Assemble the original shim and pinion gear.

3. Assemble the washer and pinion nut. tighten the nut using a breaker bar and a holding wrench until the rotational effort is 4.0–8.0 inch lbs. (0.44–.90) with the new bearings. Do not exceed this specification or a new collapsible spacer will be required to obtain the proper preload.

4. Position shims and a new O–ring onto the gear housing. Be sure to lubricate the O–rings.

5. Install the gear housing subassembly to the transfer case and tighten the bolts to 8–12 ft. lbs. (11–16 Nm).

6. Check the backlash between the drive and pinion gear. Correct backlash should be 0.004–0.006 inch. (0.10–0.15mm).

➡ **Check the gear contact tooth pattern. If a gross pattern error is detected with backlash correct, adjust the drive pinion gear shim stack. Increasing the shim stack should move the contact pattern on the drive (pull) side of the gear.**

7. Install the shift collar onto the clutch shaft.

8. Slide the ball bearing onto the input gear. Install the input gear into the transfer case. Slide the small end of the input gear into the clutch shaft.

9. Install the snapring onto the outer end of the shaft.

10. Slide the bearing outboard and install the snapring onto the inner end of the input shaft. Make certain the snaprings are completely seated in the grooves.

11. Install the 2 piece snapring into the groove for the ball bearing in the transfer case.

12. Install the bearing cap and retainer bolts. Tighten the bolts to 18–24 ft. lbs. (24–33 Nm).

13. Inspect the shift fork clips and replace as necessary. Install the shift fork onto the clutch collar.

14. Install a new O-ring onto the vacuum servo shaft. Lubricate O-ring with automatic transaxle fluid.

15. Install the vacuum servo assembly into the transfer case. Install the snapring, making certain it is fully seated in the groove.

16. Install the shift fork snaprings.

17. Apply a bead of silicone rubber sealer on the cover surface. Install the transfer case side cover and tighten the bolts to 7–12 ft. lbs. (9–16 Nm).

18. After checking the backlash, install the transfer case onto the transaxle.

19. Check all hardware for tightness. Start vehicle, and check for fluid leaks.

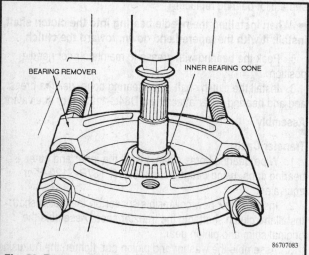

Fig. 58  Remove the inner bearing from the drive gear using a press

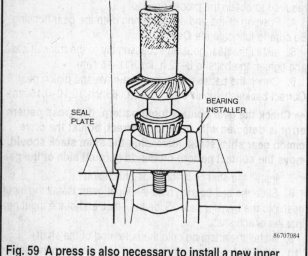

Fig. 59  A press is also necessary to install a new inner bearing cone assembly to the drive gear

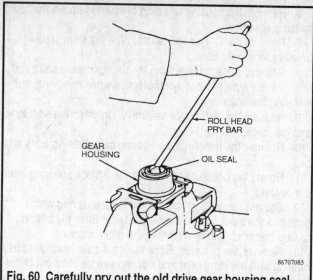

Fig. 60  Carefully pry out the old drive gear housing seal

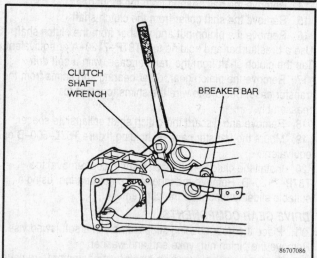

Fig. 61  A clutch shaft wrench is necessary to remove the pinion nut and washer from the clutch shaft

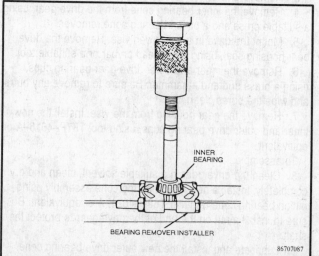

Fig. 62  Again, the press is used with a bearing remover to free the clutch shaft inner bearing

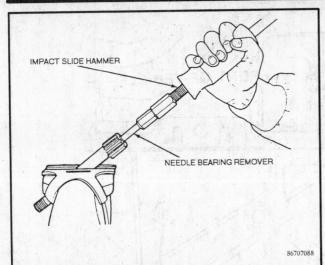

Fig. 63 Disassembling the clutch shaft needle bearings which center the input gear

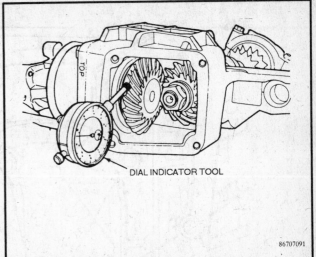

Fig. 66 Checking the backlash between the drive and pinion gear

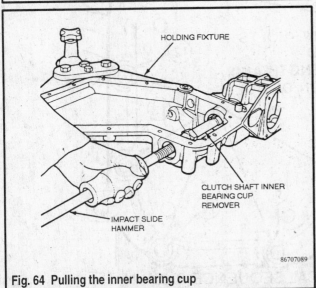

Fig. 64 Pulling the inner bearing cup

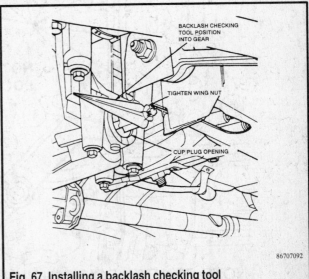

Fig. 67 Installing a backlash checking tool

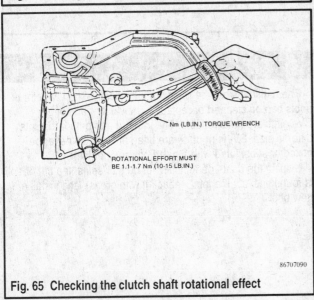

Fig. 65 Checking the clutch shaft rotational effect

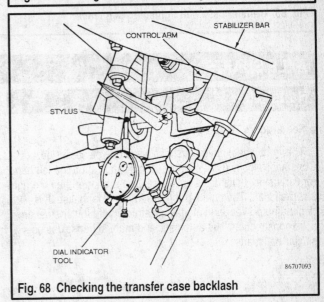

Fig. 68 Checking the transfer case backlash

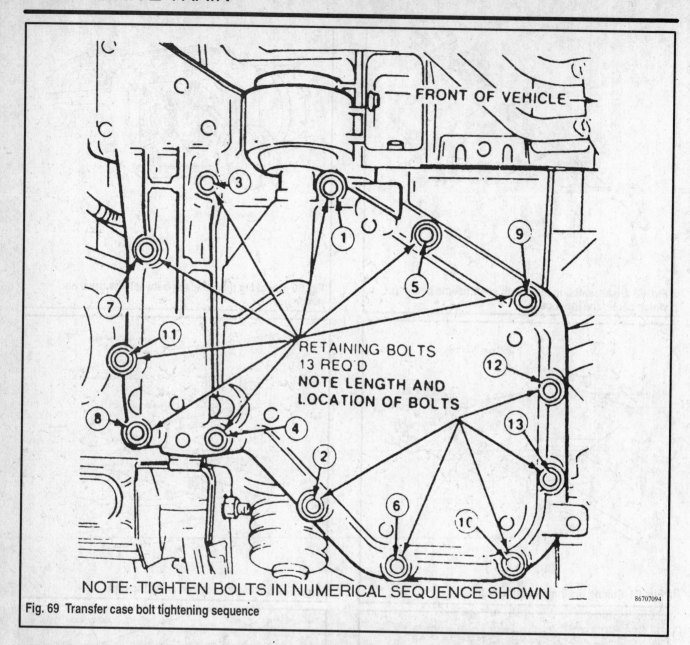

Fig. 69 Transfer case bolt tightening sequence

## AXLE SHAFTS

### Halfshafts

▶ See Figures 70 and 71

The front wheel drive halfshafts are a one piece design. Constant Velocity (CV) joint are used at each end. The left hand (driver's side) halfshaft is solid steel and is shorter than the right side halfshaft. The right hand (passenger) side halfshaft is depending on year and model, constructed of tubular steel or solid construction. The automatic and manual transaxles use similar halfshafts.

The halfshafts can be replaced individually. The CV–joint or boots can be cleaned or replaced. Individual parts of the CV–joints are not available. The inboard and outboard joints differ in size. CV–joint parts are fitted and should never be mixed or substituted with a part from another joint.

Inspect the boots periodically for cuts or splits. If a cut or split is found, inspect the joint, repack it with grease and install a new boot.

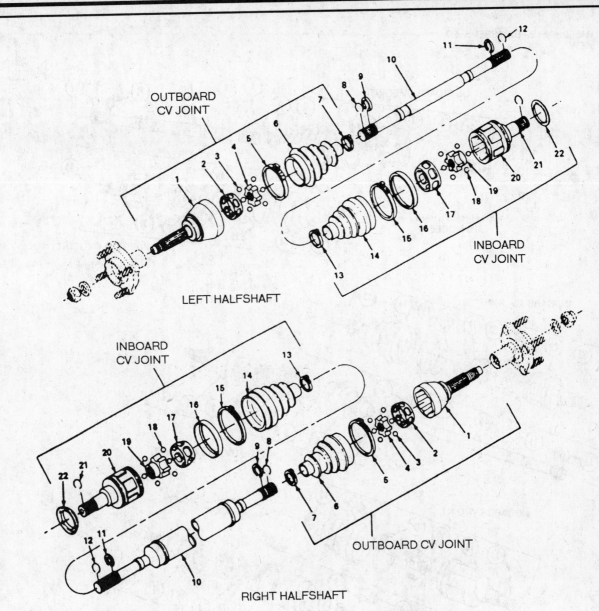

OUTBOARD
CV JOINT

INBOARD
CV JOINT

LEFT HALFSHAFT

INBOARD
CV JOINT

OUTBOARD CV JOINT

RIGHT HALFSHAFT

1 Outer bearing race and stub shaft assembly
2 Bearing cage
3 Ball bearings (6)
4 Inner bearing race
5 Boot clamp (large)
6 Boot
7 Boot clamp (small)
8 Circlip
9 Stop ring
10 Interconnecting shaft
11 Stop ring

12 Circlip
13 Boot clamp (small)
14 Boot
15 Boot clamp (large)
16 Bearing retainer
17 Bearing cage
18 Ball bearings (6)
19 Inner bearing race
20 Outer bearing race and stub shaft assembly
21 Circlip
22 Dust deflector

Fig. 70 Exploded view of the Halfshaft assembly—1984–85 vehicles

86707039

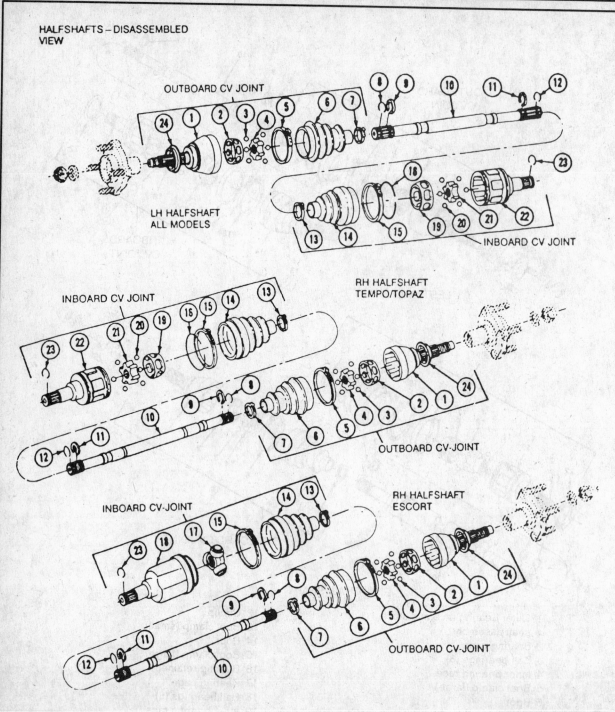

HALFSHAFTS – DISASSEMBLED VIEW

OUTBOARD CV JOINT

LH HALFSHAFT ALL MODELS

INBOARD CV JOINT

INBOARD CV JOINT

RH HALFSHAFT TEMPO/TOPAZ

OUTBOARD CV-JOINT

INBOARD CV-JOINT

RH HALFSHAFT ESCORT

OUTBOARD CV-JOINT

| | | |
|---|---|---|
| 1. Outboard joint outer race and stub shaft | 7. Boot clamp (small) | 13. Boot clamp (small) | 19. Ball cage |
| 2. Ball cage | 8. Circlip | 14. Boot | 20. Balls (6) |
| 3. Balls (6) | 9. Stop ring | 15. Boot clamp (large) | 21. Inboard joint inner race |
| 4. Outboard joint inner race | 10. Interconnecting shaft | 16. Wire ring ball retainer | 22. Inboard joint outer race and stub shaft |
| 5. Boot clamp (large) | 11. Stop ring | 17. Tripod assy | 23. Circlip |
| 6. Boot | 12. Circlip | 18. Tripod outer race | 24. Dust seal |

Fig. 71 Exploded view of the Halfshaft assembly—1986–94 vehicles

86707040

## REMOVAL & INSTALLATION

### 1984–85 Models

◆ See Figures 72, 73, 74, 75 and 76

➡ Special tools are required for removing, installing and servicing halfshafts. They are listed by descriptive name (Ford part number). Front Hub Installer Adapter (T81P–1104–A), Wheel Bolt Adapters (T81P–1104–B or T83P–1104–BH), CV–Joint Separator(T81P–3514–A), Front Hub Installer/Remover (T81P–1104–C), Shipping Plug Tool (T81P–1177–B), Dust Deflector Installer CV–Joint (T83P–3425–AH), Differential Rotator (T81P–4026–A). It is necessary to have on hand new hub nuts and new lower control arm to steering knuckle attaching nuts and bolts. Once removed, these parts must not be reused. The torque holding ability is destroyed during the removal process.

1. Loosen the front hub nut and the wheel lugs.
2. Raise and support the vehicle safely on jackstands.
3. Remove the tire and wheel assembly. Remove and discard the front hub nut. Save the washers.

➡ Halfshaft removal & installation are the same for manual and automatic transaxles EXCEPT: The configuration of the Automatic Transaxle (AT) differential case requires that the right hand halfshaft assembly be removed first. The differential service tool T81P–4026 (Differential Rotator) is then inserted to drive the left hand halfshaft from the transaxle. If only the left hand halfshaft is to be serviced, removed the right hand halfshaft from the transaxle side and support it with a length of wire. Drive the left hand halfshaft assembly from the transaxle.

4. Remove the bolt that retains the brake hose to the strut.
5. Remove the nut and bolt securing the lower ball joint and separate the joint from the steering knuckle by inserting a pry bar between the stabilizer and frame and pulling downward. Take care not to damage the ball joint boot.

➡ The lower control arm ball joint fits into a pocket formed in a plastic disc rotor shield, on some models. The shield must be carefully bent back away from the ball joint while prying the ball joint out of the steering knuckle. Do not contact or pry on the lower control arm.

6. Remove the halfshaft from the differential housing, using a pry bar. Position the pry bar between the case and the shaft and pry the joint away from the case. Do not damage the oil seal, the CV–joint boot or the CV–dust deflector. Install tool number T81P–1177–B (Shipping plug) to prevent fluid loss and differential side gear misalignment.
7. Support the end of the shaft with a piece of wire, suspending it from a chassis member.
8. Separate the shaft from the front hub using the special remover/installer tool and adapters. Instructions for the use of the tool may be found in section 8 under the Front Wheel Bearing section.

➡ Never use a hammer to force the shaft from the wheel hub. Damage to the internal parts of the CV–joint may occur.

To install:

9. Install a new circlip on the inboard CV–joint stub shaft. Align the splines of the inboard CV–joint stub shaft with the splines in the differential. Push the CV–joint into the differential until the circlip seats on the side gear. Some force may be necessary to seat the clip.
10. Carefully align the splines of the outboard CV–joint stub shaft with the splines in the front wheel hub. Push the shaft into the hub as far as possible. Install the remover/installer tool and pull the CV–stub shaft through the hole.
11. Connect the control arm to the steering knuckle and install a new mounting bolt and nut. Tighten to 37–44 ft. lbs. (50–60 Nm).
12. Connect the brake line to the strut.
13. Install the front hub washer and new hub nut. Install the tire and wheel assembly.
14. Lower the vehicle. Tighten the center hub nut to 180–200 ft. lbs. (244–271 Nm). Stake the nut using a blunt chisel.

### 1986–94 Models

#### EXCEPT ALL WHEEL DRIVE (AWD) REAR HALFSHAFTS

◆ See Figures 72, 73, 74, 75 and 76

➡ Halfshaft assembly removal and installation procedures are the same for automatic and manual transaxles, except on the automatic transaxle, the right side halfshaft must be removed first. Differential rotator tool T81P–4026–A or equivalent, is then inserted into the transaxle to drive the left side inboard CV–joint assembly from the transaxle. If only the left side halfshaft assembly is to be removed for service, remove the right side halfshaft assembly from the transaxle only. After removal, support it with a length of wire, then drive the left side halfshaft assembly from the transaxle.

1. Remove the cap from the hub and loosen the hub nut. Set the parking brake.
2. Raise and safely support the vehicle on jackstands. Remove the wheel and tire assembly. Remove the hub nut/washer and discard the nut.
3. Remove the brake hose routing clip–to–strut bolt.
4. Remove the nut from the ball joint–to–steering knuckle bolt. Using a hammer and a punch, drive the bolt from the steering knuckle and discard the bolt/nut.
5. Using a prybar, separate the ball joint from the steering knuckle. Position the end of the prybar outside of the bushing pocket to avoid damage to the bushing; be careful not to damage the ball joint or CV–joint boot.

➡ The lower control arm ball joint fits into a pocket formed in the plastic disc brake rotor shield; bend the shield away from the ball joint while prying the ball joint from the steering knuckle.

6. Using a prybar, pry the halfshaft from the differential housing. Position the prybar between the differential housing and the CV–joint assembly. Be careful not to damage the differential oil seal, case, CV–joint boot or the transaxle.

➡ Shipping plugs T81P–1177–B or equivalent, must be installed in the differential housing after halfshaft removal. Failure to do so can result in dislocation of the differential side gears. Should the gears become misaligned, the differential will have to be removed from the transaxle to re–align the gears.

7. Using a piece of wire, support the end of the shaft from a convenient underbody component.

➡ Do not allow the shaft to hang unsupported, as damage to the outboard CV–joint may result.

8. Using a front hub removal tool, press the halfshaft's outboard CV–joint from the hub.

➡ Never use a hammer or separate the outboard CV–joint stub shaft from the hub. Damage to the CV–joint internal components may result.

**To install:**

9. Install a new circlip onto the inboard CV–joint stub shaft; the outboard CV–joint stub shaft does not have a circlip. To install the circlip properly, start one end in the groove and work the circlip over the stub shaft end and into the groove; this will avoid over expanding the circlip.

10. Carefully, align the splines of the inboard CV–joint stub shaft with the splines in the differential. Push the CV–joint into the differential until the circlip is seated in the differential side gear. Use care to prevent damage to the differential oil seal.

➡ A non–metallic mallet may be used to aid in seating the circlip into the differential side gear groove; if a mallet is necessary, tap only on the outboard CV–joint stub shaft.

11. Carefully align the outboard CV–joint stub shaft splines with the hub splines and push the shaft into the hub, as far as possible; use the front hub replacer tool to firmly press the halfshaft into the hole.

12. Connect the control arm–to–steering knuckle and tighten the new nut/bolt to 40–54 ft. lbs. (54–74 Nm). A new bolt and nut must be used.

13. Position the brake hose routing clip on the suspension strut and tighten the bolt to 8 ft. lbs. (11 Nm).

14. Install the hub nut washer and a new hub nut.

15. Install the wheel/tire assembly and tighten the lug nuts to 80–105 ft. lbs. (108–144 Nm). Lower the vehicle and tighten the hub nut to 180–200 ft. lbs. (244–271 Nm).

16. Refill the transaxle and road test.

PRYBAR

EXHAUST PIPE

86707041

**Fig. 72 Carefully pry the halfshaft away from the transaxle**

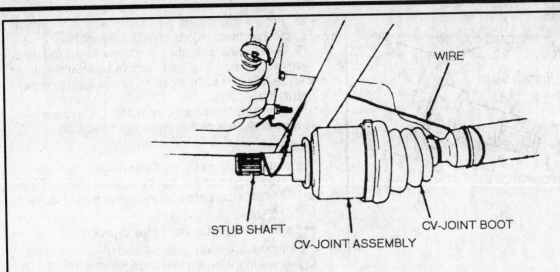

WIRE

STUB SHAFT

CV-JOINT ASSEMBLY

CV-JOINT BOOT

86707042

**Fig. 73 Support the halfshaft with wire to the vehicle body**

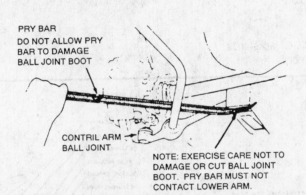

PRY BAR
DO NOT ALLOW PRY
BAR TO DAMAGE
BALL JOINT BOOT

CONTRIL ARM
BALL JOINT

NOTE: EXERCISE CARE NOT TO
DAMAGE OR CUT BALL JOINT
BOOT. PRY BAR MUST NOT
CONTACT LOWER ARM.

SEPARATING THE BALL JOINT FROM THE STEERING KNUCKLE

86707045

**Fig. 74 Use a prytool to separate the balljoint assembly from the steering knuckle**

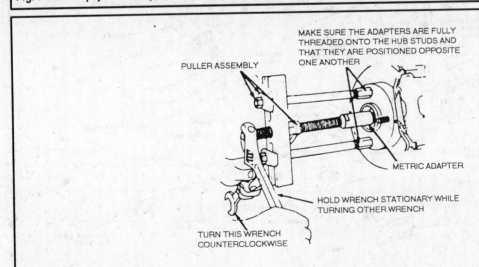

MAKE SURE THE ADAPTERS ARE FULLY
THREADED ONTO THE HUB STUDS AND
THAT THEY ARE POSITIONED OPPOSITE
ONE ANOTHER

PULLER ASSEMBLY

METRIC ADAPTER

HOLD WRENCH STATIONARY WHILE
TURNING OTHER WRENCH

TURN THIS WRENCH
COUNTERCLOCKWISE

86707043

**Fig. 75 Remove the hub from the shaft assembly using a suitable puller**

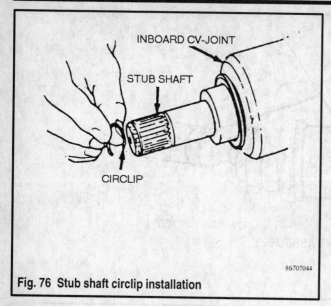

**Fig. 76 Stub shaft circlip installation**

### ALL WHEEL DRIVE REAR HALFSHAFTS

♦ **See Figure 77**

1. Raise and safely support the vehicle on jackstands. Remove the rear suspension control arm bolt.

2. Remove the outboard U–joint retaining bolts and straps. Remove the inboard U–joint retaining bolts and straps.

3. Slide the shafts together; do not allow the splined shafts to contact with excessive force. Remove the halfshafts; do not drop the halfshafts as the impact may cause damage to the U–joint bearing cups.

4. Retain the bearing cups. Inspect the U–joint assemblies for wear or damage, replace the U–joint if necessary.

### To install:

5. Install the halfshaft at the inboard U–joint; the inboard shaft has a larger diameter than the outboard shaft. Install the U–joint retaining caps and bolts and tighten to 15–17 ft. lbs. (21–23 Nm).

➡ **Be sure to apply Loctite® to the U–joint bolts.**

6. Install the halfshaft at the outboard U–joint. Install the U–joint retaining caps and bolts and tighten them to 15–17 ft. lbs. (21–23 Nm).

7. Install the rear suspension control arm and tighten the bolt to 60–86 ft. lbs. (82–116 Nm).

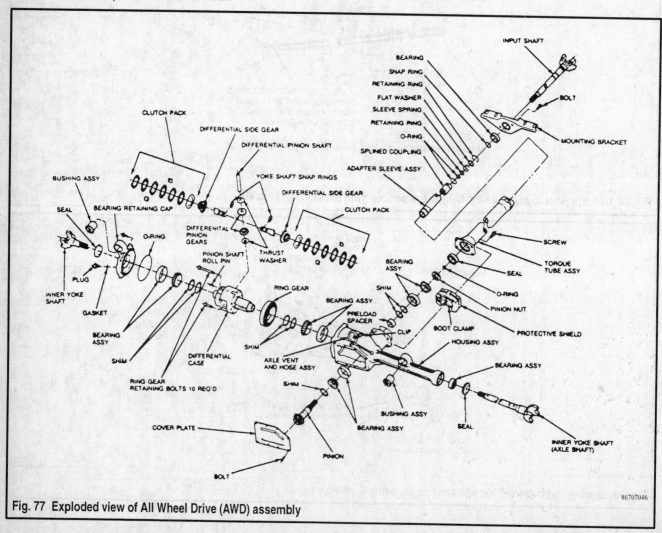

**Fig. 77 Exploded view of All Wheel Drive (AWD) assembly**

## CV–JOINT OVERHAUL

➡ When replacing a CV–boot, be aware of the transaxle type, transaxle ratio, le ratio, engine size, CV–joint type, right or left side and inboard or outboard end.

**Inboard CV–Joint Assembly**

◆ See Figures 78, 79 and 80

There are two different types of inboard CV–joints (Double Offset Joint and Tripod–Type) requiring different removal procedures.

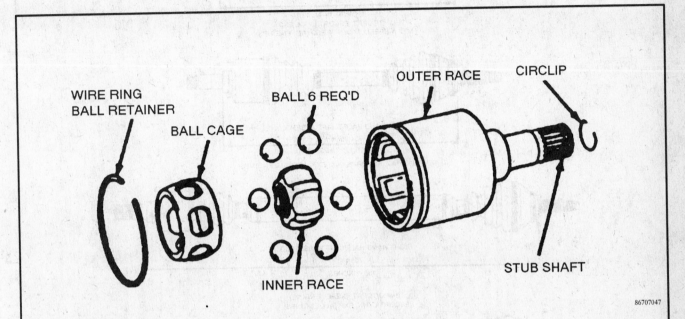

Fig. 78 Double offset CV–joint

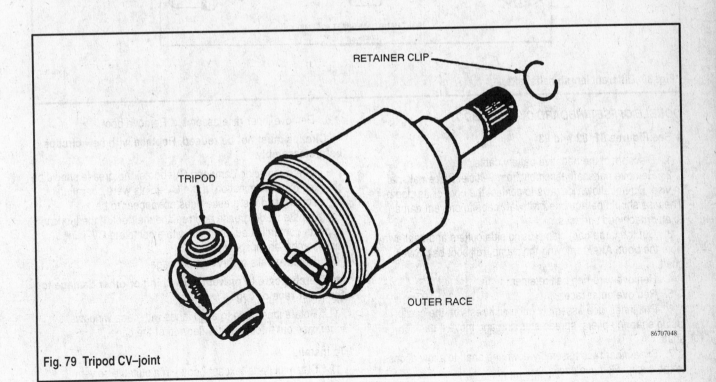

Fig. 79 Tripod CV–joint

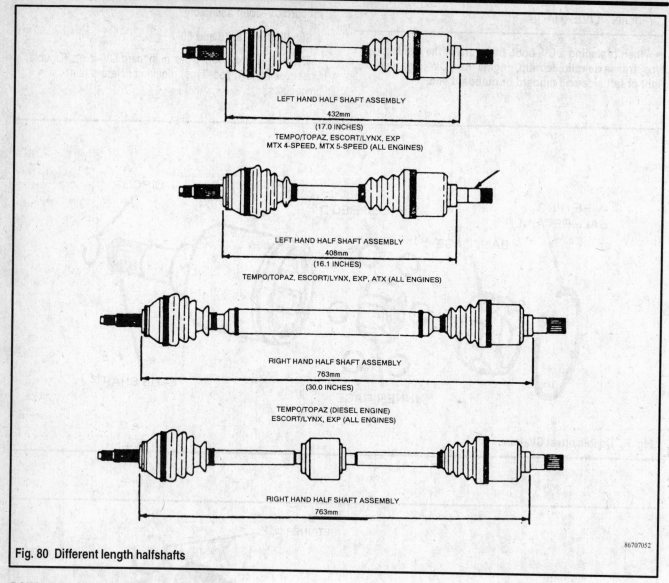

LEFT HAND HALF SHAFT ASSEMBLY
432mm
(17.0 INCHES)
TEMPO/TOPAZ, ESCORT/LYNX, EXP
MTX 4-SPEED, MTX 5-SPEED (ALL ENGINES)

LEFT HAND HALF SHAFT ASSEMBLY
408mm
(16.1 INCHES)
TEMPO/TOPAZ, ESCORT/LYNX, EXP, ATX (ALL ENGINES)

RIGHT HAND HALF SHAFT ASSEMBLY
763mm
(30.0 INCHES)
TEMPO/TOPAZ (DIESEL ENGINE)
ESCORT/LYNX, EXP (ALL ENGINES)

RIGHT HAND HALF SHAFT ASSEMBLY
763mm

86707052

**Fig. 80 Different length halfshafts**

### DOUBLE OFFSET INBOARD CV–JOINT BOOT

▶ **See Figures 81, 82 and 83**

1. Disconnect the negative battery cable.
2. Remove halfshaft assembly from vehicle. Place halfshaft in vise. Do not allow vice jaws to contact the boot or its clamp. The vise should be equipped with jaw caps to prevent damage to any machined surfaces.
3. Cut the large boot clamp using side cutters and peel away from the boot. After removing the clamp, roll boot back over shaft.
4. Remove wire ring ball retainer.
5. Remove outer race.
6. Pull inner race assembly out until it rests on the circlip. Using snapring pliers, spread stop ring and move it back on shaft.
7. Slide inner race assembly down the shaft to allow access to the circlip. Remove circlip.

8. Remove inner race assembly. Remove boot.

➡ **Circlips must not be reused. Replace with new circlips before assembly.**

9. When replacing damaged CV–boots, the grease should be checked for contamination. If the CV–joints were operating satisfactorily and the grease does not appear to be contaminated, add grease and replace the boot. If the lubricant appears contaminated, proceed with a complete CV–joint disassembly and inspection.
10. Remove balls by prying from cage.

➡ **Exercise care to prevent scratching or other damage to the inner race or cage.**

11. Rotate inner race to align lands with cage windows. Lift inner race out through the wider end of the cage.

**To install:**

12. Clean all parts (except boots) in a suitable solvent.

13. Inspect all CV–joint parts for excessive wear, looseness, pitting, rust and cracks.

➡ **CV–joint components are matched during assembly. If inspection reveals damage or wear the entire joint must be replaced as an assembly. Do not replace a joint merely because the parts appear polished. Shiny areas in ball races and on the cage spheres are normal.**

14. Install a new circlip, supplied with the service kit, in groove nearest end of shaft. Do not over–expand or twist circlip during installation.

15. Install inner race in the cage. The race is installed through the large end of the cage with the circlip counterbore facing the large end of the cage.

16. With the cage and inner race properly aligned, install the balls by pressing through the cage windows with the heel of the hand.

17. Assemble the inner race and cage assembly in outer race.

18. Push the inner race and cage assembly by hand, into the outer race. Install with inner race chamfer facing out.

19. Install the ball retainer into groove inside of outer race.

20. Install a new CV–boot.

21. Tighten the clamp securely but not to the point where the clamp bridge is cut or the boot is damaged.

22. Position stop ring and new circlip into grooves on shaft.

23. Fill the CV–joint outer race with 3.2 oz. (90 grams) of grease, then spread 1.4 oz. (40 grams) of grease evenly inside boot for a total combined fill of 4.6 oz. (130 grams).

24. With boot peeled back, install CV–joint using soft tipped hammer. Ensure splines are aligned prior to installing CV–joint onto shaft.

25. Remove all excess grease from the CV–joint external surfaces.

26. Position boot over CV–joint. Before installing boot clamp, move it in or out, as necessary, to adjust to the proper length.

➡ **Insert a suitable tool between the boot and outer bearing race and allow the trapped air to escape from the boot. The air should be released from the boot only after adjusting to the proper dimensions.**

27. Ensure the boot is seated in its groove and clamp in position.

28. Tighten clamp securely but not to the point where the clamp bridge is cut or the boot is damaged.

29. Install halfshaft assembly in vehicle.

30. Connect the negative battery cable.

### TRIPOD INBOARD CV–JOINT BOOT

▶ See Figure 84

1. Disconnect the negative battery cable.

2. Remove halfshaft assembly from vehicle. Place halfshaft in vice. Do not allow vise jaws to contact the boot or its clamp. The vise should be equipped with jaw caps to prevent damage to any machined surfaces.

3. Cut the large boot clamp using side cutters and peel away from the boot. After removing the clamp, roll boot back over shaft.

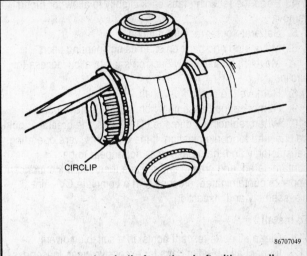

Fig. 81 Remove the circlip from the shaft with a small prytool

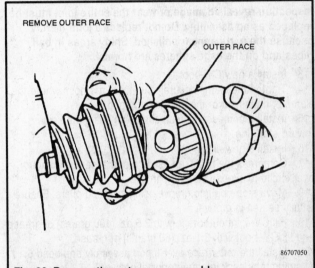

Fig. 82 Remove the outer race assembly

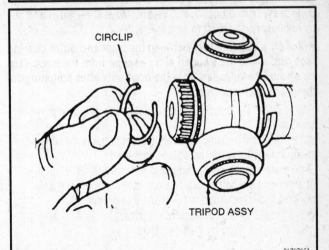

Fig. 83 Install a new circlip to the shaft. Work one end first, then the other end until in place

4. Bend the retaining tabs back slightly to allow for tripod removal.

5. Separate outer race from tripod.

6. Move stop ring back on shaft using snapring pliers.

7. Move tripod assembly back on shaft to allow access to circlip.

8. Remove the circlip from shaft.

9. Remove tripod assembly from shaft. Remove boot.

10. When replacing a damaged CV–boots, the grease should be checked for contamination. If the CV–joints were operating satisfactorily and the grease does not appear to be contaminated, add grease and replace the boot. If the lubricant appears contaminated, proceed with a complete CV–joint disassembly and inspection.

**To install:**

11. Clean all parts (except boots) in a suitable solvent.

12. Inspect all CV–joint parts for excessive wear, looseness, pitting, rust and cracks.

➡ **CV–joint components are matched during assembly. If inspection reveals damage or wear the entire joint must be replaced as an assembly. Do not replace a joint merely because the parts appear polished. Shiny areas in ball races and on the cage spheres are normal.**

13. Install a new CV–boot.

14. Tighten the clamp securely but not to the point where the clamp bridge is cut or the boot is damaged.

15. Install tripod assembly on shaft with chamfered side toward stop ring.

16. Install a new circlip.

17. Compress the circlip and slide tripod assembly forward over circlip to expose stop ring groove.

18. Move stop ring into groove using snapring pliers. Ensure it is fully seated in groove.

19. Fill CV–joint outer race with 3.5 oz. (100 grams) of grease and fill CV–boot with 2.1 oz. (60 grams) of grease.

20. Install the outer race over tripod assembly and bend 6 retaining tabs back into their original position.

21. Remove all excess grease from CV–joint external surfaces. Position boot over CV–joint. Move CV–joint in and out as necessary, to adjust to proper length.

➡ **Insert a suitable tool between the boot and outer bearing race and allow the trapped air to escape from the boot. The air should be released from the boot only after adjusting to the proper dimensions.**

22. Ensure the boot is seated in its groove and clamp in position.

23. Tighten the clamp securely but not to the point where the clamp bridge is cut or the boot is damaged.

24. Install a new circlip, supplied with service kit, in groove nearest end of shaft by starting one end in the groove and working clip over stub shaft end and into groove.

25. Install halfshaft assembly in vehicle.

26. Connect negative battery cable.

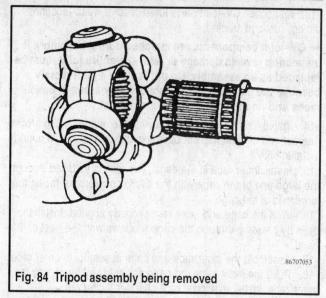

**Fig. 84 Tripod assembly being removed**

**Outboard CV–Joint Assembly**

◆ **See Figures 85, 86, 87 and 88**

1. Disconnect the negative battery cable.

2. Remove the halfshaft assembly from vehicle.

3. Place the halfshaft in vice. Do not allow vise jaws to contact the boot or its clamp. The vise should be equipped with jaw caps to prevent damage to any machined surfaces.

4. Cut the large boot clamp using side cutters and peel away from the boot. After removing the clamp, roll boot back over shaft.

5. Support the interconnecting shaft in a soft jaw vise and angle the CV–joint to expose inner bearing race.

6. Using a brass drift and hammer, give a sharp tap to the inner bearing race to dislodge the internal circlip and separate the CV–joint from the interconnecting shaft. Take care not to drop the CV–joint at separation.

7. Remove the boot.

8. When replacing damaged CV–boots, the grease should be checked for contamination. If the CV–joints were operating satisfactorily and the grease does not appear to be contaminated, add grease and replace the boot. If the lubricant appears contaminated, proceed with a complete CV–joint disassembly and inspection.

9. Remove the circlip located near the end of the shaft. Discard the circlip. Use new clip supplied with boot replacement kit and CV–joint overhaul kit.

10. Clamp CV–joint stub shaft in a vise with the outer face facing up. Care should be taken not to damage dust seal. The vise must be equipped with jaw caps to prevent damage to the shaft splines.

11. Press down on inner race until it tilts enough to allow removal of ball. A tight assembly can be tilted by tapping the inner race with wooden dowel and hammer. Do not hit the cage.

12. With cage sufficiently tilted, remove the ball from cage. Remove all 6 balls in this manner.

13. Pivot cage and inner race assembly until it is straight up and down in outer race. Align cage windows with outer race lands while pivoting the bearing cage. With the cage pivoted and aligned, lift assembly from the outer race.

14. Rotate the inner race up and out of the cage.

### To install:

15. Clean all parts (except boots) in a suitable solvent.

16. Inspect all CV–joint parts for excessive wear, looseness, pitting, rust and cracks.

➡ **CV–joint components are matched during assembly. If inspection reveals damage or wear the entire joint must be replaced as an assembly. Do not replace a joint merely because the parts appear polished. Shiny areas in ball races and on the cage spheres are normal.**

17. Apply a light coating of grease on inner and outer ball races. Install the inner race in cage.

18. Install the inner race and cage assembly in the outer race.

19. Install the assembly vertically and pivot 90 degrees into position.

20. Align cage and inner race with outer race. Tilt inner race and cage and install one of the 6 balls. Repeat this process until the remaining balls are installed.

21. Install new CV–boot.

22. Tighten clamp securely but not to the point where the clamp bridge is cut or the boot is damaged.

23. Install the stop ring, if removed.

24. Install a new circlip, supplied with the service kit, in groove nearest the end of the shaft.

25. Pack CV–joint with grease. Any grease remaining in tube should be spread evenly inside boot.

26. With the boot "peeled" back, position CV–joint on shaft and tap into position using a plastic tipped hammer.

27. Remove all excess grease from the CV–joint external surfaces.

28. Position the boot over CV–joint.

29. Ensure the boot is seated in its groove and clamp into position.

30. Tighten the clamp securely but not to the point where the clamp bridge is cut or the boot is damaged.

31. Install the halfshaft assembly in vehicle.

32. Connect the negative battery cable.

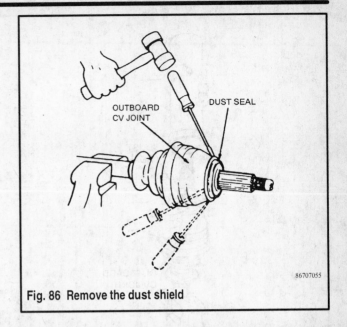

Fig. 86  **Remove the dust shield**

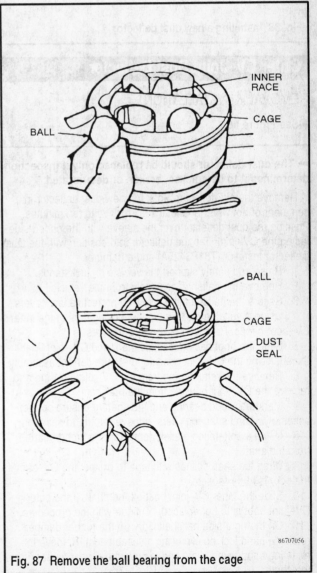

Fig. 87  **Remove the ball bearing from the cage**

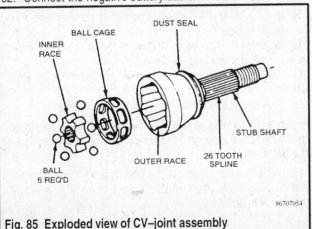

Fig. 85  **Exploded view of CV–joint assembly**

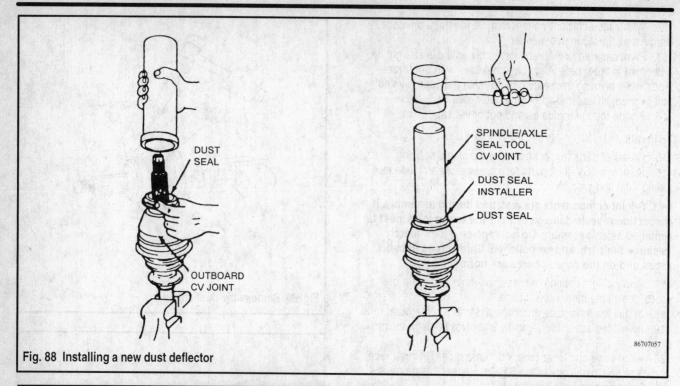

DUST
SEAL

OUTBOARD
CV JOINT

SPINDLE/AXLE
SEAL TOOL
CV JOINT

DUST SEAL
INSTALLER

DUST SEAL

86707057

**Fig. 88 Installing a new dust deflector**

## Outer CV–Joint Dust Deflector

### REMOVAL & INSTALLATION

♦ See Figure 88

➡ **The dust deflector should be replaced only if inspection determines it to be cracked, broken or deteriorated.**

Remove the old deflector. Soak the new dust deflector in a container of hot water and let it soak for five to ten minutes. Position the dust deflector over the sleeve with the ribbed side facing the CV–joint. Tap the deflector into position with the Dust Deflector Installer (T81P3425A) and a hammer.

1. Raise and safely support the vehicle on jackstands.
2. Remove the halfshaft assembly from the vehicle.
3. Secure the halfshaft in a vise with protective jaw covers.
4. Using a suitable tool, pry up the locking tabs of the inner CV–boot bands. Remove the bands with pliers.
5. Slide the boot back to expose the tripod CV–joint. Mark the shaft and the CV–joint housing to ensure correct assembly.
6. Remove the retainer ring from the CV–joint housing and remove the CV–joint housing from the halfshaft.
7. Mark the tripod bearing and the shaft to ensure correct assembly. Using snapring pliers, remove the tripod snapring.
8. Using a soft–faced mallet, gently tap the tripod bearing from the shaft.
9. Wrap the shaft splines with tape to protect the CV–boot if the boot is to be reused.
10. Slide the inner CV–joint boot off the shaft. If the outer CV–joint boot is to be replaced, continue with the procedure.
11. On the right side halfshafts, pry up the rubber damper retaining band locking clip using a suitable tool. Remove the retaining band using pliers and remove the rubber damper from the shaft.

12. Using a suitable tool, pry up the outer CV–boot band locking tabs. Remove the bands with pliers.
13. Slide the outer CV–boot off the shaft.

➡ **When replacing a damaged boot, check the grease for contamination by rubbing it between 2 fingers. Any gritty feeling indicates a contaminated CV–joint. A contaminated inner CV–joint must be completely disassembled, cleaned and inspected. The outer CV–joint is not serviceable and should be replaced as an assembly, if necessary. If the grease is not contaminated and the CV–joint has been operating satisfactorily, replace only the boot and add the required lubricant.**

**To install:**

14. Cover the halfshaft splines with tape and install the outer CV–joint boot.

➡ **The outer and inner CV–joint boots are different. Failure to correctly install the boot on the proper end of the halfshaft could lead to premature boot and/or CV–joint wear.**

15. Fill the outer CV–joint housing with the proper type and amount of lubricant.
16. Position the CV–boot. Make sure the boot is fully seated in the shaft grooves and the CV–joint housing.
17. Insert a suitable tool between the boot and the CV–joint housing to allow trapped air to escape.
18. Position new bands on the outer CV–joint boot.

➡ **Always use new bands. The bands should be mounted in the direction opposite the forward revolving direction of the halfshaft.**

19. Wrap the bands around the boot in a clockwise direction, pull them tight with pliers and bend the locking tabs to secure the bands in position.

20. Work the CV–joint through it's full range of travel at various angles. The CV–joint should flex, extend and compress smoothly.

21. On the right side halfshafts, position the rubber damper on the halfshaft. Position a new band on the damper. Pull the band tight with pliers and fold it back. Lock the end of the band by bending the locking clip.

22. Position the inner CV–joint boot on the halfshaft.

23. Align the marks on the tripod bearing and the halfshaft. Install the tripod bearing on the halfshaft. If necessary, using a soft–faced mallet, tap the bearing into place.

24. Install the snapring.

25. Fill the inner CV–joint housing with the proper type and amount of lubricant. Coat the tripod bearing with the same lubricant.

26. Position the inner CV–joint housing over the tripod bearing, making sure to align the alignment marks. Install the retainer ring in the CV–joint housing.

27. Slide the inner CV–boot in place. Make sure the boot is fully seated in the shaft grooves and in the housing.

28. Insert a suitable tool between the boot and the CV–joint housing to allow trapped air to escape.

29. Position new bands on the inner CV–joint boot.

➡ **Always use new bands. The bands should be mounted in the direction opposite the forward revolving direction of the halfshaft.**

30. Wrap the bands around the boot in a clockwise direction, pull them tight with pliers and bend the locking tabs to secure the bands in position.

31. Work the CV–joint through it's full range of travel at various angles. The CV–joint should flex, extend and compress smoothly.

32. Measure the length of the assembled halfshaft. If the length is not as specified, check the CV–joints for freedom of movement to ensure that it was assembled correctly. Repair or replace any components as necessary.

## Rear Driveshaft

The All Wheel Drive (AWD) models of the Tempo/Topaz utilize a rear driveshaft to deliver power from the transaxle to the transfer case which is mounted at the rear of the vehicle and used to drive the rear halfshafts. Serviceable U–joints are located at either end of the rear driveshaft.

### REMOVAL & INSTALLATION

1. Raise and support the rear of the vehicle safely using jackstands.

2. Matchmark the driveshaft U–joints to the companion flanges at either end.

3. Loosen the nuts and bolts holding the retaining straps to the companion flanges.

4. Remove the retaining straps from one of the companion flanges, then support the driveshaft to prevent damage to the joint on the opposite end.

5. Remove the retaining straps from the other end of the driveshaft, then remove the shaft from the vehicle.

**To install:**

6. Align the matchmarks made earlier, then install the driveshaft to one of the companion flanges. Loosely install the retaining straps using the fasteners.

### ✳✳WARNING

**Do NOT allow the shaft to hang freely from one U–joint, or the joint may become damaged.**

7. Align the matchmarks on the other end of the shaft and loosely install the retaining straps.

8. Verify proper positioning, then tighten the fasteners securing the retaining straps to the companion flanges.

9. Remove the jackstands and carefully lower the vehicle.

### U–JOINT OVERHAUL

➡ **Before starting this procedure, purchase a new set of U–joint bearings.**

1. Remove the driveshaft from the vehicle.

2. Place the driveshaft in a vise with the U–joint needing work closet to the vise.

3. Using a pair of snapring pliers, remove the 2 snaprings from the U–joint

➡ **Wear protective eyewear to shield your eyes in the event a snapring comes loose during the removal or installation.**

4. Use U–joint removal and installation tool T74P–4635–C or equivalent to press out the bearings connecting the U–joint to the driveshaft. Once the bearings are pressed out, the assembly can be separated from the driveshaft, then the bearings can be removed and discarded.

5. Remove the remaining bearing from the U–joint assembly and discard.

6. With the bearing removed, clean the remaining assembly and allow to dry.

**To install:**

7. Install the U–joint assembly to the driveshaft with 2 new bearings at either end.

8. Use the U–joint removal and installation tool T74P–4635–C or equivalent to press the bearing into place.

9. Install a snapring at either end of the U–joint assembly to secure the bearing in place.

10. Position the remaining bearings on the U–joint assembly, and hold in position.

11. While holding the bearings in place to prevent them from falling off, remove the driveshaft from the vise and install on the vehicle.

### INSPECTION

With the components of the driveshaft removed, inspect each for signs of damage or excessive wear. If the driveshaft is heavily dented, bent or shows signs of extremely damage, purchase another unit. Although this is a rare occurrence, because the driveshaft is open to the elements on the road, damage is possible.

## DIAGNOSIS AND TESTING MANUAL TRANSAXLE (MTX)

### TRANSAXLE

| CONDITION | POSSIBLE SOURCE | ACTION |
|---|---|---|
| • Clicking Noise in Reverse Gear | • Damaged or rough gears.<br><br>• Damaged linkage preventing complete gear travel. | • Replace damaged gears.<br><br>• Check for damaged or misaligned shift linkage or other causes of shift linkage travel restrictions. |
| • Gear Clash into Reverse | • Owner not familiar with manual transmission shift techniques.<br><br><br><br>• Damaged linkage preventing complete gear travel. | • Instruct customer to refer to Owner's Guide on proper shifting and the time-lapse required before a shift into reverse.<br><br>• Check for damaged or misaligned shift linkage or other causes of shift linkage bind. |
| • Gears Clash When Shifting From One Forward Gear to Another | • Improper clutch disengagement.<br><br>• Clutch disc installed improperly with damper springs toward flywheel.<br><br>• Worn or damaged shift forks, synchro-teeth (usually high mileage phenomenon). | <br><br><br><br>• Check for damage, and service or replace as required. |
| • Leaks | • Excessive amount of lubrication transaxle — wrong type.<br><br>• Other components leaking.<br><br>• False report. (Do not assume that lube on lower case surfaces is from gasket material leakage or seals).<br><br>• Worn or damaged internal components.<br><br><br><br><br><br>• Slight mist from vent. | • Check lube level and type. Fill to bottom of filler plug opening.<br><br>• Identify leaking fluid at engine, power steering, or transaxle.<br><br>• Remove all traces of lube on exposed transaxle surfaces. Operate transaxle and inspect for new leakage.<br><br>• Remove transaxle clutch housing lower dust cover and inspect for lube inside housing. Inspect for leaks at the shift lever shaft seal, differential seals and input shift shaft seal. Service as required.<br><br>• Normal condition that does not require service. If dripping, check lubricant level. |
| • Locked in One Gear — it cannot be shifted out of that gear | • Damaged external shift mechanism.<br><br>• Internal shift components worn or damaged.<br><br><br><br><br><br><br>• Synchronizer damaged by burrs which prevent sliding action. | • Check external shift mechanism for damage. Service or replace as required.<br><br>• Disconnect external shift mechanism and verify problem by trying to shift input shift rail. Remove transaxle. Inspect the problem gear, shift rails, and fork and synchronizer assemblies for wear or damage, service or replace as required.<br><br>• Replace synchronizer assembly. |
| • Noise in Neutral | • Neutral rollover rattle. | |

**TRANSAXLE — Continued**

| CONDITION | POSSIBLE SOURCE | ACTION |
|---|---|---|
| • Noisy in forward gears | • Low lubricant level. | • Fill to bottom of filler plug opening with proper lubricant (ATF). Type F. |
| | • Contact between engine/transaxle and chassis. | • Check for contact or for broken engine motor mounts. |
| | • Transaxle to engine block bolts loose. | • Tighten to specification. |
| | • Worn or damaged input/output bearings. Worn or damaged gear teeth (usually high mileage phenomenon). | • Remove transaxle. Inspect bearings and gear teeth for wear or damage. Replace parts as required. |
| | • Gear rattle. | |
| • Shifts hard | • Improper clutch disengagement. | |
| | • External shift mechanism binding. | |
| | • Clutch disc installed improperly with damper springs toward flywheel. | |
| | • Internal damage to synchronizers or shift mechanism. | • Check for damage to internal components. |
| | • Incorrect lubricant. | • Verify that ATF type lube is present. Do not use gear lube or hypoid type lubricants. |
| | • Sticking blocker ring. | |
| • Walks out of gear | • Damaged linkage preventing complete travel into gear. | • Check for damaged shift mechanism. |
| | • Floor shift stiff or improperly installed boot. | • Verify jumpout with boot removed, replace boot if necessary. |
| | • Floor shift interference between shift handle and console. | • Adjust console to eliminate interference. |
| | • Broken/loose engine mounts. | • Check for broken or loose engine mounts and service as required. |
| | • Loose shift mechanism stabilizer bar. | • Check stabilizer bar attaching bolt and torque to specification. |
| | • Worn or damaged internal components. | • Check shift forks, shift rails and shift rail detent system for wear or damage, synchronizer sliding sleeve and gear clutching teeth for wear or damage. Repair or replace as required. |
| | • Bent top gear locknut switch actuator. | • With shift lever in fourth gear, check actuator position with shift rod. Actuator should be positioned at a 90 degree angle to shift rod. Bend actuator to proper position, if required. |

86707301

**TRANSAXLE — Continued**

| CONDITION | POSSIBLE SOURCE | ACTION |
|---|---|---|
| • Will not shift into one gear — all other gears OK | • Damaged external shift mechanism. | • Check for damaged shift mechanism. Service or replace as necessary. |
| | • Floor shift. Interference between shift handle and console or floor cut out. | • Adjust console or cut out floor pan to eliminate interference. |
| | • Restricted travel of internal shift components. | • Disconnect external shift mechanism and shift the input shift rail through the gears to verify problem. Remove transaxle. Inspect fork system, synchronizer system and gear clutch teeth for restricted travel. Service or replace as required. |
| • Will not shift into reverse | • Damaged external shift mechanism. | • Check for damaged external shift mechanism. Remove shift mechanism at input shift rail and try shifting into reverse at the rail. |
| | • Worn or damaged internal components. | • Remove transaxle. Check for damaged reverse gear train, misaligned reverse relay lever, shift rail and fork system. Check the gear clutching teeth and synchronizer system for restricted travel or damage. Service or replace as required. |
| | • Normal blockout due to position of non-synchronized reverse gear components.<br>**NOTE:** This condition may occur approximately 10 percent of the time. | • Condition is considered normal and requires "double-clutching" to engage into reverse. |

**SHIFT LINKAGE**

| CONDITION | POSSIBLE SOURCE | ACTION |
|---|---|---|
| • Binding, sticking shift feel — difficult to find or engage gears, high shift efforts | • Worn, broken, missing bushings in shift rod U-joint. | • Replace shift rod. |
| | • Bent shift rod, U-joint or multi-piece bracket. | • Replace shift rod. |
| | • Bent or broken stabilizer. | • Replace support assembly. |
| | • Worn, missing stabilizer bushing. | • Replace stabilizer bushing. |
| | • Bolts holding control assembly to body J-nuts missing or loose. | • Tighten or replace bolts. |
| | • Bolt holding stabilizer bar to transaxle case missing or loose. | • Tighten or replace bolt. |
| | • Body J-nuts missing or broken. | • Replace J-nuts on seat track bracket. |
| | • Bolt, nut, and clamp washers loose at shift rod to transaxle connection. | • Tighten or replace bolt, nut and clamp washers. |
| | • Plastic control housing cracked or broken. | • Replace plastic control housing. |
| | • Plastic pivot housing on shift lever broken, cracked. | • Replace shift lever. |
| | • Shift lever pivot balls worn or loose. | • Replace shift lever. |
| | • Mounting insulators torn. | • Replace support assembly. |
| | • Shift lever loose on support assembly. | • Tighten or replace self-tapping screws. |
| | • Shift lever pivot balls worn, loose, or broken. | • Replace shift lever assembly. |
| | • Shift rod sealing boot torn. | • Replace shift rod assembly. |
| • Excessive noise, rattles, buzz or tizz | • Worn, broken, missing bushings in shift rod U-joint. | • Replace shift rod assembly. |
| | • Worn pivot balls on shift lever. | • Replace shift lever assembly. |
| | • Loose bolt, nut and clamp washers at shift rod to transaxle connection. | • Tighten or replace bolt, nut, and clamp washers. |
| | • Loose shift lever assembly. | • Tighten or replace self-tapping screws. |
| | • Loose control housing. | • Tighten self-tapping screws attaching housing to support assembly. |
| | • Loose control assembly. | • Tighten or replace bolts holding control assembly to body J-nuts. |
| | • Loose shift knob causes tizz. | • Drive knob further onto shift lever with rubber mallet. If still loose, replace boot/knob assembly. |

SHIFT LINKAGE — Continued

| CONDITION | POSSIBLE SOURCE | ACTION |
|---|---|---|
| • Excessive Noise, Rattles, Buzz or Tizz (Continued) | • Mounting insulators torn. | • Replace support assembly. |
| | • Inner shift boot torn, split. | • Replace inner sealing boot. |
| | • Stabilizer bar bushing worn or split. | • Replace stabilizer bushing. |
| | • Pivot balls on shift lever chipped, cracked. | • Replace shift lever assembly. |
| | • Crimp on shift lever improperly placed allows loose pivot ball in pivot housing. | • Replace shift lever. |
| • Shifter is Inoperative — cannot shift gears | • Bolt, nut and clamp washers loose at shift rod to transaxle connection. | • Tighten or replace bolt, nut and clamp washers. |
| | • Shifter attachment to body weld bolts loose. | • Replace or tighten bolts on body J-nuts. |
| | • Shift lever loose on stabilizer mounting bracket. | • Replace or tighten self-tapping bolts. |
| | • Shift rod broken or bent. | • Replace shift rod. |
| | • Stabilizer bar is bent. | • Replace support assembly. |
| | • Mounting insulators torn or loose. | • Replace support assembly. |
| | • Crimp holding pivot ball tight in pivot housing inadequate. | • Replace shift lever assembly. |
| • Shift Lever Feels Sloppy or Loose | • Nuts holding control assemby to body weld bolts missing or loose. | • Tighten or replace nuts. |
| | • Body J-nuts missing or broken. | • Replace J-nuts on seat track bracket. |
| | • Worn, broken or missing anti-tizz bushing. | • Replace anti-tizz bushing in shift rod assembly. |
| | • Bolt holding stabilizer bar to transaxle case missing or loose. | • Tighten or replace bolt. |
| | • Bolt, nut and clamp washers loose at shift rod to transaxle connection. | • Tighten or replace bolt, nut and clamp washers. |
| | • Stabilizer bar broken. | • Replace mounting bracket and stabilizer assembly. |
| | • Plastic control housing cracked or broken. | • Replace plastic control housing. |
| | • Mounting insulators torn or improperly riveted. | • Replace mounting bracket and stabilizer assembly. |
| | • Shift lever attaching screw loose or missing. | • Tighten or replace shift lever attaching screws. |
| | • Shift lever pivot balls worn of loose. | • Replace shift lever assembly. |
| | • Shift knob is loose on shift lever. | • Drive knob further onto shift lever with rubber mallet. If still loose, replace boot/knob assembly. |

CONSIDER THE FOLLOWING FACTORS WHEN DIAGNOSING BEARING CONDITION

1. GENERAL CONDITION OF ALL PARTS DURING DISASSEMBLY AND INSPECTION.

2. CLASSIFY THE PROBLEM WITH THE AID OF THE ILLUSTRATION.

3. DETERMINE THE CAUSE.

4. MAKE ALL SERVICES FOLLOWING RECOMMENDED PROCEDURES.

**GOOD BEARING**

**BENT CAGE**

CAGE DAMAGE DUE TO IMPROPER HANDLING OR TOOL USAGE.

REPLACE BEARING.

**BENT CAGE**

CAGE DAMAGE DUE TO IMPROPER HANDLING OR TOOL USAGE.

REPLACE BEARING.

**GALLING**

METAL SMEARS ON ROLLER ENDS DUE TO OVERHEAT, LUBRICANT PROBLEM OR OVERLOAD.

REPLACE BEARING — CHECK SEALS AND CHECK FOR PROPER LUBRICATION.

**CRACKED INNER RACE**

RACE CRACKED DUE TO IMPROPER FIT, COCKING, OR POOR BEARING SEATS.

**ETCHING**

BEARING SURFACES APPEAR GRAY OR GRAYISH BLACK IN COLOR WITH RELATED ETCHING AWAY OF MATERAIL USUALLY AT ROLLER SPACING.

REPLACE BEARINGS — CHECK SEALS AND CHECK FOR PROPER LUBRICATION.

**BRINELLING**

SURFACE INDENTATIONS IN RACEWAY CAUSED BY ROLLERS EITHER UNDER IMPACT LOADING OR VIBRATION WHILE THE BEARING IS NOT ROTATING.

REPLACE BEARING IF ROUGH OR NOISY.

**HEAT DISCOLORATION**

HEAT DISCOLORATION IS DARK BLUE RESULTING FROM OVERLOAD OR NO LUBRICANT (YELLOW OR BROWN COLOR IS NORMAL).

EXCESSIVE HEAT CAN CAUSE SOFTENING OF RACES OR ROLLERS.

TO CHECK FOR LOSS OF TEMPER ON RACES OR ROLLERS A SIMPLE FILE TEST MAY BE MADE. A FILE DRAWN OVER A TEMPERED PART WILL GRAB AND CUT METAL, WHEREAS, A FILE DRAWN OVER A HARD PART WILL GLIDE READILY WITH NO METAL CUTTING.

REPLACE BEARINGS IF OVER HEATING DAMAGE IS INDICATED. CHECK SEALS AND OTHER PARTS.

**FATIGUE SPALLING**

FLAKING OF SURFACE METAL RESULTING FROM FATIGUE.

REPLACE BEARING — CLEAN ALL RELATED PARTS.

86707310

## Troubleshooting the Manual Transmission

| Problem | Cause | Solution |
|---|---|---|
| Transmission shifts hard | • Clutch adjustment incorrect<br>• Clutch linkage or cable binding<br>• Shift rail binding | • Adjust clutch.<br>• Lubricate or repair as necessary<br>• Check for mispositioned selector arm roll pin, loose cover bolts, worn shift rail bores, worn shift rail, distorted oil seal, or extension housing not aligned with case. Repair as necessary. |
| | • Internal bind in transmission caused by shift forks, selector plates, or synchronizer assemblies<br>• Clutch housing misalignment<br><br>• Incorrect lubricant<br>• Block rings and/or cone seats worn | • Remove, dissemble and inspect transmission. Replace worn or damaged components as necessary.<br>• Check runout at rear face of clutch housing<br>• Drain and refill transmission<br>• Blocking ring to gear clutch tooth face clearance must be 0.030 inch or greater. If clearance is correct it may still be necessary to inspect blocking rings and cone seats for excessive wear. Repair as necessary. |
| Gear clash when shifting from one gear to another | • Clutch adjustment incorrect<br>• Clutch linkage or cable binding<br>• Clutch housing misalignment<br><br>• Lubricant level low or incorrect lubricant<br><br>• Gearshift components, or synchronizer assemblies worn or damaged | • Adjust clutch<br>• Lubricate or repair as necessary<br>• Check runout at rear of clutch housing<br>• Drain and refill transmission and check for lubricant leaks if level was low. Repair as necessary.<br>• Remove, disassemble and inspect transmission. Replace worn or damaged components as necessary. |
| Transmission noisy | • Lubricant level low or incorrect lubricant<br><br><br>• Clutch housing-to-engine, or transmission-to-clutch housing bolts loose<br>• Dirt, chips, foreign material in transmission<br>• Gearshift mechanism, transmission gears, or bearing components worn or damaged<br>• Clutch housing misalignment | • Drain and refill transmission. If lubricant level was low, check for leaks and repair as necessary.<br>• Check and correct bolt torque as necessary<br>• Drain, flush, and refill transmission<br>• Remove, disassemble and inspec transmission. Replace worn or damaged components as necessary.<br>• Check runout at rear face of clutch housing |

## Troubleshooting the Manual Transmission

| Problem | Cause | Solution |
|---|---|---|
| Jumps out of gear | • Clutch housing misalignment | • Check runout at rear face of clutch housing |
| | • Gearshift lever loose | • Check lever for worn fork. Tighten loose attaching bolts. |
| | • Offset lever nylon insert worn or lever attaching nut loose | • Remove gearshift lever and check for loose offset lever nut or worn insert. Repair or replace as necessary. |
| | • Gearshift mechanism, shift forks, selector plates, interlock plate, selector arm, shift rail, detent plugs, springs or shift cover worn or damaged | • Remove, disassemble and inspect transmission cover assembly. Replace worn or damaged components as necessary. |
| | • Clutch shaft or roller bearings worn or damaged | • Replace clutch shaft or roller bearings as necessary |
| Jumps out of gear (cont.) | • Gear teeth worn or tapered, synchronizer assemblies worn or damaged, excessive end play caused by worn thrust washers or output shaft gears | • Remove, disassemble, and inspect transmission. Replace worn or damaged components as necessary. |
| | • Pilot bushing worn | • Replace pilot bushing |
| Will not shift into one gear | • Gearshift selector plates, interlock plate, or selector arm, worn, damaged, or incorrectly assembled | • Remove, disassemble, and inspect transmission cover assembly. Repair or replace components as necessary. |
| | • Shift rail detent plunger worn, spring broken, or plug loose | • Tighten plug or replace worn or damaged components as necessary |
| | • Gearshift lever worn or damaged | • Replace gearshift lever |
| | • Synchronizer sleeves or hubs, damaged or worn | • Remove, disassemble and inspect transmission. Replace worn or damaged components. |
| Locked in one gear—cannot be shifted out | • Shift rail(s) worn or broken, shifter fork bent, setscrew loose, center detent plug missing or worn | • Inspect and replace worn or damaged parts |
| | • Broken gear teeth on countershaft gear, clutch shaft, or reverse idler gear | • Inspect and replace damaged part |
| | Gearshift lever broken or worn, shift mechanism in cover incorrectly assembled or broken, worn damaged gear train components | • Disassemble transmission. Replace damaged parts or assemble correctly. |

86707316

## Troubleshooting Basic Clutch Problems

| Problem | Cause |
|---|---|
| Excessive clutch noise | Throwout bearing noises are more audible at the lower end of pedal travel. The usual causes are:<br>· Riding the clutch<br>· Too little pedal free-play<br>· Lack of bearing lubrication<br>A bad clutch shaft pilot bearing will make a high pitched squeal, when the clutch is disengaged and the transmission is in gear or within the first 2″ of pedal travel. The bearing must be replaced.<br>Noise from the clutch linkage is a clicking or snapping that can be heard or felt as the pedal is moved completely up or down. This usually requires lubrication.<br>Transmitted engine noises are amplified by the clutch housing and heard in the passenger compartment. They are usually the result of insufficient pedal free-play and can be changed by manipulating the clutch pedal. |
| Clutch slips (the car does not move as it should when the clutch is engaged) | This is usually most noticeable when pulling away from a standing start. A severe test is to start the engine, apply the brakes, shift into high gear and SLOWLY release the clutch pedal. A healthy clutch will stall the engine. If it slips it may be due to:<br>· A worn pressure plate or clutch plate<br>· Oil soaked clutch plate<br>· Insufficient pedal free-play |
| Clutch drags or fails to release | The clutch disc and some transmission gears spin briefly after clutch disengagement. Under normal conditions in average temperatures, 3 seconds is maximum spin-time. Failure to release properly can be caused by:<br>· Too light transmission lubricant or low lubricant level<br>· Improperly adjusted clutch linkage |
| Low clutch life | Low clutch life is usually a result of poor driving habits or heavy duty use. Riding the clutch, pulling heavy loads, holding the car on a grade with the clutch instead of the brakes and rapid clutch engagement all contribute to low clutch life. |

## Troubleshooting Basic Automatic Transmission Problems

| Problem | Cause | Solution |
|---|---|---|
| Fluid leakage | • Defective pan gasket | • Replace gasket or tighten pan bolts |
| | • Loose filler tube | • Tighten tube nut |
| | • Loose extension housing to transmission case | • Tighten bolts |
| | • Converter housing area leakage | • Have transmission checked professionally |
| Fluid flows out the oil filler tube | • High fluid level | • Check and correct fluid level |
| | • Breather vent clogged | • Open breather vent |
| | • Clogged oil filter or screen | • Replace filter or clean screen (change fluid also) |
| | • Internal fluid leakage | • Have transmission checked professionally |
| Transmission overheats (this is usually accompanied by a strong burned odor to the fluid) | • Low fluid level | • Check and correct fluid level |
| | • Fluid cooler lines clogged | • Drain and refill transmission. If this doesn't cure the problem, have cooler lines cleared or replaced. |
| | • Heavy pulling or hauling with insufficient cooling | • Install a transmission oil cooler |
| | • Faulty oil pump, internal slippage | • Have transmission checked professionally |
| Buzzing or whining noise | • Low fluid level | • Check and correct fluid level |
| | • Defective torque converter, scored gears | • Have transmission checked professionally |
| No forward or reverse gears or slippage in one or more gears | • Low fluid level | • Check and correct fluid level |
| | • Defective vacuum or linkage controls, internal clutch or band failure | • Have unit checked professionally |
| Delayed or erratic shift | • Low fluid level | • Check and correct fluid level |
| | • Broken vacuum lines | • Repair or replace lines |
| | • Internal malfunction | • Have transmission checked professionally |

## Lockup Torque Converter Service Diagnosis

| Problem | Cause | Solution |
|---|---|---|
| No lockup | • Faulty oil pump<br>• Sticking governor valve<br>• Valve body malfunction<br>  (a) Stuck switch valve<br>  (b) Stuck lockup valve<br>  (c) Stuck fail-safe valve<br>• Failed locking clutch<br>• Leaking turbine hub seal<br>• Faulty input shaft or seal ring | • Replace oil pump<br>• Repair or replace as necessary<br>• Repair or replace valve body or its internal components as necessary<br><br><br>• Replace torque converter<br>• Replace torque converter<br>• Repair or replace as necessary |
| Will not unlock | • Sticking governor valve<br>• Valve body malfunction<br>  (a) Stuck switch valve<br>  (b) Stuck lockup valve<br>  (c) Stuck fail-safe valve | • Repair or replace as necessary<br>• Repair or replace valve body or its internal components as necessary |
| Stays locked up at too low a speed in direct | • Sticking governor valve<br>• Valve body malfunction<br>  (a) Stuck switch valve<br>  (b) Stuck lockup valve<br>  (c) Stuck fail-safe valve | • Repair or replace as necessary<br>• Repair or replace valve body or its internal components as necessary |
| Locks up or drags in low or second | • Faulty oil pump<br>• Valve body malfunction<br>  (a) Stuck switch valve<br>  (b) Stuck fail-safe valve | • Replace oil pump<br>• Repair or replace valve body or its internal components as necessary |
| Sluggish or stalls in reverse | • Faulty oil pump<br>• Plugged cooler, cooler lines or fittings<br>• Valve body malfunction<br>  (a) Stuck switch valve<br>  (b) Faulty input shaft or seal ring | • Replace oil pump as necessary<br>• Flush or replace cooler and flush lines and fittings<br>• Repair or replace valve body or its internal components as necessary |
| Loud chatter during lockup engagement (cold) | • Faulty torque converter<br>• Failed locking clutch<br>• Leaking turbine hub seal | • Replace torque converter<br>• Replace torque converter<br>• Replace torque converter |
| Vibration or shudder during lockup engagement | • Faulty oil pump<br><br>• Valve body malfunction<br><br><br>• Faulty torque converter<br>• Engine needs tune-up | • Repair or replace oil pump as necessary<br>• Repair or replace valve body or its internal components as necessary<br>• Replace torque converter<br>• Tune engine |
| Vibration after lockup engagement | • Faulty torque converter<br>• Exhaust system strikes underbody<br>• Engine needs tune-up<br>• Throttle linkage misadjusted | • Replace torque converter<br>• Align exhaust system<br>• Tune engine<br>• Adjust throttle linkage |

## Lockup Torque Converter Service Diagnosis

| Problem | Cause | Solution |
|---|---|---|
| Vibration when revved in neutral Overheating: oil blows out of dip stick tube or pump seal | • Torque converter out of balance<br>• Plugged cooler, cooler lines or fittings<br>• Stuck switch valve | • Replace torque converter<br>• Flush or replace cooler and flush lines and fittings<br>• Repair switch valve in valve body or replace valve body |
| Shudder after lockup engagement | • Faulty oil pump<br>• Plugged cooler, cooler lines or fittings<br>• Valve body malfunction | • Replace oil pump<br>• Flush or replace cooler and flush lines and fittings<br>• Repair or replace valve body or its internal components as necessary |
| | • Faulty torque converter<br>• Fail locking clutch<br>• Exhaust system strikes underbody<br>• Engine needs tune-up<br>• Throttle linkage misadjusted | • Replace torque converter<br>• Replace torque converter<br>• Align exhaust system<br>• Tune engine<br>• Adjust throttle linkage |

86707330

## Transmission Fluid Indications

The appearance and odor of the transmission fluid can give valuable clues to the overall condition of the transmission. Always note the appearance of the fluid when you check the fluid level or change the fluid. Rub a small amount of fluid between your fingers to feel for grit and smell the fluid on the dipstick.

| If the fluid appears: | It indicates: |
|---|---|
| Clear and red colored | • Normal operation |
| Discolored (extremely dark red or brownish) or smells burned | • Band or clutch pack failure, usually caused by an overheated transmission. Hauling very heavy loads with insufficient power or failure to change the fluid, often result in overheating.<br>Do not confuse this appearance with newer fluids that have a darker red color and a strong odor (though not a burned odor). |
| Foamy or aerated (light in color and full of bubbles) | • The level is too high (gear train is churning oil)<br>• An internal air leak (air is mixing with the fluid). Have the transmission checked professionally. |
| Solid residue in the fluid | • Defective bands, clutch pack or bearings. Bits of band material or metal abrasives are clinging to the dipstick. Have the transmission checked professionally. |
| Varnish coating on the dipstick | • The transmission fluid is overheating |

86707335

## AWD — VACUUM DIAGNOSIS

| CONDITION | POSSIBLE SOURCE | ACTION |
|---|---|---|
| Insufficient vacuum | • Damaged or clogged manifold fitting. | • Service or replace fitting. |
| | • Damaged hoses. | • Service as required. |
| | • Damaged or worn check valve. | • Replace/service. |
| Reservoir not maintaining vacuum | • Worn or damaged reservoir. | • Check for leak by installing a vacuum gauge at rubber tee (input to dual solenoids). Gauge should rear 54-67 kPa (16-20 inches) vacuum. |
| Dual solenoid assembly inoperative | • Damaged or worn solenoid assembly. | • Check for vacuum at solenoids as outlined. |
| No AWD engagement | • Insufficient vacuum at vacuum servo. | • Disconnect vacuum harness at single to double connector and install a vacuum gauge. With engine running and AWD switch in proper position, check for vacuum. |
| | • Damaged or worn vacuum servo. | • Place transaxle in NEUTRAL. Raise vehicle on a hoist and disconnect vacuum harness at single to double connector. Install a hand vacuum pump onto red tube connector and block off black connector. Apply 54-67 kPa (16-20 inches) vacuum at servo end of harness. While rotating front wheels, note that rear wheels also rotate. If rear wheels do not rotate, replace vacuum servo. |

86707340

## AWD — ELECTRICAL DIAGNOSIS

| CONDITION | POSSIBLE SOURCE | ACTION |
|---|---|---|
| AWD system inoperative | • Blown fuse. | • Replace fuse. |
| | • Connector at fuse panel disengaged. | • Install connector firmly into fuse panel. |
| AWD switch indicator inoperative | • Loose connection at switch. | • Push connector firmly into switch. |
| | • Worn or damaged switch. | • Replace switch. |
| AWD relay inoperative | • Poor connection at relay. | • Check connection at relay. |
| | • Open or short in harness. | • Service or replace harness as necessary. |
| | • Worn or damaged relay. | • Replace relay. |
| AWD dual solenoids inoperative | • Open or short in harness. | • Service or replace harness. |

86707341

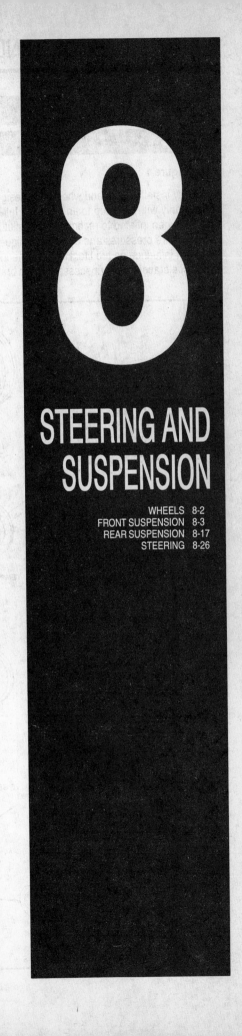

# 8

# STEERING AND SUSPENSION

# WHEELS

## Wheels

▶ **See Figure 1**

Factory installed tires and wheels are designed to operate satisfactorily with loads up to an including full–rated load capacity when inflated to recommended inflation pressures.

Correct tire pressures and driving techniques have an important influence on tire life. Heavy cornering, excessively rapid acceleration, and unnecessary sharp braking increases tire wear.

Wheels must must be replaced when they are bent, dented or heavily rusted, have air leaks or elongated bolt holes, and have excessive lateral or radial runout. Such conditions may cause high–speed vehicle vibration.

Replacement wheels must be equal to the original equipment wheels in load capacity, diameter, width, offset and mounting configuration. Improper wheels may affect wheel and bearing life, ground and tire clearance, or speedometer and odometer calibrations.

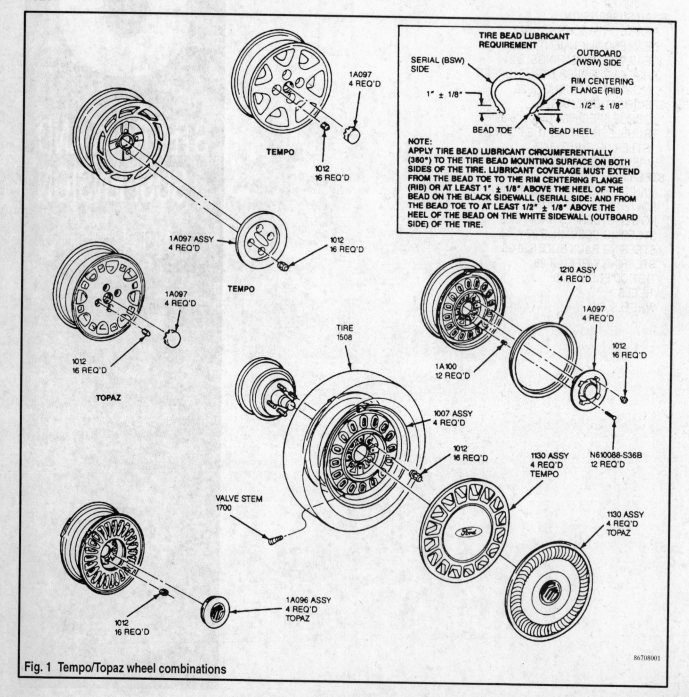

Fig. 1 Tempo/Topaz wheel combinations

## TIRE AND WHEEL BALANCE

#### ◆ See Figures 2 and 3

There are 2 types of wheel and tire balance:
- Static balance—is the equal distribution of weight around the wheel. This condition cause a bouncing action called "wheel tramp."
- Dynamic balance—is the equal distribution of weight on each side of the centerline so that when the tire spins there is no tendency for the assembly to move from side to side. This condition could cause wheel shimmy.

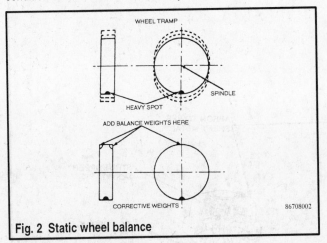

**Fig. 2  Static wheel balance**

## REMOVAL & INSTALLATION

1. Remove the hub cap nuts and hub cap, if equipped.
2. Raise and support the vehicle safely.

3. Remove the wheel lug nuts and pull the wheel off the hub or drum assembly.

**To install:**

4. Clean the dirt from the hub or drum mounting surface.
5. Place the wheel on the hub or drum assembly. Alternately tighten the nuts to specifications.
6. Lower the vehicle.
7. Install the hub cap nuts and hub cap, if equipped.
8. Before driving the vehicle, make sure the lug nuts are tight.

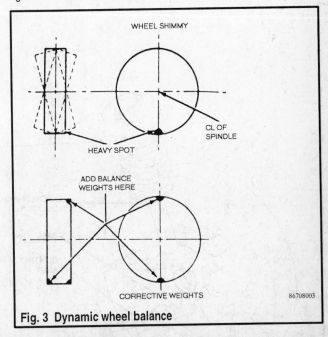

**Fig. 3  Dynamic wheel balance**

# FRONT SUSPENSION

#### ◆ See Figures 4 and 5

Your vehicle is equipped with a MacPherson strut front suspension. The strut acts upon a cast steering knuckle, which pivots on a ball joint mounted on a forged lower control arm. A stabilizer bar, which also acts as a locating link, is standard equipment. To maintain good directional stability, negative scrub radius is designed into the suspension geometry. This means that an imaginary line extended from the strut intersects the ground outside the tire patch. Caster and camber are preset and nonadjustable. The front suspension fittings are "lubed–for–life," no grease fittings are provided.

## Lower Control Arm

### REMOVAL & INSTALLATION

#### ◆ See Figures 6, 7, 8, 9, 10, 11, 12, 13 and 14

1. Raise and safely support the vehicle.
2. Remove nut from stabilizer bar end. Pull off large dished washer.
3. Remove lower control arm inner pivot nut and bolt.

4. Remove lower control arm ball joint pinch bolt. Using a suitable tool, slightly spread knuckle pinch joint and separate control arm from steering knuckle. A drift punch may be used to remove bolt.

➡ **Do not allow the steering knuckle/halfshaft to move outward. Over–extension of the tripod CV–joint could result in separation of internal parts, causing failure of the joint.**

5. Remove the nut and bolt from the rear portion of the control arm, where it attaches to the body frame.

➡ **Make sure steering column is in unlocked position. Do not use a hammer to separate ball joint from knuckle.**

6. Pry the control arm away from the frame member.
7. Remove the front sway bar mounts.
8. Lower the sway bar and sway bar assembly to the floor.
9. Pull the control arms away from the sway bar.

**To install:**

10. Grease the sway bar and bushing of the control arm where the bar slides into the arm. Push the control arm onto the sway bar.
11. Position the sway bar to the vehicle frame and secure the front sway bar bolts. Tighten bolts to 38–45 ft. lbs. (52–60 Nm).

12. Position the rear end of the control arm to the frame of the vehicle and install the nut and bolt securing the control arm to the fame. Tighten the bolts to 48–55 ft. lbs. (65–74 Nm).

13. Assemble lower control arm ball joint stud to the steering knuckle, ensuring that the ball stud groove is properly positioned, so the pinch bolt will slide through the retaining hole easily.

14. Insert a new pinch bolt and nut. Tighten to 38–45 ft. lbs. (52–60 Nm).

15. Insert stabilizer bar spacer into arm bushing.

16. Clean stabilizer bar threads to remove dirt and contamination.

17. Install and tighten sway bar nut to 48–55 ft. lbs. (65–74 Nm).

18. Lower vehicle.

19. Road test the vehicle.

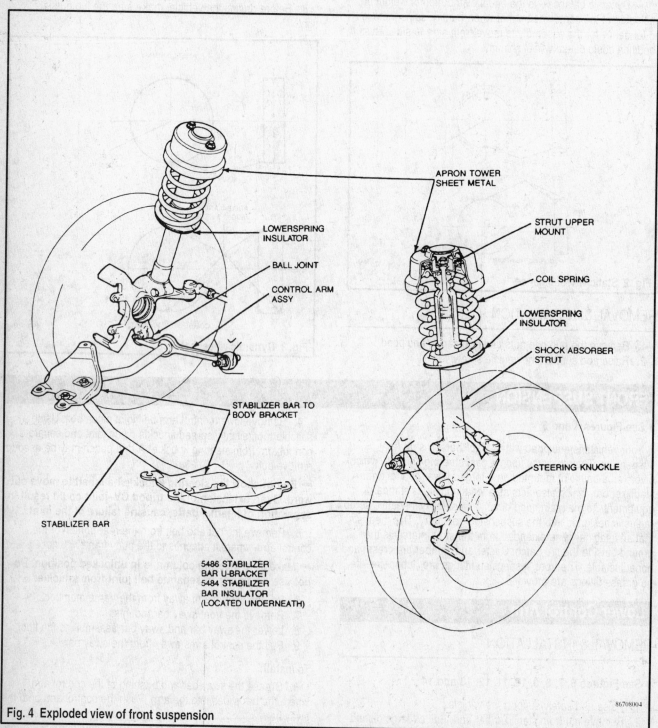

APRON TOWER SHEET METAL

STRUT UPPER MOUNT

COIL SPRING

LOWERSPRING INSULATOR

SHOCK ABSORBER STRUT

STEERING KNUCKLE

LOWERSPRING INSULATOR

BALL JOINT

CONTROL ARM ASSY

STABILIZER BAR TO BODY BRACKET

STABILIZER BAR

5486 STABILIZER BAR U-BRACKET
5484 STABILIZER BAR INSULATOR (LOCATED UNDERNEATH)

Fig. 4 Exploded view of front suspension

86708004

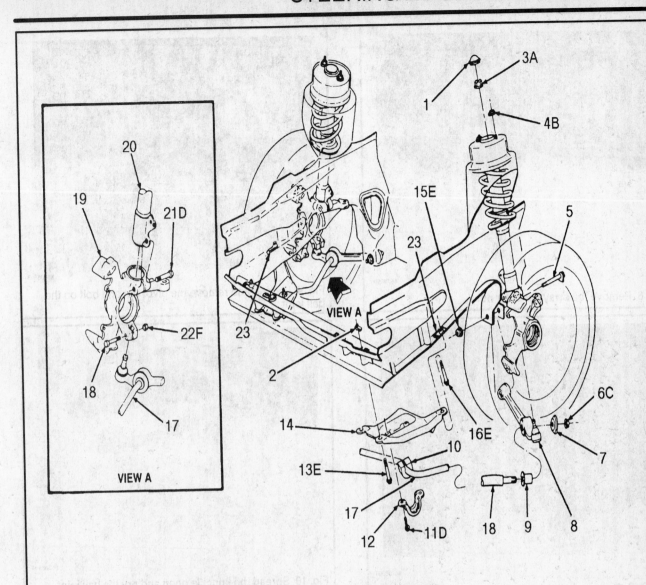

1  Cap (2 req'd)
2  Nut (4 req'd)
3A  Nut (2 req'd)
4B  Nut (4 req'd)
5  Bolt (2 req'd)
6C  Nut (2 req'd)
7  Washer (2 req'd)
8  Control arm
9  Spacer (2 req'd)
10  Bushing (2 req'd)
11D  Bolt (4 req'd)
12  U-bracket (2 req'd)
13E  Bolt (4 req'd)
14  Stabilizer bar bracket
15  Nut (2 req'd)

16E  Bolt (2 req'd)
17  Stabilizer bar
18  Bolt (2 req'd)
19  Knuckle assy
20  Strut assy
21D  Bolt (2 req'd)
22F  Nut (2 req'd)
23  Nut (2 req'd)
A  Tighten to 47-63 Nm (35-46 lb.ft.)
B  Tighten to 30-40 Nm (23-29 lb.ft.)
C  Tighten to 133-153 Nm (99-112 lb.ft.)
D  Tighten to 91-104 Nm (67-77 lb.ft.)
E  Tighten to 63-72 Nm (47-53 lb.ft.)
F  Tighten to 48-55 Nm (35-41 lb.ft.)

86708005

**Fig. 5  Front suspension hardware**

86708500

Fig. 6 Remove the sway bar outer nut

86708501

Fig. 7 Outer sway bar nut removed

86708502

Fig. 8 Remove the metal washer

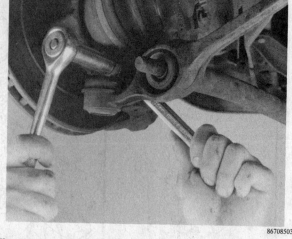

86708503

Fig. 9 Loosen and remove the pivot nut and bolt on the ball joint

86708504

Fig. 10 Spread the knuckle open and pry the ball joint away from the unit

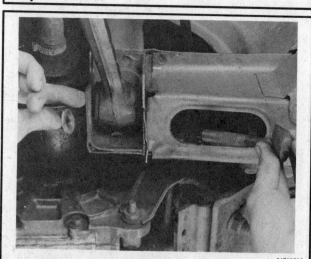

86708505

Fig. 11 Remove the nut and bolt from the rear portion of the control arm, where it mounts to the vehicle subframe

**Fig. 12 Pry the control arm out of its mount**

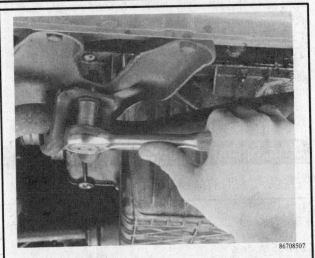

**Fig. 13 Remove the front sway bar mounts. They are located below the radiator area**

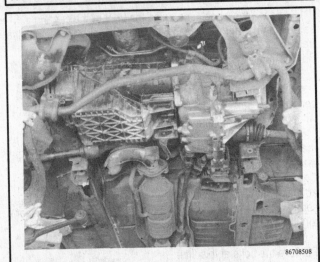

**Fig. 14 With help, lower the control arms and sway bar assembly**

## Lower Control Arm Inner Pivot Bushing

### REMOVAL & INSTALLATION

▶ See Figures 15, 16 and 17

➡ A special C–Clamp type removal/installation tool is required. See note under Stabilizer Bar for the Ford part number of this tool.

1. Raise the front of the car and safely support it on jackstands.
2. Remove the stabilizer bar–to–control arm nut and the dished washer.
3. Remove the inner control arm pivot nut and bolt. Pull the arm down from its mounting and away from the stabilizer bar.
4. Carefully cut away the retaining lip of the bushing. Use the special clamp type tool and remove the bushing.
5. Saturate the new bushing with vegetable oil and install the bushing using the special tool.
6. Position the lower control arm over the stabilizer bar and install into the inner body mounting using a new bolt and nut. Tighten the inner nut and bolt to 44–53 ft. lbs. (60–72 Nm). Tighten the stabilizer nut to 60–70 ft. lbs. (81–95 Nm). Be sure to install the dished washer ahead of the nut.

## Stabilizer Bar and/or Insulators

### REMOVAL & INSTALLATION

▶ See Figures 6, 7, 8, 13, 14, 18, 19 and 20

**1984–85 Models**

1. Raise the vehicle and support it safely. The tire and wheel assembly may be removed for convenience.
2. Remove the stabilizer bar insulator mounting bracket bolts, end nuts and washers. Remove the bar assembly.
3. Carefully cut the center mounting insulators from the stabilizers.

➡ A C–clamp type remover/installer tool is necessary to replace the control arm to stabilizer mounting bushings. The Ford part number of this tool is T81P5493A with T74P–3044–A1.

4. Remove the control arm inner pivot nut and bolt. Pull the arm down from the inner mounting and away from the stabilizer bar (if still mounted on car).
5. Remove the old bar to control arm insulator bushing with the clamp–type tool.

**To install:**

6. Use vegetable oil and saturate the new control arm bushing. Install the bushing with the clamp–type tool. Coat the center stabilizer bar bushings with a suitable lubricant. Slide the bushings into place. Install the inner control arm mounting. Tighten to 60–75 ft. lbs. (81–102 Nm).
7. Install the stabilizer bar using new insulator mounting bracket bolts. Tighten to 50–60 ft. lbs. (68–81 Nm). Install new

end nuts with the old dished washers. Tighten to 75–80 ft. lbs. (102–108 Nm).

8. Install the wheel if removed. Lower the vehicle.
9. Road test the vehicle.

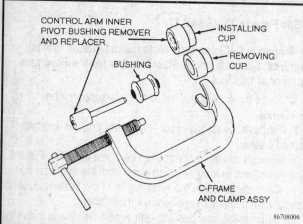

**Fig. 15 Bushing removal tool. Notice the different pieces for removing and installing the bushings**

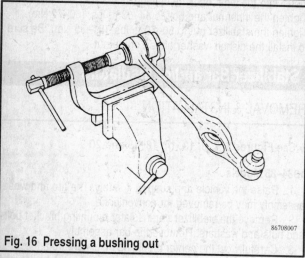

**Fig. 16 Pressing a bushing out**

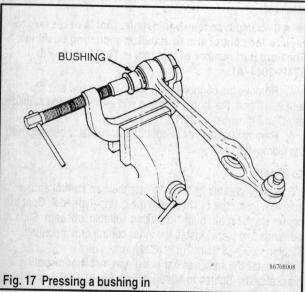

**Fig. 17 Pressing a bushing in**

### 1986–94 Models

1. Raise and safely support the vehicle.
2. Remove nut from stabilizer bar at each lower control arm and pull off large dished washer. Discard nuts.
3. Remove stabilizer bar insulator U–bracket bolts and U–brackets and remove stabilizer bar assembly. Discard bolts.

➡ **Stabilizer bar U–bracket insulators can be serviced without removing the stabilizer bar assembly.**

### To install:

4. Slide new insulators onto the stabilizer bar and position them in the approximate location.
5. Clean stabilizer bar threads to remove dirt and contamination.
6. Install spacers into the control arm bushings from forward side of control arm so washer end of spacer will seat against stabilizer bar machined shoulder and push mounting brackets over insulators.
7. Insert end of stabilizer bar into the lower control arms. Using new bolts, attach the stabilizer bar and the insulator U–brackets to the bracket assemblies. Hand start all 4 U–bracket bolts. Tighten all bolts halfway, then tighten bolts to 85–100 ft. lbs. (115–135 Nm).
8. Using new nuts and the original dished washers (dished side away from bushing), attach the stabilizer bar to the lower control arm. Tighten nuts to 98–115 ft. lbs. (132–156 Nm).
9. Lower vehicle.
10. Road test the vehicle.

## Strut, Spring and Upper Mount

### REMOVAL & INSTALLATION

◆ See Figure 21, 22, 23, 24, 25, 26 and 27

### 1984–85 Models

➡ **A coil spring compressor, Ford tool number T81P5310A, is required to compress the strut coil spring.**

1. Loosen the wheel lugs, raise the front of the car and safely support it on jackstands. Locate the jackstands under the frame jack pads, slightly behind the front wheels.
2. Remove the tire and wheel assembly.
3. Remove the brake line from the strut mounting bracket.
4. Place a floor jack or small hydraulic jack under the lower control arm. Raise the lower arm and strut as far as possible without raising the car.
5. Install the coil spring compressors. Place the top jaw of the compressors on the second coil from the top of the spring. Install the bottom jaw so that five coils will be gripped. Compress the spring evenly, from side to side, until there is about 1/8 in. (3mm) between any two spring coils. The coil spring must be compressed evenly. Always oil the compressor tool threads.
6. Two bolts secure the strut to the steering knuckle. Remove the bolts at this time.
7. Loosen, but do not remove, the top mount–to–strut tower nuts. Lower the jack supporting the lower control arm.
8. Using a soft faced hammer, tap on the steering knuckle assembly until the strut separates from the knuckle.

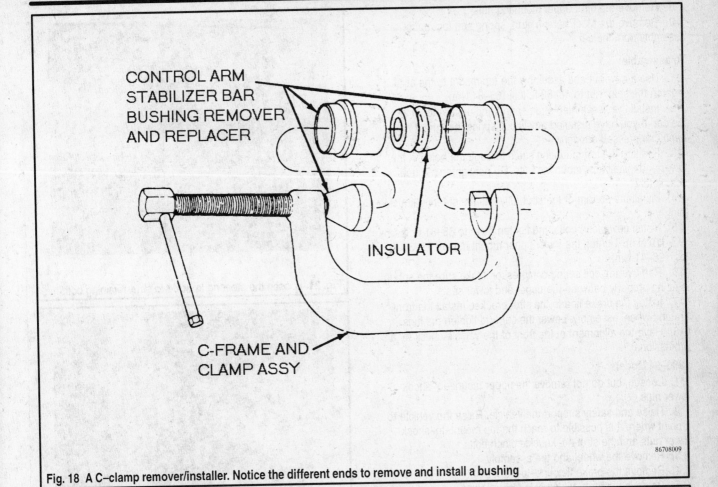

CONTROL ARM
STABILIZER BAR
BUSHING REMOVER
AND REPLACER

INSULATOR

C-FRAME AND
CLAMP ASSY

86708009

Fig. 18 A C–clamp remover/installer. Notice the different ends to remove and install a bushing

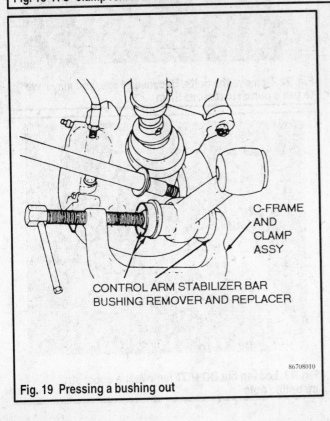

C-FRAME
AND
CLAMP
ASSY

CONTROL ARM STABILIZER BAR
BUSHING REMOVER AND REPLACER

86708010

Fig. 19 Pressing a bushing out

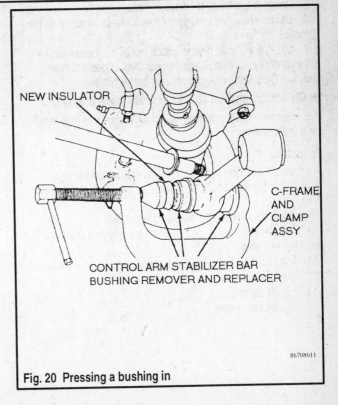

NEW INSULATOR

C-FRAME
AND
CLAMP
ASSY

CONTROL ARM STABILIZER BAR
BUSHING REMOVER AND REPLACER

86708011

Fig. 20 Pressing a bushing in

9. Remove the strut upper mounting nuts.

10. Remove the MacPherson strut, spring and top mount assembly from the car.

**To assemble:**

11. Use a new nut and assembly the top mount to the strut. Tighten the shaft nut to 48–62 ft. lbs. (65–84 Nm).

12. Install the assembled strut, spring and upper mount into the car. If you have installed a new coil spring, be sure it has been compressed enough.

13. Position the top mounting studs through the holes in the tower and install new mounting nuts. Do not tighten the nuts completely.

14. Install the bottom of the strut fully into the steering knuckle joint.

15. Install new pinch bolts and tighten them to 68–81 ft. lbs. (92–110 Nm). Tighten the tower upper mount nuts to 25–30 ft. lbs. (26–41 Nm).

16. Remove the coil spring compressor. Make sure the spring is fitting properly between the upper and lower seats.

17. Install the brake line to the strut bracket. Install the front tire and wheel assembly. Lower the car and tighten the lugs.

18. Have the alignment of the front of the vehicle check by a professional.

**1986–94 Models**

1. Loosen, but do not remove the upper mount–to–shock tower nuts.

2. Raise and safely support the vehicle. Raise the vehicle to a point where it is possible to reach the top mount–to–shock tower nuts and the strut–to–knuckle pinch bolts.

3. Remove the wheel and tire assembly.

4. Remove the brake flex line–to–strut bolt.

5. Remove the strut–to–knuckle pinch bolts.

6. Using a suitable tool, spread knuckle–to–strut pinch joint slightly.

7. Using a suitable prybar, place top of bar under fender apron and pry down on knuckle until strut separates from knuckle. Be careful not to pinch the brake hose.

➡ **Do not pry against caliper or brake hose bracket.**

8. Remove the top mount–to–shock tower nuts and remove strut from vehicle.

**To install:**

9. Install the strut assembly in vehicle. Install the top mount–to–shock tower nuts. Tighten to 25–30 ft. lbs. (37–41 Nm).

10. Slide strut mounting flange onto knuckle.

11. Install strut–to–knuckle pinch bolts. Tighten to 68–80 ft. lbs. (92–110 Nm).

12. Install brake flex line–to–strut bolt.

13. Install wheel and tire assembly.

14. Lower vehicle.

15. Check alignment.

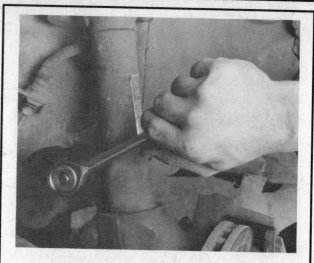

**Fig. 21 Loosen the steering knuckle to strut retaining bolts**

**Fig. 22 Remove the bolts. Because of age, you may have to use a punch to remove them**

**Fig. 23 Loosen but DO NOT remove the upper strut mounting nuts**

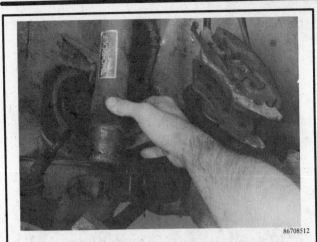

Fig. 24  Using a soft faced hammer, tap on the knuckle to separate the strut from the steering knuckle

Fig. 25  With the strut and knuckle separated, lower the jack, so the strut assembly can be removed

Fig. 26  While holding the strut from the base, remove the upper strut nuts

Fig. 27  Remove the strut from the vehicle

## STRUT OVERHAUL

▶ See Figures 28, 29, 30, 31, 32, 33 and 34

1. If not already done, use a spring compressor and compress the spring until it no longer applies pressure on the upper and lower portion of the strut.

2. While holding the strut shaft with a wrench, loosen and remove the retaining nut at the top of the assembly.

➡ Do not attempt to remove the nut without securing the shaft.

3. With the nut removed, the strut bearing cap can be taken off. Inspect the cap for wear and replace if needed.

4. Remove the spring upper perches, and as above, inspect for wear and replace if necessary.

5. Remove the spring and compressor.

6. Remove the rubber bump stop and dust cap if equipped.

7. If the strut is the type which has a cartridge installed within, loosen the upper cap and remove the cartridge.

### To install:

8. If your strut is a cartridge type, install the cartridge according to the manufacturers specifications.

9. Slide the rubber bump stop and dust cap, if equipped, on to the strut shaft.

10. Place the compressed spring on to the strut, making sure the spring is correctly seated in the perch.

11. Install the upper spring perches, being careful that they align correctly with the spring.

12. Position the upper strut bearing cap on the strut shaft. Install the washer and nut. Tighten nut to 35–50 ft. lbs. (48–68 Nm).

13. Install the strut assembly in the vehicle.

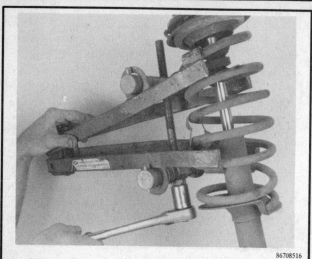

Fig. 28 With the strut assembly placed in a vise, compress the spring, if not already done

86708516

Fig. 29 Remove the nut from the upper strut bearing cap. Hold the strut shaft with a wrench while turning the nut. Remove and discard the nut

86708517

Fig. 30 With the nut removed, the upper strut bearing plate can be removed

86708518

Fig. 31 Remove the upper spring perches. Inspect the parts for sign of wear

86708519

Fig. 32 Slide the perch off the spring

86708520

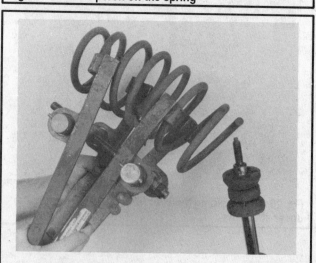

Fig. 33 Remove the spring from the strut

86708521

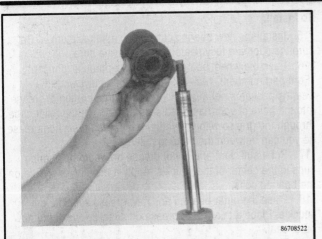

**Fig. 34 Remove the rubber bump stop and duct cap if equipped**

## Lower Ball Joints

### INSPECTION

▶ See Figure 35

1. Raise and safely support the vehicle on jackstands.
2. Have an assistant grasp lower edge of the tire and move wheel and tire assembly in and out.
3. As wheel is being moved in and out, observe lower end of knuckle and lower control arm. Any movement indicates abnormal ball joint wear.
4. If any movement is observed, install new lower control arm assembly or ball joint, as required.

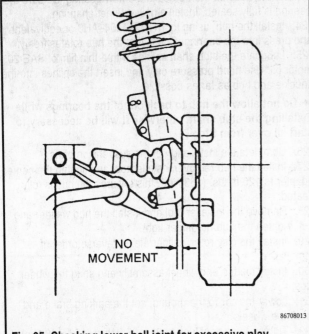

**Fig. 35 Checking lower ball joint for excessive play**

### REMOVAL & INSTALLATION

The lower ball joint is integral to the lower control assembly and cannot be serviced individually. Any movement of the lower ball joint detected as a result of inspection requires replacement of the lower control arm assembly.

1. Raise and safely support the vehicle.
2. Remove the wheel and tire assembly.
3. Remove the nut and bolt securing the ball joint to the steering knuckle.
4. Remove the nut and bolt securing the control arm to the vehicle sub frame.

**To install:**

5. Install the control arm assembly to the vehicle sub-frame using the nut and bolt. Tighten the nut to 69–86 ft. lbs. (93–117 Nm).
6. Install the lower ball joint into the steering knuckle and secure it with the nut and bolt. Tighten the nut to 32–43 ft. lbs. (43–59 Nm).
7. Install the wheel and tire assembly and lower the vehicle.
8. Road test the vehicle.

## Steering Knuckle

### REMOVAL & INSTALLATION

1. Loosen the wheel lugs. Raise and support the vehicle safely Remove the tire and wheel assembly.
2. Remove the drive axle nut.
3. Remove the cotter pin from the tie rod end stud nut and remove the nut. Use a suitable tie rod removal tool and separate the tie rod end from the steering knuckle.
4. Remove the disc brake caliper, rotor and center hub as outlined in this section. Loosen, but do not remove the top strut mounting nut.
5. Remove the lower control arm to steering knuckle pinch bolt, slightly spread the connection after the bolt has been removed.
6. Remove the strut to steering knuckle pinch bolts, slightly spread the connection after the bolts have been removed. Remove the driveaxle from the knuckle hub.
7. Remove the steering knuckle from the strut.
8. Remove the wheel bearings and rotor splash shield, as outlined in this section.

**To install:**

9. Install the rotor splash shield and wheel bearings as outlined.
10. Install the steering knuckle onto the strut. Install new pinch bolts and tighten to specifications.
11. Install the center hub onto the stub driveshaft as outlined.
12. Install the lower control arm to the knuckle. Make sure the ball joint groove is aligned so the pinch bolt can slide through. Install a new pinch bolt and tighten to specifications.
13. Install the rotor and disc brake caliper (see Section 9). Position the tie rod end into the steering knuckle, install a new

nut and tighten to specifications. Align the cotter pin slot and install a new cotter pin.

14. Install the tire and wheel assembly. Lower the vehicle and tighten the wheel lugs.

15. Road test the vehicle.

## Front Wheel Hub, Knuckle and Bearings

### REMOVAL & INSTALLATION

♦ See Figures 36, 37, and 38

**1984–85 Models**

➡ **The wheel hub and knuckle must be removed for bearing replacement or servicing. A special puller is required to remove and install the hub. (Ford Part Number T81P–1104–A, T81P–1104–C and adapters T81P–1104–B or T83P–1104–AH.) The adaptors screw over the lugs and attach to the puller, which uses a long screw attached to the end of the stub shaft to pull off or install the hub.**

1. Remove wheel cover and slightly loosen the lugs.

2. Remove the hub retaining nut and washer. The nut is crimped staked to the shaft, which means that one portion of the nut has been hit with a hammer and chisel to make the nut unround. With an unround nut, more force is needed to remove the nut. Therefore, use a socket and sufficient torque to overcome the locking force of the crimp. It would be better if you had access to an air compressor and an impact gun.

3. Raise the front of the car and support safely with jackstands. Remove the tire and wheel assembly.

4. Remove the brake caliper and disc rotor.

5. Disconnect the lower control arm and tie rod from the steering knuckle. Loosen tow top strut mounting nuts, but do not remove them. Install the hub remover/installer tool and remove the hub. If the outer bearing is seized on the hub remove it with a puller.

6. Remove the front suspension knuckle.

7. Pull out the inner grease shield, the inner seal and bearing.

8. Remove the outer grease seal and bearing.

9. If you plan to reuse the bearings, clean them in a safe solvent. After cleaning the bearings and races, carefully inspect them for damage, pitting, heat coloring etc. If damage etc. has occurred, replace all components (bearings, cups and seals). Always replace the seals with new ones. Always use a new hub nut whenever the old one has been removed.

10. If new bearings are to be used, remove the inner and outer races from the knuckle. A three jawed puller on a slide hammer will do the job.

11. Clean the interior bore of the knuckle.

12. Remove the snapring that retains the bearing in the steering knuckle.

13. Position the knuckle, outboard side up, under a hydraulic press with appropriate adapters in place, and press the bearing from the knuckle.

14. Clean the interior bore of the knuckle.

**To install:**

15. Install the new bearing cups using a suitable driver. Be sure the cups are fully seated in the knuckle bore.

16. Pack the wheel bearings with multi–purpose lubricant (Ford part number C1AZ–19590–B or the equivalent). If a bearing packer is not available, place a large portion of grease into the palm of your hand and slide the edge of the roller cage through the grease with your other hand. Work as much grease as you can between the bearing rollers.

17. Put a sufficient amount of grease between the bearing cups in the center of the knuckle. Apply a thin film of grease on the bearing cups.

18. Place the outer bearing and new grease seal into the knuckle. Place a thin film of grease on all three lips of the new outer seal.

19. Turn the knuckle over and install the inner bearing and seal. Once again, apply a thin film of grease to the three lips of the seal.

20. Install the inner grease shield. A small block of wood may be used to tap the seal into the knuckle bore.

21. Keep the knuckle in the vertical position or the inner bearing will fall out. Start the wheel hub into the outer knuckle bore and push the hub as far as possible through the outer and inner bearings by hand.

➡ **Prior to installing the hub, make sure it is clean and free from burrs. Use crocus cloth to polish the hub is necessary. It is important to use only hand pressure when installing the hub, make sure the hub is through both the outer and inner bearings.**

22. With the hub as fully seated as possible through the bearings, position the hub and knuckle to the front strut.

23. Position the knuckle, outboard side down on the appropriate adapter, then press in the new bearing. Be sure the bearing is fully seated. Install a new retainer snapring.

24. Install the hub, using tool T83T–1104–AH3 or equivalent, and press into the bearing. Check that the hub rotates freely.

25. Lubricate the stub shaft splines with a thin film of SAE 20 motor oil. Use hand pressure only and insert the splines into the knuckle and hub as far as possible.

➡ **Do not allow the hub to back out of the bearings while installing the stub shaft, otherwise it will be necessary to start all over from Step 7.**

26. Complete the installation of the suspension parts.

27. Install the hub remover/installer tool and tighten the center adapter to 120 ft. lbs. (163 Nm), this ensures the hub is fully seated.

28. Remove the installer tool and install the hub washer and nut. Tighten the hub nut finger tight.

29. Install the disc rotor, caliper etc. in reverse order of removal.

30. Install the tire and wheel assembly and snug the wheel lugs.

31. Lower the car to the ground, set the parking brake and block the wheels.

32. Tighten the wheel lugs to 80–105 ft. lbs. (108–142 Nm).

33.  Tighten the center hub nut to 180–200 ft. lbs. (244–271 Nm). DO NOT USE A POWER WRENCH TO TIGHTEN THE HUB NUT!

34.  Stake the hub nut using a rounded, dull chisel. DO NOT USE A SHARP CHISEL.

35.  Road test the vehicle.

### 1986–94 Models

1.  Remove the wheel cover/hub cover from the wheel and tire assembly and loosen the nuts.

2.  Remove hub nut retainer and washer by applying sufficient torque to nut to break the locking tab and remove hub nut retainer. The hub nut retainer must be discarded after removal.

3.  Raise and safely support the vehicle. Remove the wheel and tire assembly.

4.  Remove the brake caliper by loosening the caliper locating pins and rotating caliper off rotor starting from lower end of caliper and lifting upward. Do not remove caliper pins from caliper assembly. Lift caliper off rotor and hang it free of rotor. Do not allow caliper assembly to hang from brake hose. Support caliper assembly with a length of wire.

5.  Remove the rotor from the hub by pulling it off the hub bolts. If the rotor is difficult to remove from the hub, strike the rotor sharply between studs with a rubber or plastic hammer. If rotor will not pull off, apply rust penetrating fluid to the inboard and outboard rotor hub mating surfaces. Install a jaw puller and remove the rotor by pulling on rotor outside diameter and pushing on hub center in. If excessive force is required for removal, check rotor for lateral runout. (Lateral runout must be checked with the nuts clamping the hat section of the rotor.)

6.  With the rotor removed, unfasten the rotor splash shield.

7.  Disconnect the lower control arm and tie rod from knuckle (leave strut attached).

8.  Loosen the strut top mount-to-apron nuts.

9.  Install a suitable hub removal tool and remove hub/bearing/knuckle assembly by pushing out CV-joint outer shaft until it is free of assembly.

10.  Support the knuckle with a length of wire, then remove the strut bolt, and slide the hub/knuckle assembly off the strut.

11.  Carefully remove the support wire and transfer the hub/bearing assembly to the bench.

12.  Install a front hub puller with jaws for pulling on the knuckle bosses, and remove the hub.

➡ **When using a hub puller, ensure the shaft is centered and clears the bearing inside diameter and rests on the end face of the hub journal. This will prevent damage to the tool, hub and other suspension parts.**

13.  Remove the snapring which retains the bearing knuckle assembly and discard the snapring.

14.  Using a hydraulic press, place a suitable front bearing spacer on the hub, with the step side up toward the press. Install the bearing removal tool on the bearing inner race and press the bearing out of the knuckle.

15.  Once the bearing has been pressed out, discard the bearing.

### To install:

16.  On the bench, remove all foreign material from the knuckle bearing bore and hub bearing journal to ensure a correct seating of the new bearing.

➡ **If hub bearing journal is scored or damaged, replace the hub. Do not attempt to service. The front wheel bearings are of a cartridge design and are pregreased, sealed and require no scheduled maintenance. The bearings are preset and cannot be adjusted. If a bearing is disassembled for any reason, it must be replaced as a unit. No individual service seals, rollers or races are available.**

17.  Place a suitable bearing spacer step side down on the hydraulic press plate and position the knuckle on the spacer with the outboard side down. Position a new bearing in the inboard side of the knuckle. Install a suitable front bearing installer on bearing outer race face with the undercut side facing the bearing and press the bearing into the knuckle. Ensure that the bearing seats completely against the shoulder of the knuckle bore.

➡ **Ensure proper positioning of bearing installer during installation to prevent bearing damage.**

18.  Install a new snapring in the knuckle groove using snapring pliers.

19.  Place a suitable front bearing spacer on an arbor press plate and position the hub on the tool with lugs facing downward. Position knuckle assembly on the hub barrel with the outboard side down. Place a suitable front bearing remover on inner the race of the bearing and press down on the tool until the bearing is freely in the knuckle after installation.

20.  Suspend the hub/knuckle/bearing assembly on the vehicle with wire and attach the strut loosely to the knuckle. Lubricate the CV-joint stub shaft splines with SAE 30 weight motor oil and insert the shaft into the hub splines as far as possible using hand pressure only. Check that the splines are properly engaged.

21.  Install a suitable front hub installer and wheel bolt adapter to the hub and stub shaft. Tighten the hub installer tool to 120 ft. lbs. (162 Nm) to ensure that the hub is fully seated.

22.  Remove the tool and install a washer and new hub nut. Tighten the hub nut finger-tight.

23.  Complete installation of front suspension components.

24.  Install disc brake rotor to hub assembly.

25.  Install disc brake caliper over rotor.

26.  Ensure outer brake shoe spring end is seated under upper arm of knuckle.

27.  Install wheel and tire assembly, tightening wheel nuts finger-tight.

28.  Lower vehicle and block wheels to prevent vehicle from rolling.

29.  Tighten wheel nuts to 85–105 ft. lbs. (115–142 Nm).

30.  Manually thread hub nut retainer assembly on constant velocity output shaft as far as possible using a 30mm or 11/8 in. socket, tighten retainer assembly to 180–200 ft. lbs. (245–270 Nm).

➡ **Do not use power or impact tools to tighten the hub nut. Do not move the vehicle before retainer is tightened.**

31.  During tightening, an audible click sound will indicate proper ratchet function of the hub nut retainer. As the hub nut retainer tightens, ensure that one of the 3 locking tabs is in the slot of the CV-joint shaft. If the hub nut retainer is damaged, or more than 1 locking tab is broken, replace the hub nut retainer.

32. Install wheelcover or hub cover and lower the vehicle completely to ground.
33. Remove the wheel blocks.
34. Road test the vehicle.

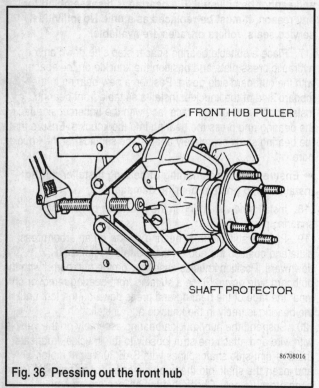

Fig. 36 Pressing out the front hub

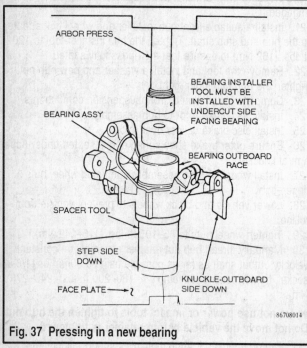

Fig. 37 Pressing in a new bearing

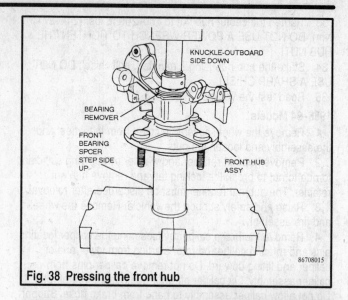

Fig. 38 Pressing the front hub

## Front End Alignment

### CASTER AND CAMBER

Caster and camber angles on your vehicle are preset at the factory and cannot be adjusted in the field. Improper caster and camber can be corrected only through replacement of worn or bent parts. The caster measurements must be made on the left hand side by turning the left hand wheel through the prescribed angle of sweep and on the right hand side by turning the right hand wheel through the prescribed angle of sweep. When using alignment equipment designed to measure caster on both the right hand and left hand side, turning only one wheel will result in a significant error in the caster angle for the opposite side.

### TOE ADJUSTMENT

▶ See Figure 39

Toe is the difference in distance between the front and the rear of the front wheels.
1. On models equipped with power steering, move the steering wheel back and forth several times until the steering wheel is in the straight–ahead or centered position.
2. Turn the engine OFF and lock the steering wheel in place using a suitable steering wheel holder.
3. Loosen the slide off the small outer boot clamp so the boot will not twist during adjustment.
4. Loosen the locknuts on the outer tie rod ends.
5. Rotate both (right and left) tie rods in exactly equal amounts during adjustment. This will keep the steering wheel centered.
6. Tighten the locknuts when the adjustment has been completed. Install and tighten the boot clamps.

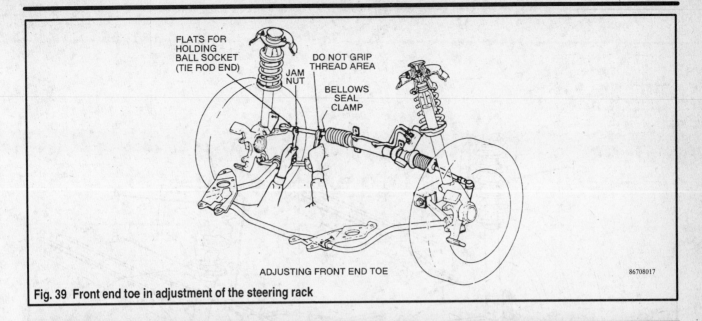

**Fig. 39 Front end toe in adjustment of the steering rack**

## REAR SUSPENSION

◆ See Figures 40, 41 and 42

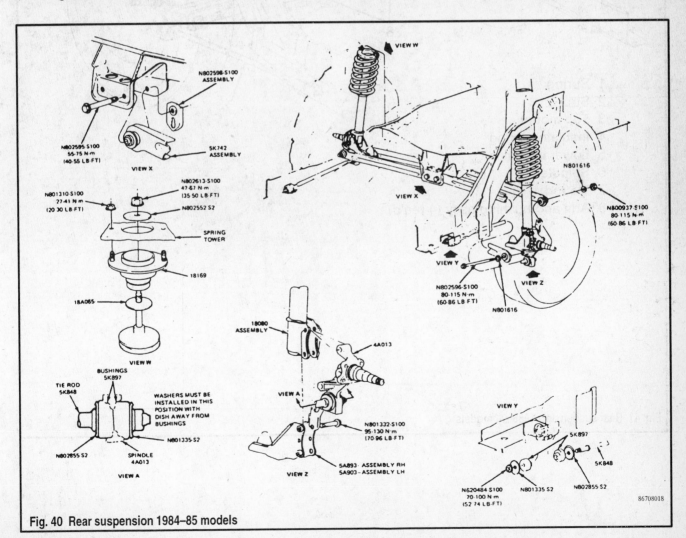

**Fig. 40 Rear suspension 1984–85 models**

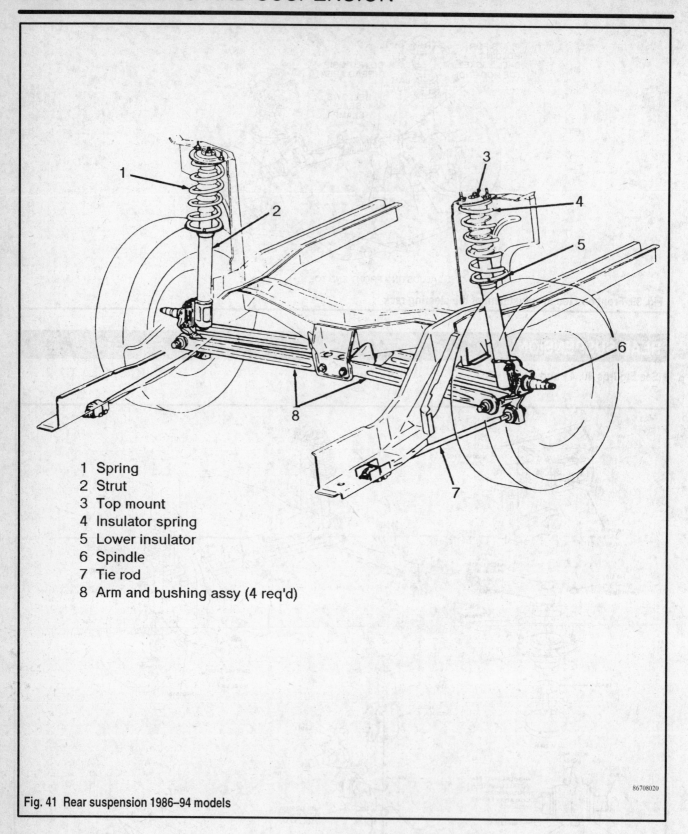

1 Spring
2 Strut
3 Top mount
4 Insulator spring
5 Lower insulator
6 Spindle
7 Tie rod
8 Arm and bushing assy (4 req'd)

**Fig. 41 Rear suspension 1986–94 models**

86708020

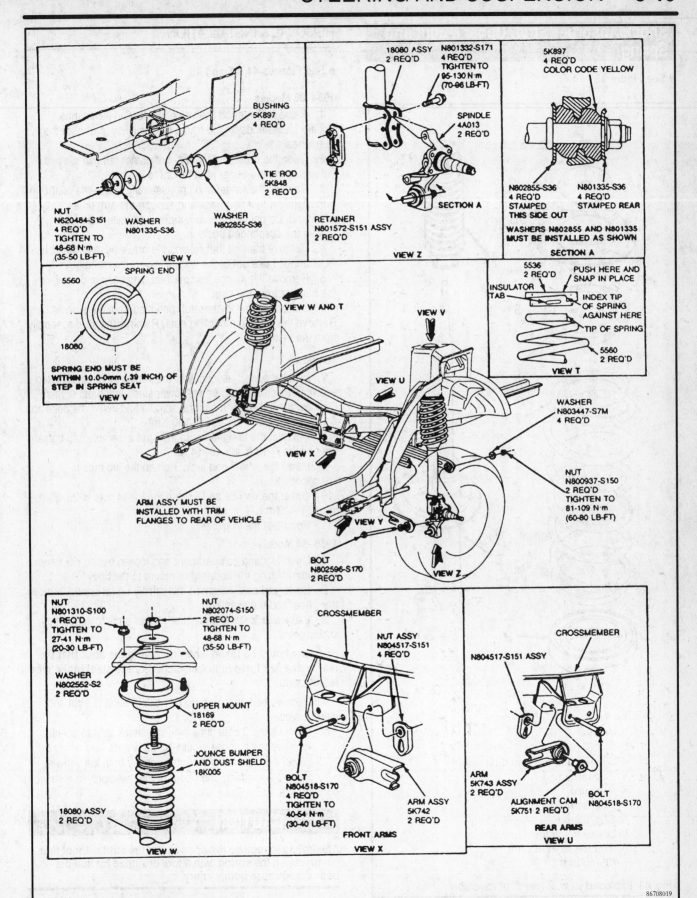

BUSHING
5K897
4 REQ'D

TIE ROD
5K848
2 REQ'D

NUT
N620484-S151
4 REQ'D
TIGHTEN TO
48-68 N·m
(35-50 LB-FT)

WASHER
N801335-S36

WASHER
N802855-S36

VIEW Y

18080 ASSY
2 REQ'D

N801332-S171
4 REQ'D
TIGHTEN TO
95-130 N·m
(70-96 LB-FT)

SPINDLE
4A013
2 REQ'D

SECTION A

RETAINER
N801572-S151 ASSY
2 REQ'D

VIEW Z

5K897
4 REQ'D
COLOR CODE YELLOW

N802855-S36
4 REQ'D
STAMPED
THIS SIDE OUT

N801335-S36
4 REQ'D
STAMPED REAR

WASHERS N802855 AND N801335
MUST BE INSTALLED AS SHOWN

SECTION A

SPRING END

5560

18080

SPRING END MUST BE
WITHIN 10.0-0mm (.39 INCH) OF
STEP IN SPRING SEAT

VIEW V

5536
2 REQ'D

INSULATOR
TAB

PUSH HERE AND
SNAP IN PLACE

INDEX TIP
OF SPRING
AGAINST HERE

TIP OF SPRING

5560
2 REQ'D

VIEW T

VIEW W AND T

VIEW V

VIEW U

WASHER
N803447-S7M
4 REQ'D

NUT
N800937-S150
2 REQ'D
TIGHTEN TO
81-109 N·m
(60-80 LB-FT)

VIEW X

ARM ASSY MUST BE
INSTALLED WITH TRIM
FLANGES TO REAR OF VEHICLE

VIEW Y

BOLT
N802596-S170
2 REQ'D

VIEW Z

NUT
N801310-S100
4 REQ'D
TIGHTEN TO
27-41 N·m
(20-30 LB-FT)

NUT
N802074-S150
2 REQ'D
TIGHTEN TO
48-68 N·m
(35-50 LB-FT)

WASHER
N802552-S2
2 REQ'D

UPPER MOUNT
18169
2 REQ'D

JOUNCE BUMPER
AND DUST SHIELD
18K005

18080 ASSY
2 REQ'D

VIEW W

CROSSMEMBER

NUT ASSY
N804517-S151
4 REQ'D

BOLT
N804518-S170
4 REQ'D
TIGHTEN TO
40-54 N·m
(30-40 LB-FT)

ARM ASSY
5K742
2 REQ'D

FRONT ARMS
VIEW X

CROSSMEMBER

N804517-S151 ASSY

ARM
5K743 ASSY
2 REQ'D

ALIGNMENT CAM
5K751 2 REQ'D

BOLT
N804518-S170

REAR ARMS
VIEW U

86708019

**Fig. 42 Rear suspension fastener list**

## Shock Absorber Strut, Upper Mount and Spring

♦ See Figure 43

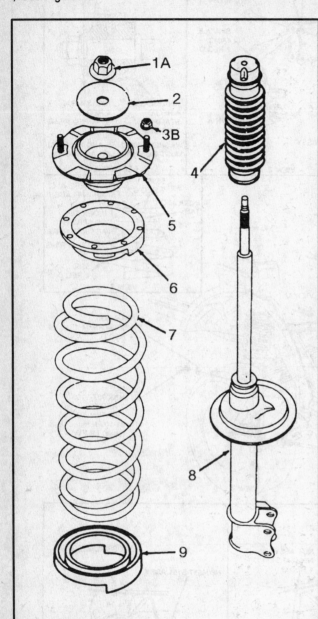

1A Nut
2 Washer
3B Nut (2 req'd)
4 Jounce bumper and dust shield
5 Top mount
6 Insulator
7 Rear spring
8 Shock strut
9 Lower insulator
A Tighten to 47-63 Nm
   (35-46 lb.ft.)

86708021

**Fig. 43 Exploded view of rear strut assembly**

## REMOVAL & INSTALLATION

♦ See Figures 44, 45 and 46

### 1984–85 Models

1. Raise and support the vehicle safely on jackstands. Position jackstands on the frame pads slightly in front of the rear wheels.
2. Open the trunk and loosen, but do not remove the two nuts retaining the upper strut mount to the body.
3. Remove the wheel and tire assembly. Raise the control arm slightly with a floor jack and support the arm on a jackstand. Do not jack the arm more than necessary. Just relieve the suspended position.
4. Remove the bolt that retains the brake hose to the strut. Position the hose out of the way of the strut assembly.
5. Remove the jounce bumper retaining bolts and remove the bumper from the strut.
6. Disconnect the lower strut mounting from the spindle. Remove the two top mounting nuts. Remove the strut assembly from the vehicle.

**To install:**

7. Install the strut assembly to the vehicle, inserting the top end first. Place the nuts on the tower studs and hand tighten. Connect the lower portion to the spindle and insert the bolts and tighten to 70–96 ft. lbs. (94.8–130 Nm).
8. Connect the brake hose to the strut assembly and tighten the bolts to 7–10 ft. lbs. (9–14 Nm).
9. Install the wheel and lugs. Tighten the lug nuts to specification.
10. Lower the vehicle and tighten the tower nuts to 25–30 ft. lbs. (34–41 Nm).
11. Road test the vehicle.

### 1986–94 Models

1. Open luggage compartment and loosen but do not remove the nuts retaining the upper strut mount to the body.
2. Raise and safely support the vehicle on jackstand, remove the wheel and tire assembly.
3. Place a jack stand under the control arms to support the suspension.

➡ **Care should be taken when removing the strut that the rear brake flex hose is not stretched or the steel brake tube is not bent.**

4. Remove bolt attaching brake hose bracket to strut and move it aside.
5. Remove the 2 bolts attaching the shock strut to spindle.
6. Remove the 2 upper mount–to–body nuts.
7. Lower and remove the strut assembly from the vehicle.
8. Place strut, spring and upper mount assembly in a spring compressor.

### ✳✳CAUTION

**Attempting to remove the spring from the strut without first compressing the spring with a tool designed for that purpose could cause bodily injury.**

➡ **Do not attempt to remove shaft nut by turning shaft and holding nut. Nut must be turned and shaft held to avoid possible fracture of shaft at base of hex.**

9. With the spring compressed, remove strut shaft–to–mount nut and then remove spring, strut and mount from compressor tool.

**To install:**

10. With the spring compressed, install spring, spring insulator, top mount and upper washer on strut shaft.

11. Ensure spring is properly located in upper and lower spring seats. The spring end must be within 0.39 in. (10mm) of the step in the spring seat.

12. Tighten shaft nut to 35–50 ft. lbs. (48–68 Nm). Use 18mm deep socket to turn the nut and 1/4 drive 8mm deep socket to hold shaft so it will not turn while tightening the nut.

13. Remove the assembled strut from the compressor, and position unit into vehicle.

14. Insert 2 upper mount studs into strut tower and hand start the new nuts. Do not tighten at this time.

15. Position spindle into lower strut mount and install 2 new bolts. Tighten to 70–96 ft. lbs. (95–130 Nm).

16. Install brake flex–hose bracket on the strut.

17. Install wheel and tire.

18. Remove jack stand and lower vehicle to the ground.

19. Tighten 2 top mount–to–body nuts to 25–30 ft. lbs. (27–41 Nm).

20. Road test the vehicle.

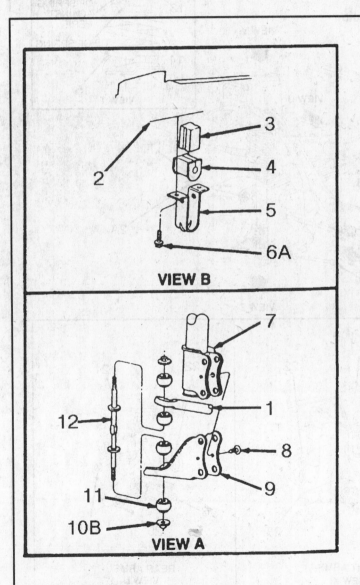

1  Rear stabilizer bar
2  Frame
3  Adapter (2 req'd)
4  Rubber Insulators (2 req'd)
5  U-brackets (2 req'd)
6A  Bolts (4 req'd)
7  Shock absorber
8  Retainers (2 req'd)
9  Support brackets (2 req'd)
10B  Nuts (4 req'd)
11  Rubber bushings (8 req'd)
12  Stabilizer bar stud and
      washer link assy
A  Tighten to 25-29 Nm (18-22 lb.ft.)
B  TIghten to 8-24 Nm (6-17 lb.ft.)

VIEW B

VIEW A

86708022

**Fig. 44  Exploded view of lower mounting assembly**

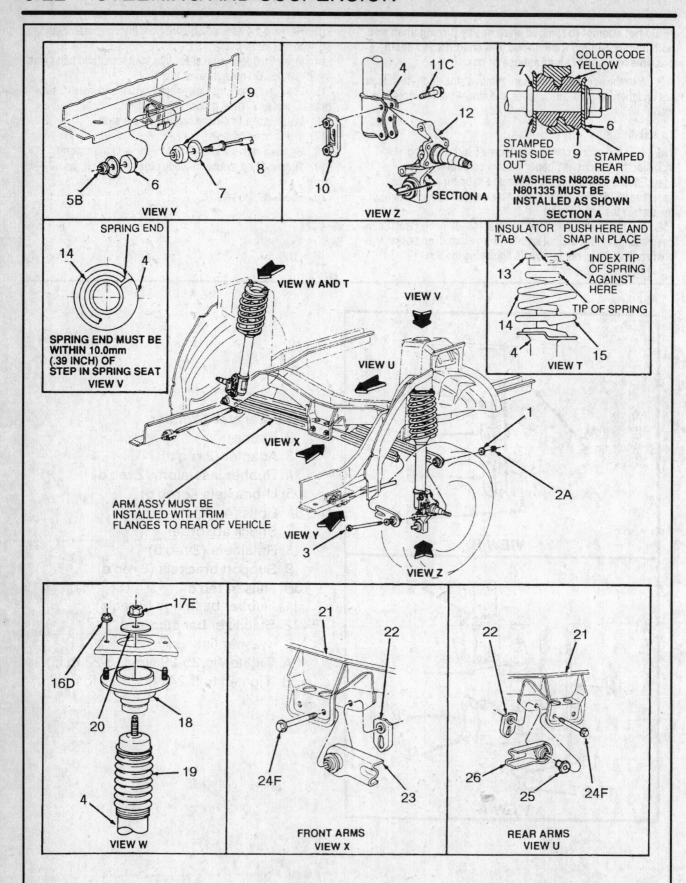

VIEW Y

9

6

5B

7

8

VIEW Z

4

11C

10

12

SECTION A

COLOR CODE YELLOW

7

6

STAMPED THIS SIDE OUT

9

STAMPED REAR

**WASHERS N802855 AND N801335 MUST BE INSTALLED AS SHOWN**
**SECTION A**

SPRING END

14

4

**SPRING END MUST BE WITHIN 10.0mm (.39 INCH) OF STEP IN SPRING SEAT**
**VIEW V**

INSULATOR TAB

PUSH HERE AND SNAP IN PLACE

INDEX TIP OF SPRING AGAINST HERE

13

14

4

TIP OF SPRING

15

**VIEW T**

VIEW W AND T

VIEW V

VIEW U

VIEW X

1

2A

ARM ASSY MUST BE INSTALLED WITH TRIM FLANGES TO REAR OF VEHICLE

VIEW Y

3

VIEW Z

17E

16D

20

18

19

4

**VIEW W**

21

22

24F

23

22

21

26

25

24F

**FRONT ARMS**
**VIEW X**

**REAR ARMS**
**VIEW U**

86708023

Fig. 45 View of upper strut assembly located in trunk compartment. Notice how similar the rear strut assembly is to the front strut

1  Washer (4 req'd)
2  Nut (2 req'd)
3  Bolt (2 req'd)
4  Strut assy (2 req'd)
5B  Nut (4 req'd)
6  Washer (4 req'd)
7  Washer (4 req'd)
8  Tie rod (2 req'd)
9  Bushing (4 req'd)
10  Retainer assy (2 req'd)
11C  Bolt (4 req'd)
12  Spindle (2 req'd)
13  Upper insulator (2 req'd)
14  Spring (2 req'd)
15  Lower insulator (2 req'd)
16D  Nut (4 req'd)

17E  Nut (2 req'd)
18  Upper mount (2 req'd)
19  Jounce bumper and dust shield
20  Washer (2 req'd)
21  Crossmember
22  Nut assy (4 req'd)
23  Front arm assy (2 req'd)
24F  Bolt (4 req'd)
25  Alignment cam (2 req'd)
26  Rear arm assy (2 req'd)
A  Tighten to 81-109 Nm (60-80 lb.ft.)
B  Tighten to 53-72 Nm (39-53 lb.ft.)
C  Tighten to 98-132 Nm (72-97 lb.ft.)
D  Tighten to 30-40 Nm (23-29 lb.ft.)
E  Tighten to 47-63 Nm (35-46 lb.ft.)
F  Tighten to 55-63 Nm (41-46 lb. ft.)

86708k23

**Fig. 46  Rear suspension parts list**

## Rear Control Arms

▶ **See Figure 47**

### REMOVAL & INSTALLATION

1. Raise and safely support the vehicle on jackstands.
2. Remove and discard the arm–to–spindle bolt and nut.
3. Remove and discard center retaining bolt and nut.
4. Remove the arm from the vehicle.

**To install:**

➡ **When installing new control arms, the bushing with the 0.39 in. (10mm) hole is installed to the center of the vehicle and the bushing with the 0.48 in. (12mm) hole is installed to the spindle. The offset on the arm must face up on the right side of the vehicle and down on the left side of the vehicle. The flange edge of the arm stamping must also face the rear of the vehicle.**

5. Position the arm at the center of vehicle and insert a new bolt and nut. Do not tighten at this time.
6. Move arm end up to spindle and insert a new bolt, washer and nut. Ensure bolt engages both the arms and spindle.
7. Tighten the arm–to–body bolt to 30–40 ft. lbs. (40–54 Nm).
8. Tighten the arm–to–spindle nut to 60–80 ft. lbs. (81–109 Nm).
9. Remove the jackstand and lower the vehicle.
10. Road test the vehicle.

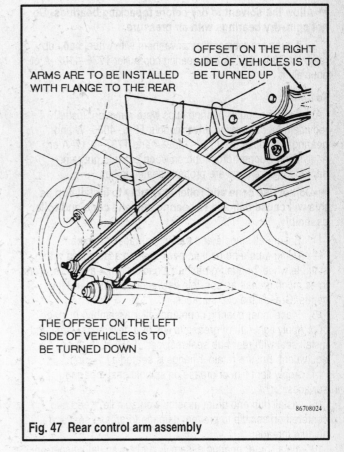

ARMS ARE TO BE INSTALLED WITH FLANGE TO THE REAR

OFFSET ON THE RIGHT SIDE OF VEHICLES IS TO BE TURNED UP

THE OFFSET ON THE LEFT SIDE OF VEHICLES IS TO BE TURNED DOWN

86708024

**Fig. 47  Rear control arm assembly**

## Rear Wheel Bearings

### REMOVAL & INSTALLATION

▶ **See Figures 48 and 49**

#### All Models except AWD Vehicles

1. Raise and safely support the vehicle on jackstands.

2. Remove wheel and tire assembly. Remove grease cap from the hub.

3. Remove the pin, nut retainer, adjusting nut and flatwasher from spindle. Discard the cotter pin.

4. Pull hub and drum assembly off spindle being careful not to drop outer bearing during removal.

5. Remove the outer bearing assembly.

6. Using a seal remover, remove and discard grease seal. Remove inner bearing assembly from hub.

7. Wipe all lubricant from spindle and inside of hub. Cover spindle with a clean cloth and vacuum all loose dust and dirt from brake assembly. Carefully remove cloth to prevent dirt from falling on spindle.

8. Clean both bearing assemblies and cups using solvent. inspect bearing assemblies and cups for excessive wear, scratches, pits or other damage. Replace all worn or damaged parts as required.

➡ **Allow the solvent to dry before repacking bearings. Do not spin–dry bearings with air pressure.**

9. If cups are replaced, remove them with wheel hub cup remover D80L–927–A and bearing cup puller T77F–1102–A or equivalent.

**To install:**

10. If inner or outer bearing cups were removed, install replacement cups using driver handle T80T–4000–W and bearing cup replacers T77F–1202–A and T73T–1217–A or equivalent. Support drum hub on wood block to pre}vent damage. Insure cups are properly seated in hub.

➡ **Do not use cone and roller assembly to install cup as this will cause damage to bearing cup and cone and roller assembly.**

11. Ensure all spindle and bearing surfaces are clean.

12. Using a bearing packer, pack bearing assemblies with a suitable wheel bearing grease. If a packer is not available, work in as much grease as possible between the rollers and the cages. Grease the cup surfaces.

13. Place inner bearing cone and roller assembly} in inner cup. Apply light film of grease to lips of a new grease seal and install seal with rear hub seal replacer T81P–1249–A or equivalent. Ensure retainer flange is seated all around.

14. Apply light film of grease on spindle shaft bearing surfaces.

15. Install hub and drum assembly on spindle. Keep hub centered on spindle to prevent damage to grease seal and spindle threads.

16. Install outer bearing assembly and keyed flat washer on spindle. Install adjusting nut finger–tight. Adjust wheel bearings. Install a new cotter pin.

17. Install wheel and tire on drum.

18. Lower vehicle.

19. Road test the vehicle.

#### All Wheel Drive (AWD) Models

1. Raise and support the vehicle safely on jackstands. Remove the tire and wheel assembly.

2. Remove the brake drum. Remove the parking brake cable from the brake backing plate.

3. Remove the brake line from the wheel cylinder. Remove the outboard U–joint retaining bolts. Remove the outboard end of the halfshaft from the wheel stub shaft yoke and wire it to the control arm.

4. Remove and discard the control arm to spindle bolt, washer and nut. Remove the tie rod nut, bushing and washer and discard the nut.

5. Remove and discard the 2 bolts retaining the spindle to the strut. Remove the spindle from the vehicle. Mount the spindle and backing plate assembly in a suitable vise.

6. Remove the cotter pin and nut attaching the stub shaft yoke to the stub shaft. Discard the cotter pin.

7. Remove the spindle and backing plate assembly from the vise. Remove the stub shaft yoke using a 2 jaw puller and shaft protector. After removing end yoke from spindle assembly, inspect the nylon bushing and replace, as necessary.

8. Position the spindle and backing plate assembly into a vise and remove the wheel stub shaft.

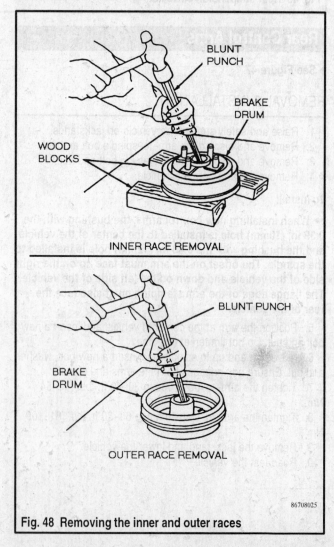

86708025

**Fig. 48 Removing the inner and outer races**

9. Remove the snapring retaining the bearing. Remove the bolts retaining the spindle to the backing plate and remove the backing plate.

10. Remove the spindle from the vise and mount it into a suitable press. With the spindle side facing upward, carefully press out the bearing from the spindle, using a driver handle and bearing cup driver. Discard the bearing after removal.

**To install:**

11. Mount the spindle in a press, spindle side facing down. Position a new bearing in the outboard side of the spindle and carefully press in the new bearing using a driver handle and bearing installer.

12. Remove the spindle from the press and mount it in a vise. Install the snapring retaining the bearing. Position the backing plate to the spindle and install the retaining bolts.

13. Install the wheel stub shaft. Install the stub shaft yoke and attaching nut. Tighten the nut to 120–150 ft. lbs. (163–203 Nm) and install a new cotter pin.

14. Remove the spindle and backing plate assembly from the vise. Position the spindle onto the tie rod and then into the strut lower bracket. Insert 2 new strut–to–spindle bolts. Do not tighten at this time.

15. Install the tie rod bushing washer and new nut. Install the new control arm to spindle bolt, washers and nut. Do not tighten them at this time.

16. Install a jack stand to support the suspension at the normal curb height before tightening the fasteners.

17. Tighten the spindle–to–strut bolts to 70–96 ft. lbs. (95–130 Nm). Tighten the tie rod nut to 52–74 ft. lbs. (70–100 Nm). Tighten the control arm to spindle nut to 60–86 ft. lbs. (81–117 Nm).

18. Position the outboard end of the halfshaft to the wheel stub shaft yoke. Install the retaining caps and bolts and tighten them to 15–17 ft. lbs. (20–23 Nm).

19. Install the brake line to the wheel cylinder. Install the parking brake cable and brake drum. Install the wheel assembly, torque the lugs nuts to 80–105 ft. lbs. (108–142 Nm).

20. Lower the vehicle and bleed the brake system. Check and adjust the toe, if necessary.

21. Road test the vehicle.

## ADJUSTMENT

➡ **The Bearings on 4WD vehicles are not adjustable.**

**All Models Except AWD**

1. Raise and safely support the vehicle.

2. Remove wheel cover or ornament and nut covers. Remove grease cap from hub.

3. Remove cotter pin and nut retainer. Discard the cotter pin.

4. Back–off adjusting nut 1 full turn. Ensure nut turns freely on spindle threads. Correct any binding condition.

5. Tighten the adjusting nut to 17–25 ft. lbs. (23–34 Nm) while rotating hub and drum assembly to seat the bearings. Loosen the adjusting nut 1/2 turn and, then tighten adjusting nut to 24–28 inch lbs. (2.7–3.2 Nm) using an inch lb. torque wrench.

6. Position adjusting nut retainer over adjusting nut so slots in nut retainer flange are in line with cotter pin hole in spline.

7. Install a new cotter pin and bend ends around retainer flange.

8. Check hub rotation. If hub rotates freely, install grease cap. If not, check bearings for damage and replace as necessary.

9. Install wheel and tire assembly, wheel cover or ornaments, and nut covers as required.

10. Lower the vehicle. Road test the car.

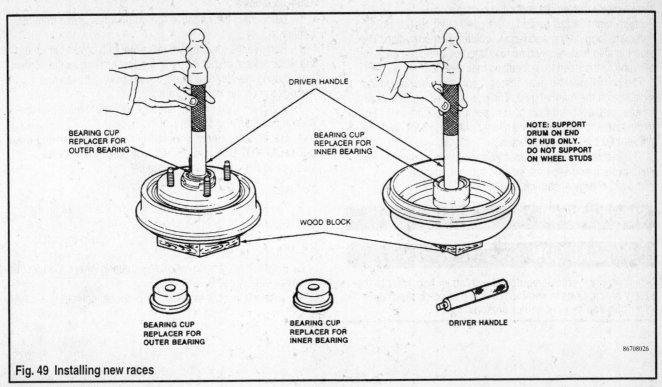

**Fig. 49　Installing new races**

## Rear End Alignment

### ADJUSTMENTS

♦ See Figure 50

➡ **Camber is factory set and cannot be adjusted.**

Toe–in and toe–out can be adjusted when it is determined that the vehicle is not within alignment specifications.

1. Loosen the bolt attaching the rear control arm to the body.
2. Rotate the alignment cam until the required alignment setting is obtained.
3. Tighten the control arm attaching bolt to 30–40 ft. lbs. (40–54 Nm).
4. Road test the vehicle.

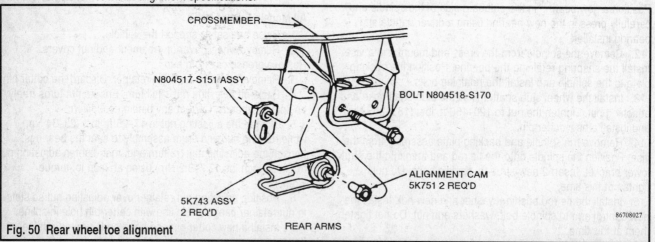

Fig. 50  Rear wheel toe alignment

## STEERING

Rack and pinion steering in either manual or power versions gives your car precise steering control. The manual rack and pinion gear is smaller and about seven and one half pounds lighten than that in any other Ford or Mercury small cars. The increased use of aluminum and the use of a one piece valve sleeve make this weight reduction possible.

Lightweight, sturdy bushings are used to mount the steering, these are long lasting and lend to quieter gear operation. The steering also features lifetime lubricated outer tie rod ends, eliminating the need for scheduled maintenance.

The power steering gear shares a common body mounting system with the manual gear. The power steering pump is of a smaller displacement than current pumps, it requires less power to operate and has streamlined inner porting to provide more efficient fluid flow characteristics.

The steering column geometry uses a double universal joint shaft system and separate column support brackets for improved energy absorbing capabilities.

## Steering Wheel

### ✳✳CAUTION

When serving vehicles equipped with an air bag, refer to the safety precautions in section 6. Failure to do so may result in air bag deployment and/or personal injury.

### REMOVAL & INSTALLATION

♦ See Figures 51 and 52

#### 1984–85 Models

1. Disconnect the negative (ground) battery cable from the battery.
2. Remove the steering wheel center hub cover. Lift up on the outer edges, do not use a sharp tool or remove the screws from behind the steering wheel cross spoke. Loosen and remove the center mounting nut.
3. Using a magic marker, scribe 2 alignment marks on the steering column and steering wheel body.
4. Remove the steering wheel with a crowfoot steering wheel puller. DO NOT USE a knock–off type puller it will cause damage to the collapsible steering column.

#### To install:

5. To reinstall the steering wheel, align the marks on the steering shaft and steering wheel. Place the wheel onto the shaft. Install a new center mounting nut. Tighten the nut to 30–40 ft. lbs. (41–54 Nm).
6. Install the center cover on the steering wheel. Connect the negative battery cable.
7. Drive the vehicle to check for proper alignment.

**1986–94 Models**

## ✳✳CAUTION

**On vehicles equipped with an air bag, the negative battery cable and backup power supply must be disconnected, before working on the system. Failure to do so may result in deployment of the air bag and possible personal injury.**

1. Disconnect the negative battery cable. On air bag equipped vehicles, disconnect the backup power supply as follows:

   a. Remove the screws retaining steering column opening cover to instrument panel and remove cover.

   b. Remove the bolts retaining bolster and remove bolster.

   c. Disconnect the connector from the backup power supply.

2. Remove the horn pad cover by removing the retaining screws from the steering wheel assembly.

➡ **The emblem assembly is removed after the horn pad cover is removed by pushing it out from the backside of the emblem.**

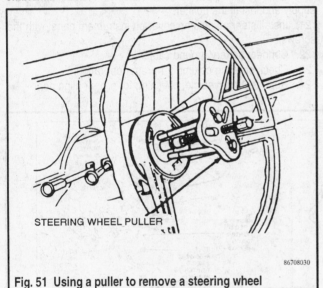

STEERING WHEEL PULLER

86708030

**Fig. 51  Using a puller to remove a steering wheel**

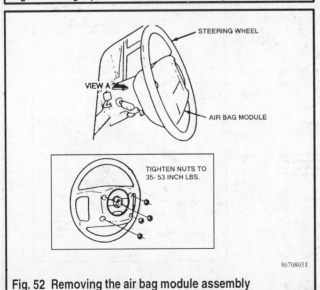

STEERING WHEEL

VIEW A

AIR BAG MODULE

TIGHTEN NUTS TO 35- 53 INCH LBS.

86708031

**Fig. 52  Removing the air bag module assembly**

3. Remove the energy absorbing foam from the wheel assembly, if equipped. Remember, the energy absorbing foam must be installed when the steering wheel is assembled. Disconnect the horn pad wiring connector.

4. If equipped with air bag restraint system, remove the 4 nuts located on the back of the steering wheel holding the air bag module to the steering wheel.

5. Lift the air bag module from the wheel and disconnect the air bag module–to–clockspring connector.

6. Loosen the steering wheel retaining bolt 4–6 turns, but do not remove. On air bag–equipped vehicles, remove the bolt completely to remove the vibration damper, then reinstall the bolt loosely on the shaft.

7. Remove the steering wheel with a suitable puller. Do not use a knock-off type puller, because it will cause damage to the collapsible steering column. Loosen the retaining bolt, grasp the rim of the steering wheel and pull the steering wheel from the upper shaft.

### To install:

8. Install the steering wheel assembly on the steering column, making sure the alignment marks are correct.

9. Install a new retaining bolt. Tighten the bolt to 23–33 ft. lbs. (31–45 Nm). On air bag equipped vehicles, install the vibration damper before installing the bolt.

10. If equipped with an air bag, connect the air bag module wire to Clockspring connector and place the module on the steering wheel with the 4 attaching nuts. Tighten the nuts to 35–53 inch lbs. (4–6 Nm).

11. On vehicles without air bag, connect the horn pad wiring connector and, if equipped, install the energy absorbing foam. Install the horn pad cover and tighten the retaining screws to 8–10 inch lbs. (0.9–1.1 Nm).

12. On air bag equipped vehicles, connect the backup power supply connector and reinstall the bolster and steering column opening cover.

13. Reconnect the negative battery cable and check the steering wheel for proper operation.

14. Drive vehicle to check for proper steering wheel alignment.

## Steering Column

### REMOVAL & INSTALLATION

▸ **See Figures 53, 54 and 55**

➡ **On air bag equipped vehicles, whenever the steering column is separated from the steering gear for any reason, the steering column must be locked to prevent the steering wheel from being rotated, which in turn will prevent damage to the air bag clockspring.**

1. Disconnect the negative battery cable.

➡ **Before disconnecting cable on air bag equipped vehicles, ensure wheels are in straight ahead position. Turn ignition switch to LOCK position and rotate steering wheel about 16 degrees counterclockwise until locked into position.**

2. Remove steering column cover on lower portion of instrument panel. On air bag equipped vehicles, remove the

bolster and disconnect the backup power supply for the air bag module.

3. Remove speed control module, if equipped.

4. Remove lower steering column shroud.

5. Loosen, but do not remove, the nuts and bolts retaining steering column to support bracket and remove upper shroud.

6. Disconnect all steering column electrical connections: ignition, wash/wipe, turn signal, key warning buzzer, speed control. On console shift automatic transaxle, remove interlock cable retaining screw and disconnect cable from steering column.

7. Loosen steering column–to–intermediate shaft clamp connection and remove bolt or nut.

8. Remove the nuts and bolts retaining steering column to support bracket.

9. Pry open steering column shaft in area of clamp on each side of bolt groove with steering column locked. Open enough to disengage shafts with minimal effort. Do not use excessive force.

10. Inspect 2 steering column bracket clips for damage. If clips have been bent or excessively distorted, they must be replaced.

**To install:**

11. Engage lower steering shaft to intermediate shaft and hand start clamp bolt and nut.

12. Align the bolts on steering column support bracket assembly with outer tube mounting holes and hand start 2 nuts.

Check for presence of the clips on outer bracket. The clips must be present to ensure adequate performance of vital parts and systems. Hand start the bolts through outer tube upper bracket and clip and into support bracket nuts. On console shift automatic transaxles, install interlock cable and retaining screw. Tighten to 30–38 inch lbs. (3.3–4.3 Nm).

13. Connect all quick–connect electrical connections: turn signal, wash/wipe, key warning buzzer, ignition, speed control and air bag clockspring connector, if equipped.

14. Install upper shroud.

15. Tighten steering column mounting nuts and bolts to 15–25 ft. lbs. (20–34 Nm).

16. On air bag equipped vehicles, unlock steering column and cycle steering wheel 1 turn left and 1 turn right to align intermediate shaft into column shaft. Power steering vehicles must have engine running.

17. Tighten steering shaft clamp nut to 20–30 ft. lbs. (27–40 Nm).

18. Install lower trim shroud with retaining screws.

19. Install speed control module, if equipped, with screws.

20. On air bag equipped vehicles, connect the backup power supply and install the bolster.

21. Install steering column cover on instrument panel with the screws.

22. Connect battery ground cable.

23. Check steering column for proper operation.

24. Road test the vehicle, checking for proper alignment.

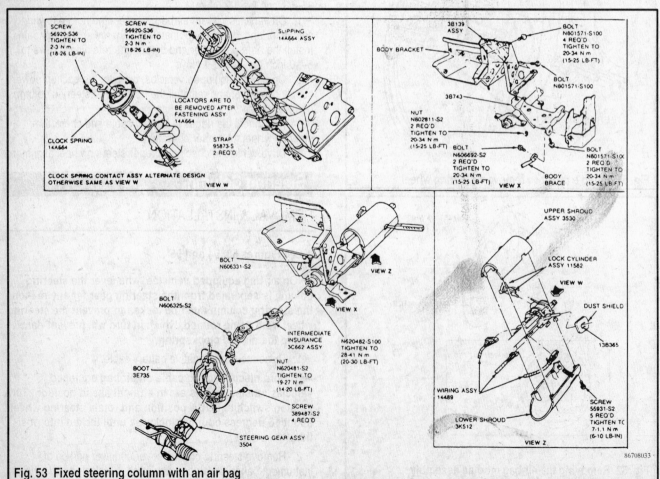

**Fig. 53 Fixed steering column with an air bag**

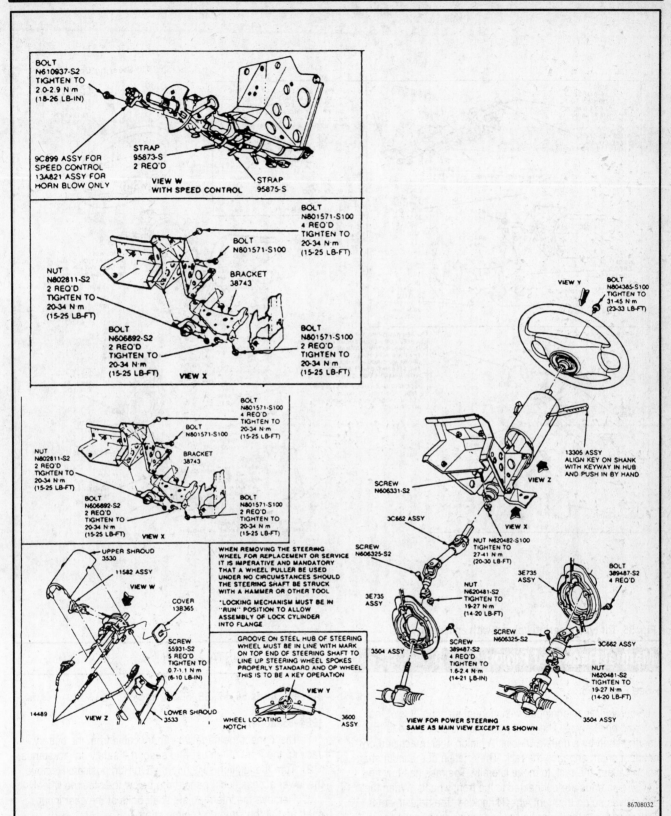

**Fig. 54 Fixed steering column without an air bag**

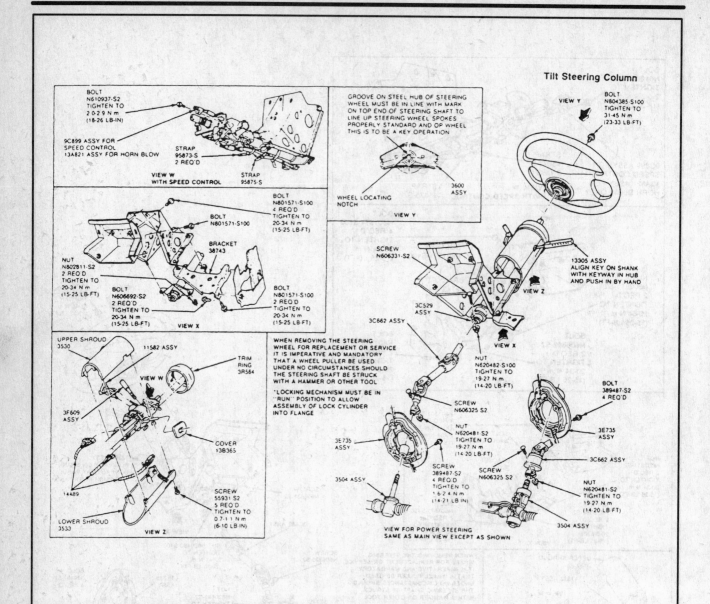

**Tilt Steering Column**

BOLT
N610937-S2
TIGHTEN TO
20-29 N·m
(18-26 LB-IN)

9C899 ASSY FOR
SPEED CONTROL
13A821 ASSY FOR HORN BLOW

STRAP
95873-S
2 REQ'D

VIEW W
WITH SPEED CONTROL

STRAP
95875-S

GROOVE ON STEEL HUB OF STEERING
WHEEL MUST BE IN LINE WITH MARK
ON TOP END OF STEERING SHAFT TO
LINE UP STEERING WHEEL SPOKES
PROPERLY STANDARD AND OP WHEEL
THIS IS TO BE A KEY OPERATION

WHEEL LOCATING
NOTCH

3600
ASSY

VIEW Y

BOLT
N804385-S100
TIGHTEN TO
31-45 N·m
(23-33 LB-FT)

VIEW Y

BOLT
N801571-S100
4 REQ'D
TIGHTEN TO
20-34 N·m
(15-25 LB-FT)

BOLT
N801571-S100

BRACKET
38743

NUT
N802811-S2
2 REQ'D
TIGHTEN TO
20-34 N·m
(15-25 LB-FT)

BOLT
N606692-S2
2 REQ'D
TIGHTEN TO
20-34 N·m
(15-25 LB-FT)

BOLT
N801571-S100
2 REQ'D
TIGHTEN TO
20-34 N·m
(15-25 LB-FT)

VIEW X

SCREW
N606331-S2

13305 ASSY
ALIGN KEY ON SHANK
WITH KEYWAY IN HUB
AND PUSH IN BY HAND

VIEW Z

3C529
ASSY

3C662 ASSY

VIEW X

NUT
N620482-S100
TIGHTEN TO
19-27 N·m
(14-20 LB-FT)

BOLT
389487-S2
4 REQ'D

UPPER SHROUD
3530

11582 ASSY

TRIM
RING
3R564

VIEW W

3F609
ASSY

COVER
13B365

14489

SCREW
55931-S2
5 REQ'D
TIGHTEN TO
0.7-1.1 N·m
(6-10 LB-IN)

LOWER SHROUD
3533

VIEW Z

WHEN REMOVING THE STEERING
WHEEL FOR REPLACEMENT OR SERVICE
IT IS IMPERATIVE AND MANDATORY
THAT A WHEEL PULLER BE USED
UNDER NO CIRCUMSTANCES SHOULD
THE STEERING SHAFT BE STRUCK
WITH A HAMMER OR OTHER TOOL

*LOCKING MECHANISM MUST BE IN
"RUN" POSITION TO ALLOW
ASSEMBLY OF LOCK CYLINDER
INTO FLANGE

SCREW
N606325-S2

NUT
N620481-S2
TIGHTEN TO
19-27 N·m
(14-20 LB-FT)

3E735
ASSY

3E735
ASSY

3C662 ASSY

SCREW
389487-S2
4 REQ'D
TIGHTEN TO
1.6-2.4 N·m
(14-21 LB-IN)

3504 ASSY

SCREW
N606325-S2

NUT
N620481-S2
TIGHTEN TO
19-27 N·m
(14-20 LB-FT)

3504 ASSY

VIEW FOR POWER STEERING
SAME AS MAIN VIEW EXCEPT AS SHOWN

86708034

**Fig. 55 Tilt type steering column with an air bag**

## Manual Rack and Pinion

♦ **See Figure 56**

If your vehicle is equipped with manual steering, it is of the rack and pinion type. The gear input shaft is connected to the steering shaft by a double U–joint. A pinion gear, machined on the input shaft, engages the rack. The rotation of the input shaft pinion causes the rack to move laterally. The rack has tow tie rods whose ends are connected to the front wheels. When the rack moves so do the front wheel knuckles. Toe adjustment is made by turning the outer tie rod ends in or out equally as required.

## REMOVAL & INSTALLATION

♦ **See Figures 56, 57, 58, 59, 60 and 61**

### 1984–85 Models

1. Disconnect the negative battery cable from the battery. Jack up the front of the car and support it safely on jackstands.
2. Turn the ignition switch to the On/Run position. Remove the lower access (kick) panel from below the steering wheel.
3. Remove the intermediate shaft bolts at the gear input shaft and at the steering column shaft.
4. Spread the slots of the clamp to loosen the intermediate shaft at both ends.
5. Remove the cotter pin from each tie rod end.

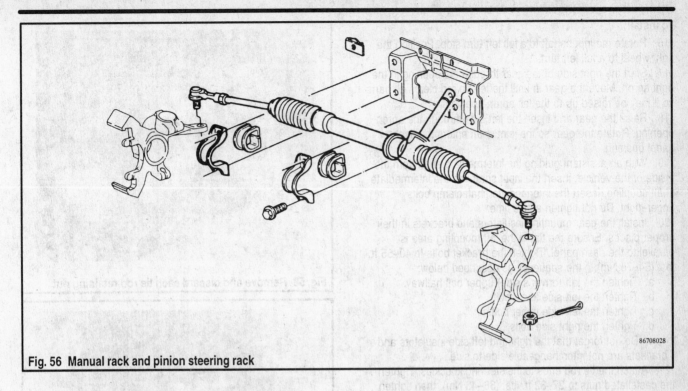

**Fig. 56 Manual rack and pinion steering rack**

6. Remove the nuts from each tie rod end and discard.

7. Separate the outer tie rod ends from the steering knuckle by using a tie rod end remover.

8. Remove the rod ends from the tie rod shafts.

9. Remove the steering rack mounting brackets and rubber mounting insulators.

10. Separate the intermediate shaft from the input shaft.

11. With some help, slowly move the steering rack to one side of the vehicle through the tie rod access hole. The rack may have to be twisted to allow the steering rod to clear the hole.

**To install:**

12. Position the gear through the splash panel and into the body opening.

13. Work the intermediate shaft into the input shaft. Secure with the nut and bolt, but do not tighten at this time.

14. Install the steering gear mounting rubber and brackets, tightening to 40–55 ft. lbs. (54–75 Nm).

15. Tighten the intermediate shaft and input shaft nut and bolt to 20–37 ft. lbs. (28–50 Nm).

16. Rotate the steering wheel so the tie rod ends move back and forth. Connect the tie rods to the spindle and tighten the nuts to 27–32 ft. lbs. (36–43 Nm).

17. Install the tie rod ends on to each steering knuckle, using new nuts. Tighten nuts to 27–32 ft. lbs. (36–43 Nm). Install new cotter pins

18. Install the lower access panel and secure with the hardware.

19. Connect the negative battery cable.

20. Turn ignition switch on and check for proper operation.

21. Lower vehicle. Have alignment checked.

**1986–94 Models**

1. Disconnect the negative battery cable.

2. Turn the ignition key to the RUN position.

3. Remove the access trim panel from below the steering column.

4. Remove the intermediate shaft bolts at the rack and pinion input shaft and the steering column shaft.

5. Spread the slots enough to loosen the intermediate shaft at both ends. They cannot be separated at this time.

6. Raise the vehicle and support it safely.

7. Separate the tie rod ends from the steering knuckles, using a suitable tool. Turn the right wheel to the full left turn position.

8. Disconnect the speedometer cable at the transaxle on automatic transaxles only.

9. Disconnect the secondary air tube at the check valve. Disconnect the exhaust system at the manifold and remove the system.

10. Remove the gear mounting brackets and insulators. Keep separated as they are not interchangeable.

11. Turn the steering wheel full left so the tie rod will clear the shift linkage during removal.

12. Separate the gear intermediate shaft, with an assistant pulling upward on the shaft from the inside of the vehicle.

➡ **Care should be taken during steering gear removal and installation to prevent tearing or damaging the steering gear bellows.**

13. Rotate the gear forward and down to clear the input shaft through the dash panel opening.

14. With the gear in the full left turn position, move the gear through the right (passenger side) apron opening until the left tie rod clears the shift linkage and other parts so it may be lowered.

15. Lower the left side of the gear assembly and remove from the vehicle.

**To install:**

16. Rotate the input shaft to a full left turn stop. Position the right wheel to a full left turn.

17. Start the right side of the gear through the opening in the right apron. Move the gear in until the left tie rod clears all parts so it may be raised up to the left apron opening.

18. Raise the gear and insert the left side through the apron opening. Rotate the gear so the joint shaft enters the dash panel opening.

19. With an assistant guiding the intermediate shaft from the inside of the vehicle, insert the input shaft into the intermediate shaft coupling. Insert the intermediate shaft clamp bolts finger–tight. Do not tighten at this time.

20. Install the gear mounting insulators and brackets in their proper places. Ensure the flat in the left mounting area is parallel to the dash panel. Tighten the bracket bolts to 40–55 ft. lbs. (54–75 Nm) in the sequence as described below:

    a. Tighten the left (driver's side) upper bolt halfway.

    b. Tighten the left side lower bolt.

    c. Tighten the left side upper bolt.

    d. Tighten the right side bolts.

    e. Do not forget that the right and left side insulators and brackets are not interchangeable side to side.

21. Attach the tie rod ends to the steering knuckles. Tighten the castellated nuts to 27–32 ft. lbs. (36–43 Nm), then tighten the nuts until the slot aligns with the cotter pin hole. Insert a new cotter pin.

22. Install the exhaust system. Install the speedometer cable, if removed.

23. Tighten the gear input shaft to intermediate shaft coupling clamp bolt first. Then, tighten the upper intermediate shaft clamp bolt. Tighten both bolts to 20–37 ft. lbs. (28–50 Nm).

24. Install the access panel below the steering column. Turn the ignition key to the OFF position.

25. Check and adjust the toe. Tighten the tie rod end jam nuts, check for twisted bellows.

26. Lower vehicle. Have toe alignment check. Road test the vehicle, checking for correct operation.

86708524

**Fig. 58 Remove and discard each tie rod retaining nut**

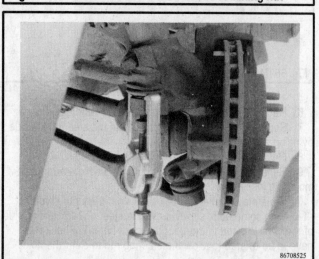

86708525

**Fig. 59 Using a tie rod remover, unfasten the tie rod from the knuckle**

86708523

**Fig. 57 Remove the cotter pin from each tie rod**

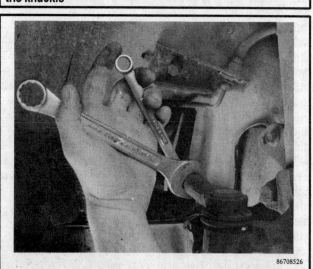

86708526

**Fig. 60 Using 2 wrenches, loosen the retaining nut to the tie rod**

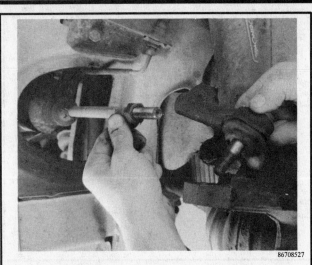

86708527

Fig. 61 Remove the tie rod from the tie rod shaft.

## ADJUSTMENTS

### Tie Rod Articulation Effort

The yoke clearance is not adjustable except when overhauling the steering gear assembly. Pinion bearing preload is not adjustable. Tie rod articulation is preset and is not adjustable. If articulation is out of specification, replace the tie rod assembly. To check tie rod articulation, proceed as follows:

1. With the tie rod end disconnected from the steering knuckle, loop a piece of wire through the hole in the tie rod end stud.
2. Insert the hook of spring scale T74P–3504–Y or equivalent, through the wire loop. Effort to move the tie rod after initial breakaway should be 0.7–5.0 lbs.

➡ Do not damage tie rod neck.

3. Replace ball joint/tie rod assembly if effort falls outside this range. Save the tie rod end for use on the new tie rod assembly.

### Rack Preload/Support Yoke

1. Remove the rack and pinion assembly from the vehicle and mount it in a suitable vice.
2. Loosen the locknut.
3. Tighten the adjusting bolt using yoke adjustment adapter T90P–3504–JH in the yoke plug to 8.7 inch lbs. (1 Nm), then loosen the adjusting bolt 10–40 degrees from that position.
4. Measure the pinion turning torque using pinion shaft adapting tool T86P–3504–K. The correct torque at the neutral position plus or minus 90 degrees should be 9–12 inch lbs. (1.0–1.3 Nm). At any other position the torque should be 14.7 inch lbs. (1.6 Nm) or less.
5. If the pinion torque is not within specification, re-adjust the adjusting bolt to achieve the correct pinion torque. Tighten the adjusting bolt locknut.

## Power Steering Rack

A rotary design control valve uses relative rotational motion of the input shaft and valve sleeve to direct fluid flow. When the steering wheel is turned, resistance of the wheels and the weight of the car cause a torsion bar to twist. The twisting causes the valve to move in the sleeve and aligns fluid passages for right/left and straight ahead position. The pressure forces on the valve and helps move the rack to assist in the turning effort. The piston is attached directly to the rack. The housing tube functions as the power cylinder. The hydraulic areas of the gear assembly are always filled with fluid. The mechanical gears are filled with grease making periodic lubrication unnecessary. The fluid and grease act as a cushion to absorb road shock.

## REMOVAL & INSTALLATION

▶ See Figure 62

1. Disconnect the negative battery cable.
2. Turn the ignition key to the RUN position.
3. Remove access panel from dash below the steering column.
4. Remove screws from steering column boot at the dash panel and slide boot up intermediate shaft.
5. Remove intermediate shaft bolt at gear input shaft and loosen the bolt at the steering column shaft joint.
6. With a suitable tool, spread the slots enough to loosen intermediates shaft at both ends. The intermediate shaft and gear input shaft cannot be separated at this time.
7. Remove the air cleaner, as required.
8. On vehicles equipped with air conditioning, wire the air conditioner liquid line above the dash panel opening. Doing so provides clearance for gear input shaft removal and installation.
9. Separate pressure and return lines at intermediate connections.
10. Disconnect the exhaust secondary air tube at check valve. Raise the vehicle and support it safely. Disconnect exhaust system at exhaust manifold.
11. Separate tie rod ends from steering knuckles.
12. Remove left tie rod end from tie rod on manual transaxle vehicles. This will allow tie rod to clear the shift linkage.

➡ Mark location of rod end prior to removal.

13. Disconnect speedometer cable at transaxle, if equipped with automatic transaxle. Remove the vehicle speed sensor.
14. Remove transaxle shift cable assembly at transaxle on vehicles equipped with automatic transaxle.
15. Turn steering wheel to full left turn stop for easier gear removal.
16. Remove screws holding the heater water tube to shake brace below the oil pan.
17. Remove nut from the lower of bolt holding engine mount support bracket to transaxle housing. Tap bolt out as far as it will go.
18. Remove the gear mounting brackets and insulators.
19. Drape cloth towel over both apron opening edges to protect bellows during gear removal.
20. Separate gear from intermediate shaft by either pushing up on shaft with a bar from underneath the vehicle while pulling the gear down or with an assistant removing the shaft from inside the vehicle.
21. Rotate gear forward and down to clear the input shaft through the dash panel opening.

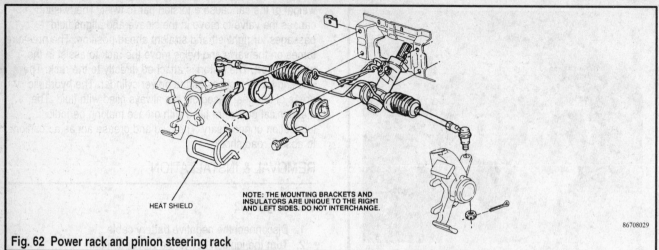

HEAT SHIELD

NOTE: THE MOUNTING BRACKETS AND INSULATORS ARE UNIQUE TO THE RIGHT AND LEFT SIDES. DO NOT INTERCHANGE.

86708029

**Fig. 62 Power rack and pinion steering rack**

22. Make sure input shaft is in full left turn position. Move gear through the right (passenger) side apron opening until left tie rod clears left apron opening and other parts so it may be lowered. Guide the power steering hoses around the nearby components as the gear is being removed.

23. Lower the left side of the gear and remove the gear out of the vehicle. Use care not to tear the bellows.

**To install:**

24. Rotate the input shaft to a full left turn stop. Position the right road wheel to a full left turn.

25. Start the right side of the gear through the opening in the right apron. Move the gear in until the left tie rod clears all parts so it may be raised up to the left apron opening.

26. Raise the gear and insert the left side through the apron opening. Move the power steering hoses into their proper position at the same time. Rotate the gear so the joint shaft enters the dash panel opening.

27. With an assistant guiding the intermediate shaft from the inside of the vehicle, insert the input shaft into the intermediate shaft coupling. Insert the intermediate shaft clamp bolts finger-tight. Do not tighten at this time.

28. Install the gear mounting insulators and brackets in their proper places. Ensure the flat in the left mounting area is parallel to the dash panel. Tighten the bracket bolts to 40–55 ft. lbs. (54–75 Nm) in the sequence as described below:

    a. Tighten the left (driver's side) upper bolt halfway.

    b. Tighten the left side lower bolt.

    c. Tighten the left side upper bolt.

    d. Tighten the right side bolts.

    e. Do not forget that the right and left side insulators and brackets are not interchangeable side to side.

29. Attach the tie rod ends to the steering knuckles. Tighten the castellated nuts to 27–32 ft. lbs. (36–43 Nm), then tighten the nuts until the slot aligns with the cotter pin hole. Insert a new cotter pin.

30. Install the engine mount nut.

31. Install the heater water tube to the shake brace.

32. Install the exhaust system. Install the speedometer cable, if removed. Install the vehicle speed sensor and the transaxle shift cable.

33. Connect the secondary air tube at the check valve. Connect the pressure and return lines at the intermediate connections or steering gear.

34. Install the air cleaner.

35. Tighten the gear input shaft to intermediate shaft coupling clamp bolt first. Then, tighten the upper intermediate shaft clamp bolt. Tighten to 20–30 ft. lbs. (27–40 Nm).

36. Install the access panel below the steering column. Turn the ignition key to the OFF position.

37. Fill the system. Check and adjust the toe. Tighten the tie rod end jam nuts to 40–50 ft. lbs. (54–68 Nm), check for twisted bellows.

38. Connect negative battery cable.

39. Have the alignment checked.

## ADJUSTMENTS

The power rack and pinion steering gear provides for only rack yoke plug preload adjustment. This adjustment can be performed only with the gear out of the vehicle. To check rack yoke plug preload, proceed as follows:

### Rack and Pinion With One–Piece Housing

1. Disconnect the negative battery cable.

2. Raise and safely support the vehicle on jackstands.

3. Remove power rack and pinion assembly from vehicle.

4. Clean exterior of steering gear thoroughly.

5. Mount steering gear in a suitable rack housing holding fixture.

➡ **Do not mount gear in vise.**

6. Do not remove external pressure lines, unless they are leaking or damaged. If these lines are removed, they must be replaced with new lines.

7. Drain the power steering fluid by rotating the input shaft lock–to–lock twice using input shaft torque adapter T81P–3504–R or equivalent. Position adapter and wrench on input shaft.

8. Loosen yoke plug locknut with yoke locknut wrench T81P–3504–G or equivalent.

9. Loosen yoke plug using yoke plug adapter T87P–3504–G or equivalent.

10. With rack at center of travel, tighten yoke plug to 44–50 inch lbs. (5.0–5.7 Nm). Clean threads of yoke plug prior to tightening to prevent a false reading.

11. install yoke plug adapter T87P–3504–G or equivalent. Mark location of zero degree mark on housing. Back off adjuster so 48 degree mark lines up with zero degree mark.

12. Place yoke locknut wrench T81P–3504–G or equivalent, on yoke plug locknut. While holding yoke plug, tighten locknut to 40–50 ft. lbs. (54–68 Nm). Do not allow yoke plug to move while tightening or preload will be affected. Check input shaft torque after tightening locknut.

13. If external pressure lines were removed, the Teflon® seal rings must be replaced. Clean out Teflon® seal shreds from housing ports prior to installation of new lines.

14. Install power rack assembly in vehicle.

15. Lower vehicle.

16. Connect negative battery cable.

17. Road test the vehicle.

### Rack and Pinion With Two–Piece Housing

1. Disconnect the negative battery cable.

2. Raise and safely support the vehicle.

3. Remove the power rack and pinion assembly from the vehicle.

4. Clean the exterior of the gear in the yoke plug area and mount the gear in a vise, gripping it near the center of the tube. Do not over–tighten.

5. Loosen and remove the yoke plug locknut.

6. Back off the yoke plug 1 turn.

7. Tighten the yoke plug to 45 inch lbs. (5.8 Nm) using yoke plug adapter T81P–3504–U or equivalent, and an inch–pound torque wrench with a full scale reading to 100 inch lbs. maximum.

8. Scribe the gear housing in line with the 0 mark on the yoke plug adapter tool.

9. Back off the yoke plug so the second mark on the yoke plug adapter tool aligns with the scribe mark on the gear housing.

10. Hold the plug, and install and tighten the locknut to 40–50 ft. lbs. (54–68 Nm) using yoke locknut wrench T81P–3504–G or equivalent.

## Power Steering Pump

## REMOVAL & INSTALLATION

### 2.0L Diesel Engine

1. Remove the drive belts.

2. On air conditioned models, remove the alternator.

3. Remove both braces from the support bracket on air conditioned models.

4. Disconnect the power steering fluid lines and drain the fluid into a suitable container.

5. Remove the four bracket mounting bolts and remove the pump and bracket assembly.

6. The pulley must be remove before the pump can be separated from the mounting bracket. Tool T65P–3A733–C or equivalent is required to remove and install the drive pulley.

### To install:

7. Install the pump and mounting bracket assembly using the 4 mounting bolts.

8. Connect the power steering fluid lines, and fill with clean fluid.

9. Install the braces if vehicle is equipped with A/C.

10. Position and secure the alternator if equipped with A/C.

11. Connect the drive belt and tension to specification.

12. Start vehicle, and check for air bubbles. Bleed if necessary.

13. Road test the vehicle.

### 2.3L and 3.0L Gasoline Engines

1. Disconnect the negative battery cable. Remove the air cleaner, thermactor air pump and belt. Remove the reservoir filler extension and cover the hole to prevent dirt from entering.

2. If equipped with EFI and remote reservoir, remove the reservoir supply hose at the pump, drain the fluid and plug or cap the opening at the pump to prevent entry of contaminants during removal.

3. From under the vehicle, loosen 1 pump adjusting bolt. Remove 1 pump to bracket mounting bolt and disconnect the fluid return line.

4. From above the vehicle, loosen 1 adjusting bolt and the pivot bolt. Remove the drive belt and the 2 remaining pump to bracket mounting bolts.

5. Remove the pump by passing the pulley through the adjusting bracket opening. Remove the pressure hose from the pump assembly.

### To install:

6. From under the vehicle, connect the pressure hose to the pump. Pass the pulley through the opening in the adjusting bracket. Install the mounting bolts and tighten to 30–45 ft. lbs. (40–62 Nm).

7. If applicable, make sure the air pump belt is on the inner power steering pump pulley groove. Install the power steering pump belt and adjust. Tighten all bolts to 30–45 ft. lbs. (40–62 Nm).

➡ **When adjusting belt tension, never pry on the pump or surrounding aluminum parts or brackets.**

8. If not equipped with a remote reservoir, install the return line to the pump.

9. From above the vehicle, install the reservoir filler neck extension, if applicable. Install the air cleaner, if applicable.

10. Install remote reservoir supply to pump on EFI/remote vehicles.

11. Fill pump or remote reservoir with fluid and check operation.

12. Start vehicle and check for air in the fluid. Bleed if necessary.

## SYSTEM BLEEDING

If air bubbles are present in the power steering fluid, bleed the system by performing the following:

1. Fill the reservoir to the proper level.

2. Operate the engine until the fluid reaches normal operating temperature (165–175°F).

3. Turn the steering wheel all the way to the left then all the way to the right several times. Do not hold the steering wheel in the far left or far right position stops.

4. Check the fluid level and recheck the fluid for the presence of trapped air. If apparent that air is still in the system, fabricate or obtain a vacuum tester and purge the system as follows:

   a. Remove the pump dipstick cap assembly.

b. Check and fill the pump reservoir with fluid to the COLD FULL mark on the dipstick.

c. Disconnect the ignition wire and raise the front of the vehicle and support safely.

d. Crank the engine with the starter and check the fluid level. Do not turn the steering wheel at this time.

e. Fill the pump reservoir to the COLD FULL mark on the dipstick. Crank the engine with the starter while cycling the steering wheel lock–to–lock. Check the fluid level.

f. Tightly insert a suitable size rubber stopper and air evacuator pump into the reservoir fill neck. Connect the ignition coil wire.

g. With the engine idling, apply a 15 in. Hg vacuum to the reservoir for 3 minutes. As air is purged from the system, the vacuum will drop off. Maintain the vacuum on the system as required throughout the 3 minutes.

h. Remove the vacuum source. Fill the reservoir to the COLD FULL mark on the dipstick.

i. With the engine idling, re–apply 15 in. Hg vacuum source to the reservoir. Slowly cycle the steering wheel to lock–to–lock stops for approximately 5 minutes. Do not hold the steering wheel on the stops during cycling. Maintain the vacuum as required.

j. Release the vacuum and disconnect the vacuum source. Add fluid, as required.

k. Start the engine and cycle the wheel slowly and check for leaks at all connections.

l. Lower the front wheels.

5. In cases of severe aeration, repeat the procedure.

6. Road test the vehicle.

## Tie Rod Ends

### REMOVAL & INSTALLATION

▶ **See Figures 58, 59, 60 and 61**

1. Raise and support the vehicle on jackstands. Remove the wheel and tire.

2. Remove and discard cotter pin and nut from worn tie rod end ball stud.

3. Scribe matchmarks on the tie rod locking nut and inner tie rod shaft. These marks will help ensure that the installation of the tie rods will be close to the original specifications.

4. Disconnect tie rod end from spindle, using tie rod end remover tool 3290–D and adapter T81P–3504–W or equivalent.

5. Holding tie rod end with a wrench, loosen tie rod jam nut.

6. When you remove the tie rod, count the number of turns it takes to remove the unit. This will be the number of turns you will apply when installing the new tie rod.

7. Grip tie rod hex flats with a pair of suitable locking pliers, and remove tie rod end assembly from tie rod. Note depth to which tie rod was located, using jam nut as a marker.

**To install:**

8. Clean tie rod threads. Apply a light coating of disc brake caliper slide grease D7AZ–19590–A or equivalent, to tie rod threads. Thread the new tie rod end on the shaft the same

number of turns, and depth. Tighten jam nut, aligning the matchmarks.

9. Place the tie rod end stud into steering spindle.

10. Install a new nut on tie rod end stud. Tighten nut to minimum specification, and continue tightening nut to align next castellation with cotter pin hole in stud. Install a new cotter pin.

11. Have the alignment checked and adjusted, if needed, by qualified professional.

## Steering Rack Boots

### REMOVAL & INSTALLATION

▶ **See Figures 63, 64 and 65**

Because the boots are rubber, salt and time can destroy them. Steering rack boots should be checked regularly and replaced when needed. A torn boot can introduce dirt and girt into the steering rack and contribute to premature rack failure.

1. Raise and support the vehicle on jackstands. Remove the wheel and tire.

2. Remove the tie rod as outlined earlier.

3. Loosen the clamp securing the inner portion of the boot to the steering rack. If equipped with power steering, remove the hoses from the boot.

4. Remove the clip from the outer portion of the boot.

5. Slide the boot off the tie rod shaft.

6. Inspect the rack shaft and clean any dirt present.

**To install:**

7. Slide the new boot on to the tie rod shaft and seat on inner portion of the rack. Tighten the clamp. Install the hose if equipped with power steering.

8. Install the clip on the outer part of the boot.

9. Install the tie rods as outlined earlier.

10. Position and secure the wheel and tire. Lower the vehicle.

11. Because the tie rods were removed, have the alignment checked.

86708528

**Fig. 63 Loosen the inner clamp, and hose fitting, then slide the boot back.**

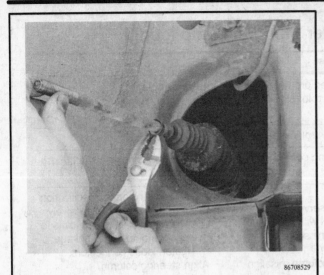

86708529

Fig. 64 Using pliers, remove the clip from the tie rod shaft

86708530

Fig. 65 Slide the boot off the shaft. Check for dirt and debris, and clean if necessary

## Troubleshooting the Power Steering Pump

| Problem | Cause | Solution |
|---|---|---|
| Chirp noise in steering pump | • Loose belt | • Adjust belt tension to specification |
| Belt squeal (particularly noticeable at full wheel travel and stand still parking) | • Loose belt | • Adjust belt tension to specification |
| Growl noise in steering pump | • Excessive back pressure in hoses or steering gear caused by restriction | • Locate restriction and correct. Replace part if necessary. |
| Growl noise in steering pump (particularly noticeable at stand still parking) | • Scored pressure plates, thrust plate or rotor<br>• Extreme wear of cam ring | • Replace parts and flush system<br><br>• Replace parts |
| Groan noise in steering pump | • Low oil level<br>• Air in the oil. Poor pressure hose connection. | • Fill reservoir to proper level<br>• Tighten connector to specified torque. Bleed system by operating steering from right to left—full turn. |
| Low pump pressure | • Extreme wear of cam ring<br>• Scored pressure plate, thrust plate, or rotor<br>• Vanes not installed properly<br>• Vanes sticking in rotor slots<br><br>• Cracked or broken thrust or pressure plate | • Replace parts. Flush system.<br>• Replace parts. Flush system.<br><br>• Install properly<br>• Freeup by removing burrs, varnish, or dirt<br>• Replace part |

86708300

## Troubleshooting the Power Steering Pump (cont.)

| Problem | Cause | Solution |
|---|---|---|
| Rattle noise in steering pump | • Vanes not installed properly<br>• Vanes sticking in rotor slots | • Install properly<br>• Free up by removing burrs, varnish, or dirt |
| Swish noise in steering pump | • Defective flow control valve | • Replace part |
| Whine noise in steering pump | • Pump shaft bearing scored | • Replace housing and shaft. Flush system. |
| Hard steering or lack of assist | • Loose pump belt<br>• Low oil level in reservoir<br>**NOTE:** Low oil level will also result in excessive pump noise<br><br>• Steering gear to column misalignment<br>• Lower coupling flange rubbing against steering gear adjuster plug<br>• Tires not properly inflated | • Adjust belt tension to specification<br>• Fill to proper level. If excessively low, check all lines and joints for evidence of external leakage. Tighten loose connectors.<br>• Align steering column<br>• Loosen pinch bolt and assemble properly<br>• Inflate to recommended pressure |
| Foaming milky power steering fluid, low fluid level and possible low pressure | • Air in the fluid, and loss of fluid due to internal pump leakage causing overflow | • Check for leaks and correct. Bleed system. Extremely cold temperatures will cause system aeriation should the oil level be low. If oil level is correct and pump still foams, remove pump from vehicle and separate reservoir from body. Check welsh plug and body for cracks. If plug is loose or body is cracked, replace body. |
| Low pump pressure | • Flow control valve stuck or inoperative<br>• Pressure plate not flat against cam ring | • Remove burrs or dirt or replace. Flush system.<br>• Correct |
| Momentary increase in effort when turning wheel fast to right or left | • Low oil level in pump<br><br>• Pump belt slipping<br>• High internal leakage | • Add power steering fluid as required<br>• Tighten or replace belt<br>• Check pump pressure. (See pressure test) |
| Steering wheel surges or jerks when turning with engine running especially during parking | • Low oil level<br>• Loose pump belt<br>• Steering linkage hitting engine oil pan at full turn<br>• Insufficient pump pressure | • Fill as required<br>• Adjust tension to specification<br>• Correct clearance<br><br>• Check pump pressure. (See pressure test). Replace flow control valve if defective. |
| Steering wheel surges or jerks when turning with engine running especially during parking (cont.) | • Sticking flow control valve | • Inspect for varnish or damage, replace if necessary |
| Excessive wheel kickback or loose steering | • Air in system | • Add oil to pump reservoir and bleed by operating steering. Check hose connectors for proper torque and adjust as required. |

86708301

## TORQUE SPECIFICATIONS

| Component | English | Metric |
|---|---|---|
| **Front Suspension** | | |
| Strut top mount-to-body: | 25–30 ft. lbs. | 34–41 Nm |
| Strut-to-top mount: | 35–50 ft. lbs. | 48–68 Nm |
| Strut-to-knuckle: | 55–81 ft. lbs. | 75–110 Nm |
| Control arm-to-body: | 48–55 ft. lbs. | 65–74 Nm |
| Control arm-to-knuckle: | 38–45 ft. lbs. | 51–61 Nm |
| Stablizer bar-to-control arm: | 98–115 ft. lbs. | 132–156 Nm |
| Stablizer bar bracket assembly-to-body: | 48–55 ft. lbs. | 65–74 Nm |
| Tie rod end-to-steering knuckle: | 28–32 ft. lbs. | 38–43 Nm |
| Left hand front engine mount-to-stablizer bar to body bracket: | 55–65 ft. lbs. | 75–88 Nm |
| **Rear Suspension** | | |
| Strut top mount-to-body: | 20–30 ft. lbs. | 27–41 Nm |
| Strut-to-top mount: | 35–50 ft. lbs. | 48–68 Nm |
| Strut-to-spindle: | 70–96 ft. lbs. | 95–130 Nm |
| Control arm-to-spindle: | 60–80 ft. lbs. | 81–109 Nm |
| Control arm-to-body: | 30–40 ft. lbs. | 40–54 Nm |
| Tie rod-to-spindle: | 52–74 ft. lbs. | 70–100 Nm |
| Tie rod-to-body: | 52–74 ft. lbs. | 70–100 Nm |
| **Steering Column** | | |
| Steering wheel bolt: | 23–33 ft. lbs. | 31–45 Nm |
| Column-to-support bracket bolt: | 15–25 ft. lbs. | 20–34 Nm |
| Intermediate shaft-to-steering gear nut and bolt: | 14–20 ft. lbs. | 19–27 Nm |
| Air bag module-to-steering wheel nuts | | |
| 1989-91: | 35–53 inch lbs. | 4–6 Nm |
| 1992-94: | 36–49 inch lbs. | 4–6 Nm |
| **Steering Gear—Rack-and-Pinion Manual** | | |
| Pinion plug: | 52–73 ft. lbs. | 70–100 Nm |
| Steering gear mounting bolts: | 40–55 ft. lbs. | 54–75 Nm |
| Tie rod end-to-spindle arm*: | 27–32 ft. lbs. | 36–43 Nm |
| Tie rod end-to-inner tie rod jam nut: | 35–50 ft. lbs. | 47–68 Nm |
| Pinion shaft-to-intermediate shaft bolts: | 20–37 ft. lbs. | 28–50 Nm |
| Ball housing-to-rack: | 50–60 ft. lbs. | 68–81 Nm |
| Yoke plug prior to 30 degrees back-off: | 40 inch lbs. | 4.5 Nm |

*Tighten to nearest cotter pin slot after tightening to minimum specifications.

86708310

## TORQUE SPECIFICATIONS

| Component | English | Metric |
|---|---|---|
| **Steering Gear—Power Rack-and-Pinion** | | |
| **TRW 2-piece Housing** | | |
| Pinion locknut: | 20–35 ft. lbs. | 27–47 Nm |
| Pinion cap: | 35–45 ft. lbs. | 47–61 Nm |
| Yoke plug locknut: | 40–50 ft. lbs. | 54–68 Nm |
| Tie rod ball housing: | 50–55 ft. lbs. | 68–75 Nm |
| Tie rod end-to-spindle arm*: | 27–32 ft. lbs. | 36–43 Nm |
| Steering gear mounting bolt: | 40–55 ft. lbs. | 54–75 Nm |
| Flex coupling-to-steering gear input shaft clamp bolt: | 20–30 ft. lbs. | 27–40 Nm |
| Tie rod-to-tie rod end jam nut: | 42–50 ft. lbs. | 57–68 Nm |

*Tighten to nearest cotter pin slot after tightening to minimum specifications.

| Component | English | Metric |
|---|---|---|
| **Steering Gear—Power Rack-and-Pinion** | | |
| **Corporate 1-piece Housing** | | |
| Pinion locknut: | 20–35 ft. lbs. | 27–47 Nm |
| Pinion cap: | 35–45 ft. lbs. | 47–61 Nm |
| Yoke plug locknut: | 40–50 ft. lbs. | 54–68 Nm |
| Tie rod ball housing: | 40–50 ft. lbs. | 54–68 Nm |
| Tie rod end-to-spindle arm*: | 27–32 ft. lbs. | 36–43 Nm |
| Steering gear mounting bolt: | 40–55 ft. lbs. | 54–75 Nm |
| Flex coupling-to-steering gear input shaft clamp bolt: | 20–30 ft. lbs. | 27–40 Nm |
| Tie rod-to-tie rod end jam nut: | 42–50 ft. lbs. | 57–68 Nm |

*Tighten to nearest cotter pin slot after tightening to minimum specifications.

86708311

## WHEEL ALIGNMENT

| Year | Model | | Caster Range (deg.) | Caster Preferred Setting (deg.) | Camber Range (deg.) | Camber Preferred Setting (deg.) | Toe-in (In.) | Steering Axis Inclination (deg.) |
|------|-------|---|------|------|------|------|------|------|
| 1984 | Tempo/Topaz | LF | 1/2P-2P | 1 1/4P | 1 1/4P-2 3/4P | 2P | 1/8N | 14 5/8 |
| | Tempo/Topaz | RF | 1/2P-2P | 1 1/4P | 3/4N-2 1/4P | 1 1/2P | 1/8N | 15 1/8 |
| | Tempo/Topaz | R | - | - | 9/16N-15/16P | 15/16N | 3/32 | - |
| 1985 | Tempo/Topaz | LF | 1/2P-2P | 1 1/4P | 1 1/4P-2 3/4P | 2P | 1/8N | 14 5/8 |
| | Tempo/Topaz | RF | 1/2P-2P | 1 1/4P | 3/4N-2 1/4P | 1 1/2P | 1/8N | 15 1/8 |
| | Tempo/Topaz | R | - | - | 9/16N-15/16P | 15/16N | 3/32 | - |
| 1986 | Tempo/Topaz [1] | LF | 1 5/8P-3 1/8P | 2 3/8P | 7/16P-1 15/16P | 1 3/16P | 3/32N | 14 21/32 |
| | Tempo/Topaz [1] | RF | 1 5/8P-3 1/8P | 2 3/8P | 0-1 1/2P | 3/4P | 3/32N | 15 3/32 |
| | Tempo/Topaz [2] | LF | 1 11/16P-3 3/16P | 2 7/16P | 13/32P-1 29/32P | 1 5/32P | 3/32N | 14 21/32 |
| | Tempo/Topaz [2] | RF | 1 11/16P-3 3/16P | 2 7/16P | 1/32N-1 15/32P | 23/32P | 3/32N | 15 3/32 |
| | Tempo/Topaz | R | - | - | 1 1/32N-15/32P | 9/32N | 0 | - |
| 1987 | Tempo/Topaz | LF | 1 11/16P-3 3/16P | 2 7/16P | 21/32P-2 5/32P | 1 13/32P | 3/32N | 14 21/32 |
| | Tempo/Topaz | RF | 1 11/16P-3 3/16P | 2 7/16P | 7/32P-1 23/32P | 31/32P | 3/32N | 15 3/32 |
| | Tempo/Topaz | R [1] | - | - | 29/32N-19/32P | 5/32N | 0 | - |
| | Tempo/Topaz | R [2] | - | - | 13/32N-1 3/32P | 11/32P | 0 | - |
| 1988 | Tempo/Topaz | LF | 1 11/16P-3 3/16P | 2 7/16P | 21/32P-2 5/32P | 1 13/32P | 3/32N | 14 21/32 |
| | Tempo/Topaz | RF | 1 11/16P-3 3/16P | 2 7/16P | 7/32P-1 23/32P | 31/32P | 3/32N | 15 3/32 |
| | Tempo/Topaz [1] | R | - | - | 29/32N-19/32P | 5/32N | 0 | - |
| | Tempo/Topaz [2] | R | - | - | 13/32N-1 3/32P | 11/32P | 0 | - |
| 1989 | Tempo/Topaz | RF | 1 11/16P-3 3/16P | 2 7/16P | 21/32P-2 5/32P | 1 13/32P | 3/32N | 14 21/32 |
| | Tempo/Topaz | LF | 1 11/16P-3 3/16P | 2 7/16P | 7/32P-1 23/32P | 31/32P | 3/32N | 15 3/32 |
| | Tempo/Topaz [1] | R | - | - | 29/32N-19/32P | 5/32N | 0 | - |
| | Tempo/Topaz [2] | R | - | - | 13/32N-1 3/32P | 11/32P | 0 | - |
| 1990 | Tempo/Topaz | LF | 1 11/16P-3 3/16P | 2 7/16P | 21/32P-2 5/32P | 1 13/32P | 3/32N | 14 21/32 |
| | Tempo/Topaz | RF | 1 11/16P-3 3/16P | 2 7/16P | 7/32P1 23/32P | 31/32P | 3/32N | 15 3/32 |
| | Tempo/Topaz [1] | R | - | - | 29/32N-19/32P | 5/32N | 0 | - |
| | Tempo/Topaz [2] | R | - | - | 13/32N-1 3/32P | 11/32P | 0 | - |
| 1991 | Tempo/Topaz | LF | 1 11/16P-3 3/16P | 2 7/16P | 21/32P-2 5/32P | 1 13/32P | 3/32N | 14 21/32 |
| | Tempo/Topaz | RF | 1 11/16P-3 3/16P | 2 7/16P | 7/32P-1 23/32P | 31/32P | 3/32N | 15 3/32 |
| | Tempo/Topaz [1] | R | - | - | 29/32N-19/32P | 5/32N | 0 | - |
| | Tempo/Topaz [2] | R | - | - | 13/32N-1 3/32P | 11/32P | 0 | - |
| 1992 | Tempo/Topaz | LF | 1 11/16P-3 3/16P | 2 7/16P | 21/32P-2 5/32P | 1 13/32P | 3/32N | 14 21/32 |
| | Tempo/Topaz | RF | 1 11/16P-3 3/16P | 2 7/16P | 7/32P-1 23/32P | 31/32P | 3/32N | 15 3/32 |
| | Tempo/Topaz [1] | R | - | - | 29/32N-19/32P | 5/32N | 0 | - |
| | Tempo/Topaz [2] | R | - | - | 13/32N-1 3/32P | 11/32P | 0 | - |
| 1993 | Tempo/Topaz | LF | 1 11/16P-3 3/16P | 2 7/16P | 21/32P-2 5/32P | 1 13/32P | 3/32N | 14 21/32 |
| | Tempo/Topaz | RF | 1 11/16P-3 3/16P | 2 7/16P | 7/32P-1 23/32P | 31/32P | 3/32N | 15 3/32 |
| | Tempo/Topaz | R | - | - | 29/32N-19/32P | 5/32P | 0 | - |
| 1994 | Tempo/Topaz | LF | 1.69P-3.19P | 2.44P | 0.66P-2.16P | 1.41P | 0.09N | 14.66 |
| | Tempo/Topaz | RF | 1.69P-3.19P | 2.44P | 0.22P-1.72P | 0.97P | 0.09N | 15.09 |

P - Positive
N - Negative
LF - Left Front
RF - Right Front
R- Rear
1  Without AWD
2  AWD

86708315

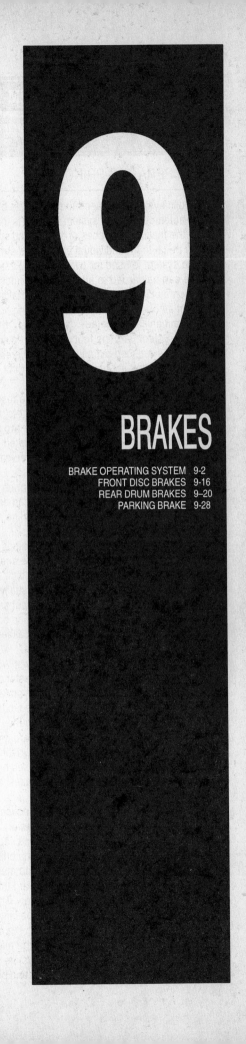

# 9

# BRAKES

# BRAKE OPERATING SYSTEM

## Understanding the Brake Hydraulic System

### BASIC OPERATING PRINCIPLES

Hydraulic systems are used to actuate the brakes of all modern automobiles. The system transports the power required to force the frictional surfaces of the braking system together from the pedal to the individual brake units at each wheel. A hydraulic system is used for two reasons. First, fluid under pressure can be carried to all parts of an automobile by small hoses, some of which are flexible, without taking up a significant amount of room or posing routing problems. Second, a great mechanical advantage can be given to the brake pedal end of the system, and the foot pressure required to actuate the brakes can be reduced by making surface area of the master cylinder pistons smaller than that of any of the pistons in the wheel cylinders or calipers.

The master cylinder consists of a double reservoir and piston assembly as well as other springs, fittings etc. Double (dual) master cylinders are designed to separate two wheels from the others. Your car's braking system is separated diagonally. That is, the right front and left rear use one reservoir and the left front and right rear use the other.

Steel lines carry the brake fluid to a point on the car's frame near each wheel. A flexible hose usually carries the fluid to the disc caliper or wheel cylinder. The flexible line allows for suspension and steering movements.

The rear wheel cylinders contain two pistons each, one at either end, which push outward in opposite directions. The front disc brake calipers contain one piston each.

All pistons employ some type of seal, usually make of rubber, to minimize fluid leakage. A rubber dust boot seals the outer end of the cylinder against dust and dirt. The boot fits around the outer end of the piston on disc brake calipers, and around the brake actuating rod on wheel cylinders.

The hydraulic system operates as follows: When at rest, the entire system, from the piston(s) in the master cylinder to those in the wheel cylinders or calipers, is full of brake fluid. Upon application of the brake pedal, fluid trapped in front of the master cylinder piston(s) is forced through the lines to the wheel cylinders. Here, it forces the pistons outward, in the case of drum brakes, and inward toward the disc, in the case of disc brakes. The motion of the pistons is opposed by return springs mounted outside the cylinders in drum brakes, and by internal springs or spring seal, in disc brakes.

Upon release of the brake pedal, a spring located inside the master cylinder immediately return the master cylinder pistons to the normal position. The pistons contain check valves and the master cylinder has compensating ports drilled in it. These are uncovered as the pistons reach their normal position. The piston check valves allow fluid to flow toward the wheel cylinders or calipers as the pistons withdraw. Then, as the return springs force the brake pads or shoes into the released position, the excess fluid reservoir through the compensating ports. It is during the time the pedal is in the released position that any fluid that has leaked out of the system will be replaced from the reservoirs through the compensating ports.

The dual master cylinder has two pistons, located one behind the other. The primary piston is actuated directly by mechanical linkage from the brake pedal. The secondary piston is actuated by fluid trapped between the two pistons. If a leak develops in front of the secondary piston, it moves forward until it bottoms against the front of the master cylinder. The fluid trapped between the piston will operate one side of the diagonal system. If the other side of the system develops a leak, the primary piston will move forward until direct contact with the secondary piston takes place, and it will force the secondary piston to actuate the other side of the diagonal system. In either case the brake pedal drops closer to the floor board and less braking power is available.

The brake system uses a switch to warn the driver when only half of the brake system is operational. This switch is located in a valve body which is mounted on the firewall or the frame below the master cylinder. A hydraulic piston receives pressure from both circuits, each circuit's pressure being applied to one end of the piston. When the pressures are in balance, the piston remains stationary. When one circuit has a leak, however, the greater pressure in the circuit during application of the brakes will push the piston to one side, closing the switch and activating the brake warning light.

In disc brake system, this valve body contains a metering valve and, in some cases, a proportioning valve or valves, The metering valve keeps pressure from traveling to the disc brakes on the front wheels until the brake shoes on the rear wheels have contacted the drums, ensuring that the front brakes will never be used alone. The proportioning valve controls the pressure to the rear brakes to avoid rear wheel lock–up during very hard braking.

Warning lights may be tested by depressing the brake pedal and holding it while opening one of the wheel cylinder bleeder screws. If this does not cause the light to go on, substitute a new lamp, make continuity checks, and finally, replace the switch as necessary.

The hydraulic system may be checked for leaks by applying pressure to the pedal gradually and steadily. If the pedal sinks very slowly to the floor, the system has a leak. This is not to be confused with a springy or spongy feel due to the compression of air within the lines. If the system leaks, there will be a gradual change in the position of the pedal with a constant pressure.

Check for leaks along all lines and at wheel cylinders or calipers. If no external leaks are apparent, the problem is inside the master cylinder.

## Disc Brakes

### BASIC OPERATING PRINCIPLES

Instead of the traditional expanding brakes that press outward against a circular drum, disc brake systems utilize a disc (rotor) with brake pads positioned on either side of it. Braking effect is achieved in a manner similar to the way you would squeeze a spinning phonograph record between your fingers. The disc (rotor) is a casting with cooling fins between the two braking surfaces. This enables air to circulate between the braking surfaces making them less sensitive to heat buildup and more resistant to fade. Dirt and water do not affect braking action since contaminants are thrown off by the centrifugal action of the rotor or scraped off by the pads. Also, the equal clamping action of the two brake pads tends to ensure uniform, straight line stops. Disc brakes are inherently self–adjusting.

Your car uses a pin slider front wheel caliper. The brake pad on the inside of the brake rotor is moved in contact with the rotor by hydraulic pressure. The caliper, which is not held in a fixed position, moves slightly, bringing the outside brake pad into contact with the disc rotor.

## Drum Brakes (Rear)

### BASIC OPERATING PRINCIPLES

Drum brakes employ two brake shoes mounted on a stationary backing plate. These shoes are positioned inside a circular drum which rotates with the wheel assembly. The shoes are held in place by springs. This allows them to slide toward the drums (when they are applied) while keeping the linings and drums in alignment. The shoes are actuated by a wheel cylinder which is mounted at the top of the backing plate. When the brakes are applied, hydraulic pressure forces the wheel cylinder's actuating links outward. Since these links bear directly against the top of the brake shoes, the tops of the shoes are then forced against the inner side of the drum. This action forces the bottoms of the two shoes to contact the brake drum by rotating the entire assembly slightly (known as servo action). When pressure within the wheel cylinder is relaxed, return springs pull the shoes back away from the drum.

The rear drum brakes on your car are designed to self–adjust themselves during application. Motion causes both shoes to rotate very slightly with the drum, rocking an adjusting lever, thereby causing rotation of the adjusting screw or lever.

## Power Brake Boosters

Power brakes operate just as standard brake systems except in the actuation of the master cylinder pistons. A vacuum diaphragm is located on the front of the master cylinder and assists the driver in applying the brakes, reducing both the effort and travel he must put into moving the brake pedal.

The vacuum diaphragm housing is connected to the intake manifold by a vacuum hose. A check valve is placed at the point where the hose enters the diaphragm housing, so that during periods of low manifold vacuum brake assist vacuum will not be lost.

Depressing the brake pedal closes off the vacuum sources and allows atmospheric pressure to enter on one side of the diaphragm. This causes the master cylinder pistons to move and apply the brakes. When the brake pedal is released, vacuum is applied to both sides of the diaphragm, and return springs return the diaphragm and master cylinder pistons to the released position. If the vacuum fails, the brake pedal rod will butt against the end of the master cylinder actuating rod, and direct mechanical application will occur as the pedal is depressed.

The hydraulic and mechanical problems that apply to conventional brake systems also apply to power brakes.

## Adjustments

### REAR DRUM BRAKES

The rear drum brakes on your vehicle are self–adjusting. The only adjustments necessary should be an initial adjustment, which is performed after new brake shoes have been installed or some type of service work has been done on the rear brake system.

➡ **After any brake service, obtain a firm brake pedal before moving the vehicle. Adjusted brakes must not drag. The wheel must turn freely. Be sure the parking brake cables are not adjusted too tightly. A special brake shoe gauge, Tool D81L–1103–A or equivalent, is necessary for making an accurate adjustment after installing new brake shoes. The special gauge measures both the drum diameter and the brake shoe setting.**

#### Vehicles Equipped with 7 in. (178mm) Brakes

Pivot the adjuster quadrant until the third or fourth notch from the outer end of the quadrant meshes with the knurled pin on the adjuster strut. Install the hub and drum.

#### Vehicles Equipped with 8 in. (203mm) Brakes

Measure and set the special brake gauge to the inside diameter of the brake drum. Lift the adjuster lever from the star–wheel teeth. Turn the star–wheel until the brake shoes are adjusted out to the shoe setting fingers of the brake gauge. Install the hub and drum.

➡ **Complete the adjustment by applying the brakes several times. After the brakes have been properly adjusted, check their operation by making several stops from varying forward speeds.**

### FRONT DISC BRAKES

Front disc brakes require no adjustment. Hydraulic pressure maintains the proper pad–to–disc contact at all times. If for any reason the brake pressure changes, check the brake fluid level or pad width.

#### Brake Pedal

The correct adjustment of the brake pedal height, free–play and reserve distance is critical to the correct operation of the brake system. These 3 measurements interrelate and should be performed in sequence.

#### Brake Pedal Reserve

1. Operate the engine at idle with the transmission in either PARK or NEUTRAL.
2. Depress the brake pedal lightly 3 to 4 times.
3. Allow 15 seconds for vacuum to replenish the booster.
4. Apply the brake pedal until it stops moving downward.
5. Hold pedal in applied position and raise engine idle to approximately 2000 rpm.

6. Release the accelerator pedal and observe that the brake pedal moves downward as the engine returns to normal idle speed.

➡ **The additional movement of the brake pedal is the result of the increased engine manifold vacuum which exerts more force on the brake booster during engine rundown.**

7. If the pedal does not move downward, check one or both of the following:

a. Check the one–way valve between the brake booster and the manifold. This valve is usually white in color, and is found in–line with the vacuum hose, near the booster. Remove the valve, and blow air through both ends of it. If the valve functions properly, air will pass through in only one direction. If air passes through in both directions, or will not pass at all, the valve should be replaced.

b. If the one–way valve is functioning properly, the rod length on the booster pump may be too long. To check and adjust this you will need to remove the master cylinder from the vehicle. Refer to the master cylinder procedure for more details. With the master cylinder removed, the rod length on the booster can be checked and/or adjusted. Refer to brake booster adjustment information for a detailed procedure.

### Brake Pedal Free Height Measurement

▶ See Figure 1

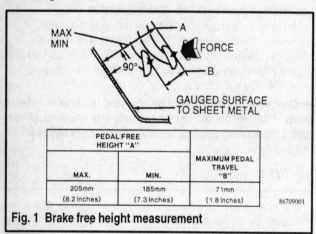

**Fig. 1 Brake free height measurement**

| PEDAL FREE HEIGHT "A" | | MAXIMUM PEDAL TRAVEL "B" |
|---|---|---|
| MAX. | MIN. | |
| 205mm (8.2 Inches) | 185mm (7.3 Inches) | 71mm (1.8 Inches) |

1. Insert a slender, sharp pointed prod through the carpet and sound deadener to dash panel metal. Measure the distance to the center of brake pedal pad on the side of the pedal pad nearest the accelerator pedal.

2. If the position of the pedal is not within specification, check brake pedal for missing, worn or damaged bushings, or loose attaching bolts, and replace if necessary.

3. If pedal free height is still out of specification, check brake pedal, booster or master cylinder to be sure the correct components are installed. Replace components as necessary.

### Brake Pedal Travel Measurement

▶ See Figure 2

1. With engine running and the transmission in PARK or NEUTRAL, block the wheels and release the parking brake.

2. Install brake pedal effort gauge 021–00001 or equivalent on the brake pedal.

3. Secure steel measuring tape to the brake pedal. Measure and record the distance from the brake pedal free height position to the reference point which is at the 6:00 position on the steering wheel rim.

4. With the steel tape hooked to the brake pedal, depress the brake pedal. Apply 25 lbs. (11.2 Nm) of load to the center of the pedal. Maintain the pedal load and measure the distance from the brake pedal to the fixed reference point on the steering wheel rim, which is parallel to the center–line of the steering column.

5. If pedal travel is more than the maximum specification on vehicles with self–adjusting drum brakes, make several reverse stops with the vehicle, with a forward stop before each to adjust the brakes. If these several stop/start attempts do not work, try another series of stop/start.

6. On self–adjusting drum brake vehicles, if the previous step did not bring the travel within specification, Remove the brake drums and visually check the adjuster. Check the brake lining for wear or damage. Replace any worn parts.

7. If the previous step does not resolve the problem, check the brake pedal assembly for missing or loose attachments.

8. If brake travel is still not within specification, bleed the brake system.

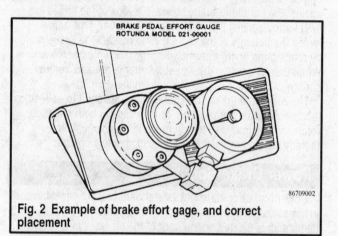

**Fig. 2 Example of brake effort gage, and correct placement**

## Brake Light Switch

### REMOVAL & INSTALLATION

▶ See Figure 3

1. Disconnect the negative battery cable.

2. Disconnect the wire harness at the connector from the switch.

➡ **The locking tab must be lifted before the connector can be removed.**

3. Remove the hairpin retainer and white nylon washer. Slide the stoplight switch and the pushrod away from the pedal. Remove the switch by sliding the switch up/down.

➡ **Since the switch side plate nearest the brake pedal is slotted, it is not necessary to remove the brake master cylinder pushrod black bushing and 1 white spacer washer nearest the pedal arm from the brake pedal pin.**

**To install:**

4. Position the switch so that the U–shaped side is nearest the pedal and directly over/under the pin. The black bushing must be in position in the push rod eyelet with the washer face on the side closest to the retaining pin.

5. Slide the switch up/down, trapping the master cylinder pushrod and black bushing between the switch side plates. Push the switch and pushrod assembly firmly towards the brake pedal arm. Assemble the outside white plastic washer to pin and install the hairpin retainer to trap the whole assembly.

➡ **Do not substitute other types of pin retainer. Replace only with production hairpin retainer.**

6. Connect the wire harness connector to the switch.
7. Connect negative battery cable.
8. Check the stoplight switch for proper operation. Stoplights should illuminate with less than 6 lbs. applied to the brake pedal at the pad.

➡ **The stoplight switch wire harness must have sufficient length to travel with the switch during full stroke at the pedal.**

Fig. 3 1985 Tempo/Topaz brake switch

## Brake Pedal

### REMOVAL & INSTALLATION

◆ **See Figure 4**

1. Disconnect battery ground cable.
2. Disconnect brake light switch harness from rear of switch.
3. Remove the pushrod retainer and nylon washer connected from the pedal to the brake booster and master cylinder. Slide the brake light switch outboard along the brake pedal pin just far enough for the outer hole of the switch frame to clear the

pin. Remove the switch by sliding it upward. Remove the black brake light switch bushing from the push rod.

4. Loosen the brake booster retaining nuts at the pedal support and slide the pushrod and inner nylon washer (on vehicles without speed control) off the pedal pin.

5. With the pedal support assembly removed, unfasten the locknut, followed by the pivot bolt, brake pedal, pivot spacer and bushing from the pedal support. Remove the speed control adapter if equipped, by unlatching the locking tab.

6. With everything disassembled, clean all the parts and replace those that are worn. Pay particular attention to the bushings.

**To install:**

7. Apply a light coat of engine oil to the bushings. Locate bushings and pivot spacer in brake pedal hub.

8. Position brake pedal in the pedal support and install pivot bolt. Install locknut and tighten to 10–20 ft. lbs. (14–27 Nm).

9. Install the inner nylon washer or speed control adapter, if equipped, and master cylinder pushrod, with the brake light switch bushing on the brake pedal pin. Position the brake light switch so that it straddles the push rod with the slot on the pedal pin and the switch outer frame hole just clearing the pin. Slide the switch down onto the pin and push rod. Slide the assembly down onto the pin and pushrod. Slide the assembly inboard toward the brake pedal arm. Install the outer nylon washer and push rod retainer. Lock retainer securely.

10. Tighten booster retaining nuts to 16–21 ft. lbs. (21–29 Nm).

11. Connect harness to stop light switch.
12. Connect battery ground cable.
13. Check pedal pressure and make sure the brake light switch works correctly before driving the vehicle.

## Master Cylinder

### REMOVAL & INSTALLATION

◆ **See Figures 5, 6 and 7**

➡ **Brake fluid acts like paint remover. Be certain not to spill brake fluid on the vehicle's painted surfaces.**

1. Disconnect the negative battery cable.
2. Disconnect any brake sensor harnesses which may be attached to the master cylinder.
3. Disconnect and plug the brake lines from the primary and secondary outlet ports of the master cylinder and pressure control valves.
4. Remove the nuts attaching the master cylinder to the brake booster assembly.
5. Slide the master cylinder forward and upward from the vehicle.

**To install:**

6. Before installation, bench bleed the new master cylinder as follows:
   a. Mount the new master cylinder in a suitable holding fixture. Be careful not to damage the housing.
   b. Fill the master cylinder reservoir with clean brake fluid.

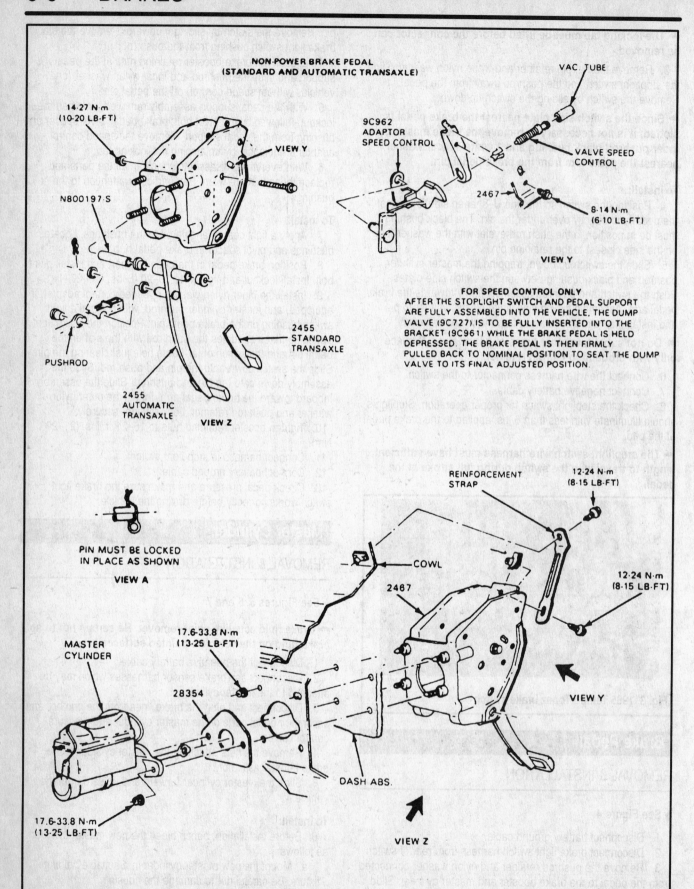

**NON-POWER BRAKE PEDAL**
(STANDARD AND AUTOMATIC TRANSAXLE)

14-27 N·m
(10-20 LB-FT)

VIEW Y

N800197-S

PUSHROD

2455
AUTOMATIC
TRANSAXLE

VIEW Z

2455
STANDARD
TRANSAXLE

VAC. TUBE

9C962
ADAPTOR
SPEED CONTROL

VALVE SPEED
CONTROL

2467

8-14 N·m
(6-10 LB-FT)

VIEW Y

**FOR SPEED CONTROL ONLY**
AFTER THE STOPLIGHT SWITCH AND PEDAL SUPPORT
ARE FULLY ASSEMBLED INTO THE VEHICLE, THE DUMP
VALVE (9C727) IS TO BE FULLY INSERTED INTO THE
BRACKET (9C961) WHILE THE BRAKE PEDAL IS HELD
DEPRESSED. THE BRAKE PEDAL IS THEN FIRMLY
PULLED BACK TO NOMINAL POSITION TO SEAT THE DUMP
VALVE TO ITS FINAL ADJUSTED POSITION.

PIN MUST BE LOCKED
IN PLACE AS SHOWN

VIEW A

REINFORCEMENT
STRAP

12-24 N·m
(8-15 LB-FT)

COWL

2467

12-24 N·m
(8-15 LB-FT)

VIEW Y

MASTER
CYLINDER

17.6-33.8 N·m
(13-25 LB-FT)

28354

DASH ABS.

17.6-33.8 N·m
(13-25 LB-FT)

VIEW Z

**Fig. 4 Brake pedal, support and master cylinder—non–vacuum type**

86709003

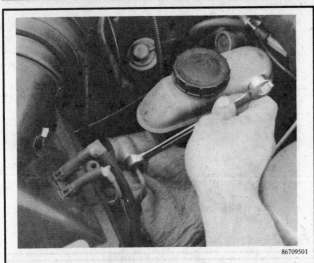

Fig. 6 Using a flare wrench, disconnect the brake lines

Fig. 5 If equipped, unplug the brake sensor

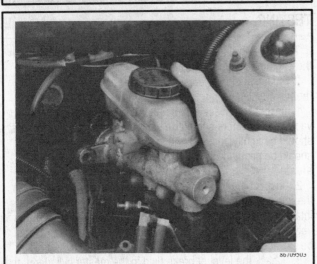

Fig. 7 With the retaining nuts removed, carefully work the master cylinder away from the studs

c. Using a suitable tool inserted into the booster pushrod cavity, carefully push the master cylinder piston in slowly. Place a container under the master cylinder to catch the fluid being expelled from the outlet ports.

d. Place a finger tightly over each outlet port and allow the master cylinder piston to return.

e. Repeat the procedure until clear fluid only is expelled from the master cylinder. Plug the outlet ports and remove the master cylinder from the holding fixture.

7. Position the master cylinder over the booster pushrod and booster mounting studs. Install the nuts and tighten to 13–25 ft. lbs. (18–33 Nm).

8. Remove the plugs individually and connect the brake lines. Tighten the fittings.

9. Make sure the master cylinder reservoir is full. Have an assistant push down on the brake pedal. When the pedal is all the way down, crack open the brake line fittings, 1 at a time, to expel any remaining air in the master cylinder and brake lines. Tighten the fittings, then have the assistant allow the brake pedal to return.

10. Repeat Step 9 until all air is expelled from the master cylinder and brake lines. Final tighten the brake line fittings to 10–18 ft. lbs. (14–24 Nm).

11. Connect the brake warning indicator connector.

12. Make sure the master cylinder reservoir is full.

13. If necessary, bleed the brake system.

14. Connect the negative battery cable. Check for fluid leaks and check for proper operation.

15. Road test the vehicle.

## OVERHAUL

▶ See Figures 8, 9, 10, 11 and 12

1. Remove master cylinder from vehicle. Clean any dirt from the body of the assembly. Place master cylinder in suitable vise. Take care not to damage the brake housing.

2. Drain any brake fluid from master cylinder and dispose of properly.

➡ **Never reuse brake fluid.**

3. Remove master cylinder reservoir from metal body.

4. Depress the primary piston and remove the snapring from the retaining groove at the end of the bore.

5. Remove the primary and secondary piston assemblies from the master cylinder. Tap open end of cylinder on the bench to remove the piston. If secondary piston does not readily come out, apply compressed air pressure to the secondary outlet port to assist removal.

6. Remove fluid control valve.

7. Wash the master cylinder body, especially the bore in clean brake fluid. Do the same to the primary and secondary pistons. Inspect the seals for cuts, nicks, scratches or other signs of wear, blistering or swelling. Replace parts as required. Inspect the master cylinder body and bore for pitting, corrosion or heavy wear characterized by scoring or galling of the metal.

**To install:**

8. Dip the piston assembly in clean brake fluid, DOT 3 or equivalent. Install the secondary (smaller) piston assembly into the bore, spring end first.
9. Install primary piston assembly, spring end first.
10. Depress primary piston and install snapring.
11. Install the fluid control valve.
12. Position and secure fluid reservoir.
13. Install master cylinder to booster. Bleed brake system.

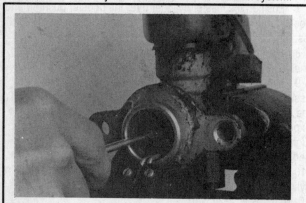

**Fig. 8 With the master cylinder in a vise, push the valve in and remove the snapring**

**Fig. 9 Snapring and seal removed**

**Fig. 10 Remove the primary valve**

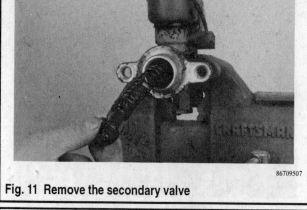

**Fig. 11 Remove the secondary valve**

**Fig. 12 A disassembled master cylinder. Notice the difference between the pistons**

## Power Brake Booster

### TESTING

The power brake booster depends on vacuum produced by the engine for proper operation.

If you suspect problems in the power brake system, check the following:

1. Inspect all hoses and hose connections. All unused vacuum connectors should be sealed. Hoses and connections should be tightly secured and in good condition. The hoses should be pliable with no holes or cracks and no collapsed areas.
2. Inspect the check valve which is located in line between the intake manifold and booster. Disconnect the hose on the intake manifold side of the valve. Attempt to blow through the valve. If air passes through the valve, it is defective and must be replaced.
3. Check the level of brake fluid in the master cylinder. If the level is low, check the system for fluid leaks.

4. Idle the engine briefly and then shut it off. Pump the brake pedal several times to exhaust all of the vacuum stored in the booster. Keep the brake pedal depressed and start the engine. The brake pedal should drop slightly, if vacuum is present after the engine is started less pressure should be necessary on the brake pedal. If no drop, or action is felt the power brake booster should be suspect.

5. With the parking brake applied and the wheels blocked, start the engine and allow to idle in PARK or NEUTRAL . Disconnect the vacuum line to the check valve on the intake manifold side. If vacuum is felt, connect the hose and repeat Step 4. Once again, if no action is felt on the brake pedal, suspect the booster.

6. Operate the engine at a fast idle for about ten seconds, shut off the engine. Allow the car to sit for about ten minutes. Depress the brake pedal with moderate force (about 20 pounds). The pedal should feel about the same as when the engine was running. If the brake pedal feels hard (no power assist) suspect the power booster.

## ADJUSTMENT

▶ **See Figures 13 and 14**

A booster that is suspected of having an improper pushrod length will react in either of the following ways:
- A long pushrod will prevent the master cylinder piston from completely releasing hydraulic pressure and cause the brakes to drag.
- A short pushrod will have excessive brake pedal travel and cause a groaning noise to come from the booster.

➡ **A home–made push rod gauge can be constructed. Refer to the diagram for dimensions.**

1. Without disconnecting the brake lines, remove the hardware securing the master cylinder to the booster, and carefully move the master cylinder out of the way. Support the master cylinder to prevent damage to the brake lines.

2. Start engine, and apply a force of 5 lbs. (2.2 Nm) to the pedal/pushrod to ensure proper pushrod placement within the booster unit.

3. Using the home–made gauge, check rod length. If adjustment is needed, grasp rod at knurled area only, and adjust nut at end of rod. After adjust has been made, check length with gauge again.

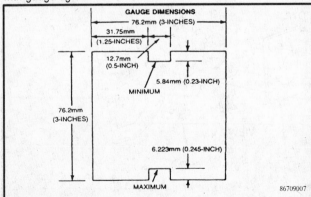

**Fig. 13 Brake booster pushrod gauge dimension. (Diagram not to scale)**

4. Install master cylinder on booster unit. Tighten securing nuts in an alternating fashion. Torque to 16–21 ft. lbs. (21–29 Nm).

5. Road test the vehicle.

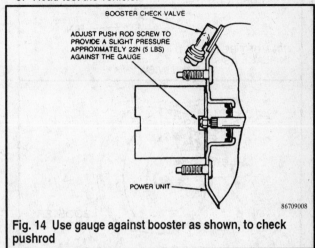

**Fig. 14 Use gauge against booster as shown, to check pushrod**

## REMOVAL & INSTALLATION

▶ **See Figures 15 and 16**

### 1984–85 Vehicles

1. Disconnect the negative battery cable.
2. Place protective aprons on the fenders of the vehicle.
3. Disconnect any sensor wire harness.
4. Carefully remove the brake lines from the primary and secondary outlet ports of the master cylinder.
5. Working from inside the car, beneath the instrument panel, remove the booster pushrod from the brake pedal.
6. Remove the master cylinder from the booster.
7. Remove the manifold vacuum hose from the booster by rotating and carefully pulling on the hose.
8. Remove the booster–to–firewall attaching bolts and remove the booster from the vehicle.

**To install:**

9. Align the pedal support and support spacer inside the vehicle. Place the booster to the firewall and install the mounting bolts.
10. Install the brake pedal pushrod and bushing. Tighten the booster–to–dash attaching nuts to 13–25 ft. lbs. (18–33 Nm).
11. Connect the manifold vacuum hose to the booster.
12. Install the master cylinder and tighten the nuts.
13. Connect the sensor wire harness.
14. Bleed the brake system.
15. Connect the negative battery cable.
16. Test the brake system to make sure that both the stoplight switch and brake booster work correctly.

### 1986–94 Vehicles

1. Disconnect the battery ground cable.
2. Place protective aprons on the fenders of the vehicle.
3. Remove any sensor wire harness.
4. Remove the primary and secondary brake lines from the master cylinder.

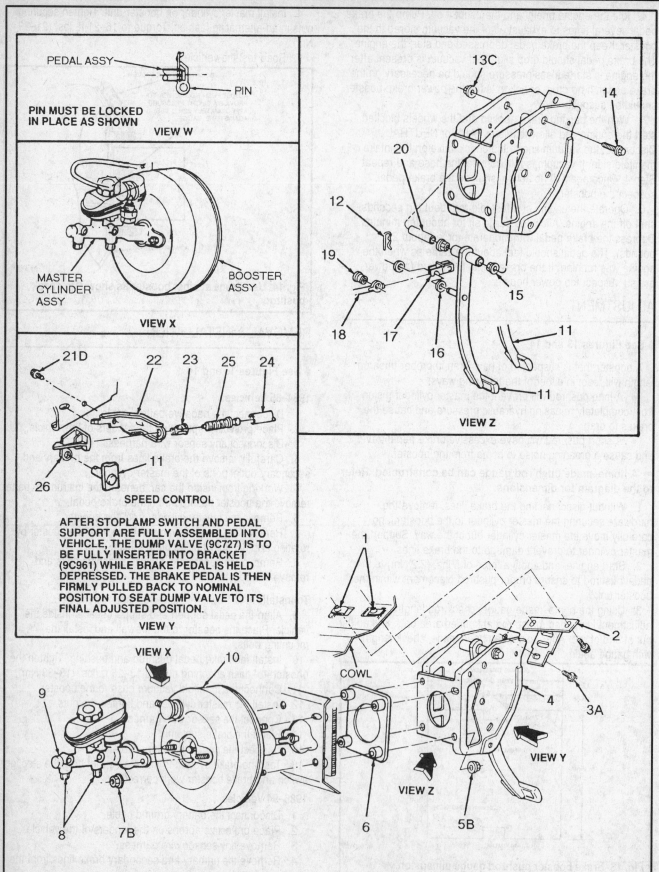

**Fig. 15 Exploded view of brake booster assembly**

| | |
|---|---|
| 1 Nut (3 req'd) | 17 Stoplamp switch assy |
| 2 Bracket | 18 Push rod assy |
| 3 Bolt (3 req'd) | 19 Bushing |
| 4 Pedal holder assembly | 20 Spacer |
| 5A Nut (4 req'd) | 21 Bolt |
| 6 Spacer | 22 Speed control vacuum valve |
| 7 Nut (2 req'd) | mounting bracket |
| 8 Pressure control valve assy | 23 Speed control vacuum valve clip |
| 9 Master cylinder assy | 24 Vacuum tube |
| 10 Booster assy | 25 Speed control metering valve |
| 11 Pedal assy | 26 Speed control vacuum valve |
| 12 Pin | actuator adapter |
| 13 Nut | A Tighten to 12-24 Nm (8-15 lb.ft.) |
| 14 Bolt | B Tighten to 21-29 Nm (16-21 lb.ft.) |
| 15 Spacer | C Tighten to 14-27 Nm (10-20 lb.ft.) |
| 16 Push rod spacer | D Tighten to 4-5 Nm (32-46 lb.in.) |

86709k04

**Fig. 16  Brake booster parts list**

5.  Remove the retaining nuts and remove the master cylinder.

6.  Working from inside the car, beneath the instrument panel, remove the booster pushrod from the brake pedal.

7.  Remove the booster retaining nuts.

8.  Disconnect the manifold vacuum hose from the booster check valve and move the booster forward until the booster studs clear the dash panel and remove the booster.

**To install:**

9.  Align the pedal support and support spacer inside the vehicle and place the booster in position on the dash panel. Hand-start the retaining nuts.

10.  Working inside the vehicle, install the pushrod and pushrod bushing on the brake pedal pin. Tighten the booster–to–dash panel retaining nuts to 13–25 ft. lbs. (18–33 Nm).

11.  Connect the manifold vacuum hose to the booster check valve using a hose clamp.

12.  Install the master cylinder according to the proper procedure.

13.  Connect the sensor harness.

14.  Bleed the brake system.

15.  Connect the negative battery cable and start the engine. Check the power brake function.

16.  If equipped with speed control, adjust the dump valve. The dump valve is located above the brake pedal, below the steering column, attached to a bracket. To adjust, proceed as follows:

a.  Firmly depress and hold the brake pedal.

b.  Push in the dump valve until the valve collar bottoms against the retaining clip.

c.  Place a 0.050–0.10 in. (1.25–2.54mm) shim between the white button of the valve and the pad on the brake pedal.

d.  Firmly pull the brake pedal rearward to its normal position, allowing the dump valve to ratchet backward in the retaining clip.

17.  Road test the vehicle

## Fluid Control Valve

The fluid control valve is located in the body of the master cylinder, just below the primary reservoir compartment. This valve is responsible for pressure relief for the large fast fill bore in the master cylinder.

### REMOVAL & INSTALLATION

▶ **See Figure 17**

1.  Remove any brake fluid from the reservoir.

2.  Remove the brake reservoir from the primary port, by carefully prying up on the reservoir. Rotate the reservoir out of the way and remove the grommet from the casting.

3.  Use a socket and remove the control valve. Inspect for contamination.

**To install:**

4.  Install new fluid control valve. Tighten valve to 8–9.6 ft. lbs. (11–13 Nm).

5.  Install the reservoir to the primary port. Add brake fluid.

6.  Bleed brake system as needed.

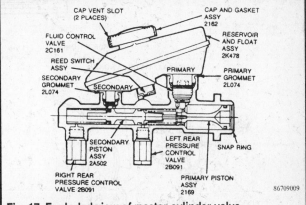

**Fig. 17  Exploded view of master cylinder valve assemblies**

## Brake Control Valve

The brake control valve is located to the left and below the master cylinder and mounted to the shock (strut) tower by a removable bracket.

### REMOVAL & INSTALLATION

◆ See Figure 18

1. Using the proper size flare wrench, disconnect the brake lines to the valve.
2. Disconnect the warning switch wiring.
3. Remove the bolt(s) retaining the valve to the mount and remove the valve.
4. Installation is in the reverse order of removal.
5. Bleed the brake system after installing the new valve.

## Pressure Differential Valve

If a loss of brake fluid occurs on either side of the diagonally split system when the brakes are applied, a piston mounted in the valve moves off center allowing the brakes on the non-leaking side of the split system to operate. When the piston moves off center a brake warning switch, located in the center of the valve body, will turn on a dash mounted warning light indicating brake problems.

After repairs are made on the brake system and the system is bled, the warning switch will reset itself, once you pump the brake pedal. The dash light should also turn OFF.

## Proportioning Valve

The dual proportioning valve, located between the rear brake system inlet and outlet port, controls the rear brake system hydraulic pressure. When the brakes are applied, the dual proportioning valve reduces pressure to the rear wheels and provides balanced braking.

### TROUBLESHOOTING

If the rear brakes lock-up during light brake application or do not lock-up under heavy braking the problem could be with the dual proportioning valve.

1. Check tires and tire pressures.
2. Check the brake linings for thickness, and for contamination by fluid, grease etc.
3. Check the brake system hoses, steel lines, calipers and wheel cylinders for leaks.
4. If none of the proceeding checks have uncovered any problems, suspect the proportioning valve.

➡ **Take the car to a qualified service center and ask them to do a pressure test on the valve. If a pressure test is not possible, replace the control valve.**

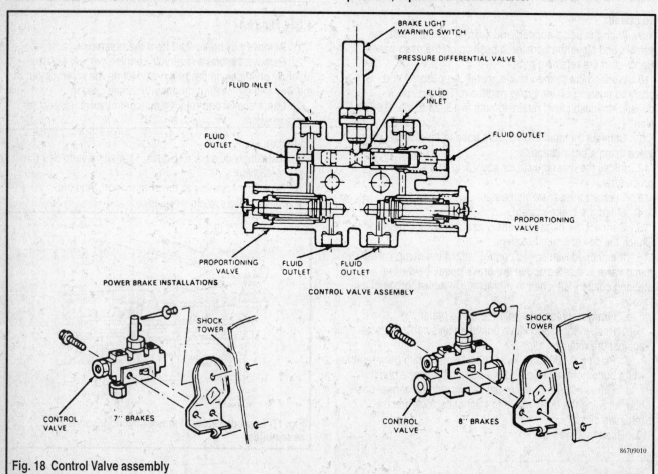

Fig. 18 Control Valve assembly

## Pressure Control Valves

There are 2 pressure control valves housed in the master cylinder assembly. The valves reduce rear brake system hydraulic pressure when the pressure exceeds a preset value. The rear brake hydraulic pressure is limited in order to minimize rear wheel skidding during hard braking.

### REMOVAL & INSTALLATION

#### ♦ See Figure 17

1. Disconnect the primary or secondary brake line, as necessary.
2. Loosen and remove the pressure control valve from the master cylinder housing.

**To install:**

3. Install the pressure control valve in the master cylinder housing port and tighten to 10–18 ft. lbs. (14–24 Nm).
4. Connect the brake line and tighten the fitting to 10–18 ft. lbs. (14–24 Nm).
5. Fill and bleed the brake system.

## Brake Tubing

The hydraulic brake lines from the master cylinder use a double wall steel tubing throughout the system with the exception of the flexible hoses at the front and rear wheels. When connecting a tube to a hose, tube connector, or brake cylinder, tighten the tube fitting nut to specifications using a flare wrench. These are available in different sizes at most automotive parts stores.

All models utilize the brake tubes with ISO flares and metric tube nuts at the master cylinder. These brake tubes are installed from the brake master cylinder to the left and right front brake hoses. The fittings at the master cylinder are either M10 or M12 metric tube nuts, where as the fitting at the front brake hoses are 3/8 in. or 3/16 in. tube nuts, used with a double flare.

When replacing a brake line, it is recommended that factory lines with machine flared ends be used. With these type lines, the connection are far superior. Also, with many factory brake lines, the line is pre–bent and therefore far easier to install.

Although factory brake line tubing is recommended, you can purchase hydraulic tubing and bend and flare the ends yourself. Refer to the section on flaring brake tubing for information on the procedure.

If brake tube replacement is required from the brake master cylinder to the left or right brake hose, the following procedure should be followed.

1. Obtain the recommended bulk 3/16 in. steel tubing and correct standard 3/8–3/16 in. tube nut. The M10 and M12 metric nuts will be reused.
2. Cut the tubing to the length required. Clean the burrs after cutting. The correct length may be obtained by measuring the removed tube using a string and adding 1/8 in. for each flare.
3. Place the removed metric tube nut on the tube. ISO flare one end of the tubing using the ISO and double flare tool kit D81L-2269-A or equivalent.
4. On the opposite end of the replacement tube, install a standard 3/8–3/16 in. tube nut and double flare tube end.

➡ Be sure to follow the flaring instructions included in the ISO and double flare tool kit D81L–2269–A or equivalent.

5. Using a bending tool of the correct diameter, bend the replacement brake tube to match the removed tube using a suitable tube bender. When the replacement brake tube is installed, maintain adequate clearance to all moving or vibrating parts.

➡ If a section of brake tubing becomes damaged, the entire section should be replaced with tubing of the same size, shape, length and material. Copper tubing should not be used in a hydraulic system. When bending the brake tubing to fit the body contours, be careful not to kink or crack the tubing.

All brake tubing should be flared properly to provide a good leakproof connection. Clean the brake tubing by flushing it with clean brake fluid before installation. When connecting a tube to a hose, tube connector or brake cylinder, tighten the tube fitting nut to specifications with a suitable torque wrench.

Always bleed the applicable primary or secondary brake system after the hose or line replacement.

### REMOVAL & INSTALLATION

1. Drain the brake reservoir of any brake fluid.
2. Using the correct size flare wrench, loosen the brake line.

➡ Because the material used to construct brake tubing is thin metal, great care should be used when removing and replacing brake lines.

3. Once the nut on the brake line is loose enough, finish loosening the nut by hand.
4. Loosen the other end of the brake line, and remove the line.
5. Clean any open connection in the brake system. Clean both ends of the new brake line. Use compressed air and blow out the line to make sure no foreign matter is in the line.

**To install:**

6. Position brake line to open end of brake system. Begin fastening the nut by hand until tight.

➡ Start any brake line nuts by hand to ensure that no nuts get cross threaded.

7. Position and install the other end of the brake line in the same manner as done above.
8. Tighten the nut.
9. Fill brake reservoir with new brake fluid.
10. Bleed brake system.

### BRAKE PIPE FLARING

#### ♦ See Figures 19 and 20

Flaring steel lines is a skill which needs to be practiced before it should be done on a line which is to be used on a vehicle. A special flaring kit with double flaring adapters is required. It is essential that the flare is formed evenly to prevent any leaks when the brake system is under pressure. Only steel lines, not copper, should be used. It is also mandatory that the flare be a double flare. With the supply of parts available today, a pre–flared steel brake line should be available to fit your lines, not copper, should be used. It is also mandatory that the flare be a double flare. With the supply of parts available today, a pre–flared steel brake line should be available to fit your needs. Due to the high pressures in the brake system and the serious injuries that could occur if the flare should fail, it is strongly advised that pre–flared lines should be installed when repairing the braking system. If a line were to leak brake fluid due to a defective flare, and the leak were to go undetected, brake failure would result.

## ✳✳WARNING

**A double flaring tool must be used to flare any brake line for the Tempo/Topaz. A single flaring tool cannot produce a flare strong enough to hold the necessary hydraulic pressure.**

➡ **If this is the first time flaring a brake line, it is strongly recommended that you try flaring on a piece of metal line before actually flaring the line to be used on the vehicle.**

1. Determine the length of metal brake line needed. Allow 1/8 in. (3.2mm) extra for each flare. Cut the metal line using only a suitable pipe cutting tool.
2. Square the end of the tube with a file and chamfer the edges. Remove any burrs.
3. Install the required fittings on the metal tube.
4. Install the flaring tool into a vise, and install the handle into the operating cam.
5. Loosen the die clamp screw and rotate the locking plate to expose the die carrier.
6. Select the required die set and install it in the carrier.
7. Insert the prepared line through the rear of the die and push forward until the line end is flush with the die face.
8. Make sure that the rear of both halves of the die are resting against the hexagon die stops. Then rotate the locking plate to the fully closed position and clamp the die firmly by tightening the clamp screw.
9. Rotate the punch turret until the appropriate size points toward the open end of the metal line to be flared.
10. Pull the operating handle against the metal line to create resistance in order to make the flare, then return the handle to the original position.
11. Release the clamp screw and rotate the locking plate to the open position.

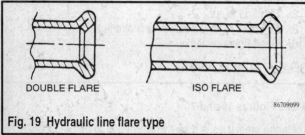

DOUBLE FLARE    ISO FLARE

86709099

Fig. 19 Hydraulic line flare type

12. Remove the die set and the metal line, then carefully separate by gently tapping both halves on the bench. Inspect the flare for the proper size and shape.

## Brake Hose

A flexible brake hose should be replaced if it shows any signs of softening, cracking or other damage. When installing a new front brake hose, 2 new sealing washers should be used.

The position of the front hose is controlled by a self indexing brass block. When attaching the block to the caliper, tighten the bolt to 30–40 ft. lbs. (41–54 Nm). Attach the intermediate bracket to the shock strut and tighten the screw. Engage the opposite end of the hose to the bracket on the body. Install the horseshoe type retaining clip and connect tube to hose with tube nut. Inspect the position of the installed hose for clearance to the other chassis components.

Positioning of rear brake hose is controlled by self–indexing the end fittings. Engage either end of the hose to the bracket on the body. Install the horseshoe type retaining clip and connect the tube to the hose with the tube fitting nut. Engage the opposite end of the hose to the bracket on the rear spindle. Install the horseshoe type retaining clip and connect the tube to hose with the tube fitting nut. Inspect the position of the installed hose for contact with other chassis parts.

### REMOVAL & INSTALLATION

◆ **See Figure 20**

1. Drain the brake reservoir of any brake fluid.
2. Using 2 correct diameter flare wrenches, Secure the nut on the metal brake line with one wrench, while turning the rubber brake hose with the other wrench.

➡ **Because the material used to construct brake tubing is thin metal, great care should be used when removing and replacing any brake line or hose.**

3. Once the nut on the brake line is loose enough, finish loosening the nut by hand.
4. Loosen the other end of the brake hose, and remove the hose.
5. Clean any open connection in the brake system. Clean both ends of the new brake hose. Use compressed air and blow out the new line to make sure no foreign matter is in the line.

**To install:**

6. Position brake line to open end of brake system. Begin fastening by hand until tight.

➡ **Start any brake fitting by hand to ensure that no cross-threading occurs.**

7. Position and install the other end of the brake line in the same manner as done above.
8. Tighten the hose ends.
9. Fill brake reservoir with new brake fluid.
10. Bleed brake system.

## Bleeding the Brake System

◆ **See Figure 21**

It is necessary to bleed the brake system of air whenever a hydraulic component, of the system, has been rebuilt or replaced, or if the brakes feel spongy during application.

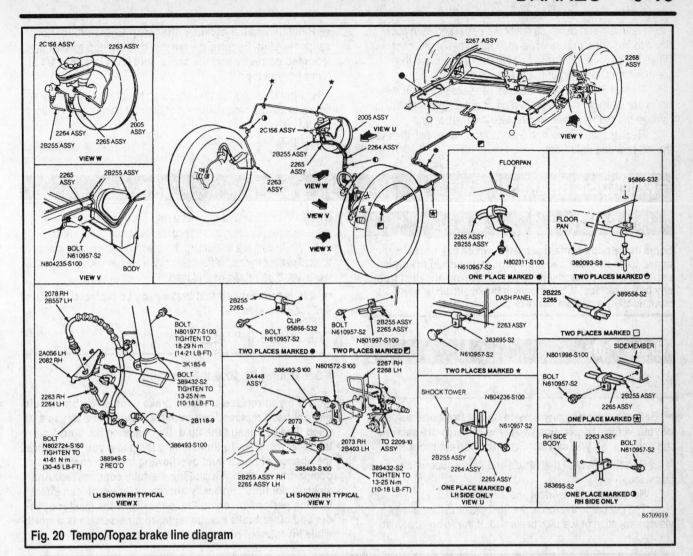

Fig. 20  Tempo/Topaz brake line diagram

Your car has a diagonally split brake system. Each side of this system must be bled as an individual system. Because of this type of system, as well as the brake line going to each individual wheel is different in length, there is a set order for bleeding a brake system.

➡ **Bleed the right rear brake, left front brake, left rear brake and right front brake. Always start with the longest line from the master cylinder first.**

### ✳✳CAUTION

When bleeding the system(s) never allow the master cylinder to run completely out of brake fluid. Always use D heavy duty brake fluid or the equivalent. Never reuse brake fluid that has been drained from the system or that has been allowed to stand in an opened container for an extended period of time. If your car is equipped with power brakes, remove the reserve vacuum stored in the booster by pumping the brake pedal several times before bleeding the brakes.

1. Clean any dirt away from the master cylinder filler cap.
2. Raise and support the car on jackstands. Make sure your car is safely supported and it is raised evenly front and rear.
3. Starting with the right rear wheel cylinder. Remove the dust cover from the bleeder screw. Place the proper size box

wrench over the bleeder fitting and attach a piece of rubber tubing (about an inch long and snug fitting) over the end of the fitting.

4. Submerge the free end of the rubber tube into a container half filled with clean brake fluid.

Fig. 21  Bleeding a front brake caliper

5. Have a friend pump up the brake pedal and then push down to apply the brakes while you loosen the bleeder screw. When the pedal reaches the bottom of its travel close the bleeder fitting before your friend release the brake pedal.

6. Repeat Step 5 until air bubbles cease to appear in the container in which the tubing is submerged. Tighten the fitting, remove the rubber tubing and replace the dust cover.

7. Repeat Steps 3 through 6 to the left front wheel, then to the left rear and right front.

➡ Refill the master cylinder after each wheel cylinder or caliper is bled. Be sure the master cylinder top gasket is mounted correctly and the brake fluid level is within 1/4 in. (6mm) of the top.

8. After bleeding the brakes, pump the brake pedal several times, to ensure proper seating of the rear linings and the front caliper pistons.

9. Road test the vehicle.

## FRONT DISC BRAKES

### ✳✳CAUTION

**Some brake pads contain asbestos, which has been determined to be a cancer causing agent. Never clean the brake surfaces with compressed air! Avoid inhaling any dust from any brake surface! When cleaning brake surfaces, use a commercially available brake cleaning solvent.**

### Brake Pads

#### INSPECTION

➡ Before attempting any service on the front brake system of your vehicle, determine what type of hardware secures the calipers, so you can purchase the correct tools.

1. Raise the front of the vehicle and safely support on jackstands.

2. Remove the front wheel and tire assemblies.

3. The cut out in the top of the front brake caliper allows visual inspection of the disc brake pad. If the lining is worn to within 1/8 in. (3mm) of the metal disc shoe (check local inspection requirements) replace all four pads (both sides).

4. While you are inspecting the brake pads, visually inspect the caliper for hydraulic fluid leaks. If a leak is visible the caliper will have to be rebuilt or replaced.

➡ It is recommended that brake pads be replaced in sets of 4, 2 for each side.

#### REMOVAL & INSTALLATION

◆ See Figures 22, 23, 24, 25 and 26

➡ When you replace the front brake pads, if the brake fluid has not been replaced within the last two years, this is a good time to change the fluid. By removing the fluid from the reservoir prior to unfastening the pads, you will reduce the chance of brake fluid overflowing into the engine compartment when the pistons are fully compressed. And since brake fluid can easily absorb water which can effect braking performance and the longevity of the master cylinder and other brake components, routine service is a worthwhile investment of time.

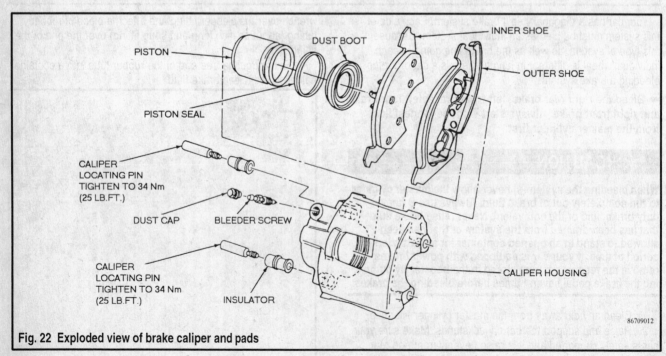

PISTON
DUST BOOT
INNER SHOE
OUTER SHOE
PISTON SEAL
CALIPER LOCATING PIN TIGHTEN TO 34 Nm (25 LB.FT.)
DUST CAP
BLEEDER SCREW
CALIPER LOCATING PIN TIGHTEN TO 34 Nm (25 LB.FT.)
INSULATOR
CALIPER HOUSING

86709012

**Fig. 22 Exploded view of brake caliper and pads**

1. If changing the brake fluid, remove the master cylinder cap and remove as much brake fluid as possible. Discard brake fluid properly.

2. Raise and safely support the vehicle on jackstands.

3. Remove the wheel and tire assembly.

4. Remove the caliper locating pins using either a hex or a Torx® socket.

5. Lift the caliper assembly from the integral knuckle and anchor plate and rotor using rotating motion. Do not pry directly against plastic piston or damage will occur.

6. Remove the outer and inner brake pads.

7. Inspect both rotor braking surfaces. Minor scoring or buildup of lining material does not require machining or replacement of rotor. Hand–sand glaze from both rotor braking surfaces using garnet paper 100–A (medium grit) or aluminum oxide 150–J (medium).

8. Suspend the caliper inside fender housing with wire. Use care not to damage caliper or stretch brake hose.

Fig. 23  With the wheel removed, use a hex or Torx® socket to remove the caliper retaining bolts

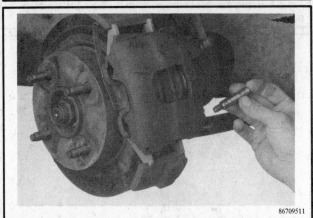

Fig. 24  Although it is not necessary to remove the retaining bolts completely, If it makes the procedure easier, the bolts will slide out.

Fig. 25  Slide the caliper and pads away from the rotor

Fig. 26  Remove the pads

**To install:**

9. Use a 4 in. C–clamp and wood block 2¾ in. x 1 in. (70mm x 25mm) and approximately ¾ in. (19mm) thick against the piston, and turn the C–clamp to seat caliper hydraulic piston in its bore.

➡ Extra care must be taken during this procedure to prevent damage to the plastic piston. Metal or sharp objects cannot come into direct contact with the piston surface or damage will result.

10. Remove all rust buildup from inside of caliper legs where the outer shoe makes contact.

11. Install the inner pad by sliding the clips into place, with the center of the pad on top of the piston. Do not bend the pad clips during installation.

12. Install the outer pad to the caliper, securing it with the clips. Ensure clips are properly seated.

13. Install the caliper over rotor.

14. Position and secure caliper locating pins.

15. If changing the brake fluid, fill the brake fluid reservoir with clean brake fluid. Bleed the brakes.

16. Check the brake fluid level in the reservoir, and adjust if needed. Install the wheel and tire assembly. Tighten wheel nuts to 80–105 ft. lbs. (109–142 Nm).

17. Connect negative battery cable.

18. Road test vehicle.

## Brake Caliper

### REMOVAL & INSTALLATION

➡ **Before removing the caliper, determine which hardware secures the caliper so you can purchase the correct tools.**

1. Disconnect the negative battery cable.

2. Raise and safely support the vehicle with jackstands.

3. Remove the wheel and tire assembly from rotor mounting face.

4. Remove as much brake fluid from the reservoir as possible.

5. Disconnect the flexible brake hose from caliper. Remove hollow retaining bolt which secures the hose to the caliper. Remove the hose assembly and plug.

6. Remove the caliper locating pins using either a hex socket or a Torx® socket.

7. Lift caliper off rotor using a rotating motion.

➡ **Do not pry directly against the plastic piston or damage to piston may occur. Inspect before installing on vehicle.**

**To install:**

8. Using a C–clamp or caliper piston push tool, return the caliper piston to the bore.

9. Position caliper assembly above rotor with anti–rattle spring under upper arm of knuckle. Install caliper over rotor. Ensure inner shoe is properly positioned.

➡ **Ensure correct caliper assembly is installed on correct knuckle. The caliper bleed screw should be positioned on top of caliper when assembled on vehicle.**

10. Lubricate locating pins and inside of insulators with silicone grease. Install locating pins through caliper insulators and into knuckle attaching holes. The caliper locating pins should be inserted and threads started by hand.

11. Using Torx® drive bit D79P–2100–T40 or equivalent, tighten caliper locating pins to 18–25 ft. lbs. (24–34 Nm).

12. Remove plug and install the brake hose to the caliper using a new gasket on each side of the fitting. Insert attaching bolt through washers and fittings. Tighten bolts to 30–40 ft. lbs. (40–54 Nm).

13. Fill master cylinder with clean brake fluid, Pump brake pedal to seat pads and pistons.

14. Bleed brake system. Replace rubber bleed screw cap after bleeding.

15. Fill master cylinder as required.

16. Install wheel and tire assembly. Tighten wheel nuts to 80–105 ft. lbs. (109–142 Nm).

17. Connect negative battery cable.

18. Pump brake pedal to check brake resistance.

19. Road test vehicle.

### OVERHAUL

◆ **See Figures 27 and 28**

1. Remove the caliper(s) from the vehicle, and place on a clean surface.

2. Before disassembly, clean any dirt from the exterior of the caliper(s).

➡ **The next step requires a controllable air source. If not available, take the caliper(s) to your local gas station and ask them to do the following step.**

3. Place a folded cloth, shop rag, etc. over the caliper piston. Apply low pressure compressed air through the brake hose hole with an air blow gun. The air pressure will force the caliper piston from its bore. If the piston is seized, tap lightly on the caliper with a plastic hammer while applying air pressure.

## ✳✳CAUTION

**Apply air pressure slowly. Pressure can built up inside the caliper and the piston may come out with considerable force. KEEP HANDS AWAY FROM PISTON.**

**Fig. 27 Using low pressure compressed air, blow piston out of bore. (protective rag removed to show procedure)**

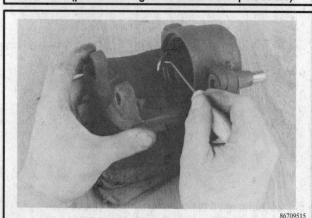

**Fig. 28 Remove seal from groove in caliper bore**

4.   Remove the dust boot and piston seal from the caliper. Clean all parts with alcohol or clean brake fluid. Blow out the passage ways in the caliper. Check the condition of the caliper bore and piston. If pitted or scored or show excessive wear, replacement will be necessary. Slight scoring in the caliper bore may be cleaned up by light honing. Replace the piston if scored.

5.   Apply a coating of brake fluid to the new caliper piston seal and caliper bore. Some rebuilding kits provide a lubricant for this purpose. Install the seal in the caliper bore, make sure it is not twisted and is firmly seated in the groove.

6.   Install the new dust seal in the caliper mounting groove.

7.   Coat the piston with clean brake fluid or brake lubricant and install in the caliper bore. Use a C–clamp to press the piston to the bottom of the bore.

8.   Install the dust boot over the piston and seat in the piston groove.

9.   Install the brake pads as outlined.

10.   Install the caliper over the rotor. Mount the caliper as described in the previous section.

11.   Install the bake hose to the caliper. Be sure to use a new gasket on each side of the hose fitting. Position and install the upper end of the hose. Take care not to twist the hose.

12.   Fill the brake fluid reservoir with new brake fluid.

13.   Bleed the brake system and centralize the brake warning switch.

14.   Install wheel and tire assembly. Tighten wheel nuts to 80–105 ft. lbs. (109–142 Nm).

15.   Check brake pedal resistance before driving

16.   Road test vehicle.

## Front Brake Disc (Rotor)

### REMOVAL & INSTALLATION

▶ **See Figures 29, 30 and 31**

1.   Disconnect the negative battery cable.

2.   Raise and safely support the vehicle with jackstands.

3.   Remove the wheel and tire assembly.

4.   Remove caliper locating pins.

5.   Lift caliper assembly from integral knuckle and rotor using rotating motion. Do not pry directly against plastic piston or damage will occur.

6.   Position caliper aside and support it with a length of wire or rubber cord, to prevent damaging caliper.

7.   Remove rotor from hub assembly by pulling it off the hub studs. Inspect the rotor and refinish or replace, as necessary. If refinishing, check the minimum thickness specification.

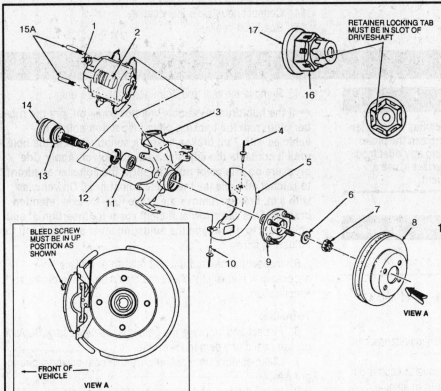

RETAINER LOCKING TAB MUST BE IN SLOT OF DRIVESHAFT

BLEED SCREW MUST BE IN UP POSITION AS SHOWN

FRONT OF VEHICLE

VIEW A

1   Bleed screw and bleed screw cap
2   Caliper assembly
3   Knuckle
4   Dust shield rivet
5   Plastic dust shield
6   Washer
7   Hub retainer
8   Rotor
9   Hub
10   Dust shield rivet
11   Cartridge bearing
12   Retainer
13   Dust seal
14   Constant velocity universal joint
15A   Caliper pin
16   Hub retainer nut
17   Flat washer
A   Tighten to 25-34 Nm (18-25 lb.ft.)

VIEW A

86709013

**Fig. 29  Exploded view of disc brake system**

86709516

Fig. 30 Remove the rotor from the assembly

86709517

Fig. 31 Assembly without rotor. Notice the caliper placement

**To install:**

8. If rotor is being replaced, remove protective coating from new rotor with carburetor degreaser. If original rotor is being installed, make sure rotor braking and mounting surfaces are clean.

9. Install rotor on hub assembly.

10. Install caliper assembly on rotor.

11. Install wheel and tire assembly. Tighten wheel nuts to 80–105 ft. lbs. (109–142 Nm).

12. Pump brake pedal prior to moving vehicle to position brake pad and check pedal resistance.

13. Bleed brakes if necessary.

14. Connect negative battery cable.

15. Road test vehicle.

## REAR DRUM BRAKES

### ✳✳CAUTION

Some brake shoes contains asbestos, which has been determined to be a cancer causing agent. Never clean the brake surfaces with compressed air! Avoid inhaling any dust from any brake surface! When cleaning brake surfaces, use a commercially available brake cleaning solvent.

### Brake Drums

#### REMOVAL & INSTALLATION

♦ See Figures 32, 33, 34, 35, 36, 37, 38, 39, 40, 41 and 42

#### Except All Wheel Drive (AWD) Vehicles

1. Raise and safely support the vehicle with jackstands.

2. Remove the wheel and tire assembly.

3. Remove the grease cap from hub. Remove the cotter pin, nut lock, adjusting nut and keyed flat washer from spindle. Remove outer bearing.

4. Remove the hub and drum assembly as a unit.

➡ If the hub/drum assembly will not come off, pry the rubber plug from the backing plate inspection hole. On vehicles with 7 in. brakes, insert a suitable tool in the hole until it contacts the adjuster assembly pivot. Apply side pressure on this pivot point to allow the adjuster quadrant to ratchet and release the brake adjustment. On vehicles with 8 in. brakes, remove the brake line–to–axle retention bracket. This will allow sufficient room for insertion of suitable tools to disengage the adjusting lever and back–off the adjusting screw.

5. Inspect the brake drum and refinish or replace, as necessary. If refinishing, check the maximum inside diameter specification.

**To install:**

6. Inspect and lubricate the bearings, as necessary. Replace grease seal if any damage is visible.

7. Clean spindle stem and apply a thin coat of wheel bearing grease.

8. Install the hub and drum assembly on spindle.

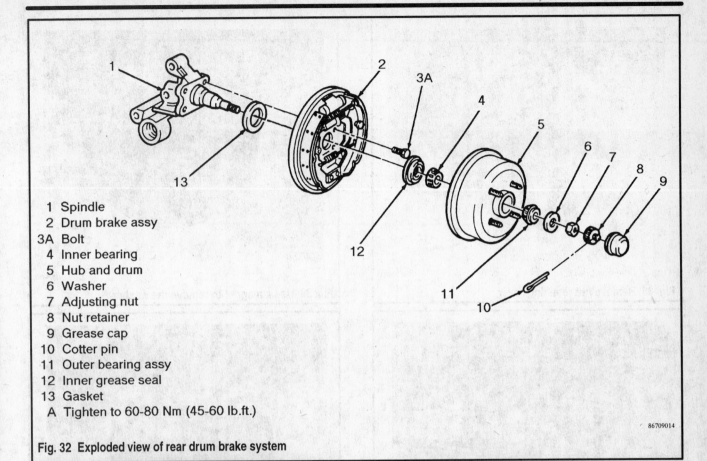

1 Spindle
2 Drum brake assy
3A Bolt
4 Inner bearing
5 Hub and drum
6 Washer
7 Adjusting nut
8 Nut retainer
9 Grease cap
10 Cotter pin
11 Outer bearing assy
12 Inner grease seal
13 Gasket
A Tighten to 60-80 Nm (45-60 lb.ft.)

86709014

**Fig. 32 Exploded view of rear drum brake system**

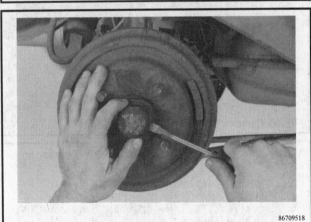

86709518

**Fig. 33 Pry dust cap away from rear drum**

86709519

**Fig. 34 Remove dust cap**

86709520

**Fig. 35 Remove cotter pin and discard**

9. Install the outer bearing into hub on spindle.
10. Install the keyed flat washer and adjusting nut. Tighten nut finger–tight.
11. Adjust wheel bearing. Install nut retainer and a new cotter pin.
12. Install grease cap.
13. Install the wheel and tire assembly. Tighten wheel nuts to 80–105 ft. lbs. (109–142 Nm).
14. Pump the brake pedal prior to moving vehicle to position brake linings.
15. Connect negative battery cable.
16. Road test vehicle.

Fig. 36 Remove nut retaining cover

Fig. 37 Unfasten the securing nut

Fig. 38 Remove the securing nut

Fig. 39 Use a magnet to remove the washer

Fig. 40 Remove the outer rear wheel bearing

Fig. 41 Rear drum installation hardware

**Fig. 42 With all the hardware removed, pull drum away from the vehicle**

86709527

### All Wheel Drive (AWD) Vehicles

1. Disconnect the negative battery cable.
2. Raise and safely support the vehicle with jackstands.
3. Remove the wheel and tire assembly.
4. Remove the spring nut and attaching screws.
5. Pull the brake drum from the hub. Inspect the drum and refinish or replace, as necessary. If refinishing, check the maximum inside diameter specification.

### To install:

6. Position the brake drum on the hub.
7. Install the drum attaching screws, and spring nut.
8. Install the wheel and tire assembly and lower the vehicle.
9. Apply the brake pedal to test the resistance.
10. Connect negative battery cable.
11. Road test vehicle.

## Brake Shoes

### REMOVAL & INSTALLATION

▶ **See Figures 43, 44, 45, 46, 47, 48, 49, 50, 51 and 52**

1. Raise and safely support the vehicle with jackstands.
2. Remove the wheel, tire, hub and finally, the drum assembly.
3. Using a spring removal tool, remove the horizontal securing spring at the top first of the assembly.
4. Pull the adjuster locking plate away from the shoes.
5. Remove the lower horizontal securing spring.

6. Unfasten one of the 2 shoe hold–down springs and remove the pin.
7. Remove the brake adjuster.
8. Remove the remaining hold down spring and clip.
9. Lift the brake shoes assembly off the backing plate and wheel cylinder assembly. Be careful not to bend adjusting lever during the removal process.
10. Remove the parking brake cable from the parking brake lever.
11. Remove the horseshoe retaining clip and spring washer and slide the lever off the parking brake lever pin on the trailing shoe.

### To install:

12. Apply a light coating of high temperature grease at the points where the brake shoes contact the backing plate.
13. Apply a light coating of lubricant to the adjuster screw threads and the socket end of the adjusting screw. Turn the adjusting screw into the adjusting pivot nut to the limit of the threads and then back–off 1/2 turn.
14. Assemble the parking brake lever to the trailing shoe by installing the spring washer and a new horseshoe retaining clip. Crimp the clip until it retains the lever to the shoe securely.
15. Attach the parking brake cable to the parking brake lever.
16. Attach the lower retracting spring to the leading and trailing shoe assemblies and install to backing plate. It will be necessary to stretch the retracting spring as the shoes are installed downward over the anchor plate to inside of shoe retaining plate.
17. Install the adjuster screw assembly between the leading shoe slot and the slot in the trailing shoe and parking brake lever. The adjuster socket end slot must fit into the trailing shoe and parking brake lever.

➡ **The adjuster socket blade is marked R or L for the right or left brake assemblies. The R or L adjuster blade must be installed with the letter R or L in the upright position, facing the wheel cylinder, on the correct side to ensure that the deeper of the 2 slots in the adjuster sockets fits into the parking brake lever.**

18. Assemble the adjuster lever in the groove located in the parking brake lever pin and into the slot of the adjuster socket that fits into the trailing shoe web.
19. Attach the upper retracting spring to the leading shoe slot. Using a suitable spring tool, stretch the other end of the spring into the notch on the adjuster lever. If the adjuster lever does not contact the star wheel after installing the spring, it is possible that the adjuster socket is installed incorrectly.
20. Inspect your work to make sure it is correct.
21. Install the hub/drum and wheel/tire assemblies and adjust the wheel bearings.
22. Lower the vehicle and check brake operation.

Rear Brake

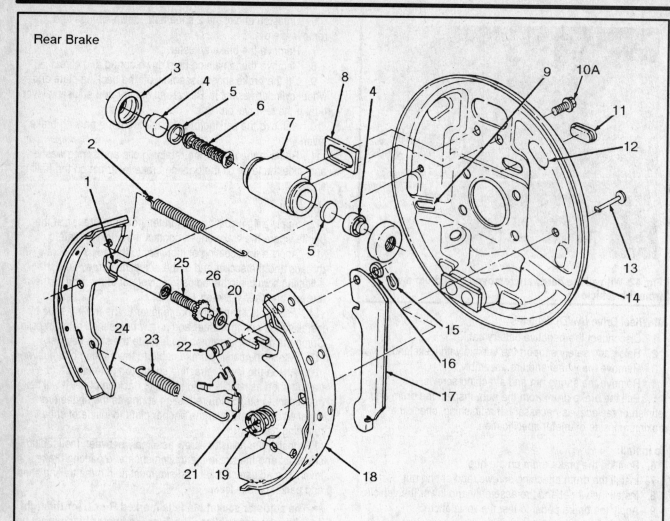

1  Adjuster pivot nut
2  Adjuster screw retracting spring
3  Boot
4  Piston and insert
5  Cup
6  Spring expander
7  Wheel cylinder
8  Wheel cylinder gasket
9  Brake lining inspection access hole
10A Wheel cylinder attaching screw
11  Access hole cover
12  Shoe adjustment access hole
13  Shoe hold-down pin
14  Backing plate

15  Parking lever retaining clip
16  Spring washer
17  Parking brake lever
18  Trailing shoe and lining
19  Shoe hold-down spring assy
20  Adjuster socket
21  Adjuster lever
22  Parking brake lever pin
23  Lower retracting spring
24  Leading shoe and lining
25  Adjusting screw
26  Washer
A  Tighten to 12-18 Nm (9-13 lb.ft.)

**Fig. 43 Exploded view of brake drum assembly**

86709015

86709528

Fig. 44 Remove the brake shoe upper retaining spring with a suitable removal tool

86709529

Fig. 45 Removed spring. Notice spring direction

86709530

Fig. 46 Removed the adjuster lock plate. Notice the direction of the tab

86709531

Fig. 47 Remove the lower retaining spring

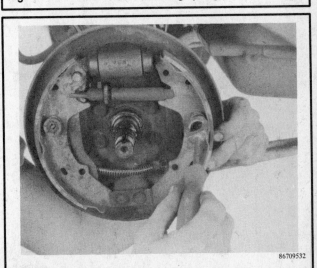

86709532

Fig. 48 Remove the hold down spring. Notice the tool used for removal

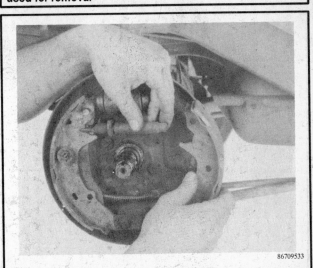

86709533

Fig. 49 Remove the shoe adjuster. Notice the direction of the adjuster spline

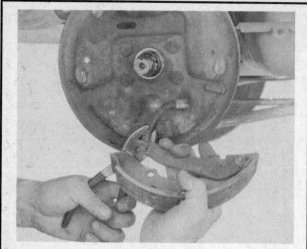

Fig. 50  Remove the hand brake cable

Fig. 51  The final shoe is removed

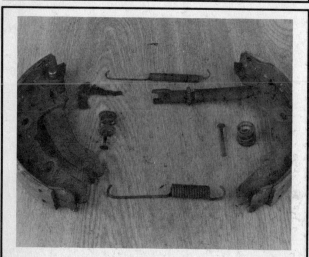

Fig. 52  The removed items of a rear drum assembly

## Wheel Cylinders

### REMOVAL & INSTALLATION

▶ **See Figures 53 and 54**

1. Raise and safely support the vehicle on jackstands. Remove wheel, hub and drum assemblies.
2. Remove as much brake fluid from the master cylinder as possible. Dispose of brake fluid properly.
3. Remove the brake shoe assembly.
4. Disconnect the brake line from wheel cylinder.
5. Remove the wheel cylinder attaching bolts and remove wheel cylinder.

➡ **Use caution to prevent brake fluid from contacting brake linings and drum braking surface. Contaminated linings must be replaced.**

6. Completely clean the brake backing plate.

**To install:**

7. Ensure that the ends of hydraulic fittings are free of foreign matter before making connections.
8. Position the wheel cylinder on backing plate and finger–tighten brake tube to cylinder.
9. Secure the cylinder to backing plate by installing attaching bolts. Tighten bolts to 8–10 ft. lbs. (10–14 Nm).
10. Tighten the tube nut fitting.
11. Install and adjust the brakes.
12. Install hub/drum and wheel assembly, making sure the bearing is secure.
13. Bleed brake system and lower the vehicle.
14. Test brake pedal resistance.
15. Road test vehicle.

### OVERHAUL

▶ **See Figures 55, 56 and 57**

1. Remove the wheel cylinder as outlined earlier.
2. Place cylinder on a clean surface and remove the rubber seals from each end of the unit.
3. Using low pressure compressed air and a rag placed over the unit, blow into the tube hole to remove the plate inside the cylinder.
4. Remove the internal seal, spring and other parts of the cylinder. Discard all the seals. Clean all parts completely, and allow to air dry.
5. Check the cylinder for signs of wear or grooving. Replace if excessive wear is present.
6. Install one internal seal to the plate and insert into cylinder.
7. Insert the spring followed by the other internal seal and plate into the open end of the cylinder. Hold the ends of the cylinder so the parts do not spring out.
8. Install the outer seals to both ends of the cylinder.
9. Position the rebuilt cylinder to the backing plate and install.

10. Install the brake shoes and drum. When complete bleed the brake system.

11. Check for proper brake pedal resistance, and road test the vehicle.

Fig. 53 Clamp brake hose and remove the brake line from the rear of the cylinder

Fig. 54 Remove the wheel cylinder from the backing plate

Fig. 55 Remove the outer wheel cylinder seal from both sides of the cylinder

Fig. 56 With low pressure compressed air, remove the plates from inside the cylinder

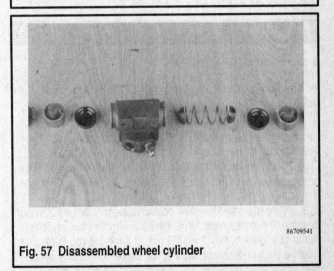

Fig. 57 Disassembled wheel cylinder

## Brake Backing Plate

### REMOVAL & INSTALLATION

1. Raise and safely support the vehicle on jackstands. Remove wheel, hub and drum assemblies.

2. Remove as much brake fluid from the master cylinder as possible. Dispose of brake fluid properly.

3. Remove the brake shoe assembly.

4. Disconnect the brake tube from wheel cylinder.

5. Remove the wheel cylinder attaching bolts and remove wheel cylinder.

➡ Use caution to prevent brake fluid from contacting brake linings and drum braking surface. Contaminated linings must be replaced.

6. Completely clean the brake backing plate.

7. Remove the bolts which secure the backing plate, and discard the bolts.

8. Remove the backing plate and foam gasket from the spindle, if equipped.

**To install:**

9. Install new foam gasket on spindle.

10. Position and install backing plate and new retaining bolts. Torque bolts to 45–60 ft. lbs. (60–80 Nm).

11. Ensure ends of hydraulic fittings are free of foreign matter before making connections.

12. Position wheel cylinder and foam seal on backing plate and finger–tighten brake tube to cylinder.

13. Secure cylinder to backing plate by installing attaching bolts. Tighten bolts to 8–10 ft. lbs. (10–14 Nm).

14. Tighten the tube nut fitting.

15. Install and adjust brakes.

16. Install hub/drum and wheel assembly, making sure the bearing is secure.

17. Bleed the brake system and lower the vehicle.

18. Test the brake pedal resistance.

19. Road test vehicle.

## PARKING BRAKE

The parking brake control is hand operated and mounted on the floor between the front seats. When the control lever is pulled up (from the floor) an attached cable applies the rear brakes. The function of the parking brake and hydraulics of the rear shoes are independent of each other.

## Adjustment

▶ See Figure 58

➡ **The rear brake shoes should be properly adjusted before adjusting the parking brake.**

1. With the engine running, apply approximately 100 lbs. pedal effort to the hydraulic service brake 3 times before adjusting the parking brake.

2. Block the front wheels and place the transaxle in N. Raise and safely support the rear of the vehicle just enough to rotate the wheels.

3. Place the parking brake control assembly in the 12th notch position, 2 notches from full application. Tighten the adjusting nut until approximately 1 in. (25mm) of threaded rod is exposed beyond the nut. Release the parking brake control and rotate the rear wheels by hand. There should be no brake drag.

4. If the brakes drag when the control assembly is fully released, or the handle travels too far on full apply, repeat the procedure and adjust the nut accordingly.

## REMOVAL & INSTALLATION

▶ See Figure 59

1. Make sure the vehicle is in a gear if equipped with a manual transaxle, or PARK if equipped with an automatic transaxle. Block the wheels.

2. Disconnect the negative battery cable.

3. Place the control assembly in the seventh notch position and remove the adjusting nut. Completely release the control assembly.

4. Remove the 2 bolts that attach the control assembly to the floor pan.

5. Remove the adjusting rod from the brake handle.

6. Disconnect the brake light and ground wire from the control assembly.

7. Remove the control assembly from the vehicle.

**To install:**

8. Install the adjusting rod into the control assembly clevis and position the control assembly on the floor pan.

9. Position and tighten the 2 retaining bolts, tightening to 13–20 ft. lbs. (17–28 Nm).

10. Install the brake light and ground wire.

11. Install the adjusting nut and adjust the parking brake.

12. Connect the negative battery cable.

13. Test brake lever to make sure both rear tire engage.

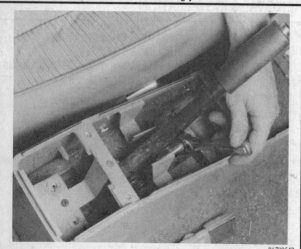

Fig. 58 Adjusting parking brake on console equipped vehicle

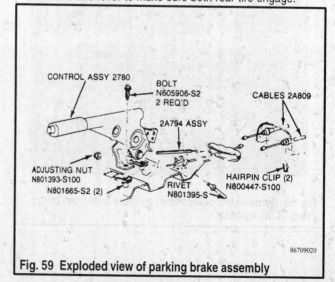

Fig. 59 Exploded view of parking brake assembly

## Cable

### REMOVAL & INSTALLATION

◗ **See Figure 60**

1. Make sure the vehicle is in a gear if equipped with a manual transaxle, or PARK if equipped with an automatic transaxle. Block the wheels.

2. Place the control assembly in seventh notch position and loosen adjusting nut. Completely release the control from the parking brake assembly.

3. Raise the vehicle and support on jackstands. Remove rear parking brake cable from equalizer.

4. Remove hairpin clip holding cable to floor vehicle pan tunnel bracket.

5. Remove wire retainer holding cable to fuel tank mounting bracket. Remove cable from wire retainer. Remove cable and clip from the fuel pump bracket.

6. Remove the screw holding the brake cable retaining clip to rear side–member. Remove the cable from the clip.

7. Remove the wheel and tire assembly and rear brake drum.

8. Disengage cable end from brake assembly parking brake lever. Depress cable prongs holding cable to the brake backing plate. Remove cable through hole in backing plate.

### To install:

9. Insert cable through hole in backing plate. Attach cable end to rear brake assembly parking brake lever.

10. Insert conduit end fitting into backing plate. Ensure retention prongs are locked into place.

➡ **When routing the brake cable, the cable must be routed over the rear suspension and inboard of the trailing arm assembly, to prevent wheel and tire interference.**

11. Insert cable into rear attaching clip and attach clip to rear side–member with screw.

12. Route cable through bracket in floorpan tunnel and install hairpin retaining clip.

13. Install cable end into equalizer.

14. Insert cable into wire retainer and snap retainer into hole in fuel tank mounting bracket. Insert cable and install clip into fuel pump bracket.

15. Install rear drum, wheel and tire assembly and wheel cover. Make sure wheel bearing is properly adjusted.

16. Lower the vehicle.

17. Adjust parking brake. Check brake pedal for proper resistance.

18. Road test vehicle.

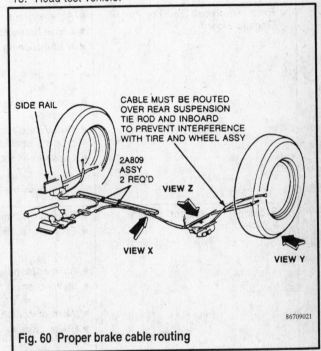

Fig. 60 Proper brake cable routing

## BRAKE SPECIFICATIONS

All measurements in inches unless noted

| Year | Model | Master Cylinder Bore | Brake Disc | | | Brake Drum Diameter | | | Minimum Lining Thickness | |
| | | | Original Thickness | Minimum Thickness | Maximum Runout | Original Inside Diameter | Max. Wear Limit | Maximum Machine Diameter | Front | Rear |
|---|---|---|---|---|---|---|---|---|---|---|
| 1984 | Tempo/Topaz | 0.828 | NA | 0.882 | 0.003 | 8.00 | 8.09 | 8.06 | 0.125 | 10 |
| 1985 | Tempo/Topaz | 0.828 | NA | 0.882 | 0.003 | 8.00 | 8.09 | 8.06 | 0.125 | 10 |
| 1986 | Tempo/Topaz | 0.828 | NA | 0.882 | 0.003 | 8.00 | 8.09 | 8.06 | 0.125 | 10 |
| 1987 | Tempo/Topaz | 0.828 | NA | 0.882 | 0.003 | 8.00 | 8.09 | 8.06 | 0.125 | 1 |
| 1988 | Tempo/Topaz | 0.828 | NA | 0.882 | 0.003 | 8.00 | 8.09 | 8.06 | 0.125 | 1 |
| 1989 | Tempo/Topaz | 0.828 | NA | 0.882 | 0.003 | 8.00 | 8.09 | 8.06 | 0.125 | 1 |
| 1990 | Tempo/Topaz | 0.828 | NA | 0.882 | 0.003 | 8.00 | 8.09 | 8.06 | 0.125 | 1 |
| 1991 | Tempo/Topaz | 1 | 0.945 | 0.882 | 0.003 | 8.06 | 8.15 | 8.12 | 0.125 | 0.060 |
| 1992 | Tempo/Topaz | 1 | 0.945 | 0.882 | 0.003 | 8.06 | 8.15 | 8.12 | 0.125 | 0.060 |
| 1993 | Tempo/Topaz | 1 | 0.945 | 0.882 | 0.003 | 8.06 | 8.15 | 8.12 | 0.125 | 0.060 |
| 1994 | Tempo/Topaz | 1 | 0.945 | 0.882 | 0.003 | 8.06 | 8.15 | 8.12 | 0.125 | 0.060 |

NA - Not Available

1　With rear disc

10　0.030 in. over rivet head; 0.062 in. if bonded lining

86709818

## BRAKE SYSTEM DIAGNOSIS AND SERVICE

| GENERAL BRAKE SYSTEM DIAGNOSIS | | |
|---|---|---|
| CONDITION | POSSIBLE SOURCE | ACTION |
| • Brakes Do Not Apply | • Insufficient brake fluid.<br>• Binding or damaged brake pedal linkage.<br>• Binding or damaged brake booster linkage. | • Add fluid, bleed system, check for leaks.<br>• Service as required.<br>• Service as required. |
| • Excessive Pedal Travel or Pedal Goes to Floor | • Air in system.<br>• Loose brake tube fittings.<br>• Malfunctioning master cylinder.<br>• Drum brakes — improperly adjusted.<br>• Loose-missing pedal bushings or fasteners.<br>• Outer shoe retainer buttons not properly seated in caliper holes.<br>• Loose front hub nut. | • Bleed system.<br>• Tighten to specification.<br>• Refer to Master Cylinder Diagnosis Chart.<br>• Check adjustment. Inspect brakes. Service as required.<br>• Replace/tighten as required.<br>• Check and service.<br>• Check bearing adjustment. If hub nut is loose or not staked, install new nut and tighten to 244-271 N·m (180-200 lb-ft) and stake. |
| • Excessive Pedal Effort to Stop Vehicle | • Binding or damaged pedal linkage.<br>• Engine vacuum loss.<br>• Booster inoperative.<br>• Malfunctioning master cylinder.<br>• Worn or contaminated linings.<br>• Brake system | • Inspect. Service as required.<br>• Check engine vacuum, and vacuum at check valve to booster. Service as required.<br>• Perform power brake function test.<br>• Refer to Master Cylinder Diagnosis Chart.<br>• Inspect. Replace if necessary.<br>• Inspect wheel cylinders or caliper pistons, restricted lines or hoses, contaminated brake fluid, improper operation of proportioning valve. Service as necessary. |
| • Spongy Pedal | • Air in system.<br>• Loose or improper brake pedal, pedal support, booster, master cylinder attachment.<br>• Malfunctioning master cylinder.<br>• Brake system.<br>• Inoperative brake adjusters. | • Bleed system.<br>• Service as required.<br>• Refer to Master Cylinder Diagnosis Chart.<br>• Inspect for damaged or distorted parts in brake caliper assemblies, cracked brake drums, mis-machined knuckle anchor plates.<br>• Service as required. |
| • Brakes Drag, Slow or Incomplete Release | • Parking brake cable out of adjustment or binding.<br>• Blocked master cylinder compensator ports.<br>• Brake adjustment (rear).<br>• Restriction in hydraulic system.<br>• Wheel cylinders or caliper piston seizure. | • Check cables for correct adjustment or bind.<br>• Refer to Master Cylinder Diagnosis Chart.<br>• Check and adjust.<br>• Check and service.<br>• Check and service. |

86709888

## BRAKE SYSTEM DIAGNOSIS AND SERVICE—CONTINUED

| GENERAL BRAKE SYSTEM DIAGNOSIS — Continued | | |
|---|---|---|
| **CONDITION** | **POSSIBLE SOURCE** | **ACTION** |
| • Noise at Wheels When Brakes are Applied — Snap or Clicks | • On drum brakes — brake shoes binding at backing plate ledges. | • Lubricate. |
| | • On drum brakes — backing plate ledges worn. | • Replace backing plate and lubricate ledges. |
| | • Loose or missing disc brake caliper attaching bolts. | • Replace missing bolts, tighten to specification. |
| | • On disc brakes — loose or missing anti-rattle clips. | • Replace. |
| | • Spiral grooves on rotor braking surface. | • Hand sand rotor to remove grooves. |
| | • Disc brake shoe end clearance in excess of 0.66mm (0.026 inch) | • Peen ends of shoes with hammer and anvil to lengthen shoe end and reinstall. Minimum clearance 0.13mm (0.005 inch). |
| • Noise at Wheels When Brakes Are Applied — Scrape or Grind | • Worn brake linings. | • Replace. Refinish drums or rotors if heavily scored. |
| | • Brake shoe interference with back of drum. Binding at backing plate guide ledges. | • Inspect. Replace as necessary. Lubricate. |
| | • Caliper to wheel or rotor interference. | • Inspect and replace as required. |
| | • Other brake system components: Warped or bent brake backing plate or splash shield, cracked drums or rotors. | • Inspect and service. |
| • Noise at Wheels When Brakes are Applied — Squeaks, Squeals, or Chatter<br><br>NOTE: Brake friction materials inherently generate noise and heat in order to dissipate energy. As a result, occasional squeal is normal, and is aggravated by severe environmental conditions such as cold, heat, wetness, snow, salt, mud, etc. This occasional squeal is not a functional problem and does not indicate any loss of brake effectiveness. | • Brake drums and linings, rotors and pads worn or scored. | • Inspect, service or replace. Lightly sand rotors. Do not machine unless heavily scored. |
| | • On disc brakes — missing or damaged brake pad insulators. | • Replace. |
| | • On disc brakes — burred or rusted calipers or knuckles. | • Clean or deburr. |
| | • Dirty, greased or glazed linings. | • Sand or replace dirty or glazed linings and lightly sand rotor braking surfaces, replace pads if contaminated. |
| | • Improper lining parts. | • Inspect for correct usage. Replace. |
| | • On drum brakes — loose lining rivets, weak, damaged or incorrect shoe retracting springs, loose or damaged shoe retaining pins, springs and clips, and grooved backing plate ledges. | • Inspect, service or replace. |

## BRAKE SYSTEM DIAGNOSIS AND SERVICE—CONTINUED

| GENERAL BRAKE SYSTEM DIAGNOSIS — Continued | | |
|---|---|---|
| **CONDITION** | **POSSIBLE SOURCE** | **ACTION** |
| • Noise at Wheels, Brakes Not Applied — Squeak or Squeal | • Wheelcover attachment. | • Seat covers with a rubber mallet. Service flanges or replace cover. |
| | • Loose wheel attaching lug nuts. | • Tighten to specification. Replace wheel if stud holes are damaged. |
| | • Bent or warped backing plate causing interference with drum or rotor. | • Service or replace. |
| | • Improper machining of drum, causing interference with backing plate or shoe. | • Replace drum. |
| | • Other brake system components: | |
| | • Loose or extra parts in brakes. | • Inspect, service, replace as required. |
| | • Drum brake adjustment too tight causing lining to glaze. | |
| | • Worn, damaged, or insufficiently lubricated wheel bearings. | |
| | • On drum brakes — weak, damaged or incorrect shoe retracting springs. | |
| | • On drum brakes — dry/grooved backing plate ledges. | |
| | • Improper positioning of shoe in caliper. | |
| | • Outside diameter of rotor rubbing caliper housing. | |
| • Noise at Wheels, Brakes Not Applied — Growling, Click or Rattle | • Stones or foreign material trapped inside wheelcovers. | • Service or replace. |
| | • Loose grease cap. (Rear only). | • Service or replace. |
| | • Loose wheel lug nuts. | • Tighten to specification. Replace if stud holes are elongated. |
| | • Disc brake caliper — loose or missing anti-rattle clips. | • Inspect, service or replace. |
| | • Drum brakes — loose parts. | • Inspect, service or replace. |
| | • Worn, damaged or dry wheel bearings. | • Inspect, lubricate or replace. |

## BRAKE SYSTEM DIAGNOSIS AND SERVICE—CONTINUED

| GENERAL BRAKE SYSTEM DIAGNOSIS — Continued | | |
|---|---|---|
| **CONDITION** | **POSSIBLE SOURCE** | **ACTION** |
| • Brakes Pull to One Side | • Unequal air pressure in tires. | • Inflate tires to correct pressure. |
| | • Grease or fluid on linings. | • Replace. |
| | • Loose or missing disc brake caliper attaching pins. | • Replace missing bolts. Tighten to specification. |
| | • Improper size or type lining on one wheel. | • Replace with correct brake lining in axle sets. |
| | • Seized wheel cylinders or calipers. | • Service or replace. |
| | • Restricted brake lines or hoses. | • Service or replace. |
| | • Loose suspension components. | • Tighten as necessary. |
| | • Other brake system components: | |
| |   • Improper adjustment of rear brake. | • Inspect, service or replace as required. |
| |   • Improper positioning of disc brake shoe and lining in the caliper. | |
| |   • Improperly adjusted, damaged or worn rear wheel bearings. | |
| |   • Distorted drum brake linings. | |
| |   • Missing, broken or stretched retracting or retaining springs and clips in drum brakes. | |
| | • Malfunctioning master cylinder. | • Refer to Master Cylinder Diagnosis chart. |
| • Brakes Grab or Lockup When Applied | • Tires worn or incorrect pressure. | • Inflate tires to correct pressure. Replace tires with worn tread. |
| | • Grease or fluid on linings — damaged linings. | • Inspect and replace as necessary. |
| | • Improper size or type of linings. | • Replace with correct brake in axle sets. |
| | • Other brake system components: | |
| |   • Bolts for caliper attachment loose or missing. | • Inspect, service or replace as required. |
| |   • Improperly adjusted parking brake. | |
| |   • Contaminated or malfunctioning fluid control valve. | • Refer to Master Cylinder Diagnosis chart. |
| • Brake Warning Lamp On | • Hydraulic system. | • Refer to Master Cylinder Diagnosis chart. |
| | • Shorted lamp circuit. | • Correct short in warning circuit. |
| | • Parking brake not returned. | • Refer to Parking Brake Will Not Release or Fully Return. |
| | • Fluid level indicator switch. | • Replace. |
| • Intermittent Loss of Pedal | • Loose front hub nut. <br>   • Improperly installed front lining. | • If hub nut is loose or not staked, install new nut and tighten to 244-271 N·m (180-200 lb-ft) and stake. |
| | • Master cylinder. | • Perform Master Cylinder Diagnosis test. |

## BRAKE SYSTEM DIAGNOSIS AND SERVICE—CONTINUED

### GENERAL BRAKE SYSTEM DIAGNOSIS — Continued

| CONDITION | POSSIBLE SOURCE | ACTION |
|---|---|---|
| • Rough Engine Idle or Stall, Brakes Applied — Power Brakes Only | • Vacuum booster. | • Check vacuum booster for internal leaks. Replace if required. |
| • Parking Brake Will Not Release or Fully Return (Manual Release) | • Cable disconnected. | • Connect or replace cable. |
| | • Control assembly binding. | • Service or replace. |
| | • Parking brake levers binding. | • Service or replace. |
| | • Rear brakes. | • Check rear brakes shoe retracting springs and parking brake levers. |

### MASTER CYLINDER DIAGNOSIS
### PEDAL GOES DOWN FAST

| TEST STEP | | RESULT ▶ | ACTION TO TAKE |
|---|---|---|---|
| A0 | VERIFY CONDITION | | |
| | • Road test vehicle and depress brake pedal. | (OK) ▶ | Vehicle OK. |
| | | (O̶K̶) ▶ | GO to A1. |
| A1 | BRAKE FLUID LEVEL | | |
| | • Check master cylinder brake fluid reservoir level. | (OK) ▶ | GO to A2. |
| | | (O̶K̶) ▶ | CHECK reservoir sealing points (use Diagnostic Technique No. 3), ADD fluid and BLEED system. REPEAT Test A0. |
| A2 | PRESSURIZE SYSTEM | | |
| | • Pump brake pedal rapidly (five times). | Pedal height builds up, then sinks. ▶ | GO to A3. |
| | | Pedal height builds up and holds. ▶ | CHECK rear brake adjustment and ADJUST if necessary. If condition still exists, BLEED system for air. REPEAT Test A0. |
| A3 | BRAKE SYSTEM LEAKS | | |
| | • Check for external brake system leaks (use Diagnostic Technique No. 1). | (OK) ▶ | GO to A4. |
| | | (O̶K̶) ▶ | SERVICE as necessary, ADD fluid and BLEED system. REPEAT Test A0. |

86709892

## BRAKE SYSTEM DIAGNOSIS AND SERVICE—CONTINUED

| MASTER CYLINDER DIAGNOSIS PEDAL GOES DOWN FAST | | | |
|---|---|---|---|
| **TEST STEP** | **RESULT** | ▶ | **ACTION TO TAKE** |
| **A4** MASTER CYLINDER BY-PASS TEST<br><br>• Test for master cylinder by-pass (use Diagnostic Technique No. 2). | | (OK) ▶ | System OK. |
| | | (ØK) ▶ | REPLACE damaged parts, ADD fluid and BLEED system. REPEAT Test A0. |

86709777

| MASTER CYLINDER DIAGNOSIS — Continued PEDAL EASES DOWN SLOWLY | | | |
|---|---|---|---|
| **TEST STEP** | **RESULT** | ▶ | **ACTION TO TAKE** |
| **B0** VERIFY CONDITION<br><br>• Check if condition occurs during actual stopping application by depressing the brake pedal while the vehicle is moving. | Condition occurs only when vehicle is stationary. | ▶ | No action required. (SEE Normal Condition No. 1.) |
| | Condition occurs while vehicle is moving and braking performance is affected. | ▶ | GO to B1. |
| **B1** BRAKE SYSTEM LEAKS<br><br>• Check for external brake system leaks. (Refer to Diagnostic Technique No. 1.) | | (OK) ▶ | GO to B2. |
| | | (ØK) ▶ | SERVICE as necessary, ADD fluid and BLEED system. REPEAT Test B0. |
| **B2** MASTER CYLINDER BY-PASS TEST<br><br>• Test for master cylinder by-pass. (Refer to Diagnostic Technique No. 2.) | | (OK) ▶ | System OK. |
| | | (ØK) ▶ | REPLACE damaged parts, ADD fluid and BLEED system. REPEAT Test B0. |

86709778

## BRAKE SYSTEM DIAGNOSIS AND SERVICE—CONTINUED

| MASTER CYLINDER DIAGNOSIS — Continued<br>PEDAL IS LOW AND/OR FEELS SPONGY | | |
|---|---|---|
| **TEST STEP** | **RESULT** ▶ | **ACTION TO TAKE** |
| **C0**  VERIFY CONDITION<br><br>• Road test vehicle and apply brake pedal. | (OK) ▶<br><br>(OK̸) ▶ | Vehicle OK.<br><br>GO to **C1**. |
| **C1**  BRAKE FLUID LEVEL CHECK<br><br>• Check master cylinder brake fluid reservoir level. | (OK) ▶<br><br>(OK̸) ▶ | GO to **C2**.<br><br>CHECK reservoir sealing points. (USE Diagnostic Technique No. 3), ADD fluid and BLEED system. |
| **C2**  FILLER CAP VENT CHECK<br><br>• Check if filler cap vent holes are clogged or dirty. | (OK) ▶<br><br>(OK̸) ▶ | GO to **C3**.<br><br>CLEAN as necessary. REPEAT Test **C0**. |
| **C3**  BLEED BRAKE SYSTEM<br><br>• Bleed brake system as outlined in this Section. | Condition corrected ▶<br><br>Condition persists ▶ | Vehicle OK.<br><br>GO to **C4**. |
| **C4**  FRONT HUB NUT CHECK<br><br>• Check front wheel hub nut for looseness or improper positioning of stake. | (OK) ▶<br><br>(OK̸) ▶ | CHECK rear brake adjustment and ADJUST if necessary. REPEAT Test **C0**.<br><br>REPLACE with new nut and stake. **Do not reuse the nut.** REPEAT Test **C0**. |

## BRAKE SYSTEM DIAGNOSIS AND SERVICE—CONTINUED

| MASTER CYLINDER DIAGNOSIS — Continued PEDAL EFFORT EXCESSIVE | | |
|---|---|---|
| **TEST STEP** | **RESULT** ▶ | **ACTION TO TAKE** |
| **D0** VERIFY CONDITION<br><br>• Depress brake pedal fully several times. | Pedal has short stroke and requires excessive effort. ▶<br><br>Pedal has long stroke and requires excessive effort. ▶ | GO to **D1**.<br><br><br>GO to **D2**. |
| **D1** FLUID CONTROL VALVE CHECK<br><br>• Check fluid control valve for contamination. (Refer to Fluid Control Valve Assembly procedure in this Section.) | (OK) ▶<br><br>(O̶K̶) ▶ | GO to **D2**.<br><br>REPLACE valve. FILL reservoir. REPEAT Test **D0**. |
| **D2** CHECK FOR PROPER VENTILATION<br><br>• Check reservoir cap vent hole for obstruction. | Unobstructed ▶<br><br>Obstructed ▶ | GO to **D3**.<br><br>SERVICE or REPLACE reservoir cap. |
| **D3** BRAKE PEDAL LINKAGE TEST<br><br>• Detach booster push rod from pedal pin and depress brake pedal fully. | Pedal moves freely. ▶<br><br><br>Condition persists. ▶ | CHECK booster vacuum availability as described under Vacuum Booster Diagnosis in this Section.<br><br>SERVICE or REPLACE brake pedal linkage. REPEAT Test **D0**. |

## BRAKE SYSTEM DIAGNOSIS AND SERVICE—CONTINUED

| MASTER CYLINDER DIAGNOSIS — Continued REAR BRAKE LOCKUP DURING LIGHT BRAKE PEDAL FORCE | | |
|---|---|---|
| **TEST STEP** | **RESULT** ▶ | **ACTION TO TAKE** |
| **E0** VERIFY CONDITION<br><br>• Road test vehicle and apply brakes lightly. | (OK) ▶<br><br>(OK̸) ▶ | Vehicle OK.<br><br>GO to **E1**. |
| **E1** TIRE INSPECTION<br><br>• Check for excessive tire wear or improper tire pressures. | (OK) ▶<br><br>(OK̸) ▶ | GO to **E2**.<br><br>SUBSTITUTE known good tires if worn. INFLATE to proper pressure. REPEAT Test **E0**. |
| **E2** BRAKE PAD INSPECTION<br><br>• Inspect brake pads for grease or fluid on linings and/or wear problems. | (OK) ▶<br><br>(OK̸) ▶ | GO to **E3**.<br><br>REPLACE if necessary. REPEAT Test **E0**. |
| **E3** PRESSURE CONTROL VALVE TEST<br><br>• Install pressure gauges in the LH front and RH rear bleeder screws. Apply 6895 kPa (1,000 psi) in the front brake system. The rear brake pressure must be between 3689-4137 kPa (535-600 psi). | (OK) ▶<br><br>(OK̸) ▶ | GO to **E4**.<br><br>REPLACE pressure control valve(s). REPEAT Test **E0**. |
| **E4** PRESSURE CONTROL VALVE TEST<br><br>• Install pressure gauges in the RH front and LH rear bleeder screws. Apply 6895 kPa (1,000 psi) in the front brake system. The rear brake pressure must be between 3689-4137 kPa (535-600 psi). | (OK) ▶<br><br>(OK̸) ▶ | INSPECT parking brake and ADJUST as required. REPEAT **E0**.<br><br>REPLACE pressure control valve(s). REPEAT Test **E0**. |

## BRAKE SYSTEM DIAGNOSIS AND SERVICE—CONTINUED

| MASTER CYLINDER DIAGNOSIS — Continued<br>EXCESSIVE AND/OR ERRATIC PEDAL TRAVEL | | |
|---|---|---|
| **TEST STEP** | **RESULT** ▶ | **ACTION TO TAKE** |
| **F0**  VERIFY CONDITION<br><br>• Road test vehicle and apply brakes slowly. | (OK) ▶<br><br>(OK̸) ▶ | GO to **F2**.<br><br>GO to **F1**. |
| **F1**  FLUID CONTROL VALVE CHECK<br><br>• Inspect fluid control valve for contamination as outlined in this Section. | (OK) ▶<br><br>(OK̸) ▶ | GO to **F2**.<br><br>REPLACE valve if necessary. REPEAT Test **F0**. |
| **F2**  ROUGH ROAD TEST<br><br>• Road test vehicle under rough road conditions. Apply brakes slowly. | (OK) ▶<br><br>(OK̸) ▶ | Vehicle OK.<br><br>GO to **F3**. |
| **F3**  WHEEL BEARING CHECK<br><br>• Check for loose wheel bearings. | (OK) ▶<br><br>(OK̸) ▶ | CHECK rotor for thickness variances. (REFER to Section 12-20 for front disc overhaul procedures.)<br><br>REPLACE wheel bearing if damaged. TIGHTEN wheel bearing assembly to specification. REPEAT Test **F0**. |

86709782

## BRAKE SYSTEM DIAGNOSIS AND SERVICE—CONTINUED

### MASTER CYLINDER DIAGNOSIS — Continued
### BRAKE WARNING LAMP ON

| TEST STEP | RESULT ▶ | ACTION TO TAKE |
|---|---|---|
| **G0** BRAKE FLUID LEVEL<br><br>• Check master cylinder brake fluid reservoir level. | (OK) ▶ | GO to **G2**. |
| | (ØK) ▶ | GO to **G1**. |
| **G1** BRAKE SYSTEM LEAKAGE<br><br>• Check reservoir sealing points and external brake system for leakage. (Refer to Diagnostic Techniques No. 1 and 3.) | (OK) ▶ | FILL reservoir. GO to **G2**. |
| | (ØK) ▶ | SERVICE as necessary, ADD fluid and BLEED system. |
| **G2** IGNITION WIRING CHECK<br><br>• Check that ignition wiring is not within a 50.8mm (2 inches) radius of the reed switch Fluid Level Indicator (FLI) assembly. | (OK) ▶ | GO to **G3**. |
| | (ØK) ▶ | REROUTE wiring as necessary. |
| **G3** FLOAT ASSEMBLY CHECK<br><br>• Check if float is stuck or if magnet is dislodged from float. | (OK) ▶ | CHECK if ignition prove out circuit is working properly. |
| | (ØK) ▶ | REPLACE reservoir assembly. |

### MASTER CYLINDER DIAGNOSIS — Continued
### RH FRONT BRAKE DRAGS

| TEST STEP | RESULT ▶ | ACTION TO TAKE |
|---|---|---|
| **H0** VERIFY CONDITION<br><br>• Road test vehicle and apply brakes. | (OK) ▶ | Vehicle OK. |
| | (ØK) ▶ | INSPECT fluid control valve for contamination. (REFER to Fluid Control Valve Assembly procedure in this Section.) REPEAT **H0**. |

## BRAKE SYSTEM DIAGNOSIS AND SERVICE—CONTINUED

### VACUUM BRAKE BOOSTER DIAGNOSIS
### EXCESSIVE BRAKE PEDAL EFFORT OR VACUUM LEAKS

| | TEST STEP | RESULT | ▶ | ACTION TO TAKE |
|---|---|---|---|---|
| **J0** | **VERIFY CONDITION** | | | |
| | • With engine off, depress and release brake pedal five times to deplete all vacuum from booster. Depress pedal, hold with light pressure. Start engine. | Pedal falls slightly, then holds (OK) | ▶ | GO to **J1**. |
| | | (OK̸) | ▶ | GO to **J3**. |
| **J1** | **VACUUM BOOSTER LEAK TEST** | | | |
| | • Run engine to medium speed, release accelerator and turn engine off. Wait 90 seconds and apply brakes. Two or more applications should be power assisted. | (OK) | ▶ | Vehicle OK. |
| | | (OK̸) | ▶ | GO to **J2**. |
| **J2** | **POWER SECTION CHECK VALVE TEST** | | | |
| | • Disconnect vacuum hose for booster check valve at manifold. Blow into hose attached to check valve. | Air passes through check valve | ▶ | INSTALL new check valve and REPEAT Test Step **J1**. |
| | | Air does not pass through check valve | ▶ | REPLACE booster. REPEAT Test Step J0. |
| **J3** | **POWER SECTION TEST** | | | |
| | • Disconnect vacuum hose from vacuum booster check valve. Run engine at idle. Check vacuum supply with a vacuum gauge. | Above 405 kPa (12 in. Hg) and booster does not operate | ▶ | REPLACE booster. REPEAT Test Step J0. |
| | | Below 405 kPa (12 in. Hg) | ▶ | REPLACE or SERVICE vacuum hose and vacuum fittings. TUNE or SERVICE engine as required. REPEAT Test Step **J0**. |

### VACUUM BRAKE BOOSTER DIAGNOSIS — Continued
### SLOW OR INCOMPLETE BRAKE PEDAL RETURN

| | TEST STEP | RESULT | ▶ | ACTION TO TAKE |
|---|---|---|---|---|
| **K0** | **VERIFY CONDITION** | | | |
| | • Run engine at fast idle. Pull brake pedal rearward with approximately 44N (10 lbs) force. Release the pedal and measure the distance to the toe board. Make a heavy brake application. Release the brake pedal and measure the pedal to toe distance. The pedal should return to its original position. | (OK) | ▶ | Vehicle OK. |
| | | (OK̸) | ▶ | GO to **K1**. |
| **K1** | **BRAKE PEDAL BINDING** | | | |
| | • Check pedal to be sure it is operating freely. | (OK) | ▶ | REPLACE booster, REPEAT Test K0. |
| | | (OK̸) | ▶ | CORRECT any sticking or binding. REPEAT Test K0. |

86709784

## BRAKE SYSTEM DIAGNOSIS AND SERVICE—CONTINUED

| | VACUUM BRAKE BOOSTER DIAGNOSIS — Continued<br>VACUUM BRAKE BOOSTER NOISE | | | |
|---|---|---|---|---|
| | **TEST STEP** | **RESULT** | ► | **ACTION TO TAKE** |
| **L0** | **VERIFY CONDITION**<br><br>• Run engine at fast idle for 10 seconds or longer. Depress brake pedal and listen for noise. Compare results with known good system. | No noise | ► | Vehicle OK. |
| | | Noise | ► | CHECK and ADJUST booster push rod as outlined in this Section. |

## TORQUE SPECIFICATIONS

| Component | English | Metric |
|---|---|---|
| Master cylinder mounting nuts: | 13–25 ft. lbs. | 18–33 Nm |
| Booster-to-dash panel: | 13–25 ft. lbs. | 18–33 Nm |
| Rear Drum Brakes | | |
|   Wheel cylinder bleeder screws: | 7.5–15 ft. lbs. | 10–20 Nm |
|   Wheel cylinder-to-backing plate screws: | 9–13 ft. lbs. | 12–18 Nm |
|   Rear brake backing plate-to-spindle: | 45–60 ft. lbs. | 60–80 Nm |
|   Wheel to hub and drum: | 85–105 ft. lbs. | 115–142 Nm |
| Front Disc Brakes | | |
|   Caliper bleeder screws: | 7.5–15 ft. lbs. | 10–20 Nm |
|   Caliper locating pin: | 18–25 ft. lbs. | 24–34 Nm |
|   Wheel nuts: | 85–105 ft. lbs. | 115–142 Nm |

## Troubleshooting the Brake System

| Problem | Cause | Solution |
|---|---|---|
| Low brake pedal (excessive pedal travel required for braking action.) | · Excessive clearance between rear linings and drums caused by inoperative automatic adjusters | · Make 10 to 15 alternate forward and reverse brake stops to adjust brakes. If brake pedal does not come up, repair or replace adjuster parts as necessary. |
| | · Worn rear brakelining | · Inspect and replace lining if worn beyond minimum thickness specification |
| | · Bent, distorted brakeshoes, front or rear | · Replace brakeshoes in axle sets |
| | · Air in hydraulic system | · Remove air from system. Refer to Brake Bleeding. |
| Low brake pedal (pedal may go to floor with steady pressure applied.) | · Fluid leak in hydraulic system | · Fill master cylinder to fill line; have helper apply brakes and check calipers, wheel cylinders, differential valve tubes, hoses and fittings for leaks. Repair or replace as necessary. |
| | · Air in hydraulic system | · Remove air from system. Refer to Brake Bleeding. |
| | · Incorrect or non-recommended brake fluid (fluid evaporates at below normal temp). | · Flush hydraulic system with clean brake fluid. Refill with correct-type fluid. |
| | · Master cylinder piston seals worn, or master cylinder bore is scored, worn or corroded | · Repair or replace master cylinder |
| Low brake pedal (pedal goes to floor on first application—o.k. on subsequent applications.) | · Disc brake pads sticking on abutment surfaces of anchor plate. Caused by a build-up of dirt, rust, or corrosion on abutment surfaces | · Clean abutment surfaces |
| Fading brake pedal (pedal height decreases with steady pressure applied.) | · Fluid leak in hydraulic system | · Fill master cylinder reservoirs to fill mark, have helper apply brakes, check calipers, wheel cylinders, differential valve, tubes, hoses, and fittings for fluid leaks. Repair or replace parts as necessary. |
| | · Master cylinder piston seals worn, or master cylinder bore is scored, worn or corroded | · Repair or replace master cylinder |
| Spongy brake pedal (pedal has abnormally soft, springy, spongy feel when depressed.) | · Air in hydraulic system | · Remove air from system. Refer to Brake Bleeding. |
| | · Brakeshoes bent or distorted | · Replace brakeshoes |
| | · Brakelining not yet seated with drums and rotors | · Burnish brakes |
| | · Rear drum brakes not properly adjusted | · Adjust brakes |

## Troubleshooting the Brake System (cont.)

| Problem | Cause | Solution |
|---|---|---|
| Decreasing brake pedal travel (pedal travel required for braking action decreases and may be accompanied by a hard pedal.) | • Caliper or wheel cylinder pistons sticking or seized<br>• Master cylinder compensator ports blocked (preventing fluid return to reservoirs) or pistons sticking or seized in master cylinder bore<br>• Power brake unit binding internally | • Repair or replace the calipers, or wheel cylinders<br>• Repair or replace the master cylinder<br><br>• Test unit according to the following procedure:<br>  (a) Shift transmission into neutral and start engine<br>  (b) Increase engine speed to 1500 rpm, close throttle and fully depress brake pedal<br>  (c) Slow release brake pedal and stop engine<br>  (d) Have helper remove vacuum check valve and hose from power unit. Observe for backward movement of brake pedal.<br>  (e) If the pedal moves backward, the power unit has an internal bind—replace power unit |
| Grabbing brakes (severe reaction to brake pedal pressure.) | • Brakelining(s) contaminated by grease or brake fluid<br>• Parking brake cables incorrectly adjusted or seized<br>• Incorrect brakelining or lining loose on brakeshoes<br>• Caliper anchor plate bolts loose<br>• Rear brakeshoes binding on support plate ledges<br><br>• Incorrect or missing power brake reaction disc<br>• Rear brake support plates loose | • Determine and correct cause of contamination and replace brakeshoes in axle sets<br>• Adjust cables. Replace seized cables.<br>• Replace brakeshoes in axle sets<br>• Tighten bolts<br>• Clean and lubricate ledges. Replace support plate(s) if ledges are deeply grooved. Do not attempt to smooth ledges by grinding.<br>• Install correct disc<br>• Tighten mounting bolts |
| Chatter or shudder when brakes are applied (pedal pulsation and roughness may also occur.) | • Brakeshoes distorted, bent, contaminated, or worn<br>• Caliper anchor plate or support plate loose<br>• Excessive thickness variation of rotor(s) | • Replace brakeshoes in axle sets<br>• Tighten mounting bolts<br>• Refinish or replace rotors in axle sets |
| Noisy brakes (squealing, clicking, scraping sound when brakes are applied.) | • Bent, broken, distorted brakeshoes<br>• Excessive rust on outer edge of rotor braking surface | • Replace brakeshoes in axle sets<br>• Remove rust |

## Troubleshooting the Brake System (cont.)

| Problem | Cause | Solution |
|---|---|---|
| Hard brake pedal (excessive pedal pressure required to stop vehicle. May be accompanied by brake fade.) | • Loose or leaking power brake unit vacuum hose<br>• Incorrect or poor quality brakelining<br>• Bent, broken, distorted brakeshoes<br>• Calipers binding or dragging on mounting pins. Rear brakeshoes dragging on support plate. | • Tighten connections or replace leaking hose<br>• Replace with lining in axle sets<br><br>• Replace brakeshoes<br>• Replace mounting pins and bushings. Clean rust or burrs from rear brake support plate ledges and lubricate ledges with molydisulfide grease.<br>**NOTE:** If ledges are deeply grooved or scored, do not attempt to sand or grind them smooth—replace support plate. |
| | • Caliper, wheel cylinder, or master cylinder pistons sticking or seized<br>• Power brake unit vacuum check valve malfunction | • Repair or replace parts as necessary<br><br>• Test valve according to the following procedure:<br>(a) Start engine, increase engine speed to 1500 rpm, close throttle and immediately stop engine<br>(b) Wait at least 90 seconds then depress brake pedal<br>(c) If brakes are not vacuum assisted for 2 or more applications, check valve is faulty |
| | • Power brake unit has internal bind | • Test unit according to the following procedure:<br>(a) With engine stopped, apply brakes several times to exhaust all vacuum in system<br>(b) Shift transmission into neutral, depress brake pedal and start engine<br>(c) If pedal height decreases with foot pressure and less pressure is required to hold pedal in applied position, power unit vacuum system is operating normally. Test power unit. If power unit exhibits a bind condition, replace the power unit. |

## Troubleshooting the Brake System (cont.)

| Problem | Cause | Solution |
|---|---|---|
| Hard brake pedal (excessive pedal pressure required to stop vehicle. May be accompanied by brake fade.) | · Master cylinder compensator ports (at bottom of reservoirs) blocked by dirt, scale, rust, or have small burrs (blocked ports prevent fluid return to reservoirs). | · Repair or replace master cylinder **CAUTION:** Do not attempt to clean blocked ports with wire, pencils, or similar implements. Use compressed air only. |
| | · Brake hoses, tubes, fittings clogged or restricted | · Use compressed air to check or unclog parts. Replace any damaged parts. |
| | · Brake fluid contaminated with improper fluids (motor oil, transmission fluid, causing rubber components to swell and stick in bores | · Replace all rubber components, combination valve and hoses. Flush entire brake system with DOT 3 brake fluid or equivalent. |
| | · Low engine vacuum | · Adjust or repair engine |
| Dragging brakes (slow or incomplete release of brakes) | · Brake pedal binding at pivot | · Loosen and lubricate |
| | · Power brake unit has internal bind | · Inspect for internal bind. Replace unit if internal bind exists. |
| | · Parking brake cables incorrrectly adjusted or seized | · Adjust cables. Replace seized cables. |
| | · Rear brakeshoe return springs weak or broken | · Replace return springs. Replace brakeshoe if necessary in axle sets. |
| | · Automatic adjusters malfunctioning | · Repair or replace adjuster parts as required |
| | · Caliper, wheel cylinder or master cylinder pistons sticking or seized | · Repair or replace parts as necessary |
| | · Master cylinder compensating ports blocked (fluid does not return to reservoirs). | · Use compressed air to clear ports. Do not use wire, pencils, or similar objects to open blocked ports. |
| Vehicle moves to one side when brakes are applied | · Incorrect front tire pressure | · Inflate to recommended cold (reduced load) inflation pressure |
| | · Worn or damaged wheel bearings | · Replace worn or damaged bearings |
| | · Brakelining on one side contaminated | · Determine and correct cause of contamination and replace brakelining in axle sets |
| | · Brakeshoes on one side bent, distorted, or lining loose on shoe | · Replace brakeshoes in axle sets |
| | · Support plate bent or loose on one side | · Tighten or replace support plate |
| | · Brakelining not yet seated with drums or rotors | · Burnish brakelining |
| | · Caliper anchor plate loose on one side | · Tighten anchor plate bolts |
| | · Caliper piston sticking or seized | · Repair or replace caliper |
| | · Brakelinings water soaked | · Drive vehicle with brakes lightly applied to dry linings |
| | · Loose suspension component attaching or mounting bolts | · Tighten suspension bolts. Replace worn suspension components. |
| | · Brake combination valve failure | · Replace combination valve |
| Noisy brakes (squealing, clicking, scraping sound when brakes are applied.) (cont.) | · Brakelining worn out—shoes contacting drum of rotor | · Replace brakeshoes and lining in axle sets. Refinish or replace drums or rotors. |
| | · Broken or loose holdown or return springs | · Replace parts as necessary |
| | · Rough or dry drum brake support plate ledges | · Lubricate support plate ledges |
| | · Cracked, grooved, or scored rotor(s) or drum(s) | · Replace rotor(s) or drum(s). Replace brakeshoes and lining in axle sets if necessary. |
| | · Incorrect brakelining and/or shoes (front or rear). | · Install specified shoe and lining assemblies |
| Pulsating brake pedal | · Out of round drums or excessive lateral runout in disc brake rotor(s) | · Refinish or replace drums, re-index rotors or replace |

86709447

# 10

# BODY AND TRIM

## EXTERIOR

➡ **To avoid damage to the Electronic Engine Control (EEC) modules and/or other electrical components or wiring, always disconnect the negative battery cable before using any electric welding equipment on the vehicle.**

### Doors

#### REMOVAL & INSTALLATION

◆ **See Figures 1 and 2**

1. Disconnect the negative battery cable.
2. Open the door and support it with Rotunda Door Rack 103–00027 or equivalent for door service.
3. Remove the trim panel, watershield, and all outside mouldings and clips if the door is to be replaced.
4. Remove all window and door latch components from the door, if the door is to be replaced.
5. Scribe marks around the hinge locations for reference during installation.
6. Remove the door hinge attaching bolts from the door and remove the door.
7. Disconnect any wiring harness connectors, if equipped.

**To install:**

8. Drill holes in replacement door, as necessary, for attaching outside moulding.
9. Position the door hinges to the vehicle and partially tighten the bolts.
10. Install the latch and window mechanism, glass and weather–stripping. Adjust the window mechanism as needed.
11. Install the exterior trim, watershield, and the interior trim.
12. Adjust the door and tighten the retaining bolts.
13. Connect the negative battery cable.
14. Open and close the door, checking for proper alignment.

#### ALIGNMENT

◆ **See Figure 3**

Adjusting the hinge affects the positioning of the outside surface of the door frame. Adjusting the latch striker affects the alignment of the door relative to the weather–stripping and the door closing characteristics.

The door latch striker pin can be adjusted laterally and vertically as well as for and aft. The latch striker should not be adjusted to correct for any door sag.

The latch striker should be shimmed to get the correct clearance, between the striker and the latch. To check this clearance, clean the latch jaws and striker area. Apply a thin layer of dark grease to the striker. As the door is closed and opened, a measurable pattern will result on the latch striker.

➡ **Use a maximum of two shims under the striker.**

The door hinges provide sufficient adjustment to correct most door misalignment conditions. The holes of the hinge and/or the hinge attaching points are enlarged or elongated to provide for hinge and door alignment.

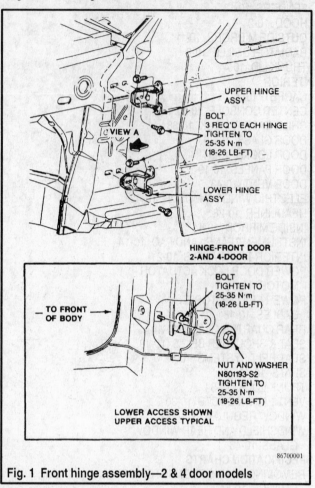

Fig. 1 Front hinge assembly—2 & 4 door models

➡ **DO NOT cover up a poor alignment with a latch striker adjustment.**

15. Determine which hinge screws must be loosened to move the door in the desired direction.
16. Loosen the hinge screws just enough to permit movement of the door with a padded pry bar.
17. Move the door the distance estimated to be necessary for a correct fit. Tighten the hinge bolts and check the door fit to be sure there is no bind or interference with the adjacent panel.

### Hood

#### REMOVAL & INSTALLATION

◆ **See Figure 4**

➡ **When removing or installing the hood, the help of an assistant is recommended.**

1. Open and support the hood.

2. Protect the body with vinyl covers or other devices to prevent damage to the paint.

3. Scribe marks around the hinge locations for reference during installation.

4. Carefully remove the attaching bolts. Be careful not to let the hood slip when the bolts are removed.

5. Remove the hood from the vehicle.

### To install:

6. Place the hood into position. Install and partially tighten attaching bolts. Adjust the hood with the reference marks and tighten the attaching bolts.

7. Check the hood for an even fit between fenders, and for flush fit with the front of the vehicle. Also, check for a flush fit with the top of the cowl and fenders. If necessary, adjust the hood latch. Remember, it is better to make numerous small adjustments, than one large adjustment.

8. Torque attaching bolts to 7–10 ft. lbs. (9–14 Nm).

## ALIGNMENT

▶ See Figure 5

The hood can be adjusted fore and aft and side to side by loosening the hood–to–hinge attaching bolts and moving the hood. To raise or lower the hood, loosen the hinge attaching bolts and raise or lower the hinge as necessary.

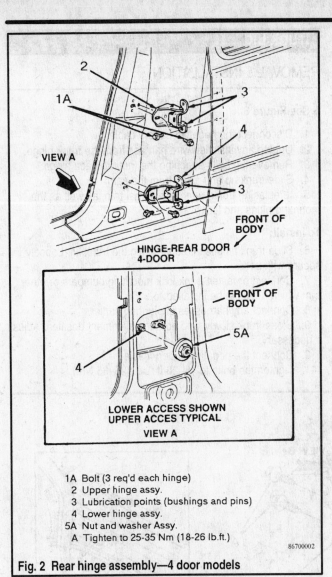

1A  Bolt (3 req'd each hinge)
 2  Upper hinge assy.
 3  Lubrication points (bushings and pins)
 4  Lower hinge assy.
5A  Nut and washer Assy.
 A  Tighten to 25-35 Nm (18-26 lb.ft.)

86700002

**Fig. 2  Rear hinge assembly—4 door models**

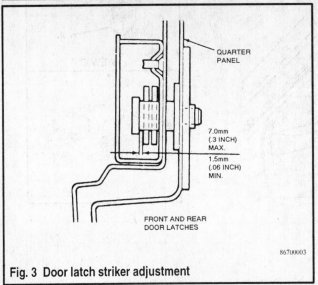

**Fig. 3  Door latch striker adjustment**

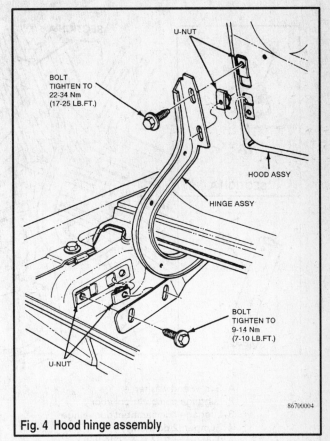

86700004

**Fig. 4  Hood hinge assembly**

The hood lock can also be moved from side–to–side as well as up and down and laterally to obtain a snug hood fit. Loosening the lock attaching screws and move as needed.

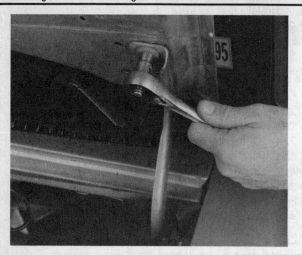

86700500

**Fig. 5 Loosen hood bolts slightly, and move in small increments**

## Trunk Lid

### REMOVAL & INSTALLATION

▶ **See Figure 6**

1. Disconnect the negative battery cable.
2. Unplug any installed wire harness from the trunk hinge.
3. Remove the bolts attaching the trunk to each hinge.
4. Slide trunk up and away from the car.
5. If replacing trunk, remove external trim, as well as the mounting plugs and lock.

**To install:**

6. Slide trunk hinges into opening in the trunk lid. Loosely secure with bolts.
7. Connect or fasten trunk lock mounting bumpers or other trim which needs to be installed.
8. Connect any harnesses unplugged earlier.
9. Close trunk slowly, and note the alignment position. Adjust if necessary.
10. Connect the negative battery cable.
11. Tighten the bolts to 18–26 ft. lbs. (25–35 Nm).

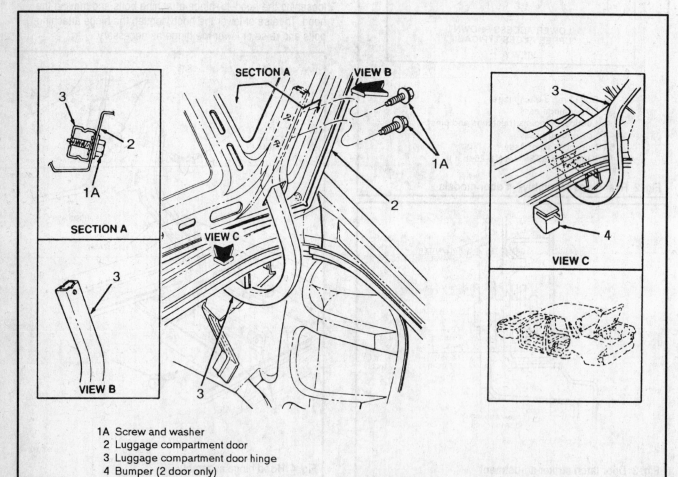

1A Screw and washer
2 Luggage compartment door
3 Luggage compartment door hinge
4 Bumper (2 door only)
A Tighten to 9-14 Nm (7-10 lb.ft.)

86700005

**Fig. 6 Trunk hinge assembly**

## ALIGNMENT

The trunk lid can be shifted fore and aft on all models as well as from side to side. The up and down adjustment can be made by loosening the hinge attaching bolts and raising or lowering the trunk.

The trunk lid should be adjusted for an even and parallel fit with the lid opening. The panel should also be adjusted up and down for a flush fit with the surrounding panels. Care should be taken not to distort or mar the the trunk lid or surrounding body panels.

## Bumpers

## REMOVAL & INSTALLATION

### Front Bumper

*1984–85 MODELS*

◆ **See Figure 7**

1. Remove all necessary trim moulding and guards from the bumper in order to gain access to the bumper retaining bolts.
2. If the vehicle is equipped with the optional (long) bumper extension assembly, remove the screws through the tab on the inside surface of the extension brackets.
3. Remove the isolator–to–reinforcement retaining nuts and remove the bumper assembly from the vehicle.

**To install:**

4. Transfer bumper guards, rub strip, extension assemblies, pads and license plate bracket, if the bumper is being replaced.
5. Position the bumper assembly to the isolators and install the attaching nuts, but do not tighten.

6. Adjust the bumper height so that the distance from the top edge to the ground is the same on both sides. The bumper should be as close to the body as possible.
7. Tighten the isolator–to–bumper bolts to 26–40 ft. lbs. (35–55 Nm).
8. On vehicles equipped with optional extension assemblies, secure the extension assembly to the fender with the retaining hardware.

*1986–94 MODELS*

◆ **See Figure 8**

1. Remove all necessary trim moulding and guards from the bumper in order to gain access to the bumper retaining bolts.
2. Support the bumper and remove the bumper–to–isolator attaching bolts.

➡ **The outboard ends of the bumper covers are attached to the fender panels by a single hidden slide attachment accessed from inside the fender.**

3. Lower the front of the bumper assembly slightly and pull the bumper away from the vehicle to disengage the side attachments.

**To install:**

4. Transfer bumper guards, rub strip, extension assemblies, pads and license plate bracket and bumper mounting brackets if the bumper is being replaced.
5. Position the bumper assembly to the vehicle while sliding the ends over the side attachments.
6. Hand start the bumper–to–isolator attaching bolts.
7. Adjust the bumper height so that the distance from the top edge to the ground is the same on both sides.
8. Tighten the isolator–to–bumper bolts to 17–25 ft. lbs. (22–33 Nm).

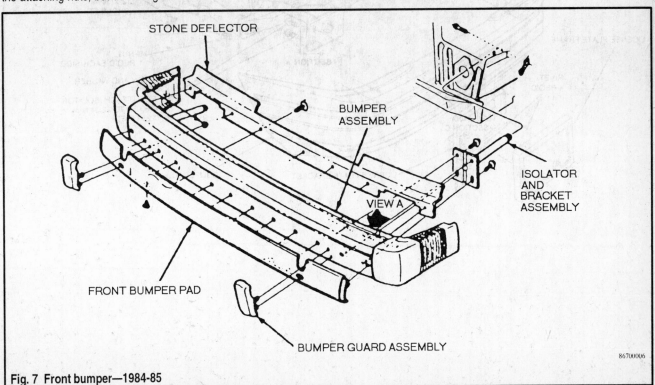

Fig. 7 Front bumper—1984-85

86700006

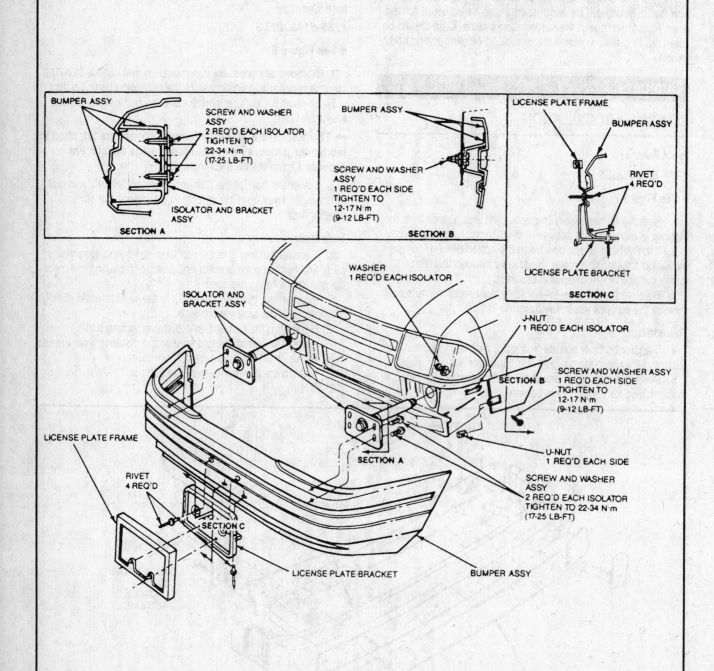

**Fig. 8 Front bumper assembly—1986–94**

### Rear Bumper

#### 1984–85 MODELS

▶ See Figure 9

1.  Remove all necessary trim moulding and guards from the bumper in order to gain access to the bumper retaining bolts.

2.  If the vehicle is equipped with the optional (long) bumper extension assemblies, remove the screws through the tab on the inside surface of the extension brackets.

3.  Remove the isolator–to–reinforcement retaining nut and remove the bumper assembly from the vehicle.

➡ **Steel and aluminum bumpers have retaining nuts at each isolator, while the light weight aluminum bumpers have one fewer retaining nut at the isolator.**

**To install:**

4.  Transfer bumper guards, rub strip, extension assemblies, pads and license plate bracket and bumper mounting brackets if the bumper is being replaced.

5.  Position the bumper assembly to the isolators and install the retaining nuts, but do not tighten.

6.  Adjust the bumper height so that the distance from the top edge to the ground is the same on both sides. The bumper should be as close to the body as possible.

7.  Tighten the isolator to bumper bolts to 26–40 ft. lbs. (35–55 Nm).

8.  On vehicles equipped with optional extension assemblies, secure the extension assembly to the fender with the retaining hardware.

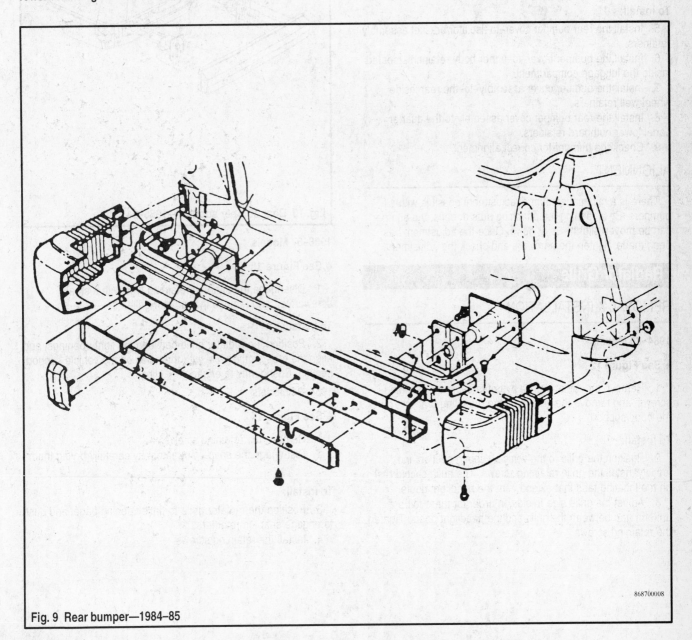

868700008

**Fig. 9 Rear bumper—1984–85**

*1986–94 MODELS*

**♦ See Figures 10 and 11**

1. Remove the rear bumper cover assembly–to–quarter the panel lower retainer. There is one on each side.

2. Remove the bumper cover assembly–to–rear inside wheel well retainers.

3. Remove the bumper cover to upper body retainers. These are located inside the luggage compartment.

➡ **On the 4 door models, the outboard ends of the bumper covers are attached to the quarter panels by a single hidden slide retainer attachment.**

4. Remove the rear bumper cover–to–isolator/ bracket assembly retainers, and remove the rear bumper assembly.

**To install:**

5. Install the rear bumper cover–to–isolator/bracket assembly retainers.

6. Install the bumper cover–to–upper body retainers, located inside the luggage compartment.

7. Install the bumper cover assembly–to–the rear inside wheel well retainers.

8. Install the rear bumper cover assembly to the quarter panel lower outboard retainers.

9. Check the bumper for correct alignment.

## ALIGNMENT

There is a minimal amount of adjustment possible with all bumpers. By loosening the attaching nuts or bolts, the bumper can be moved slightly up or down. Once the adjustment has been made, tighten the hardware and check the adjustment.

## Radiator Grille

### REMOVAL & INSTALLATION

**1984–85 Models**

**♦ See Figure 12**

1. Remove the radiator grille by unfastening the retaining screws, and remove the grille from the mounting brackets on the body support.

**To install:**

2. Position the grille to the vehicle support section and loosely install the grille retaining screws. The grille should rest on the locating tabs that extend from the headlight doors.

3. Adjust the grille side to side, in order for there to be a uniform gap between the grille and the headlight doors. Tighten the retaining screws.

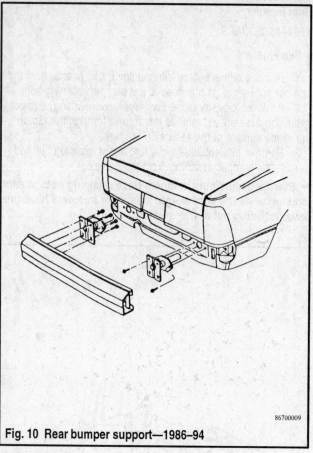

86700009

**Fig. 10 Rear bumper support—1986–94**

**1986–87 Models**

**♦ See Figure 13**

1. Disengage the snap–in retaining legs with a small screwdriver, and remove the radiator grille.

**To install:**

2. Position the radiator grille between the light openings, and align the tabs on the grille with the holes on the vehicle support section. Push firmly to engage the clips.

**1988–94 Models**

**♦ See Figure 14**

1. Remove the retaining screws.

2. Disengage the snap–in retainers by carefully prying them up.

**To install:**

3. Position the radiator grille to grille opening panel and push to engage snap–in retainers.

4. Install the retaining screws.

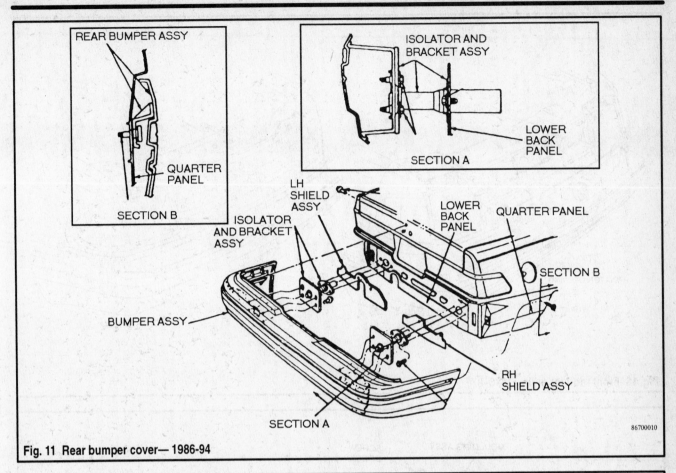

Fig. 11 Rear bumper cover— 1986-94

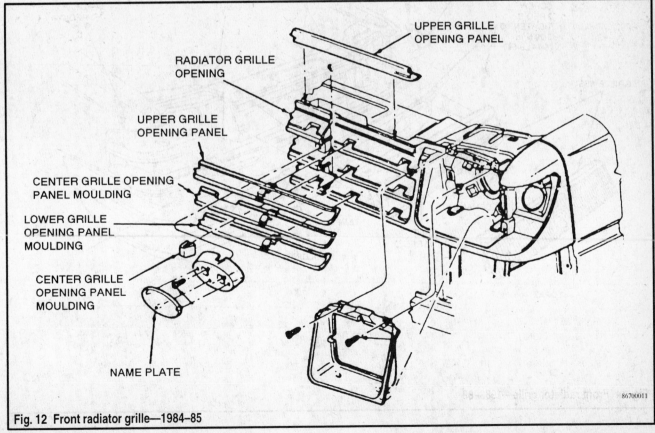

Fig. 12 Front radiator grille—1984–85

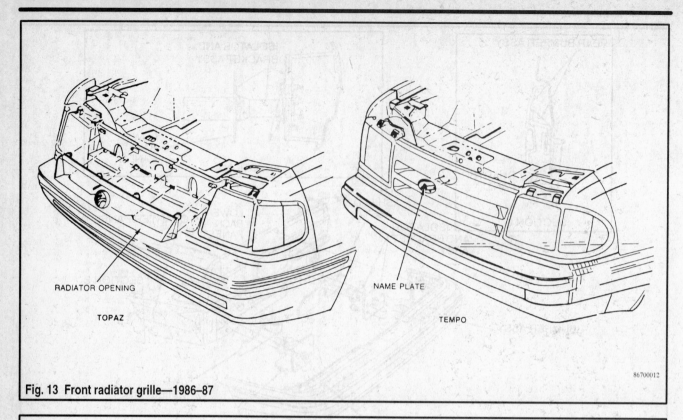

RADIATOR OPENING

TOPAZ

NAME PLATE

TEMPO

86700012

**Fig. 13 Front radiator grille—1986–87**

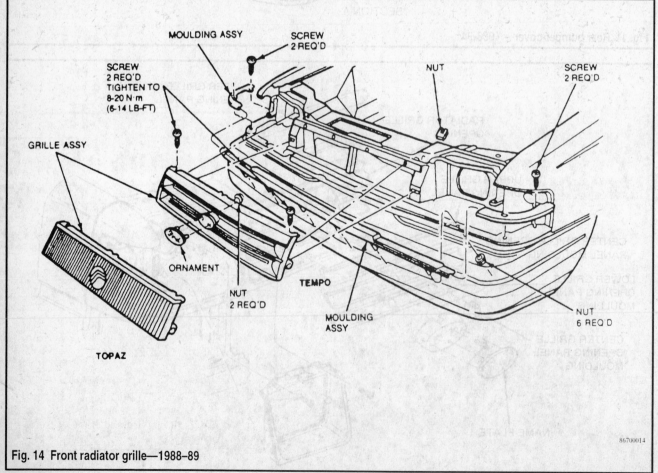

MOULDING ASSY

SCREW
2 REQ'D

SCREW
2 REQ'D
TIGHTEN TO
8-20 N·m
(6-14 LB-FT)

GRILLE ASSY

NUT

SCREW
2 REQ'D

ORNAMENT

NUT
2 REQ'D

TEMPO

MOULDING
ASSY

NUT
6 REQ'D

TOPAZ

86700014

**Fig. 14 Front radiator grille—1988–89**

## Outside Mirrors

### REMOVAL & INSTALLATION

#### Manual Mirrors

▶ **See Figure 15**

1. Remove the inside door trim panel from the door.
2. Remove the interior retaining nuts and washers from the mirror.
3. Roll the window down.
4. Lift the mirror up and out of the door.

➡ **It is recommended that when the mirror is reinstalled, a new gasket between the mirror and door be used.**

**To install:**

5. Install the mirror and gasket onto the door.
6. Install the nuts and washers, tightening the nuts to 25–36 inch lbs. (2.8–4.0 Nm).
7. Reinstall the door trim panel.

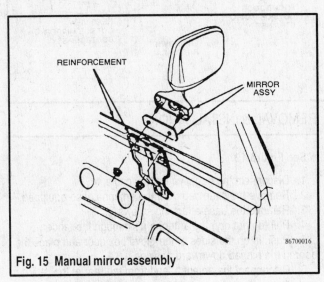

**Fig. 15 Manual mirror assembly**

#### Remote Manual Mirrors

▶ **See Figure 16**

1. Remove the set screw securing the control lever of the cable assembly to the bezel on the door trim panel.
2. Remove the interior trim panel and from the door.
3. Disengage the cable from the routing clips and guides located inside the door.
4. Remove the mirror attaching nuts and washers from the interior door.
5. Roll the window down. Remove the mirror and cable assembly from the door.

**To install:**

6. Place the remote cable into the hole on the door and position the mirror to the panel. Install the nuts and washers and tighten them to 21–39 inch lbs. (2.3–4.4 Nm).

7. Route the cable through the door into the cable guides and locating clips.
8. Check the operation of the mirror to insure that the mirror cables do not interfere with the window mechanism.
9. Install the door trim panel.
10. Place the control lever bezel onto the door trim panel and install the set screw.

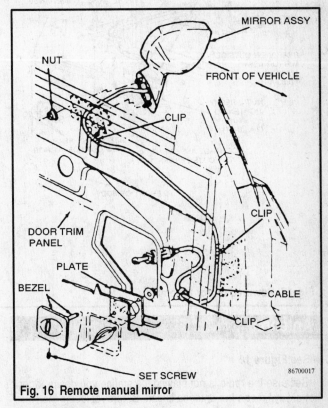

**Fig. 16 Remote manual mirror**

#### Power Mirrors

▶ **See Figure 17**

1. Disconnect the negative battery cable.
2. Remove the inside door trim panel and weather insulator from the door.
3. Disconnect the electrical connector from the mirror unit. Disengage the wire harness from the routing clips and guides inside the door.
4. Roll the window down.
5. Remove the mirror attaching nuts and washers. Remove the mirror and wire assembly from the door.

**To install:**

6. Place the wire harness into the door hole and position the mirror. Install the nuts and washers and tighten them to 35–51 inch lbs. (3.9–5.7 Nm).
7. Route the wire harness through the door into the guides and connect. Reconnect the negative battery cable.
8. Check the operation of the mirror and make sure that the mirror wires do not interfere with the window mechanism.
9. Install the door trim panel.

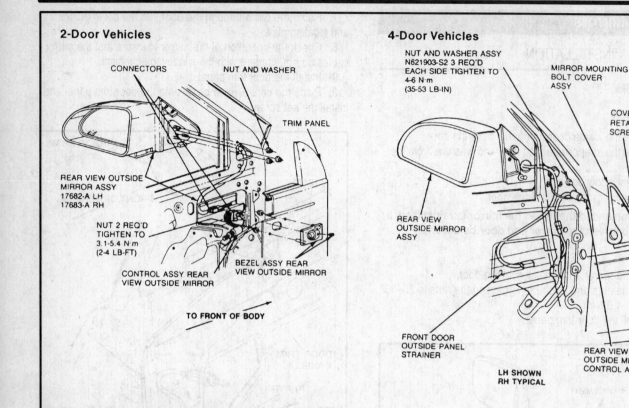

**2-Door Vehicles**

CONNECTORS

NUT AND WASHER

TRIM PANEL

REAR VIEW OUTSIDE MIRROR ASSY
17682-A LH
17683-A RH

NUT 2 REQ'D
TIGHTEN TO
3.1-5.4 N·m
(2-4 LB-FT)

CONTROL ASSY REAR VIEW OUTSIDE MIRROR

BEZEL ASSY REAR VIEW OUTSIDE MIRROR

TO FRONT OF BODY

**4-Door Vehicles**

NUT AND WASHER ASSY
N621903-S2 3 REQ'D
EACH SIDE TIGHTEN TO
4-6 N·m
(35-53 LB-IN)

MIRROR MOUNTING BOLT COVER ASSY

COVER RETAINING SCREW

TRIM PANEL

REAR VIEW OUTSIDE MIRROR ASSY

FRONT DOOR OUTSIDE PANEL STRAINER

LH SHOWN
RH TYPICAL

REAR VIEW OUTSIDE MIRROR CONTROL ASSY

86700018

**Fig. 17 Powered mirror assembly**

## Antenna

♦ See Figure 18

Because the radio is not playing the station you desire, does not always mean the antenna is bad. Before replacing the antenna, make sure the connection from the antenna to the radio is solid. Remove the antenna plug, clean the contact and plug back into the radio. Also remove the snap cap from the antenna base, and make sure the retaining screws are secure.

=86700501

**Fig. 18 The antenna mast is removed easily by unscrewing it at the base**

## REMOVAL & INSTALLATION

♦ See Figure 19

1. Disconnect the negative battery cable.
2. Remove the snap cap from the antenna, if so equipped.
3. Remove the base attaching screws.
4. Pull (do not pry) the antenna up through the fender.
5. Push in on the sides of the glove box door and place the door in the hinged downward position.
6. Disconnect the antenna lead from the rear of the radio and remove the antenna cable from the heater or air conditioning cable retaining clips.

➡ **On some models it may be necessary to remove the right side kick panel in order to gain access to some of the antenna cable retaining clips.**

7. Pull the antenna cable through the hole in the door hinge pillar and remove the antenna assembly from the vehicle.

**To install:**

8. Place the gasket on the base of the antenna and feed the wire through the fender opening. Install the antenna base onto the fender using the retaining screws.
9. Install the antenna base cap and antenna mast assembly, if so equipped.
10. Pull the antenna lead through the door hinge pillar opening. Seat the grommet by pulling the antenna through the hole from the inside of the vehicle.

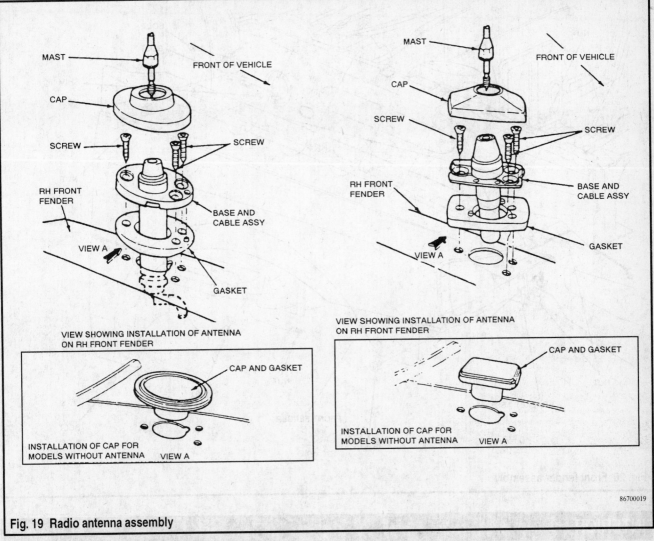

**Fig. 19 Radio antenna assembly**

11. Route the antenna cable behind the glove box, along the instrument panel and install the cable in the retaining clips from which they were removed.

12. Connect the antenna wiring connector into the back of the radio. Install the right hand kick panel, if removed.

13. Push in on the sides of the glove box door and place in the hinged upward position.

14. Connect the negative battery cable.

15. Turn on the radio and check to see that both Am and Fm stations work.

## Fenders

### REMOVAL & INSTALLATION

♦ **See Figure 20**

1. Raise and support the vehicle with jackstands.
2. Remove the wheel and tire assembly.
3. Remove the front bumper assembly.
4. Disconnect the parking lamp and headlight wiring connectors.

5. Remove the fender-to-radiator support retainer screws and bracket.

6. Remove the fender-to-splash shield retainers.

7. Remove the fender-to-rocker panel retainers.

8. Remove fender-to-door hinge retainer.

9. Remove the fender-to-engine compartment retainers and remove the fender.

**To install:**

10. Place the fender into position and hand tighten the fender to engine compartment retainers.

11. Install the fender-to-door hinge retainer.

12. Install the fender-to-rocker panel retainers.

13. Install the fender-to-splash shield retainers.

14. Install the fender-to-radiator support bracket assembly and retainers.

15. Connect the parking lamp and headlight wiring connectors to their respective lamps.

16. Close the hood and align the fender, so there is an even gap between the hood and the fender.

17. Tighten all fender hardware.

18. Install the front bumper.

19. Install the wheel and tire assembly.

20. Lower vehicle.

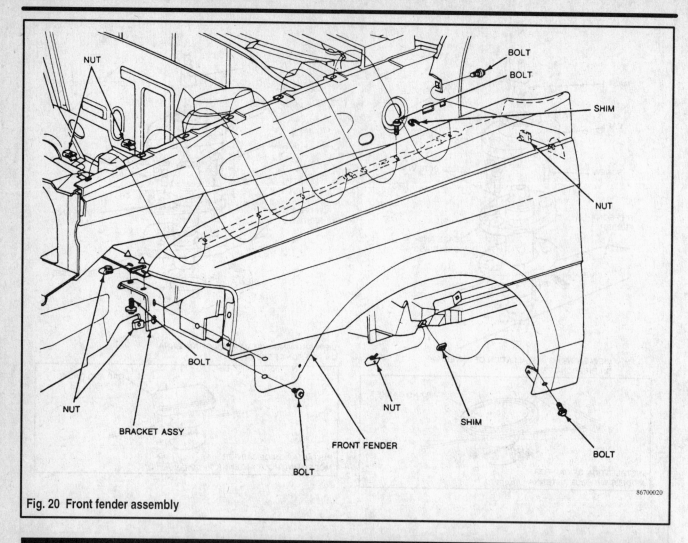

NUT

BOLT
BOLT

SHIM

NUT

NUT

BOLT

NUT

BRACKET ASSY

NUT

SHIM

FRONT FENDER

BOLT

BOLT

86700020

**Fig. 20 Front fender assembly**

## INTERIOR

### Instrument Panel and Pad

#### REMOVAL & INSTALLATION

**1984–89 Models**

◆ **See Figure 21**

1. Disconnect the negative battery cable.

2. Remove the steering column cover retaining screws and remove the cover.

3. Remove the sound insulator, if equipped.

4. On 1988–89 vehicles, remove the snap-in lower cluster finish panel to expose the retaining screws to the panel. Remove the screws and the panel

5. Identify and tag all electrical connections. Once marked, disconnect and move out of the way.

6. To remove the steering column, remove the nut and bolt at the lock collar U–joint, and the screws at the steering column bracket.

7. Remove the radio by disconnecting the wire harness and antenna.

8. On 1988–89 vehicles, disconnect the speedometer cable at the transaxle. This is necessary for added cable length when removing the cluster from the dash panel.

9. Remove the instrument cluster by removing trim panel and cluster retaining screws, identify and tag the connectors and unplug the speedometer cable at the instrument cluster.

10. Carefully pull out the cluster pack.

11. Remove the glove box hinge support screws. Depress the sides of the glove box bin and remove the glove box assembly.

12. Identify, tag and disconnect all vacuum hoses and electrical connectors, heater, A/C control cables and radio antenna cable.

13. Remove the speaker grilles and speakers.

14. Remove the instrument panel tubular brace retaining screw.

15. Remove the upper and lower instrument panel–to–cowl retaining screws.

16. Carefully remove the instrument panel from the vehicle.

**To install:**

17. Place the instrument panel into position. Install the upper and lower instrument panel–to–cowl retaining screws.

18. Install the instrument panel tubular brace retaining screw.
19. Install the speakers and speaker grilles.
20. Push the wiring harness and connectors through the dash panel, being careful not to tear any of the wire insulation on the metal.
21. Connect all vacuum hoses and electrical connectors, heater, A/C control cables and radio antenna cable on the passenger side.
22. Connect the speedometer cable to the transaxle.
23. Install the radio, connector and antenna.
24. Install the glove box assembly.
25. Install the instrument cluster and wire connectors.
26. Connect the speedometer and any other connectors unplugged earlier.
27. Secure the instrument cluster with the retaining screws. Install the trim panel around the cluster.
28. Install the sound insulator, if equipped.
29. Install the steering column opening cover.
30. Connect the negative battery cable.
31. Start vehicle and check all electrical accessaries.

### 1990–94 Models

▶ See Figure 22

1. Disconnect the negative battery cable.

2. Disconnect the speedometer at the transaxle. This is necessary for additional cable length needed to remove the cluster from the dash panel.
3. Remove the lower cluster finish panel.
4. Remove the upper and lower retaining screws to the steering column reinforcement.
5. Remove the speed control module, if equipped.
6. Loosen, but do not remove the 2 nuts and bolts retaining the steering column to the support bracket.
7. Remove the instrument cluster by unfastening the upper retaining screws, speedometer cable and connectors.
8. Remove the radio, harness and antenna.
9. Identify, tag and disconnect all vacuum hoses and electrical connectors, including heater, A/C control cables and radio antenna cable.
10. Remove the steering column–to–support bracket retaining screws and nuts.
11. Carefully, pry open the steering column shaft area of the clamp to disengage the shaft.
12. Depress the sides of the glove box bin and remove the glove box assembly.

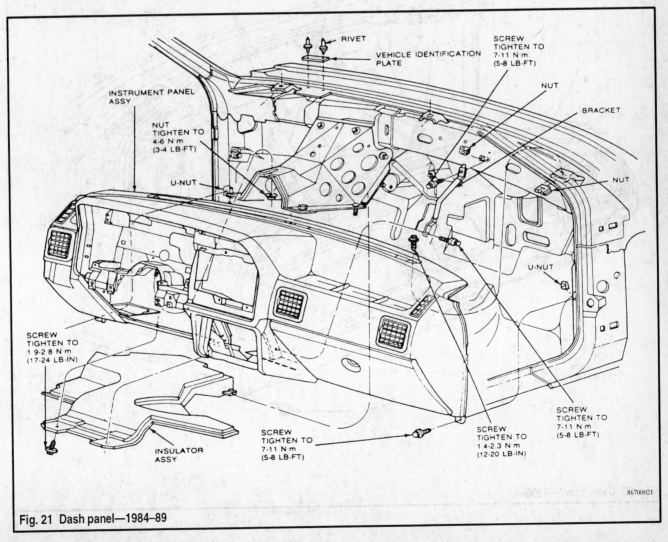

Fig. 21 Dash panel—1984–89

13. Disconnect all vacuum hoses and electrical connectors, including, heater, A/C control cables and radio antenna cable.

14. Remove the steering column support bracket retaining nut.

15. Remove the speakers and grilles.

16. Remove the instrument panel tubular brace retaining screw.

17. Remove the upper and lower instrument panel–to–cowl retaining screws and remove the instrument panel from the vehicle.

**To install:**

18. While holding the instrument panel close to the installed position, push the instrument wiring harness and connectors through the dash panel. Secure the dash panel to the cowls using the retaining screws.

19. Install the panel tubular brace using the retaining screws.

20. Install the instrument cluster, speedometer cable and electrical connectors.

21. Position the radio, and connect the wire harness and antenna.

22. Connect all vacuum hoses and electrical connectors, heater, A/C control cables and radio antenna cable.

23. Install the glove box, speakers and grilles.

24. Raise the steering column into position and engage the lower shaft to the intermediate shaft. Install the clamp bolt and nut.

25. Install the speed control module, if equipped.

26. Install the upper and lower retaining screws to column reinforcement.

27. Install the lower cluster finish panel.

28. Install the steering column cover retaining screws and remove the cover.

29. Connect the speedometer at the transaxle.

30. Connect the negative battery cable.

31. Test all electrical accessaries

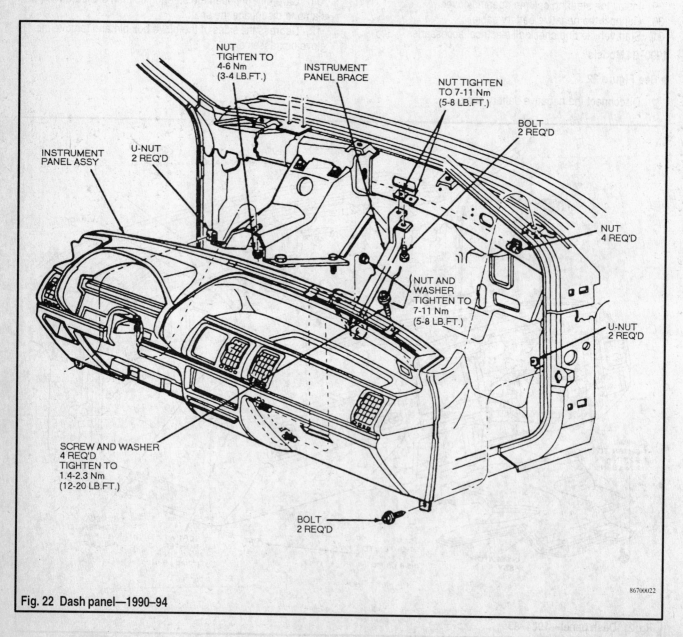

**Fig. 22 Dash panel—1990–94**

86700022

## Center Console

### REMOVAL & INSTALLATION

▶ **See Figure 23**

**With Armrest**

➡ **If equipped with ashtray/cup holder, remove now.**

1. If equipped with the shoulder belt option, remove shoulder belt anchor plug button and bolts.

2. Remove the armrest–to–rear support retaining screws, located on each side. To access the screws, the left and right belt bezel may have to be removed. Remove the armrest.

3. Remove the finish panel–to–console retaining screws. Lift panel from console.

4. Unscrew the console to center support retaining screws.

5. Lift console up. If equipped with the shoulder belt option, feed shoulder belts through openings, and remove console.

**To install:**

6. Position console between seats, with shoulder belts fed through the bezel holes on the side, if equipped.

7. Install the retaining screws in console which secure the unit to the floor.

8. Install the finish panel over the brake lever and install the retaining screws.

9. Position the console finish panel and secure with screws.

10. Pull up on emergency brake and pull on shoulder harness, if equipped, to make sure all function correctly.

11. Install any belt assemblies which were removed.

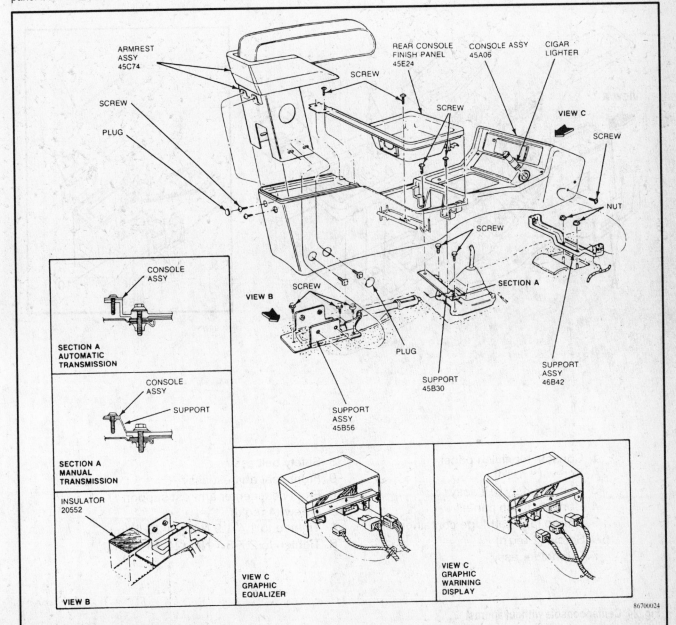

**Fig. 23 Center console with armrest**

**Without Armrest**

♦ **See Figures 24, 25, 26, 27 and 28**

➡ **If equipped with ashtray/cupholder, remove now**

1. Unfasten the shoulder belt anchor plug button and bolts.

2. Remove the screws securing the pocket at the rear of the console. Remove the pocket

3. Remove the screws securing the trim plate around the brake handle. Screws are located under the pocket, and last is under the brake handle. Remove the trim panel.

4. Remove the screws securing the console to the floor.

5. Lift console up. If equipped with the shoulder belt option, feed shoulder belts through the openings.

**To install:**

6. Position console between seats, with shoulder belts fed through the bezel holes on the side.

7. Install the retaining screws securing the unit to the floor, in front of the shifter, below the cupholder/ashtray section, if equipped.

8. Place the trim panel around the brake handle and fasten the retaining screws.

9. Install the rear pocket with the retaining screws.

10. Secure any seat belts which were removed.

11. Pull up on emergency brake and pull on shoulder harness to make sure all function correctly.

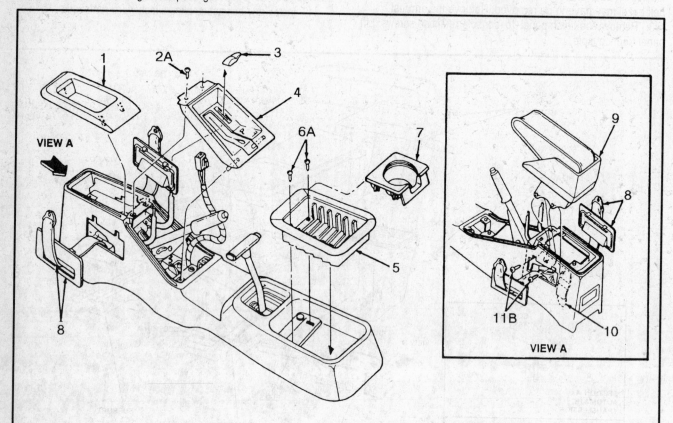

| | | |
|---|---|---|
| 1 | Console top finish panel | 8 Safety belt assy |
| 2A | Screw (2 req'd) | 9 Front seat armrest assy |
| 3 | Part of safety belt assy | 10 Front seat center armrest support |
| 4 | Console finish panel | 11B Screw (4 req'd) |
| 5 | Stereo tape cartridge container | A Tighten to 1.4-1.9 Nm (14-16 lb.in.) |
| 6A | Screw (2 req'd) | B Tighten to 2.7-3.7 Nm (24-33 lb. in.) |
| 7 | Cupholder assy | |

**Fig. 24  Center console without armrest**

86700023

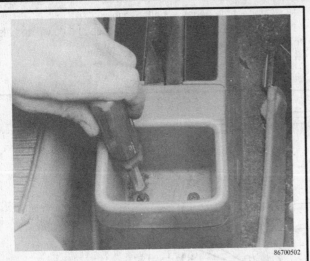

Fig. 25 Remove the screws from the rear pocket portion of the console

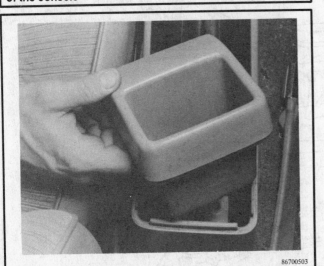

Fig. 26 Remove the pocket

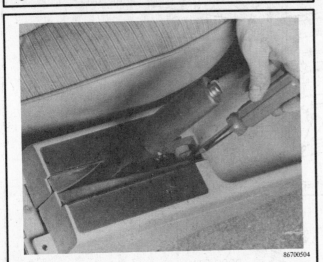

Fig. 27 Unfasten the retaining screw under the emergency brake. Do not forget the screws under the rear pocket

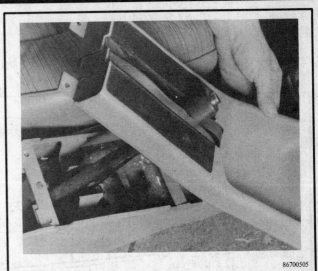

Fig. 28 Slide the piece over the brake handle

## Door Panels

### REMOVAL & INSTALLATION

♦ See Figure 29

1. Disconnect the negative battery cable.
2. Remove the window regulator handle retaining screw and remove the handle, if equipped. If the vehicle is equipped with power windows and/or power locks, remove the control panel from the door.
3. Remove the retaining screw from the armrest recess and around the edge of the door panel.
4. Remove the retaining set screw from the remote control mirror bezel. Remove the bezel, if so equipped.
5. Remove the door handle pull cap, if so equipped.
6. With a push pin tool, putty knife or similar flat tool, pry the trim panel retaining push pins from the door interior panel.

➡ Do not use the trim panel to pull the push pins from the door inner panel holes.

7. If the trim panel is to be replaced, transfer the trim panel retaining push pins to the new panel assembly. Replace any bent, broken or missing push pins.
8. If the watershield has been removed, be sure to position it correctly before installing the trim panel.

**To install:**

9. Be sure that the armrest retaining clips are properly positioned on the door inner panel.
10. Position the trim panel to the door inner panel. Route the remote control outside mirror cable through the bezel, if so equipped.
11. Position the trim panel to the door inner panel and locate the push pins in the countersunk holes. Firmly push the trim panel at the push pin locations to set each push pin.
12. Install the set screw from the remote control outside mirror bezel, if so equipped.

13. Install the trim panel retaining screws.
14. Install the door handle pull cup.
15. Install the window regulator handle, if equipped. If equipped with power windows and/or power locks, install control panel.

16. Connect the negative battery cable.
17. Test to make sure the window rolls up and down, and also that the door locks work correctly.

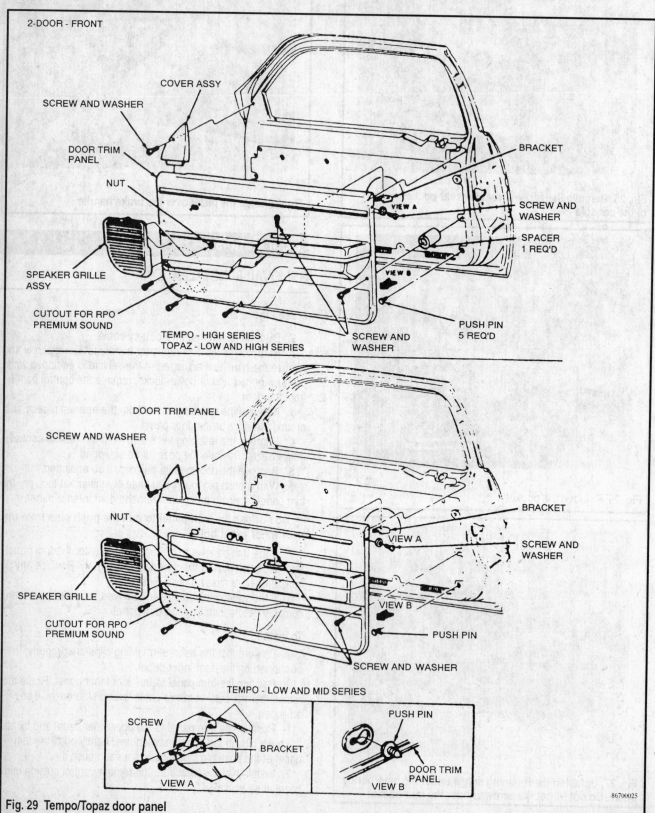

Fig. 29 Tempo/Topaz door panel

86700025

## Interior Trim Panels

### REMOVAL & INSTALLATION

Because many of the interior panels are surrounded by some type of trim work, it is important to know how to remove and install trim.

**Windshield Trim**

▶ **See Figure 30**

1. Remove the retaining screws attaching the side trim to the vehicle body. Remove the coat hook if installed. Carefully pry trim panel away from pillar.

2. Remove the screw attaching the windshield trim to the pillar.

3. Remove trim by carefully pulling toward rear of vehicle.

**To install:**

4. Position the trim panel over the windshield and secure with the retaining screw.

5. Position the pillar trim panel and secure with retaining screws.

6. Install coat hook, if equipped.

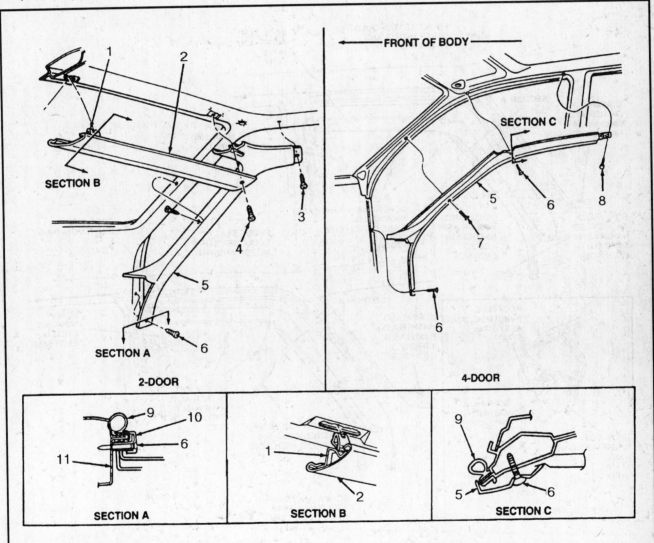

1  Retainer
2  Windshield upper moulding
3  Screw and washer assy.
4  Screw and washer ssy.
5  Windshield side moulding (4 door)
   Windshield side moulding (2 door)
6  Screw and washer assy.
7  Screw and washer assy.
8  Screw
9  Front door opening weatherstrip
10 Side moulding
11 Body pillar

Fig. 30 Windshield trim

86700026

## Rear Roof & Side Trim

♦ **See Figures 31 and 32**

1. Remove the attaching screws above door opening. Remove coat hanger, if equipped.
2. Remove the retaining screws around the rear vent window.
3. Remove the retaining screws above the rear window.
4. Begin removing the trim pieces by carefully prying each piece away from the vehicle.

**To install:**

5. Position trim panel around rear vent window.
6. Position trim above rear window, and secure with retaining screws.
7. Install trim over door opening and secure with retaining screws.
8. Install remaining retaining screws around rear vent window.
9. Install coat hook, if equipped.

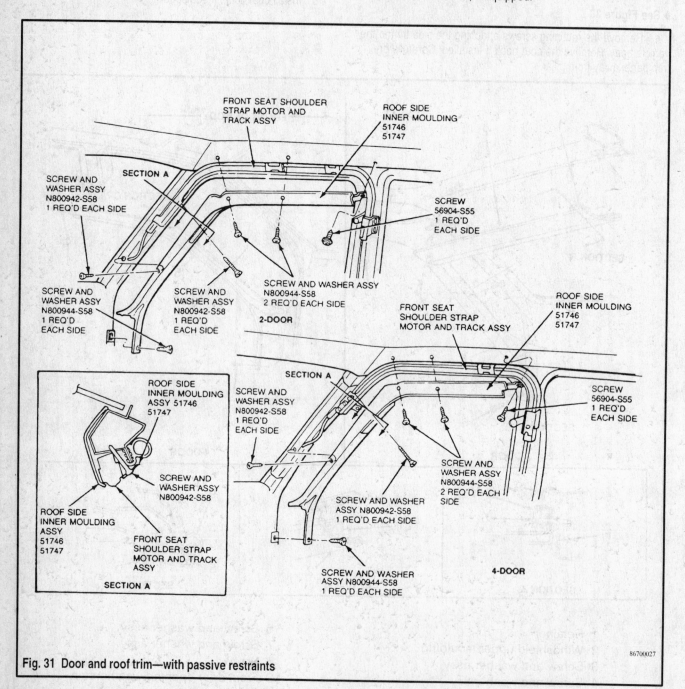

**Fig. 31 Door and roof trim—with passive restraints**

86700027

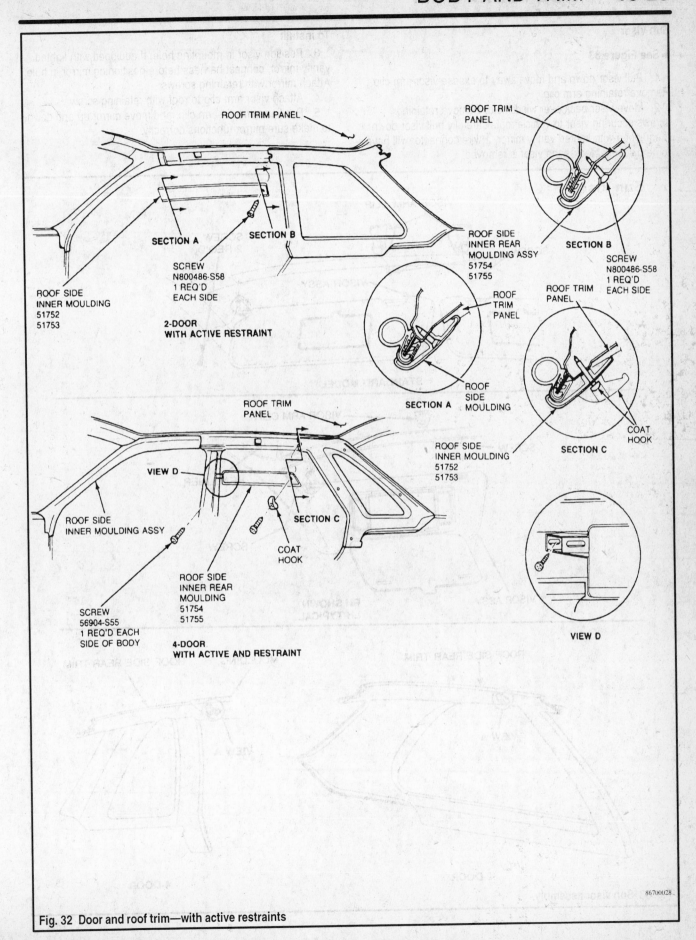

ROOF TRIM PANEL

ROOF TRIM PANEL

SECTION A

SECTION B

SCREW
N800486-S58
1 REQ'D
EACH SIDE

ROOF SIDE
INNER MOULDING
51752
51753

**2-DOOR
WITH ACTIVE RESTRAINT**

ROOF SIDE
INNER REAR
MOULDING ASSY
51754
51755

SECTION B

SCREW
N800486-S58
1 REQ'D
EACH SIDE

ROOF
TRIM
PANEL

ROOF TRIM
PANEL

SECTION A

ROOF
SIDE
MOULDING

ROOF SIDE
INNER MOULDING
51752
51753

SECTION C

COAT
HOOK

ROOF TRIM
PANEL

VIEW D

SECTION C

COAT
HOOK

ROOF SIDE
INNER MOULDING ASSY

ROOF SIDE
INNER REAR
MOULDING
51754
51755

SCREW
56904-S55
1 REQ'D EACH
SIDE OF BODY

**4-DOOR
WITH ACTIVE AND RESTRAINT**

VIEW D

**Fig. 32 Door and roof trim—with active restraints**

86700028

## Sun Visor

▶ **See Figure 33**

1. Pull visor down and move away to expose visor arm clip. Remove retaining arm clip.

2. Move visor back over windshield. Remove retaining screws securing visor to vehicle roof. Carefully pull visor down. If equipped with lighted vanity mirror, a wire connector will have to be disconnected as the visor is removed.

**To install:**

3. Position visor in mounting hole. If equipped with lighted vanity mirror, connect harness before positioning mirror in hole. Attach mirror with retaining screws.

4. Attach visor arm clip to roof with retaining screw.

5. Position mirror in arm clip, and move mirror up and down to make sure mirror functions correctly.

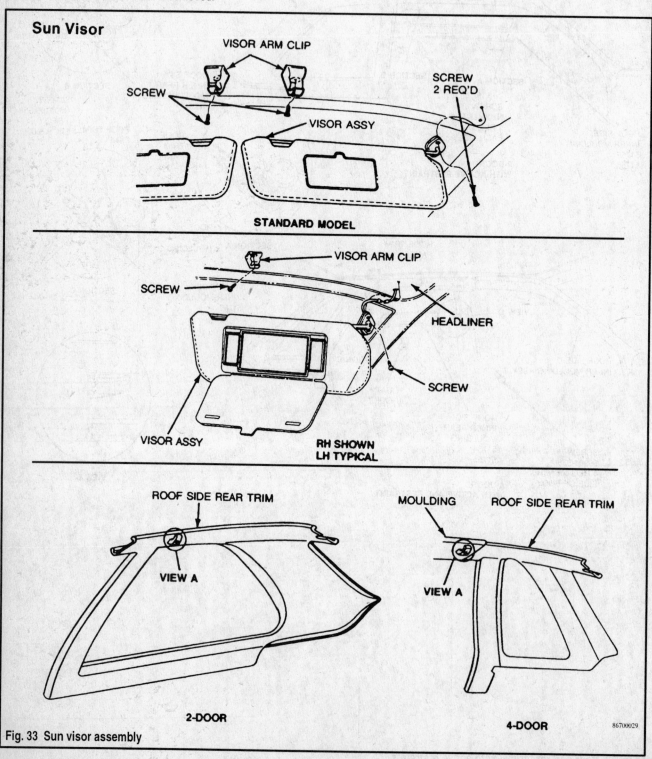

Fig. 33 Sun visor assembly

## Cowl Trim Panel

▶ **See Figure 34**

1. Remove the retaining screws. On driver's side panel, an additional screw is hidden behind hood pull handle.

2. Carefully pry panel away from vehicle. On driver's side, unfasten hood release cable from behind panel. Once clip has disengaged, remove panel from car.

## To install:

3. Position panel to body. If installing driver's side panel, make sure the hood cable has been installed to the handle. Position panel such that clip aligns with panel and push panel in.

4. Secure panel with retaining screws.

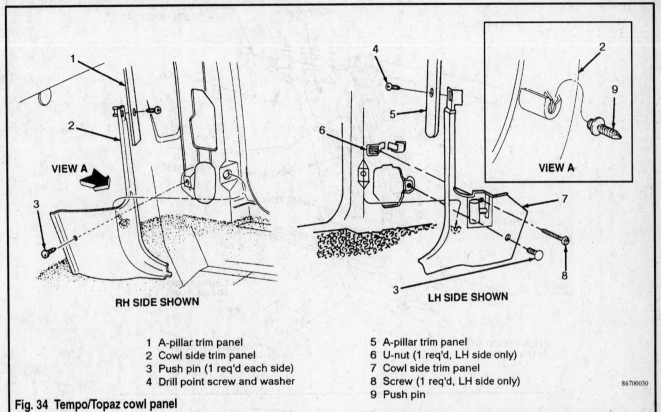

| 1 A-pillar trim panel | 5 A-pillar trim panel |
|---|---|
| 2 Cowl side trim panel | 6 U-nut (1 req'd, LH side only) |
| 3 Push pin (1 req'd each side) | 7 Cowl side trim panel |
| 4 Drill point screw and washer | 8 Screw (1 req'd, LH side only) |
| | 9 Push pin |

86700030

**Fig. 34  Tempo/Topaz cowl panel**

## Rear Package Tray

▶ **See Figure 35**

1. Remove the rear seat and cushion.

2. Remove third brake light, if equipped, by removing the screws from the side of the piece, pulling away from the tray and disconnecting the harness.

3. Remove push pins that secure panel to vehicle body.

4. Pull panel forward and up. Remove retaining bolts securing rear seat belts, and slide belts through panel.

5. Remove panel.

## To install:

6. Secure seat belts with retaining bolts.

7. Position panel, feeding seat belts through, and securing the panel with push pins.

8. Connect the third brake light harness, and fasten to vehicle with retaining screws, if equipped.

9. Install rear cushion and seat.

10. Check to make sure third brake light functions correctly.

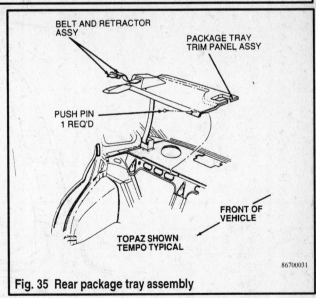

86700031

**Fig. 35  Rear package tray assembly**

**B–pillar Trim**

♦ **See Figure 36**

1. Remove upper retaining screws.
2. Carefully pull away weather–stripping around both sides of panel.
3. Pull panel up and away to remove.

**To install:**

4. Align and push panel down to secure into lower interior panel.
5. Attach weather–stripping around both edges of the door such that it holds the panel.
6. Attach retaining screws.

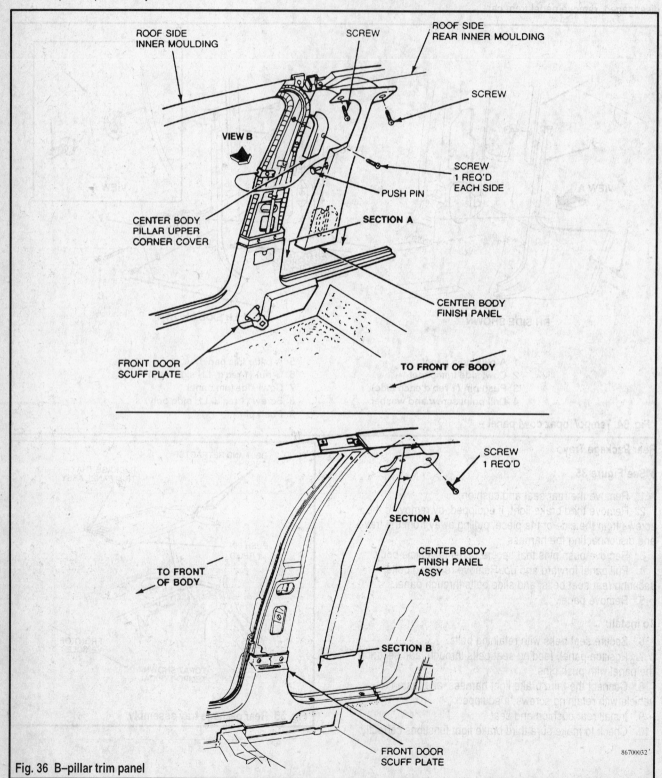

Fig. 36 B–pillar trim panel

86700032

## Lower B–pillar Trim Panel

▶ **See Figure 37**

1. On 2 door models, remove retaining screws from door sill and remove scuff panel.

2. On 4 door models, remove center panel trim.

3. On 4 door models, remove retaining screws from sill on front and rear door. Also the screws securing the panel to the center pillar.

4. Remove panel by pulling up and away.

### To install:

5. On 4 door models, position panel, and attach retaining screw to center pillar and floor sill of both doors.

6. On 4 door models, install the center pillar panel.

7. On 2 door models, position the scuff panel on the sill and secure with retaining screws.

## Quarter Trim Panel

▶ **See Figure 38**

1. Remove rear seat and cushion. Remove third brake light assembly, if equipped, by loosening the 2 screws and unplugging the harness. Remove the package tray.

2. On 4 door models, remove retaining screws and remove trim panel.

3. On 2 door models, remove armrest pad cover by removing the nuts attaching piece to panel.

4. Remove trim panel insert by prying out the trim retaining clips.

5. Remove panel by unfastening retaining screws, disconnecting the seat belt by removing it from the quarter panel and bringing it through the bezel on the panel. Remove panel from car.

### To install:

6. On 2 door models, install seat belt assembly to vehicle body. Position panel and secure with retaining screws.

7. Install trim panel insert by aligning clips with holes on the panel, and pushing on the panel to lock in place.

8. Position armrest pad cover and fasten with the nuts.

9. On 4 door models, align trim panel and secure with retaining screws.

10. Install package tray and third brake light, if equipped.

11. Secure rear seat and cushion.

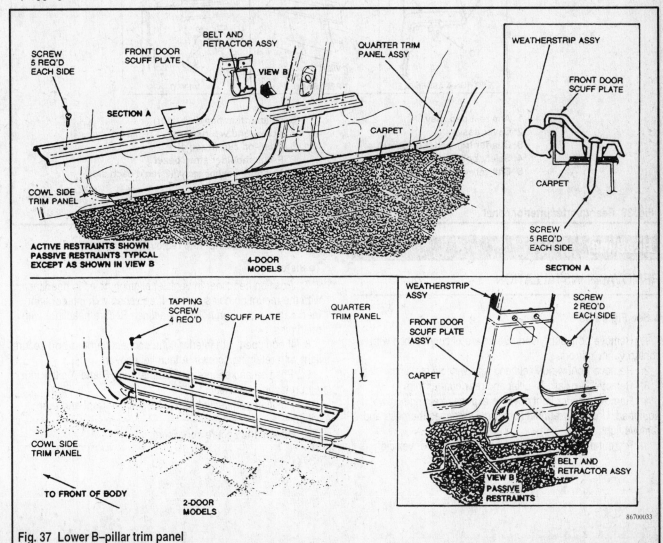

**Fig. 37 Lower B–pillar trim panel**

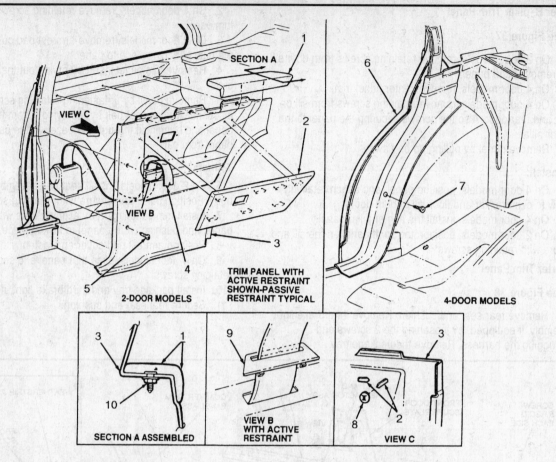

1 Arm rest pad assy.
2 Cover assy.
3 Quarter trim panel (2-door)
4 Safety belt assy.
5 Drill screw and washer assy.
6 Quarter trim panel (4-door)
7 Screw and washer assy.
8 Push-on clip (6 req'd)
9 Front shoulder strap bezel
10 Nut and washer assy. (2 req'd each side)

86700034

**Fig. 38 Rear quarter interior panel**

## Headliner

### REMOVAL & INSTALLATION

▶ See Figure 39

1. Remove both sun visors. Be aware of connections with lighted vanity mirrors.
2. Remove front windshield and rear window molding.
3. Remove A–pillar , B–pillar and rear quarter trim.
4. Remove interior light cover to expose retaining screws, if equipped. Unfasten retaining screws. Disconnect harness and remove light.
5. Pry out push pin securing headliner to roof of vehicle.

6. Balance headliner and remove from vehicle.

**To install:**

7. Position headliner in vehicle, aligning holes in headliner with the mounting holes in roof. If equipped with interior light, feed harness through hole in headliner. Secure headliner with push pins.
8. If equipped with interior light, connect harness and secure light with retaining screws. Attach light cover.
9. Position and secure rear quarter trim, B and A pillar trim with retaining screws.
10. Position and secure trim pieces above front and rear windows.
11. Attach and secure sun visors.

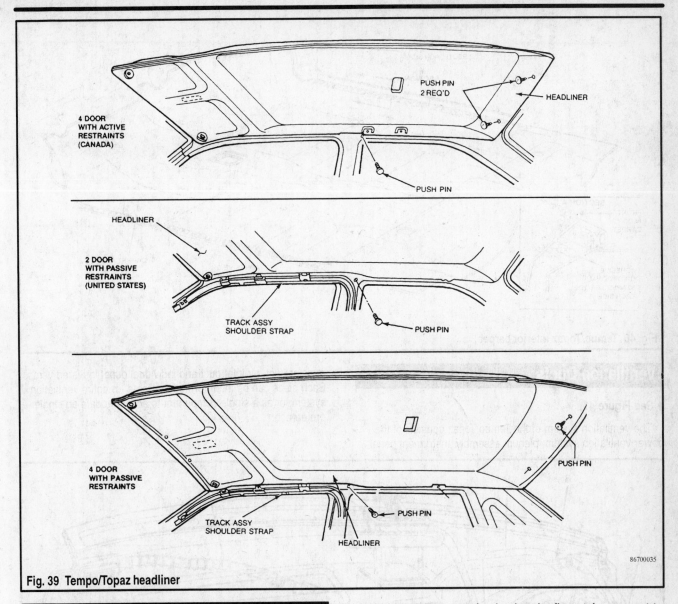

**4 DOOR WITH ACTIVE RESTRAINTS (CANADA)**

PUSH PIN 2 REQ'D

HEADLINER

PUSH PIN

**2 DOOR WITH PASSIVE RESTRAINTS (UNITED STATES)**

HEADLINER

TRACK ASSY SHOULDER STRAP

PUSH PIN

**4 DOOR WITH PASSIVE RESTRAINTS**

PUSH PIN

PUSH PIN

TRACK ASSY SHOULDER STRAP

HEADLINER

86700035

**Fig. 39 Tempo/Topaz headliner**

## Carpet

### REMOVAL & INSTALLATION

▶ **See Figure 40**

1. Remove front and rear seats.
2. Remove shift console assembly.
3. Remove scuff panels from door sills.
4. Remove cowl panels.
5. Remove retaining screws securing rear quarter trim.
6. Remove seat belts by removing retaining bolts.
7. Begin pulling up the carpet. Start from the outside and work inward. Fold carpet in and remove from vehicle.

➡ Because the carpet is glued to the floor, take care not to tear the carpet as you are pulling on it. If replacing the carpet, make sure all the carpet is removed before installing new carpet.

**To install:**

8. Check condition of glue on vehicle floor. If still tacky, it can be used again. If not tacky, apply a new coat to the floor. Position carpet and apply pressure to carpet to ensure contact with glue.
9. Connect seatbelts by securing with retaining bolts.
10. Install quarter trim panel and retaining screws.
11. Install and secure the door sill scuff panel.
12. Install the center console and secure with screws.
13. Install the front and rear seats.

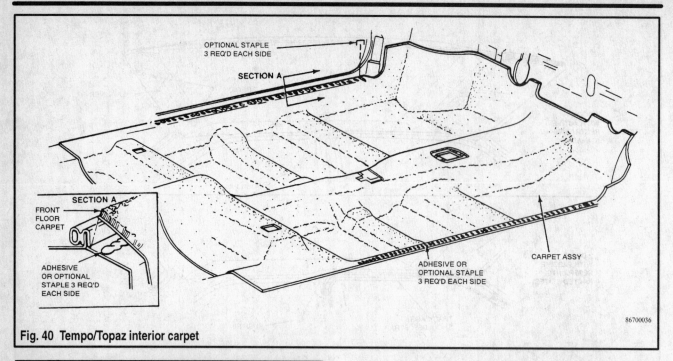

**Fig. 40 Tempo/Topaz interior carpet**

## Ventilation Ducts

♦ **See Figure 41**

The ventilation system of the Tempo/Topaz consists of the power ventilation system, plenum assembly, Instrument panel register duct, air inlet duct and individual outlet louvered vents. Each piece can be incorporated to create an entire ventilation system, or as a single component to accommodate an single preference.

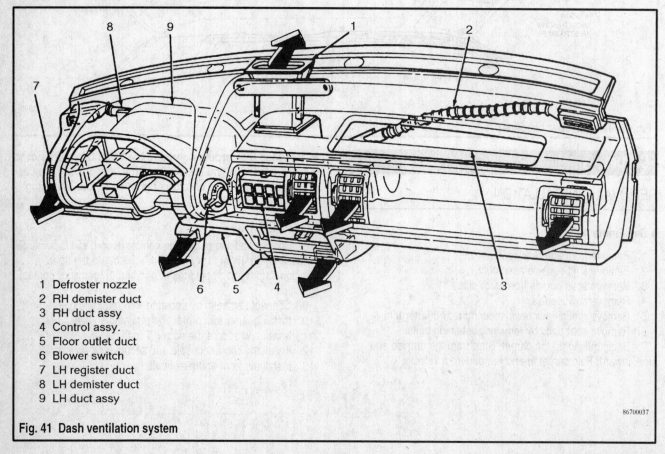

1 Defroster nozzle
2 RH demister duct
3 RH duct assy
4 Control assy.
5 Floor outlet duct
6 Blower switch
7 LH register duct
8 LH demister duct
9 LH duct assy

**Fig. 41 Dash ventilation system**

## REMOVAL & INSTALLATION

### Plenum Assembly

▶ **See Figure 42**

The plenum assembly run from the register duct in the center of the dash panel, to each individual dash vent.

1. Remove the lower portion of the dashboard, including glove box and panel below the steering wheel.
2. Remove the center console.
3. Identify, tag and remove the vacuum and electrical connections to the register duct.
4. Remove the retaining screws securing the register duct and plenum assembly to the dashboard.
5. Carefully lower and remove the register/plenum assembly.
6. Remove the retaining screws securing the register duct to the plenum assembly.

**To install:**

7. Connect and attach the plenum assembly to the register duct. Make sure the sealing gasket between the pieces is tight.
8. Raise the assembly up to the dashboard. Secure the center section with retaining screws.
9. Check and make sure that plenum assembly is mated correctly with the vents. Adjust if needed.
10. Install the remaining retaining screws.
11. Position glove box and install panel below steering wheel.
12. Run ventilation system to make sure all outlets function correctly.

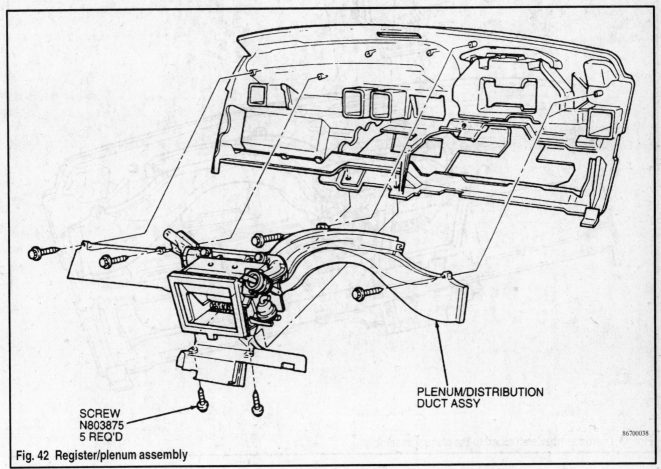

PLENUM/DISTRIBUTION DUCT ASSY

SCREW
N803875
5 REQ'D

86700038

**Fig. 42 Register/plenum assembly**

### Defroster Nozzle

▶ **See Figure 43**

The defroster nozzle is incorporated into the register duct.
1. Remove the center console.
2. Remove register/plenum assembly.
3. With the assembly out of the vehicle, remove the retaining screws securing the defroster nozzle to the register duct.

**To install:**

4. Check and make sure the gasket between the register duct and the defroster nozzle is in good shape. If not, replace gasket.
5. Position defroster nozzle to register duct and secure with retaining screws.
6. Position register/plenum assembly and secure with retaining screws.
7. Run defroster and check for leaks or weak air–flow.

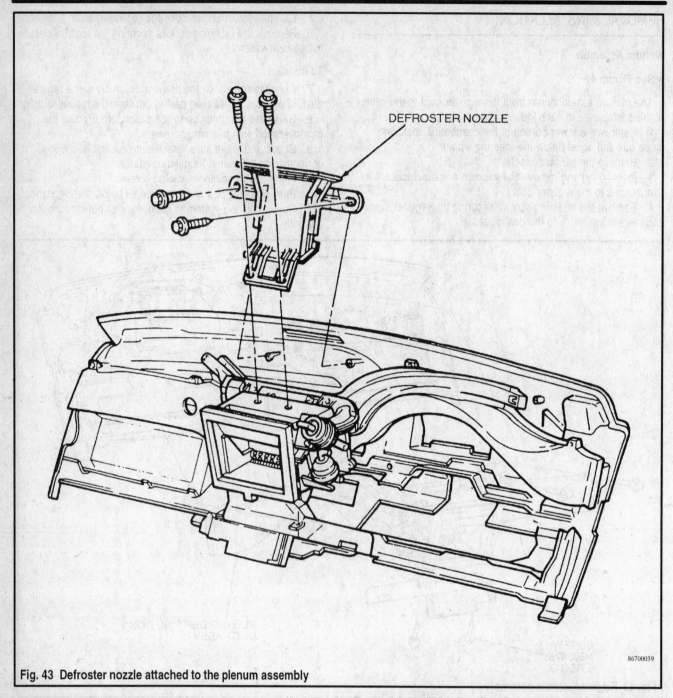

DEFROSTER NOZZLE

Fig. 43 Defroster nozzle attached to the plenum assembly

86700039

## Louvered Vents

### ▶ See Figures 44 and 45

The louvered vents control the amount of air flow as well as the direction of air flow coming from the ventilation system. These vents should be checked once a year to make sure nothing is blocking the air flow.

1. Insert a thin bladed pry–tool between the vent and dashboard.

2. Carefully work the vent assembly out of the dashboard.

3. To remove the louvered portion of the vent, proceed as follows:

   a. Insert a thin bladed pry–tool between the louvered portion and the vent housing.

   b. Carefully work the louvered portion out of the assembly. With the louver removed, the thumb wheel and outlet door are visible.

   c. Check each piece and replace broken components.

### To install:

4. If the vent has been taken apart, reassemble by positioning the outlet door and thumb wheel in the housing, and carefully applying pressure to the louver and press in the housing until it "clicks" into place.

5. Carefully work the vent assembly into the dash hole, making sure it slides into the plenum tube.

6. With all the vents installed, turn on the ventilation system and make sure that each vent works correctly.

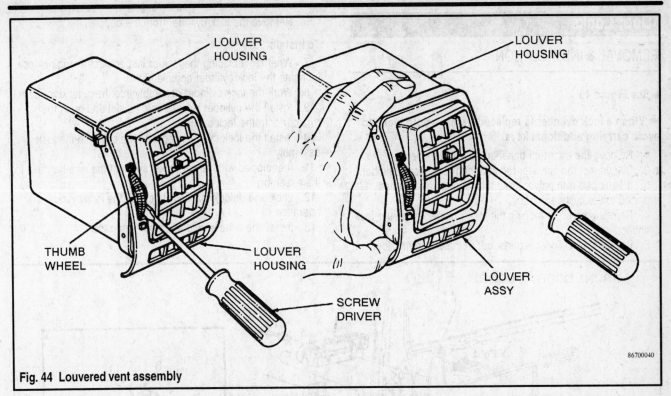

**Fig. 44 Louvered vent assembly**

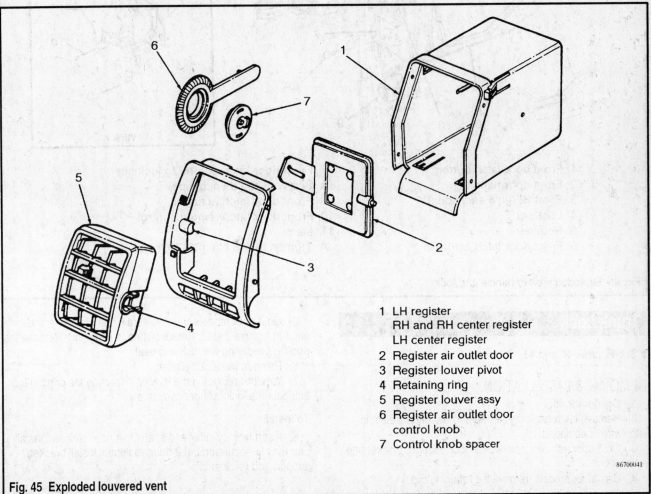

1 LH register
  RH and RH center register
  LH center register
2 Register air outlet door
3 Register louver pivot
4 Retaining ring
5 Register louver assy
6 Register air outlet door
  control knob
7 Control knob spacer

**Fig. 45 Exploded louvered vent**

## Door Locks

### REMOVAL & INSTALLATION

▶ See Figure 46

➡ **When a lock cylinder is replaced, replace both locks to avoid carrying additional keys.**

1. Remove the door trim panel and the watershield.
2. Disconnect the actuator rod attached to the lock cylinder.
3. If equipped with power locks, disconnect the harness attached to the cylinder.
4. Remove the clip attaching the lock cylinder rod to the lock cylinder.
5. Pry the lock cylinder retainer out of the slot in the door.

6. Remove the lock cylinder from the door.

**To install:**

7. Whether replacing the lock or inspecting the original lock, lubricate the lock cylinder completely.
8. Work the lock cylinder assembly into the outer door panel.
9. Install the cylinder retainer into its slot and push the retainer onto the lock cylinder.
10. Install the lock cylinder rod with the clip onto the lock assembly.
11. If equipped with power locks, connect the wire harness to the assembly.
12. Lock and unlock the door to check the lock cylinder operation.
13. Install the watershield and door trim panel.

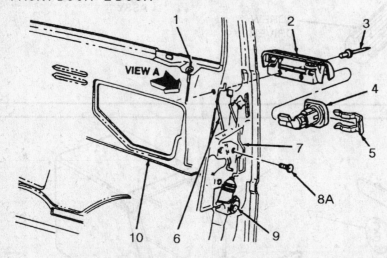
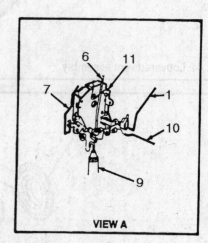

FRONT DOOR - 2 DOOR

VIEW A

VIEW A

1  Front door latch button
2  Front door handle
3  Rivet (2 req'd each side)
4  Lock set
5  Retainer
6  Front door latch actuator
7  Front door latch control to lock set
8A  Screw (3 req'd each side)
9  Front door latch actuator
10  Front door latch remote control
11  Latch
A  Tighten to 4-8 Nm (36-70 lb.in.)

86700042

**Fig. 46 Exploded view of handle and lock**

## Trunk Lock

▶ See Figures 47 and 48

### REMOVAL & INSTALLATION

1. Open trunk lid.
2. Remove latch retaining screws and disconnect electric latch wire, if equipped.
3. On 2 door vehicles, remove the lock support, bracket and retainer.
4. On 4 door models, remove the retaining clip.

5. On 4 door models, remove screw retaining plate and support to inner panel. Remove plate and support. Remove the pop rivet securing the lock and seal.
6. Remove the lock cylinder.
7. Whether replacing the lock or inspecting the original lock, lubricate the lock cylinder completely.

**To install:**

8. Insert lock cylinder and seal. On 4 door vehicles, install pop rivet to secure unit. If 2 door equipped, install bracket, support and retainer clip.

9. On 4 door models, insert and secure retaining plate and support. Install retaining screw.

10. Connect electric latch wire for trunk release, if equipped.

11. Before closing trunk, use key and make sure cylinder and lock mechanism work correctly.

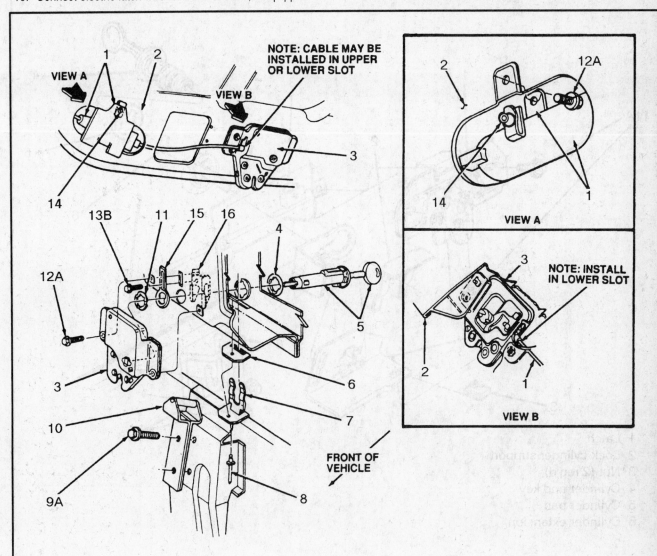

1   Luggage compartment latch solenoid assy.
2   Luggage compartment deck lid
3   Luggage compartment deck lid latch assy.
4   Luggage compartment lock cylinder pad
5   Lock and key set
6   Luggage compartment lock cylinder retaining seal
7   Luggage compartment lock cylinder retainer
8   Rivet
9A  Screw and washer assy. (2 req'd)
10  Luggage compartment latch striker assy.
11  Luggage compartment lock cylinder retaining clip
12A Screw and washer assy. (2 req'd)
13B Screw and washer assy. (1 req'd)
14  Nut (1 req'd)
15  Luggage compartment lock cylinder plate
16  Luggage compartment lock support
A   Tighten to 9-14 Nm (7-10 lb.ft.)
B   Tighten to 7-11 Nm (62-97 lb.in.)

86700044

Fig. 47 Trunk lock assembly—2-door model

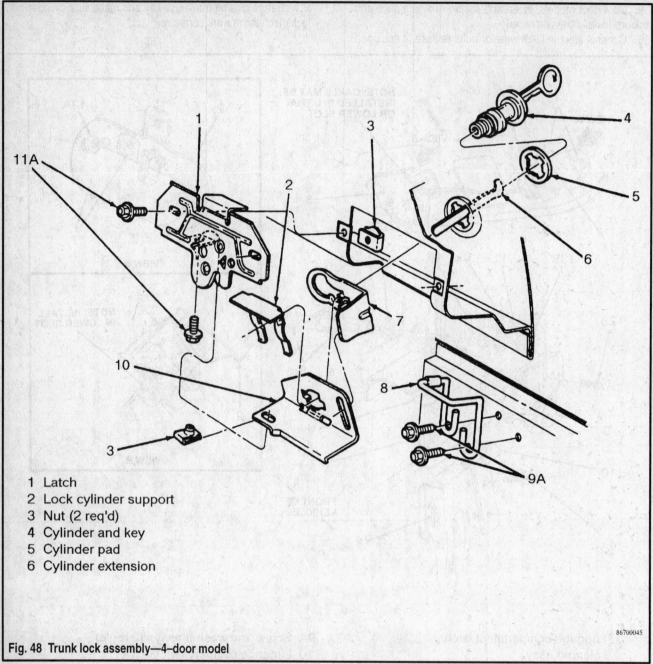

1 Latch
2 Lock cylinder support
3 Nut (2 req'd)
4 Cylinder and key
5 Cylinder pad
6 Cylinder extension

86700045

**Fig. 48 Trunk lock assembly—4–door model**

## Power Door Lock Actuator Motor

### REMOVAL & INSTALLATION

▶ **See Figures 49, 50 and 51**

1. Disconnect the negative battery cable.
2. Remove the door trim panel and the watershield.
3. Using a 1/4 in. (6mm) diameter drill bit, drill out the pop rivet attaching the actuator motor to the door body. Disconnect the wiring harness at the actuator.
4. Disconnect the actuator motor link from the door latch and remove the motor.

**To install:**

5. Check and make sure the protective rubber boot is tightly installed on the actuator motor.
6. Connect the actuator motor link to the door latch.
7. Connect the wiring harness at the actuator.
8. Install the door lock actuator motor to the door with a pop rivet, using a suitable rivet gun.

➡ **Make sure that the actuator boot is not twisted during installation. The pop rivet must be installed with the bracket base tight to the inner panel.**

9. Connect the negative battery cable. Check and make sure the actuator motors function properly.
10. Install the door trim panel and water shield.

**FRONT DOOR -2 DOOR**

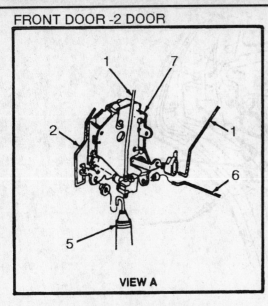

**VIEW A**

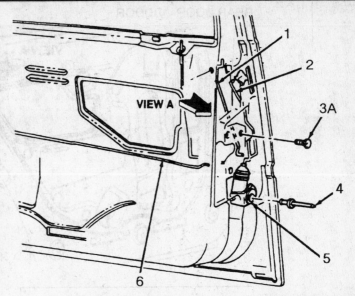

**VIEW A**

1  Front door latch actuator
2  Front door latch control to lock set
3A  Screw (3 req'd)
4  Rivet

5  Front door latch actuator
6  Front door latch remote control link
7  Latch
A  Tighten to 4-8 Nm (36-70 lb.in.)

86700046

**Fig. 49 Actuator assembly—2-door model**

---

**4-Door**

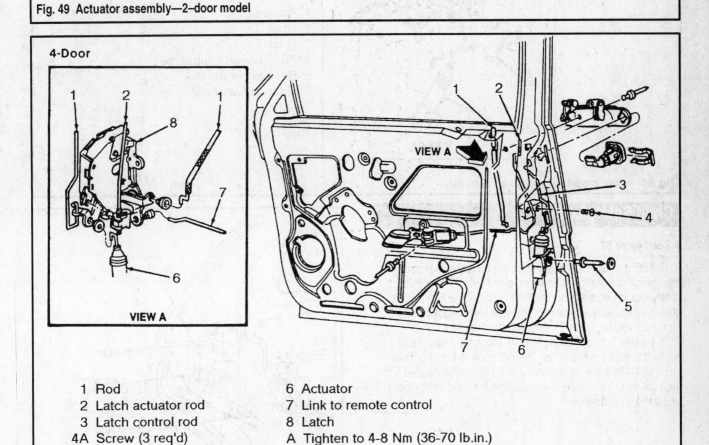

**VIEW A**

**VIEW A**

1  Rod
2  Latch actuator rod
3  Latch control rod
4A  Screw (3 req'd)
5  Rivet

6  Actuator
7  Link to remote control
8  Latch
A  Tighten to 4-8 Nm (36-70 lb.in.)

86700047

**Fig. 50 4-door model—front actuator assembly**

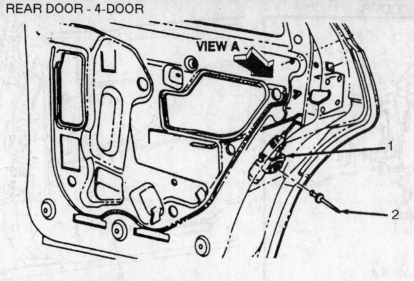

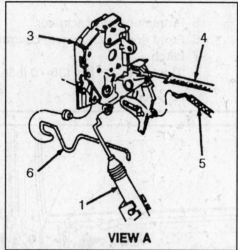

1 Actuator
2 Rivet
3 Latch
4 Push button control rod
5 Remote control link
6 Latch actuator rod

Fig. 51 4-door model—rear actuator assembly

## Child Safety Lock

▶ **See Figure 52**

The child safety lock, when used, prevents the rear doors from being opened from the inside of the vehicle. The child safety lock is designed into the rear latch bellcrank assembly. A gold colored decal is located on the rear door of a 4 door equipped vehicle, to alert the owner of this option.

To engage the child safety feature, move the lever, located below the latch assembly, up. This will prevent the door from being open from the inside, although it still can be opened from the outside of the vehicle. To disengage the child safety lock, move the lever down.

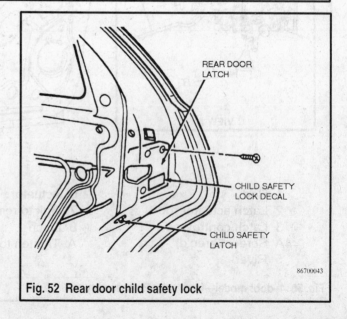

Fig. 52 Rear door child safety lock

## Door Glass

♦ **See Figures 53, 54 and 55**

### REMOVAL & INSTALLATION

1. Remove the door interior panel and watershield.
2. Remove the 2 rivets attaching the glass to the rail and bracket assembly.

➡ **Prior to the removing center pins from the rivet, it is recommended that a suitable block support be inserted between the door outer panel and the glass bracket to stabilize the glass during the rivet removal. Remove the center pin from each rivet with a drift punch. Then, using a 1/4 in.**

(6mm) diameter drill carefully drill out the remainder of each rivet as damage to the plastic glass retainer and spacer could result.

3. Remove the glass.
4. Remove the drillings and pins from the bottom of the door.

**To install:**

5. Insert the glass into the door.
6. Position the door glass to the door glass bracket and align the glass and glass bracket retaining holes
7. Install the retaining rivets.
8. Raise the glass to the full UP position.
9. Install the rear glass run retainer and rear glass rail.
10. Check the operation of the window.
11. Install the trim panel and watershield.

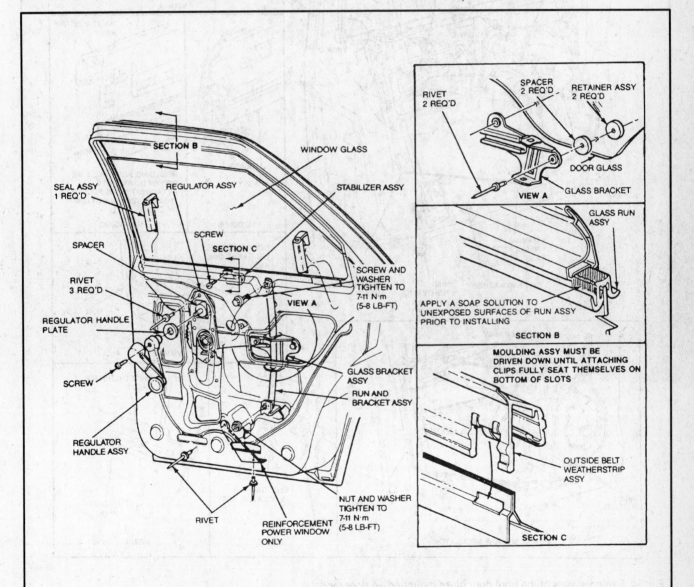

**Fig. 53 Exploded view of the rear door glass mounting—4 door model**

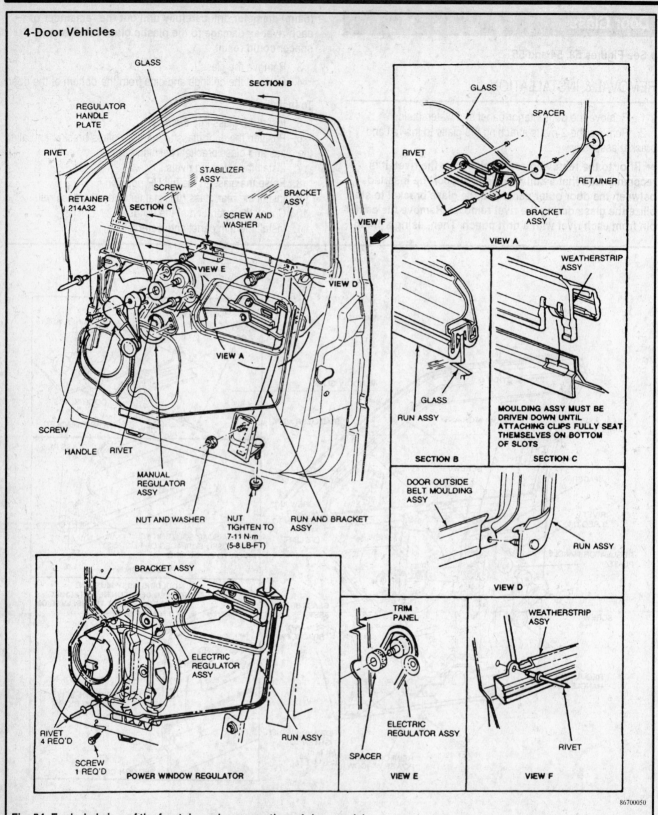

**4-Door Vehicles**

GLASS

REGULATOR HANDLE PLATE

RIVET

RETAINER 214A32

STABILIZER ASSY

SCREW

SECTION C

SECTION B

SCREW AND WASHER

BRACKET ASSY

VIEW F

VIEW E

VIEW A

VIEW D

SCREW

HANDLE

RIVET

MANUAL REGULATOR ASSY

NUT AND WASHER

NUT TIGHTEN TO 7-11 N·m (5-8 LB-FT)

RUN AND BRACKET ASSY

GLASS

SPACER

RIVET

RETAINER

BRACKET ASSY

VIEW A

WEATHERSTRIP ASSY

GLASS

RUN ASSY

MOULDING ASSY MUST BE DRIVEN DOWN UNTIL ATTACHING CLIPS FULLY SEAT THEMSELVES ON BOTTOM OF SLOTS

SECTION B

SECTION C

DOOR OUTSIDE BELT MOULDING ASSY

RUN ASSY

VIEW D

BRACKET ASSY

ELECTRIC REGULATOR ASSY

RIVET 4 REQ'D

SCREW 1 REQ'D

RUN ASSY

POWER WINDOW REGULATOR

TRIM PANEL

ELECTRIC REGULATOR ASSY

SPACER

VIEW E

WEATHERSTRIP ASSY

RIVET

VIEW F

86700050

**Fig. 54 Exploded view of the front door glass mounting—4 door model**

**2-Door Vehicles**

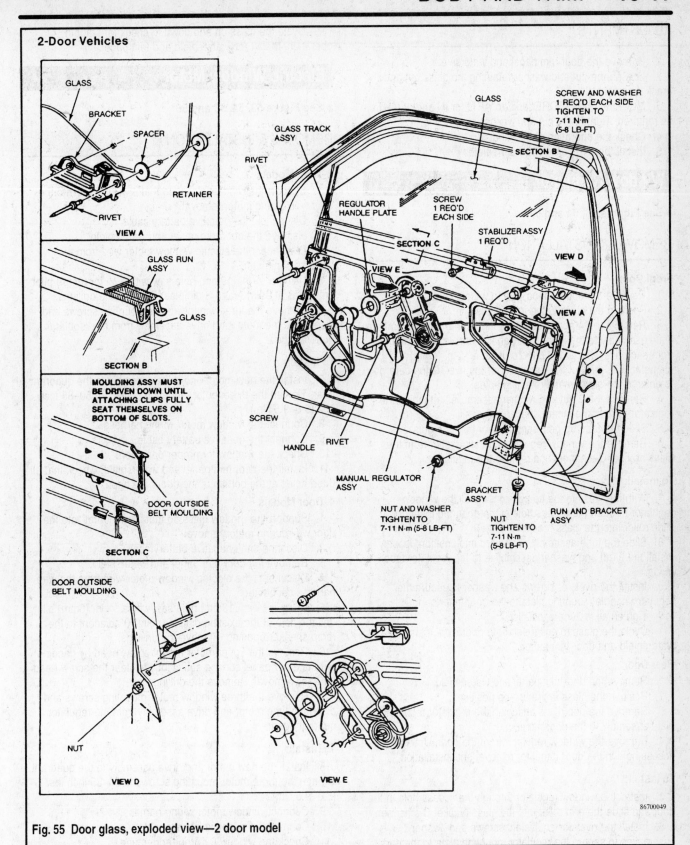

Fig. 55 Door glass, exploded view—2 door model

## ADJUSTMENTS

1. Remove the door trim panel and watershield.
2. Loosen the nut and washer retaining the glass rail and bracket assembly.
3. Move the glass "FORE" and/or "AFT" (or IN and/or OUT), as required. Tighten the nut and washer assemblies.
4. Check the operation of the window.
5. Install the trim panel and watershield.

## Window Regulator

▶ See Figures 53, 54 and 55

### REMOVAL & INSTALLATION

#### Front Door

1. Remove the door trim panel and watershield.
2. Position the glass in the full–up position.
3. Remove the 4 pop rivets attaching the regulator mounting plate assembly to the inner door panel. Remove the center pin from each rivet with a drift punch. Using a ¼ in. (6mm) diameter drill, drill out the remainder of the rivet, using care not to enlarge the sheet metal retaining holes.
4. Remove the 2 nut and washer assemblies attaching the regulator tube to the inner panel and door sill.
5. Slide the tube up between the door belt and glass.
6. Remove the window regulator arm slide/roller from the glass bracket C–channel and remove the regulator.

#### To install:

7. With the glass in the up position, install the window regulator through the access hole in the door and insert the slide roller into the glass bracket channel.
8. Slide the tube assembly downward into position, loosely install the 2 nut and washer assemblies to the regulator tube guide.
9. Install the rivets or screws and washer to secure the regulator handle mounting plate to the door inner panel.
10. Tighten all fasteners installed.
11. Cycle the glass to ensure smooth operation. Install the watershield and door trim panel.

#### Rear Door

1. Remove the door trim panel and watershield.
2. Position the glass in the full–up position.
3. Remove the pop rivets attaching the regulator mounting plate assembly to the door panel.
4. Remove the window regulator from the door. Use the access hole in the door panel for removal and installation.

#### To install:

5. Install the window regulator through the access hole in the door and slide the arm roller into the glass bracket C–channel.
6. Install the rivets or equivalent screws and washer assemblies to secure the regulator mounting plate to the door panel.

7. Cycle the glass up and down to check for smooth operation. Install the watershield and trim panel.

## Electric Window Motor

▶ See Figure 53, 54, 55 and 56

### REMOVAL & INSTALLATION

#### 2–Door Models

1. Support the window glass, so that it will not fall into the door well during motor removal.
2. Disconnect the negative battery cable.
3. Remove the door trim panel and watershield.
4. Disconnect the electric window motor wire from the harness connector.
5. Using a ¾ in. (19mm) hole saw with a ¼ in. (6mm) pilot, drill holes at point A and B dimples. Remove the drillings.
6. Remove the three window motor mounting screws and disengage the motor and drive assembly from the regulator quadrant gear.

#### To install:

7. Install the new motor and drive assembly to the quadrant gear. Tighten the three motor mounting screws to 50–85 inch lbs. (5.6–9.6 Nm).
8. Connect the window motor wiring harness.
9. Connect the negative battery cable.
10. Check the window for proper operation.
11. Install the door trim panel and watershield. Check that all drain holes at the bottom of the doors are open.

#### 4–Door Models

1. Support the window glass so that it will not fall into the door well during motor removal.
2. Disconnect the negative battery cable.
3. Remove the door trim panel and watershield.
4. Disconnect the electric window motor wire from the wire harness connector.
5. Using a ¾ in. (19mm) hole saw with a ¼ in. (6mm) pilot, drill the hole at the existing dimple (point A) adjacent to the radio speaker opening. Remove the drillings.
6. Remove the upper motor mount screw head by grinding out the inner panel surface sufficiently to clear the screw head for easy removal. Remove the drillings.
7. Remove the three window motor mounting screws and disengage the motor and drive assembly from the regulator quadrant gear.

#### To install:

8. Install the new motor and drive assembly to the quadrant. Tighten the three motor mounting screws to 50–85 inch lbs. (5.6–9.6 Nm).
9. Connect window motor wiring harness.
10. Connect the negative battery cable.
11. Check the window for proper operation.
12. Install the door trim panel and watershield. Check that all drain holes at the bottom of the doors are open.

**4–Door Rear Motor**

1. Support the glass so that it will not fall into the door well during motor removal.
2. Disconnect the negative battery cable.
3. Remove the door trim panel and watershield.
4. Disconnect the electric window motor wire from the wire harness connector.
5. Using a ¾ in. (19mm) hole saw with a ¼ in. (6mm) pilot, drill three holes in the door inner panel at the three existing dimples to gain access to the three motor and drive attaching screws. Remove the drillings.

6. Remove the three window motor mounting screws and disengage the motor and drive assembly from the regulator quadrant gear.

**To install:**

7. Install the new motor and drive assembly to the quadrant gear. Tighten the three motor mounting screws to 50–85 inch lbs. (5.6–9.6 Nm).
8. Connect window motor wiring harness.
9. Connect the negative battery cable.
10. Check the window for proper operation.
11. Install the door trim panel and watershield. Check that all drain holes at the bottom of the doors are open.

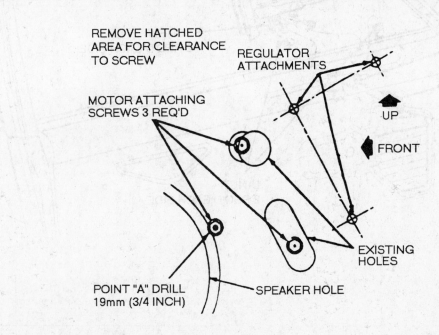

REMOVE HATCHED AREA FOR CLEARANCE TO SCREW

REGULATOR ATTACHMENTS

MOTOR ATTACHING SCREWS 3 REQ'D

UP

FRONT

EXISTING HOLES

POINT "A" DRILL 19mm (3/4 INCH)

SPEAKER HOLE

86700052

**Fig. 56  Drill holes at existing dimples—front door on 4–door model**

## Windshield and Rear Window Glass

### REMOVAL & INSTALLATION

Ford cars use a Butyl/Urethane type sealed windshield and rear window which requires the use of special tools for removal and installation. It is advised that if the windshield needs replacement, the vehicle be taken to a professional glass shop.

## Door Vent

### REMOVAL & INSTALLATION

◆ **See Figure 57**

1. Remove the door trim panel and watershield.
2. Move the glass to the full down position, and remove the window regulator handle.

3. Remove the retaining screws securing the vent frame to the door frame.
4. Remove the retaining screws attaching the vent window assembly to the inner door.
5. Remove the vent window assembly from the door by slowly working the assembly out of the door frame.

**To install:**

6. Position the vent window into the door frame. If the unit will not seat itself completely, Use a plastic " dead blow" hammer and lightly tap on the vent window frame to help move the unit into place.

➡ **The vent weather–stripping must be lubricated with a soapy solution prior to vent window installation.**

7. Loosely install all attaching screws. Roll window completely up, and tighten all retaining hardware.
8. Install the trim panel.
9. Check the operation of the window.

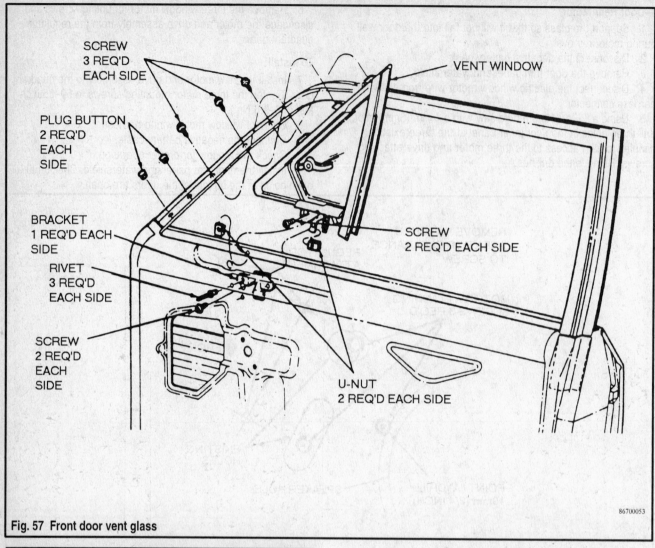

SCREW
3 REQ'D
EACH SIDE

PLUG BUTTON
2 REQ'D
EACH
SIDE

BRACKET
1 REQ'D EACH
SIDE

RIVET
3 REQ'D
EACH SIDE

SCREW
2 REQ'D
EACH
SIDE

VENT WINDOW

SCREW
2 REQ'D EACH SIDE

U-NUT
2 REQ'D EACH SIDE

86700053

**Fig. 57 Front door vent glass**

## Rear Quarter Glass

### REMOVAL & INSTALLATION

Ford cars use a Butyl/Urethane type sealed rear quarter window which requires the use of special tools for removal and installation. It is advised that if the glass needs replacement, the vehicle be taken to a professional glass shop.

## Inside Mirror

### REMOVAL & INSTALLATION

◆ **See Figure 58**

1. Loosen the mirror assembly–to–mounting bracket set screw.
2. Remove the mirror assembly by sliding upward and away from the mounting bracket.
3. Install it by attaching the mirror assembly to the mounting bracket and tighten the set screw to 10–20 inch lbs. (1.1–2.2 Nm).

➡ If the mirror bracket pad has to be removed from the windshield (or if it has fallen off), it will be necessary to use a suitable heat gun to heat the vinyl pad until vinyl softens. Peel the vinyl off the windshield and discard. Install the new one as follows.

4. Make sure glass, bracket and adhesive kit (Rearview mirror adhesive D9AZ–19554–CA or equivalent) are at least at room temperature 65–75°F (18–24°C).
5. Locate and mark the mirror mounting bracket location on the outside surface of the windshield.
6. Thoroughly clean the bonding surfaces of the glass and bracket to remove old adhesive, if reusing the old mirror bracket pad. Use a mild abrasive cleaner on the glass and fine sandpaper on the bracket to lightly roughen the surface. Wipe clean with an alcohol moistened cloth.
7. Crush the accelerator vial (part of the rearview mirror adhesive kit D9AZ–19554–CA) and apply the accelerator to the bonding surface of the bracket and windshield. Let it dry for 3 minutes.
8. Apply 2 drops of adhesive (part of the rearview mirror adhesive kit D9AZ–19554–CA) to the mounting surface of the bracket and windshield. Using a clean toothpick or a wooden

match, quickly spread the adhesive evenly over the mounting surface of the bracket.

9. Quickly position the mounting bracket on the windshield. The $^3/_8$ in. (9.5mm) circular depression in the bracket must be toward the inside of the passengers compartment. Press the bracket firmly against the windshield for one minute.

10. Allow the bond to set for five minutes. Remove any excess bonding material from the windshield with an alcohol dampened cloth.

11. Install the mirror and tighten bracket screw.

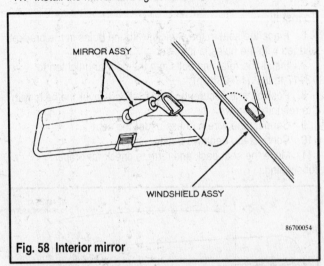

**Fig. 58 Interior mirror**

## Seats

## REMOVAL & INSTALLATION

**Manual Seats**

*FRONT*

▶ **See Figures 59, 60, 61 and 62**

1. Remove the seat track plastic shield retaining screws inside the vehicle.

2. Remove the retaining bolts securing the seat to the floor of the vehicle.

3. Carefully remove the seat from the car.

**To install:**

4. Place the seat in the vehicle, with the holes in the bracket aligned with the holes in the floor.

5. Install the retaining bolts into the floor and tighten to 13–17 ft. lbs. (17–23 Nm).

6. Position and secure the plastic shields over the bolts with the retaining screws.

7. Move the seat back and forth to check for proper functioning.

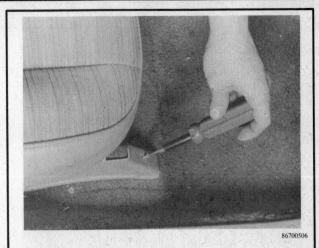

**Fig. 59 Remove the front shields.**

**Fig. 60 Remove the rear shields.**

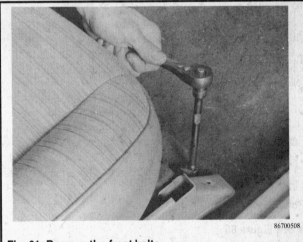

**Fig. 61 Remove the front bolts.**

**Fig. 62 Remove the rear bolts, and extract the seat from the vehicle**

### *REAR*

#### ♦ See Figures 63 and 64

1. Apply knee pressure to the lower portion of the rear seat cushion; then push rearward to disengage the seat cushion from the retainer brackets.

2. Push the safety belts through the bezels in the seat cushion.

➡ **The arm rest is not required to remove the rear seat cushion or back.**

3. Remove the rear seat cushion by first removing the safety belt assembly bolts.

4. Grasp the seat back assembly at the bottom and lift up to disengage the hanger wire from the retainer brackets.

#### To install:

5. Position the seat back in the vehicle so that hangers are engaged with the retaining brackets.

6. Install safety belt assemblies and tighten the bolts to 22–32 ft. lbs. (30–43 Nm). Install the rear seat cushion as follows:

   a. Position the seat cushion assembly into the vehicle.
   b. Insert the safety belts through the cushions.
   c. Apply knee pressure to the lower portion of the seat cushion assembly and push rearward and down to lock the seat cushion into position.
   d. Pull the rear seat cushion forward to ensure it is secured into the floor retainer.

#### Power Seats

#### ♦ See Figure 65

The driver's power seat uses a rack and pinion drive system. The 6–way power seat provides horizontal, vertical and tilt adjustments. It consists of a reversible 3 armature motor

(tri–motor), a switch and housing assembly, vertical gear drives and horizontal rack and pinion drives.

1. Disconnect the negative battery cable.

2. From under the seat, unplug the wire harness to the seat controls.

3. Remove the seat track plastic shield retaining screws inside the vehicle.

4. Remove the retaining bolts securing the seat to the floor of the vehicle.

5. Carefully remove the seat from the car.

#### To install:

6. Place the seat in the vehicle, with the holes in the bracket aligned with the holes in the floor.

7. Install the retaining bolts into the floor and tighten to 13–17 ft. lbs. (17–23 Nm).

8. Position and secure the plastic shields over the bolts with the retaining screws.

9. Connect the wire harness under the seat.

10. Connect the negative battery cable.

11. Move the seat back and forth to check for proper functioning.

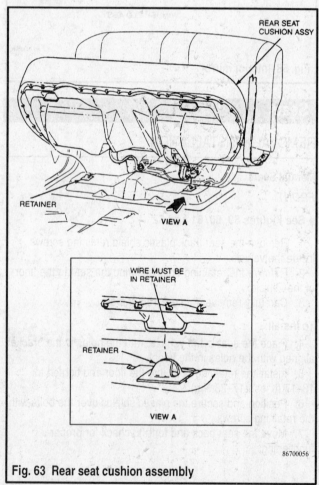

**Fig. 63 Rear seat cushion assembly**

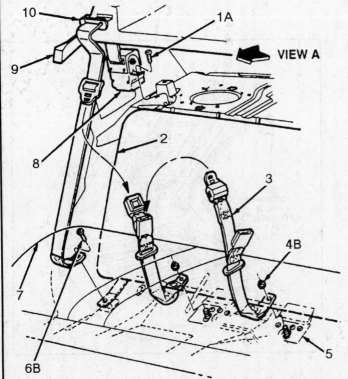
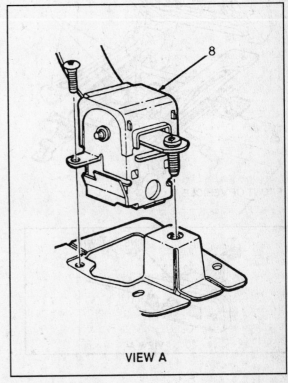

1A  Bolt
 2  Rear seat back assy.
 3  Safety belt and buckle assy.
4B  Nut
 5  Bracket assy.
6B  Bolt
 7  Rear seat cushion assy.

 8  Rear seat safety belt and
    retractor assy.
 9  Package tray trim panel
10  Bezel
 A  Tighten to 22-34 Nm (17-25 lb.ft.)
 B  Tighten to 30-43 Nm (23-31 lb.ft.)

**Fig. 64 Rear seat belt assembly**

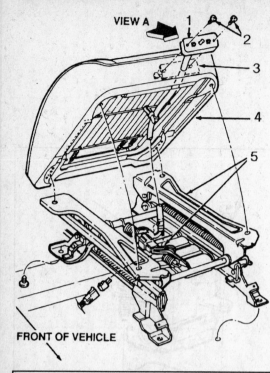

VIEW A

1 Seat control switch
2 Screw (2 req'd)
3 Bracket
4 Seat assy.
5 Seat track assy.

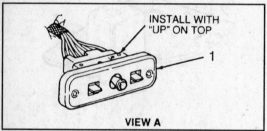

INSTALL WITH "UP" ON TOP

1

VIEW A

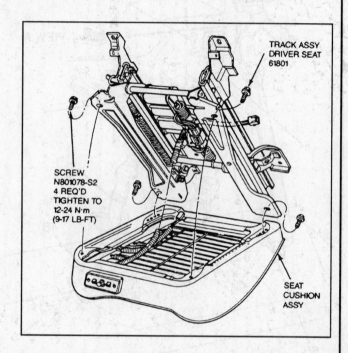

TRACK ASSY DRIVER SEAT 61801

SCREW N801078-S2 4 REQ'D TIGHTEN TO 12-24 N·m (9-17 LB-FT)

SEAT CUSHION ASSY

86700058

Fig. 65 Power seat assembly

## Power Seat Motor & Cables

### REMOVAL & INSTALLATION

▶ See Figure 65

1. Disconnect the negative battery cable.
2. Remove the seat assembly from the vehicle.
3. Remove the motor retaining bolts from the seat mounting.
4. Disconnect the housings and the cables from the motor.
5. Remove the motor assembly from the seat.

**To install:**

6. Position and secure the motor to the seat.
7. Connect the cable to the motor.

8. Install the seat in the vehicle, and test for proper functioning.

## Seat Belt Systems

### SAFETY PRECAUTIONS

- Seat belt assemblies must be installed in matched sets and must not be interchanged between vehicles. The manufacturer's identification on the label of the retractor webbing must match the identification on the buckle base.
- Sealer should be placed around all seat belt anchor bolt holes in floor pan.
- Seat belt assemblies must be replaced after they have been subjected to loading by occupants in a collision.

## Seat & Shoulder Belts

The Seat and Shoulder Belt System used on all 1984–94 vehicles is referred to as a continuous loop, single retractor restraint system.

### REMOVAL & INSTALLATION

#### Front

♦ See Figure 66

1. Remove the upper and lower trim panels from the B–pillar to expose the belt assembly.
2. To remove the upper most portion of the belt from the pillar, pry off the ring cover and unfasten the bolt.
3. Remove the retractor mounting bolt and remove the outboard belt assembly.
4. Disconnect the buzzer assembly and remove the inboard belt assembly.

#### To install:

5. Position the seat belt components in their proper location.

6. Tighten all attaching bolts to 22–32 ft. lbs. (30–45 Nm).
7. Cycle the system several times to assure proper operation of the retractor.
8. Install the upper and lower trim panels.

➡ Make sure the webbing is not twisted.

#### Rear

♦ See Figure 64

1. Remove the rear seat cushion.
2. Remove the buckle end anchor bolts, and remove the belt assembly.
3. Remove the rear seat back.
4. Remove the mounting bolts from both rear seat retractors. Remove the retractors.

#### To install:

5. Position the seat belt components in their proper location.
6. Tighten all attaching bolts to 22–32 ft. lbs. (30–45 Nm).
7. Cycle the system several times to assure proper operation of the retractor.

➡ Make sure the webbing is not twisted.

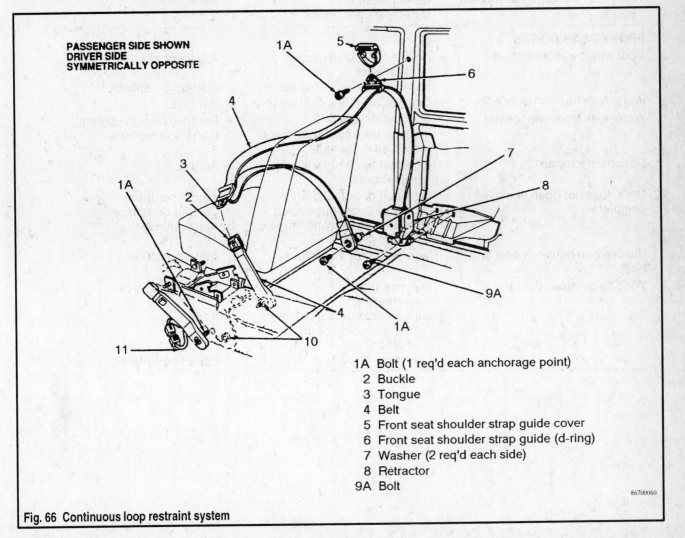

PASSENGER SIDE SHOWN
DRIVER SIDE
SYMMETRICALLY OPPOSITE

1A Bolt (1 req'd each anchorage point)
2 Buckle
3 Tongue
4 Belt
5 Front seat shoulder strap guide cover
6 Front seat shoulder strap guide (d-ring)
7 Washer (2 req'd each side)
8 Retractor
9A Bolt

86700060

Fig. 66 Continuous loop restraint system

## Hood, Trunk Lid, Hatch Lid, Glass and Doors

| Problem | Possible Cause | Correction |
|---|---|---|
| **HOOD/TRUNK/HATCH LID** | | |
| Improper closure. | • Striker and latch not properly aligned. | • Adjust the alignment. |
| Difficulty locking and unlocking. | • Striker and latch not properly aligned. | • Adjust the alignment. |
| Uneven clearance with body panels. | • Incorrectly installed hood or trunk lid. | • Adjust the alignment. |
| **WINDOW/WINDSHIELD GLASS** | | |
| Water leak through windshield | • Defective seal.<br>• Defective body flange. | • Fill sealant<br>• Correct. |
| Water leak through door window glass. | • Incorrect window glass installation.<br>• Gap at upper window frame. | • Adjust position.<br>• Adjust position. |
| Water leak through quarter window. | • Defective seal.<br>• Defective body flange. | • Replace seal.<br>• Correct. |
| Water leak through rear window. | • Defective seal.<br>• Defective body flange. | • Replace seal.<br>• Correct. |
| **FRONT/REAR DOORS** | | |
| Door window malfunction. | • Incorrect window glass installation.<br>• Damaged or faulty regulator. | • Adjust position.<br>• Correct or replace. |
| Water leak through door edge. | • Cracked or faulty weatherstrip. | • Replace. |
| Water leak from door center. | • Drain hole clogged.<br>• Inadequate waterproof skeet contact or damage. | • Remove foreign objects.<br>• Correct or replace. |
| Door hard to open. | • Incorrect latch or striker adjustment. | • Adjust. |
| Door does not open or close completely. | • Incorrect door installation.<br>• Defective door check strap.<br>• Door check strap and hinge require grease. | • Adjust position.<br>• Correct or replace.<br>• Apply grease. |
| Uneven gap between door and body. | • Incorrect door installation. | • Adjust position. |
| Wind noise around door. | • Improperly installed weatherstrip.<br>• Improper clearance between door glass and door weatherstrip.<br>• Deformed door. | • Repair or replace.<br>• Adjust.<br>• Repair or replace. |

## How to Remove Stains from Fabric Interior

For best results, spots and stains should be removed as soon as possible. Never use gasoline, lacquer thinner, acetone, nail polish remover or bleach. Use a 3' x 3" piece of cheesecloth. Squeeze most of the liquid from the fabric and wipe the stained fabric from the outside of the stain toward the center with a lifting motion. Turn the cheesecloth as soon as one side becomes soiled. When using water to remove a stain, be sure to wash the entire section after the spot has been removed to avoid water stains. Encrusted spots can be broken up with a dull knife and vacuumed before removing the stain.

| Type of Stain | How to Remove It |
|---|---|
| Surface spots | Brush the spots out with a small hand brush or use a commercial preparation such as K2R to lift the stain. |
| Mildew | Clean around the mildew with warm suds. Rinse in cold water and soak the mildew area in a solution of 1 part table salt and 2 parts water. Wash with upholstery cleaner. |
| Water stains | Water stains in fabric materials can be removed with a solution made from 1 cup of table salt dissolved in 1 quart of water. Vigorously scrub the solution into the stain and rinse with clear water. Water stains in nylon or other synthetic fabrics should be removed with a commercial type spot remover. |
| Chewing gum, tar, crayons, shoe polish (greasy stains) | Do not use a cleaner that will soften gum or tar. Harden the deposit with an ice cube and scrape away as much as possible with a dull knife. Moisten the remainder with cleaning fluid and scrub clean. |
| Ice cream, candy | Most candy has a sugar base and can be removed with a cloth wrung out in warm water. Oily candy, after cleaning with warm water, should be cleaned with upholstery cleaner. Rinse with warm water and clean the remainder with cleaning fluid. |
| Wine, alcohol, egg, milk, soft drink (non-greasy stains) | Do not use soap. Scrub the stain with a cloth wrung out in warm water. Remove the remainder with cleaning fluid. |
| Grease, oil, lipstick, butter and related stains | Use a spot remover to avoid leaving a ring. Work from the outisde of the stain to the center and dry with a clean cloth when the spot is gone. |
| Headliners (cloth) | Mix a solution of warm water and foam upholstery cleaner to give thick suds. Use only foam—liquid may streak or spot. Clean the entire headliner in one operation using a circular motion with a natural sponge. |
| Headliner (vinyl) | Use a vinyl cleaner with a sponge and wipe clean with a dry cloth. |
| Seats and door panels | Mix 1 pint upholstery cleaner in 1 gallon of water. Do not soak the fabric around the buttons. |
| Leather or vinyl fabric | Use a multi-purpose cleaner full strength and a stiff brush. Let stand 2 minutes and scrub thoroughly. Wipe with a clean, soft rag. |
| Nylon or synthetic fabrics | For normal stains, use the same procedures you would for washing cloth upholstery. If the fabric is extremely dirty, use a multi-purpose cleaner full strength with a stiff scrub brush. Scrub thoroughly in all directions and wipe with a cotton towel or soft rag. |

86700889

## GLOSSARY

**AIR/FUEL RATIO:** The ratio of air-to-gasoline by weight in the fuel mixture drawn into the engine.

**AIR INJECTION:** One method of reducing harmful exhaust emissions by injecting air into each of the exhaust ports of an engine. The fresh air entering the hot exhaust manifold causes any remaining fuel to be burned before it can exit the tailpipe.

**ALTERNATOR:** A device used for converting mechanical energy into electrical energy.

**AMMETER:** An instrument, calibrated in amperes, used to measure the flow of an electrical current in a circuit. Ammeters are always connected in series with the circuit being tested.

**AMPERE:** The rate of flow of electrical current present when one volt of electrical pressure is applied against one ohm of electrical resistance.

**ANALOG COMPUTER:** Any microprocessor that uses similar (analogous) electrical signals to make its calculations.

**ARMATURE:** A laminated, soft iron core wrapped by a wire that converts electrical energy to mechanical energy as in a motor or relay. When rotated in a magnetic field, it changes mechanical energy into electrical energy as in a generator.

**ATMOSPHERIC PRESSURE:** The pressure on the Earth's surface caused by the weight of the air in the atmosphere. At sea level, this pressure is 14.7 psi at 32°F (101 kPa at 0°C).

**ATOMIZATION:** The breaking down of a liquid into a fine mist that can be suspended in air.

**AXIAL PLAY:** Movement parallel to a shaft or bearing bore.

**BACKFIRE:** The sudden combustion of gases in the intake or exhaust system that results in a loud explosion.

**BACKLASH:** The clearance or play between two parts, such as meshed gears.

**BACKPRESSURE:** Restrictions in the exhaust system that slow the exit of exhaust gases from the combustion chamber.

**BAKELITE:** A heat resistant, plastic insulator material commonly used in printed circuit boards and transistorized components.

**BALL BEARING:** A bearing made up of hardened inner and outer races between which hardened steel balls roll.

**BALLAST RESISTOR:** A resistor in the primary ignition circuit that lowers voltage after the engine is started to reduce wear on ignition components.

**BEARING:** A friction reducing, supportive device usually located between a stationary part and a moving part.

**BIMETAL TEMPERATURE SENSOR:** Any sensor or switch made of two dissimilar types of metal that bend when heated or cooled due to the different expansion rates of the alloys. These types of sensors usually function as an on/off switch.

**BLOWBY:** Combustion gases, composed of water vapor and unburned fuel, that leak past the piston rings into the crankcase during normal engine operation. These gases are removed by the PCV system to prevent the buildup of harmful acids in the crankcase.

**BRAKE PAD:** A brake shoe and lining assembly used with disc brakes.

**BRAKE SHOE:** The backing for the brake lining. The term is, however, usually applied to the assembly of the brake backing and lining.

**BUSHING:** A liner, usually removable, for a bearing; an anti-friction liner used in place of a bearing.

**CALIPER:** A hydraulically activated device in a disc brake system, which is mounted straddling the brake rotor (disc). The caliper contains at least one piston and two brake pads. Hydraulic pressure on the piston(s) forces the pads against the rotor.

**CAMSHAFT:** A shaft in the engine on which are the lobes (cams) which operate the valves. The camshaft is driven by the crankshaft, via a belt, chain or gears, at one half the crankshaft speed.

**CAPACITOR:** A device which stores an electrical charge.

**CARBON MONOXIDE (CO):** A colorless, odorless gas given off as a normal byproduct of combustion. It is poisonous and extremely dangerous in confined areas, building up slowly to toxic levels without warning if adequate ventilation is not available.

**CARBURETOR:** A device, usually mounted on the intake manifold of an engine, which mixes the air and fuel in the proper proportion to allow even combustion.

**CATALYTIC CONVERTER:** A device installed in the exhaust system, like a muffler, that converts harmful byproducts of combustion into carbon dioxide and water vapor by means of a heat-producing chemical reaction.

**CENTRIFUGAL ADVANCE:** A mechanical method of advancing the spark timing by using flyweights in the distributor that react to centrifugal force generated by the distributor shaft rotation.

**CHECK VALVE:** Any one-way valve installed to permit the flow of air, fuel or vacuum in one direction only.

**CHOKE:** A device, usually a moveable valve, placed in the intake path of a carburetor to restrict the flow of air.

**CIRCUIT:** Any unbroken path through which an electrical current can flow. Also used to describe fuel flow in some instances.

**CIRCUIT BREAKER:** A switch which protects an electrical circuit from overload by opening the circuit when the current flow exceeds a predetermined level. Some circuit breakers must be reset manually, while most reset automatically.

**COIL (IGNITION):** A transformer in the ignition circuit which steps up the voltage provided to the spark plugs.

**COMBINATION MANIFOLD:** An assembly which includes both the intake and exhaust manifolds in one casting.

**COMBINATION VALVE:** A device used in some fuel systems that routes fuel vapors to a charcoal storage canister instead of venting them into the atmosphere. The valve relieves fuel tank pressure and allows fresh air into the tank as the fuel level drops to prevent a vapor lock situation.

**COMPRESSION RATIO:** The comparison of the total volume of the cylinder and combustion chamber with the piston at BDC and the piston at TDC.

**CONDENSER:** 1. An electrical device which acts to store an electrical charge, preventing voltage surges. 2. A radiator-like device in the air conditioning system in which refrigerant gas condenses into a liquid, giving off heat.

**CONDUCTOR:** Any material through which an electrical current can be transmitted easily.

**CONTINUITY:** Continuous or complete circuit. Can be checked with an ohmmeter.

**COUNTERSHAFT:** An intermediate shaft which is rotated by a mainshaft and transmits, in turn, that rotation to a working part.

**CRANKCASE:** The lower part of an engine in which the crankshaft and related parts operate.

**CRANKSHAFT:** The main driving shaft of an engine which receives reciprocating motion from the pistons and converts it to rotary motion.

**CYLINDER:** In an engine, the round hole in the engine block in which the piston(s) ride.

**CYLINDER BLOCK:** The main structural member of an engine in which is found the cylinders, crankshaft and other principal parts.

**CYLINDER HEAD:** The detachable portion of the engine, usually fastened to the top of the cylinder block and containing all or most of the combustion chambers. On overhead valve engines, it contains the valves and their operating parts. On overhead cam engines, it contains the camshaft as well.

**DEAD CENTER:** The extreme top or bottom of the piston stroke.

**DETONATION:** An unwanted explosion of the air/fuel mixture in the combustion chamber caused by excess heat and compression, advanced timing, or an overly lean mixture. Also referred to as "ping".

**DIAPHRAGM:** A thin, flexible wall separating two cavities, such as in a vacuum advance unit.

**DIESELING:** A condition in which hot spots in the combustion chamber cause the engine to run on after the key is turned off.

**DIFFERENTIAL:** A geared assembly which allows the transmission of motion between drive axles, giving one axle the ability to turn faster than the other.

**DIODE:** An electrical device that will allow current to flow in one direction only.

**DISC BRAKE:** A hydraulic braking assembly consisting of a brake disc, or rotor, mounted on an axle, and a caliper assembly containing, usually two brake pads which are activated by hydraulic pressure. The pads are forced against the sides of the disc, creating friction which slows the vehicle.

**DISTRIBUTOR:** A mechanically driven device on an engine which is responsible for electrically firing the spark plug at a predetermined point of the piston stroke.

**DOWEL PIN:** A pin, inserted in mating holes in two different parts allowing those parts to maintain a fixed relationship.

**DRUM BRAKE:** A braking system which consists of two brake shoes and one or two wheel cylinders, mounted on a fixed backing plate, and a brake drum, mounted on an axle, which revolves around the assembly.

**DWELL:** The rate, measured in degrees of shaft rotation, at which an electrical circuit cycles on and off.

**ELECTRONIC CONTROL UNIT (ECU):** Ignition module, module, amplifier or igniter. See Module for definition.

**ELECTRONIC IGNITION:** A system in which the timing and firing of the spark plugs is controlled by an electronic control unit, usually called a module. These systems have no points or condenser.

**END–PLAY:** The measured amount of axial movement in a shaft.

**ENGINE:** A device that converts heat into mechanical energy.

**EXHAUST MANIFOLD:** A set of cast passages or pipes which conduct exhaust gases from the engine.

**FEELER GAUGE:** A blade, usually metal, of precisely predetermined thickness, used to measure the clearance between two parts.

**FIRING ORDER:** The order in which combustion occurs in the cylinders of an engine. Also the order in which spark is distributed to the plugs by the distributor.

**FLOODING:** The presence of too much fuel in the intake manifold and combustion chamber which prevents the air/fuel mixture from firing, thereby causing a no–start situation.

**FLYWHEEL:** A disc shaped part bolted to the rear end of the crankshaft. Around the outer perimeter is affixed the ring gear. The starter drive engages the ring gear, turning the flywheel, which rotates the crankshaft, imparting the initial starting motion to the engine.

**FOOT POUND (ft. lbs. or sometimes, ft.lb.):** The amount of energy or work needed to raise an item weighing one pound, a distance of one foot.

**FUSE:** A protective device in a circuit which prevents circuit overload by breaking the circuit when a specific amperage is present. The device is constructed around a strip or wire of a lower amperage rating than the circuit it is designed to protect. When an amperage higher than that stamped on the fuse is present in the circuit, the strip or wire melts, opening the circuit.

**GEAR RATIO:** The ratio between the number of teeth on meshing gears.

**GENERATOR:** A device which converts mechanical energy into electrical energy.

**HEAT RANGE:** The measure of a spark plug's ability to dissipate heat from its firing end. The higher the heat range, the hotter the plug fires.

**HUB:** The center part of a wheel or gear.

**HYDROCARBON (HC):** Any chemical compound made up of hydrogen and carbon. A major pollutant formed by the engine as a byproduct of combustion.

**HYDROMETER:** An instrument used to measure the specific gravity of a solution.

**INCH POUND (inch lbs.; sometimes in.lb. or in. lbs.):** One twelfth of a foot pound.

**INDUCTION:** A means of transferring electrical energy in the form of a magnetic field. Principle used in the ignition coil to increase voltage.

**INJECTOR:** A device which receives metered fuel under relatively low pressure and is activated to inject the fuel into the engine under relatively high pressure at a predetermined time.

**INPUT SHAFT:** The shaft to which torque is applied, usually carrying the driving gear or gears.

**INTAKE MANIFOLD:** A casting of passages or pipes used to conduct air or a fuel/air mixture to the cylinders.

**JOURNAL:** The bearing surface within which a shaft operates.

**KEY:** A small block usually fitted in a notch between a shaft and a hub to prevent slippage of the two parts.

**MANIFOLD:** A casting of passages or set of pipes which connect the cylinders to an inlet or outlet source.

**MANIFOLD VACUUM:** Low pressure in an engine intake manifold formed just below the throttle plates. Manifold vacuum is highest at idle and drops under acceleration.

**MASTER CYLINDER:** The primary fluid pressurizing device in a hydraulic system. In automotive use, it is found in brake and hydraulic clutch systems and is pedal activated, either directly or, in a power brake system, through the power booster.

**MODULE:** Electronic control unit, amplifier or igniter of solid state or integrated design which controls the current flow in the ignition primary circuit based on input from the pick–up coil. When the module opens the primary circuit, high secondary voltage is induced in the coil.

**NEEDLE BEARING:** A bearing which consists of a number (usually a large number) of long, thin rollers.

**OHM:** ($\Omega$) The unit used to measure the resistance of conductor–to–electrical flow. One ohm is the amount of resistance that limits current flow to one ampere in a circuit with one volt of pressure.

**OHMMETER:** An instrument used for measuring the resistance, in ohms, in an electrical circuit.

**OUTPUT SHAFT:** The shaft which transmits torque from a device, such as a transmission.

**OVERDRIVE:** A gear assembly which produces more shaft revolutions than that transmitted to it.

**OVERHEAD CAMSHAFT (OHC):** An engine configuration in which the camshaft is mounted on top of the cylinder head and operates the valve either directly or by means of rocker arms.

**OVERHEAD VALVE (OHV):** An engine configuration in which all of the valves are located in the cylinder head and the camshaft is located in the cylinder block. The camshaft operates the valves via lifters and pushrods.

**OXIDES OF NITROGEN (NOx):** Chemical compounds of nitrogen produced as a byproduct of combustion. They combine with hydrocarbons to produce smog.

**OXYGEN SENSOR:** Used with the feedback system to sense the presence of oxygen in the exhaust gas and signal the computer which can reference the voltage signal to an air/fuel ratio.

**PINION:** The smaller of two meshing gears.

**PISTON RING:** An open–ended ring which fits into a groove on the outer diameter of the piston. Its chief function is to form a seal between the piston and cylinder wall. Most automotive pistons have three rings: two for compression sealing; one for oil sealing.

**PRELOAD:** A predetermined load placed on a bearing during assembly or by adjustment.

**PRIMARY CIRCUIT:** The low voltage side of the ignition system which consists of the ignition switch, ballast resistor or resistance wire, bypass, coil, electronic control unit and pick–up coil as well as the connecting wires and harnesses.

**PRESS FIT:** The mating of two parts under pressure, due to the inner diameter of one being smaller than the outer diameter of the other, or vice versa; an interference fit.

**RACE:** The surface on the inner or outer ring of a bearing on which the balls, needles or rollers move.

**REGULATOR:** A device which maintains the amperage and/or voltage levels of a circuit at predetermined values.

**RELAY:** A switch which automatically opens and/or closes a circuit.

**RESISTANCE:** The opposition to the flow of current through a circuit or electrical device, and is measured in ohms. Resistance is equal to the voltage divided by the amperage.

**RESISTOR:** A device, usually made of wire, which offers a preset amount of resistance in an electrical circuit.

**RING GEAR:** The name given to a ring–shaped gear attached to a differential case, or affixed to a flywheel or as part of a planetary gear set.

**ROLLER BEARING:** A bearing made up of hardened inner and outer races between which hardened steel rollers move.

**ROTOR:** 1. The disc–shaped part of a disc brake assembly, upon which the brake pads bear; also called, brake disc. 2. The device mounted atop the distributor shaft, which passes current to the distributor cap tower contacts.

**SECONDARY CIRCUIT:** The high voltage side of the ignition system, usually above 20,000 volts. The secondary includes the ignition coil, coil wire, distributor cap and rotor, spark plug wires and spark plugs.

**SENDING UNIT:** A mechanical, electrical, hydraulic or electromagnetic device which transmits information to a gauge.

**SENSOR:** Any device designed to measure engine operating conditions or ambient pressures and temperatures. Usually electronic in nature and designed to send a voltage signal to an on–board computer, some sensors may operate as a simple on/off switch or they may provide a variable voltage signal (like a potentiometer) as conditions or measured parameters change.

**SHIM:** Spacers of precise, predetermined thickness used between parts to establish a proper working relationship.

**SLAVE CYLINDER:** In automotive use, a device in the hydraulic clutch system which is activated by hydraulic force, disengaging the clutch.

**SOLENOID:** A coil used to produce a magnetic field, the effect of which is to produce work.

**SPARK PLUG:** A device screwed into the combustion chamber of a spark ignition engine. The basic construction is a conductive core inside of a ceramic insulator, mounted in an outer conductive base. An electrical charge from the spark plug wire travels along the conductive core and jumps a preset air gap to a grounding point or points at the end of the conductive base. The resultant spark ignites the fuel/air mixture in the combustion chamber.

**SPLINES:** Ridges machined or cast onto the outer diameter of a shaft or inner diameter of a bore to enable parts to mate without rotation.

**TACHOMETER:** A device used to measure the rotary speed of an engine, shaft, gear, etc., usually in rotations per minute.

**THERMOSTAT:** A valve, located in the cooling system of an engine, which is closed when cold and opens gradually in response to engine heating, controlling the temperature of the coolant and rate of coolant flow.

**TOP DEAD CENTER (TDC):** The point at which the piston reaches the top of its travel on the compression stroke.

**TORQUE:** The twisting force applied to an object.

**TORQUE CONVERTER:** A turbine used to transmit power from a driving member to a driven member via hydraulic action, providing changes in drive ratio and torque. In automotive use, it links the driveplate at the rear of the engine to the automatic transmission.

**TRANSDUCER:** A device used to change a force into an electrical signal.

**TRANSISTOR:** A semi–conductor component which can be actuated by a small voltage to perform an electrical switching function.

**TUNE–UP:** A regular maintenance function, usually associated with the replacement and adjustment of parts and components in the electrical and fuel systems of a vehicle for the purpose of attaining optimum performance.

**TURBOCHARGER:** An exhaust driven pump which compresses intake air and forces it into the combustion chambers at higher than atmospheric pressures. The increased air pressure allows more fuel to be burned and results in increased horsepower being produced.

**VACUUM ADVANCE:** A device which advances the ignition timing in response to increased engine vacuum.

**VACUUM GAUGE:** An instrument used to measure the presence of vacuum in a chamber.

**VALVE:** A device which control the pressure, direction of flow or rate of flow of a liquid or gas.

**VALVE CLEARANCE:** The measured gap between the end of the valve stem and the rocker arm, cam lobe or follower that activates the valve.

**VISCOSITY:** The rating of a liquid's internal resistance to flow.

**VOLTMETER:** An instrument used for measuring electrical force in units called volts. Voltmeters are always connected parallel with the circuit being tested.

**WHEEL CYLINDER:** Found in the automotive drum brake assembly, it is a device, actuated by hydraulic pressure, which, through internal pistons, pushes the brake shoes outward against the drums.

MASTER
INDEX